June 11–15, 2012
London, England, UK

Association for
Computing Machinery

Advancing Computing as a Science & Profession

SIGMETRICS'12

Proceedings of the ACM SIGMETRICS/PERFORMANCE Joint International Conference on

Measurement and Modeling of Computer Systems

Sponsored by:

ACM SIGMETRICS & IFIP

Association for
Computing Machinery

Advancing Computing as a Science & Profession

The Association for Computing Machinery
2 Penn Plaza, Suite 701
New York, New York 10121-0701

ISBN: 978-1-4503-1097-0 (Digital)

ISBN: 978-1-4503-1733-7 (Print)

Additional copies may be ordered prepaid from:

ACM Order Department
PO Box 30777
New York, NY 10087-0777, USA

Phone: 1-800-342-6626 (USA and Canada)
+1-212-626-0500 (Global)
Fax: +1-212-944-1318
E-mail: acmhelp@acm.org
Hours of Operation: 8:30 am – 4:30 pm ET

Printed in the USA

Foreword

It's a great pleasure to welcome you to the 12th joint ACM SIGMETRICS and IFIP PERFORMANCE International Conference, hosted by the Department of Computing, Imperial College London – one week after the Queen's Silver Jubilee celebrations and six weeks before the 2012 Olympic Games, just the other side of Town. In fact we chose these dates so as to avoid clashing with Her Majesty's special week, which might have been compromised by an event of such stature!

This year's conference enhances the tradition of both of its constituents' being the premier fora for state-of-the-art research in performance modeling and measurement techniques, tools and applications in the American and Europe continents, respectively. We have assembled a superb technical program with 31 full papers of the highest quality and 23 posters highlighting innovative research; further details are provided in the Program Chairs' Welcome that follows. Contributors come from 18 different countries in 3 continents; 49 papers have (co-)authors from academic institutions and 22 have industrial (co-)authors. This year we have increased the numbers of Tutorials and Workshops. On Monday, 11th June there are five tutorials and two workshops: the ever-popular GreenMetrics and, for the first time, W-PIN. My thanks to Cati Lladó for her organizing the tutorials and expanding this aspect of the conference. On Friday we have three more innovative Workshops: the long-established MAMA, a new one PADE and a Hands-on Tutorial-Workshop NetFPGA. We hope as many of you as possible will take advantage of these excellent satellite events.

My grateful thanks go to many individuals, including all of the organizing committee, who have made this conference possible, and our industrial sponsors AT&T, HP Labs, IBM, Microsoft Research, Nokia, Google, Netapp, VMware, Facebook, NEC, NSF, Computer Performance Foundation and Imperial College London. The Program Chairs, Martin Arlitt and Giuliano Casale, complemented each other well and could not have been more diligent in their rigorous management of the paper selection process. Their collaboration was exceptionally harmonious and resulted in one of the most effective, systematic and efficient Program Committee meetings I have ever seen. This took place at Columbia University, New York City, in February and I thank Gil Zussman for his organization of this. Locally, I thank Tony Field and Teresa Ng for working with me on the finances, Uli Harder for being a patient and effective webmaster as well as local arrangements chair, ably assisted by Gareth Jones and our fountain of local knowledge, Ann Halford. Finally I am very grateful to two consecutive Heads of Department – Professors Jeff Magee and Susan Eisenbach – not only for allowing our event to take place during term but also offering financial support.

Finally, we have a fine student program organized by Jia Wang of AT&T. As well as extremely generous tutorial rates for students, there is a student poster competition, complete with prize for the best poster, a "jobs fair" and a special outing to a research and development facility. I sincerely hope that you will find this conference and its associated events interesting, thought-provoking, productive and generally enjoyable – and that you meet old friends, make new ones and find time to enjoy some of the many delights that the great city of London has to offer.

Peter Harrison, *Imperial College London*
General Chair

Message from Program Co-Chairs

Welcome to London in this Olympic year, and to *ACM SIGMETRICS/Performance 2012,* the 12th Joint International Conference on Measurement and Modeling of Computer Systems! This joint venue occurs every three years, bringing together the flagship conferences of ACM SIGMETRICS and the IFIP Working Group 7.3 into a forum that attracts top quality papers in performance evaluation. This year's program includes a set of excellent contributions covering topics in scheduling, networking, pricing, data centers, graphs, sampling, ranking, epidemics, characterization, load balancing, and of course computer system performance.

As in past editions of the conference, the paper selection process was highly competitive. A total of 203 papers were submitted. All submissions were evaluated through a double-blind process that ensured anonymity of both authors and reviewers. Each paper received at least four reviews from program committee (PC) members not in conflict of interest with the authors. In some cases, additional reviews from experts outside the PC were solicited. The paper selection process culminated in the PC meeting at Columbia University in New York, on February 2–3, 2012. 31 full papers were selected for inclusion in the final program, leading to a competitive acceptance rate of 15%. Additionally, 23 thought-provoking submissions were selected for poster presentation. We are extremely grateful to the PC members and external reviewers for providing a total of 866 reviews, for exchanging hundreds of comments in the active online discussions and PC meeting, and for their help in the shepherding process. We would also like to thank all the authors who submitted papers: their efforts and enthusiasm truly represent the soul of this conference.

We are very grateful to Peter Harrison, Gil Zussman, Gareth Gale, Y. Charlie Hu, Samuel Kounev, Anirban Mahanti, Uli Harder, Gareth Jones, Urtzi Ayesta, Kimberley Keeton, Dan Rubinstein, Walter Willinger, Patrick Thiran, Carey Williamson, Jeff Mogul, Eddie Kohler, and the student volunteers at Columbia University and Imperial College London. Their assistance was fundamental in a variety of tasks, including organizing and running the PC meeting, configuring and using the conference submission site, preparing the proceedings, advertising the conference, and last but not least, hosting the conference.

We hope that you will find this year's program stimulating and highly innovative. Enjoy!

Martin Arlitt, *HP Labs and University of Calgary*
Giuliano Casale, *Imperial College London*
Program Co-Chairs

Table of Contents

Tutorials

SIGMETRICS/Performance 2012 Conference Organization

General Chair: Peter Harrison *(Imperial College London, United Kingdom)*

Program Chairs: Martin Arlitt *(HP Labs, USA and University of Calgary, Canada)*
Giuliano Casale *(Imperial College London, United Kingdom)*

Finance Chair: Tony Field *(Imperial College London, United Kingdom)*

Tutorial Chair: Catalina Lladó *(UIB, Palma De Mallorca, Spain)*

Publication Chair: Urtzi Ayesta *(LAAS-CNRS, France)*

Local Arrangements Chairs: Uli Harder *(Imperial College London, United Kingdom)*
Gareth Jones *(Imperial College London, United Kingdom)*

Publicity Chairs: Y. Charlie Hu *(Purdue University, USA)*
Samuel Kounev *(KIT, Germany)*
Anirban Mahanti *(NICTA, Australia)*

Student Activities Chair: Jia Wang *(AT&T Labs – Research, USA)*

Program Committee: Tarek Abdelzaher *(University of Illinois at Urbana-Champaign, USA)*
Jussara Almeida *(Universidade Federal de Minas Gerais, Brazil)*
Urtzi Ayesta *(LAAS-CNRS, France)*
Paul Barford *(University of Wisconsin, USA)*
Sem Borst *(Eindhoven University of Technology, The Netherlands, and Bell Labs, Alcatel-Lucent, USA)*
Ana Busic *(INRIA and ENS Paris, France)*
Niklas Carlsson *(Linköping University, Sweden)*
Augustin Chaintreau *(Columbia University, USA)*
Abhishek Chandra *(University of Minnesota, USA)*
Florin Ciucu *(TU Berlin/Deutsche Telekom Laboratories, Germany)*
Mark Crovella *(Boston University, USA)*
Grzegorz Czajkowski *(Google, USA)*
Susanna Donatelli *(Università di Torino, Italy)*
John Douceur *(Microsoft Research, USA)*
Derek Eager *(University of Saskatchewan, Canada)*
Vijay Erramilli *(Telefonica Research, Spain)*
Anja Feldmann *(TU Berlin/Deutsche Telekom Laboratories, Germany)*
Ayalvadi Ganesh *(University of Bristol, United Kingdom)*
Erol Gelenbe *(Imperial College London, United Kingdom)*
Leana Golubchik *(University of Southern California, USA)*
Ajay Gulati *(VMware, USA)*
Varun Gupta *(Google, USA)*

Program Committee (continued):

Mor Harchol-Balter *(Carnegie Mellon University, USA)*
Nidhi Hegde *(Technicolor, France)*
Jane Hillston *(University of Edinburgh, United Kingdom)*
Y. Charlie Hu *(Purdue University, USA)*
Canturk Isci *(IBM T. J. Watson Research Center, USA)*
Alain Jean-Marie *(LIRMM and INRIA, France)*
Terence Kelly *(HP Labs, USA)*
Peter Key *(Microsoft Research, United Kingdom)*
William Knottenbelt *(Imperial College London, United Kingdom)*
Dejan Kostic *(EPFL, Switzerland)*
Samuel Kounev *(KIT, Germany)*
Diwakar Krishnamurthy *(University of Calgary, Canada)*
Catalina Lladó *(UIB, Palma De Mallorca, Spain)*
John C.S. Lui *(Chinese University of Hong Kong, Hong Kong)*
Qin Lv *(University of Colorado at Boulder, USA)*
Anirban Mahanti *(NICTA, Australia)*
Arif Merchant *(Google, USA)*
Rudesindo Nunez-Queija *(University of Amsterdam & CWI, The Netherlands)*
Mark Oskin *(University of Washington, USA)*
Andrew Rice *(University of Cambridge, United Kingdom)*
Alma Riska *(EMC, USA)*
Thomas Sandholm *(HP Labs, USA)*
Jiri Schindler *(NetApp, USA)*
Abhishek Sharma *(NEC Labs America, USA)*
Evgenia Smirni *(The College of William & Mary, USA)*
Alex Snoeren *(University of California San Diego, USA)*
Mark Squillante *(IBM T. J. Watson Research Center, USA)*
Christopher Stewart *(Ohio State University, USA)*
Y.C. Tay *(National University of Singapore, Singapore)*
Don Towsley *(University of Massachusetts, USA)*
Andy Tucker *(NetApp, USA)*
Mustafa Uysal *(VMware, USA)*
Benny Van Houdt *(University of Antwerp, Belgium)*
Milan Vojnovic *(Microsoft Research, United Kingdom)*
Jia Wang *(AT&T Labs - Research, USA)*
Adam Wierman *(California Institute of Technology, USA)*
Murray Woodside *(Carleton University, Canada)*
Jun Xu *(Georgia Tech, USA)*
Li Zhang *(IBM T. J. Watson Research Center, USA)*
Xiaoyun Zhu *(VMware, USA)*
Gil Zussman *(Columbia University, USA)*

Additional reviewers:

David Aikema
Gianfranco Balbo
Marco Beccuti
Andrey Bernstein
Deepavali Bhagwat
Berk Birand
Fabian Brosig
Michael Chien-Chun Hung
Juan F. Perez
Giuliana Franceschinis
Rossano Gaeta
Sebastià Galmés
Anshul Gandhi
Paolo Giacomazzi
Maria Gorlatova
Marco Grangetto
Marco Gribaudo
David Hay
Richard Hayden
Jung Ho Ahn
Andras Horvath
Nikolaus Huber
Victor Jimenez
Rouven Krebs
Jon Lenchner
Sung-Han Lin
Alex Liu
Zhenming Liu
Lei Lu
Moray McLaren
Aleksandar Milenkoski
Iqbal Mohomed
Naveen Muralimanohar
Qais Noorshams
Dejan Novakovic
Rasha Osman
Ranjan Pal
Michal Papež
Stan Park
Greg Pink
Roger Piqueras Jover
Bruno Ribeiro
Giancarlo Ruffo
Piotr Rygielski
Renato Santos
Michael Schapira
Mike Schlansker
Simon Schubert
Gadiel Seroussi
Kai Song
Jason Sonnek
Simon Spinner
Nedeljko Vasic
Bo-Chun Wang
Chengwei Wang
Praveen Yalagandula
Feng Yan
Yuan Yao
Stefano Zanero
Alex Zhang

SIGMETRICS/Performance 2012 Sponsors & Supporters

Sponsors:

Supporters:

Performance Implications of Flash and Storage Class Memories

Naresh M. Patel
NetApp Inc.
495 East Java Drive
Sunnyvale, CA 94089
naresh@netapp.com

Categories and Subject Descriptors
C.4 [Performance of Systems]: Performance Attributes

General Terms
Performance, Design, Economics

Keywords
Storage systems, performance, analytical modeling, flash-memory

1. INTRODUCTION

The storage industry has seen incredible growth in data storage needs by both consumers and enterprises. Long-term technology trends mean that the data deluge will continue well into the future. These trends include the big-data trend (driven by data mining analytics, high-bandwidth needs, and large content repositories), server virtualization, cloud storage, and Flash. We will cover how Flash and storage class memories (SCM) interact with some of these major trends from a performance perspective.

Within the Flash trend we include both NAND Flash (including potential 3D variants) and follow-on SCM technologies. Flash and SCM have some similar properties: nonvolatile storage, long retention times, and wear-out of physical locations. In addition, Flash devices are composed of a set of erase blocks, and each erase block contains a fixed set of pages (for example, a 4K page is the minimum size of a Flash read). Each erase block must be written sequentially, and once all erase blocks are used, some have to be "cleaned" of all valid pages before being rewritten. SCM devices are simpler to use because they allow bit-level writes just like DRAM. From a hardware technology perspective, the storage devices record digital ones and zeros by changing some physical attribute, such as amount of electrical charge, resistance level, or magnetic orientation. As semiconductor process geometries shrink, it is becoming challenging to reliably distinguish the charge level (currently down to a double-digit number of electrons) in a Flash cell. Other SCM technologies rely on other physical attributes that are more reliable at smaller process geometries. Their relatively high write endurance and bit addressability make them more suitable for main memory applications. Two types of SCMs—phase change memory (PCM) and spin-torque transfer (STT) magnetic RAM ([1] and [2])—are likely to gain traction in niche applications initially. PCM is attempting to be a better Flash solution whereas STT SCM is competing to replace DRAM.

SIGMETRICS'12, June 11–15, 2012, London, England, UK.
ACM 978-1-4503-1097-0/12/06.

2. PERFORMANCE VS. CAPACITY TIERS AND SIMPLICITY

SCMs have the potential to radically change the system architecture of storage systems. For decades, we have been accustomed to IT architectures with host/compute servers, networking, and storage arrays, all of which are often separate buying decisions in different IT organizations. Simplicity of data management across multiple layers is vital because people costs dominate and the risk of errors needs to be minimized.

Flash can be leveraged in various ways in each layer. For low latency access to large amounts of data, it can be in the host or in the network layer. In the storage array, Flash can be used as a part of a storage pool or a cache to improve latency characteristics and overall cost. By closely coupling Flash with main memory, Flash can act as a large extended memory cache. Flash-based solid-state drives (SSDs) can also be used as an alternative storage location for hot data that would otherwise reside in hard disk drives (HDDs). In either case, Flash absorbs the hot data accesses and thereby allows HDDs to store much colder data. With Flash replacing HDDs, the next-generation SCM technologies have a chance of replacing DRAM.

For multi-tenant storage, sharing HDDs is a problem for mixed I/Os because of the significant performance difference between random and sequential I/Os. Flash does not have such a large performance disparity and therefore makes it easier to meet service-level objectives at the same cost. We believe that each layer will require dynamic optimization of the mix of shared storage resources. For storage, we evaluate different architectures by using three categories: performance (cost per IOPS, cost per GB/s, latency, and IOPS per watt); capacity (cost per TB, thin provisioning, dedupe, compression); and simplicity (cost of maintenance at scale, nondisruptive operations, scalability). The simplicity aspect suggests that systems will require little admin involvement and some degree of automated self-tuning via built-in performance models.

In a best-of-breed architecture, we see the emergence of tiers optimized for different cost/performance metrics. Using Flash, the system can be optimized for performance by keeping frequently accessed data close to compute nodes, thereby creating an *IOPS* or *performance tier*. For colder data, optimizing the system for capacity creates a *capacity tier*, which still needs Flash but is dominated by HDDs. With SCM, the workload patterns between the performance tier and the capacity tier are likely to change. For example, after returning from a power outage, most of the system state remains intact and a reboot may involve less data transfer. All of this increased complexity needs to be hidden from the user to keep things simple in multi-tenant systems. This increases the need for analytical models that run in real time and provide dynamic insight into system operation.

3. MODELING CHALLENGES AND OPPORTUNITIES FOR FLASH AND SCM

Flash and SCM devices have some very different properties and the newly created architectures are still evolving. This raises some challenges and opportunities for performance modeling of the workload and system resources. The multi-tenant workloads, each with their own service level objective, are distributed over multiple layers with many large caches. This suggests a need for an efficient way to determine working set sizes and data content characteristics. On the resource modeling side, these new devices have very different aging characteristics and solutions.

Analytical models and simulation both provide great insight into how the system performs. One could argue that analytical models are compact enough to run alongside the real system, provided they can be sufficiently accurate and incur low system overhead (perhaps by utilizing on-chip parallel graphics hardware). Typically, performance evaluation involves a fair amount of workload characterization as well as resource modeling. Although detailed workload modeling is sometimes given insufficient attention, it is critical to provide accurate assessment of system performance. In practice, workloads described by a simple arrival rate with Poisson assumptions are often inadequate because real systems exhibit other distributions and dependencies in the time series [3]. Data content aspects such as dedupability (the amount of duplicate blocks written to and read from the storage system) and compressibility are also important factors. The big-data demand is so great that storage space efficiency remains important as storage hardware costs (cost per TB) come down with higher capacity HDDs. In the performance tier, one can imagine that deduplication and compression are important trade-offs between CPU resources and Flash/SCM space usage. Deduplication is a relatively new factor to consider in workload characterization and an area in which we need to build better understanding at some level of abstraction.

Given a good understanding of the new workload, we will need models of the resources [4]. For Flash, the resource characteristics are relatively simple, but the layer of software called the Flash translation layer (FTL) is fairly complex and not well understood via models (although [5] is a good starting point). Some abstract model of the FTL would help make sense of the proliferation of FTLs we see today. For the new SCM devices, simple abstract models would suffice. These would be convenient for storage architects who are designing systems in general, enabling them to execute low-overhead models directly in the running system. For example, consider a hybrid SSD and HDD storage system with a blended response time distribution with two modes; a simple metric of interest could be the latency of a single-threaded application that is issuing one class of requests to the system. Although closed-form solutions are elegant and useful for insight, many of the resource models for these new architectures would work well via numerical or symbolic computational techniques.

4. SUMMARY

Flash is being deployed in different parts of the storage stack and SCMs are poised to change storage architectures in a big way. Together these technologies are changing the rules of the game with respect to random IOPS and performance. A new architecture is emerging with distinct performance and capacity tiers optimized for different metrics but working together for system-wide multi tenant storage. These trends are creating new challenges and opportunities for performance in terms of workload characterization and resource modeling. Although the focus of the industry is mostly about building great products, the industry relies on the universities to do the cutting-edge research and to further our understanding of new nonvolatile memory architectures. As with all promising memory technologies in the past, there are many competing technologies, and it is better for all when the best technology is evaluated fairly in terms of performance capabilities. With all the disruptive technologies becoming available in the near future, it's a great time to be in the storage business.

5. ACKNOWLEDGEMENTS

I would like to thank the NetApp Engineering team, the NetApp Advanced Technology Group and the Office of the CTO at NetApp for helping to put this together. Kaladhar Voruganti reviewed an early draft and provided valuable feedback.

6. REFERENCES

[1] Benjamin C. Lee, Engin Ipek, Onur Mutlu, and Doug Burger. 2009. Architecting phase change memory as a scalable dram alternative. *SIGARCH Comput. Archit. News* 37, 3 (June 2009), 2-13. DOI=10.1145/1555815.1555758 http://doi.acm.org/10.1145/1555815.1555758

[2] Adrian M. Caulfield, Joel Coburn, Todor Mollov, Arup De, Ameen Akel, Jiahua He, Arun Jagatheesan, Rajesh K. Gupta, Allan Snavely, and Steven Swanson. 2010. Understanding the Impact of Emerging Non-Volatile Memories on High-Performance, IO-Intensive Computing. In *Proceedings of the 2010 ACM/IEEE International Conference for High Performance Computing, Networking, Storage and Analysis* (SC '10). IEEE Computer Society, Washington, DC, USA, 1-11. DOI=10.1109/SC.2010.56 http://dx.doi.org/10.1109/SC.2010.56

[3] P. G. Harrison, S. K. Harrison, N. M. Patel, and S. Zertal. 2012. Storage workload modelling by hidden Markov models: Application to Flash memory. *Perform. Eval.* 69, 1 (January 2012), 17-40. DOI=10.1016/j.peva.2011.07.022 http://dx.doi.org/10.1016/j.peva.2011.07.022

[4] P. G. Harrison, N. M. Patel, and S. Zertal. 2010. Response time distribution of flash memory accesses. *Perform. Eval.* 67, 4 (April 2010), 248-259. DOI=10.1016/j.peva.2009.10.003. http://dx.doi.org/10.1016/j.peva.2009.10.003

[5] Simona Boboila and Peter Desnoyers. 2011. Performance models of flash-based solid-state drives for real workloads. In *Proceedings of the 2011 IEEE 27th Symposium on Mass Storage Systems and Technologies* (MSST '11). IEEE Computer Society, Washington, DC, USA, 1-6. DOI=10.1109/MSST.2011.5937227 http://dx.doi.org/10.1109/MSST.2011.5937227

Keynote

High-Performance Computing in Mobile Services

Zhen Liu
Nokia Research Center

Abstract

With the ever increasing popularity of smart phones, mobile services have been evolving rapidly to allow users to enjoy localized and personalized experiences. Users can discover local information and keep connected with family and friends on the go, and ultimately to experience the convergence of cyber space and physical world where digital technologies are interwoven into the day-to-day life.

A pivotal component of such a cyber-physical convergence is the contextual intelligence. The extraction and dissemination of contextual information around users is the key for the cyber capabilities to be applied to physical activities and for the cyber world to better reflect the physical reality.

In this talk, we shall address some issues arising from context-based mobile services. In particular, we discuss how mobility impacts contextual relevancy and personalization in mobile services. The relevancy and timeliness of contextual information not only are essential for these services to deliver great user experiences, but also put significant computation pressure on service infrastructure that processes continuous data streams in real time and disseminate relevant data to a large amount of mobile users.

This talk will explore the challenges and opportunities for high-performance computing in mobile services. Based on key findings from large-scale mobile measurement data, the talk will analyze the tradeoff of different computing architectures, present case studies of scalable system design and implementation for personalized mobile services, and conclude with open challenges for the broad research community in performance measurement and modeling.

ACM Classifier: C.4Computer Systems Organization, PERFORMANCE OF SYSTEMS

SIGMETRICS'12, June 11–15, 2012, London, England, UK.
ACM 978-1-4503-1097-0/12/06.

Delay Tails in MapReduce Scheduling

Jian Tan, Xiaoqiao Meng, Li Zhang
IBM T. J. Watson Research
Hawthorne, NY 10562
{tanji,xmeng,zhangli}@us.ibm.com

ABSTRACT

MapReduce/Hadoop production clusters exhibit heavy-tailed characteristics for job processing times. These phenomena are resultant of the workload features and the adopted scheduling algorithms. Analytically understanding the delays under different schedulers for MapReduce can facilitate the design and deployment of large Hadoop clusters. The map and reduce tasks of a MapReduce job have fundamental difference and tight dependence between them, complicating the analysis. This also leads to an interesting starvation problem with the widely used Fair Scheduler due to its greedy approach to launching reduce tasks. To address this issue, we design and implement Coupling Scheduler, which gradually launches reduce tasks depending on map task progresses. Real experiments demonstrate improvements to job response times by up to an order of magnitude.

Based on extensive measurements and source code investigations, we propose analytical models for the default FIFO and Fair Scheduler as well as our implemented Coupling Scheduler. For a class of heavy-tailed map service time distributions, i.e., regularly varying of index $-\alpha$, we derive the distribution tail of the job processing delay under the three schedulers, respectively. The default FIFO Scheduler causes the delay to be regularly varying of index $-\alpha+1$. Interestingly, we discover a criticality phenomenon for Fair Scheduler, the delay under which can change from regularly varying of index $-\alpha$ to $-\alpha+1$, depending on the maximum number of reduce tasks of a job. Other more subtle behaviors also exist. In contrast, the delay distribution tail under Coupling Scheduler can be one order lower than Fair Scheduler under some conditions, implying a better performance.

Categories and Subject Descriptors

G.3 [**Probability and Statistics**]: *Queueing Theory, Stochastic Processes*; D.2.8 [**Software Engineering**]: Metrics—*complexity measures, performance measures*

SIGMETRICS '12, June 11–15, 2012, London, England, UK.

General Terms

Performance, Design, Algorithms, Theory, Experimentation

Keywords

MapReduce, Hadoop, Fair Scheduler, Coupling Scheduler, Processor Sharing, First In First Out, Heavy-tails

1. INTRODUCTION

MapReduce is a popular programming framework that can parallelize large data processing on a cluster. This framework and its implementations, Google's MapReduce [6] and the open source project Hadoop [9], have attracted increasing attention. To reduce operational costs, organizations often deploy MapReduce in a shared cluster, e.g., the Datawarehouse Hadoop cluster at Facebook contains $2,000$ machines and receives on average $25,000$ MapReduce jobs per day in 2010. Due to the large number of jobs sharing limited resources, an efficient job scheduler is critical for improving system performance and resource utilization. Fair Scheduler (FAIR) [1, 27], as the de facto industry standard, is one of the most widely used schedulers in practice; other schedulers also exist, including the default First In First Out (FIFO) Scheduler, Capacity Scheduler [2], FLEX Scheduler [23] and variations [10, 18].

Hadoop scheduling mechanism

A MapReduce job consists of a map phase and a reduce phase. Each phase is executed by multiple affiliated tasks. The input data of a job is split into small fixed size chunks. Each map task processes one data chunk and generates intermediate results in key-value pairs. Reduce tasks fetch these results according to keys through a copy/shuffle phase, during which the key-value pairs are sorted and merged. Only after receiving all the intermediate results from every map task can a reduce task start the reduce phase. MapReduce jobs are submitted to the job tracker running on the master node. Other nodes are slave nodes, with each having a task tracker that periodically sends status information to the job tracker via heartbeats every few seconds. In response, a scheduler on the job tracker assigns tasks to slave nodes, as illustrated in Fig. 1.

As pointed out in [23], in current practice, map and reduce tasks are scheduled separately by assigning map and reduce slots on slave nodes, with each slot holding at most one task. For Fair Scheduler, once the map tasks of a job generate a certain amount of intermediate results, the reduce tasks are launched in a greedy fashion to the maximum. This is due to

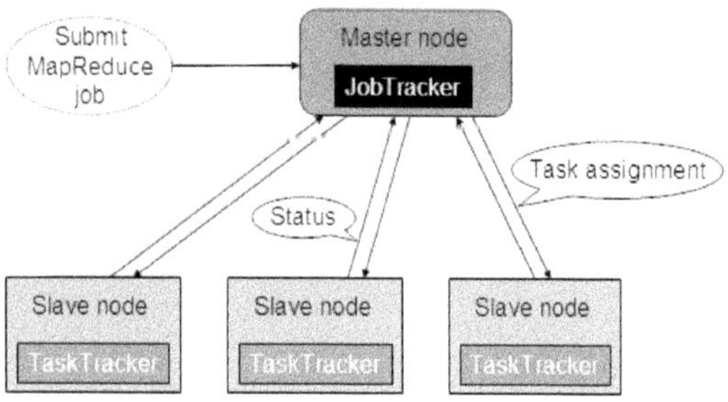

Figure 1: Illustration of the heartbeat mechanism

the consideration that the intermediate results generated by map tasks may have data that needs to be fetched by every reducer of the same job. Thus, overlapping the copy/shuffle phases of reduce tasks and the execution of map tasks can reduce the job processing delays.

As already recognized in [23, 27], the fundamental interdependence between map and reduce tasks can lead to starvation. Map tasks run independently and each completes quickly. However, reducers are long-running tasks as the copy/shuffle phase requires the outputs from all the mappers. More importantly, in most of the current implementations, a long job that has launched a reducer will not release the occupied slot until its reduce phase completes, which may starve other jobs whose mappers have finished. This problem is more pronounced when Fair Scheduler launches reducers in a greedy manner. Fig. 2 illustrates the problem: a large job 1 greedily takes all the reduce slots after job 2 completes; even though a small job 3 can start its mappers upon submission, it has to wait until the reducers of job 1 complete before launching its own reducers. This

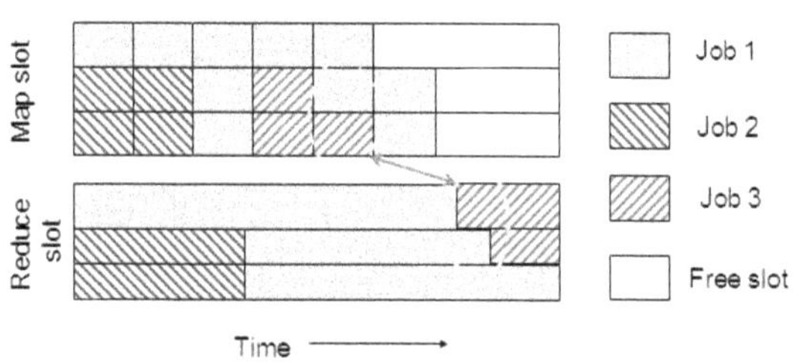

Figure 2: Starvation problem

starvation problem can yield interesting new analytic results that are presented in Section 3.2. As a solution, a copy-compute splitting mechanism [27] has been implemented in Fair Scheduler [1], which, however, does not fully resolve this issue. Ideally, a stop-and-resume control may solve this problem, which nevertheless incurs large overhead [27].

To further alleviate this problem, we design and implement Coupling Scheduler [20], which, among other new features, launch reducers gradually by coupling the progresses of map and reduce tasks of the same job. It is based on the intuition that allocating excess resources to reducers without balancing with the mapper progress of the same job is likely to result in resource underutilization. Experiments demonstrate improvements to job response times by up to an order of magnitude. Existing schedulers, e.g., Fair Scheduler [1], have already implemented a way to postpone the launch of reducers until mappers generate a certain amount of intermediate results. However this approach still greedily takes all the reduce slots whenever possible. In contrast, our unique way of gradually launching reducers depending on the map progress according to a functional relationship allows the possibility of reserving reduce slots for other jobs. More importantly, it enables new ways to form cooperation between mappers and reducers to jointly optimize data locality, which is to move computation close to data. Initially both mappers and reducers do not know their optimal placement with the common goal for better data locality; as the job evolves, new run-time information becomes available such that mappers and reducers can alternatively optimize step by step depending on the decisions taken by the other phase. A full description of this scheduler is presented in [20].

Heavy-tailed characteristics

Empirical trace studies on a production MapReduce cluster reveal the heavy-tailed characteristics of the workload [12]. In addition, typical MapReduce work flows consist of small jobs after large ones [5]. Therefore, scheduling disciplines that dedicate the whole computing resources to a long job, such as FIFO, may delay the processing of other small ones that arrive later. This motivates the design of schedulers (e.g., Fair Scheduler and Capacity Scheduler) that allow resource sharing among jobs. Up to now, most of the performance studies of MapReduce are through either experiments [17] or trace-driven simulations [21]. It still remains untouched how to analytically characterize the job processing delays under different schedulers.

Summary of contributions

Based on extensive measurements and source code investigations, we propose analytical models for the default FIFO, Fair Scheduler and Coupling Scheduler, respectively. For the latter two schedulers, we model mappers by a processor sharing queue and reducers by a multi-server queue with complicated and dependent scheduling behaviors.

Our first contribution is in theory. For a class of heavy-tailed map service time distributions, i.e., regularly varying of index $-\alpha$, we derive the distribution tail of the job processing delay under the three schedulers, respectively. For Fair and Coupling schedulers, MapReduce is one of the widely used systems that have characteristics similar to both processor sharing and FIFO (precisely it is a "water filling" like policy as explained in Section 2.2.2; see a related model in [8]). The classic result developed by A. G. Pakes shows that a FIFO discipline causes the delay to be regularly varying of index $-\alpha+1$. Intuitively, a long delay is caused by the fact that an arrival sees the residual time of a large job in the line under FIFO. If MapReduce only has mappers without reducers, the insights derived by R. Núñez-Queija show that when the map queue adopts processor sharing, the delay is regularly varying of index $-\alpha$. The long delay is due to a large job sharing the limited resource with other jobs, which has an equivalent service rate equal to the residual capacity. The presence of reduce tasks fundamentally changes the model and yields interesting new analytical results that require novel proof methods.

Due to the tight dependence between map and reduce tasks, we discover an intriguing criticality phenomenon for Fair Scheduler caused by the starvation problem. The delay can change from regularly varying of index $-\alpha$ to $-\alpha+1$, depending on the maximum number of reducers of a job. Other more subtle behaviors also exist; see Theorem 4. Informally, if jobs can claim reduce slots more than a critical value, then the large delay is due to a long job that has arrived earlier and claimed a large number of reduce slots, under which the delay is of the same order $-\alpha + 1$ as the residual service requirement. However, if the number of reduce tasks per job is strictly smaller than the critical value, then a large job that arrives earlier can not block the system, under which a long delay is resultant from the fact that this job of index $-\alpha$ itself is long. Under more restrictive conditions, we also derive the exact asymptotics. From an engineering perspective, our result provides insights on how to size system resources above the critical value such that the computing cluster operates in a benign point. It also shows that the job processing delay distribution under Coupling Scheduler can have an order gain under some conditions.

Our second contribution is an implementation of Coupling Scheduler for Hadoop. Fig 3 plots the job processing times

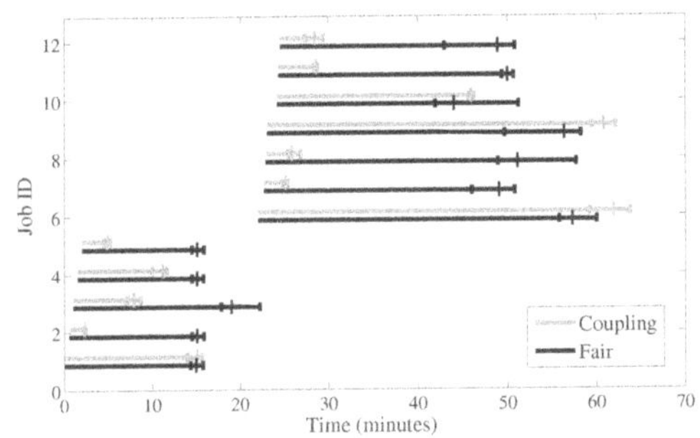

Figure 3: Compare job processing times

when repeating 12 jobs 5 times under Fair and Coupling schedulers with identical configurations. Each line depicts the starting time and the minimum, mean and maximum delays for 5 different trials, where the three vertical lines from left to right represent the minimum, mean and maximum, respectively. On average the job response times decrease by 47% in this experiment, with some jobs, e.g., job 2, 7, 8, 11 and 12, decreasing by even more than 83%. The details are described in Section 4. Note that Coupling Scheduler contains a number of other new design ideas that can contribute to the performance improvement, e.g., wait scheduling for reduce tasks, peeking algorithm for map tasks, balancing performance goals; see [20] for a complete description.

2. SCHEDULING MODELS

By collecting measurements from experiments conducted on our Hadoop testbed and investigating the source code, we characterize the scheduling properties for the default FIFO Scheduler, the popular Fair Scheduler and our proposed Coupling Scheduler in Subsection 2.1. Using these observations, we propose models in Subsection 2.2.

2.1 Measurements

We conduct a set of experiments to illustrate the differences between the three schedulers. In each experiment, we submit eight identical Grep jobs. Each job counts the number of words that begin with letters from 'a' to 'f' in Wikipedia Free Encyclopedia (28G bytes). We plot the number of running map and reduce tasks for every job along the time. These eight jobs are submitted one after the other, with time interval 5 minutes for the first 4 jobs and 1 minute for the last 4 jobs. Each job contains 427 mappers and 7 reducers on 7 slave nodes. In our configuration, each slave node has 4 map slots and 1 reduce slot. Thus, the total number of mappers and reducers that can run simultaneously is 28 and 7, respectively.

2.1.1 FIFO Scheduler

First, we investigate the default FIFO Scheduler. We plot the task assignment along the time in Fig. 4. Each colored line corresponds to one submitted job. As shown in the figure, eight jobs are processed in the order of the submission times. Thus, a large job can cause long delays for later short ones. This fact motivates the design of Fair Scheduler [27].

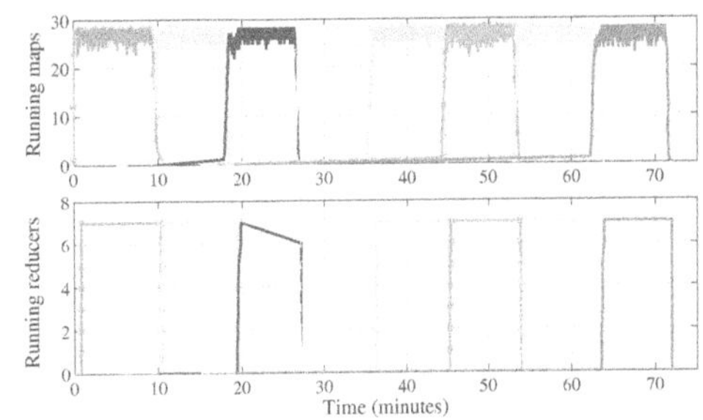

Figure 4: Task assignment with FIFO Scheduler

2.1.2 Fair Scheduler

Due to its popularity, next we study Fair Scheduler. As shown in Fig. 5, the first job is allocated all 28 mappers until the second job arrives. Then the first two jobs equally share all the map slots until the third job arrives. On the other hand, the first job is allocated all 7 reducers until its completion at around 16.0 minutes. Compared with the sharing of map slots, the second and the third job are not able to get a share of the reduce slots upon arrival. They are allocated 4 and 3 reducers only after the first job completes. The process continues in this fashion until all jobs complete.

Based on these observations, we model the map phase by the processor sharing discipline. This is appropriate in environments with small map tasks and a large number of processing nodes. The Fair Scheduler can assign different weights to jobs in a configuration file, leading to generalized processor sharing. Throughout this paper, we assume the weight assignments for all jobs are equal.

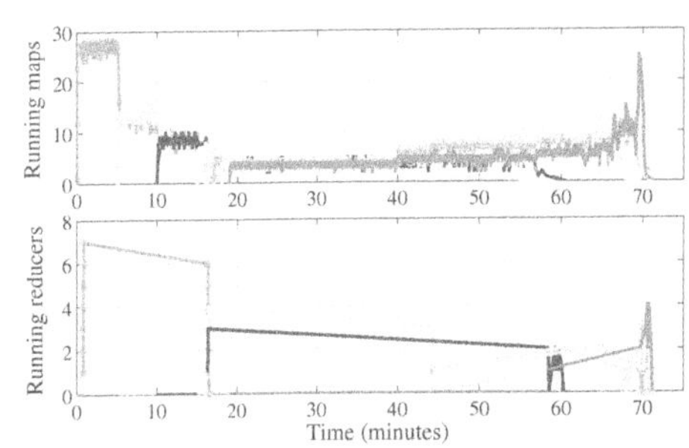

Figure 5: Task assignment with Fair Scheduler

The reducers need to be modeled differently, since they have the following three distinguishing features. 1) Reducers take a long time to finish, since the copy/shuffle phase spans over the whole map service time. Once launched, a reducer sticks to a slot until it completes. 2) Fair Scheduler greedily allocates the available reduce slots fairly to the jobs that still run on the cluster. 3) If there are not enough reduce slots, then jobs submitted earlier have higher priority. For example, even though all jobs are submitted before time 19.0 minutes, job 8 can only start its reducers around time 59.0 minutes, later than job 6 and 7 due to lack of reduce slots.

2.1.3 Coupling Scheduler

We observe two aspects of the Fair Scheduler that can be improved. First, reducers are launched greedily regardless of map task progresses. Even when the mappers of a job stop temporarily, say, due to job arrivals of higher priority, this job can still claim/hold reduce slots and starve others. Second, Fair Scheduler only considers data locality for mappers and ignores that the intermediate data generated from mappers also need to be fetched by reducers, through either networks or local disks. The placement of mappers determines where the intermediate data are stored. In turn, the placement of reducers impacts how map outputs are fetched. The greedy approach to launching reducers [1] at the beginning can make wrong placement decisions due to unawareness of the evolving job dynamics.

To this end, we resort to a different approach to launch reducers gradually according to the progress of the mappers. For typical workloads of Hadoop that consist of small jobs after large ones [12], gradually launching reducers of large jobs can reserve reduce slots that may be used by small jobs that arrive later. In addition, it enables new possibilities to form cooperation between map and reduce phases: as new run-time information becomes available mappers and reducers can alternatively optimize step by step depending on the decisions taken by the other phase [20]. Specifically, for $f : [0, 1] \to [0, 1]$ with $y = f(x)$, when a job finishes a fraction x of mappers, a fraction y of reducers of the same job can be launched if possible. If the reduce progress lags behind the map progress, then this job should have a better chance to launch reducers; otherwise, it should not acquire more reduce slots. We repeat the same experiment as in Fig. 5 and plot the task assignments under Coupling Scheduler in Fig. 6 for an implementation that takes $f(x) = cx$ for some $c > 0$.

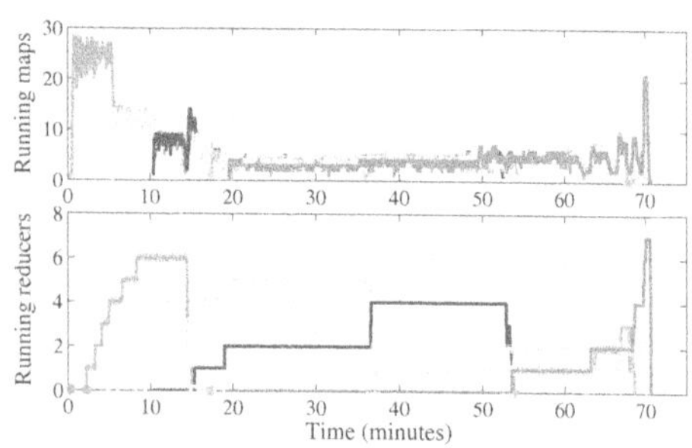

Figure 6: Task assignment with Coupling Scheduler

2.2 Model description

In this section, we propose analytic models to investigate the delay performance based on the observations from Section 2.1. We begin with common settings and then describe other aspects pertaining to different schedulers in Sections 2.2.1 and 2.2.2.

I) Job submissions: job arrivals are modeled by a Poisson process, where the interarrival times $\{A_i\}_{i>-\infty}$ are assumed to be exponentially distributed with rate λ.

II) Map tasks: the map phase is modeled by a $M/G/1$ queue, with scheduling disciplines specified in Sections 2.2.1 and 2.2.2. A job has multiple map tasks and these map tasks in their entirety are called the map service of a job. The i.i.d. sequence $\{B_i\}_{i>-\infty}$, which is independent of other random variables, represents the map service times, where $B_i \overset{d}{=} B$ ("$\overset{d}{=}$" means equal in distribution) is the total map service time of job i if the whole cluster is dedicated to serve job i exclusively. Let $\rho = \lambda\mathbb{E}[B]$.

Empirical trace studies of production MapReduce clusters reveal the heavy-tailed statistical characteristics of the job processing times [12]. Additionally, extensive measurements on modern data networks have shown that file sizes follow Pareto distributions [7]. Since the number of mappers of a job is proportional to its input file size (the ratio is the block size of HDFS file system), we can argue that the map service time distribution is also heavy-tailed. Specifically, we consider an important class of heavy-tailed distributions that are called regularly varying [3].

Definition 1. A random variable B is called regularly varying with index $-\alpha$ (denoted by $B \in \mathcal{R}_\alpha$) if

$$\mathbb{P}[B > x] = l(x)/x^\alpha, \; x \geq 0, \; \alpha \geq 0, \quad (1)$$

where $l(x)$ is slowly varying, i.e., $\lim_{x\to\infty} l(kx)/l(x) = 1$ for all $k > 0$.

III) Reduce tasks: let r be the total number of reduce slots in the cluster and R_i the number of reduce tasks of job i. As soon as the jth reduce task of job i finishes the copy/shuffle phase, it takes time C_i^j to process the reduce phase. Since the copy/shuffle phase of a job overlaps in time with its map phase, we assume that they complete at the same time. If not, then we can think that the beginning part of the time in C_i^j is actually spent for processing the copy/shuffle phase, which still fits the model.

Definition 2. Let $\{R, R_i\}$ and $\{C, C_i^j\}$, $i, j > -\infty$ be two sequences of mutually independent i.i.d. random variables that are independent of other random variables.

Remark 1. Statistical studies show that 91% of the MapReduce jobs fall into the map-only and map-mostly category and only 7% of the jobs are reduce-mostly [12]. Thus, for most jobs the real reduce function takes much less time than the map service. If C is also heavy-tailed, the job processing time may be dominated by either the map or the reduce phase, depending on which one has a heavier distribution tail. However, in view of the statistical report in [12] and to reduce the complexity of the analysis, we introduce the following two different assumptions in subsequent studies.

I. C is light-tailed, i.e, $\mathbb{E}[e^{\theta C}] < \infty$ for some $\theta > 0$.

II. $C \equiv 0$.

Note that for the case $C \equiv 0$ reduce tasks still exist but only take time 0 to finish. This assumption captures the impact from starvation, since the starvation problem still persists because of the copy/shuffle phase when $C \equiv 0$; see Fig. 2.

Definition 3. Let $\{T_i\}_{i>-\infty}$ be the processing time of job i. For better clarification, we replace T_i by T_i^d to denote the processing time under the default FIFO Scheduler, T_i^f under Fair Scheduler and T_i^c under Coupling Scheduler.

2.2.1 Default FIFO Scheduler

For the default FIFO Scheduler, the map queue is first in first out. Since the reduce function can only start when the whole map service completes, we model the default FIFO Scheduler by a tandem queue, as shown in Fig. 7. It assumes that both the map queue and the reduce queue can take at most one job simultaneously. This assumption is true in many scenarios, including the one in Fig. 4. However, in practice there are moments that multiple jobs can be in service at the same time, e.g., when the number of mappers of a job is smaller than or not a multiple of the number of map slots in the system. These will not impact the asymptotic results, since MapReduce jobs often have many mappers processed in multiple "map waves" on a cluster [12] and thus the number of mappers can be sandwiched between two multiples of the number of map slots in the system.

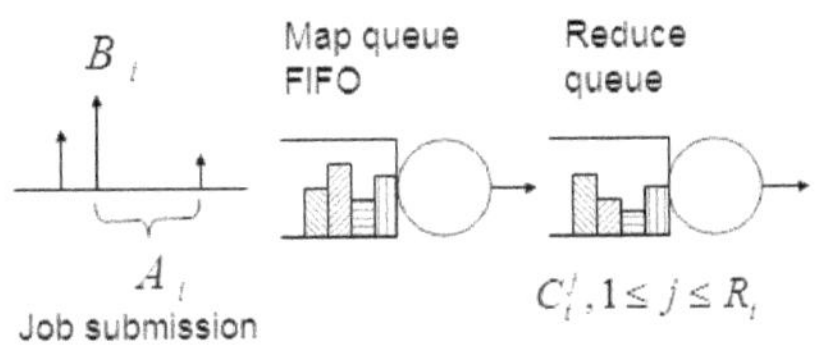

Figure 7: FIFO Scheduler for MapReduce

When $C \equiv 0$, the model reduces to a FIFO single queue. We quote the result by A. Pakes [16] in the following proposition.

Proposition 1. *If $B \in \mathcal{R}_\alpha$, $\alpha > 1$, $\rho < 1$ and $C \equiv 0$, then, as $x \to \infty$,*

$$\mathbb{P}[T^d > x] \sim \frac{1}{1/\lambda - \mathbb{E}[B]} \int_x^\infty \mathbb{P}[B > u]du \sim \frac{1}{(1/\lambda - \mathbb{E}[B])(\alpha - 1)} \frac{l(x)}{x^{\alpha-1}},$$

where $T^d \stackrel{d}{=} T_i^d$ for all i.

When $\mathbb{E}[C] > 0$, we can derive the following result.

Theorem 1. *If $B \in \mathcal{R}_\alpha$, $\alpha > 1$, $\rho < 1$ and $\lambda(\mathbb{E}[B] + \mathbb{E}\left[\lceil R/r \rceil \max_{1\le j\le r} C_0^j\right]) < 1$, then, as $x \to \infty$,*

$$\frac{1}{1/\lambda - \mathbb{E}[B]} \le \lim_{x\to\infty} \mathbb{P}[T^d > x] \left(\int_x^\infty \mathbb{P}[B > u]du \right)^{-1} \le \frac{1}{1/\lambda - \mathbb{E}[B] - \mathbb{E}\left[\lceil R/r \rceil \max_{1\le j\le r} C_0^j\right]}.$$

Proof. Setting $C \equiv 0$ gives a lower bound to $\mathbb{P}[T^d > x]$, which is directly implied by Proposition 1. The upper bound can be derived by requiring that at most one job shall be served in the system and when a job is in service all other jobs have to wait. This requirement yields another FIFO queue, with new service time of job i no more than $B_i + \sum_{k=1}^{\lceil R_i/r \rceil} \max_{(k-1)r+1\le j\le kr} C_i^j$, where $\lceil R_i/r \rceil$ represents the number of reduce waves of job i. Applying Proposition 1 yields the upper bound. □

2.2.2 Fair and Coupling schedulers

The default FIFO Scheduler may not work well since a long job can exclusively take the computing resource on the cluster, and cause large delays for other jobs. This is the exact reason why schedulers that can share the resource among multiple jobs have been designed. These types of schedulers have complicated dependence between map and reduce phases due to sharing activities.

Upon the submission of a new job, its mappers join the map queue and its reducers join the reduce queue, as shown in Fig. 8. Note that the map and reduce queues are not in tandem, since a job needs to claim reduce slots upon arrival. It is because each mapper generates intermediate results that need to be fetched by every reducer. Copying and sorting the intermediate results takes time. Overlapping the map phase and the copy/shuffle phase saves time. A reducer can start its real reduce function only after its whole map service completes. Therefore, the reduce queue is not work-conserving.

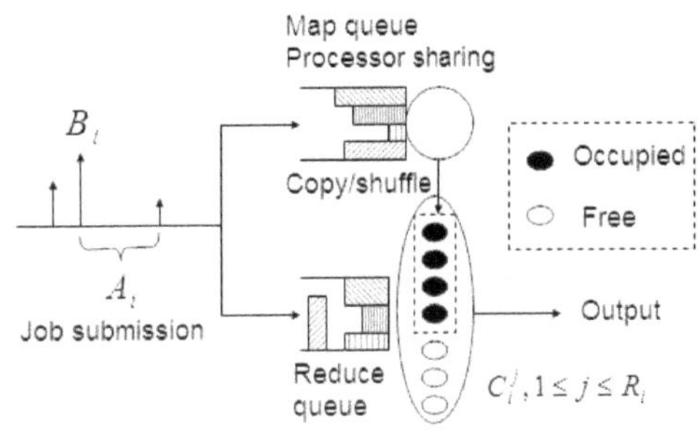

Figure 8: Fair/Coupling Scheduler for MapReduce

We assume that the map queue schedules according to the processor sharing discipline, under which all jobs in map phase are simultaneously in service and each receives the same fraction of service. Denote by $R_i(t)$ the number of running reducers of job i at time t.

- Fair Scheduler: When available reduce slots exist, all of them will be allocated to existing jobs such that the assignments $R_i(t)$ for all i present in the queue are as close as possible with constraints $R_i(t) \le R_i$. When tie breaking is needed, preferences are given according to the order of job arrival times. This scheme is similar to "water filling" (or max-min fairness), as shown in Fig. 9. The black areas represent the running reducers of the four jobs. The available reduce slots, represented by the grey areas, are assigned to job 2, 3, 4.

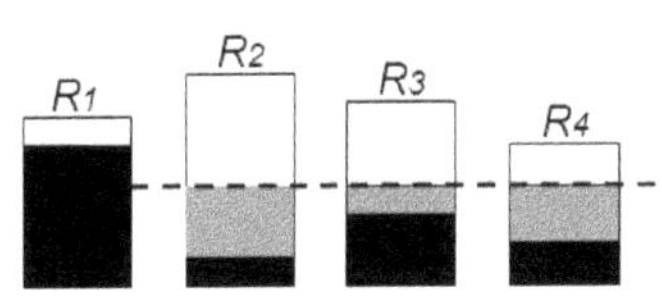

Figure 9: Water filling

- Coupling Scheduler: Let $\phi_i(t) \in [0, 1]$ be the fraction of map service that job i finishes at time t. Define $\bar{R}_i(t) = \lfloor R_i f(\phi_i(t)) \rfloor$. Then, replace R_i by $\bar{R}_i(t)$ (shown in Fig. 9) and conduct the same type of "water filling" as in Fair Scheduler.

When MapReduce jobs do not have the reduce phase, it simply reduces to a M/GI/1 processor sharing queue. The asymptotic insensitivity of the sojourn time distribution for the processor sharing discipline was first derived in the following theorem under some restrictive conditions [15]; see [4, 11] for the result under more general conditions. When in stationarity, $T_i^m \stackrel{d}{=} T^m$ where T_i^m is the processing time of job i. Recall that $\rho \triangleq \lambda\mathbb{E}[B]$.

THEOREM 2. *If $B \in \mathcal{R}_\alpha$, $\alpha > 1$ and $\rho < 1$, then, as $x \to \infty$,*

$$\mathbb{P}[T^m > x] \sim \mathbb{P}[B > (1-\rho)x].$$

With reduce phase, the distinguishing characteristics of map and reduce tasks and the dependence between them yield interesting new analytical results presented in Section 3.

3. MAIN RESULTS

In this section, we first establish the stationarity of the model by explicitly identifying regeneration points. Then, we analyze the tail distribution of the job processing time under Fair and Coupling schedulers, respectively. For the results under FIFO Scheduler see Section 2.2.1.

3.1 Regeneration and stationarity

MapReduce model is close to a two-station tandem queue with some intriguing differences. Though conditions $\rho < 1$ and $\lambda\mathbb{E}[R]\mathbb{E}[C] < r$ ensure that both the map and reduce queue do not blow, they do not directly imply the stationarity of $\{T_i\}_{i>-\infty}$. Identifying the regeneration points in this process allows one to harness the full force of the renewal theory. For example, if the time points when any job sees an empty system upon arrival are positive regenerative, then using the results on positive recurrent regenerative process (e.g., see Theorem 17 on p.112 in [25]), we know the existence of a stationary version of $\{T_i\}_{i>-\infty}$. However, in general these time points may not exist, since the system may be never empty after the start [14].

Regeneration in tandem FIFO queues was first studied in [14], which was generalized to a tandem queue with a multiserver system at each station in [19]. The analysis in [14, 19] relies on constructing a Harris-ergodic Markov chain with i.i.d. service times at each station. In the MapReduce model, the map queue uses processor sharing and the reduce queue is non-work-conserving with complicated task assignments. Therefore, we give a direct proof of the stationarity under the more restrictive condition $\rho < 1$ and $\lambda\mathbb{E}[R]\mathbb{E}[C] < r(1-\rho)$. Our initial efforts suggest that the proof is more involved under $\rho < 1$ and $\lambda\mathbb{E}[R]\mathbb{E}[C] < r$.

THEOREM 3. *If $\rho < 1$ and $\lambda\mathbb{E}[R]\mathbb{E}[C] < r(1-\rho)$, then the time points when any job sees an empty system upon arrival are positive regenerative, and $\{T_i\}_{i>-\infty}$ can reach stationarity, with $T_i^f \stackrel{d}{=} T^f$ and $T_i^c \stackrel{d}{=} T^c$ for all i.*

PROOF. Let $\{P_i\}$ and $\{I_i\}$ be the sequences of busy and idle periods of the map queue. For Poisson arrivals, the condition $\rho < 1$ ensures that $\mathbb{E}[P_i] < \infty$ [25]. Additionally, I_i are i.i.d. exponential random variables, which are independent from the i.i.d. busy periods P_i. Let N_i be the number of jobs that arrive to the system in the busy period P_i and V_i the workload added to the reduce queue during the busy period P_i. Then, $N_i \stackrel{d}{=} N$ and

$$V_i \stackrel{d}{=} \sum_{k=1}^{N_i}\sum_{j=1}^{R_k} C_k^j. \qquad (2)$$

Our proof relies on constructing a new system, where all reduce tasks can only be processed in the idle periods $\{I_i\}$, as illustrated in Fig. 10. An important feature of the reduce

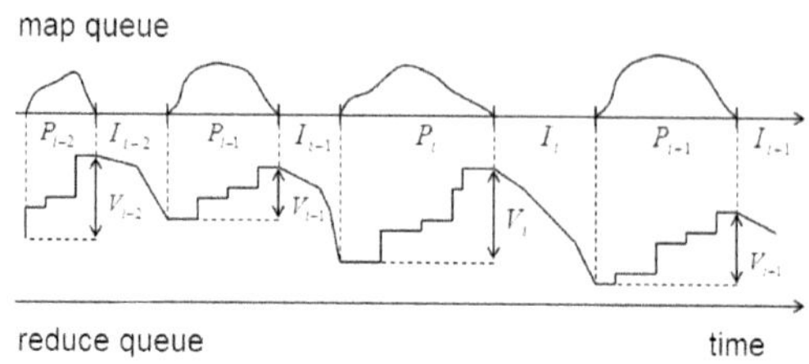

Figure 10: Construct a new system

queue under both Fair and Coupling schedulers is that it is impossible to have a pending reduce task and an idle reduce slot simultaneously in the new system, which can happen in the original system though. Because C_i^j are i.i.d., though the order of serving reduce tasks changes under different schedulers, the stochastic behavior is the same as a FIFO queue. Furthermore, we assume that all of the reduce tasks arriving in busy period P_i will be assigned to the same server in the reduce queue. Thus, if taking all the busy periods P_i away and concatenating the idle periods I_i, we obtain a GI/GI/r queue for the reduce queue, with i.i.d. inter-arrival times I_i and i.i.d. service requirements $V \stackrel{d}{=} V_i$.

It is clear that the workload of the map queue is identical in the two systems. However, the total workload in the reduce queue of the newly constructed system is always no less than that of the original system in the stochastic ordering under the i.i.d. assumption on C_i^j; see Equation (9) in [24]. Here we emphasize that the constructed system only provides an upper bound in the stochastic ordering and it does not necessarily hold pathwise [24]. Because of this property, if the time points when any job sees an empty system upon arrival in the new system are positive regenerative, the original system is also positive regenerative. Therefore, we only need to prove the regeneration for the new system.

Applying $\mathbb{E}[N_i] = 1/(1-\rho)$ and Wald's identity to (2) yields $\lambda\mathbb{E}[V_i] < r$, which, in conjunction with $\mathbb{P}[I_i > V_i] > 0$, ensures that the total workload in the reduce queue reaches zero infinitely often with a finite expected time between two consecutive visits to an empty state [22]. Using Theorems 17 and 20 of Chapter 2 in [25] and noting that the renewal cycle is nonlattice, we prove the theorem. □

3.2 Fair Scheduler

This section focuses on Fair Scheduler. We first study the criticality phenomena in Section 3.2.1 for general C. Then, we derive the exact asymptotic result for the delays in Section 3.2.2 under the restrictive condition $C \equiv 0$; see Remark 1 on this condition.

3.2.1 Criticality phenomena

We derive the logarithmic asymptotic results for studying the criticality phenomena in the following theorem. Recall that r is the total number of reduce slots in the cluster.

THEOREM 4. *When the system is stationary with $B \in \mathcal{R}_\alpha, \alpha > 1$and $\lambda\mathbb{E}[R]\mathbb{E}[C] < r$, $\rho < 1$, we obtain:*

1. *If $\mathbb{P}[R > r - \lambda\mathbb{E}[R]\mathbb{E}[C]] > 0$, then*

$$\lim_{x\to\infty} \frac{\log \mathbb{P}\left[T^f > x\right]}{\log x} = -\alpha + 1. \tag{3}$$

2. *If $\mathbb{P}[R < r - \lambda\mathbb{E}[R]\mathbb{E}[C]] = 1$ and $\alpha > 3$, then*

$$\mathbb{P}\left[T^f > x\right] \sim \mathbb{P}[B > (1-\rho)x], \tag{4}$$

implying

$$\lim_{x\to\infty} \frac{\log \mathbb{P}\left[T^f > x\right]}{\log x} = -\alpha.$$

3. *If $1 < \alpha \le k^*/(k^*-1)$, $k^* \ge 2$ and $\mathbb{P}[r/(k^*-1) > R \ge r/k^*] = 1$, $C \equiv 0$, then*

$$\lim_{x\to\infty} \frac{\log \mathbb{P}\left[T^f > x\right]}{\log x} = -k^*(\alpha - 1). \tag{5}$$

Remark 2. After slightly modifying the proof of (4), we can prove the same result under the more relaxed condition $\mathbb{P}[R < r - \lambda\mathbb{E}[R]\mathbb{E}[C]] = 1$ and $\alpha > (3+\sqrt{5})/2$ or $\mathbb{P}[R < (r - \lambda\mathbb{E}[R]\mathbb{E}[C])(\alpha-2)/(\alpha-1)] = 1$ and $\alpha > 2$. Since the proof is not as clean as the case for $\alpha > 3$ and the space is limited, we only present the current one.

Remark 3. A careful investigation of the proof reveals the large delay of a job under consideration in (3) is resultant from that this job is blocked by a long job that has already arrived at the system earlier. In addition, the number of reduce slots held by this long job is larger than the critical value $r - \lambda\mathbb{E}[R]\mathbb{E}[C]$, thus the number of remaining available reduce slots is less than $\lambda\mathbb{E}[R]\mathbb{E}[C]$. Under this condition the reduce queue is unstable and will keep growing until this long job completes. Therefore, the reduce queue is blocked by the long job, which causes the starvation problem discussed in the introduction. Thus, approximately the processing time T^f is of the order of the residual map service time B^e, which is defined by

$$\mathbb{P}[B^e > x] \triangleq \int_x^\infty \frac{\mathbb{P}[B > u]}{\mathbb{E}[B]} du, x \ge 0. \tag{6}$$

When B is regularly varying with index $-\alpha$, B^e is regularly varying with index $-\alpha+1$, which implies (3). The exact asymptotic of T^f is derived in Theorem 5. On the other hand, when the number of reduce slots required by each job is strictly smaller than the critical value $r - \lambda\mathbb{E}[R]\mathbb{E}[C]$, the reduce queue will not be blocked under the technical condition $\alpha > 3$, and the long delay of a job is caused by the fact that this job itself is long. Due to processor sharing of the map queue, we know (4) by Proposition 1.

To prove the theorem, we need the following two lemmas.

LEMMA 1. *If the system is stationary with $\lambda\mathbb{E}[R]\mathbb{E}[C] < r$, $\rho < 1$, $\mathbb{E}[e^{\theta C}] < \infty$, $\mathbb{E}[e^{\theta R}] < \infty$ for some $\theta > 0$, then, the total workload W_0^r in the reduce queue observed by job 0 satisfies that for any $\epsilon > 0$ there exists $h > 0$,*

$$\mathbb{P}[W_0^r > x] \le h/x^{\alpha-1-\epsilon}. \tag{7}$$

LEMMA 2. *If the map queue has k permanent jobs with infinite map service requirements and job i has a map service $B_i \wedge (\epsilon x)$ for $i \ge -\tau$ and 0 for $i < -\tau$, $\tau > 0$, where $y \wedge z \triangleq \min\{y, z\}$, then, the residual busy period $P_0^{(r,\epsilon x)}$ in the map queue when it has at least $k+1$ jobs and the total workload $W_0^{(r,\epsilon x)}$ in the reduce queue observed by job 0 for all jobs excluding the k permanent ones satisfy that, for any $\beta > 0$ there exists $\epsilon > 0$ such that*

$$\mathbb{P}[P_0^{(r,\epsilon x)} + W_0^{(r,\epsilon x)} > x] = O\left(1/x^\beta\right). \tag{8}$$

PROOF OF LEMMA 1. Our proof is based on constructing a new system that is similar to the one in Fig. 10 in the proof of Theorem 3. The difference is that the reduce queue can still work during the idle periods I_i after postponing the processing of the reduce tasks of a job to the end of the busy period of the map queue that contains the submission time of this job. That is why we only need the condition $\lambda\mathbb{E}[R]\mathbb{E}[C] < r$. In addition, we assign successive workloads V_i cyclically to the r servers, where workloads V_{kr+j} are assigned to server $j, 1 \le j \le r$. Recall that all the tasks belong to the workload V_i will be assigned to the same server. In this construction the map service of any job completes before its reduce tasks start. By the same approach as in [24], we can prove that the new task assignment increases the total workload in the stochastic ordering compared to the original queue (see Equation (9) in [24]).

In the original system, denote by P_0 the busy period that contains the submission time of job 0, and by W_{-1}^b the reduce workload observed immediately after the end of the busy period P_{-1}. In addition, denote by $P_0^{(e)}$ the elapsed time between the beginning of the busy period P_0 and the time when job 0 is submitted. Correspondingly, we let $W_0^{(e)}$ be the total workload added to the reduce queue and $N_0^{(e)}$ the number of jobs submitted during $P_0^{(e)}$. Therefore, we obtain

$$W_0^r \le W_{-1}^b + W_0^{(e)}. \tag{9}$$

First we study W_{-1}^b. Let $C([0,t])$ be the number of Poisson arrivals on interval $[0,t]$. Observe

$$\begin{aligned}\mathbb{P}[N_i > x] &\le \mathbb{P}[N_i > x, P_i > (1-\epsilon)x/\lambda] + \\ &\qquad \mathbb{P}[N_i > x, P_i \le (1-\epsilon)x/\lambda] \\ &\le \mathbb{P}[P_i > (1-\epsilon)x/\lambda] + \\ &\qquad \mathbb{P}\left[C([0,(1-\epsilon)x/\lambda] > x\right], \end{aligned} \tag{10}$$

which, noting that $P_i \in \mathcal{R}_\alpha$ [28] and $\mathbb{P}[C([0,(1-\epsilon)x/\lambda] > x] < he^{-\delta x}$ for some h, δ, implies $\mathbb{P}[N > x] \lesssim 1/x^{\alpha-\epsilon}$ for any $\epsilon > 0$. This result shows, by (2) and conditions $\mathbb{E}[e^{\theta C}] < \infty$, $\mathbb{E}[e^{\theta R}] < \infty$,

$$\mathbb{P}[V > x] \lesssim 1/x^{\alpha-\epsilon}. \tag{11}$$

In the new system, if we observe at the ends of the busy periods $\{P_i\}$, each of the r servers of the reduce queue forms a GI/G/1 FIFO queue with arrival interval equal in distribution to $\sum_{k=1}^r (I_k + P_{k+1})$ due to cyclic job assignments and i.i.d. service requirements equal in distribution to V. Now, using the classic result by A. Pakes [16] (see Proposition 1), we can prove that for any $\epsilon > 0$ there exists $h > 0$ such that the workloads $W_1(-1), W_2(-1), \cdots, W_r(-1)$ observed on the r servers of the reduce queue immediately after the end of the busy period P_{-1} satisfy

$$\mathbb{P}[W_j(-1) > x] \le h_1/x^{\alpha-1-\epsilon},$$

for all $1 \le j \le r$ and some $h_1 > 0$, which, by noting that $\mathbb{P}[W_{-1}^b > x] \le \sum_{j=1}^{r} \mathbb{P}[W_j(-1) > x/r]$, proves

$$\mathbb{P}[W_{-1}^b > x] \le h_2/x^{\alpha-1-\epsilon}, \quad \text{for some } h_2 > 0. \tag{12}$$

Under (1), it has been shown that, e.g., by Lemma 3.3 in [11], for any $\epsilon > 0$ there exists $h > 0$ such that

$$\mathbb{P}[P_0^{(e)} > x] \le h/x^{\alpha-1-\epsilon}. \tag{13}$$

This result, by noting that $W_0^{(e)} \stackrel{d}{=} \sum_{k=1}^{N_0^{(e)}} \sum_{j=1}^{R_k} C_k^j$ where $\sum_{j=1}^{R_k} C_k^j$ is light-tailed and applying the same arguments in (10) and (11), implies

$$\mathbb{P}[W_0^{(e)} > x] \le h_2/x^{\alpha-1-\epsilon}, \quad \text{for some } h_2 > 0. \tag{14}$$

Combining (9), (12) and (14) finishes the proof of (7). □

Proof of Lemma 2. We only need to prove the result when the system is in stationarity with $\tau \to \infty$, since $W_0^{(r,\epsilon x)}$ and $P_0^{(r,\epsilon x)}$ increase as τ increases [13]; see the arguments below. First, we construct a new map queue (called A) using a similar approach as in the proof of Lemma 3.3 in [11]. It is fed by two processes: (1) the arrivals of the original M/GI/1 queue with k permanent jobs, and (2) a fluid process of a constant rate ϵ, $0 < \epsilon < (1-\rho)/(k+1)$. The second process is served with rate 1 only when the first process does not have any other map service except the k permanent ones; otherwise the second process receives no service. Let W_2 be the stationary workload of the second process and W be the total workload excluding the k permanent jobs in the newly constructed map queue seen by job 0. Clearly, $W_2 \le W$.

Next, for the input processes of queue A, we run a second map queue (called B) simultaneously by allocating $(k+1)\epsilon$ capacity to serve the second process and the remaining $1-(k+1)\epsilon$ capacity to serve the first process. Let $N_A(t)$ and $N_B(t)$ be the number of map services excluding the k permanent ones running in queue A and B at time t, respectively. We show that this new scheme yields an upper bound to W.

This can be proved by checking: 1) if a map service is still working in queue A, then it is also unfinished in queue B, implying $N_A(t) \le N_B(t)$; 2) at any time the workload in queue B for all the jobs present in queue A excluding the k permanent ones is processed with a rate $\mu_B(t)$ no larger than the rate $\mu_A(t)$ of queue A. The result is immediate when $N_A(t) = 0$. Assuming $N_B(t) \ge N_A(t) \ge 1$ for all $t \le t_0$, we obtain, due to processor sharing, $\mu_A(t) = N_A(t)/(N_A(t)+k)$. In the meanwhile $\mu_B(t) = (1-(k+1)\epsilon)N_A(t)/(N_B(t)+k)+\epsilon$. Since $x/(x+k)$ is increasing for $x > 0$, we obtain $\mu_B(t) \le \mu_A(t)$. Using induction proves the result for all t.

Thus,

$$\mathbb{P}[W_2] \le \mathbb{P}[W > x] \le \mathbb{P}[W_{B\wedge\epsilon x}^{1-(k+1)\epsilon} > x], \tag{15}$$

where $W_{B\wedge\epsilon x}^{1-(k+1)\epsilon}$ is the stationary workload in queue B. Using the insensitivity result in [26], we obtain that

$$W_{B\wedge\epsilon x}^{1-(k+1)\epsilon} = \sum_{i=1}^{N} (B_i \wedge \epsilon x)^{(e)}, \tag{16}$$

where $(B_i \wedge \epsilon x)^{(e)}$ is the residual of $B_i \wedge \epsilon x$ and $\mathbb{P}[N = n] = \left(\prod_{l=1}^{k}(n+l)/l\right)\rho^n / \sum_{i=0}^{\infty}\left(\prod_{l=1}^{k}(i+l)/l\right)\rho^i$. Using (16) and repeating the arguments in the proof of Lemma 3.2 in [11] (essentially it only needs N to be light-tailed), we can prove that, for any $\beta > 0$ there exists $\epsilon > 0$ such that

$$\mathbb{P}[W_{B\wedge\epsilon x}^{1-(k+1)\epsilon} > x] = O\left(1/x^{\beta}\right). \tag{17}$$

Now, note that the workload of the second process in queue A is exactly that of the fluid queue with an On-Off server. The Off periods correspond to the busy periods of the first process in queue A. Therefore,

$$\mathbb{P}[W_2 > x] \ge \mathbb{P}[N \ge 1]\mathbb{P}\left[P^{(e,\epsilon x)} > x/\epsilon\right], \tag{18}$$

which, in conjunction with (15), (16) and (17), proves

$$\mathbb{P}[P_0^{(r,\epsilon x)} > x] = O\left(1/x^{\beta}\right). \tag{19}$$

Using the preceding result and repeating the arguments for (9) proves $\mathbb{P}[W_0^{(r,\epsilon x)} > x] = O\left(1/x^{\beta}\right)$, which, in conjunction with (19), finishes the proof of (8). □

Proof of Theorem 4. For Poisson arrivals, we can assume that job 0 arrives at time 0, with map service time B_0, reducer number R_0 and processing times C_0^j. In addition, we can also assume that job 0 arrives in the busy period P_0 of the map queue with $P_0^{(r)}$ denoting the residual time. The total workload in the reduce queue observed by job 0 is W_0^r.

I) We begin with proving (3) for Fair Scheduler. First, we prove the upper bound. Notice that though the reduce queue is not FIFO, due to the water filling characteristics of the scheme (see Section 2.2.2), at least one unfinished reducer from a running job that arrives earlier is assigned with a higher priority at any time for all jobs. Therefore, the total processing time T_0 of job 0 has an upper bound

$$T_0 \le P_0^{(r)} + W_0^r + \sum_{j=1}^{R_0} C_0^j, \tag{20}$$

since its map service completes before $P_0^{(r)}$ and its reducers take time less than $W_0^r + \sum_{j=1}^{R_0} C_0^j$. This result, using Lemma 3.3 in [11], Lemma 1, conditions $\mathbb{E}[e^{\theta C_0}] < \infty$, $\mathbb{E}[e^{\theta R_0}] < \infty$, and passing $\epsilon \to 0$, implies that

$$\overline{\lim_{x\to\infty}} \frac{\log \mathbb{P}[T_0 > x]}{\log x} \le -\alpha + 1. \tag{21}$$

Next, we prove the lower bound for (3). For $x > 0$ and $H_1 > H_2 > 0$, we consider the map service times $B_{-i}, \lceil H_2 x\rceil + 1 \le i \le \lfloor H_1 x \rfloor$ that arrives before time 0. Let $\mathcal{A}_{-i}$ be the event that job $-i$ arrives to the system and finds that the system is empty. Furthermore, we denote by X_i the time between the arrival point of job $-i$ and 0.

If job $-i$ finds the system empty upon arrival and $R_{-i} \ge r^* \triangleq r - \lambda\mathbb{E}[R]\mathbb{E}[C] + \epsilon$, $\epsilon > 0$, then job $-i$ can immediately take the required reduce slots due to the greedy approach of Fair Scheduler. Thus, the number of remaining reduce slots is less than $\lambda\mathbb{E}[R]\mathbb{E}[C] - \epsilon$. Note that $\mathbb{P}[R > r^*] > 0$ since R only takes integer values and $\mathbb{P}\left[R > r - \lambda\mathbb{E}[R]\mathbb{E}[C]\right] > 0$.

More importantly, if $B_{-i} > x + X_i, x \ge 0$, then, even dedicating the whole map service capacity to job $-i$, when job 0 arrives, the remaining service time of job $-i$ is at least x. In addition, before job $-i$ finishes, the available reduce slots is less than $\lambda\mathbb{E}[R]\mathbb{E}[C] - \epsilon$. Recall that the reduce queue is not work conserving and has r servers. If we combine all the r servers into one big server which is r times faster, the workload in the reduce queue can be only smaller. Now, even when the total workload of the reduce tasks from all jobs other than job $-i$ are combined and served by the big server, the reduce queue still grows with a positive drift larger than $\epsilon > 0$, since it satisfies $\lambda\mathbb{E}[R]\mathbb{E}[C] - (r - R_{-i}) > \epsilon$.

Using Loynes's scheme [13], we obtain that the reduce workload $W_r(-i)$ excluding that of job $-i$ seen by job 0 satisfies

$$\mathbb{P}[W_r(-i) \leq i(1-\epsilon)\epsilon/\lambda, R_{-i} > r^*]$$
$$\leq \mathbb{P}\left[\sum_{k=1}^{i-1}\left(\lambda \sum_{j=1}^{R_{-k}} C^j_{-k} - (r - r^*)\lambda A_{-k+1}\right)\right.$$
$$\left.\leq (i-1)(1-\epsilon)\epsilon\right] \times \mathbb{P}[R_{-i} > r^*],$$

which, by Chernoff bound, implies $\mathbb{P}[W_r(-i) \leq (i-1)(1-\epsilon)\epsilon/\lambda, R_{-i} > r^*] \leq h_3 e^{-\delta_3 i}$, for some $h_3, \delta_3 > 0$. Since $i > \lceil H_2 x \rceil + 1$, choosing $H_2 > k\lambda/((1-\epsilon)\epsilon)$ with $k > 0$ yields $\mathbb{P}[W_r(-i) \leq kx, R_{-i} > r^*] \leq h_3 e^{-\delta_3 x}$. Because of the multiple servers and the water filling scheme, only part of the workload from $W_r(-i)$ will be assigned on the same server as that of job 0 which need to finish before job 0; let it be $V_r(-i)$. Using the "essential lemma" (Lemma 2) in [13] that bounds the workload differences between multiple servers, and the arguments similar to (10) to characterize the number of reducers that have higher priorities than those of job 0, we can prove, for some $h, \delta > 0$, by choosing k large enough,

$$\mathbb{P}[V_r(-i) \leq x, R_{-i} > r^*] \leq he^{-\delta x}. \quad (22)$$

Furthermore, the preceding arguments imply

$$\bigcup_{i=\lceil H_2 x\rceil+1}^{\lfloor H_1 x \rfloor} \{\{B_{-i} > X_i + x, R_{-i} > r^*, V_r(-i) > x\} \cap \mathcal{A}_{-i}\}$$
$$\subseteq \{T_0 > x\}. \quad (23)$$

Now we show that these events

$$\{B_{-i} > X_i + x, R_{-i} > r^*, V_r(-i) > x\} \cap \mathcal{A}_{-i}, \quad (24)$$

where $\lceil H_2 x \rceil + 1 \leq i \leq \lfloor H_1 x \rfloor$, are disjoint. If not, then there exist $\lceil H_2 x\rceil + 1 \leq i < j \leq \lfloor H_1 x \rfloor$ such that both $\{B_{-i} > X_i + x, R_{-i} > r^*, W_r(-i) > x\} \cap \mathcal{A}_{-i}$ and $\{B_{-j} > X_j + x, R_{-j} > r^*, W_r(-j) > x\} \cap \mathcal{A}_{-j}$ occur. However, notice that job $-i$ will not finish before time 0, and thus $\mathcal{A}_j$ can not happen, which contradicts the assumption.

Based on (23) and the preceding arguments, we obtain

$$\mathbb{P}[T_0 > x] \geq$$
$$\sum_{i=\lceil H_2 x\rceil+1}^{\lfloor H_1 x \rfloor} \mathbb{P}[\{B_{-i} > X_i + x, R_{-i} > r^*, V_r(-i) > x\} \cap \mathcal{A}_{-i}]$$
$$= \sum_{i=\lceil H_2 x\rceil+1}^{\lfloor H_1 x \rfloor} (\mathbb{P}[B_{-i} > X_i + x] \, \mathbb{P}[R_{-i} > r^*]$$
$$- \mathbb{P}[V_r(-i) \leq x, R_{-i} > r^*]) \times \mathbb{P}[\mathcal{A}_{-i}], \quad (25)$$

where the last equality uses the independence assumption.

In addition, we can lower bound $\mathbb{P}[B_{-i} > X_i + x]$ by

$$\mathbb{P}[B_{-i} > i(1+\epsilon)\mathbb{E}[X_1] + x] - \mathbb{P}[X_i > i(1+\epsilon)\mathbb{E}[X_1]] \quad (26)$$

where, by Chernoff bound, we obtain $\mathbb{P}[X_i > i(1+\epsilon)\mathbb{E}[X_1]] < h_4 e^{-\delta_4 i}$ for some $h_4, \delta_4 > 0$ with $\lceil H_2 x \rceil + 1 \leq i \leq \lfloor H_1 x \rfloor$.

Theorem 3 implies $\mathbb{P}[\mathcal{A}_{-i}] > 0$, which, in conjunction with (25), $\mathbb{P}[R_{-i} > r^*] > 0$ and recalling (22), (26), yields that, for some $h, H > 0$, $\mathbb{P}[T_0 > x]$ is lower bounded by

$$h \sum_{i=\lceil H_2 x\rceil+1}^{\lfloor H_1 x \rfloor} \mathbb{P}[B_{-i} > i(1+\epsilon)\mathbb{E}[X_1] + x] - xHe^{-\delta x}$$
$$\geq h \int_{\lceil H_2 x \rceil + 2}^{\lfloor H_1 x \rfloor} \mathbb{P}[B_{-i} > u(1+\epsilon)/\lambda + x] \, du - xHe^{-\delta x}.$$

By properties of regularly varying functions [3], the preceding inequality implies the lower bound

$$\lim_{x \to \infty} \frac{\log \mathbb{P}[T^f > x]}{\log x} \geq -\alpha + 1. \quad (27)$$

Combining (21) and (27) finishes the proof of (3).

II) Now we prove (4). Let T_0^m be the total processing time of the map service of job 0. By Theorem 2, we obtain

$$\mathbb{P}[T_0^m > x] \sim \mathbb{P}[B_0 > (1-\rho)x], \quad (28)$$

which, noting that $T_0 \geq T_0^m$, proves the lower bound.

Next, we focus on the upper bound. For $x > 0$, $H > 0$ and $0 < \epsilon < \alpha - 1$, we consider the map service times $B_{-i}, 1 \leq i \leq \lfloor x^{1+\eta} \rfloor$, $\eta > 0$ that arrives before time 0. Since $R < r - \lambda\mathbb{E}[R]\mathbb{E}[C]$ almost surely and R only takes integer values, there exists $\epsilon > 0$ such that $\mathbb{P}[R \leq r^*] = 1$ where $r^* \triangleq \lfloor r - \lambda\mathbb{E}[R]\mathbb{E}[C] - \epsilon \rfloor$. Before job $-\lfloor x^{1+\eta} \rfloor$ arrives, we only use $r - r^*$ number of reduce slots to serve all the jobs. Let $W^{r-r^*}_{-\lfloor x^{1+\eta} \rfloor}$ be the total workload and $P^{(r)}_{-\lfloor x^{1+\eta} \rfloor}$ the residual time of the busy period observed by job $-\lfloor x^{1+\eta} \rfloor$ upon arrival in this new map queue. Since $\lambda\mathbb{E}[R]\mathbb{E}[C] < r - r^*$, by Lemma 1, we have

$$\mathbb{P}\left[W^{r-r^*}_{-\lfloor x^{1+\eta} \rfloor} > x\right] \leq \frac{h}{x^{\alpha-1-\epsilon}}. \quad (29)$$

Let $W^P_{-\lfloor x^{1+\eta} \rfloor}$ be the workload injected into the reduce queue during $P^{(r)}_{-\lfloor x^{1+\eta} \rfloor}$. Using the arguments for (11) and (13), (29), we obtain, for $W^\circ_\epsilon \triangleq W^{r-r^*}_{-\lfloor x^{1+\eta} \rfloor} + W^P_{-\lfloor x^{1+\eta} \rfloor} + \epsilon P^{(r)}_{-\lfloor x^{1+\eta} \rfloor}$,

$$\mathbb{P}[W^\circ_\epsilon > x] = O\left(1/x^{\alpha-1-\epsilon}\right). \quad (30)$$

Define $N_x = \sum_{i=1}^{\lfloor x^{1+\eta} \rfloor} \mathbf{1}\{B_{-i} > \epsilon x\}$. Thus, for $\delta > 0$, we obtain, using a union bound,

$$\mathbb{P}[T_0 > x] \leq \mathbb{P}\left[T_0 > x, W^\circ_\epsilon \leq x^{1+\delta}, N_x \leq 1\right]$$
$$+ \mathbb{P}[W^\circ_\epsilon > x^{1+\delta}] + \mathbb{P}[N_x \geq 2]$$
$$\triangleq P_1 + P_2 + P_3. \quad (31)$$

Choosing $\delta = (1+2\epsilon)/(\alpha - 1 - \epsilon)$ in (30) yields

$$P_2 = \mathbb{P}\left[W^\circ_\epsilon > x^{1+\delta}\right] = O\left(1/x^{\alpha+\epsilon}\right). \quad (32)$$

For $0 < \epsilon < (\alpha-2)/3$ and $\eta = (\alpha - 2 - 3\epsilon)/2$, we have

$$P_3 \leq \binom{x^{1+\eta}}{2} (\mathbb{P}[B > \epsilon x])^2 = O\left(1/x^{\alpha+\epsilon}\right). \quad (33)$$

Next we study P_1. Since $N_x \leq 1$, there is at most one job whose map service is larger than ϵx after job $-\lfloor x^{1+\eta} \rfloor$ arrives and before time 0. We use the reserved r^* reduce slots to serve the reduce tasks of the job whose map service is larger than ϵx; note that it can not claim more than r^*

number of reduce slots. The remaining $r - r^*$ reduce slots only serve the workload $W^{r-r^*}_{-\lfloor x^{1+\eta}\rfloor}$ and the reduce tasks of the jobs $B_i \mathbf{1}\{B_i \leq \epsilon x\}$, $-\lfloor x^{1+\delta}\rfloor \leq i \leq -1$.

Since $\lambda\mathbb{E}[R]\mathbb{E}[C] < r - r^*$, there exists $\epsilon > 0$ such that $\lambda\mathbb{E}[R]\mathbb{E}[C] < (r - r^*)(1-\epsilon)$. We can allocate ϵ fraction of capacity on one reduce server to process the workload $W^{r}_{-\lfloor x^{1+\eta}\rfloor}$ and only use the remaining capacity $1-\epsilon$ on each of the $r - r^*$ reduce servers to process the reduce tasks of job i, $-\lfloor x^{1+\eta}\rfloor \leq i \leq -1$. After time 0 we assign workloads $V_i, i \geq 0$ cyclically to the $r - r^*$ servers with all the tasks belong to V_i being assigned to the same server after being postponed to the end of P_i. Using the same arguments in the proof of Lemma 1, we know that the new task assignment gives an upper bound to W_0^r in the stochastic ordering.

Due to starvation, the processing of $W^{r-r^*}_{-\lfloor x^{1+\eta}\rfloor}$ can be delayed but no longer than time $P^{(r)}_{-\lfloor x^{1+\eta}\rfloor}$. In the newly constructed system, the workload $W^{r-r^*}_{-\lfloor x^{1+\eta}\rfloor}$ will complete before time 0 if $W^{r-r^*}_{-\lfloor x^{1+\eta}\rfloor} + W^P < \epsilon\left(X_{\lfloor x^{1+\eta}\rfloor} - P^{(r)}_{-\lfloor x^{1+\eta}\rfloor}\right)$ (equivalently, $W^\circ_\epsilon < \epsilon X_{\lfloor x^{1+\eta}\rfloor}$), where $X_{\lfloor x^{1+\eta}\rfloor}$ is the time between the arrival point of job $-\lfloor x^{1+\eta}\rfloor$ and 0. When $\alpha > 3$, we can prove that $x^{1+\delta} = o\left(x^{1+\eta}\right)$ for ϵ small enough, implying, for some $h, \delta_h > 0$,

$$\mathbb{P}\left[\epsilon X_{\lfloor x^{1+\eta}\rfloor} \leq x^{1+\delta}\right] \leq h e^{-\delta_h x}. \tag{34}$$

The last inequality holds because $X_{\lfloor x^{1+\eta}\rfloor} \stackrel{d}{=} \sum_{i=1}^{\lfloor x^{1+\eta}\rfloor} Y_i$ where Y_i are i.i.d. exponential random variables with parameter λ. If $N_x \leq 1$, let $\tilde{P}_0^{(r)}$ be the residual time of the busy period for all jobs excluding job 0 and the one whose map service is larger than ϵx as well as the k permanent ones in the map queue observed by job 0. The arguments before (20) yield

$$T_0 \leq T_0^m + \tilde{P}_0^{(r)} + W_0^r + \sum_{j=1}^{R_0} C_0^j. \tag{35}$$

When $N_x \leq 1$ and $W^\circ_\epsilon < \epsilon X_{\lfloor x^{1+\eta}\rfloor}$, applying Lemma 2 with $k = 2$ (treating job 0 and the one whose map service is larger than ϵx as two permanent jobs) and $\tau = \lfloor x^{1+\eta}\rfloor$, we obtain that, for any $\beta > 0$, there exists $\epsilon > 0$ such that

$$\mathbb{P}[\tilde{P}_0^{(r)} + W_0^r > x] = O\left(1/x^\beta\right). \tag{36}$$

Observe

$$P_1 \leq \mathbb{P}\left[T_0 > x, W^\circ_\epsilon \leq x^{1+\delta} < \epsilon X_{\lfloor x^{1+\eta}\rfloor}, N_x \leq 1\right] + \mathbb{P}[\epsilon X_{\lfloor x^{1+\eta}\rfloor} \leq x^{1+\delta}],$$

which, in conjunction with (31), (32), (33), (34), (35) (36) and passing $\epsilon \to 0$, finishes the proof of (4).

III) Last we prove (5). For the map queue, it is known [25] that, due to processor sharing, the number N_0 of unfinished map services in the system immediately before time 0 satisfies $\mathbb{P}[N_0 \geq n] = \rho^n$. Furthermore, given $N_0 = n$, the remaining service times B^e_{-i} of the ith job observed immediately before time 0 are i.i.d. with $B^e_{-i} \stackrel{d}{=} B^e$. Denote by $\tilde{B}^{k,n}$ the kth largest value in $\{B^e_{-i}\}_{1\leq i\leq n}$ with $\tilde{B}^{k,n} = 0$ for $k > n$ and $\tilde{T}^{k,n}$ its remaining processing time after 0. If there are exactly k^* jobs in the system observed by job 0 then all the reduce slots will be taken by these jobs since $\mathbb{P}[r/(k^*-1) > R \geq r/k^*] = 1$. Therefore, for any $\epsilon > 0$ there exists $h > 0$ such that $\mathbb{P}[T_0^f > x]$ is lower bounded by

$$\mathbb{P}\left[N_0 = k^*, \min_{1\leq i\leq N_0}\{B^e_{-i}\} > x\right] \geq \frac{h}{x^{k^*(\alpha-1+\epsilon)}}. \tag{37}$$

Regarding the upper bound, we observe that, for $H > 0$,

$$\begin{aligned}\mathbb{P}[T_0 > x] &\leq \mathbb{P}\left[T_0 > x, \tilde{B}^{k^*,N_0} > \epsilon x, N_0 \leq H\log x\right]\\ &+ \mathbb{P}\left[T_0 > x, \tilde{T}^{k^*,N_0} \leq x, \tilde{B}^{k^*,N_0} \leq \epsilon x, N_0 \leq H\log x\right]\\ &+ \mathbb{P}\left[\tilde{T}^{k^*,N_0} > x, \tilde{B}^{k^*,N_0} \leq \epsilon x, N_0 \leq H\log x\right]\\ &+ \mathbb{P}[N_0 > H\log x] \triangleq P_1 + P_2 + P_3 + P_4.\end{aligned} \tag{38}$$

Since N_0 follows a geometric distribution and

$$\begin{aligned}P_1 &\leq \mathbb{P}\left[\tilde{B}^{k^*,N_0} > \epsilon x, N_0 \leq H\log x\right]\\ &\leq (H\log x)^{k^*}\left(\mathbb{P}[B^e > \epsilon x]\right)^{k^*},\end{aligned}$$

we obtain, for H and h large enough,

$$P_1 + P_4 \leq h/x^{k^*(\alpha-1-\epsilon)}. \tag{39}$$

For P_2, note $\{T_0 > x, \tilde{T}^{k^*,N_0} \leq x\} \subseteq \{T_0^m > x\}$ when $C \equiv 0$; otherwise if $T_0^m \leq x$ then $T_0 > x$ can not occur when $\tilde{T}^{k^*,N_0} \leq x$. Applying Theorem 2 yields $P_2 = O\left(1/x^{\alpha - k^*\epsilon}\right)$, which, by $\alpha - k^*\epsilon \geq k^*(\alpha - 1 - \epsilon)$, implies

$$P_2 \leq h_\epsilon/x^{k^*(\alpha-1-\epsilon)}. \tag{40}$$

Last we study P_3. Due to processor sharing, we can upper bound $\tilde{T}^{k^*,N_0}$ using the min-plus identify in [11],

$$\tilde{T}^{k^*,N_0} \leq \sum_{i=1}^{N_0}\left(B^e_{-i} \wedge \tilde{B}^{k^*,N_0}\right) + \sum_{i=1}^{N(\tilde{B}^{k^*,N_0})} B_i \wedge \tilde{B}^{k^*,N_0},$$

where $N(\tilde{B}^{k^*,N_0})$ is the number of new jobs arriving to the system during $\left(0, \tilde{T}^{k^*,N_0}\right]$. Thus, for $0 < \delta < 1-\rho$, $0 < \epsilon < 1$ and $\delta_\epsilon \triangleq (1-\rho-\delta)$, P_3 is upper bounded by

$$\begin{aligned}&\mathbb{P}\left[\tilde{T}^{k^*,N_0}(1-\rho-\delta) > \delta_\epsilon x, \tilde{B}^{k^*,N_0} \leq \epsilon x, N_0 \leq H\log x\right]\\ &\leq \mathbb{P}\left[\sum_{i=1}^{N\left(\tilde{T}^{k^*,N_0}\right)} B_i \wedge (\epsilon x) - (\rho+\delta)\tilde{T}^{k^*,N_0} > \frac{\delta_\epsilon x}{2}\right]\\ &\quad + \mathbb{P}\left[\sum_{i=1}^{H\log x} B^e_{-i} \wedge (\epsilon x) > \frac{\delta_\epsilon x}{2}\right].\end{aligned}$$

In addition, for any $\beta > 0$ there exists $\epsilon > 0$ such that $\mathbb{P}\left[\sum_{i=1}^{H\log x} B^e_{-i} \wedge (\epsilon x) > \delta_\epsilon x/2\right] = O\left(1/x^\beta\right)$. Therefore,

$$P_3 \leq \mathbb{P}\left[\sup_{t\geq 0}\left(\sum_{i=1}^{N(t)} B_i \wedge (\epsilon x) - (\rho+\delta)t\right) > \frac{\delta_\epsilon x}{2}\right] + O\left(\frac{1}{x^\beta}\right)$$

which, by Lemma 3.2 in [11], implies, for ϵ small enough,

$$P_3 = O\left(1/x^{k^*(\alpha-1-\epsilon)}\right). \tag{41}$$

Combining (38), (39), (40) and (41) yields the upper bound, which, using (37) and passing $\epsilon \to 0$ proves (5). □

3.2.2 *Exact asymptotic*

The preceding section only derives the logarithmic asymptotics of T^f. The exact asymptotics under general C and R is difficult to obtain since the reduce queue has multiple servers that are not work-conserving and a job has a random number of reduce tasks. However, under the condition $C \equiv 0$ (see Remark 1 for the comments on this condition), we can prove the following asymptotic result. See the technical report for the proof.

THEOREM 5. *If the system is stationary with* $\rho < 1$, $\mathbb{P}[R \geq r] > 0$, $\alpha > 3$ *and* $C \equiv 0$, *then,*

$$\mathbb{P}[T^f > x] \sim \frac{\lambda \mathbb{P}[R \geq r]}{1-\rho} \int_{(1-\rho)x}^{\infty} \mathbb{P}[B > x] dx$$
$$\sim \frac{\lambda \mathbb{P}[R \geq r]}{(\alpha - 1)(1-\rho)^{\alpha}} \frac{l(x)}{x^{\alpha-1}}. \quad (42)$$

Remark 4. This result is contrasted to the one with conditions $\mathbb{P}[R < r] = 1$ and $C \equiv 0$ (a special case of (4)), under which we have

$$\mathbb{P}[T^f > x] \sim \mathbb{P}[B > (1-\rho)x] \sim \frac{1}{(1-\rho)^{\alpha}} \frac{l(x)}{x^{\alpha}}.$$

Now, we provide the intuition behind the result (42). The long delay $T_0 > x$ is caused by a large job that arrives at time $-y$ with a map service larger than $(1-\rho)(x+y)$ and reduce tasks no less than r, as illustrated in Fig. 11. Due to

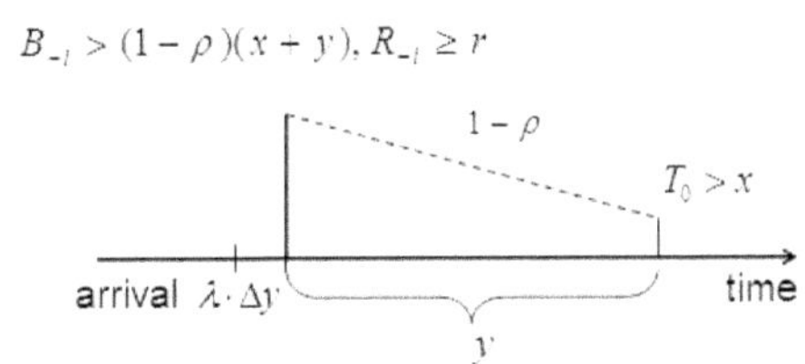

Figure 11: Illustration of one large job

processor sharing, the remaining workload of job $-i$ drains with rate $1-\rho$. Since a job arrives to the system in the interval $(y - \Delta y, y)$ with probability $\lambda \Delta y$, we obtain

$$\mathbb{P}[T_0 > x] \approx \int_0^{\infty} \mathbb{P}[R \geq r] \mathbb{P}[B > (1-\rho)(x+y)] \lambda dy,$$

which yields (42).

3.3 Coupling Scheduler

Coupling Scheduler launches reducers gradually depending on the map task progress according to a functional relationship $y = f(x)$. Thus, it should be viewed as a class of disciplines. For example, $f(x) = \mathbf{1}\{x > \tau\}, \tau \geq 0$ exactly characterizes Fair Scheduler (this paper assumes $\tau = 0$), which is a special case of Coupling Scheduler. In principle, we can investigate the delay tails with Coupling Scheduler for scenarios including both $C \equiv 0$ and $\mathbb{E}[C] > 0$, as studied in Theorem 4.

However, we only state the following result due to the limited space. If $B \in \mathcal{R}_{\alpha}, \alpha > 2$, $\rho < 1$, $C \equiv 0$, $R_i \leq r$ and $f(x) < 1$ for all $0 \leq x < 1$, then, using Coupling Scheduler, we obtain

$$\mathbb{P}[T^c > x] \sim \mathbb{P}[B > (1-\rho)x],$$

which implies $\lim_{x \to \infty} \log \mathbb{P}[T^c > x] / \log x = -\alpha$.

Under the preceding conditions with $\mathbb{P}[R_i = r] > 0$, we can prove $\lim_{x \to \infty} \log \mathbb{P}[T^f > x] / \log x = -(\alpha - 1)$ using Fair Scheduler. This result demonstrates an order gain for Coupling Scheduler under certain conditions. In general, an order gain is not always attainable, but a constant gain is still possible.

4. EXPERIMENTS

We compare the job processing times using both Coupling Scheduler and Fair Scheduler on our test bed with 1 master node and 7 slave nodes. The same sequence of 12 jobs is repeated 5 times, and across the five experiments the job submission times are kept the same. To be fair, the system parameters with these two schedulers are configured identical with 4 map slots and 2 reduce slots per node. For the input files, we download Wikipedia Free Encyclopedia (28G, named WikiInput). In addition, we generate two files (named Random05, Random10) of size 0.5G, 1.0G bytes, respectively, where each line of these two files only contains a randomly generated 10 digit integer, and build two files (named RandomPair1 and RandomPair2 of size 15G and 29G bytes, respectively) using the Hadoop example code RandomWriter.

The trace study on a production MapReduce cluster shows that most of the jobs are map intensive and typical work flows contain large jobs followed by small ones [12]. Therefore we submit jobs that exhibit these statistical characteristics, with both map intensive jobs (e.g., Grep and QuasiMonteCarlo) and copy/shuffle intensive jobs (e.g., sort). The details are presented in Table 1: the third column (Time) lists the job submission times in minutes and the fourth (M) and fifth (R) columns contain the number of map and reduce tasks of each job.

Table 1: MapReduce jobs

JobID	Job description	Time	M	R	W_C	W_F
01	Grep [a-g][a-z]* wikiInput	0.00	427	14	0.00	0.00
02	Grep [1-2]* random05	0.50	8	2	0.00	12.42
03	WordCount wikiInput	1.00	15	1	0.00	10.22
04	QuasiMonteCarlo	1.50	10	1	0.00	4.33
05	Grep [1-2]* random10	2.00	15	2	0.00	9.22
06	Sort randomPair2	20.33	352	14	10.22	0.00
07	Grep [1-4]* random05	21.00	8	2	0.00	23.03
08	Grep [1-2]* random10	21.17	15	2	0.00	21.63
09	Sort randomPair1	21.33	224	14	16.91	14.60
10	RandomWriter	22.50	70	0	0.00	0.00
11	Grep [1-2]* random10	22.67	15	2	0.00	20.07
12	Grep [1-5]* random05	22.83	8	2	0.00	21.20

In order to demonstrate the performance improvement from mitigating the starvation problem, we introduce the starvation time for a given job, W_C under Coupling Scheduler and W_F under Fair Scheduler, respectively. The starvation time of a job is defined as the average of the set of durations from the completion time of its map service to the starting times of each of its reduce tasks that are launched after the map service completes. Fig. 3 in Section 1 plots the starting time point as well as the minimum, mean and maximum processing times for each job. In this case Coupling Scheduler, compared to Fair Scheduler, can greatly expedite the processing of all jobs (e.g., 10 times for job 7) except job 6 and 9 which have 10% increase in the processing times. Table 1 contains the values for W_C and W_F, which clearly explain that job 2, 3, 7, 8, 11, 12 run much faster under Coupling Scheduler due to the largely reduced starvation times.

5. CONCLUSION

By conducting extensive measurements and investigating the source code, we propose an analytically tractable model to study the job processing delay distribution for MapReduce under different schedulers, including the default FIFO Scheduler and the popular Fair Scheduler. Interestingly, Fair Scheduler exhibits an intriguing criticality phenomenon because of the greedy approach to launching reduce tasks. The system can experience a delay distribution of a different order when the maximum number of reduce tasks of a job exceeds a critical value. To mitigate this problem, we design and implement Coupling Scheduler, which gradually launches reduce tasks depending on the progress of the map tasks that belong to the same job. Under certain conditions, Coupling Scheduler can result in an order gain to the delay distribution compared to Fair Scheduler. This order gain is not always attainable under general conditions, but a constant gain is still possible.

6. REFERENCES

[1] Fair Scheduler, `http://hadoop.apache.org/mapreduce/docs/r0.21.0/fair_scheduler.html`.

[2] Capacity Scheduler, `http://hadoop.apache.org/mapreduce/docs/r0.21.0/capacity_scheduler.html`.

[3] N. H. Bingham, C. M. Goldie, and J. L. Teugels. *Regular Variation*, volume 27. Cambridge University Press, 1987.

[4] S. C. Borst, O. J. Boxma, R. Núñez-Queija, and A. P. Zwart. The impact of the service discipline on delay asymptotics. *Performance Evaluation*, 54(2):175–206, 2003.

[5] Y. Chen, A. Ganapathi, R. Griffith, and R. H. Katz. The case for evaluating MapReduce performance using workload suites. In *Proceedings of the 19th IEEE International Symposium on Modeling, Analysis and Simulation of Computer and Telecommunication Systems (MASCOTS)*, July 2011.

[6] J. Dean and S. Ghemawat. Mapreduce: simplified data processing on large clusters. *Commun. ACM*, 51:107–113, January 2008.

[7] A. B. Downey. The structural cause of file size distributions. In *Proceedings of ACM SIGMETRICS 2001*, pages 328–329, New York, NY, USA, 2001.

[8] V. Gupta and M. Harchol-Balter. Self-adaptive admission control policies for resource-sharing systems. In *Proceedings of ACM SIGMETRICS 2009*, pages 311–322, Seattle, WA, USA, 2009.

[9] Hadoop. `http://hadoop.apache.org`.

[10] M. Isard, V. Prabhakaran, J. Currey, U. Wieder, K. Talwar, and A. Goldberg. Quincy: fair scheduling for distributed computing clusters. In *Proceedings of the ACM SIGOPS 22nd symposium on Operating systems principles*, SOSP '09, pages 261–276, New York, NY, USA, 2009.

[11] P. Jelenković and P. Momčilović. Large deviation analysis of subexponential waiting times in a processor-sharing queue. *Mathematics of Operations Research*, 28(3):587–608, 2003.

[12] S. Kavulya, J. Tan, R. Gandhi, and P. Narasimhan. An analysis of traces from a production mapreduce cluster. In *Proceedings of the 2010 10th IEEE/ACM International Conference on Cluster, Cloud and Grid Computing*, CCGRID '10, pages 94–103, Washington, DC, USA, 2010.

[13] R. M. Loynes. The stability of a queue with non-independent inter-arrival and service times. *Proc. Cambridge Philos. Soc.*, 58:497–520, 1962.

[14] E. Nummelin. Regeneration in tandem queues. *Advances in Applied Probability*, 13(1):221–230, 1981.

[15] R. Núñez-Queija. *Processor-Sharing Models for Integrated-Service Networks*. PhD thesis, Eindhoven University of Technology, 2000.

[16] A. G. Pakes. On the tails of waiting-time distributions. *Journal of Applied Probability*, 12:555–564, 1975.

[17] A. Pavlo, E. Paulson, A. Rasin, D. J. Abadi, D. J. DeWitt, S. Madden, and M. Stonebraker. A comparison of approaches to large-scale data analysis. In *Proceedings of the 35th ACM SIGMOD international conference on Management of data*, pages 165–178, New York, NY, USA, 2009.

[18] T. Sandholm and K. Lai. Dynamic proportional share scheduling in hadoop. In *Proceedings of the 15th international conference on job scheduling strategies for parallel processing*, JSSPP'10, pages 110–131, Berlin, Heidelberg, 2010. Springer-Verlag.

[19] K. Sigman. Regeneration in tandem queues with multiserver stations. *Journal of Applied Probability*, 25(2):391–403, 1988.

[20] J. Tan, X. Meng, and L. Zhang. Coupling task progress for mapreduce resource-aware scheduling. Technical report, IBM T. J. Watson Research Center, Hawthorne, New York, July 2011.

[21] G. Wang, A. R. Butt, P. Pandey, and K. Gupta. Using realistic simulation for performance analysis of mapreduce setups. In *Proceedings of the 1st ACM workshop on Large-Scale system and application performance*, LSAP '09, pages 19–26, New York, NY, USA, 2009.

[22] W. Whitt. Embedded renewal processes in the GI/G/s queue. *Journal of Applied Probability*, 9(3):650–658, 1972.

[23] J. Wolf, D. Rajan, K. Hildrum, R. Khandekar, V. Kumar, S. Parekh, K.-L. Wu, and A. Balmin. Flex: A slot allocation scheduling optimizer for mapreduce workloads. In *Middleware 2010*, volume 6452 of *Lecture Notes in Computer Science*, pages 1–20. Springer Berlin/Heidelberg, 2010.

[24] R. W. Wolff. An upper bound for multi-channel queues. *Journal of Applied Probability*, 14(4):884–888, 1977.

[25] R. W. Wolff. *Stochastic Modeling and Theory of Queues*. Prentice Hall, 1989.

[26] S. Zachary. A note on insensitivity in stochastic networks. *Journal of Applied Probability*, 44(1):238–248, 2007.

[27] M. Zaharia, D. Borthakur, J. S. Sarma, K. Elmeleegy, S. Shenker, and I. Stoica. Job scheduling for multi-user mapreduce clusters. Technical Report UCB/EECS-2009-55, EECS Department, University of California, Berkeley, April 2009.

[28] A. P. Zwart. Tail asymptotics for the busy period in the GI/G/1 queue. *Mathematics of Operations Research*, 26(3):485–493, 2001.

Optimal Queue-Size Scaling in Switched Networks

Devavrat Shah
MIT, LIDS
Cambridge, MA 02139, USA
devavrat@mit.edu

Neil Walton
University of Amsterdam
1012 ZA Amsterdam
The Netherlands
n.s.walton@uva.nl

Yuan Zhong
MIT, LIDS
Cambridge, MA 02139, USA
zhyu4118@mit.edu

ABSTRACT

We consider a switched (queueing) network in which there are constraints on which queues may be served simultaneously; such networks have been used to effectively model input-queued switches and wireless networks. The scheduling policy for such a network specifies which queues to serve at any point in time, based on the current state or past history of the system. In the main result of this paper, we provide a new class of online scheduling policies that achieve optimal average queue-size scaling for a class of switched networks including input-queued switches. In particular, it establishes the validity of a conjecture (documented in [24]) about optimal queue-size scaling for input-queued switches.

Categories and Subject Descriptors

C.2.1 [**Network Architecture and Design**]: Packet Switching Networks; G.3 [**Probability and Statistics**]: Markov Processes, Queueing Theory, Stochastic Processes

General Terms

Algorithms, Performance, Theory

Keywords

Switched Network, Markov Chain, Large Deviations, Emulation, Heavy Traffic, Store-and-Forward

1. INTRODUCTION.

A switched network consists of a collection of, say N, queues, operating in discrete time. At each time slot, queues are offered service according to a *service schedule* chosen from a specified finite set, denoted by $\mathcal{S}$. The rule for choosing a schedule from $\mathcal{S}$ at each time slot is called the *scheduling policy*. New work may arrive to each queue at each time slot exogenously and work served from a queue may join another queue or leave the network. We shall restrict our attention, however, to the case where work arrives in the form of unit-sized packets, and once it is served from a queue, it leaves the network, i.e., the network is single-hop.

Switched networks are special cases of what Harrison [12] calls "stochastic processing networks". Switched networks are general enough to model a variety of interesting applications. For example, they have been used to effectively model input-queued switches, the devices at the heart of high-end Internet routers, whose underlying silicon architecture imposes constraints on which traffic streams can be transmitted simultaneously [8]. They have also been used to model multihop wireless networks in which interference limits the amount of service that can be given to each host [31]. Finally, they can be instrumental in finding the right operational point in a data center [27].

In this paper, we consider *online* scheduling policies, that is, policies that only utilize historical information (i.e., past arrivals and scheduling decisions). The performance objective of interest is the total queue size or total number of packets waiting to be served in the network on average (appropriately defined). The questions that we wish to answer are: (a) what is the minimal value of the performance objective among the class of online scheduling policies, and (b) how does it depend on the network structure, $\mathcal{S}$, as well as the effective load.

Consider a work-conserving M/D/1 queue with a unit-rate server in which unit-sized packets arrive as a Poisson process with rate $\rho \in (0,1)$. Then, the average queue size scales[1] as $1/(1-\rho)$. Such scaling dependence of the average queue size on $1/(1-\rho)$ (or the inverse of the *gap*, $1-\rho$, from the load to the capacity) is a universally observed behavior in a large class of queueing networks. In a switched network, the scaling of the average total queue size ought to depend on the number of queues, N. For example, consider N parallel M/D/1 queues as described above. Clearly, the average total queue size will scale as $N/(1-\rho)$. On the other hand, consider a variation where all of these queues pool their resources into a single server that works N times faster. Equivalently, by a time change, let each of the N queues receive packets as an independent Poisson process of rate ρ/N, and each time a common unit-rate server serves a packet from one of the non-empty queues. Then, the average total queue size scales as $1/(1-\rho)$. Indeed, these are instances of switched networks that differ in their scheduling

SIGMETRICS'12, June 11–15, 2012, London, England, UK.

[1]In this paper, by scaling of quantity we mean its dependence (ignoring universal constants) on $\frac{1}{1-\rho}$ and/or the number of queues, N, as these quantities become large. Of particular interest is the scaling of $\rho \to 1$ and $N \to \infty$, in that order.

set $\mathcal{S}$, which leads to different queue-size scalings. Therefore, a natural question is the determination of average queue-size scaling in terms of $\mathcal{S}$ and $(1-\rho)$, where ρ is the effective load. In the context of an n-port input-queued switch with $N = n^2$ queues, the optimal scaling of average total queue size has been conjectured to be $n/(1-\rho)$, that is, $\sqrt{N}/(1-\rho)$ [24].

As the main result of this paper, we propose a new online scheduling policy for any single-hop switched network. This policy effectively emulates an insensitive bandwidth sharing network with a product-form stationary distribution with each component of this product-form behaving like an M/M/1 queue. This crisp description of stationary distribution allows us to obtain precise bounds on the average queue sizes under this policy. This leads to establishing, as a corollary of our result, the validity of the conjecture stated in [24] for input-queued switches. In general, it provides explicit bounds on the average total queue size for any switched network. Furthermore, due to the explicit bound on the stationary distribution of queue sizes under our policy, we are able to establish a form of large-deviations optimality of the policy for *any* single-hop switched network.

We note that the validity of the conjecture in [24] for input-queued switches, stating that optimal average total queue size scales as $\sqrt{N}/(1-\rho)$, is a significant improvement over the best known bounds of $O(N/(1-\rho))$ (due to the moment bounds of [20] for the maximum weight policy) or $O\left(\frac{\sqrt{N}\log N}{(1-\rho)^2}\right)$ (obtained by using a batching policy [21]).

Our analysis consists of two principal components. Firstly, a scheduling mechanism that is able to emulate, in discrete time, any continuous-time bandwidth allocation within a bounded degree of error. This scheduler maintains a continuous-time queueing process and tracks its own queue size process. If, valued under a certain decomposition, the gap between the idealized continuous-time process and the real queueing process becomes too large then an appropriate schedule is allocated. Secondly, we implement specific bandwidth allocation named the store-and-forward allocation policy (SFA). This policy was first considered by Massoulié (see page 63, sec 3.4.1 [22]), and was consequently discussed in Section 3.4 of Proutière's thesis [22]. It was shown to be insensitive with respect to phase-type service distributions in works by Bonald and Proutière [3, 4]. The insensitivity of this policy for general service distributions was established by Zachary [37]. The Store-and-Forward bandwidth allocation policy is closely related to classical product-form multiclass queueing network, which have highly desirable queue-size scalings. By emulating these queueing networks, we are able to translate results which render optimal queue-size bounds for a switched network.

We make two remarks here. First, the focus of this paper is on policies that achieve provably (close-to-)optimal performance bounds, but not on their implementation complexity. While the design of low-complexity, and hence practically implementable, scheduling policies with provably optimal performance remains an important challenge, we believe that our result is a substantial advancement in this direction. Second, besides classical product-form queueing networks, SFA is also closely related to the so-called proportionally fair bandwidth allocation (see, for example, [16]), and their relationship is explored in [34]. Proportional fairness can be viewed as a low-complexity approximation to SFA, and it is natural to conjecture that a version of proportional fairness is optimal for a large class of switched networks, including the input-queued switch. See Section 3 for more discussions.

1.1 Organization.

In Section 2, we specify a stochastic switched network model. In Section 3, we discuss related works. Section 4 details the necessary background on the insensitive store-and-forward bandwidth allocation (SFA) policy. The main result of the paper is presented and proved in Section 5. We first describe the policy for single-hop switched networks, and state our main result, Theorem 5.2. This is followed by a discussion of the optimality of the policy. We then provide a proof of Theorem 5.2. A discussion of directions for future work is provided in Section 6.

Notation.

Let $\mathbb{Z}_+ = \{0, 1, 2, \dots\}$ be the set of non-negative integers, $\mathbb{R}$ the set of real numbers, and $\mathbb{R}_+ = \{x \in \mathbb{R} : x \geqslant 0\}$.

We will reserve bold letters for vectors in $\mathbb{R}^N$, where N is the number of queues. For example, $\mathbf{x} = [x_n]_{1\leqslant n\leqslant N}$. Superscripts on vectors are used to denote labels, not exponents, except where otherwise noted; thus, for example, $(\mathbf{x}^0, \mathbf{x}^1, \mathbf{x}^2)$ refers to three arbitrary vectors. Let $\mathbf{0}$ be the vector of all 0s, and $\mathbf{1}$ be the vector of all 1s. The vector $\mathbf{e}_i$ is the ith unit vector, with all components being 0 but the ith component equal to 1. We use the norm $|\mathbf{x}| = \max_n |x_n|$. For vectors $\mathbf{u}$ and $\mathbf{v}$, and functions $f : \mathbb{R} \to \mathbb{R}$, we let $\mathbf{u}\cdot\mathbf{v} = \sum_{n=1}^N u_n v_n$, $\mathbf{uv} = [u_n v_n]_{1\leqslant n\leqslant N}$, and $f(\mathbf{u}) = \left[f(u_n)\right]_{1\leqslant n\leqslant N}$, and let matrix multiplication take precedence over dot product so that

$$\mathbf{u}\cdot\mathbf{A}\mathbf{v} = \mathbf{u}\cdot(\mathbf{A}\mathbf{v}) .$$

For a set $\mathcal{S} \subset \mathbb{R}^N$, denote its convex hull by $\langle\mathcal{S}\rangle$.

2. SWITCHED NETWORK MODEL.

We now introduce the switched network model. Section 2.1 describes the general system model, Section 2.2 lists the probabilistic assumptions about the arrival process, and Section 2.3 introduces some useful definitions.

2.1 Queueing dynamics.

Consider a collection of N queues. Let time be discrete, and indexed by $\tau \in \{0, 1, \dots\}$. Let $Q_i(\tau)$ be the amount of work in queue $i \in \{1, \dots, N\}$ at time slot τ. Following our general notation for vectors, we write $\mathbf{Q}(\tau)$ for $[Q_i(\tau)]_{1\leqslant i\leqslant N}$. The initial queue sizes are $\mathbf{Q}(0)$. Let $A_i(\tau)$ be the total amount of work arriving to queue i, and $B_i(\tau)$ be the cumulative potential service to queue n, up to time τ, with $\mathbf{A}(0) = \mathbf{B}(0) = \mathbf{0}$.

We first define the queueing dynamics for a single-hop switched network. Defining $d\mathbf{A}(\tau) = \mathbf{A}(\tau+1) - \mathbf{A}(\tau)$ and $d\mathbf{B}(\tau) = \mathbf{B}(\tau+1) - \mathbf{B}(\tau)$, the basic Lindley recursion that we will consider is

$$\mathbf{Q}(\tau+1) = \left[\mathbf{Q}(\tau) - d\mathbf{B}(\tau)\right]^+ + d\mathbf{A}(\tau) \qquad (1)$$

where the operation $[\cdot]^+$ is applied componentwise. The fundamental switched network constraint is that there is some finite set $\mathcal{S} \subset \mathbb{R}_+^N$ such that

$$d\mathbf{B}(\tau) \in \mathcal{S}, \quad \text{for all } \tau. \qquad (2)$$

For the purpose of this work, we shall focus on $\mathcal{S} \subset \{0, 1\}^N$. We will refer to $\boldsymbol{\sigma} \in \mathcal{S}$ as a schedule, and $\mathcal{S}$ as the set of allowed schedules. In the applications in this paper, the schedule is chosen based on current queue sizes, which is why it is natural to write the basic Lindley recursion as (1) rather than the more standard $[\mathbf{Q}(\tau) + d\mathbf{A}(\tau) - d\mathbf{B}(\tau)]^+$.

For the analysis in this paper, it is useful to keep track of two other quantities. Let $Z_i(\tau)$ be the cumulative amount of idling at queue n, defined by $\mathbf{Z}(0) = \mathbf{0}$ and

$$d\mathbf{Z}(\tau) = \left[d\mathbf{B}(\tau) - \mathbf{Q}(\tau)\right]^+, \tag{3}$$

where $d\mathbf{Z}(\tau) = \mathbf{Z}(\tau+1) - \mathbf{Z}(\tau)$. Then, (1) can be rewritten as

$$\mathbf{Q}(\tau) = \mathbf{Q}(0) + \mathbf{A}(\tau) - \mathbf{B}(\tau) + \mathbf{Z}(\tau). \tag{4}$$

Also, let $S_{\boldsymbol{\sigma}}(\tau)$ be the cumulative amount of time that is spent on using schedule $\boldsymbol{\sigma}$ up to time τ, so that

$$\mathbf{B}(\tau) = \sum_{\boldsymbol{\sigma} \in \mathcal{S}} S_{\boldsymbol{\sigma}}(\tau)\boldsymbol{\sigma}. \tag{5}$$

A policy that decides which schedule to choose at each time slot $\tau \in \mathbb{Z}_+$ is called a *scheduling policy*. In this paper, we will be interested in online scheduling policies. That is, the scheduling decision at time τ will be based on historical information, i.e., the cumulative arrival process $\mathbf{A}(\cdot)$ till time τ.

2.2 Stochastic model.

We shall assume that the exogeneous arrival process for each queue is independent and Poisson. Specifically, unit-sized packets arrive to queue i as a Poisson process of rate λ_i. Let $\boldsymbol{\lambda} = [\lambda_i]_{i=1}^N$ denote the vector of all arrival rates. The results presented in this paper extend to more general arrival process with i.i.d. interarrival times with finite means, using a *Poissonization* trick. We discuss this extension in Section 6.

2.3 Useful quantities.

We shall assume that the scheduling constraint set $\mathcal{S}$ is *monotone*. This is captured in the following assumption.

ASSUMPTION 2.1 (MONOTONICITY). *If $\mathcal{S}$ contains a schedule, then $\mathcal{S}$ also contains all of its sub-schedules. Formally, for any $\boldsymbol{\sigma} \in \mathcal{S}$, if $\boldsymbol{\sigma}' \in \{0,1\}^N$ and $\boldsymbol{\sigma}' \leqslant \boldsymbol{\sigma}$ component-wise, then $\boldsymbol{\sigma}' \in \mathcal{S}$.*

Without loss of generality, we will assume that each unit vector $\mathbf{e}_i$ belongs to $\mathcal{S}$. Next, we define some quantities that will be useful in the remainder of the paper.

DEFINITION 2.2 (ADMISSIBLE REGION). *Let $\mathcal{S} \subset \{0,1\}^N$ be the set of allowed schedules. Let $\langle\mathcal{S}\rangle$ be the convex hull of $\mathcal{S}$, i.e.,*

$$\langle\mathcal{S}\rangle = \left\{\sum_{\boldsymbol{\sigma}\in\mathcal{S}} \alpha_{\boldsymbol{\sigma}}\boldsymbol{\sigma} : \sum_{\boldsymbol{\sigma}\in\mathcal{S}} \alpha_{\boldsymbol{\sigma}} = 1, \text{ and } \alpha_{\boldsymbol{\sigma}} \geqslant 0 \text{ for all } \boldsymbol{\sigma}\right\}.$$

Define the admissible region $\mathcal{C}$ *to be*

$$\mathcal{C} = \{\boldsymbol{\lambda} \in \mathbb{R}_+^N : \boldsymbol{\lambda} \leqslant \boldsymbol{\sigma} \text{ componentwise, for some } \boldsymbol{\sigma} \in \langle\mathcal{S}\rangle\}.$$

Note that under Assumption 2.1, the capacity region $\mathcal{C}$ and the convex hull $\langle\mathcal{S}\rangle$ of $\mathcal{S}$ coincide.

Given that $\langle\mathcal{S}\rangle$ is a polytope contained in $[0,1]^N$, there exists an integer $J \geqslant 1$, a matrix $\mathbf{R} \in \mathbb{R}_+^{J\times N}$, and a vector $\mathbf{C} \in \mathbb{R}_+^J$ such that

$$\langle\mathcal{S}\rangle = \left\{\mathbf{x} \in [0,1]^N : \mathbf{R}\mathbf{x} \leqslant \mathbf{C}\right\}. \tag{6}$$

We call J the *rank* of $\langle\mathcal{S}\rangle$ in the representation (6). When it is clear from the context, we simply call J the rank of $\langle\mathcal{S}\rangle$. Note that this rank may be different from the rank of matrix $\mathbf{R}$. Our results will exploit the fact that the rank J may be an order of magnitude smaller than N.

DEFINITION 2.3 (STATIC PLANNING PROBLEMS AND LOAD). *Define the static planning optimization problem* PRIMAL($\boldsymbol{\lambda}$) *for $\boldsymbol{\lambda} \in \mathbb{R}_+^N$ to be*

$$\text{minimize} \quad \sum_{\boldsymbol{\sigma}\in\mathcal{S}} \alpha_{\boldsymbol{\sigma}} \tag{7}$$

$$\text{subject to} \quad \boldsymbol{\lambda} \leqslant \sum_{\boldsymbol{\sigma}\in\mathcal{S}} \alpha_{\boldsymbol{\sigma}}\boldsymbol{\sigma}, \tag{8}$$

$$\alpha_{\boldsymbol{\sigma}} \in \mathbb{R}_+, \text{ for all } \boldsymbol{\sigma} \in \mathcal{S}. \tag{9}$$

Define the load induced by $\boldsymbol{\lambda}$, denoted by $\rho(\boldsymbol{\lambda})$, as the value of the optimization problem PRIMAL($\boldsymbol{\lambda}$).

Note that $\boldsymbol{\lambda}$ is admissible if and only if $\rho(\boldsymbol{\lambda}) \leqslant 1$. It also follows immediately from Definition 2.3 that

$$\rho(\boldsymbol{\lambda}) = \inf\left\{\gamma \geqslant 0 : \mathbf{R}\boldsymbol{\lambda} \leqslant \gamma\mathbf{C}\right\},$$

and $\boldsymbol{\lambda}$ is admissible if and only if $\mathbf{R}\boldsymbol{\lambda} \leqslant \mathbf{C}$, component-wise.

The following is a simple and useful property of $\rho(\cdot)$: for any $\mathbf{a}$, $\mathbf{b} \in \mathbb{R}_+^N$,

$$\rho(\mathbf{a} + \mathbf{b}) \leqslant \rho(\mathbf{a}) + \rho(\mathbf{b}). \tag{10}$$

2.4 Motivating example.

An Internet router has several input ports and output ports. A data transmission cable is attached to each of these ports. Packets arrive at the input ports. The function of the router is to work out which output port each packet should go to, and to transfer packets to the correct output ports. This last function is called *switching*. There are a number of possible switch architectures; we will consider the commercially popular input-queued switch architecture.

Figure 1 illustrates an input-queued switch with three input ports and three output ports. Packets arriving at input k destined for output ℓ are stored at input port k, in queue $Q_{k,\ell}$, thus there are $N = 9$ queues in total. (For this example, it is more natural to use double indexing, e.g., $Q_{3,2}$, whereas for general switched networks it is more natural to use single indexing, e.g., Q_i for $1 \leqslant i \leqslant N$.)

The switch operates in discrete time. At each time slot, the switch fabric can transmit a number of packets from input ports to output ports, subject to the two constraints that each input can transmit at most one packet, and that each output can receive at most one packet. In other words, at each time slot the switch can choose a *matching* from inputs to outputs. The schedule $\boldsymbol{\sigma} \in \mathbb{R}_+^{3\times 3}$ is given by $\sigma_{k,\ell} = 1$ if input port k is matched to output port ℓ in a given time slot, and $\sigma_{k,\ell} = 0$ otherwise. The matching constraints require that $\sum_{m=1}^{3} \sigma_{k,m} \leqslant 1$ for $k = 1,2,3$, and $\sum_{m=1}^{3} \sigma_{m,\ell} \leqslant 1$ for $\ell = 1,2,3$. Figure 1 shows two possible matchings. On the left-hand side, the matching allows a packet to be transmitted from input port 3 to output port 2, but since $Q_{3,2}$ is empty, no packet is actually transmitted.

In general, for an n-port switch, there are $N = n^2$ queues. The corresponding schedule set $\mathcal{S}$ is defined to be

$$\left\{\boldsymbol{\sigma} \in \{0,1\}^{n\times n} : \sum_{m=1}^{n} \sigma_{k,m} \leqslant 1, \sum_{m=1}^{n} \sigma_{m,\ell} \leqslant 1, 1 \leqslant k,\ell \leqslant n\right\}.$$

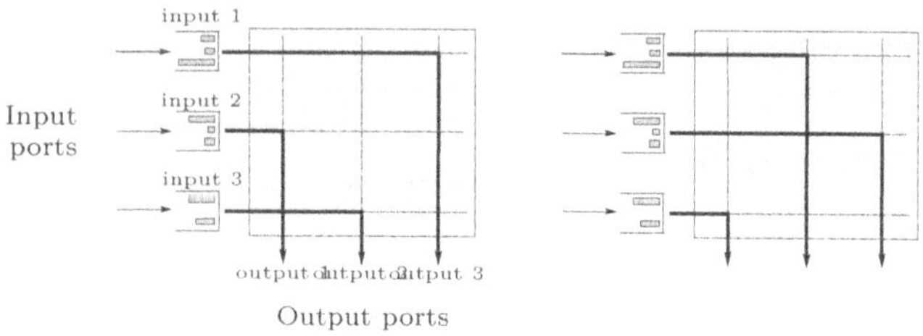

Figure 1: An input-queued switch, and two example matchings of inputs to outputs.

It can be checked that $\mathcal{S}$ is *monotone*. Furthermore, due to Birkhoff-von Neumann Theorem, [2, 33], the convex hull $\langle\mathcal{S}\rangle$ of $\mathcal{S}$ is given by

$$\Big\{\mathbf{x} \in [0,1]^{n\times n} : \sum_{m=1}^{n} x_{k,m} \leqslant 1, \sum_{m=1}^{n} x_{m,\ell} \leqslant 1, 1 \leqslant k, \ell \leqslant n\Big\}.$$

That is, the rank of $\langle\mathcal{S}\rangle$ is less than or equal to $2n = 2\sqrt{N}$ for an n-port switch. Finally, given an arrival rate matrix[2] $\boldsymbol{\lambda} \in [0,1]^{n\times n}$, $\rho(\boldsymbol{\lambda})$ is given by

$$\rho(\boldsymbol{\lambda}) = \max_{1\leqslant k,\ell\leqslant n} \Big\{ \sum_{m=1}^{n} \lambda_{k,m}, \sum_{m=1}^{n} \lambda_{m,\ell} \Big\}.$$

3. RELATED WORKS.

The question of determining the optimal scaling of queue sizes in switched networks, or more generally, stochastic processing networks, has been an important intellectual pursuit for more than a decade. The complexity of the generic stochastic processing network makes this task extremely challenging. Therefore, in search of tractable analysis, most of the prior work has been on trying to understand optimal scaling and scheduling policies for *scaled* systems: primarily, with respect to fluid and heavy-traffic scaling.

In heavy-traffic analysis, one studies the queue-size behavior under a diffusion (or heavy-traffic) scaling. This regime was first considered by Kingman [18]; since then, a substantial body of theory has developed, and modern treatments can be found in [11, 5, 36, 35]. Stolyar [30] has studied a class of myopic scheduling policies, known as the maximum weight policy, introduced by Tassiulas and Ephremides [31], for a generalized switch model in the diffusion scaling. In a general version of the maximum weight policy, a schedule with maximum weight is chosen at each time step, with the weight of a schedule being equal to the sum of the weights of the queues chosen by that schedule. The weight of a queue is a function of its size. In particular, for the choice of one parameter class of functions parameterized by $\alpha > 0$, $f(x) = x^{\alpha}$, the resulting class of policies are called the maximum weight policies with parameter $\alpha > 0$, and denoted as MW-α.

In [30], a complete characterization of the diffusion approximation for the queue-size process was obtained, under a condition known as *"complete resource pooling"*, when the network is operating under the MW-α policy, for any $\alpha > 0$. This condition effectively requires that there exists a scheduling policy which is able to balance the weights of all the heavily loaded queues. Stolyar [30] showed the remarkable result that the limiting queue-size vector lives in a one-dimensional state space. Operationally, this means that all one needs to keep track of is the one-dimensional total amount of work in the system (called the *rescaled workload*), and at any point in time one can assume that the individual queues have all been balanced. Furthermore, it was established that a max-weight policy minimizes the rescaled workload induced by any policy under the heavy-traffic scaling (with complete resource pooling). Dai and Lin [6, 7] have established that a similar result holds (with complete resource pooling) in the more general setting of a stochastic processing network. In summary, under the complete resource pooling condition, the results in [30, 6, 7] imply that the performance of the maximum weight policy in an input-queued switch, or more generally in a stochastic processing network, is always optimal (in the diffusion limit, and when each queue size is approriately weighted). These results suggest that the average total queue size scales as $1/(1-\rho)$ in the $\rho \to 1$ limit. However, such analyses do not capture the dependence on the network scheduling structure $\mathcal{S}$. Essentially, this is because the complete resource pooling condition reduces the system to a one-dimensional space (which may be highly dependent on a network's structure), and optimality results are then initially expressed with respect to this one-dimensional space.

Motivated to capture the dependence of the queue sizes on the network scheduling structure $\mathcal{S}$, a heavy-traffic analysis of switched networks with multiple bottlenecks (without resource pooling) was pursued by Shah and Wischik [28]. They established the so-called multiplicative state space collapse, and identified a member, denoted by MW-0^+ (obtained by taking $\alpha \to 0$), of the class of maximum-weight policies as optimal with respect to a critical fluid model. In a more recent work, Shah and Wischik [27] established the optimality of MW-0^+ with respect to overloaded fluid models as well. However, this collection of works stops short of establishing optimality for diffusion scaled queue-size processes.

Finally, we take note of the work by Meyn [19], which establishes that a class of generalized maximum weight policies achieve logarithmic (in $1/(1-\rho)$) regret with respect to an optimal policy under certain conditions.

In a related model — the bandwidth-sharing network model — Kang et al. [15] have established a diffusion approximation for the proportionally fair bandwidth allocation policy, assuming a technical "local traffic" condition, but without assuming complete resource pooling[3]. They show that the resulting diffusion approximation has a product-form stationary distribution. Shah et al. [25] have recently established that this product-form stationary distribution is indeed the limit of the stationary distributions of the original stochastic model (an interchange-of-limits result). As a consequence, if one could utilize a scheduling policy in a switched network that corresponds to the proportionally fair policy, then the resulting diffusion approximation will have a product-form stationary distribution, as long as the effective network scheduling structure $\mathcal{S}$ (precisely $\langle\mathcal{S}\rangle$) satisfies the "local traffic condition". Now, proportional fairness is a continuous-time rate allocation policy that usually requires rate allocations that are a convex combination of multiple schedules. In a switched network, a policy must operate in

[2]not a vector, for notational convenience, as discussed earlier

[3]Kang et al. [15] assume that critically loaded traffic is such that all the constraints are saturated simultaneously.

discrete time and has to choose one schedule at any given time from a finite discrete set $\mathcal{S}$. For this reason, proportional fairness cannot be implemented directly. However, a natural randomized policy inspired by proportional fairness is likely to have the same diffusion approximation (since the fluid models would be identical, and the entire machinery of Kang et al. [15], building upon the work of Bramson [5] and Williams [36], relies on a fluid model). As a consequence, if $\mathcal{S}$ (more accurately, $\langle\mathcal{S}\rangle$) satisfies the "local traffic condition", then effectively the diffusion-scaled queue sizes would have a product-form stationary distribution, and would result in bounds similar to those implied by our results. In comparison, our results are non-asymptotic, in the sense that they hold for any admissible load, they have a product-form structure, and they do not require technical assumptions such as the 'local traffic condition'. Furthermore, such generality is needed because there are popular examples, such as the input-queued switch, that do *not* satisfy the 'local traffic condition'.

We note that Stolyar [29] and Venkataramanan and Lin [32] established that the maximum weight policy with weight parameter $\alpha > 0$, MW-α, optimizes the tail exponent of the $1+\alpha$ norm of the queue-size vector. However, it does not characterize the tail exponent explicitly. See [23] which has the best known *explicit* bounds on the tail exponent.

In the context of input-queued switches, the example that has primarily motivated this work, the policy that we propose has the average total queue size bounded within factor 2 of the same quantity induced by *any* policy, in the heavy-traffic limit. Furthermore, this result does not require conditions like complete resource pooling. More generally, our policy provides non-asymptotic bounds on queue sizes for every arrival rate and switch size. The policy even admits exponential tail bounds with respect to the stationary distribution; and the exponent of these tail bounds is *optimal*. These results are significant improvements on the state-of-the-art bounds for best performing policies for input-queued switches. As noted in the introduction, our bound on the average total queue size is $\sqrt{N}$ times better than the existing bound for the maximum-weight policy, and $\log N/(1-\rho)$ times better than that for the batching policy in [21]. (Here N is the number of queues, and ρ the system load.) For more details of these results, see [24].

For a generic switched network, our policy induces average total queue size that scale linearly with the *rank* of $\langle\mathcal{S}\rangle$, under the diffusion scaling. This is in contrast to the best known bounds, such as those for maximum weight policy, where the average queue-size scales as N, under the diffusion scaling. Therefore, whenever the *rank* of $\langle\mathcal{S}\rangle$ is smaller than N (the number of queues), our policy provides tighter bounds. Under our policy, queue sizes admit exponential tail bounds. The bound on the distribution of queue-sizes under our policy leads to an explicit characterization of the tail exponent, which is optimal for any single-hop switched network.

4. INSENSITIVITY IN STOCHASTIC NETWORKS.

This section recalls the background on insensitive stochastic networks that underlies the main results of this work. We shall focus on descriptions of the insensitive bandwidth allocation in so-called bandwidth-sharing networks operating in continuous time. Justifications of claims made in this section are omitted in the interest of space.

We consider a bandwidth-sharing network operating in continuous time with capacity constraints. The particular bandwidth-sharing policy of interest is the so-called "store-and-forward allocation (SFA)," introduced by Bonald and Proutière [4]. We shall use the SFA as an idealized policy to design online scheduling policies for switched networks. We now describe the precise model, the SFA policy, and what we know about its performance.

Model.

Let time be continuous and indexed by $t \in \mathbb{R}_+$. Consider a network with $J \geqslant 1$ resources indexed from $1, \dots, J$. Let there be N routes, and suppose that each *packet* on route i consumes an amount $R_{ji} \geqslant 0$ of resource j, for each $j \in \{1, 2, \dots, J\}$. Let $\mathcal{K}$ be the set of all resource-route pairs (j, i) such that route i uses resource j, i.e., $\mathcal{K} = \{(j,i) : R_{ji} > 0\}$. Without loss of generality, we assume that for each $i \in \{1, 2, \dots, N\}$, $\sum_{j=1}^{J} R_{ji} > 0$. Let $\mathbf{R}$ be the $J \times N$ matrix with entries R_{ji}. Let $\mathbf{C} \in \mathbb{R}_+^J$ be a positive *capacity* vector with components C_j. For each route i, *packets* arrive as an independent Poisson process of rate λ_i. Packets arriving on route i require a unit amount of service, deterministically.

We denote the number of packets on route i at time t by $M_i(t)$, and define the queue-size vector at time t by $\mathbf{M}(t) = [M_i(t)]_{i=1}^N \in \mathbb{Z}_+^N$. Each packet gets service from the network at a rate determined according to a bandwidth-sharing policy. Once a packet receives its total (unit) amount of service, it departs the network.

We consider online, myopic bandwidth allocations. That is, the bandwidth allocation at time t only depends on the queue-size vector $\mathbf{M}(t)$. When there are m_i packets on route i, that is, if the vector of packets is $\mathbf{m} = [m_i]_{i=1}^N$, let the total bandwidth allocated to route i be $\phi_i(\mathbf{m}) \in \mathbb{R}_+$. We consider a processor-sharing policy, so that each packet on route i is served at rate $\phi_i(\mathbf{m})/m_i$, if $m_i > 0$. If $m_i = 0$, let $\phi_i(\mathbf{m}) = 0$. If the *bandwidth vector* $\boldsymbol{\phi}(\mathbf{m}) = [\phi_i(\mathbf{m})]_{i=1}^N$ satisfies the capacity constraints

$$\mathbf{R}\boldsymbol{\phi}(\mathbf{m}) \leqslant \mathbf{C}, \quad \text{component-wise,} \tag{11}$$

for all $\mathbf{m} \in \mathbb{Z}_+^N$ then, in light of Definition 2.2, we say that $\boldsymbol{\phi}(\cdot)$ is an *admissible bandwidth allocation*. A Markovian description of the system is given by a process $\mathbf{X}(t)$ which contains the queue-size vector $\mathbf{M}(t)$ along with the residual workloads of the set of packets on each route.

Now, on average, λ_i units of work arrive to route i per unit time. Therefore, in order for the Markov process $\mathbf{X}(\cdot)$ to be positive (Harris) recurrent, it is necessary that

$$\mathbf{R}\boldsymbol{\lambda} \;<\; \mathbf{C}, \quad \text{component-wise.} \tag{12}$$

All such $\boldsymbol{\lambda} = [\lambda_i]_{i=1}^N \in \mathbb{R}_+^N$ will be called *strictly admissible*, in the same spirit as the admissible region for a switched network.

Store-and-Forward Allocation (SFA) policy.

We describe the store-and-forward allocation policy that was first considered by Massoulié and later analysed in the thesis of Proutière [22]. Bonald and Proutière [4] established that it induces product-form stationary distributions and is insensitive with respect to phase-type service distributions. This policy is shown to be *insensitive* for general service time distributions, including the deterministic service considered here, by Zachary [37]. The relation between this policy, the proportionally fair allocation, and multiclass queueing networks is discussed in depth by Walton [34] and Kelly et al. [16]. The insensitivity property implies that the invariant measure of the process $\mathbf{M}(t)$ only depends on the parameters $\boldsymbol{\lambda} = [\lambda_i]_{i=1}^N \in \mathbb{R}_+^N$, and no other aspects of the stochastic description of the system.

We, first, give an informal motivation for SFA. SFA is closely related to quasi-reversible queueing networks. Consider a continuous-time multi-class queueing network (without scheduling constraints) consisting of processor sharing queues indexed by $j \in \{1, ..., J\}$ and job types indexed by the routes $i \in \{1, ..., N\}$. Each route i job has a service requirement R_{ji} at each queue j, and a fixed service capacity C_j is shared between jobs at the queue. Here each job will sequentially visit all the queues (so called store-and-forward) and will visit each queue a fixed number of times. If we assume jobs on each route arrive as a Poisson process, then the resulting queueing network will be stable for all strictly admissible arrival rates. Moreover, each stationary queue will be independent with a queue size that scales, with its load ρ, as $\rho/(1-\rho)$. For further details, see Kelly [17]. So, assuming each queue has equal load, the total number of jobs within the network is of the order $J\rho/(1-\rho)$. In other words, these networks have the stability and queue-size scaling that we require, but they do not obey the necessary scheduling constraints (11). However, these networks do emit an admissible schedule on average. For this reason, we consider SFA which, given the number of jobs on each route, allocates the average rate that jobs are transferred through this multi-class network. Next, we describe this policy (using notations similar to those used in [16, 34]).

Given $\mathbf{m} \in \mathbb{Z}_+^N$, define

$$U(\mathbf{m}) = \Big\{ \tilde{\mathbf{m}} = (\tilde{m}_{ji} : (j,i) \in \mathcal{K}) \in \mathbb{Z}_+^{|\mathcal{K}|} : \sum_{j:j\in i} \tilde{m}_{ji} = m_i \text{ for all } 1 \leqslant i \leqslant N \Big\}.$$

For $\mathbf{L} \in \mathbb{Z}_+^J$, we also define

$$V(\mathbf{L}) = \Big\{ \tilde{\mathbf{m}} = (\tilde{m}_{ji} : (j,i) \in \mathcal{K}) \in \mathbb{Z}_+^{|\mathcal{K}|} : \sum_{i:i\ni j} \tilde{m}_{ji} = L_j \text{ for all } 1 \leqslant j \leqslant J \Big\}.$$

Here, by notation $j \in i$ (and $i \ni j$) we mean $R_{ji} > 0$. The notation $i \ni j$ is used when we consider a collection of i satisfying this condition for a given j. For each $\tilde{\mathbf{m}} \in U(\mathbf{m})$, we exploit notation somewhat and define

$$\tilde{m}_j = \sum_{i:j\in i} \tilde{m}_{ji}, \text{ for all } j \leqslant J.$$

Also define

$$\binom{\tilde{m}_j}{\tilde{m}_{ji} : i \ni j} = \frac{\tilde{m}_j!}{\prod_{i:j\in i} (\tilde{m}_{ji}!)}.$$

For $\mathbf{m} \in \mathbb{Z}_+^N$, we define $\Phi(\mathbf{m})$ as

$$\Phi(\mathbf{m}) = \sum_{\tilde{\mathbf{m}} \in U(\mathbf{m})} \prod_{j \in J} \left(\binom{\tilde{m}_j}{\tilde{m}_{ji} : i \ni j} \prod_{i:j\in i} \left(\frac{R_{ji}}{C_j} \right)^{\tilde{m}_{ji}} \right). \quad (13)$$

We shall define $\Phi(\mathbf{m}) = 0$ if any of the components of $\mathbf{m}$ is negative. The store-and-forward allocation (SFA) assigns rates according to the function $\boldsymbol{\phi} : \mathbb{Z}_+^N \to \mathbb{R}_+^N$ so that for any $\mathbf{m} \in \mathbb{Z}_+^N$, $\boldsymbol{\phi}(\mathbf{m}) = (\boldsymbol{\phi}_i(\mathbf{m}))_{i=1}^N$, with

$$\boldsymbol{\phi}_i(\mathbf{m}) = \frac{\Phi(\mathbf{m} - \mathbf{e}_i)}{\Phi(\mathbf{m})}, \quad (14)$$

where, recall that $\mathbf{m} - \mathbf{e}_i$ is the same as $\mathbf{m}$ at all but the ith component; its ith component equals $m_i - 1$. The bandwidth allocation $\phi(m)$ is the stationary throughput of jobs on the routes of a multi-class queueing network (described above), conditional on there being $\mathbf{m}$ jobs on each route.

A priori it is not clear if the above described bandwidth allocation is even admissible (i.e., satisfies (11)). This can be argued as follows. The $\boldsymbol{\phi}(\mathbf{m})$ can be related to the stationary throughput of a multi-class network with a finite number of jobs, $\mathbf{m}$, on each route. Under this scenario (due to finite number of jobs), each queue must be stable. Therefore, the load on each queue, $\mathbf{R}\boldsymbol{\phi}(\mathbf{m})$, must be less than the overall system capacity $\mathbf{C}$. That is, the allocation is admissible. The precise argument along these lines is provided in, for example [16, Corollary 2] and [34, Lemma 4.1].

The SFA induces a product-form invariant distribution for the number of packets waiting in the bandwidth-sharing network and is insensitive. We summarize this in the following result.

THEOREM 4.1. *Consider a bandwidth-sharing network with* $\mathbf{R}\boldsymbol{\lambda} < \mathbf{C}$. *Under the SFA policy described above, the Markov process* $\mathbf{X}(t)$ *is positive (Harris) recurrent and* $\mathbf{M}(t)$ *has a unique stationary probability distribution* $\boldsymbol{\pi}$ *given by*

$$\boldsymbol{\pi}(\mathbf{m}) = \frac{\Phi(\mathbf{m})}{\Phi} \prod_{i=1}^N \lambda_i^{m_i}, \quad \textit{for all } \mathbf{m} \in \mathbb{Z}_+^N, \quad (15)$$

where

$$\Phi = \prod_{j=1}^J \left(\frac{C_j}{C_j - \sum_{i:i\ni j} R_{ji}\lambda_i} \right) \quad (16)$$

is a normalizing factor. Furthermore, in steady state, the residual workload of each packet in the network is uniformly distributed on $[0,1]$ *and is conditionally independent from the residual workloads of other packets, when we condition on the number of packets on each route of the network.*

Note that statements similar to Theorem 4.1 have appeared in other works, for example, [3], [34, Proposition 4.2] and [16]. Theorem 4.1 is a summary of these statements.

The following property of the stationary distribution $\boldsymbol{\pi}$ described in Theorem 4.1 that will be useful.

PROPOSITION 4.2. *Consider the setup of Theorem 4.1 and let* $\boldsymbol{\pi}$ *be as described by* (15). *Define a measure* $\tilde{\boldsymbol{\pi}}$ *on* $\mathbb{Z}_+^{|\mathcal{K}|}$ *as follows: for* $\tilde{\mathbf{m}} \in \mathbb{Z}_+^{|\mathcal{K}|}$,

$$\tilde{\boldsymbol{\pi}}(\tilde{\mathbf{m}}) = \frac{1}{\Phi} \prod_{j=1}^J \left(\binom{\tilde{m}_j}{\tilde{m}_{ji} : i \ni j} \prod_{i:j\in i} \left(\frac{R_{ji}\lambda_i}{C_j} \right)^{\tilde{m}_{ji}} \right). \quad (17)$$

Then, for any $L \in \mathbb{Z}_+$,

$$\boldsymbol{\pi}\Big(\Big\{\mathbf{m} : \sum_{i=1}^N m_i = L\Big\}\Big) = \tilde{\boldsymbol{\pi}}\Big(\Big\{\tilde{\mathbf{m}} : \sum_{j=1}^J \tilde{m}_j = L\Big\}\Big). \quad (18)$$

Finally, we relate the distribution $\tilde{\pi}$ to the stationary distribution of an insensitive multiclass queueing network with a product-form stationary distribution and geometrically distributed queue sizes.

PROPOSITION 4.3. *Consider the distribution $\tilde{\pi}$ defined in (17). Then, for any $\mathbf{L} = (L_1, \ldots, L_J) \in \mathbb{Z}_+^J$,*

$$\tilde{\pi}(\tilde{m}_1 = L_1, \ldots, \tilde{m}_J = L_J) \overset{(a)}{=} \sum_{(\tilde{m}_{ji}) \in V(\mathbf{L})} \tilde{\pi}((\tilde{m}_{ji}))$$
$$= \prod_{j=1}^{J} \tilde{\rho}_j^{L_j}(1 - \tilde{\rho}_j), \qquad (19)$$

where $\tilde{\rho}_j = \left(\sum_{i:i\ni j} R_{ji}\lambda_j\right)/C_j$.

5. MAIN RESULT: A POLICY AND ITS PERFORMANCE

In this section, we describe an online scheduling policy and quantify its performance in terms of explicit, closed-form bounds on the stationary distribution of the induced queue sizes. Section 5.1 describes the policy for a generic switched network and provides the statement of the main result. Section 5.2 discusses its implications. Specifically, it discusses (a) the optimality of the policy for any single-hop switched network with respect to exponential tail bounds, and (b) the optimality of the policy for a class of switched networks, including input-queued switches, with respect to the average total queue size. Section 5.3 proves the main result stated in Section 5.1.

5.1 A policy for switched networks.

The basic idea behind the policy, to be described in detail shortly, is as follows. Given a switched network, denoted by **SN**, with constraint set $\mathcal{S}$ and N queues, let $\langle \mathcal{S} \rangle$ have rank J and representation (cf. (6))

$$\langle \mathcal{S} \rangle = \{\mathbf{x} \in [0,1]^N : \mathbf{Rx} \leqslant \mathbf{C}\}, \quad \mathbf{R} \in \mathbb{R}_+^{J \times N}, \ \mathbf{C} \in \mathbb{R}_+^J.$$

Now consider a virtual bandwidth-sharing network, denoted by **BN**, with N routes corresponding to each of these N queues. The resource-route relation is determined precisely by the matrix $\mathbf{R}$; and the J resources have capacities given by $\mathbf{C}$. Both networks, **SN** and **BN** are fed identical arrivals. That is, whenever a packet arrives to queue i in **SN**, a packet is added to route i in **BN** at the same time. The main question is that of determining a scheduling policy for **SN**; this will be derived from **BN**. Specifically, the **BN** will operate under the insensitive SFA policy described in Section 4. Due to Theorem 4.1 as well as Propositions 4.2 and 4.3, this will induce a desirable stationary distribution of queue sizes in **BN**. Therefore, if we could use the rate allocation of **BN**, that is, the policy SFA, directly in **SN**, it would give us a desired performance in terms of the stationary distribution of the induced queue sizes. Now the rate allocation in **BN** is such that the instantaneous rate is always inside $\langle \mathcal{S} \rangle$. However, it could change all the time and need not utilize points of $\mathcal{S}$ as rates. In contrast, in **SN** we require that the rate allocation can change only once per discrete time slot and it must always employ one of the generators of $\langle \mathcal{S} \rangle$, that is, a schedule from $\mathcal{S}$. The key to our policy is an effective way to emulate the rate allocation of **BN** under SFA (or for that matter, any admissible bandwidth allocation) by utilizing schedules from $\mathcal{S}$ in an online manner and with the discrete-time constraint. We will see shortly that this emulation policy relies on $\mathcal{S}$ being monotone (cf. Assumption 2.1).

To that end, we describe this emulation policy. Let us start by introducing some useful notation. Let $\mathbf{A}(\cdot) = (A_i(\cdot))$ be the vector of exogenous, independent Poisson processes according to which unit-sized packets arrive to both **BN** and **SN**, simultaneously. Recall that $A_i(\cdot)$ is a Poisson process with rate λ_i. Let $\mathbf{M}(t) = (M_i(t))$ denote the vector of numbers of packets waiting on the N routes in **BN** at time $t \geqslant 0$. In **BN**, the services are allocated according to the SFA policy described in Section 4. Let $\Lambda^{\text{SFA}}(\cdot) = (\Lambda_i^{\text{SFA}}(\cdot)) \in \mathbb{R}_+^N$ denote the cumulative amount of service allocated to the N routes in **BN** under the SFA policy: $\Lambda_i^{\text{SFA}}(t)$ denotes the total amount of service allocated to all packets on route i during the interval $[0,t]$, for $t \geqslant 0$, with $\Lambda_i^{\text{SFA}}(0) = 0$ for $1 \leqslant i \leqslant N$. By definition, all components of $\Lambda^{\text{SFA}}(\cdot)$ are non-decreasing and Lipschitz continuous. Furthermore, $(\Lambda^{\text{SFA}}(t+s) - \Lambda^{\text{SFA}}(t))/s \in \langle \mathcal{S} \rangle$ for any $t \geqslant 0$ and $s > 0$. Recall that the (right-)derivative of $\Lambda^{\text{SFA}}(\cdot)$ is determined by $\mathbf{M}(\cdot)$ through the function $\phi(\cdot)$ as defined in (14).

Now we describe the scheduling policy for **SN** that will rely on $\Lambda^{\text{SFA}}(\cdot)$. Let $\mathbf{B}(\tau) = (B_i(\tau))$ denote the cumulative amount of service allocated in **SN** by the scheduling policy up to time slot $\tau \geqslant 0$, with $\mathbf{B}(0) = \mathbf{0}$. The scheduling policy determines how $\mathbf{B}(\cdot)$ is updated. Let $\mathbf{Q}(\tau) = (Q_i(\tau))$ be the queue sizes measured at the end of time slot τ. Let service be provided according to the scheduling policy instantly at the begining of a time slot. Thus, the scheduling policy decides the schedule $d\mathbf{B}(\tau) = \mathbf{B}(\tau+1) - \mathbf{B}(\tau) \in \mathcal{S}$ at the very beginning of time slot $\tau+1$. This decision is made as follows. Let $\mathbf{D}(\tau) = \Lambda^{\text{SFA}}(\tau) - \mathbf{B}(\tau)$. We will see shortly that by virtue of our policy, $\mathbf{D}(\tau) \geqslant d\mathbf{B}(\tau)$, and hence $\mathbf{D}(\tau) \geqslant \mathbf{0}$, for all time τ. This fact will be key for many subsequent proofs. Let $\rho(\mathbf{D}(\tau))$ be the optimal objective value in the optimization problem PRIMAL($\mathbf{D}(\tau)$) defined in (7). In particular, there exists a non-negative combination of schedules in $\mathcal{S}$ such that

$$\sum_{\sigma \in \mathcal{S}} \tilde{\alpha}_\sigma \boldsymbol{\sigma} \geqslant \mathbf{D}(\tau), \quad \text{and} \quad \sum_{\sigma \in \mathcal{S}} \tilde{\alpha}_\sigma = \rho(\mathbf{D}(\tau)). \qquad (20)$$

We claim that in fact, we can find non-negative numbers α_σ, $\boldsymbol{\sigma} \in \mathcal{S}$, such that

$$\sum_{\sigma \in \mathcal{S}} \alpha_\sigma \boldsymbol{\sigma} = \mathbf{D}(\tau), \quad \text{and} \quad \sum_{\sigma \in \mathcal{S}} \alpha_\sigma = \rho(\mathbf{D}(\tau)). \qquad (21)$$

This is formalized in the following lemma.

LEMMA 5.1. *Let $\mathbf{D} \in \mathbb{R}_+^N$ be a non-negative vector. Consider the static planning problem* PRIMAL($\mathbf{D}$) *defined in (7). Let the optimal objective value to* PRIMAL($\mathbf{D}$) *be* $\rho(\mathbf{D})$. *Then there exist $\alpha_\sigma \geqslant 0$, $\boldsymbol{\sigma} \in \mathcal{S}$, such that (21) hold.*

The proof of the lemma relies on Assumption 2.1. The detail of the proof is provided in [26].

There could be many possible non-negative combinations of $\mathbf{D}(\tau)$ satisfying (21). If there exists non-negative numbers α_σ, $\boldsymbol{\sigma} \in \mathcal{S}$, satisfying (21) with $\alpha_{\sigma'} \geqslant 1$ for some $\boldsymbol{\sigma}' \in \mathcal{S}$, then choose $\boldsymbol{\sigma}'$ as the schedule: set $d\mathbf{B}(\tau) = \boldsymbol{\sigma}'$. If no such decomposition exists for $\mathbf{D}(\tau)$, then set $d\mathbf{B}(\tau) = \tilde{\boldsymbol{\sigma}}$, where $\tilde{\boldsymbol{\sigma}}$ is a solution (ties broken arbitrarily) of

$$\text{maximize} \ \sum_i \sigma_i \quad \text{over} \quad \boldsymbol{\sigma} \in \mathcal{S}, \ \boldsymbol{\sigma} \leqslant \mathbf{D}(\tau). \qquad (22)$$

Note that $\mathbf{0}$ is a feasible solution for the above problem as $\mathbf{0} \in \mathcal{S}$ and $\mathbf{0} \leqslant \mathbf{D}(\tau)$. Observe also that for all time τ, $d\mathbf{B}(\tau) \leqslant \mathbf{D}(\tau)$.

The above is a complete description of the scheduling policy. Observe that it is an online policy, as the virtual network **BN** can be simulated in an online manner, and, given this, the scheduling decision in **SN** relies only on the history of **BN** and **SN**. The following result quantifies the performance of the policy.

THEOREM 5.2. *Given a strictly admissible arrival rate vector* $\boldsymbol{\lambda}$, *with* $\rho(\boldsymbol{\lambda}) < 1$, *under the above described policy, the switched network* ***SN*** *is positive recurrent and has a unique stationary distribution. Let* $\tilde{\rho}_j = \left(\sum_i R_{ji}\lambda_i\right)/C_j$, $j = 1, 2, \ldots, J$ *be as in Proposition 4.3. With respect to this stationary distribution, the following properties hold:*

1. *The expected total queue size is bounded as*

$$\mathbb{E}\Big[\sum_{i=1}^{N} Q_i\Big] \leqslant \frac{1}{2}\left(\sum_{j=1}^{J} \frac{\tilde{\rho}_j}{1-\tilde{\rho}_j}\right) + K(N+2), \quad (23)$$

where $K = \max_{\boldsymbol{\sigma}\in\mathcal{S}}\left(\sum_i \sigma_i\right)$.

2. *The distribution of the total queue size has an exponential tail with exponent given by*

$$\lim_{L\to\infty} \frac{1}{L} \log \mathbb{P}\Big(\sum_{i=1}^{N} Q_i \geqslant L\Big) = \max_{j=1,\ldots,J} \log \tilde{\rho}_j. \quad (24)$$

5.2 Optimality of the policy.

This section establishes the optimality of our policy for input-queued switches, both with respect to expected total queue size scaling and tail exponent. The policy produces an optimal tail exponent for any single-hop switched network.

Scaling of queue sizes.

We start by formalizing what we mean by the optimality of expected queue sizes and of their tail exponents. We consider policies under which there is a well-defined limiting stationary distribution of the queue sizes for all $\boldsymbol{\lambda}$ such that $\rho(\boldsymbol{\lambda}) < 1$. Note that the class of policies is not empty; indeed, the maximum weight policy and our policy are members of this class. With some abuse of notation, let $\boldsymbol{\pi}$ denote the stationary distribution of the queue-size vector under the policy of interest. We are interested in two quantities:

1. *Expected total queue size.* Let $\bar{Q}$ be the expected total queue size under the stationary distribution $\boldsymbol{\pi}$, defined by

$$\bar{Q} = \mathbb{E}_{\boldsymbol{\pi}}\Big[\sum_i Q_i\Big].$$

Note that by ergodicity, the time average of the total queue size and the expected total queue size under $\boldsymbol{\pi}$ are the same quantity.

2. *Tail exponent.* Let $\beta_L(Q), \beta_U(Q) \in [-\infty, 0]$ be the lower and upper limits of the tail exponent of the total queue size under $\boldsymbol{\pi}$ (possibly $-\infty$ or 0), respectively, defined by

$$\beta_L(Q) = \liminf_{\ell\to\infty} \frac{1}{\ell} \log \mathbb{P}_{\boldsymbol{\pi}}\Big(\sum_i Q_i \geqslant \ell\Big), \quad (25)$$

and $$\beta_U(Q) = \limsup_{\ell\to\infty} \frac{1}{\ell} \log \mathbb{P}_{\boldsymbol{\pi}}\Big(\sum_i Q_i \geqslant \ell\Big). \quad (26)$$

If $\beta_L(Q) = \beta_U(Q)$, then we denote this common value by $\beta(Q)$.

We are interested in policies that can achieve minimal $\bar{Q}$ and $\beta(Q)$. For tractability reasons, we focus on the *scaling* of these quantities with respect to $\mathcal{S}$ (equivalently, N) and $\rho(\boldsymbol{\lambda})$, as $1/(1-\rho(\boldsymbol{\lambda}))$ and N increase. Now, for different $\boldsymbol{\lambda}'$ and $\boldsymbol{\lambda}$, it is possible that $\rho(\boldsymbol{\lambda}) = \rho(\boldsymbol{\lambda}')$, but the scaling of $\bar{Q}$, for example, could be wildly different. For this reason, we consider the worst possible dependence on $1/(1-\rho)$ and N among all $\boldsymbol{\lambda}$ with $\rho(\boldsymbol{\lambda}) = \rho$.

Note that we are considering scalings with respect to two quantities ρ and N, and we are interested in two limiting regimes $\rho \to 1$ and $N \to \infty$. The optimality of average queue-size stated here is with respect to the order of limits $\rho \to 1$ and then $N \to \infty$. As noted in [24], taking the limits in different orders could potentially result in different limiting behaviors of the object of interest, e.g., $\bar{Q}$. For more discussions, see Section 6. It should be noted, however that the optimality of the tail exponent holds for *any* ρ and N.

Optimality of the tail exponent.

Here we establish the optimality of the tail exponent for any single-hop switched network under our policy. Consider any policy under which there exists a well-defined limiting stationary distribution of the queue sizes for all $\boldsymbol{\lambda}$ such that $\rho(\boldsymbol{\lambda}) < 1$. Let $\boldsymbol{\pi}_0$ denote the stationary distribution of queue sizes under this policy. The optimality of the tail exponent under our policy is an immediate consequence of the following lemma.

LEMMA 5.3. *Let* $\boldsymbol{\pi}_0$ *and* $\boldsymbol{\lambda}$ *be as described. Let* $\tilde{\rho}_1, \ldots, \tilde{\rho}_J$ *be as defined in* (4.3). *Then under* $\boldsymbol{\pi}_0$,

$$\liminf_{\ell\to\infty} \frac{1}{\ell} \log \mathbb{P}_{\boldsymbol{\pi}_0}\left(\sum_i Q_i \geqslant \ell\right) = \max_{j=1,2,\ldots,J} \log \tilde{\rho}_j.$$

PROOF. Recall that $\tilde{\rho}_j = \left(\sum_i R_{ji}\lambda_i\right)/C_j$, for $j = 1, 2, \ldots, J$, under the representation

$$\langle\mathcal{S}\rangle = \left\{\mathbf{x} \in [0,1]^N : \mathbf{R}\mathbf{x} \leqslant \mathbf{C}\right\}.$$

Without loss of generality, suppose that $\tilde{\rho}_1 = \max_{j=1,2,\ldots,J} \tilde{\rho}_j$. We now lower bound the total queue size stochastically by that of an $M/D/1$ queue. Consider an $M/D/1$ queue where the arrival rate is $\tilde{\rho}_1$, and the service capacity has a deterministic rate of 1. Since in the original network, this service capacity has to be shared among the queues, $\sum_i Q_i$ stochastically dominates this $M/D/1$ queue. Now the stationary distribution of this $M/D/1$ queue has a tail exponent $\log \tilde{\rho}_1$, which provides a lower bound on the same quantity in the original network, under $\boldsymbol{\pi}_0$. □

Input-queued switches.

Here we argue the optimality of our policy for input-queued switches. As discussed above, the scaling of tail exponent is optimal under our policy for any switched networks, and hence for input-queued switches. We would argue the optimal scaling of the average total queue size under our policy for input-queued switches. To that end, as argued in Shah et al. [24], when all input and output ports approach critical load, the average total queue size under any policy for input-queued switch must scale at least as fast as $\sqrt{N}/(1-\rho)$, for any n-port switch with $N = n^2$ queues.

For completeness, we include the proof for this lower bound here. As in Section 2.4, we use double indexing.

LEMMA 5.4. *Consider a n-port input-queued switch, with an arrival rate vector* $\boldsymbol{\lambda}$. *Suppose that the loads on all input and output ports are* ρ, *i.e.,* $\sum_{k=1}^{n} \lambda_{k,\ell} = \sum_m \lambda_{\ell,m} = \rho$, *for all* $\ell \in \{1, 2, \ldots, n\}$, *where* $\rho \in (0,1)$. *Consider any policy under which the queue-size process has a well-defined limiting stationary distribution, and let this distribution be denoted by* $\boldsymbol{\pi}_0$. *Then under* $\boldsymbol{\pi}_0$, *we must have*

$$\mathbb{E}_{\boldsymbol{\pi}_0}\left[\sum_{k,\ell=1}^{n} Q_{k,\ell}\right] \geqslant \frac{n\rho}{2(1-\rho)}.$$

PROOF. We consider the sums of queue sizes at each output port, i.e., the quantities $\sum_{k=1}^{n} Q_{k,\ell}$ for each $\ell \in \{1, 2, \ldots, n\}$. Since at most one packet can depart at each time slot, $\sum_{k=1}^{n} Q_{k,\ell}$ stochastically dominates the queue size in an $M/D/1$ system, with arrival rate ρ and deterministic service rate 1. Therefore, for each $\ell \in \{1, 2, \ldots, n\}$,

$$\mathbb{E}_{\boldsymbol{\pi}_0}\left[\sum_{k=1}^{n} Q_{k,\ell}\right] \geqslant \frac{\rho}{2(1-\rho)}.$$

Here, $\frac{\rho}{2(1-\rho)}$ is the expected queue size in steady state in an $M/D/1$ system. Summing over ℓ gives us the desired bound. □

The optimality in terms of the average total queue size is a direct consequence of Theorem 5.2 and Lemma 5.4.

COROLLARY 5.5. *Consider the same setup as in Lemma 5.4. Then in the heavy-traffic limit* $\rho \to 1$, *our policy is 2-optimal in terms of the average total queue size. More precisely, consider the expected total queue size in the diffusion scale in steady state, i.e.,* $(1-\rho)\bar{Q}$. *Then*

$$\limsup_{\rho \to 1} (1-\rho)\bar{Q} \leqslant n$$

under our policy, and

$$\liminf_{\rho \to 1} (1-\rho)\bar{Q} \geqslant \frac{n}{2}$$

under any other policy.

PROOF. Lemma 5.4 implies that

$$\liminf_{\rho \to 1} (1-\rho)\bar{Q} \geqslant \frac{n}{2}$$

under any policy. For the upper bound, note that by Theorem 5.2, under our policy,

$$\bar{Q} \leqslant \frac{J}{2(1-\rho)} + (N+2)K.$$

For input-queued switches, $J \leqslant 2n$, as remarked in Section 5.2, $N = n^2$, and $K = n$. Therefore, we have that under our policy, the expected total queue size scales as

$$\bar{Q} \leqslant \frac{n}{1-\rho} + (n^2+2)n. \tag{27}$$

Now consider the steady-state heavy-traffic scaling $(1-\rho)\mathbf{Q}$. We have that

$$(1-\rho)\bar{Q} \leqslant n + (1-\rho)(n^2+2)n. \tag{28}$$

The term $(1-\rho)(n^2+2)n$ goes to zero as $\rho \to 1$, and hence under our policy,

$$\limsup_{\rho \to 1} (1-\rho)\bar{Q} \leqslant n.$$

□

Our policy is not optimal in terms of the average total queue size, in general switched networks. In cases where $J >> N$, the moment bounds for the maximum-weight policy give tighter upper bounds. For more discussions, see Section 6.

5.3 Proof of Theorem 5.2.

The proof is divided in three parts. The first part describes a sample-path-wise relation between $\mathbf{Q}(\cdot)$ and $\mathbf{M}(\cdot)$, which implies that $\mathbf{Q}(\cdot)$ is essentially dominated by $\mathbf{M}(\cdot)$ at all times. Note that this domination is a distribution-free statement. The second part utilizes this fact to establish the positive recurrence of the **SN** Markov chain. Given the technical nature of the second part, we skip the detail, which can be found in [26]. The third part, as a consequence of the first two parts, and using Theorem 4.1, establishes the quantitative claims in Theorem 5.2.

Part 1. Dominance. We start by establishing that the queue sizes $\mathbf{Q}(\cdot)$ of **SN** are effectively dominated by the workloads $\mathbf{W}(\cdot)$ of **BN** at all times. We state this result formally in Proposition 5.8, which is a consequence of Lemmas 5.6 and 5.7 below.

LEMMA 5.6. *Consider the evolution of queue sizes in both* ***BN*** *and* ***SN*** *networks fed by identical arrival process. Initially,* $\mathbf{Q}(0) = \mathbf{M}(0) = \mathbf{0}$. *Let* $\mathbf{W}(\tau) = (W_i(\tau))$ *denote the amount of unfinished work in all* N *queues under the* ***BN*** *network at time* τ. *Then for any* $\tau \geqslant 0$ *and* $1 \leqslant i \leqslant N$,

$$Q_i(\tau) \leqslant W_i(\tau) + D_i(\tau) \leqslant M_i(\tau) + D_i(\tau), \tag{29}$$

where $\mathbf{D}(\tau) = \Lambda^{SFA}(\tau) - \mathbf{B}(\tau)$ *is as described in Section 5.1.*

PROOF. Consider any $i \in \{1, 2, \ldots, N\}$ and $\tau \geqslant 0$. From (4), in **SN**,

$$Q_i(\tau) = A_i(\tau) - B_i(\tau) + Z_i(\tau), \tag{30}$$

where $Z_i(\tau)$ is the cumulative amount of idling at the ith queue in **SN**. In a similar manner, in **BN**,

$$W_i(\tau) = A_i(\tau) - \Lambda_i^{\text{SFA}}(\tau) + \hat{Z}_i(\tau), \tag{31}$$

where $\hat{Z}_i(\tau)$ is the cumulative amount of idling for the ith queue in **BN**. Since by construction, $\mathbf{D}(\tau) = \Lambda^{\text{SFA}}(\tau) - \mathbf{B}(\tau)$, and $\mathbf{D}(\tau) \geqslant \mathbf{0}$, we have that

$$B_i(\tau) \leqslant \Lambda_i^{\text{SFA}}(\tau) \leqslant B_i(\tau) + D_i(\tau). \tag{32}$$

By definition, the instantaneous rate allocation to the ith queue satisfies $\frac{d}{dt^+}\Lambda_i^{\text{SFA}}(t) = 0$ if $W_i(t) = 0$ (equivalently, if $M_i(t) = 0$) for any $t \geqslant 0$. Therefore, $\hat{Z}_i(\tau) = 0$. On the other hand, by Skorohod's map,

$$\begin{aligned} Z_i(\tau) &= \sup_{0 \leqslant s \leqslant \tau} \left[B_i(s) - A_i(s)\right]^+ \\ &\leqslant \sup_{0 \leqslant s \leqslant \tau} \left[\Lambda_i^{\text{SFA}}(s) - A_i(s)\right]^+ \\ &= \hat{Z}_i(\tau). \end{aligned} \tag{33}$$

From (32) and (33), it follows that

$$\begin{aligned} Q_i(\tau) &= A_i(\tau) - B_i(\tau) + Z_i(\tau) \\ &\leqslant A_i(\tau) - \Lambda_i^{\mathrm{SFA}}(\tau) + D_i(\tau) + Z_i(\tau) \\ &\leqslant A_i(\tau) - \Lambda_i^{\mathrm{SFA}}(\tau) + D_i(\tau) + \widehat{Z}_i(\tau) \\ &= W_i(\tau) + D_i(\tau). \end{aligned} \tag{34}$$

Since the workload at the ith queue equals the total amount of unfinished work for all of the $M_i(\tau)$ packets waiting at the ith queue, and since each packet has at most a unit amount of unfinished work, $W_i(\tau) \leqslant M_i(\tau)$. □

LEMMA 5.7. *Let* $\mathbf{D}(\tau)$ *be as in Lemma 5.6. For all* $\tau \geqslant 0$, $\rho(\mathbf{D}(\tau)) \leqslant N+2$. *In particular,*

$$\sum_i D_i(\tau) \leqslant K(N+2), \quad \textit{where} \quad K = \max_{\sigma \in \mathcal{S}} \sum_i \sigma_i. \tag{35}$$

PROOF. This result is established as follows. First, observe that $\mathbf{D}(0) = \mathbf{0}$ and therefore $\rho(\mathbf{D}(0)) = 0$. Next, we show that $\rho(\mathbf{D}(\tau+1)) \leqslant \rho(\mathbf{D}(\tau)) + 1$. That is, $\rho(\mathbf{D}(\cdot))$ can at most increase by 1 in each time slot. And finally, we show that it cannot increase once it exceeds $N+1$. That is, if $\rho(\mathbf{D}(\tau)) \geqslant N+1$, then $\rho(\mathbf{D}(\tau+1)) \leqslant \rho(\mathbf{D}(\tau))$. This will complete the proof.

We start by establishing that $\rho(\mathbf{D}(\cdot))$ increases by at most 1 in unit time. By definition,

$$\begin{aligned} \mathbf{D}(\tau+1) &= \Lambda^{\mathrm{SFA}}(\tau+1) - \mathbf{B}(\tau+1) \\ &= \Lambda^{\mathrm{SFA}}(\tau) - \mathbf{B}(\tau) \qquad (36) \\ &\quad + \Big(\Lambda^{\mathrm{SFA}}(\tau+1) - \Lambda^{\mathrm{SFA}}(\tau) - d\mathbf{B}(\tau)\Big) \\ &= \mathbf{D}(\tau) + d\Lambda^{\mathrm{SFA}}(\tau) - d\mathbf{B}(\tau) \\ &= \Big(\mathbf{D}(\tau) - d\mathbf{B}(\tau)\Big) + d\Lambda^{\mathrm{SFA}}(\tau), \qquad (37) \end{aligned}$$

where $d\Lambda^{\mathrm{SFA}}(\tau) = \Lambda^{\mathrm{SFA}}(\tau+1) - \Lambda^{\mathrm{SFA}}(\tau)$. As remarked earlier, $d\mathbf{B}(\tau) \leqslant \mathbf{D}(\tau)$ component-wise. Therefore, by (10) it follows that

$$\rho\big(\mathbf{D}(\tau+1)\big) \leqslant \rho\big(\mathbf{D}(\tau) - d\mathbf{B}(\tau)\big) + \rho(d\Lambda^{\mathrm{SFA}}(\tau)).$$

Note that $\rho(d\Lambda^{\mathrm{SFA}}(\tau)) \leqslant 1$ because the instantaneous service rate under SFA is always admissible. Since $\mathbf{D}(\tau) \geqslant \mathbf{D}(\tau) - d\mathbf{B}(\tau) \geqslant \mathbf{0}$, any feasible solution to PRIMAL $\big(\mathbf{D}(\tau)\big)$ is also feasible to PRIMAL $\big(\mathbf{D}(\tau) - d\mathbf{B}(\tau)\big)$, and hence

$$\rho\big(\mathbf{D}(\tau) - d\mathbf{B}(\tau)\big) \leqslant \rho\big(\mathbf{D}(\tau)\big).$$

Hence it follows that

$$\rho\big(\mathbf{D}(\tau+1)\big) \leqslant \rho\big(\mathbf{D}(\tau)\big) + 1. \tag{38}$$

Next, we shall argue that if $\rho(\mathbf{D}(\tau)) \geqslant N+1$, then $\rho(\mathbf{D}(\tau+1)) \leqslant \rho(\mathbf{D}(\tau))$. To that end, suppose that $\rho(\mathbf{D}(\tau)) \geqslant N+1$. Now $\frac{1}{\rho(\mathbf{D}(\tau))}\mathbf{D}(\tau) \in \langle \mathcal{S} \rangle$. Note that $\langle \mathcal{S} \rangle$ is a convex set in a N-dimensional space with extreme points contained in $\mathcal{S}$. Therefore, by Carathéodory's theorem, $\frac{1}{\rho(\mathbf{D}(\tau))}\mathbf{D}(\tau)$ can be written as a convex combination of at most $N+1$ elements in $\mathcal{S}$. That is, there exists $\alpha_k \geqslant 0$ with $\sum_{k=1}^{N+1} \alpha_k = 1$, and $\boldsymbol{\sigma}^k \in \mathcal{S}$, $k \in \{1, 2, \ldots, N+1\}$, such that

$$\frac{1}{\rho(\mathbf{D}(\tau))}\mathbf{D}(\tau) = \sum_{k=1}^{N+1} \alpha_k \boldsymbol{\sigma}^k. \tag{39}$$

Therefore, there exists some $k^* \in \{1, 2, \ldots, N+1\}$, such that $\alpha_{k^*} \geqslant 1/(N+1)$. Since $\rho(\mathbf{D}(\tau)) \geqslant N+1$, $\rho(\mathbf{D}(\tau))\alpha_{k^*} \geqslant 1$.

That is, $\mathbf{D}(\tau)$ can be written as a convex combination of elements from $\mathcal{S}$ with one of them, $\boldsymbol{\sigma}^{k^*}$, having an associated coefficient that satisfies $\rho(\mathbf{D}(\tau))\alpha_{k^*} \geqslant 1$, as required. In this case, we have

$$\mathbf{D}(\tau) - \boldsymbol{\sigma}^{k^*} = \sum_{k=1, k \neq k^*}^{N+1} \rho(\mathbf{D}(\tau))\alpha_k \boldsymbol{\sigma}^k + (\rho(\mathbf{D}(\tau))\alpha_{k^*} - 1)\boldsymbol{\sigma}^{k^*}. \tag{40}$$

Therefore,

$$\rho\Big(\mathbf{D}(\tau) - \boldsymbol{\sigma}^{k^*}\Big) \leqslant \rho(\mathbf{D}(\tau)) - 1. \tag{41}$$

Our scheduling policy chooses such a schedule, i.e., $\boldsymbol{\sigma}^{k^*}$; that is, $d\mathbf{B}(\tau) = \boldsymbol{\sigma}^{k^*}$. Therefore,

$$\mathbf{D}(\tau+1) = \mathbf{D}(\tau) - \boldsymbol{\sigma}^{k^*} + d\Lambda^{\mathrm{SFA}}(\tau). \tag{42}$$

By another application of (10) it follows that

$$\begin{aligned} \rho(\mathbf{D}(\tau+1)) &\leqslant \rho(\mathbf{D}(\tau) - \boldsymbol{\sigma}^{k^*}) + \rho(d\Lambda^{\mathrm{SFA}}(\tau)) \\ &\leqslant \rho(\mathbf{D}(\tau)) - 1 + 1, \\ &= \rho(\mathbf{D}(\tau)), \end{aligned} \tag{43}$$

where again we have used the fact that $\rho(d\Lambda^{\mathrm{SFA}}(\tau)) \leqslant 1$, due to the feasibility of SFA policy and (41). This establishes that $\rho(\mathbf{D}(\tau)) \leqslant N+2$ for all $\tau \geqslant 0$. That is, for each $\tau \geqslant 0$, there exist $\alpha_{\boldsymbol{\sigma}} \geqslant 0$ for all $\boldsymbol{\sigma} \in \mathcal{S}$, $\sum_{\boldsymbol{\sigma}} \alpha_{\boldsymbol{\sigma}} \leqslant N+2$ and

$$\mathbf{D}(\tau) \leqslant \sum_{\boldsymbol{\sigma}} \alpha_{\boldsymbol{\sigma}} \boldsymbol{\sigma}. \tag{44}$$

Therefore,

$$\begin{aligned} \sum_i D_i(\tau) &= \mathbf{D}(\tau) \cdot \mathbf{1} \\ &\leqslant \sum_{\boldsymbol{\sigma}} \alpha_{\boldsymbol{\sigma}} \boldsymbol{\sigma} \cdot \mathbf{1} \\ &\leqslant \Big(\sum_{\boldsymbol{\sigma}} \alpha_{\boldsymbol{\sigma}}\Big)\Big(\max_{\sigma \in \mathcal{S}} \sum_i \sigma_i\Big) \\ &\leqslant (N+2)K, \end{aligned} \tag{45}$$

where $K = \max_{\boldsymbol{\sigma} \in \mathcal{S}} \sum_i \sigma_i$. This completes the proof of Lemma 5.7. □

Lemma 5.6 and 5.7 together imply the following proposition.

PROPOSITION 5.8. *Let* $\mathbf{Q}(\cdot)$, $\mathbf{W}(\cdot)$ *and* $\mathbf{M}(\cdot)$ *be as in Lemma 5.6. Then*

$$\sum_{i=1}^N Q_i(\tau) \leqslant \sum_{i=1}^N W_i(\tau) + K(N+2) \leqslant \sum_{i=1}^N M_i(\tau) + K(N+2), \tag{46}$$

where $K = \max_{\boldsymbol{\sigma} \in \mathcal{S}} \Big(\sum_{i=1}^N \sigma_i\Big)$.

PROOF. We obtain the bounds (46) by summing inequality (29) over $i \in \{1, 2, \ldots, N\}$, and using the bound (35). □

Part 2. Positive recurrence. See [26].

Part 3. Completing the proof. The positive recurrence of the Markov chain $\mathbf{X}(\cdot)$ implies that it possesses a unique stationary distribution and it is ergodic. Let $\overline{W} =$

$\mathbb{E}_\pi\left[\sum_{i=1}^N W_i\right]$, where, similar to Lemma 5.6, W_i is the steady-state workload on queue i in **BN**. Define $\bar{M}$ similarly. By ergodicity, the time average of the total queue size equals the expected total queue size in steady state, i.e., $\bar{Q}$, and similarly for $\bar{W}$. Therefore, by Proposition 5.8,

$$\bar{Q} \leqslant \bar{W} + K(N+2).$$

We now claim that

$$\bar{W} \leqslant \frac{1}{2}\left(\sum_{j=1}^J \frac{\tilde{\rho}_j}{1-\tilde{\rho}_j}\right).$$

First, we have that

$$\bar{M} \leqslant \sum_{j=1}^J \frac{\tilde{\rho}_j}{1-\tilde{\rho}_j}.$$

By Propositions 4.2 and 4.3, $\bar{M}$ is the sum of J independent geometric random variables, with parameters $1-\tilde{\rho}_1, 1-\tilde{\rho}_2, \ldots, 1-\tilde{\rho}_J$. Hence, in fact, we have

$$\bar{M} = \sum_{j=1}^J \frac{\tilde{\rho}_j}{1-\tilde{\rho}_j}.$$

By Theorem 4.1, the individual residual workload in steady state is independent from the number of packets in the network, and is uniformly distributed on $[0,1]$. Therefore, $\bar{W} = \frac{1}{2}\bar{M}$, and the claim is proved.

We now establish the tail exponent in (24). By Lemma 5.3,

$$\beta_L(\mathbf{Q}) \geqslant \max_{j=1,2,\ldots,J} \log \tilde{\rho}_j,$$

so we only need to show that

$$\beta_U(\mathbf{Q}) \leqslant \max_{j=1,2,\ldots,J} \log \tilde{\rho}_j,$$

where $\beta_L(\mathbf{Q})$ and $\beta_U(\mathbf{Q})$ are defined in (25) and (26) respectively.

First note that $\beta_U(\mathbf{Q}) \leqslant \beta_U(\mathbf{M})$, where $\mathbf{M}$ is the queue-size vector of the virtual system **BN**. This is because, by Proposition 5.8,

$$\sum_{i=1}^N Q_i(\tau) \leqslant \sum_{i=1}^N M_i(\tau) + K(N+2),$$

deterministically and for all times τ. Thus, in steady state, $\sum_{i=1}^N Q_i$ is upper bounded by $\sum_{i=1}^N M_i(\tau) + K(N+2)$, deterministically. Since $K(N+2)$ is a constant, $\sum_{i=1}^N M_i(\tau) + K(N+2)$ and $\sum_{i=1}^N M_i(\tau)$ have the same tail exponent. This establishes that $\beta_U(\mathbf{Q}) \leqslant \beta_U(\mathbf{M})$.

We now consider $\beta_U(\mathbf{M})$. As noted earlier, in steady state, $\mathbf{M}$ is the sum of J independent geometric random variables, with parameters $1-\tilde{\rho}_1, 1-\tilde{\rho}_2, \ldots, 1-\tilde{\rho}_J$. The following lemma states that the tail exponent of the sum of these J geometric random variables is upper bounded by $\max_{j=1,2,\ldots,J} \log \tilde{\rho}_j$.

LEMMA 5.9. *Let M be the sum of J independent geometric random variables, with parameters $1-\tilde{\rho}_1, \ldots, 1-\tilde{\rho}_J$ respectively, where $\tilde{\rho}_j \in [0,1)$ for all $j \in \{1,2,\ldots,J\}$. Then we have*

$$\limsup_{\ell\to\infty} \frac{1}{\ell} \log \mathbb{P}(M \geqslant \ell) \leqslant \max_{j=1,2,\ldots,J} \log \tilde{\rho}_j.$$

The detailed proof is provided in [26].

In conclusion,

$$\beta_U(\mathbf{Q}) \leqslant \beta_U(\mathbf{M}) = \max_{j=1,2,\ldots,J} \log \tilde{\rho}_j.$$

6. DISCUSSION.

We presented a novel scheduling policy for a generic single-hop switched network model. The policy, in effect, emulates the so-called Store-and-forward (SFA) continuous-time bandwidth-sharing policy. The insensitivity property of SFA along with the relation of its stationary distribution with that of multi-class queueing network leads to the explicit characterization of the stationary distribution of queue sizes induced by our policy. This allows us to establish the optimality of our policy in terms of tail exponent for any single-hop switched network and that with respect to the average total queue size for a class of switched networks, including the input-queued switches. As a consequence, this settles a conjecture stated in [24]. On the technical end, a key contribution of the paper is creating a discrete-time scheduling policy from a continuous-time rate allocation policy, and this on its own may be of potential interest in other domains of applications.

The switched network model considered here requires the arrival processes to be Poisson. However, this is not a major restriction, due to a *Poissonization* trick considered, for example in [9] and [14]: all arriving packets are first passed through a 'regularizer', which emits packets according to a Poisson process with a rate that lies between the arrival rate and the network capacity. This leads to the arrivals being effectively Poisson, as seen by the system with a somewhat higher rate — by choosing the rate of 'regularizer' so that the effective gap to the capacity, i.e., $(1-\rho)$, is decreased by factor 2.

The scheduling policy that we propose is not optimal for general switched networks. For example, in the context of ad-hoc wireless networks, in the independent-set model, there are as many constraints as the number of edges in the interference graph, which is often much larger than the number of nodes. Under our policy, the average total queue size would scale with the number of edges, whereas maximum-weight policy achieves a scaling with the number of nodes.

There are many possible directions for future research. One direction is the search for low-complexity and optimal scheduling policies. In the context of input-queued switches, our policy has a complexity that is exponential in N, the number of queues, because one has to compute the sum of exponentially many terms at every time instance. This begs the question of finding an optimal policy with polynomial complexity in N. One candidate is the MW-α policies, which has polynomial complexity, but their optimality appears difficult to analyze. Another possible candidate could be, as discussed in the introduction, a (randomized) version of proportional fairness.

Acknowledgements.

Devavrat Shah and Yuan Zhong would like to thank John Tsitsiklis for a careful reading of the paper which has helped improve the readability, for his insights and support of this project. They would also like to acknowledge the support of NSF TF collaborative project and NSF CNS CAREER project.

7. REFERENCES

[1] S. Asmussen. *Applied probability and queues.* Second edition, Springer Verlag, 2003.

[2] G. Birkhoff. Tres observaciones sobre el algebra lineal. *Univ. Nac. Tucuman Rev. Ser. A*, 5:147–151, 1946.

[3] T. Bonald and A. Proutiére. Insensitivity in processor-sharing networks. *Performance Evaluation*, 49(1-4):193–209, 2002.

[4] T. Bonald and A. Proutiére. Insensitive bandwidth sharing in data networks. *Queueing systems*, 44(1):69–100, 2003.

[5] M. Bramson. State space collapse with application to heavy traffic limits for multiclass queueing networks. *Queueing Systems*, 30:89–148, 1998.

[6] J. G. Dai and W. Lin. Maximum pressure policies in stochastic processing networks. *Operations Research*, 53(2), 2005.

[7] J. G. Dai and W. Lin. Asymptotic optimality of maximum pressure policies in stochastic processing networks. *The Annals of Applied Probability*, 18(6), 2008.

[8] J. G. Dai and B. Prabhakar. The throughput of switches with and without speed-up. In *Proceedings of IEEE Infocom*, pages 556–564, 2000.

[9] A. El Gamal, J. Mammen, B. Prabhakar, and D. Shah. Optimal throughput-delay scaling in wireless networks – part ii: Constant-size packets. *Information Theory, IEEE Transactions on*, 52(11):5111–5116, 2006.

[10] S. Foss and T. Konstantopoulos. An overview of some stochastic stability methods. *Journal of Operations Research, Society of Japan*, 47(4), 2004.

[11] J. M. Harrison. Balanced fluid models of multiclass queueing networks: A heavy traffic conjecture. *Stochastic Networks*, 71:1–20, 1995. IMA Volumes in Mathematics and Its Applications.

[12] J. M. Harrison. Brownian models of open processing networks: canonical representation of workload. *The Annals of Applied Probability*, 10:75–103, 2000. Also see [13].

[13] J. M. Harrison. Correction to [12]. *The Annals of Applied Probability*, 13:390–393, 2003.

[14] S. Jagabathula and D. Shah. Optimal delay scheduling in networks with arbitrary constraints. In *Proceedings of the 2008 ACM SIGMETRICS*, pages 395–406. ACM, 2008.

[15] W. Kang, F. Kelly, N. Lee, and R. Williams. State space collapse and diffusion approximation for a network operating under a fair bandwidth sharing policy. *The Annals of Applied Probability*, 2009.

[16] F. Kelly, L. Massoulié, and N. Walton. Resource pooling in congested networks: proportional fairness and product form. *Queueing Systems*, 63(1):165–194, 2009.

[17] F. P. Kelly. *Reversibility and Stochastic Networks.* Wiley, Chicester, 1979.

[18] J. F. C. Kingman. On queues in heavy traffic. *Journal of the Royal Statistical Society, series B*, 24(2):383–392, 1962.

[19] S. Meyn. Stability and asymptotic optimality of generalized maxweight policies. *SIAM J. Control and Optimization*, 2008.

[20] S. Meyn and R. Tweedie. *Markov chains and stochastic stability.* Springer New York, 1993.

[21] M. Neely, E. Modiano, and Y. Cheng. Logarithmic delay for n× n packet switches under the crossbar constraint. *IEEE/ACM Transactions on Networking (TON)*, 15(3):657–668, 2007.

[22] A. Proutiére. *Insensitivity and stochastic bounds in queueing networks–Applications to flow level traffic modelling in telecommunication networks.* PhD thesis, Ecoloe Doctorale de l'Ecole Polytechnique, 2003.

[23] D. Shah, J. N. Tsitsiklis, and Y. Zhong. Qualitative properties of α-weighted scheduling policies. In *ACM SIGMETRICS Performance Evaluation Review*, volume 38, pages 239–250. ACM, 2010.

[24] D. Shah, J. N. Tsitsiklis, and Y. Zhong. Optimal scaling of average queue sizes in an input-queued switch: an open problem. *Queueing Systems*, 68(3-4):375–384, 2011.

[25] D. Shah, J. N. Tsitsiklis, and Y. Zhong. Qualitative properties of alpha-fair policies in bandwidth sharing network. *Unpublished, available on arxiv.org*, 2011.

[26] D. Shah, N. Walton, and Y. Zhong. Optimal queue-size scaling in switched networks. `http://arxiv.org/pdf/1110.4697v1.pdf`.

[27] D. Shah and D. Wischik. Fluid models of congestion collapse in overloaded switched networks. *Queueing Systems*, 69(2):121–143, 2011.

[28] D. Shah and D. Wischik. Switched networks with maximum weight policies: Fluid approximation and state space collapse. *The Annals of Applied Probability*, 2011.

[29] A. Stolyar. Large deviations of queues sharing a randomly time-varying server. *Queueing Systems*, 59(1):1–35, 2008.

[30] A. L. Stolyar. MaxWeight scheduling in a generalized switch: State space collapse and workload minimization in heavy traffic. *The Annals of Applied Probability*, 14(1):1–53, 2004.

[31] L. Tassiulas and A. Ephremides. Stability properties of constrained queueing systems and scheduling policies for maximum throughput in multihop radio networks. *IEEE Transactions on Automatic Control*, 37:1936–1948, 1992.

[32] V. Venkataramanan and X. Lin. Structural properties of LDP for queue-length based wireless scheduling algorithms. In *Proceedings of Allerton*, 2007.

[33] J. von Neumann. A certain zero-sum two-person game equivalent to the optimal assignment problem. *In Contributions to the theory of games*, 2, 1953.

[34] N. Walton. Proportional fairness and its relationship with multi-class queueing networks. *The Annals of Applied Probability*, 19(6):2301–2333, 2009.

[35] W. Whitt. *Stochastic-Process Limits.* Springer, 2001.

[36] R. J. Williams. Diffusion approximations for open multiclass queueing networks: sufficient conditions involving state space collapse. *Queueing Systems*, 30:27–88, 1998.

[37] S. Zachary. A note on insensitivity in stochastic networks. *Journal of applied probability*, 44(1):238–248, 2007.

Minimizing Slowdown in Heterogeneous Size-Aware Dispatching Systems

Esa Hyytiä
Aalto University, Finland
esa@comnet.tkk.fi

Samuli Aalto
Aalto University, Finland
samuli@comnet.tkk.fi

Aleksi Penttinen
Aalto University, Finland
aleksi.penttinen@aalto.fi

ABSTRACT

We consider a system of parallel queues where tasks are assigned (dispatched) to one of the available servers upon arrival. The dispatching decision is based on the full state information, i.e., on the sizes of the new and existing jobs. We are interested in minimizing the so-called mean slowdown criterion corresponding to the mean of the sojourn time divided by the processing time. Assuming no new jobs arrive, the shortest-processing-time-product (SPTP) schedule is known to minimize the slowdown of the existing jobs. The main contribution of this paper is three-fold: 1) To show the optimality of SPTP with respect to slowdown in a single server queue *under Poisson arrivals*; 2) to derive the so-called size-aware value functions for M/G/1-FIFO/LIFO/SPTP *with general holding costs* of which the slowdown criterion is a special case; and 3) to utilize the value functions to derive efficient dispatching policies so as to minimize the mean slowdown in a heterogeneous server system. The derived policies offer a significantly better performance than e.g., the size-aware-task-assignment with equal load (SITA-E) and least-work-left (LWL) policies.

Categories and Subject Descriptors

D.4.8 [**Performance**]: Queueing Theory; G.3 [**Probability and Statistics**]: Queueing Theory; F.2.2 [**Nonnumerical Algorithms and Problems**]: Sequencing and Scheduling

Keywords

Task Assignment, M/G/1, policy improvement, MDP

1. INTRODUCTION

Dispatching problems arise in many contexts such as manufacturing sites, web server farms, super computing systems, and other parallel server systems. In a dispatching system jobs are assigned upon arrival to one of the several queues as illustrated in Fig. 1. Such systems involve two decisions: (i) *dispatching policy* α chooses the server, and (ii) *scheduling discipline* the order in which the jobs are served. The dispatching decisions are irrevocable, i.e., it is not possible to move a job to another queue afterwards. In the literature, the dispatching problems and their solutions differ with respect to (i) optimization objective, (ii) available information, and (iii) scheduling discipline used in the servers.

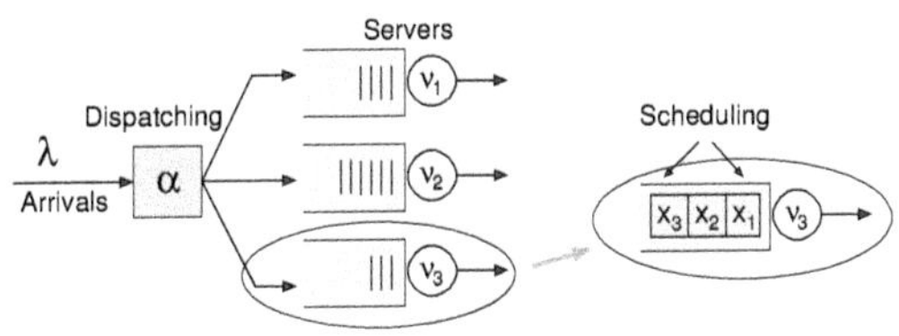

Figure 1: A dispatching system with m = 3 servers.

Although the literature has generally addressed the mean sojourn time (i.e., response time) as the optimization objective, also other performance metrics can be relevant. One such metric is the *slowdown*[1] of a job, defined as the ratio of the sojourn time and the processing time (service requirement) [17, 9, 1]. The slowdown criterion combines *efficiency* and *fairness* and stems from the idea that *longer jobs can tolerate longer sojourn time.* The optimal scheduling discipline in this respect for a single server queue and a fixed number of jobs is the so-called *shortest-processing-time-product*[2] (SPTP) discipline [31], where the index of a job is the product of the initial and remaining service requirements and the job with the smallest index is served first. With aid of Gittins index, we show that SPTP minimizes the mean slowdown in single server queues also in the dynamic case of Poisson arrivals, i.e., it is the optimal discipline for an M/G/1 queue with respect to the slowdown.

Then we derive value functions with respect to *arbitrary job specific holding costs* for an M/G/1 with the first-in-first-out (FIFO), the last-in-first-out (LIFO), the shortest-processing-time (SPT), the shortest-remaining-processing-time (SRPT) and SPTP scheduling disciplines, where the last three are size-aware. A value function essentially characterizes the queue state in terms of the expected costs in infinite time horizon for a fixed scheduling discipline. In this respect, our work generalizes the results of [20] to arbitrary job specific holding cost rates, and includes also the analysis of the slowdown specific SPTP scheduling discipline.

[1]Yang and de Veciana refer to the slowdown as the bit-transmission delay (BTD) [31].
[2]Wierman et al. refer to SPTP as the RS policy, a product of the remaining size and the original size [29].

Finally, we apply the derived value functions to the dispatching problem so as to minimize the mean slowdown when the scheduling disciplines in each queue are fixed. We assume that the dispatcher is fully aware of the state of the system, i.e., of the tasks in each queue and their remaining service requirements. By starting with an arbitrary state-independent policy, we carry out the first-policy-iteration (FPI) step of the Markov decision processes (MDP) and obtain efficient state-dependent dispatching policies.

The rest of the paper is organized as follows. In Section 2, we consider a single M/G/1 queue with respect to slowdown criterion, and prove the optimality of SPTP. In Section 3, we derive the size-aware value functions with respect to arbitrary job specific holding cost rates for FIFO, LIFO and SPTP. (SPT and SRPT are given in [19]). The single queue scheduling related results are utilized in Section 4 to derive efficient dispatching policies, which are then evaluated in Section 5. Section 6 concludes the paper.

1.1 Related Work

FIFO is perhaps the most common scheduling discipline due to its nature and ease of implementation. Other common disciplines are LIFO, SPT and SRPT. As for the objective, minimization of the mean sojourn time has been a popular choice. Indeed, SPT and SRPT, respectively, are the optimal non-preemptive and preemptive schedules with this respect [26]. For a recent survey on fairness and other scheduling objectives in a single server queue we refer to [28].

In the context of dispatching problems, FIFO has been studied extensively in the literature since the early work by Winston [30], Ephremides et al. [8], and others. Often the number of tasks per server is assumed to be known, cf., e.g., *join-the-shortest-queue* (JSQ) dispatching policy [30]. Even though FIFO queues have received the most of the attention, also other scheduling disciplines have been studied. For example, Gupta et. al consider JSQ with *processor-sharing* (PS) scheduling discipline in [12].

Only a few optimality results are known for the dispatching problems. Assuming exponentially distributed interarrival times and job sizes, [30] shows that JSQ with FIFO minimizes the mean waiting time when the number in each queue is available. Also [8] argues for the optimality of JSQ/FIFO when the number in each queue is available, while the Round-Robin (RR), followed by FIFO, is shown to be the optimal policy when it is only known that the queues were initially in the same state. [25] proves that RR/FIFO is optimal with the absence of queue length information if the job sizes have a non-decreasing hazard function. The RR results were later generalized in [24]. Whitt [27], on the other hand, provides several counterexamples where JSQ/FIFO policy fails. Crovella et al.[6] and Harchol-Balter et al. [14] assume that the dispatcher is aware of the size of a new job, but not of the state of the FIFO queues, and propose policies based on job size intervals (e.g., short jobs to one queue, and the rest to another). Feng et al. [10] later showed that such a policy is the optimal size-aware state-independent dispatching policy for homogeneous servers.

Also the MDP framework lends itself to dispatching problems. Krishnan [23] has utilized it in the context of parallel M/M/s-FIFO servers so as to minimize the mean sojourn time, similarly as Aalto and Virtamo [3] for the traditional M/M/1 queue. Recently, FIFO, LIFO, SPT and SRPT queues were analyzed in [20] with a general service time distribution. Similarly, PS is considered in [22, 21]. The key idea with the above work is to start by an arbitrary state-independent policy, and then carry out FPI step utilizing the value functions (relative values of states).

2. M/G/1 QUEUE AND SLOWDOWN

In this section we consider a single M/G/1 queue with arrival rate λ. The service requirements are i.i.d. random variables $X_i \sim X$ with a general distribution.

We define the *slowdown* of a job as a ratio of the sojourn time T to the service requirement X,

$$\gamma \triangleq \frac{T}{X},$$

where one is generally interested in its mean value $\mathrm{E}[\gamma]$. Also other similar definitions exist. In the context of distributed computing, Harchol-Balter defines the slowdown as the "wall-time" divided by the CPU-time in [15]. Another common convention is to consider the ratio of the waiting time to the processing time (see, e.g., [13]), which is a well-defined quantity for non-preemptive systems. These different definitions, however, are essentially the same.

For non-preemptive work conserving policies, the sojourn time in queue comprises the initial waiting time W and the consequent processing time X. Thus, the mean slowdown is

$$\mathrm{E}[\gamma] = \mathrm{E}[\frac{W+X}{X}] = 1 + \mathrm{E}[W/X].$$

Waiting time with FIFO is independent of the job size X, and with aid of Pollaczek-Khinchin formula one obtains [13],

$$\mathrm{E}[\gamma] = 1 + \mathrm{E}[W] \cdot \mathrm{E}[X^{-1}] = 1 + \frac{\lambda\,\mathrm{E}[X^2]}{2(1-\rho)} \cdot \mathrm{E}[X^{-1}], \quad (1)$$

which underlines the fact that the mean slowdown may be infinite for a stable queue as $\mathrm{E}[X^{-1}] = \infty$ for many common job size distributions, e.g., for an exponential distribution.

The mean slowdown in an M/G/1 queue with preemptive LIFO and PS disciplines is a constant for all job sizes,

$$\mathrm{E}[\gamma \mid X = x] = \frac{1}{1-\rho}. \quad (2)$$

Comparison of (1) and (2) immediately gives:

COROLLARY 1. *FIFO is a better scheduling discipline than LIFO in an M/G/1 queue with respect to slowdown iff*

$$2\,\mathrm{E}[X] > \mathrm{E}[X^2] \cdot \mathrm{E}[X^{-1}]. \quad (3)$$

2.1 Shortest-Processing-Time-Product (SPTP)

In [31], Yang and de Veciana introduced the *shortest-processing-time-product* (SPTP) scheduling discipline, which will serve the job i^* such that

$$i^* = \arg\min_i \Delta_i^* \Delta_i,$$

where Δ_i^* and Δ_i denote, respectively, the initial and remaining service requirement of job i. Yang and de Veciana were able to show that SPTP is optimal with respect to the mean slowdown $\mathrm{E}[\gamma]$ in a transient system where all jobs are available at time 0 and no new jobs arrive thereafter (i.e., a *myopic* approach). SPTP can be seen as the counterpart of the SRPT[3] when instead of minimizing the mean sojourn time, one is interested in minimizing the mean slowdown.

We argue below that SPTP is the optimal scheduling discipline also in the corresponding dynamic system with Poisson arrivals. That is, we show that SPTP is optimal with respect to the slowdown in the M/G/1 queue. Our proof is based on the Gittins index approach.

2.2 Gittins Index

Consider an M/G/1 queue with *multiple* job classes k, $k = 1,\dots,K$. Let λ_k denote the class-k arrival rate, and $p_k = \lambda_k/\lambda$ the probability that an arriving job belongs to class k. In addition, let X_k denote the generic service time related to class k. The total load is denoted by $\rho = \lambda_1 \mathrm{E}[X_1] + \dots + \lambda_K \mathrm{E}[X_K]$. We assume that $\rho < 1$. The *Gittins index* [11, 2] for a class-k job with attained service a is defined by

$$G_k(a) = \sup_{\delta>0} w_k \frac{\mathrm{P}\{X_k - a \le \delta \mid X_k > a\}}{\mathrm{E}[\min\{X_k - a, \delta\} \mid X_k > a]},$$

where w_k is the holding cost rate related to class k. Note that, in addition to the attained service a, the Gittins index is based on the (class-specific) distribution of the service time, but not on the service time itself. The *Gittins index policy* will serve the job i^* such that

$$i^* = \arg\max_i G_{k_i}(a_i),$$

where k_i refers to the class and a_i to the attained service of job i. Let T_k denote the sojourn time of a class-k job. We recall the following optimality result proved by Gittins [11, Theorem 3.28].

THEOREM 1. *Consider an M/G/1 multi-class queue. The Gittins index policy minimizes the mean holding costs,*

$$\sum_k p_k w_k \mathrm{E}[T_k],$$

among the non-anticipating scheduling policies.

The non-anticipating policies are only aware of the attained service times a_i of each job i and the service time distributions (but not on the actual service times). So, in general, non-anticipating policies do not know the remaining service times implying that, e.g., SPTP does not belong to non-anticipating disciplines. However, there is one exception: If the service times X_k are deterministic, $\mathrm{P}\{X_k = x_k\} = 1$, then the remaining service times $x_k - a_k$ are available for the non-anticipating policies (with probability 1). In such a case, all policies are non-anticipating.

2.3 Optimality of SPTP

Consider now an M/G/1 queue with a *single* class and load $\rho < 1$. Let X and T denote, respectively, the generic service and sojourn times of a job. In addition, let $\tau(x)$ denote the conditional mean sojourn time of a job with service time x,

$$\tau(x) \triangleq \mathrm{E}[T \mid X = x].$$

Assume first that the support of the service time distribution is finite. In other words, there are $x_1 < \ldots < x_K$ such that $\sum_k \mathrm{P}\{X = x_k\} = 1$. The following result is an immediate consequence of Theorem 1 as soon as we associate class k with the jobs with the same service time requirement x_k. Note that the Gittins index is now clearly given by

$$G_k(a) = \frac{w_k}{x_k - a}$$

with the optimal δ equal to $x_k - a$.

COROLLARY 2. *Consider an M/G/1 queue for which the support of the service time distribution is finite. Among all scheduling policies, the mean holding costs,*

$$\sum_k \mathrm{P}\{X = x_k\} w_k \tau(x_k),$$

are minimized by the policy that will serve job i^* such that

$$i^* = \arg\min_i \frac{\Delta_i}{w_{k(i)}}$$

where $k(i)$ and Δ_i denote the class and the remaining service requirement of job i.

In particular, if we choose $w_k = 1/x_k$, we see that the mean slowdown is minimized by SPTP:

COROLLARY 3. *Consider an M/G/1 queue for which the support of the service time distribution is finite. SPTP minimizes the mean slowdown $\mathrm{E}[\gamma]$ among all scheduling policies.*

Since any service time distribution can be approximated with an arbitrary precision by discrete service time distributions, we expect that the above result holds also for general service time distributions. Note also that the choice $w_k = 1$, for all k, results in the well-known optimality result of SRPT with respect to the mean sojourn time.

3. VALUE FUNCTIONS FOR M/G/1

In this section we analyze a single M/G/1 queue in isolation with FIFO, LIFO, and SPTP scheduling disciplines and derive expressions for the size-aware value functions *with respect to arbitrary job specific holding costs.* The corresponding results for SPT and SRPT are also given in [19]. As special cases, one trivially obtains the value functions with respect to the mean sojourn time and the mean slowdown. Thus, these results generalize the corresponding results in [20], where the size-aware value functions with respect to sojourn time are given (except for SPTP).

Holding cost model

Consider an M/G/1 queue with an arbitrary but fixed work conserving scheduling discipline and load $\rho < 1$. Each existing task incurs costs at some *task specific holding cost rate* denoted by B_i for job i. Assume that B_i are i.i.d. random variables, $B_i \sim B$. However, B_i may depend on the corresponding service requirement X_i. Both the service requirement and the holding cost become known upon arrival.

The cumulative cost during $(0, t)$ for an initial state $\mathbf{z}$ is

$$V_{\mathbf{z}}(t) \triangleq \int_0^t \sum_{i\in\mathcal{N}_{\mathbf{z}}(s)} B_i \, ds,$$

where $\mathcal{N}_{\mathbf{z}}(s)$ denotes the set of tasks present in the system at time s. Similarly, the long-term mean cost rate is

$$r_{\mathbf{z}} \triangleq \lim_{t\to\infty} \frac{1}{t} \mathrm{E}[V_{\mathbf{z}}(t)] = \lim_{t\to\infty} \frac{1}{t} \mathrm{E}[\int_0^t \sum_{i\in\mathcal{N}_{\mathbf{z}}(s)} B_i \, ds],$$

[3]Note that defining an index policy with indices Δ_i, Δ_i^* and $\sqrt{\Delta_i \Delta_i^*}$ gives SRPT, SPT and SPTP, respectively, where $\sqrt{\Delta_i \Delta_i^*}$ corresponds to the geometric mean of Δ_i and Δ_i^*.

which for an ergodic Markovian system reads

$$r = \lim_{t\to\infty} \mathrm{E}[\sum_{i\in\mathcal{N}_a(t)} B_i].$$

The value function $v_{\mathbf{z}}$ is defined as the expected deviation from the mean cost rate in infinite time-horizon,

$$v_{\mathbf{z}} \triangleq \lim_{t\to\infty} \mathrm{E}[V_{\mathbf{z}}(t) - r\cdot t].$$

A value function characterizes how expensive it is to start from each state. In our setting, it enables one to compute the expected cost of admitting a job with size x and holding cost rate b to a queue, which afterwards behaves as an M/G/1 queue with the given scheduling discipline:

$$\omega_{\mathbf{z}}(x,b) \triangleq v_{\mathbf{z}\oplus(x,b)} - v_{\mathbf{z}}, \tag{4}$$

where $\mathbf{z}\oplus(x,b)$ denotes the state resulting from adding a new job (x,b) in state $\mathbf{z}$. In Section 4 we will carry out the FPI step in the context of dispatching problem, for which a corresponding value function is a prerequisite.

Size dependent holding cost

In general, the holding cost rate b can be arbitrary, e.g., a class-specific i.i.d. random variable. However, in two important special cases, mean sojourn time and mean slowdown, it depends solely on the service requirement x, $b=c(x)$:

mean sojourn time:	$c(x)=1$
mean slowdown:	$c(x)=1/x$

In equilibrium, the average cost *per job* is $\mathrm{E}[c(X)\cdot T]$. Using Little's result, we have for the *mean cost rate*,

$$r = \lambda\,\mathrm{E}[c(X)\cdot T] = \begin{cases} \lambda\,\mathrm{E}[T] = \mathrm{E}[N], & \text{for } c(x)=1,\\ \lambda\,\mathrm{E}[\gamma], & \text{for } c(x)=1/x.\end{cases}$$

where $\mathrm{E}[N]$ denotes the mean number in the system.

3.1 M/G/1-FIFO Queue

Next we derive the size-aware value function for an M/G/1-FIFO queue with respect to arbitrary job specific holding costs. To this end, let $\mathbf{z} = ((\Delta_1,b_1);\ldots;(\Delta_n,b_n))$ denote the remaining service requirements (measured in time) Δ_i and the corresponding *holding cost rates* b_i at state $\mathbf{z}$. The total rate at which costs are accrued at given state $\mathbf{z}$ is thus the sum $\sum_i b_i$. Job 1 is currently receiving service and job n is the latest arrival. The total backlog is denoted by $u_{\mathbf{z}}$,

$$u_{\mathbf{z}} = \sum_{i=1}^{n} \Delta_i.$$

PROPOSITION 1. *For the size-aware relative value in an M/G/1-FIFO queue with respect to arbitrary job specific holding costs it holds that*

$$v_{\mathbf{z}} - v_0 = \sum_{i=1}^{n}\left(b_i\sum_{j=1}^{i}\Delta_j\right) + \frac{\lambda\cdot\mathrm{E}[B]}{2\,(1-\rho)}u_{\mathbf{z}}^2 \tag{5}$$

where $\mathrm{E}[B]$ *is the mean holding cost rate for all later jobs.*

PROOF. We compare two systems with the same arrival patterns, System 1 initially in state $\mathbf{z}$ and System 2 initially empty. The two systems behave equivalently after System 1 becomes empty. The cost incurred by the current n jobs, present only in System 1, is already fixed as

$$h_1 = \sum_{i=1}^{n}\left(b_i\sum_{j=1}^{i}\Delta_j\right).$$

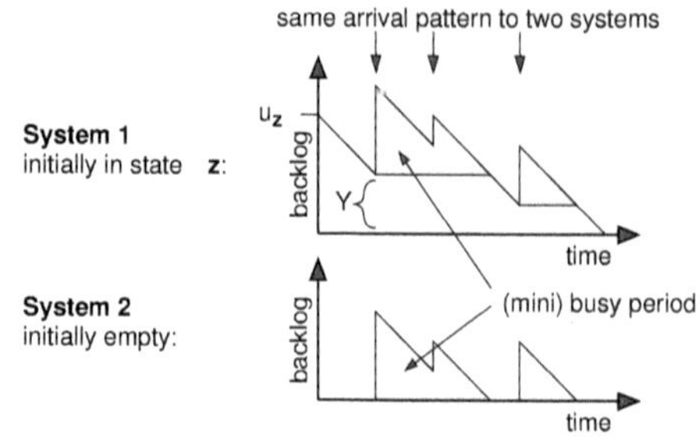

Figure 2: Derivation of the value function in an M/G/1-FIFO queue.

The later arriving jobs encounter a longer waiting time in System 1. The key observation here is that these jobs experience an additional delay of Y in System 1 when compared to System 2, as is illustrated in Fig. 2. Otherwise the sojourn times are equal. On average $\lambda u_{\mathbf{z}}$ (mini) busy periods occur before System 1 becomes empty. These busy periods are independent and on average $1/(1-\rho)$ jobs are served during each of them. The average additional waiting time is $\mathrm{E}[Y] = u_{\mathbf{z}}/2$. Therefore, the later arriving jobs incur on average

$$h_2 = \frac{\lambda\cdot\mathrm{E}[B]}{2\,(1-\rho)}u_{\mathbf{z}}^2$$

higher holding cost in System 1 than in System 2. Total cost difference is h_1+h_2, which completes the proof. □

COROLLARY 4. *The mean cost in terms of sojourn time due to accepting a job with size x to a size-aware M/G/1-FIFO queue initially at state $\mathbf{z}$ is*

$$\omega_{\mathbf{z}}(x) = x + u_{\mathbf{z}} + \frac{\lambda}{2(1-\rho)}(2\,u_{\mathbf{z}}\,x + x^2).$$

COROLLARY 5. *The mean cost in terms of slowdown due to accepting a job with size x to a size-aware M/G/1-FIFO queue initially at state $\mathbf{z}$ is*

$$\omega_{\mathbf{z}}(x) = 1 + \frac{u_{\mathbf{z}}}{x} + \frac{\lambda\cdot\mathrm{E}[X^{-1}]}{2(1-\rho)}(2u_{\mathbf{z}}x + x^2). \tag{6}$$

In both cases, it is implicitly assumed that the question about the admittance is a one-time operation and the future behavior of the queue is according to the standard M/G/1-FIFO. The proofs follow trivially from (4) and (5).

3.2 M/G/1-LIFO Queue

Next we derive the size-aware value function for the LIFO scheduling discipline. We let $\mathbf{z} = ((\Delta_1,b_1);\ldots;(\Delta_n,b_n))$ denote the state of the system with n jobs, where Δ_i denotes the remaining service requirement (measured in time) and b_i the *holding cost rate* of job i. Job 1 is the latest arrival and currently receiving service (if any), i.e., without new arrivals the jobs are processed in the natural order: $1,2,\ldots,n$.

PROPOSITION 2. *For the size-aware relative value in a preemptive M/G/1-LIFO queue with respect to arbitrary job specific holding cost it holds that*

$$v_{\mathbf{z}} - v_0 = \frac{1}{1-\rho} \sum_{i=1}^{n} \left(b_i \sum_{j=1}^{i} \Delta_j \right). \tag{7}$$

PROOF. We compare System 1 initially in state $\mathbf{z}$ and System 2 initially empty. The current state bears no meaning for the future arrivals with preemptive LIFO, and thus the difference in the expected costs is equal to the cost the current n jobs in System 1 incur:

$$v_{\mathbf{z}} - v_0 = \sum_{i=1}^{n} b_i \, \mathrm{E}[R_i],$$

where R_i denotes the remaining sojourn time of job i [20],

$$\mathrm{E}[R_i] = \frac{\sum_{j=1}^{i} \Delta_j}{1-\rho},$$

which completes the proof. □

For the mean sojourn time, the holding cost rate is constant $b_i = 1$ and a sufficient state description is $(\Delta_1, \ldots, \Delta_n)$.

COROLLARY 6. *The cost in terms of sojourn time due to accepting a job with size x to a size-aware preemptive M/G/1-LIFO queue at state $\mathbf{z}$ is*

$$\omega_{\mathbf{z}}(x) = \frac{1}{1-\rho}(n+1)x.$$

For the slowdown, the initial service requirements define the holding costs and a sufficient state description is $\mathbf{z} = ((\Delta_1, \Delta_1^*), .., (\Delta_1, \Delta_1^*))$, where Δ_i and Δ_i^* denote the remaining and initial service requirement of job i, so that the holding cost of job i is $b_i = 1/\Delta_i^*$:

COROLLARY 7. *The cost in terms of slowdown due to accepting a job with size x to a size-aware preemptive M/G/1-LIFO queue at state $\mathbf{z}$ is*

$$\omega_{\mathbf{z}}(x) = \frac{1}{1-\rho} \left(1 + \sum_{i=1}^{n} x/\Delta_i^* \right). \tag{8}$$

The proofs follow trivially from (7) and from definition (4). Note that $\omega_{\mathbf{z}}(x)$ with (preemptive) LIFO does not depend on the remaining service times Δ_i due to the preemption.

3.3 M/G/1-SPTP Queue

Next we derive the corresponding size-aware value function for the SPTP scheduling discipline. The state description for SPTP is $\mathbf{z} = ((\Delta_1, \Delta_1^*, b_1), \ldots, (\Delta_n, \Delta_n^*, b_n))$, where, without loss of generality, we assume a decreasing priority order, $\Delta_i \Delta_i^* < \Delta_{i+1} \Delta_{i+1}^*$, i.e., the job 1 (if any) is currently receiving service. Then, $u_{\mathbf{z}}(h)$ denotes the amount of work with a higher priority than h,

$$u_{\mathbf{z}}(h) \triangleq \sum_{i:\Delta_i \Delta_i^* < h} \Delta_i.$$

Let $\lambda(x)$, $m(x)$ and $\rho(x)$ denote the arrival rate, mean job size and offered load due to jobs shorter than x,

$$\begin{aligned} \lambda(x) &\triangleq \lambda \, \mathrm{P}\{X < x\}, \\ m(x) &\triangleq \mathrm{E}[X \mid X < x], \\ \rho(x) &\triangleq \lambda \textstyle\int_0^x t\, f(t)\, dt, \end{aligned} \tag{9}$$

where $f(x)$ denotes the job size pdf.

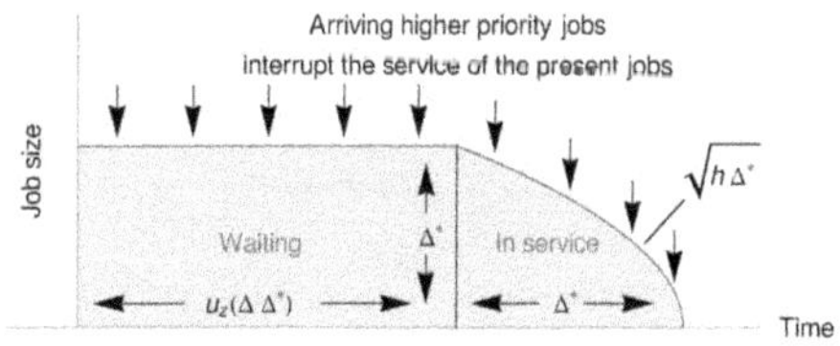

Figure 3: Remaining sojourn time of an (Δ, Δ^*)-job in an M/G/1-SPTP queue.

LEMMA 1. *The mean remaining sojourn time of a (Δ, Δ^*)-job in an M/G/1-SPTP queue initially in state $\mathbf{z}$ is given by*

$$\mathrm{E}[R_{\mathbf{z}}(\Delta, \Delta^*)] = \frac{u_{\mathbf{z}}(\Delta\Delta^*)}{1-\rho(\sqrt{\Delta\Delta^*})} + \frac{2}{\Delta^*} \int_0^{\sqrt{\Delta\Delta^*}} \frac{x\, dx}{1-\rho(x)}. \tag{10}$$

PROOF. Let k denote the (Δ, Δ^*)-job, whose remaining sojourn time depends on the initial and later arriving higher priority work. We can assume that the latter are served immediately according to LIFO, thus triggering mini busy periods. Let $h = h(t)$ denote the remaining service time of job k at (virtual) time t, where we have omitted these mini busy periods from the time axis. During $0 < t < u_{\mathbf{z}}(\Delta\Delta^*)$, job k is waiting and $h = \Delta$, but as the service begins $h \to 0$ linearly. The later arriving higher priority jobs shorter than $\sqrt{h\Delta^*}$ constitute an inhomogeneous Poisson process with rate $\lambda(\sqrt{h\Delta^*})$, as illustrated in Fig. 3. The mean duration of a mini busy period is (cf. the mean busy period in M/G/1),

$$D(h) \triangleq \frac{m(\sqrt{h\,\Delta^*})}{1-\rho(\sqrt{h\,\Delta^*})}.$$

The mean waiting time before job k receives service for the first time is $u_{\mathbf{z}}(\Delta\Delta^*) + \lambda(\sqrt{h\Delta^*})\, u_{\mathbf{z}}(\Delta\Delta^*) \cdot D(\Delta)$, which gives the first term in (10).

The service time Δ and the additional delays during the service are on average

$$\Delta + \int_0^{\Delta} \lambda(\sqrt{h\,\Delta^*}) \cdot D(h)\, dh;$$

refer to the "in service" region of Fig. 3. Change of integration variable, $x = \sqrt{h\,\Delta^*}$ then gives the second term in (10), which completes the proof. □

Even though SPTP explicitly tries to minimize the mean slowdown, we derive next a general expression for the value function with arbitrary job specific holding costs:

PROPOSITION 3. *For the size-aware relative value in an M/G/1-SPTP queue with respect to arbitrary job specific holding costs it holds that*

$$\begin{aligned} v_{\mathbf{z}} - v_0 = &\sum_{i=1}^{n} b_i \left(\frac{\sum_{j=1}^{i-1} \Delta_j}{1-\rho(\tilde{\Delta}_i)} + \frac{2}{\Delta_i^*} \int_0^{\tilde{\Delta}_i} \frac{x\, dx}{1-\rho(x)} \right) \\ &+ \frac{\lambda}{2} \sum_{i=0}^{n} \Bigg[(\sum_{j=1}^{i} \Delta_j)^2 \int_{\tilde{\Delta}_i}^{\tilde{\Delta}_{i+1}} \frac{b(x)\, f(x)}{(1-\rho(x))^2}\, dx \; + \\ &\sum_{j=i+1}^{n} (\Delta_j^*)^{-2} \int_{\tilde{\Delta}_i}^{\tilde{\Delta}_{i+1}} \frac{x^4\, b(x)\, f(x)}{(1-\rho(x))^2}\, dx \Bigg] \end{aligned} \tag{11}$$

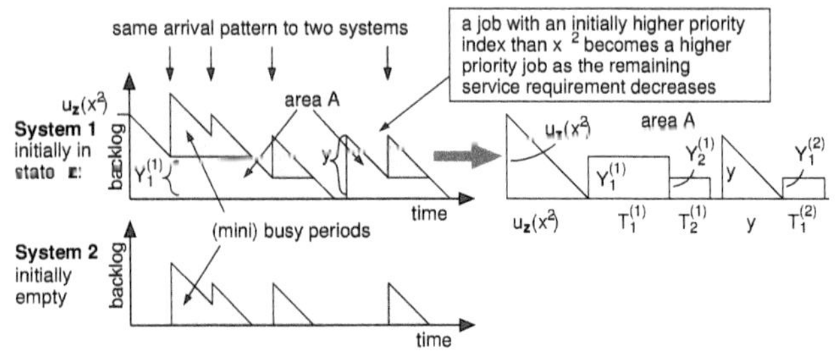

Figure 4: Derivation of the value function for an M/G/1-SPTP queue with respect to slowdown.

where $b(x) \triangleq \mathrm{E}[B \mid X = x]$ *and*

$$\tilde{\Delta}_i = \begin{cases} 0, & i = 0 \\ \sqrt{\Delta_i \Delta_i^*}, & i = 1, \ldots, n \\ \infty, & i = n+1. \end{cases}$$

PROOF. The relative value comprises the mean holding cost h_1 accrued by the current n tasks in state $\mathbf{z}$,

$$\mathbf{z} = ((\Delta_1, \Delta_1^*, b_1), \ldots, (\Delta_n, \Delta_n^*, b_n)),$$

and the difference in costs accrued by the later arriving jobs, h_2, $v_{\mathbf{z}} - v_0 = h_1 + h_2$. The first summation over n gives h_1, i.e., it follows from multiplying (10) with the job specific holding cost b_i and adding over all i.

The latter integral corresponds to h_2 where the accrued costs are conditioned on the size x of an arriving job. The corresponding arrival rate is $\lambda f(x)\, dx$. The mean difference in sojourn time experienced by an arriving job with size x is accrued during the initial waiting time – once a job enters the service for the first time its mean remaining sojourn time is the same in both systems. The initial waiting time is a function of higher priority workload upon arrival, denoted by $U_{\mathbf{z}}(x^2, t)$ for an initial state $\mathbf{z}$ at arrival time t. In particular, the mean (initial) waiting time is simply $\mathrm{E}[U_{\mathbf{z}}(x^2, t)]/(1 - \rho(x))$, which gives

$$h_2 = \lambda \int_0^\infty \frac{f(x)}{1 - \rho(x)} \left(\mathrm{E}[U_{\mathbf{z}}(x^2, t) - U_0(x^2, t)]\right) dx.$$

Next we refer to Fig. 4 and observe that $U_{\mathbf{z}}(x^2, t) - U_0(x^2, t)$ in the integrand corresponds to area A. This area consists of one $u_{\mathbf{z}}(x^2)$ triangle, followed by N_0 rectangles, and similar sequences starting with a x^2/Δ_i^* triangle for $\{i : \Delta_i \Delta_i^* > x^2\}$, each followed by N_i rectangles. The N_i are random variables corresponding to the number of mini busy periods during the service time of a particular triangle. The first triangle corresponds to the initially higher priority workload $u_{\mathbf{z}}(x^2)$, and the latter to the jobs with initially lower priority, i.e., to jobs i with $\Delta_i \Delta_i^* > x^2$. At some point in time, the remaining service requirement of such a job i decreases to $y_i = x^2/\Delta_i^*$ and its priority index drops below x^2. For a sequence starting with a y-triangle, the number of mini busy periods (rectangles) obeys Poisson distribution with mean $\lambda(x)\, y$. The height of a rectangle is uniformly distributed in $(0, y)$ having the mean $y/2$ (property of Poisson process), while the width corresponds to the duration of a busy period in a work conserving M/G/1 queue having the mean $m(x)/(1 - \rho(x))$. Thus, the mean total area is

$$\frac{y^2}{2} + \lambda(x) y \cdot \frac{y}{2} \cdot \frac{m(x)}{1 - \rho(x)} = \frac{y^2}{2(1 - \rho(x))}.$$

Therefore,

$$h_2 = \frac{\lambda}{2} \int_0^\infty \frac{b(x)\, f(x)}{(1 - \rho(x))^2} \left(u_{\mathbf{z}}(x^2)^2 + \sum_{i:\Delta_i \Delta_i^* > x^2} \left(\frac{x^2}{\Delta_i^*}\right)^2 \right) dx,$$

where $b(x) = \mathrm{E}[B \mid X = x]$ factor in the numerator corresponds to the mean holding cost of an x-job. For each interval $x \in (\tilde{\Delta}_i, \tilde{\Delta}_{i+1})$, $u_{\mathbf{z}}(x^2) = \sum_{j=1}^{i-1} \Delta_j$ and

$$\sum_{j:\Delta_j \Delta_j^* > x^2} \left(\frac{x^2}{\Delta_j^*}\right)^2 = x^4 \sum_{j=i+1}^{n} (\Delta_j^*)^{-2},$$

and integration in $n + 1$ parts completes the proof. □

Recall that with respect to the mean sojourn time, $b_i = 1$ and $b(x) = 1$, while for the slowdown criterion, $b_i = 1/\Delta_i^*$ and $b(x) = 1/x$. Hence, (11) allows one to compute the mean cost $\omega_{\mathbf{z}}(x)$ due to accepting a given job in terms of sojourn time or slowdown. We omit the explicit expression for $\omega_{\mathbf{z}}(x)$ for brevity.

The corresponding value functions for SPT and SRPT are derived in [19]. The numerical evaluation of the value function for SPTP, SPT and SRPT is not as unattractive as it first may seem. Basically one needs to be able to compute integrals of form

$$F_k(x) = \int_0^x \frac{t^k\, b(t)\, f(t)}{(1 - \rho(t))^2}\, dt, \text{ and } G_d(x) = \int_0^x \frac{t^d}{1 - \rho(t)}\, dt,$$

where $k = 0, 2, 4$ and $d = 0, 1$ depending on the discipline. Thus, e.g., a suitable interpolation of the $F_k(x)$ and $G_d(x)$ enables on-line computation of the value function.

4. DISPATCHING PROBLEM

Next we utilize the results of Section 3 in the dispatching problem with parallel servers and focus solely on minimizing the mean slowdown. The dispatching system illustrated in Fig. 1 comprises m servers with service rates $\nu_1, \ldots, \nu_m$. Jobs arrive according to a Poisson process with rate λ and their service requirements are i.i.d. random variables with a general distribution. The jobs are served according to a given scheduling discipline (e.g., FIFO) in each server.

The slowdown for an isolated queue was defined as the sojourn time T divided by the service requirement X [17] (both measured in time), $\gamma = T/X$. However, as we consider heterogeneous servers with rates ν_i, the service requirement X of size Y job (measured, e.g., in bytes) is no longer unambiguous but a server specific quantity,

$$X_i = Y/\nu_i.$$

Therefore, for a dispatching system we compare the sojourn time T to the hypothetical service time if all capacity could be assigned to process a given job [7],

$$\gamma^* \triangleq \frac{T}{Y/\sum_i \nu_i}.$$

The relationship between the queue i specific slowdown γ and the system wide slowdown γ^* is $\gamma^* = \gamma \cdot (\sum_j \nu_j)/\nu_i$.

4.1 Random Dispatching Policies

The so-called Bernoulli splitting assigning jobs independently in random using probability distribution $(p_1, \ldots, p_m)$ offers a good state-independent basic dispatching policy. Due to Poisson arrivals, each queue also receives jobs according to a Poisson process with rate $p_i\,\lambda$.

DEFINITION 1 (RND-ρ). *The* RND-ρ dispatching policy *balances the load equally by setting* $p_i = \nu_i / \sum_j \nu_j$.

As an example, the mean slowdown in a preemptive LIFO or PS queue with RND-ρ policy is,

$$\mathrm{E}[\gamma^*] = \Big(\sum_j \nu_j\Big) \frac{m}{\sum_j \nu_j - \lambda\,\mathrm{E}[Y]},$$

where the denominator corresponds to the excess capacity. Thus, with RND-ρ and LIFO queues, the slowdown criterion is m times higher when m servers are used instead of a single fast one irrespectively of the service rate distribution ν_i.

For identical servers, $\nu_1 = \nu_2 = \ldots = \nu_m$, the RND-$\rho$ dispatching policy reduces to RND-U:

DEFINITION 2 (RND-U). *The RND-U dispatching policy assigns jobs randomly in uniform using* $p_i = 1/m$.

RND-U is obviously the optimal random policy in case of identical servers.

In general, the optimal splitting probabilities depend on the service time distribution and the scheduling discipline. For the preemptive LIFO (and PS) server systems the mean slowdown with a random dispatching policy is given by

$$\mathrm{E}[\gamma^*] = \Big(\sum_j \nu_j\Big) \sum_{i=1}^{m} \frac{p_i}{\nu_i - p_i \cdot \lambda\,\mathrm{E}[Y]},$$

where $\sum_j \nu_j$ is a constant that can be neglected when optimizing the p_i.

DEFINITION 3 (RND-OPT). *The optimal random dispatching policy for LIFO/PS queues, referred to as RND-opt, splits the incoming tasks using the probability distribution,*

$$p_i = \frac{\nu_i - \sqrt{\nu_i}\,G}{\lambda\,\mathrm{E}[Y]}, \quad \textit{where } G = \frac{\sum_i \nu_i - \lambda\,\mathrm{E}[Y]}{\sum_i \sqrt{\nu_i}}.$$

The result is easy to show with the aid of Lagrange multipliers. We note that when some servers are too slow, the above gives infeasible values for some p_i, in case of which one simply excludes the slowest server from the solution and recomputes a new probability distribution. This is repeated until a feasible solution is found. A more explicit formulation is given in [5, 18]. RND-opt is insensitive to the job size distribution and optimal only for LIFO and PS.

Pollaczek-Khinchin mean value formula enables one to analyze FIFO queues and, e.g., to write an expression for the mean slowdown with RND-ρ. Also the optimal splitting probabilities can be computed numerically for an arbitrary job size distribution. According to (1), the mean slowdown in each queue depends on the mean waiting time $\mathrm{E}[W_i]$ and $\mathrm{E}[X_i^{-1}]$, where the latter is assumed to exist and to be finite. Hence, the optimal probability distribution with respect to slowdown is the same as with the mean sojourn time.

Similarly, the mean sojourn time in SPT and SRPT queues is known which allows a numerical optimization of the splitting probabilities. For simplicity, we consider only RND-ρ and RND-opt in this paper as compact closed form expressions for the p_i are only available for these.

4.2 SITA-E Dispatching Policy

With FIFO queues, a state-independent dispatching policy known as the size-interval-task-assignment (SITA) has proven to be efficient especially with heavy-tailed job size distributions [6, 14, 4]. The motivation behind SITA is to segregate the long jobs from the short ones. Reality, however, is more complicated and segregating the jobs categorically can also give suboptimal results [16]. Here we assume $\nu_1 \geq \nu_2 \geq \ldots \geq \nu_m$ and a continuous job size distribution with pdf $f(x)$.

DEFINITION 4 (SITA). *A SITA policy is defined by disjoint job size intervals* $\{(\xi_0, \xi_1],\ (\xi_1, \xi_2],\ \ldots,\ (\xi_{m-1}, \xi_m]\}$, *and assigns a job with size x to server i iff* $x \in (\xi_{i-1}, \xi_i]$.

Without loss of generality, one can assume that $\xi_0 = 0$ and $\xi_m = \infty$. Note that in contrast to random policies, SITA assumes that the dispatcher is aware of the size of the new job. In this paper, we limit ourselves to SITA-E, where E stands for *equal load*. That is, the size intervals are chosen in such a way that the load is balanced between the servers.

DEFINITION 5 (SITA-E). *With SITA-E dispatching policy the thresholds ξ_i are defined in such a way that*

$$\frac{1}{\nu_i} \int_{\xi_{i-1}}^{\xi_i} x\,f(x)\,dx = \frac{1}{\nu_j} \int_{\xi_{j-1}}^{\xi_j} x\,f(x)\,dx, \qquad \forall\, i, j.$$

Thus, similarly as RND-ρ, also the SITA-E policy is insensitive to the arrival rate λ.

4.3 Improved Dispatching Policies

The important property the above state-independent dispatching policies have is that the arrival process to each queue is a Poisson process. Consequently, the value functions derived earlier allow us to quantify the value function of the whole system. With a slight abuse of notation,

$$v_{\tilde{\mathbf{z}}} - v_{\mathbf{0}} = \sum_{i=1}^{m} (v_{\mathbf{z}_i}^{(i)} - v_0^{(i)}),$$

where $v_{\mathbf{z}_i}^{(i)}$ denotes the relative value of queue i in state $\mathbf{z}_i$, and $\tilde{\mathbf{z}} = (\mathbf{z}_1, \ldots, \mathbf{z}_m)$ the state of the whole system.

Policy Improvement by Role Switching

One interesting opportunity to utilize the relative values is to *switch* the roles of two queues [20]. Namely, with an arbitrary state-independent policy one can switch the input processes of any two identical servers at any moment, and effectively end up to a new state of the same system. Despite its limitation (identical servers), *switching* is an interesting policy improvement method that requires little additional computation. The switch should only be carried out when the new state has lower expected future costs, i.e. when for some $i \neq j$, the rates are equal, $\nu_i = \nu_j$, and

$$v_{(\mathbf{z}_1,\ldots,\mathbf{z}_i,\ldots\mathbf{z}_j,\ldots,\mathbf{z}_m)} < v_{(\mathbf{z}_1,\ldots,\mathbf{z}_j,\ldots\mathbf{z}_i,\ldots,\mathbf{z}_m)}.$$

Carrying out this operation whenever a new job has arrived to the system reduces the state-space by *removing* such states for which a better alternative to continue exists. Formally, let $\pi(\tilde{\mathbf{z}})$ denote the set of feasible permutations of the queues' roles, where the input processes between identical servers are switched. Then, the optimal state-space reduction, implicitly defining a new policy, is given by

$$\tilde{\mathbf{z}} \leftarrow \operatorname*{argmin}_{\tilde{\mathbf{z}}' \in \pi(\tilde{\mathbf{z}})} v_{\tilde{\mathbf{z}}'}.$$

To elaborate this, consider a RND-ρ/LIFO system. In this case, (7) implies that switching the roles of any two identical queues makes no difference to the relative value.

In contrast, with FIFO discipline the interesting quantity from (5) for two identical servers i and j is identified to be

$$C_{ij} \triangleq \frac{\lambda_i \, \mathrm{E}[B_i]}{1-\rho_i} \cdot u_{\mathbf{z}_j}^2.$$

Switching the input processes between queues i and j leads to a state with a lower relative value if $C_{ii}+C_{jj} > C_{ij}+C_{ji}$. Again, with RND-$\rho$ the factor $\lambda_i \, \mathrm{E}[B_i]/(1-\rho_i)$ is a constant for any two identical servers and switching provides no gain. However, with SITA-E, even though the denominator $1-\rho_i$ is a constant, the numerator is not. Let X_i denote a job size in queue i. Then $\mathrm{E}[X_i] < \mathrm{E}[X_{i+1}]$, and therefore $\lambda_i > \lambda_{i+1}$. Moreover, $\mathrm{E}[1/X_i] > \mathrm{E}[1/X_{i+1}]$, yielding

$$\lambda_i \, \mathrm{E}[1/X_i] > \lambda_{i+1} \, \mathrm{E}[1/X_{i+1}].$$

Consequently, with the *SITA-E with switch* policy, the optimal permutation, after inserting a new job to a queue, is the one with increasing backlogs for identical servers:

DEFINITION 6 (SITA-Es). *SITA-E with switch dispatching policy behaves similarly as SITA-E with a distinction that after each task assignment the queues are permutated in such a way that $u_{\mathbf{z}_i} \le u_{\mathbf{z}_{i+1}}$ for all identical servers i and $i+1$.*

Policy Improvement by FPI

The *first-policy-iteration* (FPI) is a general method of the MDP framework to improve any given policy. We apply it to the dispatching problem [20]. Suppose that the scheduling discipline in each queue is fixed and that a state-independent basic dispatching policy would assign a new job to some queue. Given the relative values and the expected cost associated with accepting the job to each queue, we can carry out FPI: we deviate from the default action if the expected cost is smaller with some other action, thereby decreasing the expected cumulative costs in infinite time horizon.

Let λ_i denote the arrival rate to queue i according to the basic dispatching policy, and Y_i the corresponding job size. With a state-independent policy, accepting a job to queue i does not affect the future behavior of the other queues. Thus, the cost of assigning a job with size y to queue i is

$$\omega_{\bar{\mathbf{z}}}(y,i) = \omega^*_{\mathbf{z}_i}(y).$$

where $\omega^*_{\mathbf{z}_i}(y)$ is the mean admittance cost of a job with size y (measured, e.g., in bytes) to queue i, where its service requirement (measured in time) would be y/ν_i. For slowdown, we have an elementary relation

$$\omega^*_{\mathbf{z}_i}(y) = \frac{\sum_j \nu_j}{\nu_i} \cdot \omega_{\mathbf{z}_i}(y/\nu_i).$$

For *FIFO queues*, (6) gives

$$\omega^*_{\mathbf{z}_i}(y) = \big(\sum_j \nu_j\big)\left(\frac{1}{\nu_i}+\frac{u_{\mathbf{z}_i}}{y}+\frac{\lambda_i \, \mathrm{E}[Y_i^{-1}]}{2}\cdot\frac{2u_{\mathbf{z}_i}y+y^2/\nu_i}{\nu_i-\lambda_i \, \mathrm{E}[Y_i]}\right).$$

For *preemptive LIFO* queues, (8) similarly gives

$$\omega^*_{\mathbf{z}_i}(y) = \big(\sum_j \nu_j\big)\frac{1+(y/\nu_i)\sum_{j=1}^{n_i} 1/\Delta^*_{i,j}}{\nu_i-\lambda_i \, \mathrm{E}[Y_i]},$$

where n_i denotes the number of jobs in queue i and $\Delta^*_{i,j}$ the initial service requirement (in time) of job j in queue i. According to the FPI principle, one simply chooses the queue with the smallest (expected) cost,

$$\alpha_{\bar{\mathbf{z}}}(y) \triangleq \operatorname*{argmin}_i \, \omega^*_{\mathbf{z}_i}(y). \qquad (12)$$

We refer to these improved dispatching policies simply as the *FPI-p policy*, where p denotes the basic dispatching policy, e.g., RND-opt or RND-ρ, where for brevity reasons the RND prefix is often omitted. Note that the factor $\sum_j \nu_j$ in both expressions is a common constant for all queues.

In a symmetric case of m identical servers and the RND-U basic policy, a corresponding FPI-based policy reduces to a well-known dispatching policy, i.e., with FIFO queues, FPI yields LWL, and with LIFO, the Myopic policy (see Table 1). Moreover, given additionally a constant job size, then in case of LIFO queues one ends up with the JSQ policy. In general, for constant job sizes the slowdown objective reduces to the minimization of the mean sojourn time.

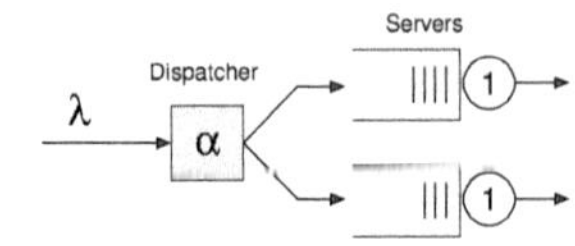

(a) Two identical servers

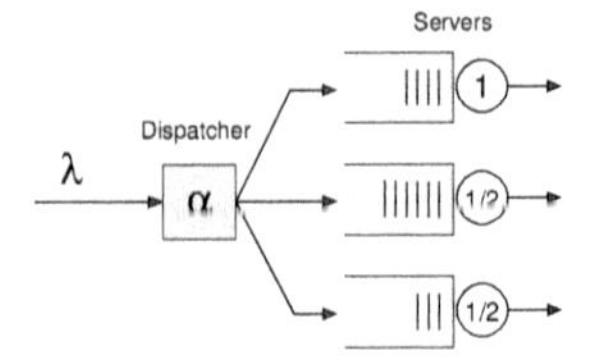

(b) Three heterogeneous servers

Figure 5: Example dispatching systems.

5. NUMERICAL EXAMPLES

Let us next evaluate by means of numerical simulations the improved dispatching policies derived in Section 4. To this end, we have chosen to consider two elementary server systems that are illustrated in Fig 5:

(a) Two identical servers with rates $\nu_1 = \nu_2 = 1$,

(b) Three heterogeneous servers with rates $\nu_1 = 1$ and $\nu_2 = \nu_3 = 1/2$.

Thus, the total service rate in both systems is equal to 2. We compare the mean slowdown performance of the FPI policies against several well-known heuristic dispatching policies, including the state-independent policies RND-opt, RND-ρ and SITA-E. The somewhat more sophisticated least-work-left (LWL) policies choose the queue with the least amount of unfinished work (backlog). The difference between the LWL policies is that LWL$^-$ considers the situation without the new job, and LWL$^+$ afterwards. With identical servers the LWL policies are equivalent. JSQ chooses the queue with the least number of jobs. With the LWL and JSQ, the ties are broken in favor of a faster server. The Myopic policy assumes in a greedy fashion that no further jobs arrive and chooses the queue which minimizes the immediate cost the known jobs accrue. All policies are listed in Table 1.

In many real-life settings, the job sizes have been found to exhibit a heavy-tailed behavior, (cf., e.g., file sizes in the Internet). Thus, in most examples we assume a *bounded Pareto distribution* with pdf

$$f(x) = \frac{\alpha k^\alpha}{1-(k/p)^\alpha}\, x^{-\alpha-1}, \quad k \le x \le p, \qquad (13)$$

where $(k,p,\alpha) = (0.33959, 1000, 1.5)$ so that $\mathrm{E}[X] \approx 1$. This job size distribution is particularly suitable for SITA-E.

RND-ρ	state-independent random policy with load balancing
RND-opt	state-independent random policy minimizing the mean slowdown (assumes LIFO/PS)
SITA-E	state-independent size-interval-task-assignment with equal loads (optionally, with switch)
Round-Robin	assigns arriving tasks sequentially to servers [8]
LWL$^-$	least-work-left, assigns a job to server with the least amount unfinished work upon arrival
LWL$^+$	same as LWL$^-$ but based on the unfinished work (in time) including the new job [20]
JSQ	join-the-shortest-queue, i.e., the one with the least number of jobs [30]
Myopic	minimize the mean slowdown on condition that no further jobs arrive
FPI	first policy iteration on the state-independent RND-ρ, RND-opt and SITA-E policies

Table 1: Dispatching policies evaluated in the numerical examples.

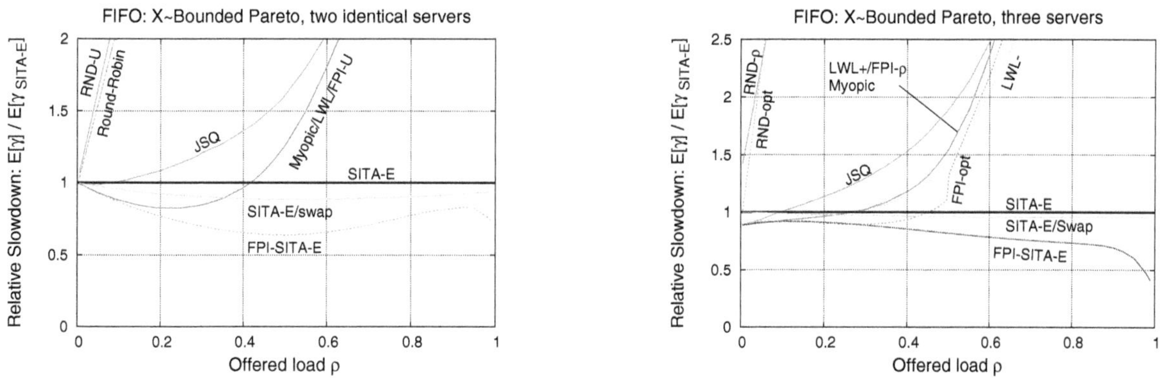

Figure 6: Numerical results with two identical (left) and three heterogeneous servers having rates $\nu = (1, 0.5, 0.5)$ (right). The scheduling discipline is FIFO and jobs sizes obey bounded Pareto distribution.

5.1 FIFO

First we assume that servers operate under the FIFO scheduling discipline and job sizes obey the bounded Pareto distribution (13). With FIFO, the departure time gets fixed at dispatching and the Myopic policy corresponds to selfish users choosing the queue that guarantees the shortest sojourn time, i.e., LWL$^+$. Similarly, LWL$^-$ is equivalent to an $M/G/m$ system with a single shared queue.

Two identical servers

Fig. 6 (left) depicts the results with two identical servers with rates $\nu_1 = \nu_2 = 1$. The x-axis corresponds to the offered load ρ and the y-axis to the relative mean slowdown, $\mathrm{E}[\gamma]/\mathrm{E}[\gamma_{\text{SITA-E}}]$, i.e., the comparison is against SITA-E. We find that the policies appear to fall in one of the three groups with respect to slowdown: SITA policies form the best group, other queue state-dependent policies the next, and RND-U and Round-Robin have the worst performance. Especially, FPI-SITA-E outperforms the other policies by a significant margin, including the other SITA policies. Note also that when ρ is small, the sensible state-dependent policies utilize idle servers better than, e.g., SITA-E.

Fig. 7 illustrates SITA-E and FPI-SITA-E in the same setting at an offered load of $\rho = 0.5$. The x- and y-axes correspond to the backlog in Queue 1 and Queue 2, respectively, and the z-axis to the maximum job size a given policy assigns to Queue 1. With SITA-E, this threshold is constant, while FPI-SITA-E changes the threshold dynamically. One observes that as a result of FPI, Queue 1 has become a "high-priority" queue where no jobs are accepted whenever Queue 1 has more unfinished work than Queue 2. Similarly, when Queue 2 has a long backlog, the threshold for assigning a job to Queue 1 becomes higher with FPI than with SITA-E.

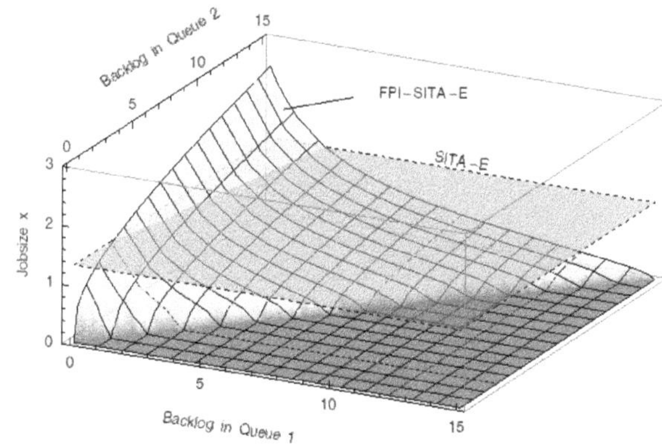

Figure 7: SITA-E and FPI-SITA-E policies in the setting of two identical FIFO queues, bounded Pareto distributed job sizes and offered load $\rho = 0.5$. x- and y-axes correspond to the backlog in Queue 1 and Queue 2, respectively, and z-axis to the maximum job size that a policy assigns to Queue 1.

Three heterogeneous servers

Consider next the asymmetric setting comprising one primary server with service rate $\nu_1 = 1$ and two secondary servers with rates $\nu_2 = \nu_3 = 1/2$. Fig. 6 (right) illustrates the results from a numerical simulation.

The state-independent random policies are much worse than the other policies. However, state-independent SITA-E again proves out to be better than the state-dependent policies JSQ, LWL$^-$, LWL$^+$, Myopic, FPI-ρ and FPI-opt. The gain from switching the roles of the queues (SITA-E vs. SITA-Es) is smaller in this case due to the fact that we may

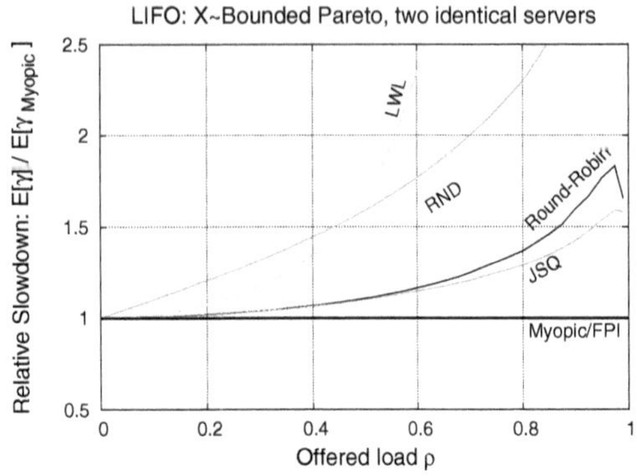

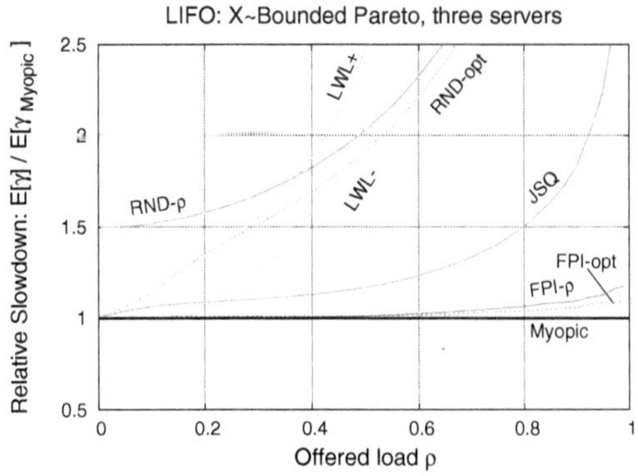

Figure 8: Numerical results with preemptive LIFO scheduling discipline for two identical (left) servers with rates $\nu_1 = \nu_2 = 1$, and three heterogeneous servers with rates $\nu_1 = 1$ and $\nu_2 = \nu_3 = 1/2$.

only switch the roles of the two slower queues having the same service rate $\nu = 0.5$. As expected, the FPI-SITA-E policy yields a significantly lower mean slowdown than any other policy especially under a heavy load.

Based on the results, one can assume that the relative values obtained for the random policies simply do not capture the situation sufficiently well, while SITA-E is already a good dispatching policy, and FPI then leads to "adaptive" size intervals.

5.2 Preemptive LIFO

Next we assume that the servers are bound to operate under LIFO, which, as mentioned, has a reasonably robust performance with respect to the mean slowdown. Job sizes are again assumed to obey the bounded Pareto distribution.

Two identical servers

Fig. 8 (left) illustrates the performance with respect to the slowdown criterion for two identical servers. On x-axis is again the offered load ρ and y-axis corresponds to the relative mean slowdown (here comparison is against the Myopic policy). One can identify three performance groups: RND and LWL form the worst performing group, then come Round-Robin and JSQ, and the Myopic and FPI-RND policy achieve the lowest mean slowdown.

Three heterogeneous servers

Fig. 8 (right) illustrates the simulation results in the asymmetric setting comprising one primary server with service rate $\nu_1 = 1$ and two secondary servers with rates $\nu_2 = \nu_3 = 1/2$. In this case, the Myopic approach is the optimal (among the candidates) while both FPI policies attain almost identical mean slowdown. Even though the value function for the Myopic policy is not available for us, one can estimate the relative values by means of simulation and carry out the policy improvement numerically. However, in this paper we do not pursue into this direction.

Server constellations

In Fig. 9 we compare the mean slowdown between different server constellations assuming the preemptive LIFO scheduling discipline. The y-axis represents the relative performance when compared to the two server system. To no surprise, when the load is small or moderate, a single server system achieves the lowest mean slowdown. However, as the load increases more, first the two server system becomes optimal, and then eventually the three server system takes the lead. This is due to the fact that at higher load levels, the correct dispatching decisions allow one to serve more expensive jobs faster. One interesting research question indeed is that given a total capacity budget, what is the optimal server constellation so as to minimize the mean slowdown.

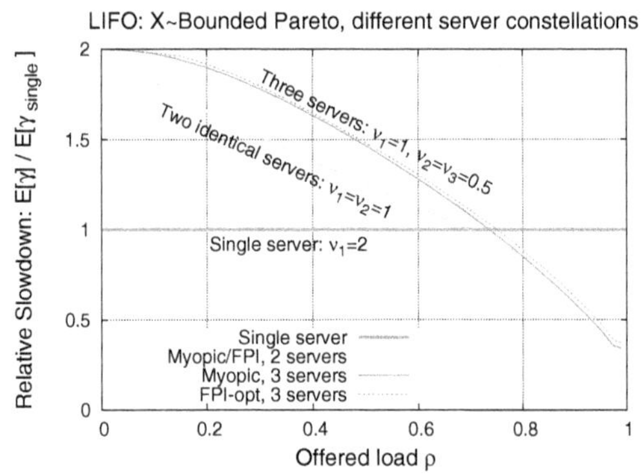

Figure 9: Comparison of the chosen server constellations with an equal total capacity: i) single server, ii) two identical servers, and iii) three servers.

5.3 SPTP

Finally, let us consider the SPTP scheduling discipline that is the natural choice when minimizing the mean slowdown (see Section 2). The job sizes are again assumed to obey the bounded Pareto distribution. Fig. 10 (left) illustrates the slowdown performance with the two identical servers. Interestingly, LWL becomes even weaker than RND-U as the offered load increases. Myopic and FPI-RND achieve the lowest mean slowdown.

In the case of three heterogeneous servers, the situation is again more challenging and the numerical results are depicted in Fig. 10 (right). At low levels of load, RND-opt is a surprisingly good choice, suggesting that SPTP manages to locally "correct" the occasional suboptimal decisions. When the load increases, the LWL policies become weak again. The Myopic policy shows a robust and good performance at all levels of offered load. However, the FPI policies, and FPI-opt in particular, achieve the lowest mean slowdown which is significantly better than with any other policy when $\rho > 0.5$.

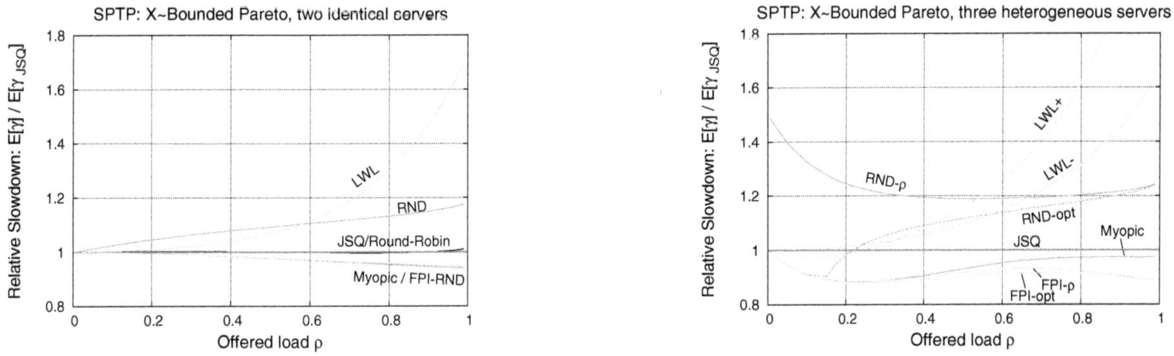

Figure 10: Numerical results with SPTP for two identical (left) and three heterogeneous servers (right).

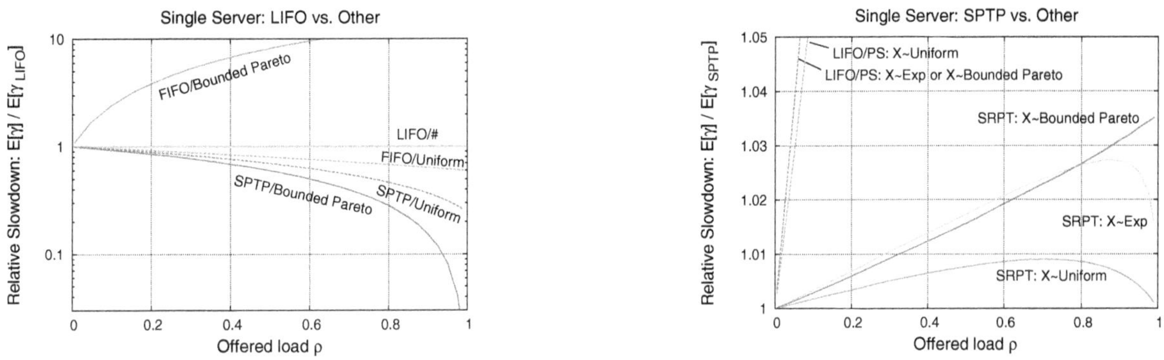

Figure 11: Comparison of different scheduling disciplines in a single server queue. FIFO is better than LIFO with some job size distributions (left). SPTP is only marginally better than SRPT (right).

5.4 Comparison of scheduling disciplines

So far we have fixed a scheduling discipline and evaluated different dispatching policies. Here we give a brief comparison of different scheduling disciplines with respect to the slowdown metric. Job sizes obey either (a) uniform distribution, $Y \sim \mathrm{U}(0.5, 1.5)$, or (b) the bounded Pareto distribution, both having the same mean, $\mathrm{E}[Y] = 1$.

First we consider a *single server queue*. Fig. 11 (left) depicts a comparison against LIFO with the same job size distribution on the logarithmic scale. In accordance with (3), FIFO is better than LIFO with uniform job size distribution, and with the bounded Pareto distribution the situation is the opposite. SPTP is clearly the best in both cases. In Fig. 11 (right), the reference level is the mean slowdown with SPTP. Here we have included also SRPT, which turns out to be only marginally better than SRPT, as observed also in [29]. LIFO and PS are significantly worse.

Fig. 12 illustrates the relative performance between different scheduling disciplines and dispatching policies in the heterogeneous three server dispatching system. SRPT is not included as its performance is very similar to SPTP. The reference level is the mean slowdown a JSQ/FIFO (left) and JSQ/LIFO (right) achieve. FPI manages to outperform the corresponding JSQ policy in all cases. Especially with the bounded Pareto distributed job sizes, FPI/LIFO performs rather well when compared to JSQ/LIFO. SPTP is clearly superior scheduling discipline in both cases, as expected.

In general, the scheduling discipline seems to have a stronger influence to the performance than the dispatching policy.

6. CONCLUSIONS

This work generalizes the earlier results of the size-aware value functions with respect to the sojourn time for M/G/1 queues with FIFO and LIFO to a general job specific holding cost. Additionally, we have considered the SPTP scheduling discipline, the optimality of which with Poisson arrivals was also established. As an important special case, one obtains the *slowdown criterion*, where the holding cost is inversely proportional to the job's (original) size. These results were then utilized in developing robust policies for dispatching systems. In particular, the value functions enable the policy improvement step for an arbitrary state-independent dispatching policy such as Bernoulli-splitting. The derived dispatching policies were shown to perform well by means of simulations. The highest improvements were often obtained in a more challenging heterogeneous setting with unequal service rates. Also the SPTP scheduling discipline outperformed the other by a clear margin in the examples, except the SRPT discipline, which appears to offer a rather similar performance in terms of slowdown and sojourn time.

7. REFERENCES

[1] S. Aalto, U. Ayesta, S. Borst, V. Misra, and R. Núñez-Queija. Beyond processor sharing. *SIGMETRICS Perform. Eval. Rev.*, 34:36–43, 2007.

[2] S. Aalto, U. Ayesta, and R. Righter. On the Gittins index in the M/G/1 queue. *Queueing Systems*, 63(1-4):437–458, 2009.

[3] S. Aalto and J. Virtamo. Basic packet routing problem. In *NTS-13*, Trondheim, Norway, Aug. 1996.

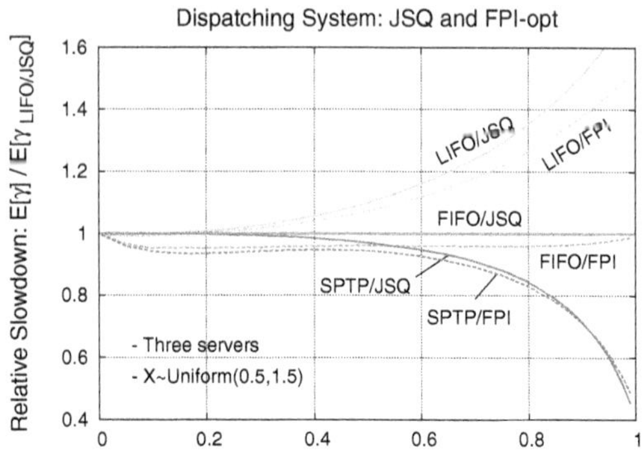

(a) $X \sim \mathrm{U}(0.5, 1.5)$

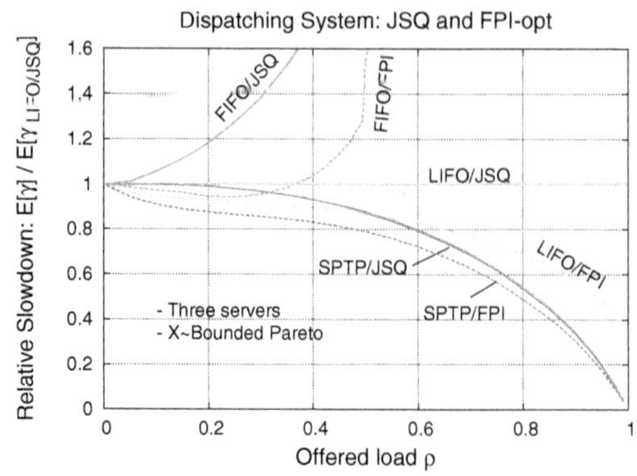

(b) $X \sim$ Bounded Pareto

Figure 12: Heterogeneous dispatching system with different scheduling disciplines.

[4] E. Bachmat and H. Sarfati. Analysis of SITA policies. *Performance Evaluation*, 67(2):102–120, 2010.

[5] C. E. Bell and J. Shaler Stidham. Individual versus social optimization in the allocation of customers to alternative servers. *Management Science*, 29(7):831–839, July 1983.

[6] M. E. Crovella, M. Harchol-Balter, and C. D. Murta. Task assignment in a distributed system: Improving performance by unbalancing load. In *ACM SIGMETRICS*, pages 268–269, June 1998.

[7] A. Downey. A parallel workload model and its implications for processor allocation. In *IEEE HPDC'97*, pages 112–123, Aug. 1997.

[8] A. Ephremides, P. Varaiya, and J. Walrand. A simple dynamic routing problem. *IEEE Transactions on Automatic Control*, 25(4):690–693, Aug. 1980.

[9] H. Feng and V. Misra. Mixed scheduling disciplines for network flows. *SIGMETRICS Perform. Eval. Rev.*, 31:36–39, Sept. 2003.

[10] H. Feng, V. Misra, and D. Rubenstein. Optimal state-free, size-aware dispatching for heterogeneous M/G/-type systems. *Perform. Eval.*, 62(1-4), 2005.

[11] J. Gittins. *Multi-armed Bandit Allocation Indices.* Wiley, 1989.

[12] V. Gupta, M. Harchol-Balter, K. Sigman, and W. Whitt. Analysis of join-the-shortest-queue routing for web server farms. *Performance Evaluation*, 64(9-12):1062–1081, Oct. 2007.

[13] M. Harchol-Balter. Task assignment with unknown duration. *J. ACM*, 49(2):260–288, Mar. 2002.

[14] M. Harchol-Balter, M. E. Crovella, and C. D. Murta. On choosing a task assignment policy for a distributed server system. *Journal of Parallel and Distributed Computing*, 59:204–228, 1999.

[15] M. Harchol-Balter and A. B. Downey. Exploiting process lifetime distributions for dynamic load balancing. *ACM Transactions on Computer Systems*, 15(3):253–285, Aug. 1997.

[16] M. Harchol-Balter, A. Scheller-Wolf, and A. R. Young. Surprising results on task assignment in server farms with high-variability workloads. In *ACM SIGMETRICS*, pages 287–298, 2009.

[17] M. Harchol-Balter, K. Sigman, and A. Wierman. Asymptotic convergence of scheduling policies with respect to slowdown. *Perform. Eval.*, 49(1-4):241–256, Sept. 2002.

[18] M. Haviv and T. Roughgarden. The price of anarchy in an exponential multi-server. *Oper. Res. Lett.*, 35(4):421–426, 2007.

[19] E. Hyytiä, S. Aalto, and A. Penttinen. Minimizing slowdown in heterogeneous size-aware dispatching systems (full version). Technical report, Mar. 2012. arXiv:1203.5040.

[20] E. Hyytiä, A. Penttinen, and S. Aalto. Size- and state-aware dispatching problem with queue-specific job sizes. *European Journal of Operational Research*, 217(2):357–370, Mar. 2012.

[21] E. Hyytiä, A. Penttinen, S. Aalto, and J. Virtamo. Dispatching problem with fixed size jobs and processor sharing discipline. In *ITC'23*, SFO, USA, Sept. 2011.

[22] E. Hyytiä, J. Virtamo, S. Aalto, and A. Penttinen. M/M/1-PS queue and size-aware task assignment. *Performance Evaluation*, 68(11):1136–1148, Nov. 2011.

[23] K. R. Krishnan. Joining the right queue: a state-dependent decision rule. *IEEE Transactions on Automatic Control*, 35(1):104–108, Jan. 1990.

[24] Z. Liu and R. Righter. Optimal load balancing on distributed homogeneous unreliable processors. *Operations Research*, 46(4):563–573, 1998.

[25] Z. Liu and D. Towsley. Optimality of the round-robin routing policy. *Journal of Applied Probability*, 31(2):466–475, June 1994.

[26] L. Schrage. A proof of the optimality of the shortest remaining processing time discipline. *Operations Research*, 16(3), 1968.

[27] W. Whitt. Deciding which queue to join: Some counterexamples. *Oper. Res.*, 34(1):55–62, 1986.

[28] A. Wierman. Fairness and scheduling in single server queues. *Surveys in Operations Research and Management Science*, 16(1):39–48, 2011.

[29] A. Wierman, M. Harchol-Balter, and T. Osogami. Nearly insensitive bounds on SMART scheduling. In *ACM SIGMETRICS*, pages 205–216, 2005.

[30] W. Winston. Optimality of the shortest line discipline. *Journal of Applied Probability*, 14:181–189, 1977.

[31] S. Yang and G. de Veciana. Size-based adaptive bandwidth allocation: optimizing the average QoS for elastic flows. In *IEEE INFOCOM*, 2002.

Bipartite Graph Structures for Efficient Balancing of Heterogeneous Loads

M. Leconte
Technicolor - INRIA
mathieu.leconte@inria.fr

M. Lelarge
INRIA - École Normale Supérieure
marc.lelarge@ens.fr

L. Massoulié
Technicolor
laurent.massoulie@technicolor.com

ABSTRACT

This paper considers large scale distributed content service platforms, such as peer-to-peer video-on-demand systems. Such systems feature two basic resources, namely storage and bandwidth. Their efficiency critically depends on two factors: (i) content replication within servers, and (ii) how incoming service requests are matched to servers holding requested content. To inform the corresponding design choices, we make the following contributions.

We first show that, for underloaded systems, so-called *proportional content placement* with a simple greedy strategy for matching requests to servers ensures full system efficiency provided storage size grows logarithmically with the system size. However, for constant storage size, this strategy undergoes a phase transition with severe loss of efficiency as system load approaches criticality.

To better understand the role of the matching strategy in this performance degradation, we characterize the asymptotic system efficiency under an *optimal* matching policy. Our analysis shows that –in contrast to greedy matching– optimal matching incurs an inefficiency that is exponentially small in the server storage size, even at critical system loads. It further allows a characterization of content replication policies that minimize the inefficiency. These optimal policies, which differ markedly from *proportional placement*, have a simple structure which makes them implementable in practice.

On the methodological side, our analysis of matching performance uses the theory of local weak limits of random graphs, and highlights a novel characterization of matching numbers in bipartite graphs, which may both be of independent interest.

Categories and Subject Descriptors

C.2.4 [**Computer-Communication Networks**]: Distributed Systems

General Terms

Theory, Performance

Keywords

Content Delivery Networks, Random Graphs, Matchings, Content Placement Policies

1. INTRODUCTION

The surge in consumption of video over the Internet necessitates massive bandwidth provisioning. At the same time, storage is extremely cheap. Extensive replication of content not only within data centers, but also at the periphery of the network, e.g. in users' computers, can thus be envisioned to leverage uplink bandwidth available from users' homes. *People's CDN* is one particular commercial initiative in this direction; the massively popular *PPLive* peer-to-peer system for video-on-demand is another example of this approach.

Such systems feature two key resources, namely storage and bandwidth. Ideally, one would like to utilize storage by pre-loading content replicas at individual servers, in such a way that bandwidth of all servers is available to serve any incoming request. In other words, a challenge in engineering such systems is to create content replicas so that bandwidth can be used maximally. Several strategies for content replication have been considered: uniform replication does not discriminate between contents; proportional replication tunes the number of replicas to the average number of requests, and automatically arises at cache memories when the so-called random-useful cache eviction method is used (it is also approximately achieved by the classical least-recently-used eviction rule [21]).

Our first objective is to develop a clear understanding of the relative merits of distinct replication strategies in the context of large-scale distributed server platforms. We also aim at characterizing the amount of storage necessary to remove the *content bottleneck*, i.e. for what amount of storage is the system service capacity only constrained by its overall bandwidth? These properties certainly depend both on the content replication strategy and on the algorithm used to match incoming service requests to servers capable of treating these requests.

To this end, we develop performance models based on bipartite graphs (Section 2). To motivate our main results, in Section 3 we first consider simple strategies for these two design issues, namely proportional replication and greedy online matching. Regarding proportional replication, using simple large-deviations estimates (Chernoff bounds) we show that a limited amount of storage (logarithmic in system size) suffices to absorb all requests in *sub-critical scenarios*, where the system is under-loaded. In other words, the content bottleneck is removed under these assumptions. However, these analysis techniques are not powerful enough to characterize system performance under critical or super-critical load. We also establish through mean field analysis that system inefficiency is exponentially small in the amount of storage per server, provided the system is not critically loaded. In contrast, the performance degrades significantly at critical loads.

We thus turn to other analysis tools to bound the best possible inefficiency under general replication strategies and system loads. In Section 4, we exploit recent advances [17, 12] in the application of the *cavity method* from statistical physics to obtain explicit characterizations of the optimal system capacity under given replication strategies (Theorem 2). We also establish a novel characterization of the matching numbers in finite bipartite graphs (Theorem 1) which helps explain the formulas of Theorem 2. In addition, this result suggests that the applicability of the cavity method could be extended to broad classes of bipartite random graph models beyond locally tree-like graphs, as it was recently observed in related frameworks by [7] and [5].

We then leverage these tools to revisit our initial questions in Section 5. There, we establish that system inefficiency under optimal matching is exponentially small in storage space, and this even at criticality, for a large class of replication policies which includes uniform and proportional. We furthermore identify the best replication policies; they have a simple distinct structure for each of the three possible system regimes, namely sub-critical, critical and super-critical. We review related work in Section 6 and conclude in Section 7.

2. SYSTEM MODEL AND STATISTICAL ASSUMPTIONS

In this section we introduce the bipartite graph representation of the system on which our analysis is based. We also describe some statistical assumptions on the contents and the replication policies at the servers, as well as the random graph models that they induce.

2.1 Content-server graph

We are given a collection of n contents and m servers. Each server is storing replicas of a subset of the contents. We assume that all servers have an identical storage capacity $d \in \mathbb{N}$, i.e. each server is capable of storing d different contents at then same time. Such a system can be represented by a bipartite graph $G = (C \cup S, E)$ where:

- the set C represents the contents and is of cardinality n;
- the set S represents the servers and is of cardinality m;
- there is an (undirected) edge $(cs) \in E$ whenever server s stores a replica of content c.

We denote by ∂c or ∂s the neighborhood of c or s, i.e. the set of neighbors in G of c or s. Hence, ∂c is the set of servers that hold a replica of content c, and ∂s is the set of contents of which server s stores a replica. The degree of a node $s \in S$ is exactly $d = |\partial s|$, while the degree of a node $c \in C$ is equal to the total number of replicas of content c in the system. In Section 2.2, we will explain how the graph G is constructed. Before, we describe how the natural constraints on the service of requests can be seen on the graph G.

We let $b_c \in \mathbb{N}$ be the number of requests made for content $c \in C$. Such a request for content c can be served only by a server having content c stored on disk, i.e. a request for content c can only be served by a neighbor of c in the bipartite graph G. Moreover, we assume in this paper that servers can serve at most one request at a time, although an analysis could be attempted using similar methods when servers have a larger service capacity. Hence, if a request for a content c is assigned to server $s \in \partial c$, then server s becomes unavailable for all the contents in $\partial s \backslash c$, where $\partial s \backslash c$ is a short-hand notation for $\partial s \setminus \{c\}$.

We are now ready to define an allocation which represents a possible assignement of requests to servers. Given a bipartite graph $G = (C \cup S, E)$, and a vector $B = (b_c)_{c \in C}$, an allocation is a subset of edges $A \subseteq E$ such that

- each server in S is adjacent to at most one edge in A, as a server is able to serve at most one request.
- each content c in C is adjacent to at most b_c edges in A: it would make no sense to dedicate more servers to the service of content c than there are requests for c.

The total number of requests satisfied by an allocation A is simply given by the cardinality $|A|$ of the set A since if edge $(cs) \in A$ one request for content c is served by server s. The maximum size of such an allocation for a given graph G is denoted by $M(G, B)$. In the particular case where $b_c = 1$ for all contents $c \in C$, an allocation of G is what is classically known as a *matching*, and $M(G, B) = M(G)$ is then the *matching number* of G.

We define the load of the system as ratio of the total number of requests summed over all contents and the total service capacity summed over all servers, thus $\rho = \sum_c b_c/m$. If $\rho < 1$ (resp. $\rho > 1$, $\rho = 1$), we say that the system is under-loaded (resp. over-loaded, critical). Clearly, in the under-loaded regime not all servers can be assigned to a request, while in the over-loaded regime not all requests can be serviced. Hence, we have $|A| \leq \min\left(\sum_{c \in C} b_c, m\right)$ and we define the inefficiency of an allocation A as the quantity $\gamma_A = \rho \wedge 1 - |A|/m \geq 0$, where $\rho \wedge 1 = \min(\rho, 1)$. In the under-loaded regime, the inefficiency represents the ratio of the total number of unallocated requests divided by the total number of servers. In the over-loaded regime, the inefficiency represents the fraction of unallocated servers.

The objective is to minimize the inefficiency of the allocations output by the matching algorithm on the graph determined by the replication policy. This could result in a joint optimization problem of both the matching scheme and the replication strategy, however for tractability reasons we will consider the two problems separately. This leads to two design questions, namely: (i) find a replication policy that minimizes the minimal inefficiency over the resulting graph G, given by $\gamma_{G,B} = \rho \wedge 1 - M(G, B)/m$; (ii) find a matching algorithm which is simple and whose inefficiency approaches as close as possible to $\gamma_{G,B}$ for graphs G (and B) of interest. We will deal with both questions in the sequel.

Note that the problem of finding a maximum allocation in a finite bipartite graph is known to be of strongly polynomial complexity [4], using a strongly polynomial algorithm for maximum flow problems by [20]. There may nontheless exist lower-complexity methods, that yield comparable performance for the graphs of interest.

2.2 Random graph models

The large scale of the system as well as the uncertainty ahead of time in the number of requests for each content make it hopeless to design with too much precision the joint constitution of the caches of all the servers, i.e. deciding jointly of each and every edges in the bipartite graph G. Indeed, we will be interested in a regime where the number of contents n and the number of servers m tend to infinity together, with $\frac{m}{n} \to \beta \in \mathbb{R}_+$. In this regime, it seems plausible that there will be little fine-tuned cooperation among the servers, and they will thus essentially make independent choices for their cache based on the available statistics on the requests. Of course, allowing more cooperation between servers could only improve the performance and would arguably be even more realistic, however one would have to precisely define the extent of cooperation that is reasonable; we will not deal with such issues in this paper. We will also assume that the storage size d of each server does not scale with n. Indeed the point of having a large number of servers is precisely that the storage size of each server does not need to scale with the size of the system.

We now present the most simple model we will use in this paper, which represents a situation where no information on the requests is available to the servers: in this case, each server picks d contents uniformly at random among all contents and independently of the other servers. Then, the distribution of the number of replicas of a given content, i.e. its degree in the graph G is a Binomial random variable with parameters m and $\frac{d}{n}$. Hence in the regime where n tends to infinity with $m/n \to \beta$ while d is kept fixed, the distribution of the degree of a content in G tends to a Poisson distribution with mean $d\beta$. Note that even if the degrees of the contents are not independent for any fixed n, the degrees become k-wise independent for any $k = o(n)$ in the limit when n tends to infinity [6]. We will refer to this model as the *single class model*. In Section 3, we will moreover use a Poisson distribution of parameter λ for the number of requests in order to analyze the performance of a simple greedy algorithm for matching requests to servers.

Of course, in a real system, the contents are not all of the same popularity, and we may consider prioritizing replication of more popular contents at the servers. In such a system the number of requests for a content and its number of replicas would not be independent as in the previous example; however the servers may not have full information ahead of time about the number of requests for each content and they may have to rely only on a coarse-grained estimate of the popularity of the contents.

We model this situation by partitioning the set of all contents into *popularity classes*. Specifically, we let class i contain a fraction α_i of all contents and we assume that the number of requests for the contents in class i are independent and identically distributed with a Poisson distribution with mean λ_i. Servers do not distinguish between contents within the same popularity class, but they may favor some classes with respect to others. For example, we can let servers assign independently contents to each memory slot in the following way: the server first chooses a class of content, for example picking class i with probability θ_i; then it picks a particular content within that class uniformly at random. Then, the number of replicas and number of requests for a content are independent given its class. Moreover in the large n limit, they are distributed as two independent Poisson random variables: the number of replicas having mean $\beta d\theta_i/\alpha_i =: \beta_i d$ and the number of requests having mean λ_i. Of course, other types of content popularity distributions could be of interest (notably Zipf-like distributions), however the model considered here is particularly suited for investigating how to adapt the replication policy to the popularity of contents, i.e. how to choose the θ_i's as a function of the α_i's and λ_i's. It will be used for that purpose in Section 5. We call this model the *multi-class model*.

3. CANDIDATE STRATEGIES

In this section we consider easily implementable candidates for the replication policy and matching algorithm. Their analysis will serve as a point of comparison to determine whether more advanced strategies are needed or not. We first consider the so-called proportional placement policy, which maintains for each content a number of replicas proportional to its popularity, and then a simple online matching algorithm that iteratively makes random assignements of requests to available servers.

3.1 Proportional placement

Assume that the numbers of requests b_c for content c are mutually independent over all $c \in C$, b_c having a Poisson distribution with parameter $\lambda_c \geq \underline{\lambda}$ for some fixed parameter $\underline{\lambda} > 0$. Based on knowledge of the λ_c's only (and not of the b_c's), the replication problem consists in determining the number of replicas d_c of each item c and their placement onto servers. A candidate strategy consists in taking the number of replicas d_c deterministic and proportional to the *expected* number of requests λ_c: $d_c \approx (\beta d)\lambda_c/\lambda$, where $\lambda = n^{-1}\sum_{c=1}^{n}\lambda_c$. The system is then sub-critical if the following stability condition holds, that the expected number of requests be smaller than the number of servers, which reads

$$\delta := \beta - \lambda > 0, \tag{1}$$

where we introduced notation δ for the stability margin $\beta - \lambda$. In this context we have the following:

PROPOSITION 1. *Assuming $\delta > 0$ and proportional placement is used, all requests can be met with high probability if the storage space per server d satisfies $d \geq \Omega(\log(n))$.*

As a corollary, this result implies that the inefficiency of proportional placement is equal to 0 a.s. for d logarithmic in the number of contents n in the system, i.e. $\mathbb{E}[\gamma_{G,B}] = 0$ for $d \geq \Omega(\log(n))$ when G is chosen according to the proportionnal placement rule (and B is drawn as explained before).

PROOF. For each content c and each of the corresponding b_c requests, we can split the request equally into d_c subrequests of size $1/d_c$. To a given server s with corresponding collection ∂s of stored items, for each item $c \in \partial s$ we associate b_c sub-requests to that particular server. Then a service of all requests will be feasible provided that for each such server $s \in \{1, \dots, \beta n\}$ one has

$$\sum_{c \in \partial s} \frac{b_c}{d_c} \leq 1. \tag{2}$$

Indeed, this mapping of sub-requests to servers would constitute a fractional matching of requests, and an integral matching would therefore exist, by the total unimodularity of the adjacency matrix of the graph G.

Calling $\mathcal{A}_s$ the event corresponding to Condition (2) and $\mathcal{A}_s^{\mathsf{c}}$ its complement, Chernoff's inequality yields

$$\begin{aligned}\mathbb{P}(\mathcal{A}_s^{\mathsf{c}}) &\le \exp\left(-\sup_{\theta>0}\left[\theta - \sum_{c\in\partial s}\log \mathbb{E}e^{\theta(b_c/d_c)}\right]\right)\\ &= \exp\left(-\sup_{\theta>0}\left[\theta - \sum_{c\in\partial s}\lambda_c\left(-1+e^{\theta/d_c}\right)\right]\right).\end{aligned}$$

Note that $d_c \ge d\beta\lambda_c/\lambda - 1 \ge \lambda_c d\left(1+\frac{\delta}{2\lambda}\right)$ for d large enough, namely for $d \ge 2\lambda/(\delta\underline{\lambda})$. Replacing d_c by this corresponding lower bound in the above expression, we obtain

$$\mathbb{P}(\mathcal{A}_s^{\mathsf{c}}) \le \exp\left(-\sup_{\theta>0}\left[\theta - \sum_{c\in\partial s}\lambda_c\left(-1+e^{\theta'/\lambda_c}\right)\right]\right),$$

where we introduced the notation $\theta' := \theta\lambda/(d(\lambda+\delta/2\lambda))$. It is readily checked that the function $\lambda_c \to \lambda_c\left(-1+e^{\theta'/\lambda_c}\right)$ is decreasing in λ_c, and is thus upper-bounded by its value at $\underline{\lambda}$ for all $\lambda_c \ge \underline{\lambda}$. Using the fact that the cardinality of ∂s is precisely d, this then entails

$$\begin{aligned}\mathbb{P}(\mathcal{A}_s^{\mathsf{c}}) &\le e^{-\sup_{\theta>0}\left[\theta - d\underline{\lambda}\left(-1+e^{\theta\lambda/(d\underline{\lambda}(\delta/2+\lambda))}\right)\right]}\\ &= e^{-d\underline{\lambda}h(1+\delta/(2\lambda))},\end{aligned}$$

where $h(x) := x\log(x) - x + 1$ is the Cramér transform of a unit rate Poisson random variable. It follows that

$$\mathbb{P}(\mathcal{A}_s^{\mathsf{c}}) \le n^{-\alpha\underline{\lambda}h(1+\delta/(2\lambda))}$$

for $d \ge \alpha\log(n)$. Thus, provided

$$\alpha > \frac{1}{\underline{\lambda}h(1+\delta/(2\lambda))}, \tag{3}$$

by the union bound the probability that at least one event $\mathcal{A}_s$ fails is $o(1)$. Consequently, under the stability assumption (1), for popularities lower-bounded by $\underline{\lambda} > 0$, all requests are met with high probability as $n \to \infty$ provided

$$d \ge \max(\alpha\log(n), 2\lambda/(\delta\underline{\lambda})),$$

where constant α verifies (3). □

This result indicates that a logarithmic storage size d suffices to meet all the requests, provided one uses the above proportional placement. Note also that proportional placement is robust, in the sense that this feasibility property does not depend on the particular way in which content replicas are co-located within servers so long as one does not replicate content more than once at a single server.

Nevertheless, several questions of interest remain open. In particular, the above argument does not say what happens when the stability margin δ becomes small: indeed, for small δ, the lower bound (3) on α is $\Theta(\delta^{-2})$, and it is thus not clear how this replication policy behaves in a near-critical regime $\delta \to 0$. In addition, it does not say how many requests remain unmatched under storage size restrictions, for instance for constant rather than logarithmic d. Moreover, it states the existence of a matching, but does not address whether such a matching is easy to find. The first two of these three questions will be addressed in Section 5.

3.2 Online matching algorithm

We now study the performance of a simple online algorithm for matching incoming requests to servers. For simplicity we consider the single-class model, where all contents have the same popularity, and servers choose uniformly at random which content they store.

We consider the following algorithm: pick a request at random and match it, if possible, to an unmatched server chosen uniformly at random among all unmatched servers storing the corresponding content; otherwise the request is discarded and all further requests for the same content will be rejected as well. We call such contents *depleted* contents (as opposed to *available* contents).

We adopt a temporal view of this process, assuming that a request arrives at every time step and is for a content chosen uniformly at random. As soon as a request arrives, the algorithm checks whether it can be matched to a server or not; as this does not require knowledge of the requests that will arrive at later time steps, we say this algorithm is *online*. After λn time steps, the number of requests for the contents will be independent Poisson random variables of parameter λ, as required.

Let γ be the limit of the inefficency of the online algorithm as $n \to \infty$. We then have the following:

PROPOSITION 2. *For $\rho \neq 1$, the inefficiency γ verifies*

$$\gamma \le \exp\left(-d\beta|\rho - 1|(1+o(1))\right),$$

where the $o(1)$ is with respect to the storage capacity d. In the critical regime $\rho = 1$,

$$\gamma = \frac{\log 2}{d\beta} + o(1/d).$$

Thus, online matching incurs severe performance degradation at criticality, compared to the under-loaded and overloaded regimes. This will be contrasted with the properties of optimal matching in Section 5.

The remainder of this section describes the main steps in the proof of the Proposition 2 above.

3.2.1 Mean field analysis of online matching

We let X_t^n be the number of matched servers at time t and Y_t^n be the number of contents for which at least one request has already been discarded by time t. It can be easily verified that $(X_t^n, Y_t^n)_{t\in\mathbb{N}}$ is a Markov chain. Indeed, it is enough to check that the induced subgraph on the $n-Y_t^n$ available contents and the $m-X_t^n$ unmatched servers is still distributed according to the same random graph model, i.e. every unassigned server stores exactly d available contents (because it cannot store depleted contents as those would not be depleted otherwise) and the set of contents stored by an unmatched server is chosen uniformly at random among the subsets of size d of the set of available contents. The correct distribution of number of requests for each content is ensured by the random uniform choice of a content among all contents for each incoming request.

The one-step transition probabilities of the Markov chain are as follows:

$$(X_{t+1}^n, Y_{t+1}^n) = \begin{cases} (X_t^n, Y_t^n) & \text{w.p. } \frac{Y_t^n}{n} \\ (X_t^n, Y_t^n+1) & \text{w.p. } \frac{n-Y_t^n}{n}p_{x,y} \\ (X_t^n+1, Y_t^n) & \text{w.p. } \frac{n-Y_t^n}{n}(1-p_{x,y}) \end{cases}$$

where $p_{x,y}$ is the probability that no unmatched server stores a particular available content given $X_t^n = x$ and $Y_t^n = y$. We have

$$p_{x,y} = \left(\frac{\binom{n-y-1}{d}}{\binom{n-y}{d}} \right)^{m-x} \sim_{n\to\infty} e^{-d\frac{m-x}{n-y}}.$$

In the limit $n \to \infty$, we use mean field techniques to approximate the Markov chain $(X_t^n, Y_t^n)_t$ by the solution of differential equations. We define $x(t)$ and $y(t)$ as candidate approximations of $\frac{X_{tn}^n}{n}$ and $\frac{Y_{tn}^n}{n}$ respectively, by setting: $x(0) = y(0) = 0$ and $x(t), y(t)$ are given by the following differential equations:

$$\dot{x} = (1-y)\left(1 - e^{-d\frac{\beta - x}{1-y}}\right) \quad (4)$$

$$\dot{y} = (1-y)e^{-d\frac{\beta-x}{1-y}} \quad (5)$$

Classical results of Kurtz [11] then imply the following

LEMMA 1. *Almost surely, we have*

$$\lim_{n\to\infty} \frac{1}{n}(X_{\lambda n}^n, Y_{\lambda n}^n) = (x(\lambda), y(\lambda)).$$

The limiting inefficiency γ of the online algorithm is thus given by $\gamma = \rho \wedge 1 - x(\lambda)/\beta$. While the above differential equations do not admit closed form solutions, it is possible to derive explicit upper and lower bounds based on more tractable ODE's, which become accurate for large d. We defer this part of the proof to the appendix.

4. OPTIMAL MATCHING

In this section, we compute the size of a maximum allocation $M(G, B)$ and hence the inefficiency $\gamma_{G,B}$ of the graph for the models presented in Section 2.2. Our first main result shows that $M(G, B)$ can be expressed in terms of 'local contributions' for any bipartite graph G and any numbers of requests B. This expression turns out to be 'continuous' in the large n limit and converge a.s. to a deterministic quantity for random graphs drawn according to the models of Section 2.2, which allows us to compute explicitly the asymptotic for the maximum number of requests satisfied.

4.1 Finite bipartite graphs

We focus here on finite bipartite deterministic graphs. The results obtained in this subsection are meant to help understand Theorem 2 on which the analysis in Section 5 builds.

We will need to introduce some notations to state the results of this section. First-of-all, recall from Section 2.1 that $G = (C \cup S, E)$ is a finite bipartite graph and b_c is the number of requests for content $c \in C$. An allocation A is a subset of edges of G which satisfies some degree constraints at the vertices of G: in the subgraph $(C \cup S, A)$ where only edges in A are kept, each node $c \in C$ has degree at most b_c and each node $s \in S$ has degree at most 1. We define $b_s = 1$ for all $s \in S$ to ease the definition of quantities that are similar for contents and servers, so that the vector $(b_v)_{v\in C\cup S}$ represents the degree constraints for the allocation A.

The characterization of $M(G, B)$ that we will obtain here involves a message passing algorithm between the vertices of G, which can be seen to be the well-known *belief propagation* algorithm from statistical physics [15, 16]. We will not expand on the links with belief propagation as this is not the purpose of this paper and no prior knowledge of the related literature will be needed here.

As neighboring vertices in G will be sending messages to each other, and although the original graph G is not oriented, it is convenient to associate to each edge $(cs) \in E$ two oriented edges denoted by $c \to s$ and $s \to c$. We let $\overrightarrow{E}$ be the set of oriented edges of G. In what follows a vector $I \in \{0,1\}^{\overrightarrow{E}}$ will be interpreted as a set of (binary) messages $I_{x\to y} \in \{0,1\}$ along oriented edges $x \to y \in \overrightarrow{E}$. We say that $I_{x\to y}$ is the message from x to y. For a given oriented edge $x \to y$, we define the local operator which takes as arguments all incoming messages to x except the one coming from y:

$$\mathcal{P}_{x\to y}\left((I_{z\to x})_{z\in\partial x\setminus y}\right) = \mathbf{1}\left(\sum_{z\in\partial x\setminus y} I_{z\to x} < b_x\right). \quad (6)$$

By convention, if x is a leaf in the graph G, i.e. y is the only neighbor of x, we set $\mathcal{P}_{x\to y} = 1$.

If J is a vector in $\{0,1\}^{\overrightarrow{E}}$ and L is a subset of $\overrightarrow{E}$, we write J_L for the vector induced by J on $\{0,1\}^L$ and $|J_L| = \sum_{\vec{e}\in L} J_{\vec{e}}$. Also, for $x \in V$, let $\overrightarrow{\partial x}$ be the set of edges directed towards x. It will be convenient to see the local operator $\mathcal{P}_{x\to y}$ as an operator from $\{0,1\}^{\overrightarrow{E}}$ to $\{0,1\}$, although it depends only on a few component of the input. Namely, with these notations, for $I \in \{0,1\}^{\overrightarrow{E}}$, we can rewrite (6) as: $\mathcal{P}_{x\to y}(I) = \mathbf{1}\left(|I_{\overrightarrow{\partial x}}| - I_{y\to x} < b_x\right)$. It is now easy to define a global operator on the graph G, denoted $\mathcal{P}_G : \{0,1\}^{\overrightarrow{E}} \to \{0,1\}^{\overrightarrow{E}}$, which performs simultaneously the action of all the local operators $\mathcal{P}_{x\to y}$ for all x, y, so that $J = \mathcal{P}_G(I)$ is defined by: $J_{x\to y} = \mathcal{P}_{x\to y}(I)$. In words, the action of $\mathcal{P}_G$ on messages I is as follows: for each oriented edge $x \to y$, return a message 0 on this edge if the sum of the incoming messages to x from neighbors different from y is at least b_x and return a message 1 otherwise.

The global operator $\mathcal{P}_G$ was introduced in [12], where it was shown that in the special case where G is a finite tree (i.e. acyclic graph) there is a unique fixed point to the operator $\mathcal{P}_G$ (obtained by iterating it) and the size of the maximum allocation can be computed from this fixed point. Here we show that this result is indeed correct for a much larger class of graphs, namely for any bipartite graph.

THEOREM 1. *Consider a finite, bipartite graph $G = (C \cup S, E)$ with $b_c \in \mathbb{N}$ for $c \in C$. We define the function F^S : $\{0,1\}^{\overrightarrow{E}} \to \mathbb{N}$ by*

$$F^S(I) = \sum_{s\in S} \mathbf{1}(|I_{\overrightarrow{\partial s}}| > 0) + \sum_{c\in C} b_c \mathbf{1}\left(\sum_{s\in\partial c} \mathcal{P}_{s\to c}(I) > b_c\right).$$

Then, we have

$$M(G, B) = \inf_{I = \mathcal{P}_G \circ \mathcal{P}_G(I)} F^S(I). \quad (7)$$

We use the superscript S for the function F^S to emphasize the fact that F^S actually depends only on messages incoming to nodes in S. Indeed, if we denote by $I_{C\to S}$ those messages, applying once the operator $\mathcal{P}_G$ to these messages give a set of messages from nodes in S to nodes in C that we denote with a slight abuse of notation: $J_{S\to C} = \mathcal{P}_G(I_{C\to S})$. Now if I is a solution of the fixed point equation $I = \mathcal{P}_G \circ \mathcal{P}_G(I)$, we must also have $\mathcal{P}_G(J_{S\to C}) = I_{C\to S}$. For such an I, if we consider the messages $K \in \{0,1\}^{\vec{E}}$ defined by: $K_{C\to S} = I_{C\to S}$ and $K_{S\to C} = J_{S\to C}$, we have $K = \mathcal{P}_G(K)$. Moreover since $F^S(K)$ depends only on $K_{C\to S}$, we have $F^S(K) = F^S(I)$. Hence we proved that

$$M(G,B) = \inf_{I=\mathcal{P}_G(I)} F^S(I). \quad (8)$$

But if $I = \mathcal{P}_G(I)$, the expression of $F^S(I)$ simplifies to

$$F^S(I) = \sum_{s\in S} \mathbf{1}\left(|I_{\vec{\partial s}}| > 0\right) + \sum_{c\in C} b_c \mathbf{1}\left(|I_{\vec{\partial c}}| > b_c\right).$$

Now if the graph G is a finite tree, it is easy to see that there is indeed a unique solution to the fixed point equation $I = \mathcal{P}_G(I)$, so that our Theorem 1 recovers Proposition 3 in [12]. However, extending this result to general bipartite graphs is non-trivial and requires dealing with possibly multiple solutions to the fixed point equation. We give a full proof in Section 4.3.

4.2 Asymptotics for large graphs

We now explain how the previous results allow to deal with random graphs model as described in Section 2.2 in the large n limit. We follow the approach of [12] based on the objective method developed by Aldous and Steele [3] and adapt it to our framework.

We are now given a sequence of bipartite graphs $G_n = (C_n \cup S_n, E_n)$ with $|C_n| = n$ and $|S_n| = \lfloor \beta n \rfloor$ and a sequence of vectors $B_n = (b_c^n)_{c\in C_n}$. We are interested in computing the limit

$$\lim_{n\to\infty} \frac{M(G_n, B_n)}{|S_n|}.$$

Of course, this limit might exist only if the sequence of graphs G_n does converge. In our case, sequences of random graphs as described in Section 2.2 have been extensively studied in the random graphs literature [6] and are known to be locally tree-like: with high probability, there is no cycle in a ball of fixed radius around a vertex chosen at random. The notion of local weak convergence [3] makes rigorous the fact that the sequence of graphs we consider in this paper converges to trees. More precisely, pick a vertex in G_n uniformly at random and call it the root. Then the local neighborhood of the root converges for the local weak convergence towards a probability distribution concentrated on rooted (possibly infinite) trees.

We now need to adapt the analysis done for finite graphs in Section 4.1 to the framework of possibly infinite graphs. We start with the following simple observation: let A^* be a maximum allocation of a finite graph G with constraints B, then

$$\frac{M(G,B)}{|S|} = \frac{1}{|S|}\sum_{s\in S} \mathbf{1}(s \text{ belongs to an edge of } A^*).$$

Now the right-hand part has a very natural probabilistic interpretaion. First consider the deterministic function mapping S to $\{0,1\}$, defined by $\mathbf{1}(s$ belongs to an edge of $A^*)$. Denote by R a node taken uniformy at random in S. We can rewrite the expression as

$$\frac{M(G,B)}{|S|} = \mathbb{E}^S\left[\mathbf{1}(R \text{ belongs to an edge of } A^*)\right], \quad (9)$$

where $\mathbb{E}^S$ is the expectation with respect to the uniform distribution over the set S. The local weak convergence directly tells us that this expectation converges to the corresponding expectation on the infinite graph provided the function $\mathbf{1}(R$ belongs to an edge of $A^*)$, which takes as input a bipartite graph $G = (C\cup S, E)$ rooted at $R \in S$ and a vector B, is continuous (with respect to the adequate topology for local weak convergence). This fact is not at all obvious and follows from [17] and [12]. Note first that the global operator $\mathcal{P}_G$ is perfectly well-defined for any locally finite graph, i.e. a graph in which each node has a finite degree. However, in an infinite setting the fixed point equation $I = \mathcal{P}_G(I)$ might not have a solution, so that it is not possible to extend the expression (8) to the infinite framework. However, Proposition 5 in [12] shows that our Theorem 1 extends nicely to the infinite framework as follows: dividing by $|S|$ the expression of F^S, we get

$$\begin{aligned}
\mathcal{F}^S(I) &= \frac{1}{|S|}F^S(I)\\
\mathcal{F}^S(I) &= \mathbb{E}^S\left[\mathbf{1}(|I_{\vec{\partial R}}| > 0)\right]\\
&\quad + \frac{|C|}{|S|}\mathbb{E}^C\left[b_R \mathbf{1}\left(\sum_{s\in\partial R} \mathcal{P}_{s\to R}(I) > b_R\right)\right]
\end{aligned}$$

where $\mathbb{E}^S$ has been defined in (9) and $\mathbb{E}^C$ is the expectation with respect to R being taken uniformly at random in the set C. For the sequence of graph G_n that we are interested in, we have $\frac{|C_n|}{|S_n|} \to \frac{1}{\beta}$ and $\mathbb{E}^{S_n}$ and $\mathbb{E}^{C_n}$ converges locally weakly to $\mathbb{E}^S$ and $\mathbb{E}^C$ on the (possibly infinite) limit graph G. We are now ready to extend Theorem 1 to the following proposition:

PROPOSITION 3. *For a sequence of bipartite graphs G_n converging locally weakly to a tree G with root R, we define*

$$\begin{aligned}
\mathcal{F}^S(I) &= \mathbb{E}^S\left[\mathbf{1}(|I_{\vec{\partial R}}| > 0)\right] \quad (10)\\
&\quad + \frac{1}{\beta}\mathbb{E}^C\left[b_R \mathbf{1}\left(\sum_{s\in\partial R} \mathcal{P}_{s\to R}(I) > b_R\right)\right]
\end{aligned}$$

Then we have

$$\lim_{n\to\infty} \frac{|M(G_n, B_n)|}{|S_n|} = \inf_{I=\mathcal{P}_G\circ\mathcal{P}_G(I)} \mathcal{F}^S(I), \quad (11)$$

where the fixed point I should not depend on the root R of G.

We can now use the markovian nature of the limiting tree in our case to compute the right expression in (11). Indeed, using the recursive structure of the tree, the fixed point equation $I = \mathcal{P}_G\circ\mathcal{P}_G(I)$ becomes a simple fixed point equation on probability distributions. More precisely, since G is now random, the variables $I_{x\to y}$ are also random and, being $\{0,1\}$-valued, are Bernoulli random variables. Moreover all the messages incoming to a vertex are independent thanks to the branching property of the limiting tree G. For simplicity, we consider the single class model, so that the limiting tree is a simple branching process with two types of nodes: nodes in S have a fixed degree d in the tree, while nodes in C have a random degree following a Poisson distribution with mean $d\beta$. In this case, we have two types of messages -those going from a vertex in S to a vertex in C and those going from a vertex in C to a vertex in S- and we need to compute their probability distributions, i.e. the corresponding parameter of the Bernoulli random variable associated to each of these messages. We denote by $I^{C\to S}$

and $I^{S\to C}$ Bernoulli random variables with respective parameter $p_{C\to S}$ and $p_{S\to C}$ corresponding to messages from C to S and S to C respectively. The values of $p_{C\to S}$ and $p_{S\to C}$ are now given by the fixed point equation $I = \mathcal{P}_G \circ \mathcal{P}_G(I)$ which gives here the following fixed point equation for the distributions of $I^{C\to S}$ and $I^{S\to C}$:

$$\begin{aligned} I^{S\to C} &\stackrel{d}{=} \mathbf{1}\left(\sum_{i=1}^{d-1} I_i^{C\to S} < 1\right) \\ I^{C\to S} &\stackrel{d}{=} \mathbf{1}\left(\sum_{i=1}^{\tilde{D}} I_i^{S\to C} < \tilde{B}\right), \end{aligned}$$

where the $I_i^{C\to S}$'s (resp. $I_i^{S\to C}$'s) are i.i.d. with the same law as $I_i^{C\to S}$ (resp. $I_i^{S\to C}$), $\tilde{D}$ is a Poisson random variable with parameter $d\beta$ (so that $\tilde{D}+1$ corresponds to the edge-biased degree distribution of a random content) and $\tilde{B}$ is a Poisson random variable with parameter λ (corresponding to the number of requests for a content).

Taking the expectation of these equations give:

$$\begin{aligned} p_{S\to C} &= (1-p_{C\to S})^{d-1} \\ p_{C\to S} &= \mathbb{P}\left(\text{Bin}(\tilde{D}, p_{S\to C}) < \tilde{B}\right), \end{aligned}$$

where $\text{Bin}(n,p)$ is a Binomial random variable with parameters n and $p \in [0,1]$. We can now use (10) to compute the function $\mathcal{F}^S$ as follows:

$$\begin{aligned} \mathcal{F}^S(I) &= \mathbb{E}\left[\mathbf{1}(\text{Bin}(d, p_{C\to S}) > 0)\right] \\ &\quad + \frac{1}{\beta}\mathbb{E}\left[B\mathbf{1}\left(\text{Bin}(\tilde{D}, p_{S\to C}) > \tilde{B}\right)\right], \end{aligned}$$

where we used the same notation as above and used the fact that the degree of a node in S (resp. C) is d (resp. a random Poisson variable with mean $d\beta$). It is convenient at this stage to introduce the following function from $[0,1]^2 \to \mathbb{R}$:

$$\begin{aligned} \mathcal{F}^S(p,q) &= \mathbb{E}\left[\mathbf{1}(\text{Bin}(d, p) > 0)\right] \\ &\quad + \frac{1}{\beta}\mathbb{E}\left[B\mathbf{1}\left(\text{Bin}(\tilde{D}, q) > \tilde{B}\right)\right], \end{aligned}$$

so that $\mathcal{F}^S(I) = \mathcal{F}^S(p_{C\to S}, p_{S\to C})$. We can now specialize Proposition 3 to our setting and obtain:

THEOREM 2. *For a sequence of random graphs G_n as described in Section 2.2, we have*

$$\lim_{n\to\infty} \frac{M(G_n, B_n)}{|S_n|} = \inf \mathcal{F}^S(p,q),$$

where the infimum is taken over pairs (p,q) satisfying

$$\begin{aligned} p &= \mathbb{P}\left(Bin(\tilde{D}, q) < \tilde{B}\right) \\ q &= (1-p)^{d-1}, \end{aligned}$$

where $(\tilde{D}+1, \tilde{B})$ is distributed as the edge-biased joint number of (replicas, request) of a random content, i.e. $(\tilde{D}+1, \tilde{B})$ is distributed as the joint number of (replicas, request) of the content adjacent to an edge chosen uniformly *at random among all edges of the graph.*

4.3 Proof of Theorem 1

The proof of Theorem 1 requires a basic result of graph theory. Note that in Equation (7), the left-hand side is the maximum size of an allocation whereas the right-hand side is a minimum. This kind of min-max relations is ubiquitous in matching theory [13]. In particular, for finite bipartite graphs, the size of a maximum allocation equals the minimum weight of a vertex cover. Recall that a vertex cover of a graph $G = (V, E)$ is a set of vertices $U \subset V$ such that any edge of G is incident to at least one vertex in U. The weight of a vertex cover is simply the sum of the weights of the vertices (in our case, the weights are the b_v's, equal to 1 if $v \in S$ and to b_c if $v = c \in C$.). The Koenig-Hall's theorem [13] for bipartite graphs states

$$M(G,B) = \min_{X\subseteq C}\left(|\partial X| + \sum_{c\in\overline{X}} b_c\right) \qquad (12)$$

where ∂X is the set of vertices with a neighbor in X and $\overline{X} = C \setminus X$. Clearly isolated vertices do not contribute to $M(G,B)$ and can be ignored so that $\overline{X} \cup \partial X$ is a vertex cover of G (because $\partial\overline{X} \subset \partial(\overline{X})$) with weight $|\partial X| + \sum_{c\in\overline{X}} b_c$.

The proof of Theorem 1 follows then from the two following steps: we first show how to construct from $I = \mathcal{P}_G(I)$ a vertex cover with weight $F^S(I)$ which is by previous min-max relation an upper bound for $M(G,B)$. Then, we show how to construct from a particular maximum allocation A a fixed point $I^A = \mathcal{P}_G(I^A)$ such that $F^S(I^A) = |A| = M(G,B)$, so that $M(G,B)$ is an upper bound for $\inf_{I=\mathcal{P}_G(I)} F^S(I)$.

4.3.1 *To each fixed point a vertex cover*

For any $I \in \{0,1\}^{\vec{E}}$, we consider the following subset V^I of vertices of G: for $s \in S$, $c \in C$,

$$\begin{aligned} s \in V^I &\Leftrightarrow |I_{\vec{\partial s}}| > 0 \\ c \in V^I &\Leftrightarrow |I_{\vec{\partial c}}| > b_c. \end{aligned}$$

LEMMA 2. *If $I = \mathcal{P}_G(I)$, then the associated subset of vertices V^I defined above is a vertex cover of G.*

PROOF. Towards a contradiction, suppose there exists an edge $(cs) \in E$, with $c \in C$ and $s \in S$, which is not covered by V^I, i.e. such that $s \notin V^I$ and $c \notin V^I$. From the definition of V^I, the fact that $s \notin V^I$ implies that $|I_{\vec{\partial s}}| = 0$ so that in particular $I_{c\to s} = 0$ and then, using the fact that $I = \mathcal{P}_G(I)$, we get $I_{s\to c} = \mathbf{1}(|I_{\vec{\partial s}}| - I_{c\to s} < 1) = 1$. On the other hand, $c \notin V^I$ implies that $|I_{\vec{\partial c}}| \le b_c$ so that $I_{c\to s} = \mathbf{1}(|I_{\vec{\partial c}}| - I_{s\to c} < b_c) = 1$, a contradiction. □

It only remains to check that the weight of V^I is equal to $F^S(I)$. This is easily obtained by noting that the term $\sum_{s\in S}\mathbf{1}\left(|I_{\vec{\partial s}}| > 0\right)$ in $F^S(I)$ is the total weight of the vertices in $S \cap V^I$, and the term $\sum_{c\in C} b_c \mathbf{1}\left(|I_{\vec{\partial c}}| > b_c\right)$ in $F^S(I)$ is the total weight of the vertices in $C \cap V^I$. Since for finite bipartite graphs, the weight of any vertex cover is an upper bound on $M(G,B)$, it follows that :

$$M(G,B) \le \inf_{I=\mathcal{P}_G(I)} F^S(I) \qquad (13)$$

4.3.2 *To a maximum allocation a fixed point*

In this section we want to find an $I \in \{0,1\}^{\vec{E}}$ that is invariant by $\mathcal{P}_G$ and such that $F^S(I) = M(G,B)$.

We start with equation (12). Note that there are no edges between vertices in X and $\overline{\partial X}$ (but there are possibly edges between $\overline{X}$ and ∂X). In particular, if A^X (resp. $A^{\overline{X}}$) is an allocation on $G[X \cup \partial X]$ (resp. $G[\overline{X} \cup \overline{\partial X}]$), the induced graph of G on the set of vertices $X \cup \partial X$ (resp. $\overline{X} \cup \overline{\partial X}$), then $A^X \cap A^{\overline{X}} = \emptyset$ so that $A = A^X \cup A^{\overline{X}}$ is an allocation of G. Let X be a subset of C that achieves the minimum in equation (12). Let A^X (resp. $A^{\overline{X}}$) be a maximum allocation on $G[X \cup \partial X]$ (resp. $G[\overline{X} \cup \overline{\partial X}]$). Then $|A^X| \le |\partial X|$ and $|A^{\overline{X}}| \le \sum_{c \in \overline{X}} b_c$. There is a vertex cover of $G[X \cup \partial X]$ with weight $|A^X|$ and a vertex cover of $G[\overline{X} \cup \overline{\partial X}]$ with weight $|A^{\overline{X}}|$. The union of these vertex covers is a vertex cover of G, so that $|A^X| + |A^{\overline{X}}| \ge M(G, B)$ and finally $|A^X| = |\partial X|$ and $|A^{\overline{X}}| = \sum_{c \in \overline{X}} b_c$. Hence we defined a maximum allocation A such that with $I^A_{c \to s} = I^A_{s \to c} = \mathbf{1}((cs) \in A)$, we have

$$\forall s \in \partial X, \quad \sum_{c \in \partial s} I^A_{c \to s} = 1$$
$$\forall c \in \overline{X}, \quad \sum_{s \in \partial c} I^A_{s \to c} = b_c,$$

and for $u \in \overline{X}$ and $v \in \partial X$, we have

$$I^A_{u \to v} = I^A_{v \to u} = 0. \tag{14}$$

We now define the sequence of messages $I^{A,k}$ along the directed edges of G in the following manner: $I^{A,0} = I^A$ and for $k \ge 0$, $I^{A,k+1} = \mathcal{P}_G(I^{A,k})$.

LEMMA 3. *For all $u \in \partial X \cup \overline{X}$, the sequences $(I^{A,k}_{u \to v})$ are non-increasing in k for all v. For all $u \in X \cup \overline{\partial X}$, the sequences $(I^{A,k}_{u \to v})$ are non-decreasing in k for all v.*

PROOF. Note that if $u \in \partial X \cup \overline{X}$, then $|I^A_{\vec{\partial u}}| = b_u$ so that $I^{A,1}_{u \to v} = \mathbf{1}\left(|I^A_{\vec{\partial u}}| - I^A_{v \to u} < b_u\right) = I^A_{v \to u} = I^A_{u \to v}$. Now if $u \in X \cup \overline{\partial X}$, then we simply have $I^{A,1}_{u \to v} \ge I^A_{u \to v}$. In particular if $u \in \overline{X}$ and $v \in \partial X$, we have $I^{A,1}_{u \to v} = I^{A,1}_{v \to u} = I^A_{u \to v} = I^A_{v \to u} = 0$. The lemma follows then by induction on k. Indeed, the induction hypothesis implies that for $u \in \overline{X}$ and $v \in \partial X$, we have $I^{A,k}_{u \to v} = I^{A,k}_{v \to u} = 0$ by (14). Hence the $(k+1)$-th messages from $u \in \partial X \cup \overline{X}$ to v are obtained from the k-th messages from $v \in X \cup \overline{\partial X}$ by applying the decreasing map $\mathcal{P}_G$ and vice-versa. □

Lemma 3 allows to define $I^{A,\infty} = \lim_k I^{A,k}$ and to get the following inequalities:

$$\forall u \in \partial X \cup \overline{X}, \quad I^{A,\infty}_{u \to v} \le I^A_{u \to v},$$
$$\forall u \in X \cup \overline{\partial X}, \quad I^{A,\infty}_{u \to v} \ge I^A_{u \to v}.$$

Moreover we clearly have $I^{A,\infty} = \mathcal{P}_G(I^{A,\infty})$. We now compute $F^S(I^{A,\infty})$ that we decompose in two terms:

$$\begin{aligned}\Sigma_1 &= \sum_{s \in S} \mathbf{1}\left(|I^{A,\infty}_{\vec{\partial s}}| > 0\right) \\ &= |\partial X| + \sum_{s \in \overline{\partial X}} \mathbf{1}\left(|I^{A,\infty}_{\vec{\partial s}}| > 0\right),\end{aligned}$$

and

$$\begin{aligned}\Sigma_2 &= \sum_{c \in C} b_c \mathbf{1}\left(|I^{A,\infty}_{\vec{\partial c}}| > b_c\right) \\ &= \sum_{c \in \overline{X}} b_c \mathbf{1}\left(|I^{A,\infty}_{\vec{\partial c}}| > b_c\right).\end{aligned}$$

Note that for any $c \in \overline{X}$, we have $|I^{A,\infty}_{\vec{\partial c}}| \ge b_c$. Indeed if $|I^{A,\infty}_{\vec{\partial c}}| > b_c$, then $I^{A,\infty}_{c \to s} = 0$ for all s, whereas if $|I^{A,\infty}_{\vec{\partial c}}| = b_c$, then $I^{A,\infty}_{c \to s} = I^{A,\infty}_{s \to c}$. Hence we have

$$\sum_{c \in X} b_c \mathbf{1}\left(|I^{A,\infty}_{\vec{\partial c}}| = b_c\right) = \sum_{s \in \overline{\partial X}} \mathbf{1}\left(|I^{A,\infty}_{\vec{\partial s}}| > 0\right)$$

so that we get,

$$\begin{aligned}\Sigma_1 + \Sigma_2 &= |\partial X| + \sum_{c \in \overline{X}} b_c \mathbf{1}\left(|I^{A,\infty}_{\vec{\partial c}}| \ge b_c\right) \\ &= |\partial X| + \sum_{c \in \overline{X}} b_c = M(G, B).\end{aligned}$$

As a consequence, we directly get

$$M(G, B) \ge \inf_{I = \mathcal{P}_G(I)} F^S(I),$$

which with (13) concludes the proof.

5. PERFORMANCE OF REPLICATION POLICIES

We now apply the previous result to the model with K content classes, where class i contains a fraction α_i of all contents and the number of requests for each content in this class is Poisson with parameter λ_i. Recall that d is the degree of all servers and β is the ratio of number of servers to number of contents.

We consider here the couple (G, B), of the infinite graph G together with the corresponding vector of number of requests B, that is the limit in local weak sense of sequences of graphs drawn from the multi-class model presented in Section 2.2. Hence, we assume that the number of replicas for each type i content is also Poisson, with parameter $d\beta_i$ for non-negative β_i verifying $\sum_{i=1}^K \alpha_i \beta_i = \beta$. A particular example is the proportional replication strategy mentioned in Section 3, for which $\beta_i = \lambda_i / \rho$.

We express performance in terms of the asymptotic inefficiency $\gamma_{G,B} := \min(\rho, 1) - f$, where f is the limiting fraction of matched servers in a maximum allocation. Indeed, the asymptotic behavior of γ_{G_n, B_n} for (G_n, B_n) following the multi-class model will almost surely be given by $\gamma_{G,B}$, according to Theorem 2.

The explicit expression for $\gamma_{G,B}$ can be obtained straightforwardly from Theorem 2, however it is hard to gain insights from the expression obtained. Thus, we look at the behavior as d tends to infinity, as we did in Section 3 for the candidate strategies:

PROPOSITION 4. *Under the multi-class model, in which within class i the number of requests is Poisson with mean λ_i and the number of replicas is Poisson with mean $d\beta_i$, and assuming that $\beta_i > 0$ for all $i \in 1, \ldots, K$, the asymptotic inefficiency $\gamma_{G,B}$ verifies*

$$\frac{\log(\gamma_{G,B})}{d} \xrightarrow{d \to \infty} \begin{cases} -\inf_i \beta_i \text{ if } \rho < 1, \\ \log\left(\sum_{i=1}^K \frac{\alpha_i \beta_i}{\beta} e^{-\lambda_i}\right) \text{ if } \rho > 1, \\ \max\left(-\inf_i \beta_i, \log\left(\sum_{i=1}^K \frac{\alpha_i \beta_i}{\beta} e^{-\lambda_i}\right)\right) \\ \text{if } \rho = 1. \end{cases} \tag{15}$$

First-of-all, it is quite remarkable in the proposition above that the asymptotic inefficiency as $d \to \infty$ is explained only by very local and individual situations. Indeed, $\exp(-d\beta_i)$ is the probability that a content of class i is not replicated in any server cache, and similarly $\left(\sum_{i=1}^{K} \theta_i e^{-\lambda_i}\right)^d$ is the probability that a server stores only replicas of contents which have not been requested at all. Hence, asymptotically, the only noticeable cause for inefficiencies in under-loaded regime (when anyway not all servers can be busy) is contents that are stored nowhere; in over-loaded regime (when it is not possible to satisfy all requests) the only visible inefficiency comes from servers that store only unrequested contents; and in critically loaded systems, inefficiency is due almost only to the dominant of these two effects.

Let us then first comment the implications of this result before turning to its proof. First, we observe an exponential decay of the inefficiency in d for any positive β_i's, *even* at criticality. This is in sharp contrast with the performance of online matching as discussed in Section 3, for which inefficiency decays polynomially in d for $\rho = 1$. It is also a robustness property, in that this qualitative behaviour does not depend on the precise values of the β_i's.

Second, it is possible to pick replication ratios β_i that improve upon proportional replication (for which $\beta_i = \lambda_i/\rho$). Indeed, it follows at once from (15) that in under-load $\rho < 1$, for large d, inefficiency is minimized by setting $\beta_i \equiv \beta$ for all i, i.e. by not discriminating replication between classes. It is also easy to show that in over-load $\rho > 1$, the corresponding exponent in (15) is minimized by shifting replicas towards the most popular class i^* such that $\lambda_{i^*} = \max_i \lambda_i$. As for the critical case, it can be shown that the corresponding exponent is minimized by equalizing all the coefficients β_i for $i \neq i^*$ in such a way that the two expressions $-\inf_i \beta_i$ and $\log(\sum_i (\alpha_i \beta_i)/\beta e^{-\lambda_i})$ are equal. We summarize these statements by the following

Corollary 1. *Under the multi-class model, we have the following optimal asymptotic inefficiencies:*

$$\lim_{d\to\infty} \frac{1}{d} \log(\gamma_{G,B}) = \begin{cases} -\beta & \text{if } \rho < 1, \\ -\sup_i \lambda_i & \text{if } \rho > 1, \\ -\beta^- & \text{if } \rho = 1, \end{cases} \tag{16}$$

where β^- is the unique solution x in $[0, \beta]$ to the equation

$$x = \beta \frac{e^{-x} - e^{-\lambda_{i^*}}}{\sum_i \alpha_i \left(e^{-\lambda_i} - e^{-\lambda_{i^*}}\right)}.$$

The corresponding optimal replication factors β_i are given by

$$\begin{array}{ll} \beta_i \equiv \beta & \text{if } \rho < 1, \\ \beta_{i^*} = \frac{\beta}{\alpha_{i^*}},\ \beta_i = 0,\ i \neq i^* & \text{if } \rho > 1, \\ \beta_{i^*} = \frac{\beta - \beta^-(1-\alpha_{i^*})}{\alpha_{i^*}},\ \beta_i = \beta^-,\ i \neq i^* & \text{if } \rho = 1. \end{array} \tag{17}$$

Figure 1 illustrates the inefficiency exponents for various replication policies in a two-class scenario, with two classes of equal sizes ($\alpha_1 = \alpha_2$), respective popularities $\lambda_1 = 3$ and $\lambda_2 = 1$, and the content/server ratio therefore governs the load of the system according to $\rho = 2/\beta$. the fraction of replicas that correspond to a content of class i is given by $\theta_i = \alpha_i \beta_i / \beta$. As we vary θ_1, we span replication policies from uniform at $\theta_1 = 1/2$ to proportional at $\theta_1 = 0.75$ to extreme unbalance at $\theta_1 = 1$. The curves represent the inefficiency exponents for various values of d, namely $d = 2, 5, 15$. We also represent the optimal value of θ_1 and the corresponding exponent in the limit $d \to \infty$, as characterized in the previous corollary.

We observe in particular how the optimal value for finite d approaches this limiting value: for d as small as 15, the asymptotic evaluations are already reasonably accurate. Note however that for the super-critical case, one should not take $\theta_2 = 0$ for any finite d, as is illustrated by the drop in the exponent of the right-most curve.

Proof. (of Proposition 4): The fraction of matched servers is given by Theorem 2 and we need to explicitely compute the function $\mathcal{F}^S(p,q)$ in our setting. We still denote by $(\tilde{D}+1, \tilde{B})$ the edge-biased joint number of (replicas,requests) of a random content. Under the present assumptions, with probability α_i, the pair $(\tilde{D}+1, \tilde{B})$ is distributed as two independent Poisson random variables with respective means $(\beta_i d, \lambda_i)$. Hence a simple computation shows that

$$\begin{aligned} \mathcal{F}^S(p,q) = \ & 1 - (1-q)^d \\ & + \textstyle\sum_i \frac{\alpha_i \lambda_i}{\beta} \mathbb{P}(\mathrm{Poi}(\beta_i dp) \geq \mathrm{Poi}(\lambda_i) + 2), \end{aligned} \tag{18}$$

where $\mathrm{Poi}(\lambda)$ is a Poisson random variable with mean λ and all Poisson random variables appearing in the expression are independent. The fraction of matched servers is given by taking the infimum of this expression over p and q satisfying:

$$q = (1-p)^{d-1}, \tag{19}$$

and

$$p = \frac{1}{\beta} \sum_i \alpha_i \beta_i \mathbb{P}(\mathrm{Poi}(\beta_i dq) < \mathrm{Poi}(\lambda_i)). \tag{20}$$

We now consider the fixed points of (19,20) in the regime of large d. First, if p is bounded away from zero, by (19), q is exponentially small in d. Plugging this into (20), we find that there is indeed a fixed point such that

$$\begin{aligned} p &\sim \textstyle\sum_i \frac{\alpha_i \beta_i}{\beta} \left(1 - e^{-\lambda_i}\right), \\ q &\sim \left(\textstyle\sum_i \frac{\alpha_i \beta_i}{\beta} e^{-\lambda_i}\right)^{d(1+o(1))}. \end{aligned} \tag{21}$$

Next consider the case where p goes to zero with d. Then necessarily by (20), qd is large, and $p = e^{-\Theta(qd)}$. Plugging this into (19) we obtain

$$q = (1 - e^{-\Theta(qd)})^{d-1}.$$

Assume then that $qd = O(\log(d))$. This would entail that $q \to 0$, and hence $(1-p)^d \to 0$; the corresponding evaluation (18) would be equivalent to $1 + \sum_i \alpha_i \lambda_i / \beta$ which is larger than 1, and hence cannot be the minimal evaluation. We can thus assume $qd \gg \log(d)$. Then by (20), it follows that $p = o(1/d)$, so that by (19), $q \sim 1$. Thus the only other meaningful fixed point to consider satisfies

$$\begin{aligned} p = \ & \textstyle\sum_i \frac{\alpha_i \beta_i}{\beta} e^{-\beta_i d(1+o(1))} = e^{-\inf_i \beta_i d(1+o(1))}, \\ q = \ & 1 - e^{-\inf_i \beta_i d(1+o(1))}. \end{aligned} \tag{22}$$

It remains to evaluate Expression (18) at the two meaningful fixed points (21,22). Considering first (21), the last term in (18) is of order $(dq)^2$, which is negligible compared to the first term $(1-p)^d$. This yields the first evaluation

$$f_1 = 1 - \exp\left(d \log\left(\sum_i \frac{\alpha_i \beta_i}{\beta} e^{-\lambda_i}\right)\right). \tag{23}$$

Considering next plugging (22) into (18). The term $(1-p)^d$ and the last term of (18) are equivalent to 1 and ρ respectively, up to corrections of order $e^{-d \inf_i \beta_i (1+o(1))}$. This concludes the proof. □

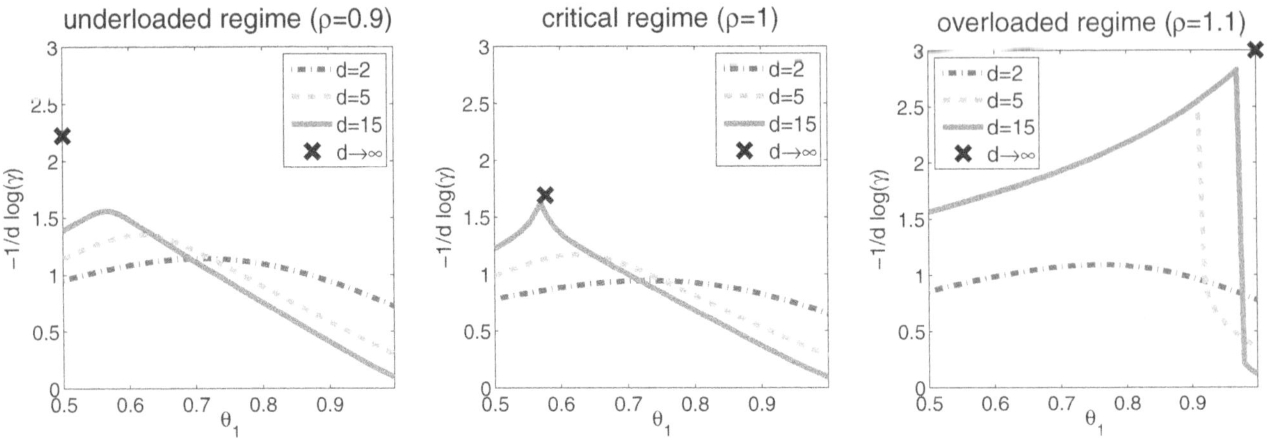

Figure 1: Inefficiency exponential-decay exponents as a function of the fraction of storage space allocated to contents of the first class in under-loaded, critical, and over-loaded regimes.

6. RELATED WORK

The question of how to replicate content in distributed systems is related to the general problem of *facility location* (see e.g. Vazirani [22] Chapter 24). The latter has received considerable attention from the standpoint of algorithmic complexity and approximability. The version that we consider here is atypical in that it features capacity constraints on the locations (the servers), and stochastic demand. Also, we aim at characterizing simple, easily implementable strategies with good performance for practical workloads rather than placement algorithms with low worst-case complexity.

There is a rich literature on cache management strategies motivated by server memory and web cache management, one abstract version of which is the so-called paging problem (see e.g. Albers [2]). In this context, the main focus has been on characterization of hit rates, focusing on the temporal properties of streams of requests. Capacity limits at the servers are typically not considered in these models, while they are essential for the application scenarios we consider.

Our present motivation, namely efficient use of servers' bandwidth through adequate replication, has been considered in the specific context of Peer-to-Peer systems, in a number of recent papers [21, 8, 18, 19, 23, 24]. In [21, 8], an argument is made for the proportional replication policy based on the analysis of delay in a queueing model of performance. More recently, [19] also argue in favour of proportional replication by considering a loss network model of performance. [18] and [8] propose replication policies that are oblivious to content popularity. The first considers stochastic delay performance models, and the second deterministic conditions on request arrivals to guarantee feasibility of service. The two articles [23, 24] are closer to our motivation in that they revisit the proportional placement strategy, to which they propose alternatives. Their modeling approach however significantly differs from ours.

The main result on asymptotic characterization of matching density, Theorem 2, is a direct consequence of the recent paper [12], itself building on recent works [7, 17] on the rigorous use of the so-called *cavity method* of statistical physics for the characterization of asymptotics in large random graphs. The version we provide for finite graphs, Theorem 1, is novel and sheds new light on the particular form of the formula in Theorem 2. It also hints at possible generalizations of the cavity method to bipartite graphs, whereas it has been rigorously applied in the context of matchings only to tree-like graphs so far.

Finally, there is a rich body of literature on load balancing algorithms, which in our context would correspond to the question of forming a particular matching, given content replication. One strand of research has considered simple one shot comparisons of several assignments, e.g. the power of two choices paradigm as surveyed in [14]. A more recent strand [9], [10], has considered the so-called Cuckoo-hashing method, by which requests get assigned irrespective of whether the target server is free or not; if not, the current job at the server is pushed to another server, and so on. These two approaches are in a sense intermediate between the online method we considered in Section 3 and an optimal assignment as characterized and discussed in Sections 4-5. Their performance has however not been studied in contexts with heterogeneity both in the replications and numbers of requests. We view such a study as a promising future work, which could build on our present analysis of optimal matching density .

7. CONCLUSION

Motivated by the performance of large-scale distributed server systems, we developed an analysis of optimal matching performance for heterogeneous loads and replication policies. Our results show (i) robustness of optimal matching performance to replication strategies, with an inefficiency that is exponentially small in the server storage capacity; (ii) possibility to improve upon proportional replication, with explicit identification of target replication strategies, depending on the criticality of the system load; and (iii) the need to go beyond simple greedy matching in order to approach these ideal matching inefficiencies. On the methodological side, we build on recent advances on the so-called cavity method, and use it to obtain novel performance formulas.

Moreover, we extend previous characterizations of maximum matchings from finite trees to finite bipartite graphs. This points the way to further extensions of the cavity method.

8. ACKNOWLEDGMENTS

The second author acknowledges the support of the French Agence Nationale de la Recherche (ANR) under reference ANR-11-JS02-005-01 (GAP project).

9. REFERENCES

[1] S. Abramsky, C. Gavoille, C. Kirchner, F. M. auf der Heide, and P. G. Spirakis, editors. *ICALP 2010*, volume 6198 of *Lecture Notes in Computer Science*. Springer, 2010.

[2] S. Albers, L. Favrholdt, and O. Giel. On paging with locality of reference. *Journal of Computer and System Sciences*, 70:145–175, 2005.

[3] D. Aldous and J. M. Steele. The objective method: probabilistic combinatorial optimization and local weak convergence. In *Probability on discrete structures*, volume 110 of *Encyclopaedia Math. Sci.*, pages 1–72. Springer, Berlin, 2004.

[4] R. P. Anstee. A polynomial algorithm for b-matchings: an alternative approach. *Inform. Process. Lett.*, 24(3):153–157, 1987.

[5] M. Bayati, C. Borgs, J. Chayes, and R. Zecchina. Belief propagation for weighted b-matchings on arbitrary graphs and its relation to linear programs with integer solutions. *SIAM Journal on Discrete Mathematics*, 25(2):989–1011, 2011.

[6] B. Bollobás. *Random Graphs*. Cambridge University Press, 2001.

[7] C. Bordenave, M. Lelarge, and J. Salez. Matchings on infinite graphs. *ArXiv e-prints*, Feb. 2011.

[8] Y. Boufkhad, F. Mathieu, F. de Montgolfier, D. Perino, and L. Viennot. Achievable catalog size in peer-to-peer video-on-demand systems. In *Proc. of IPTPS*, 2008.

[9] M. Dietzfelbinger, A. Goerdt, M. Mitzenmacher, A. Montanari, R. Pagh, and M. Rink. Tight thresholds for cuckoo hashing via xorsat. In Abramsky et al. [1], pages 213–225.

[10] N. Fountoulakis and K. Panagiotou. Orientability of random hypergraphs and the power of multiple choices. In Abramsky et al. [1], pages 348–359.

[11] T. Kurtz. *Approximation of Population Processes*. CBMS-NSF Regional Conference Series in Applied Mathematics, 1981.

[12] M. Lelarge. A new approach to the orientation of random hypergraphs. *available at: http://www.di.ens.fr/ lelarge/*, 2012.

[13] L. Lovász and M. D. Plummer. *Matching theory*, volume 121 of *North-Holland Mathematics Studies*. North-Holland Publishing Co., Amsterdam, 1986. Annals of Discrete Mathematics, 29.

[14] M. Mitzenmacher, A. Richa, and R. Siaraman. The power two random choices: a survey of techniques and results. In *Handbook of randomized computing*, volume 1, 2001.

[15] J. Pearl. Reverend bayes on inference engines: A distributed hierarchical approach. In *Proceedings of the American Association of Artificial Intelligence National Conference on AI*, pages 133–136, Pittsburgh, PA, 1982.

[16] J. Pearl. *Probabilistic reasoning in intelligent systems: networks of plausible inference*. Morgan Kaufmann Publishers Inc., San Francisco, CA, USA, 1988.

[17] J. Salez. The cavity method for counting spanning subgraphs subject to local constraints. *ArXiv e-prints*, Mar. 2011.

[18] K. Suh, C. Diot, J. Kurose, L. Massoulie, C. Neumann, D. Towsley, and M. Varvello. Push-to-peer video-on-demand system: Design and evaluation. *IEEE Journal on Selected Areas in Communications*, 25(9):1706–1716, 2007.

[19] B. Tan and L. Massoulié. Optimal content placement for peer-to-peer video-on-demand systems. In *Proceedings of IEEE Infocom*, 2011.

[20] É. Tardos. A strongly polynomial algorithm to solve combinatorial linear programs. *Operations Research*, 34(2):pp. 250–256, 1986.

[21] S. Tewari and L. Kleinrock. On fairness, optimal download performance and proportional replication in peer-to-peer networks. In *Proc. of IFIP Networking*, 2005.

[22] V. Vazirani. *Approximation Algorithms*. Springer, 2003.

[23] W. Wu and J. Lui. Exploring the optimal replication strategy in p2p-vod systems: Characterization and evaluation. In *Proceedings of IEEE Infocom*, 2011.

[24] Y. Zhou, T. Z. J. Fu, and D. Ming Chiu. Statistical modeling and analysis of p2p replication to support vod service. In *Proceedings of IEEE Infocom*, 2011.

10. APPENDIX:

Online algorithm analysis

Letting $u = d\frac{\beta - x}{1-y}$, we obtain

$$\begin{aligned} \dot{u} &= ue^{-u} + de^{-u} - d \quad (24) \\ \gamma &= \rho \wedge 1 - 1 + \frac{u(\lambda)}{d\beta}(1 - y(\lambda)) \end{aligned}$$

To find a good surrogate for u, note first that u is a decreasing function, because $e^u \dot{u} = u + d - de^u \leq -(d-1)u$. Also, the term ue^{-u} is always small compared to the others when d is large.

It suggests that the behavior of u for large d should be captured by the solution to the following equation:

$$\begin{aligned} \dot{v} &= d(e^{-v} - 1) \quad (25) \\ v(0) &= u(0) = d\beta \end{aligned}$$

A change of variables leads to

$$v(t) = \log\left(1 + e^{d(\beta - t)}(1 - e^{-d\beta})\right)$$

Note that, at all time, we have $v \leq u$, because the functions are continuous and $\dot{v} \leq \dot{u}$ whenever $v = u$.

We then have

LEMMA 4. *In the regime $\rho < 1$, the solution of equations (4)-(5) satisfies*

$$\gamma \leq \rho(\beta + 1)e^{-d\beta(1-\rho)}$$

PROOF. At all time, $d\beta \geq u \geq d\beta(1-\rho)$, thus $\dot{u} \leq d\left((\beta+1)e^{-d\beta(1-\rho)} - 1\right)$. We immediately obtain

$$\begin{aligned} u(\lambda) &\leq d\beta(1-\rho) + d\lambda(\beta+1)e^{-d\beta(1-\rho)} \\ \gamma &= \rho - 1 + \frac{1}{d\beta}u(\lambda)(1 - y(\lambda)) \leq \rho(\beta+1)e^{-d\beta(1-\rho)} \end{aligned}$$

□

LEMMA 5. *In the regime $\rho = 1$, the solution of equations (4)-(5) satisfies*

$$\gamma \leq \frac{\log 2}{d\beta} + o(1/d)$$

PROOF. Let $c > 1$. $u(0) = d\beta$ so there exists $0 < T_d \leq \lambda$ such that $u \geq c \log d$ on $[0, T_d]$ and $u \leq c \log d$ on $(T_d, \lambda]$ for large enough d. Furthermore, $\dot{u} \geq -d$, so we always have $T_d \geq \beta - \frac{c \log d}{d}$ for d large enough. Then, on $[0, T_d]$, we have

$$\dot{u} \leq \beta d^{1-c} + d(e^{-u} - 1) \leq \beta d^{1-c} + \dot{v}$$

and, on $(T_d, \rho]$,

$$\dot{u} \leq c \log d + \dot{v}$$

We obtain an upper-bound on $u(\lambda)$:

$$\begin{aligned} u(\lambda) &\leq v(\lambda) + T_d\beta d^{1-c} + (\lambda - T_d)c \log d \\ &\leq \log(2 - e^{-d\beta}) + \beta d^{1-c}\lambda + \frac{c^2 \log^2 d}{d} \end{aligned}$$

As $c > 1$,

$$\begin{aligned} \gamma &\leq \frac{\log 2}{d\beta} + d^{-c}\rho + \frac{c^2 \log^2 d}{d^2\beta^2} \\ &= \frac{\log 2}{d\beta} + o(1/d) \end{aligned}$$

□

LEMMA 6. *In the regime $\rho = 1$, the solution of equations (4)-(5) satisfies*

$$\gamma \geq \frac{\log 2}{d\beta} + o(1/d)$$

PROOF. As $y + x \leq \lambda$, it follows that $y \leq \beta\gamma \leq \frac{\log 2}{d} + o(1/d)$. Hence,

$$\begin{aligned} \gamma &\geq \frac{1}{d\beta}\log(2 - e^{-d\beta})\left(1 - \frac{\log 2}{d} + o(1/d)\right) \\ &= \frac{\log 2}{d\beta} + o(1/d) \end{aligned}$$

□

As upper- and lower-bound coincide, we actually have that $\gamma = \frac{\log 2}{d\beta} + o(\frac{1}{d}) \sim_{d\infty} v(\lambda)$.

LEMMA 7. *In the regime $\rho > 1$, the solution of equations (4)-(5) satisfies*

$$\gamma \leq \frac{\log 2}{d^2\beta}e^{-(d-1)\beta(\rho-1)}(1 + o(1))$$

PROOF. We already know that $u(\beta) = \frac{\log 2}{d\beta} + o(\frac{1}{d})$, so we can focus on the time interval $[\beta, \lambda]$. For d large enough and for all $t \geq \beta$, as u is decreasing, u is strictly less than 1. Then,

$$\dot{u} \leq u + d(1 - u + \frac{u^2}{2} - 1) = -(d-1)u + d\frac{u^2}{2}$$

As u is actually much smaller than 1 in the range $[\beta, \lambda]$, we can guess that the influence of the term in u^2 will be small compared to that of the term in u, and that we did not lose much by neglecting higher order terms.

Let z such that $z(\beta) = u(\beta)$ and $\dot{z} = -(d-1)z + d\frac{z^2}{2}$. At $u = z$, we have $\dot{u} \leq \dot{z}$, so $u \leq z$ on $[\beta, \lambda]$, and z is decreasing on $[\beta, \lambda]$ for d large enough.

As long as $z \neq 0$ and $z \neq 2(1 - \frac{1}{d})$,

$$\dot{z} = -(d-1)z + d\frac{z^2}{2} \Leftrightarrow \frac{\dot{z}}{d-1}\left(\frac{1}{z - 2(1 - \frac{1}{d})} - \frac{1}{z}\right) = 1$$

Integrating from λ to β, we obtain

$$\begin{aligned} \frac{1}{d-1}\left[\log\left(z - 2(1 - \frac{1}{d})\right)\right]_\beta^\lambda - \frac{1}{d-1}\left[\log z\right]_\beta^\lambda &= \lambda - \beta \\ \frac{1}{d-1}\log\frac{1 - \frac{z(\lambda)}{2(1-\frac{1}{d})}}{1 - \frac{u(\beta)}{2(1-\frac{1}{d})}} + \frac{1}{d-1}\log\frac{u(\beta)}{z(\lambda)} &= \lambda - \beta \end{aligned}$$

As $0 < z(\lambda) < u(\beta) = \frac{\log 2}{d} + o(\frac{1}{d})$, the first term is $o(1)$. Thus, we obtain

$$\begin{aligned} u(\lambda) &\leq z(\lambda) = u(\beta)e^{-(d-1)\beta(\rho-1)+o(1)} \\ &= \frac{\log 2}{d}e^{-(d-1)\beta(\rho-1)}(1 + o(1)) \end{aligned}$$

and also

$$\gamma \leq \frac{\log 2}{d^2\beta}e^{-(d-1)\beta(\rho-1)}(1 + o(1))$$

□

Workload Analysis of a Large-Scale Key-Value Store

Berk Atikoglu
Stanford, Facebook
atikoglu@stanford.edu

Yuehai Xu
Wayne State, Facebook
yhxu@wayne.edu

Eitan Frachtenberg*
Facebook
etc@fb.com

Song Jiang
Wayne State
sjiang@wayne.edu

Mike Paleczny
Facebook
mpal@fb.com

ABSTRACT

Key-value stores are a vital component in many scale-out enterprises, including social networks, online retail, and risk analysis. Accordingly, they are receiving increased attention from the research community in an effort to improve their performance, scalability, reliability, cost, and power consumption. To be effective, such efforts require a detailed understanding of realistic key-value workloads. And yet little is known about these workloads outside of the companies that operate them. This paper aims to address this gap.

To this end, we have collected detailed traces from Facebook's Memcached deployment, arguably the world's largest. The traces capture over 284 billion requests from five different Memcached use cases over several days. We analyze the workloads from multiple angles, including: request composition, size, and rate; cache efficacy; temporal patterns; and application use cases. We also propose a simple model of the most representative trace to enable the generation of more realistic synthetic workloads by the community.

Our analysis details many characteristics of the caching workload. It also reveals a number of surprises: a GET/SET ratio of 30:1 that is higher than assumed in the literature; some applications of Memcached behave more like persistent storage than a cache; strong locality metrics, such as keys accessed many millions of times a day, do not always suffice for a high hit rate; and there is still room for efficiency and hit rate improvements in Memcached's implementation. Toward the last point, we make several suggestions that address the exposed deficiencies.

Categories and Subject Descriptors

C.2.4 [**Distributed Systems**]: Distributed Databases; D.4.8 [**Performance**]: Modeling and Prediction; D.4.2 [**Storage Management**]: Distributed Memories

*Corresponding author.

Keywords

Workload Analysis, Workload modeling, Key-Value Store

1. INTRODUCTION

Key-value (KV) stores play an important role in many large websites. Examples include: Dynamo at Amazon [15]; Redis at GitHub, Digg, and Blizzard Interactive [27]; Memcached at Facebook, Zynga and Twitter [18, 26]; and Voldemort at Linkedin [1]. All these systems store ordered (*key, value*) pairs and are, in essence, a distributed hash table.

A common use case for these systems is as a layer in the data-retrieval hierarchy: a cache for expensive-to-obtain values, indexed by unique keys. These values can represent any data that is cheaper or faster to cache than re-obtain, such as commonly accessed results of database queries or the results of complex computations that require temporary storage and distribution.

Because of their key role in large website performance, KV stores are carefully tuned for low response times and high hit rates. But like all caching heuristics, a KV-store's performance is highly dependent on its workload. It is therefore imperative to understand the workload's characteristics. Additionally, analyzing and understanding large-scale cache workloads can also: provide insights into topics such as the role and effectiveness of memory-based caching in distributed website infrastructure; expose the underlying patterns of user behavior; and provide difficult-to-obtain data and statistical distributions for future studies.

In this paper, we analyze five workloads from Facebook's Memcached deployment. Aside from the sheer scale of the site and data (over 284 billion requests over a period of 58 sample days), this case study also introduces to the community several different usage scenarios for KV stores. This variability serves to explore the relationship between the cache and various data domains: where overall site patterns are adequately handled by a generalized caching infrastructure, and where specialization would help. In addition, this paper offers the following key contributions and findings:

1. A workload decomposition of the traces that shows how different applications of Memcached can have extreme variations in terms of read/write mix, request sizes and rates, and usage patterns (Sec. 3).

2. An analysis of the caching characteristics of the traces and the factors that determine hit rates. We found that different Memcached pools can vary significantly in their locality metrics, but surprisingly, the best predictor of hit rates is actually the pool's size (Sec. 6).

3. An examination of various performance metrics over time, showing diurnal and weekly patterns (Sec. 3.3, 4.2.2, 6).

4. An analytical model that can be used to generate more realistic synthetic workloads. We found that the salient size characteristics follow power-law distributions, similar to other storage and Web-serving systems (Sec. 5).

5. An exposition of a Memcached deployment that can shed light on real-world, large-scale production usage of KV-stores (Sec. 2.2, 8).

The rest of this paper is organized as follows. We begin by describing the architecture of Memcached, its deployment at Facebook, and how we analyzed its workload. Sec. 3 presents the observed experimental properties of the trace data (from the request point of view), while Sec. 4 describes the observed cache metrics (from the server point of view). Sec. 5 presents a simple analytical model of the most representative workload. The next section brings the data together in a discussion of our results, followed by a section surveying previous efforts on analyzing cache behavior and workload analysis.

2. MEMCACHED DESCRIPTION

2.1 Architecture

Memcached[1] is a simple, open-source software package that exposes data in RAM to clients over the network. As data size grows in the application, more RAM can be added to a server, or more servers can be added to the network. Additional servers generally only communicate with clients. Clients use consistent hashing [9] to select a unique server per *key*, requiring only the knowledge of the total number of servers and their IP addresses. This technique presents the entire aggregate data in the servers as a unified distributed hash table, keeps servers completely independent, and facilitates scaling as data size grows.

Memcached's interface provides the basic primitives that hash tables provide—insertion, deletion, and retrieval—as well as more complex operations built atop them.

Data are stored as individual items, each including a key, a value, and metadata. Item size can vary from a few bytes to over 100 KB, heavily skewed toward smaller items (Sec. 3). Consequently, a naïve memory allocation scheme could result in significant memory fragmentation. To address this issue, Memcached adopts a slab allocation technique, in which memory is divided into slabs of different sizes. The slabs in a class store items whose sizes are within the slab's specific range. A newly inserted item obtains its memory space by first searching the slab class corresponding to its size. If this search fails, a new slab of the class is allocated from the heap. Symmetrically, when an item is deleted from the cache, its space is returned to the appropriate slab, rather than the heap. Memory is allocated to slab classes based on the initial workload and its item sizes, until the heap is exhausted. Consequently, if the workload characteristics change significantly after this initial phase, we may find that the slab allocation is inappropriate for the workload, resulting in memory underutilization.

[1] `http://memcached.org/`

Table 1: Memcached pools sampled (in one cluster). These pools do not match their UNIX namesakes, but are used for illustrative purposes here instead of their internal names.

Pool	Size	Description
USR	few	user-account status information
APP	dozens	object metadata of one application
ETC	hundreds	nonspecific, general-purpose
VAR	dozens	server-side browser information
SYS	few	system data on service location

A new item arriving after the heap is exhausted requires the eviction of an older item in the appropriate slab. Memcached uses the Least-Recently-Used (LRU) algorithm to select the items for eviction. To this end, each slab class has an LRU queue maintaining access history on its items. Although LRU decrees that any accessed item be moved to the top of the queue, this version of Memcached coalesces repeated accesses of the same item within a short period (one minute by default) and only moves this item to the top the first time, to reduce overhead.

2.2 Deployment

Facebook relies on Memcached for fast access to frequently-accessed values. Web servers typically try to read persistent values from Memcached before trying the slower backend databases. In many cases, the caches are demand-filled, meaning that generally, data is added to the cache after a client has requested it and failed.

Modifications to persistent data in the database often propagate as deletions (invalidations) to the Memcached tier. Some cached data, however, is transient and not backed by persistent storage, requiring no invalidations.

Physically, Facebook deploys front-end servers in multiple datacenters, each containing one or more *clusters* of varying sizes. Front-end clusters consist of both Web servers, running primarily HipHop [31], and caching servers, running primarily Memcached. These servers are further subdivided based on the concept of *pools*. A pool is a partition of the entire key space, defined by a prefix of the key, and typically represents a separate application or data domain. The main reason for separate domains (as opposed to one all-encompassing cache) is to ensure adequate quality of service for each domain. For example, one application with high turnover rate could evict keys of another application that shares the same server, even if the latter has high temporal locality but lower access rates. Another reason to separate domains is to facilitate application-specific capacity planning and performance analysis.

In this paper, we describe traces from five separate pools—one trace from each pool (traces from separate machines in the same pool exhibit similar characteristics). These pools represent a varied spectrum of application domains and cache usage characteristics (Table 1). One pool in particular, ETC, represents general cache usage of multiple applications, and is also the largest of the pools; the data collected from this trace may be the most applicable to general-purpose KV-stores.

The focus of this paper is on workload characteristics, patterns, and relationships to social networking, so the exact details of server count and components have little relevance here. It is important to note, however, that all Memcached instances in this study ran on identical hardware.

2.3 Tracing Methodology

Our analysis called for complete traces of traffic passing through Memcached servers for at least a week. This task is particularly challenging because it requires nonintrusive instrumentation of high-traffic volume production servers. Standard packet sniffers such as tcpdump[2] have too much overhead to run under heavy load. We therefore implemented an efficient packet sniffer called *mcap*. Implemented as a Linux kernel module, mcap has several advantages over standard packet sniffers: it accesses packet data in kernel space directly and avoids additional memory copying; it introduces only 3% performance overhead (as opposed to tcpdump's 30%); and unlike standard sniffers, it handles out-of-order packets correctly by capturing incoming traffic after all TCP processing is done. Consequently, mcap has a complete view of what the Memcached server sees, which eliminates the need for further processing of out-of-order packets. On the other hand, its packet parsing is optimized for Memcached packets, and would require adaptations for other applications.

The captured traces vary in size from $3TB$ to $7TB$ each. This data is too large to store locally on disk, adding another challenge: how to offload this much data (at an average rate of more than $80,000$ samples per second) without interfering with production traffic. We addressed this challenge by combining local disk buffering and dynamic offload throttling to take advantage of low-activity periods in the servers.

Finally, another challenge is this: how to effectively process these large data sets? We used Apache HIVE[3] to analyze Memcached traces. HIVE is part of the Hadoop framework that translates SQL-like queries into MapReduce jobs. We also used the Memcached "stats" command, as well as Facebook's production logs, to verify that the statistics we computed, such as hit rates, are consistent with the aggregated operational metrics collected by these tools.

3. WORKLOAD CHARACTERISTICS

This section describes the observed properties of each trace in terms of the requests that comprise it, their sizes, and their frequencies.

3.1 Request Composition

We begin by looking at the basic data that comprises the workload: the total number of requests in each server, broken down by request types (Fig. 1). Several observations delineate the different usage of each pool:

USR handles significantly more GET requests than any of the other pools. GET operations comprise over 99.8% of this pool's workload. One reason for this is that the pool is sized large enough to maximize hit rates, so refreshing values is rarely necessary. These values are also updated at a slower rate than some of the other pools. The overall effect is that USR is used more like RAM-based persistent storage than a cache.

APP has high GET rates too—owing to the popularity of this application—but also a large number of DELETE operations. DELETE operations occur when a cached database entry is modified (but not required to be set again in the cache). SET operations occur when the Web servers add a value to the cache. The relatively high number of DELETE operations show that this pool represents database-backed values that are affected by frequent user modifications.

[2]`http://www.tcpdump.org/`
[3]`http://hive.apache.org/`

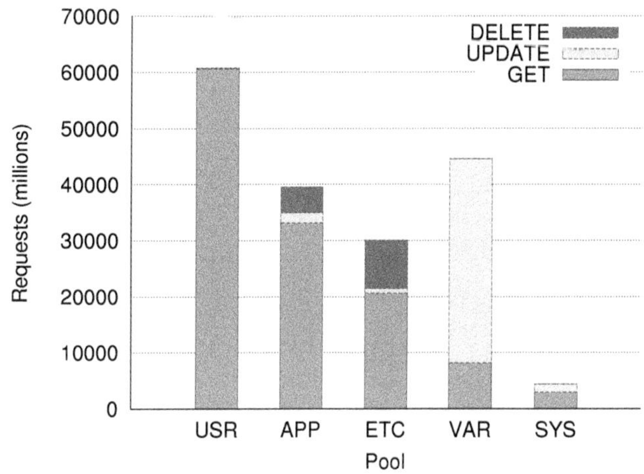

Figure 1: Distribution of request types per pool, over exactly 7 days. UPDATE commands aggregate all non-DELETE writing operations, such as SET, REPLACE, etc.

ETC has similar characteristics to APP, but with an even higher rate of DELETE requests (of which some may not be currently cached). ETC is the largest and least specific of the pools, so its workloads might be the most representative to emulate. Because it is such a large and heterogenous workload, we pay special attention to this workload throughout the paper.

VAR is the only pool sampled that is write-dominated. It stores short-term values such as browser-window size for opportunistic latency reduction. As such, these values are not backed by a database (hence, no invalidating DELETEs are required). But they change frequently, accounting for the high number of UPDATEs.

SYS is used to locate servers and services, not user data. As such, the number of requests scales with the number of servers, not the number of user requests, which is much larger. This explains why the total number of SYS requests is much smaller than the other pools'.

It is interesting to note that the ratio of GETs to UPDATEs in ETC (approximately $30 : 1$) is significantly higher than most synthetic workloads typically assume (Sec. 7). For demand-filled caches like USR, where each miss is followed by an UPDATE, the ratios of GET to UPDATE operations mentioned above are related to hit rate in general and the sizing of the cache to the data in particular. So in theory, one could justify any synthetic GET to UPDATE mix by controlling the cache size. But in practice, not all caches or keys are demand-filled, and these caches are already sized to fit a real-world workload in a way that successfully trades off hit rates to cost.

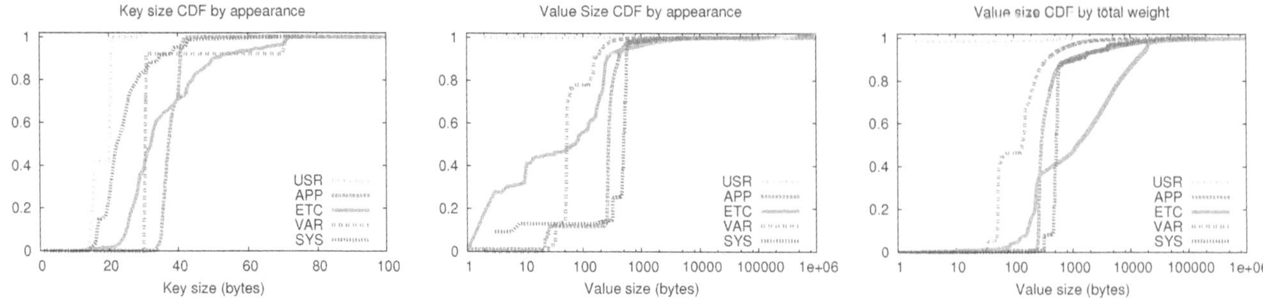

Figure 2: Key and value size distributions for all traces. The leftmost CDF shows the sizes of keys, up to Memcached's limit of $250\,B$ (not shown). The center plot similarly shows how value sizes distribute. The rightmost CDF aggregates value sizes by the total amount of data they use in the cache, so for example, values under $320\,B$ or so in SYS use virtually no space in the cache; $320\,B$ values weigh around 8% of the data, and values close to $500\,B$ take up nearly 80% of the entire cache's allocation for values.

3.2 Request Sizes

Next, we look at the sizes of keys and values in each pool (Fig. 2), based on SET requests. All distributions show strong modalities. For example, over 90% of APP's keys are 31 bytes long, and values sizes around $270\,B$ show up in more than 30% of SET requests. USR is the most extreme: it only has two key size values ($16\,B$ and $21\,B$) and virtually just one value size ($2\,B$). Even in ETC, the most heterogeneous of the pools, requests with 2-, 3-, or 11-byte values add up to 40% of the total requests. On the other hand, it also has a few very large values (around $1MB$) that skew the weight distribution (rightmost plot in Fig. 2), leaving less caching space for smaller values.

Small values dominate all workloads, not just in count, but especially in overall weight. Except for ETC, 90% of all cache space is allocated to values of less than $500\,B$. The implications for caching and system optimizations are significant. For example, network overhead in the processing of multiple small packets can be substantial, which explains why Facebook coalesces as many requests as possible in as few packets as possible [9]. Another example is memory fragmentation. The strong modality of each workload implies that different Memcached pools can optimize memory allocation by modifying the slab size constants to fit each distribution. In practice, this is an unmanageable and unscalable solution, so instead Memcached uses many (44) slab classes with exponentially growing sizes, in the hope of reducing allocation waste, especially for small sizes.

3.3 Temporal Patterns

To understand how production Memcached load varies over time, we look at each trace's transient request rate over its entire collection period (Fig. 3). All traces clearly show the expected diurnal pattern, but with different values and amplitudes. If we increase our zoom factor further (as in the last plot), we notice that traffic in ETC bottoms out around 08:00 and has two peaks around 17:00 and 03:00. Not surprisingly, the hours immediately preceding 08:00 UTC (midnight in Pacific Time) represent night time in the Western Hemisphere.

The first peak, on the other hand, occurs as North America starts its day, while it is evening in Europe, and continues until the later peak time for North America. Although different traces (and sometimes even different days in the same trace) differ in which of the two peaks is higher, the entire period between them, representing the Western Hemisphere day, sees the highest traffic volume. In terms of weekly patterns, we observe a small traffic drop on most Fridays and Saturdays, with traffic picking up again on Sundays and Mondays.

The diurnal cycle represents load variation on the order of 2×. We also observe the presence of traffic spikes. Typically, these can represent a swift surge in user interest on one topic, such as occur with major news or media events. Less frequently, these spikes stem from programmatic or operational causes. Either way, the implication for Memcached development and deployment is that one must budget individual node capacity to allow for these spikes, which can easily double or even triple the normal peak request rate. Although such budgeting underutilizes resources during normal traffic, it is nevertheless imperative; otherwise, the many Web servers that would take to this sudden traffic and fail to get a prompt response from Memcached, would all query the same database nodes. This scenario could be debilitating, so it must remain hypothetical.

4. CACHE BEHAVIOR

The main metric used in evaluating cache efficacy is hit rate: the percentage of GET requests that return a value. The overall hit rate of each server, as derived from the traces and verified with Memcached's own statistics, are shown in Table 2. This section takes a deeper look at the factors that influence these hit rates and how they relate to cache locality, user behavior, temporal patterns, and Memcached's design.

Table 2: Mean cache hit rate over entire trace.

Pool	APP	VAR	SYS	USR	ETC
Hit rate	92.9%	93.7%	98.7%	98.2%	81.4%

4.1 Hit Rates over Time

When looking at how hit rates vary over time (Fig. 4), almost all traces show diurnal variance, within a small band of a few percentage points. USR's plot is curious: it appears to be monotonically increasing (with diurnal undulation). This behavior stems from the usage model for USR. Recall

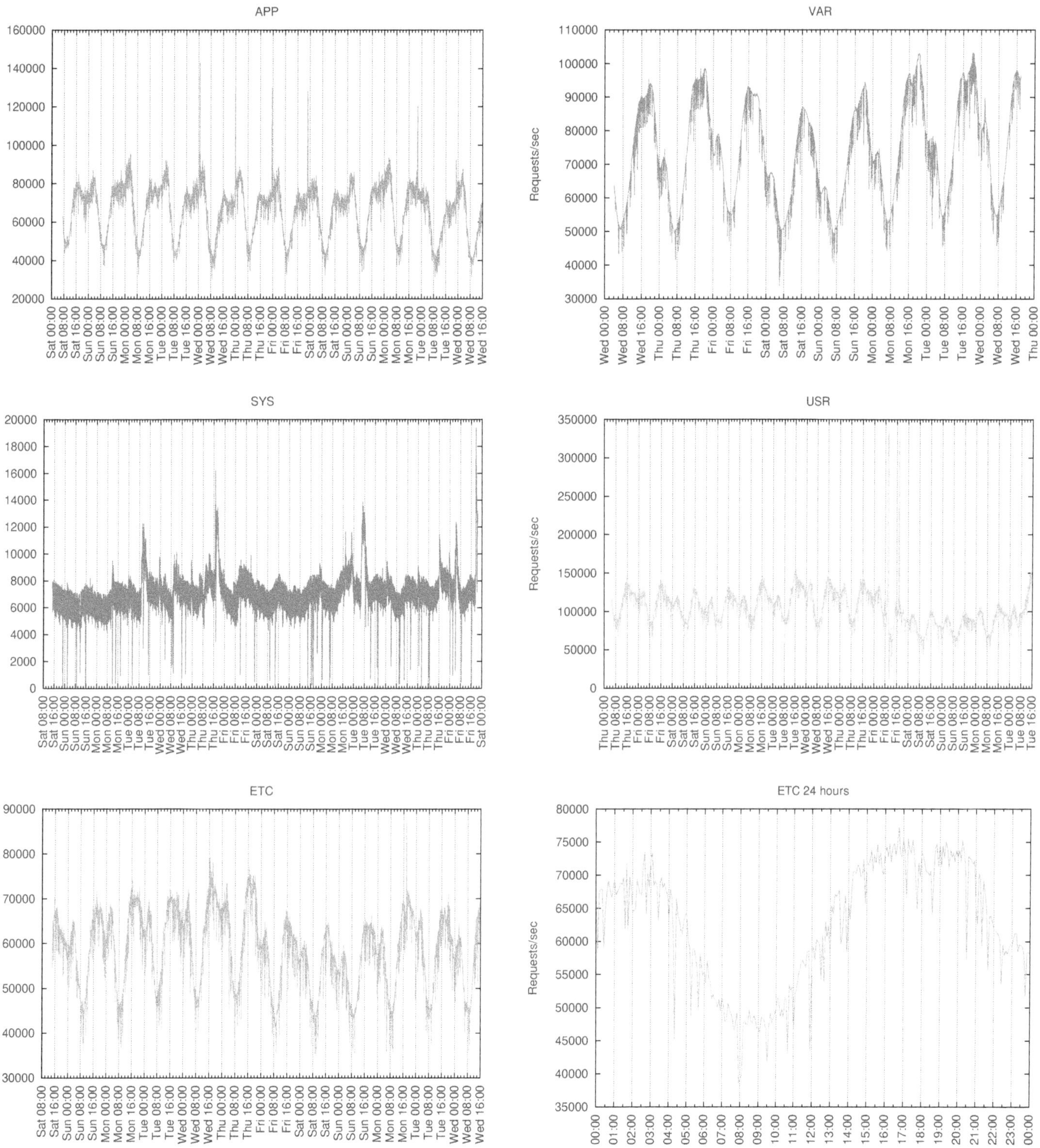

Figure 3: Request rates at different dates and times of day, Coordinated Universal Time (UTC). Each data point counts the total number of requests in the preceding second. Except for USR and VAR, different traces were collected in different times. The last plot zooms in on a 24-hour period from the ETC trace for greater detail.

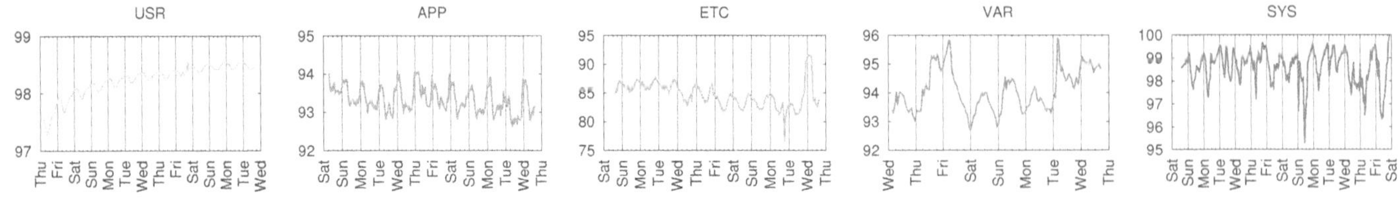

Figure 4: GET hit rates over time for all pools (days start at midnight UTC).

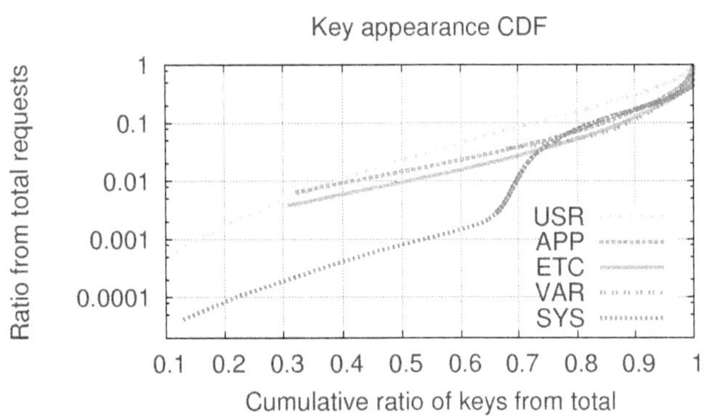

Figure 5: CDFs of key appearances, depicting how many keys account for how many requests, in relative terms. Keys are ranked from least popular to most popular.

from Sec. 2.2 that USR is sized large enough to minimize the number of misses—in other words, to contain almost all possible keys. When a USR Memcached server starts, it contains no data and misses on all requests. But over time, as clients add values to it while the pressure to evict is nonexistent, hit rates climb upwards. Thus, USR's transient hit rate is correlated not only with time of day, but primarily with the server's uptime, reaching 99.8% after several weeks.

Like USR, SYS has a relatively bounded data domain, so it can easily be sized to keep hit rates high and stable. But unlike the other four workloads, SYS does not react directly to user load, so its performance is less cyclical and regular.

4.2 Locality Metrics

This section looks at three ways to measure locality in GET requests: (1) how often and how much some keys repeat in requests; (2) the amount of unique keys and how it varies over time; and (3) reuse period, as a measure of temporal locality.

These metrics, unlike hit rates, are an inherent property of the request stream of each pool; changing the server's hardware or server count will not affect them. Consequently, this data could provide insights toward the workload, in isolation of implementation choices.

4.2.1 Repeating Keys

We start by looking at the distribution of key repeats (Fig. 5). All workloads exhibit the expected long-tail distributions, with a small percentage of keys appearing in most of the requests, and most keys repeating only a handful of times. So, for example, 50% of ETC's keys occur in only 1% of all requests, meaning they do not repeat many times, while a few popular keys repeat in millions of requests per day. This high concentration of repeating keys provides the justification for caching them in the first place.

All curves are remarkably similar, except for SYS's, which has two distinct sections. The first, up to about 65% of the keys, represents keys that are repeated infrequently—conceivably those that are retrieved when one or more clients start up and fill their local cache. The second part, representing the last 25% of keys and more than 90% of the requests, may account for the normal SYS scenario, when a value is added or updated in the cache and all the clients retrieve it.

4.2.2 Locality over Time

It is also interesting to examine how key uniqueness varies over time by counting how many keys *do not* repeat in close time proximity (Fig. 6). To interpret this data, note that a lower percentage indicates that fewer keys are unique, and therefore suggests a higher hit rate. Indeed, note that the diurnal dips correspond to increases in hit rates in Fig. 4.

An immediately apparent property is that in any given pool, this percentage remains relatively constant over time—especially with hour-long bins, with only small diurnal variations and few spikes. Data for 5-minute bins are naturally noisier, but even here most samples remain confined to a narrow range. This suggests that different pools have not only different traffic patterns, but also different caching properties that can benefit from different tuning, justifying the choice to segregate workloads to pools.

Each pool exhibits its characteristic locality band and average. SYS's low average rate of 3.3% unique keys per hour, for example, suggests that different clients request roughly the same service information. In contrast, USR's much higher average rate of 34.6% unique keys per hour, suggests that the per-user data it represents spans a much more disparate range . Generally, we would assume that lower bands translate to higher overall hit rates, all other things being equal. This turns out not to be the case. In fact, the Pearson correlation coefficient between average unique key ratios with 60-minute bins (taken from Fig. 6) and the average hit rates (Table 2) is negative as expected, but small: −0.097. Indeed not all other things are equal, as discussed in Sec. 4.1.

Comparing 5-minute bins to hour-long bins reveals that unique keys in the former appear in significantly higher concentrations than in the latter. This implies a rapid rate of decay in interest in most keys. But does this rate continue to drop very fast over a longer time window? The next section sets out to answer this question.

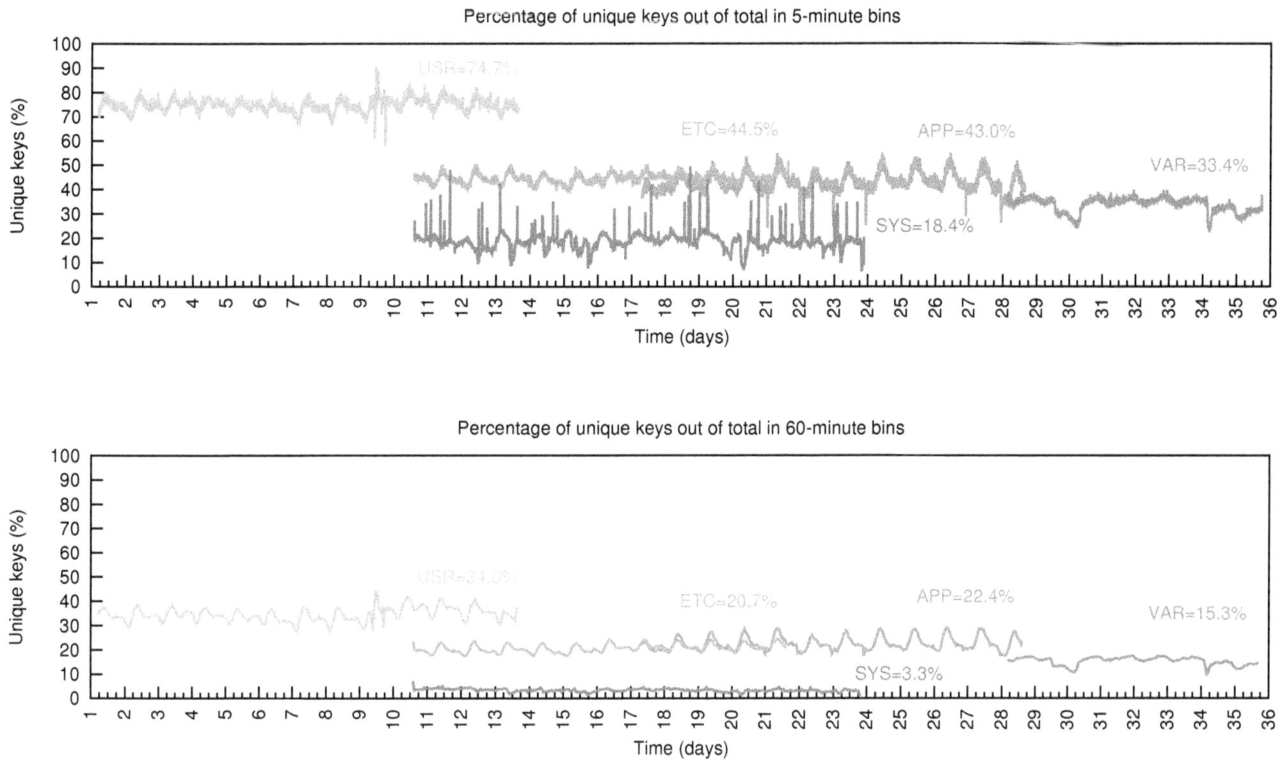

Figure 6: Ratio of unique keys over time. Each data point on the top (bottom) plot shows how many unique keys were requested in the preceding 5 (60) minutes, as percentage of all keys. The label for each pool, at the top right corner of the data, also includes the average ratio throughout the entire pool's trace.

4.2.3 Temporal Locality: Reuse Period

Temporal locality refers to how often a key is re-accessed. One metric to quantify temporal locality of any given key is the reuse period—the time between consecutive accesses to the key. Fig. 7 counts all key accesses in the five traces, and bins them according to the time duration from the previous key's access. Unique keys (those that do not repeat at all within the trace period) are excluded from this count.

The answer to the question from the previous section is therefore positive: count of accesses in each reuse period continues to decay quickly after the first hour. For the ETC trace, for example, 88.5% of the keys are reused within an hour, but only 4% more within two, and within six hours, 96.4% of all nonunique keys have already repeated. It continues to decay at a slower rate. This access behavior suggests a pattern for Facebook's users as well, with some users visiting the site more frequently than others and reusing the keys associated with their accounts. Another interesting sub-pattern occurs every day. Note the periodic peaks on even 24 hours in four of the five traces, especially in the VAR pool that is associated with browser usage. These peaks suggest that a noteworthy number of users log in to the site at approximately the same time of day each time. Once more, these increased-locality indications also correspond to increased hit rates in Fig. 4.

As in the previous section, the SYS pool stands out. It does not show the same 24-hour periodicity, because its keys

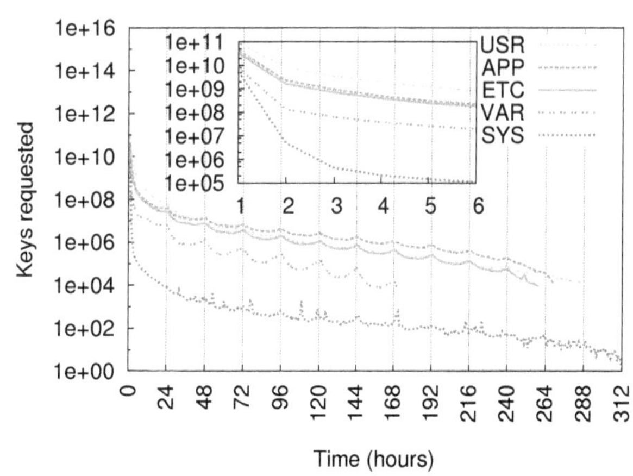

Figure 7: Reuse period histogram per pool. Each hour-long bin n counts keys that were first requested n hours after their latest appearance. The inset zooms in on the five hours after the first.

relate to servers and services, not users. It also decays precipitously compared to the others. As in Sec. 4.2.1, we find that since its data are cached locally by clients, it is likely that most of SYS's GET requests represent data that are newly available, updated or expired from the client cache; these are then requested by many clients concurrently. This would explain why 99.9% of GET requests are repeated within an hour of the first key access. Later, such keys would be cached locally and accessed rarely, perhaps when a newly added client needs to fill its own cache.

Nevertheless, there is still value in reuse period to predict hit rates. Since all pools have sufficient memory for over an hour of fresh data, the percentage of keys reused within an hour correlates positively with the overall hit rates in Table 2 (with a Pearson coefficient of 0.17). The correlation is stronger—with a coefficient of 0.44—if we omit USR and SYS, which have atypical cache behavior (minimum evictions in the former and local caching in the latter).

4.3 Case Study: ETC Hit Rates

We turn our attention to ETC's hit/miss rates, because frequent misses can noticeably hurt user experience. At this point, one might expect ETC's hit rate to exceed the 96% 6-hour key-reuse rate, since it is provisioned with more than enough RAM to store the fresh data of the preceding 6 hours. Unfortunately, this is not the case, and the observed hit rate is significantly lower at 81%. To understand why, we analyzed all the misses in the last 24 hours of the trace (Table. 3). The largest number of misses in ETC comes from keys that are accessed for the first time (at least in a 10-day period). This is the long tail of the locality metrics we analyzed before. Sec. 4.2.1 showed that ≈ 50% of ETC's keys are accessed in only 1% of requests, and therefore benefit little or not at all from a demand-filled cache. The many deletions in the cache also hinder the cache's efficacy. ETC is a very diverse pool with many applications, some with limited reusability. But the other half of the keys that show up in 99% of the requests are so popular (some repeating millions of times) that Memcached can satisfy over 4 in 5 requests to the ETC pool.

Table 3: Miss categories in last 24 hours of the ETC trace. Compulsory misses count GETs with no matching SET in the preceding 10 days (meaning, for all practical purposes, new keys to the cache). Invalidation misses count GETs preceded by a matching DELETE request. Eviction misses count all other missing GETs.

Miss category	Compulsory	Invalidation	Eviction
Ratio of misses	70%	8%	22%

5. STATISTICAL MODELING

This section describes the salient workload characteristics of the ETC trace using simple distribution models. The ETC trace was selected because it is both the most representative of large-scale, general-purpose KV stores, and the easiest to model, since it is not distorted by the idiosyncratic aberrations of application-specific pools. We also think that its mixed workload is easier to generalize to other general-purpose caches with a heterogeneous mix of requests and sizes. The more Facebook-specific workloads, such as USR or SYS, may be interesting as edge cases, but probably not so much as models for synthetic workloads.

The functional models presented here prioritize parsimonious characterization over fidelity. As such, they obviously do not capture all the nuances of the trace, such as its bursty nature or the inclusion of one-off events. But barring access to the actual trace, they can serve the community as a better basis for synthetic workload generation than assumptions based on guesswork or small-scale logs.

Methodology

We modeled independently the three main performance properties that would enable simple emulation of this trace: key sizes, value sizes, and inter-arrival rates. The rate and ratio between GET/SET/DELETE requests can be derived from Sec. 3.1. For cache analysis, additional properties can be gleaned from Sec. 4.

To justify the assumption that the three properties are independent, we picked a sample of 1,000,000 consecutive requests and measured the Pearson coefficient between each pair of variables. The pairwise correlations, as shown in Table 4, are indeed very low.

Table 4: Pearson correlation coefficient between each two pair of modeled variables.

Variable pair	Correlation
Inter-arrival gap ↔ Key size	−0.0111
Inter-arrival gap ↔ Value size	0.0065
Key size ↔ Value size	−0.0286

We created functional models by fitting various distributions (such as Weibull, Gamma, Extreme Value, Normal, etc.) to each data set and choosing the distribution that minimizes the Kolmogorov-Smirnov distance. All our data resemble power-law distributions, and fit the selected models quite well, with the exception of a handful of points (see Fig. 8). To deal with these outliers and improve the fit, we removed these points as necessary and modeled the remaining samples. The few removed points are tabulated separately as a histogram, so a more accurate synthetic workload of the entire trace should combine the functional model with the short list of value-frequency outliers.

Key-Size Distribution

We found the model that best fits key sizes in bytes (with a Kolmogorov-Smirnov distance of 10.5) to be Generalized Extreme Value distribution with parameters $\mu = 30.7984$, $\sigma = 8.20449$, $k = 0.078688$. We have verified that these parameters remain fairly constant, regardless of time of day.

Value-Size Distribution

We found the model that best fits value sizes in bytes (with a Kolmogorov-Smirnov distance of 10.5), starting from 15 bytes, to be Generalized Pareto with parameters $\theta = 0$, $\sigma = 214.476$, $k = 0.348238$ (this distribution is also independent of the time of day). The first 15 values of length and probabilities can be modeled separately as a discrete probability distribution whose values are given in Table 5.

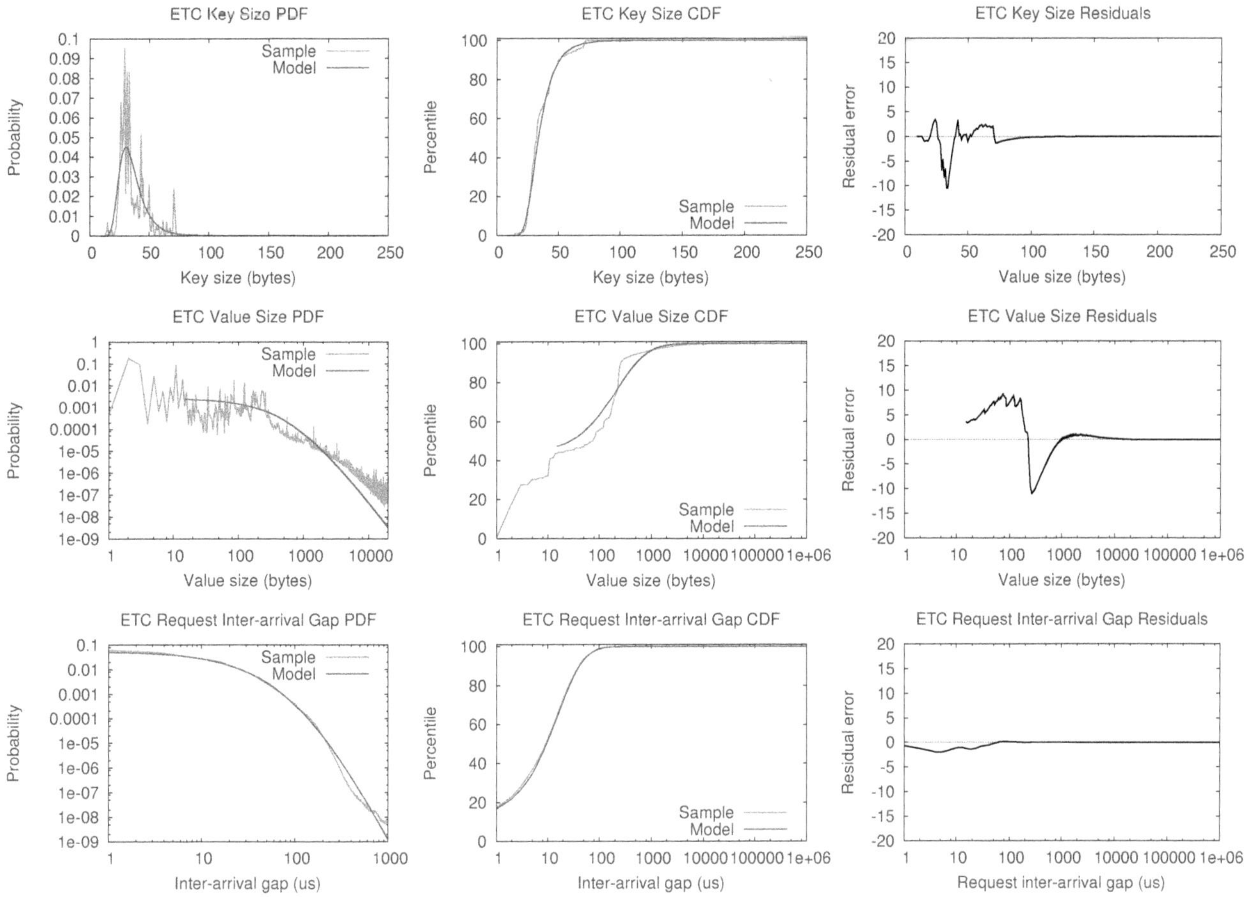

Figure 8: PDF (left), CDF (middle), and CDF residuals (right) plots for the distribution of ETC's key size (top), value size (center). and inter-arrival gap (bottom). Note that some axes are logarithmic, and that PDF plots limit the X-axis to area of interest for greater detail.

Table 5: Probability distribution for first few value lengths, in bytes.

Value size	Probability
0	0.00536
1	0.00047
2	0.17820
3	0.09239
4	0.00018
5	0.02740
6	0.00065
7	0.00606
8	0.00023
9	0.00837
10	0.00837
11	0.08989
12	0.00092
13	0.00326
14	0.01980

Inter-arrival Rate Distribution

We found the model that best describes the time gap in microseconds between consecutive received requests (with a Kolmogorov-Smirnov distance of 2.0) to be Generalized Pareto with parameters $\theta = 0$, $\sigma = 16.0292$, $k = 0.154971$, starting from the second value.

One excluded point from this model is the first value, representing a gap of $0\,\mu sec$ (in other words, multiple requests at the same microsecond time slot), with a probability of 0.1159. This is likely an artifact of our measurement granularity and aggregation by the network stack, and not of concurrent requests, since they are all serialized by the single networking interface.

In addition, the model is most accurate up to about a gap of $1000\,\mu sec$. But the total number of sampled points not covered by this model (i.e., those requests that arrive more than $1msec$ after the previous request) represents less than 0.002% of the total samples and their residual error is negligible.

Unlike the previous two distributions, inter-arrival rate—the reciprocal function of offered load—is highly dependent on time of day, as evident in Fig. 3. For those wishing to capture this diurnal variation, this complete-trace model may be too coarse. To refine this distribution, we divided the

Table 6: Hourly distributions for inter-arrival gap. The columns represent (in order): start time of each hourly bin (in UTC), the two Generalized Pareto parameters (with $\theta = 0$), the fraction of samples under $1\,\mu s$ gap , and the Kolmogorov-Smirnov distance of the fit.

Time	σ	k	$< 1\,\mu s$	KS
0:00	16.2868	0.155280	0.1158	2.18
1:00	15.8937	0.141368	0.1170	2.14
2:00	15.6345	0.137579	0.1174	2.09
3:00	15.7003	0.142382	0.1174	2.16
4:00	16.3231	0.160706	0.1176	2.32
5:00	17.5157	0.181278	0.1162	2.52
6:00	18.6748	0.196885	0.1146	2.64
7:00	19.5114	0.202396	0.1144	2.64
8:00	20.2050	0.201637	0.1123	2.58
9:00	20.2915	0.193764	0.1116	2.46
10:00	19.5577	0.178386	0.1122	2.35
11:00	18.2294	0.161636	0.1130	2.17
12:00	17.1879	0.140461	0.1138	2.00
13:00	16.2159	0.119242	0.1146	1.88
14:00	15.6716	0.104535	0.1152	1.76
15:00	15.2904	0.094286	0.1144	1.72
16:00	15.2033	0.096963	0.1136	1.72
17:00	14.9533	0.098510	0.1140	1.74
18:00	15.1381	0.096155	0.1128	1.67
19:00	15.3210	0.094156	0.1129	1.65
20:00	15.3848	0.100365	0.1128	1.68
21:00	15.7502	0.111921	0.1127	1.80
22:00	16.0205	0.131946	0.1129	1.96
23:00	16.3238	0.147258	0.1148	2.14

raw data into 24 hourly bins and modeled each separately. Fortunately, they all fit a Generalized Pareto distribution with $\theta = 0$ rather well. The remaining two parameters are distributed over time in Table. 6.

6. DISCUSSION

One pertinent question is, what are the factors that affect and predict hit rates? Since all hosts have the same amount of RAM, we should be able to easily explain the relative differences between different traces using the data we gathered so far on locality. But as Sec. 4 discusses, hit rates do not actually correlate very well with most locality metrics, but rather, correlates inversely with the size of the pool (compare Tables 1 and2). Does correlation imply causation in this case?

Probably not. A more likely explanation invokes a third, related parameter: the size of the application domain. Both in USR's and SYS's cases, these sizes are more or less capped, and the bound is small enough that a limited number of servers can cover virtually the entire domain, so locality no longer plays a factor. On the other extreme, ETC has a varying and growing number of applications using it, some with unbounded data. If any single application grows enough in importance to require a certain quality of service, and has the size limitations to enable this quality, given enough servers, then it is separated out of ETC to its own pool. So the applications that end up using ETC are precisely those that cannot or need not benefit from hit-rate guarantees.

Nevertheless, improving hit rates is important for these applications, or we would not need a cache in the first place. One way to improve ETC's hit rates, at least in theory, is to increase the total amount of RAM (or servers) in the pool so that we can keep a longer history. But in practice, beyond a couple of days' worth of history, the number of keys that would benefit from the longer memory is vanishingly small, as Fig. 7 shows. And of course, adding hardware adds cost.

A more fruitful direction may be to focus on the cache replacement policy. Several past studies demonstrated replacement policies with reduced eviction misses, compared to LRU, such as LIRS [19]. Table 3 puts an upper limit on the number of eviction misses that can be eliminated, at around 22%, meaning that eviction policy changes could improve hit rates by another $0.22 \times (1 - 0.814) = 4.1\%$. This may sound modest, but it represents over 120 million GET requests per day per server, with noticeable impact on service latency. Moreover, the current cache replacement scheme and its implementation are suboptimal when it comes to multithreaded performance [9], with its global lock protecting both hash table and slab LRUs. We therefore perceive great potential in alternative replacement policies, not only for better hit rates but also for better performance.

Another interesting question is whether we should optimize Memcached for hit rates or byte hit rates. To answer it, we estimated the penalty of each miss in the ETC workload, by measuring the duration between the missing GET and the subsequent SET that reinstates the value (presumably, the duration represents the time cost to recalculate the value, and is already highly optimized, emphasizing the importance of improved hit rates). We found that it is roughly proportional to the value size, so whether we fill the cache with few large items or many small items of the same aggregate size should not affect recalculation time much. On the other hand, frequent misses do noticeably increase the load on the back-end servers and hurt the user experience, which explains why this cache does not prioritize byte hit rate. Memcached optimizes for small values, because they are by far the most common values. It may even be worthwhile to investigate not caching large objects at all, to increase overall hit rates.

7. RELATED WORK

To the best of our knowledge, this is the first detailed description of a large-scale KV-store workload. Nevertheless, there are a number of related studies on other caching systems that can shed light on the relevance of this work and its methodology.

The design and implementation of any storage or caching system must be optimized for its workload to be effective. Accordingly, there is a large body of work on the collection, analysis, and characterization of the workloads on storage systems, including enterprise computing environments [2, 20, 21] and high-performance computing environments [11, 22, 30]. The observations can be of great importance to system design, engineering, and tuning. For example, in a study on file system workloads for large-scale scientific computing applications, Wang et. al. collected and analyzed file accesses on an 800-node cluster running the Lustre file system at Lawrence Livermore National Laboratory [30]. One of their findings is that in some workloads, small requests account for more than 90% of all requests, but almost all data are accessed by large requests. In a study on file system workloads across different environments, Roselli et. al. found that even small caches can produce a high hit rate, but larger caches would have diminishing returns [28], similar to our conclusions on the ETC workload (Sec. 4.3).

In the work describing Facebook's photo storage system [8], the authors presented statistics of I/O requests for the photos, which exhibit clear diurnal patterns, consistent with our observations in this paper (Sec. 3.3).

Web caches are widely deployed as a caching infrastructure for speeding up Internet access. Their workloads have been collected and analyzed in Web servers [6, 25], proxies [5, 10, 16], and clients [7, 12]. In a study of requests received by Web servers, Arlitt and Williamson found that 80% of requested documents are smaller than $\approx 10KB$. However, requests to these documents generate only 26% of data bytes retrieved from the server [6]. This finding is consistent with the distribution we describe in Sec. 3.2

In an analysis of traces of client-side requests, Cunha et. al. show that many characteristics of Web use can be modeled using power-law distributions, including the distribution of document sizes, the popularity of documents, the distribution of user requests for documents, and the number of references to documents as a power law of their overall popularity rank (Zipf's law) [12]. Our modeling work on the ETC trace (Sec. 5) also shows power-law distributions in most request properties.

In light of the increasing popularity and deployment of KV-stores, several schemes were proposed to improve their performance, energy efficiency, and cost effectiveness [4, 9, 15, 26, 29]. Absent well-publicized workload traces, in particular large-scale production traces, many works used hypothetical or synthetic workloads [29]. For example, to evaluate SILT, a KV-store design that constructs a three-level store hierarchy for storage on flash memory with a memory based index, the authors assumed a workload of 10% PUT and 90% GET requests using $20B$ keys and $100B$ values, as well as a workload of 50% PUT and 50% GET requests for $64B$ KV pairs [23]. Andersen et. al. used queries of constant size ($256B$ keys and $1KB$ values) in the evaluation of FAWN, a KV-store designed for nodes consisting of low-power embedded CPUs and small amounts of flash storage [4]. In the evaluation of CLAM, a KV-store design that places both hash table and data items on flash, the authors used synthetic workloads that generate keys from a random distribution and a number of artificial workload mixes [3]. There are also some studies that used real workloads in KV-store evaluations. In two works on flash-based KV store-design, Debnath et. al. adopted workloads from online multi-player gaming and a storage de-duplication tool from Microsoft [13, 14]. Amazon's production workload was used to evaluate its Dynamo KV store, Dynamo [15]. However, these papers did not specifically disclose the workload characteristics.

Finally, there are multiple studies offering analytical models of observed, large-scale workloads. Of those, a good survey of the methods is presented in Lublin's and Feitelson's analysis of supercomputer workloads [17, 24].

8. CONCLUSION AND FUTURE WORK

This paper presented a dizzying number of views into a very large data set. Together, these views tell a coherent story of five different Memcached workloads at Facebook. We have ETC, the largest and most heterogeneous of the five. It has many keys that are requested millions of times a day, and yet its average hit rate is only 81.4% because half of its keys are accessed infrequently, and because a few large values take up a disproportionate amount of the storage. We have APP, which represents a single application and consequently has more uniform objects: 90% of them have roughly the same size. It also mirrors the interest of Facebook's users in specific popular objects, as evidenced in load spikes that are accompanied by improved locality metrics. We have VAR, a transient store for non-persistent performance data. It has three times as many writes as reads and 70% of its keys occur only once. But its 94% hit rate provides noticeable improvements to the user experience. We have USR, which is more like a RAM-based store for immutable two-byte values than a cache. It may not be the best fit for Memcached, but its overall data size is small enough that even a few Memcached servers can deliver a hit rate of 98.2%. And finally, we have SYS, another RAM-based storage that exhibits unique behavior, because its clients already cache its data. They only access SYS when new data or new clients show up, resulting in a low request rate and a nearly bimodal distribution of temporal locality: either a key is accessed many times in a short period, or virtually not at all.

This study has already answered pertinent questions to improve Facebook's Memcached usage. For example, Fig. 7 shows the relatively marginal benefit of significantly increasing the cache size for the ETC pool. As another example, the analysis in Sec. 6 demonstrated both the importance of increasing Memcached's hit rate, especially on larger data, as well as the upper bound on the potential increase.

The data presented here can also be used as a basis for new studies on key-value stores. We have also provided a simple analytical model of ETC's performance metrics to enable synthetic generation of more representative workloads. The treatment of workload modeling and synthetic load generation in this paper only scratches the surface of possibility, and deserves its own focus in a following publication. We plan to focus on this area and model the remaining workload parameters for ETC (such as key reuse), and other workloads as well. With these models, we would like to create representative synthetic load generators, and share those with the community.

We would also like to see improvements in the memory allocation model so that more room is saved for items in high demand. Areas of investigation include an adaptive slab allocation, using no slabs at all, or using prediction of item locality based on the analysis in this study.

Finally, we are looking into replacing Memcached's replacement policy. LRU is not optimal for all workloads, and can be quite slow. We have already started prototyping alternative replacement schemes, and the initial results are encouraging.

Acknowledgements

We would like to thank Marc Kwiatkowski for spearheading this project and Mohan Srinivasan for helping with the kernel module. We are also grateful for the valuable feedback provided by the following: Goranka Bjedov, Rajiv Krishnamurthy, Rajesh Nishtala, Jay Parikh, and Balaji Prabhakar.

9. REFERENCES

[1] http://voldemort-project.com.

[2] AHMAD, I. Easy and efficient disk I/O workload characterization in VMware ESX server. In *Proceedings of IEEE International Symposium on Workload Characterization* (Sept. 2007).

[3] ANAND, A., MUTHUKRISHNAN, C., KAPPES, S., AKELLA, A., AND NATH, S. Cheap and large CAMs for high performance data-intensive networked systems. In *Proceedings of the 7th USENIX conference on Networked Systems Design and Implementation* (Apr. 2010).

[4] ANDERSEN, D. G., FRANKLIN, J., KAMINSKY, M., PHANISHAYEE, A., TAN, L., AND VASUDEVAN, V. FAWN: a fast array of wimpy nodes. In *Proceedings of the 22nd ACM SIGOPS Symposium on Operating Systems Principles (SOSP)* (Big Sky, Montana, 2009), ACM, pp. 1–14.

[5] ARLITT, M., FRIEDRICH, R., AND JIN, T. Workload characterization of a web proxy in a cable modem environment. *ACM SIGMETRICS - Performance Evaluation Review 27* (1999), 25–36.

[6] ARLITT, M. F., AND WILLIAMSON, C. L. Internet web servers: Workload characterization and performance implications. *IEEE/ACM Transactions on Networking 5* (October 1997), 631–645.

[7] BARFORD, P., BESTAVROS, A., BRADLEY, A., AND CROVELLA, M. Changes in web client access patterns. In *World Wide Web Journal, Special Issue on Characterization and Performance Evaluation* (1999).

[8] BEAVER, D., KUMAR, S., LI, H. C., SOBEL, J., AND VAJGEL, P. Finding a needle in haystack: Facebook's photo storage. In *Proceedings of the 10th USENIX Symposium on Operating Systems Design and Implementation* (Oct. 2010).

[9] BEREZECKI, M., FRACHTENBERG, E., PALECZNY, M., AND STEELE, K. Many-core key-value store. In *Proceedings of the Second International Green Computing Conference* (Orlando, FL, Aug. 2011).

[10] BRESLAU, L., CAO, P., FAN, L., PHILLIPS, G., AND SHENKER, S. Web caching and zipf-like distributions: Evidence and implications. In *Proceedings of the 18th Annual IEEE International Conference on Computer Communications* (1999).

[11] CARNS, P., LATHAM, R., ROSS, R., KAMIL ISKRA, S. L., AND RILEY, K. 24/7 characterization of petascale I/O workloads. In *Proceedings of the 4th Workshop on Interfaces and Architectures for Scientific Data Storage* (Nov. 2009).

[12] CUNHA, C. R., BESTAVROS, A., AND CROVELLA, M. E. Characteristics of WWW client-based traces. In *Technical Report TR-95-010, Boston University Department of Computer Science,* (July 1995).

[13] DEBNATH, B. K., SENGUPTA, S., AND LI, J. Flashstore: High throughput persistent key-value store. *Proceedings of 36th International Conference on Very Large Data Bases (VLDB) 3*, 2 (2010).

[14] DEBNATH, B. K., SENGUPTA, S., AND LI, J. SkimpyStash: RAM space skimpy key-value store on flash-based storage. In *Proceedings of the Annual ACM SIGMOD Conference* (June 2010), pp. 25–36.

[15] DECANDIA, G., HASTORUN, D., JAMPANI, M., KAKULAPATI, G., PILCHIN, A., SIVASUBRAMANIAN, S., VOSSHALL, P., AND VOGELS, W. Dynamo: Amazon's highly available key-value store. In *Proceedings of the 21st ACM SIGOPS Symposium on Operating Systems Principles (SOSP)* (Stevenson, WA, 2007), pp. 205–220.

[16] DUSKA, B. M., MARWOOD, D., AND FEELEY, M. J. The measured access characteristics of world-wide web client proxy caches. In *Proceedings of USENIX Symposium of Internet Technologies and Systems* (Dec. 1997).

[17] FEITELSON, D. G. Workload modeling for performance evaluation. In *Performance Evaluation of Complex Systems: Techniques and Tools*, M. C. Calzarossa and S. Tucci, Eds., vol. 2459 of *Lecture Notes in Computer Science*. Springer-Verlag, Sept. 2002, pp. 114–141. www.cs.huji.ac.il/~feit/papers/WorkloadModel02chap.ps.gz.

[18] FITZPATRICK, B. Distributed caching with memcached. *Linux Journal*, 124 (Aug. 2004), 72–78. www.linuxjournal.com/article/7451?page=0,0.

[19] JIANG, S., AND ZHANG, X. LIRS: an efficient low inter-reference recency set replacement policy to improve buffer cache performance. In *Proceedings of the 2002 ACM SIGMETRICS international conference on Measurement and modeling of computer systems* (2002), SIGMETRICS'02, ACM, pp. 31–42.

[20] KAVALANEKAR, S., WORTHINGTON, B., ZHANG, Q., AND SHARDA, V. Characterization of storage workload traces from production windows servers. In *Proceedings of IEEE International Symposium on Workload Characterization* (Sept. 2008).

[21] KEETON, K., ALISTAIR VEITCH, D. O., AND WILKES, J. I/O characterization of commercial workloads. In *Proceedings of the 3rd Workshop on Computer Architecture Evaluation using Commercial Workloads* (Jan. 2000).

[22] KIM, Y., GUNASEKARAN, R., SHIPMAN, G. M., DILLOW, D. A., ZHANG, Z., AND SETTLEMYER, B. W. Workload characterization of a leadership class storage cluster. In *Proceedings of Petascale Data Storage Workshop* (Nov. 2010).

[23] LIM, H., FAN, B., ANDERSEN, D. G., AND KAMINSKY, M. Silt: A memory-eficient, high-performance key-value store. In *Proceedings of the 23rd ACM Symposium on Operating Systems Principles* (Oct. 2011).

[24] LUBLIN, U., AND FEITELSON, D. G. The workload on parallel supercomputers: Modeling the characteristics of rigid jobs. *Journal of Parallel and Distributed Computing 63*, 11 (Nov. 2003), 1105–1122. www.cs.huji.ac.il/~feit/papers/Rigid01TR.ps.gz.

[25] MANLEY, S., AND SELTZER, M. Web facts and fantasy. In *Proceedings of USENIX Symposium on Internet Technologies and Systems* (Dec. 1997).

[26] PETROVIC, J. Using Memcached for data distribution in industrial environment. In *Proceedings of the Third International Conference on Systems* (Washington, DC, 2008), IEEE Computer Society, pp. 368–372.

[27] REDDI, V. J., LEE, B. C., CHILIMBI, T., AND VAID, K. Web search using mobile cores: Quantifying and mitigating the price of efficiency. In *Proceedings of the 37th International Symposium on Computer Architecture (ISCA)* (June 2010), ACM. portal.acm.org/citation.cfm?id=1815961.1816002.

[28] ROSELLI, D., LORCH, J. R., AND ANDERSON, T. E. A comparison of file system workloads. In *Proceedings of the 2000 USENIX Annual Technical Conference* (June 2000).

[29] VASUDEVAN, V. R. *Energy-Efficient Data-intensive Computing with a Fast Array of Wimpy Nodes*. PhD thesis, Carnegie Mellon University, Oct. 2011.

[30] WANG, F., XIN, Q., HONG, B., MILLER, E. L., LONG, D. D. E., BRANDT, S. A., AND MCLARTY, T. T. File system workload analysis for large scientific computing applications. In *Proceedings of 21st IEEE / 12th NASA Goddard Conference on Mass Storage Systems and Technologies* (Apr. 2004).

[31] ZHAO, H. HipHop for PHP: Move fast. https://developers.facebook.com/blog/post/358/, Feb. 2010.

A First Look at Cellular Machine-to-Machine Traffic – Large Scale Measurement and Characterization

M. Zubair Shafiq† Lusheng Ji‡ Alex X. Liu† Jeffrey Pang‡ Jia Wang‡
†Department of Computer Science and Engineering, Michigan State University, East Lansing, MI, USA
‡AT&T Labs – Research, Florham Park, NJ, USA
{shafiqmu,alexliu}@cse.msu.edu, {lji,jeffpang,jiawang}@research.att.com

ABSTRACT

Cellular network based Machine-to-Machine (M2M) communication is fast becoming a market-changing force for a wide spectrum of businesses and applications such as telematics, smart metering, point-of-sale terminals, and home security and automation systems. In this paper, we aim to answer the following important question: Does traffic generated by M2M devices impose new requirements and challenges for cellular network design and management? To answer this question, we take a first look at the characteristics of M2M traffic and compare it with traditional smartphone traffic. We have conducted our measurement analysis using a week-long traffic trace collected from a tier-1 cellular network in the United States. We characterize M2M traffic from a wide range of perspectives, including temporal dynamics, device mobility, application usage, and network performance. Our experimental results show that M2M traffic exhibits significantly different patterns than smartphone traffic in multiple aspects. For instance, M2M devices have a much larger ratio of uplink to downlink traffic volume, their traffic typically exhibits different diurnal patterns, they are more likely to generate synchronized traffic resulting in bursty aggregate traffic volumes, and are less mobile compared to smartphones. On the other hand, we also find that M2M devices are generally competing with smartphones for network resources in co-located geographical regions. These and other findings suggest that better protocol design, more careful spectrum allocation, and modified pricing schemes may be needed to accommodate the rise of M2M devices.

Categories and Subject Descriptors

C.2.3 [**Computer System Organization**]: Computer Communication Networks—*Network Operations*

Keywords

Cellular Network, M2M, Mobility, Network Performance

SIGMETRICS'12, June 11–15, 2012, London, England, UK.

1. INTRODUCTION

Smart devices that function without direct human intervention are rapidly becoming an integral part of our lives. Such devices are increasingly used in applications such as telehealth, shipping and logistics, utility and environmental monitoring, industrial automation, and asset tracking. Compared to traditional automation technologies, one major difference for this new generation of smart devices is how tightly they are coupled into larger scale service infrastructures. For example, in logistic operations, the locations of fleet vehicles can be tracked with Automatic Vehicle Location (AVL) devices such as the CalAmp LMU-2600 [7] and uploaded into back-end automatic dispatching and planning systems for real-time global fleet management. More and more emerging technologies also heavily depend on these smart devices. For instance, a corner stone for the Smart Grid Initiative is the capability of receiving and controlling individual customer's power usage on a real-time and wide-area basis through devices such as the electric meters equipped with Trilliant CellReader [21] modules.

This kind of leap in technology would not be possible without the support of wide area wireless communication infrastructure, in particular cellular data networks. It is estimated that there are already tens of millions of such smart devices connected to cellular networks world wide and within the next 3-5 years this number will grow to hundreds of millions [3, 4]. This represents a substantial growth opportunity for cellular operators as mobile phone penetration rate increase is flattening in the developed world [10, 23].

M2M devices and smartphones share the same network infrastructure, but current cellular data networks are primarily designed, engineered, and managed for smartphone usage. Given that the population of cellular M2M devices may soon eclipse that of smartphones, a logical question to ask is: What are the challenges cellular network operators may face in trying to accommodate traffic from both smartphones and M2M devices? Existing configurations may not be optimized to support M2M devices. In addition, M2M devices may compete with smartphones and impose new demand on shared resources. Hence, to answer this question, it is crucial to understand the M2M traffic patterns and how they are different from traditional smartphone traffic. The knowledge of traffic patterns can reveal insights for better management of shared network resources and ensuring best service quality for both types of devices.

In this paper, we take a first look at M2M traffic on a commercial cellular network. Our goal is to understand the characteristics of M2M traffic, in particular, whether and how they differ from those of smartphones. To the best of our knowledge, our study is the first to investigate the characteristics of traffic generated by M2M devices. We summarize our key contributions below.

- **Large Scale Measurement:** We conduct the first large scale measurement study of cellular M2M traffic. For our study, we have collected anonymized IP-level traffic traces from the core network of a tier-1 cellular network in the United States. This trace covers all states in the United States during one week in August 2010. This trace contains M2M traffic from millions of devices belonging to more than 150 hardware models. In addition, we have also collected anonymized traffic traces from millions of smartphones from the same cellular network. Overall, we find that M2M devices generate significantly less traffic compared to smartphones. Furthermore, in our trace, we observe that the number of M2M devices is also significantly smaller than the number of smartphones. However, the number of new M2M devices and their total traffic volume is increasing at a very rapid pace. In fact, a longitudinal comparison of M2M traffic in this cellular network showed that total M2M traffic volume has increased more than 250% in 2011. In comparison, Cisco reported that mobile data traffic grew only 132% in 2011, which is almost half of the increase observed for M2M traffic [5]. Consequently, it is important to understand the peculiarities of M2M traffic, especially its contrast to the traditional smartphone traffic, for future network engineering. In this study, we compare M2M and smartphone traffic in the following aspects: aggregate volume, volume time series, sessions, mobility, applications, and network performance.
- **Aggregate Traffic Volume:** We jointly study the distribution of aggregate uplink and downlink traffic volume. Our major finding is that, though M2M devices do not generate as much traffic as smartphones, they have a much larger ratio of uplink to downlink traffic volume compared to smartphones. Since existing cellular data protocols support higher capacity in the downlink than the uplink, *our finding suggests that network operators need careful spectrum allocation and management to avoid contention between low volume, uplink-heavy M2M traffic and high volume, downlink-heavy smartphone traffic.*
- **Traffic Volume Time Series:** We analyze the traffic volume time series of M2M devices and smartphones. Our analysis shows that different M2M device models exhibit different diurnal behaviors than smartphones. However, some M2M device models do share similar peak hours as smartphones. Hence, *M2M traffic imposes new requirements on the shared network resources that need to be considered in capacity planning, where network is usually provisioned according to peak usage.* Another finding from time series analysis is that some M2M device models generate traffic in a synchronized fashion (like a botnet [20]), which can result in denial of service due to limited radio spectrum. Therefore, *M2M protocols should randomize such network usage to avoid congesting the radio network.*
- **Traffic Sessions:** To understand the usage behavior of individual devices, we conduct session-level traffic analysis in terms of active time, session length, and session inter-arrival time. We find that high traffic volume does not always correlate with more active time. *This finding calls for new billing schemes, which go beyond per-byte charging models.* We also find that M2M devices have different session length and inter-arrival time characteristics compared to smartphones. *This finding can be utilized by device manufacturers to improve battery management and by network operators to optimize radio network parameters for M2M devices.*
- **Device Mobility:** We compare the mobility characteristics of M2M devices and smartphones from individual device and network perspectives. We find that M2M devices, with a few exceptions, are less mobile than smartphones. We also find that M2M and smartphone traffic competes for network resources in co-located geographical regions. *This finding indicates that careful network resource allocation is required to avoid contention between low-volume M2M traffic and high-volume smartphone traffic.*
- **Application Usage:** We also study the contribution of different applications to the aggregate traffic volume of M2M devices and smartphones. *We find that M2M traffic mostly uses non-standard and custom application protocols, which is undesirable because it is difficult for network operators to understand and mitigate adverse effects from these protocols compared to standard protocols.*
- **Network Performance:** The network performance results of M2M traffic, in terms of packet loss ratio and round trip time, show strong dependency on device radio technology (2G or 3G) and expected device environment (*e.g.* indoors vs. outdoors). *This implies that network operators must continue to support and improve legacy networks for M2M devices even as smartphones move to 4G technologies.*

The rest of this paper proceeds as follows. We first provide details of our collected trace in Section 2. Sections 3–8 present measurement analysis of M2M traffic and compare them to traditional smartphone traffic. Finally, we review the related work in Section 9 and conclude in Section 10.

2. DATA

2.1 Data Set

The data used in this study is collected from a nation-wide cellular operator in the United States that provides 2G and 3G cellular data services. It supports GPRS, EDGE, UMTS, and HSPA technologies. Architecturally, the portion of its network that supports cellular data service is organized in two tiers. The lower tier, the radio access network, provides wireless connectivity to user devices, and the upper tier, the core network, interfaces the cellular data network with the Internet. More details about cellular data network architecture can be found in prior literature such as [2].

The data collection apparatus that produced the trace used in our study is deployed at all links between Serving Gateway Support Nodes (SGSN) and Gateway GRPS Support Nodes (GGSN) in the core network. This apparatus is capable of anonymously logging session level traffic information at 5 minute intervals for all IP data traffic between cellular devices and the Internet. In other words, each record in the trace is a 5-minute traffic volume summary aggregated by unique device identifier and application category. Each record also contains the cell location of the device at the start of the session. Each record is originally timestamped according to the standard coordinated universal time (UTC), which is then converted to the local time at the device for our analysis. This trace was collected during one complete week in August 2010. Geographically, the trace covers the whole United States. Applications are identified using a combination of port information, HTTP host and user-agent information, and other heuristics [9]. More information about the data collection system can be found in [9, 18].

2.2 M2M Device Categorization

The data set contains traffic records for all cellular devices, so we first need to separate M2M devices from the rest. Furthermore, because M2M devices are usually developed for specific applications, significant behavioral differences are expected between M2M devices for different target applications. Thus, it is reasonable to sub-divide M2M devices into categories based on their intended application to better understand the unique traffic characteristics of different M2M categories. We start this process by identifying the hardware model of each cellular device using the device's Type Allocation Code (TAC), which is part of the unique identifier of each cellular device. Although the records in our data set are anonymized, the TAC portion of the unique ID is retained. Thus, the hardware model of each cellular device is obtained by consulting the TAC database of the GSM Association.

Because there is no rigorous definition for M2M devices or standard ways for determining their application categories, and many devices have multiple uses, knowing the device model is not sufficient for identifying a device with certainty as M2M device nor for identifying its M2M category. Towards this end, we adopt the device classification scheme of a major cellular service provider as a base template for categorizing M2M devices [1]. To supplement and verify this template, we also use public information such as production brochures and specification sheets. In total, we have classified more than 150 device models as M2M devices, and further divide them into the following 6 categories.

1) Asset Tracking: These M2M devices are used to remotely track objects like cargo containers and other shipments. These devices are often coupled with other sensors for tasks like temperature and pressure measurement. In our trace, about 18% devices belong to this category.

2) Building Security: These M2M devices are typically used to manage door access and security cameras. In our trace, about 14% devices belong to this category.

3) Fleet: These M2M devices are used to monitor vehicle locations, arrivals, and departures and provide real-time access to critical operational data for logistic service providers. In our trace, about 51% devices belong to this category.

4) Modem: These M2M devices are used as generic cellular communication modems with embedded system data input and output ports such as serial, I2C, analog, and digital. They provide network connectivity for customized solutions. In our trace, about 9% devices belong to this category.

5) Metering: These M2M devices are mostly used for remote measurement and monitoring in agricultural, environmental, and energy applications. In our trace, about 6% devices belong to this category.

6) Telehealth: These M2M devices are mostly used for remote measurement and monitoring in healthcare applications. In our trace, about 2% devices belong to this category.

We acknowledge that due to lack of more detailed usage information and ambiguity in device registry databases, our classification may contain some errors. To limit such errors, we try to be as conservative as possible when deciding whether to include a M2M device model in our study. For example, cellular routers are generally excluded from this study because the actual end devices behind these routers

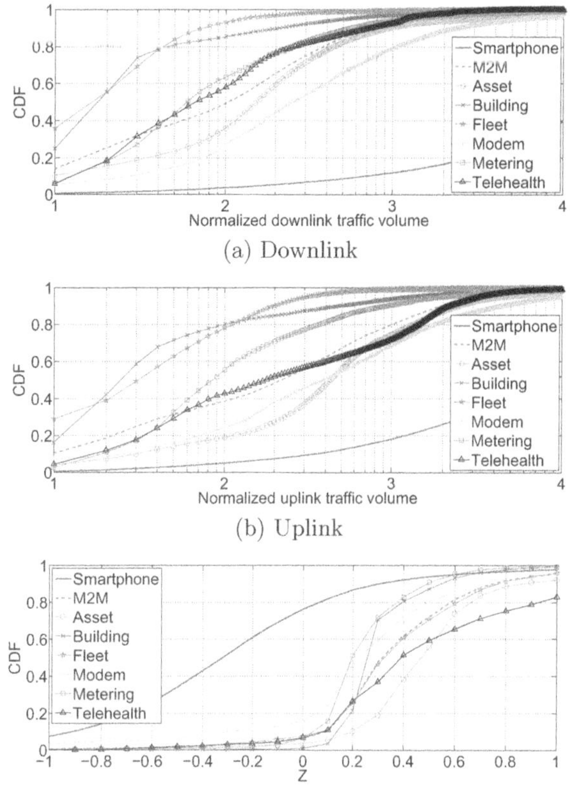

(a) Downlink

(b) Uplink

(c) Ratio: log(Uplink/Downlink)

Figure 1: CDFs of aggregate downlink and uplink traffic volume.

cannot be identified. For cellular modems and modules, we exclude models with data interfaces likely used by modern day computers such as USB, PCI Express, and miniPCI but keep those with UART, SPI, and I2C interfaces. For the sake of comparing M2M and typical human-generated traffic characteristics, we have also included in our study traffic records from a uniformly sampled set of smartphone models, covering millions of smartphone devices.

In the following sections, based on this collected trace, we conduct a detailed analysis of M2M traffic characteristics and compare them with those of the smartphones found in the same trace. The traffic characteristics analyzed in this paper include aggregate data volume, volume time series, session analysis, mobility, application usage, and network performance.

3. AGGREGATE TRAFFIC VOLUME

When a new technology emerges and it has to share resources with existing parties, a natural first question is the level of competition and how different parties can better coexist. This is why we first study and compare the distribution of aggregate traffic volume for M2M devices and smartphones. Moreover, we also investigate whether the long established perception of traffic volume being downlink heavy remains true for M2M devices [15].

Figure 1 shows the cumulative distribution functions (CDFs) of downlink and uplink normalized traffic volume for M2M devices and smartphones separately. To normalize traffic volume, we divided the maximum observed volume by an arbitrary constant. For M2M, we show both the distributions for all M2M devices together and for each M2M category. We first notice that different device categories exhibit strong diversity in aggregate downlink and uplink traffic volume distributions. However, we do observe a consistent relative ordering of CDFs for different device categories. We note that the average aggregate downlink and uplink traffic volume for smartphones is several orders of magnitude larger compared to all M2M device categories. Within M2M device categories, modem category has the largest downlink traffic volume, followed by asset category; whereas, building security and fleet categories have the smallest downlink traffic volume. A similar ordering is also observed for uplink traffic volume.

We now study the distribution of ratios of uplink traffic volume to downlink traffic volume. For the sake of clarity, we plot the ratios after taking their logarithm, denoted by Z. The positive values of Z represent more uplink traffic volume than downlink traffic volume and its negative values represent more downlink traffic volume than uplink traffic volume. It is not surprising that approximately 80% of smartphone devices have $Z \leq 0$; thereby, indicating larger downlink traffic volumes. However, this trend is reversed by large margin for all M2M device categories, which all have $Z > 0$ for more than 80% of devices indicating larger uplink traffic volumes. This finding provides another evidence that M2M traffic has significantly different characteristics compared to traditional smartphone traffic. Comparing different M2M device categories, we observe that building and metering categories have the lowest average Z values; whereas, asset and telehealth have the highest average Z values. Such differences provide insight into the functionality of M2M device categories.

Summary: Overall, the average per-device traffic volume of M2M devices is much smaller than that of smartphones. However, the strength of M2M devices is really in the size of their population. As M2M population continues to increase, how network operators efficiently support a large number of low volume devices will become an important issue. Our finding that M2M traffic has a much larger ratio of uplink to downlink traffic volume compared to smartphone traffic shows that M2M devices act more as "content producers" than "content consumers", unlike traditional smartphone devices. Interestingly, this difference coincides with the paradigm shift in web and mobile computing towards user-centric content generation. The momentum of such a shift may eventually question the assumptions for optimization approaches exploiting downlink asymmetry of network traffic [14].

4. TRAFFIC VOLUME TIME SERIES

Having gained an understanding of aggregated M2M traffic volume, the next step is to study the temporal dynamics of M2M traffic volume. It would be interesting to know whether M2M devices exhibit similar daily diurnal pattern as smartphones. One particular use of such information is to evaluate the potential benefits of incentive programs such as billing discounts encouraging non-peak time usage. Time series analysis is also helpful for gaining insights into the operations of M2M devices.

As mentioned in Section 2, the logged traffic records contain timestamps at 5-minute time resolution. Therefore, we can separately construct averaged traffic volume time series for smartphones and all M2M device categories. We plot these averaged uplink and downlink traffic volume time series in Figure 2. While the daily diurnal pattern is evident

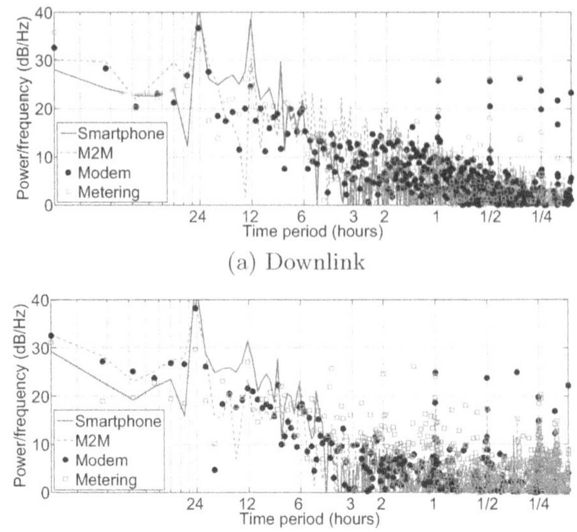

(a) Downlink

(b) Uplink

Figure 3: Periodograms containing power spectral density estimate of traffic volume time series.

for both aggregate M2M and smartphone traffic, the comparison of Figures 2(a) and (b) reveals the following two interesting differences. First, the volume of downlink traffic dominates that of uplink traffic for smartphones, whereas these are fairly equal in M2M traffic time series. This finding follows our earlier observations in Section 3. Second, we also observe that peaks in smartphone traffic time series are wider, starting in the morning and prolonging up to mid-night, whereas peaks in M2M traffic time series are narrower, ending by the evening time; and M2M traffic volume exhibits significant reduction during weekend compared to weekdays while smartphone traffic volume remains virtually unchanged. It appears that smartphone traffic time series is coupled with human "waking" hours while M2M traffic time series is coupled with human "working" hours. This is a strong indication that currently a majority of M2M devices are employed for business use. They are not yet in the mainstream for residential users, or as tightly integrated into people's daily life as smartphones.

We have also separately plotted averaged uplink and downlink traffic volume time series for all M2M device categories in Figures 2(c)–(h). We observe strong diurnal variations for all M2M device categories. However, the weekday-weekend pattern comparison reveals different results for most M2M categories, illustrating that M2M categories indeed behave vastly differently from each other due to the different applications they serve. The previously mentioned association of M2M traffic time series with daily business activity cycle is highlighted the most by Figure 2(d) (Building), where each working day pattern displays not only elevated volume during working hours but also two peaks which in time coincide with the beginning and the end of typical business hours. Contrastingly, we see that there is virtually no difference in traffic volume for the metering category for different days.

Frequency Analysis: On a finer scale, we observe repetitive spikes in time series of most M2M device categories. To investigate these high frequency spikes in more detail, we plot the periodograms of some downlink and uplink traffic volume time series in Figures 3(a) and (b), respectively.

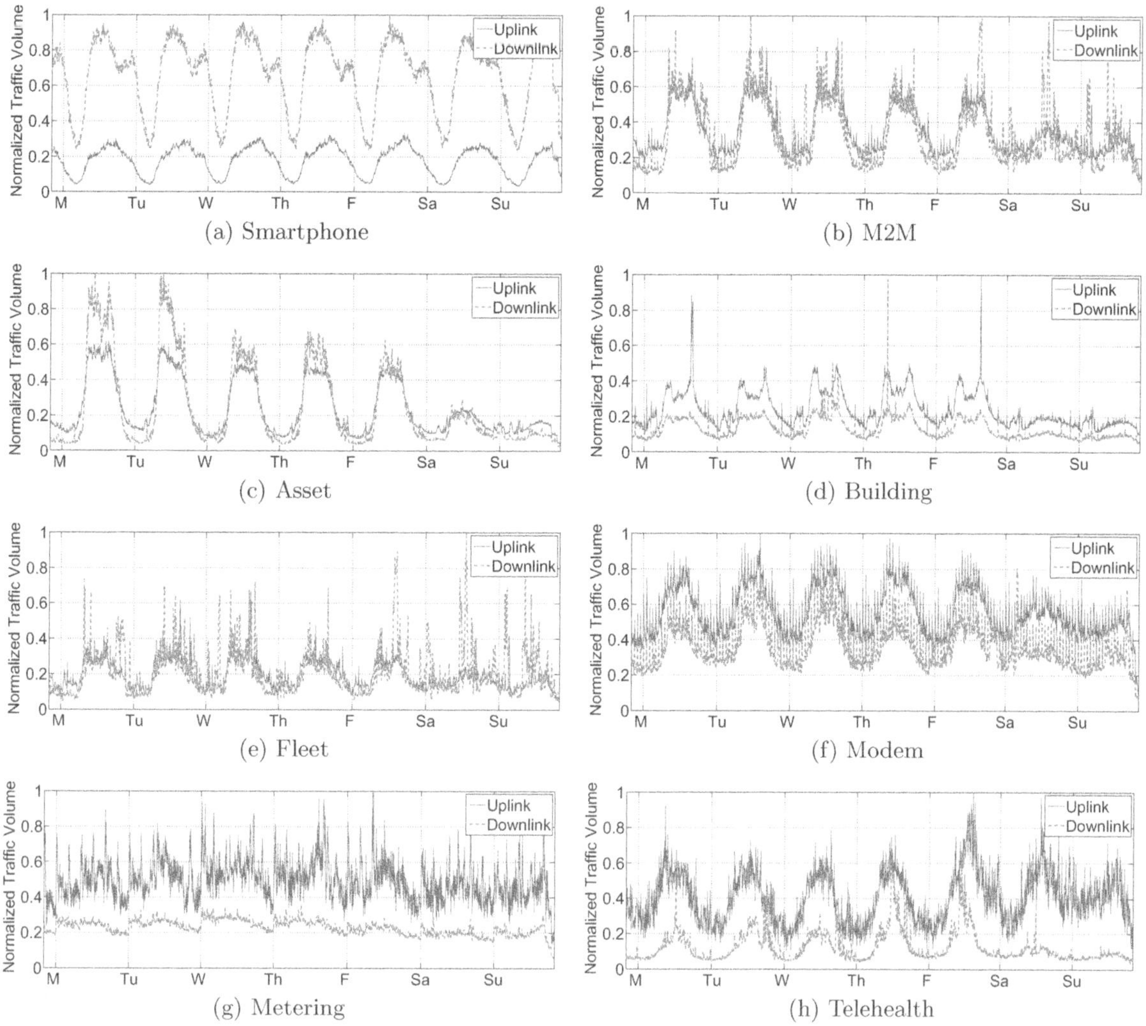

Figure 2: Downlink and uplink traffic volume time series.

The periodogram is an estimate of power spectral density, or frequency spectrum, of a given signal and is defined as:

$$S(f) = \frac{1}{F_s N}\left|\sum_{k=1}^{N} x_k e^{-j(2\pi f/F_s)k}\right|^2,$$

where f is the frequency in Hertz, N is the total number of signal samples, and F_s is the sampling frequency [19]. In this study, we have $F_s = 5$ minutes and $N = 2,016$. The x-axis in Figure 3 represents time period on logarithm scale and y-axis represents power in decibels (dB) for each frequency. We observe distinct spikes in the periodograms corresponding to multiple time periods, *e.g.* 1 hour, 30 minutes, and 15 minutes, strongly suggesting the timer-driven nature of many M2M operations. The perfect alignment of the spikes in Figure 2(f) and (g) to one, half, and quarter hour marks in time also suggests that these timers are highly synchronized.[1] Such synchronized communication by large number of devices is highly undesirable both for the M2M application service providers and cellular network operators because it may create disruptive congestion at various locations in the infrastructure. It is noteworthy that such sub-hour frequency components are absent for smartphone traffic time series, highlighting peculiar nature of M2M traffic.

Time Series Clustering: Until now we have only examined the averaged time series for M2M device categories. To gain more fine-grained insights, we construct more than 150 M2M device model traffic time series from our trace, each representing averaged time series of individual devices of respective device models at 5-minute time resolution. Likewise, we construct individual device traffic time series at the same time resolution. However, the time series of individual devices at 5-minute time resolution over the duration of one week are less useful because they are highly sparse. To reduce their sparsity, we change the time resolution to 1 hour and also average them across all days. Therefore, the time series of individual devices each contain 24 data points representing hourly time series averaged over all days of the week.

With these two sets of time series (device models and individual devices) at hand, we now aim to find some structure across them by clustering together similar traffic time se-

[1]For a causal analysis of the spikes in Figure 2, we have manually analyzed the traffic logs for potential patterns. Our analysis showed that all spikes are caused by coordinated activities from thousands of devices belonging to the same device models, not by a small number of "outliers". For instance, spikes for modem category are caused by traffic belonging to thousands of modem devices of a particular model exactly at hour marks.

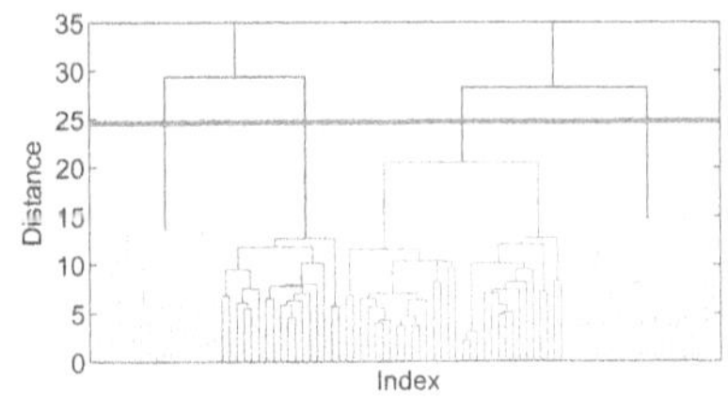

(a) Device model

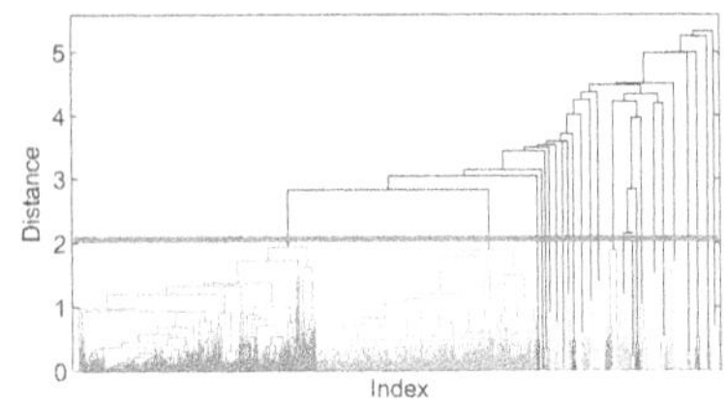

(b) Individual device

Figure 4: Dendrograms for hierarchical clustering.

ries. The notion of similarity is not obvious for time series because a pair of time series may exhibit different levels of similarity at different time scales. Therefore, we are required to examine each pair of traffic time series at multiple time scales. In this paper, we utilize discrete wavelet transform to analyze and compute similarity score between time series at multiple time scales [8]. We then utilize hierarchical clustering to group time series into distinct clusters [13].

Figure 4(a) shows the dendrogram for hierarchical clustering of M2M device model traffic volume time series. The x-axis represents the indices of time series and y-axis represents the l^2 norm distance metric. In the dendrogram, we visually observe an obvious grouping of device models into well-separated clusters. Using the Davies-Bouldin index [13], the optimal number of clusters is selected to be four for M2M device model dendrogram. The Davies-Bouldin index is known to result in compact and well-separated clusters. Similarly, Figure 4(b) shows the dendrogram for hierarchical clustering of individual device traffic volume time series. We observe a different structure in this dendrogram as compared to the one in Figure 4(a). Here we note that the bottom-right of the tree contains several clusters, each containing one or a small number of individual device time series. Intuitively, these small clusters potentially represent outliers whose distance to other clusters is fairly large. We visually observe two clusters on the bottom-left of Figure 4(b), each containing a major chunk of time series. After separating out the sparse outlying clusters, these two clusters are selected as optimal by the Davies-Bouldin index. To further study the clusters identified using the abovementioned methodology, we plot their centroids with pointwise standard deviations in Figures 5 and 6. In these figures, the dark red lines represent the centroids, the blue lines represent point-wise standard deviations, and the light red lines in the background represent the member time series for each cluster.

Figure 5 shows device model clusters where we label the identified centroids based on two of their temporal characteristics: traffic volume and diurnal variations. We label a cluster centroid as high volume if its average normalized daily peak volume for weekdays is more than ≈ 0.5. Otherwise, the cluster centroid is labeled as low volume. Similarly, we

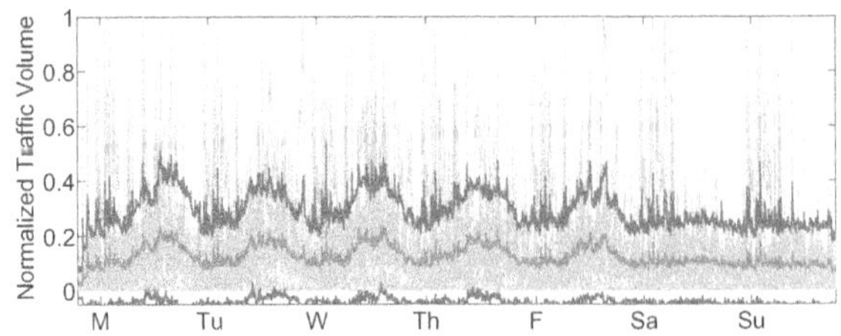

(a) Low Volume-Low Diurnality (LV-LD)

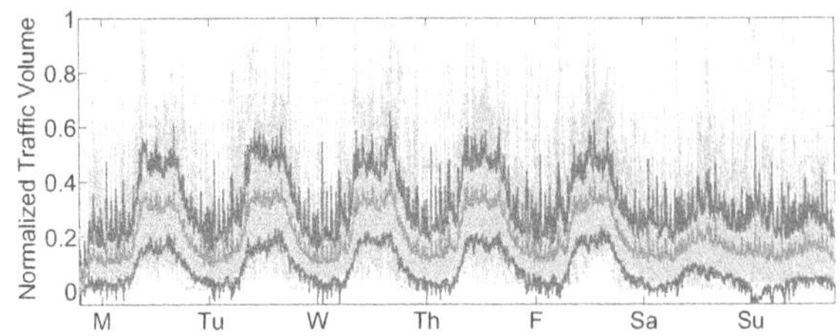

(b) Low Volume-High Diurnality (LV-HD)

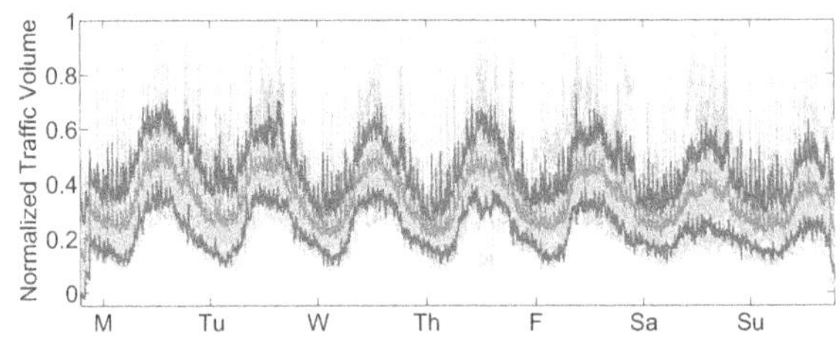

(c) High Volume-Low Diurnality (HV-LD)

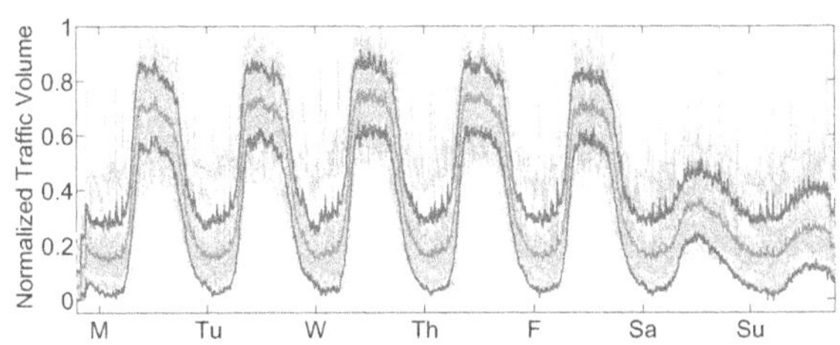

(d) High Volume-High Diurnality (HV-HD)

Figure 5: Cluster centroids identified using device models traffic time series.

label the cluster centroids based on the diurnal variations in the following way. Let DI denote the diurnality coefficient, and $V_{max}(d)$, $V_{min}(d)$, and $V_{avg}(d)$ denote the maximum, minimum, and average traffic volumes, respectively, on day d of a traffic time series spanning $|D|$ days. The diurnality coefficient is quantified as:

$$DI = \frac{1}{|D|} \sum_{\forall d \in D} \frac{V_{max}(d) - V_{min}(d)}{V_{avg}(d)}.$$

If the diurnality coefficient of a cluster centroid is more than 1.0 then it is labeled as high diurnality. Otherwise, it is labeled as low diurnality. Using this labeling methodology, we label the identified clusters as low volume-low diurnality (LV-LD), low volume-high diurnality (LV-HD), high volume-low diurnality (HV-LD), and high volume-high diurnality (HV-HD). We now study the composition of these labeled clusters with respect to the categories defined in Section 2. Table 1 shows the composition of the identified clusters across all categories and the largest value in every row is marked as bold. We note that asset tracking and fleet device models mostly belong to HV-HD cluster. Furthermore, we note that building security and telehealth device

Table 1: **Composition of device model clusters.**

	LV-LD %	LV-HD %	HV-LD %	HV-HD %
Asset	13.1	16.1	23.5	**33.3**
Building	13.1	**19.3**	11.7	0.0
Fleet	26.2	29.2	5.9	**61.2**
Modem	34.5	25.8	**47.1**	5.5
Metering	**13.1**	3.2	5.9	0.0
Telehealth	0.0	**6.4**	5.9	0.0

models mostly belong to LV-HD cluster. These observations follow our intuition that the activity of these device models is tightly coupled with human activities. They also indicate that building security and telehealth device models tend to generate low traffic volume. Similarly, we observe that metering device models mostly belong to LV-LD cluster. This observation follows our earlier finding from Figure 3 that metering devices tend to download or upload data after periodic time intervals throughout the day. Finally, we observe that modem device models mostly belong to HV-LD clusters. Similar to metering device models, modem device models also tend to generate traffic after periodic time intervals throughout the day resulting in low diurnality.

For individual device traffic volume time series clustering, we identified a handful number of outlier clusters and two main clusters containing a majority of devices. We plot the centroids of two main clusters and one of the outlier clusters in Figure 6. The cluster centroid in Figure 6(a) shows strong diurnal behavior with higher traffic volume during day time as compared to night time; therefore, we label this cluster as diurnal. On the other hand, the cluster centroid in Figure 6(b) does not show any diurnal characteristics and is labeled as flat. We also show an outlier cluster in Figure 6(c), which consists of devices generating traffic volume spikes at late night. To gain insights from the clustering results of individual device traffic volume time series, we study their composition across various M2M device categories. Table 2 shows the cluster composition results with the largest value in every row marked as bold. We have similar observations for device level clustering as we previously had for device model traffic volume time series clustering. For instance, asset tracking and fleet devices mostly belong to the diurnal cluster. Modem, metering, and telehealth devices, with spiky traffic volume time series, mostly belong to the outlier cluster. Finally, building security devices mostly belong to the flat cluster. The individual device level clustering results further improve the confidence of our understanding about the behavior of M2M devices.

Summary: In this section, we have presented time series analysis for M2M traffic volume. Just like that of smartphones, M2M traffic volume also exhibits strong daily diurnal pattern. However, M2M traffic volume peaks correspond to people's working hours while smartphone traffic volume peaks correspond to waking hours, which indicates that a majority of M2M devices are employed for business use. The overlap between M2M peaks and smartphone peaks suggests that incentive based leverage mechanism such as off-peak time pricing for encouraging better sharing of network capacity can be beneficial. We have also investigated fine-grained features in traffic volume time series for different categories and uncovered the differences in behaviors among different M2M categories. For example unlike other M2M categories, metering devices show only weak diurnal pattern, suggesting that the traditional approach of scheduling service down time in early morning hours may not be the best for them. Finally, the surprising discovery of synchronized communication among M2M devices highlights the importance of developing and imposing standard traffic protocols and randomization methods.

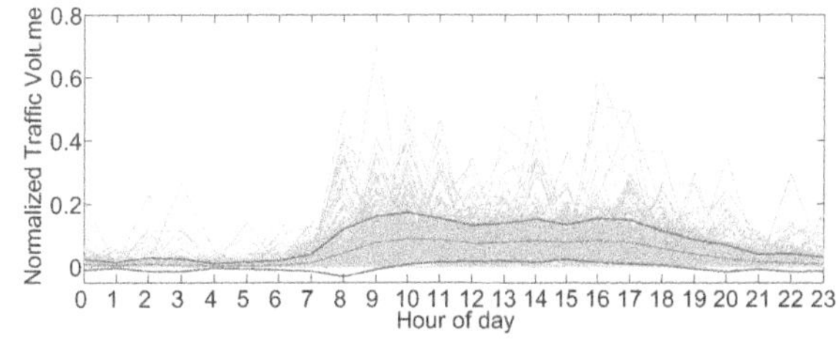

(a) Diurnal

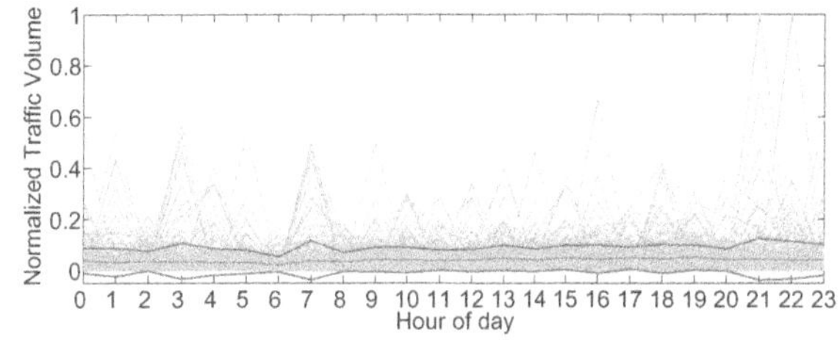

(b) Flat

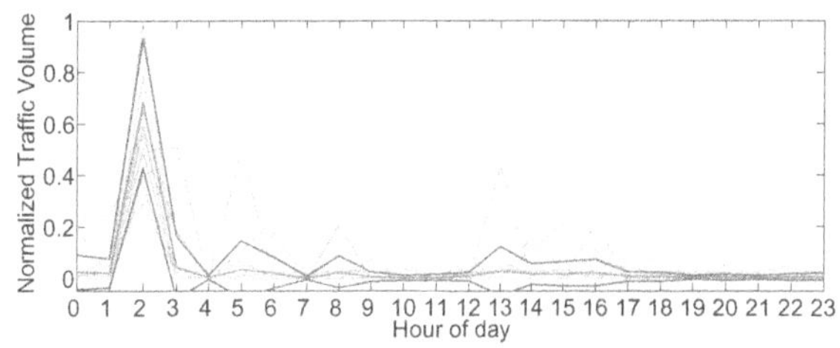

(c) An outlier cluster

Figure 6: Cluster centroids identified using individual device traffic time series.

Table 2: Composition of individual device time series clusters.

	Diurnal %	Flat %	Outlier %
Asset	**16.9**	15.7	4.8
Building	11.8	**19.1**	15.7
Fleet	**57.1**	47.5	44.6
Modem	8.3	11.1	**12.0**
Metering	2.3	3.8	**9.6**
Telehealth	3.6	2.8	**13.3**

5. SESSION ANALYSIS

We now analyze and compare session-level traffic characteristics of M2M devices and smartphones. Understanding session duration and inter-arrival distribution is a time honored tradition for the telecommunication industry because they are important inputs for network resource planning and management. Such information is valuable for cellular network operators too because device active time corresponds more closely to radio resource usage than aggregate traffic volume [17]. Moreover, being able to accurately estimate session timing parameters not only improves radio resource use efficiency for cellular operators, it also helps M2M service providers to better design their devices and protocols for better battery management.

Towards this end, we first formally define a session and then study different metrics based on session-level information. A flow consists of all packets in a given transport layer connection, including TCP and UDP. To study characteristics of flows at a given time resolution, we need to define equally-spaced time bins denoted by Δ_i where $i = 1, 2, ...$ and $|\Delta|$ denotes the magnitude of time bin and i is the index variable. Recall from Section 2 that the smallest available time resolution in our traffic trace is 5 minutes; therefore, we use $|\Delta| = 5$ minutes for the rest of this section. We look at flow arrivals in 5 minute time bins as a binary random process, which is denoted by $\{F_t : t \in T, F \in \{0, 1\}\}$ and where 0 and 1 respectively denote absence or presence of flow arrival, respectively. We now define a session as a run of flow arrivals in consecutive time bins, where a flow spanning multiple time bins is marked for all time bins during its span. A session is denoted by $S_{\{t_x(i), t_y(i)\}}$, where $t_x(i)$ and $t_y(i)$ are the times corresponding to the first flow arrival and the last flow arrival of i-th session. In the following text, we separately investigate several metrics that capture diverse characteristics of the session arrival process.

Active Time: The first metric that we study is device active time, denoted by T_{active}, which is the total amount of time in our week-long trace when a device has traffic. In our study, it is calculated by multiplying number of unique time bins in which we have at least one flow arrival by the bin duration. Using this metric, we are primarily interested in studying the impact of devices on the network in terms of radio channel occupation. Note that a given time bin may have multiple flow arrivals but they are all mapped to 1. Mathematically, active time is defined as:

$$T_{active} = \sum_{\forall t \in T} F_t \text{ (counts)} = \sum_{\forall t \in T} F_t * |\Delta| \text{ (time units)}.$$

In Figure 7(a), we plot the CDFs of active time for smartphones and all M2M categories defined in Section 2. The x-axis represents active time, which ranges from a minimum of $|\Delta| = 5$ minutes to a maximum of one week (*i.e.* the duration of trace collection). We first observe significant diversity in active time of devices of smartphone and all M2M categories. Our second observation is that smartphones tend to have significantly more active time compared to all M2M device categories. The median active time for smartphones is approximately 2 days, which is approximately 30% of the total trace time duration. It is important to note that active time cannot be accurately related to the interaction time of users with smartphones because of the following two reasons. First, users can interact with smartphone without actually generating network traffic, *e.g.* playing offline games. Second, some applications may generate background traffic when the user may not be actually interacting with the smartphone. We also observe diversity in the distributions of active time across M2M device categories. Modem and asset tracking categories, with high aggregate traffic volume per device, have the largest active time values among all categories. It is noteworthy that the fleet category, despite small aggregate traffic volume per device, have above average active time values. This observation suggests that fleet devices tend to generate well spread out traffic across different time bins. We have also verified this conjecture from the data. Finally, telehealth and metering devices have the smallest active time among all M2M device categories.

Average Session Length: Another important metric that we study is called average session length L_{avg}, which is defined as the average count of consecutive time bins with flow arrivals. Mathematically, for a device with n sessions L_{avg} is defined as:

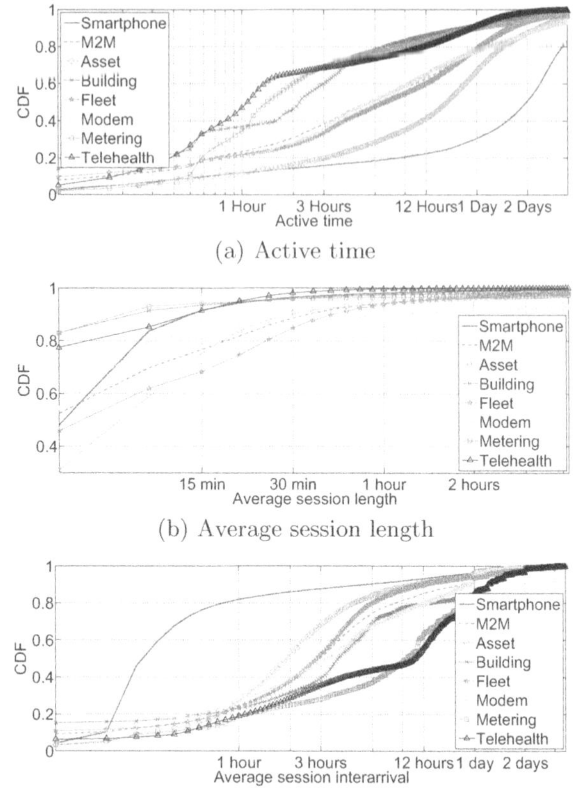

(a) Active time

(b) Average session length

(c) Average session inter-arrival time

Figure 7: CDFs of active time, average session length, and session inter-arrival.

$$L_{avg} = \sum_{i=1}^{n} \frac{t_y(i) - t_x(i) + 1}{n}.$$

Note that session lengths are potentially inflated because session timeouts may be missed due to the coarse measurement granularity. Figure 7(b) shows the CDFs of average session length for M2M devices and smartphones. We note that a significant chunk of devices for all categories have average session lengths smaller than or equal to 5 minutes (left most points). However, remaining devices do have average session lengths significantly larger than the minimum value. For instance, 10% devices of modem category have average session lengths larger than one hour, which reflects the way these devices operate. It is also interesting to note that smartphones typically have significantly smaller average session lengths compared to asset tracking, fleet, and modem categories. Among M2M categories, telehealth, metering, and building security have the smallest average session lengths.

Average Session Inter-arrival: We also study the average session inter-arrival metric, which is defined as the average of inter-arrival times between consecutive sessions. Using the earlier notion, we can mathematically define average session inter-arrival T_{avg} as follows:

$$T_{avg} = \sum_{i=1}^{n-1} \frac{t_x(i+1) - t_y(i)}{n-1}.$$

Figure 7(c) shows the CDFs of average session inter-arrival for smartphone and M2M categories. We observe an approximately opposite trend as compared to active time and average session length for M2M device categories. For instance, metering and telehealth categories, with relatively small active time and average session lengths, have relatively large average session inter-arrival time with median values of approximately 9 hours. On the other hand, asset tracking and fleet categories have relatively relatively small average session inter-arrival time with median values of less than 3 hours. Smartphones tend to have even smaller average session inter-arrival time, where approximately 80% of devices have less than one hour average session inter-arrival time.

Summary: Once again, M2M traffic sessions exhibit rather different characteristics from smartphone traffic sessions. Overall M2M devices are active for traffic for much less time than smartphones. M2M traffic sessions occur much less frequently. It is especially worth noting that 3 out of 6 M2M categories have about 80% of the devices with average session time lasting less than 5 minutes. This indicates that byte volume of data traffic for these devices is likely not an accurate reflection of their network resource use due to disproportional amount of control plane overhead for establishing and tearing down short sessions. The large differences between different M2M categories also advocate for differentiated radio resource control configurations for different categories.

6. MOBILITY

In this section, we study and compare the mobility characteristics and geographical distribution of M2M devices and smartphones. Mobility patterns for different devices, constructed from our nation-wide trace, helps establishing an understanding for how much they move. Understanding mobility patterns for different devices has a direct impact on network resource planning. More importantly, we are interested in investigating how the locations of M2M device population are distributed relative to those of smartphones. Previously in Section 4, we have discovered that M2M traffic volume peaks overlap with those of smartphones in time. Here we investigate whether they also overlap in space.

It is important to note that cell identifiers derived from information collected within the core network are not considered an accurate approximation for device location. This is because many low-level radio access network operations such as handoffs of mobile devices between cells are not exposed to the core network. However, we consider such inaccuracy acceptable for three reasons. First, Xu *et al.* reported that although cell-sector information collected from the core network is not exact for the purpose of being used as device location, the median error is < 1 kilometer [25]. Second, we do not use the locations of the cell tower to proximate user device locations. We simply count the number of unique cells a device is involved with. Finally, the scope of our study covers the whole United States, compared to which cell-level errors at kilometer scale are rather minor.

Device Mobility: Figure 8 shows the CDFs of unique cells for different M2M device categories and smartphones. We observe that devices of M2M categories appear across less unique cells compared to smartphone devices, with the exception of asset tracking category. This is expected because asset tracking devices are typically connected to automotive vehicles for transportation of goods. We also note that while we might intuitively believe that asset tracking and fleet devices are more mobile than the average smartphone, our results show that the difference is insubstantial. Furthermore, as expected, we observe that building security and metering devices appear across the least number of unique cells.

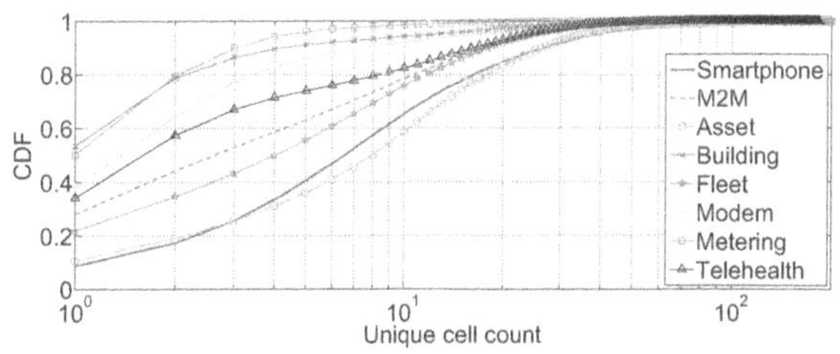

Figure 8: CDFs of unique cells for smartphone and M2M categories.

Geographical Distribution: We now investigate the geographical distribution of M2M traffic. Towards this end, we first plot the Voronoi diagrams for traffic volume of cell-level aggregated M2M and smartphone traffic in Figure 9. The geographical region shown in this figure covers more than 1 million square kilometers, spanning multiple states in the United States. Note that the cells in the Voronoi diagram cover varying geographical areas and their colors represent the traffic volume. The clusters of cells covering small geographical areas appear around major population centers. From the perspective of network operators, we are interested in identifying locations with highest traffic volume for smartphones and M2M devices and how closely located they are. Furthermore, we want to identify geographical dependencies among the locations with highest traffic volume for M2M devices and smartphones. The three possible types of geographical dependencies between two sets of locations are: attraction, repulsion, and independence. Attraction or repulsion between two sets of location respectively indicate correlation or anti-correlation, whereas independence indicates no correlation at all.

A well-known method to characterize geographical dependency between two sets of points is based on the nearest neighbor statistics [6]. Specifically, for two sets of points i and j, we can define $G_{ij}(h)$ as the probability that the distance from a randomly selected point i to the nearest event j is less then or equal to h. Likewise, we can define $F_j(h)$ as the probability that the nearest point j to a random point is less then or equal to h. If the two sets of points are geographically independent then $G_{ij}(h) = F_j(h)$. Given i and j respectively point to the top-10% locations for M2M and smartphone traffic in terms of traffic volume, Figure 10(a) plots G_{ij} (Smartphone-M2M) and F_j (Point-M2M) for varying values of h. A theoretical Poisson line is also plotted for reference, which indicates the expected pattern if both sets of points are independently distributed as homogeneous Poisson processes. We observe that both G_{ij} and F_j significantly depart from the theoretical Poisson line and they are also not close to each other. This observation indicates that the point sets i and j do not follow homogeneous Poisson distribution and are also not independently distributed of each other. The question remains if the point sets show attraction or repulsion to each other. This question is also addressed by the relative positioning of G_{ij} and F_j lines, where G_{ij} line rises above F_j. This pattern shows that we have more than expected high volume M2M locations nearest to high volume smartphone locations. This indicates that these point sets are attracted to each other.

Another well-known method to study the geographical dependency of two point sets i and j, called cross-L, is based on Ripley's cross-K function [6]. It is denoted by $\hat{L}_{ij}(h) - h$ and is defined as:

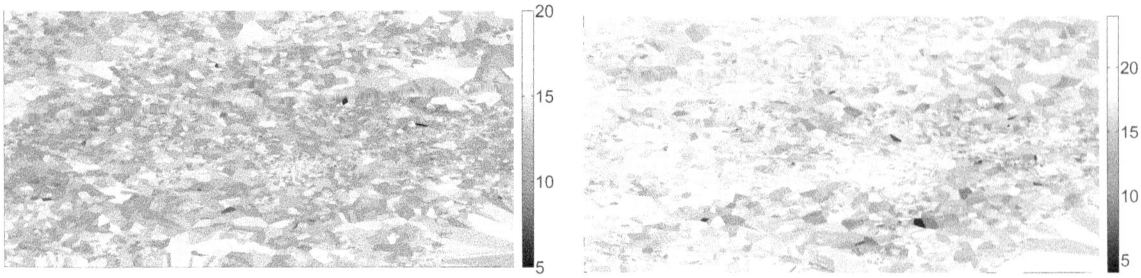

(a) Aggregate M2M (b) Smartphone

Figure 9: Geographical distribution of aggregate M2M and Smartphone traffic volume.

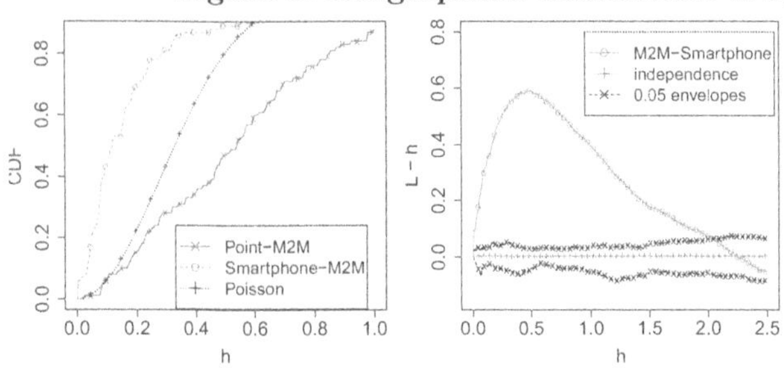

(a) Nearest Neighbor (b) Cross-L

Figure 10: Point pattern interaction analysis for high volume M2M and Smartphone cell locations.

$$\hat{L}_{ij}(h) - h = \sqrt{\frac{\hat{K}_{ij}(h)}{\pi}} - h,$$

where $\hat{K}_{ij}$ is the empirical Ripley's cross-K function and h denotes the distance. The empirical Ripley's cross-K function is defined as:

$$\hat{K}_{ij} = E(\#\text{ type } j \text{ points} \leq h \text{ from an arbitrary } i \text{ point})/\lambda_j.$$

Here λ_j is the average intensity of point set j and $E(.)$ is the expectation operator. Positive and negative values of $\hat{L}_{ij}(h) - h$ respectively indicate attraction and repulsion between two point sets. The co-independence is indicated if the $\hat{L}_{ij}(h) - h$ remains between the estimated confidence envelope lines for co-independent homogeneous Poisson processes. This method overcomes one limitation of the nearest neighbor analysis that it is not restricted to only considering the closest points. However, it is also limited because it gives us the average impression of all points in the data set and may overlook small-scale local dependencies. Figure 10(b) shows the plot of $\hat{L}_{ij}(h) - h$ for varying values of h. We again observe a significant attraction pattern between high volume M2M and smartphone traffic locations. The above-mentioned two sets of experiments jointly provide a strong evidence that high volume M2M and smartphone traffic locations are attracted to each other.

Summary: Most M2M devices are more likely to remain within a smaller geographical area compared to smartphones, with the exception of asset tracking devices. On the other hand, the geographical distribution of M2M device population, especially those with high traffic volume, exhibits "attraction" to high volume smartphone devices. In other words, the information provided by the analysis of mobility characteristics of M2M devices is mixed for network operators. While M2M devices are less mobile, which suggests that service optimization is easier to conduct because it only involves a small area, the co-location of high volume M2M devices with smartphone devices brings more chance for congestion in such areas.

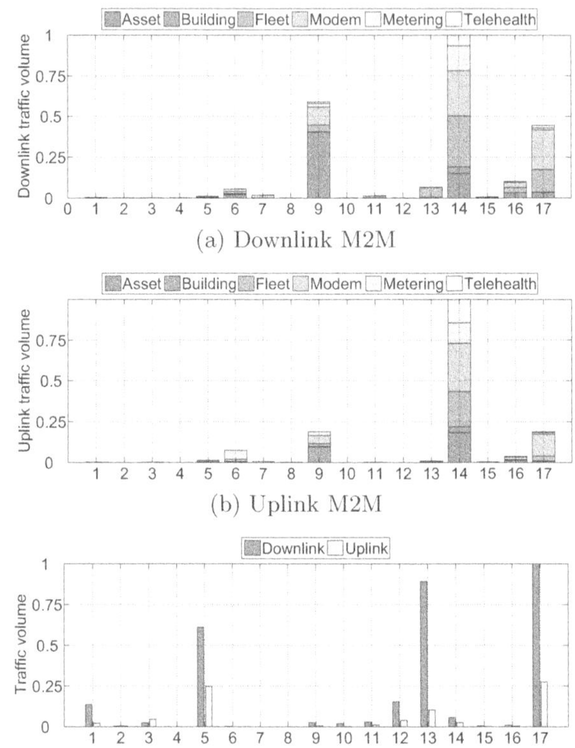

(a) Downlink M2M

(b) Uplink M2M

(c) Smartphone

Figure 11: Traffic application distributions of M2M device categories and smartphone. The application indices along x-axis are: (1) `appstore`, (2) `jabber`, (3) `mms`, (4) `navigation`, (5) `email`, (6) `ftp`, (7) `gaming`, (8) `im`, (9) `miscellaneous`, (10) `optimization`, (11) `p2p`, (12) `apps`, (13) `streaming`, (14) `unknown`, (15) `voip`, (16) `vpn`, and (17) `web`.

7. APPLICATION USAGE

So far in this study we have treated all data bits equally, simply all as "traffic volume". However, the truth is that not all bits are equal. For example, a bit that is part of an 8-bit encoding of a temperature reading has higher information density than a bit in an image of a thermometer that displays the temperature. In this section, we make an attempt for looking into how M2M devices use data traffic by finding out the applications that M2M data traffic belong to.

Recall from Section 2 that traffic records in our data set are tagged with application identifiers. These identifiers cover traffic of 17 different application realms, including HTTP, email (POP, IMAP, *etc.*), and all common video streaming protocols (HTTP streaming, flash, *etc.*), all of which make up the majority of smartphone traffic volume.

Using this application classification, we can compute application distribution of traffic volume for M2M device categories. We observe that most of the flows, up to 95%, in our logged trace use TCP. This observation is in accordance with the findings reported in prior literature [12, 16]. We provide the averaged uplink and downlink application distribution of traffic volume for M2M device categories in Figure 11. To first average a device category, we take the ratio of the sum of traffic volume of all devices and the total number of devices. We then normalize the averaged traffic application volumes by their maximum value. Figures 11(a) and (b) show that the traffic of all device categories mostly belongs to unknown or miscellaneous realms. This indicates that M2M devices typically use custom protocols that are either not identified by our application classification methodology, mentioned in Section 2, or they use atypical protocols.

It is interesting to compare application distribution of M2M traffic with that of smartphone traffic shown in Figure 11(c). As expected, smartphone traffic mostly belongs to web browsing, audio and video streaming, and email applications. This is in sharp contrast to what we have observed for M2M traffic. Another interesting aspect for Figure 11 is that M2M traffic has approximately similar uplink and downlink traffic volume for most categories and applications while smartphones have more downlink traffic volume than uplink traffic volume across all applications. This result echoes what we discovered in Sections 3 and 4, yet with details along one more dimension – applications.

Summary: M2M devices mostly use non-standard application protocols. This makes it more difficult for network operators to mitigate adverse effects from these protocols compared to the standard ones such as HTTP. Towards this end, better standardization of M2M protocols would certainly be a mutually beneficial solution for both M2M application service providers and cellular network operators.

8. NETWORK PERFORMANCE

We now characterize the network performance of M2M traffic. We examine network performance in terms of round trip time (RTT) and packet loss ratio, both of which provide us unique perspectives of network performance.

Round Trip Time: RTT is an important metric for network performance evaluation and is a key performance indicator that quantifies delay in cellular networks. The RTT metric is especially important for M2M applications that are real-time critical. It is important to note that RTT measurements can be potentially biased by differences in the paths between different cellular devices and the external servers they communicate with. For this study, we only have RTT measurements for TCP flows, which are estimated by the time duration between the trace collecting apparatus seeing a SYN packet and its corresponding ACK packet in the TCP handshake. Figure 12(a) shows the CDFs of the median RTTs experienced by each device for smartphones and all M2M device categories. We observe that all M2M device categories experience larger RTT compared to smartphones. Furthermore, within M2M device categories, telehealth devices have smaller RTT than all other categories. Our manual investigation of hardware specifications showed that smartphones and telehealth devices are mostly equipped with 3G modems, in contrast to other categories that typically rely on 2G modems. 2G RTTs are larger due to longer delays on the air interface, which explains these observations.

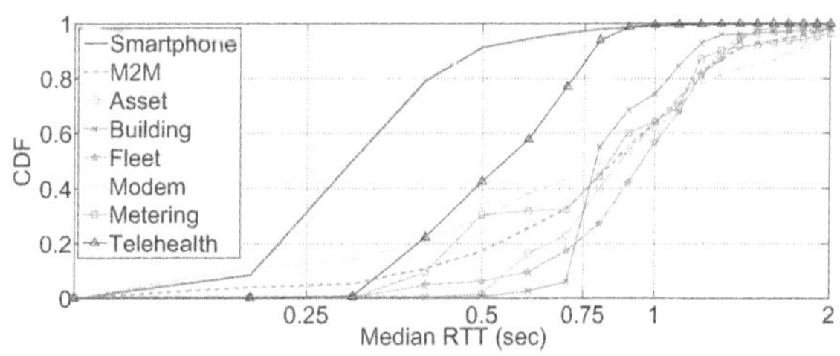

(a) Round trip time

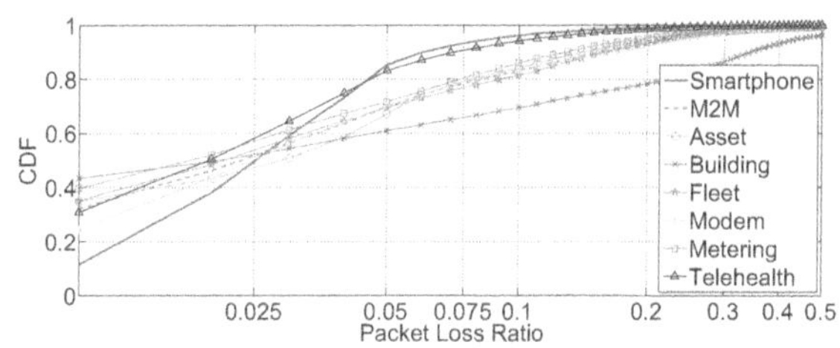

(b) Packet loss ratio

Figure 12: CDFs of round trip time and packet loss ratio.

Packet Loss Ratio: Packet loss ratio is a key performance indicator metric that quantifies reliability in cellular networks. We estimate the packet loss ratio as the ratio of observed TCP payload bytes to the observed TCP sequence number range, summed over all TCP flows. Since most packet loss occurs in the radio access network (RAN) and our measurement point is in between the RAN and the Internet, this metric effectively estimates the downlink packet loss ratio. Figure 12(b) shows the CDFs of packet loss ratio for smartphones and all M2M device categories. Similar to the CDFs of RTT shown in Figure 12(a), we observe differences for packet loss ratio distribution in terms of third and fourth quartile values, where smartphones and telehealth devices experience at least an order of magnitude lower loss ratios than other M2M device categories due to a larger ratio of 3G to 2G modems. We also observe that building security devices have much higher third and fourth quartile loss ratios than other M2M devices, despite using similar technologies. This may be due to the placement of these devices indoors where the signal quality is poorer.

Summary: M2M traffic's network performance also differs from that of smartphones. The RTT of M2M traffic is significantly larger than smartphone traffic. Careful inspection of the hardware specifications of M2M devices reveals that M2M devices generally fall behind smartphones in choice of cellular technology. A majority of M2M devices still use 2G technologies such as GPRS and EDGE. Although 2G technologies are often adequate for M2M communication in terms of data rates, such lagging does present a challenge for cellular operators because they would need to maintain older generation services, instead of repurposing 2G spectrum for newer technologies of higher spectral efficiency. M2M traffic also generally has higher packet loss ratios. This is probably due to poor deployment location choices for which the likely reasons are application specific location requirements or the lack of user interface that clearly displays cellular signal strength.

9. RELATED WORK

To our best knowledge, this paper presents the first study on characterizing M2M traffic patterns. Prior related work only focuses on characterizing general Internet traffic in cellular networks. Due to lack of space, we briefly describe only prominent related work below.

General Smartphone Usage: Falaki *et al.* conducted a measurement study of smartphone usage [11]. They collected data from smartphones of 255 users with only Android and Windows Mobile platforms. The results of their experimental studies indicate significant diversity among smartphone usage of different users. In contrast to this work on smartphone activities, our work focuses on M2M data traffic analysis as seen by the cellular network. Furthermore, the scale of our study, in terms of the number of unique device models, is several orders of magnitude larger.

Smartphone Apps: In [24], Xu *et al.* characterized usage patterns of smartphone apps in a 3G cellular network. They observed that different types of apps had different diurnal and mobility patterns. Similarly, we observe different diurnal and mobility patterns for different M2M device models. In contrast to their study, we find that most M2M applications use custom protocols that are not identifiable using the traffic classification technique used in [24]. Thus, M2M traffic is a disjoint set of traffic from smartphone app traffic.

Cellular Devices: In [18], Shafiq *et al.* studied the temporal dynamics and distribution of applications in Internet traffic of cellular devices. The authors only studied characteristics of 3 cellular device families in their measurement analysis, whereas we study characteristics of more than 150 M2M device models. Furthermore, we additionally explore Internet traffic dynamics of M2M devices along the dimensions of mobility, network performance, and session-level analysis.

Mobility and Network Performance: In another recent related work, Tso *et al.* evaluated network performance of users in different mobility scenarios in a cellular network [22]. They collected network performance data for 4 laptops, 4 modems, and 4 smartphones. Similar to our analysis, they also studied the network performance metrics such as round trip time and loss rate. In contrast to this work on network performance in different mobility scenarios, our work focuses on large scale characterization of traffic from more than 150 M2M device models.

10. CONCLUSIONS

This paper presents the first attempt to characterize M2M traffic in cellular data networks. Our study was based on a week long traffic trace collected from a major cellular service provider's core network in the United States. In our analysis, we compared M2M and smartphone traffic in several aspects including temporal traffic patterns, device mobility, application usage, and network performance. We found that although M2M devices have different traffic patterns from smartphones, they are generally competing with smartphones for shared network resources. Our findings presented in this paper have important implications on cellular network design, management, and optimization. Through better understanding of M2M traffic, cellular service providers can improve resource allocation mechanisms and develop better billing strategies for different categories of M2M devices. The methodology developed in this paper for M2M traffic analysis is generic and can also be deployed for more general cellular traffic analyses.

Acknowledgements

We thank our shepherd, Anirban Mahanti, and the anonymous reviewers for their useful feedback on this paper.

11. REFERENCES

[1] AT&T specialty vertical devices. www.rfwel.com/support/hw-support/ATT_Specialty VerticalDevices.pdf.

[2] *Evolved Cellular Network Planning and Optimization for UMTS and LTE.*

[3] 3G machine-to-machine (M2M) communications: Cellular 3G, WiMAX, and municipal Wi-Fi for M2M applications. Technical report, ABIresearch, 2007.

[4] The global wireless M2M market. Technical report, Berg Insight, December 2010.

[5] Cisco visual networking index: Global mobile data traffic forecast update, 2011-2016. White Paper, 2012.

[6] R. S. Bivand, E. J. Pebesma, and V. Gomez-Rubio. *Applied Spatial Data Analysis with R.* Springer, 2008.

[7] CalAmp. LMU-2600 GPRS fleet tracking unit. http://www.calamp.com/ pdf/LMU-2600.pdf.

[8] P. Chaovalit, A. Gangopadhyay, G. Karabatis, and Z. Chen. Discrete wavelet transform-based time series analysis and mining. *ACM Computing Surveys*, 43(2), 2011.

[9] J. Erman, A. Gerber, M. T. Hajiaghayi, D. Pei, and O. Spatscheck. Network-aware forward caching. In *WWW*, 2009.

[10] Z. M. Fadlullah, M. M. Fouda, N. K. A. Takeuchi, N. Iwasaki, and Y. Nozaki. Toward intelligent machine-to-machine communications in smart grid. *IEEE Communications Magazine*, 49(4):60–65, 2011.

[11] H. Falaki, R. Mahajan, S. Kandula, D. Lymberopoulos, R. Govindan, and D. Estrin. Diversity in smartphone usage. In *MobiSys*, 2010.

[12] A. Gerber, J. Pang, O. Spatscheck, and S. Venkataraman. Speed testing without speed tests: Estimating achievable download speed from passive measurements. In *ACM IMC*, 2010.

[13] N. Grira, M. Crucianu, and N. Boujemaa. Unsupervised and semi-supervised clustering: A brief survey. Report of the MUSCLE European Network of Excellence (FP6), 2004.

[14] L. K. Law, S. V. Krishnamurthy, and M. Faloutsos. Capacity of hybrid cellular-ad hoc data networks. In *INFOCOM*, 2008.

[15] Z. Moczar and S. Molnar. Comparative traffic analysis study of popular applications. In *International Conference on Energy-aware Communications*, 2011.

[16] U. Paul, A. P. Subramanian, M. M. Buddhikot, and S. R. Das. Understanding traffic dynamics in cellular data networks. In *INFOCOM*, 2011.

[17] F. Qian, Z. Wang, A. Gerber, Z. M. Mao, S. Sen, and O. Spatscheck. Characterizing radio resource allocation for 3G networks. In *ACM IMC*, 2010.

[18] M. Z. Shafiq, L. Ji, A. X. Liu, and J. Wang. Characterizing and modeling Internet traffic dynamics of cellular devices. In *ACM SIGMETRICS*, 2011.

[19] P. Stoica and R. L. Moses. *Introduction to Spectral Analysis.* Prentice Hall, 1997.

[20] P. Traynor, M. Lin, M. Ongtang, V. Rao, T. Jaeger, P. McDaniel, and T. L. Porta. On cellular botnets: measuring the impact of malicious devices on a cellular network core. In *ACM CCS*, 2009.

[21] Trilliant. CellReader digital cellular meters. http://www.trilliantinc.com/ products/cellreader/.

[22] F. P. Tso, J. Teng, W. Jia, and D. Xuan. Mobility: A double-edged sword for HSPA networks. In *MobiHoc*, 2010.

[23] I. T. Union. World telecommunication/ICT indicators database 2011. http://www.itu.int/ITU-D/ict/ publications/world/world.html, 2011.

[24] Q. Xu, J. Erman, A. Gerber, Z. M. Mao, J. Pang, and S. Venkataraman. Identifying diverse usage behaviors of smartphone apps. In *ACM IMC*, 2011.

[25] Q. Xu, A. Gerber, Z. M. Mao, and J. Pang. AccuLoc: Practical localization of peformance measurement in 3G networks. In *ACM MobiSys*, 2011.

Bundling Practice in BitTorrent: What, How, and Why

Jinyoung Han
Seoul National University
Seoul, Korea
jyhan@mmlab.snu.ac.kr

Seungbae Kim
KIITC
Daejeon, Korea
sbkim@itc.kaist.ac.kr

Taejoong Chung
Seoul National University
Seoul, Korea
tjchung@mmlab.snu.ac.kr

Ted "Taekyoung" Kwon*
Seoul National University
Seoul, Korea
tkkwon@snu.ac.kr

Hyun-chul Kim*
Sangmyung University
Cheonan, Korea
hkim@smu.ac.kr

Yanghee Choi
Seoul National University
Seoul, Korea
yhchoi@snu.ac.kr

ABSTRACT

We conduct comprehensive measurements on the current practice of content bundling to understand the structural patterns of torrents and the participant behaviors of swarms on one of the largest BitTorrent portals: The Pirate Bay. From the datasets of the 120 K torrents and 14.8 M peers, we investigate what constitutes torrents and how users participate in swarms from the perspective of bundling, across different content categories: Movie, TV, Porn, Music, Application, Game and E-book. In particular, we focus on: (1) how prevalent content bundling is, (2) how and what files are bundled into torrents, (3) what motivates publishers to bundle files, and (4) how peers access the bundled files. We find that over 72% of BitTorrent torrents contain multiple files, which indicates that bundling is widely used for file sharing. We reveal that profit-driven BitTorrent publishers who promote their own web sites for financial gains like advertising tend to prefer to use the bundling. We also observe that most files (94%) in a bundle torrent are selected by users and the bundle torrents are more popular than the single (or non-bundle) ones on average. Overall, there are notable differences in the structural patterns of torrents and swarm characteristics (i) across different content categories and (ii) between single and bundle torrents.

Categories and Subject Descriptors

C.2.4 [**Computer Communication Networks**]: Distributed Systems - *Distributed Applications*

General Terms

Measurement

*Corresponding Authors: Ted "Taekyoung" Kwon (tkkwon@snu.ac.kr) and Hyun-chul Kim (hkim@smu.ac.kr)

Keywords

Peer-to-Peer, BitTorrent, Content Bundling

1. INTRODUCTION

According to Sandvine's report on Global Internet phenomena in Fall 2011, BitTorrent is responsible for a substantial amount of the Internet traffic, representing one-half to one-fifth of all the upstream traffic and one-sixth to one-fifteenth of all the downstream traffic depending on geographical regions during peak period [6]. The huge success of BitTorrent is attributed to the attractive properties of its swarming operations [16, 21, 24]. First, the swarming technique scales well even in the presence of flash crowds for popular files. Second, cooperation among peers in a swarm stimulated by the tit-for-tat incentive mechanism improve the overall system performance like throughput. Third, the tit-for-tat mechanism also addresses the free-riding problem.

This in turn has attracted the research community to investigate BitTorrent's behavior in terms of throughput, fairness and incentive issues, revealing valuable insights into the performance aspects of BitTorrent [15, 16, 21, 24, 27]. However, most of these studies paid little attention to the internal structures of the torrents[1] (e.g., how many files are bundled in a torrent), rendering the following research questions under-appreciated by the research community: *How are torrents structured by human beings, and for what purposes? Are there any differences in the way people participate in the swarms depending on the structures of the torrents?*

We argue that understanding the structural patterns of torrents and the participant behaviors of swarms in BitTorrent with empirically-grounded evidence is important for BitTorrent stakeholders: (i) how BitTorrent service providers deal with bundling to improve the system performance, and (ii) how content providers publish torrents, especially for their financial incentives. Also, understanding and modeling how a BitTorrent-like system works from a socio-economic perspective can be linked to the research efforts in social studies and economics by addressing the following questions: "how, and for what purposes, are constituent files (component goods) bundled/packaged by people (sellers), and how peers (market consumers) respond to them?"

[1] A torrent refers to a single file or multiple files that are downloaded collectively in a swarm. In this paper, a torrent and a swarm are used interchangeably; the former focuses on files, while the latter focuses on users.

To our knowledge, this measurement study is the first attempt to address the aforementioned questions with data from a large-scale BitTorrent system from the perspective of content bundling. Here, bundling [19] is a common strategy in which a publisher packages multiple files into a single torrent, which is disseminated by a single swarm, instead of disseminating individual files via separate swarms. A torrent in BitTorrent can contain either a single file or a bundle of files. If a torrent consists of a bundle of files, BitTorrent allows a user to download an arbitrary subset of the torrent.

Recently, bundling in BitTorrent has gained increasing attention, as it can mitigate the availability problem of unpopular files [18, 19] as well as reduce download times [9, 17–19, 29, 32]. However, despite the increasing interest in content bundling in BitTorrent, there have been few efforts to empirically investigate the practice of content bundling in P2P systems. This leaves researchers uncertain of how to make assumptions on bundling strategies and/or user's accesses to bundles.

This paper seeks to bridge the gap by conducting a large scale measurement on one of the largest BitTorrent portals: The Pirate Bay [5]. We have collected datasets that contain the information on 120,550 torrents, 3,163,685 files, and 14,822,261 users, which are comprehensively analyzed. In particular, we focus on: (1) how prevalent content bundling is, (2) how and what files are bundled into torrents, (3) what motivates publishers to bundle files, and (4) how users access the bundled files.

We highlight the main contributions and key findings of this paper as follows:

1. This is the first comprehensive measurement study on content bundling practice in BitTorrent. We examine the structural patterns of and users' behavior with bundle torrents[2], in comparison to single ones. We also make our developed codes and datasets online at: `http://mmlab.snu.ac.kr/traces/bundling`.

2. We find that over 72% of BitTorrent torrents contain multiple files, which indicates that bundling is prevalent.

3. We reveal that 41% of the bundle torrents consist of multiple independent yet related content files (e.g., different episodes of the same TV show), while the other 59% of the bundle torrents consist of a single main file (e.g., a movie video) and supplementary files (e.g., subtitles).

4. We find that the bundle torrents are more popular (2.1 times) than the single ones on average.

5. We observe that most files (94%) in a bundle torrent are selected by users on average.

6. To answer what motivates publishers to bundle files, we investigate top-20 publishers for each content category in single and bundle torrents, respectively, who contribute roughly 41% of all the torrents in our datasets. We observe that 68% of the bundle torrents are published by profit-driven publishers who seek financial gains, while only 34% of the single torrents are published by profit-driven ones. This signifies that profit-driven publishers tend to adopt the bundling strategy in BitTorrent.

7. Most of our findings lead to the following question, which provides us a socio-economic point of view on BitTorrent publishing: *what are the main incentives of content bundling in BitTorrent? How do users respond?* Our empirically grounded answers are, (i) BitTorrent publishers prefer to upload bundled torrents (72%),(ii) content bundling in BitTorrent is mainly (68%) driven by financial incentives of the publishers, which can be linked to the studies in the economics literature [7, 8, 12, 26, 30], and (iii) bundle torrents are more popular (2.1 times) than the single ones to BitTorrent users.

[2]Throughout this paper, a bundle torrent refers to a torrent which contains multiple files, while a single torrent contains only a single file.

We organize this paper as follows. After reviewing related work in Section 2, we first present the measurement methodology in Section 3. We then show how prevalent bundling is and what files constitute torrents in Section 4. In Section 5, we analyze the characteristics of bundle torrents. We next reveal what motivates publishers to bundle files in Section 6, followed by the analysis of user access patterns in Section 7. After discussing the implications of bundling practice in Section 8, we conclude the paper in Section 9.

2. RELATED WORK

Sharing multiple torrents: Many studies on BitTorrent have focused on the advantages of users participating in multiple torrents simultaneously [11, 13, 20, 22, 31]. Note that they do not differentiate single torrents and bundle torrents. Guo *et al.* found that 85% of users concurrently access multiple torrents [13]. Yang *et al.* [31] proposed an incentive mechanism for users remaining as seeds in a subset of torrents when a user downloads multiple torrents. That is, each user calculates the aggregated download rate in a *cross-torrent* fashion in the peer selection phase, so that a user can get additional credits by participating in another torrent as a seed. Piatek *et al.* [22] also suggested a scheme that propagates peer reputations to encourage users to exchange file pieces across torrents. Sirivianos *et al.* [28] proposed a credit-based incentive scheme to stimulate more cooperation across torrents. Peterson *et al.* [20] proposed a swarm coordination system that optimally allocates the upload bandwidth of seeds among the multiple torrents to optimize the download performance. Dán *et al.* [11] explored the performance benefits achieved by dynamically merging or splitting swarms of the same content file. These studies on how to leverage multiple torrents/swarms pay no attention to whether a torrent has a single file or multiple files. In contrast, we focus on bundling, which allows peers to share multiple files in a single swarm.

Bundling in BitTorrent: Recently, Menasche *et al.* [18, 19] theoretically showed that bundling can mitigate the availability problem by combining multiple unpopular files into a single swarm. Tian *et al.* studied the performance issues in downloading files of a bundle torrent in a concurrent or sequential way with the assumption that files in a bundle torrent are highly interest-correlated [29]. Carlsson *et al.* [9] proposed a dynamic bundling strategy in which peers are assigned to download complementary contents (files or parts of files) at the time they decide to download a particular file.

Based on the dynamic bundling strategy, Zhang *et al.* [32] designed and implemented a system that can support dynamic bundling in practice. Lev-tov *et al.* [17] proposed a dynamic file selection and download strategy (among files contained in a bundle torrent) to reduce download times, where they assumed that each peer is interested in downloading only a small subset of the bundled files. While these studies were looking at potential benefits that may arise from bundling, our focus is to empirically study the current practice of bundling in BitTorrent.

Incentives of content publishing in BitTorrent: Recently, Cuevas *et al.* [10] studied the incentives of content publishing in BitTorrent from a socio-economic viewpoint, by categorizing publishers into profit-driven, altruistic, and fake ones. Here, we investigate what kind of contents are published depending on the three publisher types, and how many torrents are contributed by each publisher type from the perspective of bundling.

Bundling in economics: Product bundling is a common marketing strategy. In the economics literature, bundling strategies have been proposed as a mechanism to increase sales, extend monopoly power, and smooth demands across multiple goods [7, 12, 26, 30]. This strategy is very common in almost every business; e.g., in the cable television industry (e.g., many TV channels are often combined into a single package), in the music industry where multiple songs are combined into a single album, and in the fast food industry in which multiple foods are packaged into a combo meal. Furthermore, the bundling strategy is also widely used to promote a main product by adding supplementary items (e.g., the "free gift with purchase" concept [25] in the cosmetic industry, or a software package that contains a main software and everything it needs to operate in the software industry [23]). For the information goods that have almost zero cost to be replicated, bundling is a useful strategy to increase sales as well [8]. To distribute files as information goods, BitTorrent already supports bundling. This is the first comprehensive measurement study on the current practice of bundling in the BitTorrent ecosystem.

3. METHODOLOGY

We conduct a measurement study on one of the largest BitTorrent portal, The Pirate Bay (TPB) [5], one of the most popular torrent hosting sites. For the purpose of data collection, we developed a BitTorrent monitoring agent to keep track of each swarm by modifying the Azureus [3] client software. We also developed a torrent crawling agent to timely fetch newly released ".torrent" files by using an RSS feed[3] from TPB. (We can fetch all the published torrents by using the RSS feeds from TPB.)

Figure 1 illustrates the overall measurement framework. An RSS notification of a new torrent triggers our crawling agent to immediately retrieve its publisher's username and to request the .torrent file. By analyzing the .torrent file, the monitoring agents contact trackers through the BitTorrent Tracker protocol [2] to retrieve the lists of peers. The monitoring agents also leverage the Peer EXchange (PEX) protocol [4] to discover more peers not found via the trackers.

[3]TPB offers an RSS feed to announce a newly published torrent. The RSS feed provides information such as content category, content size, and publisher's username for the new torrent.

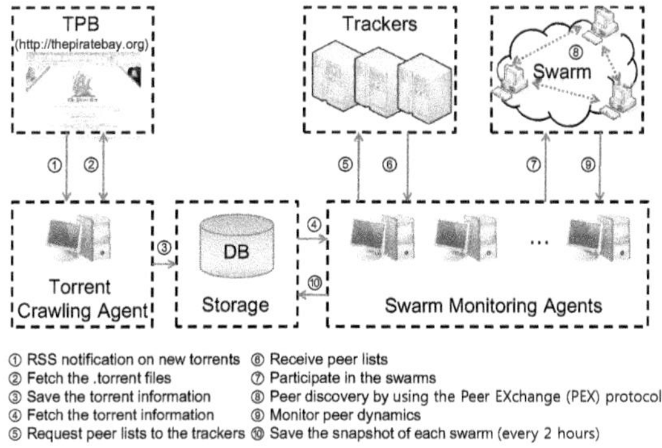

Figure 1: Measurement framework.

After finding the peers in each swarm, the monitoring agents begin monitoring each swarm. In this way, we periodically (once every two hours) obtain the snapshot of each swarm by exploiting trackers and peers. That is, the *swarm datasets* record which pieces of the file(s) are being downloaded by each peer in the swarm at the moment. For each torrent, the *torrent datasets* consist of its .torrent information, category given at TPB, publisher's username, and published time.

3.1 Torrent Datasets

Our torrent datasets have been collected for 77 days from February 14 to May 1, 2011. The crawling agent fetched torrent data of 120,550 torrents from TPB[4], which contains 3,163,685 files whose total volume is around 120 TB. Throughout this paper, we investigate the bundling practice of the seven major (91% and 90% in terms of the torrent counts and data volume, respectively) content categories given by TPB: Movie, TV, Porn, Music, Application, Game and E-book. The percentage of each category in terms of the number of torrents and the volume of torrents is shown in Table 1. The other torrents belonging to unknown or marginal categories are not considered in this paper.

Table 1: Percentage of the number of (1st row) and the total volume of (2nd row) torrents in each category

Movie	TV	Porn	Music	App	Game	E-book
31%	18%	15%	11%	8%	5%	3%
42%	18%	13%	4%	4%	9%	1%

3.2 Swarm Datasets

For the torrents discovered between March 25 and April 26, we have periodically (once every two hours) captured swarm snapshots, to investigate access pattern of peers participating in the swarms. We restrict the swarm dataset collection and analysis to those of the torrents collected between March 25 and April 26, due to the performance limitations of our monitoring facilities, which consist of 14 desktop PCs (admittedly research-grade). Consequently, we have captured swarm snapshots of 43,837 torrents, in which 14,822,261 peers were exchanging 1,301,354 files.

[4]The average number of daily published torrents in TPB is around 1.6 K.

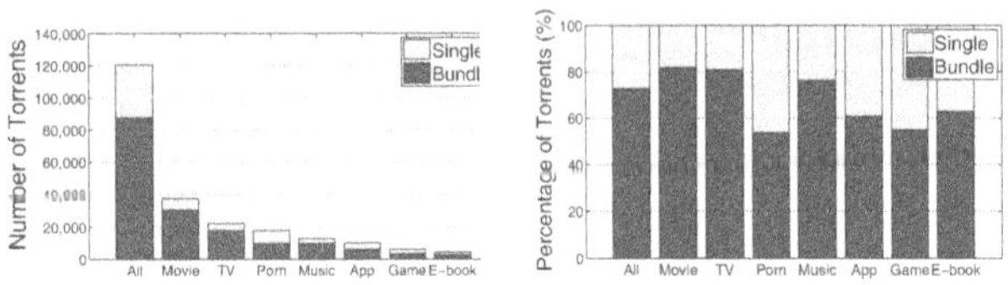

(a) The numbers of single and bundle torrents.

(b) Percentage of torrents counts of single and multi torrents.

Figure 2: Bundling is widely used in BitTorrent.

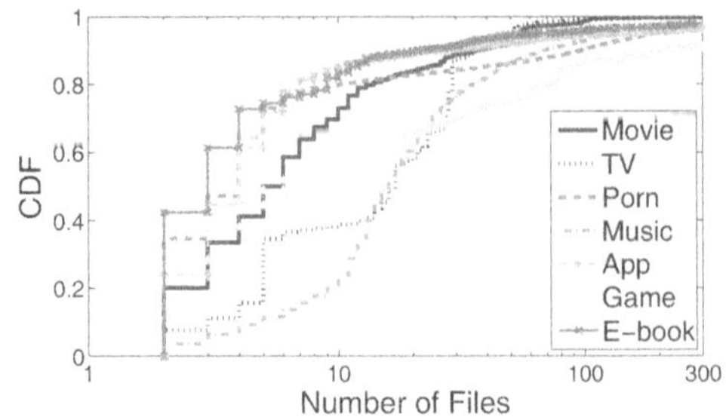

Figure 4: Number of files in a bundle torrent.

Notice that the torrent dataset is used in Sections 4, 5, and 6 for investigating bundling patterns from the perspective of publishers, while the swarm dataset is used in Section 7 for investigating the bundling patterns and user access patterns together from the perspectives of publishers and users.

4. SINGLE VS. BUNDLE

In this section, we seek to answer the following questions: (1) to what extent content bundling is prevalent in BitTorrent, and (2) how and what files are bundled into torrents, particularly in terms of the number, volume, and types of files. Note that we focus on the comparison between single and bundle torrents in this analysis. Recall that the torrent datasets of 120,550 torrents are used here.

4.1 Bundling is widespread

To analyze how prevalent content bundling is in BitTorrent, we compare bundle torrents with single ones in terms of the number of torrents and the volume of torrents. Note that the volume of torrents is the total size of files of the given torrents. Figure 2 shows that over 72% of the torrents contain multiple files, which means content bundling is widely used. In the Music category, around 80% of the torrents use bundling, which indicates that BitTorrent users often share a collection of music files from the same genre, player, composer, or album. Likewise, over 80% of the torrents in the Movie category use bundling, mostly because users often package: (i) multiple movie files of the same series (e.g., sequels), or (ii) a main video file and other supplementary files like subtitles. Meanwhile, around 60% of the torrents in the Application and Game categories contain multiple files (e.g., installation files and subsidiary files such as how-to documents), while the other torrents (40%) have a single installation file.

We next compare the volume of single and bundle torrents in Figure 3. The average size of a bundle torrent (1.2 GB on average) is approximately twice as large as that of a single one (0.6 GB on average) as shown in Figure 3(a). In the Movie category, the average size of a bundle torrent (1.4 GB) is not so higher than that of a single one (1.2 GB), while the average size of a bundle torrent in the other categories is significantly higher (mostly more than 2 times) than that of a single one. This is because a Movie bundle torrent usually consists of a large video file with smaller supplementary files like subtitles, to be detailed in Section 5. Figures 3(b) and 3(c) show that the volume of bundle torrents outweighs that of single ones; the volume of bundle torrents across the seven categories accounts for over 80% of the volume of total torrents that we investigated. The volume of all the torrents reaches around 120 TB.

4.2 How files are bundled

In this subsection, we investigate the number of files and their file extensions (e.g., avi, jpg, mp3) in single and bundle torrents to understand the internal structures of the torrents. Our torrent dataset consists of 120,550 torrents, which contain 3,163,685 files with 5,538 different file extensions. Among them, the total number of files contained in 87,430 bundle torrents is 3,130,565; i.e., 36 files per bundle torrent on average.

The number of files in a bundle torrent: Figure 4 shows the CDF of the number of files in a bundle torrent across different categories of torrents. As shown in Figure 4, bundle torrents of the Music category contain significantly more files than those of the other categories; around 80% of Music bundle torrents contain more than 10 files. In contrast, 73% of E-book bundle torrents contain 4 files or less. Around 70% of TV bundle torrents contain 5 to 30 files because users often package and share the series of the same TV drama (e.g., 22 episodes of "*Gossip Girl*" season-3 or 24 episodes of "*24*" season-4). Note that in the Porn bundle torrents, around 80% contain 7 files or less, while over 10% contain 100 files or more.

File extension analysis: Table 2 shows the top 3 file extensions in the single and bundle torrents, respectively. In the Movie category, although the number of .avi files in bundle torrents is placed third, the volume of the .avi files ranks top. Note that the file extension .txt ranking second in the Movie bundle torrents is often used for promoting web sites to be discussed in Section 6. In the Porn category, around 92% of files contained in bundle torrents are with .jpg extension, which means publishers of those files often bundle a lot of pornographic pictures into a torrent. However, video files account for more than 90% of the total volume of all files contained in the Porn bundle torrents, since the size of video files are much larger than that of images. Notice that most of the top 3 file extensions in terms of the number and the volume of files in the single torrents in the Movie, TV, and Porn categories are those of video files. The bias toward the video files in these three categories is also significant in the bundle torrents when we look at the volume percentages of file extensions in Table 2. In the Music and E-book categories, .mp3 files and .pdf files are dominant in terms of both number and volume, respectively. Interestingly, the .avi file extension ranks second in terms of volume in Music single torrents, which are music-video files. In the Application and Game categories, there are numerous file extensions; however, the volume of .exe, .iso, and .rar files is dominant. Note that most of the high rank file types are

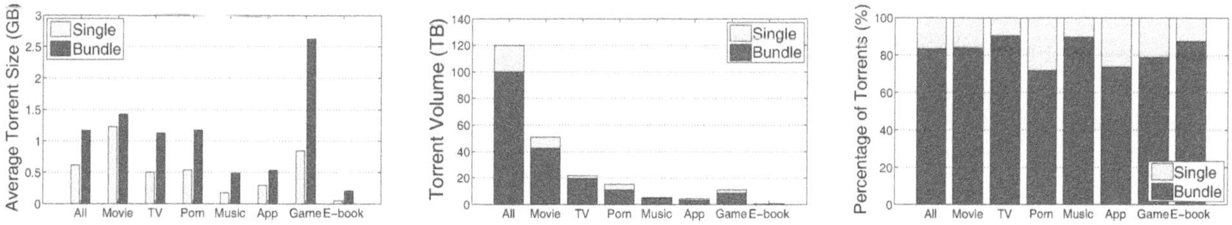

(a) Average torrent size in each category.

(b) Total volume of single and bundle torrents in each category.

(c) Percentage of the volume of single and bundle torrents in each category.

Figure 3: Volume of bundle torrents is substantially larger than that of the single ones.

Table 2: Top 3 file extensions in single (S) and bundle (B) torrents in terms of number and volume, repectively

Type		S-Rank1(%)	S-Rank2(%)	S-Rank3(%)	B-Rank1(%)	B-Rank2(%)	B-Rank3(%)
All	Number	avi(32)	rar(14)	wmv(14)	jpg(24)	mp3(12)	rar(10)
	Volume	avi(37)	wmv(15)	rar(11)	avi(36)	rar(14)	vob(9)
Movie	Number	avi(68)	rar(9)	mkv(8)	rar(30)	txt(11)	avi(9)
	Volume	avi(61)	wmv(14)	iso(8)	avi(41)	vob(15)	rar(14)
TV	Number	avi(65)	mkv(16)	mp4(13)	rar(47)	avi(11)	txt(8)
	Volume	avi(52)	mkv(26)	mp4(13)	avi(46)	rar(19)	mkv(16)
Porn	Number	wmv(49)	avi(21)	mp4(15)	jpg(92)	avi(2)	wmv(2)
	Volume	wmv(53)	mp4(19)	avi(19)	avi(49)	wmv(31)	mp4(7)
Music	Number	mp3(59)	avi(15)	mp4(9)	mp3(77)	jpg(6)	wma(3)
	Volume	mp3(24)	avi(17)	iso(15)	mp3(47)	vob(27)	avi(5)
App	Number	rar(45)	exe(22)	zip(17)	wav(5)	jpg(5)	exe(4)
	Volume	rar(39)	iso(35)	zip(8)	iso(39)	rar(12)	exe(10)
Game	Number	rar(46)	exe(21)	zip(13)	wav(11)	png(5)	rar(3)
	Volume	rar(48)	iso(27)	exe(10)	rar(24)	iso(16)	mpq(5)
E-book	Number	pdf(70)	rar(14)	zip(5)	pdf(28)	jpg(18)	doc(7)
	Volume	pdf(50)	rar(22)	zip(14)	pdf(63)	rar(11)	djvu(5)

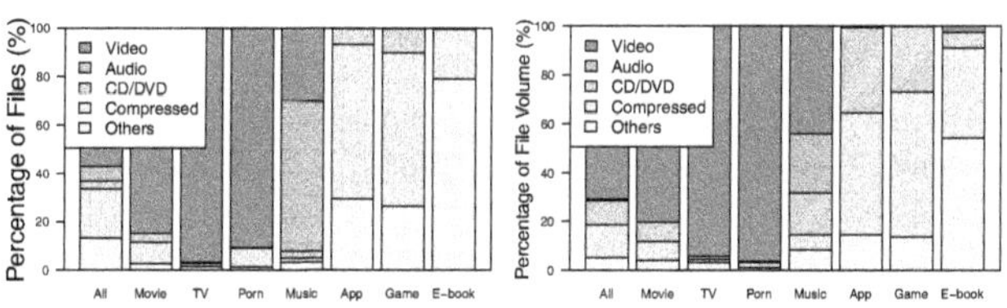

(a) Percentage of the number of file types in single torrents.

(b) Percentage of the volume of file types in single torrents.

Figure 5: Percentage of file types for single torrents in terms of number and volume.

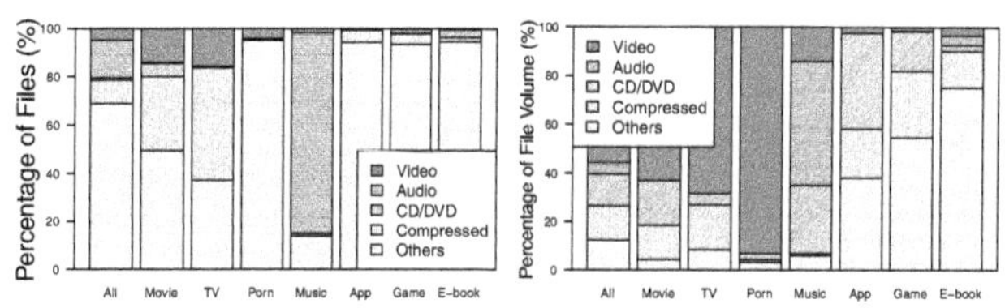

(a) Percentage of the number of file types in bundle torrents.

(b) Percentage of the volume of file types in bundle torrents.

Figure 6: Percentage of file types for bundle torrents in terms of number and volume.

linked to the main files of the torrents to be discussed in Section 5.

Video, audio, cd/dvd, and compressed files analysis: From the above results, we note that video, audio, cd/dvd, and compressed files are major file types constituting torrents. Thus, we plot the percentage of the numbers and volume of the file types in single and bundle torrents in Figures 5 and 6, respectively. Notice that we consider compressed files as single files and do not investigate what files are contained in the compressed files because it is not easy to identify what files are contained in the compressed files until we actually download them, which might be illegal. As shown in Figures 5 and 6, the numbers of compressed files account for approximately 20% and 10% across all the categories of the single and bundle torrents, respectively. In the Application and Game categories, notice that over 60% of the single torrents in terms of number are compressed mainly for installation purposes. Along the same line, the volume of cd/dvd images is substantial in both single and bundle torrents. Figures 5(b) and 6(b) show that the volume of video files accounts for over 70% in the single torrents but less than 60% in the bundle ones. The number and volume of video files are dominant in the Movie, TV, and Porn categories in the single torrents. However, the number and volume of video files in Movie and TV categories in the bundle torrents show a less portion than those in the single torrents. Note that the number of video files in Porn bundle torrents shows a small portion compared to that of video files in single ones because porn publishers often bundle a lot of pornographic pictures into a torrent. Interestingly, (music) video files account for around 45% of the total volume of all files in the Music single torrents.

5. MAIN FILE ANALYSIS IN BUNDLING

In this section, we investigate how many *"main files"* are included in each bundle torrent. Here a main file is the primary media file in a torrent; other supplementary files in the torrent are not counted as main files. For example, an .avi file in a Movie torrent or an .mp3 file in a Music torrent is the main file. Note that there may be multiple main files in a torrent; if a publisher bundles two episodes of a TV drama, there are two main files in the torrent.

5.1 Identifying Main Files

When we identify main files, we first consider the torrent categories and file extensions as shown in Table 3. In addition, we examine file names to further refine our identification; for instance, a file whose name contains special keywords such as "sample" or "trailer" is excluded.

We then count the number of main files in each torrent. A torrent containing k main files is denoted by "bundle-k." Bundle-k ($k > 1$) can be linked to a bundling strategy that packages multiple products into a single combined product. On the other hand, bundle-1 can be linked to another bundling strategy that promotes a main product by adding supplementary items (e.g., the "free gift with purchase" concept [25] in the cosmetic industry). As mentioned earlier, we exclude torrents with the compressed files. We also exclude the torrents in the Game and Application categories because it is difficult to identify their main files. Note that a bundle-1 torrent contains a main file with other supplementary files, while a single torrent has only a single file.

Table 3: File extensions identified as main files in five categories

Category	File extensions
Movie	avi, wmv, mkv, mp4, vob, mpg, mov, ...
Porn	jpg, avi, asf, wmv, mpg, mkv, gif, ...
TV	avi, mkv, mp4, mpg, mov, m4v, wmv, ...
Music	mp3, m4a, wma, flac, m3u, mp4, wav, ...
E-book	pdf, epub, mobi, dvju, ps, ...

5.2 Constituents of Bundle-k

Bundle-1 versus bundle-k: Figure 7 shows the percentage of bundle-1 and bundle-k ($k > 1$) torrents in all the bundle torrents in terms of the number and volume of torrents. As shown in Figure 7(a), the bundle-1 torrents account for 59% across all the categories, which means users often use a torrent to share only a single main file. However, in the Music category, around 92% of the torrents have multiple music files, which means a Music bundle torrent is mostly used to offer several music files as one combined product like a single music album. The number of bundle-1 torrents in the Movie category accounts for around 88% of that of all the Movie bundle torrents, which indicates that users often

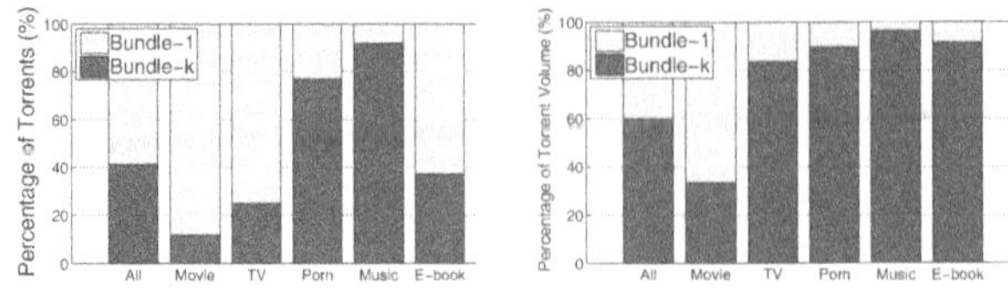

(a) Percentage of numbers of bundle-1 and bundle-k (k>1) torrents.
(b) Percentage of volume of bundle-1 and bundle-k (k>1) torrents.

Figure 7: Comparison between bundle-1 and bundle-k (k>1) torrents.

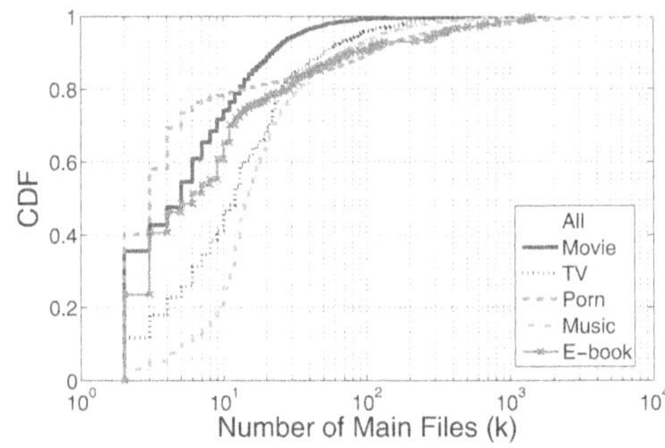

Figure 8: CDF of bundle-k torrents (k>1).

share a single movie file with supplementary files such as subtitles. Figure 7(b) shows that the volume of bundle-k ($k > 1$) is around 60% on average. Note that the volume of bundle-k ($k > 1$) torrents in the TV category accounts for around 83% of that of all the TV bundle torrents even though the number of bundle-k ($k > 1$) torrents is less than 25%. This is because users often bundle a large number of episodes into a bundle-k ($k > 1$) torrent in the TV category.

The number of main files in a bundle-k (k>1): To analyze how many main files are included in a bundle torrent depending on the categories, we plot the CDF of bundle-k ($k > 1$) in Figure 8. Porn torrents exhibit interesting phenomena; 40% of torrents have two main files (mostly video files), and 11% of the torrents have 100 main files or more (mostly image files), which explains the heavy tail distribution. E-book torrents have a similar but weak pattern to the Porn ones; 24% of torrents contain only two main files and 9% of torrents have 100 main files or more. In the Movie category, around 74% of torrents have 10 main files or less, which reflects that a movie series normally has less than 10 episodes. On the other hand, 60% of the TV torrents have 10 episodes or more since a TV series typically consists of more than 10 episodes. Similarly, the number of main files in a Music torrent falls between 10 and 100 with 74% probability.

A torrent size versus the number of main files in a bundle-k: To analyze the correlation between the torrent size and the number of main files (i.e., k of bundle-k) in a torrent, we adopt Pearson's correlation coefficient [14], denoted by ρ. Figure 9 shows the torrent sizes of bundle-k torrents as k increases. The ρ values of the Movie, TV, Porn, Music, and E-book categories are 0.372, 0.746, 0.056, 0.434, and 0.501, respectively. Except for Porn category, a positive correlation between the torrent size and the number of main

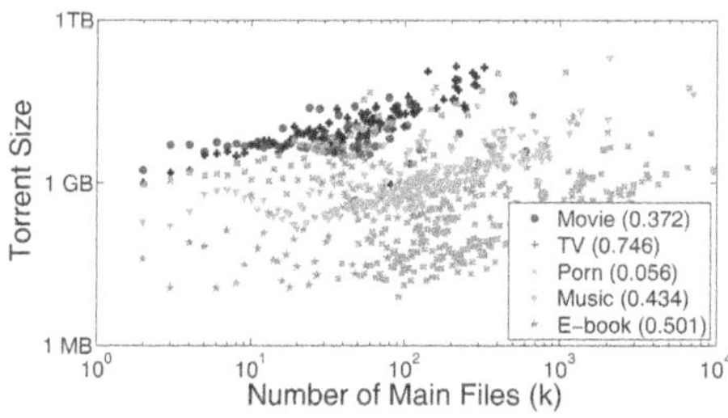

Figure 9: The torrent size and k is highly correlated in all the categories except for Porn.

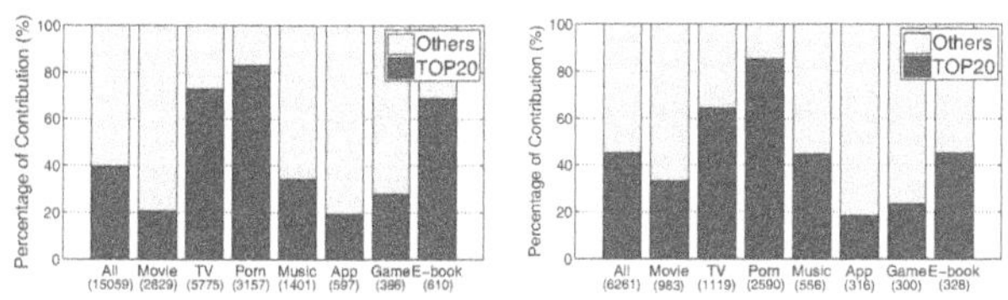

(a) Percentage of the number of torrents of the top-20 publishers and the others in single torrents.

(b) Percentage of the number of torrents of the top-20 publishers and the others in bundle torrents.

Figure 10: Top-20 publishers contribute a significant number of torrents depending on each content category. The numbers below each category indicates the number of torrents published by the top-20 publishers.

files is found in all the categories. Especially, the correlation is relatively stronger in the TV, Music, and E-book categories because files are typically of the similar size; e.g., an avi file of a TV drama is around 700 MB, an mp3 file of a song is around 10 MB, and a pdf file of an E-book is around 2 MB. The correlation in the Movie category is somewhat weaker since the sizes of .vob files vary diversely according to their included functions like DVD menu or captions. Note that there is a negligible correlation in the Porn category because pictures and videos are two major disparate elements, which are mixed into a torrent without any regular pattern.

6. PUBLISHER ANALYSIS

In this section, we study publishers in BitTorrent from a socio-economic point of view by unravelling who publishes bundle or single torrents and why. To this end, we first divide publishers into three types based on the purposes of content publishing [10]: (1) *fake* publishers who publish fake contents, (2) *profit-driven* publishers who usually promote their own web sites for financial gains like advertising, and (3) *altruistic* publishers. We also investigate the level of contribution (i.e., the number of published torrents) of publishers in each type and whether and how they publish torrents across multiple content categories.

6.1 Classifying Publishers

Fake publishers publish "fake" contents. They often inject malware into files or make garbage files with catchy titles (e.g., recently released popular movies such as "The Green Hornet" or "Black Swan" as of April, 2011) or intriguing titles (e.g., adult movies); these publishers appear to be malicious users to disseminate malware or be associated with antipiracy agencies to hinder the distribution of copyrighted content [10]. The administrators of TPB remove the accounts of publishers and their published torrents on TPB when they are reported as fake publishers from other users.

Profit-driven publishers publish contents for financial incentives. They often promote one or more web sites with financial incentives [10]. Profit-driven publishers usually use major BitTorrent portals such as TPB as a platform to advertise their profitable web sites (e.g., BitTorrent portals that are associated with private trackers or adult sites) to users. For this purpose, they publish popular torrents where they attach URLs of their web sites in various manners: (i) textbox in the web page associated with each published content, (ii) title of a text file (mostly .txt, .nfo, and .html files), (iii) title of a .torrent file, and (iv) title of a main file.

Altruistic publishers publish contents only for sharing. They neither promote any web site nor distribute fake contents.

In order to systematically classify publishers, we take following steps:

1. **Checking publisher's account:** We first check whether the account of each publisher is removed from TPB or not after the observation period. If the account is removed and their associated torrents uploaded by the publisher are not available on TPB, we conclude the publisher is a fake one. We double check the account of the publisher in the Suprbay forum[5] where users report fake publishers on TPB.

2. **Checking web pages:** When the account is available, we next examine the textbox in the web page associated with each published torrents. If there are any URLs on the textbox, we identify them as profit-driven publishers.

3. **Checking files:** We then examine whether any file in a torrent has a URL information to be advertised. If so, we classify them as profit-driven publishers. We also investigate the titles of torrents. If there are any URLs to advertise specific web sites or private trackers embedded in the titles, the publishers are classified as profit-driven ones.

4. The remaining publishers are classified as altruistic publishers because they do not seem to promote any URL nor upload fake contents.

6.2 Contribution of Top-20 Publishers

Using the above methodology, we classify the top-20 publishers in terms of the number of published torrents for each content category in single and bundle torrents, respectively, into three publisher types. There would be total $20 \times 7 \times 2$ (= 280) publishers; however there are total 242 publishers since some publishers are overlapping. Although the top-20 publishers in the single torrents account only for 2.7%, 7.0%, 9.6%, 4.6%, 1.8%, 2.6%, and 6.7% of the total number of publishers in the Movie, TV, Porn, Music, Application, Game, and E-book categories, respectively, they contribute a substantial portion of torrents as shown in Figure 10(a). Likewise, the top-20 publishers in the bundle torrents account only for 1.0%, 3.2%, 9.7%, 1.7%, 1.4%, 2.6%, and 10.5% of the total number of publishers in the Movie, TV,

[5]https://forum.suprbay.org

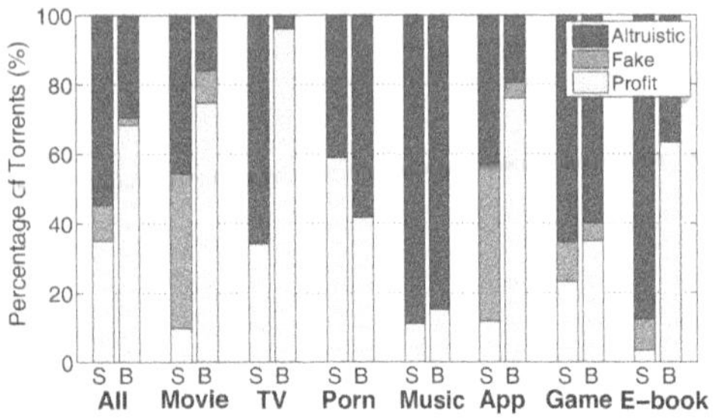

Figure 11: Percentage of the number of torrent of each publisher type in single (S) and bundle (B) torrents.

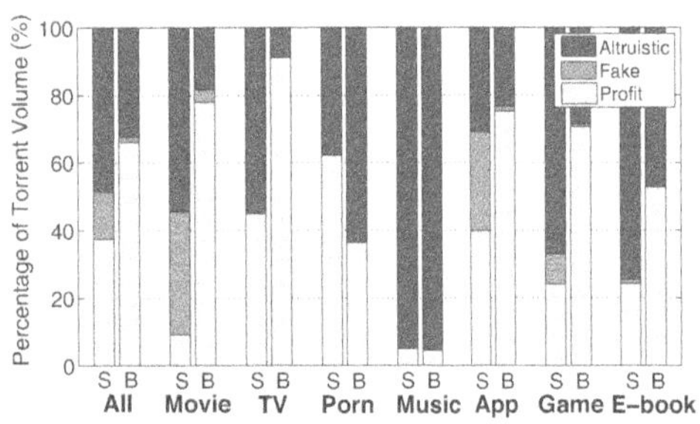

Figure 12: Percentage of the volume of torrent of each publisher type in single (S) and bundle (B) torrents.

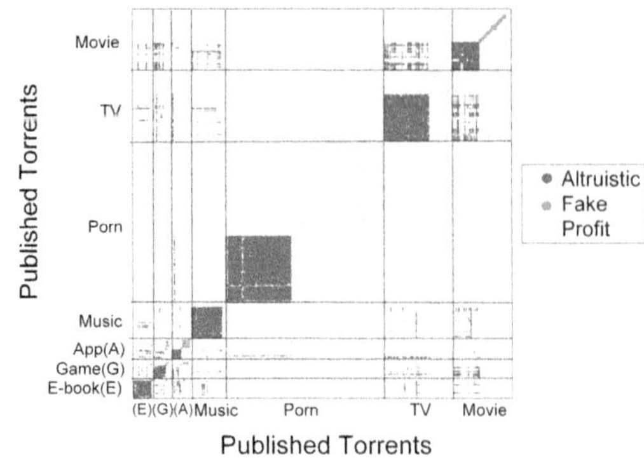

Figure 13: Cross-category publishing of each publisher in single torrents.

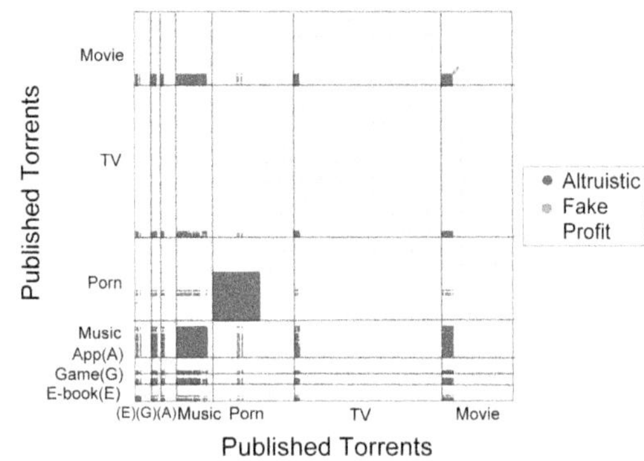

Figure 14: Cross-category publishing of each publisher in bundle torrents.

Porn, Music, Application, Game, and E-book categories, respectively, but they contribute a significant portion of torrents as well as shown in Figure 10(b). Note that the top-20 publishers in the bundle torrents contribute around 73%, 83%, and 69% of all the bundle torrents in the TV, Porn and E-book categories, respectively. Overall, the top-20 publishers across the seven categories contribute roughly 41% of all the single and bundle torrents in our torrent datasets.

Figures 11 and 12 show the percentage of contribution for each publisher type in terms of number and volume of all the torrents, respectively. Interestingly, the contribution of the profit-driven publishers is significant (around 68%) in bundle torrents while the contribution of the profit-driven publishers in single torrents accounts only for around 34%; profit-driven publishers tend to prefer to upload the bundle torrents. Especially, the percentage of the number of torrents of the profit-driven publishers is higher in the Movie (75%), TV (96%), Application (76%), and E-book (63%) categories. This is because profit-driven publishers often use the additional text files such as .txt, .nfo, and .html files to promote their web sites. When we look at the bundle torrents of profit-driven publishers only, the numbers of .txt files account for 11%, 9%, 11%, and 16% of the files in the bundle torrents in these four categories, respectively. Note that .txt file extension of the bundle torrents ranks third (5%) in terms of the number of file extensions across seven categories. However, the torrents in the Porn category exhibit a different pattern; the percentage of contribution of profit-driven publishers in single torrents is higher than the one in bundle torrents since they usually use the textbox in the web pages to advertise their URLs instead of using additional text files.

Fake publishers exhibit also interesting patterns. As shown in Figures 11 and 12, the percentage of their contribution in single torrents is higher than the one in the bundle torrents; they tend to prefer to upload single torrents. This is because fake publishers have no reason to bundle additional text files; they just inject "fake" files instead of original files. Note that the contribution of the fake publishers (especially in the single torrents) in the Movie and Application categories is higher than the ones in the others since they try to hinder the distribution of copyrighted movie contents and to disseminate malware, respectively. We also find that file extensions published by fake publishers are mostly .avi, .rar, and .exe files. This is because fake publishers try to attract users by .avi movie files with catchy titles in Movie torrents or infect users by .exe executable files in Application torrents. Also .rar files are widely used to hide their fake contents both in the Movie and Application categories.

In summary, we show that a significant amount (68%) of bundling is done by profit-driven publishers. From this result, we conclude that bundling in BitTorrent is mainly driven by financial considerations, which can be linked to the bundling in economics [7,12,26,30]. In other words, the publishers who have financial considerations often adopt the bundling strategy in BitTorrent. Later, we will investigate how users respond to the bundling practices in Section 7.

6.3 Cross-category Publishing of Top-20 Publishers

In this subsection, we examine whether and how the top-20 publishers publish torrents across multiple content cat-

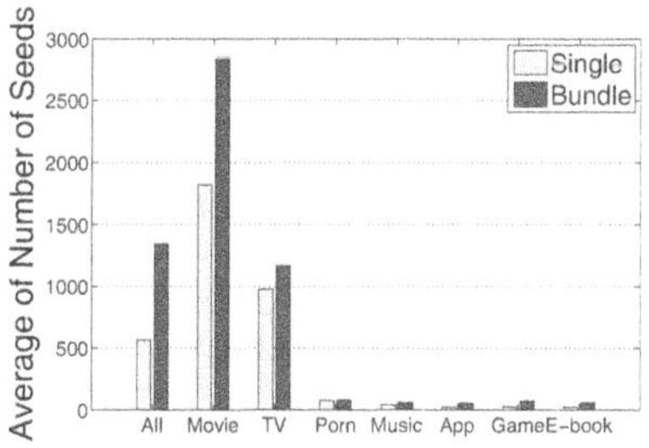

(a) Average of peak number of seeds over all the swarms

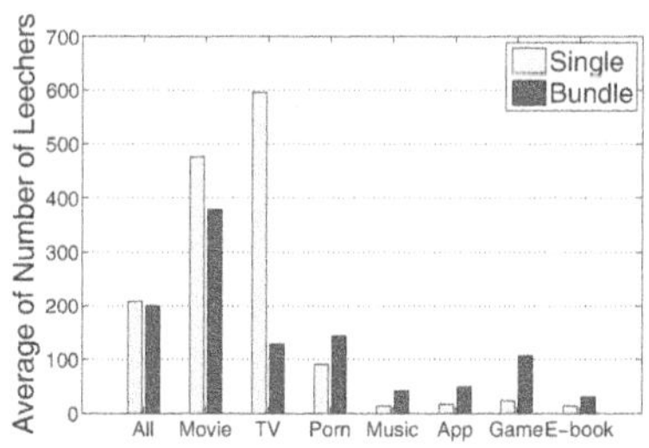

(b) Average of peak number of leechers over all the swarms

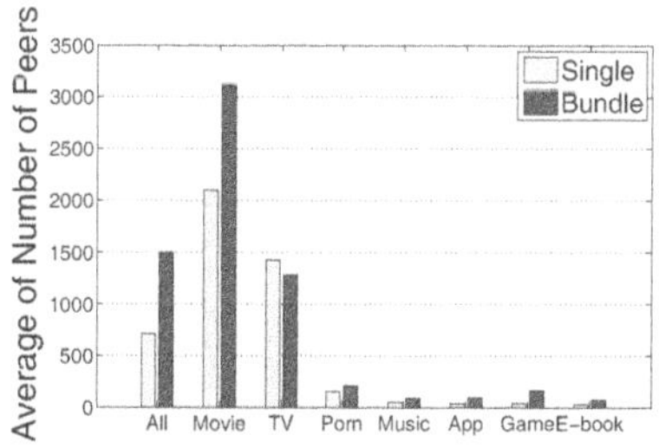

(c) Average of peak number of peers over all the swarms

Figure 15: Bundle swarms are more popular than single ones on average.

egories in single and bundle torrents, respectively. To this end, we examine the number of published torrents across the different content categories in our torrent datasets.

Figures 13 and 14 show whether a publisher, who published a torrent in a content category, also publishes another in the other categories. That is, a color pixel at (x, y) represents whether the publisher of torrent x in the horizontal axis also publish torrent y in the vertical axis. We enumerate each torrent according to the seven categories and three publisher types in the horizontal and vertical axes. Figure 14 shows that profit-driven publishers in bundle torrents often publish torrents in other content categories. For example, a profit-driven publisher in the TV category has a strong tendency of publishing torrents in the Porn and Movie categories as well. On the contrary, profit-driven publishers in single torrents mostly publish torrents only in a single category (mostly Porn) as shown in Figure 13 because profit-driven publishers who publish single Porn torrents often use the textbox in the webpage rather than the advertisement text files. Interestingly, altruistic publishers of the single and bundle torrents in the Porn category mostly focus on the Porn category alike while the other altruistic publishers (not in the Porn category) publish torrents across multiple categories. This indicates that altruistic Porn publishers are solely interested in uploading the Porn contents.

7. USER ACCESS PATTERN ANALYSIS

In this section, we address the following questions. Do users prefer to download bundle torrents over single ones? Are bundle torrents more available than single ones in practice? Is there a correlation between the popularity and the number of main files? Do users actually prefer to download all the files in a bundle torrent? To answer these questions, we investigate user access patterns in terms of multiple metrics: (1) popularity is the number of seeds, leechers, and peers (i.e., both seeds and leechers) in a swarm at peak time, (2) area popularity is the summation of the periodically sampled numbers of peers during the swarm's lifetime, (3) availability is the average of the sum of the number of seeds and the fraction of the file(s) in leechers in a swarm during its lifetime [1], (4) seed ratio is the fraction of time with at least one seed available over the swarm's lifetime [19], and (5) file selection ratio is the ratio of the number of files requested by users to the number of all the files in a bundle torrent. Here, a swarm's lifetime is from the moment of the first seed to the moment of the last seed and no seed appears after the moment. As we focus on user behaviors here, single

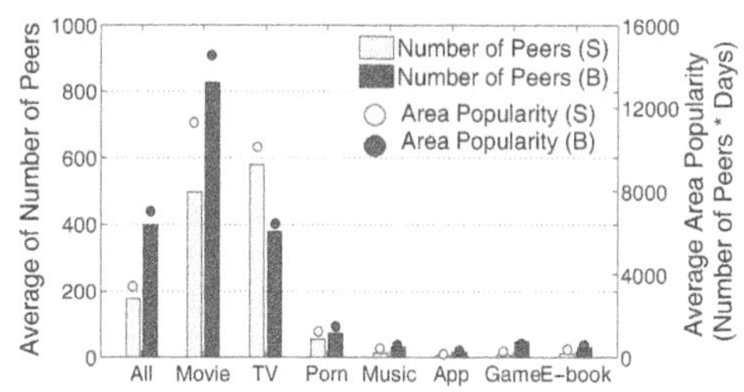

Figure 16: Average of number of peers during swarm's lifetime and average area popularity of single (S) and bundle (B) swarms in each category.

swarms and bundle swarms are mostly used instead of single torrents and bundle torrents, respectively. Note that we use the 33 days' swarm datasets of the 43,837 torrents collected from March 25 to April 26 for this analysis, as explained in Section 3.2.

7.1 Popularity Analysis

We first measure the popularity of the single and bundle swarms in terms of the number of seeds, leechers, and peers (i.e., both seeds and leechers) at peak time in Figure 15. Figure 15(a) shows the average of the peak number of seeds of all the swarms in each category. Notice that the average of the seed popularity of bundle swarms is around 2.4 times as large as that of the single ones. In other words, the bundle swarms are likely to be more available, and hence support faster download. Note that the average of the seed popularity in Movie bundle swarms reaches almost 3000. Figure 15(b) shows the average of the peak number of leechers of all the swarms in each category. Notice that the averages of the leecher popularity of single swarms in the Movie and TV categories are higher than those of bundle swarms. Interestingly, the average of the leecher popularity of the TV single swarms is 4.7 times as large as that of the TV bundle ones. This is due to the timing-sensitive nature of the TV drama; a single torrent containing a new episode aired this week is usually much more popular than a bundle torrent containing multiple old episodes of the same TV drama. On the other hand, the average of the leecher popularity of single swarms in the other categories (except for TV and Movie) is smaller than that of bundle ones. Finally, Figure 15(c) shows that the average of the peer popularity of bundle swarms is 2.1 times larger than that of the single ones.

Additionally, we estimate the "*Area Popularity*" which

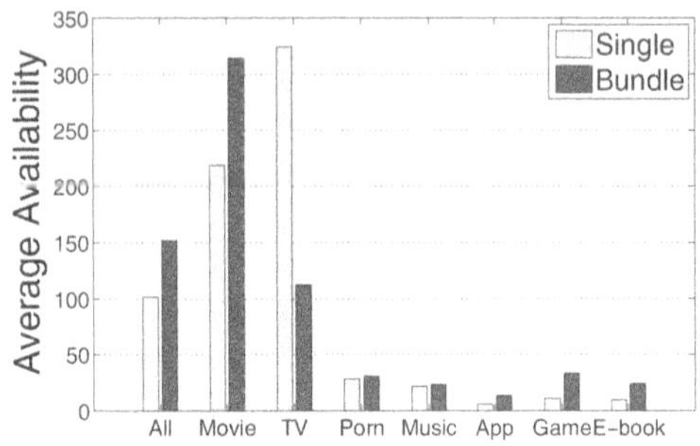

Figure 17: Average of availability of single and bundle swarms in each category.

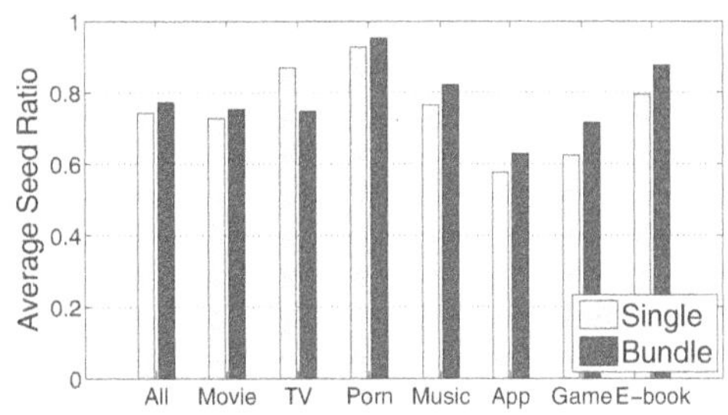

Figure 18: Average of seed ratio of single and bundle swarms in each category.

reflects not only the instantaneous popularity but also the popularity over time. The *Area Popularity* of swarm s can be calculated as follows:

$$Area\ Popularity\ (s) = \sum_{lifetime\ of\ s} P(s,t)$$

where $P(s,t)$ is the periodically measured number of peers in swarm s at time t. Figure 16 shows that the average of number of peers during swarm's lifetime and area popularity in bundle swarms are larger than those in single ones across all the categories except for TV, which is consistent with Figure 15(c).

7.2 Availability Analysis

We then analyze the availability of single and bundle swarms. While some studies (e.g., [19]) define the availability as the existence of seeds, our definition also accounts for the union of file pieces that leechers have in a swarm. For example, if there are two seeds and the portion of pieces of leechers in a swarm is 75% of the whole content file(s), the availability is 2.75. Many BitTorrent clients also use this definition [1]. Figure 17 shows that the bundle swarms are mostly more available than the single ones except for TV, which is in line with the average of number of peers during swarm's lifetime in Figure 16.

Finally, we show the seed ratio, the fraction of time with at least one seed available over the swarm's lifetime [19] in Figure 18. The seed ratio of the bundle swarms is slightly higher than that of the single ones across all the categories except for TV, which is somewhat in line with Figure 17. Interestingly, the seed ratio of the Porn category is significantly high (around 0.95).

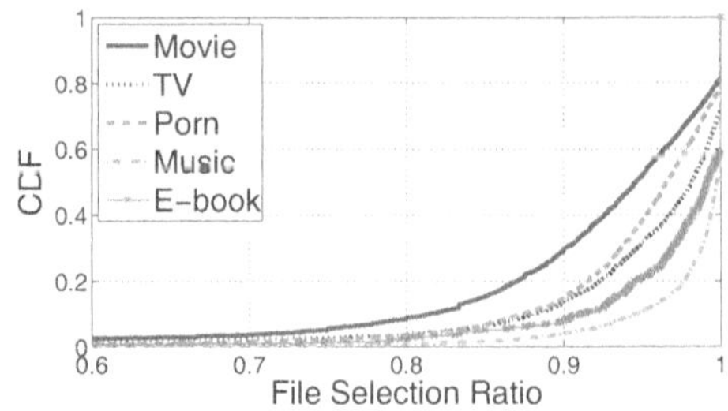

Figure 19: Ratio of the number of files requested in a bundle swarm. Over 94% of all the files in a bundle torrent are selected on average.

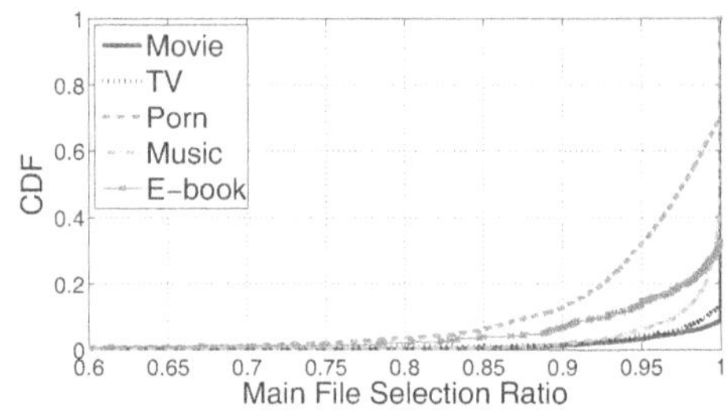

Figure 20: Ratio of the number of main files requested in a bundle swarm. Over 98% of all the main files in a bundle torrent are selected on average.

7.3 The Number of Files Requested by Users in a Bundle Torrent

We next analyze the ratio of the number of files requested by users in a bundle torrent. In the BitTorrent software, users can select any subset of the bundled files. Figures 19 and 20 show the ratio of the numbers of files and main files requested by users to the numbers of all the files and all the main files in a bundle torrent, respectively. As shown in Figure 19, over 94% files in a bundle torrent are selected on average by users. Furthermore, almost every main file (over 98% on average) in a bundle torrent is selected by users in Figure 20. Especially, all the files are selected in 42% of bundle torrents in the Music category. On the other hand, all the files are selected in only 19% of bundle torrents in the Movie category. This is because users often deselect non-main files in Movie bundle torrents. Interestingly, however, all the main files in 91% of Movie bundle torrents are selected by users; users prefer to download all the main video files because they are usually related (e.g., Shrek 1 and Shrek 2). The ratio of the main files requested by users in the Porn category is relatively lower than that in the other categories as shown in Figure 20; (i) main files in the same torrent are often disparate like video and image and (ii) the relation of main files is usually weak. Overall, the selection ratio of the main files is higher than that of all files (i.e., main and non-main files) across all the categories.

7.4 Swarm Behaviors versus Bundle-k

Popularity versus number of main files: We first analyze the correlation between the number of main files (i.e., k in bundle-k) in a torrent and the number of peers in its swarm at peak time. Figure 21 shows the number of peers that access a bundle-k torrent at peak time as k in-

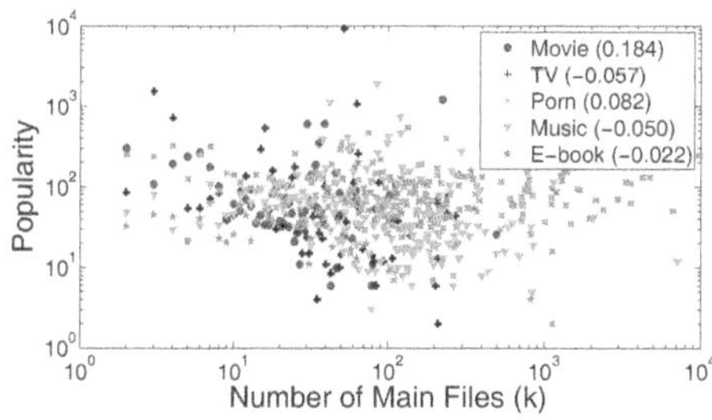

Figure 21: Popularity versus Bundle-k.

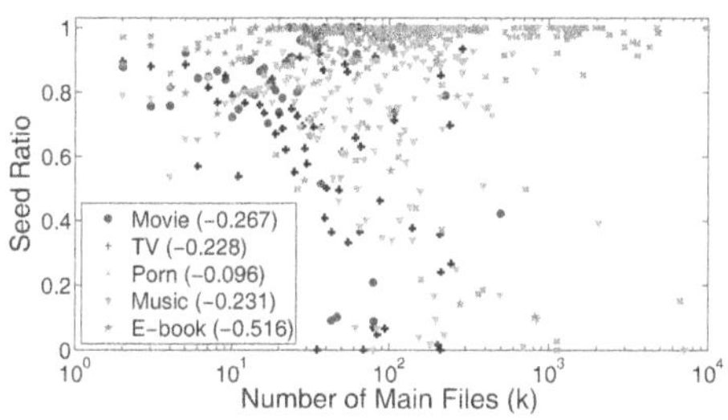

Figure 22: Seed ratio versus Bundle-k.

creases. To quantify the correlation, we again calculate the Pearson's correlation coefficient ρ. As shown in Figure 21, the ρ values of the Movie, TV, Porn, Music, and E-book categories are 0.184, -0.057, 0.082, -0.050, and -0.022, respectively. The correlation in the Movie category is slightly positive since users tend to download a torrent containing multiple episodes of the same movie series. However, k in bundle-k torrents has no strong correlation with the popularity of the torrent across all the categories except for Movie.

Seed ratio versus number of main files: We then analyze the correlation between k and the seed ratio of the swarm. Figure 22 shows the seed ratio as k increases. The ρ values of the Movie, TV, Porn, Music, and E-book categories are -0.267, -0.228, -0.096, -0.231, and -0.516, respectively. Figure 22 is not in line with Figure 21. Overall, there is clear negative correlation between the seed ratio and k except for Porn. This is because seeds may not prefer to stay in the swarm since the seeding overhead worsens as the torrent size increases, which is consistent with Section 5 (See Figure 9). However, there is negligible correlation in the Porn category as well since correlation between the torrent size and k is insignificant as shown in Figure 9.

Main file selection ratio versus number of main files: We finally analyze the correlation between k and the ratio of main files requested by users in a bundle-k torrent. As shown in Figure 23, the ρ values of the Movie, TV, Porn, Music, and E-book categories are -0.002, -0.240, -0.056, -0.398, and -0.478, respectively. Interestingly, there is significant negative correlation in the TV, Music and E-book categories; users prefer not to download all the main files in a bundle-k as k increases, but to download only a small subset of interested main files such as recent TV episodes and personally favorite songs. On the contrary, there is no clear correlation in the Movie category. This is mainly because all the main files are selected by users in 91% of Movie bundle torrents as shown in Figure 20. Note that there is also negligible correlation between the features of Porn torrents and k when we look at Figures 9, 21, 22, and 23. This implies

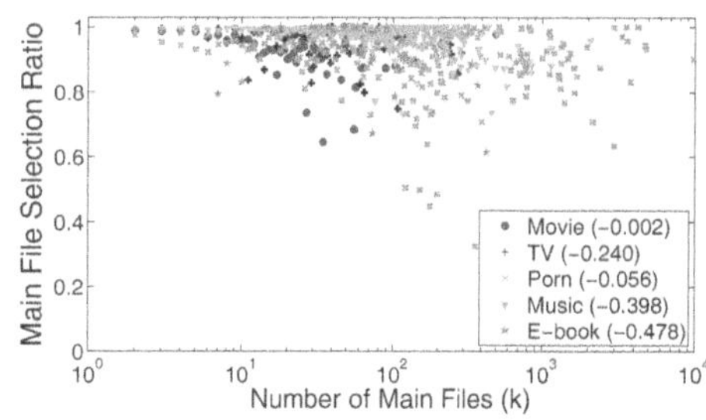

Figure 23: Main file selection ratio versus Bundle-k.

that porn users tend to be indifferent to the number of main files.

8. DISCUSSIONS

This paper is motivated by the following question: *How can we understand bundling in BitTorrent?* Specifically, we investigate the bundling practice in BitTorrent from the following perspective: Are similar patterns to the bundling in economics observed in bundling in BitTorrent? Our empirically grounded answer is that we can observe a similar trend between the bundling in economics [7, 8, 12, 26, 30] and the bundling in BitTorrent: (i) bundling in BitTorrent is mainly (68%) driven by financial considerations, and (ii) current bundling practice in BitTorrent adopts both of the bundling cases: (a) multiple comparable products are combined into a single package, and (b) supplementary items are added to a main product. We believe that the analysis of the bundling practice can give insights to content providers for making their marketing/publishing strategies. For instance, using bundling with additional text files to advertise their profitable web sites can be an advertising business model to the content providers, which is similar to the marketing strategy using leaflets.

Some theoretical studies [9, 17–19, 29] suggest that bundling can improve the content availability and reduce download times. However, to exploit the above advantages in real environment, P2P/BitTorrent service providers need to consider how they effectively constitute bundles and to predict how users participate in the swarms of the bundle. We expect that our empirical analysis of the bundling practice can be a reference for P2P/BitTorrent service providers. For example, a small number of files (say, less than 15) need to be bundled into a torrent in the E-book category if the average seed ratio is required to be over 85% since the seed ratio significantly decreases as the number of main files increases (See Figure 22). Another example is that if a P2P/BitTorrent service provider wants to maintain the main file selection ratio over 98% in the TV category, less than 10 files need to be bundled into a torrent (See Figure 23).

While the bundling strategy is mainly adopted by firms in traditional businesses for increasing sales, e.g., extending monopoly power and smoothing demands across multiple goods [7, 12, 26, 30], this paper shows that bundling is actively adopted by anonymous publishers as well. Interestingly, there are notable similarities between the bundling in BitTorrent and traditional businesses. Further studies on the links between the BitTorrent and business practices may be interesting.

9. CONCLUSIONS

We conducted comprehensive measurements on the bundling practice to understand the structural patterns of torrents and the participant behaviors of swarms in BitTorrent. From the datasets of the BitTorrent files and swarm dynamics, we analyzed: (1) how prevalent content bundling is, (2) how and what files are bundled into torrents, (3) what motivates publishers to bundle files, and (4) how peers access the bundled files. We first found that bundling is widespread for file sharing. We observed that 41% of the bundle torrents consist of multiple main files, while the other 59% of the bundle torrents consist of a single main file and supplementary files. We also observed that most files (94%) in a bundle torrent are selected by users and the bundle torrents are more popular than the single ones on average. We further revealed that bundling in BitTorrent is mainly (68%) driven by financial incentives, which can be linked to the bundling in economics.

10. ACKNOWLEDGMENTS

We owe special thanks to Dr. Anirban Mahanti and anonymous reviewers for their thorough and helpful feedback, which was tremendously vital to significantly improve the contents and presentation of this paper. This work was supported by the KCC (Korea Communications Commission), Korea, under the R&D program supervised by the KCA (Korea Communications Agency) (KCA-2012-11-911-05-002). The ICT at Seoul National University provided research facilities for this study.

11. REFERENCES

[1] Availability, vuze. `http://wiki.vuze.com/w/Availability`.

[2] Bittorrent tracker protocol. `http://wiki.theory.org/BitTorrent_Tracker_Protocol`.

[3] Open sourced bittorrent client, vuze. `http://www.vuze.com`.

[4] Peer exchange. `http://en.wikipedia.org/wiki/Peer_exchange`.

[5] The pirate bay. `http://thepiratebay.org/`.

[6] Sandvine global internet phenomena report: Fall 2011. `http://www.sandvine.com/news/global_broadband_trends.asp`.

[7] W. J. Adams and J. L. Yellen. Commodity bundling and the burden of monopoly. *Quarterly Journal of Economics*, 90(3):475–498, 1976.

[8] Y. Bakos and E. Brynjolfsson. Bundling information goods: Pricing, profits, and efficiency. *Management Science*, 45(12):1613–1630, 1999.

[9] N. Carlsson, D. L. Eager, and A. Mahanti. Using torrent inflation to efficiently serve the long tail in peer-assisted content delivery systems. In *IFIP Networking*, 2010.

[10] R. Cuevas, M. Kryczka, A. Cuevas, S. Kaune, C. Guerrero, and R. Rejaie. Is content publishing in bittorrent altruistic or profit-driven? In *ACM CoNEXT*, 2010.

[11] G. Dán and N. Carlsson. Dynamic swarm management for improved bittorrent performance. In *IPTPS*, 2009.

[12] R. Fuerderer, A. Herrmann, and G. Wuebker. *Optimal Bundling: Marketing Strategies for Improving Economic Performance*. Springer, 1999.

[13] L. Guo, S. Chen, Z. Xiao, E. Tan, X. Ding, and X. Zhang. Measurements, analysis, and modeling of bittorrent-like systems. In *ACM IMC*, 2005.

[14] R. Joseph Lee and N. W. Alan. Thirteen ways to look at the correlation coefficient. *The American Statistician*, 42(1):59–66, 1988.

[15] A. Legout, N. Liogkas, E. Kohler, and L. Zhang. Clustering and sharing incentives in bittorrent systems. In *ACM SIGMETRICS*, 2007.

[16] A. Legout, G. Urvoy-Keller, and P. Michiardi. Rarest first and choke algorithms are enough. In *ACM IMC*, 2006.

[17] N. Lev-tov, N. Carlsson, Z. Li, C. Williamson, and S. Zhang. Dynamic file-selection policies for bundling in bittorrent-like systems. In *IEEE IWQOS*, 2010.

[18] D. S. Menasche, G. Neglia, D. Towsley, and S. Zilberstein. Strategic reasoning about bundling in swarming systems. In *IEEE GameNets*, 2009.

[19] D. S. Menasche, A. A. Rocha, B. Li, D. Towsley, and A. Venkataramani. Content availability and bundling in swarming systems. In *ACM CoNEXT*, 2009.

[20] R. S. Peterson and E. G. Sirer. Antfarm: efficient content distribution with managed swarms. In *USENIX NSDI*, 2009.

[21] M. Piatek, T. Isdal, T. Anderson, A. Krishnamurthy, and A. Venkataramani. Do incentives build robustness in bittorrent. In *USENIX NSDI*, 2007.

[22] M. Piatek, T. Isdal, A. Krishnamurthy, and T. Anderson. One hop reputations for peer to peer file sharing workloads. In *USENIX NSDI*, 2008.

[23] E. W. Pugh. Origins of software bundling. *IEEE Annals of the History of Computing*, 24(1):57–58, 2002.

[24] D. Qiu and R. Srikant. Modeling and performance analysis of bittorrent-like peer-to-peer networks. In *ACM SIGCOMM*, 2004.

[25] P. Raghubir. Free gift with purchase: Promoting or discounting the brand? *Journal of Consumer Psychology*, 14(1-2):181–186, 2004.

[26] M. A. Salinger. A graphical analysis of bundling. *Journal of Business*, 68(1):85–98, 1995.

[27] A. Sherman, J. Nieh, and C. Stein. Fairtorrent: bringing fairness to peer-to-peer systems. In *ACM CoNEXT*, 2009.

[28] M. Sirivianos, J. Han, P. Rex, and C. X. Yang. Free-riding in bittorrent networks with the large view exploit. In *IPTPS*, 2007.

[29] Y. Tian, D. Wu, and K.-W. Ng. Analyzing multiple file downloading in bittorrent. In *IEEE ICCP*, 2006.

[30] R. B. Wilson. Strategic models of entry deterrence. *Handbook of Game Theory with Economic Applications*, 1(1):305–329, 1992.

[31] Y. Yang, A. L. H. Chow, and L. Golubchik. Multi-torrent: A performance study. In *IEEE MASCOTS*, 2008.

[32] S. Zhang, N. Carlsson, D. Eager, Z. Li, and A. Mahanti. Towards a dynamic file bundling system for large-scale content distribution. In *IEEE MASCOTS*, 2011.

Energy-Efficient Congestion Control

Lingwen Gan
EE, California Institute of Technology
lgan@caltech.edu

Anwar Walid
Alcatel-Lucent Bell Labs
anwar@research.bell-labs.com

Steven H. Low
CMS & EE, California Institute of Technology
slow@caltech.edu

ABSTRACT

Various link bandwidth adjustment mechanisms are being developed to save network energy. However, their interaction with congestion control can significantly reduce throughput, and is not well understood. We firstly put forward an easily implementable link dynamic bandwidth adjustment (DBA) mechanism, and then study its iteration with congestion control. In DBA, each link updates its bandwidth according to an integral control law to match its average buffer size with a target buffer size. We prove that DBA reduces link bandwidth without sacrificing throughput—DBA only turns off excess bandwidth—in the presence of congestion control. Preliminary ns2 simulations confirm this result.

Categories and Subject Descriptors

C.2.1 [**Computer-Communication Networks**]: Network Architecture and Design—*Distributed networks*

Keywords

bandwidth adjustment, congestion control, stability.

1. INTRODUCTION

Energy efficiency is becoming one of the main design criterias in the information and communication industry, from hardware design (devices to systems) to software configuration (e.g., virtualization), and to service deployment. While significant advances in semiconductor technology have led to decrease in power consumption per byte transmission, the power efficiency is starting to plateau and the demand for greater bandwidth is leading to an overall increase in energy consumption [10]. The level of energy consumption in information and communication industry is growing exponentially at an annual rate of 15%. This trend could lead to significant cost increase to network operators [10, 13]. Therefore, there is a need to reduce energy consumption through other power management technologies. In fact, there have been ongoing efforts to develop mechanisms to reduce network energy consumption by opportunistically turning off or slowing down network devices during periods of low traffic loads. Sleep-mode operations have been proposed at various network layers, and dynamic resource adjustment is being facilitated by voltage and frequency scaling techniques [12].

SIGMETRICS'12, June 11–15, 2012, London, England, UK.

Today's core networks have large link bandwidths with low utilization levels (30-40%) [11], providing opportunities for turning off excess bandwidth and saving energy, especially when traffic loads follow diurnal pattern, and link utilization level is low during off-peak hours. Turning off excess bandwidth may be achieved by turning off one or more of the parallel links between routers, or slowing down a particular link. With current technology, power consumption in backbone routers and their line cards is essentially load-independent and therefore selective application of sleep mode is more feasible during periods of low utilization—[11, 13]. In core networks, pairs of routers are typically connected by multiple physical links, called a link bundle, and the bundle is used as a logical link for routing purposes. Link bundling, standardized in IEEE 802.1AX [11], facilitates incremental bandwidth upgrade and prolongs the lifetime of a router. Furthermore, individual link components of a bundle may be selectively turned off to provide graceful bandwidth adjustment and energy savings during low traffic loads without affecting the topology. In the future, application of frequency and voltage scaling could facilitate fine-grain adjustment of the bandwidth of each individual link component.

TCP is the dominant transport layer protocol on the Internet, and all energy saving mechanisms in the network can interact with TCP in intricate ways. Link bandwidth adjustment can lead to serious TCP throughput reduction and instability if it is not done in concert with the dynamics of TCP and active queue management, which is often represented by random early discard (RED). The objective of the paper is to study energy-saving bandwidth adjustment mechanisms in the presence of TCP/RED.

The contribution of this paper are mainly three folds. First, we propose a dynamic bandwidth adjustment (DBA) mechanism that updates the bandwidth with local buffer information, thus easy to implement. Each link uses an integral control law to match its average buffer size with some moving target buffer size. The target buffer size is a function of the bandwidth, and corresponds to a chosen queueing delay. Second, we prove the following results regarding the joint dynamic of TCP/RED/DBA.

- TCP/RED/DBA is globally stable if network delay is negligible. At steady state, excess bandwidth is turned off, and throughput is preserved.
- The steady-state TCP source rates and link bandwidths solve an optimization problem, which we call the network surplus maximization problem.
- TCP/RED/DBA is locally stable if network delay is bounded and link dynamics are sufficiently slow.

Third, we evaluate the performance of DBA through ns2 simulations, and confirm that DBA turns off excess bandwidth without reducing throughput.

The rest of the paper is structured as follows. In section

2, we introduce some preliminaries including the network model and the utility maximization framework. In section 3, we propose a dynamic bandwidth adjustment (DBA) mechanism, and give its implementations. We analyze the steady state and transient stability of TCP/RED/DBA in section 4, and provide ns2 simulations in section 5.

2. PRELIMINARIES

Consider a network that consists of a set $\mathcal{L} := \{1, \ldots, L\}$ of unidirectional links and a set $\mathcal{N} := \{1, \ldots, N\}$ of sources. For each link $l \in \mathcal{L}$, let $\mathcal{N}_l$ denote the set of sources that traverse it. For each source $i \in \mathcal{N}$, let $\mathcal{L}_i$ denote the set of links on its path to the destination. Then $i \in \mathcal{N}_l$ is equivalent to $l \in \mathcal{L}_i$ for any $i \in \mathcal{N}$ and any $l \in \mathcal{L}$. We make the following assumptions on the links and sources.

Assumption 1. *Each link $l \in \mathcal{L}$ can set its bandwidth c_l to any value in the range $C_l := [c_l^{min}, c_l^{max}]$.*

Link bandwidth may be adjusted by assuming that the link is in fact a link bundle, as described in the introduction, and an individual link component may be put to sleep or turned off to control the total bandwidth of the bundle. Alternatively, the bandwidth of a link may be adjusted with voltage and frequency scaling technology. We assume continuous bandwidth levels in the theoretical framework, and discuss discrete bandwidth levels in the implementation in section 3.2, and in the simulations in section 5.

Assumption 2. *Each source $i \in \mathcal{N}$ can set its rate x_i to any value in the range $\mathcal{X}_i := [0, x_i^{max}]$.*

Each source i is associated with a transmission window w_i, and transmits roughly w_i unacknowledged bits at any given time. Let τ_i denote the round-trip time (RTT) for source i, then source rate x_i is roughly given by $x_i = w_i/\tau_i$. Though TCP only controls x_i through adjusting w_i, we assume that TCP can control x_i explicitly as in [1, 2].

Define routing entries

$$R_{li} := \begin{cases} 1 & \text{if } i \in \mathcal{N}_l \\ 0 & \text{otherwise} \end{cases}, \quad l \in \mathcal{L},\ i \in \mathcal{N},$$

then the traffic y_l on link l is

$$y_l = \sum_{i \in \mathcal{N}_l} x_i = \sum_{i \in \mathcal{N}} R_{li} x_i, \quad l \in \mathcal{L}.$$

We use lower case letter without subscript to denote a column vector of the corresponding quantity. For example, x denotes $(x_1, \ldots, x_N)^T$ and c denotes $(c_1, \ldots, c_L)^T$.

Table 1: List of Symbols

i	a source, $i \in \mathcal{N} = \{1, \ldots, N\}$
l	a link, $l \in \mathcal{L} = \{1, \ldots, L\}$
c_l	capacity of link l
x_i	rate of source i
R_{li}	routine entry, $R_{li} = 1$ if source i passes link l, and 0 otherwise
y_l	traffic on link l
b_l	average buffer size on link l
p_l	packet drop probability on link l
q_i	end-to-end packet loss probability for source i
U_i	utility function of source i
$\tilde{b}_l(c_l)$	target buffer size of link l
d_l	target queueing delay of link l
$\tilde{p}_l(c_l)$	packet drop probability corresponding to $\tilde{b}_l$
V_l	cost function of link l

2.1 Traditional Congestion Control

There are two types of congestion control: loss-based congestion control and delay-based congestion control, and we focus on loss-based congestion control in this paper. In loss-based congestion control, links drop packets to reflect their buffer occupancy, and sources adjust their transmission rates to respond to their end-to-end packet loss.

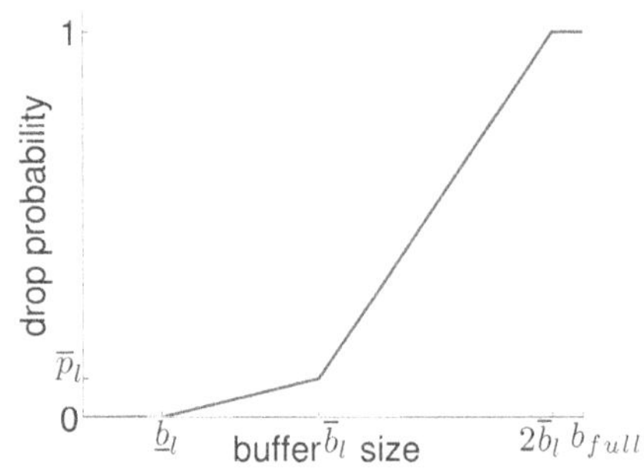

Figure 1: Packet drop probability for RED.

We consider active queue management link control, in particular the random early discard (RED) mechanism. In RED, a link l keeps track of its average buffer size b_l,[1] and drops packets with probability (see Figure 1)

$$p_l = \begin{cases} 0 & \text{if } b_l \le \underline{b}_l \\ \gamma_l (b_l - \underline{b}_l) & \text{if } \underline{b}_l < b_l \le \bar{b}_l \\ \eta_l b_l - (1 - 2\bar{p}_l) & \text{if } \bar{b}_l < b_l \le 2\bar{b}_l \\ 1 & \text{if } b_l > 2\bar{b}_l \end{cases},$$

where $\underline{b}_l$, $\bar{b}_l$, $\bar{p}_l$ are design parameters and $\gamma_l = \frac{\bar{p}_l}{\bar{b}_l - \underline{b}_l}$, $\eta_l = \frac{1-\bar{p}_l}{\bar{b}_l}$ are the corresponding slopes. As its buffer builds up, a link drops more and more packets, guiding the sources to reduce their transmission rates. In practice, TCP/RED often gets unstable when $b_l > \bar{b}_l$, and the parameters $\bar{p}_l$, $\bar{b}_l$, $\underline{b}_l$ are designed empirically or adaptively (ARED [14]) to avoid such instability. Hence, the model

$$p_l = \begin{cases} 0 & \text{if } b_l \le \underline{b}_l \\ \gamma_l (b_l - \underline{b}_l) & \text{if } \underline{b}_l < b_l \le \bar{b}_l \end{cases} \tag{1}$$

suffices for our study. In prior works (for example, [2]), the following simpler model

$$p_l = \gamma_l b_l \tag{2}$$

is often used. Model (2) neglects the region $[0, \underline{b}_l]$ on which $p_l = 0$, for the convenience of analysis. We will generally use model (2), but use the more precise model (1) to derive an important result: we can reduce the bandwidth without sacrificing throughput. Basically, after reducing the bandwidth, average buffer size b_l at non-bottleneck links increases. But if b_l is still below $\underline{b}_l$, the corresponding p_l remains zero. Consequently, sources will not observe additional packet loss, and throughput will be preserved.

We consider TCP source control. In TCP Reno, a widely used loss-based TCP, a source generally increases its window size by 1 packet per round-trip time and halves its window size after a packet loss. For each source i, the end-to-end

[1] Average buffer size is the average of instantaneous buffer size over a moving time window of typically 500ms.

packet loss probability q_i it observes is given by

$$q_i = 1 - \prod_{l \in \mathcal{L}_i} (1 - p_l) \approx \sum_{l \in \mathcal{L}_i} p_l = \sum_{l \in \mathcal{L}} R_{li} p_l.$$

The approximation is due to the fact that $\sum_{l \in \mathcal{L}_i} p_l \ll 1$, i.e., in practice, the end-to-end packet loss probability is very small. At steady state, source i transmits at rate [7]

$$x_i = \begin{cases} x_i^{max} & \text{if } q_i < q_i^{min} \\ f_i(q_i) & \text{if } q_i \geq q_i^{min} \end{cases}, \quad (3)$$

where $f_i : [q_i^{min}, \infty) \to (0, x_i^{max}]$ is strictly decreasing, and determined by the TCP protocol source i uses. For example,

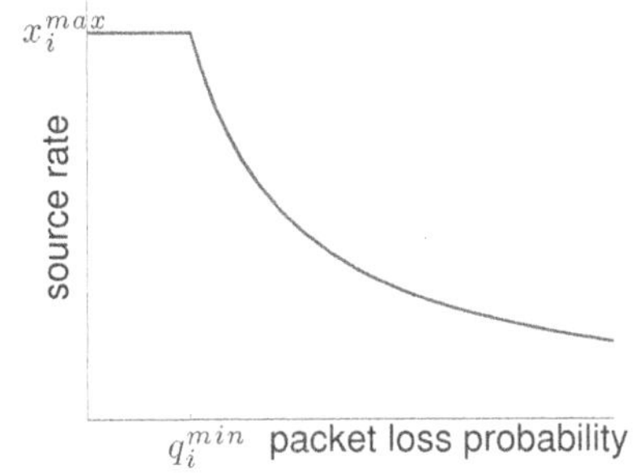

Figure 2: Source rate.

$f_i(q_i) = \frac{1}{\tau_i}\sqrt{\frac{3}{2q_i}}$ for TCP Reno, inversely proportional to the round-trip time τ_i, and decreases as loss q_i increases. Noting that (3) captures the stationary relationship between q_i and x_i for all TCP protocols, we use it for the sake of generality. Associate a utility function [7]

$$U_i(x_i) := \int^{x_i} f_i^{-1}(x)dx$$

with each source $i \in \mathcal{N}$, then (3) is equivalent to

$$x_i = \begin{cases} x_i^{max} & \text{if } q_i < U_i'(x_i^{max}) \\ U_i'^{-1}(q_i) & \text{if } q_i \geq U_i'(x_i^{max}) \end{cases}. \quad (4)$$

Since f_i^{-1} is strictly decreasing and positive for $x_i \leq x_i^{max}$, U_i is strictly concave and increasing. For instance, $U_i(x_i) = -\frac{3}{2\tau^2}\frac{1}{x_i}$ for TCP Reno [7].

2.2 Network Utility Maximization

For each link l, its average buffer size b_l updates as[2]

$$\dot{b}_l = \begin{cases} 0 & \text{if } b_l = 0 \ \& \ y_l < c_l \\ y_l - c_l & \text{otherwise} \end{cases}. \quad (5)$$

Using model (2) for p_l, (5) is equivalent to

$$\dot{p}_l = \begin{cases} 0 & \text{if } p_l = 0 \ \& \ y_l < c_l \\ \gamma_l(y_l - c_l) & \text{otherwise} \end{cases}. \quad (6)$$

Discrete version of (6) and (4) is proven to solve the following *network utility maximization* (NUM) problem [2]

$$\text{NUM} \begin{cases} \max\limits_{x_i \in \mathcal{X}_i} & \sum\limits_{i \in \mathcal{N}} U_i(x_i) \\ \text{s.t.} & y_l \leq c_l, \ l \in \mathcal{L}. \end{cases}$$

[2]We do not distinguish between instantaneous buffer size and average buffer size in this paper.

Let x^{NUM} denote the solution to NUM with $c_l = c_l^{max}$ for all l, then x^{NUM} is the steady-state source rate for TCP/RED. Let y^{NUM} denote the traffic corresponding to x^{NUM}.

3. BANDWIDTH ADJUSTMENT

In this section, we propose a dynamic bandwidth adjustment mechanism, and give its detailed implementations.

3.1 Algorithm

The objective of energy-efficient congestion control is to achieve the same throughput as traditional congestion control, while consuming less energy by turning off excess bandwidth. Conceptually, we can achieve this by finding x^{NUM} and reducing the bandwidth c to the traffic y^{NUM}. However, measuring the traffic on a link is expensive. In practice, a link only knows its own buffer size. To conclude, energy-efficient congestion control has the following objectives:

- achieves the source rate x^{NUM};
- reduces link bandwidth c to traffic rate y^{NUM};
- uses local buffer information to update c.

We maintain the existing TCP/RED architecture, and introduce bandwidth updates. Noting that the only available information is its buffer size, a link l compares its average buffer size b_l with a moving target $\tilde{b}_l(c_l)$, and updates its bandwidth proportional to their difference according to the following *dynamic bandwidth adjustment* (DBA) mechanism:

$$\dot{c}_l = \begin{cases} 0 & \text{if } c_l = c_l^{min} \ \& \ b_l < \tilde{b}_l(c_l) \\ & \text{or } c_l = c_l^{max} \ \& \ b_l > \tilde{b}_l(c_l) \\ \alpha_l\left(b_l - \tilde{b}_l(c_l)\right) & \text{otherwise} \end{cases}. \quad (7)$$

Design parameter $\alpha_l > 0$ characterizes bandwidth dynamic speed, and its value will be discussed in section 3.2. We can interpret (7) as a truncated integral control law with a moving target. If b_l exceeds $\tilde{b}_l$, bandwidth is increased to clear the buffer, and vice versa. At equilibrium, we expect $b_l = \tilde{b}_l(c_l)$. If the target $\tilde{b}_l$ is a constant, then queueing delay generally increases as we decrease bandwidth, and quality of service can be degraded. In order to limit the queueing delay, $\tilde{b}_l$ should decrease as c_l decreases. If throughput y_l is time invariant, the corresponding phase plot is shown in Figure 3: bandwidth c_l converges to the throughput y_l, and buffer size b_l equals its target $\tilde{b}_l(c_l)$ at convergence. However, y_l will react to link buffer dynamics due to TCP, calling for more detailed study, which is given in section 4.

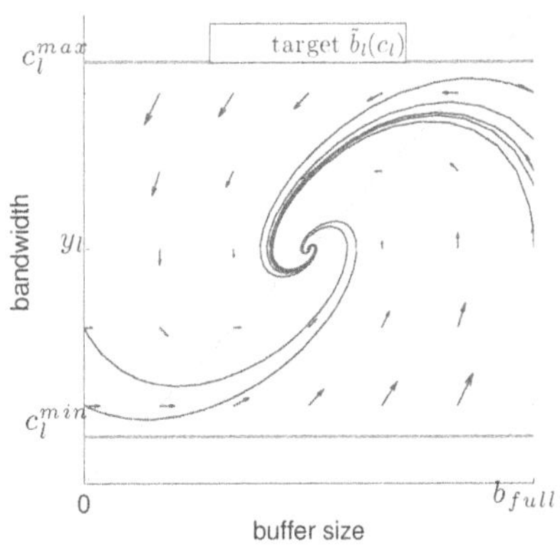

Figure 3: Phase plot of (b_l, c_l) for constant traffic y_l.

3.2 Implementation

In this section, we give the implementations of DBA. For ease of presentation, we consider a single link l. Recall that c_l, b_l, and $\tilde{b}_l(c_l)$ denote the bandwidth, average buffer size, and target buffer size of link l respectively. For notational brevity, we will drop the subscript l in this section.

We set $\tilde{b}(c) = dc$, where d is called *target queueing delay* and satisfies $d < \underline{b}/c^{max}$, so that the moving target $\tilde{b}$ is always below $\underline{b}$. Then, at steady state, packet drop probability $p_l = 0$ if link l is not at its full bandwidth.[3] Consequently, either a link is at its full bandwidth, or it will not drop any packet. Hence, end-to-end loss probability q_i is not increased after we reduce the bandwidth. As a result, source rates won't be reduced. A rigorous statement is provided in Theorem 1. Noting that queueing delay on non-bottleneck links increases by d, we should set d small for quality of service consideration. A typical value is $d = 1ms$.

Algorithm 1 Continuous DBA

At epoch $k \in \mathbb{Z}$, input $c[k-1]$, $b[k-1]$.

1. Integral law.

   if $\left|\frac{b[k-1]}{dc[k-1]} - 1\right| \le \epsilon$ **then**

   $c \leftarrow c[k-1] + \delta_1 \frac{b[k-1]-dc[k-1]}{T}$;

   else

   $c \leftarrow c[k-1] + \delta_2 \frac{b[k-1]-dc[k-1]}{T}$;

   end if

2. Lower and upper bounds.

   if $c > c^{max}$ **then**

   $c \leftarrow c^{max}$;

   else

   if $c < c^{min}$ **then**

   $c \leftarrow c^{min}$;

   end if

   end if

3. Switching.

   $c[k] \leftarrow c$;

Return $c[k]$ as the link bandwidth during $[kT, (k+1)T)$.

Bandwidth c should be updated periodically. Though current technology supports switching each physical interface (for instance, an optical cable) between idle and sleep states within 1ms, the updating period T should be much larger than 1ms to reduce switching overhead. On the other hand, the period T cannot be too large, in order to remain responsive to traffic increases. A typical value is $T = 100$ms. Assume bandwidth updates at epochs $t = kT, k \in \mathbb{Z}$, and define $c[k] := c(kT)$ as the bandwidth at epoch k (then $c[k]$ is also the bandwidth during $[kT, (k+1)T)$). Similarly, define $b[k] := b(kT)$, $\tilde{b}[k] := \tilde{b}(kT) = dc(kT)$ as the average buffer size and target buffer size at epoch k. If we discretize (7) and neglect the lower and upper bounds on c, we get

$$c[k+1] = c[k] + T\alpha(b[k] - \tilde{b}[k]),\ k \in \mathbb{Z}.$$

Assuming static traffic y, static target buffer size $\tilde{b}$, and $c[k] = y$, then if we set $\alpha = \frac{1}{T^2}$, we have $b[k+2] = \tilde{b}$. Hence, α is on the order of $1/T^2$, and we update c as

$$c[k+1] = c[k] + \delta\frac{b[k] - \tilde{b}[k]}{T},\ k \in \mathbb{Z},$$

where δ is a damping parameter and resides in $(0, 1]$. On one hand, we need small δ to guarantee local stability of TCP/RED/DBA (Theorem 4); on the other hand, we need big δ to avoid long transients. We balance this by using different δ in different buffer regions. We set a threshold $\epsilon > 0$. If the relative deviation $\left|b/\tilde{b} - 1\right| \le \epsilon$, we use a small δ_1 for local stability. If $\left|b/\tilde{b} - 1\right| > \epsilon$, we use a big δ_2 to shorten the transient. Typical values are $\epsilon = 0.1$, $\delta_1 = 0.04$, and $\delta_2 = 0.2$. Recall that d, T, ϵ, δ_1 and δ_2 are design parameters, and we summarize the continuous dynamic bandwidth adjustment (continuous DBA) mechanism in Algorithm 1.

Bandwidth levels are far from continuous in practice. Assume that a link has N bandwidth levels

$$c_1 < c_2 < \cdots < c_N.$$

To protect throughput, we choose a bandwidth c_k such that $c_k \ge y^{\text{NUM}} > c_{k-1}$. Since excess bandwidth $c_k - y^{\text{NUM}}$ will probably make $b < \tilde{b}$, we set a hysteresis buffer region $[\underline{b}, \tilde{b}]$ in which we do not reduce c. How to set $\underline{b}$ is beyond the scope of this paper, and we pick $\underline{b} = \tilde{b}/2$ in this paper for simplicity. The discrete dynamic bandwidth adjustment algorithm—given in Algorithm 2—exploits stochasticity to mimic continuous DBA. Recall that d, T, ϵ, and δ_2 are design parameters and we set $\underline{b} = \frac{1}{2}\tilde{b}$.

Algorithm 2 Discrete DBA

At epoch $k \in \mathbb{Z}$, input $c[k-1]$, $b[k-1]$.

1. Integral law.

   $c \leftarrow c[k-1] + \delta_2 \frac{b[k-1]-dc[k-1]}{T}$;

2. Lower and upper bounds.

   if $c > c^{max}$ **then**

   $c \leftarrow c^{max}$;

   else

   if $c < c^{min}$ **then**

   $c \leftarrow c^{min}$;

   end if

   end if

3. Stochastic round off.

   $i \leftarrow \text{argmin}\{i \in \{1, \ldots, N-1\}\ :\ c_i \le c \le c_{i+1}\}$;

   $p \leftarrow \frac{c_{i+1}-c}{c_{i+1}-c_i}$;

   $c \leftarrow \begin{cases} c_i & \text{with probability } p \\ c_{i+1} & \text{with probability } 1-p \end{cases}$;

4. Hysteresis.

   if $\frac{1}{2}dc[k-1] \le b[k-1] \le dc[k-1]$ **then**

   $c \leftarrow c[k-1]$;

   end if

5. Switching.

   $c[k] \leftarrow c$;

Return $c[k]$ as the link bandwidth during $[kT, (k+1)T)$.

It can be verified that the expectation $E(c)$ does not change during step 3. Besides, c coming from step 1 is equal to the result of continuous DBA when $\left|\frac{b[k-1]}{dc[k-1]} - 1\right| > \epsilon$. Hence, discrete DBA will hopefully mimic continuous DBA. We will further explore this in section 5.2.

4. ANALYSIS

There are mainly two questions to answer: will traffic y oscillate, and how much throughput reduction will be incurred. Oscillation of y leads to poor quality of service, and might

[3] At steady state, $c_l \neq c_l^{max}$ implies $b_l \le \tilde{b}_l$. Since $\tilde{b}_l < \underline{b}_l$, we have $b_l < \underline{b}_l$, which implies $p_l = 0$.

be induced by the interaction between DBA and TCP/RED. Supporting traffic is the primal goal of the network, hence it would be undesirable if DBA seriously reduce throughput. We answer these two questions in this section.

4.1 Global Stability without Network Delay

Recall that p_l, b_l, x_i and c_l denotes packet drop probability, average buffer size, source rate, and bandwidth respectively. We start with equations (1), (5), (4), and (7) to study the dynamic of TCP/RED/DBA, and call them the *synchronous model* (SM).

Synchronous Model (SM):

$$p_l = \begin{cases} 0 & \text{if } b_l \le \underline{b}_l \\ \gamma_l(b_l - \underline{b}_l) & \text{if } \underline{b}_l < b_l \le \bar{b}_l \end{cases} \quad (1)$$

$$\dot{b}_l = \begin{cases} 0 & \text{if } b_l = 0 \;\&\; y_l < c_l \\ y_l - c_l & \text{otherwise} \end{cases} \quad (5)$$

$$x_i = \begin{cases} x_i^{max} & \text{if } q_i < U_i'(x_i^{max}) \\ U_i'^{-1}(q_i) & \text{if } q_i \ge U_i'(x_i^{max}) \end{cases} \quad (4)$$

$$\dot{c}_l = \begin{cases} 0 & \begin{array}{l}\text{if } c_l = c_l^{min} \;\&\; b_l < \tilde{b}_l \\ \text{or } c_l = c_l^{max} \;\&\; b_l > \tilde{b}_l\end{array} \\ \alpha_l\left(b_l - \tilde{b}_l(c_l)\right) & \text{otherwise} \end{cases} \quad (7)$$

To model RED, we use the more precise equation (1) rather than (2), since the fact that we set $\tilde{b}_l < \underline{b}_l$ can only be captured by (1). We model the dynamics of average buffer size b_l by the dynamics (5) of instantaneous buffer size for simplicity. The actual dynamics of b_l should be a low-pass filtered version of (5). As mentioned in section 2.1, the model (4) we adopt for TCP captures the stationary relationship between source rate and end-to-end packet loss for a generic TCP protocol. To analyze the stability of a specific TCP protocol, we should change to its specific dynamic equation. The dynamic model (7) for c_l is exact for continuous DBA. Note that Model SM does not capture network delay, which we will consider in section 4.3.

According to SM, source rate and link bandwidth converge globally to a unique equilibrium. At the equilibrium, excess bandwidth is completely turned off while source rate is preserved as if DBA has not been implemented. A rigorous statement is given in Theorem 1.

Theorem 1. *Let $(x(t), c(t), b(t), p(t))$ be an arbitrary trajectory generated by SM, then*

$$x(t) \to x^{NUM}, \quad c(t) \to \max\{c^{min}, y^{NUM}\}$$

as $t \to \infty$ provided the following conditions hold:

C1 $\tilde{b}_l'(c_l) = d_l > 0$ *for* $l \in \mathcal{L}$ *and* $c_l \in \mathcal{C}_l$.

C2 $\tilde{b}_l(c_l^{max}) < \underline{b}_l$ *for* $l \in \mathcal{L}$.

C3 $U_i''(x_i) \le -u < 0$, $\forall i \in \mathcal{N}$, $\forall x_i \in \mathcal{X}_i$.

By the design of DBA, Conditions C1 and C2 hold automatically since we set $\tilde{b}_l(c_l) = d_l c_l$ with $d_l c_l^{max} < \underline{b}_l$. The utility function U_i is strictly concave so that $U_i''(x_i) < 0$, and Condition C3 holds since $\mathcal{X}_i$ is bounded for each i.

The fact that $x(t) \to x^{\text{NUM}}$ implies no traffic oscillation and zero throughput reduction, and the fact that $c(t) \to \max\{c^{min}, y^{\text{NUM}}\}$ implies zero excess bandwidth at steady state. The proof of Theorem 1 is presented in Appendix A.

4.2 Network Surplus Maximization

The reason DBA reduces c without sacrificing x is that there is a nonempty interval $[0, \underline{b}_l]$ over which p_l is zero. This feature is captured in (1). Without this feature, i.e., $\underline{b}_l = 0$, (1) reduces to (2), which we will use to simplify Model SM. Noting that (2) gives a bijective mapping between b_l and p_l, we can substitute b_l by p_l to reduce the state space dimension. Define $\tilde{p}_l(c_l) := \gamma_l \tilde{b}_l(c_l)$ as the packet drop probability corresponding to $\tilde{b}_l$, and call its integral

$$V_l(c_l) := \int_{c_l^{min}}^{c_l} \tilde{p}_l(c)dc$$

the cost function of link l. Note that $V_l(c_l)$ comes from the moving target buffer size $\tilde{b}_l(c_l)$ we set, and is strictly convex and increasing. By substituting b_l by p_l, the dynamics (7) for c_l is equivalent to

$$\dot{c}_l = \begin{cases} 0 & \begin{array}{l}\text{if } c_l = c_l^{min} \;\&\; p_l < V_l'(c_l) \\ \text{or } c_l = c_l^{max} \;\&\; p_l > V_l'(c_l)\end{array} \\ \beta_l\left(p_l - V_l'(c_l)\right) & \text{otherwise} \end{cases}, \quad (8)$$

where $\beta_l := \alpha_l/\gamma_l$. Then, Model SM is simplified as below.

Simplified Synchronous Model (SSM):

$$\dot{p}_l = \begin{cases} 0 & \text{if } p_l = 0 \;\&\; y_l < c_l \\ \gamma_l(y_l - c_l) & \text{otherwise} \end{cases} \quad (6)$$

$$x_i = \begin{cases} x_i^{max} & \text{if } q_i < U_i'(x_i^{max}) \\ U_i'^{-1}(q_i) & \text{if } q_i \ge U_i'(x_i^{max}) \end{cases} \quad (4)$$

$$\dot{c}_l = \begin{cases} 0 & \begin{array}{l}\text{if } c_l = c_l^{min} \;\&\; p_l < V_l'(c_l) \\ \text{or } c_l = c_l^{max} \;\&\; p_l > V_l'(c_l)\end{array} \\ \beta_l\left(p_l - V_l'(c_l)\right) & \text{otherwise} \end{cases} \quad (8)$$

Definition 1. A point (x, c, p) is an equilibrium for SSM, provided that at (x, c, p), $\dot{p} = 0$, $\dot{c} = 0$ according to (6) and (8), and (x, p) satisfy (4).

Then the steady states of TCP/RED/DBA are equilibrium points for SSM. Similar to NUM for traditional congestion control, we are able to show that steady state of TCP/RED/DBA solves the following *network surplus maximization* (NSM) problem

$$\textbf{NSM} \begin{cases} \max\limits_{x_i \in \mathcal{X}_i, c_l \in \mathcal{C}_l} & \sum\limits_{i \in \mathcal{N}} U_i(x_i) - \sum\limits_{l \in \mathcal{L}} V_l(c_l) \\ \text{s.t.} & y_l \le c_l, \; l \in \mathcal{L}. \end{cases}$$

A rigorous statement is given in Theorem 2. Let (x^*, c^*) denote the unique solution to NSM,[4] and y^* the corresponding traffic throughput. Since V_l is strictly increasing, $c^* = y^*$ if there is no lower bound on c.

Theorem 2. *Equilibrium points of SSM exist, and a point (x, c, p) is an equilibrium point for SSM if and only if (x, c, p) is primal dual optimal for NSM.*

Theorem 2 connects NSM with TCP/RED/DBA, just like the relationship between NUM and TCP/AQM. It implies that we can study the steady-state traffic throughput and link bandwidth of TCP/RED/DBA by solving NSM. The proof of Theorem 2 is based on the duality theory [8, Chapter 5], and omitted due to page limit. Theorem 3 says that TCP/RED/DBA converges globally to its unique steady state (x^*, c^*).

[4] Since U_i are strictly concave for all i and V_l are strictly convex for all l, solution to NSM is unique.

Theorem 3. *Let $(x(t), c(t), p(t))$ be an arbitrary trajectory generated by SSM. Then the source rate $x(t)$ and bandwidth $c(t)$ converge to (x^*, c^*) as $t \to \infty$ if the following conditions hold:*

C3 $U_i''(x_i) \leq -u < 0$, $\forall i \in \mathcal{N}$, $\forall x_i \in \mathcal{X}_i$.

C4 $V_l''(c_l) \geq v > 0$, $\forall l \in \mathcal{L}$, $\forall c_l \in \mathcal{C}_l$.

Condition C3 has already been justified in the discussion after Theorem 1. Condition C4 also holds since $V_l''(c_l) = d_l\gamma_l > 0$ for all l and all c_l. Theorem 3 implies that SSM is globally stable, and solves NSM. The proof of theorem 3 is based on the uniqueness of (x^*, c^*) and contraction-type analysis shown in appendix B. Contraction-type analysis can be found in many references including [3].

4.3 Local Stability with Delay

We proved global convergence to (x^*, c^*) without considering network delay in section 4.2, and will study local stability of (x^*, c^*) under network delay in this section. We add link to source and source to link delays to SSM. For each source link pair $(i, l) \in \mathcal{N} \times \mathcal{L}$, if $l \in \mathcal{L}_i$, let $\tau_{il}(t)$ and $\tau_{li}(t)$ denote the feedforward delay from source i to link l and the feedback delay from link l to source i at time t respectively; if $l \notin \mathcal{L}_i$, define $\tau_{li}(t) = \tau_{il}(t) = 0$ for all t. Then link $l \in \mathcal{L}$ in fact observes traffic

$$\hat{y}_l(t) = \sum_{i \in \mathcal{N}_l} x_i(t - \tau_{il}(t)) = \sum_{i \in \mathcal{N}} R_{li} x_i(t - \tau_{il}(t)), \quad (9)$$

and updates its drop probability according to

$$\dot{p}_l = \begin{cases} 0 & \text{if } p_l = 0 \ \& \ \hat{y}_l < c_l \\ \gamma_l(\hat{y}_l - c_l) & \text{otherwise} \end{cases}. \quad (10)$$

Source $i \in \mathcal{N}$ in fact observes congestion level

$$\hat{q}_i(t) = \sum_{l \in \mathcal{L}_i} p_l(t - \tau_{li}(t)) = \sum_{l \in \mathcal{L}} R_{li} p_l(t - \tau_{li}(t)), \quad (11)$$

and updates its rate as

$$x_i = \begin{cases} x_i^{max} & \text{if } \hat{q}_i < U_i'(x_i^{max}) \\ U_i'^{-1}(\hat{q}_i) & \text{if } \hat{q}_i \geq U_i'(x_i^{max}) \end{cases}. \quad (12)$$

We do not model the delay from a link to itself since it is much shorter, and come to the following simplified asynchronous model (SAM).

Simplified Asynchronous Model (SAM):

$$\dot{p}_l = \begin{cases} 0 & \text{if } p_l = 0 \ \& \ \hat{y}_l < c_l \\ \gamma_l(\hat{y}_l - c_l) & \text{otherwise} \end{cases} \quad (10)$$

$$x_i = \begin{cases} x_i^{max} & \text{if } \hat{q}_i < U_i'(x_i^{max}) \\ U_i'^{-1}(\hat{q}_i) & \text{if } \hat{q}_i \geq U_i'(x_i^{max}) \end{cases} \quad (12)$$

$$\dot{c}_l = \begin{cases} 0 & \begin{array}{l} \text{if } c_l = c_l^{min} \ \& \ p_l < \tilde{p}_l \\ \text{or } c_l = c_l^{max} \ \& \ p_l > \tilde{p}_l \end{array} \\ \beta_l\left(p_l - \tilde{p}_l(c_l)\right) & \text{otherwise} \end{cases} \quad (8)$$

Definition 2. A point (x, c, p) is an equilibrium for SAM, provided that at (x, c, p), $\dot{p} = 0$, $\dot{c} = 0$ according to (10) and (8), and (x, p) satisfy (12).

It is not difficult to show that SSM and SAM have the same equilibrium points. Hence, Theorem 2 holds for SAM as well as SSM. Let (x^e, c^e, p^e) be an equilibrium point for SAM, then $(x^e, c^e) = (x^*, c^*)$—the solution to NSM—according to Theorem 2. We study local stability near (x^*, c^*) through linearization. Neglect the dynamics of $\tau_{il}(t)$ and $\tau_{li}(t)$ when linearizing (9) and (11) around (x^e, c^e, p^e) as in [5], i.e., treat them as static, and denote the respective values by τ_{il} and τ_{li}. For each source $i \in \mathcal{N}$, its round-trip time τ_i is equal to the sum of source to link delay τ_{il} and link to source delay τ_{li}, for all link l on its path, i.e.,

$$\tau_{il} + \tau_{li} = \tau_i, \ i \in \mathcal{N}, l \in \mathcal{L}_i.$$

Then, we are able to show that (x^*, c^*) is locally stable, if round-trip times are bounded and link price dynamics and link bandwidth dynamics are not too fast.

Theorem 4. *(x^*, c^*) is locally asymptotically stable for SAM, provided the following conditions hold:*

C3 $U_i''(x_i) \leq -u < 0$, $\forall i \in \mathcal{N}$, $\forall x_i \in \mathcal{X}_i$.

C4 $V_l''(c_l) \geq v > 0$, $\forall l \in \mathcal{L}$, $\forall c_l \in \mathcal{C}_l$.

C5 $\tau_i \leq \tau$ *for all* $i \in \mathcal{N}$.

C6 $\gamma_l < \frac{u}{NL\tau}$ *for each* $l \in \mathcal{L}$.

C7 $\beta_l < \frac{\pi(\pi-2)}{4\tau^2\gamma_l}$ *for each* $l \in \mathcal{L}$.

Conditions C3 and C4 have been justified in the discussions after Theorem 1 and Theorem 3. Condition C5 holds since network delay is typically below several hundred milliseconds in real networks. β and γ are design parameters we choose. A smaller γ leads to a slower dynamic in p, and a smaller β leads to a slower dynamic in c. By damping the dynamics, Conditions C6 and C7 can be satisfied. Hence, Theorem 4 implies that we can slow down link dynamics to guarantee local stability of (x^*, c^*). Theorem 4 also implies that the larger the network delay τ, the more likely instability occurs, since the upper bounds for β and γ are inversely proportional to τ. The proof of Theorem 4 is based on the generalized Nyquist theorem [4], and shown in Appendix C.

5. SIMULATION

We evaluate the performance of the dynamic bandwidth adjustment (DBA) mechanisms using the network topology in Figure 4. There are 40 TCP Reno sources connected to a shared link through 1Mb/s access links. To investigate how DBA reacts to traffic changes, we assume that 20 of the TCP sources are long-lived, while the other 20 TCP sources are active only from 200s to 250s. The number of TCP connections change abruptly at 200s and 250s, making bandwidth adjustment more challenging. Since the analysis in section 4 only deals with TCP traffic, we also investigate the impact of non-TCP traffic by introducing 20Mb/s UDP constant-bit-rate traffic in the period 350 ~ 400s.

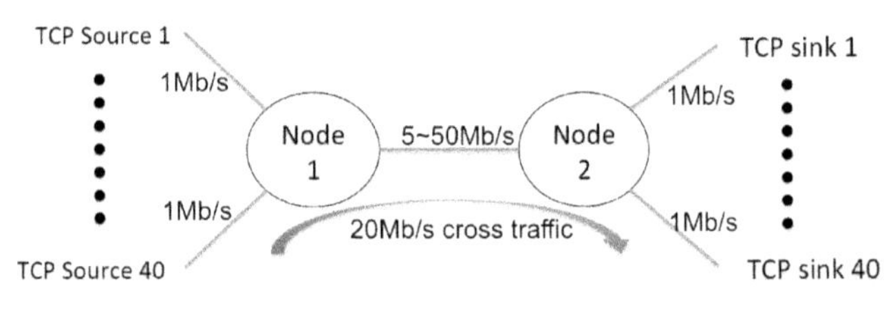

Figure 4: There are 20 long-lived TCP connections and 20 short-lived TCP connections, which start at 200s and end at 250s. There is also 20Mb/s constant-bit-rate UDP cross traffic from 350*s* to 400*s*.

We compare the following settings for the shared link.

1. The shared link has static bandwidth of 50Mb/s.
2. The shared link has dynamic bandwidth with continuous levels ranging from 5Mb/s to 50Mb/s. Continuous

DBA, with parameters $T = 100\text{ms}$, $d = 1\text{ms}$, $\epsilon = 0.1$, $\delta_1 = 0.04$, and $\delta_2 = 0.2$, is implemented to adjust the bandwidth.

3. The shared link has dynamic bandwidth with discrete levels 5Mb/s, 10Mb/s, ..., 50Mb/s. Discrete DBA, with the same parameters as in setting 2, is implemented to adjust the bandwidth.

All the simulations in this paper use ns-allinone-2.34 on Mac OS X Lion 10.7.2.

5.1 Continuous DBA

Figure 5 shows the traffic throughput and link bandwidth on the shared link, in the static bandwidth setting (no DBA) and continuous bandwidth setting (continuous DBA). All TCP sources use TCP/Reno (loss-based), and have 50ms round-trip time. Due to the 1Mb/s access links (red links in Figure 4), each TCP connection takes up at most 1Mb/s bandwidth. Hence, throughput never reaches maximum bandwidth (50Mb/s) on the shared link. The low utilization level of the shared link provides an opportunity to save energy (by decreasing bandwidth) without reducing the throughput, and continuous DBA effectively exploits this opportunity.

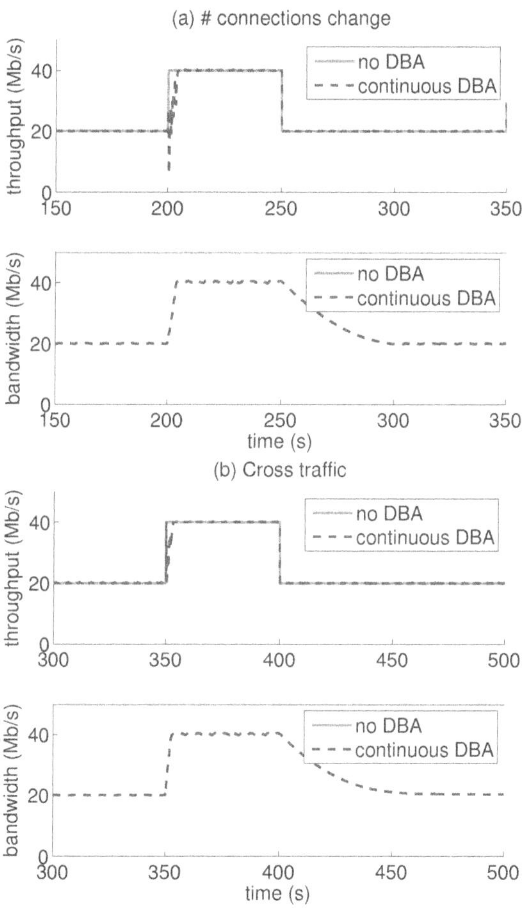

Figure 5: There are 40 TCP connections with $50ms$ RTT. 20 of the TCP connections are long-lived while the other 20 are active only from $200s$ to $250s$. Additional 20Mb/s UDP constant-bit-rate cross traffic comes at $350s$ and leaves at $400s$.

The following observations can be made from Figure 5.

- At steady state, the throughput is the same for both settings (no DBA and continuous DBA), even with the presence of non-TCP traffic.
- In the continuous DBA setting, when traffic (abruptly) increases (due to the increase in TCP connections or injection of cross traffic), the bandwidth increases fast. Hence, the effect of DBA is transparent to the TCP sources.
- In the continuous DBA setting, when traffic (abruptly) decreases (due to the decrease in TCP connections or removal of cross traffic), the bandwidth decreases slowly.
- In the continuous DBA setting, link bandwidth equals throughput at steady state.

As we observed, the bandwidth ramps up fast, but ramps down slowly. Fast ramping up makes DBA transparent to the TCP sources, and slow ramping down helps preserving network performance. We now give the reason for the fast ramping up and slow ramping down in DBA. When $c < y$, buffer b can reach its full size b_{full}, and

$$c[k+1] - c[k] \leq \delta_2 \frac{b_{full} - \tilde{b}[k]}{T}.$$

When $c > y$, b can only decrease to 0, and

$$c[k] - c[k+1] \leq \delta_2 \frac{\tilde{b}[k]}{T}.$$

Since $\tilde{b} < \underline{b} \ll b_{full}$, the ramping down speed has a much smaller upper bound than the ramping up speed. Furthermore, since $\tilde{b} = dc$, the smaller d, the slower c can decrease. When cross traffic goes away at $400s$, excess bandwidth clears the buffer to 0 almost instantaneously. Taking average buffer size b to be 0, the dynamics in (7) reduces to

$$\dot{c} = -\delta_2 \frac{\tilde{b}}{T^2} = -\frac{\delta_2 d}{T^2} c.$$

Bandwidth exponentially decays with time constant

$$\frac{T^2}{\delta_2 d} = \frac{(0.1s)^2}{0.2 \times 1ms} = 50s,$$

and it should take

$$50s \times \ln\left(\frac{40}{20}\right) = 34.7s$$

for c to decrease from 40Mbps to 20Mbps, in accordance with the simulation result in Figure 5. We come to the following conclusions for the transients of continuous DBA:

- steady-state is (locally) stable;
- bandwidth ramps up very fast;
- bandwidth ramps down slowly and exponentially, with a time constant inversely proportional to the target queueing delay d.

We provide below two ways to decrease the bandwidth faster to save more energy.

- Increase d. This leads to larger RTT and affects quality of service. Note that $d < \underline{b}_l / c_l^{max}$, otherwise packet loss kicks in to reduce traffic throughput dramatically.
- Increase δ. However, increasing δ potentially results in instability according to Theorem 4.

5.2 Discrete DBA

Section 5.1 evaluates the performance of continuous DBA, which provides an "upper bound" on what is achievable. In practice, bandwidth levels are discrete, and we may incur performance loss due to this restriction. This motivates us to evaluate discrete DBA in this section.

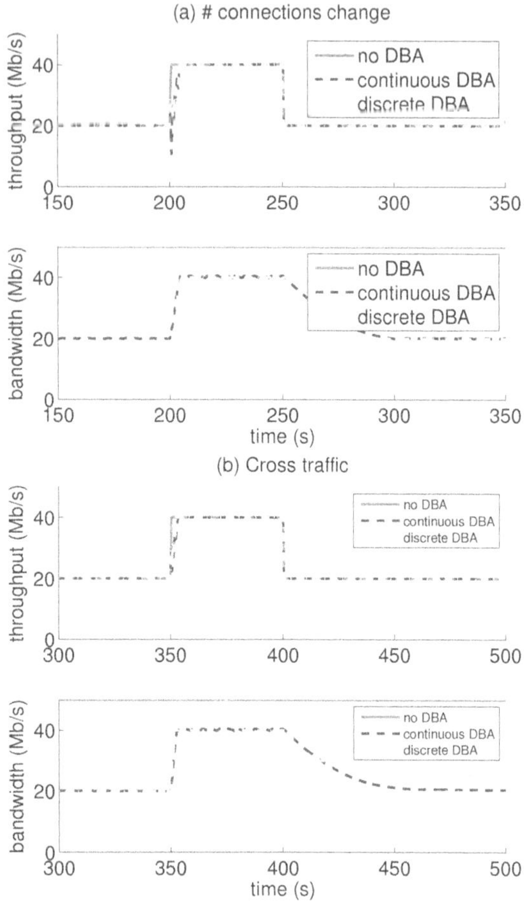

Figure 6: There are 40 TCP connections with $50ms$ RTT. 20 of the TCP connections are long-lived while the other 20 are active only from $200s$ to $250s$. Additional 20Mb/s UDP constant-bit-rate cross traffic comes at $350s$ and leaves at $400s$.

Figure 6 shows the throughput and bandwidth for all three settings (no DBA, continuous DBA, and discrete DBA) under the same setup as Figure 5. It can be concluded that

- discrete DBA still preserves throughput;
- the bandwidth trajectory generated by discrete DBA roughly follows that of continuous DBA;
- the bandwidth trajectory generated by discrete DBA oscillates around that of continuous DBA—while staying above most of the time—at a low frequency.

Since discrete DBA only has few bandwidth levels to choose from, oscillation around optimal bandwidth is hardly avoidable. Spending most of the time above optimal bandwidth is what we prefer, since traffic protection is of primal concern. In fact, this is achieved by setting hysteric target buffer $[\underline{b}, \tilde{b}]$.

On average, link bandwidth is updated only once every multiple seconds. Frequent link bandwidth updating will cause high overhead that prohibits implementation, and discrete DBA reduces the number of bandwidth updates by exploiting randomness. At each decision epoch, bandwidth is only updated with a small probability. For instance, at $25Mb/s$, the bandwidth switches to $20Mb/s$ with probability 1% (assuming empty buffer). Hence, it takes

$$\frac{1}{0.01}T \approx 10s$$

per update on average. Go on improving the performance of discrete DBA is a topic of our ongoing research.

5.3 Long Network Delay

As network delay increases, stability of flow control becomes more challenging, as reflected in Conditions C6 and C7. This motivates us to evaluate the impact of long network delay.

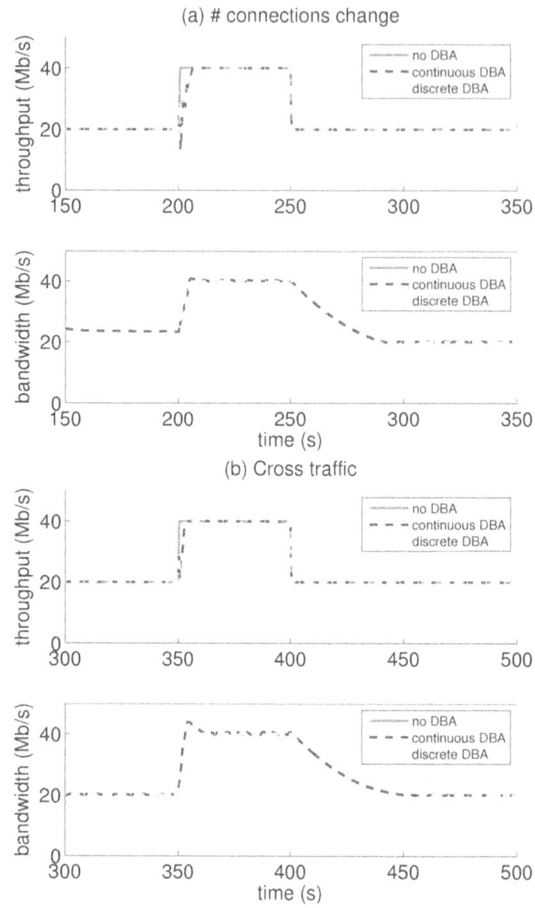

Figure 7: There are 40 TCP connections with $100ms$ RTT. 20 of the TCP connections are long-lived while the other 20 are active only from $200s$ to $250s$. Additional 20Mb/s UDP constant-bit-rate cross traffic comes at $350s$ and leaves at $400s$.

Figure 7 shows the throughput and bandwidth for all three settings (no DBA, continuous DBA, and discrete DBA) under the same setup as Figure 6, except that the RTT for each flow is 100ms rather than 50ms. It can be seen that the performance of DBA is almost unaffected: the traffic throughput is still as if no DBA is implemented; excess bandwidth is completely turned off at steady state for continuous DBA; bandwidth of discrete DBA follows the bandwidth of continuous DBA.

6. CONCLUSION

We have proposed easily implementable dynamic bandwidth adjustment (DBA) mechanisms that update link bandwidth with local buffer information. We proved global stability of TCP/RED/DBA if network delay is negligible, and local stability if network delay is bounded and link dynamics are sufficiently slow. We also proved that DBA turns off excess bandwidth without reducing throughput, and this is confirmed by ns2 simulations. With a simplified model for RED, we proved that TCP/RED/DBA solves an optimization problem—which we call the network surplus maximization problem—that is similar to the well-known network utility maximization problem.

7. REFERENCES

[1] F. P. Kelly, A. Maulloo, and D. Tan, "Rate control for communication networks: shadow prices, proportional fairness and stability," *Journal of Operations Research Society*, vol. 49, no. 3, 1998, pp. 237-252.

[2] S. H. Low and D. E. Lapsley, "Optimization flow control, I: basic algorithm and convergence," *IEEE/ACM Transactions on Networking*, vol. 7, no. 6, 1999, pp. 861-874.

[3] W. Lohmiller and J. E. Lapsley, "On contraction analysis for nonlinear systems," *Automatica*, vol. 34, no. 6, 1998, pp. 683-696.

[4] F. Paganini, Z. Wang, J. C. Doyle and S. H. Low, "Congestion control for high performance, stability, and fairness in general networks," *IEEE/ACM Transactions on Networking*, vol. 13, no. 1, 2005, pp. 43-56.

[5] S. H. Low, F. Paganini, J. Wang, and J. C. Doyle, "Linear stability of TCP/RED and a scalable control," *Computer Networks Journal*, vol. 14, no. 5, 2003, pp. 633-647.

[6] D. X. Wei, C. Jin, S. H. Low and S. Hegde, "FAST TCP: motivation, architecture, algorithms, performance," *IEEE/ACM Transactions on Networking*, vol. 15, no. 4, 2006, pp. 1246-1259.

[7] S. H. Low, "A duality model of TCP and queue management algorithms," *IEEE/ACM Transactions on Networking*, vol. 11, no. 4, 2003, pp. 525-536.

[8] S. Boyd and L. Vandenberghe, "Convex optimization," Cambridge University Press, 2004.

[9] J. He, M. Chiang, and J. Rexford, "Can congestion control and traffic engineering be at odds," *in Proceedings of the IEEE GLOBECOM*, 2006.

[10] J. Chabarek, J. Sommers, P. Barford, C. Estan, D. Tsiang, and S. Wright, " Power awareness in network design and routing," *IEEE INFOCOM*, 2008.

[11] W. Fisher, M. Suchara, and J. Rexford, "Greening backbone networks: reducing energy consumption by shutting off cables in bundled links," *in Proceedings of the first ACM SIGCOMM workshop on Green networking. ACM*, 2010, pp. 29-34.

[12] S. Nedevschi, L. Popa, G. Iannaccone, S. Ratnasamy, and D. Wetherall, "Reducing network energy consumption via sleeping and rate-adaptation," *in Proceedings of the 5th USENIX Symposium on Networked Systems Design and Implementation. USENIX Association*, 2008, pp. 323-336.

[13] L. Liu and B. Ramamurthy, "Rightsizing Bundle Link Capacities for Energy Savings in the Core Network", *IEEE GLOBECOM*, 2011.

[14] A. Francini, "Beyond RED: periodic early detection for on-chip buffer memories in network elements", *IEEE International conference on high performance switching and routing*, 2011.

APPENDIX

A. PROOF OF THEOREM 1

Convergence of $\dot{x}(t)$ to 0.

Lemma 1. *For each $i \in \mathcal{N}$, if $U_i''(x_i) \le -u_i \le 0$ for all x_i in $\mathcal{X}_i$, then the inequalities*

$$|\dot{q}_i(t)| \ge u_i|\dot{x}_i(t)|, \; \dot{q}_i(t)\dot{x}_i(t) \le -u_i|\dot{x}_i(t)|^2. \qquad (13)$$

hold for all t.

PROOF. $|\dot{q}_i| \ge |U_i''(x_i)\dot{x}_i| = u_i|\dot{x}_i|$, the rest is omitted. □

Lemma 2. *If condition C3 holds, then the inequality*

$$\sum_l \dot{p}_l(t)\dot{y}_l(t) \le -u\sum_i \dot{x}_i(t)^2$$

hold for all t.

PROOF.

$$\begin{aligned}\sum_l \dot{p}_l\dot{y}_l &= \sum_l \dot{p}_l \sum_i R_{li}\dot{x}_i = \sum_i \dot{x}_i \sum_l R_{li}\dot{p}_l \\ &= \sum_i \dot{x}_i\dot{q}_i \le -\sum_i u_i\dot{x}_i^2. \qquad \square\end{aligned}$$

Define indicators 1_l as

$$1_l(t) := \begin{cases} 1 & \text{if } b_l(t) > \underline{b}_l \text{ or } b_l(t) = \underline{b}_l \;\&\; \dot{b}_l \ge 0 \\ 0 & \text{otherwise} \end{cases},$$

for $l \in \mathcal{L}$, then $1_l = 0 \Rightarrow (p_l = 0 \;\&\; \dot{p}_l = 0)$ and $1_l = 1 \Rightarrow \dot{p}_l = \gamma_l\dot{b}_l$. We compute

$$\frac{d}{dt}\dot{p}_l^2 = 2\dot{p}_l\ddot{p}_l = 2\dot{p}_l\gamma_l\ddot{b}_l = 2\gamma_l\dot{p}_l(\dot{y}_l - \dot{c}_l),$$

$$\begin{aligned}1_l\alpha_l\gamma_l\frac{d}{dt}(b_l - \tilde{b}_l)^2 &= 2\alpha_l\gamma_l(b_l - \tilde{b}_l)(\dot{b}_l - \tilde{b}_l'(c_l)\dot{c}_l)1_l \\ &= 2\alpha_l\gamma_l\dot{b}_l 1_l(b_l - \tilde{b}_l) - 2d_l\gamma_l\dot{c}_l^2 1_l \\ &= 2\alpha_l\dot{p}_l(b_l - \tilde{b}_l) - 2d_l\gamma_l\dot{c}_l^2 1_l.\end{aligned}$$

Then we have

$$\begin{aligned}&\frac{1}{\gamma_l}\frac{d}{dt}\dot{p}_l^2 + 1_l\alpha_l\gamma_l\frac{d}{dt}(b_l - \tilde{b}_l)^2 \\ =\;& 2\dot{p}_l(\dot{y}_l - \dot{c}_l) + 2\alpha_l(b_l - \tilde{b}_l)\dot{p}_l - 2d_l\gamma_l\dot{c}_l^2 1_l \\ =\;& 2\dot{p}_l\dot{y}_l + 2\dot{p}_l(\alpha_l(b_l - \tilde{b}_l) - \dot{c}_l) - 2d_l\gamma_l\dot{c}_l^2 1_l.\end{aligned}$$

For each link l, let

$$(t_{2k-1}^l, t_{2k}^l) \subseteq [0, \infty), k \ge 1$$

denote the time segments on which $1_l = 1$ (t_k^l can be ∞). For convenience, we assume that $b_l(0) = \underline{b}_l$ for all $l \in \mathcal{L}$ in the rest of the proof. Extension to other initial points of b is similar. We ignore the superscript l when there is no confusion. Then 1) $t_1 = 0$; 2) $b_l = \underline{b}_l$ at t_k if $t_k \ne \infty$; 3) $b_l \ge \underline{b}_l > \tilde{b}_l(c_l)$ on (t_{2k-1}, t_{2k}) and 4) $\dot{c}_l \ge 0$ on (t_{2k-1}, t_{2k}). Note that on (t_{2k-1}, t_{2k}), $\dot{c}_l = 0$ if and only if $c_l = c_l^{max}$, and $\dot{c}_l > 0$ otherwise. If c_l reaches c_l^{max} on (t_{2k-1}, t_{2k}), define s_{2k} as the first time it attains c_l^{max}. Then we have 1) $c_l = c_l^{max}$ on (s_{2k}, t_{2k}), 2) $\dot{c}_l = \alpha_l(b_l - \tilde{b}_l)$ on (t_{2k-1}, s_{2k}), and

$$\begin{aligned}&\int_{t_{2k-1}}^{t_{2k}} 2\dot{p}_l(\alpha_l(b_l - \tilde{b}_l) - \dot{c}_l)dt \\ =\;& \int_{s_{2k}}^{t_{2k}} 2\gamma_l\dot{b}_l\alpha_l(b_l - \tilde{b}_l(c_l^{max}))dt \\ =\;& \alpha_l\gamma_l\left(b_l^2(t_{2k}) - b_l^2(s_{2k})\right) - 2\alpha_l\gamma_l\tilde{b}_l(c_l^{max})\left(b_l(t_{2k}) - b_l(s_{2k})\right) \\ =\;& \alpha_l\gamma_l\left(\underline{b}_l - b_l(s_{2k})\right)\left(\underline{b}_l + b_l(s_{2k}) - 2\tilde{b}_l(c_l^{max})\right) \le 0.\end{aligned}$$

If c_l does not reach c_l^{max} on (t_{2k-1}, t_{2k}), the integration above is obviously 0 since $\dot{c}_l = \alpha_l(b_l - \tilde{b}_l)$ on (t_{2k-1}, t_{2k}). Hence,

$$\begin{aligned}
&\int_0^\infty 2\dot{p}_l(\alpha_l(b_l - \tilde{b}_l) - \dot{c}_l)dl \\
&= \sum_{k\geq 1}\int_{t_{2k-1}}^{t_{2k}} 2\dot{p}_l(\alpha_l(b_l - \tilde{b}_l) - \dot{c}_l)dt \leq 0.
\end{aligned}$$

We also have

$$\begin{aligned}
&\int_{t_{2k-1}}^{t_{2k}} \left(-2d_l\gamma_l 1_l\dot{c}_l^2\right) dt \\
&= -2d_l\alpha_l\gamma_l \int_{t_{2k-1}}^{t_{2k}} \dot{c}_l(b_l - \tilde{b}_l)dt \\
&\leq -2d_l\alpha_l\gamma_l \int_{t_{2k-1}}^{t_{2k}} \dot{c}_l(\underline{b}_l - \tilde{b}_l)dt \\
&= d_l\alpha_l\gamma_l \left(d_l c_l^2 - 2\underline{b}_l c_l\right)|_{t_{2k-1}}^{t_{2k}} \\
&= \alpha_l\gamma_l \left(d_l c_l - \underline{b}_l\right)^2|_{t_{2k-1}}^{t_{2k}}.
\end{aligned}$$

Hence,

$$\int_0^\infty \left(-2d\gamma_l 1_l\dot{c}_l^2\right) dt \leq \alpha_l\gamma_l \sum_{k\geq 1} \left(d_l c_l - \underline{b}_l\right)^2|_{t_{2k-1}}^{t_{2k}}.$$

We have

$$\begin{aligned}
&\int_0^\infty \frac{d}{dt}\left(\frac{1}{\gamma_l}\dot{p}_l^2 + \alpha_l\gamma_l(b_l - \tilde{b}_l)^2\right) dt \\
&= \alpha_l\gamma_l \sum_{k\geq 1}(b_l - \tilde{b}_l)^2|_{t_{2k}}^{t_{2k+1}} \\
&\quad + \int_0^\infty \left(2\dot{p}_l\dot{y}_l + 2\dot{p}_l(\alpha_l(b_l - \tilde{b}_l) - \dot{c}_l) - 2d\gamma_l\dot{c}_l^2 1_l\right) dt \\
&\leq \alpha_l\gamma_l \sum_{k\geq 1}(\underline{b}_l - \tilde{b}_l)^2|_{t_{2k}}^{t_{2k+1}} + 2\int_0^\infty \dot{p}_l\dot{y}_l dt \\
&\quad + \alpha_l\gamma_l \sum_{k\geq 1}\left(d_l c_l - \underline{b}_l\right)^2|_{t_{2k-1}}^{t_{2k}} \\
&= 2\int_0^\infty \dot{p}_l\dot{y}_l dt - \alpha_l\gamma_l\left(\tilde{b}_l(0) - \underline{b}_l\right)^2.
\end{aligned}$$

Sum up the previous inequality for all $l \in \mathcal{L}$ yields

$$\begin{aligned}
&\int_0^\infty \frac{d}{dt}\sum_l\left(\frac{1}{\gamma_l}\dot{p}_l^2 + \alpha_l\gamma_l(b_l - \tilde{b}_l)^2\right) dt \\
&\leq 2\int_0^\infty \sum_l \dot{p}_l\dot{y}_l dt - \sum_l \alpha_l\gamma_l(\underline{b}_l - \tilde{b}_l(0))^2 \\
&\leq -\sum_l \alpha_l\gamma_l(\underline{b}_l - \tilde{b}_l(0))^2 - 2u\sum_i\int_0^\infty \dot{x}_i^2 dt.
\end{aligned}$$

Since the left hand side is finite,

$$\int_0^\infty \dot{x}_i^2 dt$$

is finite for all i. Since $\dot{x}_i$ is Lipschitz, $\dot{x}_i \to 0$ as $t \to \infty$.

Convergence of $x(t)$ *to* x^{NUM}.

Define the set

$$\mathcal{S} := \{(x, c, p, b) \mid \dot{x} = 0 \text{ according to Model SM}\},$$

and $\mathcal{M}$ its largest invariant set. Then starting from any element $(x, c, p, b) \in \mathcal{M}$, x and y are time-invariant. If $y_l > c_l^{max}$ for some $l \in \mathcal{L}$, then $b_l(t)$ blows up, driving x_i to 0 for $i \in \mathcal{N}_l$, contradict with $\dot{x} = 0$. Hence, $y_l \leq c_l^{max}$ for $l \in \mathcal{L}$ on $\mathcal{M}$. Each link l has a state (c_l, b_l) and constant control input y_l. From the phase plot in Figure 3, it is not difficult to show that (c_l, b_l) will converge to some equilibrium point (c_l^e, b_l^e). Let p_l^e be the packet drop probability corresponding to b_l^e. By checking the KKT conditions, (x, p^e) is primal dual optimal for Problem NUM with $c_l = c_l^{max}$ for all $l \in \mathcal{L}$. Hence, $x = x^{\text{NUM}}$. Now we have shown that $x \in \mathcal{M} \Rightarrow x = x^{\text{NUM}}$. Similar to Lasalle's theorem, we can show that $(x(t), c(t), p(t), b(t)) \to \mathcal{M}$. Consequently, $x(t) \to x^{\text{NUM}}$ as $t \to \infty$.

Convergence of $c(t)$ *to* $\max\{c^{min}, y^{\text{NUM}}\}$.

Consider each link l as an autonomous system with state (c_l, b_l) and input y_l. According to the phase plot in Figure 3, the system of link l is globally asymptotically stable with constant input y_l.[5] Since $x(t) \to x^{\text{NUM}}$, $y_l \to y_l^{\text{NUM}}$ for all l. If the input is y_l^{NUM}, the unique equilibrium point (c_l^e, b_l^e) satisfies that $c_l^e = \max\{c_l^{min}, y_l^{\text{NUM}}\}$. Consequently, $c_l(t) \to \max\{c_l^{min}, y_l^{\text{NUM}}\}$ as $t \to \infty$ for all $l \in \mathcal{L}$.

This completes the proof of Theorem 1.

B. PROOF OF THEOREM 3

Let (x^*, c^*, p^*) be an equilibrium for Model SSM, $(x(t), c(t), p(t))$ be an arbitrary trajectory generated by SSM. Define $\delta x(t) := x(t) - x^*$, $\delta c(t) := c(t) - c^*$, $\delta p(t) := p(t) - p^*$ as the deviation of the trajectory from the equilibrium.

Lemma 3. *For each $i \in \mathcal{N}$, if*

$$U_i''(x_i) \leq -u_i \leq 0, \ \forall x_i \in \mathcal{X}_i,$$

then

$$|\delta q_i(t)| \geq u_i|\delta x_i(t)|, \ \delta q_i(t)\delta x_i(t) \leq -u_i(\delta x_i(t))^2 \qquad (14)$$

for all t.

PROOF. For brevity, we abbreviate the argument t. We only show proof for the case $\delta x_i \leq 0$. Proof for the case $\delta x_i \geq 0$ is similar. If $\delta x_i = 0$, (14) is satisfied. Otherwise,

$$x_i^{min} \leq x_i < x_i^* \leq x_i^{max}.$$

It follows that

$$q_i \geq U_i'(x_i) > U_i'(x_i^*) \geq q_i^*,$$

and

$$\begin{aligned}
\delta q_i &\geq U_i'(x_i) - U_i'(x_i^*) = \int_{x_i}^{x_i^*} -U_i''(x)dx \\
&\geq \int_{x_i}^{x_i^*} u_i dx = -u_i\delta x_i.
\end{aligned}$$

It follows that (14) is satisfied. □

Define $B := \text{diag}(\beta_1, \ldots, \beta_L)$, $\Gamma := \text{diag}(\gamma_1, \ldots, \gamma_L)$. Since $\gamma_l > 0$, $\beta_l > 0$ for all $l \in \mathcal{L}$, diagonal matrices B and Γ are positive definite.

Lemma 4. *For each $l \in \mathcal{L}$,*

$$\begin{aligned}
\frac{d}{dt}\left(\frac{(p_l - p_l^*)^2}{\gamma_l}\right) &\leq 2(p_l - p_l^*)(y_l - c_l) \qquad (15)\\
&\leq 2\delta p_l(\delta y_l - \delta c_l). \qquad (16)
\end{aligned}$$

[5]When the input y_l is time-invariant, the dynamic of link l can be shown in a 2-dimensional phase plot, from which its global asymptotical stability is obvious.

PROOF. For each $l \in \mathcal{L}$, define

$$[a]_0 := \begin{cases} 0 & \text{if } p_l = 0 \ \&\ a < 0 \\ a & \text{otherwise} \end{cases},$$

then

$$\begin{aligned} \frac{d}{dt}\left(\frac{(p_l - p_l^*)^2}{\gamma_l}\right) &= \frac{2}{\gamma_l}(p_l - p_l^*)\dot{p}_l \\ &= \frac{2}{\gamma_l}(p_l - p_l^*)\left[\gamma_l(y_l - c_l)\right]_0 \\ &= 2(p_l - p_l^*)\left[y_l - c_l\right]_0 \end{aligned}$$

If $[y_l - c_l]_0 = y_l - c_l$, (15) is satisfied with equality. Otherwise, $[y_l - c_l]_0 = 0$, $p_l = 0$ and $y_l < c_l$. It follows that the left hand side of (15) is zero, and the right hand side of (15) is non-negative. Hence, (15) is always satisfied. Besides,

$$\begin{aligned} & 2(p_l - p_l^*)(y_l - c_l) \\ = \ & 2\delta p_l(y_l - y_l^* + c_l^* - c_l) + 2\delta p_l(y_l^* - c_l^*) \\ = \ & 2\delta p_l(\delta y_l - \delta c_l) + 2p_l(y_l^* - c_l^*) - 2p_l^*(y_l^* - c_l^*) \\ \leq \ & 2\delta p_l(\delta y_l - \delta c_l). \end{aligned}$$

The last inequality holds since $p_l^*(y_l^* - c_l^*) = 0$, $p_l \geq 0$, and $y_l^* \leq c_l^*$. □

Lemma 5. *For each $l \in \mathcal{L}$, if*

$$V_l''(c_l) \geq v_l \geq 0, \ \forall c_l \in C_l,$$

then

$$\frac{d}{dt}\left(\frac{(c_l - c_l^*)^2}{\beta_l}\right) \leq 2(c_l - c_l^*)(p_l - V_l'(c_l)) \quad (17)$$

$$\leq 2\delta c_l \delta p_l - 2v_l(\delta c_l)^2. \quad (18)$$

PROOF. For each $l \in \mathcal{L}$, define

$$[a]_{c_l^{min}}^{c_l^{max}} := \begin{cases} 0 & \text{if } c_l = c_l^{min} \ \&\ a < 0 \\ & \text{or } c_l = c_l^{max} \ \&\ a > 0 \\ a & \text{otherwise} \end{cases},$$

then,

$$\begin{aligned} \frac{d}{dt}\left(\frac{(c_l - c_l^*)^2}{\beta_l}\right) &= \frac{2}{\beta_l}(c_l - c_l^*)\dot{c}_l \\ &= \frac{2}{\beta_l}(c_l - c_l^*)\left[\beta_l(p_l - V_l'(c_l))\right]_{c_l^{min}}^{c_l^{max}} \\ &= 2(c_l - c_l^*)\left[p_l - V_l'(c_l)\right]_{c_l^{min}}^{c_l^{max}} \end{aligned}$$

If $[p_l - V_l'(c_l)]_{c_l^{min}}^{c_l^{max}} = p_l - V_l'(c_l)$, (17) is satisfied with equality. Otherwise, $[p_l - V_l'(c_l)]_{c_l^{min}}^{c_l^{max}} = 0$, the left hand side of (17) is zero. Besides, either $p_l > V_l'(c_l)$, $c_l = c_l^{max}$ or $p_l < V_l'(c_l)$, $c_l = c_l^{min}$. For both cases, the right hand side of (17) is non-negative. Hence, (17) is always satisfied. Besides,

$$\begin{aligned} & 2(c_l - c_l^*)(p_l - V_l'(c_l)) \\ = \ & 2\delta c_l(p_l - p_l^* + V_l'(c_l^*) - V_l'(c_l)) + 2\delta c_l(p_l^* - V_l'(c_l^*)) \\ \leq \ & 2\delta c_l \delta p_l + 2\delta c_l(V_l'(c_l^*) - V_l'(c_l)) \\ = \ & 2\delta c_l \delta p_l + 2\delta c_l \int_{c_l}^{c_l^*} V_l''(c)dc \\ \leq \ & 2\delta c_l \delta p_l + 2\delta c_l \int_{c_l}^{c_l^*} v_l dc \\ = \ & 2\delta c_l \delta p_l - 2v_l(\delta c_l)^2. \end{aligned}$$

Hence, (18) holds. □

Lemma 6. *If Conditions C3 and C4 hold, then*

$$\begin{aligned} & \frac{d}{dt}\left[\begin{pmatrix} \delta p \\ \delta c \end{pmatrix}^T \begin{pmatrix} \Gamma^{-1} & 0 \\ 0 & B^{-1} \end{pmatrix} \begin{pmatrix} \delta p \\ \delta c \end{pmatrix}\right] \\ \leq \ & -2\sum_{i \in \mathcal{N}} u(\delta x_i)^2 - 2\sum_{l \in \mathcal{L}} v(\delta c_l)^2. \end{aligned} \quad (19)$$

PROOF. If Conditions C3 and C4 hold, then

$$\begin{aligned} & \frac{d}{dt}\left[\begin{pmatrix} \delta p \\ \delta c \end{pmatrix}^T \begin{pmatrix} \Gamma^{-1} & 0 \\ 0 & B^{-1} \end{pmatrix} \begin{pmatrix} \delta p \\ \delta c \end{pmatrix}\right] \\ = \ & \sum_{l \in \mathcal{L}} \frac{d}{dt}\left(\frac{(p_l - p_l^*)^2}{\gamma_l}\right) + \sum_{l \in \mathcal{L}} \frac{d}{dt}\left(\frac{(c_l - c_l^*)^2}{\beta_l}\right) \\ \leq \ & \sum_{l \in \mathcal{L}} 2\delta p_l(\delta y_l - \delta c_l) + \sum_{l \in \mathcal{L}} 2\left(\delta c_l \delta p_l - v(\delta c_l)^2\right) \\ = \ & 2\sum_{l \in \mathcal{L}} \delta p_l \delta y_l - 2\sum_{l \in \mathcal{L}} v(\delta c_l)^2 \\ = \ & 2\sum_{i \in \mathcal{N}} \delta x_i \delta q_i - 2\sum_{l \in \mathcal{L}} v(\delta c_l)^2 \\ \leq \ & -2\sum_{i \in \mathcal{N}} u(\delta x_i)^2 - 2\sum_{l \in \mathcal{L}} v(\delta c_l)^2. \end{aligned}$$

The first inequality is due to (16) and (18), and the second inequality is due to (14). □

Proof of Theorem 3.

For brevity, define $z := (\delta p^T, \delta c^T)^T$, $M := \text{diag}(\Gamma^{-1}, B^{-1})$. Then (19) implies that

$$\begin{aligned} & \int_0^\infty \frac{d}{dt}\left(z^T M z\right) dt \\ \leq \ & -2u\sum_{i \in \mathcal{N}} \int_0^\infty (\delta x_i)^2 dt - 2v\sum_{l \in \mathcal{L}} \int_0^\infty (\delta c_l)^2 dt. \end{aligned}$$

Since the left hand side is bounded and δx_i is Lipschitz, we have $\delta x_i(t) \to 0$ as $t \to \infty$ for all $i \in \mathcal{N}$. Similarly, $\delta c_l(t) \to 0$ as $t \to \infty$ for all $l \in \mathcal{L}$. As $\delta x(t)/\delta c(t)$ denotes the deviation from $x(t)/c(t)$ to x^*/c^*, source rate $x(t)$ and link bandwidth $c(t)$ converge to the unique solution (x^*, c^*) to NSM. □

C. PROOF OF THEOREM 4

Let (x^*, c^*, p^*) be an equilibrium for Model SAM, then it's also an equilibrium for Model SSM, and primal dual optimal point for Problem NSM. Let $(x(t), c(t), p(t))$ be an arbitrary trajectory generated by SAM, and define $\delta x(t) := x(t) - x^*$, $\delta c(t) := c(t) - c^*$, $\delta p(t) := p(t) - p^*$ as the deviation from the trajectory to the equilibrium point (x^*, c^*, p^*).

We use the generalized Nyquist theorem to show local stability of (x^*, c^*). We first linearize dynamic equations (8,10,12) near (x^*, c^*, p^*), and then derive the loop transfer matrix. In the end, we evaluate the eigenvalues of the loop transfer matrix and show that they will not encircle the -1 point as frequency goes from $-\infty$ to ∞, if the conditions in Theorem 4 holds.

Linearization.

For each link $l \in \mathcal{L}$, c_l is restricted to the region $[c_l^{min}, c_l^{max}]$. If the constraint is active, c_l will be fixed at either c_l^{min} or c_l^{max}. Effectively, it is equivalent to c_l being static, and we only need to linearize (8) for the links that c_l is not static. For the same reason, we only linearize (10) and (12) for the links and sources that p_l and x_i are not effectively static. Without loss of generality, we assume that all links and sources are not effectively static, leading us to

$$\begin{aligned}
\dot{\delta c_l}(t) &= \beta_l(\delta p_l(t) - v_l \delta c_l(t)),\ l \in \mathcal{L}, \quad (20)\\
\dot{\delta p_l}(t) &= \gamma_l \left(\sum_{i \in \mathcal{N}} R_{li} \delta x_i(t-\tau_{il}) - \delta c_l(t) \right),\ l \in \mathcal{L}, (21)\\
\delta x_i(t) &= -u_i \sum_{l \in \mathcal{L}} R_{li} \delta p_l(t - \tau_{li}),\ i \in \mathcal{N}, \quad (22)
\end{aligned}$$

where $v_l := V_l''(c_l^*)$ for $l \in \mathcal{L}$ and $u_i := -1/U_i''(x_i^*)$ for $i \in \mathcal{N}$.

Loop Transfer Matrix.

Let $R(s)$ denote the $L \times N$ matrix whose (l,i) entry is given by $R_{li}(s) := R_{li}\exp(-s\tau_{il})$. Let $X(s)$, $P(s)$, $C(s)$ denote the Laplacian transformation of $\delta x(t)$, $\delta p(t)$, and $\delta c(t)$ respectively. Define $U := \mathrm{diag}(u_1, \ldots, u_N)$, $V := \mathrm{diag}(v_1, \ldots, v_L)$. Equation (20) implies

$$C(s) = \mathrm{diag}\left(\frac{\beta_l}{s + \beta_l v_l}\right) P(s).$$

Equation (21) implies

$$sP(s) = \Gamma R(s) X(s) - \Gamma C(s).$$

Equation (22) implies

$$\begin{aligned}
X_i(s) &= -u_i \sum_{l \in \mathcal{L}} R_{li} P_l(s) \exp(-s\tau_{li})\\
&= -u_i \exp(-s\tau_i) \sum_{l \in \mathcal{L}} R_{li} P_l(s) \exp(s\tau_{il})
\end{aligned}$$

for $i \in \mathcal{N}$. Hence,

$$X(s) = -\mathrm{diag}\left(u_i e^{-s\tau_i}\right) R^T(-s) P(s).$$

It is not difficult to show that the loop transfer matrix is

$$L(s) = \frac{1}{s}\Gamma R(s) \mathrm{diag}\left(u_i e^{-s\tau_i}\right) R^T(-s) + \mathrm{diag}\left(\frac{\beta_l \gamma_l}{s(s+\beta_l v_l)}\right).$$

Eigenvalues.

Define matrices

$$A := \mathrm{diag}\left(\frac{u_i e^{-jw\tau_i}}{jw}\right),\ D := \mathrm{diag}\left(\frac{\beta_l \gamma_l}{jw(jw + \beta_l v_l)}\right).$$

Let λ denote an arbitrary eigenvalue of $L(jw)$, and z its corresponding eigenvector. To this end, abbreviate $R(jw)$ as R, and use the superscript H to denote conjugate transpose, then

$$\begin{aligned}
\lambda z &= (\Gamma R A R^H + D) z,\\
\lambda z^H \Gamma^{-1} z &= z^H (R A R^H + \Gamma^{-1} D) z,\\
\lambda &= \frac{z^H R A R^H z}{z^H \Gamma^{-1} z} + \frac{z^H \Gamma^{-1} D z}{z^H \Gamma^{-1} z}.
\end{aligned}$$

Define

$$\lambda_1 := \frac{z^H R A R^H z}{z^H \Gamma^{-1} z},\ \lambda_2 := \frac{z^H \Gamma^{-1} D z}{z^H \Gamma^{-1} z},$$

then $\lambda = \lambda_1 + \lambda_2$. Denote $\xi := R^H z$, then

$$\|\xi\|^2 = z^H R R^H z \le LN \|z\|^2.$$

Condition C3 implies that $u_i \le 1/u$. Define $\gamma := \max_{l \in \mathcal{L}}\{\gamma_l\}$, $f_i := \frac{e^{-jw\tau_i}}{jw\tau_i}$, then

$$\begin{aligned}
\lambda_1 &= \frac{\xi^H A \xi}{z^H \Gamma^{-1} z}\\
&\in [0,1] * \gamma \frac{\xi^H A \xi}{z^H z}\\
&\subseteq [0,1] * \gamma L N \frac{\xi^H A \xi}{\xi^H \xi}\\
&= [0, \gamma L N] * \frac{\sum_{i \in \mathcal{N}} u_i \tau_i f_i \|\xi_i\|^2}{\sum_{i \in \mathcal{N}} \|\xi_i\|^2}\\
&= \left[0, \frac{\gamma L N \tau}{u}\right] * \sum_{i \in \mathcal{N}} \frac{u u_i \tau_i \|\xi_i\|^2}{\sum_{j \in \mathcal{N}} \tau \|\xi_j\|^2} f_i\\
&\subseteq [0,1] * \sum_{i \in \mathcal{N}} \frac{u u_i \tau_i \|\xi_i\|^2}{\sum_{j \in \mathcal{N}} \tau \|\xi_j\|^2} f_i.
\end{aligned}$$

Since $\tau_i \le \tau$, $u u_i \le 1$ for all $i \in \mathcal{N}$, λ_1 lies in the convex hull of $\{0, f_1, \ldots, f_N\}$. Define $d_l := \frac{\beta_l \gamma_l}{jw(jw + \beta_l v_l)}$ for all $l \in \mathcal{L}$, then d_l lies in the third orthant for all $w > 0$, and

$$\lambda_2 = \sum_{l \in \mathcal{L}} \frac{\|z_l\|^2/\gamma_l}{\sum_{k \in \mathcal{L}} \|z_k\|^2/\gamma_k} d_l$$

lies in the convex hull of $\{d_1, \ldots, d_L\}$.

Proof of Theorem 4.

When $0 < w < \frac{\pi}{2\tau}$, f_i is in the third orthant for all $i \in \mathcal{N}$. Hence, λ_1 is in the third orthant. Since d_l is also in the third orthant for all $l \in \mathcal{L}$ and all $w > 0$, λ_2 is in the third orthant. Hence, $\lambda = \lambda_1 + \lambda_2$ is in the third orthant when $0 < w < \frac{\pi}{2\tau}$.

When $w \ge \frac{\pi}{2\tau}$, Condition C7 implies that

$$|d_l| \le \frac{\beta_l \gamma_l}{\frac{\pi}{2\tau}\sqrt{\left(\frac{\pi}{2\tau}\right)^2 + (\beta_l v_l)^2}} \le \frac{4\tau^2}{\pi^2}\beta_l \gamma_l < 1 - \frac{2}{\pi}.$$

Hence, $|\lambda_2| < 1 - \frac{2}{\pi}$. Note that λ_1 lies in the shaded area in Figure 8, and λ_2 lies in the third orthant. $|\lambda_2| \ge 1 - \frac{2}{\pi}$ is necessary for λ to wind the -1 point. Hence, λ does not wind the -1 point when $w \ge \frac{\pi}{2\tau}$.

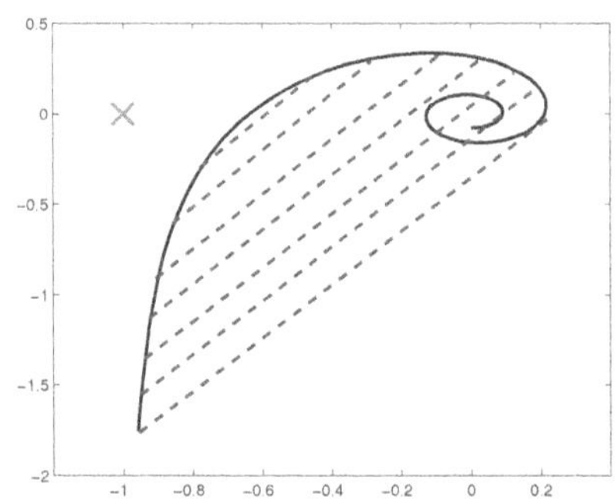

Figure 8: Nyquist plot for $f_i, i \in \mathcal{N}$.

Hence, λ does not wind the -1 point as w goes from 0 to ∞. Similarly, λ does not cross the -1 point as w goes from $-\infty$ to 0. Since λ is an arbitrary eigenvalue of the loop transfer matrix, the equilibrium point (x^*, c^*, p^*) is locally asymptotically stable by the generalized Nyquist theorem.□

Uniform Approximation of the Distribution for the Number of Retransmissions of Bounded Documents*

Predrag R. Jelenković
Department of Electrical Engineering
Columbia University, New York, NY 10027
predrag@ee.columbia.edu

Evangelia D. Skiani
Department of Electrical Engineering
Columbia University, New York, NY 10027
valia@ee.columbia.edu

ABSTRACT

Retransmission-based failure recovery represents a primary approach in existing communication networks, on all protocol layers, that guarantees data delivery in the presence of channel failures. Contrary to the traditional belief that the number of retransmissions is geometrically distributed, a new phenomenon was discovered recently, which shows that retransmissions can cause long (-tailed) delays and instabilities even if all traffic and network characteristics are light-tailed, e.g., exponential or Gaussian. Since the preceding finding holds under the assumption that data sizes have infinite support, in this paper we investigate the practically important case of bounded data units $0 \leq L_b \leq b$. To this end, we provide an explicit and uniform characterization of the entire body of the retransmission distribution $\mathbb{P}[N_b > n]$ in both n and b. This rigorous approximation clearly demonstrates the previously observed transition from power law distributions in the main body to exponential tails. The accuracy of our approximation is validated with a number of simulation experiments. Furthermore, the results highlight the importance of wisely determining the size of data units in order to accommodate the performance needs in retransmission-based systems. From a broader perspective, this study applies to any other system, e.g., computing, where restart mechanisms are employed after a job processing failure.

Categories and Subject Descriptors

G.3 [**Probability And Statistics**]: Probabilistic algorithms; C.4 [**Performance of Systems**]: Performance Attributes; H.4 [**Information Systems Applications**]: Miscellaneous

General Terms

Algorithms, Performance, Theory

*This work is supported by the National Science Foundation grant number 0915784.

Keywords

Retransmissions, restarts, channel with failures, truncated distributions, power laws, Gamma distributions, heavy-tailed distributions, light-tailed distributions.

1. INTRODUCTION

Failure recovery mechanisms are employed in almost all engineering systems since complex systems of any kind are often prone to failures. One of the most straightforward and widely used failure recovery mechanism is to simply restart the system and all of the interrupted jobs from the beginning after a failure occurs. It was first recognized in [5, 13] that such mechanisms may result in long-tailed (power law) delays even if the job sizes and failure rates are exponential. In [7], it was noted that the same mechanism is at the core of modern communication networks where retransmissions are used on all protocol layers to guarantee data delivery in the presence of channel failures. Furthermore, [7] shows that the power law number of retransmissions and delay occur whenever the hazard functions of the data and failure distributions are linearly proportional. Hence, power laws may arise even if the data and channel failure distributions are both Gaussian. In particular, retransmission phenomena can lead to zero throughput and system instabilities, and therefore need to be carefully considered for the design of fault tolerant systems.

More specifically, in communication networks, retransmissions represent the basic building blocks for failure recovery in all network protocols that guarantee data delivery in the presence of channel failures. These types of mechanisms have been employed on all networking layers, including, for example, Automatic Repeat reQuest (ARQ) protocol (e.g., see Section 2.4 of [3]) in the data link layer where a packet is resent automatically in case of an error; contention based ALOHA type protocols in the medium access control (MAC) layer that use random backoff and retransmission mechanism to recover data from collisions; end-to-end acknowledgement for multi-hop transmissions in the transport layer; HTTP downloading scheme in the application layer, etc. It has been shown that several well-known retransmission based protocols in different layers of networking architecture can lead to power law delays, e.g., ALOHA type protocols in MAC layer [8] and end-to-end acknowledgements in transport layer [6, 9] as well as in other layers [7].

Traditionally, retransmissions were thought to follow light-tailed distributions (with rapidly decaying tails), namely geometric, which requires the further assumption of independence between data (packet) sizes and transmission error probability. However, these two are often highly correlated in most communication systems, meaning that longer data units have higher probability of error, thus violating the independence assumption. Recent work [7, 8] has shown that, when the data size distribution has infinite support, all retransmission-based protocols could cause heavy-tailed behavior and possibly result in zero throughput, regardless of how light-tailed the distributions of data sizes and channel failures are. Nevertheless, in reality, packet sizes are upper bounded by the maximum transmission unit. For example, WaveLAN's maximum transfer unit is 1500 bytes. This fact motivates us to investigate the transmission of bounded data and approximate uniformly the entire body of the resulting retransmission distribution as it transits from the power law to the exponential tail.

We use the following generic channel with failures [7] to model the preceding situations. This model was first introduced (for $U_i = 0$) in [5] in a different application context. The channel dynamics is described as an on-off process $\{(A, U), (A_i, U_i)\}_{i\geq 1}$ with alternating periods when channel is available A_i and unavailable U_i, respectively; $(A, A_i)_{i\geq 1}$ and $(U, U_i)_{i\geq 1}$ are two independent sequences of i.i.d random variables. In each period of time that the channel becomes available, say A_i, we attempt to transmit the data unit of random size L_b. We focus on the situation when the data size has finite support on interval $[0, b]$. If $L_b < A_i$, we say that the transmission is successful; otherwise, we wait for the next period A_{i+1} when the channel is available and attempt to retransmit the data from the beginning. It was first recognized in [5] that this model results in power law distributions when the distributions of $L \equiv L_\infty$ and A have a matrix exponential representation, and this result was rigorously proved and further generalized in [7, 9, 2].

It was discovered in [7] that bounded data units result in truncated power law distributions for the number of retransmissions, see Example 3 in [7]. Such distributions are characterized by a power law main body and an exponentially bounded tail. However, the exponential behavior appears only for very small probabilities, often meaning that the number of retransmissions of interest may fall inside the region of the distribution that behaves as a power law. It was argued in Example 3 of [7] that the power law region will grow faster than exponential if the distributions of A and L_b are lighter than exponential. This phenomenon was further studied in [14], where partial approximations of the distribution of the number of retransmissions on the logarithmic and exact scales were provided in Theorems 1 and 3 of [14], respectively. In this paper, we present a uniform characterization of the entire body of such a distribution, both on the logarithmic as well as the exact scale.

Specifically, let N_b represent the number of retransmissions (until successful transmission) of a bounded random data unit of size $L_b \in [0, b]$ on the previously described channel. In order to study the uniform approximation in both n and b we construct a family of variables L_b, such that $\mathbb{P}[L_b \leq x] = \mathbb{P}[L \leq x]/\mathbb{P}[L \leq b]$, for $0 \leq x \leq b$ when $L = L_\infty$ is fixed. This scaling of L_b was also used in [14]. For the logarithmic scale, our result stated in Theorem 2, provides a uniform characterization of the entire body of $\log \mathbb{P}[N_b > n]$, i.e., informally

$$\log \mathbb{P}[N_b > n] \approx -\alpha \log n + n \log \mathbb{P}[A \leq b]$$

for all n and b sufficiently large. Note that the first term in the preceding approximation corresponds to the power law part $n^{-\alpha}$ of the distribution, while the second part describes the exponential (geometric $\mathbb{P}[A \leq b]^n$) tail. Hence, it may be natural to define the transition point n_b from the power law to the exponential tail as a solution to $n_b \log \mathbb{P}[A \leq b] \approx \alpha \log n_b$.

In addition, under more restrictive assumptions, we discover a new exact asymptotic formula for the retransmission distribution that works uniformly for all large n, b. Surprisingly, the approximation admits an explicit form (see Theorems 3 and 4)

$$\mathbb{P}[N_b > n] \approx \frac{\alpha}{n^\alpha \ell(n \wedge \mathbb{P}[A > b]^{-1})} \int_{-n \log \mathbb{P}[A \leq b]}^{\infty} e^{-z} z^{\alpha - 1} dz, \tag{1.1}$$

where $x \wedge y = \min(x, y)$ and $\ell(\cdot)$ is a slowly varying function; note that the preceding integral is the incomplete Gamma function $\Gamma(x, \alpha)$.

Clearly, when $-n \log \mathbb{P}[A \leq b] \downarrow 0$, the preceding approximation converges to a true power law $\Gamma(\alpha + 1)/(\ell(n) n^\alpha)$. And, when $-n \log(\mathbb{P}[A < b]) \uparrow \infty$, approximation (1.1), by the property $\Gamma(x, \alpha) \approx e^{-x} x^{\alpha - 1}$ as $x \to \infty$, has a geometric leading term $\mathbb{P}[A \leq b]^n$. Interestingly, when α is an integer, one can compute the exact expression for $\mathbb{P}[N_b > n]$ under more restrictive assumptions, see Proposition 2.2. Furthermore, our results show that the length of the power law region increases as the corresponding distributions of L and A assume lighter tails. All of the preceding results are validated via simulation experiments in Section 3. It is worth noting that our asymptotic approximations are in excellent agreement with the simulations.

This uniform approximation allows for a characterization of the entire body of the distribution $\mathbb{P}[N_b > n]$, so that one can explicitly estimate the region where the power law phenomenon arises. Introducing the relationship between n and $\mathbb{P}[A > b]$ also provides an assessment method of efficiency and is important for diminishing the power law effects in order to achieve high throughput. Basically, when the power law region is significant, it could lead to nearly zero throughput ($\alpha < 1$), implying that the system parameters should be more carefully adjusted in order to meet the new requirements. On the contrary, if the exponential tail dominates, the system performance is more desirable. Our analytical work could be applicable in network protocol design, possibly including packet fragmentation techniques [10, 11] and failure-recovery mechanisms. In particular, since we know the entire body of the distribution, we could approximate the mean value of N_b, and thus, via Wald's identity, the mean delay and throughput.

Also, from an engineering perspective, our results further suggest that careful re-examination and possible redesign of retransmission based protocols in communication networks might be necessary. Specifically, current engineering trends towards infrastructure-less, error-prone wireless technology encourage the study of highly variable systems with frequent failures. Hence, our results could be of potential use in improving the design of future complex and failure-prone systems.

The rest of the paper is organized as follows. After a detailed description of the channel model in the next Subsection 1.1, we present our main results in Section 2. Then, we conclude the paper with Section 3 that contains simulation examples to verify our theoretical work, which is followed by Section 4, where we include some of the technical proofs.

1.1 Description of the Channel

In this section, we formally describe our model and provide necessary definitions and notation. Consider transmitting a generic data unit of random size L_b over a channel with failures. Without loss of generality, we assume that the channel is of unit capacity. The channel dynamics is modeled as an on-off process $\{(A_i, U_i)\}_{i\geq 1}$ with alternating independent periods when channel is available A_i and unavailable U_i, respectively. In each period of time that the channel becomes available, say A_i, we attempt to transmit the data unit and, if $A_i > L_b$, we say that the transmission was successful; otherwise, we wait for the next period A_{i+1} when the channel is available and attempt to retransmit the data from the beginning. A sketch of the model depicting the system is drawn in Figure 1.

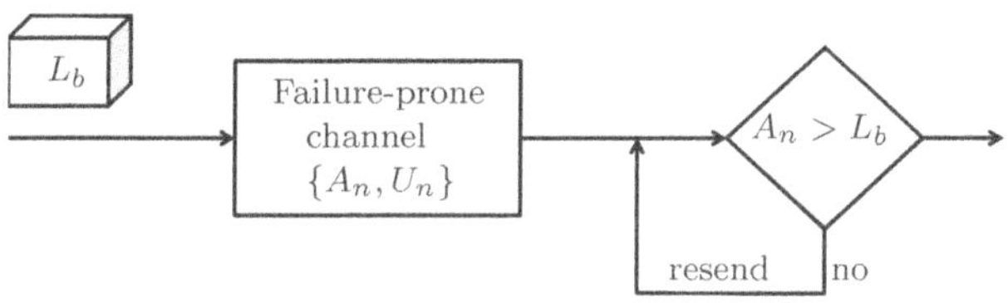

Figure 1: Packets sent over a channel with failures

Assume that $\{U, U_i\}_{i\geq 1}$ and $\{A, A_i\}_{i\geq 1}$ are two mutually independent sequences of i.i.d. random variables.

Definition 1.1 *The total number of (re)transmissions for a generic data unit of length L_b is defined as*

$$N_b \triangleq \inf\{n : A_n > L_b\}$$

We denote the complementary cumulative distribution functions for A and L, respectively, as

$$\bar{G}(x) \triangleq \mathbb{P}[A > x]$$

and

$$\bar{F}(x) \triangleq \mathbb{P}[L > x],$$

where L is a generic random variable that is used to define the distribution of L_b.

Throughout the paper we assume that $\bar{G}(x)$ and $\bar{F}(x)$ are absolutely continuous and have infinite support, i.e., $\bar{G}(x) > 0$ and $\bar{F}(x) > 0$ for all $x \geq 0$. Then, the distribution of L_b is defined as

$$\mathbb{P}[L_b \leq x] = \frac{\mathbb{P}[L \leq x]}{\mathbb{P}[L \leq b]}, \quad 0 \leq x \leq b. \tag{1.2}$$

To avoid trivialities, we always assume $\mathbb{P}[L \leq b] > 0$.

In this paper we use the following standard notations. For any two real functions $a(t)$ and $b(t)$ and fixed $t_0 \in \mathbb{R}\bigcup\{\infty\}$, we use $a(t) \sim b(t)$ as $t \to t_0$ to denote $\lim_{t\to t_0} a(t)/b(t) = 1$. Similarly, we say that $a(t) \gtrsim b(t)$ as $t \to t_0$ if $\liminf_{t\to t_0} [a(t)/b(t)] \geq 1$; $a(t) \lesssim b(t)$ has a complementary definition.

2. MAIN RESULTS

In this section, we present our main results. Under mild conditions, we first prove a general upper bound for the distribution of N_b in Proposition 2.1. Next, we show that $-\log \mathbb{P}[N_b > n]$ is actually a power law in the region where $n/\log n \leq o(1/\bar{G}(b))$, which represents the main body of the distribution, see Theorem 1. Then, in Theorem 2, we present our first main result, which under more stringent assumptions, characterizes the entire body of the distribution on the logarithmic scale uniformly for all large n and b, i.e., informally we show that

$$\log \mathbb{P}[N_b > n] \approx -\alpha \log n + n \log \mathbb{P}[A \leq b],$$

as previously mentioned in the introduction. Our results on the exact asymptotics are given in the next Subsection 2.1 in Theorems 3 and 4.

Recall that the distribution of L_b has finite support on $[0, b]$, given by (1.2). First, we prove the following general upper bound.

Proposition 2.1 *Assume that*

$$\log \mathbb{P}[L > x] \lesssim \alpha \log \mathbb{P}[A > x] \quad \text{as } x \to \infty$$

and let b_0 be such that $\mathbb{P}[L \leq b_0] > 0$, then for any $\epsilon > 0$, there exists n_0, such that, for all $n \geq n_0, b \geq b_0$,

$$\log \mathbb{P}[N_b > n] \leq (1 - \epsilon)\left[n \log \mathbb{P}[A \leq b] - \alpha \log n\right].$$

PROOF. See Section 4. □

Next, we determine the region where the power law asymptotics holds on the logarithmic scale.

Theorem 1 *If*

$$\log \mathbb{P}[L > x] \sim \alpha \log \mathbb{P}[A > x] \quad \text{as } x \to \infty, \tag{2.1}$$

then, for any $\epsilon > 0$, there exist positive n_0, δ, such that for all $n \geq n_0$, $n\mathbb{P}[A > b] \leq \delta \log n$, we have

$$\left|\frac{-\log \mathbb{P}[N_b > n]}{\alpha \log n} - 1\right| \leq \epsilon. \tag{2.2}$$

PROOF. See Section 4. □

Remark 1 Note that this result extends the region of validity of Theorem 1(i) in [14] since $\delta \log n/\bar{G}(b) >> \bar{G}(b)^{-\eta}, 0 < \eta < 1$. In addition, $n/\log n \leq o(1/\bar{G}(b))$ can be shown to be the largest region where the power law asymptotics holds.

Next, one can easily characterize the logarithmic asymptotics of the very end of the exponential tail of $\mathbb{P}[N_b > n]$ for small b and large n. In particular, for fixed b, it can be shown that $\log \mathbb{P}[N_b > n] \sim n \log(1 - \bar{G}(b))$ as $n \to \infty$, see Theorem 1 in [14].

However, our main goal in this paper is to determine the entire body of the distribution of $\mathbb{P}[N_b > n]$ uniformly in n and b. To this end, in the region where $n\bar{G}(b) > \delta \log n$, we need more restrictive assumptions than in (2.1) in order to approximate $\log \mathbb{P}[N_b > n]$. The reason why this is the case is that $\mathbb{P}[N_b > n]$ behaves like a power law in the region where $n/\log n << 1/\bar{G}(b)$, while for $n/\log n >> 1/\bar{G}(b)$, it follows essentially a geometric distribution. Hence, more restrictive assumptions are required since the geometric distribution is much more sensitive to the changes in its parameters (informally, $((1+\epsilon)x)^{-\alpha} \approx x^{-\alpha}$ but $e^{-(1+\epsilon)x} \not\approx e^{-x}$).

Definition 2.1 *A function $\ell(x)$ is slowly varying if $\ell(x)/\ell(\lambda x) \to 1$ as $x \to \infty$ for any fixed $\lambda > 0$.*

We also assume that functions $\ell(x)$ are positive and bounded on finite intervals.

Theorem 2 *If* $\mathbb{P}[A > x] = \ell(\mathbb{P}[L > x]^{-1})\mathbb{P}[L > x]^{1/\alpha}$, $\alpha > 0$, $x \geq 0$, $\ell(x)$ *slowly varying, then for any* $\epsilon > 0$*, there exist* n_0, b_0*, such that for all* $n \geq n_0, b \geq b_0$,

$$\left|\frac{-\log \mathbb{P}[N_b > n]}{-n\log \mathbb{P}[A \leq b] + \alpha \log n} - 1\right| \leq \epsilon.$$

Remark 2 Note that the statement of this theorem can be formulated in an equivalent form

$$\left|\frac{-\log \mathbb{P}[N_b > n]}{n\mathbb{P}[A > b] + \alpha \log n} - 1\right| \leq \epsilon,$$

since $-n\log \mathbb{P}[A \leq b] \approx n\mathbb{P}[A > b]$ for large b.

Remark 3 This theorem unifies and extends Theorem 1 in [14]. In particular, it proves the result uniformly in n and b, while Theorem 1 in [14] characterized the initial power law part of the distribution ($n \leq \bar{G}(b)^{-\eta}, 0 < \eta < 1$) and the very end with exponential tail (fixed b, $n \to \infty$).

PROOF. The case where $n \leq \delta \log n/\bar{G}(b)$ is already covered by Theorem 1 since for δ sufficiently small, $\alpha \log n \leq -n\log(1-\bar{G}(b)) + \alpha \log n \leq (\alpha+\epsilon)\log n$. Hence, it remains to prove the result for $n \geq \delta \log n/\bar{G}(b)$. To this end, observe that

$$\begin{aligned}\mathbb{P}[N_b > n] &= \mathbb{E}[1 - \bar{G}(L_b)]^n \\ &= \int_0^b \left(1 - \ell(\bar{F}(x)^{-1})\bar{F}(x)^{\frac{1}{\alpha}}\right)^n \frac{dF(x)}{F(b)},\end{aligned}$$

and by $F(b) \leq 1$ and the absolute continuity of $F(x)$,

$$\begin{aligned}\mathbb{P}[N_b > n] &\geq \int_{\bar{F}(b)}^1 \left(1 - \ell(z^{-1})z^{\frac{1}{\alpha}}\right)^n dz \\ &\geq \int_{\bar{F}(b)}^{\lambda\bar{F}(b)} \left(1 - \ell(z^{-1})z^{\frac{1}{\alpha}}\right)^n dz,\end{aligned}$$

where $\lambda > 1$ is chosen so that $\lambda\bar{F}(b) \leq 1$, since $\bar{F}(b) < 1$. Now, we can use the slowly varying property of $\ell(x)$ in the region $\{\bar{F}(b)^{-1}, \lambda^{-1}\bar{F}(b)^{-1}\}$ and thus, for b_0 large enough, $b \geq b_0$,

$$\mathbb{P}[N_b > n] \geq \int_{\bar{F}(b)}^{\lambda\bar{F}(b)} \left(1 - (1-\epsilon)\ell(\bar{F}(b)^{-1})z^{\frac{1}{\alpha}}\right)^n dz.$$

Then, by changing variables $u = (1-\epsilon)\ell\left(\bar{F}(b)^{-1}\right) z^{1/\alpha}$ and setting $C_{b,\epsilon}^{1/\alpha} = (1-\epsilon)\ell(\bar{F}(b)^{-1})$, we obtain

$$\begin{aligned}\mathbb{P}[N_b > n] &\geq \int_{(1-\epsilon)\ell(\bar{F}(b)^{-1})\bar{F}(b)^{\frac{1}{\alpha}}}^{\lambda^{1/\alpha}(1-\epsilon)\ell(\bar{F}(b)^{-1})\bar{F}(b)^{\frac{1}{\alpha}}} (1-u)^n \frac{\alpha u^{\alpha-1}}{C_{b,\epsilon}} du \\ &= \frac{\alpha}{C_{b,\epsilon}} \int_{(1-\epsilon)\bar{G}(b)}^{\lambda^{1/\alpha}(1-\epsilon)\bar{G}(b)} (1-u)^n u^{\alpha-1} du,\end{aligned}$$

where $\bar{G}(b) = \ell(\bar{F}(b)^{-1})\bar{F}(b)^{\frac{1}{\alpha}}$ from our main assumption.

Now, if $\alpha \geq 1$, $u^{\alpha-1}$ is monotonically increasing and thus

$$\begin{aligned}\mathbb{P}[N_b > n] &\geq \frac{\alpha(1-\epsilon)^{\alpha-1}\bar{G}(b)^{\alpha-1}}{C_{b,\epsilon}} \int_{(1-\epsilon)\bar{G}(b)}^{\lambda^{1/\alpha}(1-\epsilon)\bar{G}(b)} (1-u)^n du \\ &= \frac{\alpha(1-\epsilon)^{\alpha-1}\bar{G}(b)^{\alpha-1}}{C_{b,\epsilon}} \frac{(1-u)^{n+1}}{n+1}\Big|_{\lambda^{1/\alpha}(1-\epsilon)\bar{G}(b)}^{(1-\epsilon)\bar{G}(b)} \\ &= \frac{\alpha(1-\epsilon)^{\alpha-1}\bar{G}(b)^{\alpha-1}}{C_{b,\epsilon}(n+1)} \Big[\left(1-(1-\epsilon)\bar{G}(b)\right)^{n+1} \\ &\qquad -(1-\lambda^{1/\alpha}(1-\epsilon)\bar{G}(b))^{n+1}\Big] \\ &= \frac{\alpha(1-\epsilon)^{\alpha-1}\bar{G}(b)^{\alpha-1}\left(1-(1-\epsilon)\bar{G}(b)\right)^{n+1}}{C_{b,\epsilon}(n+1)} \\ &\quad \times \left(1 - \left[\frac{1-\lambda^{1/\alpha}(1-\epsilon)\bar{G}(b)}{1-(1-\epsilon)\bar{G}(b)}\right]^{n+1}\right) \\ &\geq \frac{\alpha(1-\epsilon)^{\alpha}\bar{G}(b)^{\alpha-1}}{C_{b,\epsilon}(n+1)} \left(1-(1-\epsilon)\bar{G}(b)\right)^{n+1} \quad (2.3)\end{aligned}$$

The last inequality is implied by standard limit $(1-y/n)^n \to e^{-y}$ as $n \to \infty$, i.e.,

$$\begin{aligned}\lim_{n\to\infty}\left(\frac{1-\lambda^{1/\alpha}(1-\epsilon)\bar{G}(b)}{1-(1-\epsilon)\bar{G}(b)}\right)^{n+1} &= \lim_{n\to\infty}\frac{e^{-\lambda^{1/\alpha}(1-\epsilon)(n+1)\bar{G}(b)}}{e^{-(1-\epsilon)(n+1)\bar{G}(b)}} \\ &= \lim_{n\to\infty} e^{-(\lambda^{1/\alpha}-1)(1-\epsilon)(n+1)\bar{G}(b)} = 0,\end{aligned}$$

since $\lambda^{1/\alpha} > 1$ and the assumption $n\bar{G}(b) \geq \delta \log n$.

Then, using the standard property of slowly varying functions (see [4]) that $\ell(x) \leq Hx^{\eta}$, for any $\eta > 0$ and some sufficiently large constant H, we derive $C_{b,\epsilon}/(1-\epsilon)^{\alpha} = \ell(\bar{F}(b)^{-1})^{\alpha} \leq \sqrt{H}\bar{F}(b)^{-\epsilon(1-\alpha\epsilon)} \leq H\bar{G}(b)^{-\epsilon\alpha}$ and thus, by (2.3), obtain

$$\begin{aligned}\mathbb{P}[N_b > n] &\geq \frac{\alpha\bar{G}(b)^{\alpha-1+\epsilon\alpha}}{(n+1)H}\left(1-(1-\epsilon)\bar{G}(b)\right)^{n+1} \\ &= \frac{\alpha_H\bar{G}(b)^{\alpha-1+\epsilon\alpha}}{n+1}\left(1-(1-\epsilon)\bar{G}(b)\right)^{n+1},\end{aligned}$$

where we define $\alpha_H = \alpha/H$. Next, by taking the logarithm,

$$\begin{aligned}\log \mathbb{P}[N_b > n] &\geq \log \alpha_H + (\alpha(1+\epsilon)-1)\log \bar{G}(b) \\ &\quad + (n+1)\log(1-(1-\epsilon)\bar{G}(b)) - \log(n+1) \\ &\geq \log \alpha_H - (\alpha(1+\epsilon)-1)\log n \\ &\quad + (\alpha(1+\epsilon)-1)\log(\delta \log n) \\ &\quad + (n+1)\log(1-(1-\epsilon)\bar{G}(b)) - \log(1+\epsilon)n,\end{aligned}$$

where in the last inequality we used $\log \bar{G}(b) \geq \log(\delta \log n) - \log n$. Then, we can pick n_0 such that, for all $n \geq n_0$, $\log(\delta \log n) \geq (\log(1+\epsilon) - \log \alpha_H)/(\alpha(1+\epsilon)-1)$. Hence,

$$\begin{aligned}\log \mathbb{P}[N_b > n] &\geq -\alpha(1+\epsilon)\log n + (n+1)\log(1-(1-\epsilon)\bar{G}(b)) \\ &\geq -\alpha(1+\epsilon)\log n + n(1+\epsilon)\log(1-\bar{G}(b)) \\ &= -(1+\epsilon)\left(\alpha \log n - n\log(1-\bar{G}(b))\right).\end{aligned}$$

Finally, dividing by $(\alpha \log n - n\log(1-\bar{G}(b))) > 0$ yields

$$\frac{\log \mathbb{P}[N_b > n]}{\alpha \log n - n\log(1-\bar{G}(b))} \geq -(1+\epsilon)$$

Symmetric arguments hold for the case where $\alpha < 1$. We omit the details. □

2.1 Exact Asymptotics

In this section, under more restrictive assumptions, we derive the exact approximation for $\mathbb{P}[N_b > n]$ that works uniformly for all n, b sufficiently large (Theorems 3 and 4). Although some of the assumptions can be relaxed, we refrain from such generalizations here in order to gain analytical tractability. Interestingly enough, this characterization is explicit in that

$$\mathbb{P}[N_b > n] \approx \frac{\alpha}{n^\alpha \ell(n \wedge \mathbb{P}[A > b]^{-1})} \int_{-n \log \mathbb{P}[A \le b]}^{\infty} e^{-z} z^{\alpha-1} dz, \tag{2.4}$$

where $x \wedge y = \min(x, y)$ and $\ell(\cdot)$ is slowly varying. Implicitly, the argument of $\ell(x)$ is altered depending on whether $n\mathbb{P}[A > b] \le C$ or $n\mathbb{P}[A > b] > C$ for some constant C. Hence, we can choose $C = 1$ since $\ell(n \wedge 1/\mathbb{P}[A > b]) \approx \ell(n \wedge C/\mathbb{P}[A > b])$ for large n, b. Note that when $-n \log \mathbb{P}[A \le b] \downarrow 0$, the power law dominates, whereas when $-n \log \mathbb{P}[A \le b] \to \infty$, the integral determines the tail with the geometric (exponential) leading term.

We would like to point out that approximation (2.4) actually works well when $\mathbb{P}[A > b]^{-1}$ is large rather than simply b; this can be concluded by examining the proofs of the theorems in this section. Hence, formula (2.4) can be accurate for relatively small values of b provided that A is light-tailed. This may be the reason why we obtain such accurate results in our simulation examples in Section 3 for $b \le 10$.

First, in Theorem 3, we precisely describe the region where the distribution of N_b exhibits the power law behavior, $n\mathbb{P}[A > b] \le C$, for any fixed constant C. Then, Theorem 4 covers the remaining region, $n\mathbb{P}[A > b] > C$, where $\mathbb{P}[N_b > n]$ approaches the geometric tail. Proposition 2.3 gives an explicit exact asymptote for the exponential tail with b possibly small and $n \to \infty$.

Theorem 3 *Let $\mathbb{P}[L > x]^{-1} = \ell(\mathbb{P}[A > x]^{-1})\mathbb{P}[A > x]^{-\alpha}$, $\alpha > 0$, $x \ge 0$, and $C > 0$ be a fixed constant. Then, for any $\epsilon > 0$, there exists n_0 such that for all $n \ge n_0$, and $n\mathbb{P}[A > b] \le C$,*

$$\left| \frac{\mathbb{P}[N_b > n] n^\alpha \ell(n)}{\alpha \Gamma(-n \log \mathbb{P}[A \le b], \alpha)} - 1 \right| \le \epsilon, \tag{2.5}$$

where $\Gamma(x, \alpha)$ is the incomplete Gamma function defined as $\int_x^\infty e^{-z} z^{\alpha-1} dz$.

PROOF. This result can be proved using similar techniques as in [9]. We omit the details. □

Remark 4 Related result was derived in Theorem 3 of [14] where it was required that $n \le \bar{G}(b)^{-\eta}, 0 < \eta < 1$. Note that here we broaden the region where the result holds by requiring $n \le C/\bar{G}(b)$, which is larger than $n \le \bar{G}(b)^{-\eta}$. Furthermore, this is the largest region where the exact power law asymptotics $O(n^{-\alpha}/\ell(n))$ holds since for $n\bar{G}(b) > C$, $\Gamma(n\bar{G}(b), \alpha) \le \Gamma(C, \alpha) \to 0$ as $C \to \infty$.

Remark 5 Note here that the incomplete Gamma function $\Gamma(\alpha, x) = \int_x^\infty z^{\alpha-1} e^{-z} dz$ can be easily computed using the well known asymptotic approximation (see Sections 6.5.32 in [1]), as $x \to \infty$,

$$\Gamma(\alpha, x) \sim x^{\alpha-1} e^{-x} \left[1 + \frac{\alpha - 1}{x} + \frac{(\alpha-1)(\alpha-2)}{x^2} + \dots \right].$$

Now, we characterize the remaining region where $n\mathbb{P}[A > b] > C$. Informally speaking, this is the region where $\mathbb{P}[N_b > n]$ has a lighter tail converging to the exponential when $n >> \bar{G}(b)^{-1}$. In the following theorem, we need more restrictive assumptions for $\ell(x)$; see the discussion before Theorem 2. In particular, we assume that $\ell(x)$ is slowly varying, eventually differentiable and monotonic.

Theorem 4 *Assume that $\mathbb{P}[L > x]^{-1} = \ell(\mathbb{P}[A > x]^{-1})\mathbb{P}[A > x]^{-\alpha}, \alpha > 0, x \ge 0$, where $\ell(x)$ is such that $\ell(x \log x)/\ell(x) \to 1$, as $x \to \infty$ and let $C > \alpha > 0$ be a fixed constant. Then, for any $\epsilon > 0$, there exist b_0, n_0, such that for all $n \ge n_0, b \ge b_0, n\mathbb{P}[A > b] > C$,*

$$\left| \frac{\mathbb{P}[N_b > n] n^\alpha \ell(\mathbb{P}[A > b]^{-1})}{\alpha \Gamma(-n \log \mathbb{P}[A \le b], \alpha)} - 1 \right| \le \epsilon. \tag{2.6}$$

Remark 6 Note that many slowly varying functions satisfy the condition $\ell(x \log x)/\ell(x) \to 1$, as $x \to \infty$. For example, it is easy to check that $(\log x)^\beta, (\log \log x)^\beta, \beta > 0$, and $e^{(\log x)^\gamma}, 0 < \gamma < 1$, satisfy the preceding condition.

Remark 7 Observe that Theorems 3 and 4 cover the entire distribution $\mathbb{P}[N_b > n]$ for all large n and b. Interestingly, the formula for the approximation is the same except for the argument of the slowly varying part, which equals to n and $\mathbb{P}[A > b]^{-1}$, respectively. Furthermore, when $n\mathbb{P}[A > b] = C$ the formulas are asymptotically identical as $\ell(n) \sim \ell(\mathbb{P}[A > b]^{-1})$ as $n \to \infty$ and $n\mathbb{P}[A > b] = C$.

PROOF. Recall that

$$\begin{aligned} \mathbb{P}[N_b > n] &= \mathbb{E}[1 - \bar{G}(L_b)]^n \\ &= \int_0^b (1 - \bar{G}(x))^n \frac{dF(x)}{F(b)} \\ &= \int_0^{x_0} (1 - \bar{G}(x))^n \frac{dF(x)}{F(b)} \\ &\quad + \int_{x_0}^b (1 - \bar{G}(x))^n \frac{dF(x)}{F(b)}. \end{aligned} \tag{2.7}$$

Next, without loss of generality, we assume that $\ell(x)$ is eventually non-decreasing. Now, from the fact that $\ell(x)$ is eventually differentiable ($x \ge x_0$) and slowly varying, it is easy to show that $\ell'(x)x/\ell(x) \to 0$ as $x \to \infty$. Hence, using the preceding observation, it follows that $d\bar{F}(x) = (1 + o(1))\alpha \bar{G}(x)^{\alpha-1} \ell^{-1}(1/\bar{G}(x)) d\bar{G}(x)$ as $x \to \infty$. Thus, for the upper bound we have

$$\begin{aligned} &\mathbb{P}[N_b > n] \\ &\le (1 - \bar{G}(x_0))^n - (1+\epsilon)^{1/2} \int_{x_0}^b (1 - \bar{G}(x))^n \frac{\alpha \bar{G}(x)^{\alpha-1} d\bar{G}(x)}{\ell(1/\bar{G}(x)) F(b)} \\ &= (1 - \bar{G}(x_0))^n + (1+\epsilon)^{1/2} \int_{\bar{G}(b)}^{\bar{G}(x_0)} (1 - z)^n \frac{\alpha z^{\alpha-1} dz}{\ell(1/z) F(b)} \\ &\le (1 - \bar{G}(x_0))^n + \frac{\alpha (1+\epsilon)^{1/2}}{F(b) \ell(1/\bar{G}(x_0))} \int_{\bar{G}(b)}^1 (1 - z)^n z^{\alpha-1} dz, \end{aligned} \tag{2.8}$$

where the equality follows from the absolute continuity of $G(x)$ and change of variables, whereas the last inequality follows from the monotonicity of $\ell(x)$. Next, by changing the variables $z = 1 - e^{-u/n}$, we compute the integral in (2.8)

$$\int_{-n\log(1-\bar{G}(b))}^{\infty} \frac{e^{-u(n+1)/n}(1-e^{-u/n})^{\alpha-1}}{n} du \leq \int_{-n\log(1-\bar{G}(b))}^{\infty} \frac{e^{-u}(1-e^{-u/n})^{\alpha-1}}{n} du,$$

where for the inequality we use $e^{-u/n} \leq 1$. Thus, for $\alpha \geq 1$, from the preceding expression using the inequality $1-e^{-x} \leq x$, for $x \geq 0$, and since $\ell(x\log x)/\ell(x) \to 1$, we obtain the upper bound for (2.8)

$$\begin{aligned}\mathbb{P}[N_b > n] &\leq (1-\bar{G}(x_0))^n + \\ &\frac{\alpha(1+\epsilon)}{F(b)n\ell(1/\bar{G}(b))} \int_{-n\log(1-\bar{G}(b))}^{\infty} e^{-u}\left(\frac{u}{n}\right)^{\alpha-1} du \\ &= (1-\bar{G}(x_0))^n + \\ &\frac{\alpha(1+\epsilon)}{F(b)n^\alpha\ell(1/\bar{G}(b))} \int_{-n\log(1-\bar{G}(b))}^{\infty} e^{-u}u^{\alpha-1} du \\ &\leq e^{-n\bar{G}(x_0)} + \\ &\frac{\alpha(1+\epsilon)}{F(b)n^\alpha\ell(1/\bar{G}(b))}\Gamma(-n\log(1-\bar{G}(b)),\alpha).\end{aligned}$$

Now, from the continuity of $\bar{G}(x)$, we can pick x_0 such that $\bar{G}(x_0) = -\bar{G}(b)\log\bar{G}(b)$ and observe that

$$\frac{\mathbb{P}[N_b > n]n^\alpha\ell(1/\bar{G}(b))}{\alpha\Gamma(-n\log(1-\bar{G}(b)),\alpha)} \leq \frac{e^{-n\bar{G}(x_0)}n^\alpha\ell(1/\bar{G}(b))}{\alpha\Gamma(-n\log(1-\bar{G}(b)),\alpha)} + \frac{1}{F(b)}.$$

Next, we show that the first expression on the right is negligible. Observe that $\Gamma(-n\log(1-\bar{G}(b)),\alpha) \geq \Gamma((1-\delta)n\bar{G}(b),\alpha)$ for b large enough. Then, using the asymptotics $\Gamma(u,\alpha) \sim u^{\alpha-1}e^{-u}$ as $u \to \infty$, we have

$$\sup_{u>C} \frac{u^{\alpha-1}e^{-u(1-\delta)}}{\Gamma((1-\delta)u,\alpha)} < \infty.$$

From the preceding bounds and letting $u = n\bar{G}(b)$, we have

$$\frac{\mathbb{P}[N_b > n]n^\alpha\ell(1/\bar{G}(b))}{\alpha\Gamma(-n\log(1-\bar{G}(b)),\alpha)} \leq O\left(\frac{e^{-u(\log(1/\bar{G}(b))-1)}n^\alpha}{(n\bar{G}(b))^{\alpha-1}\bar{G}(b)^\delta}\right) + \frac{1}{F(b)}, \tag{2.9}$$

where we use the properties of the slowly varying functions [see Theorem 1.5.6 in [4]], $\ell(x) \geq x^{-\delta}$, for x large and $\delta > 0$, to upper bound $\ell(1/\bar{G}(b))$. Now, we pick b_0 large enough such that $\delta\log(\bar{G}(b)^{-1}) - 1 = \delta_{\epsilon,\beta} > 0$. Therefore, the preceding expression inside $O(\cdot)$ in (2.9) is upper bounded by

$$\begin{aligned}&(1+\epsilon)\frac{e^{-u\delta_{\epsilon,\beta}}\bar{G}(b)^{u(1-\delta)}n}{\bar{G}(b)^{\alpha-1+\delta}} \\ &= (1+\epsilon)ue^{-u\delta_{\epsilon,\beta}}\bar{G}(b)^{u(1-\delta)-\alpha-\delta} \\ &\leq \sup_{u\geq 0} ue^{-u\delta_{\epsilon,\beta}}(1+\epsilon)\bar{G}(b)^{C(1-\delta)-\alpha-\delta},\end{aligned}$$

where we are using our assumption that $u > C$. Also, since $C > \alpha$, we can pick $\delta = (C-\alpha)/(2(C+1))$. And thus, for b_0 large enough, $O(\sup_{u\geq 0} ue^{-u\delta_{\epsilon,\beta}}(1+\epsilon)\bar{G}(b)^{(C-\alpha)/2}) \leq \epsilon$. Hence,

$$\frac{\mathbb{P}[N_b > n]n^\alpha\ell(1/\bar{G}(b))}{\alpha\Gamma(-n\log(1-\bar{G}(b)),\alpha)} \leq \epsilon + (1+\epsilon) = 1 + 2\epsilon,$$

which completes the proof after replacing ϵ with $\epsilon/2$.

Next, we prove the lower bound starting from (2.7). Proceeding with similar arguments as in the proof for the upper bound, we obtain

$$\begin{aligned}&\mathbb{P}[N_b > n] \\ &\geq -(1-\epsilon)^{1/2}\int_{x_0}^{b}(1-\bar{G}(x))^n\frac{\alpha\bar{G}(x)^{\alpha-1}d\bar{G}(x)}{\ell(1/\bar{G}(x))F(b)} \\ &= (1-\epsilon)^{1/2}\int_{\bar{G}(b)}^{\bar{G}(x_0)}(1-z)^n\frac{\alpha z^{\alpha-1}dz}{\ell(1/z)F(b)} \\ &\geq \frac{\alpha(1-\epsilon)^{1/2}}{F(b)\ell(1/\bar{G}(b))}\int_{-(n+1)\log(1-\bar{G}(b))}^{-(n+1)\log G(x_0)}\frac{e^{-u}(1-e^{-\frac{u}{n+1}})^{\alpha-1}}{n+1}du,\end{aligned}$$

where we use the monotonicity of $\ell(x)$. Next, using the inequality $(1-e^{-x}) \geq (1-\delta)x$, for some $\delta > 0$ and all $x \geq 0$ small enough, we have

$$\begin{aligned}&\mathbb{P}[N_b > n-1] \\ &\geq \frac{\alpha(1-\epsilon)^{1/2}(1-\delta)^{\alpha-1}}{F(b)\ell(1/\bar{G}(b))n}\int_{-n\log(1-\bar{G}(b))}^{-n\log G(x_0)} e^{-u}\left(\frac{u}{n}\right)^{\alpha-1}du \\ &= \frac{\alpha(1-\epsilon)}{F(b)n^\alpha\ell(1/\bar{G}(b))}\int_{-n\log(1-\bar{G}(b))}^{-n\log G(x_0)} e^{-u}u^{\alpha-1}du \\ &= \frac{\alpha(1-\epsilon)}{F(b)n^\alpha\ell(1/\bar{G}(b))}\left[\int_{-n\log(1-\bar{G}(b))}^{\infty} e^{-u}u^{\alpha-1}du \right. \\ &\qquad \left. - \int_{-n\log G(x_0)}^{\infty} e^{-u}u^{\alpha-1}du\right]\end{aligned}$$

where we set $(1-\delta)^{\alpha-1} = (1-\epsilon)^{1/2}$. Then, by continuity, we pick x_0 such that $\Gamma(-n\log G(x_0),\alpha) \leq \epsilon\Gamma(-n\log G(b),\alpha)$ and thus

$$\frac{\mathbb{P}[N_b > n]n^\alpha\ell(1/\bar{G}(b))}{\alpha\Gamma(-n\log(1-\bar{G}(b)),\alpha)} \geq (1-\epsilon).$$

Now, if $\alpha < 1$, the lower bound follows similarly as the preceding upper bound while for the upper bound we use symmetric arguments. □

From the preceding two theorems we observe that $\mathbb{P}[N_b > n]$ behaves as a true power law when $n\mathbb{P}[A > b] \to 0$ ($n << \mathbb{P}[A > b]^{-1}$) and has an exponential tail (geometric) when $n\mathbb{P}[A > b] \to \infty$ ($n >> \mathbb{P}[A > b]^{-1}$). More specifically:

(i) If $n\mathbb{P}[A > b] \to 0$, then clearly $-n\log\mathbb{P}[A \leq b] \to 0$ and we have by Theorem 3, as $n \to \infty, n\mathbb{P}[A > b] \to 0$,

$$\mathbb{P}[N_b > n] \sim \frac{\alpha}{\ell(n)n^\alpha}\Gamma(\alpha) = \frac{\Gamma(\alpha+1)}{\ell(n)n^\alpha}.$$

(ii) If $n\mathbb{P}[A > b] \to \infty$, then $-n\log\mathbb{P}[A \leq b] \to \infty$ and thus, as $n \to \infty, b \to \infty, n\mathbb{P}[A > b] \to \infty$,

$$\mathbb{P}[N_b > n] \sim \frac{\alpha}{\ell(1/\bar{G}(b))n}\bar{G}(b)^{\alpha-1}(1-\bar{G}(b))^n,$$

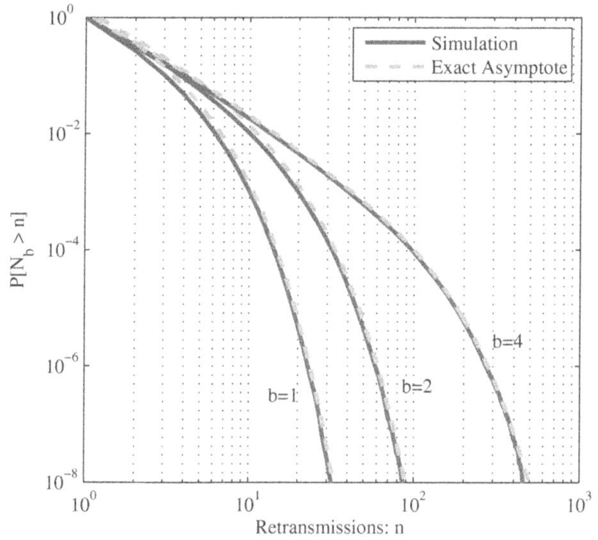

Figure 2: *Example 1(a). Exact asymptotics for $\alpha > 1$.*

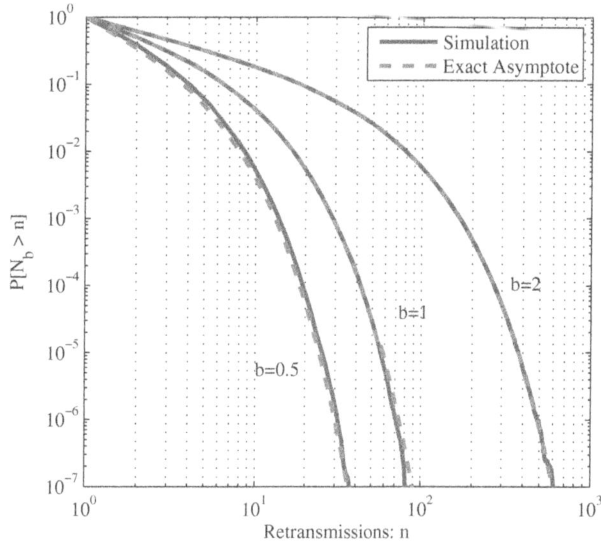

Figure 3: *Example 1(b). Exact asymptotics for $\alpha < 1$.*

which follows from Theorem 4 and the asymptotic expansion of the Gamma function (see Remark 5 of Theorem 3).

Interestingly, one can compute the distribution of $\mathbb{P}[N_b > n]$ exactly when the parameter α takes integer values.

Proposition 2.2 *If $\mathbb{P}[L > x] = \mathbb{P}[A > x]^\alpha$, for all $x \geq 0$ and α is a positive integer, then*

$$\mathbb{P}[N_b > n] = \frac{1}{\mathbb{P}[L \leq b]} \sum_{i=1}^{\alpha} \frac{\alpha!\, n!\, \mathbb{P}[A > b]^{\alpha-i}}{(\alpha - i)!(n+i)!} \mathbb{P}[A \leq b]^{n+i}.$$

PROOF. It follows directly from (2.7) using integration by parts. □

Finally, in the following proposition, we describe the tail of $\mathbb{P}[N_b > n]$ for fixed and possibly small b. Furthermore, the assumptions of this proposition could be weakened at the expense of additional technical complications, which we avoid here for reasons of simplicity.

Proposition 2.3 *Let b be fixed. If $\mathbb{P}[L > x] = \mathbb{P}[A > x]^\alpha$, $\alpha > 0$, $x \geq 0$, then*

$$\mathbb{P}[N_b > n] \sim \frac{\alpha}{\mathbb{P}[L \leq b]} \frac{\mathbb{P}[A > b]^{\alpha-1}\mathbb{P}[A \leq b]^{n+1}}{n+1} \quad \text{as } n \to \infty.$$

PROOF. See Section 4. □

3. SIMULATION EXPERIMENTS

In this section, we illustrate the validity of our theoretical results with simulation experiments. In all of the experiments, we observed that our exact asymptotics is literally indistinguishable from the simulation. In the following examples, we present the simulation experiments resulting from 10^8 (or more) independent samples of $N_{b,i}$, $1 \leq i \leq 10^8$. This number of samples was needed to ensure at least 100 independent occurrences in the lightest end of the tail that is presented in the figures ($N_{b,i} \geq n_{\max}$), thus providing a good confidence interval.

Example 1. This example illustrates the exact asymptotics presented in Theorems 3 and 4, i.e., approximation (2.4), which combines the results from both theorems. We assume that L and A follow exponential distributions with parameters $\lambda = 2$ and $\mu = 1$, respectively. It is thus clear that $\bar{F}(x) = e^{-2x} = \bar{G}(x)^\alpha$, where $\alpha = 2$ and $\ell(x) \equiv 1$. Now, approximation (2.4) states that $\mathbb{P}[N_b > n]$ is given by $(1 - e^{-2b})^{-1} 2n^{-2}\Gamma(ne^{-b}, 2)$. Note that we added a factor $\mathbb{P}[L \leq b]^{-1} = (1 - e^{-2b})^{-1}$, as in Propositions 2.2 and 2.3, for increased precision when b is small; we add such a factor to approximation (2.4) in other examples as well. We simulate different scenarios when the data sizes L_b are upper bounded by b equal to 1, 2 and 4. The simulation results are plotted on log-log scale in Fig. 2.

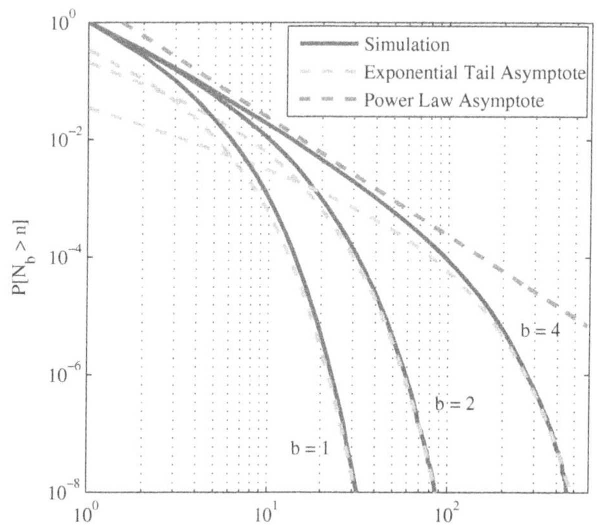

Figure 4: *Example 2. Exponential tail asymptotics.*

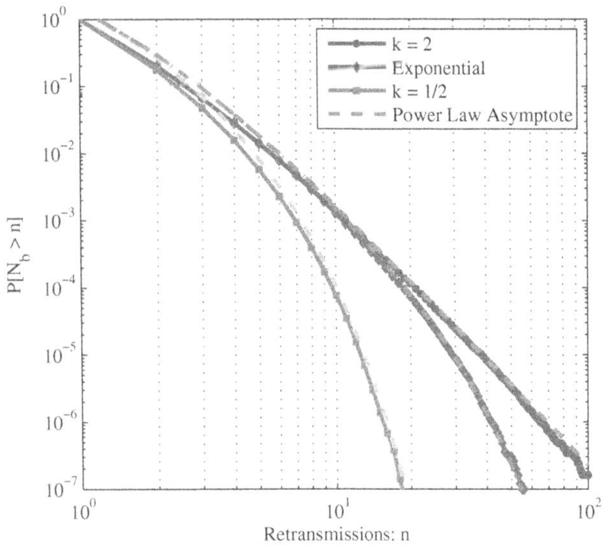

Figure 5: *Example 3. Power law region increases for lighter tails of L, A.*

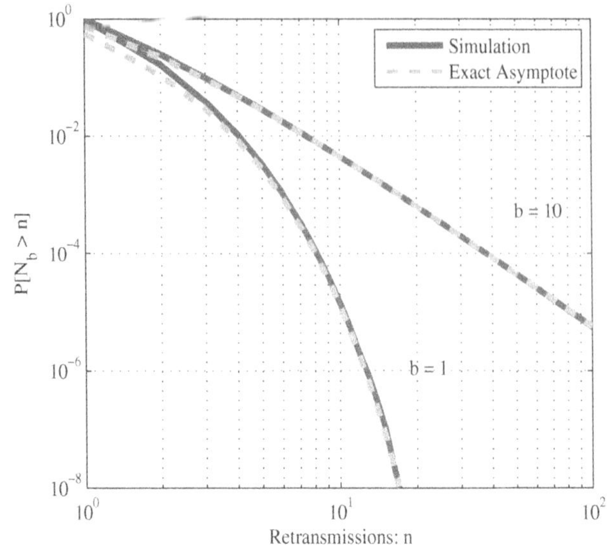

Figure 6: *Example 4. Exact asymptotics where $\mathbb{E}A > \mathbb{E}L_b$.*

From Fig. 2, we observe that the numerical asymptote approximates the simulation exactly for all different scenarios, even for very small values of n (large probabilities). We further validate our approximation by considering scenarios where L, A are exponentially distributed but $\alpha < 1$; in fact, this case tends to induce longer delays due to larger average data size compared to the channel availability periods. In this case, we obtain $\alpha = 0.5$ by assuming $\lambda = 1$ and $\mu = 2$. Again, the simulation results and the asymptotic formulas are basically indistinguishable for all n, as illustrated in Fig. 3.

For both cases, we deduce that for b small the power law asymptotics covers a smaller region of the distribution of N_b and, as n increases, the exponential tail becomes more evident and eventually dominates. As b becomes large - recall that $b \to \infty$ corresponds to the untruncated case where the power law phenomenon arises - the exponential tail becomes less distinguishable.

Example 2. This example demonstrates the exact asymptotics for the exponential tail as $n \to \infty$ and b is fixed, as in Proposition 2.3. Note that this proposition gives the exact asymptotic formula for the region $n \gg 1/\bar{G}(b)$ and lends merit to our Theorems 2 and 4. Informally, we could say that a point n_b such that $-n_b \log(1 - \bar{G}(b)) \approx n_b\bar{G}(b) = \alpha \log n_b$ represents the transition from power law to the exponential tail. We assume that L, A are exponentially distributed with $\lambda = 2$ and $\mu = 1$ (as in the first case of Example 1). Roughly speaking, we can see from Fig. 4 that the exponential asymptote appears to fit well starting from $n_b \approx \alpha e^b$, i.e., $n_b \approx 6, 15, 100$ for $b = 1, 2, 4$, respectively.

Example 3. This example highlights the importance of the distribution type of channel availability periods $\bar{G}(x) = \mathbb{P}[A > x]$. We consider some fixed b, namely $b = 8$ and assume that the matching between data sizes and channel availability, as defined in Theorems 3 and 4, is determined by the parameter $\alpha = 4$. We assume Weibull[1] distributions for L, A with the same index k and μ_L, μ_A respectively, such that $\alpha = (\mu_A/\mu_L)^k$. The simulations include three different cases for the aforementioned distributions: Weibull with index $k = 1$ (exponential) where $\mu_L = 1$ and $\mu_A = 4$, Weibull (normal-like) with index $k = 2$ ($\mu_L = 1, \mu_A = 2$) and Weibull with $k = 1/2$ ($\mu_L = 1, \mu_A = 16$). Fig. 5 illustrates the exact asymptotics from equation (2.4), shown with the lighter dashed lines; the main power law asymptote appears in the main body of all three distributions. We observe that heavier distributions (Weibull with $k = 1/2$) correspond to smaller regions for the power law main body of the distribution $\mathbb{P}[N_b > n]$. On the other hand, the case with the lighter Gaussian like distributions for $k = 2$ follows almost entirely the power law asymptotics in the region presented in Fig. 5. This increase in the power law region can be inferred from our theorems, which show that the transition from the power law main body to the exponential tail occurs roughly at $n_b \approx \bar{G}(b)^{-1}$. Hence, the lighter the tail of the distribution of A, the larger the size of the power law region.

Example 4. In this example, we deal with the case where the system availability periods are longer than the mean size of the data. This is true for a system that does not fail frequently and the packet sizes are small on average, where one would expect high throughput and lighter distributions for the retransmissions. However, our simulations demonstrate the dominant power law body when b is larger than the mean data size, i.e., we allow longer, albeit infrequent, packets to be transmitted over the channel. In this scenario, L, A are both exponentially distributed with $\lambda = 5$ and $\mu = 1$, yielding $\mathbb{E}L_b \approx 0.2 << \mathbb{E}A = 1$. Fig. 6 indicates the emergence of the power law in the main body of the distribution when the value of b is larger, namely $b = 10$. On the other hand, when $b = 1$, the exponential tail dominates and the power law basically disappears. From Fig. 6, we can

[1] In general, a Weibull distribution with index k has a complementary cumulative distribution function $\mathbb{P}[X > x] = e^{-(x/\mu)^k}$, where μ is the parameter that determines the mean.

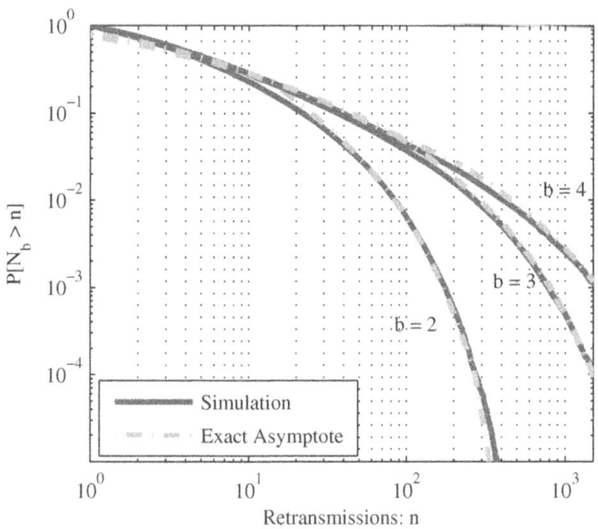

Figure 7: *Example 5(a). Uniform approximation from (2.4) for the case where L follows the Gamma distribution.*

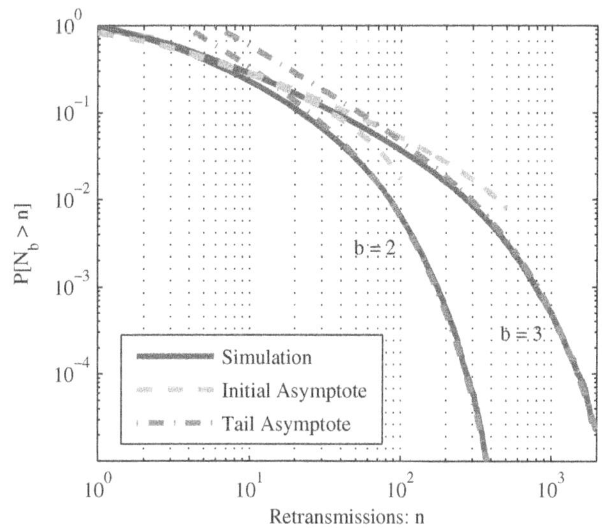

Figure 8: *Example 5(b). The asymptotes from Theorems 3 and 4 for the case where L follows the Gamma distribution.*

verify that, for even a small number of retransmissions, e.g., $n = 10$, $\mathbb{P}[N_b > 10]$ increases from 10^{-5} to roughly 10^{-2} - an almost 1000-fold increase - as b grows from 1 to 10. This dramatic change of the distribution of N_b for relatively modest increase of the maximum data size b emphasizes the importance of carefully adjusting the data characteristics (e.g., fragmentation) to the channel statistics.

Example 5. In this last example, we study the case where there is a more general functional relationship between the distributions of availability periods A and data sizes L, as Theorems 3 and 4 assume. In particular, we consider the case $\bar{F}(x) = \bar{G}(x)^\alpha/\ell(\bar{G}(x)^{-1})$, where $\ell(x)$ is slowly varying. We validate the approximation (2.4) in this more general setting.

In particular, the availability periods A are exponentially distributed with parameter μ while the data sizes L follow the Gamma distribution with parameters (λ, k); the tail of the Gamma distribution function is defined as $\lambda^k\Gamma(k)^{-1}\int_x^\infty e^{-\lambda x}x^{k-1}dx = \Gamma(\lambda x, k)/\Gamma(k)$ and, therefore, the tail distribution of L can be approximated by $\bar{F}(x) \sim (\lambda^{k-1}/\Gamma(k))\, x^{k-1}e^{-\lambda x}$ for large x. We can easily verify that $\bar{F}(x) = f(\mu^{-1}\log \bar{G}(x)^{-1})\bar{G}(x)^\alpha$, where $\alpha = \lambda/\mu$ and

$$f(x) = \lambda^{k-1}\Gamma(k)^{-1}\int_0^\infty e^{-z}(z/\lambda + x)^{k-1}dz.$$

Hence, the slowly varying function in Theorems 3 and 4 is $\ell(x) = 1/f(\mu^{-1}\log x)$. Also, from the preceding integral representation for $f(x)$, it can be easily shown that $\ell(x) \approx \Gamma(k)\alpha^{1-k}\log^{1-k}x$, which is indeed slowly varying, and $\bar{F}(x) \approx (\alpha^{k-1}/\Gamma(k))\log(\bar{G}(x)^{-1})^{k-1}\bar{G}(x)^\alpha$. We take $\lambda = 2, k = 2$ and $\mu = 2$ and run simulations for $b = \{2, 3, 4\}$. In Fig. 7, we demonstrate the results using the approximation (2.4). Surprisingly, our analytic approximation works nicely even for small values of n and b although the conditions in our theorems require n and b to be large.

In Fig. 8, we elaborate on the preceding example. To this end, we plot two asymptotes: (i) the 'Initial Asymptote' corresponding to the power law asymptote provided by Theorem 3 and (ii) the 'Tail Asymptote' from Theorem 4. Combining the two, we derive the approximation (2.4), as we have already shown in Fig. 7. Hereby, we see from Fig. 8 that both asymptotes are needed to approximate the entire distribution well, i.e., the 'Initial Asymptote' fits well the first part of the distribution, whereas the 'Tail Asymptote' is inaccurate in the beginning but works well for the tail. Recall that these two asymptotes differ only in the argument of the slowly varying function $\ell(\cdot)$, which is equal to n for the 'Initial Asymptote' and $\bar{G}(b)^{-1}$ for the tail.

4. PROOFS

In this section, we present the proofs of Propositions 2.1, 2.3 and Theorem 1.

PROOF. Proof of Proposition 2.1.
By assumption, there exists $0 < \epsilon < 1$ such that for all $x > x_\epsilon$

$$\bar{F}(x) \le \bar{G}(x)^{\alpha(1-\epsilon)}. \tag{4.1}$$

Next, since $\mathbb{P}[N_b > n | L_b] = (1 - \bar{G}(L_b))^n$,

$$\begin{aligned}
\mathbb{P}[N_b > n] &= \mathbb{E}[1 - \bar{G}(L_b)]^n \\
&= \mathbb{E}[1 - \bar{G}(L_b)]^{n(1-\epsilon+\epsilon)} \\
&= (1 - \bar{G}(b))^{n(1-\epsilon)}\Big[\mathbb{E}[1 - \bar{G}(L_b)]^{n\epsilon}1(L_b \le x_0) \\
&\qquad + \mathbb{E}[1 - \bar{G}(L_b)]^{n\epsilon}1(L_b > x_0)\Big] \\
&\le (1 - \bar{G}(b))^{n(1-\epsilon)}\Big[(1 - \bar{G}(x_0))^{n\epsilon} \\
&\qquad + \int_{x_0}^b (1 - \bar{G}(x))^{n\epsilon}\frac{dF(x)}{F(b)}\Big] \\
&\le (1 - \bar{G}(b))^{n(1-\epsilon)} \\
&\quad \times \left[\eta_{x_0}^{n\epsilon} + \int_0^b \left(1 - \bar{F}(x)^{\frac{1}{\alpha(1-\epsilon)}}\right)^{n\epsilon}\frac{dF(x)}{F(b)}\right],
\end{aligned}$$

where $\eta_{x_0} = 1 - \bar{G}(x_0)$ and the last inequality follows from (4.1).

Now, by extending the preceding integral to ∞, we obtain

$$\begin{aligned}\mathbb{P}[N_b > n] &\le \frac{1}{F(b)}(1-\bar{G}(b))^{n(1-\epsilon)}\Big[\eta_{x_0}^{n\epsilon}F(b) \\ &\quad + \int_0^\infty \Big(1-\bar{F}(x)^{\frac{1}{\alpha(1-\epsilon)}}\Big)^{n\epsilon} dF(x)\Big] \\ &= \frac{1}{F(b)}(1-\bar{G}(b))^{n(1-\epsilon)} \\ &\quad \times \Big[\eta_{x_0}^{n\epsilon}F(b) + \mathbb{E}\Big(1-\bar{F}(L)^{\frac{1}{\alpha(1-\epsilon)}}\Big)^{n\epsilon}\Big] \\ &\le \frac{1}{F(b)}(1-\bar{G}(b))^{n(1-\epsilon)} \\ &\quad \times \Big[\eta_{x_0}^{n\epsilon}F(b) + \mathbb{E}\, e^{-n\epsilon \bar{F}(L)^{\frac{1}{\alpha(1-\epsilon)}}}\Big],\end{aligned}$$

where we use the elementary inequality $1 - x \le e^{-x}$, $x \ge 0$, and thus

$$\mathbb{P}[N_b > n] \le \frac{(1-\bar{G}(b))^{n(1-\epsilon)}}{F(b)}\Big[\eta_{x_0}^{n\epsilon}F(b) + \mathbb{E}\, e^{-n\epsilon U^{\frac{1}{\alpha(1-\epsilon)}}}\Big], \tag{4.2}$$

where $\bar{F}(L) = U$ is uniformly distributed on $[0, 1]$ by Proposition 2.1 in Chapter 10 of [12].

Next, we upper bound the expectation in the preceding expression by

$$\begin{aligned}\mathbb{E}\, e^{-n\epsilon U^{\frac{1}{\alpha(1-\epsilon)}}} &= \int_0^1 e^{-x^{\frac{1}{\alpha(1-\epsilon)}} n\epsilon} dx \\ &= \int_0^{n\epsilon} \frac{\alpha(1-\epsilon)}{(n\epsilon)^{\alpha(1-\epsilon)}} e^{-z} z^{\alpha(1-\epsilon)-1} dz \\ &\le \frac{\alpha(1-\epsilon)}{(n\epsilon)^{\alpha(1-\epsilon)}} \int_0^\infty e^{-z} z^{\alpha(1-\epsilon)-1} dz \\ &= \frac{\alpha(1-\epsilon)}{(n\epsilon)^{\alpha(1-\epsilon)}} \Gamma(\alpha(1-\epsilon)),\end{aligned}$$

which follows from the definition of the Gamma function $\Gamma(a) = \int_0^\infty e^{-t}t^{a-1}dt$. Therefore, by replacing the preceding bound in (4.2), we obtain

$$\mathbb{P}[N_b > n] \le (1-\bar{G}(b))^{n(1-\epsilon)}\Big[\eta_{x_0}^{n\epsilon} + \frac{H_\epsilon}{n^{\alpha(1-\epsilon)}}\Big],$$

where $H_\epsilon = \alpha(1-\epsilon)\Gamma(\alpha(1-\epsilon))\epsilon^{-\alpha(1-\epsilon)}/F(b_0)$. Now, for any $\epsilon > 0$, we can choose n_0, such that for all $n \ge n_0$, $\eta_{x_0}^{n\epsilon} \le \epsilon H_\epsilon n^{-\alpha(1-\epsilon)}$, so that

$$\begin{aligned}\mathbb{P}[N_b > n] &\le (1-\bar{G}(b))^{n(1-\epsilon)}\Big[\epsilon\frac{H_\epsilon}{n^{\alpha(1-\epsilon)}} + \frac{H_\epsilon}{n^{\alpha(1-\epsilon)}}\Big] \\ &= (1-\bar{G}(b))^{n(1-\epsilon)}\frac{H_\epsilon}{n^{\alpha(1-\epsilon)}}(1+\epsilon).\end{aligned}$$

And by taking the logarithm in the preceding expression, we obtain

$$\begin{aligned}\log \mathbb{P}[N_b > n] &\le \log(H_\epsilon(1+\epsilon)) + n(1-\epsilon)\log(1-\bar{G}(b)) \\ &\quad - \alpha(1-\epsilon)\log n \\ &= \log(H_\epsilon(1+\epsilon)) \\ &\quad + (1-\epsilon)\left[n\log(1-\bar{G}(b)) - \alpha\log n\right].\end{aligned}$$

Next, since $-n\log(1-\bar{G}(b)) > 0$ and $\alpha \log n \ge 0$, $n \ge 1$,

$$\begin{aligned}\frac{\log \mathbb{P}[N_b > n]}{-n\log(1-\bar{G}(b)) + \alpha\log n} &\le \frac{\log H_\epsilon}{-n\log(1-\bar{G}(b)) + \alpha\log n} \\ &\quad - (1-\epsilon) \\ &\le \frac{\log H_\epsilon}{\alpha \log n} - (1-\epsilon).\end{aligned}$$

Since $\alpha\log n$ is increasing in n, we can choose n_0 such that for any $n \ge n_0$, $\log H_\epsilon/\alpha\log n \le \epsilon$, and thus,

$$\frac{\log \mathbb{P}[N_b > n]}{-n\log(1-\bar{G}(b)) + \alpha\log n} \le -(1-2\epsilon),$$

which completes the proof by replacing ϵ with $\epsilon/2$. □

PROOF. Proof of Theorem 1.
Note that the upper bound follows from Proposition 2.1. For the lower bound, we have, for $x \ge x_0$,

$$\begin{aligned}\mathbb{P}[N_b > n] &= \mathbb{E}[1-\bar{G}(L_b)]^n \\ &\ge \mathbb{E}[1-\bar{F}(L_b)^{\frac{1}{\alpha(1+\epsilon)}}]^n \\ &\ge \int_{x_0}^b \Big(1-\bar{F}(x)^{\frac{1}{\alpha(1+\epsilon)}}\Big)^n \frac{dF(x)}{F(b)} \\ &= \int_{\bar{F}(b)^{\frac{1}{\alpha(1+\epsilon)}}}^{\bar{F}(x_0)^{\frac{1}{\alpha(1+\epsilon)}}} (1-z)^n z^{\alpha(1+\epsilon)-1}\frac{\alpha(1+\epsilon)dz}{F(b)},\end{aligned}$$

where the last equality follows from the absolute continuity of $F(x)$ and change of variables. Next, by setting $z = 1 - e^{-u/n}$, and $\alpha_\epsilon = \alpha(1+\epsilon)$ we obtain

$$\mathbb{P}[N_b > n] \ge \frac{\alpha_\epsilon}{F(b)n}\int_{-n\log\left(1-\bar{F}(b)^{\frac{1}{\alpha_\epsilon}}\right)}^{-n\log\left(1-\bar{F}(x_0)^{\frac{1}{\alpha_\epsilon}}\right)} e^{-u(n+1)/n}(1-e^{-\frac{u}{n}})^{\alpha_\epsilon - 1}du.$$

Now, by continuity, for any $\delta > 0$, we can choose x_0 such that $-\log(1-\bar{F}(x_0)^{1/\alpha_\epsilon}) = \delta$, implying

$$\mathbb{P}[N_b > n] \ge \frac{\alpha_\epsilon(1-\delta)}{F(b)n}\int_{\delta\log n}^{\delta n} e^{-u}(1-e^{-\frac{u}{n}})^{\alpha_\epsilon-1}du,$$

where we use our assumption $n\bar{G}(b) \le \delta\log n$ to upper bound the lower limit of the integral; for the last inequality, note that $e^{-u/n} \ge 1-u/n \ge (1-\delta)$. Next, by $F(b) < 1$ and using $1-e^{-y} \ge (1-\delta)y$, for all y small enough, it follows that

$$\begin{aligned}\mathbb{P}[N_b > n] &\ge \frac{\alpha_\epsilon(1-\delta)^{\alpha_\epsilon}}{n^{\alpha_\epsilon}}\int_{\delta\log n}^{\delta n} e^{-u}u^{\alpha_\epsilon-1}du \\ &\ge \frac{\alpha_\epsilon(1-\delta)^{\alpha_\epsilon}h_\epsilon}{n^{\alpha_\epsilon}}(\log n)^{\alpha_\epsilon-1}\int_{\delta\log n}^{(1+\epsilon)\delta\log n} e^{-u}du \\ &= \frac{\alpha_\epsilon(1-\delta)^{\alpha_\epsilon}h_\epsilon}{n^{\alpha_\epsilon}}(\log n)^{\alpha_\epsilon-1}n^{-\delta}\left(1-n^{-\delta\epsilon}\right),\end{aligned}$$

where in the second inequality we use $n \ge (1+\epsilon)\log n$ for n large and the monotonicity of $u^{\alpha_\epsilon - 1}$; also, we set $h_\epsilon =$

$\max(1,(1+\epsilon)^{\alpha_\epsilon-1})$. Therefore, for n large such that $n^{-\delta\epsilon} < \delta$, we obtain the lower bound

$$\mathbb{P}[N_b > n] \geq \frac{\alpha_\epsilon(1-\delta)^{\alpha_\epsilon+1}h_\epsilon}{n^{\alpha_\epsilon}}\frac{(\log n)^{\alpha_\epsilon-1}}{n^\delta}.$$

Now, $\log n \geq \log n_0$ and we can choose $\delta < \epsilon\alpha$, such that $1/n^\delta \geq 1/n^{\epsilon\alpha}$, implying

$$\mathbb{P}[N_b > n] \geq \frac{h_{\epsilon,\delta}}{n^{\alpha(1+2\epsilon)}},$$

where we set $h_{\epsilon,\delta} = \alpha_\epsilon(1-\delta)^{\alpha_\epsilon+1}h_\epsilon(\log n_0)^{\alpha_\epsilon-1}$. And by taking the logarithm, we obtain

$$\log\mathbb{P}[N_b > n] \geq \log h_{\epsilon,\delta} - \alpha(1+2\epsilon)\log n.$$

Finally, since $\log n$ is increasing in n, we can choose n_0 such that for all $n \geq n_0$, $\alpha\epsilon\log n \geq -\log h_{\epsilon,\delta}$, i.e.,

$$\log\mathbb{P}[N_b > n] \geq -\alpha(1+3\epsilon)\log n,$$

which completes the proof by replacing ϵ with $\epsilon/3$. □

PROOF. Proof of Proposition 2.3.
Similarly as before, by the assumption,

$$\begin{aligned}\mathbb{P}[N_b > n] &= \mathbb{E}[1-\bar{G}(L_b)]^n\\ &= \mathbb{E}[1-\bar{F}(L_b)^{\frac{1}{\alpha}}]^n\\ &= \int_0^b\left(1-\bar{F}(x)^{\frac{1}{\alpha}}\right)^n\frac{dF(x)}{F(b)}.\end{aligned}$$

And by setting $\bar{F}(x)^{\frac{1}{\alpha}} = z$, we obtain

$$\begin{aligned}\mathbb{P}[N_b > n] &= \int_{\bar{F}(b)^{\frac{1}{\alpha}}}^1(1-z)^n z^{\alpha-1}\frac{\alpha dz}{F(b)}\\ &= \frac{\alpha}{F(b)}\int_{\bar{G}(b)}^1(1-z)^n z^{\alpha-1}dz,\end{aligned}$$

following the assumption $\bar{G}(x)^\alpha = \bar{F}(x)$. Next, we break the preceding integral into two parts

$$\begin{aligned}\mathbb{P}[N_b > n] = \frac{\alpha}{F(b)}\Bigg[&\int_{\bar{G}(b)}^{\bar{G}(b)(1+\epsilon)}(1-z)^n z^{\alpha-1}dz\\ &+\int_{\bar{G}(b)(1+\epsilon)}^1(1-z)^n z^{\alpha-1}dz\Bigg].\end{aligned}$$

To obtain the lower and upper bounds, we consider two different cases for α.
(i) If $\alpha \geq 1$,

$$\mathbb{P}[N_b > n] \geq \frac{\alpha}{F(b)}\bar{G}(b)^{\alpha-1}\int_{\bar{G}(b)}^{\bar{G}(b)(1+\epsilon)}(1-z)^n dz.$$

since $z^{\alpha-1}$ is monotonically increasing. Then,

$$\begin{aligned}&\mathbb{P}[N_b > n]\\ &\geq \frac{\alpha}{F(b)}\bar{G}(b)^{\alpha-1}\left|-\frac{(1-z)^{n+1}}{n+1}\right|_{\bar{G}(b)}^{\bar{G}(b)(1+\epsilon)}\\ &= \frac{\alpha\bar{G}(b)^{\alpha-1}}{F(b)(n+1)}\left[(1-\bar{G}(b))^{n+1}-(1-\bar{G}(b)(1+\epsilon))^{n+1}\right]\\ &= \frac{\alpha\bar{G}(b)^{\alpha-1}(1-\bar{G}(b))^{n+1}}{F(b)(n+1)}\left[1-\left(\frac{1-\bar{G}(b)(1+\epsilon)}{1-\bar{G}(b)}\right)^{n+1}\right].\end{aligned}$$

Next, by recalling that $(1-\bar{G}(b)(1+\epsilon))/(1-\bar{G}(b)) < 1$ and b is fixed, we have as $n \to \infty$,

$$\mathbb{P}[N_b > n] \gtrsim \frac{\alpha}{F(b)}\frac{\bar{G}(b)^{\alpha-1}(1-\bar{G}(b))^{n+1}}{n+1}. \tag{4.3}$$

Also, for the upper bound,

$$\begin{aligned}\mathbb{P}[N_b > n] \leq \frac{\alpha}{F(b)}\Bigg[&(\bar{G}(b)(1+\epsilon))^{\alpha-1}\int_{\bar{G}(b)}^{\bar{G}(b)(1+\epsilon)}(1-z)^n dz\\ &+\int_{\bar{G}(b)(1+\epsilon)}^1(1-z)^n dz\Bigg],\end{aligned} \tag{4.4}$$

since $z^{\alpha-1} \leq 1$. Next, we evaluate the expression in the brackets,

$$\begin{aligned}&(\bar{G}(b)(1+\epsilon))^{\alpha-1}\left.\frac{(1-z)^{n+1}}{n+1}\right|_{\bar{G}(b)(1+\epsilon)}^{\bar{G}(b)}+\left.\frac{(1-z)^{n+1}}{n+1}\right|_1^{\bar{G}(b)(1+\epsilon)}\\ &= \frac{\bar{G}(b)^{\alpha-1}(1+\epsilon)^{\alpha-1}}{n+1}\left[(1-\bar{G}(b))^{n+1}-(1-\bar{G}(b)(1+\epsilon))^{n+1}\right]\\ &\quad+\frac{(1-\bar{G}(b)(1+\epsilon))^{n+1}}{n+1}\\ &= \frac{(1-\bar{G}(b))^{n+1}}{n+1}\\ &\quad\times\left[\bar{G}(b)^{\alpha-1}(1+\epsilon)^{\alpha-1}\left(1-\left(\frac{1-\bar{G}(b)(1+\epsilon)}{1-\bar{G}(b)}\right)^{n+1}\right)\right.\\ &\quad\left.+\left(\frac{1-\bar{G}(b)(1+\epsilon)}{1-\bar{G}(b)}\right)^{n+1}\right].\end{aligned}$$

Similarly as before, $(1-\bar{G}(b)(1+\epsilon))/(1-\bar{G}(b)) < 1$ and by taking the limit as $n \to \infty$ in (4.4), we have

$$\mathbb{P}[N_b > n] \lesssim \frac{\alpha}{F(b)}\frac{\bar{G}(b)^{\alpha-1}(1-\bar{G}(b))^{n+1}(1+\epsilon)^{\alpha-1}}{n+1}.$$

Therefore, by letting $\epsilon \to 0$,

$$\mathbb{P}[N_b > n] \lesssim \frac{\alpha}{F(b)}\frac{\bar{G}(b)^{\alpha-1}(1-\bar{G}(b))^{n+1}}{n+1}. \tag{4.5}$$

Finally, by equations (4.3) and (4.5), we have

$$\mathbb{P}[N_b > n] \sim \frac{\alpha}{F(b)}\frac{\bar{G}(b)^{\alpha-1}(1-\bar{G}(b))^{n+1}}{n+1}.$$

(ii) If $\alpha \leq 1$, similar arguments work, we omit the details. □

5. ACKNOWLEDGMENTS

The authors are grateful to Sem Borst and the anonymous reviewers for their helpful comments.

6. REFERENCES

[1] M. Abramowitz and I. A. Stegun. *Handbook of Mathematical Functions with Formulas, Graphs, and Mathematical Tables.* Dover, New York, 1964.

[2] S. Asmussen, P. Fiorini, L. Lipsky, T. Rolski, and R. Sheahan. Asymptotic behavior of total times for jobs that must start over if a failure occurs. *Mathematics of Operations Research*, 33(4):932–944, November 2008.

[3] D. P. Bertsekas and R. Gallager. *Data Networks.* Prentice Hall, 2nd edition, 1992.
[4] N. H. Bingham, C. M. Goldie, and J. L. Teugels. *Regular Variation.* Cambridge University Press, 1987.
[5] P. M. Fiorini, R. Sheahan, and L. Lipsky. On unreliable computing systems when heavy-tails appear as a result of the recovery procedure. *SIGMETRICS Performance Evaluation Review*, 33(2):15–17, December 2005.
[6] P. R. Jelenković and J. Tan. Are end-to-end acknowlegements causing power law delays in large multi-hop networks? In *14th Informs Applied Probability Conference*, Eindhoven, The Netherlands, July 2007.
[7] P. R. Jelenković and J. Tan. Can retransmissions of superexponential documents cause subexponential delays? In *Proceedings of IEEE INFOCOM'07*, pages 892–900, Anchorage, AK, May 2007.
[8] P. R. Jelenković and J. Tan. Is ALOHA causing power law delays? In *Proeedings of the 20th International Teletraffic Congress, Ottawa, Canada ; Lecture Notes in Computer Science, No 4516, Springer-Verlag*, pages 1149–1160, June 2007.
[9] P. R. Jelenković and J. Tan. Characterizing heavy-tailed distributions induced by retransmissions. 2007, Eprint arXiv: 0709.1138v2.
[10] P. R. Jelenković and J. Tan. Dynamic packet fragmentation for wireless channels with failures. In *Proceedings of the 9th ACM International Symposium on Mobile Ad Hoc Networking and Computing*, Hong Kong, May 2008.
[11] J. Nair, M. Andreasson, L. Andrew, S. Low, and J. Doyle. File fragmentation over an unreliable channel. In *Proceedings of IEEE INFOCOM'10*, pages 1–9, San Diego, CA, March 2010.
[12] S. M. Ross. *A First Course in Probability.* Prentice Hall, 6th edition, 2002.
[13] R. Sheahan, L. Lipsky, P. M. Fiorini, and S. Asmussen. On the completion time distribution for tasks that must restart from the beginning if a failure occurs. *SIGMETRICS Performance Evaluation Review*, 34(3):24–26, December 2006.
[14] J. Tan and N. Shroff. Transition from heavy to light tails in retransmission durations. In *Proceedings of IEEE INFOCOM'10*, pages 1–9, San Diego, CA, March 2010.

Fluid Limit of an Asynchronous Optical Packet Switch with Shared per Link Full Range Wavelength Conversion

Benny Van Houdt
Department of Mathematics and Computer Science, University of Antwerp - IBBT, Belgium
benny.vanhoudt@ua.ac.be

Luca Bortolussi
Department of Mathematics and Computer Science, University of Trieste, Italy
luca@dmi.units.it

ABSTRACT

We consider an asynchronous all optical packet switch (OPS) where each link consists of N wavelength channels and a pool of $C \leq N$ full range tunable wavelength converters. Under the assumption of Poisson arrivals with rate λ (per wavelength channel) and exponential packet lengths, we determine a simple closed-form expression for the limit of the loss probabilities $P_{loss}(N)$ as N tends to infinity (while the load and conversion ratio $\sigma = C/N$ remains fixed). More specifically, for $\sigma \leq \lambda^2$ the loss probability tends to $(\lambda^2 - \sigma)/\lambda(1+\lambda)$, while for $\sigma > \lambda^2$ the loss tends to zero. We also prove an insensitivity result when the exponential packet lengths are replaced by certain classes of phase-type distributions.

A key feature of the dynamical system (i.e., set ... that describes the limit behavior of this OPS switc... its right-hand side is discontinuous. To prove th... gence, we therefore had to generalize some existing ... the setting of piece-wise smooth dynamical system...

Categories and Subject Descriptors

C.4 [**Performance of Systems**]: Modeling Te...
G.3 [**Probability and Statistics**]: Queueing Theory

General Terms

Performance, Theory

Keywords

Fluid limit, optical packet switch, wavelength conversion

1. INTRODUCTION

All optical packet switches (OPS) differ from traditional switches in that they avoid the need to perform any opto-electronic translations, as such they are a good candidate for future ultra-fast communications. As opposed to electronic switches where packets can be buffered (in RAM memory) for an arbitrary amount of time to avoid congestion, there exists no form of optical memory with the same capabilities for OPS switches. The lack of optical buffers may therefore be regarded as one of the main challenges faced when designing an OPS switch.

Congestion in OPS switches, which occurs whenever multiple packets want to make simultaneous use of the same wavelength on an output port, can be addressed by (a combination of) the following three methods: deflection routing, fiber delay line (FDL) buffers and tunable wavelength converters (TWCs). In case of deflection routing, part of the congested traffic is simply routed to another output port (using the same wavelength), causing additional load in the net- ...rdered arrival of packets at the destination nodes, ... delays. As such it is not regarded as a viable so- ...ept for low load scenarios [24]. FDL buffers [8, 20] ...me form of buffering, as they allow delays of op- ...ls by an amount of time chosen from a predefined ...t. TWCs on the other hand try to avoid conges- ...nverting an optical signal from one (congested) ...h to another (available) wavelength. Switch archi- ...hat rely solely on TWCs may be regarded as the ...nd more popular solutions for contention resolution in OPS networks [2].

An OPS switch using TWCs can operate either in a synchronous or asynchronous fashion, and uses either a shared per node (SPN) or shared per link (SPL) architecture. In a synchronous switch, time is slotted and packets arrive at slot boundaries, while the packet lengths are multiples of the fixed slot length. The synchronous operation may simplify the design of the switching matrix, but requires strict packet synchronization and alignment [1]. Asynchronous networks are often considered as a more natural choice for IP networks due to its variable length data packets [2]. An SPN architecture implies that there is a single pool of TWCs that is shared among all the output ports/links, while in case of SPL, each output port/link has its own set of TWCs. The shared use of the TWCs in an SPN architecture may result in a multiplexing gain, but also adds complexity to the switching matrix.

The TWCs may provide limited- or full-range wavelength conversion. A TWC is called a full-range converter, if it can convert an incoming packet from any incoming wavelength to any output wavelength. If the output wavelength range is limited (typically to a number of adjacent wavelengths), a TWC is referred to as a limited-range TWC. Finally, an OPS switch is said to support either partial or full conversion. Full conversion implies that there are as many

TWCs as there are output wavelengths, while partial conversion means that there are fewer TWCs (which is typically the case for economical reasons). When the switch uses an SPL architecture, where N represents the number of output wavelengths and C the number of TWCs per port/link, the ratio $\sigma = C/N$ is termed the conversion ratio (where $0 < \sigma < 1$).

Our contribution.

In this paper we study the loss probability of an asynchronous switch with shared per link, full-range converters that supports partial wavelength conversion. We derive a closed-form expression for the packet loss probability when the number of wavelengths N becomes large in case of Poisson arrivals with rate $\lambda < 1$ and exponential packet lengths with rate $\mu = 1$. More specifically, we prove that the loss probability tends to zero as N tends to infinity, as long as the conversion ratio $\sigma \geq \lambda^2$. Further, if $\sigma < \lambda^2$, the loss probability converges to $(\lambda^2 - \sigma)/\lambda(1+\lambda)$ as N tends to infinity. This result is established as follows:

1. We introduce a set of ordinary differential equations (ODEs) that describe the evolution of the fluid limit of the system. One of the main characteristics of this set of ODEs is that the right-hand side is discontinuous (and therefore clearly not Lipschitz as required when relying on the work of Kurtz [11,16]).
2. We reformulate the set of ODEs as a differential inclusion and prove that it has a unique solution for any initial value.
3. We show that all the trajectories of the unique solution are regular, as such the results presented in [6] imply that the sample paths of length t for the finite system converge to the trajectory of the fluid limit.
4. We prove that the unique solution of the differential inclusion has a unique fixed point.
5. The unique fixed point is shown to be a global attractor.
6. We show that the support of the steady state measures of the finite systems converges to the unique fixed point.

In fact, to establish 6. a more general result for piece-wise smooth (PWS) dynamical systems is proven that can be used for other problem settings, as such the paper also contains a methodological contribution.

Further, the same results are also established for phase-type distributed packet lengths, except that the unique fixed point was proven to be a global attractor for a limited range of the conversion ratio σ only. These results indicate that the loss probability becomes insensitive to the packet length distribution as the number of wavelengths N grows.

Related work.

There have been various performance studies of all optical switches (see [1,2,19,22,23]), of which the two most related studies are [1,19]. The switch architecture considered in [1] is identical to the one in this paper, i.e., it considers an asynchronous switch with shared per link full-range converters that supports partial wavelength conversion. A numerical approach to compute the blocking probability was presented for both Poisson and MAP arrivals [18] (which is a class of arrival processes that contains the Markov modulated Poisson process [13] as a special case), while the packet lengths were assumed to be exponential. The sensitivity with respect to the packet length distribution was investigated by means of simulation only as the numerical approach presented does not scale well in case of more general packet lengths, e.g., phase-type [17]. Simulation results for deterministic and order-2 hyperexponential distributions, indicated that the blocking probability is nearly insensitive to the packet length distribution in case of Poisson arrivals.

In this paper we focus on the system with Poisson arrivals only and determine the loss probability in closed-form when the number of wavelengths N tends to infinity. We further prove that the switch performance does indeed become insensitive to the packet length distribution as N tends to infinity in case of order-2 hyperexponential distributions (for most of the σ values).

The study presented in [19] is also strongly related to the current paper, as it analyzes a similar synchronous switch. The arrival process considered is a discrete-time MAP arrival process and the packet lengths are multiples of the slot length and have a general distribution with finite support (which is a subclass of the discrete-time phase-type distributions). The authors also study the switch behavior as the number of wavelengths N becomes large and rely on the framework developed in [7]. More specifically, the limiting system is described by a set of difference equations that were solved numerically and for which a unique fixed point was shown to exist in case the arrival process is a superposition of N Bernoulli processes with parameter p (one for each wavelength on the output port). However, no proof was provided that this fixed point is a global attractor or that the limit of the steady state distributions for the finite systems can be expressed through this fixed point. Under the assumption that both these results can be proven, the authors showed that the loss rate decreases to zero if and only if $\sigma \geq \rho^2(1-1/E[L])$, where $\rho = pE[L]$ and $E[L]$ is the mean packet length expressed in slots. If we decrease the slot length to zero, meaning ρ remains fixed and $E[L]$ tends to infinity, the Bernoulli process with parameter p becomes Poisson with rate $\lambda = p$ and the formula reduces to $\sigma \geq \rho^2$, which is in agreement with the result presented in this paper as $E[L]$ was set equal to 1.

Finally, we note that, based on simulation experiments, insensitivity of the loss probability with respect to the packet length distribution for OPS switches with a large number of wavelengths was also conjectured in [23].

2. ANALYTICAL MODEL

This section discusses the analytical model used to assess the loss probability in an asynchronous OPS switch with an SPL architecture with full-range TWCs. Due to the SPL architecture, we can focus on the behavior of a single, tagged output port/link. This link contains N wavelengths and has its own pool of $C < N$ TWCs, where $\sigma = C/N$ is the conversion ratio. We assume that packets destined for the tagged link arrive according to a Poisson process with rate λN. More specifically, for all $w \in \{1, \ldots, N\}$, we assume that the packets destined for the tagged output port that arrive on wavelength w form a Poisson process with rate

$\lambda < 1$. For the packet lengths we consider both exponential as well as phase-type (PH) distributed packet lengths.

An order m phase-type distribution is characterized by a stochastic $1 \times m$ vector α (with entries $\alpha_1, \ldots, \alpha_m$) and an $m \times m$ sub-generator matrix T. Let X_{ij} represent the (i,j)-th element of a matrix X, then $T_{ij} \geq 0$ for $i \neq j$ and $T_{ii} < 0$. Further, let e denote a *column* vector with all its entries equal to one, then $T^* = -Te \geq 0$. Let Z be a phase-type random variable with representation (α, T), then $P[Z > t] = \alpha \exp(Tt)e$ and $E[Z] = \alpha(-T)^{-1}e$. In other words, Z can be regarded as the time until absorption in a continuous time Markov chain with $m+1$ states and rate matrix Q given by

$$Q = \begin{bmatrix} T & T^* \\ 0 & 0 \end{bmatrix},$$

where the initial state is sampled according to the probability vector α. The exponential distribution with mean $1/\mu$ is obtained by setting $m = 1$, $\alpha = 1$ and $T = -\mu$. Notice, any order $m > 1$ PH distribution with $T^* = \mu e$ also represents the exponential distribution with mean $1/\mu$ (in a redundant manner). Throughout the paper we set the mean packet length $1/\mu = \alpha(-T)^{-1}e$ equal to one.

Given the above assumptions on the arrival process and packet lengths, it is clear that we can analyze the switch performance by means of the following $2m$ dimensional Markov chain $\{(W^{(N)}(t), C^{(N)}(t))\}_{t \geq 0}$, where

$$W^{(N)}(t) = (W_1^{(N)}(t), \ldots, W_m^{(N)}(t))$$

and

$$C^{(N)}(t) = (C_1^{(N)}(t), \ldots, C_m^{(N)}(t)).$$

Let $W_i^{(N)}(t)$ denote the number of wavelengths in use on the tagged link that do *not* require a TWC, while the phase of the packet that is being transmitted is i at time t. Similarly, $C_i^{(N)}(t)$ represents the number of wavelengths in use that *make use* of a TWC, while the phase of the packet that is being transmitted is i at time t.

For exponential packet lengths this Markov chain becomes 2 dimensional and the following events can take place. The transmission of a packet may end on one of the wavelengths in use, causing $W^{(N)}(t)$ or $C^{(N)}(t)$ to decrease by one. These events occur at rate $W^{(N)}(t)$ and $C^{(N)}(t)$, respectively. Arrivals occur at each channel and they form a Poisson input process with rate λ. If an arrival does not require a TWC (because its incoming wavelength is still available at the output link), then $W^{(N)}(t)$ is increased by one. This happens at rate $\lambda(N - W^{(N)}(t) - C^{(N)}(t))$. On the other hand, if an arrival happens on a busy wavelength, then it is redirected to a TWC, provided that there are wavelengths available, $W^{(N)}(t) + C^{(N)}(t) < N$, and that there is a TWC available, $C^{(N)}(t) < C = \sigma N$. This kind of arrival increases $C^{(N)}(t)$ by one, and it occurs with rate $\lambda(W^{(N)}(t) + C^{(N)}(t))$, so that the total arrival rate (if channels and TWC are available) is $N\lambda$.

We can determine the steady state of the above 2 dimensional Markov chain by means of efficient numerical techniques [1, 15] for systems with as many as a few hundred wavelengths. Further, even replacing the Poisson arrivals by MAP arrivals as in [1] requires little extra effort. For (non-redundant) phase-type distributions of order 2 (or higher) these numerical techniques are only effective to analyze systems with a small number of wavelengths (which explains why [1] relied on simulation experiments to investigate the sensitivity of the packet length distribution).

Our objective is to derive a closed-form expression for the loss probability when the number of wavelengths N becomes large. Thus, we are interested in the limit behavior of the loss probability $P_{loss}(N)$, when N goes to infinity. To this end we study the scaled process $\{(W^{(N)}(t), C^{(N)}(t))/N\}_{t \geq 0}$ as N goes to infinity. Although it is not hard to show that the set of Markov chains $\{(W^{(N)}(t)/N, C^{(N)}(t)/N)\}_{t \geq 0}$, for $N \geq 1$, form a set of density dependent Markov processes as defined by Kurtz [11], it will become apparent that the right-hand side of the set of ordinary differential equations (ODEs) is in our case discontinuous (hence, not Lipschitz). This implies that we cannot rely on the results in [4, 11] to guarantee convergence and interchangeability of the limits.

3. EXPONENTIAL PACKET LENGTHS

In this section we consider exponential packet lengths with mean 1. Thus, $\{(W^{(N)}(t), C^{(N)}(t))\}_{t \geq 0}$ is a 2 dimensional Markov chain, where $W^{(N)}(t)$ is the number of the wavelengths in use at time t that do not make use of a TWC, while $C^{(N)}(t)$ the number of the wavelengths in use that also occupy a TWC. Let $w(t) = W^{(N)}(t)/N$ be the fraction of wavelengths in use that do not make use of a TWC at time t and $c(t) = C^{(N)}(t)/N$ the fraction of wavelengths in use at time t that uses a TWC (i.e., $c(t)/\sigma$ is the fraction of busy TWCs) and let N go to infinity. Given the possible events discussed in Section 2, we obtain the following set of differential equations in case of exponential packet lengths

$$\begin{aligned} \frac{d}{dt} w(t) &= \lambda(1 - w(t) - c(t)) - w(t), \\ \frac{d}{dt} c(t) &= \lambda(w(t) + c(t)) 1_{[w(t)+c(t)<1 \text{ and } c(t)<\sigma]} - c(t), \end{aligned} \quad (1)$$

where $1_A = 1$ if A is true and $1_A = 0$ otherwise. If we denote this system of ODEs as $\frac{d}{dt}(w(t), c(t)) = F(w(t), c(t))$, then F is clearly not Lipschitz on $S = \{(w,c) | 0 \leq w, c \leq 1, w + c \leq 1, c \leq \sigma\}$ due to the presence of the indicator function $1_{[w(t)+c(t)<1 \text{ and } c(t)<\sigma]}$. This implies that we cannot rely on the convergence results of Kurtz and Benaïm [4, 11]. Moreover, the Picard-Lindelöf theorem [21] no longer guarantees that a unique solution for $(w(t), c(t))$ exists given an arbitrary $(w(0), c(0)) \in S$.

To deal with the presence of this indicator function, we will replace the above system of discontinuous ODEs by the differential inclusion [9]

$$\frac{d}{dt}(w(t), c(t)) = \bar{F}(w(t), c(t)),$$

where $\bar{F}(w, c)$ is a set-valued function defined as

$$\bar{F}(w, c) = \begin{cases} \{F(w, c)\} & w + c \neq 1 \text{ and } c \neq \sigma, \\ \text{co}(f_1(w, c), f_2(w, c)) & w + c = 1 \text{ or } c = \sigma, \end{cases} \quad (2)$$

where co denotes the convex closure of a set and

$$\begin{aligned} f_1(w, c) &= (\lambda - \lambda c - (1 + \lambda)w, \lambda w - (1 - \lambda)c), \\ f_2(w, c) &= (\lambda - \lambda c - (1 + \lambda)w, -c). \end{aligned} \quad (3)$$

Note, the *row* vector $f_1(w(t), c(t))$ and $f_2(w(t), c(t))$ denotes the rate of change of $(w(t), c(t))$ if we replace the indicator function in (1) by one and zero, respectively.

3.1 Solutions, fixed points and global attraction

In this section we prove the following theorem. We start by looking at the solution of the set of ODEs without the indicator function and discuss its influence afterwards.

THEOREM 1. *The differential inclusion* $\frac{d}{dt}(w(t), c(t)) = \bar{F}(w(t), c(t))$ *defined by (2) has a unique (Filippov*[1]*) solution* $(w(t), c(t))$ *for any initial value* $(w(0), c(0)) \in S$. *There exists a unique fixed point* π *in* S *given by*

$$(\frac{\lambda(1-\sigma)}{1+\lambda}, \sigma)$$

for $\sigma \leq \lambda^2$ *and*

$$(\lambda(1-\lambda), \lambda^2)$$

for $\sigma > \lambda^2$. *Further,* π *is a global attractor, i.e., all the trajectories starting from* $(w(0), c(0)) \in S$ *converge towards* π.

No boundaries.

We start by considering the set of ODEs (1) without the indicator function $1_{[w(t)+c(t)<1 \text{ and } c(t)<\sigma]}$. This equation can be written in matrix form as

$$\frac{d}{dt}(w(t), c(t)) = (w(t), c(t)) \underbrace{\begin{bmatrix} -(1+\lambda) & \lambda \\ -\lambda & \lambda - 1 \end{bmatrix}}_{\text{matrix } A} + (\lambda, 0).$$

As a result, the unique solution of the initial value problem defined by the above set of ODEs can be written as

$$(w(t), c(t)) = (\lambda, 0)(-A)^{-1}(I - e^{tA}) + (w(0), c(0))e^{tA}.$$

As -1 is an eigenvalue of A with multiplicity 2, the matrix exponential e^{tA} becomes zero as t goes to infinity. This implies that all the trajectories converge to

$$(\lambda(1-\lambda), \lambda^2) = (\lambda, 0)(-A)^{-1}.$$

Further, using

$$e^{tA} = e^{-t} \begin{bmatrix} 1 - \lambda t & -\lambda t \\ \lambda t & 1 + \lambda t \end{bmatrix},$$

we find that

$$\begin{aligned} w(t) &= \lambda(1-\lambda) - e^{-t}(\lambda(1 - \lambda(1+t))) \\ &+ e^{-t}((1-\lambda t)w(0) - \lambda t c(0)), \\ c(t) &= \lambda^2 - e^{-t}(\lambda^2(1+t) - \lambda t w(0) - (1+\lambda t)c(0)). \end{aligned} \quad (4)$$

[1]A Filippov solution is an absolutely continuous function, therefore almost everywhere differentiable, in contrast with solutions of ODE with Lipschitz continuous right-hand side, which are of class at least $\mathcal{C}^1$.

Boundary behavior.

To examine the behavior of the differential inclusion at the boundaries $\{(w, c)|w + c = 1\}$ and $\{(w, c)|c = \sigma\}$, we use the following methodology outlined in [6,9]. Let $\mathcal{R}_1$ and $\mathcal{R}_2$ be two regions separated by a smooth boundary $\mathcal{H}$. More specifically, $\mathcal{H} = \{(w, c)|h(w, c) = 0\}$, with h a function with continuous second order derivatives such that

$$\mathcal{R}_1 = \{(w, c)|h(w, c) < 0\},$$

and

$$\mathcal{R}_2 = \{(w, c)|h(w, c) > 0\}.$$

Further, the normal vector $n(w, c)$ should be well-defined on $\mathcal{H}$ and is assumed to point into $\mathcal{R}_1$. Denote the limit of $\bar{F}$ in $(w, c) \in \mathcal{H}$ as $f_1(w, c)$ ($f_2(w, c)$) if (w, c) is approached from within $\mathcal{R}_1$ ($\mathcal{R}_2$).

According to [6,9], the behavior of a solution of the differential inclusion that starts from $(w, c) \in \mathcal{H}$ is determined by the values of the scalar products

$$f_1(w, c)n(w, c) \text{ and } f_2(w, c)n(w, c),$$

where $n(w, c)$ was denoted as a column vector. If both are positive (negative), a *transversal crossing* is said to occur, that is, the solution will move into $\mathcal{R}_1$ ($\mathcal{R}_2$). Thus, if a trajectory hits $\mathcal{H}$ in such a point (w, c) (from within $\mathcal{R}_2$), the trajectory crosses $\mathcal{H}$. If $f_1(w, c)n(w, c)$ (or $f_2(w, c)n(w, c)$) is zero, we have a *tangential crossing* along $f_2(w, c)$ (or $f_1(w, c)$). Finally, if $f_1(w, c)n(w, c) < 0$ and $f_2(w, c)n(w, c) > 0$, we get a *(stable) sliding motion* along $\mathcal{H}$, meaning the solution follows the surface $\mathcal{H}$ (as long as these conditions remain valid). The precise trajectory of the sliding motion is discussed further on. We also note that the differential inclusion is known to have a unique solution if we start in $(w, c) \in \mathcal{H}$ provided that either $f_1(w, c)n(w, c) < 0$ or $f_2(w, c)n(w, c) > 0$ for all $(w, c) \in \mathcal{H}$ [12].

Assume we start from $(w(0), c(0)) \in S = \{(w, c)|0 \leq w, c \leq 1, w + c \leq 1, c \leq \sigma\}$. The boundary ∂S of S is the union of four line segments: $L_1 = \{(w, c)|w = 0, 0 \leq c \leq \sigma\}$, $L_2 = \{(w, c)|0 \leq w \leq 1, c = 0\}$, $L_3 = \{(w, c)|w + c = 1, 0 \leq c \leq \sigma\}$ and $L_4 = \{(w, c)|0 \leq w \leq 1 - \sigma, c = \sigma\}$. $\bar{F}$ is continuous on L_1 and L_2 and it is easy to see that the drift points towards the interior of S. The line L_3 is part of the smooth surface $\mathcal{H}$ defined by setting $h(w, c) = 1 - w - c$ and f_1 and f_2 as in (3). Clearly, the transposed normal vector $n^T(w, c) = (-1, -1)/\sqrt{2}$ and therefore $f_1(w, c)n(w, c) = (1-\lambda)/\sqrt{2} > 0$ and $f_2(w, c)n(w, c) = (w + c)/\sqrt{2} = 1/\sqrt{2} > 0$ for $(w, c) \in \mathcal{H}$. In other words, if we start on the line segment L_3, we immediately move into S and never hit this boundary again.

The behavior at the boundary $c = \sigma$ is somewhat more involved. First define $\mathcal{H}$ by letting $h(w, c) = \sigma - c$ and f_1 and f_2 as in (3). The transposed normal vector $n^T(w, c) = (0, -1)$, meaning $f_1(w, c)n(w, c) = -\lambda w + (1 - \lambda)\sigma$ and $f_2(w, c)n(w, c) = \sigma > 0$. Notice, the latter expression guarantees the uniqueness of the solution. Thus, if $w \leq (1 - \lambda)\sigma/\lambda$ we get a crossing into $\mathcal{R}_1$, otherwise we get a sliding motion along the line $\mathcal{H} = \{(w, c)|c = \sigma\}$. Notice, if $\sigma > \lambda$, then $w < (1 - \lambda)\sigma/\lambda$ holds for all $w < 1 - \sigma$, meaning there is no sliding motion on L_4 either.

Limit behavior of trajectories.

We will distinguish two cases: $\sigma \leq \lambda^2$ and $\lambda^2 < \sigma \leq 1$. In the first case, we can partition the line segment $L_4 = \{(w, c)|c = \sigma, 0 < w < 1 - \sigma\}$ into two disjoint pieces

$L_{4,1} = \{(w,c)|c = \sigma, 0 < w \leq (1-\lambda)\sigma/\lambda\}$ and $L_{4,2} = \{(w,c)|c = \sigma, (1-\lambda)\sigma/\lambda < w < 1\}$. The above discussion indicated that if we start on $L_{4,1}$, we cross into S. Further, as $f_1(w,c)n(w,c) \geq 0$ on $L_{4,1}$, we can never hit $L_{4,1}$ from the interior of S. Next, recall that the drift close to the three other boundaries points inwards and that all the trajectories starting in the interior of S move towards the fixed point $(\lambda(1-\lambda), \lambda^2)$, which is located outside of the interior of S if $\sigma \leq \lambda^2$. Thus, the line segment $L_{4,2}$ is eventually hit by all the trajectories starting in S.

When $L_{4,2}$ is hit, a sliding motion starts. As explained in [6,9], the evolution of the sliding motion is determined by the differential equation $\frac{d}{dt}(w(t), c(t)) = g(w(t), c(t))$, where $g(w,c)$ is the linear combination of $f_1(w,c)$ and $f_2(w,c)$ such that $g(w,c)$ is tangential to $\mathcal{H}$. In other words, on $L_{4,2}$ we have

$$g(w,c) = (\lambda - \lambda\sigma - (1+\lambda)w, 0).$$

Thus, if we hit $L_{4,2}$ below $w^* = \lambda(1-\sigma)/(1+\lambda)$, we slide upwards, otherwise we slide downwards. Note that (w^*, σ) is part of $L_{4,2}$ if and only if $\sigma < \lambda^2$ (it lies on the boundary between $L_{4,1}$ and $L_{4,2}$ if $\sigma = \lambda^2$). Further, if we start in $(w(0), \sigma) \in L_{4,2}$ then

$$w(t) = \frac{\lambda(1-\sigma)}{1+\lambda}(1 - \exp(-(1+\lambda)t)) + \exp(-(1+\lambda)t)w(0).$$

In conclusion, if $\sigma \leq \lambda^2$ we hit $L_{4,2}$ after a finite amount of time and start an infinite slide towards

$$(\frac{\lambda(1-\sigma)}{1+\lambda}, \sigma),$$

which is therefore a global attractor of the differential inclusion starting from any $(w(0), c(0)) \in S$.

When $\lambda^2 < \sigma \leq 1$, the fixed point $(\lambda(1-\lambda), \lambda^2)$ of the system without the indicator function, lies in the interior of S. As before we can partition the line L_4 into $L_{4,1}$ and $L_{4,2}$, where $L_{4,1}$ cannot be reached from the interior of S. The line $L_{4,2}$ can still be hit from the interior of S and a sliding motion starts when it is hit. Further, the motion is still described by the function g defined before and is downwards as (w^*, σ) lies in the interior of $L_{4,1}$. Therefore, the slide will end (after a finite amount of time) at $((1-\lambda)\sigma/\lambda, \sigma)$ by a tangential crossing into S. Now, if we set $(w(0), c(0)) = ((1-\lambda)\sigma/\lambda, \sigma)$ in the system without boundaries, (4) implies that

$$c(t) = \lambda^2 + e^{-t}(\sigma - \lambda^2)(1+t).$$

Hence, the value of $c(t)$ decreases towards λ^2 and the line $L_{4,2}$ is therefore hit at most once. The point

$$(\lambda(1-\lambda), \lambda^2),$$

is therefore a global attractor of the differential inclusion starting from any $(w(0), c(0)) \in S$.

3.2 Limit results

Our next objective is to prove the following theorem:

THEOREM 2. *For $N \geq 1$, consider the sequence of Markov chains $(W^{(N)}(t), C^{(N)}(t))$, and let π be the unique fixed point defined in Theorem 1, then*

$$\lim_{N\to\infty} \lim_{t\to\infty} \|(W^{(N)}(t)/N, C^{(N)}(t)/N) - \pi\| = 0 \text{ in probability.}$$

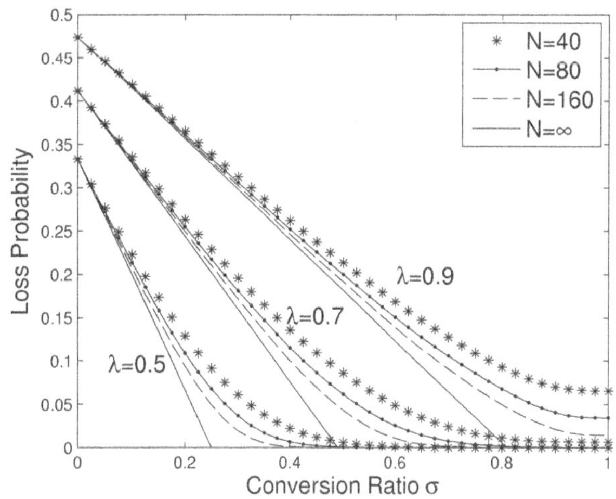

Figure 1: Comparison of loss probability $P_{loss}(N)$ for $N = 40, 80$ and 160 wavelengths per link with the fluid limit

We will prove a more general result for piece-wise smooth (PWS) dynamical systems in Section 5, which will be valid for any PWS that satisfies the four required assumptions H0 to H3 introduced in Section 5. Given the results in the previous section, it is clear that H1 to H3 are satisfied in case of exponential packet lengths and therefore Theorem 5 applies.

As the loss probability can be determined as 1 minus the ratio between the output and input rate of the switch, the previous theorem indicates that the loss probability behaves as follows:

COROLLARY 1. *Under Poisson arrivals with rate $\lambda < 1$ (per wavelength) and exponential packet lengths with mean 1, the limit of the loss probability $P_{loss}(N)$ in an asynchronous OPS switch with an SPL architecture, full range TWCs and a conversion ratio σ equals*

$$\lim_{N\to\infty} P_{loss}(N) = \frac{\lambda - \pi e}{\lambda} = 0,$$

for $\sigma > \lambda^2$ and

$$\lim_{N\to\infty} P_{loss}(N) = \frac{\lambda - \pi e}{\lambda} = \frac{\lambda^2 - \sigma}{\lambda(1+\lambda)},$$

for $0 \leq \sigma \leq \lambda^2$.

In other words, if σ exceeds λ^2, the loss probability decreases to zero as in the Erlang loss model (which corresponds to the case where $\sigma = 1$) and in the limit a fraction $1 - \lambda^2/\sigma$ of the TWCs remains idle. When $\sigma \leq \lambda^2$, all the TWC are occupied and the remaining fraction $(1-\sigma)$ of wavelengths act as a set of independent $M/M/1/1$ queues, meaning each is occupied with probability $\lambda/(1+\lambda)$. If we provision a conversion ratio of $\sigma = \eta\lambda^2$, with $\eta \leq 1$, one finds that the loss rate becomes $(1-\eta)\lambda/(1+\lambda)$. In other words, when a link is equipped with a pool of TWCs with $\sigma = \eta\lambda^2$, the loss probability diminishes by a factor $(1-\eta)$ when compared to a switch without TWCs (i.e., when $\sigma = 0$).

In Figure 1 we compare the loss probability $P_{loss}(N)$ for $N = 40, 80$ and 160 with the fluid limit for three different loads $\lambda = 0.5, 0.7$ and 0.9 (where the numerical approach

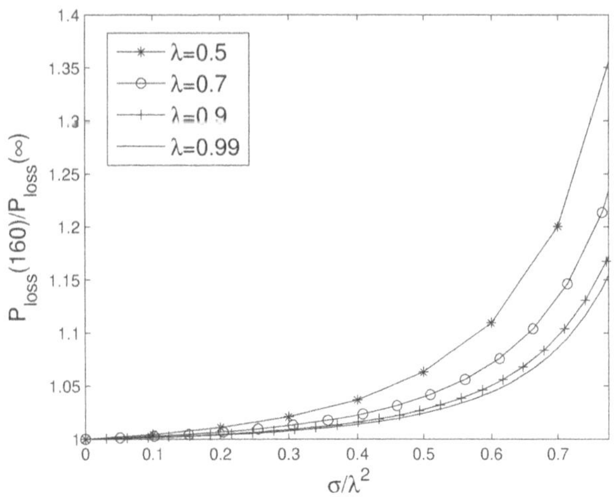

Figure 2: Comparison of ratio $P_{loss}(N)/P_{loss}(\infty)$ for $N = 160$ wavelengths per link with the fluid limit for different loads λ

of [15] was used to obtain the loss for finite N). Commercial DWDM systems with as many as 160 wavelengths are currently on the market (by the Infinera Corporation), though they still rely on opto-electronic translations to store packets in electronic RAM memory. These results confirm the convergence to the fluid limit. We also note that the convergence is slower for σ values close to λ^2. Figure 2 indicates that the accuracy tends to improve with the load λ for σ/λ^2 fixed. As σ/λ^2 approaches one, the ratio $P_{loss}(N)/P_{loss}(\infty)$ tends to infinity as $P_{loss}(\infty)$ tends to zero.

Notice that the slower convergence near λ^2 can be possibly connected to the fact that for $\sigma = \lambda^2$ the limit system undergoes a boundary equilibrium bifurcation [10], in which the limit loss probability (as a function of σ) has a discontinuity in the derivative, absent in the curves for $P_{loss}(N)$, for finite N (cf. Figure 1).

4. PHASE-TYPE PACKET LENGTHS

In this section we consider the same optical switch, but assume that the packet lengths are distributed according to a phase-type distribution with an order m representation (α, T). Recall that the matrix T is an $m \times m$ subgenerator, this implies that there exists a $\tau_1 < 0$, such that τ_1 is an eigenvalue of T and for any other eigenvalue τ_i of T, for $i = 2, \ldots, m$, the real part $Re(\tau_i) \leq \tau_1$. We also assume that the mean packet length $1/\mu$, which can be computed as $\alpha(-T)^{-1}e$, is equal to 1. For technical reasons that will become apparent further on, we will assume that $T^* = -Te > 0$ in all its entries. This is for instance the case for hyperexponential distributions, but not for an Erlang-k distribution with $k > 1$. However, it should be clear that any phase-type distribution for which Te is zero in some of its entries can be approximated arbitrarily close by one for which $-Te > 0$. For further use let T_i^* be the i-th entry of the *column* vector T^*.

We denote $w_i(t)$ as the fraction of wavelengths in use that are in phase i and that do not require a converter and $c_i(t)$ as the fraction of wavelengths in use requiring a converter that are in phase i, for $i = 1, \ldots, m$. We also denote $w(t) = (w_1(t), \ldots, w_m(t))$ and $c(t) = (c_1(t), \ldots, c_m(t))$. The set of ODEs given by (1) is now replaced by

$$\begin{aligned}
\frac{d}{dt}w_i(t) &= \lambda(1 - w(t)e - c(t)e)\alpha_i + \sum_{j \neq i} w_j(t)T_{ji} \\
&\quad - \sum_{j \neq i} w_i(t)T_{ij} - w_i(t)T_i^*, \\
\frac{d}{dt}c_i(t) &= \lambda(w(t)e + c(t)e)\alpha_i 1_{[w(t)e+c(t)e<1 \text{ and } c(t)e<\sigma]} \\
&\quad + \sum_{j \neq i} c_j(t)T_{ji} - \sum_{j \neq i} c_i(t)T_{ij} - c_i(t)T_i^*, \qquad (5)
\end{aligned}$$

for $i = 1, \ldots, m$, where $T^* = -Te$. These equations can be further simplified by noting that $T_{ii} = -\sum_{j \neq i} T_{ij} - T_i^*$.

The set-valued function $\bar{F}(w_1, \ldots, w_m, c_1, \ldots, c_m)$ needed for the differential inclusion is given by

$$\bar{F}(w,c) = \begin{cases} \{F(w,c)\} & we + ce \neq 1 \text{ and } ce \neq \sigma, \\ \text{co}(f_1(w,c), f_2(w,c)) & we + ce = 1 \text{ or } ce = \sigma, \end{cases} \qquad (6)$$

where $w = (w_1, \ldots, w_m)$ and $c = (c_1, \ldots, c_m)$,

$$f_1(w,c) = (\lambda\alpha + w(T - \lambda e\alpha) - c\lambda e\alpha, w\lambda e\alpha + c(T + \lambda e\alpha)) \qquad (7)$$

and

$$f_2(w,c) = (\lambda\alpha + w(T - \lambda e\alpha) - c\lambda e\alpha, cT). \qquad (8)$$

4.1 Solutions, fixed points and global attraction

We start by proving the theorem below for phase-type distributed packet lengths. The issue of whether the unique fixed point is also a global attractor is addressed in Appendix A, where we prove several results for certain subclasses of the set of phase-type distributions and certain ranges of the conversion ratio σ. A general proof for the complete class of phase-type distributions (with $T^* > 0$) and all possible σ values is currently still lacking.

THEOREM 3. *The differential inclusion* $\frac{d}{dt}(w(t), c(t)) = \bar{F}(w(t), c(t))$ *defined by (2) for phase-type distributed packet lengths with representation* (α, T) *and* $T^* > 0$*, has a unique solution* $(w(t), c(t))$ *for any initial value* $(w(0), c(0)) \in S$. *Further, there exists a unique fixed point* π *in* S *given by*

$$\left(\frac{\lambda(1-\sigma)}{1+\lambda}\theta, \sigma\theta\right)$$

for $\sigma \leq \lambda^2$ *and*

$$(\lambda(1-\lambda)\theta, \lambda^2\theta)$$

for $\sigma > \lambda^2$*, where* θ *is the stochastic row vector given by* $\theta = \alpha(-T)^{-1}$.

No boundaries.

Consider the set of ODEs (5) after removing the indicator function $1_{[w(t)e+c(t)e<1 \text{ and } c(t)e<\sigma]}$. This equation can clearly be written in matrix form as

$$\frac{d}{dt}(w(t), c(t)) = (w(t), c(t)) \underbrace{\begin{bmatrix} T - \lambda e\alpha & \lambda e\alpha \\ -\lambda e\alpha & T + \lambda e\alpha \end{bmatrix}}_{\text{matrix } A} + (\lambda\alpha, 0),$$

where we used the fact that $T_{ii} = -\sum_{j \neq i} T_{ij} - T_i^*$. As a result, the unique solution of the initial value problem defined by the above set of ODEs can be written as

$$(w(t), c(t)) = (\lambda\alpha, 0)(-A)^{-1}(I - e^{tA}) + (w(0), c(0))e^{tA}.$$

As

$$\det(A - \tau I) = \det\left(\begin{bmatrix} T - \tau I & \lambda e\alpha \\ T - \tau I & T + \lambda e\alpha - \tau I \end{bmatrix}\right) = \det\left(\begin{bmatrix} T - \tau I & \lambda e\alpha \\ 0 & T - \tau I \end{bmatrix}\right),$$

we see that if τ is an eigenvalue of T with multiplicity n, then τ is also an eigenvalue of A with multiplicity $2n$. As the real part of all the eigenvalues of T is negative, so is the real part of all the eigenvalues of A and therefore the matrix exponential e^{tA} becomes zero as t goes to infinity. This implies that all the trajectories converge to

$$(\lambda(1 - \lambda)\theta, \lambda^2\theta) = (\lambda\alpha, 0)(-A)^{-1},$$

where $\theta = \alpha(-T)^{-1}$ is a stochastic vector such that $\theta(T + T^*\alpha) = 0$ (θ is stochastic as the mean service time $\alpha(-T)^{-1}e$ equals one). The i-th entry of θ represents the probability that a wavelength is in phase i provided that it is in use, as it is the invariant vector of the rate matrix $T + T^*\alpha$. Note, the above fixed point lies in the interior of S if and only if $\sigma < \lambda^2$ (as in the exponential case).

Boundary behavior.

Assume we start from $(w(0), c(0)) \in S = \{(w, c)|0 \leq w_i, c_i \leq 1, i = 1, \ldots, m, we + ce \leq 1, ce \leq \sigma\}$. The boundary ∂S of S is the union of the surfaces: $\{(w, c)|w_i = 0\}$, $\{(w, c)|c_i = 0\}$, for $i = 1, \ldots, m$, $\{(w, c)|we + ce = 1\}$ and $\{(w, c)|ce = \sigma\}$. F is continuous on the first $2m$ surfaces and it is easy to see that the drift points towards the interior of S. The surface $\{(w, c)|we + ce = 1\}$ can be defined as a smooth surface $\mathcal{H}$ by letting $h(w, c) = 1 - we - ce$ and f_1 and f_2 as in (7) and (8). Clearly, the transposed normal vector $n^T(w, c) = (-e^T, -e^T)/\sqrt{2m}$ and therefore

$$f_1(w, c)n(w, c) = ((w + c)T^* - \lambda)/\sqrt{2m}$$

and

$$f_2(w, c)n(w, c) = (w + c)T^*/\sqrt{2m}$$

for $(w, c) \in \mathcal{H}$. By the assumption that $T^* > 0$, we see that $f_2(w, c)n(w, c) > 0$, which guarantees the uniqueness of the solution if we start on the surface $\mathcal{H}$. The value of $(w + c)T^* - \lambda$ can become negative if at least one of the entries of T^* is less than λ, that is, if the rate of completion in some phase i is less than λ. In this case $\mathcal{H}$ contains a region where a sliding motion occurs, while otherwise a (transversal) crossing occurs in each point $(w, c) \in \mathcal{H}$.

To understand the behavior during the sliding motion on $\mathcal{H}$, we note that any convex combination $\eta f_1(w, c) + (1 - \eta)f_2(w, c)$, with $we + ce = 1$, is of the form $(wT, cT + \eta\lambda\alpha)$. Such a combination is tangential to $\mathcal{H}$ if $wTe + cTe + \eta\lambda\alpha e = 0$, meaning $g(w, c)$ is obtained by setting $0 \leq \eta = (w + c)T^*/\lambda \leq 1$ (during the slide). The sliding motion is therefore described by

$$\frac{d}{dt}(w(t), c(t)) = (w(t), c(t))\begin{bmatrix} T & T^*\alpha \\ 0 & T + T^*\alpha \end{bmatrix}.$$

Hence, if the sliding motion lasts indefinitely, $(w(t), c(t))$ converges towards $(0, \theta)$. However $\theta T^* = -\theta(Te) = \alpha e = 1$, which indicates that $(0 + \theta)T^* - \lambda = 1 - \lambda > 0$. This means that $(0, \theta)$ is a point of transversal crossing and the sliding motion must therefore end at some point where $(w + c)T^* = \lambda$, which results in a tangential crossing (along $f_2(w, c)$). We should note that we may hit the surface $\{(w, c)|ce = \sigma\}$ before this crossing takes place (if $\sigma < 1$). In the latter case, it is worth noting that no sliding motion occurs on the intersection of these two surfaces due to the assumption that $T^* > 0$ (which guarantees that $we + ce$ immediately becomes less than one when ce becomes σ).

We now proceed with the boundary behavior at $\{(w, c)| ce = \sigma\}$. We set $h(w, c) = \sigma - ce$ and f_1 and f_2 as in (7) and (8). The transposed normal vector $n^T(w, c) = (0, -e^T)/\sqrt{m}$, meaning

$$f_1(w, c)n(w, c) = (-\lambda(we) - \lambda\sigma + cT^*)/\sqrt{m}$$

and

$$f_2(w, c)n(w, c) = cT^*/\sqrt{m} > 0,$$

due to the assumption that $T^* > 0$. Note, the latter expression once again guarantees the uniqueness of the solution. If $cT^* < \lambda(we + \sigma)$ we get a sliding motion, otherwise a (transversal) crossing into $\mathcal{R}_1$ occurs. To understand the behavior of the sliding motion we note that any convex combination $\eta f_1(w, c) + (1 - \eta)f_2(w, c)$, with $ce = \sigma$, is of the form $(\lambda(1 - \sigma)\alpha + w(T - \lambda e\alpha), cT + \eta\lambda(we + \sigma)\alpha)$. Such a combination is tangential to $\mathcal{H}$ if $cTe + \eta\lambda(we + \sigma)\alpha e = 0$, meaning $g(w, c)$ is obtained by setting $0 \leq \eta = cT^*/(\lambda(we + \sigma)) \leq 1$ (during the slide). The sliding motion is therefore described by

$$\frac{d}{dt}(w(t), c(t)) = (w(t), c(t))\begin{bmatrix} T - \lambda e\alpha & 0 \\ 0 & T + T^*\alpha \end{bmatrix} + (\lambda(1 - \sigma)\alpha, 0).$$

Thus, if the slide lasts indefinitely, $(w(t), c(t))$ converges to

$$(-\lambda(1 - \sigma)\alpha(T - \lambda e\alpha)^{-1}, \sigma\theta).$$

The vector $\alpha(T - \lambda e\alpha)^{-1}$ can be further simplified using the Sherman-Morrison formula, which states that $(A + uv^T)^{-1} = A^{-1} - (A^{-1}uv^TA^{-1})/(1 + v^TA^{-1}u)$, where u is a column vector and v^T a row vector of the appropriate size. That is, by setting $A = T$, $u = (-\lambda e)$ and $v^T = \alpha$ and using the fact that $\alpha(-T)^{-1}e = 1$, we find that $-\alpha(T - \lambda e\alpha)^{-1} = \theta/(1 + \lambda)$. Thus, if the slide lasts indefinitely, $(w(t), c(t))$ converges to

$$(\frac{\lambda(1 - \sigma)}{1 + \lambda}\theta, \sigma\theta).$$

One easily checks that the condition $f_1(w, c)n(w, c) = cT^* - \lambda(we + \sigma) \leq 0$ holds in this fixed point if and only if $\sigma \leq \lambda^2$. In other words, this point lies in the region (or on the boundary) of the area where the sliding motion occurs if and only if $\sigma \leq \lambda^2$ (as in the exponential case).

4.2 Limit results

In this section we identify some cases where the loss probability can be proven to become insensitive to the packet length distribution. Given the results in Sections 4.1 and 5, the final step exists in proving that the unique fixed point π is a global attractor. Various results for different ranges of σ and sub-classes of the class of phase-type distributions are presented in Appendix A. More specifically, the results in Appendix A show that the unique fixed point is a global attractor if $\sigma > \lambda/\min_i T_i^*$ or $\sigma < \lambda^2/(\max_i T_i^*)^2$

for any phase-type distribution with $T^* > 0$. For any hyperexponential distribution, $\sigma > \lambda^2/\min_i T_i^*$ or $\sigma < \lambda^2(1-\lambda)/(\max_i T_i^* - \lambda)$ suffices, while for order-2 hyperexponential distributions having $\sigma > \lambda^2$ is also sufficient.

In this section we will focus on the set of hyperexponential distributions of order-2 only, meaning with probability α_1 the packet length is exponential with parameter μ_1 and with probability $1-\alpha_2$ it is exponential with parameter μ_2. Note, as the mean packet length is one, we may assume without loss of generality that $\mu_1 \leq 1 \leq \mu_2$. Due to Theorems 3, 8, 10 and 5; as well as the equality $\theta T^* = \alpha(-T)^{-1}(-T)e = 1$, we obtain the following generalization of Corollary 1:

COROLLARY 2. *Under Poisson arrivals with rate $\lambda < 1$ (per wavelength) and order-2 hyperexponential packet durations with mean 1, the limit of the loss probability $P_{loss}(N)$ in an asynchronous OPS switch with an SPL architecture, full range TWCs and a conversion ratio σ equals*

$$\lim_{N\to\infty} P_{loss}(N) = \frac{\lambda - \pi\begin{pmatrix} T^* \\ T^* \end{pmatrix}}{\lambda} = 0,$$

for $\sigma > \lambda^2$ and

$$\lim_{N\to\infty} P_{loss}(N) = \frac{\lambda - \pi\begin{pmatrix} T^* \\ T^* \end{pmatrix}}{\lambda} = \frac{\lambda^2 - \sigma}{\lambda(1+\lambda)},$$

for $0 \leq \sigma < \lambda^2(1-\lambda)/(\mu_2 - \lambda)$.

Note, as $\mu_2 > 1$ for non-exponential distributions, insensitivity remains an open issue for $\sigma \in [\lambda^2(1-\lambda)/(\mu_2-\lambda), \lambda^2]$. Extensive numerical experiments seem to indicate that π is also a global attractor when σ is part of this region, but we did not manage to come up with a formal proof thus far.

Hyperexponential distributions of order 2 are often used when fitting the first two moments of a distribution as they can match both the mean $1/\mu$ and squared coefficient of variation (SCV) for any $SCV \geq 1$. The set of order-2 hyperexponential distributions was also used in [1] to investigate the impact of the packet length distribution on the loss probability. Simulation experiments in case of Poisson arrivals indicated that for general σ the loss probability of an OPS with $N = 32$ wavelengths per link *is* sensitive to the packet length distribution as opposed to the extreme cases $\sigma = 0$ or 1. In other words, the loss probability for non-exponential packet lengths deviates from the one with exponential packet lengths especially under low load and a moderate number of TWCs. However, the difference is not substantial and the authors state that *one can still make use of exponential packet length distributions for approximating the behavior of non-exponential packet lengths.* Corollary 2 shows that these simulation results are not a coincidence. The system may not be insensitive for finite N, but it becomes insensitive as N tends to infinity.

5. STEADY STATE LIMIT OF PIECE-WISE SMOOTH DYNAMICAL SYSTEMS

The purpose of this section is to prove a theorem for the steady state limit behavior of a sequence $X^{(N)}(t)$ of CTMCs converging to the solution of a piecewise smooth dynamical system (PWS), for any finite time horizon. A PWS is characterized by an ODE of the form $\frac{d}{dt}x(t) = F(x(t))$ with $F : E \to \mathbb{R}^n$ and $E \subset \mathbb{R}^n$. Further, there exist a finite number of domains $\mathcal{R}_i$, $i = 1, \ldots, s$, such that F can be extended to a smooth (or at least Lipschitz) function on the closure $\bar{\mathcal{R}}_i$ and $\bar{E} \subseteq \cup \bar{\mathcal{R}}_i$. Note, F may be discontinuous on the union of the boundaries of $\mathcal{R}_i$.

Similarly to the ODE limit case, we will prove that, if the PWS has a unique globally attracting equilibrium, then the steady state behavior of the sequence of CTMCs will be a point mass concentrated in such an equilibrium. In case the sequence of CTMC models a constant population in terms of the occupancy measure, then the theorem will provide the equilibrium distribution of each CTMC being in each state for large N. In order to prove this theorem, we need to introduce a few concepts and some additional regularity hypothesis on the PWS.

We now fix the notation and introduce the main hypothesis on the sequence of CTMCs.

H0: $X^{(N)}(t)$ is a sequence of CTMC on normalized population counts, i.e., with increments of order $\Theta(\frac{1}{N})$ and exit rate bounded by a $\Theta(N)$ constant. If the total population remains equal to N for all $t \geq 0$, then $X^{(N)}(t)$ is the occupancy measure. Furthermore, $X^{(N)}(t)$ has density dependent rates, so that the drift $F^{(N)}(x)$ is independent of N and equal to $F(x)$.

Let $\mathcal{S}^{(N)}$ be the state space of the N-th CTMC, and let $E \subset \mathbb{R}^n$ be the closure of the union of all domains $\mathcal{S}^{(N)}$: $E = cl(\bigcup_{N\in\mathbb{N}} \mathcal{S}^{(N)})$. Let the discontinuous vector field F be such that no trajectory starting in E can ever leave E.

H1: The PWS $\frac{dx(t)}{dt} = F(x(t))$ has a unique solution for any initial point $x_0 \in E$.

The hypothesis H1 implies that solutions of the PWS are defined in E for all $t \geq 0$. This property, combined with uniqueness, makes it possible to define a notion of (*forward*) flow also for the PWS: let $\phi_t(x)$, $t \geq 0$, be the point reached at time t by the PWS starting at x at time 0. Furthermore, we can show the following:

LEMMA 1. *If H0 and H1 holds, then $\phi_t(x) : E \to E$ is continuous for every $t > 0$.*

PROOF. The proof relies on properties of a generalization of the notion of flow for differential inclusions [3], of which PWS are a proper subclass. Let $F : E \to \mathcal{P}(E)$ be a set valued map, where $\mathcal{P}(E)$ is the power set of E, associating a convex and compact set $F(x)$ of E with any point $x \in E$. Furthermore, assume that F is upper semi-continuous, i.e., for each open neighborhood V of $F(x)$, there exists an open neighborhood U of x such that $F(U) \subseteq V$. Notice that if $F(x) = \{y\}$ is a singleton, the definition of upper semi-continuity reduces to the standard definition of continuity. A differential inclusion is an equation of the form $\frac{dx(t)}{dt} \in F(x(t))$, whose solutions are absolute continuous functions satisfying point-wise the inclusion. If F is upper semi-continuous, then solutions exist for any initial point. Hence, we can define the semi-flow of the differential inclusion, which is a set-valued map $\phi_T(x_0) = \{x(T) \mid x(0) = x_0,\ x(t) \text{ solution of } \frac{dx(t)}{dt} \in F(x(t))\}$. It turns out that, if F is upper semi-continuous, then so is ϕ_T, provided solutions are defined up to time T [3].

Given a PWS system, it is easy to convert it to a differential inclusion, along the lines of (2). For a more precise statement, see [3, 9]. Therefore, we can conclude that the flow of our PWS system is an upper semi-continuous function, hence a posteriori continuous, as H1 implies that ϕ_T is a point-value function. □

We now require an additional hypothesis, related to the behavior of the PWS at the discontinuity surfaces, which is required to apply the convergence theorem of [6].

H2: The trajectories $x(t)$ of the PWS $\frac{dx(t)}{dt} = F(x(t))$ are *regular*, i.e., they satisfy:

1. for each initial state $x_0 \in E$, the number of *discontinuous events*, i.e., changes of vector field like transversal crossing and points in which sliding motion starts or terminates, is bounded.
2. sliding motion happens only on single discontinuity surfaces $\mathcal{H}_i$, with both vector fields having a non-null normal component to $\mathcal{H}_i$. It never happens on the intersection of more than one discontinuity surface. It can end either when the normal component of one vector field becomes zero (first order exit conditions), or when trajectories intersect another discontinuity surface. In this case, we can have transversal crossing confined to discontinuity surfaces.

Hypothesis H2 is needed as it allows us to properly define a Filippov solution for the PWS. In fact, sliding motion happening on $k > 1$ surfaces cannot be defined by the Filippov approach, as there are 2^k coefficients needed to construct the sliding vector field, but only $k+1$ equations to constrain them. However, solutions of the PWS may still be defined in the context of differential inclusions (and convergence proved [14]), but they may be difficult to compute and not necessarily unique.

Given that the flow function $\phi_t(x)$ is well defined in each point x and continuous, hence a fortiori measurable, we can define a concept of invariant measure for $\phi_t(x)$ similarly to ODE flows: a probability measure μ on E is invariant for ϕ if and only if $\mu(A) = \mu(\phi_t^{-1}(A) \cap E)$ for each Borel measurable set $A \subseteq E$. The intersection with E is needed because flows pointing inwards E at its boundary will leave E if we reverse time. Notice that the flow of a PWS may not be time-reversible: if we invert time for stable sliding motion, we obtain an unstable sliding motion, for which trajectories are not uniquely defined.

We recall now some notions about sequences of measures that will be needed in the following. We refer the reader to [5] for any additional detail.

A sequence of probability measures $\mu^{(N)}$ on E converges weakly to a probability measure μ if and only if, for all bounded continuous functions $g : E \to \mathbb{R}$,

$$\int_E g(x)\mu^{(N)}(dx) \to \int_E g(x)\mu(dx).$$

The weak convergence provides the space of probability measures on E with a topology, called the weak topology.

A sequence of measures is *tight* if and only if, for each $\varepsilon > 0$ there exists a compact set K_ε such that, for each $N \geq 0$, $\mu_N(K_\varepsilon) > 1 - \varepsilon$. If $E \subseteq \mathbb{R}^n$ (so that it is a Polish space), then each sequence of measures on E is tight if and only if it is *relatively compact*, i.e., if and only if it has a subsequence converging to a probability measure μ. Notice that this is trivially the case whenever E is a bounded subset of $\mathbb{R}^n$.

We will now state the key lemma that provides convergence of invariant measures. It is essentially a straightforward adaption of Corollary 3.2 of [4]. Before that, we recall the following limit theorem:

THEOREM 4 (SEE [6, 14]). *Let $X^{(N)}(t)$ be the sequence of CTMCs and $\phi_t(x_0)$ be the trajectory of the PWS starting at x_0, and assume that $X^{(N)}(0)$ converges to x_0 in probability. If the PWS satisfies H0 to H2, then, for any $T > 0$, $\sup_{t \leq T} \|X^{(N)}(t) - \phi_t(x_0)\| \to 0$ in probability.*

As a corollary, it obviously holds that $\mathbb{P}\{\|X^{(N)}(T) - \phi_T(x_0)\| > \varepsilon\} \to 0$ for any fixed time T.

LEMMA 2. *Let $\mu^{(N)}$ be an invariant measure of $X^{(N)}(t)$, and assume E is bounded. Furthermore, assume that the flow $\phi_t(x)$ of the PWS defined by $X^{(N)}(t)$ satisfies H1 and H2. Then, any limit measure μ of the sequence $\mu^{(N)}$ is an invariant measure of $\phi_t(x)$.*

PROOF. The proof proceeds as in [4]. First, note that as E is bounded, the sequence of invariant measures $\mu^{(N)}$ is tight, hence relatively compact, so that the set of limits points of $\mu^{(N)}$ is not empty (that is, there exists a measure μ such that a subsequence of $\mu^{(N)}$ converges weakly to μ). Let μ be one such limit point. By possibly passing to a subsequence of $\mu^{(N)}$, we can assume that μ is the limit of $\mu^{(N)}$.

Let g be any bounded continuous function on E. As E is bounded, g is uniformly continuous on E. Now, due to the invariance of $\mu^{(N)}$, for each $T > 0$ we have:

$$\int_E \mathbb{E}_x[g(X^{(N)}(T))]\mu^{(N)}(dx) = \int_E g(x)\mu^{(N)}(dx). \quad (9)$$

Now, as g is uniformly continuous in E, for each $\delta > 0$ there is an $\eta > 0$ such that, if $\|u - v\| < \eta$ then $\|g(u) - g(v)\| < \delta$ for each $u, v \in E$. Recalling that $\phi_T(E) \subseteq E$, it holds that

$$\begin{aligned}
&\|\mathbb{E}_x[g(X^{(N)}(T)) - g(\phi_T(x))]\| = \\
&\quad \|\mathbb{E}_x[(g(X^{(N)}(T)) - g(\phi_T(x)))1_{\|X^{(N)}(T)-\phi_T(x)\|\leq\eta}] \\
&\quad \mathbb{P}\{\|X^{(N)}(T) - \phi_T(x)\| \leq \eta\} + \\
&\quad \mathbb{E}_x[(g(X^{(N)}(T)) - g(\phi_T(x)))1_{\|X^{(N)}(T)-\phi_T(x)\|>\eta}] \\
&\quad \mathbb{P}\{\|X^{(N)}(T) - \phi_T(x)\| > \eta\}\| \\
&\quad \leq \delta + 2\|g\|\mathbb{P}\{\|X^{(N)}(T) - \phi_T(x)\| > \eta\}.
\end{aligned}$$

Therefore,

$$\begin{aligned}
&\left\| \int_E \mathbb{E}_x[g(X^{(N)}(T))]\mu^{(N)}(dx) - \int_E g(\phi_T(x))\mu^{(N)}(dx) \right\| \\
&\quad \leq \int_E \left\| \mathbb{E}_x[g(X^{(N)}(T)) - g(\phi_T(x))] \right\| \mu^{(N)}(dx) \\
&\quad \leq \delta + 2\|g\| \int_E \mathbb{P}\{\|X^{(N)}(T) - \phi_T(x)\| > \eta\}\mu^{(N)}(dx).
\end{aligned}$$

Exploiting the fact that μ is the limit of $\mu^{(N)}$, and by Theorem 4 and (9), we have that

$$\left\| \int_E g(\phi_T(x))\mu(dx) - \int_E g(x)\mu(dx) \right\| \leq \delta,$$

which, by the arbitrariness of δ and g, proves the lemma. To see why this is the case, observe that if $I_A(x)$ is the indicator function of a (measurable) set $A \subseteq E$, then $I_A(G(x))$ is the indicator function of $G^{-1}(A)$. If we could use I_A in place of g in the previous inequality, we would have concluded. To show this, fix an open set A and approximate I_A by the sequence of continuous functions $g_\varepsilon = \min\{1, d(x, A^c)/\varepsilon\}$. As g_ε converges monotonically to I_A, by the monotone convergence theorem [5] $\int_E g_\varepsilon(x) \to \int_E I_A(x)$, hence invariance holds for open sets. Furthermore, it can then be extended to all measurable sets by a straightforward application of the π-λ theorem [5]. □

Notice that in the previous proof, we used continuity of ϕ only implicitly, to ensure that $g \circ \phi_T$ is integrable. However, the previous proof can be easily extended to unbounded domains E, just requiring tightness of the sequence of measures $\mu^{(N)}$. This allows to restrict the integral on a compact set K, introducing only a small error. In this case, however, continuity of ϕ_T has a crucial role, to ensure that the image of any compact set is compact, so that the uniform continuity argument can be applied on compact neighbors of $\phi_T(K)$.

Now we are almost ready to state the limit theorem about steady states. We just need an additional hypothesis on the PWS flow:

H3: The PWS system has a unique globally attracting fixed point, hence for all $x \in E$, $\lim_{t\to\infty} \phi_t(x) = x^*$.

Hypothesis H3 immediately implies the following

PROPOSITION 1. *A PWS satisfying H0 to H3 has a unique invariant measure $\mu = \delta_{x^*}$, equal to the Dirac delta measure on the global equilibrium x^*.*

PROOF. Due to *H3*, for any ball $B_\varepsilon(x^*)$ of radius ε centered in x^*, there is a $t > 0$ such that $\phi_t(E) \subseteq B_\varepsilon(x^*)$, hence $\phi_t^{-1}(B_\varepsilon(x^*)) \cap E = E$. If μ is an invariant measure, it therefore satisfies $\mu(B_\varepsilon(x^*)) = 1$ for any $\varepsilon > 0$. But the only measure with this property is δ_{x^*}. □

We can now state the following result, which is a generalization of Theorem 2:

THEOREM 5. *Let $X^{(N)}(t)$ be a sequence of irreducible CTMCs satisfying hypothesis H0, and let $\mu^{(N)}$ be their unique invariant measure. Let F be the drift of the sequence, defining a PWS on E with flow $\phi_t(x)$ satisfying H1 to H3, and let x^* be its globally attracting fixed point. Let $X^{(N)}(0) \to x_0 \in E$ in probability, then*

$$\lim_{N\to\infty} \lim_{t\to\infty} \|X^{(N)}(t) - x^*\| = 0 \quad \textit{in probability.}$$

PROOF. Consider the sequence of CTMC invariant measures $\mu^{(N)}$ and let μ be a limit point. By Lemma 2 and Proposition 1, $\mu = \delta_{x^*}$. Therefore, the set of limit points of $\mu^{(N)}$ contains a single point, hence the whole sequence $\mu^{(N)}$ converges weakly to δ_{x^*}. Therefore, $\lim_{t\to\infty} X^{(N)}(t)$ converges in distribution, for N going to infinity, to x^*. But as x^* is deterministic, it converges also in probability [5]. □

Acknowledgements

Luca Bortolussi has done part of this work while visiting on sabbatical the Laboratory for Foundations of Computer Science at the University of Edinburgh.

6. REFERENCES

[1] N. Akar, E. Karasan, and K. Dogan. Wavelength converter sharing in asynchronous optical packet/burst switching: an exact blocking analysis for markovian arrivals. *IEEE Journal on Selected Areas in Communications*, 24:69–80, 2006.

[2] N. Akar, Ezhan Karasan, and Carla Raffaelli. Fixed point analysis of limited range share per node wavelength conversion in asynchronous optical packet switching systems. *Photon. Netw. Commun.*, 18(2):255–263, 2009.

[3] J. Aubin and A. Cellina. *Differential Inclusions.* Springer-Verlag, 1984.

[4] M. Benaïm. Recursive algorithms, urn processes and chaining number of chain recurrent sets. *Ergodic Theory and Dynamical Systems*, 18:53–87, 1998.

[5] P. Billingsley. *Probability and Measure.* John Wiley and Sons, 1979.

[6] L. Bortolussi. Hybrid limits of continuous time Markov chains. In *Proc. of QEST 2011*, pages 3–12, Aachen, Germany, 2011.

[7] J. Le Boudec, D. McDonald, and J. Mundinger. A generic mean field convergence result for systems of interacting objects. In *Proc. of QEST 2007*, pages 3–15, Edinburgh, UK, 2007.

[8] F. Callegati. Optical buffers for variable length packet switching. *IEEE Communications Letters*, 4:292–294, 2002.

[9] J. Cortes. Discontinuous dynamical systems: A tutorial on solutions, nonsmooth analysis, and stability. *IEEE Control Systems Magazine*, pages 36–73, 2008.

[10] M. di Bernardo, C.J. Budd, A.R. Champneys, and P. Kowalczyk. *Piecewise-smooth dynamical systems: Theory and Applications.* Springer, 2007.

[11] S. N. Ethier and T. C. Kurtz. *Markov processes: characterization and convergence.* Wiley, 1986.

[12] A. Filippov. *Differential equations with discontinuous right-hand sides.* Mathematics and its Applications. Kluwer Academic, 1988.

[13] W. Fischer and K. Meier-Hellstern. The Markov-modulated poisson process (MMPP) cookbook. *Performance Evaluation*, 18(2):149 – 171, 1993.

[14] N. Gast and B. Gaujal. Mean field limit of non-smooth systems and differential inclusions. *SIGMETRICS Perform. Eval. Rev.*, 38:30–32, October 2010.

[15] D.P. Gaver, P.A. Jacobs, and G. Latouche. Finite Birth-and-Death models in randomly changing environments. *Adv. in Appl. Probab.*, 16:715–731, 1984.

[16] T. Kurtz. *Approximation of population processes.* Society for Industrial and Applied Mathematics, 1981.

[17] G. Latouche and V. Ramaswami. *Introduction to Matrix Analytic Methods and stochastic modeling.* SIAM, Philadelphia, 1999.

[18] D.M. Lucantoni. New results on the single server queue with a batch Markovian arrival process. *Stochastic Models*, 7(1):1–46, 1991.

[19] J. F. Pérez and B. Van Houdt. A mean field model for an optical switch with a large number of wavelengths

and centralized partial conversion. *Performance Evaluation*, 67:1044–1058, Nov 2010.

[20] W. Rogiest, J. Lambert, D. Fiems, B. Van Houdt, H. Bruneel, and C. Blondia. A unified model for synchronous and asynchronous FDL buffers allowing closed-form solution. *Performance Evaluation*, 66:343–355, 2009.

[21] W. Rudin. *Principles of Mathematical Analysis*. McGraw-Hill, 1976.

[22] L. Xu, H. Perros, and G. N. Rouskas. A queueing network model of an edge optical burst switching node. In *Proceedings of the IEEE Infocom 2003*, 2003.

[23] L. Xu, H. Perros, and G. N. Rouskas. Performance analysis of an edge optical burst switching node with a large number of wavelengths. *Performance Evaluation*, 64:315–346, 2007.

[24] S. Yao, B. Mukherjee, S. J. B. Yoo, and S. Dixit. All-optical packet-switched networks: a study of contention-resolution schemes in an irregular mesh network with variable-sized packets. In *Proc. of OPTICOMM 2000*, 2000.

APPENDIX

A. PHASE-TYPE PACKET LENGTHS AND GLOBAL ATTRACTION

In this Appendix we prove that the unique fixed point π introduced in Theorem 3 is a global attractor for certain subclasses of the set of phase-type distributions and certain ranges of σ. We consider two cases: π lies in the interior of S, that is, $\sigma > \lambda^2$, and π is part of the boundary $\{(w,c)|ce = \sigma\}$, i.e., $\sigma \leq \lambda^2$. For the phase-type distribution (α, T), recall that we assumed that $T^* > 0$. Further, $\min_i T_i^* \leq 1 \leq \max_i T_i^*$ with equalities only for representations of the exponential distribution (because the mean packet length is defined as one).

A.1 Case 1: $\sigma > \lambda^2$

In this section we establish three results: one for general phase-type distributions, one for hyperexponential (HE) distributions and finally one for order-2 HE distributions. Note, the first result is trivial if $\lambda \geq \min_i T_i^*$.

THEOREM 6. *For $\sigma > \lambda/\min_i T_i^*$, the fixed point $\pi = (\lambda(1-\lambda)\theta, \lambda^2\theta)$ is a global attractor of the set of ODEs given by (5) for any phase-type distribution with $T^* > 0$.*

PROOF. From Section 4.1, we know that the sliding motion on the surface $\{(w,c)|we + ce = 1\}$ only occurs on the region that bounds S if one of the entries of T^* is less than λ. Thus, the motion on the part of $\{(w,c)|we + ce = 1\}$ that bounds S is transversal. Further, a sliding motion on the surface of $\{(w,c)|ce = \sigma\}$ only occurs if $cT^* \leq \lambda(we + \sigma) \leq \lambda$. As $ce = \sigma$, $cT^* \geq \sigma(\min_i T_i^*)$ which implies that a sliding motion cannot occur if $\sigma > \lambda/\min_i T_i^*$. In other words, the boundary of S cannot be reached from the interior and if we start on the boundary we immediately move into the interior of S. Therefore, all trajectories starting in S will converge to $((1-\lambda)\lambda\theta, \lambda^2\theta)$. $\square$

For a HE distribution T is diagonal and $\alpha > 0$. Further, let $\mu_i = -T_{ii}$ and assume without loss of generality that $\mu_1 < \mu_2 < \ldots < \mu_m$.

Define the function $V(w,c)$ from $\mathbb{R}^{2m}$ to $\mathbb{R}$ such that

$$V(w(t), c(t)) = (w(t) + c(t))v,$$

where v is a right-eigenvector of T such that $\alpha v > 0$, $Tv = \tau v$ with $\tau < 0$ a real eigenvalue of T. Notice, as T is a sub-generator, such an eigenvalue always exists (e.g., τ_1).

LEMMA 3. *For any phase-type distribution with $T^* > 0$ and any $\epsilon > 0$, there exists a $t_0 > 0$ such that*

$$V(w(t), c(t)) < \lambda\theta v,$$

for all $t > t_0$.

PROOF. In the interior of S, we find that

$$\frac{d}{dt}V(w(t), c(t)) = (w(t)+c(t))Tv+\lambda\alpha v = \tau(w(t)+c(t))v+\lambda\alpha v.$$

Thus, if $(w(t) + c(t))v > \lambda\theta v = -\lambda\alpha v/\tau$, we see that

$$\frac{d}{dt}V(w(t), c(t)) < -\lambda\alpha v + \lambda\alpha v = 0.$$

Similarly, $(w(t)+c(t))v < \lambda\theta v$ implies that $\frac{d}{dt}V(w(t), c(t)) > 0$. Hence, $(w(t)+c(t))v$ converges towards $\lambda\theta v$ in the interior of S. During the sliding motion on $\{(w,c)|we + ce = 1\}$ we find that

$$\frac{d}{dt}V(w(t), c(t)) = \tau(w(t) + c(t))v + (w(t) + c(t))T^*\alpha v.$$

Thus, if $(w(t) + c(t))v > \lambda\theta v = -\lambda\alpha v/\tau$ we have

$$\frac{d}{dt}V(w(t), c(t)) < ((w(t) + c(t))T^* - \lambda)\alpha v.$$

As $(w(t) + c(t))T^* - \lambda < 0$ is required during the sliding motion, we find that $(w(t) + c(t))v$ decreases towards $\lambda\theta v$ during the sliding motion. Note, when $(w(t)+c(t))v < \lambda\theta v$, the above equation only indicates that $\frac{d}{dt}V(w(t), c(t)) > ((w(t) + c(t))T^* - \lambda)\alpha v$, which is a negative number, so $(w(t) + c(t))v$ can also decrease. Finally, for the sliding motion on $\{(w,c)|ce = \sigma\}$, one readily checks that

$$\frac{d}{dt}V(w(t), c(t)) = \tau(w(t) + c(t))v + (c(t)T^* - \lambda(w(t)e + \sigma))\alpha v + \lambda\alpha v,$$

which yields

$$\frac{d}{dt}V(w(t), c(t)) < (c(t)T^* - \lambda(w(t)e + \sigma))\alpha v < 0,$$

during the sliding motion provided that $(w(t)+c(t))v > \lambda\theta v$. In conclusion, when $V(w(t), c(t)) - \lambda\theta v > 0$, for $(w(t), c(t)) \in S$, it will decrease towards zero. $\square$

In case of HE distributions we can set $v = e_i$ (a vector of zeros with a one in position i) and $\tau = T_{ii}$, for any $i = 1, \ldots, m$.

COROLLARY 3. *For any hyperexponential distribution and any $\epsilon > 0$, there exists a $t_0 > 0$ such that*

$$w_i(t) + c_i(t) < \lambda\theta_i + \epsilon/m,$$

for all $t > t_0$ and $i \in \{1, \ldots, m\}$. Hence, $w(t)e + c(t)e < \lambda + \epsilon$ for $t > t_0$.

THEOREM 7. *For $\sigma > \lambda^2/\min_i T_i^*$, the fixed point $\pi = (\lambda(1-\lambda)\theta, \lambda^2\theta)$ is a global attractor of the set of ODEs given by (5) for any hyperexponential distribution.*

PROOF. If we set $\epsilon < 1 - \lambda$ in Corollary 3, we find that $w(t)e + c(t)e < 1$ after time t_0, meaning we cannot hit the surface $\{(w, c)|we + ce = 1\}$ after time t_0. On the surface $\{(w, c)|ce = \sigma\}$ the value of $c(t)T^*$ is still lower bounded by $\sigma(\min_i T_i^*) = \sigma\mu_1$, but now for $t > t_0$, $\lambda(w(t)e + \sigma)$ can upper bounded by $\lambda(\lambda + \epsilon)$. Thus, for any $\sigma > \lambda^2/\mu_1$, we can set $\epsilon < \sigma\mu_1/\lambda - \lambda$ to guarantee that no sliding motion on $\{(w, c)|ce = \sigma\}$ can occur after time t_0. □

THEOREM 8. *For $\sigma > \lambda^2$, the fixed point $\pi = (\lambda(1 - \lambda)\theta, \lambda^2\theta)$ is a global attractor of the set of ODEs given by (5) for any order-2 hyperexponential distribution.*

PROOF. The drift of $c_i(t)$ in the interior of S can be written as

$$\frac{d}{dt}c_i(t) = -\mu_i c_i(t) + \lambda(w(t) + c(t))e\alpha_i.$$

If $c_i(t) = \lambda^2\theta_i + \delta = \lambda^2\alpha_i/\mu_i + \delta$, for $\delta > 0$, then Corollary 3 implies

$$\frac{d}{dt}c_i(t) < -\delta + \lambda\epsilon\alpha_i,$$

after time t_0. Hence, for $c_i(t) > \lambda^2\theta_i$, $c_i(t)$ decreases after time t_0 (in the interior of S).

Further, during the slide on $\{(w, c)|ce = \sigma\}$, the drift

$$\frac{d}{dt}c_i(t) = -\mu_i c_i(t) + \left(\sum_{i=1}^{m} c_i(t)\mu_i\right)\alpha_i.$$

For HE distributions of order 2 (with $\mu_1 < \mu_2$), we have $\alpha_2 = 1 - \alpha_1$ and $c_2(t) = \sigma - c_1(t)$ during the slide, which implies

$$\begin{aligned}
\frac{d}{dt}c_1(t) &= \sigma\mu_2\alpha_1 - c_1(t)(\alpha_2\mu_1 + \alpha_1\mu_2),\\
\frac{d}{dt}c_2(t) &= \sigma\mu_1\alpha_2 - c_2(t)(\alpha_1\mu_2 + \alpha_2\mu_1).
\end{aligned}$$

As $\alpha_1/\mu_1 + \alpha_2/\mu_2 = 1$ and $\theta_1 = \alpha_1/\mu_1$, we find that if $c_i(t)$ differs from $\sigma\theta_i$, $c_i(t)$ approaches $\sigma\theta_i$ during the slide on $\{(w, c)|ce = \sigma\}$ (for any t).

Hence, for $\sigma > \lambda^2$ and any $\epsilon_2 > 0$, there exists a $t_1 > t_0$ such that $c_1(t)$ is upper bounded by $\sigma\theta_1 + \epsilon_2$ for $t > t_1$. This indicates that $c(t)T^*$ can be lower bounded by $\sigma + \delta$ for any $\delta > 0$ after time t_1. Repeating the arguments in Theorem 7 with this improved lower bound on $c(t)T^*$ for order-2 HE distributions, suffices to complete the proof. □

A.2 Case 2: $\sigma \le \lambda^2$

In this section we establish a result for any phase-type distribution as well as one for the class of HE distributions.

THEOREM 9. *For $\sigma < \lambda^2/(\max_i T_i^*)^2$, the fixed point $\pi = (\lambda(1-\sigma)\theta/(1+\lambda), \sigma\theta)$ is a global attractor of the set of ODEs given by (5) for any phase-type distribution with $T^* > 0$.*

PROOF. During the slide on $\{(w, c)|ce = \sigma\}$, we observe that

$$\frac{d}{dt}w(t)e = -w(t)T^* - \lambda w(t)e + \lambda(1 - \sigma).$$

As $w(t)T^* \le w(t)e(\max_i T_i^*)$,

$$\frac{d}{dt}w(t)e \ge -w(t)e(\lambda + \max_i T_i^*) + \lambda(1 - \sigma).$$

The derivative of $w(t)e$ is therefore positive if $w(t)e < \lambda(1 - \sigma)/(\lambda + \max_i T_i^*)$. For the motion in the interior of S, we see that

$$\frac{d}{dt}w(t)e = -w(t)T^* - \lambda w(t)e + \lambda(1 - c(t)e),$$

where $c(t)e < \sigma$. Hence, by the same argument the derivative of $w(t)e$ is also positive in the interior of S if $w(t)e < \lambda(1-\sigma)/(\lambda+\max_i T_i^*)$. On the surface $\{(w, c)|we+ce = 1\}$, we have $w(t)e \ge (1 - \sigma) > \lambda(1 - \sigma)/(\lambda + \max_i T_i^*)$. This allows us to conclude that for any $\epsilon > 0$, there exists a $\bar{t}$ such that for all $t > \bar{t}$

$$w(t)e > \frac{\lambda(1 - \sigma)}{\lambda + \max_i T_i^*} - \epsilon.$$

When combined with the inequality $c(t)T^* \le \sigma \max_i T_i^*$, this indicates that $c(t)T^* \ge \lambda(w(t)e + \sigma)$ cannot hold after time $\bar{t}$ if

$$\begin{aligned}
\sigma(\max_i T_i^*) &< \lambda(\frac{\lambda(1 - \sigma)}{\lambda + \max_i T_i^*} - \epsilon + \sigma)\\
\Leftrightarrow \quad \sigma &< \left(\frac{\lambda}{\max_i T_i^*}\right)^2 (1 - \epsilon(\lambda + \max_i T_i^*)/\lambda).
\end{aligned}$$

Thus, with a properly chosen ϵ, we may conclude that any sliding motion on the surface $\{(w, c)|ce = \sigma\}$ that starts after time $\bar{t}$ will last indefinitely for $\sigma < (\lambda/\max_i T_i^*)^2$. □

THEOREM 10. *For $\sigma < \lambda^2(1-\lambda)/(\max_i T_i^* - \lambda)$, the fixed point $\pi = (\lambda(1 - \sigma)\theta/(1 + \lambda), \sigma\theta)$ is a global attractor of the set of ODEs given by (5) for any hyperexponential distribution.*

PROOF. The drift of $w_i(t)$ in the interior of S can be written as

$$\frac{d}{dt}w_i(t) = -\mu_i w_i(t) - \lambda(w(t) + c(t))e\alpha_i + \lambda\alpha_i.$$

Hence, if $w_i(t) = \lambda(1 - \lambda)\theta_i - \delta$, for some $\delta > 0$, then

$$\frac{d}{dt}w_i(t) > \delta - \lambda\epsilon\alpha_i,$$

after time t_0, due to Corollary 3. Meaning, if $w_i(t) < \lambda(1 - \lambda)\theta_i$, then $w_i(t)$ increases after time t_0 (in the interior of S). For the drift of $w_i(t)$ during the slide on $\{(w, c)|ce = \sigma\}$, we observe that

$$\frac{d}{dt}w_i(t) = -\mu_i w_i(t) - \lambda w(t)e\alpha_i + \lambda(1 - \sigma)\alpha_i.$$

Hence, after time t_0 we get

$$\frac{d}{dt}w_i(t) > -\mu_i w_i(t) + \lambda(1 - \lambda)\alpha_i - \lambda\epsilon\alpha_i,$$

by noting that $w(t)e < \lambda - \sigma + \epsilon$. Thus, if $w_i(t) < \lambda(1-\lambda)\theta_i$, $w_i(t)$ will increase after time t_0. This allow us to conclude that for any $\epsilon_2 > 0$ there exists a $t_2 > t_0$, such that $w(t)e$ is lower bounded by $\lambda(1-\lambda)-\epsilon_2$. The expression $\lambda(w(t)e+\sigma)$ is therefore lower bounded by $\lambda^2(1 - \lambda) + \lambda\sigma - \lambda\epsilon_2$. As $c(t)T^*$ is upper bounded by $\sigma \max_i T_i^*$, we find that the unique fixed point is a global attractor for any HE distribution with $\sigma < \lambda^2(1 - \lambda)/(\max_i T_i^* - \lambda)$. □

Towards Optimal Error-Estimating Codes through the Lens of Fisher Information Analysis

Nan Hua
School of Computer Science
Georgia Institute of Technology
nanhua@cc.gatech.edu

Ashwin Lall
Department of Math and Computer Science
Denison University
lalla@denison.edu

Baochun Li
Department of Electrical and Computer Engineering
University of Toronto
bli@eecg.toronto.edu

Jun (Jim) Xu
School of Computer Science
Georgia Institute of Technology
jx@cc.gatech.edu

ABSTRACT

Error estimating coding (EEC) has recently been established as an important tool to estimate bit error rates in the transmission of packets over wireless links, with a number of potential applications in wireless networks. In this paper, we present an in-depth study of error estimating codes through the lens of Fisher information analysis and find that the original EEC estimator fails to exploit the information contained in its code to the fullest extent. Motivated by this discovery, we design a new estimator for the original EEC algorithm, which significantly improves the estimation accuracy, and is empirically very close to the Cramer-Rao bound. Following this path, we generalize the EEC algorithm to a new *family* of algorithms called gEEC (generalized EEC). These algorithms can be tuned to hold 25-35% more information with the same overhead, and hence deliver even better estimation accuracy—close to optimal, as evidenced by the Cramer-Rao bound. Our theoretical analysis and assertions are supported by extensive experimental evaluation.

Categories and Subject Descriptors

E.4 [**Coding and Information Theory**]: Error control codes; C.2.1 [**Computer-Communication Networks**]: Network Architecture and Design - Wireless communication

General Terms

Algorithms, Theory

Keywords

Error Estimating Coding, Fisher Information

1. INTRODUCTION

Estimating the bit error rate (BER) in packets transmitted over wireless networks has been established as an important research problem in the seminal work of Chen *et al.* [3]. It was shown in [3] that, if the BER in packets can be accurately estimated, important operations in wireless networks such as packet re-scheduling, routing, and carrier selection can all be performed with greater efficiency. A simple and elegant technique, called error estimating codes (EEC), was hence proposed in [3] to estimate this BER. The basic idea of EEC is to have the transmitter send a small error estimating codeword along with each packet that will allow the number of bits in the packet flipped during the (wireless) transmission (i.e., the BER) to be inferred at the receiver. Using an EEC of $O(\log n)$ bits for a packet n bits long, their technique guarantees that the estimated BER falls within $1 \pm \epsilon$ of the actual BER with probability at least $1 - \delta$, where ϵ and δ are tunable parameters that can be made arbitrarily small at the cost of increased constant factor in $O(\log n)$, the coding overhead.

A natural question to ask is whether EEC achieves the best tradeoff between space ($O(\log n)$) and estimation accuracy ((ϵ, δ) guarantee) in solving the BER estimation problem. Our earlier work [6] has answered this question definitively. In [6], we prove that at least $\Omega(\log n)$ bits are needed to achieve an (ϵ, δ)-approximation and EEC is therefore asymptotically optimal. However, we also show that EEC has not achieved the optimal tradeoff down to the constant factor, by proposing a different coding algorithm, called the *Enhanced Tug-of-War* (EToW) sketch, that can achieve the same (ϵ, δ)-approximation with a code size 60% smaller than that used by EEC.

In this work, we follow up with a deeper and more important question of why EEC has not achieved the desired optimal space-accuracy tradeoff. Is it because its encoding algorithm has not packed as much information into the codewords as possible (i.e., inefficient encoding), or because its decoding algorithm has not made full use of information packed into these codewords (i.e., inefficient decoding), or both? This question is important because EEC is simpler and "cleaner" (to be explained shortly) than EToW, and if we can somehow bring its efficiency to be on par with or exceed that of EToW, it will likely be the preferred solution to the BER estimation problem. In an effort to thoroughly answer this question in this work, we have made the following two major contributions.

First, we demonstrate that EEC decoding is inefficient by deriving the amount of Fisher information contained in EEC codewords and showing that the variance of the estimator used in EEC encoding is much larger than the corresponding Cramer-Rao bound. We then propose a new estimator that achieves a significantly higher estimation accuracy and is provably near-optimal by almost matching the Cramer-Rao bound. Our experiments show that this new estimator allows us to reduce the coding overhead by as much as two to three times while achieving the same BER estimation accuracy. More importantly, EEC with this new estimator performs almost as well as EToW, with the same coding overhead. Another salient property of this new estimator is that its variance can be approximated by a closed-form formula, making it much easier to parameterize the EEC algorithm (i.e., to "tune") for optimal estimation accuracies (i.e., minimum variance) under various bit error models.

Second, we proceed to investigate whether there are inefficiencies with the encoding part of EEC. This question is, however, much harder to answer definitively because existing lower-bound techniques, rooted in the theory of communication complexity [7], only allow us to establish asymptotic space lower bounds such as the aforementioned $\Omega(\log n)$ bound. We try instead to compare the encoding efficiency, i.e., the amount of Fisher information per code bit, of EEC with that of EToW. It turns out that we got more than what we had bargained for. In an effort to derive the Fisher information formula of EToW, we have discovered that EEC and EToW can be viewed as different instances of a unified coding framework that we call generalized EEC (gEEC). In other words, gEEC can be parameterized into both EEC and EToW, and EEC can be viewed as a "degenerate" case of gEEC.

This generalization makes it easier for us to analyze and improve the designs of both EEC and EToW for two reasons. First, we need only design a single optimal decoder (i.e., estimator) for gEEC, which applies to both EEC and EToW, instead of one for each. This decoder is a Maximum Likelihood Estimator (MLE) with the Jeffreys prior, which in the case of EEC is the aforementioned estimator, and in the case of EToW performs better than a different estimator we developed for EToW in [6]. Second, the Fisher information formula derived for gEEC, which is in a closed form of matrix computations, applies to both EEC and EToW. However, we still derive the Fisher information formula of EEC separately in Section 3 because the derivations in this degenerate case are much simpler than those of gEEC, resulting in a closed-form formula (as the matrices degenerate into 1×1 scalars), and shed some insight on the roles that key parameters play in the formula that can get obscured in the general case. Through this unified framework of gEEC, we found that some parameterization of gEEC (similar to EToW, but not needing the extra error detection bits) can contain around 25% more information than the pure EEC scheme. This information gain cannot be fully decoded through EToW's decoder, but is achievable by gEEC's decoder.

The remainder of this paper is organized as follows. In Section 2 we discuss the related work most pertinent to this paper. In Section 3 we provide the Fisher information analysis of the original EEC algorithm. In Section 4, we propose the generalized EEC scheme and provide the corresponding analysis and estimator design. We evaluate the performance numerically as well as experimentally in Section 5. We give our conclusions in Section 6.

2. BACKGROUND AND RELATED WORK

In this section, we introduce some background on Fisher information and the Cramer-Rao bound, and briefly survey their applications in network measurement studies. We also briefly describe two prior approaches (EEC and EToW) for solving the BER estimation problem.

2.1 Fisher Information and Cramer-Rao Bound

In information theory and mathematical statistics, Fisher information quantifies the amount of information an observable parameterized random variable $X(\theta)$ carries about its unknown parameter θ. (Our description closely follows [4]; please consult it for more background on this topic.) In our context, the error estimating codewords and sketches correspond to random variable $X(\theta)$ and θ corresponds to the BER we would like to estimate in a received packet. The probability function of $X(\theta)$ takes the form $f(x;\theta)$. When θ is viewed as a constant and x as a variable, $f(x;\theta)$ is the probability density (or mass) of the random variable X conditional on the value of θ; When θ is viewed as a variable and x as a constant on the other hand, $f(x;\theta)$ is the likelihood function of θ, that is, the likelihood of the parameter taking value θ when the observed value of X is x. Fisher information of $X(\theta)$, which is a function of θ, is defined as

$$\mathbf{J}(\theta) \triangleq \mathbf{E}_\theta\left[\frac{\partial}{\partial\theta}\log f(X;\theta))\right]^2. \quad (1)$$

Fisher information $\mathbf{J}(\theta)$ is an important quantity because it determines the minimum variance achievable by any unbiased estimator of θ given an observation of $X(\theta)$, through the Cramer-Rao lower bound (CRLB):

$$\mathbf{MSE}[\hat{\theta}] = \mathbf{Var}[\hat{\theta}] \geq \frac{1}{\mathbf{J}(\theta)}. \quad (2)$$

If a biased estimator of θ with bias $b(\theta)$ is used instead, we have a slightly different inequality:

$$\mathbf{MSE}[\hat{\theta}] \geq \frac{(1+b'(\theta))^2}{\mathbf{J}(\theta)} + b(\theta)^2. \quad (3)$$

While it is possible for a biased estimator to "beat" the Cramer-Rao bound for unbiased estimators (Formula (2)) when θ takes certain values (over which $b'(\theta)$ takes negative values), that biased estimator is not a clear winner since bias comes at a cost and may not be desirable to many applications.

In the context of this work, where the goal is to measure the "scale" of the bit error rate θ, the statistics of the relative error $\frac{\hat{\theta}-\theta}{\theta}$ and the log-difference $\log\hat{\theta} - \log\theta$ are more important. In particular, we prefer to use the statistics of the log-difference rather than the relative ratio to evaluate the performance of an estimator, since it assigns higher penalty to large deviations, making the comparison fairer for this application setting. For example, suppose the real value of θ is 0.1, and three large-deviation estimates are 0.05, 0.19 and 0.01, then the penalty for the last one will be much larger if measured by $\log\hat{\theta}$'s statistics. However, when measured by the relative error, the penalties of the latter two are the same and just around twice of the first.

The C-R bound for both $\frac{\hat{\theta}-\theta}{\theta}$ and $\log\hat{\theta} - \log\theta$ can be derived from (2) and the results are as follows:

$$\mathbf{Var}\left[\frac{\hat{\theta}-\theta}{\theta}\right] = \mathbf{Var}\left[\frac{\hat{\theta}}{\theta}\right] \geq \frac{1}{\theta^2 J(\theta)}. \quad (4)$$

$$\mathbf{Var}\left[\log\hat{\theta} - \log\theta\right] = \mathbf{Var}\left[\log\hat{\theta}\right] \geq \frac{1}{\theta^2 J(\theta)}. \quad (5)$$

Interestingly, they are bounded by the same value, $\theta^2 J(\theta)$. The second inequality (5) is derived by a transformation from (2). In other words, $\theta^2 J(\theta)$ is the Fisher information of $\log \theta$. We will use $\theta^2 J(\theta)$ frequently throughout the paper since it will directly determine the bound of the relative error/log difference.[1]

The maximum likelihood estimator (MLE) of θ, defined as $\hat{\theta}_{MLE} \triangleq \arg\max_\theta\{f(x;\theta)\}$, is known to be asymptotically normal (denoted as $N(*,*)$) under certain regularity conditions [8] and has the following distribution:

$$\hat{\theta}_{MLE} \sim N\left(\theta, \frac{1}{tJ(\theta)}\right), \tag{6}$$

where t here denotes the number of repeated independent experiments and $J(\theta)$ denotes the Fisher information contributed from each experiment. Hence the Cramer-Rao lower bound is (asymptotically) reached by the MLE.

Fisher information and Cramer-Rao bound analysis has been used in a few previous works on network measurement in the literature. It has been used by Ribeiro *et al.* [9] to derive the minimum number of samples needed for accurately estimating flow size distributions from outputs of a packet sampling process (e.g., sampled Cisco NetFlow). They also proposed an unbiased MLE estimator for this estimation problem that empirically matches the Cramer-Rao bound. This work was followed up in [10] by Tune *et al.* who demonstrated through Fisher information analysis that samples collected by flow sampling, which is much more expensive computationally, are more information-rich, in terms of Fisher information per bit, than packet sampling. They then proposed a new hybrid sampling technique called *dual sampling* that combines the advantages of both flow and packet sampling. Fisher information analysis is also used in recent work [11] to compare the information-richness of the samples collected by a few packet sampling and sketching techniques for the purpose of estimating flow size distributions.

2.2 Error Estimating Codes (EEC)

In EEC [3], the codeword for a packet consists of a set of $m = ab$ parity bits $z_1, z_2, ..., z_m$. They form a groups of size b each, $\{z_1, z_2, ..., z_b\}$, $\{z_{b+1}, z_{b+2}, ..., z_{2b}\}$, ..., $\{z_{(a-1)b+1}, z_{(a-1)b+2}, ..., z_{ab}\}$. Each parity bit z_i that belongs to group j (i.e., $(j-1)*b+1 \leq i \leq jb$) is calculated as the XOR of a set of $l_i = 2^j - 1$ bits uniformly (pseudo-)randomly sampled *with replacement* from the packet (viewed as a bit array). For example, in [3], a typical configuration of EEC scheme uses 9 groups (i.e., $a = 9$) of 32 parity bits (i.e., $b = 32$) each. In the following, we refer to each such group as a *level* to be consistent with the terms used in [3]. The codeword thus computed will be sent along with the packet to the receiver. Note the encoding scheme of EEC has some flavor of Low Density Parity Check (LDPC) codes although its parity check matrix is not strictly sparse as some of the rows can have as many as 2^a (including the parity check bit itself) ones in it, and in LDPC, no bit will be sampled more than once, which may happen in EEC due to its sampling with replacement nature.

Upon the receipt of a packet and its codeword (possibly with one or more bits flipped during transmission), the receiver will multiply them (viewed as a vector) by the same parity check matrix[2] and infer the BER from the outcome of this multiplication, which is often referred to as a *syndrome vector* in coding theory literature. From the syndrome vector, the inference algorithm (i.e., the decoder) used in [3] first decides on the group (i.e., level) of parity check bits that are expected to provide the best estimation accuracy. Then BER will be estimated *only* from the corresponding syndrome bits within that group. Such a commonsensical decoding procedure is however not optimal because other layers (groups) of parity bits, especially the neighboring layers, can provide much additional information to BER estimation, but are ignored by the decoder used in [3], as we will show shortly.

2.3 Enhanced Tug-of-war (EToW)

The Tug-of-war sketch (ToW) [1] is a sketch data structure (it can be viewed as an exotic type of error-correction code) originally proposed for estimating the L_2 norm of a single data stream. ToW can be extended for solving the problem of estimating BER, which is *almost* the same as that of measuring the Hamming distance and equivalently the L_2 norm between two binary vectors. A codeword in ToW, also referred to as a *sketch*, consists of a set of sub-sketches. In the context of this problem, in which all data items are binary, the value of each ToW sub-sketch is set to the number of 1's minus the number of 0's in the binary vector that results from XOR-ing the packet $\vec{b}$, viewed as a binary vector, bitwise with a pseudorandomly[3] generated binary vector. This bitwise exclusive-OR operation is mathematically equivalent to a projection of the vector $\vec{b}$ over a random direction (vector) $\vec{s}$, i.e. the inner product of $\vec{b}$ and $\vec{s}$. When comparing the Hamming distance between two binary data vector $\vec{b}$ and $\vec{b'}$, we can use the difference between their random projections $X = \vec{b}\cdot\vec{s} - \vec{b'}\cdot\vec{s}$ to estimate the norm of $\vec{b} - \vec{b'}$. Notice that the sketch (random projections) is much smaller in size ($O(log(n))$) than the length of original data vector (n) and hence is a succinct coding of data.

In the Enhanced ToW (EToW) scheme proposed in [6], this sketch is sent along with the packet to the receiver. Upon the receipt of the packet, which may have one or more bits flipped during transmission, the receiver will compute a new sketch from the packet received by projecting it over the same set of random directions (vectors). Then a decoder extended from the inference algorithm used in [1] will examine the differences between the sketch computed by the sender (and sent along with the packet) and the new sketch computed from the received packet, to arrive at a BER estimate.

The Enhanced ToW proposed in [6] extended ToW to make it appropriate and more space-efficient for BER estimation in the follow three ways. **First**, each sub-sketch in the original ToW scheme is encoded as a $\log_2(n)$-bit integer, where n is the maximum packet size in bits, so that no "overflow" can happen. However, since this difference (between the number of 1's and the number of 0's) is statistically much smaller than the maximum value n and in fact has mean 0, it makes sense to use "just enough" bits instead of $\log_2(n)$ to encode it. After all, these sub-sketches (differences) need to be sent along with the packet over wireless networks (the target network applications of error estimating codes) and in wireless communications, every bit counts! Therefore, in EToW, "barely enough" bits are allocated for each sub-sketch so that there is a very small probability (say 0.05) for overflows to happen. When an overflow happens, the most significant bit(s) are truncated. While this situation may sound disastrous to readers, it is in fact not that bad for two reasons: (1) most other sub-sketches have no overflows and can help correct the situation, and (2) the overflow situation most likely also occurs in the sub-sketch computed from the received packet and it is the difference between the sub-sketches

[1]There is another concept called relative Fisher information established in information theory which is not related to anything here.
[2]Both the sender and the receiver know this matrix.

[3]Both the sender and the receiver know how to generate the pseudorandom vectors. The pseudorandom vectors for computing different sub-sketches are mutually independent.

(likely both truncated) that counts. **Second**, the sketch sent along with the packet may itself be corrupted during transmission, which is a situation that ToW needs not worry about in its data streaming contexts. In EToW, lightweight error-detection codes are used to provide special protection to the sketch so that the receiver knows which sub-sketches are corrupted and can exclude them from BER estimation. **Third**, unlike in ToW, where bits are sampled with probability 1 (*without replacement*) to produce the random projection, in EToW, bits are sampled with probability less than 1 *with replacement* and only those sampled bits are used to produce the sub-sketch through the aforementioned random projection process. While such a sampling process was adopted in the EToW paper [6] purely for performance (i.e., BER estimation accuracy) considerations, it has the following two unintended (and perhaps desirable) consequences for this work: (1) While the Fisher information analysis of ToW is impossible due to its sampling without replacement nature, that of EToW is mathematically manageable. (2) EToW's adoption of sampling with replacement makes it possible for us to unify EToW with EEC, which samples bits also with replacement, through our gEEC (generalized EEC) framework, to be described in Section 4. With these three enhancements, EToW achieves 50-70% reduction in coding overhead, compared with an EEC scheme with similar BER estimation accuracy, as shown in [6].

3. FISHER INFORMATION ANALYSIS OF EEC

In this section, we analyze the Fisher information contained in an EEC codeword. Since each bit in an EEC codeword is generated in the same way independent of each other, it suffices to analyze the contribution from each bit. The Fisher information of the codeword is simply the sum of the Fisher information contained in each bit.

Throughout this paper, we will use notation $\tilde{z}_i$'s to denote the codeword bits (sent along with the packet) received (hence subjected to transmission errors), and use z_i''s to denote the codeword bits calculated from the packet received. In the EEC scheme, z_i and z_i' are the parity bits of the l_i bits on the same locations of the original and the received packets. The receiver computes their difference $X_i = \tilde{z}_i \oplus z_i'$, $i = 1, 2, \ldots, m$, and infers the error rate θ from the X_i's.

3.1 Fisher Information Contained in each EEC bit

To simplify the exposition, we first perform the Fisher information analysis under the unrealistic assumption that the codeword is immune from corruption during transmission. In this case, $\tilde{z}_i$'s, the codeword bits received, are the same as z_i's, the codeword bits sent. We will then handle the more realistic case, without immunity, at the end of this section.

3.1.1 The case with "immunity"

Recall X_i defined above indicates whether or not the i_{th} parity equation holds. In the case with immunity, the likelihood function of observing $X_i = 1$ (i.e., odd number of bits "flipped" during transmission among the set of bits sampled) is as follows:

$$\begin{aligned} f(X_i = 1, \theta) &= \Pr(X_i = 1|\theta) & (7)\\ &= \sum_{j=0}^{2j+1 \leq l_i} \binom{l_i}{2j+1} \theta^{2j+1}(1-\theta)^{l_i-2j-1} \\ &= \frac{1-(1-2\theta)^{l_i}}{2}. & (8) \end{aligned}$$

The Fisher information contained in each X_i can be calculated as follows:

$$\begin{aligned} J_i^{EEC}(\theta) &= \mathbf{E}_\theta[(\frac{\partial}{\partial\theta}\log f(X_i;\theta))^2] & (9)\\ &= \Pr(X_i = 1|\theta)(\frac{\partial}{\partial\theta}\log f(X_i = 1;\theta))^2 \\ &\quad + \Pr(X_i = 0|\theta)(\frac{\partial}{\partial\theta}\log f(X_i = 0;\theta))^2 \\ &= \frac{1-(1-2\theta)^{l_i}}{2}\left(\frac{2l_i(1-2\theta)^{l_i-1}}{1-(1-2\theta)^{l_i}}\right)^2 \\ &+ \frac{1+(1-2\theta)^{l_i}}{2}\left(-\frac{2l_i(1-2\theta)^{l_i-1}}{1+(1-2\theta)^{l_i}}\right)^2 \\ &= \frac{4l_i^2(1-2\theta)^{2l_i-2}}{1-(1-2\theta)^{2l_i}}. & (10) \end{aligned}$$

Before we aggregate Fisher information contributed by all the codeword bits, we would like to highlight some nice properties of the derived Fisher information for a single bit (10). For convenience of comparisons, we define the Fisher information (of $\log\theta$) of each bit as $\eta(l_i, \theta)$:

$$\begin{aligned} \theta^2 J_i^{EEC}(\theta) &= \frac{4\theta^2 l_i^2(1-2\theta)^{2l_i-2}}{1-(1-2\theta)^{2l_i}} & (11)\\ &\triangleq \eta(l_i, \theta). & (12) \end{aligned}$$

As we explained earlier, this is inversely proportional to the Cramer-Rao bound of the relative variance. The larger $\eta(l, \theta)$, the tighter the bound of the relative error (and the log-difference) that can be achieved.

Values of $\eta(l_i, \theta)$ for various l_i (number of bits sampled) values are plotted in Figure 1. We can see that the $\eta(l, \theta)$ curves corresponding to different l values are actually very similar in shape to each other. A larger parity group size l is better for estimating smaller θ values and vice versa. These curves also have similar "heights" except when l gets really small (targeting extremely high BER close to the maximum possible value of 0.5). This means that the "peak estimation powers" of different parity bits are about the same. The maximum (i.e., "height") of each curve is always reached around $\theta = 0.4/l$, which means the parity bit computed from l sampled bits yields the best estimation for θ when θ is around $0.4/l$.

We can even quantify how much "information about θ" flows into the whole estimation spectrum by the following integral formula, which is the area covered by the FI(rel) curves in Figure 1:

$$\mathbf{S^J}(l) = \int_0^{0.5} \theta^2 J(l, \theta) d\log\theta \qquad (13)$$

In (13), the upper limit of the integral is 0.5 is because all formulas derived above (starting from (8)) are only valid when θ is less than or equal to 0.5.

From a practical perspective, an integral over the full spectrum might not be too useful since practical applications might be only interested in a particular range of spectrum rather than a full spectrum, such as $[10^{-3}, 0.15]$ proposed in [3]. Moreover, maintaining accuracy over a certain threshold might be even more practical than an integral. However, we find $\mathbf{S^J}$ is still a very good indicator of performance since it remains almost the same for EEC bits with different parameter l, which is not surprising since the Fisher information curves are similar to each other in shape and hence the "area under" the curves are also close to one another. In Figure 1, we list the values of $\mathbf{S^J}(l)$ of different l's in the legend, where constant $C = \frac{1}{24}\pi^2 \approx 0.4112$, which is a provable limit of $\mathbf{S^J}(l)$ when l goes infinity. When l increases, $\mathbf{S^J}(l)$ gets closer to C. In other

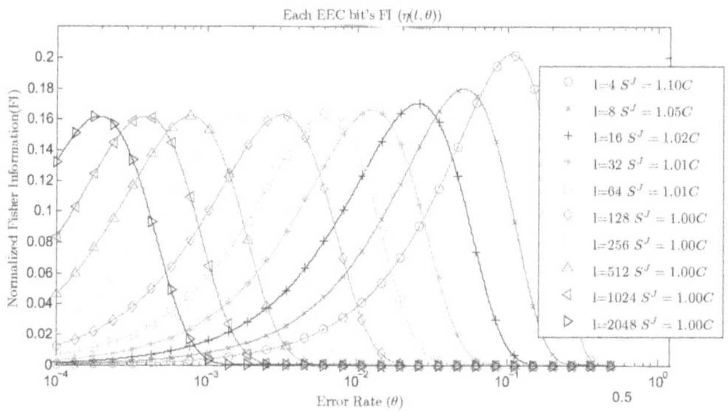

Figure 1: Fisher Information (of $\log\theta$) of each EEC bit in function of l and θ

words, the total information $\mathbf{S^J}$ contributed by each bit is all on the same scale and almost invariant to parameter l. In Section 5.1, we will see that this criteria $\mathbf{S^J}$ helps us to differentiate the strengths of different schemes and guides us in selecting better schemes.

3.1.2 The case without "immunity"

We proceed to perform the Fisher information analysis of EEC when the codeword sent along with the packet is no longer assumed to be immune from corruptions during transmission. The amount of Fisher information contained in each parity bit X_i can be derived as in (14). We omit the details of this derivation since it is a special case of the Fisher information analysis (without "immunity") in the gEEC framework in Section 4.2. Note that, unlike the case with "immunity" where the analysis rigorously holds, the analysis for the case without "immunity" only rigorously holds when i.i.d. random binary errors are assumed or random placement of bits are assumed.

$$\theta^2 J_i^{EEC}(\theta) = \frac{4(l_i+1)^2(1-2\theta)^{2l_i}}{1-(1-2\theta)^{2l_i+2}} \quad (14)$$

Notice that the RHS of (14) is equal to $\eta(l_i+1,\theta)$, only slightly different from (10).

3.2 Combining the contributions of the different levels of bits

Since all parity bit are calculated from independent samples with replacement and hence each of them is independent of every other, the Fisher information of the codeword is simply the sum of their Fisher information together:

$$J^{EEC}(\theta) = \sum_{i=1}^{m} J_i^{EEC}(\theta). \quad (15)$$

In Figure 2, we plot the Cramer-Rao bound of the EEC scheme with the typical configuration (9 levels, 32 bits per level) and we also plot the Cramer-Rao bound of schemes with only one level of 32 bits. From Figure 2, we can see that after using the information of all levels, the estimation accuracy has the potential to be considerably improved. In other words, suppose there are two optimal estimators, the first can use only the information contained in one level of bits, while the second can use the information contained in all levels. Then the variance of the first estimator will be four times as large as compared to the second for most θ values. This means the codeword size has to be four times as large for the first estimator to match the second in estimation accuracy.

In the design of the original estimator in [3], they first identify the level of bits likely to be the most accurate for estimating θ and then only use that level of bits for estimation. Hence only one level of information is used in the final estimate. In Section 3.5 of the technical report [2], the authors have proposed an improved estimator that can make use of two neighboring levels of parity bits. In Figure 2, we use $\hat{\theta}_1$ to denote the original one proposed in [3] and use $\hat{\theta}_2$ to denote the improved version proposed in [2]. We can see that neither estimator is close to the Cramer-Rao bound corresponding to the amount of Fisher information contained in such one or two levels of bits (In other words, their estimators have not made full use of even the information contained in such one or two levels of bits) and far from the Cramer-Rao bound corresponding to the Fisher information of all the codeword bits. We note that when θ is larger than 0.15, the relative MSE falls below the Cramer-Rao bound; This is because the estimator is actually very biased in that region. According to (3), this might lead to smaller MSE.

3.3 MLE estimator for EEC scheme

In this section, we present our MLE decoder that matches the Cramer-Rao bound, shown in the following formula.

$$\begin{aligned}\hat{\theta}_{MLE} &= \arg\max_{\theta}\{\sum_{i=1}^{m}\log\Pr(X_i|\theta)\} \quad (16)\\ &= \arg\max_{\theta}\{\sum_{i=1}^{m}\log\frac{1-(1-2\theta)^{l_i}}{1+(1-2\theta)^{l_i}}X_i \quad (17)\\ &\quad +\log(1+(1-2\theta)^{l_i})\} \quad (18)\end{aligned}$$

It has been discovered in [5] that the non-informative prior, Jefferys invariant prior, can remove the $O(\frac{1}{N})$ component in bias for the family of exponential models. Here, although the likelihood function is not a closed-form distribution, we find that Jeffreys prior will help the MLE estimator to achieve better results. The MLE with the Jefferys prior, denoted as $\hat{\theta}_{MLE_j}$, is

$$\begin{aligned}\hat{\theta}_{MLE_j} &= \arg\max_{\theta}\{\sum_{i=1}^{m}\log\Pr(X_i|\theta)+\frac{1}{2}\log J(\theta)\}\\ &= \arg\max_{\theta}\{\sum_{i=1}^{m}\log\frac{1-(1-2\theta)^{l_i}}{1+(1-2\theta)^{l_i}}(X_i-\frac{1}{2})\\ &\quad +\log(2l_i(1-2\theta)^{l_i-1})\}.\end{aligned}$$

Here $p(\theta)\sim\sqrt{J(\theta)}$, where $p(\theta)$ is the a priori distribution of the parameter θ and $J(\theta)$ is the Fisher information calculated in (15). Note that the MLE with Jefferys prior will still asymptotically reach the Cramer-Rao bound.

4. DESIGN AND FISHER INFORMATION ANALYSIS OF GENERALIZED EEC (GEEC)

In the previous section, we showed through Fisher information analysis that the original decoder for EEC used in [3] is far from optimal and our new decoder is near-optimal (by almost matching the Cramer-Rao bound) given the amount of Fisher information contained in an EEC codeword. Now we would like to find out whether the EEC encoding scheme is efficient enough by comparing its Fisher information (per bit) with that of EToW. How-

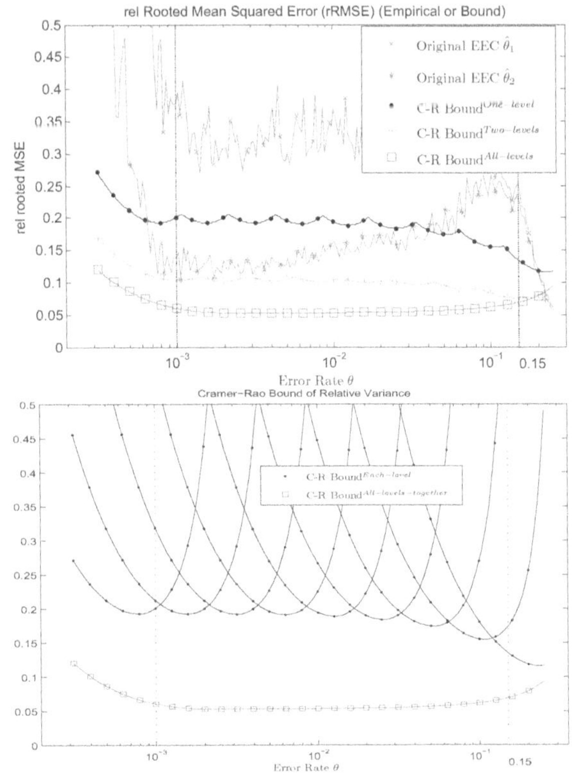

Figure 2: the empirical performance of EEC's original estimators and the associated Cramer-Rao Bound (all levels, each level, and the envelope of only one level/two levels). The EEC scheme is composed by nine levels and 32 bits each level.

ever, when we were performing the Fisher information analysis of EToW, we discovered a generalized EEC (gEEC) scheme that can be parameterized into both EEC and EToW. Fisher information analysis of EToW can thus be generalized to that of gEEC so we shift our "target" for comparison to gEEC. Through this unified framework of gEEC, we have found that some parameterizations of the gEEC family contain 25% or more Fisher information per bit in their codewords than EEC. In other words, the EEC encoding scheme is not very efficient either. The discovery of gEEC is important also for another reason: We have discovered a unified decoder (estimator) for gEEC that is near-optimal (by almost matching the Cramer-Rao bound) and when parameterized into EToW, is more accurate than the original EToW decoder proposed in [6]. Strictly speaking, it is not the clear winner however since the original EToW decoder has much lower computational and storage complexities.

The rest of the section is organized as follows. In Section 4.1, we briefly describe the gEEC encoding scheme by highlighting its differences from and connections to both EToW and EEC. In Section 4.2, we proceed to perform the Fisher information analysis of its codeword and design its estimator. We will see the gEEC decoder that almost matches the Cramer-Rao bound in Section 5.2.

4.1 The gEEC Encoding

A gEEC codeword (called *sketch*) of a packet (viewed as binary vector $\vec{b}$) consists of m sub-sketches $z_1, z_2, \ldots, z_m$. The value of sub-sketch z_i is set to the number of 1's contained in the binary vector generated by sampling l_i bits from the packet *with replacement*, which we refer to as $\vec{b_i}$, and then XOR-ing it with a pseudo random vector $\vec{s_i}$ bitwise. This operation is the same as in EToW, except that in EToW the value of z_i is set to the half of the difference between the number of 1's and the number of 0's. It can be shown that these two types of encodings can be made equally efficient and statistically equivalent with respect to the truncation operations (described shortly) with proper parameterizations.

The main difference between EToW and gEEC is that all $l_i's$ have to take the same value in EToW. This is not an artificially crafted difference because EToW's decoder, inherited from ToW and based on the method of moments, imposes this equal length requirement, while the new decoder we propose for gEEC that we will describe in Section 4.2.2, does not have such a requirement due to its MLE nature. Like in EToW, we use barely enough bits to encode each sub-sketch and "overflows" are handled in the same way through truncation. Moreover, different from EToW which needs extra checking bits to detect corruption inside the sketch, we will see that the estimators provided the gEEC's framework have built-in capability to decode the sketches which might suffer corruption in the case without "immunity".

The precise definition of z_i in gEEC scheme is as follows:

$$z_i = \sum_{j=1}^{l_i} (b_{i,j} \oplus \frac{1+s_{i,j}}{2}) \pmod{K_i}, \qquad (19)$$

where $K_i = 2^{k_i}$, k_i is the number of bits allocated to sub-sketch z_i. Each $s_{i,j}$ is a pre-computed pseudo-random number uniformly and independently selected from $\{-1, 1\}$, the same as the definition in the tug-of-war sketch [1, 6]. The function $\frac{1+s_{i,j}}{2}$ maps $s_{i,j}$ from $\{-1, 1\}$ to $\{0, 1\}$.

As shown below, the nature of the definition above is a random projection of $\vec{s_i}$ (only different from the $\vec{b_i} \cdot \vec{s_i}$ by a pseudo-random constant, i.e. a number that is the same in both sender and receiver):

$$z_i = \sum_{j=1}^{l_i} (b_{i,j} \oplus \frac{1+s_{i,j}}{2}) \qquad (20)$$

$$= \sum_{j=1}^{l_i} \frac{1+(2b_{i,j}-1)s_{i,j}}{2} \qquad (21)$$

$$= \vec{b_i} \cdot \vec{s_i} - \frac{1}{2}\vec{1} \cdot \vec{s_i} + \frac{l_i}{2}. \qquad (22)$$

It can be shown that when we allocate only 1 bit for each sub-sketch, the sketch becomes a parity array and in this case gEEC "degenerates" into a scheme statistically equivalent to EEC with the same l_i values. We can also see that gEEC becomes statistically equivalent to EToW without sketch protection (explained next) when $l_i's$ are set to the same value.

4.2 Fisher information analysis

In this section, we analyze the Fisher information contained in each gEEC codeword. Recall from Sec. 2.3 that in EToW we need to protect the sketch against corruptions during transmission using lightweight error-detection codes. We will show no such protection is needed in gEEC because, unlike the EToW decoder, the proposed MLE decoder for gEEC is robust against such corruptions. In order to simplify the presentation of the analysis, we first analyze the Fisher information of a gEEC codeword assuming that the codeword is immune from corruption during transmission in Section 4.2.1 and then show how to remove this assumption in Section 4.2.2.

4.2.1 The case with "immunity"

Like in Section 3, we use $\vec{b_i'}$ to denote the set of bits sampled *with replacement* from the packet received (subject to corruptions during transmission) that are used to compute the i_{th} sub-sketch z'_i at the receiver side, and use $\vec{b_i}$ to denote the corresponding set of bits sampled from the packet sent (can be different from $\vec{b_i'}$ due to corruptions during transmission) that are used to compute the i_{th} sub-sketch z_i at the receiver side. In this section, we derive the Fisher information of the sketch under the aforementioned immunity assumption that these sub-sketches z_1, z_2, ..., z_m will arrive at the receiver without having any of their bits corrupted during transmission.

The receiver can calculate the difference X_i between z'_i and z_i

$$X_i \triangleq z'_i - z_i (\text{mod } K), i \in [m] \tag{23}$$

Here $K = 2^k$ where k is the number of bits we allocate to each sub-sketch. The effect of the aforementioned (possible) overflow and resulting truncation is reflected in "modulo K". It can be shown that this observation X_i is the following function of the error vector $\vec{e_i}$ (the difference vector between $\vec{b_i}$ and $\vec{b_i'}$), where s_i is the aforementioned pseudorandom vector over which the sampled bit vectors $\vec{b_i}$ and $\vec{b_i'}$ are linearly projected:

$$\begin{aligned} X_i &= \vec{b_i} \cdot \vec{s_i} - \vec{b'}_i \cdot \vec{s_i} (\text{mod } K), \text{due to (22)} & (24)\\ &= \vec{e_i} \cdot \vec{s_i} (\text{mod } K). & (25) \end{aligned}$$

Since observations X_1, X_2, ..., X_m are independent random variables, the likelihood function of the random vector $\langle X_1, X_2, ..., X_m \rangle$ is the product of the likelihood functions of these random variables. The likelihood function of X_i (for arbitrary i) can be derived as follows.

For convenience, we drop the subscript from X_i and denote it simply as X. In the following we will derive the probability mass function (PMF) of X, which takes values from the set of $K = 2^k$ integers $\{0, 1, ..., K-1\}$. It can be shown that its PMF can be determined by a K-dimensional vector $\vec{\gamma}(\theta, l) \equiv \langle \gamma_0(\theta, l), \gamma_1(\theta, l), ..., \gamma_K(\theta, l) \rangle$ where $\gamma_i(\theta, l) \equiv \Pr(X = i | \theta, l)$, $i \in [0, 1, ..., K-1]$. Note that each scalar γ_i is a function of the error rate θ and the number of bits sampled l (here the subscript i is dropped from l_i). We show that $\vec{\gamma}(\theta, l)$ can be computed from the following recurrence relation.

LEMMA 1.

$$\vec{\gamma}(\theta, l)_{1\times K} = \vec{\gamma}(\theta, l-1)_{1\times K} \mathbf{M}(\theta)_{K\times K}, \tag{26}$$

where

$$\mathbf{M}(\theta) = \begin{bmatrix} 1\text{-}\theta & \theta/2 & \cdots 0 \cdots & & & \theta/2 \\ \theta/2 & 1\text{-}\theta & \theta/2 & \cdots 0 \cdots & & \\ & \theta/2 & 1\text{-}\theta & \theta/2 & \cdots 0 \cdots & \\ & \cdots & & & \cdots & \\ & \cdots 0 \cdots & & \theta/2 & 1\text{-}\theta & \theta/2 \\ \theta/2 & & \cdots 0 \cdots & & \theta/2 & 1\text{-}\theta \end{bmatrix}_{K\times K} \tag{27}$$

The initial condition for the above is

$$\vec{\gamma}(\theta, 0) = [1, 0 \cdots, 0]_{1\times K}. \tag{28}$$

PROOF. Let $\vec{e} = \langle e_1, e_2, \cdots, e_l \rangle$ and $\vec{s} = \langle s_1, s_2, \cdots, s_l \rangle$. We define the following interim random variables Y_j, $j = 0, \cdots, l$:

$$Y_j = \sum_{k=1}^{j} e_k s_k. \tag{29}$$

Clearly, $X = Y_l (\text{mod } K)$. Due to the sampling with replacement policy, the increment in each step $\Delta Y_j = Y_{j+1} - Y_j = e_{j+1} s_{j+1}$ is independent of every other. Hence the random variables $\{Y_j\}_{0\le j\le l}$ make up a Markov chain. In each step, with probability $1-\theta$ an unchanged bit is selected and hence $\Delta Y_j = 0$; with probability θ a changed bit is selected, and half of these increments are $+1$ and the other half -1 since s_k is uniformly at random from $\{-1, 1\}$.

Hence the distribution of ΔY_j is:

$$\Delta Y_j = \begin{cases} -1 & \text{with prob } \theta/2, \\ 0 & \text{with prob } 1-\theta, \\ 1 & \text{with prob } \theta/2. \end{cases} \tag{30}$$

Mapping $\{Y_j\}_{0\le j\le l}$ into the finite field Z_K, formula (30) becomes the transition matrix, which is the circular matrix M defined in (27). □

To allow for efficient matrix computation, $\mathbf{M}(\theta)$ can be diagonalized as follows.

$$\mathbf{M}(\theta) = \frac{1}{K} \mathbf{\Omega}' Diag(d_0, d_1, \ldots, d_{K-1}) \mathbf{\Omega} \tag{31}$$

where $\Omega = \{\omega_{ik}\}$, $\omega_{ik} = \exp(\frac{2\pi ikj}{K})$, j is the imaginary unit, and $d_i = 1 - \alpha_i\theta$, $\alpha_i = 2\sin^2(i\pi/K)$, which is actually the Fourier transform matrix.

Considering that $\vec{\gamma}(\theta, 0) = [1, 0 \cdots, 0]_{1\times K}$, we have

$$\begin{aligned} \vec{\gamma}(\theta, l) &= [1, 0, \cdots, 0] \mathbf{M}(\theta)^l \\ &= \frac{1}{K} [1, 0, \cdots, 0] \mathbf{\Omega}' Diag(d_0^l, d_1^l, \ldots, d_{K-1}^l) \mathbf{\Omega} \\ &= \frac{1}{K} [d_0^l, d_1^l, \ldots, d_{K-1}^l] \mathbf{\Omega}. \end{aligned} \tag{32}$$

The Fisher information of the gEEC sketch can be calculated as follows:

$$\begin{aligned} J(\theta, l) &= E_\theta(\frac{\partial}{\partial\theta} \log f(X_i; \theta))^2 \\ &= \sum_{j=0}^{K-1} \gamma_j(\theta) (\frac{\mathrm{d}}{\mathrm{d}\theta} \log(\gamma_j(\theta)))^2 \\ &= \sum_{j=0}^{K-1} \frac{l^2 \{[0, \alpha_1 d_1^{l-1}, \ldots, \alpha_K d_{K-1}^{l-1}] \mathbf{\Omega}\}_j^2}{K\{[d_0^l, d_1^l, \ldots, d_{K-1}^l] \mathbf{\Omega}\}_j}, \end{aligned} \tag{33}$$

where γ_j denotes the jth item in vector $\vec{\gamma}$ and $\{\vec{v}\}_j$ denotes the jth item in vector $\vec{v}$.

It can be shown that when we set k to 1 (so that gEEC degenerates into EEC), formula (33), the Fisher information of gEEC codeword is equal to formula (10), that of EEC.

4.2.2 The case without immunity

In the previous section, we have performed an Fisher information analysis of gEEC under the assumption that the codewords (sketches) sent along with the packets are not subject to corruptions during transmission (i.e., "with immunity"). In reality, these codewords are certainly not immune to bit errors. In this section, we perform the Fisher information anaysis without this "immunity assumption".

Suppose the sender sends out a sub-sketch z_i and the receiver receives $\tilde{z}_i$. Now $\tilde{z}_i$ may differ from z_i as the "immunity" has been taken away. Having no knowledge of z_i, the receiver has to use $\tilde{z}_i$ and z_i' computed from the received packet to infer the bit error rate θ. The conditional (upon θ) joint probability mass function of $\langle \tilde{z}_i, z_i' \rangle$ is shown as follows. For ease of notation, we remove the subscript i from the notations and get:

$$\Pr(\check{z}, z'|\theta) \propto \sum_{z=0}^{K-1} \Pr(z, \check{z}|\theta) \Pr(z'|\theta, z)$$
$$\propto \sum_{z=0}^{K-1} \Pr(z) \Pr(\check{z}|\theta, z) \Pr(z'|\theta, z). \quad (34)$$

Note that the formula (34) above only holds under the assumption that the binary error flips on sketch bits and the error flips on data bits are independent, i.e., $\check{z} \perp z'|\theta, z$, which requires either that the binary errors are i.i.d. distributed inside the sketch or that the locations of all bits participating including the sketch bits are all sampled with replacement from the packet, which is not possible to be strictly guaranteed in reality. Hence, we readily admit that, different from the analysis for the case with "immunity" which is rigorously held, the analysis for the case without "immunity" does not model reality perfectly, though we believe that it should be very close.

The matrix representation of (34) is as follows:

$$\mathbf{P}(\theta)^{final}_{K \times K} \propto \mathbf{\Lambda M}(\theta)^{l} \mathbf{T}(\theta)_{K \times K}, \quad (35)$$

In (35), matrix $\mathbf{M}$ corresponds to $\Pr(z'|\theta, z)$ and can be calculated using (31). Matrix $\mathbf{\Lambda}$ is a diagonal matrix and corresponds to $\Pr(z)$. Its diagonal elements can also be calculated using (32) with $\theta = 1$. We acknowledge that an ulterior motive for us to define z_i as the number of 1's, rather than the number of 1's minus the number of 0's, in the bitwise-XOR of $\vec{b_i}$ and $\vec{s_i}$, is that it makes these formulae much "cleaner".

Matrix $\mathbf{T}$ is the transition matrix that corresponds to $\Pr(\check{z}, \check{q}|\theta, z)$. Each of its entry T_{ij} is defined as follows:

$$\mathbf{T}_{i,j} = \theta^{d_{ij}}(1-\theta)^{k-d_{ij}}, \quad (36)$$

where d_{ij} is the Hamming distance between the binary representation of i and j.

All entries in (35) are differentiable and the Fisher information can be derived in a way similar to (33). In the interest of space the final Fisher information formula is omitted here.

Note that when $k = 1$, gEEC degenerates to EEC, and the final Fisher information formula can be shown to be equivalent to EEC's Fisher information formula (14).

4.3 Our MLE Estimators

In this section, we derive the MLE decoder for gEEC that perform much better than both EEC and EToW decoders, as we will show in Sec. 5.2. Again, we first derive it for the easier case with "immunity" and then proceed to take the "immunity" away.

In the case with "immunity", our observations are X_i, which is the difference between each pair of $\check{z}_i$ and z'_i, $i = 1, 2, ..., m$, and our goal is to estimate θ. The maximum likelihood estimator is

$$\hat{\theta}_{MLE} = \arg\max_{\theta}\{\sum_{i=1}^{m} \log\{\vec{\gamma}(\theta, l_i)\}_{X_i}\} \quad (37)$$

Here $\{\vec{\gamma}(\theta, l_i)\}_{X_i}$ denotes the X_i^{th} scalar in $\vec{\gamma}$ and $\vec{\gamma}(\theta, l)$ and $J(\theta, l)$ have both been derived earlier. The MLE estimator with Jeffreys prior (MLE-J) is

$$\hat{\theta}_{MLE-J} = \arg\max_{\theta}\{\frac{1}{2}\log J(\theta) + \sum_{i=1}^{m} \log\{\vec{\gamma}(\theta, l_i)\}_{X_i}\} \quad (38)$$

We introduce $MLE-J$ because it performs better than the plain vanilla MLE empirically, which will show in Section 5.2.

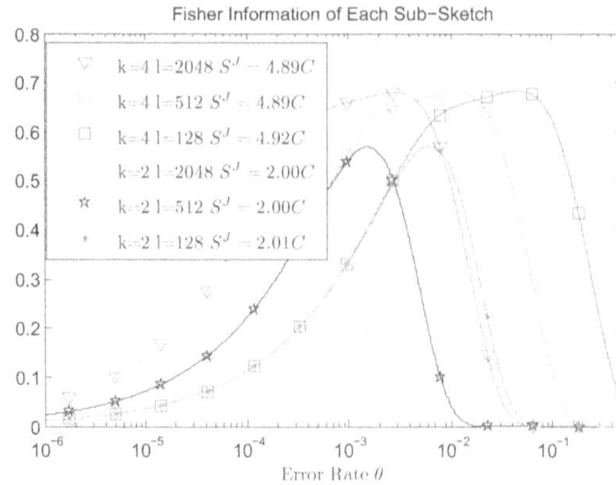

Figure 3: gEEC's Fisher information: Relationship to l and k in the case with immunity assumption

Similar to (38), the MLE estimator with Jeffreys prior for the case without immunity is

$$\hat{\theta} = \arg\max_{\theta}\left\{\frac{1}{2}\log J(\theta) + \sum_{i=1}^{m} \log\{\mathbf{P}(\theta, l_i)\}_{\check{z}_i, z'_i}\right\}, \quad (39)$$

where $\{\mathbf{P}(\theta, l_i)\}_{\check{z}_i, z'_i}$ denotes the $(\check{z}_i, z'_i)^{\text{th}}$ entry in the probability matrix $\mathbf{P}$.

This estimator will also be evaluated empirically in Section 5.2.

5. NUMERICAL AND EMPIRICAL RESULTS

In this section, we present an extensive array of numerical results for gEEC's Fisher information, as well as an empirical evaluation of gEEC's estimators with different configurations. Note that both EEC and EToW are just two of the sub-families in the gEEC family.

5.1 Fisher Information contained in the gEEC Family

Fisher information contained in each gEEC's sub-sketch is determined by two factors: the sampling group size l and the binary width k. For convenience, this is denoted as gEEC(l, k), and a sketch composed of m such sub-sketches is denoted by gEEC(m, l, k).

In Figure 3, we show the impact of different l's and k's in the case with immunity. We observe that, similar to Figure 1, the parameter l only "shifts" the curve. The larger l, the more resolution on lower θ's, while the total amount of "information flow" S^J remains almost the same. The parameter k, on the other hand, expands the "span" of the curve, leading to a wider spread of the estimation power on the spectrum.

To compare the total amount of "information flow" of different parameterizations more conveniently, we also list the value S^J—the area covered by each curve as defined in (13)—of each parameterization in the legend of the figure, where the constant C is $\frac{\pi^2}{24} \approx 0.4112$, the lower limit of the area covered by the EEC bit's Fisher information curve, as discussed in Section 3. Based on the S^J values in Figure 3, we conclude that $k = 2$ is not able to bring any additional benefit. In contrast, one sub-sketch with $k = 4$ can gain more information over 4 independently coded EEC bits.

The next question we ask is: How much information is lost due to the contamination of the sketch? To measure this, we plot the Fisher information curve with $k = 4$ or 6 and $l = 2048$, 512 or

	Case with immunity			Case without immunity		
k	l=128	l=512	l=2048	l=128	l=512	l=2048
2	1.00	1.00	1.00	1.00	1.00	1.00
3	1.12	1.12	1.11	1.08	1.10	1.11
4	1.23	1.22	1.22	1.13	1.18	1.21
5	1.24	1.31	1.31	1.16	1.20	1.26
6	1.05	1.30	1.37	1.19	1.21	1.27
7	0.90	1.14	1.36	1.22	1.24	1.27

Table 1: The total information gain $\frac{S^J}{kC}$ ($C = \frac{1}{24}\pi^2$)

128 in Figure 4. We observe that the Fisher information curve is impacted only when θ is not small and the loss of information is also modest. For some cases, such as $k = 6$ and $l = 128$, the total information is improved even when the sketch is subject to errors.

We summarize the impact of l and k's on S^J by listing the $\frac{1}{kC}S^J$ values of different parameterizations in Table 1. From the perspective of total information gain S^J, more bits per sub-sketch usually improves the gain. We see that $k = 5$ gives around 25% more information per bit in the contaminated case, which can be translated to a similar ratio of reduction of the sketch size to achieve the same variance bound. It can be also shown that the performance of one sub-sketch with $k = 5$ can dominate six one-bit sub-sketches together.

However, a larger k is not always better. The larger k gets, the wider the span of the resolution curve gets, which might cover more range than needed. If l is small (for better resolution on large θ's), k should not need to be too large, otherwise it will be wasteful (such as the $k = 6$ and $l = 128$ case in the table). For a typical EEC application in wireless communications where the primary target parameter range is $[10^{-3}, 0.15]$, the span of $k = 5$ (or 6) would be sufficient. Moreover, a large k will mean a higher implementation cost for a relatively modest gain, which will be discussed soon.

5.2 Empirical Evaluation of Estimators

We now present an empirical evaluation of gEEC's estimators. We aim to use the figures in Figures 5,6,7 to answer two questions: (1) How far is the estimator's real performance from the theoretical results? and (2) How does this compare with previously proposed solutions? Each value in igures 5,6,7 is obtained with 1000 runs in our simulations, in the case without immunity.

The comparison metrics that we use are the relative mean squared error (rMSE, defined as $\overline{\frac{1}{\theta}(\hat{\theta} - \theta)^2}$), the mean squared error of $\log \hat{\theta}$ (defined as $\overline{(\log \hat{\theta} - \log \theta)^2}$)), the ratio of large errors (the ratio of $\hat{\theta}$ that are larger than 2θ or smaller than $\theta/2$), and the relative bias ($\overline{\frac{\hat{\theta}}{\theta}} - 1$).As discussed in Section 2.1, although the Cramer-Rao lower bound for the relative MSE of $\hat{\theta}$ (4) and the MSE of $\log \hat{\theta}$ (5) are the same, we prefer to use the statistics of $\log \hat{\theta}$ for comparison since it allocates larger penalty to large deviations.

In Figure 5, we compare the performance of the original 288-bit EEC scheme with original estimators with two gEEC configurations, gEEC$(16, 768, 5)$ and gEEC$(16, 768, 6)$, whose total transmission costs are 80 and 96 bits, respectively. We see that our new sketches perform very well in $[0.001, 0.15]$ with much less transmission overhead than the original EEC, while the performance of the original EEC's estimator varies, especially when measured by harsher criteria such as the MSE of $\log \hat{\theta}$ and the ratio of large errors.

In Figure 6, we compare the performance of the four estimators of two schemes, the original EEC and gEEC$(56, 512, 5)$. All four estimators are derived from the newly proposed gEEC framework, two of which use the Jeffreys prior and the other two do not. We can see that the estimators with Jeffreys prior are generally better in the range where θ is relatively large and the inherent resolution of the scheme is relatively weak, no matter if measured by MSE or by bias. Since estimators with Jeffereys prior are usually empirically better, we always use that version in other comparisons.

In Figure 7, we compare the performance of four schemes, the original EEC, gEEC$(56, 512, 5)$, gEEC$(56, 768, 6)$ and EToW$(56, 768)$ with 5-bits per sub-sketch and 1-bit for detecting corruption, the transmission cost of which are almost the same. The first three use gEEC's MLE estimator with Jeffreys prior, while the last one uses EToW's moment-based estimator. Comparing these figures with Figure 5, we can see that, with the same transmission cost, the estimation accuracy is substantially improved. Moreover, we can see that the gEEC$(56, 512, 5)$ and gEEC$(56, 768, 6)$'s performance are generally better than the others. In a wide range they can achieve around a 30-50% reduction of MSE, compared with the EEC scheme with our new estimator. This is not surprising since we have already seen that a larger k can bring a modest improvement of estimation accuracy. We also observe that EToW's performance is only slightly worse, except when θ is close to or larger than 0.1.

Comparing the curves in Figure 5 and Figure 6, we can see that when the total number of sketches is large, the MLE estimator's performance is nearly equal to the Cramer-Rao lower bound, and its bias is also reduced as seen by comparing Figure 5(d) and Figure 5(d). Note that sometime the MSE of $\log \theta$ or rMSE might be below the Cramer-Rao bound when bias is high, which is possible since all curves of Cramer-Rao bound presented in the figures are for the unbiased estimator.

To summarize our comparisons above, our estimators, especially the ones with Jeffreys prior, can almost achieve the Cramer-Rao bound empirically. On one hand, gEEC$(16, 768, 5)$ (which is also EToW's scheme, just without EToW's extra error detection bit) can achieve a similar level of performance as the original EEC scheme with only one-fourth of the sketch size; on the other hand, with the same budget of transmission cost, the estimation accuracy of the original EEC scheme (288 bit design) can be greatly improved by our new estimators, and our gEEC design can achieve around 30% additional gain of estimation accuracy. Compared to the EToW's performance, the gEEC's performance is still better, especially in the range that θ is relatively large.

5.3 Implementation Cost of Estimators and Selection of Parameters

All presentations thus far have focused on the estimation performance. However, the implementation and the computation costs should also be considered. In practice, the MLE estimator can be implemented as table-based lookup. Whether or not it is enhanced by the Jeffreys prior, the MLE estimator can be transformed in this way:

$$\hat{\theta}_{MLE} = \arg\max_{\theta}\{\mathrm{A}(\theta)\mathrm{Y} + \mathrm{B}(\theta)\}, \tag{40}$$

where each entry of Y indicates the count of one particular type of sub-sketch equals to one particular value. $\mathrm{A}(\theta)$ and $\mathrm{B}(\theta)$ are determined by

We can implement (40) as a linear transform of $\mathbf{Y}$, i.e. $\mathbf{A}_{d_1 \times d_2}\mathbf{Y}_{d_2 \times 1} + \mathbf{B}_{d_1 \times 1}$ and then find the maximum of the result. Here $\mathbf{A}_{d_1 \times d_2}$ and $\mathbf{B}_{d_1 \times 1}$ are both pre-calculated matrixes.

One of $\mathbf{A}$'s dimensions, d_1, is determined by the size of candidate θ's. For most practical EEC applications, d_1 in the order of

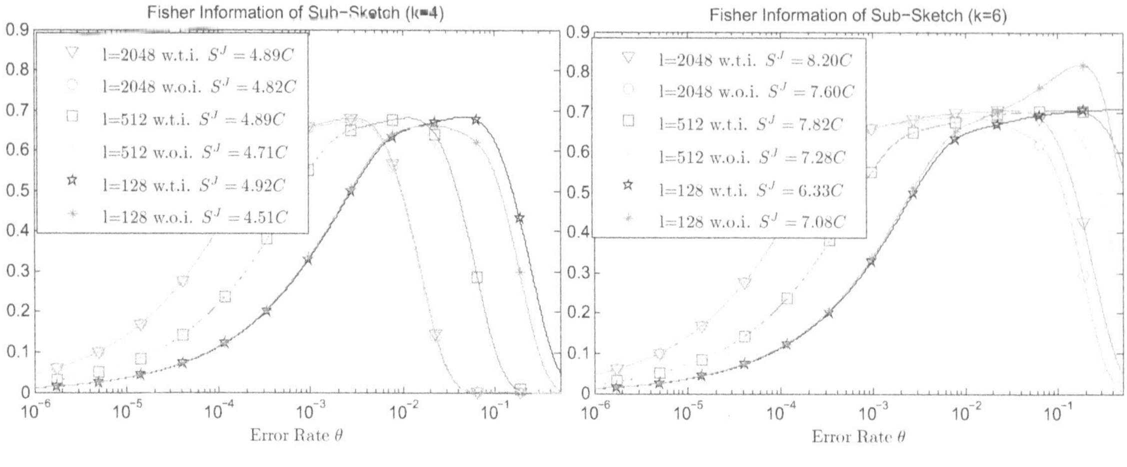

Figure 4: gEEC's Fisher information: Relationship to l and k in the cases with and without immunity (denoted as $w.t.i.$ and $w.o.i.$ respectively in the legend)

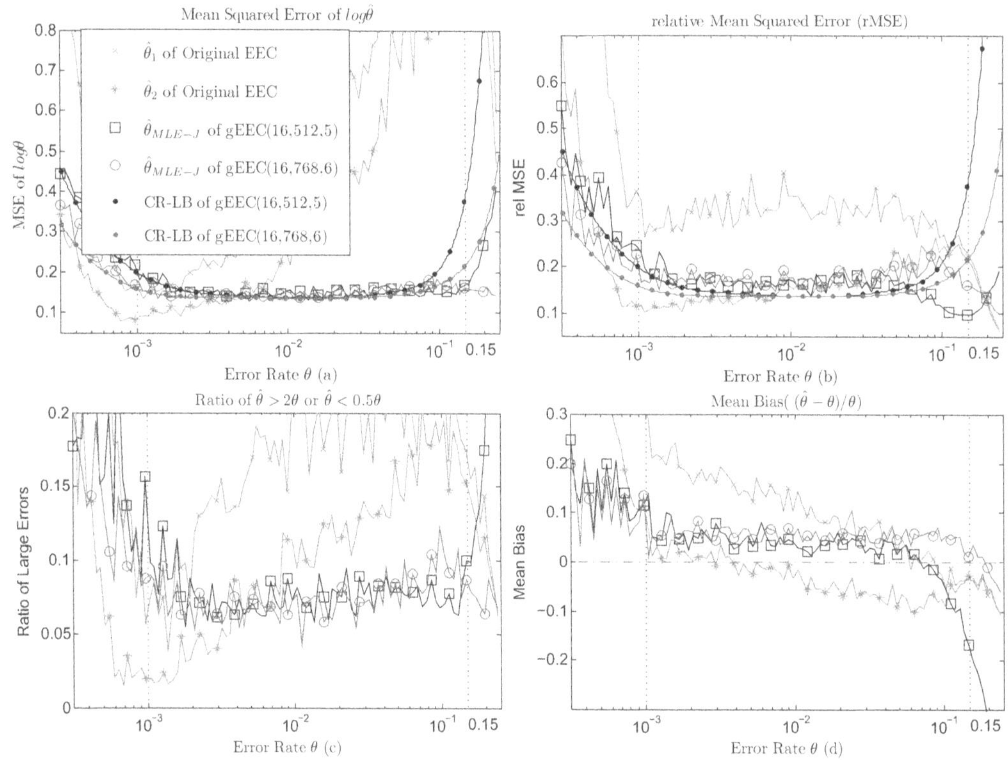

Figure 5: Empirical Results of Estimators: Compare the performance of original EEC (with original estimator) and two gEEC schemes (with much smaller size, 80 and 96 bits respectively), in the case without "immunity".

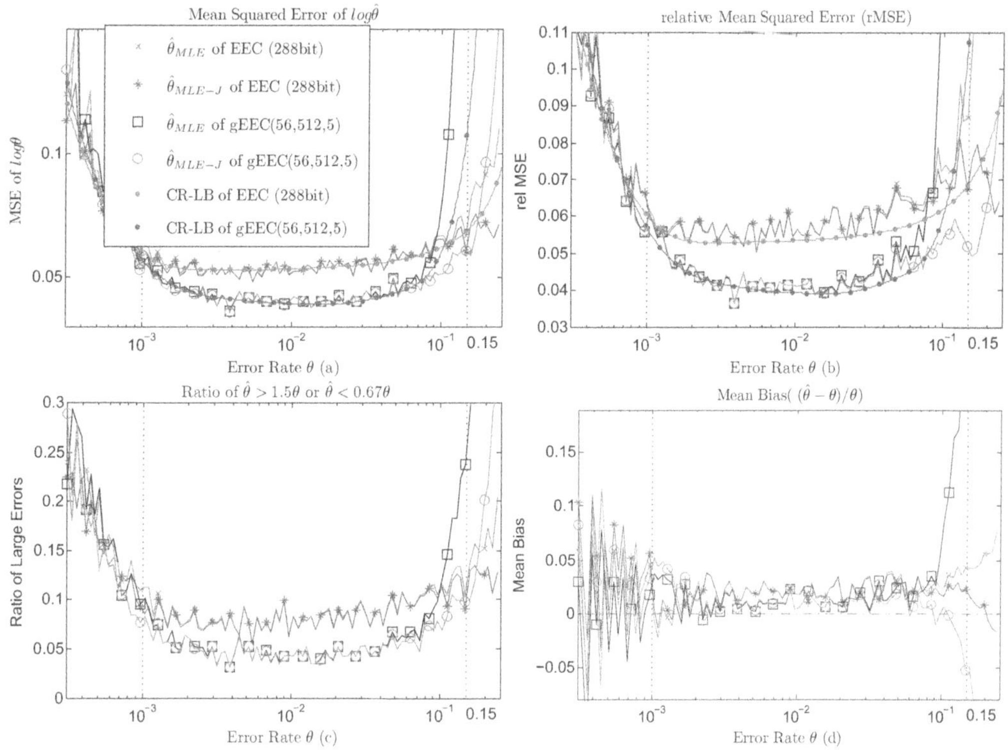

Figure 6: Empirical Results of Estimators: Compare the performance of two types of gEEC estimators (with or without Jeffrey's prior) on three schemes including the original EEC scheme, in the case without "immunity".

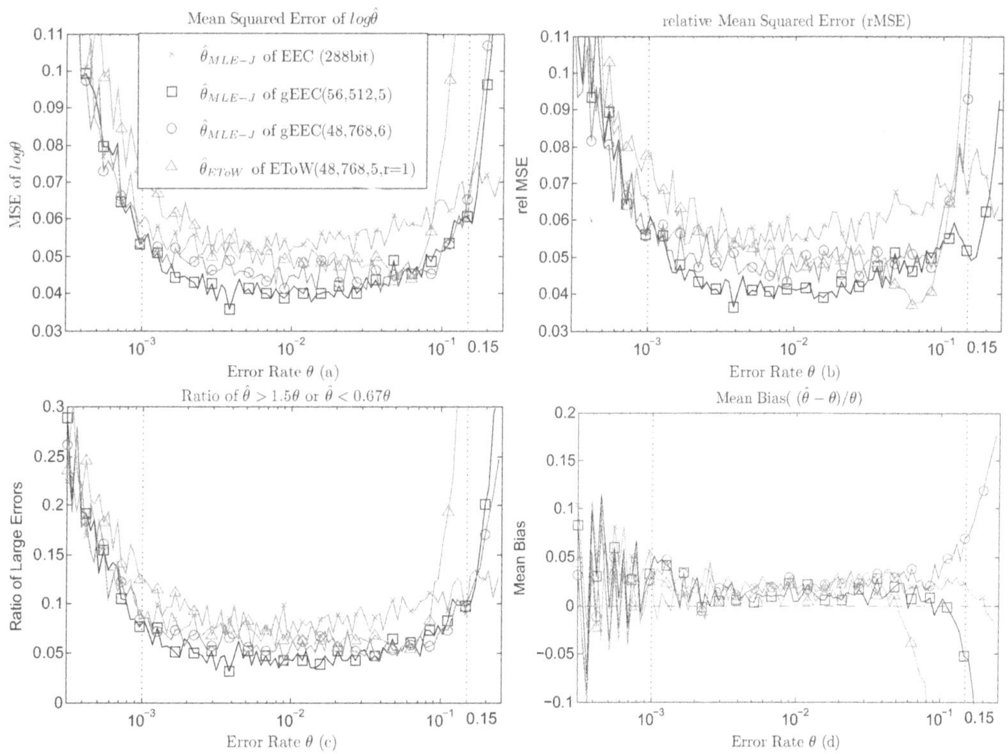

Figure 7: Empirical Results of Estimators: Compare the performance of four schemes (original EEC, gEEC(56,512,5),gEEC(48,768,6) and EToW), with almost the same size and using gEEC's estimator with Jeffrey's prior, in the case without "immunity".

hundreds is sufficient since it will be wasteful if it becomes more fine-grained than the spectrum of estimation.

A's other dimension, d_2, corresponding to the length of **Y**, depends on the design of the sketch. Suppose the codeword is composed of c types of sub-sketches: m_1 gEEC(l_1, k_1) sub-sketches, m_2 gEEC(l_2, k_2) sub-sketches, $\ldots, m_c$ gEEC(l_c, k_c) sub-sketches. In the case of "immunity" where the estimator can directly infer from the difference between $\tilde{z}_i$ and z_i', d_2 equals to $\sum_{i=1}^{c}(2^{k_i}-1)$. In the case without "immunity," d_2 equals to $\sum_{i=1}^{c}(2^{2k_i}-1)$, since in such a case the estimator should directly infer from the pair of $\tilde{z}_i$ and z_i' and hence the table size is squared.

On one hand, the MLE estimator above can be implemented with an extremely low cost, when all sub-sketches' k parameters equal 1, which means the scheme degenerates to the original EEC scheme. In this case, the matrix **A** can be as small as 9×100 (say, d_2=100). Moreover, some iterative methods similar to the bisection method can be employed to further reduce the number of multiplication, add and compare operations to about 90. Furthermore, since our estimator has strong built-in capability to combine the information from different levels, it can be shown that a 3-level, 96-bit-per-level design performs very closely to a 9-level 32-bit design, which can reduce the number of the sub-sketch types and hence even further reduce the cost by two-thirds.

On the other hand, as shown by previous evaluation results, larger values of k in the sub-sketch, such as 5 or 6, can generally bring around 25% of additional improvement of estimation accuracy, at the cost of thousands times higher cost in the storage and the lookups in tables **A** and **B**. The computation cost actually remains almost the same since **X** is sparse, and we can implement the linear transform by summing up only few rows. Hence, the applicability of this improvement depends on the application scenario, since a lookup table of several hundreds KB might be a very small cost for some applications, but infeasible for others. Also, note that as discussed in Sec. 5.1, a large k might not be necessary if the target range of parameters is not so wide.

There are two middle paths between the cases above. One way is to use the combinations of several sub-sketches with $k = 3$ or 4 and different l's, the cost of which is much smaller than $k = 5$ since the table size increases exponentially ($O(2^{2k})$) in the case without immunity, while the scheme can still receive some gain on estimation accuracy. Another way is to use the EToW's scheme and estimator proposed in [6], whose implementation cost is much lower, though performance is also weaker, especially when the error rate θ is large.

In summary, the gEEC framework can be easily and flexibly configured for different requirements of estimation accuracy. All guidelines discussed in this section not only hold for θ in the range $[0.001, 0.15]$, but also for the other arbitrary ranges as needed.

6. CONCLUSION

The seminal work of Chen *et al.* [3] has opened the door for the design of high-quality error estimating codes, with applications towards improving wireless network performance. Chen *et al.* [3] designed an exceedingly simple code for estimating bit error rates in packets being transmitted, and it is an open—yet challenging—question whether this code is optimal in practice.

In this paper, we have systematically investigated the design space of error estimating codes, stemming from the natural question whether EEC achieves the best tradeoff between the space and estimation accuracy in estimating bit error rates. Along the path of our exploration using Fisher information analysis, we have demonstrated that EEC decoding is inefficient, and proposed a new estimator (decoder) that achieves a significantly higher accuracy. While investigating whether EEC encoding is efficient, we have developed a generalized coding framework, called generalized EEC, in which existing designs, such as EEC and EToW, are just degenerate cases. Using this unified framework, we found that some parameterization of gEEC similar to EToW can contain around 25% more information than the pure EEC scheme. To our knowledge, our work represents the first systematic study of the non-asymptotic optimality of error estimating codes.

Acknowledgement: The work of Hua and Xu is supported in part by the US National Science Foundation through grants CNS 0905169 and CNS 0910592.

7. REFERENCES

[1] ALON, N., GIBBONS, P. B., MATIAS, Y., AND SZEGEDY, M. Tracking join and self-join sizes in limited storage. *J. Comput. Syst. Sci. 64*, 3 (2002), 719–747.

[2] CHEN, B., ZHOU, Z., ZHAO, Y., AND YU, H. Technical report: Efficient error estimating coding: feasibility and applications.

[3] CHEN, B., ZHOU, Z., ZHAO, Y., AND YU, H. Efficient error estimating coding: feasibility and applications. In *SIGCOMM* (2010), pp. 3–14.

[4] COVER, T. M., AND THOMAS, J. A. *Elements of information theory (2. ed.)*. Wiley, 2006.

[5] FIRTH, D. Bias reduction of maximum likelihood estimates. *Biometrika 80*, 1 (1993), 27–38.

[6] HUA, N., LALL, A., LI, B., AND XU, J. A simpler and better design of error estimating coding. In *IEEE INFOCOM* (2012).

[7] KUSHILEVITZ, E., AND NISAN, N. *Communication complexity*. Cambridge University Press, 1997.

[8] LEHMANN, E., AND CASELLA, G. *Theory of Point Estimation, 2nd edition*. Springer, 1998.

[9] RIBEIRO, B. F., TOWSLEY, D. F., YE, T., AND BOLOT, J. Fisher information of sampled packets: an application to flow size estimation. In *Internet Measurement Conference* (2006), pp. 15–26.

[10] TUNE, P., AND VEITCH, D. Towards optimal sampling for flow size estimation. In *Internet Measurement Conference* (2008), pp. 243–256.

[11] TUNE, P., AND VEITCH, D. Sampling vs sketching: An information theoretic comparison. In *INFOCOM* (2011), pp. 2105–2113.

How Well Can Congestion Pricing Neutralize Denial of Service Attacks?

Ashish Vulimiri
University of Illinois at Urbana-Champaign
Urbana IL USA
vulimir1@illinois.edu

Gul A. Agha
University of Illinois at Urbana-Champaign
Urbana IL USA
agha@illinois.edu

P. Brighten Godfrey
University of Illinois at Urbana-Champaign
Urbana IL USA
pbg@illinois.edu

Karthik Lakshminarayanan
Google Inc.
Mountain View CA USA
klkarthik@gmail.com

ABSTRACT

Denial of service protection mechanisms usually require classifying malicious traffic, which can be difficult. Another approach is to price scarce resources. However, while congestion pricing has been suggested as a way to combat DoS attacks, it has not been shown quantitatively how much damage a malicious player could cause to the utility of benign participants. In this paper, we quantify the protection that congestion pricing affords against DoS attacks, even for powerful attackers that can control their packets' routes. Specifically, we model the limits on the resources available to the attackers in three different ways and, in each case, quantify the maximum amount of damage they can cause as a function of their resource bounds. In addition, we show that congestion pricing is provably superior to fair queueing in attack resilience.

Categories and Subject Descriptors

C.2.1 [**Computer-Communication Networks**]: Network Architecture and Design

Keywords

Congestion pricing, Denial of Service, DoS, Security

1. INTRODUCTION

Denial of service (DoS) attacks are a recurring problem for servers and network links on the Internet [22]. In a 2010 survey of 118 network operators, 104 (94%) reported experiencing at least one DoS attack per month, with 8 of these reporting being the target of more than 500 attacks per month [1]. The network may be even more vulnerable in future Internet architectures that support source-controlled routing [38, 37, 25, 11]: such architectures can improve performance and reliability, but may let attackers target weak links or construct long paths that use large aggregate bandwidth.

Most past DoS defenses use filters or capabilities to reduce the volume of malicious traffic (see [19] and references therein). However, because attackers may masquerade as legitimate users, classifying traffic as malicious can be difficult. Some classification approaches exist [39, 23, 36, 24, 12] but they do not help against sophisticated application-level attacks [7, 32, 31] which generate traffic which is difficult to distinguish from legitimate requests. In this paper, we focus on mechanisms that do not require classification.

Without classification, a simple approach to limit damage is *fair queueing* (FQ): partition each congested resource among currently-active users equally [26], or using some weighted fairness rule [33]. However, because FQ acts on each resource in isolation and at a specific moment in time, FQ still allows attackers to grab disproportionately large amounts of resources by requesting many different resources across space, or continually requesting resources across time.[1] A more robust approach is to combine FQ with rationing by *limiting the volume* of data that users can send across time; for example an ISP might limit a user's total transfer volume over each month [6]. Thus, an attacker (such as a bot) is limited in the volume of resources it can send, but it can still cause *disproportionate damage* by always requesting those resources when they most negatively impact others (e.g., during natural or attacker-created periods of high utilization). A third approach is requiring all users to produce *proof of work*, such as computational [8] or bandwidth work [35, 17]. However, this imposes an additional cost on

[1] And even in the absence of malicious behavior, FQ does not maximize total utility, since it does not take the users' heterogeneous internal valuations of the network resources into account.

SIGMETRICS'12, June 11–15, 2012, London, England, UK.

all users, which may be quite significant on resource-limited nodes (e.g., mobile devices with constrained batteries).

The natural economic solution to these problems is *congestion pricing*, in which users expose their valuations to the network through an auction mechanism. Network resources are priced, and all users — legitimate and malicious — pay for what they use. While human users might be averse to fine-grained congestion payments, it is not necessary to involve individuals. For example, monetary congestion payments could be implemented between ISPs (effectively congestion-weighting the payments that already occur between ISPs), or in a cloud computing environment, where dynamically-variable resource pricing for tenants is already common [9] (and where some tenants may have incentive to carry out DoS-style attacks against other tenants [28]). Alternately, rather than directly corresponding to money, congestion payments could constitute abstract "credits" used only for resource utilization accounting during periods of network congestion. Users could be given a monthly allotment of credits from ISPs.

Congestion pricing has been extensively studied as a mechanism to optimize resource utilization among self-interested but otherwise benign users [16, 14], and a practical protocol implementation of a kind of congestion pricing has been proposed [5]. It is intuitively clear that congestion pricing should provide resilience against DoS attacks, but while interest has been expressed in using it as a DoS defense [4], the behavior of congestion pricing in the presence of malicious players has not been *quantified.*

In this paper, we address the following question quantitatively: *To what extent can congestion pricing neutralize denial of service attacks?* We follow a game-theoretic model of Kelly [16] and Johari and Tsitsiklis [14], but we add malicious players to the game. In our model, the *network* collects payments from users and allocates bandwidth in proportion to their payments; *benign* users selfishly bid for routes to maximize their utility; and a *malicious* user acts to minimize the utility of the benign users. Our main technical contribution is an extension of the analysis of [14] to malicious utility functions. The key difficulty is that the attacker's desire to minimize benign users' utility introduces an additional coupling between the users' utilities that past work does not handle.

Our analysis demonstrates that an attacker can inflict damage on a congestion-priced network, but this damage is provably limited. We show this under three scenarios describing the attacker's flow of funds.

First, we consider a scenario in which attackers have access to an unlimited amount of money but only spend it as long as they receive a sufficient rate of return. We show that if an attacker is willing to pay up to $\$\sigma$ to cause a \$1 loss to the utility of the benign users, it cannot degrade the benign users' utility by more than a fraction $\frac{\sigma}{\sigma+1}$ or 25%, whichever is higher. This result applies to the protection of individual servers or an entire network (with possibly multiple congested resources) where users can choose any routes.

Second, we show a stronger result in the case that congestion pricing uses actual monetary transfer and the goal is to bound the total utility of all *legitimate entities* — that is, the benign users and the network (which receives payments from the benign users and the attacker). In this scenario, the attacker's payments partially offset the damage it can cause. We show that in this case the attacker can cause the total utility to fall 25% below optimal, but never more, regardless of its strategy.

And third, we study a case that models attacks from a limited-size botnet of captured user machines. The attackers have limited funds since spending too much would exhaust the bots' budgets and/or increase the chance that they are detected as bots (when their congestion-spending begins to exceed a normal machine's profile). However, the attackers might spend funds in a bursty manner, and thus at any given moment might spend a very large amount. To model this, we limit the attackers to total payment M over some time period (e.g., a month) while benign users in total spend B in that time period. Note that these budgets could represent a monthly allotment of congestion credits imparted to the users by their ISPs, rather than monetary payments. In this model, assuming that the network contains only a single bottleneck resource (a link or server) and that all the benign users have homogeneous utility functions, we show that the benign users' utility is at least $B/(B+M)$. In other words, attackers cannot arrange their bids to cause damage disproportionate to their funds. We conjecture that the same bound applies in more general settings.[2]

We also show that under these assumptions congestion pricing is strictly superior to fair queueing in terms of attack resilience. Congestion pricing can result in arbitrarily higher total utility even when the network uses both FQ and per-user volume limits.

To summarize, the main contributions of this paper are as follows:

1. We quantify the maximum amount of damage an attacker can inflict on a congestion-priced network, under three scenarios limiting the attacker's payments.

2. We demonstrate that congestion pricing outperforms approaches based on fair queueing.

We next present our model (§2), our results on congestion pricing (§3) and on a comparison with fair queueing (§4), discuss some natural questions about our results and deployment of congestion pricing in general (§5), present related work (§6) and conclude (§7). Appendices A and B present proofs for the results in, respectively, §3 and §4.

2. MODEL

2.1 Congestion Pricing

Suppose we have $R = B + M$ users,[3] B of them benign, M malicious. The users share a network in which each of n directed links l has fixed capacity C_l. The network uses the per-link variant of Kelly's [16, 14] market mechanism to partition the link capacities across its users: users buy bandwidth from individual links separately, and the bandwidth division at each link is governed by a proportional allocation mechanism. If user r pays the link l a price p_{lr}, the bandwidth x_{lr} it is allocated at l is given by

$$x_{lr} = \frac{p_{lr}}{\sum_{s=1}^{R} p_{ls}} C_l = \frac{p_{lr}}{P_l} C_l$$

[2]We note however that the fact that the attacker cannot cause the 25% loss present in the earlier scenarios stems from the assumption that the benign users have homogeneous utility functions.

[3]We use the terms "user" and "player" interchangeably.

where P_l is the sum of all the payments received by link l (see [14] for a refinement to handle the case $P_l = 0$).

Each benign user b is attempting to transmit data to some destination in the network. We denote the aggregate end-to-end throughput available to b at time t by f_b. f_b is the result of a max-flow computation on b's bandwidth allocations at the individual links.

Associated with each of the benign users b is a throughput-utility function U_b that assigns a monetary value to b's aggregate bandwidth allocation f_b. Following [14], the net utility Q_b of this user is the difference between its throughput-utility and its outgoing payments:

$$Q_b = U_b(f_b) - \sum_{l=1}^{n} p_{lb}$$

We use three models of behavior for the malicious users, corresponding to the three scenarios described in the introduction (§1).

In the **strategic model**, the malicious users are players in the game that act selfishly so as to minimize the sum of the throughput-utilities of all the benign players. We define the utility of each malicious player m as

$$Q_m = -\sigma_m \sum_{b=1}^{B} U_b(f_b) - \sum_{l=1}^{n} p_{lm}$$

where the *spite coefficient* σ_m indicates that the malicious user is willing to pay \$$\sigma_m$ to see a \$1 degradation in the utilities of the benign players.

In the **Byzantine model**, we allow the malicious players to play an arbitrary, but fixed, combination of prices $\vec{p_m}$ at the links in the network. This model is stronger than the other two since we do not restrict the malicious player to strategies that myopically optimize a specific utility function.

Finally, in the **fixed-ratio model**, the malicious user attempts to minimize the total throughput-utility $\sum_b U_b$ of all the benign users, subject to the constraint that it can spend no more than a constant k times what the average benign user spends. As discussed in §1, this models the botnet setting, where the malicious user is operating by hijacking resources from some of the benign users.

While our results for the strategic and the Byzantine models (§3) are quite general, and apply in arbitrary network topologies for a large class of benign users' utility functions, our results for the fixed-ratio model (discussed in §4 in the context of a comparison with fair queueing) assume a more restricted setting. However, we conjecture that the bounds we discuss continue to apply in more general scenarios.

Without loss of generality, we will assume there is exactly one malicious user (i.e., $M = 1$). Multiple malicious players can all be combined into a single powerful player with a large value for σ_m, $\vec{p_m}$, or k.

2.2 Fair Queueing

As noted in the introduction, in this paper we present results describing both the absolute efficiency of congestion pricing in the presence of malicious behavior, as well as its relative performance compared to network-implemented fair queueing.

Our analytical models of network and benign user behavior for fair queueing (FQ) will closely parallel what was defined above for congestion pricing (CP), the differences being that (i) the network now accepts bandwidth demands directly from the users, instead of asking for payments; and (ii) user demands are served according to the max-min fairness rule, instead of proportional fairness.

We will compare CP and FQ in the botnet scenario (the third of the three scenarios discussed in §1). We assume that the malicious user is operating by hijacking resources from some number M of benign users. Thus, in CP, if the average benign user spends \$$x$, the malicious user can spend up to \$$Mx$ (this is the *fixed-ratio* model we discussed earlier, with $k = \frac{M}{B}$). In FQ, the malicious user can pretend to be up to M benign users.

Given resource bounds, the single-shot version of the game (which we have been considering so far) is trivially characterized – all the users simply spend their entire budget in the lone round of the game. In the multiple-round setting, the answer is less clear: attackers may choose, for example, to spend funds in a bursty manner in order to maximize damage when the network is vulnerable. Our analysis will show that with congestion pricing the same performance bounds as in the single-shot game apply in a more general multiple-round setting.

2.3 Metrics

As noted in §1, we study two metrics. First, the *total throughput-utility of all the benign players* is given by $L = \sum_b U_b(f_b)$ and represents the value of the network's service to benign users, ignoring payments.

Second, the *total utility of all the legitimate entities* in the system (i.e., all benign users and the network) is the sum of the net utilities of all the benign users and the total payment received by the network and is given by

$$\begin{aligned} U &= \left(\sum_b Q_b(f_b)\right) + \left(\sum_{l,b} p_{lb} + \sum_l p_{lm}\right) \\ &= L + \sum_l p_{lm}. \end{aligned}$$

Unlike L, in U we subtract what the benign users pay (inside the Q_b quantities), and add the payments the network receives. Most of these quantities cancel each other, so that the net change from L to U is that U includes the price the malicious users pay to the network. U essentially measures how well the malicious users' payments offset the damage they cause to the benign users.

We compare the values of U and L across three scenarios: *opt*, in which the network is controlled by an optimal controller that has perfect knowledge of the state of the entire system; *ben*, in which the benign players interact selfishly but the malicious players are not present in the system; and *mal*, in which the benign and malicious players all interact with each other. We use subscripts to identify scenarios (e.g. L_{mal}, U_{opt}). L and U are different only when the malicious user is present – i.e., only in the scenario *mal*.

3. CONGESTION PRICING

In this section we quantify the absolute efficiency of the market in the presence of malicious behavior. We start by establishing bounds in the special case when the network consists of a single shared link (§3.1) and then show that the same bounds apply in arbitrary networks (§3.2). The proofs of these results are in Appendix A.

3.1 Single Link

Before discussing our results, we first summarize the analysis by Johari and Tsitsiklis [14] of single-link games with only benign players.

THEOREM 3.1 (JOHARI AND TSITSIKLIS [14]). *Consider the set of all single-link games with $n > 1$ players, all benign, in which all $U_b(f_b)$ are non-negative, and strictly concave, strictly increasing and continuously differentiable in p_b*[4]*. Then:*

- *Each such game has a unique pure Nash equilibrium.*
- *In any such game, $\frac{L_{ben}}{L_{opt}} > \frac{3}{4}$, and this bound is tight, in that for all ϵ sufficiently small, there is always a game with $\frac{L_{ben}}{L_{opt}} = \frac{3}{4} + \epsilon$. In particular, for all $n > 1$, there is always a game $Benign_n^{opt}$ with n benign players for which $\frac{L_{ben}}{L_{opt}} = \frac{3n-4}{4n-6}$.*

Byzantine model

We start by considering the Byzantine model (which allows the malicious player arbitrary behavior) and bound the amount of damage the attacker can inflict on the total utility of all the legitimate entities in the system.

THEOREM 3.2. *Consider the set of all Byzantine-model single-link games in which every benign user's throughput-utility $U_b(f_b)$ is non-negative, and strictly concave, non-decreasing and continuously differentiable in $\vec{p_b}$. Then:*

- *Each such game has a unique pure Nash equilibrium.*
- *In any such game,*

$$\frac{U_{mal}}{U_{opt}} \geq \frac{3}{4} \quad \text{and} \quad \frac{U_{mal}}{U_{ben}} \geq \frac{3}{4}.$$

  These bounds are tight.

In other words, the attacker can cause U to fall 25% below U_{opt} or U_{ben}, but no more. Note also that since $U = L +$ (total price paid by the malicious player), U and L coincide when there are no malicious players in the system – which is the case in the scenarios *ben* and *opt*. Therefore, the second part of the theorem, in a sense, generalizes the known result that $\frac{U_{ben}}{U_{opt}} = \frac{L_{ben}}{L_{opt}} \geq \frac{3}{4}$ in games without malicious players.

Discussion

The restrictions on throughput-utility functions $U_b(f_b)$ bear some discussion. The non-negativity and non-decreasing restrictions simply say that the network's service never actively *hurts* the user and that having the option to send more data is never bad. These would appear to apply to all reasonable situations. The concavity assumption says that the user experiences either linear utility from more bandwidth, or diminishing returns. This does not include all real-world applications, but note that *even without malicious players*, only this class of utility functions has been analyzed [14].

Our proof of this theorem first establishes the existence of Nash equilibria using an adaptation of the earlier proof (originally due to Hajek and Gopalakrishnan [13]) for the case when all the players are benign. The key difficulty is that while in the original result all the players myopically optimize their own utilities, in our setting we have an additional player (the malicious player) whose own utility is a function of everyone else's utilities. This introduces an additional degree of coupling that needs to be handled specially. We then compute the listed bounds on the social utility U by constructing optimization problems to which they are the solutions. We show examples of how the computation might proceed in specific games later on in this section.

A potential issue with this result is that while we show that the malicious users have to pay enough to significantly offset the damage they cause, it is nevertheless true that their payments go to the *network operators*, and not directly to the *victims* of the attack. This distinction might not always be significant — for instance, in the simple case of protecting a single constrained resource (e.g. a server or data center), the resource owner can sell service itself without mediation from the network. But even if the network is a separate party, it may be possible for the network to pass on the benefits of these payments to its (non-malicious) end-users – either directly, in the form of a refund, or indirectly, such as through capacity augmentation. However, analyses of such approaches are beyond the scope of this paper. Note also that our results for the other two attacker models do quantify, in absolute terms, the actual amount of damage any given attacker can cause to the network's benign users.

Strategic model

By the definition of the Byzantine model, it follows that the stated bounds on the social utility apply in any pure equilibrium of any game in which the benign users' utility functions satisfy the conditions listed in Theorem 3.2, irrespective of the malicious user's utility function. The existence of a pure equilibrium isn't guaranteed, however. A sufficient condition is for the malicious user's utility to be concave in its payment. The requirements listed below in Theorem 3.3 essentially describe a special case of this condition.

In the strategic model, the same $\frac{3}{4}$ bound applies to the total utility, and we additionally bound the throughput utility L. However, as noted, we require stronger restrictions on the utility functions in order to guarantee the existence of an equilibrium.

THEOREM 3.3. *In the strategic model, if each $U_b(f_b)$ is non-negative, strictly concave and non-decreasing in $\vec{p_b}$, and strictly convex and non-increasing in $\vec{p_m}$, and the malicious player has spite coefficient σ_m, then:*

- *Each game has a unique pure Nash equilibrium.*
- $\frac{L_{mal}}{L_{opt}} \geq \min\left\{\frac{3}{4}, \frac{1}{1+\sigma_m}\right\}$
- *For any value of σ_m, $\frac{U_{mal}}{U_{opt}} \geq \frac{3}{4}$ and $\frac{U_{mal}}{U_{ben}} \geq \frac{3}{4}$.*

All the stated bounds are tight.

In the case of a single bottleneck link and in series-parallel networks, an example class of throughput-utility functions that satisfies the requirements are those of the form $U(x) = ax^d$, $a > 0$, $0 < d \leq 1$. We conjecture but have not proved that this is true for general networks as well.

The proof of this theorem proceeds along the same lines as the proof of Theorem 3.3.

[4]While U_b itself takes real arguments, the expression $U_b(f_b) = U_b(\frac{p_b}{P})$ is a vector function that depends on the bids of all players

Examples

Suppose we have a link with capacity 1 unit and consider the two-player game with one benign player b with utility $U_b(x_b) = x_b$, and one strategic malicious player m with spite coefficient σ_m. This simple example happens to demonstrate the worst case values of many of the metrics listed above. We now compute these metrics explicitly.

In both the optimal allocation and the scenario in which the malicious user is not present in the system, the entire link capacity would be allocated to the lone benign user. Thus, U_{opt} and U_{ben} (and hence L_{opt} and L_{ben}) are both equal to $U_b(1) = 1$.

Now suppose the malicious user does participate. Since in an equilibrium we must have $\frac{\partial Q_b}{\partial p_b} = 0 = \frac{\partial Q_m}{\partial p_m}$, we find that

$$p_b = \frac{\sigma_m}{(\sigma_m+1)^2},\ p_m = \frac{\sigma_m^2}{(\sigma_m+1)^2}$$

and that the bandwidth allocations are

$$x_b = \frac{1}{1+\sigma_m},\ x_m = \frac{\sigma_m}{1+\sigma_m}$$

Therefore, $L_{mal} = U_b(x_b) = \frac{1}{1+\sigma_m}$, and $U_{mal} = U_b(x_b) + p_m = \frac{1+\sigma_m+\sigma_m^2}{1+2\sigma_m+\sigma_m^2}$. U_{mal} is smallest when $\sigma_m = 1$, at which point its value is $\frac{3}{4}$. Observe that these match the worst case values listed in Theorem 3.3.

Now consider the game [14] which is the example of worst case behavior in games without malicious users. This game consists of one user (call it user 1) with utility $U(x) = x$ and infinitely many players each with utility $U(x) = \frac{x}{2}$. The optimal allocation would allot the entire link capacity to user 1 since that user values bandwidth the most, so that $U_{opt} = 1$. But in the Nash equilibrium, it can be shown that only half the capacity would go to user 1, and the other half would be split equally amongst all the other (infinitely many) players, so that $U_{ben} = 1 \cdot \frac{1}{2} + \frac{1}{2} \cdot \frac{1}{2} = \frac{3}{4}$.

We now show that U_{mal} in this game is also $\frac{3}{4}$ if we introduce a malicious user with spite coefficient $\sigma_m = 1$. That is, this game is another example in which $\frac{U_{mal}}{U_{opt}}$ exhibits its worst-case value. This is fairly easy to see — in this game, the malicious user essentially ends up pricing the infinitesimal players out of the system, and we are again left with the same two-player game we considered above, where we already noted that the value was $\frac{3}{4}$. Note, however, that $\frac{U_{mal}}{U_{ben}} = \frac{\frac{3}{4}}{\frac{3}{4}} = 1 > \frac{3}{4}$; $\frac{U_{mal}}{U_{ben}}$ does not display worst-case behaviour in this game. In fact, having started at a point where the Nash equilibrium was as far as possible from optimal, the attacker is unable to do further damage.

3.2 General Topology

We now need to show that the bounds we have listed in the single-link case also apply in arbitrary topologies. It turns out that the proof in [14] of an analogous result for games without malicious players can be adapted to this end as long as we can prove that the metrics $\frac{U_{mal}}{U_{opt}}$ and $\frac{U_{mal}}{U_{ben}}$ lie between 0 and 1 (as does the metric $\frac{L_{ben}}{L_{opt}}$ in games without malicious players). As a result, the same bounds we show in Theorems 3.2 and 3.3 apply to the case of arbitrary topologies. Appendix A.3 discusses the details and proofs.

4. THE BOTNET MODEL AND COMPARISON WITH FAIR QUEUEING

We now quantify the performance of congestion pricing (CP) in the Botnet model and show how it compares against fair queueing (FQ). In this section, we restrict ourselves to the special case when the network consists of a single bottleneck resource – without loss of generality, we will assume this bottleneck resource is a single shared link. Before discussing our general analytical results (§4.2) we start by describing a simple example showing why CP can outperform FQ (§4.1).

4.1 Example

Consider the following scenario, which describes a special case of our results for illustrative purposes. Suppose we have a population of $N = B + M$ users (B benign, M bots controlled by an attacker) that interact with the network, a single shared link of capacity 1 unit, over a long period of time. Suppose that most of the time the benign users place a very small value on network access, so that they would use the network if it were available, but would back off on observing a non-trivial amount of contention. However, every once in a while, the users experience some high-demand event that causes them to place a very high value on network access. A concrete example of a situation that fits this model would be for users to be executing background jobs (such as software update downloads) most of the time, but having to occasionally also execute human-facing tasks (such as webpage downloads).

Assume for the sake of simplicity that each (benign) user only experiences one of these high-demand events over the entire timeline, and that no two users experience high-demand events at the same point in time.

Simple unmodified fair-queueing performs rather poorly in this scenario, even in the absence of an attack. There is no incentive for any of the users (benign or malicious) to request any less than $\frac{1}{N}$ of the entire network capacity in each round. In particular, there is no incentive for any of the other users to back off when someone experiences a high-demand event. Therefore, the high-demand events – the only network events on which any user places value – all observe poor performance.

Now suppose we augment the fair-queued network with a volume-limiting mechanism which restricts the total amount of traffic any user can send over the entire timeline. Suppose the timeline is T rounds long. Ideally, if all the users were benign, we would want each of them to receive a bandwidth allocation of:

- $\frac{1}{N}$ in each of the $T - N$ rounds in which none of the users was experiencing a high-demand event
- 1 in the 1 round in which that user was experiencing a high-demand event
- 0 in the $N - 1$ rounds in which one of the other users was experiencing a high-demand event

Suppose we throttle users so that they can send no more than

$$(T-N) \cdot \frac{1}{N} + 1 \cdot 1 + 0 \cdot (N-1) = \frac{T}{N}$$

units of traffic over the entire timeline.

This still does not solve the problem: this is exactly the amount of traffic that users send out with unmodified fair-queueing. Users do not know (or necessarily care) when some other user is experiencing a high-demand event, and will continue to request significant amounts of network capacity in each round, whether they currently require it or not. But even if we can somehow ensure that the benign users in the system back off during high-demand events, there is no incentive for the malicious users to do so. The attacker can choose to concentrate exclusively on the points of time at which the network is experiencing a high-demand event and request high bandwidth during those times. Even if this slightly decreases the amount of traffic it can request at every other point in time, this is still a net gain for the attacker since the benign users place a low value on network access during these times anyway. Thus in this case a benign user would receive a bandwidth allocation of $\frac{1}{N}$ during a high-demand event if none of the users backed off, and $\frac{1}{M+1}$ if only the bots refused to back off.

Suppose now that the network implements congestion pricing. Every user is constrained to spend the same total amount of money over the entire timeline – call this amount 1 unit. In the absence of an attack, each user would spend small δ-amounts at each point in time in time at which it isn't experiencing a high-demand event, and a slightly higher amount when it is (just enough to drive the price of network usage high enough so that everyone else backs off).

Now consider how an attacker might affect the system. In order to cause the maximum amount of damage, the attacker should focus its resources on the B points of time at which high-demand events occur. It might choose to split its payment equally across each of these events (paying $\frac{M}{B}$ units at each of them), or it might target a specific user and spend its entire budget during that user's high-demand event. The damage it can cause in either case is limited; we look at the first here.

When a benign user observes contention (caused by the attacker) during a high-demand event, it can ramp up the amount it pays. If the value it places on network access during low-demand conditions is sufficiently low, it would simply redirect its payments so that it spends its entire budget (1 unit) during the high-demand event. The amount of bandwidth it then receives during the event is $\frac{1}{1+\frac{M}{B}} = \frac{B}{B+M}$, significantly larger than both the $\frac{1}{N}$ it would receive with unmodified fair-queueing and the $\frac{1}{1+M}$ it would receive in the best case with fair-queueing with volume limits. It does lose whatever value it would have gained at the other points in time (in low-demand conditions) but, by definition, this value is very small anyway, so that this ultimately represents a significant net gain for the benign user.

The reason congestion pricing outperforms fair queueing is that congestion pricing allows the benign players to pay more and therefore obtain a preferential bandwidth allocation during the periods of time at which they want to use the network the most – or, in other words, when their utility functions are the steepest. By treating all the users identically at every point in time, fair queueing, in effect, allows an attacker to cause damage disproportionate to its resources.

The scenario described here can be modeled more formally by defining a steep, high-value utility function for users that are experiencing a high-demand event and a slow-growing, low-value function for those that aren't. Values such as the δ in the above discussion fall out naturally from the rates of growth and the absolute values of these two functions. We omit the details.

4.2 Analytical Results

Proofs for these results are in Appendix B.

We first note the following simple result, which states that even in the absence of malicious behavior, CP is strictly better than FQ when the benign users have non-identical utilities.

THEOREM 4.1. *In every one-round single-link game in which all the players are benign and have concave, non-decreasing and non-negative utility functions, the net social utility* L_{ben}^{CP} *when the link implements congestion pricing is always at least the net social utility* L_{ben}^{FQ} *when the link implements fair queueing – that is,*

$$L_{ben}^{CP} \geq L_{ben}^{FQ}$$

The inequality is strict if the users have non-identical bandwidth allocations in the congestion pricing Nash equilibrium.[5]

Since our goal is to compare how CP and FQ are affected by malicious behavior, we will try to control for this advantage that CP has. In what follows, we will assume that in each round all active benign users have identical utility functions – in this case, both CP and FQ perform equally well (and induce Nash equilibria in which the link capacity is divided equally between the users in each round) in the absence of malicious behavior.

Formally, we have a multi-round, single-link game, with a population of B benign users and 1 malicious user controlling M bots, in which in each round t each of the n_t active benign users has the same throughput utility U^t. As in Theorem 3.3, we will require that each $U^t(x_{bt})$ be non-negative, strictly concave and non-decreasing in p_{bt}, and strictly convex and non-increasing in p_{mt}. As earlier, each active benign user b tries to optimize

$$Q_b^t(x_{bt}) = U^t(x_{bt}) - p_{bt}$$

However, now the malicious player seeks to

$$\text{minimize} \sum_t \sum_b U^t(x_{bt})$$

subject to the constraint

$$\sum_t p_{mt} \leq \frac{M}{B} \sum_t \sum_b p_{bt}$$

where B is the total size of the benign user population. This constraint essentially states that the malicious user cannot, in total, spend more than M times what the average benign user pays. Note that we only constrain the *total* amount of money the malicious user can spend – it is free to try to time its payments to maximize the damage it inflicts on the network (for example, by targeting the network in its periods of highest demand). We now show that the attacker cannot use this freedom to cause damage higher than the fraction of the total monetary resources it has available to it. Essentially, the payoff the attacker would receive from targeting the network at its most loaded is balanced by the high cost of participating in the congestion pricing market in high-demand conditions.

[5]Note that with simple fair queueing with no other constraints, there is nothing stopping every user from asking for the entire link capacity. Since the link does not differentiate between users, fair queueing would, therefore, end up alloting every user the same amount of bandwidth.

THEOREM 4.2. *In the game defined above,*

1. *If the network uses CP,* $\frac{L_{mal}}{L_{opt}} \geq \frac{1}{1+\frac{M}{B}} = \frac{B}{B+M}$. *This bound is tight, and is achieved in any one-round game in which all the benign users have (identical) linear utilities.*
2. *FQ allows the malicious user to obtain a fraction* $\frac{M}{M+n_t}$ *of the link capacity in each round* t. *This is strictly worse than CP unless every benign user participates in every round* ($\forall t.n_t = B$).

We have yet to analytically characterize how fair-queueing would perform if, in addition, traffic volume limits are imposed on all the users (because of technical difficulties induced by the max-min fairness rule used in fair-queueing). However, as the example discussed in the previous subsection shows, there are reasonable scenarios where volume limiting improves fair queueing by very little, if at all.

5. DISCUSSION

We answer here several natural questions about the results discussed in this paper and about deployment of congestion pricing in general.

Q. If the network has enough information about user identity to implement congestion pricing, isn't the DoS problem already solved?

A. No. First, implementing congestion pricing does not necessarily require that information about user identity be communicated. In Re-feedback [5], for example, each node only needs knowledge of a packet's previous hop, rather than the identity of the source, thus revealing no more information about the source of user traffic to any node in the network than the Internet does today.

Second, perfect information about user identity would not be sufficient to protect against DoS, either. Attackers have been known to initiate sophisticated application-level DoS attacks, generating requests that are hard to tell apart from legitimate traffic [32, 7]. In a case [31] from 2003, an attacker using a botnet to target a specific host started out using a simple SYN flood, but moved on to a sophisticated HTTP-level attack (sending out repeated requests for large images that could not be distinguished from the requests coming in from regular users) once the victim implemented SYN-flood countermeasures. The attack ultimately caused an estimated $2 million dollars worth of damage. The 2010 Arbor Networks survey [1] suggests application-level attacks are quite common, with more than 80% of respondents reporting HTTP-level attacks.

Q. Can per-packet congestion pricing scale to a large network?

A. One option is Re-feedback [5] which could be applied to implement congestion pricing at the packet level via lightweight non-cryptographic exchanges only between neighboring routers. However, the market mechanisms considered in this paper can be implemented at other levels of granularity, such as per user or between ISPs [34].

Of course, Internet-scale deployment of network layer changes is never easy. But we argue that congestion pricing is a plausible approach in targeted environments were changes are possible, perhaps including billing models between ISPs, or in cloud computing environments.

Q. Would human users be averse to being billed at a variable rate for each packet?

A. Not necessarily. For example, users have, in the past, accepted demand-based pricing for utilities such as electricity [3].

But more importantly, human users need not be directly involved in congestion pricing. The mechanics could be easily hidden from users by giving them a fixed budget per month, as is currently done for bandwidth by many Internet and cellular service providers, so that congestion pricing would only affect users that go over their monthly "congestion budget". Alternately, the mechanism could be used only between ISPs, or in a cloud computing environment where dynamically-variable resource pricing for tenants is already common [9] and human customers are not directly involved. Note that ISPs already commonly use pricing that penalizes peak loads by pricing at the 95th percentile of usage [27]; CP is effectively a more (economically) efficient version of this mechanism.

Q. Wouldn't users infected by bots end up paying for network usage which they did not initiate?

A. True. But we argue that this is *beneficial* because it changes the incentive structure, encouraging those who can do something about the problem to address it. In the current Internet, DoS attacks already cause a negative economic effect, in the form of a loss of service for the victim; congestion pricing shifts some of these effects from the victims to the parties that are (directly or indirectly) responsible. In particular, congestion pricing encourages:

1. *ISPs* to be more concerned about rogue activity on their networks (to reduce customer complaints);
2. *users and software vendors* to be more diligent in preventing and identifying malicious end-host behavior; and
3. *botmasters* to send less attack traffic in order to remain undetected.

6. RELATED WORK

DoS mitigation

Perhaps the simplest way to protect against DoS attacks is to increase service capacity, but this can be expensive and infeasible on short time scales. A second approach is to classify traffic as valid or malicious [39, 23, 36, 24, 12] and use this classification to reduce the volume of malicious traffic either by filtering malicious traffic or authorizing valid traffic (see [19, 20] and references therein). These methods have the disadvantages of imperfect classification [39, 23, 36], difficulty dealing with legitimate traffic not directly originated by humans [24, 12], and an inability to deal with sophisticated application-level attacks [32, 7, 31].

In *proof-of-work* schemes such as computational puzzles [8] or bandwidth work [35, 17], the network allots service to its users according to how much of their own local resources they are willing to spend — a kind of proxy for dollar payments. This approach is problematic, since

1. It wastes resources.
2. Local computational resources may not be reasonable as a proxy for monetary valuation when the users are

heterogeneous – for example, CPU proof-of-work would allow an attacker using a desktop to overwhelm a network of mobile users.

3. The relation between local computation and actual monetary worth is not straightforward – the opportunity cost for the user of using local resources for network payments depends heavily on precisely what else the user wants to do locally.

The congestion pricing approach we use does not suffer from these problems, since we use direct *payments* rather than proof-of-work. However, considering the simplicity of proof-of-work schemes, it might still be useful to characterize their DoS resilience formally. We believe the model we use in this paper is general enough that it can be adapted to achieve this characterization – we leave that to future work.

Congestion pricing has been primarily studied as a way to allocate bandwidth among legitimate selfish users [16, 5]. [21] shows through a simulation-based study that load-based pricing can protect individual servers against simple flooding attacks.

Game-theoretic analysis of congestion

Our basic game model is the market mechanism constructed by Kelly [16] for *elastic* traffic. The elastic traffic model assumes that the bandwidth requirement of each user is not static and that the users would, in general, be willing to pay more for larger bandwidth allocations. In a game-theoretic analysis of this model, Johari and Tsitsiklis [14] have shown that the efficiency of the market mechanism cannot fall more than 25% below optimal. This paper extends this analysis to games in which some of the users are malicious and seek to minimize the utility of the selfish (but benign) users in the system.

An alternate model is the *inelastic* traffic model [30], which assumes that the bandwidth requirement of each user is a fixed constant, but that the latency of each link is variable and that it increases as the congestion at the link increases. Recent work has studied the effect of malice on unpriced networks assuming an inelastic traffic model [2, 15, 10, 29]. In particular, Babaioff et al. [2] demonstrated that the amount of damage caused by a malicious user in an unpriced source routed network can potentially be unbounded in an arbitrary network, and Roth [29] analyzed the special case of linear congestion games and showed that the maximum amount of damage an attacker might cause can be bounded in terms of system and network parameters such as the diameter of the network and the slope of the latency functions.

We are not aware of any work studying the effects of malicious behaviour on priced networks with either the inelastic or the elastic traffic models.

7. CONCLUSION AND FUTURE WORK

Our analysis has shown that congestion pricing is a promising approach to mitigate denial of service attacks. This work points to two major directions in the future: game theoretic analysis of other DoS defense mechanisms, and the implications of congestion pricing.

The basic model we use is fairly general and can be adapted to study other forms of network and user behavior, and other DoS mitigation strategies. For example, our game-theoretic approach may be able to analyze the efficacy of the proof-of-work approach, or derive requirements on the accuracy and precision of traffic classifiers. As another example, our analysis did not treat the network itself as a strategic agent, and simply assumed that it would honestly implement the Kelly [16] pricing mechanism. Recent work by Kuleshov and Vetta [18] has shown how the game-theoretic network description considered in this paper can be extended to model the network as a rational agent. Other network models, such as the inelastic traffic model from §6, can also be analyzed in a game-theoretic setting.

In addition to the technical concerns, some of which are considered in this paper, congestion pricing also raises numerous questions that are economic and even societal in nature. For instance: (1) How does pricing affect the network's incentives to improve its resource provisiong? (2) If congestion pricing is implemented using actual monetary transfers, what happens to the payments that the users make to the network? Can they be refunded, somehow, without compromising the users' incentive to behave responsibly?

8. REFERENCES

[1] Worldwide Infrastructure Security Report Vol. VI, 2010. Arbor Networks.

[2] M. Babaioff, R. Kleinberg, and C. H. Papadimitriou. Congestion games with malicious players. In *EC '07: Proceedings of the 8th ACM conference on Electronic Commerce*, pages 103–112, New York, NY, USA, 2007. ACM.

[3] G. Barbose, C. Goldman, and B. Neenan. A survey of utility experience with real-time pricing. Technical Report LBNL-54238, Lawrence Berkeley National Laboratory, 2004. `http://eetd.lbl.gov/ea/ems/reports/54238.pdf`.

[4] B. Briscoe. Using self-interest to prevent malice; Fixing the denial of service flaw of the Internet. In *Proc Workshop on the Economics of Securing the Information Infrastructure*, Oct. 2006.

[5] B. Briscoe, A. Jacquet, C. Di Cairano-Gilfedder, A. Salvatori, A. Soppera, and M. Koyabe. Policing congestion response in an internetwork using re-feedback. *ACM SIGCOMM*, 35(4):288, 2005.

[6] Comcast Acceptable Use Policy. `http://www.comcast.com/Corporate/Customers/Policies/HighSpeedInternetAUP.html`.

[7] S. de Vries. Application level DoS attacks. Technical report, Corsaire, April 2004. `http://research.corsaire.com/whitepapers/technical.html`.

[8] C. Dwork and M. Naor. Pricing via processing or combatting junk mail. In *CRYPTO '92: Proceedings of the 12th Annual International Cryptology Conference on Advances in Cryptology*, pages 139–147, London, UK, 1993. Springer-Verlag.

[9] Amazon EC2 spot instances. `http://aws.amazon.com/ec2/spot-instances/`.

[10] M. Gairing. Malicious Bayesian congestion games. In *Proc. of the 6th Workshop on Approximation and Online Algorithms*, pages 119–132, 2008.

[11] P. B. Godfrey, I. Ganichev, S. Shenker, and I. Stoica. Pathlet routing. In *ACM SIGCOMM*, 2009.

[12] R. Gummadi, H. Balakrishnan, P. Maniatis, and S. Ratnasamy. Not-a-bot: improving service availability in the face of botnet attacks. In *NSDI'09:*

Proceedings of the 6th USENIX symposium on Networked systems design and implementation, 2009.

[13] B. Hajek and G. Gopal. Do greedy autonomous systems make for a sensible Internet? In *Conference on Stochastic Networks*, Stanford University, 2002.

[14] R. Johari and J. N. Tsitsiklis. Efficiency loss in a network resource allocation game. *Mathematics of Operations Research*, 29(3):407–435, 2004.

[15] G. Karakostas and A. Viglas. Equilibria for networks with malicious users. *Math. Program.*, 110(3):591–613, 2007.

[16] F. P. Kelly. Charging and rate control for elastic traffic. *European Transactions on Telecommunications*, 8:33–57, 1997.

[17] S. Khanna, S. S. Venkatesh, O. Fatemieh, F. Khan, and C. A. Gunter. Adaptive selective verification. *IEEE Conference on Computer Communications (INFOCOM '08)*, April 2008.

[18] V. Kuleshov and A. Vetta. On the efficiency of markets with two-sided proportional allocation mechanisms. In *Proceedings of the Third International Symposium on Algorithmic Game Theory (SAGT '10)*, Athens, Greece, October 2010.

[19] X. Liu, X. Yang, and Y. Lu. To filter or to authorize: Network-layer DoS defense against multimillion-node botnets. *ACM SIGCOMM*, 38(4):195–206, 2008.

[20] X. Liu, X. Yang, and Y. Xia. NetFence: preventing Internet denial of service from inside out. In *ACM SIGCOMM*, 2010.

[21] D. Mankins, R. Krishnan, C. Boyd, J. Zao, and M. Frentz. Mitigating distributed denial of service attacks with dynamic resource pricing. In *ACSAC '01: Proceedings of the 17th Annual Computer Security Applications Conference*, page 411, Washington, DC, USA, 2001. IEEE Computer Society.

[22] D. McPherson. Fire or DDoS - which is more probable?, January 2010. http://asert.arbornetworks.com/2010/01/fire-or-ddos-which-is-more-probable.

[23] J. Mirkovic and P. Reiher. D-WARD: A source-end defense against flooding denial-of-service attacks. *IEEE Trans. Dependable Secur. Comput.*, 2(3):216–232, 2005.

[24] W. Morein, A. Stavrou, D. Cook, A. Keromytis, V. Misra, and D. Rubenstein. Using graphic Turing tests to counter automated DDoS attacks against web servers. In *Proceedings of the 10th ACM conference on Computer and communications security*, page 19. ACM, 2003.

[25] M. Motiwala, M. Elmore, N. Feamster, and S. Vempala. Path splicing. In *ACM SIGCOMM*, 2008.

[26] J. Nagle. On packet switches with infinite storage. *Communications, IEEE Transactions on*, 35(4):435 – 438, Apr. 1987.

[27] A. M. Odlyzko. Internet pricing and the history of communications. *Computer Networks and ISDN Systems*, 36:493–517, 2001.

[28] T. Ristenpart, E. Tromer, H. Shacham, and S. Savage. Hey, you, get off of my cloud: exploring information leakage in third-party compute clouds. In *Proceedings of the 16th ACM conference on Computer and communications security*, CCS '09, pages 199–212, New York, NY, USA, 2009. ACM.

[29] A. Roth. The price of malice in linear congestion games. In *Proceedings of the 4th International Workshop on Internet and Network Economics*, WINE '08, pages 118–125, Berlin, Heidelberg, 2008. Springer-Verlag.

[30] T. Roughgarden. *Selfish Routing and the Price of Anarchy*. The MIT Press, 2005.

[31] SecurityFocus. FBI busts alleged DDoS mafia. `http://www.securityfocus.com/news/9411`.

[32] M. Srivatsa, A. Iyengar, J. Yin, and L. Liu. A middleware system for protecting against application level denial of service attacks. In M. van Steen and M. Henning, editors, *Middleware 2006*, volume 4290 of *Lecture Notes in Computer Science*, pages 260–280. Springer Berlin / Heidelberg, 2006.

[33] D. Stiliadis and A. Varma. Latency-rate servers: a general model for analysis of traffic scheduling algorithms. *Networking, IEEE/ACM Transactions on*, 6(5):611 -624, Oct. 1998.

[34] V. Valancius, N. Feamster, R. Johari, and V. Vazirani. MINT: A market for Internet transit. In *ACM ReArch*, 2008.

[35] M. Walfish, M. Vutukuru, H. Balakrishnan, D. Karger, and S. Shenker. DDoS defense by offense. In *ACM SIGCOMM*, 2006.

[36] H. Wang, D. Zhang, and K. G. Shin. Change-point monitoring for the detection of DoS attacks. *IEEE Trans. Dependable Secur. Comput.*, 1(4):193–208, 2004.

[37] X. Yang, D. Clark, and A. Berger. NIRA: a new inter-domain routing architecture. *IEEE/ACM Transactions on Networking*, 15(4):775–788, 2007.

[38] X. Yang and D. Wetherall. Source selectable path diversity via routing deflections. In *ACM SIGCOMM*, 2006.

[39] G. Zhang, S. Jiang, G. Wei, and Q. Guan. A prediction-based detection algorithm against distributed denial-of-service attacks. In *IWCMC '09: Proceedings of the 2009 International Conference on Wireless Communications and Mobile Computing*, pages 106–110, New York, NY, USA, 2009. ACM.

APPENDIX

A. PROOFS OF RESULTS IN §3

We establish Theorem 3.3 first, and then derive Theorem 3.2 from it.

A.1 Single Link: Strategic Model (Thm 3.3)

We discuss each of the assertions in the theorem in turn.

Nash Equilibrium

THEOREM A.1. *Any game with utility functions satisfying the constraints listed in Theorem 3.3 has a unique pure Nash equilibrium.*

PROOF. Our proof adapts the demonstration by Hajek and Gopalakrishnan [13] of a similar result for games consisting solely of benign players. The primary difficulty in this adaptation lies in handling an additional coupled constraint introduced by the presence of the malicious player.

First note that in any Nash equilibrium, at least two users must participate in the system (i.e., must have positive bid values) – in any situation in which only one or zero users have positive bids, at least one user in the system has incentive to deviate. This ensures that (i) the market operates according to the proportional allocation mechanism (the base case when $P = 0$ does not apply), (ii) each x_i is strictly increasing as a function of p_i, and whenever positive is strictly decreasing as a function of p_u for $u \neq i$, and that (iii) no one user is allocated the entire link capacity.

Now, as noted in Theorem 3.3, we assume that the expression $U_i(x_i)$ is strictly concave and strictly increasing in p_i, guaranteeing that the same properties hold for Q_i. Further, since each U_i is also assumed to be strictly convex and strictly decreasing in p_m, $Q_m = -\sigma_m \sum_i U_i - p_m$ must again be strictly concave and strictly increasing in p_m[6]. Therefore, $\vec{p} = (p_u)$ is a Nash equilibrium for the given game iff for all users u

$$\frac{\partial Q_u}{\partial p_u} = 0 \quad \text{if } p_u > 0$$
$$\frac{\partial Q_u}{\partial p_u} \leq 0 \quad \text{if } p_u = 0$$

Computing these partial derivatives and simplifying using properties (ii) and (iii) listed above, we find that these conditions are equivalent to requiring that $\vec{p}$ satisfy

$$U_i'(x_i)\left(1 - \frac{x_i}{C}\right) = \frac{P}{C} \quad \text{if } x_i > 0, \text{ for } i = 1 \dots n$$
$$U_i'(0) \leq \frac{P}{C} \quad \text{if } x_i = 0, \text{ for } i = 1 \dots n$$
$$\sum_{i=1}^{n} x_i + x_m = 1$$
$$\sum_{i=1}^{n} \frac{x_i}{1 - x_i} = \frac{1}{\sigma_m} \quad \text{if } x_m > 0$$
$$\sum_{i=1}^{n} \frac{x_i}{1 - x_i} \leq \frac{1}{\sigma_m} \quad \text{if } x_m = 0$$

It is fairly easy to verify that $\vec{p}$ satisfies these requirements iff the allocations x_i it induces are a solution to the following optimization problem (see [13] for a more detailed exposition in the purely benign setting)

$$\begin{aligned} \text{minimize} \quad & \sum_i \hat{U}_i(x_i) \\ \text{subject to} \quad & x_i \geq 0 \quad \text{for } i = 1 \dots n \\ & \sum_{i=1}^{n} x_i \leq C \\ & \sum_{i=1}^{n} \frac{x_i}{1 - x_i} \leq \frac{1}{\sigma_m} \\ & \text{at most one of the last two inequalities} \\ & \text{being strict} \\ \text{where} \quad & \hat{U}_i \text{ is an antiderivative of } U_i \end{aligned}$$

The objective function is identical to the one used in [13], where it is shown that it must be strictly concave and strictly increasing in each argument. Now note that the constraints listed above delineate a non-empty, convex and compact feasible region. Therefore, this optimization problem must have a unique solution, the bandwidth allocations in which define the unique pure equilibrium of the game. □

The detailed derivation above (as well as in what follows) is necessary; the results cannot be derived more directly from those of Johari and Tsitsiklis [14]. Consider for example the following possible proof of the above theorem:

"Add a large positive constant K to the malicious user's utility function. Since K is a constant, it does not change the equilibrium state. Every player's utility now satisfies all the conditions required by Theorem 3.1 (which summarizes the results of Johari and Tsitsiklis [14]), with the malicious player now effectively becoming just another benign player. The existence of the Nash equilibrium now follows directly."

The problem with this argument is that the results of Johari and Tsitsiklis [14] cannot be applied in this way. While the new set of utility functions does satisfy all the conditions listed explicitly in Theorem 3.1, it fails an implicit structural requirement. The results of Johari and Tsitsiklis [14] assume that every player's net utility function has the form [U(bandwidth allocated) – price paid]: that is, that every player's utility depends only on its own bandwidth allocation and its own payment. But in our case the malicious player's utility is a function of everyone else's payments and everyone else's utilities.

Note also that even if the above argument were valid, it could not be extended to derive the bounds listed in this paper. Consider for instance the case $\sigma_m = 1$. Now all Theorem 3.1 would imply is

$$\frac{(K - \sum_b U_b) + \sum_b U_b}{K} > \frac{3}{4} \iff 1 > \frac{3}{4}$$

which is less than helpful.

Observe that the constraints in Theorem A.1 characterize the unique equilibrium entirely in terms of the marginal utilities (the first derivatives of the utility functions). Therefore, given a game with arbitrary utility functions, we can always construct an equivalent game with linear utility functions that has the same equilibrium allocations – essentially, replace each utility function with its tangent at the equilibrium point. Now, since each utility function $U_i(x_i)$ is assumed to be concave, we must have

$$U_i'(x_i)(x_i - 0) \leq U_i(x_i) - U_i(0)$$

Since both our metrics essentially try to minimize $\sum_i U_i(x_i)$, this shows that it is sufficient to consider only games with linear utility functions (see [14] for a more formal proof). Further, it can easily be shown [14] that if the throughput-utilities are all non-negative, worst-case behaviour will be observed in games in which all the utility functions pass through the origin (i.e., $U_i(0) = 0$).

Therefore, when computing values for our metrics, we will assume, without loss of generality, that all utility functions are of the form $U_i(x_i) = a_i x_i$, $a_i > 0$ a constant.

Bounding $\frac{L_{mal}}{L_{opt}}$

THEOREM A.2. *In any game in which the malicious player has spite coefficient σ_m and in which $p_m > 0$ in the unique*

[6]Note that we only actually require that the *aggregate* function $\sum_i U_i$ satisfies the convexity and monotonicity requirements. Requiring that each *individual* U_i does so too is a sufficient (but not necessary) condition for ensuring this.

equilibrium, $\frac{L_{mal}}{L_{opt}} \geq \frac{1}{1+\sigma_m}$*, and there is always one such game in which equality is achieved.*

PROOF. As was noted above, it is sufficient to consider just the class of games with linear utility functions passing through the origin. Suppose we have n benign users, each with utility function of the form $U_i(x_i) = a_i x_i$. The optimal allocation (the one that maximizes the social utility $\sum_i a_i x_i$) simply allocates the entire capacity to the user v with highest marginal utility a_v. Without loss of generality, we may assume that $v = 1$ (else we can just reorder the players).

Our goal now is to find a combination of utility functions (that is, a combination of a_i values) that minimizes the ratio $\frac{\sum_i a_i x_i}{a_1 C}$. Note that the x_i are dependent variables – each combination of a_i completely determines the unique Nash equilbrium allocations x_i. Conversely, given any reasonable combination of bandwidth allocations x_i, we can always find a combination of linear utility functions for which this allocation is the equilibrium. Therefore, we may also recast our problem in terms of an optimization over the space of all reasonable flows. In what follows, we shall use this second formulation (which happens to be more concise than the first).

Adding in all the constraints on the Nash equilibrium and simplifying, our optimization problem translates to

$$\text{minimize} \quad \frac{1-x_1}{\sigma_m} \tag{1}$$

$$\text{subject to} \quad 0 \leq x_i \leq x_1 \quad \text{for i = 2,...,n} \tag{2}$$

$$\sum_{i=1}^{n} x_i < 1 \tag{3}$$

$$\sum_{i=1}^{n} \frac{x_i}{1-x_i} = \frac{1}{\sigma_m} \tag{4}$$

Note that we essentially need to maximize x_1 subject to the given constraints. Considering constraint (4), and noting that the other constraints imply that we must have $0 \leq x_i < 1$ for all i, we see that x_1 is maximized when $x_1 = \frac{1}{1+\sigma_m}$ and all other x_i are 0 – that is, when we only effectively have one benign player in the game. The minimum possible value of $\frac{L_{mal}}{L_{opt}}$, which is the solution to this optimization problem, is therefore $\frac{1-\frac{\sigma_m}{1+\sigma_m}}{\sigma_m} = \frac{1}{1+\sigma_m}$.

This bound is tight – it is achieved in the two player game defined by one benign player with throughput-utility $U(x) = x$ and one malicious player with spite coefficient σ_m. □

Recall that in games without malicious players, the least possible value of $\frac{L_{ben}}{L_{opt}}$, $\frac{3n-4}{4n-6}$ in an n-player game (note that $\lim_{n\to\infty} \frac{3n-4}{4n-6} = \frac{3}{4}$), is achieved in a game that we refer to as $Benign_n^{opt}$ (see Theorem 3.1).

LEMMA 1. *If* $\sigma_m < \frac{1}{2}$*, the malicious user has no incentive to participate in the game* $Benign_n^{opt}$ *for any* $n \geq 2$*; that is, if a malicious player* m *with this value of* σ_m *were to be added to this game,* p_m *would be* 0.

PROOF. We first describe $Benign_n^{opt}$ in full. The game includes one benign player with utility $U(x) = x$ and $n-1$ benign players each with utility $U(x) = \frac{x}{2-\frac{1}{n-1}}$. In the equilibrium, the first player is allocated half the capacity of the link and the remaining half of the capacity is split uniformly across all the other players.

Since we have shown that all games with malicious players have unique Nash equilibria, it is sufficient to show that the throughput allocation in the previous paragraph satisfies all the conditions for a Nash equilibrium with $p_m = 0$ when the malicious user is added to the system. The only new constraint is the one based on the marginal utility of the malicious player – it is sufficient to show that $\sum_i \frac{x_i}{1-x_i} < \frac{1}{\sigma_m}$.

Now for this throughput allocation, we have

$$\begin{aligned} \sum_i \frac{x_i}{1-x_i} &= \frac{\frac{1}{2}}{1-\frac{1}{2}} + (n-1)\frac{\frac{1}{2(n-1)}}{1-\frac{1}{2(n-1)}} \\ &= 1 + \frac{1}{2-\frac{1}{n-1}} \\ &\leq 2 \text{ (equality at n = 2)} \\ &< \frac{1}{\sigma_m} \text{ when } \sigma_m < \frac{1}{2} \end{aligned}$$

□

COROLLARY 1. *Consider the game obtained by adding a malicious player with spite coefficient* $\sigma_m < \frac{1}{2}$ *to* $Benign_n^{opt}$*. In this game,* $\frac{L_{mal}}{L_{opt}} = \frac{U_{mal}}{U_{opt}} = \frac{L_{ben}}{L_{opt}} = \frac{3n-4}{4n-6}$.

PROOF. Observe that the definitions of $\frac{L_{mal}}{L_{opt}}$, $\frac{U_{mal}}{U_{opt}}$ and $\frac{L_{ben}}{L_{opt}}$ all coincide in games in which no malicious players participate. The result now follows from Lemma 1. □

THEOREM A.3. *In any game satisfying the constraints listed in Theorem 3.3,* $\frac{L_{mal}}{L_{opt}} \geq \min\left\{\frac{3}{4}, \frac{1}{1+\sigma_m}\right\}$*. Further, this bound is tight for any value of* σ_m.

PROOF. Let $part_m(\sigma_m)$ denote the minimum possible value of $\frac{L_{mal}}{L_{opt}}$ over the set of games in Theorem 3.3 in which the malicious user has spite coefficient σ_m and participates in the game ($p_m > 0$), and $nopart_m(\sigma_m)$ the minimum possible value of $\frac{L_{mal}}{L_{opt}}$ over the games in which the malicious user has a spite coefficient σ_m and does not participate ($p_m = 0$). Now, for any fixed σ_m, the minimum possible value of $\frac{L_{mal}}{L_{opt}}$ over the entire set of games is the smaller of $part_m(\sigma_m)$ and $nopart_m(\sigma_m)$.

Theorem A.2 shows that for any σ_m, $part_m(\sigma_m) = \frac{1}{1+\sigma_m}$, and that there is a game which achieves this value. Theorem 3.1 shows that $nopart_m(\sigma_m)$ is bounded below by $\frac{3}{4}$, and Lemma 1 shows that the bound is tight as long as $\sigma_m < \frac{1}{2}$.

The result now follows by noting that:

1. For $\sigma_m > \frac{1}{3}$, $\frac{1}{1+\sigma_m} < \frac{3}{4}$. As we have just discussed, the $\frac{1}{1+\sigma_m}$ bound is exact – there is a game achieving this value.

2. If $\sigma_m \leq \frac{1}{3}$, $\frac{1}{1+\sigma_m} \geq \frac{3}{4}$, and further $\sigma_m < \frac{1}{2}$, ensuring that Lemma 1 applies, and that, therefore, the bound of $\frac{3}{4}$ holds and is tight.

□

Bounding $\frac{U_{mal}}{U_{opt}}$ and $\frac{U_{mal}}{U_{ben}}$

LEMMA 2. *If* $\sigma_m \geq 1$*, the malicious user always participates in the game – that is,* $p_m > 0$.

PROOF. We start by assuming that $p_m = 0$ and establish a contradiction to the equilibrium requirement $\sum_i \frac{x_i}{1-x_i} \leq \frac{1}{\sigma_m}$.

If $p_m = 0$, $\sum_{i=1}^n x_i = 1$. Under this constraint, $\sum_i \frac{x_i}{1-x_i}$ is minimized by the symmetric allocation which sets $x_i = \frac{1}{n}$ for all i. Therefore,

$$\sum_i \frac{x_i}{1-x_i} \geq \frac{n \times \frac{1}{n}}{1-\frac{1}{n}} = \frac{1}{1-\frac{1}{n}} > 1 \geq \frac{1}{\sigma_m}$$

□

THEOREM A.4. *In any game with $\sigma_m \geq 1$, $\frac{U_{mal}}{U_{opt}} \geq \frac{\sigma_m^2+\sigma_m+1}{\sigma_m^2+2\sigma_m+1}$. Further, this bound is tight – for any value of σ_m, there is a game that achieves this bound.*

PROOF. Proceeding along the lines of Theorem A.2, we find that the minimum possible value of $\frac{U_{mal}}{U_{opt}}(\sigma_m)$ is the solution to the optimization problem

$$\text{minimize} \quad (1-x_1)\left[\frac{1}{\sigma_m} + 1 - \sum_{i=1}^n x_i\right] \tag{5}$$

$$\text{subject to} \quad 0 \leq x_i \leq x_1 \quad \text{for i} = 2,\ldots,\text{n} \tag{6}$$

$$\sum_{i=1}^n x_i < 1 \tag{7}$$

$$\sum_{i=1}^n \frac{x_i}{1-x_i} = \frac{1}{\sigma_m} \tag{8}$$

First fix the value of x_1. It can be shown (by induction on the number of players) that, ignoring constraints (6) and (7), the objective is minimized when all x_i $(i \neq 1)$ are equal. The values of all these x_i can be computed explicitly in terms of x_1 using (8).

It can also be shown that this solution satisfies constraints (6) and (7) iff

$$\frac{1}{1+n\sigma_m} \leq x_1 \leq \frac{1}{1+\sigma_m}$$

Since x_1 cannot exceed $\frac{1}{1+\sigma_m}$ without violating constraint (8), we only need to consider the following two cases:

1. $x_1 < \frac{1}{1+n\sigma_m}$

   Let *obj* denote the objective function. We must have

$$\begin{aligned} obj &\geq (1-x_1)\left(\frac{1}{\sigma_m} + 1 - nx_1\right) \quad \text{(by (6))} \\ &> \left(1 - \frac{1}{1+n\sigma_m}\right)\left(\frac{1}{\sigma_m} + 1 - \frac{n}{1+n\sigma_m}\right) \\ &= \frac{n + n\sigma_m + n^2\sigma_m^2}{1 + 2n\sigma_m + n^2\sigma_m^2} \end{aligned}$$

   This last value is minimized by $n = 1$, at which point its value is $\frac{1+\sigma_m+\sigma_m^2}{1+2\sigma_m+\sigma_m^2}$.

2. $\frac{1}{1+n\sigma_m} \leq x_1 \leq \frac{1}{1+\sigma_m}$

   In this case the objective can be expressed as a univariate function of x_1 using the solution described above. The first derivative test can be used to establish that when $\sigma_m \geq 1$, the objective is monotonically decreasing in x_1 over the range listed in the case assumption. Therefore, the objective is minimized when $x_1 = \frac{1}{1+\sigma_m}$, implying that $x_i = 0$ for $i \neq 1$, and this minimum value is $\frac{1+\sigma_m+\sigma_m^2}{1+2\sigma_m+\sigma_m^2}$.

We therefore find that the optimal value is $\frac{\sigma_m^2+\sigma_m+1}{\sigma_m^2+2\sigma_m+1}$, and that, as in Theorem A.2, this optimal value is attained in a two-player game with one benign player with throughput-utility $U(x) = x$ and one malicious player with spite coefficient σ_m. □

Let $LowerBound_{\frac{mal}{opt}}(\sigma_m)$ denote the minimum possible value of $\frac{U_{mal}}{U_{opt}}$ over the set of all games in which the malicious user has spite coefficient σ_m. Define $LowerBound_{\frac{mal}{ben}}(\sigma_m)$ analogously.

LEMMA 3. *$\sigma_m = 1$ must minimize $LowerBound_{\frac{mal}{opt}}(\sigma_m)$. That is,*
$LowerBound_{\frac{mal}{opt}}(\sigma_m) \geq LowerBound_{\frac{mal}{opt}}(1) = \frac{3}{4}$.

PROOF. When $\sigma_m = 1$, the net utility of the malicious player is given by

$$Q_m = -\sum_i U_i - p_m$$

That is, the malicious user acts so as to minimize the value of $(\sum_i U_i + p_m)$. But this is exactly the numerator of the metric $\frac{U_{mal}}{U_{opt}}$. Therefore, for any given combination of throughput utilities for the benign players, $\frac{U_{mal}}{U_{opt}}$ is minimized when the malicious player has $\sigma_m = 1$, and thus the metric $LowerBound_{\frac{mal}{opt}}$ over the entire set of games must also be minimized by $\sigma_m = 1$. □

COROLLARY 2.

$$\begin{aligned} &\min_{\sigma_m > 0} LowerBound_{\frac{mal}{ben}}(\sigma_m) \\ &= \min_{\sigma_m > 0} LowerBound_{\frac{mal}{opt}}(\sigma_m) \\ &= LowerBound_{\frac{mal}{ben}}(1) \\ &= LowerBound_{\frac{mal}{opt}}(1) \\ &= \frac{3}{4} \end{aligned}$$

PROOF. Note that in any game, it follows directly from the definitions that $\frac{U_{mal}}{U_{ben}} \geq \frac{U_{mal}}{U_{opt}}$. Now, by Lemma 3 and Theorem A.4, $\min_{\sigma_m} LowerBound_{\frac{mal}{opt}}(\sigma_m)$ is achieved at $\sigma_m = 1$ in a game with exactly one benign player, and in such games, when the malicious players are removed, the social utility is the same in both the optimal and the equilibrium allocations. The result now follows from Lemma 3. □

A.2 Single Link: Byzantine Model (Thm 3.2)

Observe that the results in this theorem hold for a wider range of the benign users' utility functions than in the strategic model (cf. Theorem 3.3). The additional constraints in Theorem 3.3 were necessary to ensure the existence of an equilibrium, as noted in §3.

The existence of a unique Nash equilibirum in these games can be established using a proof that is more or less identical to the one in Theorem A.1. We omit the details.

Further, it can be shown that, as in the strategic model, it is sufficient to consider just the class of games in which the benign users' throughput-utilities are all linear functions passing through the origin when establishing bounds on $\frac{U_{mal}}{U_{opt}}$ and $\frac{U_{mal}}{U_{ben}}$. The fact that the same bound as in the strategic model ($\frac{3}{4}$) applies here now follows from the following observation.

THEOREM A.5. *Consider the class of games in which the benign users' throughput-utilities are all linear functions passing through the origin. The strategic and the Byzantine models are interchangeable in these games; it is always possible to replace a strategic malicious player with an equivalent Byzantine player (and vice-versa) without changing the prices paid by any of the players (benign or malicious) – and thus without changing the value of the $\frac{U_{mal}}{U_{opt}}$ or $\frac{U_{mal}}{U_{ben}}$ metrics.*

PROOF. The proof in the forward direction is trivial. Suppose the malicious player pays p_m in the equilibrium in a strategic model game. Then we may simply replace this player with a Byzantine malicious player that always pays p_m without affecting any of the equilibrium conditions.

Now for the reverse direction, suppose we have a game with a Byzantine malicious player that pays p_m, and that $\langle x_1, \ldots, x_n \rangle$ represent the bandwidth allocations to all the benign players in the equilibrium. Then it is easy to see that replacing the malicious player with a strategic player whose σ_m value is given by equation (8) preserves the prices paid by and the throughputs allocated to all the players in the system. □

A.3 General Topology

As noted in §3.2, the proof in [14] of an analogous result for games without malicious players can be adapted to show that the bounds in the single-link case extend to arbitrary topologies once we establish the following intermediate result, which states that the $\frac{U_{mal}}{U_{opt}}$ and $\frac{U_{mal}}{U_{ben}}$ metrics in games with malicious players lie between 0 and 1, as does the $\frac{L_{ben}}{L_{opt}}$ metric in games with only benign players.

LEMMA 4. *Consider any single-link game with $n \geq 1$ benign users, each of whose throughput utilities U_i are of the form $a_i x_i$, $a_i > 0$ a constant, and one Byzantine malicious player which plays the fixed price p_m. The social utility $U_{mal} = \sum_b U_b(x_b) + p_m$ in the unique pure Nash equilibirum in this game is not more than the social utility in the optimal allocation.*

PROOF. Proceeding as in Theorem A.4 and simplifying, we find that we essentially need to

$$\text{prove that } (1 - x_1)\left[x_m + \sum_{i=1}^{n} \frac{x_i}{1 - x_i}\right] \leq 1 \quad (9)$$

$$\text{subject to } 0 \leq x_i \leq x_1 < 1 \quad \text{for i} = 2, \ldots, \text{n} \quad (10)$$

$$\sum_{i=1}^{n} x_i + x_m = 1 \quad (11)$$

This is true since

$$\begin{aligned} LHS &\leq (1 - x_1)\left[\frac{x_m}{1 - x_1} + \sum_{i=1}^{n} \frac{x_i}{1 - x_i}\right] && \text{(by (10))} \\ &\leq (1 - x_1)\left[\frac{x_m}{1 - x_1} + \sum_{i=1}^{n} \frac{x_i}{1 - x_1}\right] && \text{(by (10))} \\ &= (1 - x_1)\left[\frac{x_m + \sum_{i=1}^{n} x_i}{1 - x_1}\right] \\ &= 1 && \text{(by (11))} \end{aligned}$$

□

However, we note that in order to guarantee stability in the strategic model, we require the presence of a virtual agent operated by the network controller that plays a small ϵ price at each link (ϵ can be arbitrarily small). This is needed to handle the resource allocation at links which are not bottlenecked – the ϵ-player essentially soaks up all the excess capacity in such links. Johari and Tsitsiklis [14] considered this ϵ-player in games without malicious players, and showed that the need for it could be removed by using an expanded version of the market mechanism in which players send auxiliary information (along with the prices) to the links – this enables the players to obtain non-zero bandwidth allocations from non-bottleneck links even with a zero price payment. However, this expanded mechanism does not work in the presence of malicious behavior.

B. PROOFS OF RESULTS IN § 4

PROOF OF THEOREM 4.1. Suppose we have a $B > 1$ player game, and assume WLOG that the link has capacity 1 unit. Let U_b and x_b denote respectively the throughput utility function and bandwidth allocation in the congestion pricing Nash equilibrium of user b, and let P denote the total payment to the link from all the users in the equilibrium.

Suppose A of the B players received non-zero bandwidth allocations in the congestion pricing NE. Order the players so that these are the players numbered 1 through A. Now

$$\begin{aligned} &\sum_{b=1}^{B} U_b(x_b) - U_b(\frac{1}{B}) \\ &= \sum_{b=1}^{A}\left[U_b(x_b) - U_b(\frac{1}{B})\right] + \sum_{b=A+1}^{B}\left[U_b(0) - U_b(\frac{1}{B})\right] \\ &\geq \sum_{b=1}^{A}\left[U_b^{'}(x_b)\left(x_b - \frac{1}{B}\right)\right] + \sum_{b=A+1}^{B}\left[U_b^{'}(0)\left(0 - \frac{1}{B}\right)\right] \\ &\geq \sum_{b=1}^{A} \frac{x_b - \frac{1}{B}}{1 - x_b} P - \sum_{b=A+1}^{B} P\left(0 - \frac{1}{B}\right) \\ &\geq \sum_{b=1}^{A} \frac{x_b - \frac{1}{B}}{1 - \frac{1}{B}} P - \sum_{b=A+1}^{B} P\frac{1}{B} \\ &= \frac{1 - \frac{A}{B}}{1 - \frac{1}{B}} P - (B - A)\frac{1}{B} P \\ &\geq 0 \end{aligned}$$

where the first inequality step uses the concavity of the U_b, the second uses the first derivative characterization of the

Nash equilibrium (see Theorem A.1), and the third follows from a simple analysis of the two cases $x_b < \frac{1}{B}$ and $x_b \geq \frac{1}{B}$.

Following the proof, it is easy to see that equality occurs only if $A = B$ and $x_b = \frac{1}{B}$ for all b. □

PROOF OF THEOREM 4.2.

Proof of part 1. First note that our argument in Appendix A for restricting our attention to linear utility functions continues to apply here – given any game with arbitrary concave utility functions, there is a corresponding game with the same equilibrium payments and bandwidth allocations but in which (i) the benign users all have linear utilities, and (ii) the values of the social utility metrics we try to bound are no better than they were in the original game. Hence we will assume that each of the n_t benign users in round t has the utility function $U^t(x) = a_t x$. Further, we will assume WLOG that the link has capacity 1 unit.

Constructing a first-derivative formulation as in the proof of Theorem A.2, we find that the required worst-case value of $\frac{L_{mal}}{L_{opt}}$ is the solution to

$$\begin{aligned}
\text{minimize} \quad & \frac{\sum_t n_t a_t x_{bt}}{\sum_t a_t} \\
\text{subject to} \quad & a_t(1 - x_{bt}) = P_t \\
& n_t a_t x_{bt} = \lambda P_t \quad \text{if} \quad p_{mt} > 0 \\
& \qquad\quad \leq \lambda_t P_t \quad \text{if} \quad p_{mt} = 0 \\
& \sum_t p_{mt} \leq \frac{M}{B} \sum_t n_t p_{bt} \\
& P_t = n_t p_{bt} + P_t \\
& p_{bt} \geq 0, p_{mt} \geq 0
\end{aligned}$$

We first consider the case when $\forall t. p_{mt} > 0$. Writing $r_t = n_t a_t x_{bt}$, noting that the inequality constraint on the malicious player's budget would be an equality constraint in any solution to the minimization problem (there is no reason for the malicious player to spend less than it is allowed to), and simplifying, we find that the solution to the above problem is lower-bounded by the solution to[7]

$$\begin{aligned}
\text{minimize} \quad & \frac{\sum_t r_t}{\sum_t a_t} \\
\text{subject to} \quad & \sum_t r_t = \left(\frac{M}{B} + 1\right) \sum_t \frac{r_t^2}{a_t} \\
& 0 < r_t < a_t
\end{aligned}$$

It can now be shown that the solution to this problem is $\frac{1}{1+\frac{M}{B}}$, obtained by setting $r_t = \frac{1}{1+\frac{M}{B}} a_t$.

The fact that this bound is the actual lower bound (and that it is tight) follows by noting that it is achieved in any single-round game with linear utility functions.

Finally, we need to justify the assumption that $\forall t. p_{mt} \neq 0$ – that is, that the malicious player does not gain by, for example, concentrating its entire budget on one round of the game. This can be done by proving, using induction, that the malicious player would always cause no more damage than the $\frac{1}{1+\frac{M}{B}}$ ratio above if it did so.

Proof of part 2. As noted in footnote 5, in simple fair queueing with no other constraints, there is nothing stopping every user from asking for the entire link capacity. Thus the link would be forced to allocate all requesting users an equal amount of bandwidth. The result follows trivially. □

[7]Lower-bounded since the constraints we're placing on r_t are potentially looser than in the original problem

Pricing Cloud Bandwidth Reservations under Demand Uncertainty

Di Niu, Chen Feng, Baochun Li
Department of Electrical and Computer Engineering
University of Toronto
{dniu, cfeng, bli}@eecg.toronto.edu

ABSTRACT

In a public cloud, bandwidth is traditionally priced in a pay-as-you-go model. Reflecting the recent trend of augmenting cloud computing with bandwidth guarantees, we consider a novel model of cloud bandwidth allocation and pricing when explicit bandwidth reservation is enabled. We argue that a tenant's utility depends not only on its bandwidth usage, but more importantly on the portion of its demand that is satisfied with a performance guarantee. Our objective is to determine the optimal policy for pricing cloud bandwidth reservations, in order to maximize social welfare, i.e., the sum of the expected profits that can be made by all tenants and the cloud provider, even with the presence of demand uncertainty. The problem turns out to be a large-scale network optimization problem with a coupled objective function. We propose two new distributed solutions — based on chaotic equation updates and cutting-plane methods — that prove to be more efficient than existing solutions based on consistency pricing and subgradient methods.

In addition, we address the practical challenge of forecasting demand statistics, required by our optimization problem as input. We propose a factor model for near-future demand prediction, and test it on a real-world video workload dataset. All included, we have designed a fully computerized trading environment for cloud bandwidth reservations, which operates effectively at a fine granularity of as small as ten minutes in our trace-driven simulations.

Categories and Subject Descriptors

K.6.2 [**Installation Management**]: Pricing and resource allocation; Performance and usage measurement; G.3 [**Probability and Statistics**]: Time series analysis

General Terms

Algorithms, Economics, Measurement, Performance

Keywords

Cloud Computing, Bandwidth Pricing, Distributed Optimization, Prediction, Time Series

1. INTRODUCTION

Cloud computing delivers *Infrastructure as a Service* (IaaS) that integrates computation, storage and network resources in a virtualized environment. It represents a new business model where applications as *tenants* of the cloud can dynamically reserve *instances* on demand. However, a major risk to these tenants using cloud services is that unlike CPU and memory, bandwidth is not guaranteed in current-generation cloud platforms (e.g., Amazon EC2), leading to unpredictable network performance [6, 20]. A lack of bandwidth guarantee impedes cloud adoption by applications that require such guarantees, such as transaction processing web applications [14] and video-on-demand (VoD) applications [4]. The utility of tenants running these applications depends not only on the bandwidth usage, but more importantly on how many of their end-user requests are served with guaranteed performance.

With an ever-increasing demand for performance predictability, a recent trend in networking research is to augment cloud computing to explicitly account for network resources. In fact, datacenter engineering techniques have been developed to expand the tenant-cloud interface to allow bandwidth reservation for traffic flowing from a virtual machine (VM) in the cloud to the Internet [7, 12]. We envision that in future cloud platforms, bandwidth reservation will be a value-added feature that attracts tenants who seek bandwidth guarantees.

Unfortunately, even with cloud bandwidth reservation enabled, due to demand uncertainty, it is still difficult for a tenant to predict how much bandwidth it needs at a particular time. The usual approach of over-provisioning incurs high costs to tenants and does not really provide quantitative service guarantees. To promote guaranteed services, we believe that a new cloud service model should be introduced, in which a tenant simply needs to specify a percentage of its (bandwidth) demand to be served with guaranteed performance, which we call the *guaranteed portion*, while the rest of its demand will be served with best effort. It is then the cloud provider's responsibility to satisfy the guaranteed portion of the tenant with a high probability. Since the cloud provider has vast historical workload data, it can leverage statistical learning to predict tenant demands and make actual bandwidth reservations for the tenants.

In this paper, we study how to price the above guaranteed service. It is worth noting that usage-based pricing (pay-as-you-go) is not suitable for pricing bandwidth guarantees. For example, it is more costly to guarantee the performance of a tenant with bursty demand than a tenant with constant demand, even if they have incurred the same usage (number of bytes transferred). As a result, on top of the *usage fee*, the cloud should charge each tenant an extra *reservation fee*, depending on its unique demand statistics. Our objective is to fairly set such reservation fees, with the following challenges. *First of all*, the cloud provider usually multiplexes tenant demands to save the service cost. Due to resource sharing, the absolute amount of bandwidth reserved for each tenant is unknown. It is a challenging question to find out each tenant's fair share in the aggregate service cost. *Second*, a pricing policy, when imposed to the market, may affect tenants demand; such demand change in turn affects pricing decisions, leading to potentially unstable iterations.

To overcome these difficulties, we define the reservation fee of each tenant as a function of its specified *guaranteed portion* instead of the absolute amount of bandwidth reserved. We also express each tenant's utility as a function of its *guaranteed portion*, which essentially measures the Quality of Service (QoS) at the tenant. Under this new model of pricing and utility, each tenant will choose a guaranteed portion to maximize its *surplus*, which is its utility minus price. Note that in reality, a tenant may choose a guaranteed portion *close to* 1 instead of being 1 out of cost concerns, while having the remaining demand served with best effort.

We study a cloud provider whose objective is to maximize the *social welfare* of the system, i.e., the total expected tenant utility under demand uncertainty minus the aggregate service cost. Although the cloud cannot know the exact form of utility at each tenant, it can affect each tenant's choice of guaranteed portion through pricing, and thus control the social welfare achieved. To handle the coupled cost function (due to multiplexing), we propose a novel algorithm based on *chaotic equation updates*, for which we provide a sufficient convergence condition. We further propose a distributed version of the *cutting-plane method* with guaranteed convergence. These methods are *step-size-free* and proved to be more efficient than traditional subgradient methods in simulations. In addition, we give explicit solutions to optimal pricing under certain special cases and point out the dependence of reservation pricing on demand statistics such as burstiness and covariances.

Since a main duty of the cloud provider is to reserve bandwidth for the tenants, demand forecast constitutes an important part in the reservation-based service. Toward this end, we propose a factor model to predict the expectations as well as covariances of tenant demands in the near future, based on principal component analysis (PCA). Finally, we evaluate the proposed algorithms on the workload traces of a real-world VoD system called *UUSee* [3]. We conduct trace-driven simulations of bandwidth reservation and algorithmic pricing based on demand prediction. The system is shown to operate effectively at a fine granularity (of as small as 10 minutes).

The remainder of the paper is organized as follows. We review related work in Sec. 2, and present our system model in Sec. 3. We formulate the problem of social welfare maximization in Sec. 4, where we outline the condition for optimal pricing and discuss its economic implications. To solve the optimal pricing problem distributively, in Sec. 5, we propose two algorithms: *chaotic price update* and the *distributed cutting-plane method*, and study their convergence performance. In Sec. 6, we present our statistical methods for demand forecast. We conduct trace-driven simulations in Sec. 7, and conclude the paper in Sec. 8.

2. BACKGROUND AND RELATED WORK

Cloud computing, e.g., Amazon EC2, is usually offered with usage-based pricing (pay-as-you-go) [6, 11]. Different from pay-as-you-go, resource reservation involves paying a negotiated cost to have the resource over a time period, whether or not the resource is used. Although suitable for delay-insensitive applications, pay-as-you-go is insufficient as a business model for bandwidth-intensive and quality-stringent applications like VoD, since no performance guarantees are provided in general.

The good news is that cloud bandwidth reservation is becoming technically feasible. There have been proposals on datacenter traffic engineering to offer elastic bandwidth guarantees for egress traffic from virtual machines (VMs) [12]. The idea of virtual networks has also been proposed to connect the VMs of the same tenant in a virtual network with bandwidth guarantees [7, 12]. Further, explicit rate control has been proposed to apportion bandwidth according to flow deadlines [22]. Such research progress has made the cloud more attractive to bandwidth-intensive applications such as video-on-demand and MapReduce computations that rely on the network to transfer large amounts of data at high rates [25]. Netflix, as a major VoD provider, moved its data store and video encoding and streaming servers to Amazon AWS [2] in 2010 [4].

To support guaranteed cloud services, we need new policies to price not only the bandwidth usage but also bandwidth reservations. Our pricing model is partially inspired by pricing electric power consumption and capacity reservation under demand uncertainty [19]. However, due to the computing capability and abundant workload data in the cloud, our bandwidth reservation pricing theory is essentially a distributed optimization problem based on statistical learning. Amazon Cluster Compute [1] allows tenants to reserve, at a high cost, a dedicated 10 Gbps network with no multiplexing. Instead of provisioning a fixed amount of capacity, we believe that tenants should be allowed to specify a guaranteed portion of demand, as a way to control QoS level, while cloud providers should dynamically vary bandwidth reservations based on demand predictions. Our approach has the unique advantage that tenants are exempted from demand estimation, for which they do not have expertise. In contrast, the cloud can easily access tenant demand history from online monitoring, and is computationally capable of accurate demand forecast.

Since pricing guaranteed portions critically depends on accurate estimates of demand statistics, we target applications with predictable demands, such as video access. As measurements show that video workload demonstrates regular diurnal periodicity [5, 17, 23, 24], various techniques have recently been proposed to forecast large-scale VoD traffic. Seasonal ARIMA models have been introduced in [16, 17] to predict non-stationary demand evolution at a fine granularity. Principal component analysis (PCA) has been proposed in [13] to extract video demand evolution patterns over longer periods (of weeks or months) and forecast coarse-grained daily populations. We combine the strengths of both approaches by finding the common factors driving the demand evolution of all tenants using PCA at a fine granularity. We then make predictions for individual tenants as regressions from factor forecasts obtained from seasonal ARIMA models. Unlike [13], our approach makes short-term predictions with a lead time of 10 minutes, enabling autoscaling of resource allocation.

Our optimal pricing algorithms are related to network utility maximization (NUM), which has been extensively studied in the past, with various distributed algorithms proposed. See [10, 18] for thorough surveys. Most of these algorithms assume no coupling in the objective function, and thus cannot be applied to our problem with a coupled cost term. One existing approach to handle coupled objectives is called *consistency pricing* [10, 21], which is based on dual decomposition and subgradient methods. However, subgradient methods suffer from the curse of step sizes, in that small steps incur big delays (many rounds of message exchanges between the cloud and tenants), while big steps yield big optimality gaps. Varying step sizes strategically is difficult in reality. In this paper, we propose two *step-size-free* algorithms: 1) chaotic price update, 2) the cutting-plane method. The first one is based on iterative equation updates instead of decomposition and achieves rapid convergence under certain conditions. The second is a search algorithm with a guaranteed convergence speed.

3. A NEW TENANT-CLOUD AGREEMENT

Our system model is a generalization of the operation mode of the current cloud. Current cloud providers charge tenants a *usage fee* based on the number of bytes transferred in the past hour, and do not provide bandwidth guarantees. We extend this model to allow tenants to make reservations for bandwidth guarantees explicitly. The system operates on a short-term basis, e.g., based on hours or tens of minutes. At the beginning of each short period, each tenant specifies a *guaranteed portion* to guard against performance risks. The cloud decides the actual bandwidth reservation for tenants through demand estimation based on workload analysis, and charges both a usage and reservation fee. We now describe our system model in detail.

We consider one such short period, where N bandwidth-sensitive tenants are present. Suppose that in this period, tenant i's bandwidth demand is a random variable D_i (Mbps) with mean $\mu_i = \mathbf{E}[D_i]$ and variance $\sigma_i^2 = \mathbf{Var}[D_i]$. We assume the cloud can predict μ_i and σ_i based on demand history and share them to tenant i before the period starts. In our proposed market, the key commodity traded is a notion called the *guaranteed portion* instead of the absolute amount of bandwidth. Specifically, the tenants and cloud will comply to the following service agreement $\mathcal{S}_i(w_i, \epsilon, R_i)$:

- Before the period starts, each tenant i specifies a *guaranteed portion* $w_i \in [0, 1]$;
- The cloud guarantees w_i fraction of demand D_i with a high probability $1 - \epsilon$; outage is allowed to happen with a small probability ϵ, during which the bandwidth allocated to tenant i is limited to R_i.

The parameters ϵ and R_i are a part of a service level agreement (SLA) advertised by the cloud provider. We introduce the *risk factor* ϵ because for random demand, regardless of how much bandwidth is allocated, there exists a small risk of resource shortage.

Let q_i denote the actual bandwidth usage (realized data rate) in this period. Under a guaranteed portion w_i, service $\mathcal{S}_i(w_i, \epsilon, R_i)$ is supposed to lead to the following actual usage of tenant i:

$$q_i(w_i) = \begin{cases} w_i D_i, & \text{w.p. } 1-\epsilon, \\ \min\{w_i D_i, R_i\}, & \text{w.p. } \epsilon, \end{cases} \tag{1}$$

i.e., with probability $1 - \epsilon$ the actual usage q_i is a realization of w_i fraction of its demand D_i, while during outage (which happens with a small probability ϵ), the actual usage q_i is rationed by R_i.

Clearly, tenant i will choose w_i based on both the utility U_i and the price of guaranteeing w_i portion of its demand D_i. Unlike most prior work on network utility maximization [10] that assumes the utility U_i depends on a single variable such as rate, we model utility $U_i(q_i, D_i)$ of tenant i as a function of both actual usage q_i and the demand D_i. For example, a video content provider (or a VoD company) may have a linear utility gain (or revenue) $\alpha_i q_i$ from usage q_i and a convexly increasing utility loss $e^{A_i(D_i - q_i)}$ for the denied requests $D_i - q_i$, with α_i, A_i being tenant-specific parameters:

$$U_i\big(q_i(w_i), D_i\big) = \alpha_i q_i(w_i) - e^{A_i(D_i - q_i(w_i))}, \tag{2}$$

where the utility loss term can model the reputation degradation and potential revenue loss due to unfulfilled demand[1]. We assume U_i is *concave* and *monotonically increasing* in q_i.

The price for tenant i to use service $\mathcal{S}_i(w_i, \epsilon, R_i)$ is divided into two parts: a *usage fee* and a *reservation fee*. As most current cloud providers do, we assume uniform pricing for usage: each tenant pays $\$p$ for every unit bandwidth consumed. As a key departure from current clouds, we introduce a reservation fee, which is a function of the guaranteed portion instead of the absolute amount of bandwidth reservation: each tenant i is charged a price of $\$k_i w_i$ for having w_i portion of its demand guaranteed. We price the guaranteed portion w_i rather than the absolute bandwidth, because tenants usually have no idea about how much bandwidth they need. Instead, they can intuitively know how much percentage of guarantee is desired. This new business model frees each tenant from the computational burden of demand prediction: it simply submits its desired guaranteed portion w_i, while the cloud provider computes the actual bandwidth reservation as well as decides the reservation fee $k_i w_i$ for each tenant.

We define the *surplus* of tenant i as its utility minus its price:

$$S_i(w_i, p, k_i) := U_i\big(q_i(w_i), D_i\big) - p q_i - k_i w_i. \tag{3}$$

Given prices p and k_i, a rational tenant will choose a w_i to maximize its surplus S_i. Tenant i will not always choose $w_i = 1$ because when its demand is bursty, the price to guarantee 100% of D_i may be high. In this case, tenant i will choose a w_i close to 1 instead of being exactly 1, while the rest of its demand $(1 - w_i)D_i$ will be served with best efforts.

Based on tenant-specified guaranteed portions $w_1, \ldots, w_N$, the cloud should guarantee the demands $w_1 D_1, \ldots, w_N D_N$ for service. Denote $\mathbf{w} := [w_1, \ldots, w_N]^\mathsf{T}$. To realize the above service guarantees, the cloud provider needs to reserve a total *bandwidth capacity* of $K(\mathbf{w})$. Depending on the technology used, the value of K could vary significantly from one case to another. For example, a simple non-multiplexing technology is to reserve R_i capacity for each tenant i individually such that demand $w_i D_i$ is satisfied with high probability, i.e.,

$$\Pr(w_i D_i > R_i) < \epsilon, \tag{4}$$

and correspondingly, reserve capacity $K = \sum_i R_i$ in total. In contrast, a multiplexing technology will reserve capacity K for the tenants altogether such that the aggregate demand is satisfied with high probability, i.e.,

$$\Pr(\sum_i w_i D_i > K) < \epsilon, \tag{5}$$

and during outage (when $\sum_i w_i D_i > K$), the usage q_i of tenant i is rationed to R_i with $\sum_i R_i = K$. In both cases, K is an implicit function of $\mathbf{w}$ defined by the probabilistic constraints (4) and (5), respectively. To determine $K(\mathbf{w})$, the cloud provider must estimate the future demand statistics of all the tenants, and convert tenant-specified guaranteed portions $\mathbf{w}$ into the actual total bandwidth reservation K.

Similarly, the cloud provider has two kinds of service costs: usage and reservation costs. We assume tier-1 ISPs charge the cloud provider $\$b$ for every unit bandwidth actually used. Furthermore, reserving bandwidth capacity K will incur a reservation cost of $\$c(K)$. Due to multiplexing gain, to guarantee a similar service level, multiplexing will incur a lower K and thus a lower reservation cost $c(K)$ than without multiplexing.

[1]Even though the cloud provider may still be able to fulfill $D_i - q_i$ in a best-effort fashion, the tenant will have no knowledge if this is the case, and will not be able to factor it into its expected utility.

We define the *cloud profit* Π as the difference between its total revenue and total cost, i.e.,

$$\Pi(\mathbf{w}) := \sum_i \left(pq_i(w_i) + k_i w_i\right) - c\left(K(\mathbf{w})\right) - \sum_i bq_i(w_i). \quad (6)$$

4. PRICING TOWARDS SOCIAL WELFARE MAXIMIZATION

We study a cloud provider as a social planner whose objective is to maximize *social welfare* $W(\mathbf{w})$, which is defined as the total tenant utility minus the total service cost:

$$W(\mathbf{w}) := \sum_i U_i - c\left(K(\mathbf{w})\right) - \sum_i bq_i(w_i)$$
$$= \Pi(\mathbf{w}) + \sum_i S_i(w_i, p, k_i) \quad (7)$$

Under *random demands*, the cloud aims to decide a set of optimal guaranteed portions $\mathbf{w}^* = [w_1^*, \ldots, w_N^*]^\mathsf{T}$ for the tenants to maximize the *expected social welfare* by solving

$$\begin{array}{ll}\max_{\mathbf{w}} & E[W(\mathbf{w})] \\ \text{s.t.} & \mathbf{0} \preceq \mathbf{w} \preceq \mathbf{1}.\end{array} \quad (8)$$

To solve (8), we first derive the expected social welfare in a simple *approximated* form. Note that $\mathbf{E}\left[U_i\right]$ is bounded as follows:

$$\mathbf{E}[U_i] \geq (1-\epsilon)\mathbf{E}[U_i(w_i D_i, D_i)] + \epsilon\mathbf{E}[U_i(0, D_i)],$$
$$\mathbf{E}[U_i] \leq (1-\epsilon)\mathbf{E}[U_i(w_i D_i, D_i)] + \epsilon\mathbf{E}[U_i(R_i, D_i)].$$

When the risk factor ϵ is small, we have

$$\mathbf{E}\left[U_i(q_i, D_i)\right] \approx (1-\epsilon)\mathbf{E}\left[U_i(w_i D_i, D_i)\right]. \quad (9)$$

To simplify notations, we define

$$\overline{U}_i(w_i) := \mathbf{E}\left[U_i(w_i D_i, D_i)\right], \quad (10)$$

which turns out to be *monotonically increasing* and *concave* in w_i under very mild technical conditions. Similarly, the expected usage of tenant i is

$$\mathbf{E}\left[q_i(w_i)\right] \approx (1-\epsilon)\mathbf{E}\left[w_i D_i\right] = (1-\epsilon) w_i \mu_i. \quad (11)$$

Therefore, the expected surplus of tenant i is

$$\mathbf{E}\left[S_i(w_i, p, k_i)\right] = \mathbf{E}\left[U_i\right] - p\mathbf{E}\left[q_i\right] - k_i w_i$$
$$= (1-\epsilon)\left(\overline{U}_i(w_i) - p w_i \mu_i\right) - k_i w_i, \quad (12)$$

and the expected profit of the cloud provider is

$$\mathbf{E}[\Pi(\mathbf{w})] = (p-b)(1-\epsilon)\sum_i w_i \mu_i + \sum_i k_i w_i - c\left(K(\mathbf{w})\right). \quad (13)$$

Substituting the above into (7) gives the *expected social welfare* as

$$\mathbf{E}[W(\mathbf{w})] = (1-\epsilon)\sum_i \left(\overline{U}_i(w_i) - b w_i \mu_i\right) - c\left(K(\mathbf{w})\right). \quad (14)$$

4.1 An Equivalent Pricing Problem

In reality, although the cloud provider has full knowledge about its service cost $c(K(\mathbf{w}))$, it does not know the utility function of each tenant. In other words, maximizing $E[W(\mathbf{w})]$ in terms of $\mathbf{w}$ requires the cloud to know the utility U_i of each tenant and is infeasible. We now convert problem (8) into an equivalent pricing problem.

Note that the expected social welfare is also the sum of the expected cloud profit and the total expected tenant surplus, i.e.,

$$E[W(\mathbf{w})] = \mathbf{E}[\Pi(\mathbf{w})] + \sum_i \mathbf{E}[S_i(w_i, p, k_i)]. \quad (15)$$

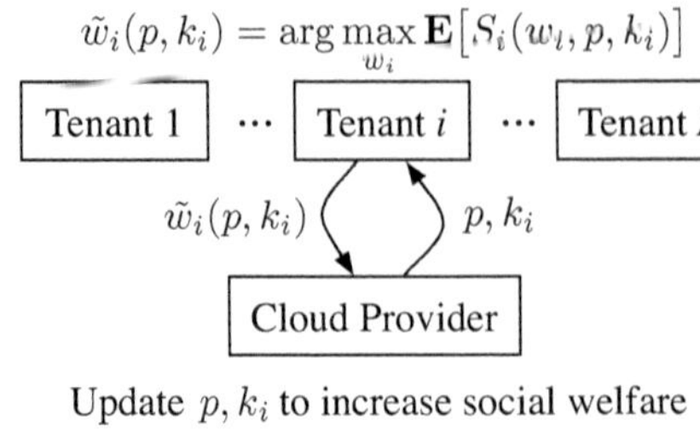

Figure 1: Iterative updates of prices and guaranteed portions.

Furthermore, when charged with prices p, k_i and facing a random demand D_i, a rational tenant will choose a guaranteed portion $\tilde{w}_i$ to maximize its expected surplus, i.e.,

$$\tilde{w}_i = \arg\max_{w_i} \mathbf{E}\left[S_i(w_i, p, k_i)\right], \quad (16)$$

which defines an implicit function $\tilde{w}_i(p, k_i)$ of the prices. The cloud can affect guaranteed portion choices $\tilde{\mathbf{w}} = [\tilde{w}_1, \ldots, \tilde{w}_N]^\mathsf{T}$ via appropriate choices of prices p, $k_1, \ldots, k_N$, and control the corresponding expected social welfare $\mathbf{E}[W(\tilde{\mathbf{w}})]$.

Therefore, the social welfare maximization problem (8) is converted into an equivalent **optimal pricing problem**:

$$\max_{p, k_1, \ldots, k_N} E[W(\tilde{\mathbf{w}})] = \mathbf{E}[\Pi(\tilde{\mathbf{w}})] + \sum_i \mathbf{E}[S_i(\tilde{w}_i, p, k_i)], \quad (17)$$

which, by combining (14) and (17), can be rewritten as

$$\max_{p, k_1, \ldots, k_N} (1-\epsilon)\sum_i \left(\overline{U}_i(\tilde{w}_i) - b\tilde{w}_i \mu_i\right) - c\left(K(\tilde{\mathbf{w}})\right), \quad (18)$$

where $\tilde{w}_i = \tilde{w}_i(p, k_i)$ is determined distributively by each tenant i via surplus maximization (16). Such a distributed optimization is illustrated in Fig. 1. Now the cloud provider does not need to know U_i: it simply charges tenant i the usage price p and reservation price k_i, and expect a $\tilde{w}(p, k_i)$ chosen by tenant i.

We denote the **optimal prices** that solve problem (18) as p^*, k_1^*, $\ldots$, k_N^*. The optimal pricing problem (18) is equivalent to the original problem (8), because by adjusting p and k_i, $\tilde{w}_i(p, k_i)$ can take any value in $[0, 1]$. In other words, the guaranteed portion $\tilde{w}_i(p^*, k_i^*)$ chosen by tenant i under optimal pricing p^*, k_i^* is exactly the guaranteed portion w_i^* that maximizes the expected social welfare, i.e., we have

$$w_i^* = \tilde{w}_i(p^*, k_i^*). \quad (19)$$

Therefore, once a set of optimal prices is obtained, we essentially have found a *decentralized solution* to expected social welfare maximization (8), which was originally impossible to solve.

Nonetheless, the optimal pricing problem (18) is not easy to solve either. At a first glance, (18) can be understood as a network utility maximization (NUM) problem [10] that may be solved via decomposition among the tenants. A closer look at (18) suggests that the term $c(K(\tilde{\mathbf{w}}))$ in the objective function may be coupled among all $\tilde{w}_i$'s, so that (18) cannot be decomposed into a set of subproblems, each solved at a tenant distributively. Coupling happens in the cost term when the cloud multiplexes tenant demands and books a capacity $K(\mathbf{w})$ for the aggregated demand. As shown in Fig. 1, the key to the solution is that the cloud provider must be able to update p and k_i towards the direction that increases $\mathbf{E}[W(\tilde{\mathbf{w}})]$. And a good price update algorithm should require fewer rounds of message-passing between the cloud and tenants before reaching optimality.

Before presenting the distributed solutions to (18) in Sec. 5, let us first provide a number of insights on how to make pricing policies, by checking the KKT conditions [8] that the optimal prices $p^*, k_1^*, \ldots, k_N^*$ must satisfy.

Proposition 1. *The optimal prices $p^*, k_1^*, \ldots, k_N^*$ must satisfy*

$$(1-\epsilon)(p^*-b)\mu_i + k_i^* - c'\big(K(\tilde{\mathbf{w}})\big)\cdot \frac{\partial K}{\partial w_i}\bigg|_{\mathbf{w}=\tilde{\mathbf{w}}} = 0, \quad \forall i, \quad (20)$$

where $\tilde{\mathbf{w}} = [\tilde{w}_1, \ldots, \tilde{w}_N]^\mathsf{T}$ with $\tilde{w}_i = \tilde{w}_i(p^*, k_i^*)$ given by (16).

Proof: Please refer to our technical report [15] for the proof. □

An inspection of (20) reveals that one set of optimal prices is

$$\begin{cases} p^* = b, \\ k_i^* = \partial c\big(K(\mathbf{w})\big)/\partial w_i\big|_{\mathbf{w}=\tilde{\mathbf{w}}}, \quad \forall i. \end{cases} \quad (21)$$

Although (21) is not the only set of optimal prices, our finding complies with the economic intuition that a welfare-maximizing cloud provider should charge marginal cost for both traffic usage and guaranteed reservation. In (21), we can also observe that k_i^* depends on $\tilde{\mathbf{w}}$, which in turn depends on $p, k_1^*, \ldots, k_N^*$. Due to such coupling, (21) is not yet a closed-form solution for the reservation price k_i^*.

4.2 No Multiplexing vs. Multiplexing All

To draw insights, we take a look at two special service technologies that may be adopted by the cloud: non-multiplexing and multiplexing across *all* the tenants. For simplicity, we assume a linear reservation cost (which will be relaxed later): $c(K) = \beta K$.

When multiplexing is not used, we can derive the optimal prices in a closed form from (21). Without multiplexing, recall that the capacity R_i is reserved for each tenant i individually, such that $\Pr(w_i D_i > R_i) < \epsilon$ and $K = \sum_i R_i$. When D_i is a Gaussian random variable (this assumption will be verified in Sec. 6), it is easy to check that

$$R_i(w_i) = \big(\mu_i + \theta(\epsilon)\sigma_i\big)w_i, \quad (22)$$

where $\theta(\epsilon) = F^{-1}(1-\epsilon)$ is a constant, with $F(\cdot)$ being the CDF of normal distribution $\mathcal{N}(0,1)$. Since the cost function is naturally decoupled among tenants, according to (21), the optimal prices are immediately given in a closed form by $p^* = b$ and

$$k_i^* = \beta\big(\mu_i + \theta(\epsilon)\sigma_i\big), \quad \forall i. \quad (23)$$

When multiplexing is used, however, optimal prices have no explicit solutions. Recall that with multiplexing, a capacity K is reserved to accommodate all the tenants together, such that the aggregate (instead of individual) demand is satisfied with high probability: $\Pr(\sum_i w_i D_i > K) < \epsilon$.

Since the random demands $D_1, \ldots, D_N$ of different tenants may be correlated, we denote ρ_{ij} the correlation coefficient of D_i and D_j, with $\rho_{ii} \equiv 1$. For convenience, let $\boldsymbol{\mu} = [\mu_1, \ldots, \mu_N]^\mathsf{T}$ and $\boldsymbol{\Sigma} = [\sigma_{ij}]$ be the $N \times N$ symmetric demand *covariance matrix*, with $\sigma_{ii} = \sigma_i^2$ and $\sigma_{ij} = \rho_{ij}\sigma_i\sigma_j$ for $i \neq j$.

Under Gaussian demands, K can be written as

$$\begin{aligned} K(\mathbf{w}) &= \mathbf{E}\big[\textstyle\sum_i w_i D_i\big] + \theta(\epsilon)\sqrt{\mathbf{Var}\big[\textstyle\sum_i w_i D_i\big]} \\ &= \boldsymbol{\mu}^\mathsf{T}\mathbf{w} + \theta(\epsilon)\sqrt{\mathbf{w}^\mathsf{T}\boldsymbol{\Sigma}\mathbf{w}}. \end{aligned} \quad (24)$$

Substituting the above $K(\mathbf{w})$ into (21) gives $p^* = b$ and

$$k_i^* = \beta\left(\mu_i + \theta(\epsilon)\cdot \frac{\partial\sqrt{\mathbf{w}^\mathsf{T}\boldsymbol{\Sigma}\mathbf{w}}}{\partial w_i}\bigg|_{\mathbf{w}=\mathbf{w}^*}\right), \quad \forall i, \quad (25)$$

where $w_i^* = \tilde{w}_i(p^*, k_i^*)$. Clearly, with multiplexing, k_i^* is not given in a closed form yet, due to the coupled cost function.

We note that whether with or without multiplexing, $K(\mathbf{w})$ is a convex function and so is $c(K(\mathbf{w}))$. In fact, we can relax the linear cost assumption $c(K) = \beta K$, as long as $c\big(K(\mathbf{w})\big)$ is *strictly convex and monotonically increasing* for each $w_i \in [0,1]$.

There is an interesting connection between the non-multiplexing and multiplexing cases: the optimal solution for non-multiplexing can be used to bound the optimal solution for the multiplexing case. Specifically, the optimal prices $\{k_i^*\}$ of non-multiplexing upper-bound $\{k_i^*\}$ of the multiplexing case, whereas the optimal portions $\{w_i^*\}$ of non-multiplexing lower-bound $\{w_i^*\}$ of the multiplexing case. This is intuitive because multiplexing leads to a reduced cost $c(K)$, stimulating tenants to increase their choices of the guaranteed portion. The proof of this connection involves the use of Cauchy-Schwarz inequality and is omitted due to space limits. We will use this connection in our distributed algorithms.

4.3 Economic Implications

Condition (20) has several economic implications, which apply to a general cost function, although we may use the non-multiplexing case for explanation due to its simplicity.

First, merely adopting a usage price p cannot maximize social welfare: when $k_i = 0$ for all i, there is no p that can satisfy (20). In other words, a positive reservation fee $k_i > 0$ is necessary to achieve welfare optimality, since in the presence of demand uncertainty, only k_i can incorporate a risk factor (e.g., σ_i in (23)) into pricing. This reveals that current cloud bandwidth pricing schemes are inefficient in terms of providing service guarantee against demand fluctuation. On the other hand, a usage price p is not necessary: even if $p = 0$, the expected welfare is maximized as long as k_i satisfies (20). In this case, the reservation fee can be raised to compensate the loss from no usage fee.

Furthermore, *heterogeneous* reservation prices $k_1, \ldots, k_N$ are necessary to achieve optimality, each k_i depending on the statistical characteristics of tenant i's demand D_i. This conforms to the intuition that tenants have different degrees of demand volatility, incurring different costs for service guarantees. For example, without multiplexing, k_i depends on σ_i in (23): the more bursty a tenant's demand D_i, the more capacity that must be reserved to guard against fluctuation, and thus the higher the price. In contrast, in terms of usage pricing, it is efficient enough to charge a homogeneous price p for every unit bandwidth consumed.

5. DISTRIBUTED SOLUTIONS

As has been noted, the main challenge to solving the optimal pricing problem (18) is that the reservation cost $c\big(K(\mathbf{w})\big)$ is coupled among all the tenants and is not decomposable in general. One existing approach to handle coupled objective functions is to find the dual problem of (18) and to decompose the dual among all the tenants and the cloud provider by introducing auxiliary variables. Such an approach is called *consistency pricing* [10, 21]. Subgradient methods are among the most popular techniques to update the prices towards the optimality of dual problems. However, they suffer from the curse of step sizes. For the final output to be close to the optimality, subgradient methods choose small step sizes to update k_i, leading to slow convergence and many iterations of message-passing between the cloud and tenants.

In this paper, we propose two novel *step-size-free* algorithms for price updates that can quickly converge to the optimality of (18). The first algorithm, called *Chaotic Price Update*, does not rely on decomposition at all: instead, it resorts to iterative equation updates based on the KKT conditions (20). The second algorithm, called the *Cutting-Plane Method*, relies on dual decomposition but does not update k_i using step sizes: it is essentially a search algorithm

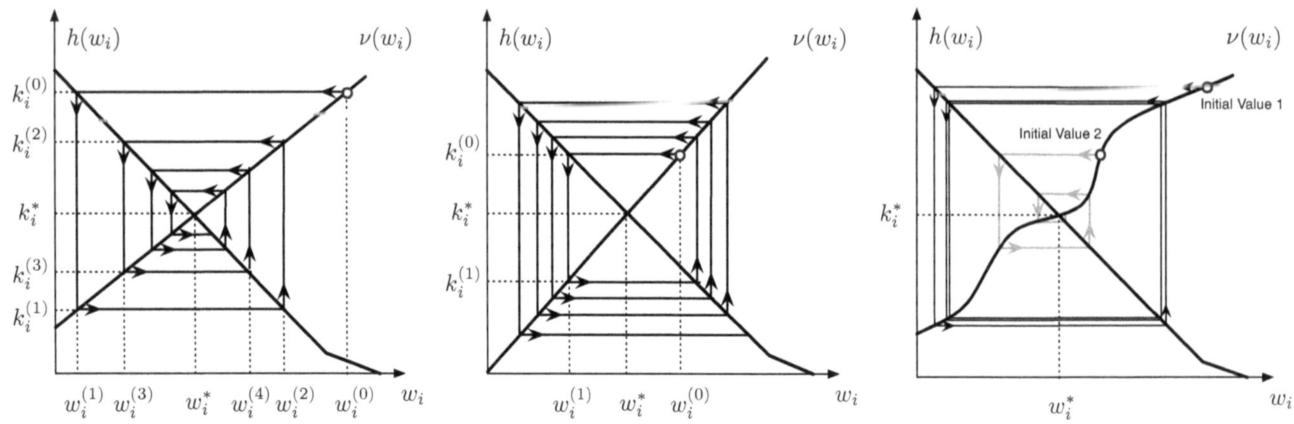

(a) Convergence to Global Optimality (b) Divergence (c) 1: Periodic; 2: Converging.

Figure 2: Behavior of price update based on chaotic equations in a one dimensional case. "o" represents the starting point $(w_i^{(0)}, k_i^{(0)})$.

that locates $\{k_i^*\}$ until it is confined in a small region. We give a sufficient condition under which chaotic price update can achieve rapid convergence. The cutting-plane method, which is guaranteed to converge, is used to compensate chaotic price update when the latter is not converging. Note that our algorithms apply to a general convex cost function $c(K(\mathbf{w}))$ (in terms of $\mathbf{w}$) under any service technology (e.g., multiplexing tenant demands in groups).

5.1 Chaotic Price Update

Chaotic price update is based on alternated phases of price updates via the cost-price relationship (20) and the tenant surplus maximization equation (16).

Chaotic Price Update. Denote $\mathbf{w}^{(t)} := [w_1^{(t)}, \ldots, w_N^{(t)}]^\mathsf{T}$. Set $p \equiv b$. Set $k_i^{(0)} := \beta(\mu_i + \theta(\epsilon)\sigma_i)$ for all i and $\mathbf{w}^{(0)} = \mathbf{1}$. For $t = 0, 1, \ldots,$ repeat

(1) **Distributed Surplus Maximization.** Pass p and $k_i^{(t)}$ to each tenant i, which returns:

$$w_i^{(t+1)} := \arg\max_{0 \le w_i \le 1} \mathbf{E}\big[S_i(w_i, p, k_i^{(t)})\big], \quad \forall i. \tag{26}$$

(2) **Price Update.** Set

$$k_i^{(t+1)} := c'\big(K(\mathbf{w}^{(t+1)})\big) \cdot \frac{\partial K(\mathbf{w})}{\partial w_i}\bigg|_{\mathbf{w}=\mathbf{w}^{(t+1)}}, \quad \forall i. \tag{27}$$

(3) If $\|\mathbf{w}^{(t+1)} - \mathbf{w}^{(t)}\| \le \xi$, return $\mathbf{w}^* = \mathbf{w}^{(t+1)}$, $k_i^* = k_i^{(t+1)}$.

The above algorithm starts by setting $k_i^{(0)}$ to be the k_i^* in the cost function without multiplexing. It then updates k_i and w_i alternately by setting the current prices $k_i^{(t)}$ to be the marginal reservation cost with the current $\mathbf{w}^{(t)}$, and by collecting the next $\mathbf{w}^{(t+1)}$ from tenants who maximize their surpluses given the current prices. Applying the KKT conditions to (16), step (1) can also be viewed as solving an equation

$$(1-\epsilon)\overline{U}_i'(w_i^{(t+1)}) = p(1-\epsilon)\mu_i + k_i^{(t)}, \tag{28}$$

for $w_i^{(t+1)}$. Since each tenant maximizes its expected surplus locally, the cloud provider does not have to know the utility function of each tenant, leading to an iterative distributed solution.

Compared with Lagrangian dual decomposition based on consistency pricing [10,21], chaotic price update represents a new way of handling coupled objectives. Since price updates are based on equation (27) rather than on updating Lagrangian multipliers, the algorithm is not concerned with the choice of step sizes that are required by subgradient methods.

We observe that the sequence $\{k_i^{(t)}\}$ produced by equations (27) and (28) could demonstrate significantly different behavior under different initial values $w_i^{(0)}$ and different forms of utility and cost functions. In other words, our algorithm demonstrates *chaotic* behavior, whose eventual outcome is sensitive to initial conditions and the structure of updating equations.

Our objective going forward is to analyze the behavior of $\{k_i^{(t)}\}$ and $\{\mathbf{w}^{(t)}\}$ and find out the conditions under which the algorithm can achieve fast convergence. To simplify notations, we define

$$h_i(w_i) \equiv (1-\epsilon)\big(\overline{U}_i'(w_i) - b\mu_i\big), \tag{29}$$

$$\nu_i(\mathbf{w}) \equiv \frac{\partial c\big(K(\mathbf{w})\big)}{\partial w_i}. \tag{30}$$

Recall that $\mathbf{w}^* := [w_1^*, \ldots, w_N^*]^\mathsf{T}$, where $w_i^* = \tilde{w}_i(p^*, k_i^*)$ is the guaranteed portion chosen by tenant i under optimal pricing. By the definition of $\mathbf{w}^*$, the optimality condition is

$$h_i(w_i^*) = k_i^* = \nu_i(\mathbf{w}^*), \quad \forall i. \tag{31}$$

Since we have set $p \equiv b$, (28) can be written as

$$h_i(w_i^{(t+1)}) := (1-\epsilon)\big(\overline{U}_i'(w_i^{(t+1)}) - b\mu_i\big) = k_i^{(t)}. \tag{32}$$

Thus, the **updating rules** (27) and (28) in chaotic price update can be rewritten as

$$h_i(w_i^{(t+1)}) = k_i^{(t)} = \nu_i(\mathbf{w}^{(t)}), \quad \forall i. \tag{33}$$

Let us illustrate the algorithm behavior using the special case of a *single* tenant. There are three scenarios where the algorithm can produce dramatically different results, as shown in Fig. 2. Since utility $u_i(w_i)$ is strictly concave and monotonically increasing in $[0,1]$, and cost $c\big(K(\mathbf{w})\big)$ is strictly convex and monotonically increasing in $[0,1]$, we have for all i:

$$\begin{cases} h_i(w_i) > -b\mu_i,\ h_i'(w_i) < 0, & \forall w_i \in [0,1] \\ \nu_i(\mathbf{w}) > 0,\ \frac{\partial \nu_i(\mathbf{w})}{\partial w_i} > 0, & \forall \mathbf{w} : \mathbf{0} \preceq \mathbf{w} \preceq \mathbf{1}. \end{cases} \tag{34}$$

All three cases in Fig. 2 satisfy (34). In Fig. 2(a), $\{w_1^{(t)}\}$ always converges to w_1^* for any initial value $w_1^{(0)} \in [0,1]$, whereas in

Fig. 2(b), $\{w_1^{(t)}\}$ always diverges regardless of its initial starting point. In Fig. 2(c), however, the behavior of $\{w_1^{(t)}\}$ critically depends on its initial value $w_1^{(0)}$. If $w_1^{(0)}$ takes "initial value 1", $w_1^{(t)}$ will eventually hop between two values alternately, without being able to approach w_1^*. On the other hand, if $w_1^{(0)}$ takes "initial value 2", $w_1^{(t)}$ will converge to w_1^*.

We now give a sufficient condition for the convergence of chaotic price update in Theorem 1.

Theorem 1. *If for each $i = 1, \ldots, N$, we have*

$$(1-\epsilon)\left|\overline{U}_i''(w_i)\right| > \frac{\partial^2 c(K(\mathbf{w}))}{\partial w_i^2}, \tag{35}$$

for all $\mathbf{w}$ *between* $\mathbf{w}^{(0)} = \mathbf{1}$ *and* $\mathbf{w}^{(1)}$, *then using chaotic price update,* $k_i^{(t)}$ *converges to* k_i^* *and* $w_i^{(t)}$ *converges to* w_i^*.

Proof: Please refer to our technical report [15] for the proof. □

The economic implication behind Theorem 1 is that the algorithm will converge when *the marginal utility gain decreases faster than the marginal cost increases*, as w_i increases. This technical assumption can be easily justified, since the marginal cost $c'(K) = \beta$ for adding network capacity (routers and switches) is decreasing at a fast pace in our economy.

From the Proof of Theorem 1 in our technical report [15], the convergence speed of $\{k_i^{(t)}\}$ in chaotic price update is dictated by $P_i(w_i^*)$ and $Q_i(w_i^*)$, which depend on $h_i(w_i)$ and $\nu_i(\mathbf{w})$, the marginal utility gain and marginal cost in terms of w_i. Intuitively speaking, the larger the gap between the rates at which the marginal utility gain decreases and the marginal cost increases, the faster the convergence speed. As a result, in systems where $\left|\overline{U}_i''(w_i)\right|$ exceeds $\partial^2 c(K(\mathbf{w}))/\partial w_i^2$ by a substantial margin, the step-size-oblivious chaotic price update can achieve extremely fast convergence.

5.2 The Cutting-Plane Method

Chaotic price update achieves fast convergence when condition (35) is met. A natural question arises: *Can we design an algorithm that is step-size-free while converging under a wider range of conditions?* Now we present such an algorithm that converges for arbitrary concave utility function $\overline{U}_i(w_i)$ and arbitrary convex cost function $c(K(\mathbf{w}))$, with a *guaranteed* convergence speed. Our basic idea is to apply the *cutting-plane method* [8] to the dual problem of social welfare maximization, leading to an alternative formulation of the optimal pricing problem.

5.2.1 Dual Problem of Social Welfare Maximization

We introduce the dual problem of social welfare maximization, following the framework of consistency pricing [10, 21]. Note that the social welfare maximization problem (8) can be rewritten as

$$\begin{array}{ll} \max_{\mathbf{w},\mathbf{v}} & (1-\epsilon)\sum_i \left(\overline{U}_i(w_i) - bw_i\mu_i\right) - c(K(\mathbf{v})) \\ \text{s.t.} & \mathbf{w} = \mathbf{v}, \end{array} \tag{36}$$

where the auxiliary vector $\mathbf{v}$ is introduced to facilitate *dual decomposition*. To derive the dual problem of (36), we define the *Lagrangian*

$$\begin{aligned} L(\mathbf{w},\mathbf{v},\mathbf{k}) &= (1-\epsilon)\sum_i \left(\overline{U}_i(w_i) - bw_i\mu_i\right) - c(K(\mathbf{v})) \\ &\quad + \mathbf{k}^{\mathsf{T}}(\mathbf{v}-\mathbf{w}) \\ &= (1-\epsilon)\sum_i \left(\overline{U}_i(w_i) - bw_i\mu_i\right) - \sum_i k_i w_i \\ &\quad + \sum_i k_i v_i - c(K(\mathbf{v})). \end{aligned} \tag{37}$$

Here k_i is the *Lagrange multiplier* associated with the ith equality constraint $w_i = v_i$; k_i can be interpreted as a *consistency price*, as it will eventually steer v_i towards w_i, as explained in [10, 21].

The *Lagrange dual function* is

$$q(\mathbf{k}) = \sup_{\mathbf{w},\mathbf{v}} L(\mathbf{w},\mathbf{v},\mathbf{k}), \tag{38}$$

and the *dual problem* of social welfare maximization (36) is

$$\min_{\mathbf{k}} \; q(\mathbf{k}). \tag{39}$$

Note that there is no duality gap between the dual problem (39) and primal problem (36) by the *strong duality theorem* [8], since the primal problem is convex optimization for any concave $\overline{U}_i(w_i)$ and convex $c(K(\mathbf{v}))$. As a result, it suffices to solve the dual problem instead of the primal problem.

In fact, the dual problem (39) is preferable because it enables distributed algorithms due to a natural decomposition of $q(\mathbf{k})$:

$$\begin{aligned} q(\mathbf{k}) = & \sum_i \sup_{w_i} \Big((1-\epsilon)\left(\overline{U}_i(w_i) - bw_i\mu_i\right) - k_i w_i \Big) \\ & + \sup_{\mathbf{v}} \Big(\sum_i k_i v_i - c(K(\mathbf{v})) \Big). \end{aligned}$$

This dual decomposition "decouples" the objective function $q(\mathbf{k})$ so that the value of $q(\mathbf{k})$ can be found by solving a surplus maximization problem at each tenant i:

$$\max_{w_i} \; (1-\epsilon)\left(\overline{U}_i(w_i) - bw_i\mu_i\right) - k_i w_i, \quad \text{for all } i, \tag{40}$$

and a profit maximization problem at the cloud provider:

$$\max_{\mathbf{v}} \sum_i k_i v_i - c(K(\mathbf{v})). \tag{41}$$

As these subproblems are independent of each other, the dual problem enables distributed solutions by charging each tenant a reservation price k_i and usage price $p = b$ (the revenue and cost related to *usage* cancel each other in (41)). In contrast, the primal problem (36) is not decomposable because of the coupled term $c(K(\mathbf{v}))$.

5.2.2 Distributed Solutions via Cutting Planes

A traditional subgradient method will find a subgradient $\mathbf{g_k}$ of $q(\mathbf{k})$ at point $\mathbf{k}$, and update the prices $\mathbf{k}$ using this subgradient times a small step size. For example, one of such subgradients is given as below:

Lemma 1. *For any point $\mathbf{k} \in \mathbb{R}^N$, let the vector $\tilde{\mathbf{w}} = [\tilde{w}_i]$ be the optimal solutions to problem (40) and $\tilde{\mathbf{v}}$ be the optimal solution to problem (41). That is,*

$$\tilde{w}_i = \arg\max_{w_i} \; (1-\epsilon)\left(\overline{U}_i(w_i) - bw_i\mu_i\right) - k_i w_i, \quad \forall i, \tag{42}$$

$$\tilde{\mathbf{v}} = \arg\max_{\mathbf{v}} \sum_i k_i v_i - c(K(\mathbf{v})). \tag{43}$$

Then a subgradient of $q(\mathbf{k})$ at point $\mathbf{k}$ is given by $\mathbf{g_k} = \tilde{\mathbf{v}} - \tilde{\mathbf{w}}$.

Proof: Please refer to our technical report [15] for the proof. □

However, to ensure the convergence speed, the subgradient method requires tuning the step sizes strategically, which is difficult to implement in reality. In contrast, the cutting-plane method is step-size-free: it is essentially a *search algorithm* based on the following fact (see [8] for a proof):

Lemma 2. *Let vector $\mathbf{g_k} \in \mathbb{R}^N$ be a subgradient of the objective function $q(\mathbf{k})$ at point $\mathbf{k} \in \mathbb{R}^N$, i.e., $\mathbf{g_k}$ must satisfy*

$$q(\mathbf{x}) \geq q(\mathbf{k}) + \mathbf{g_k}^{\mathsf{T}}(\mathbf{x}-\mathbf{k}), \quad \forall \mathbf{x} \in \mathbb{R}^N. \tag{44}$$

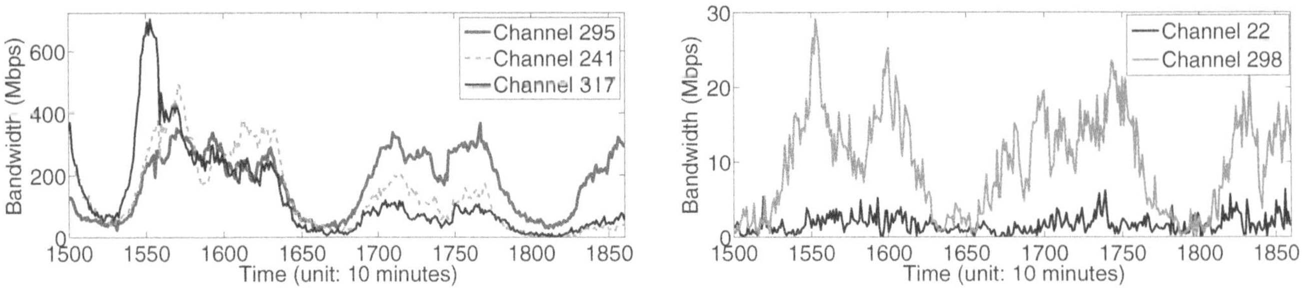

(a) Three large channels

(b) Two small channels

Figure 3: Bandwidth consumption time series of 5 representative channels over a 2.5-day period.

Let $\mathbf{k}^*$ *be the optimal solution of the dual problem (39). Then* $\mathbf{k}^*$ *satisfies* $\mathbf{g}_{\mathbf{k}}^{\mathsf{T}}(\mathbf{k}^* - \mathbf{k}) \leq 0$.

Lemma 2 implies that if we know a point $\mathbf{k}$ with its subgradient $\mathbf{g}_{\mathbf{k}}$, we can confine our search for $\mathbf{k}^*$ within the half-space $\{\mathbf{x} : \mathbf{g}_{\mathbf{k}}^{\mathsf{T}}(\mathbf{x} - \mathbf{k}) \leq 0\}$, since the other half-space does not contain $\mathbf{k}^*$. Hence, we can locate $\mathbf{k}^*$ up to a certain accuracy by iteratively ruling out a sufficient number of half-spaces, as described below.

The Cutting-Plane Method. Set $\mathbf{k}^{(0)} = \mathbf{k}^{**}$, where $\mathbf{k}^{**}$ is an optimal solution for the non-multiplexing case. Set the initial polyhedron to be $\mathcal{P}_0 = \{\mathbf{k}|\mathbf{0} \preceq \mathbf{k} \preceq \mathbf{k}^{(0)}\}$. It is clear that $\mathcal{P}_0$ contains an optimal solution $\mathbf{k}^*$. For $t = 1, 2, \ldots$, repeat:

(1) Choose a point $\mathbf{k}^{(t)}$,which is the center of gravity of $\mathcal{P}_{t-1}$, denoted $\mathbf{k}^{(t)} = \mathrm{CG}(\mathcal{P}_{t-1})$;

(2) Finding a subgradient $\mathbf{g}_{\mathbf{k}^{(t)}}$ of $q(\mathbf{k})$ at $\mathbf{k}^{(t)}$;

(3) If $\|\mathbf{g}_{\mathbf{k}^{(t)}}\|_\infty \leq \xi_1$, return $\mathbf{k}^{(t)}$; else, continue;

(4) Add a new cutting plane $\mathbf{g}_{\mathbf{k}^{(t)}}^{\mathsf{T}}(\mathbf{k} - \mathbf{k}^{(t)}) \leq 0$ to form the new polyhedron

$$\mathcal{P}_t := \mathcal{P}_{t-1} \cap \{\mathbf{k}|\mathbf{g}_{\mathbf{k}^{(t)}}^{\mathsf{T}}(\mathbf{k} - \mathbf{k}^{(t)}) \leq 0\}. \quad (45)$$

Intuitively speaking, the above algorithm attempts to shrink the volume of polyhedron $\mathcal{P}_t$ that contains the optimal solution $\mathbf{k}^*$ one iteration after another, until $\mathbf{k}^*$ is contained in a trivially small ball. In Step (2), the subgradient can be found using Lemma 2.

Now we can quantify the communication cost of the above algorithm — a crucial factor in a cloud environment. Since $\mathbf{k}^{(t)}$ is the center of gravity of $\mathcal{P}_{t-1}$, about half of the uncertainty is ruled out in each iteration. It can be proved that

$$\mathbf{vol}(\mathcal{P}_t) \leq \left(1 - \frac{1}{e}\right) \mathbf{vol}(\mathcal{P}_{t-1}) \approx 0.63 \cdot \mathbf{vol}(\mathcal{P}_{t-1}). \quad (46)$$

Therefore, the above algorithm converges *exponentially* fast. Furthermore, Lemma 2 shows that, in order to obtain a subgradient $\mathbf{g}_{\mathbf{k}^{(t)}}$ at $\mathbf{k}^{(t)}$, the cloud provider can simply charge each tenant a usage fee $p = b$ and a reservation fee $k_i = k_i^{(t)}$, and expect a return $\tilde{w}_i$ from each tenant i; it obtains $\tilde{\mathbf{v}}$ locally. Such price notification and response are performed in each iteration for all the tenants in parallel. In other words, each execution of Step (2) introduces only one *round* of message passing between the cloud and tenants. Since cloud-tenant communication happens only in Step (2), the total rounds of message-passing can be bounded as follows:

Proposition 2. *If the cutting-plane method terminates when the diameter of the smallest Euclidean ball that contains* $\mathcal{P}_t$ *is no greater than d, then in the worst case, the cutting-plane method requires*

$$R = 1.51N \log_2 \left(\frac{\max_i k_i^{(0)}}{d} \right) \quad (47)$$

rounds of message passing between the cloud and tenants.

The above proposition is a well-known property of the cutting-plane method [8]. In contrast, the worst-case communication cost of subgradient methods are of the form $O(N \times 1/\alpha)$, where α is the step size. Clearly, if d is comparable to α, the cutting-plane method may lead to much faster convergence due to the $\log_2(\cdot)$ operation.

It is worth noting that finding the center of gravity $\mathrm{CG}(\mathcal{P}_{t-1})$ requires heavy computation. However, computation cost does not pose a challenge for data centers that have superior computing power, whereas communication cost (convergence speed) is the major bottleneck. The cutting-plane method converges faster, reducing the rounds of message passing between tenants and the cloud, yet at the expense of computational cost. Such a property is in fact desirable in the cloud. To summarize, the cutting-plane method converges for arbitrary concave utility $\overline{U}_i(w_i)$ and convex cost $c(K(\mathbf{w}))$, and can be used to compensate chaotic price update when the latter is not converging.

6. DEMAND STATISTICS ESTIMATION WITH A FACTOR MODEL

Recall that both algorithms for finding the optimal pricing policy need $\boldsymbol{\mu}$, $\boldsymbol{\sigma}$ and $\boldsymbol{\Sigma}$ as inputs: μ_i and σ_i are used for the surplus maximization at each tenant i in (26) and (42), while the demand covariance matrix $\boldsymbol{\Sigma}$ is used to calculate the service cost $c(K(\mathbf{w}))$ in the presence of multiplexing in (27) and (43).

In this section, we address the practical issue of predicting demand statistics based on demand history, which can be obtained from cloud monitoring services such as Amazon CloudWatch [2] at a fine granularity (e.g., at a frequency of 5 minutes in CloudWatch). As has been mentioned, in this paper, we target applications whose bandwidth demand patterns are tractable and predictable to some extent. Video access is one example of such applications, with clear diurnal patterns and the time-of-the-day effect [17], in the sense that a popular video almost always sees its peak (or trough) demand around the same time of day.

Our study is based on a large dataset collected from thousands of on-demand video channels in a commercial VoD system [3] during the 2008 Summer Olympics. The video genres are not limited to Olympics, but range from TV episodes to sports and from movies

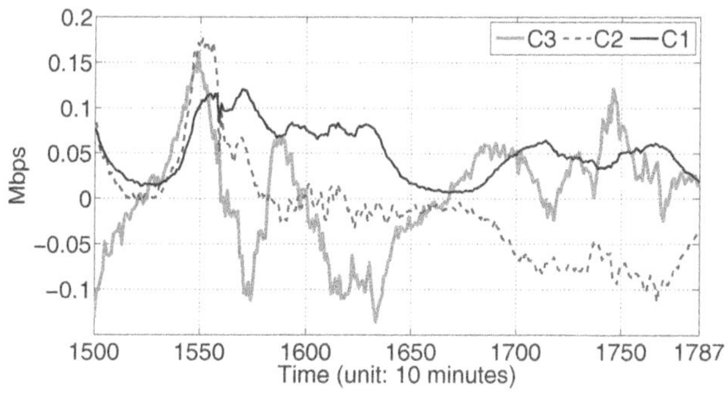

Figure 4: The first 3 principal components C_1—C_3 in bandwidth consumption series of 468 channels during 2 days via principal component analysis.

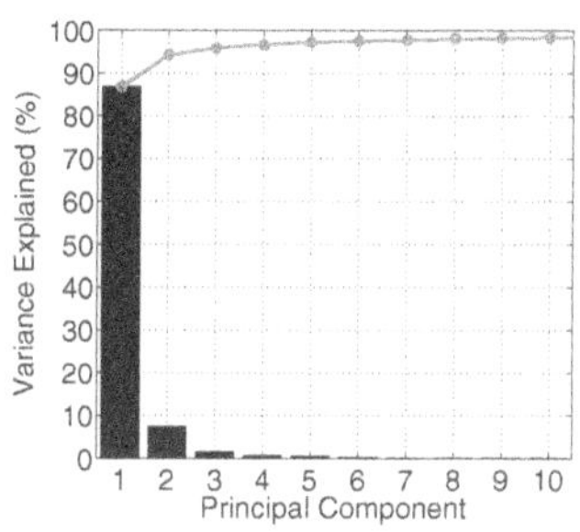

Figure 5: Variance explained in bandwidth consumption series of 468 channels in 2 days.

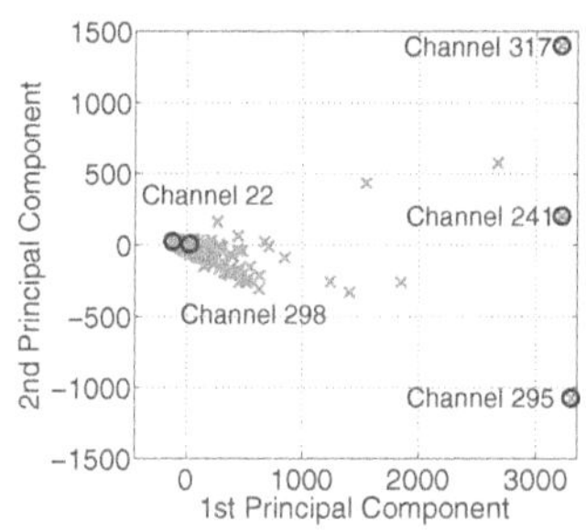

Figure 6: Data projected onto the first 2 principal components. Each point is one of the 468 channels.

to news. Fig. 3 shows the aggregate bandwidth demand in each channel for 5 representative channels over a 2.5-day period.

We have four observations about the dataset. *First*, the workload dataset consists of a large number of small unpopular channels, such as those in Fig. 3(b), dominated by a small number of large popular channels, such as those in Fig. 3(a). *Second*, there is a diurnal periodicity in the access pattern of each video channel. *Third*, a channel's popularity evolution may follow some trends over days. For example, bandwidth consumption in channels 241 and 317 exhibits a downward trend over the 2.5 days in Fig. 3(a), with 144 time periods representing one day. Finally, both the diurnal periodicity and daily trends become vague in small channels, such as in channel 22 in Fig. 3(b).

Our prior work has proposed to use seasonal ARIMA processes to predict bandwidth series in each individual channel [17] at a fine granularity of 10 minutes. The prediction is based on a regression of historical demand in the most recent time periods, as well as demand around the same time in previous days. However, this method has a shortcoming that a separate statistical model needs to be trained for every channel and thus does not scale to a large number of channels. Also, this approach performs poorly for small channels, e.g., channel 22, or ill-behaved channels, e.g., channel 317. In both types of channels, the daily repetition pattern is obscured by various random factors.

To tackle these problems, we use a *factor model* to account for demand evolutions, i.e., the demand series $\{D_i(t)\}$ of each channel i can be viewed as driven by M uncorrelated underlying factors $C_1(t), \ldots, C_M(t)$ with a zero-mean random shock $e(t)$:

$$D_i(t) = \alpha_{i1}C_1(t) + \ldots + \alpha_{iM}C_M(t) + e(t), \quad \forall i. \qquad (48)$$

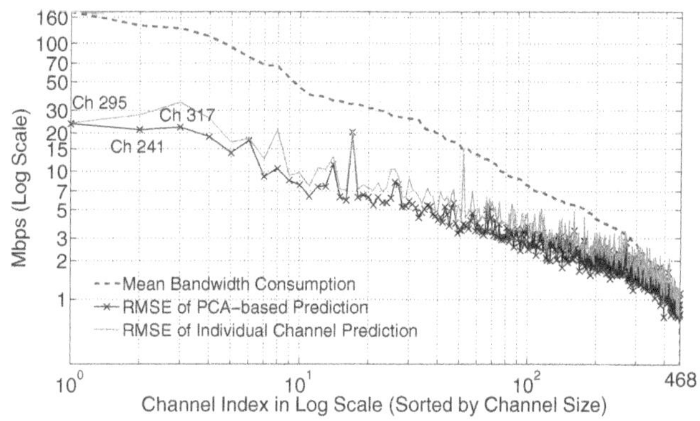

Figure 7: Root mean squared errors (RMSEs) of the two prediction methods over test period 1680-1860 (1.25 days), compared to mean bandwidth consumption in each channel. The three largest channels are channels 295, 241 and 317.

If the coefficients $\alpha_{i1}, \ldots, \alpha_{iM}$ can be learned statistically, we will be able to forecast $\{D_i(t)\}$ by predicting factor movements first. As noted from Fig. 3, channel demands exhibit co-movements. This inspires us to mine the factors while learning their coefficients from the collective demand history of *all* the channels.

We use principal component analysis (PCA) to find such underlying factors. Given N demand series $\{D_1(t)\}, \ldots, \{D_N(t)\}$, PCA applies an orthogonal transformation to these N demand series to obtain a small number of uncorrelated time series $\{C_1(t)\}$, ..., $\{C_M(t)\}$ called the *principal components*. This transformation is defined in such a way that data projected onto the first principal component has as high a variance as possible (that is, accounts for as much of the variability in data as possible), and each succeeding component in turn has the highest variance possible.

We perform PCA for all the 468 channels that are online in a 2-day period (time 1500-1787). Fig. 4 plots the first 3 principal component series in the data. We can see the first component C_1 explains the diurnal periodicity shared by all the channels. The second component C_2 accounts for the downward daily trend, which is salient in channel 317 as popularity diminishes and less salient in channel 295. A further check of Fig. 5 reveals that the first 10 principal component series explain 99% of the data variability, which are sufficient to model the factors underlying all the demand evolution.

However, different channels have different dependencies on each factor. Fig. 6 shows the 468 demand series projected onto the first 2 components, i.e., the point $(\alpha_{i1}, \alpha_{i2})$ for all i. Without surprise, the dependence on the first component, α_{i1}, indicates how large the channel is. In contrast, the dependence on the second component, α_{i2}, accounts for how fast end-users may lose interest in channel i. Channel 295 has a low α_{i2}, indicating almost no decrease in popularity over days. Channel 241 has a moderate α_{i2}, showing a slightly downward trend. Channel 317 has a large α_{i2}, exhibiting a dramatic decrease of popularity just on the second day.

To predict the demand means $\boldsymbol{\mu}(t)$ and covariances $\boldsymbol{\Sigma}(t)$ for $\{D_i(t) : i = 1, \ldots, N\}$ at time t, we first predict the principal components $C_1(t), \ldots, C_M(t)$ for $M = 10$ based on the history and obtain forecasts about their means $\hat{\mathbf{C}}(t) = [\hat{C}_1(t), \ldots, \hat{C}_M(t)]^\mathsf{T}$ and their covariances $\hat{\boldsymbol{\Sigma}}_C(t)$. We further predict the error series $e(t)$ to obtain its forecast $\hat{e}(t)$ and error variance $\hat{\sigma}_e^2(t)$. Note that $\hat{\boldsymbol{\Sigma}}_C(t)$ is a diagonal matrix because the principal components are uncorrelated. Denote the coefficient matrix as $\mathbf{A}_{N\times M} = [\alpha_{im}]$,

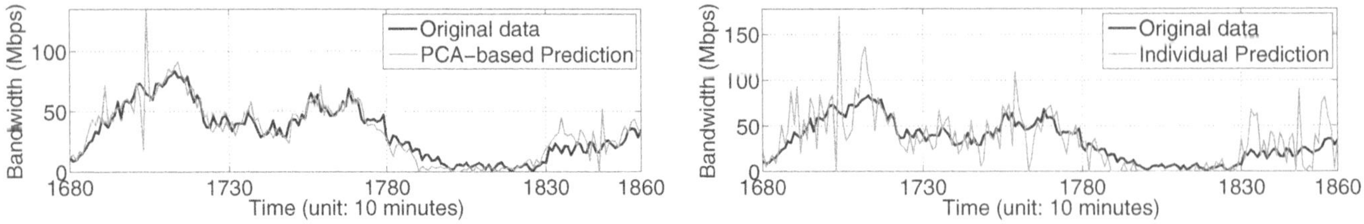

Figure 8: 10-minute-ahead conditional mean prediction in channel 172 over a test period of 1.25 days.

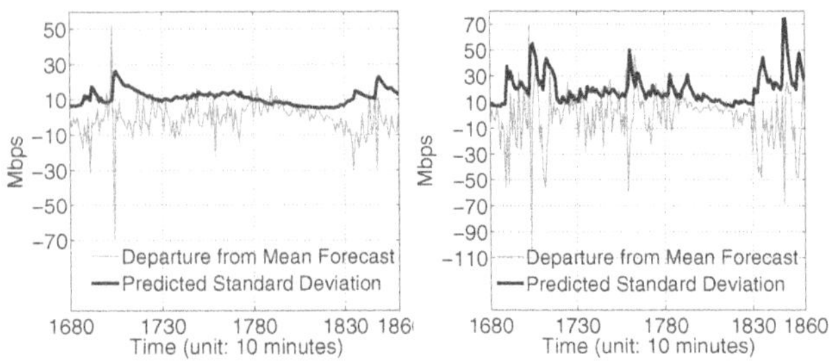

(a) PCA-based Prediction (b) Individual Prediction

Figure 9: The departure of actual bandwidth consumption from its conditional mean forecast and the predicted standard deviation of bandwidth consumption in channel 172.

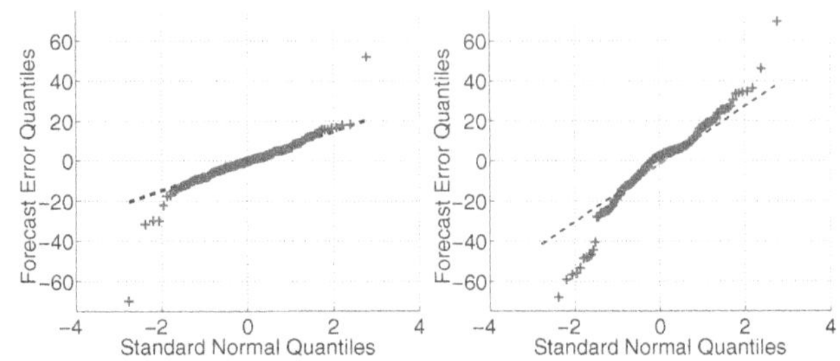

(a) PCA-based Prediction (b) Individual Prediction

Figure 10: Q-Q plot of conditional mean forecast errors in channel 172 over the test period 1680-1860 (1.25 days), in reference to Gaussian quantiles.

$i = 1, \ldots, N$, $m = 1, \ldots, M$. We can therefore forecast $\boldsymbol{\mu}(t)$ and $\boldsymbol{\Sigma}(t)$ as

$$\hat{\boldsymbol{\mu}}(t) = \mathbf{A}\hat{\mathbf{C}}(t) + \hat{e}(t) \cdot \mathbf{1}, \tag{49}$$

$$\hat{\boldsymbol{\Sigma}}(t) = \mathbf{A}\hat{\boldsymbol{\Sigma}}_C(t)\mathbf{A}^{\mathsf{T}} + \hat{\sigma}_e^2(t) \cdot [\mathbf{1}, \ldots, \mathbf{1}], \tag{50}$$

where $\mathbf{1}$ is an all-one column vector of length N and $[\mathbf{1}, \ldots, \mathbf{1}]$ is an all-one matrix of size $N \times N$.

We model each principal component series using a low-order seasonal AIRMA model [9]. Since $\{C_1(t)\}$ clearly shows daily periodicity, we model $\{C_1(t) - C_1(t-144)\}$ as an ARMA$(1,1)$ process, so that the forecast $\hat{C}_1(t)$ is regressed from both the previous value $C_1(t-1)$, the values one day before $C_1(t-144)$, $C_1(t-145)$, and random noise terms. All other components $\{C_i(t)\}$ for $i \geq 2$ do not exhibit periodicity. We thus use ARMA$(1,1)$ processes to model these principal components. The conditional variances of all the component series are forecasted using GARCH$(1,1)$ models [9, 16]. Since the components are orthogonal, we do not need to forecast their covariances. For details of using seasonal AIRMA models and GARCH models for video traffic forecast, please refer to [16, 17].

We compare PCA-based prediction with individual channel prediction over a test period of 1.25 days. Each prediction is made based on the training data of only the previous 1.25 days, which are a little more than one day to incorporate periodicity. The root mean squared errors (RMSEs) of both approaches for all the 468 channels are summarized in Fig. 7. The channel indices are sorted in descending order of the channel size. We can see that the PCA-based approach outperforms individual predictions regardless of channel sizes. For large channels, the ratio of RMSE over mean bandwidth consumption is less than 15% in most cases using the PCA-based approach.

To zoom in, we take channel 172 as an example. Fig. 8 compares the conditional mean predictions produced by the PCA-based approach with those produced by individual prediction. We observe that individual prediction tends to oscillate drastically, while the PCA-based approach can better identify both periodicity and downward trends. One reason is that the driving factors found by PCA are weighted averages over all the channels, with channel-specific erratic noises smoothed out, exhibiting co-movements of all the channels.

The standard deviation forecast of channel 172 is plotted in Fig. 9. Even though there is a big gap between real demand and its conditional mean forecast around time 1700, the GARCH$(1,1)$ model is able to forecast a larger demand variance at this time, which will be leveraged by the cloud to allocate more capacity to guard against performance risks, using the technologies in Sec. 4.2. It is worth noting that we do not assume that demand can always be perfectly forecasted: the entire point of variance or volatility forecast via GARCH is to estimate the deviation of actual demand from the conditional mean prediction and enable risk management in a probabilistic sense. Fig. 10 shows the Q-Q plot of forecast errors. We observe that with PCA, the actual demand will oscillate around its conditional mean forecast more like a Gaussian process. This also substantiates the belief that each D_i behaves like a Gaussian random variable.

Last but not least, the PCA-based approach has a lower complexity: it involves training a seasonal ARIMA model for each of the 10 principal components, together with finding these components from the 468 channels using PCA. Once the models are trained, forecasting is simply a linear regression with negligible running time. In contrast, individual prediction has to train a seasonal ARIMA model for each of the 468 channels separately, leading to a much higher complexity.

7. TRADING SIMULATIONS

In this section, we simulate a computerized bandwidth reservation and trading environment based on our proposed algorithms. The simulation operates in rounds of 10 minutes. Before the start

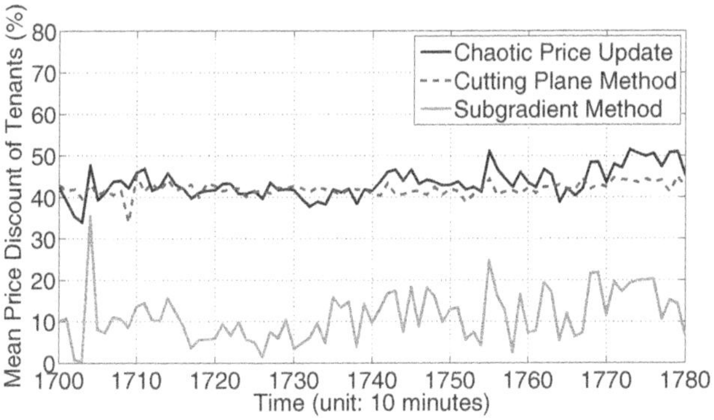

Figure 11: The mean price discount of all 100 tenants vs. time.

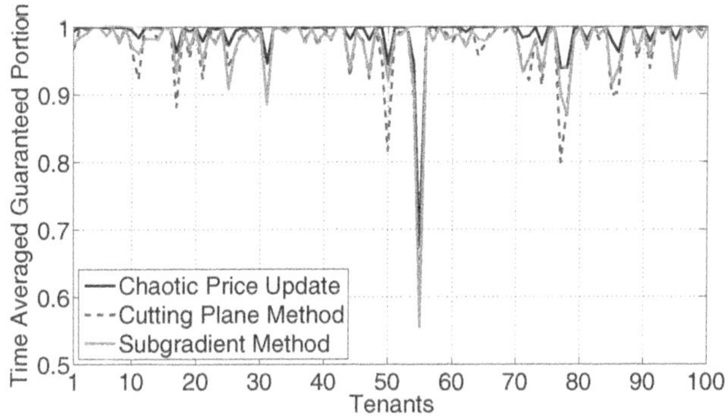

Figure 12: The guaranteed portion of each tenant averaged over all test periods 1700-1780.

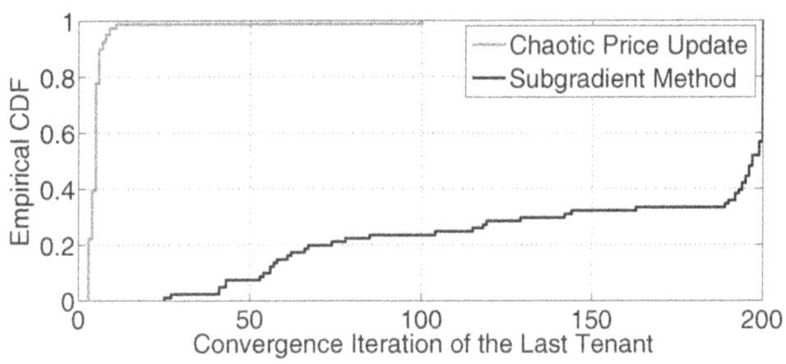

Figure 13: The CDF of the maximum convergence iteration of all tenants in each test period.

of each 10-minute period, the cloud provider has predicted the demand mean and covariances in this period and informed each tenant i about its specific μ_i and σ_i. When the period starts, the distributed price negotiation process immediately starts until convergence. Since in our particular problem, the cloud provider has superior computation power (even for finding polyhedra centroid), the delay is mainly due to the iterative message passing of prices and guaranteed portions between tenants and the cloud. We compare three algorithms: chaotic price update, the cutting-plane method and subgradient method, in terms of the convergence speed and optimization accuracy.

We consider 100 video channels of different sizes and statistics in the UUSee demand traces over a test period of 810 minutes. We assume each channel is a *tenant* that relies on the cloud for servicing the video requests from its end-users. We input such demand traces to our pricing framework and check the algorithm efficiency in the challenging case that prediction and optimization are to be carried out every 10 minutes. If the algorithms work for a 10-minute frequency, they will be competent for lower operating frequencies, such as on an hourly basis. We consider utility functions of the form (2). Under a Gaussian approximation of D_i, each tenant will have an expected utility

$$\mathbf{E}[U_i(w_i)] = \alpha_i w_i \mu_i - e^{A_i(1-w_i)\mu_i + \frac{1}{2}A_i^2(1-w_i)^2\sigma_i^2}. \quad (51)$$

The first term on the righthand side corresponds to the expected revenue of each tenant made from serving the demand $w_i D_i$, while the second term models a reputation loss which is convex and increasing in terms of the unfulfilled demand. In our simulation, we set $\alpha_i = 1$ and $A_i = 0.5$. Since different tenants have different μ_i and σ_i, their utilities are heterogeneous. We set the marginal cost of allocating bandwidth capacity to be $\beta := c'(K) = 0.5$, and assume that the cloud provider has an outage probability of $\epsilon = 0.01$.

We set the algorithm termination conditions as follows. In each iteration, if the change in either w_i, k_i or g_i ($\mathbf{g}_{\mathbf{k}^{(t)}} = [g_1^{(t)}, \ldots, g_N^{(t)}]$) is below some threshold, its w_i is not updated (using message-passing). Chaotic price update will stop if $|w_i^{(t)} - w_i^{t-1}| < 0.01$ or it has run for 100 iterations. The cutting-plane method will stop if $|k_i^{(t)} - k_i^{t-1}| < 0.05$ or it has run for 100 iterations. The subgradient method, as the benchmark, will stop if $|g_i^{(t)} - g_i^{(t-1)}| < 0.05$. In order to be generous to the benchmark algorithm, we set the maximum number of iterations for the subgradient method to 200. Note that in the subgradient method, the step size of price updates cannot be too small, which incurs slow convergence; it cannot be too big either, in which case the final output will be far away from the real optimal value. We optimize such a step size and set it to 0.1 for price updates. The other two algorithms are step-size-free.

We first compare the algorithm outputs upon termination. Note that with multiplexing, the final optimal price k_i^* for each tenant i should be lower than its initial value $k_i^{(0)} = \beta(\mu_i + \theta(\epsilon)\sigma_i)$, which is also the optimal price without multiplexing. We define $1 - k_i^*/k_i^{(0)}$ as the price discount that tenant i enjoys from multiplexing. Fig. 11 plots the mean price discount averaged over all the tenants in each test period. We observe that both chaotic price update and the cutting-plane method bring more discounts to tenants than the subgradient method. We further check the mean guaranteed portion chosen by each tenant averaged over all test periods in Fig. 12, which shows that most tenants choose a guaranteed portion close to 1 and the three algorithms are close to each other. This means although the three algorithms may reach a similar level of social welfare, the subgradient algorithm is not so good at fine-tuning the optimal prices for tenants with a guaranteed portion close to 1.

Finally, we check the communication overhead of all three algorithms. We define an iteration of message passing as a round-trip communication in which the cloud provider passes the prices to a tenant, which returns a chosen guaranteed portion. We observe that for chaotic price update, the convergence iteration of the last tenant (worst-case convergence iteration) in each test period is almost always less than 10. The CDF of the worst-case convergence iteration of chaotic price update is plotted in Fig. 13. In the same figure, we can observe that 40% of the time, the subgradient method needs 200 rounds to converge, while 60% of the time, it converges between 25 and 200 rounds. The cutting plane method always takes 100 rounds to converge, which are half of the maximum rounds needed by the subgradient method.

Taking both performance and speed into consideration, chaotic price update largely outperforms the other two. The cutting-plane method can also achieve better performance than the subgradient method with better price discounts reached within 100 rounds. Therefore, a practical strategy is to use chaotic price update first, and if it does not converge in 20 rounds, switch to the cutting-plane or subgradient method.

8. CONCLUDING REMARKS

Current-generation cloud computing platforms do not provide bandwidth guarantees, impeding the cloud adoption by tenants running QoS sensitive applications. Recent advancements in datacenter engineering augment the cloud-tenant interface with bandwidth reservation enabled. As bandwidth reservation becomes technically feasible, new models are needed to price the bandwidth guarantees to compensate the pay-as-you-go model which only prices the usage. In this paper, we propose a guaranteed cloud service model, where each tenant does not have to estimate the absolute amount of bandwidth it needs to reserve—it simply specifies a percentage of its demand from end-users that it wishes to serve with guaranteed performance, which we call the guaranteed portion, while the rest of the demand will be served with best efforts as the current cloud providers do. The cloud provider will estimate tenant demands through workload analysis and guarantee the performance in a probabilistic sense. The above process is repeated in small periods such as hours or tens of minutes.

Our main contribution is to fairly price such guaranteed services in each period. In contrast to the uniform usage pricing model, we price bandwidth reservations heterogeneously for tenants based on their workload statistics such as burstiness and correlation. It turns out to be computational challenge to find the optimal prices that maximize the expected social welfare under demand uncertainty. To address this challenge, we propose two novel distributed algorithms based on iterative equation updates and cutting-plane methods, which are oblivious to the choice of step sizes. We also propose practical algorithms to predict demand statistics based on a factor model. Trace-driven simulations show that both algorithms achieve faster convergence and better performance than subgradient methods. Given the abundant computing power and workload data in the cloud, our bandwidth reservation and algorithmic pricing system operates effectively at a fine granularity of as small as 10 minutes.

9. REFERENCES

[1] Amazon Cluster Compute, 2011. http://aws.amazon.com/ec2/hpc- applications/.

[2] Amazon Web Services. http://aws.amazon.com/.

[3] UUSee Inc. [Online]. Available: http://www.uusee.com.

[4] Four Reasons We Choose Amazon's Cloud as Our Computing Platform. *The Netflix "Tech" Blog*, Dec. 14 2010.

[5] D. Applegate, A. Archer, V. G. S. Lee, and K. Ramakrishnan. Optimal Content Placement for a Large-Scale VoD System. In *Proc. ACM International Conference on Emerging Networking Experiments and Technologies (CoNEXT)*, 2010.

[6] M. Armbrust, A. Fox, R. Griffith, A. D. Joseph, R. Katz, A. Konwinski, G. Lee, D. Patterson, A. Rabkin, I. Stoica, and M. Zaharia. A View of Cloud Computing. *Communications of the ACM*, 53(4):50–58, 2010.

[7] H. Ballani, P. Costa, T. Karagiannis, and A. Rowstron. Towards Predictable Datacenter Networks. In *Proc. of SIGCOMM'11*, Toronto, ON, Canada, 2011.

[8] D. P. Bertsekas, A. Nedic, and A. E. Ozdaglar. *Convex Analysis and Optimization*. Athena Scientific, 2003.

[9] G. E. P. Box, G. M. Jenkins, and G. C. Reinsel. *Time Series Analysis: Forecasting and Control*. Wiley, 2008.

[10] M. Chiang, S. H. Low, A. R. Calderbank, and J. C. Doyle. Layering as optimization decomposition: A mathematical theory of network architectures. *Proceedings of the IEEE*, 95(1):255 – 312, Jan. 2007.

[11] R. L. Grossman. The Case for Cloud Computing. *IT Professional*, 11(2):23–27, March-April 2009.

[12] C. Guo, G. Lu, H. J. Wang, S. Yang, C. Kong, P. Sun, W. Wu, and Y. Zhang. SecondNet: a Data Center Network Virtualization Architecture with Bandwidth Guarantees. In *Proc. of ACM International Conference on Emerging Networking Experiments and Technologies (CoNEXT)*, 2010.

[13] G. Gürsun, M. Crovella, and I. Matta. Describing and Forecasting Video Access Patterns. In *Proc. of IEEE INFOCOM Mini-Conference*, 2011.

[14] D. Kossmann, T. Kraska, and S. Loesing. An Evaluation of Alternative Architectures for Transaction Processing in the Cloud. In *Proc. of International Conference on Management of Data (SIGMOD)*, 2010.

[15] D. Niu, C. Feng, and B. Li. Pricing Cloud Bandwidth Reservations under Demand Uncertainty. Technical report, University of Toronto, 2012 http://iqua.ece.toronto.edu/~bli/papers/dniu-priceBR12.pdf.

[16] D. Niu, B. Li, and S. Zhao. Understanding Demand Volatility in Large VoD Systems. In *Proc. of the 21st International workshop on Network and Operating Systems Support for Digital Audio and Video (NOSSDAV)*, 2011.

[17] D. Niu, Z. Liu, B. Li, and S. Zhao. Demand Forecast and Performance Prediction in Peer-Assisted On-Demand Streaming Systems. In *Proc. of IEEE INFOCOM Mini-Conference*, 2011.

[18] D. Palomar and M. Chiang. A tutorial on decomposition methods for network utility maximization. *IEEE J. on Sel. Areas in Communications*, 24(8):1439 – 1451, Aug. 2006.

[19] J. C. Panzar and D. S. Sibley. Public Utility Pricing under Risk: The Case of Self-Rationing. *The American Economic Review*, 68(5):888–895, Dec. 1978.

[20] J. Schad, J. Dittrich, and J.-A. Quiane-Ruiz. Runtime Measurements in the Cloud: Observing, Analyzing, and Reducing Variance. In *Proc. of VLDB*, 2010.

[21] C. W. Tan, D. Palomar, and M. Chiang. Distributed optimization of coupled systems with applications to network utility maximization. In *Proc. of IEEE International Conference on Acoustics, Speech and Signal Processing*, Toulouse, France, May 2006.

[22] C. Wilson, H. Ballani, T. Karagiannis, and A. Rowstron. Better Never Than Late: Meeting Deadlines in Datacenter Networks . In *Proc. of SIGCOMM*, 2011.

[23] C. Wu, B. Li, and S. Zhao. Multi-Channel Live P2P Streaming: Refocusing on Servers. In *Proc. of IEEE INFOCOM*, 2008.

[24] H. Yin, X. Liu, F. Qiu, N. Xia, C. Lin, H. Zhang, V. Sekar, and G. Min. Inside the Bird's Nest: Measurements of Large-Scale Live VoD from the 2008 Olympics. In *Proc. ACM Internet Measurement Conference (IMC)*, 2009.

[25] M. Zaharia, A. Konwinski, A. D. Joseph, Y. Katz, and I. Stoica. Improving MapReduce Performance in Heterogeneous Environments. In *Proc. of OSDI*, 2008.

Temperature Management in Data Centers: Why Some (Might) Like It Hot

Nosayba El-Sayed Ioan Stefanovici George Amvrosiadis Andy A. Hwang
Bianca Schroeder
Department of Computer Science
University of Toronto
{nosayba, ioan, gamvrosi, hwang, bianca}@cs.toronto.edu

ABSTRACT

The energy consumed by data centers is starting to make up a significant fraction of the world's energy consumption and carbon emissions. A large fraction of the consumed energy is spent on data center cooling, which has motivated a large body of work on temperature management in data centers. Interestingly, a key aspect of temperature management has not been well understood: controlling the setpoint temperature at which to run a data center's cooling system. Most data centers set their thermostat based on (conservative) suggestions by manufacturers, as there is limited understanding of how higher temperatures will affect the system. At the same time, studies suggest that increasing the temperature setpoint by just one degree could save 2–5% of the energy consumption.

This paper provides a multi-faceted study of temperature management in data centers. We use a large collection of field data from different production environments to study the impact of temperature on hardware reliability, including the reliability of the storage subsystem, the memory subsystem and server reliability as a whole. We also use an experimental testbed based on a thermal chamber and a large array of benchmarks to study two other potential issues with higher data center temperatures: the effect on server performance and power. Based on our findings, we make recommendations for temperature management in data centers, that create the potential for saving energy, while limiting negative effects on system reliability and performance.

Categories and Subject Descriptors

B.8 [**Hardware**]: Performance and Reliability—*Temperature*; C.4 [**Computer Systems Organization**]: Performance of Systems—*Temperature*

Keywords

Data Center, Temperature, Reliability, Performance, Energy, LSE, Hard Drive, Memory, DRAM, CPU, Fans

SIGMETRICS'12, June 11–15, 2012, London, England, UK.

1. INTRODUCTION

Data centers have developed into major energy hogs. The world's data centers are estimated to consume power equivalent to about seventeen 1,000 MW power plants, equaling more than 1% of total world electricity consumption, and to emit as much carbon dioxide as all of Argentina [17]. More than a third, sometimes up to one half of a data center's electricity bill is made up by electricity for cooling [6, 19]. For instance, for a data center consisting of 30,000 square feet and consuming 10MW, the yearly cost of running the cooling infrastructure can reach up to $4-8 million [23].

Not surprisingly, a large body of research has been devoted to reducing cooling cost. Approaches that have been investigated include, for example, methods to minimize air flow inefficiencies [23, 35], load balancing and the incorporation of temperature awareness into workload placement in data centers [7, 25, 28, 33], and power reduction features in individual servers [14, 15].

Interestingly, one key aspect in the thermal management of a data center is still not very well understood: controlling the setpoint temperature at which to run a data center's cooling system. Data centers typically operate in a temperature range between 20C and 22C, some are as cold as 13C degrees [8, 29]. Due to lack of scientific data, these values are often chosen based on equipment manufacturers' (conservative) suggestions. Some estimate that increasing the setpoint temperature by just one degree can reduce energy consumption by 2 to 5 percent [8, 9]. Microsoft reports that raising the temperature by two to four degrees in one of its Silicon Valley data centers saved $250,000 in annual energy costs [29]. Google and Facebook have also been considering increasing the temperature in their data centers [29].

While increasing data center temperatures might seem like an easy way to save energy and reduce carbon emissions, it comes with some concerns, the most obvious being its impact on system reliability. Unfortunately, the details of how increased data center temperatures will affect hardware reliability are not well understood and existing evidence is contradicting. A recent study [35] indicated that in order to avoid thermal redlining, a typical server needs to have the air temperature at its front inlets be in the range of 20C – 30C. Every 10C increase over 21C decreases the reliability of long-term electronics by 50% [24]. Other studies show that a 15C rise increases hard disk drive failure rates by a factor of two [4, 10]. On the other hand, a recent Google study [26] suggests that *lower* temperatures are actually more detrimental to disk reliability than higher temperatures.

Other possible concerns of increasing data center temper-

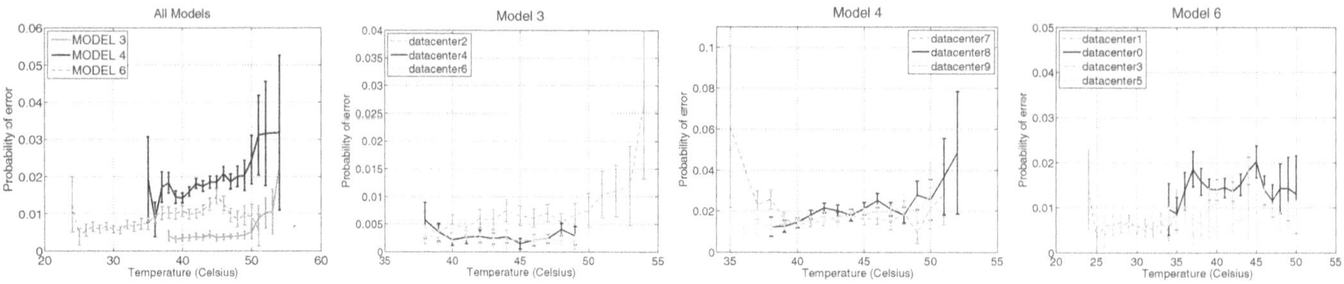

Figure 1: The monthly probability of LSEs as a function of temperature. In the three plots for individual models each line corresponds to the measurement from a different data center.

atures include the effect on server performance, as many servers employ techniques such as CPU or memory throttling when temperatures reach a critical threshold, and the effect on server energy consumption, as increased temperatures will lead to increases in power leakage and higher (server internal) fan speeds.

The goal of this paper is to provide a better understanding of the issues involved in raising data center temperatures. As a first contribution, in Section 2 we perform a detailed study of the effect of temperature on hardware reliability by analyzing a large amount of field data. The data comes from three different organizations spanning several dozen data centers and covers a diverse set of common reliability issues, including hard disk failures, latent sector errors in hard disks, uncorrectable errors in DRAM, DRAM replacements, and general node outages. In Section 3 we perform an experimental study using a testbed based on a thermal chamber and a large set of different workloads to better understand the effects that temperature has on the performance and power usage of systems. Finally, in Section 4 we use the results of our study to derive some insights and guidelines for running data centers at higher temperatures, while limiting the impact on system performance and reliability.

2. TEMPERATURE AND RELIABILITY

We begin our study by analyzing a diverse set of field data collected at different organizations and data centers to better understand the effect of temperature on various aspects of hardware reliability. We first focus on two specific hardware components, hard disks and DRAM, since these are among the most frequently replaced components in modern data centers [30, 31]. In Sections 2.1 and 2.2, we study two common failure modes of hard disks, latent sector errors and complete disk failures, respectively, before moving to DRAM reliability in Section 2.3. Then, in Section 2.4 we use data on node outages in data centers to study the effect of temperature on overall server reliability.

2.1 Temperature and latent sector errors

2.1.1 Background and data

Latent sector errors (LSEs) are a common failure mode, where individual sectors on a disk become inaccessible, and the data stored on them is lost (unless the system can use redundancy mechanisms to recover it). LSEs happen at a significant rate in the field [5, 26], with 3-4% of all drives experiencing them at some point in their life, and are expected to grow more common as disk capacities increase. While recent work [5] has studied the prevalence and some statistical properties of LSEs, there is no prior work on how temperature affects this important error condition.

To study the effect of temperature on the prevalence of LSEs, we obtained data collected from January 2007 to May 2009 at 7 different data centers (DCs) at Google covering three different disk models. For each of the disks, we have monthly reports of the average (internal) disk temperature and temperature variance in that month, the count of latent sector errors, the number of read and write operations during that month, and the age of the disk. All data were collected by polling the disks' internal self-monitoring facility (SMART). The measurement infrastructure and methodology Google uses to collect such data are described in Pinheiro et al. [26]. The table below summarizes our data:

Model ID	#DCs	#Disks	#Disk Months	Avg. monthly LSE probability
3	3	18,692	300,000	0.0063
4	3	17,515	300,000	0.0177
6	4	36,671	300,000	0.0067

2.1.2 Analysis

Figure 1 (far left) shows for each of the three models the monthly probability of a disk experiencing an LSE as a function of the average temperature. The error bars in this figure (and in all other figures in this work) are computed using a 95% confidence level; larger bars for higher temperatures are due to lack of data. Since there are many data center-specific factors beyond temperature that might affect reliability (workload, humidity, power spikes, handling procedures, etc), we also break down the results for each model by data center. The three rightmost graphs in Figure 1 show the monthly LSE probabilities for the three models, where each line corresponds to a different data center.

As one might expect, we observe a trend of increasing LSE rates as temperature rises. However, the magnitude of increase is much smaller than expected based on common models and estimates, in particular when isolating the instances of LSEs per model per data center. Models for the effect of temperature on hardware components usually assume an exponential increase in failures as a function of temperature (based on the Arrhenius equation [16]), and predict roughly doubling failure rates for every 10-15C increase in temperature [4, 10, 35]. Visual inspection of our graphs shows for only 5 out of the 10 model/data center combinations a clear increase in errors with temperature: model 3, data center 2; model 4, data centers 8 and 9; model 6, data centers 3 and 5. We also observe that the increase in error rates tends to be linear, rather than exponential, except for very high temperatures (above 50C).

To formalize our observation above, we fitted two different

Model	DC	Monthly Probability	Linear fit a1	Linear fit a2	Linear fit SSE	Exponential fit b1	Exponential fit b2	Exponential fit SSE
3	2	$7.99 \cdot 10^{-3}$	$-2.726 \cdot 10^{-2}$	$7.664 \cdot 10^{-4}$	$2.331 \cdot 10^{-4}$	$2.561 \cdot 10^{-1}$	$-1.637 \cdot 10^{+2}$	$2.402 \cdot 10^{-4}$
	4	$2.93 \cdot 10^{-3}$	$7.519 \cdot 10^{-3}$	$-1.055 \cdot 10^{-4}$	$1.157 \cdot 10^{-5}$	$6.613 \cdot 10^{-4}$	$6.192 \cdot 10^{+1}$	$1.112 \cdot 10^{-5}$
	6	$2.51 \cdot 10^{-3}$	$7.322 \cdot 10^{-3}$	$-1.111 \cdot 10^{-4}$	$2.328 \cdot 10^{-6}$	$3.730 \cdot 10^{-4}$	$8.092 \cdot 10^{+1}$	$2.402 \cdot 10^{-6}$
4	7	$2.06 \cdot 10^{-2}$	$6.517 \cdot 10^{-2}$	$-1.025 \cdot 10^{-3}$	$1.720 \cdot 10^{-3}$	$3.624 \cdot 10^{-3}$	$7.054 \cdot 10^{+1}$	$1.595 \cdot 10^{-3}$
	8	$2.28 \cdot 10^{-2}$	$-5.614 \cdot 10^{-2}$	$1.755 \cdot 10^{-3}$	$3.994 \cdot 10^{-4}$	$5.256 \cdot 10^{-1}$	$-1.429 \cdot 10^{+2}$	$3.920 \cdot 10^{-4}$
	9	$1.73 \cdot 10^{-2}$	$-2.346 \cdot 10^{-2}$	$9.482 \cdot 10^{-4}$	$6.192 \cdot 10^{-5}$	$1.955 \cdot 10^{-1}$	$-1.047 \cdot 10^{+2}$	$6.218 \cdot 10^{-5}$
6	0	$1.43 \cdot 10^{-2}$	$8.730 \cdot 10^{-3}$	$1.317 \cdot 10^{-4}$	$1.282 \cdot 10^{-4}$	$2.543 \cdot 10^{-2}$	$-2.481 \cdot 10^{+1}$	$1.275 \cdot 10^{-4}$
	1	$6.67 \cdot 10^{-3}$	$1.067 \cdot 10^{-2}$	$-1.356 \cdot 10^{-4}$	$7.784 \cdot 10^{-5}$	$4.695 \cdot 10^{-3}$	$8.477 \cdot 10^{+0}$	$7.944 \cdot 10^{-5}$
	3	$7.61 \cdot 10^{-3}$	$-4.752 \cdot 10^{-3}$	$3.616 \cdot 10^{-4}$	$2.918 \cdot 10^{-5}$	$3.131 \cdot 10^{-2}$	$-4.863 \cdot 10^{+1}$	$3.235 \cdot 10^{-5}$
	5	$7.10 \cdot 10^{-3}$	$-1.001 \cdot 10^{-2}$	$3.934 \cdot 10^{-4}$	$3.586 \cdot 10^{-5}$	$1.180 \cdot 10^{-1}$	$-1.236 \cdot 10^{+2}$	$3.820 \cdot 10^{-5}$

Table 1: Parameters from fitting linear and exponential models to monthly LSE probabilities as a function of avg. temperature.

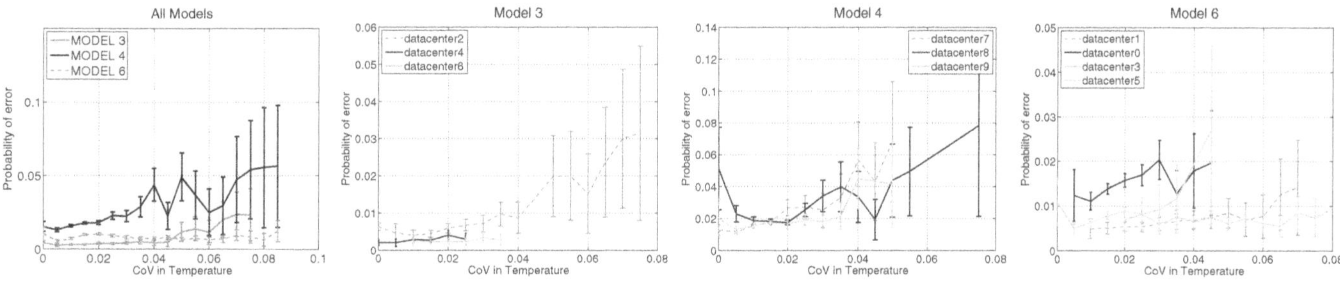

Figure 2: The monthly probability of LSEs as a function of variability in temperature, measured by the coefficient of variation. In the three plots for individual models each line corresponds to the measurement from a different data center.

models to the data. The first is a simple linear model, i.e. we try to model the error rate y as a function of temperature t as $y = a_1 + a_2 \cdot t$. Since one of the most common models for effects of temperature on hardware reliability, the Arrhenius model, is an exponential one, we also fit an exponential model to our data, i.e. we model the failure rate y as a function of temperature t as follows: $y = a_1 \cdot e^{-a_2/t}$. The detailed results (including values for the parameters a_1, a_2, b_1, b_2, and the corresponding sum of squared errors (SSE)) are presented in Table 1. We find that in all cases the linear model provides a fit of comparable or even better accuracy, as measured by the SSE. The only exception is model 3, data center 2, where the exponential model provides a better fit. We attribute this to the sudden increase in LSEs for temperatures above 50C. When repeating our analysis for only data points below 50C, also for model 3, data center 2, the linear model provides a better fit.

Observation 1: For the temperature range that our data covers with statistical significance ($< 50C$), the prevalence of latent sector errors increases much more slowly with temperature, than reliability models suggest. Half of our model/data center pairs show no evidence of an increase, while for the others the increase is linear rather than exponential.

In addition to comparing the quality of the linear versus the exponential fit, it is interesting to look at the slope of the linear increase in errors (parameter a_2), i.e. the rate at which errors increase. One interpretation of a_2 is that it gives the additional fraction of drives that will develop LSEs for each 1 degree increase in temperature, e.g. $a_2 = 0.01$ means that for a 1 degree increase in temperature an additional 1% of the drive population in a data center would develop LSEs in a given month (that would not have had LSEs otherwise). We find that for 4 of the 10 model/data center combinations a_2 actually has a small negative value, indicating a small decrease in error rates with temperature. For the remaining positive values, it is important to put the value of a_2 in relation to the average probability of a drive developing an LSE (provided in the third column in Table 1). Studying the values of a_2 for those cases where it is positive, we see that a_2 is always at least an order of magnitude smaller than the average LSE probability for that model/data center combination. That means the fraction of drives in the population that will develop LSEs due to a one degree increase in temperature, will be an order of magnitude smaller than the average observed in the dataset. However, an increase in the range of ten degrees or more in data center temperature would probably warrant some extra measures to protect against data loss due to LSEs.

In addition to the average temperature that a drive is exposed to, another important factor is the variability in temperature, since large variations in temperature can negatively affect IT equipment. To study the impact of temperature variability on LSEs we plot the monthly LSE probabilities as a function of the coefficient of variation (CoV) [1] (see Figure 2). We chose the CoV, rather than variance or standard deviation, since it is normalized by the mean. A positive correlation between LSEs and temperature variance could just be due to the positive correlation between LSEs and mean temperature. Figure 2 shows a clear increase in LSE probabilities with increasing CoV for all models. We verify those visual trends by fitting a linear model to capture the relationship between LSEs and the CoV, and find a positive slope (a_2) for all model/data center pairs.

Observation 2: The variability in temperature tends to have a more pronounced and consistent effect on LSE rates than mere average temperature.

Our analysis so far has exclusively focused on the probability of a drive developing LSEs. Another interesting question is whether higher temperature leads to a higher number of LSEs, once a drive starts developing LSEs. To answer

[1] Recall that the coefficient of variation is defined as the standard deviation divided by the mean.

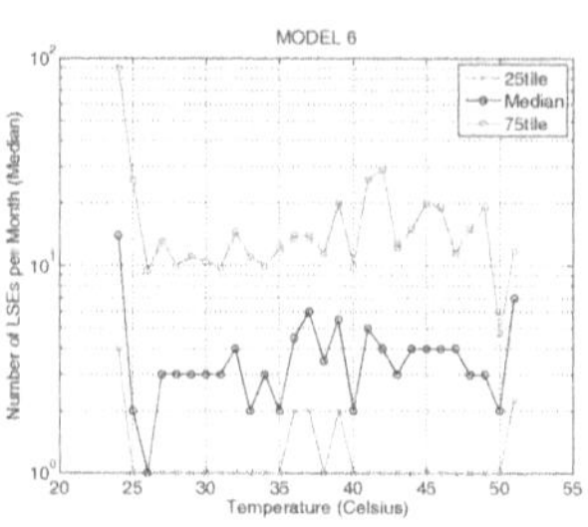

Figure 3: The quartiles of number of LSEs for drives with LSEs as a function of temperature.

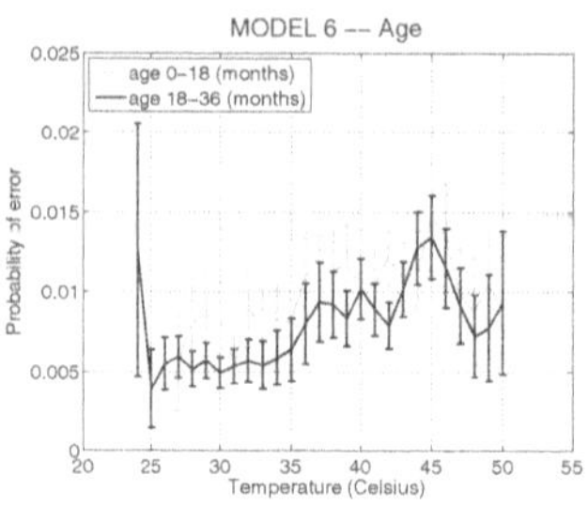

Figure 4: The monthly probability of LSEs as a function of temperature by drive age.

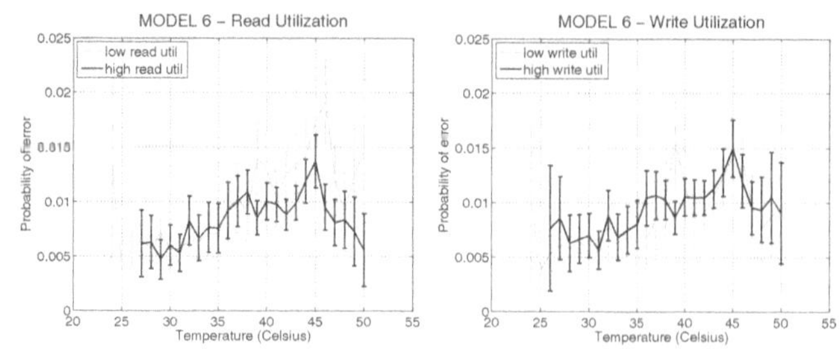

Figure 5: The monthly probability of LSEs as a function of temperature for drives with high and low write loads (right) and read loads (left).

this question Figure 3 plots for those disk months that have errors the 25th and 75th percentile, and the mean. (We only include results for model 6, all others have comparable trends). We focus on the quartiles, rather than the mean, since we find the mean number of LSEs to be highly variable and hence easily biased by outliers. We observe that the line for all quartiles is flat, indicating that hotter drives with errors do not experience a higher frequency of errors than colder drives with errors.

Observation 3: Higher temperatures do not increase the expected number of LSEs once a drive develops LSEs, possibly indicating that the mechanisms that cause LSEs are the same under high or low temperatures.

Figure 1 provides another interesting observation: The rate of LSEs for the same model can vary greatly across data centers. For example, model 3's error rate is significantly higher (more than 2x difference) for data center 2 than for the other data centers, and model 6's error rates are significantly higher for data center 0 than for other data centers (again, more than 2x difference). This brings up the question whether factors, such as environmental conditions or the age or usage of a drive affect how it reacts to temperature. While we have no data on environmental factors, such as humidity or the quality of the power, we have information on the age of each drive and its utilization and study the effect of those factors in Figures 4 and 5.

Our study of age and temperature in Figure 4 focuses on model 6, since the disks for this model span the widest range in age. We divide the drives into two groups, those that are less than 18 months old and those that are 18-36 months old, and plot LSE probabilities as a function of temperature separately for each group. We find that both lines show similar trends with no evidence that older drives are more sensitive to higher temperatures.

Observation 4: Within a range of 0-36 months, older drives are not more likely to develop LSEs under temperature than younger drives.

Figure 5 studies the effect of workload intensity. Figure 5 (left) divides disks into two groups, one with high read utilization and one with low read utilization, and plots the LSE probabilities separately for the two groups. We measure read utilization by the number of read operations per month and assign a disk to the low read utilization group if the number of read operations is below the median for the dataset, and to the high read utilization group otherwise. Figure 5 (right) performs the corresponding analysis for write utilization. Results are shown for model 6 only, but trends were similar for other models as well.

We find that drives with higher utilization are not more sensitive to higher temperatures. That is an interesting result beyond the study of temperature effects, as it has been an open question as to how workload intensity affects LSEs. Methods that are intended to protect against data loss due to LSEs, such as running a periodic "scrubber" that reads the entire disk to proactively detect LSEs, place additional load on a system, and a concern is that this added load might increase the rate of LSEs. Our results indicate that such worries are, likely, unfounded.

Observation 5: High utilization does not increase LSE rates under temperatures.

To add statistical rigour to Observations 4 and 5, we performed an ANOVA test. The results indicate no correlation between LSEs and write utilization. There is evidence for a correlation with read utilization and age, however this is due to drives with *lower* read utilization and *lower* age experiencing slightly increased rates of LSEs.

2.2 Temperature and disk failures

2.2.1 Background and data

Hard disk failures include any kind of disk problems that are considered serious enough to replace the disk in question. Hard disk failures are a serious condition since they create the potential for data loss and happen at a significant rate: typically 1-5% of drives in a data center need to be replaced in a given year [26, 31]. The only existing work that includes trends for the effect of temperature on hard disk failures based on field data is the work by Pinheiro et al. [26]. Surprisingly, this work found a strong *drop* in disk failure rates with *increasing* temperature, except for very high temperatures (above 45C). This is in contrast with common reliability models, which estimate disk failure rates to increase exponentially with temperature.

The goal of this section is to revisit the question of how temperature affects disk failure rates. In addition to obtaining a more conclusive answer to this question, we also look at the question from a broader angle, studying the effect of utilization, differences between models and data centers, and the age of a disk. For our study, we have obtained data on disk replacements collected from January 2007 to May 2009 at 19 different data centers (DCs) at Google covering 5 different disk models. For each disk we know the age of the disk, the average temperature and average utilization over

		All temperatures								< 50'C Temperatures						
Model	DC	Monthly Prob. ($\cdot 10^{-3}$)	Linear fit a1 ($\cdot 10^{-3}$)	Linear fit a2 ($\cdot 10^{-4}$)	Linear fit SSE ($\cdot 10^{-6}$)	Exponential fit b1 ($\cdot 10^{-2}$)	Exponential fit b2	Exponential fit SSE ($\cdot 10^{-6}$)	Monthly Prob. ($\cdot 10^{-3}$)	Linear fit a1 ($\cdot 10^{-3}$)	Linear fit a2 ($\cdot 10^{-5}$)	Linear fit SSE ($\cdot 10^{-6}$)	Exponential fit b1 ($\cdot 10^{-4}$)	Exponential fit b2	Exponential fit SSE ($\cdot 10^{-7}$)
1	9	2.82	−6.387	1.958	6.357	3.242	−116.7	6.702	2.47	0.02274	5.315	1.844	45.88	−29.34	18.96
	13	3.79	−7.253	2.273	5.110	4.057	−116.4	5.241	3.34	0.2640	6.499	1.348	79.08	−41.24	13.52
2	3	3.32	−6.602	2.157	12.30	4.500	−123.3	12.69	2.87	−0.02586	6.384	5.376	94.40	−56.07	55.32
	9	3.09	−8.462	2.485	15.56	6.065	−142.5	16.37	2.75	−1.297	8.807	9.901	96.89	−60.98	102.1
4	8	1.07	−0.523	0.3841	1.996	0.7987	−84.98	2.168	1.07	−1.032	5.201	1.421	129.0	−102.4	15.93
	15	1.64	−4.042	1.481	5.488	4.093	−128.8	5.607	1.41	−3.813	14.15	5.399	353.2	−123.9	56.82
6	0	0.625	0.5464	0.025	0.3250	0.076	−7.242	0.3340	0.625	0.5464	0.2496	0.325	7.600	−7.242	3.340
	1	0.869	0.9486	−0.0183	0.9065	0.06928	7.947	0.9194	0.869	0.9486	−0.1833	0.9065	6.928	7.947	9.194
	2	0.919	2.559	−0.455	0.7095	0.0179	54.33	0.8768	0.919	2.559	−4.555	0.7095	1.798	54.33	8.768
	3	1.45	−1.172	0.5886	6.440	0.3750	−45.18	7.123	1.20	2.117	−2.123	0.9326	5.812	30.03	9.105

Table 2: Parameters from fitting a linear and an exponential model to monthly disk failures as a function of avg. temperature.

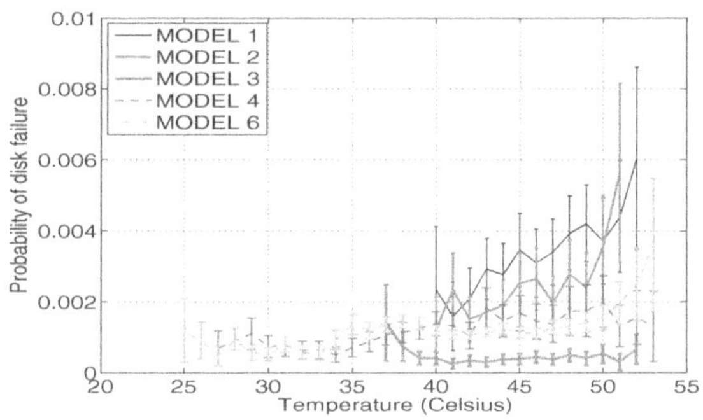

Figure 6: The monthly probability of a disk failure as a function of temperature separated by disk model.

the observation period as reported by the drive's SMART system, and whether the disk was replaced during the observation period. While the time period is different from the study in [26] (there is actually no overlap in time), the measurement methodology and infrastructure used to collect the data is the same as the one Google used in their study.

The following table provides some summary information.

Model	#DCs	#Disks	#Disk Months	Monthly disk fail prob.
1	5	7972	173,945	0.0028
2	4	5906	143,456	0.0023
3	5	93498	752,579	0.0004
4	3	69421	829,859	0.0011
6	5	95226	2,953,123	0.0012

2.2.2 *Analysis*

Figure 6 plots the monthly failure rate for each of the five models averaged across all data centers. Except for one model (model 3) we observe increasing failure rates with rising temperature. However, we observe that the increase in failures with temperature tends to be linear rather than exponential, except for very high temperatures (above 50C). We validate this observation by fitting a linear and an exponential model to the data, following the same methodology as described in Section 2.1. Results are shown in Table 2. Since the slope of the curves tends to change for very high temperatures, we also repeated the analysis by including only data points below 50C (see right half of Table 2). We find that in all cases the linear model provides a significantly better fit than the exponential model.

As explained in Section 2.1, when studying the rate at which failures increase with temperature (as given by the a_2 parameter) it is important to put the amount of increase in failures, in relation to the average failure rate in a system. When looking at the values for a_2 when fitting the linear model to data points below 50C (see Table 2), we notice that for all model/data center combinations a_2 is by two orders of magnitude smaller than the average failure rate (with the exception of one data point, model 4, data center 15). While average monthly failure rates are typically on the order of 0.1-0.2%, the additional fraction of drives one would expect to fail for each degree increase in temperature is on the order of one thousandth of a percent.

Observation 6: For temperatures below 50C, disk failure rates grow more slowly with temperature than common models predict. The increase tends to be linear rather than exponential, and the expected increase in failure rates for each degree increase in temperature is small compared to the magnitude of existing failure rates.

We also note that, unlike the Google study [26], we do not see a general trend for higher failure rates at lower temperatures. For example, the Google study reports more than a 50% drop in failure rate when moving from 25 to 35C. We believe that the reason is the aggregation of data for different models and data centers in the same curve in [26]. Since different drive models run at different temperatures (due to differences in their design) and different drive models can also vary greatly in their failure rate, it is possible that the data points at the lower end of the temperature spectrum contain more drives of a model that happened to run colder and have higher failure rates, hence biasing the results.

As was the case for LSEs, we find that for the same model, the monthly failure probabilities can vary greatly across data centers, even for the same temperature. (Full per-data-center graphs for disk failures are included in the tech-report [13]). This points to other factors, beyond temperature, that have an equally strong or stronger effect on disk lifetimes and motivates us to study two possible factors that we have data on: age and utilization. We followed the same methodology as for LSEs, and divided the drives for each model into those with high and low read utilization, high and low write utilization, and based on age. We found that the behavior of a drive under temperature did not change depending on either utilization or age (with statistically significant data only up to 36 months).

Observation 7: Neither utilization nor the age of a drive significantly affect drive failure rates as a function of temperature.

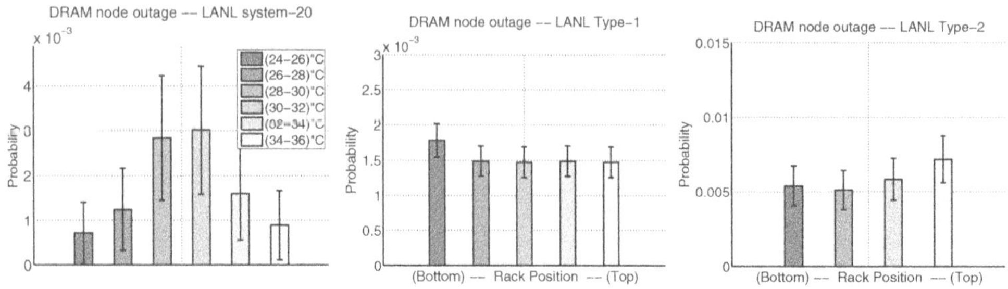

Figure 7: Probability of node outages at LANL due to DRAM problems as a function of temperature (left) and rack positions as a proxy for temperature (middle, right).

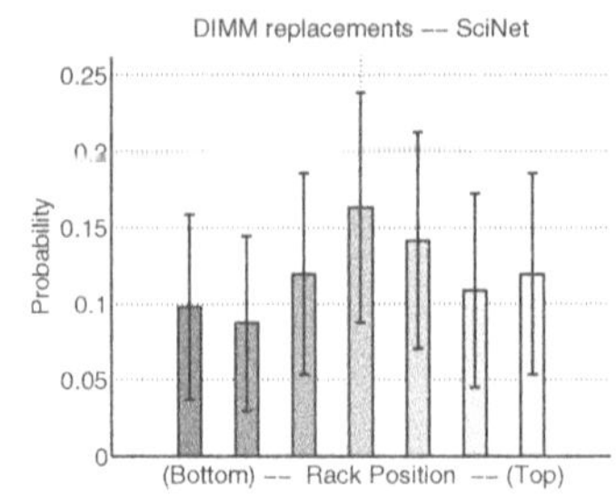

Figure 8: DIMM replacements at SciNet.

2.3 Temperature and DRAM reliability

2.3.1 *Background and data*

In this section, we study how temperature affects the reliability of DRAM, which is one of the most commonly replaced hardware components in data centers and the most common hardware related cause of node outages [30, 31]. DRAM has two different error modes: correctable errors (CEs), where a bit on a DRAM chip is flipped, but can be corrected with internal error correcting codes (ECC); and uncorrectable errors (UEs), where multiple bits are flipped, and the number of erroneous bits is too large for the ECC to correct, causing a machine crash or shutdown. CEs can be caused, by external disturbances, such as cosmic rays, or by hardware defects, such as a stuck bit. UEs usually involve underlying hardware defects, since it is highly unlikely that cosmic rays would simultaneously flip a large enough number of bits to cause an uncorrectable error. Therefore in many data centers it is a common policy to immediately replace a DRAM DIMM after the first occurrence of a UE.

Work in [32] looked at correctable errors in DRAM and showed that their frequency goes up with temperature, but found that this correlation disappears once one controls for utilization. In this section, we ask how temperature affects the long-term reliability of DRAM, rather than the likelihood of transient problems, i.e. do higher temperatures increase the rate at which DRAM wears out and needs to be replaced. We study the long-term reliability of DRAM by analyzing data on DIMM replacements, data on node outages that were attributed to DRAM, and data on uncorrectable errors (since the latter two tend to be indicative of hardware problems and typically lead to replacement of a DIMM). We have collected data from three different sources:

Google: Google routinely collects data on the occurrence of correctable and uncorrectable errors in all of their data centers, as well as periodic temperature measurements based on sensors on the motherboard. An overview of Google's measurement infrastructure is provided in [32]. For our study we have obtained data for a sample set of Google's systems, comprising a dozen different data centers. The data centers are based on five different hardware platforms, where a hardware platform is defined by the motherboard and memory generation. Details on the hardware platforms are considered confidential and we hence just refer to them as Platforms A, B, C, D, E, F.

Los Alamos National Lab (LANL): LANL has made available data on node outages for more than 20 of their high-performance computing clusters, including information on the root cause of an outage and the duration of the outage. The data can be downloaded from LANL's web page [1] and a more detailed description of the data and systems can be found in [30]. Uncorrectable DRAM errors are one of the most common root causes for node outages, and in this section we use only the subset of the data that consists of node outages due to DRAM.

For one of LANL's clusters periodic temperature measurements from a motherboard sensor are available, allowing us to directly study the relationship between temperature and outages. We refer to this system as LANL-system-20, since the ID for this system on LANL's web page is 20. For another 12 clusters information on the data center layout is available, including each node's position in a rack. We use rack position as a proxy for temperature, since due to the cooling system design in those clusters the top of the rack tends to be hotter than the bottom. We have verified that this is the case by analyzing the data for LANL-system-20, where actual temperature measurements are available, and found a difference of 4C between the top and bottom of the rack. The 12 clusters are based on two different hardware platforms, which we refer to as *LANL-Type-1* and *LANL-Type-2*.

LANL-Type-1 comprises seven clusters at LANL totalling 2720 nodes and 20880 processors. The nodes in the system are SMPs with 4 processors per node and are all based on the same hardware platform. The data for these systems spans the years 2002-2008 and corresponds to systems with IDs 3,4,5,6,18,19, and 20 on the LANL web page.

LANL-Type-2 comprises six clusters at LANL totalling 1664 nodes and 3328 processors. The nodes are SMPs with 2 processors per node and the data for these systems spans the years 2003-2008. The data is also available at LANL's web page and corresponds to the systems with IDs 9,10,11,12,13, and 14 on the web page.

SciNet-GPC: The SciNet High Performance Computing Consortium provides computing facilities to researchers in Canada. Their General Purpose Cluster (GPC) is currently the largest supercomputer in the country [2]. We obtained parts replacement data from this system which is manually entered by an administrator when broken hardware is replaced. The replacement log we obtained spans 19 months. The GPC consists of 3870 IBM iDataPlex nodes grouped into 45 racks. Each node contains 2 Intel Xeon E5540 CPUs totaling 8 cores and 16GB of ECC memory.

2.3.2 *Analysis*

Figures 7 show the monthly probability for node outages at LANL that are attributed to memory as a function of

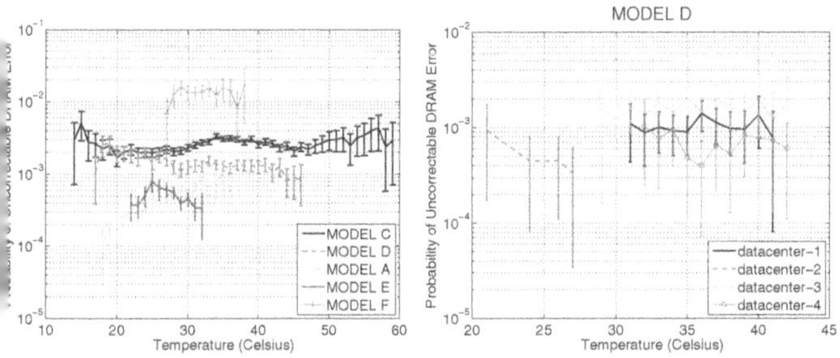

Figure 9: Probability of uncorrectable DRAM errors at Google as a function of temperature.

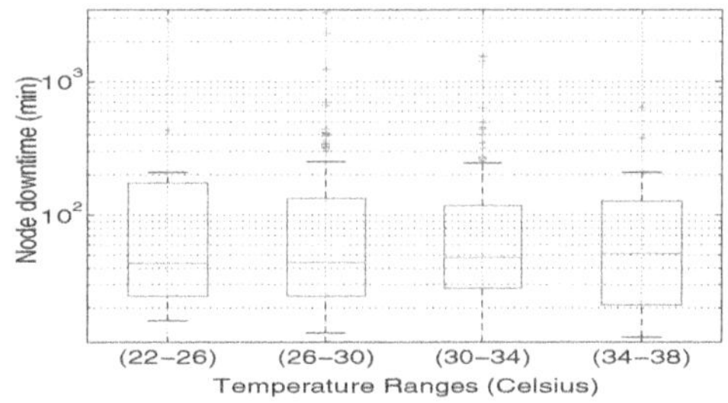

Figure 10: Box plots for per node downtime as a function of temperature.

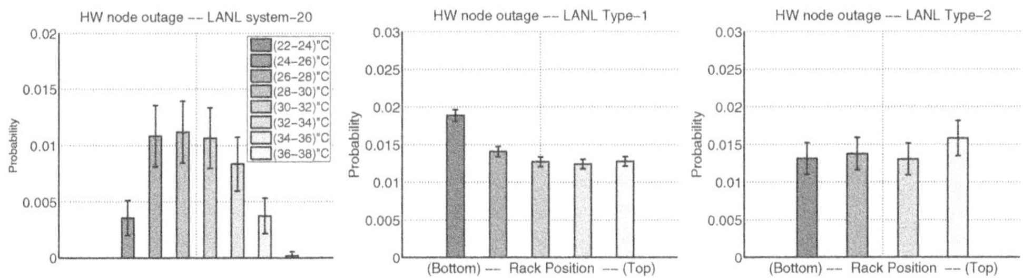

Figure 11: Probability of node outages at LANL as a function of temperature (left) and rack positions as a proxy for temperature (middle, right).

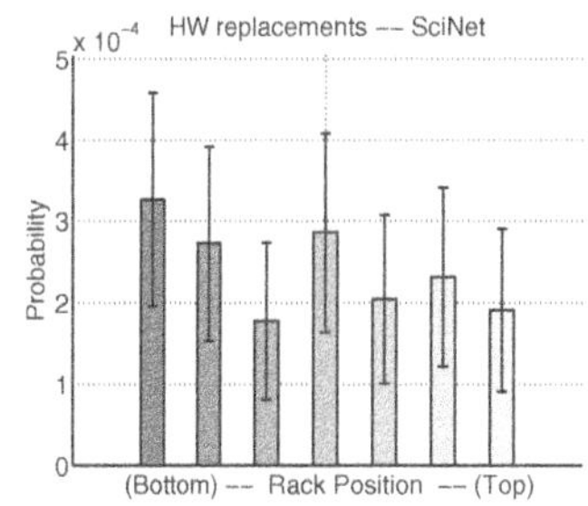

Figure 12: Probability of hardware replacements at SciNet.

the node's average temperature. In Figure 7 (left) we us the data for LANL-system-20, which has actual temperature measurements, and for Figure 7 (middle,right) we use the server's position in a rack as a proxy for temperature for LANL-Type-1 and LANL-Type-2 systems. We find that none of the graphs shows clear evidence for increasing rate of node outages with increasing temperatures.

Results are similar for hardware replacement rates at SciNet. Figure 8 shows a node's monthly probability of requiring a DIMM replacement as a function of its position in the rack. Again, we see no evidence of higher failure rates for higher (and hence hotter) rack positions.

Unfortunately, due to the size of the datasets the error bars in those graphs are relatively high. We therefore turn to the Google data on uncorrectable errors, which is a larger data set. Figure 9 (left) shows the monthly probability of an uncorrectable DRAM error for the five different hardware platforms at Google. We observe that for two of the models, model C and model F, error rates remain stable throughout the available range of temperature data (which is quite large ranging from 15C to 60C). Maybe surprisingly, model D and model A show contradicting trends, with the former exhibiting decreasing rates as temperature increases and the latter showing increasing rates as temperature rises. To investigate the possible cause we break down the data by data center. Figure 9 (right) shows the resulting breakdown by data center for model D. We find that the error rates for individual data centers are mostly flat with temperature, with the exception of one data center (datacenter-2). It is the aggregation of data from different data centers that creates those apparently contradicting trends. Similarly, we observe for model A that higher temperature points are biased by one data center that is running at a higher temperature and tends to have generally higher error rates (even for low temperatures).

Observation 8: We do not observe evidence for increasing rates of uncorrectable DRAM errors, DRAM DIMM replacements or node outages caused by DRAM problems as a function of temperature (within the range of temperature our data comprises).

2.4 Temperature and node outages

2.4.1 *Background and data*

Rather than focusing on a particular hardware component, this section looks at overall system reliability and availability as a function of temperature. For our study we use data from two different sources. The first source comprises the LANL datasets LANL-Type-1 and LANL-Type-2. Rather than focusing on records of node outages due to DRAM, we now include in our analysis any node outage that was attributed to a hardware problem. The second dataset is the SciNet-GPC replacement data, but rather than focusing on DRAM replacements we consider replacements of any hardware components.

2.4.2 *Analysis*

Figure 11 shows the effect of temperature on the rate of node outages at LANL. Figure 11 (left) shows the monthly probability of a node outages as a function of the node's average temperature for system 20 in the LANL data set, as for this system temperature measurements are available. Figure 11 (middle, right) show the monthly probability of a node outages as a function of a node's position in the rack (bottom to top position, i.e. colder to hotter) for LANL-Type-1 and LANL-Type-2 systems. We observe within the temperature range that our data spans no indication that hotter nodes have a higher probability of failing than colder nodes. Results are similar for hardware replacements observed at SciNet (Figure 12): no indication that nodes at

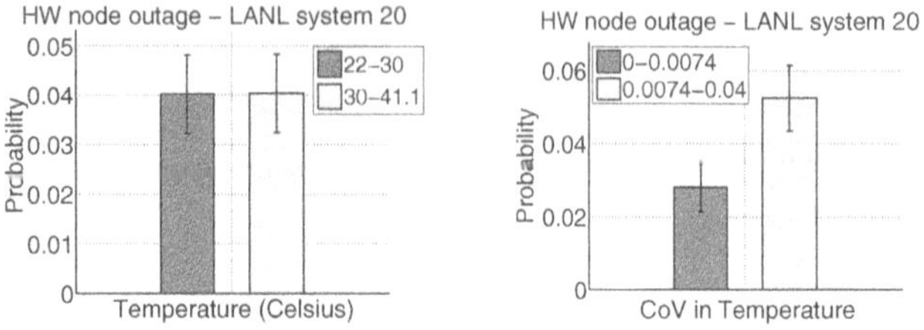

Figure 13: Probability of node outages by temperature (left) and by coefficient of variation (right).

the top of the rack experience more hardware replacements than those at the bottom of the rack.

For the LANL data, we also have information on the length of a node outage, i.e. how long did it take to bring the node back up. Figure 10 shows box plots [2] for the total amount of downtime experienced by a node per month for system 20. We find that the downtime experienced by hot nodes does not differ significantly from the downtime experienced by cold nodes, as both medians and lower and upper quartiles of downtime tend to be similar.

Observation 9: We observe no evidence that hotter nodes have a higher rate of node outages, node downtime or hardware replacements than colder nodes.

One might ask whether node outages might be more strongly affected by variability in temperature, rather than average temperature. The only dataset that allows us to study this question is the LANL data for system 20. Figure 13 (right) shows the monthly probability of a node outage for LANL-system-20 as a function of the coefficient of variation in temperature. The figure compares the node outage probability for the top 50% of nodes with the highest CoV and the bottom 50% of nodes with lowest CoV. We observe that nodes with a higher CoV in temperature have significantly increased rates of node outages. For comparison, we also plotted the probability of node outages as a function of average temperature in the same way (Figure 13 (left)) and observe no difference between hot and cold nodes.

Observation 10: We find that high variability in temperature seems to have a stronger effect on node reliability than average temperature.

3. OTHER CONCERNS WITH HIGH TEMPERATURES

Beyond potentially affecting server reliability, there are other concerns with raising data center temperatures. Higher temperatures might affect server performance, increase a server's energy consumption, and lead to smaller safety margins in case of AC or fan failures. We are studying each of these concerns in the remainder of this section.

3.1 Temperature and performance

While it is widely known that higher temperatures might negatively affect the reliability and lifetime of hardware devices, less attention is paid to the fact that high temperatures can also negatively affect the *performance* of systems. For example, in order to protect themselves against a possibly increasing rate of LSEs, some hard disk models enable Read-after-Write (RaW) when a certain temperature threshold is reached. Under RaW, every write to the disk is converted to a Write Verify command, or a Write followed by a Verify operation, reading the sector that has just been written and verifying its contents [36, 37] [3]. Also, when CPU and memory temperatures reach a certain threshold, most advanced servers employ CPU throttling (dynamic voltage frequency scaling) and memory throttling (of the memory bus).

Unfortunately, features such as RaW are often considered trade secrets and are not well documented. In fact, even within a company manufacturing hardware those features and associated parameters are regarded confidential and not shared outside product groups. The goal in this part of our work is to investigate experimentally how performance of different components changes with increasing temperatures.

3.1.1 Experimental setup

To study the performance of a server under increasing ambient temperatures, we set up a testbed using a thermal chamber. The thermal chamber is large enough to fit an entire server inside it, and allows us to exactly control temperature within a range of $-10C$ to $60C$ with a precision of $0.1C$. How ambient temperature affects the temperature of server-internal components depends on many factors, including the design of the cooling system and the server and rack architecture. Therefore, instead of directly predicting the impact of data center ambient temperature on a system, we present our results as a function of the temperature of server internal components.

The server we use in our study is a Dell PowerEdge R710, a model that is commonly used in data center server racks. The server has a quad-core 2.26 GHz Intel Xeon 5520 with 8MB L3, with 16GB DDR3 ECC memory, running Ubuntu 10.04 Server with the 2.6.32-28-server Linux kernel. We also equipped the server with a large variety of different hard disk drives, including both SAS and SATA drives and covering all major manufacturers:

Manufacturer	Model	Interface	Capacity	RPM
Hitachi	Deskstar	SATA	750GB	7200
Western Digital	Caviar	SATA	160GB	7200
Seagate	Barracuda	SATA	1TB	7200
Seagate	Constellation	SAS	500GB	7200
Seagate	Cheetah	SAS	73GB	15000
Fujitsu	MAX3073RC	SAS	73GB	15000
Hitachi	Ultrastar	SAS	300GB	15000

We use a wide range of workloads in our experiments, including a set of synthetic microbenchmarks designed to stress different parts of the system, and a set of macrobenchmarks aiming to model a number of real world applications:

STREAM: A microbenchmark measuring bandwidth of sequential memory accesses [20]. We used an implementation from the lmbench suite [21, 34] and benchmarked the performance of accessing 4GB of memory.

GUPS: Microbenchmark that measures memory random accesses, in giga-updates-per-second, as defined by the High Performance Computing Challenge [27]. We tested the performance of 8KB-chunk updates randomly to 4GB of memory.

Dhrystone: A well-known microbenchmark that evaluates the CPU performance for integer operations [40].

[2] Recall that in a box plot the bottom and top of the box are always the 25th and 75th percentile, respectively, and the band near the middle of the box is always the 50th percentile (the median).

[3] Note that Write Verify is not specified in the ATA standard, which might explain the absence of a performance hit for most SATA drives, in the following subsections.

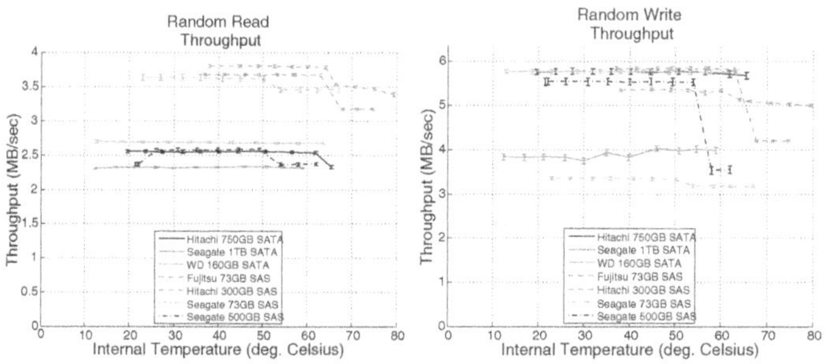

Figure 14: Disk throughput under a synthetic random read and random write workload, respectively, as a function of disk internal temperature. Results for sequential read and sequential write workloads were comparable.

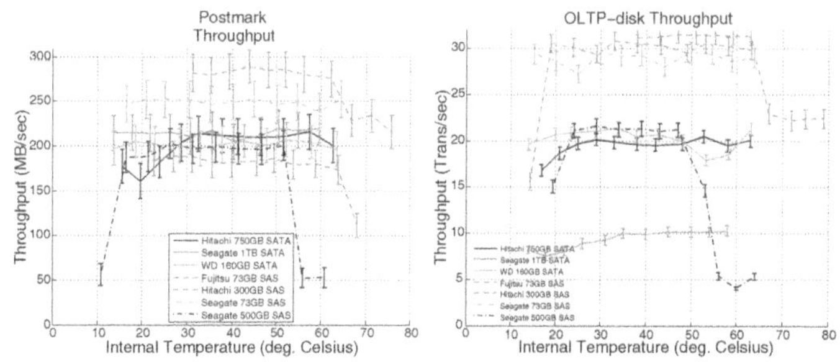

Figure 15: Throughput under two different I/O intensive workloads (Postmark, OLTP-disk) as a function of disk internal temperature.

Whetstone: A well-known CPU benchmark for floating-point performance [11]. Our implementations of *Dhrystone* and *Whetstone* were obtained from the Unixbench suite [22].

Random-Read/Write: A synthetic workload comprised of independent 64KB read (or write) requests issued back-to-back at random disk sectors.

Sequential-Read/Write: Since a pure sequential workload would stress the on-disk cache, we opt for a synthetic workload with a high degree of sequentiality, instead. We pick a random disk sector, and issue back-to-back 64KB read (or write) requests on consecutive sectors for 8MB following the initial request.

OLTP-Mem: We configured TPC-C [38], a commonly used database benchmark modeling on-line transaction processing (OLTP), with 30 warehouses resulting in a 3GB *memory-resident* database.

OLTP-Disk: Models the same workload as *OLTP-Mem*. To make the workload I/O-bound, we configured the database with 70 warehouses (7GB), using 4GB RAM.

DSS-Mem: We configured TPC-H [39], a commonly used database benchmark modeling decision support workloads (DSS), with a 1GB memory-resident MySQL InnoDB database.

DSS-Disk: Another TPC-H based workload, this time configured with a database of 10GB and a 3.4GB buffer pool, resulting in a disk-bound workload.

PostMark [18]: A common file system benchmark, which we configured to generate $50-5000$KB files, and modified it to avoid using the OS cache entirely, so that all transactions are directed to disk.

BLAST [3]: An application used by computational biology researchers, acting as a high-performance computing benchmark that stresses both the CPU and memory. We used the parallel *mpiBLAST* implementation [12] and ran 10 representative queries on a 5GB library.

3.1.2 Temperature and disk performance

To study the effect of temperature on disk performance, we ran our disk-bound workloads against each of the drives in our testbed, while placing the drive in the heat chamber and gradually increasing the temperature inside the chamber. The two graphs in Figure 14 show the results for the random-read and random-write microbenchmarks, as a function of the drive internal temperatures, as reported by the drives' SMART statistics. (Results for sequential-read and sequential-write were similar and are omitted for lack of space). We observe that all SAS drives and one SATA drive (the Hitachi Deskstar) experience some drop in throughput for high temperatures. The drop in throughput is usually in the 5-10% range, but can be as high as 30%. Because of the fact that the throughput drop for a drive happens consistently at the same temperature, rather than randomly or gradually, and that none of the drives reported any errors, we speculate that it is due to protective mechanisms enabled by the drive. For example, in the case of the write workloads (which show a more significant drop in throughput) this drop in throughput might be due to the enabling of features such as RaW.

An interesting question is: at what temperature does the throughput start to drop? We observe in Figure 14 drops at either around 50C (for the Seagate SAS drives) or 60C (for the Fujitsu and Hitachi SAS drives). However, these are disk internal temperatures. When translating them to ambient temperatures (inside the heat chamber) we observe a drop in throughput for temperatures as low as 40C (for the Seagate 73GB and Hitachi SAS drives), 45C for the Fujitsu and Seagate 500GB SAS drives, and 55C for the Hitachi Deskstar, ranges that are significantly lower than the maximum of 50-60C that manufacturers typically rate hard disks for. (A full graph mapping internal to ambient temperatures is included in the tech-report [13]). While data centers will rarely run at an average inlet temperature of 40C or above, most data centers have hot spots (see Section 3.3), which are significantly hotter than the rest of the data center, and which might routinely reach such temperatures.

Figure 15 shows how temperature affects the throughput of two of our disk-intensive applications, Postmark and OLTP-disk. We observe similar trends as for the microbenchmarks, with throughput drops at the same temperature point. However, the magnitude of lost throughput tends to be bigger, typically in the 10-20% range, sometimes as high as 40-80%. The drops observed for DSS-disk looked more similar in magnitude to those for the synthetic benchmarks.

3.1.3 Temperature and CPU/memory performance

Most enterprise class servers support features to protect the CPU and memory subsystem from damage or excessive errors due to high temperatures. These include scaling of the CPU frequency, reducing the speed of the memory bus, and employing advanced error correcting codes (ECC) for DRAM. For example, our server supports a continuous range of CPU frequencies, bus speeds of either 800MHz or 1066MHz, and three memory protection schemes: single-

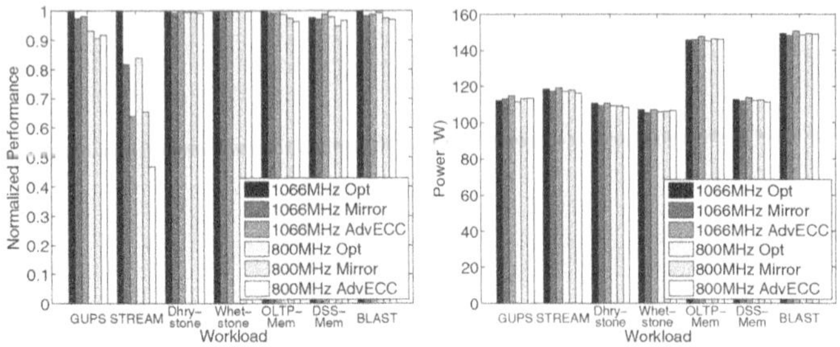

Figure 16: The effect of memory error protection and bus speed on performance (left) and power consumption (right).

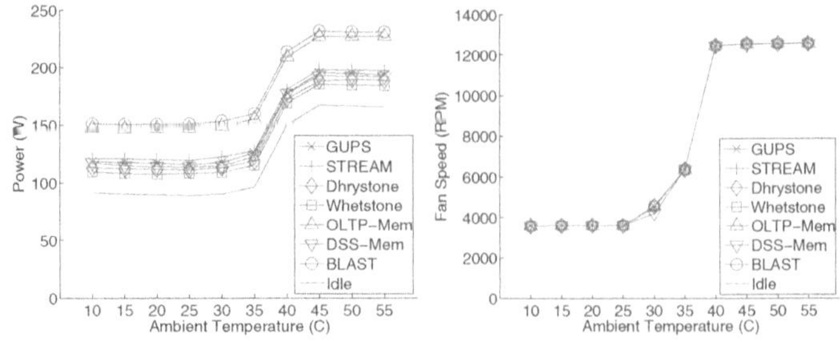

Figure 17: The effect of ambient temperature on power consumption (left) and server fan speeds (right).

error-correction and double-error-detection (SEC-DED), advanced ECC (AdvEcc), which allows the detection and correction of multi-bit errors, and mirroring, which provides complete redundancy. Server manuals tend to be purposely vague as to when such features are enabled (CPU and memory bus throttling can be automatically activated by the server), or possible performance impact. In particular, for the memory options it is difficult to predict how they affect performance and power consumption. Since running data centers at higher temperatures might necessitate the use of such features more frequently, we use our testbed to study their impact on performance and power consumption.

For the temperature range we experimented with (heat chamber temperatures up to 55C, significantly higher than the 35C inlet temperature at which most servers are rated) we did not observe any throttling triggered by the server. To study the effect of different memory features, we manually configure the server to run with different combinations of memory bus speed (800MHz vs. 1066MHz) and ECC schemes (SEC-DED, AdvEcc, Mirror). The effect on throughput for the different benchmarks is shown in Figure 16 (left). Throughput is normalized by the maximum attainable throughput, i.e. the throughput achieved when combining a 1066MHz bus speed with the SEC-DED ECC scheme. The results for the two microbenchmarks designed to stress the memory (GUPS and Stream) show that drops in throughput can potentially be huge. Switching to the lower bus speed can lead to a 20% reduction in throughput. The effect of the ECC scheme is even bigger: enabling AdvECC can cost 40% in throughput. The combination of features can cause a drop of more than 50%. For the macrobenchmarks modeling real-world applications the difference in throughput is (not surprisingly) not quite as large, but can reach significant levels at 3–4%. We also measured the server's power consumption (Figure 16 (right)), and found that the impact of memory configurations on server power is small (1-3%) compared to the increases we will observe in the next section during increasing temperatures.

3.2 Increased server energy consumption

Increasing the air intake temperature of IT equipment can have an impact on the equipment's power dissipation. Many IT manufacturers start to increase the speed of internal cooling fans once inlet air temperatures reach a certain threshold to offset the increased ambient air temperature. Also, leakage power of a processor increases with higher temperatures, and can make up a significant fraction of a processor's total power consumption. To study the effect of increasing ambient temperatures on a server's power consumption, we repeated all our earlier experiments with a power meter attached to our server and, in addition, monitored fan speeds.

Figure 17 (left) shows the server's power usage as a function of the ambient (thermal chamber) temperature for the CPU and memory intensive workloads. While the absolute energy used by different workloads varies widely, we observe the same basic trend for all workloads: power consumption stays constant up to 30C and then begins to continually increase, until it levels off at 40C. The increase in power consumption is quite dramatic: up to 50%.

An interesting question is whether this increase in power comes from an increase in fan speed (something that can be controlled by the server) or from increased leakage power (which is governed by physical laws). Unfortunately, it is not possible to measure leakage power directly. Nevertheless, there is strong evidence that the increase in power is dominated by fan power: Figure 17 (right) plots the fan speed as a function of the ambient temperature for all workload experiments. We observe that, the temperature thresholds we notice for which fan speeds increase, line up exactly with the temperatures at which when power consumption increases. We also observe that power consumption levels off once fan speeds level off, while leakage power would continue to grow with rising temperatures.

Observation 11: As ambient temperature increases, the resulting increase in power is significant and can be mostly attributed to fan power. In comparison, leakage power is negligible.

An interesting observation is that power usage starts to increase at the same ambient temperature point for all workloads, although server internal temperatures vary widely across workloads, which means fan speeds increase based on ambient rather than internal temperature. For example, CPU core temperature is more than 20C higher for BLAST and OLTP-Mem than for most other workloads. That means for many workloads the server internal temperatures are still quite low (less than 40C) when the fan speeds start to increase. In particular, we observe that for an idle server, the temperature measured at CPU and memory is still at a very modest 25-30C [4] when the fan speeds start to increase. (The tech-report [13] contains detailed graphs for CPU and memory temperatures for all workloads.) This is an important observation, since most servers in data centers spend a large fraction of their lives idle.

Observation 12: Smart control of server fan speeds is imperative to run data centers hotter. A significant fraction of the observed increase in power dissipation in our exper-

[4]For reference, DRAM, for example, is typically rated for up to 95C.

iments could likely be avoided by more sophisticated algorithms controlling the fan speeds.

3.3 Reduced safety margins

One concern with increasing data center temperatures is that most data centers tend to have hot spots that are significantly hotter than the average temperature in the facility. When raising the temperature setpoint in a data center's cooling system, it is important to also keep in mind how this will affect the hottest part of the system, rather than just the system average. In addition to hot spots, another concern are reduced safety margins: most servers are configured with a critical temperature threshold and will shut down when that threshold is reached, in order to avoid serious equipment damage. As the ambient temperature in a data center increases, equipment will be operating closer to the maximum temperature, reducing the time available to shut down a server cleanly or take protective measures in the case of data center events, such as AC or fan failures.

To better understand temperature imbalances we analyzed the differences in temperature within the data centers in our datasets. We study the distribution of per-disk temperatures in different data centers at Google (using the dataset from Section 2.1) and the per-node temperatures for nodes in LANL's system 20 (using the dataset from Section 2.3). We consider how much hotter the disk/node in the 95th and 99th percentile of the distribution in the data center is, compared to the median disk/node.

Interestingly, the trends for temperature imbalances are very similar across data centers, despite the fact that they have been designed and managed by independent entities. We find that for all of Google's data centers in our study, and LANL's system 20, the node/disk in the 95th percentile is typically around 5 degrees C hotter than the median node/disk, and that the 99th percentile is around 8–10 degrees hotter than the median node/disk. (The tech-report [13] includes full CDFs of the per node/disk distribution).

Observation 13: The degree of temperature variation across the nodes in a data center is surprisingly similar for all data centers in our study. The hottest 5% nodes tend to be more than 5C hotter than the typical node, while the hottest 1% nodes tend to be more than 8–10C hotter.

4. SUMMARY AND IMPLICATIONS

Increasing data center temperatures creates the potential for large energy savings and reductions in carbon emissions. Unfortunately, the pitfalls possibly associated with increased data center temperatures are not very well understood, and as a result most data centers operate at very conservative, low temperature levels. This work sheds some light on the issues involved in raising data center temperatures, and comes to some surprising conclusions.

Based on our study of data spanning more than a dozen data centers at three different organizations, and covering a broad range of reliability issues, we find that the effect of high data center temperatures on system reliability are smaller than often assumed. For some of the reliability issues we study, namely DRAM failures and node outages, we do not find any evidence for a correlation with higher temperatures (within the range of temperatures in our datasets). For those error conditions that show a correlation (latent sector errors in disks and disk failures), the correlation is much weaker than expected. For (device internal) temperatures below 50C, errors tend to grow linearly with temperature, rather than exponentially, as existing models suggest.

It is important to note that this does not mean that high temperatures have no effect on hardware reliability or that the Arrhenius model is flawed. But it might mean that the effects of other factors dominate failure rates. The Arrhenius model tries to solely capture the effect of heat on hardware components without taking into account other possible factors that impact hardware reliability in the field. Anecdotal evidence from discussions with data center operators suggests for example that poor handling procedures for equipment are a major factor in the field (which is hard to capture in measurement data). Our results indicate that, all things considered, the effect of temperature on hardware reliability is actually weaker than commonly thought.

We also find that, rather than average temperature, the variability in temperature might be the more important factor. Even failure conditions, such as node outages, that did not show a correlation with temperature, did show a clear correlation with the variability in temperature. Efforts in controlling such factors might be more important in keeping hardware failure rates low, than keeping temperatures low.

We also make some observations that might be helpful in protecting against temperature-induced hardware issues. The error mode that was most strongly correlated with high temperatures are LSEs. Common method for protecting against data loss due to LSEs include Read-after-Write and periodic "scrubbing" of the hard disk to proactively detect such errors. In experiments with our testbed based on a thermal chamber, we observe evidence that (enterprise class) hard disks do employ mechanisms, such as RaW, but we find that they tend to kick in only at very high temperatures and are associated with significant performance penalties. On the other hand, we find that one of the concerns often associated with scrubbing does not seem to be a valid concern in practice, which might make scrubbing the better approach to defend against LSEs: some fear that the extra workload placed on a drive by the scrub process might lead to early wear-out of the drive, but we see no correlation between a drive's workload intensity and it's failure probability.

Our encouraging results on the impact of temperature on hardware reliability move the focus to other potential issues with increasing data center temperatures. One such issue is an increase in the power consumption of individual servers as inlet air temperatures go up. The two most commonly cited reasons for such an increase are increased power leakage in the processor and increased (server internal) fan speeds. Our experimental results show that power leakage seems to be negligible compared to the effect of server fans. In fact, we find that even for relatively low ambient temperatures (on the orders that are commonly found in the hotter areas of an otherwise cool data center) fan power consumption makes up a significant fraction of total energy consumption. Much of this energy might be spent unnecessarily, due to poorly designed algorithms for controlling fan speed.

We would oversimplify the problem if we tried to make generalized recommendations or predictions on what exactly data center temperatures should be and how much energy precisely could be saved. The answer to these questions will depend on too many factors, that are data center or application specific. However, we see our results as strong evidence that most organizations could run their data centers hotter than they currently are without making significant sacrifices in system reliability. We hope that this paper will motivate future work in this area and encourage more organizations to share field data or results from analyzing their data.

5. ACKNOWLEDGMENTS

We would like to thank Google for hosting the last author of this paper as a visiting faculty in the System Health Group during the summer of 2009. In particular, we thank Wolf-Dietrich Weber for his efforts in making the data available for us and Chris Mayfield who provided scripts to extract some of the data. We would like to thank the members of SciNet, in particular Chris Loken and Ching-Hsing Yu, for providing us with the data from their GPC system. And we would like to thank LANL for making their data publicly available, and in particular Gary Grider and James Nunez who helped answer our questions about the data. We would also like to thank Jiri Schindler for the ideas for some of the thermal chamber experiments and the anonymous reviewers for their detailed feedback, especially our shepherd Abhishek Sharma. This work has been funded by an NSERC discovery grant and a Netapp Faculty Fellowship.

6. REFERENCES

[1] Operational Data to Support and Enable Computer Science Research, Los Alamos National Laboratory. http://institute.lanl.gov/data/fdata/.

[2] SciNet. http://www.scinet.utoronto.ca/.

[3] S. F. Altschul, W. Gish, W. Miller, E. W. Myers, and D. J. Lipman. Basic local alignment search tool. *Journal of Molecular Biology*, 215(3):403–410, 1990.

[4] D. Anderson, J. Dykes, and E. Riedel. More than an interface—SCSI vs. ATA. In *Proc. of FAST 2003*.

[5] L. N. Bairavasundaram, G. R. Goodson, S. Pasupathy, and J. Schindler. An Analysis of Latent Sector Errors in Disk Drives. In *Proc. of SIGMETRICS'07*, 2007.

[6] C. Belady, A. Rawson, J. Pfleuger, and T. Cader. The Green Grid Data Center Power Efficiency Metrics: PUE & DCiE. Technical report, Green Grid, 2008.

[7] D. J. Bradley, R. E. Harper, and S. W. Hunter. Workload-based power management for parallel computer systems. *IBM J.Res.Dev.*, 47:703–718, 2003.

[8] J. Brandon. Going Green In The Data Center: Practical Steps For Your SME To Become More Environmentally Friendly. *Processor*, 29, Sept. 2007.

[9] California Energy Commission. Summertime energy-saving tips for businesses. *consumerenergycenter.org/tips/business_summer.html.*

[10] G. Cole. Estimating drive reliability in desktop computers and consumer electronics systems. TP-338.1. Seagate. 2000.

[11] H. J. Curnow, B. A. Wichmann, and T. Si. A synthetic benchmark. *The Computer Journal*, 19:43–49, 1976.

[12] A. E. Darling, L. Carey, and W.-c. Feng. The design, implementation, and evaluation of mpiblast. In *In Proc. of ClusterWorld 2003*, 2003.

[13] N. El-Sayed, I. Stefanovici, G. Amvrosiadis, A. A. Hwang, and B. Schroeder. Temperature management in data centers: Why some (might) like it hot. Technical Report TECHNICAL REPORT CSRG-615, University of Toronto, 2012.

[14] K. Flautner and T. Mudge. Vertigo: automatic performance-setting for linux. In *Proc. of OSDI*, 2002.

[15] A. Gandhi, M. Harchol-Balter, R. Das, and C. Lefurgy. Optimal power allocation in server farms. In *Proc. of Sigmetrics '09*, 2009.

[16] JEDEC Global Standards for the Microelectronics Industry. Arrhenius equation for reliability. *http://www.jedec.org/standards-documents/dictionary/terms/arrhenius-equation-reliability.*

[17] J. M. Kaplan, W. Forrest, and N. Kindler. Revolutionizing data center energy efficiency. Technical report, McKinsey & Company, July 2008.

[18] J. Katcher. Postmark: a new file system benchmark. Network Appliance Tech Report TR3022, Oct. 1997.

[19] Lawrence Berkeley National Labs. Benchmarking Data Centers. *http://hightech.lbl.gov/benchmarking-dc.html*, December 2007.

[20] J. D. McCalpin. Memory bandwidth and machine balance in current high performance computers. *IEEE Comp. Soc. TCCA Newsletter*, pages 19–25, Dec. 1995.

[21] L. McVoy and C. Staelin. lmbench: portable tools for performance analysis. In *Proc. of USENIX ATC*, 1996.

[22] D. C. Niemi. Unixbench. *http://www.tux.org/pub/tux/niemi/unixbench/.*

[23] C. D. Patel, C. E. Bash, R. Sharma, and M. Beitelmal. Smart cooling of data centers. In *Proc. of IPACK*, 2003.

[24] M. Patterson. The effect of data center temperature on energy efficiency. In *Proc. of ITHERM*, May 2008.

[25] E. Pinheiro, R. Bianchini, E. V. Carrera, and T. Heath. Load balancing and unbalancing for power and performance in cluster-based systems. In *Proc. of Workshop on Compilers and Operating Systems for Low Power (COLP)*, 2001.

[26] E. Pinheiro, W. D. Weber, and L. A. Barroso. Failure trends in a large disk drive population. In *Proc. of Usenix FAST 2007.*

[27] S. J. Plimpton, R. Brightwell, C. Vaughan, K. Underwood, and M. Davis. A Simple Synchronous Distributed-Memory Algorithm for the HPCC RandomAccess Benchmark. In *IEEE Cluster Computing*, Sept. 2006.

[28] K. Rajamani and C. Lefurgy. On evaluating request-distribution schemes for saving energy in server clusters. In *Proc. of the IEEE ISPASS*, 2003.

[29] Rich Miller. Google: Raise your data center temperature. *http://www.datacenterknowledge.com/archives/2008/10/14/google-raise-your-data-center-temperature/*, 2008.

[30] B. Schroeder and G. Gibson. A large-scale study of failures in high-performance computing systems. In *Proc. of DSN'06*, 2006.

[31] B. Schroeder and G. A. Gibson. Disk failures in the real world: What does an MTTF of 1,000,000 hours mean to you? In *Proc. of USENIX FAST*, 2007.

[32] B. Schroeder, E. Pinheiro, and W.-D. Weber. DRAM errors in the wild: a large-scale field study. In *Proc. of SIGMETRICS '09*, 2009.

[33] R. Sharma, C. Bash, C. Patel, R. Friedrich, and J. Chase. Balance of power: dynamic thermal management for internet data centers. *IEEE Internet Computing*, 9(1):42–49, 2005.

[34] C. Staelin. Lmbench3: Measuring scalability. Technical report, HP Laboratories Israel, 2002.

[35] R. F. Sullivan. Alternating Cold and Hot Aisles Provides More Reliable Cooling for Server Farms. In *Uptime Institute*, 2000.

[36] T10 Technical Committee. SCSI Block Commands – 3, Rev.25. Work. Draft T10/1799-D, ANSI INCITS.

[37] T13 Technical Committee. ATA 8 - ATA/ATAPI Command Set, Rev.4a. Work. Draft T13/1699-D, ANSI INCITS.

[38] Transaction Processing Performance Council. TPC Benchmark C - Rev. 5.11. Standard, Feb. 2010.

[39] Transaction Processing Performance Council. TPC Benchmark H - Rev. 2.14.2. Standard, June 2011.

[40] R. P. Weicker. Dhrystone: a synthetic systems programming benchmark. *Communications of the ACM*, 27(10):1013–1030, Oct. 1984.

Renewable and Cooling Aware Workload Management for Sustainable Data Centers*

Zhenhua Liu[$], Yuan Chen[†], Cullen Bash[†], Adam Wierman[$],
Daniel Gmach[†], Zhikui Wang[†], Manish Marwah[†], Chris Hyser[†]
[$]California Institute of Technology, Pasadena, CA, USA, E-mail: {zhenhua, adamw}@caltech.edu
[†]HP Labs, Palo Alto, CA, USA, E-mail: firstname.lastname@hp.com

ABSTRACT

Recently, the demand for data center computing has surged, increasing the total energy footprint of data centers worldwide. Data centers typically comprise three subsystems: IT equipment provides services to customers; power infrastructure supports the IT and cooling equipment; and the cooling infrastructure removes heat generated by these subsystems. This work presents a novel approach to model the energy flows in a data center and optimize its operation. Traditionally, supply-side constraints such as energy or cooling availability were treated independently from IT workload management. This work reduces electricity cost and environmental impact using a holistic approach that integrates renewable supply, dynamic pricing, and cooling supply including chiller and outside air cooling, with IT workload planning to improve the overall sustainability of data center operations. Specifically, we first predict renewable energy as well as IT demand. Then we use these predictions to generate an IT workload management plan that schedules IT workload and allocates IT resources within a data center according to time varying power supply and cooling efficiency. We have implemented and evaluated our approach using traces from real data centers and production systems. The results demonstrate that our approach can reduce both the recurring power costs and the use of non-renewable energy by as much as 60% compared to existing techniques, while still meeting the Service Level Agreements.

Categories and Subject Descriptors

C.0 [**Computer Systems Organization**]: General

Keywords

sustainable data center, renewable energy, demand shaping, scheduling, cooling optimization

1. INTRODUCTION

Data centers are emerging as the "factories" of this generation. A single data center requires a considerable amount of electricity and data centers are proliferating worldwide as a result of increased demand for IT applications and services. As a result, concerns about the growth in energy usage and emissions have led to social interest in curbing their energy consumption. These concerns have led to research efforts in both industry and academia. Emerging solutions include the incorporation of renewable on-site energy supplies as in Apple's new North Carolina data center, and alternative cooling supplies as in Yahoo's New York data center. The problem addressed by this paper is how to use these resources most effectively during the operation of data centers.

Most of the efforts toward this goal focus on improving the efficiency in one of the three major data center silos: (i) IT, (ii) cooling, and (iii) power. Significant progress has been made in optimizing the energy efficiency of each of the three silos enabling sizeable reductions in data center energy usage, e.g., [1, 2, 3, 4, 5, 6, 7, 8]; however, the integration of these silos is an important next step. To this end, a second generation of solutions has begun to emerge. This work focuses on the integration of different silos [9, 10, 11, 12]. An example is the dynamic thermal management of air-conditioners based on load at the IT rack level [9, 13]. However, to this point, supply-side constraints such as renewable energy and cooling availability are largely treated independently from workload management such like scheduling. Particularly, current workload management are not designed to take advantage of time variations in renewable energy availability and cooling efficiencies. The work in [14] integrates power capping and consolidation with renewable, but they do not shift workloads to align power demand with renewable supply.

The potential of integrated, dynamic approaches has been realized in some other domains, e.g., cooling management solutions for buildings that predict weather and power prices to dynamically adapt the cooling control have been proposed [15]. The goal of this paper is to start to realize this potential in data centers. Particularly, the potential of an integrated approach can be seen from the following three observations:

First, most data centers support a range of IT workloads, including both critical interactive applications that run 24x7 such like Internet services, and delay tolerant, batch-style applications as scientific applications, financial analysis, and image processing, which we refer to as batch workloads or batch jobs. Generally, batch workloads can be scheduled to run anytime as long as they finish before deadlines. This enables significant flexibility for workload management.

Second, the availability and cost of power supply, e.g., renewable energy supply and electricity price, is often dynamic over time, and so dynamic control of the supply mix can help reduce CO_2 emissions and offset costs. Thus, thoughtful workload management can have a great impact on energy usage and costs by scheduling batch workloads in a manner that follows the renewable availability.

Third, many data centers nowadays are cooled by multiple means through a cooling micro grid combining traditional mechanical chillers, airside economizers, and waterside econ-

*This work is done during Zhenhua Liu's internship at HP Labs. Zhenhua Liu and Adam Wierman are partly supported by NSF grant CNS 0846025 and DoE grant DE-EE0002890.

SIGMETRICS'12, June 11–15, 2012, London, England, UK.

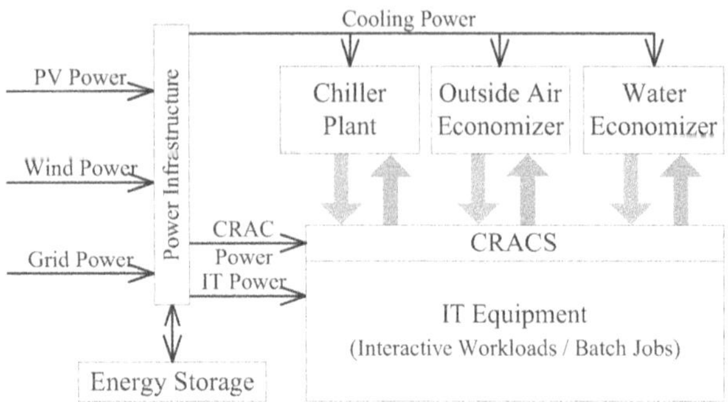

Figure 1: Sustainable Data Center

omizers. Within a micro grid, each cooling approach has a different efficiency and capacity that depends on IT workload, cooling generation mechanism and external conditions including outside air temperature and humidity, and may vary with the time of day. This provides opportunities to optimize cooling cost by "shaping" IT demand according to time varying cooling efficiency and capacity.

The three observations above highlight that there is considerable potential for integrated management of the IT, cooling, and power subsystems of data centers. Providing such an integrated solution is the goal of this work. Specifically, we provide a novel workload scheduling and capacity management approach that integrates energy supply (renewable energy supply, dynamic energy pricing) and cooling supply (chiller cooling, outside air cooling) into IT workload management to improve the overall energy efficiency and reduce the carbon footprint of data center operations.

A key component of our approach is demand shifting, which schedules batch workloads and allocates IT resources within a data center according to the availability of renewable energy supply and the efficiency of cooling. This is a complex optimization problem due to the dynamism in the supply and demand and the interaction between them. To see this, given the lower electricity price and temperature of outside air at night, batch jobs should be scheduled to run at night; however, because more renewable energy like solar is available around noon, we should do more work during the day to reduce electricity bill and environmental impact.

At the core of our design is a model of the costs within the data center, which is used to formulate a constrained convex optimization problem. The workload planner solves this optimization to determine the optimal demand shifting. The optimization-based workload management has been popular in the research community recently, e.g., [16, 17, 18, 19, 3, 11, 20, 21]. The key contributions of the formulation considered here compared to the prior literature are (i) the addition of a detailed cost model and optimization of the cooling component of the data center, which is typically ignored in previous designs; (ii) the consideration of both interactive and batch workloads; and (iii) the derivation of important structural properties of the optimal solutions to the optimization.

In order to validate our integrated design, we have implemented a prototype of our approach for a data center that includes solar power and outside air cooling. Using our implementation, we perform a number of experiments on a real testbed to highlight the practicality of the approach (Section 5). In addition to validating our design, our experiments are centered on providing insights into the following questions:

(1) How much benefit (reducing electricity bill and environmental impact) can be obtained from our renewable and cooling-aware workload management planning?

(2) Is net-zero[1] grid power consumption achievable?

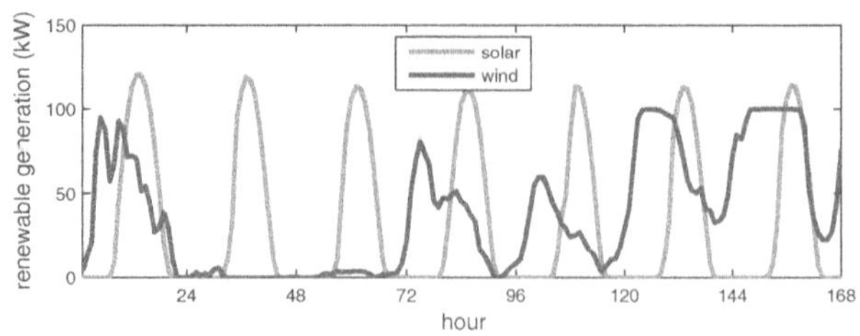

Figure 2: One week renewable generation

(3) Which renewable source is more valuable? What is the optimal renewable portfolio?

2. SUSTAINABLE DATA CENTER OVERVIEW

Figure 1 depicts an architectural overview of a sustainable data center. The *IT equipment* includes servers, storage and networking switches that support applications and services hosted in the data center. The *power infrastructure* generates and delivers power for the IT equipment and cooling facility through a power micro grid that integrates grid power, local renewable generation such as photovoltaic (PV) and wind, and energy storage. The *cooling infrastructure* provides, delivers and distributes the cooling resources to extract the heat from the IT equipment. In this example, the cooling capacity is delivered to the data center through the Computer Room Air Conditioning (CRAC) Units from the cooling micro grid that consists of air economizer, water economizer and traditional chiller plant. We discuss these three key subsystems in detail in the following sections.

2.1 Power Infrastructure

Although renewable energy is in general more sustainable than grid power, the supply is often time varying in a manner that depends on the source of power, location of power generators, and the local weather conditions. Figure 2 shows the power generated from a 130kW PV installation for an HP data center and a nearby 100kW wind turbine in California, respectively. The PV generation shows regular variation while that from the wind is much less predictable. How to manage these supplies is a big challenge for application of renewable energy in a sustainable data center.

Despite the usage of renewable energy, data centers must still rely on non-renewable energy, including grid power and on-site energy storage, due to availability concerns. Grid power can be purchased at either a pre-defined fixed rate or an on-demand time-varying rate, and Figure 3 shows an example of time-varying electricity price over 24 hours. There might be an additional charge for the peak demand.

Local energy storage technologies can be used to store and smooth out the supply of power for a data center. A variety of technologies are available [22], including flywheels, batteries, and other systems. Each has its costs, advantages and disadvantages. Energy storage is still quite expensive and there is power loss associated with energy conversion and charge/discharge. Hence, it is critical to maximize the use of the renewable energy that is generated on site. An ideal scenario is to maximize the use of renewable energy while minimizing the use of storage.

2.2 Cooling Supply

Due to the ever-increasing power density of IT equipment in today's data centers, a tremendous amount of electricity is used by the cooling infrastructure. According to [23], a

[1]By "net-zero" we mean that the total energy usage over a fixed period is less than or equal to the local total renewable generation during that period. Note that this does not mean that no power from the grid is used during this period.

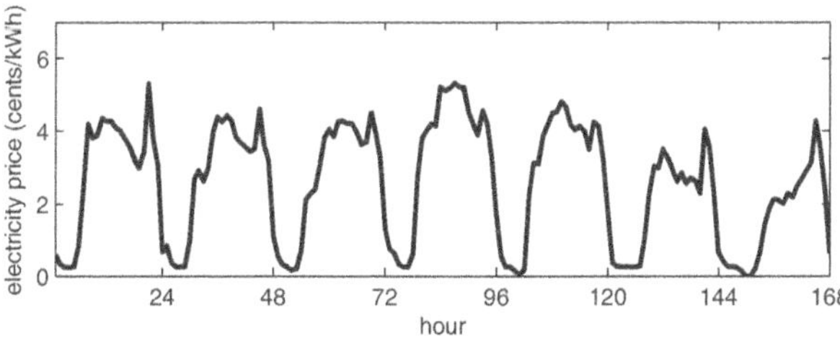

Figure 3: One week real-time electricity price

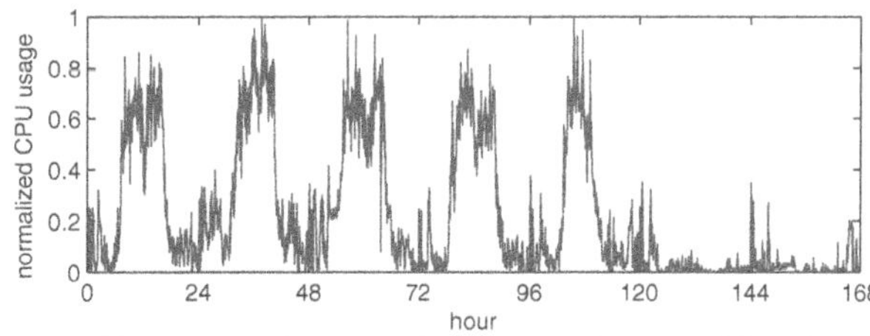

Figure 4: One week interactive workload

significant amount of data center power goes to the cooling system (up to 1/3) including CRAC units, pumps, chiller plant and cooling towers.

Lots of work has been done to improve the cooling efficiency through, e.g., smart facility design, real-time control and optimization [8, 7]. Traditional data centers use chillers to cool down the returned hot water from CRACs via mechanical refrigeration cycles since they can provide high cooling capacity continuously. However, compressors within the chillers consume a large amount of power [24, 25]. Recently, "chiller-less" cooling technologies have been adopted to remove or reduce the dependency on mechanical chillers. In the case with water-side economizers, the returned hot water is cooled down by components such as dry coolers or evaporative cooling towers. The cooling capacity may also be generated from cold water from seas or lakes. In the case of air economizers, cold outside air may be introduced after filtering and/or humidification/de-humidification to cool down the IT equipment directly while hot air is rejected into the environment.

However, these so-called "free" cooling approaches are actually not free [24]. First, there is still a non-negligible energy cost associated with these approaches, e.g., blowers driving outside air through data center need to work against air flow resistance and therefore consume power. Second, the efficiency of these approaches is greatly affected by environmental conditions such as ambient air temperature and humidity, compared with that of traditional approaches based on mechanical chillers. The cooling efficiency and capacity of the economizers can vary widely along with time of the day, season of the year, and geographical locations of the data centers. These approaches are usually complemented by more stable cooling resources such as chillers, which provides opportunities to optimize the cooling power usage by "shaping" IT demand according to cooling efficiencies.

2.3 IT Workload

There are many different workloads in a data center. Most of them fit into two classes: interactive, and non-interactive or batch. The interactive workloads such as Internet services or business transactional applications typically run 24x7 and process user requests, which have to be completed within a certain time (response time), usually within a second. Non-interactive batch jobs such as scientific applications, financial analysis, and image processing are often delay tolerant and can be scheduled to run anytime as long as progress can be made and the jobs finish before the deadline (completion time). This deadline is much more flexible (several hours to multiple days) than that of interactive workload. This provides great optimization opportunities for workload management to "shape" non-interactive batch workloads based on the varying renewable energy and cooling supply.

Interactive workloads are characterized by stochastic properties for request arrival, service demand, and Service Level Agreements (SLAs, e.g., thresholds of average response time or percentile delay). Figure 4 shows a 7-day normalized CPU usage trace for a popular photo sharing and storage web service, which has more than 85 million registered users in 22 countries. We can see that the workload shows significant variability and exhibits a clear diurnal pattern, which is typical for data center interactive workloads.

Batch jobs are defined in terms of total resource demand (e.g, CPU hours), starting time, completion time as well as maximum resource consumption (e.g., a single thread program can use up to 1 CPU). Conceptually, a batch job can run at anytime on many different servers as long as it finishes before the specified completion time. Our integrated management approach exploits this flexibility to make use of renewable energy and efficient cooling when available.

3. MODELING AND OPTIMIZATION

As discussed above, time variations in renewable energy supply availability and cooling efficiencies provide both opportunities and challenges for managing IT workloads in data centers. In this section, we present a novel design for renewable and cooling aware workload management that exploits opportunities available to improve the sustainability of data centers. In particular, we formulate an optimization problem for adapting the workload scheduling and capacity allocation to varying supply from power and cooling infrastructure.

3.1 Optimizing the cooling substructure

We first derive the optimal cooling substructure when multiple cooling approaches are available in the substructure. We consider two cooling approaches: the outside air cooling which supplies most of the cooling capacity, and cooling through mechanical chillers which guarantees availability of cooling capacity. By exploring the heterogeneity of the efficiency and cost of the two approaches, we represent the minimum cooling power of the substructure as a function of the IT heat load.

In the following discussion, we define *cooling coefficient* as the cooling power divided by the IT power to represent the cooling efficiency. By cooling capacity we mean how much heat the cooling system can extract from the IT equipment and reject into the environment. In the case of outside air cooling, the cold air from outside is assumed pushed into the return ends of the CRAC units while the hot air from the outlets of the server racks is exhausted to the ambient environment through ducts.

Outside Air Cooling

The energy usage of outside air cooling is mainly the power consumed by blowers, which can be approximated as a cubic function of the blower speed [26, 24]. We assume that capacity of the outside air cooling is under tight control, e.g., through blower speed tuning, to avoid over-provisioning. Then the outside air capacity is equal to the IT heat load at the steady state when the latter does not exceed the total air cooling capacity. Based on basic heat transfer theory [27], the cooling capacity is proportional to the air volume flow rate. The air volume flow rate is approximately proportional to blower speed according to the general fan laws [26, 24]. Therefore, outside air cooling power can be defined as a function of IT power d as $f_a(d) = kd^3, 0 \le d \le \overline{d}, k > 0$, which is a convex function. The parameter k depends on the temperature difference, $(t_{RA} - t_{OA})$, based again on heat transfer

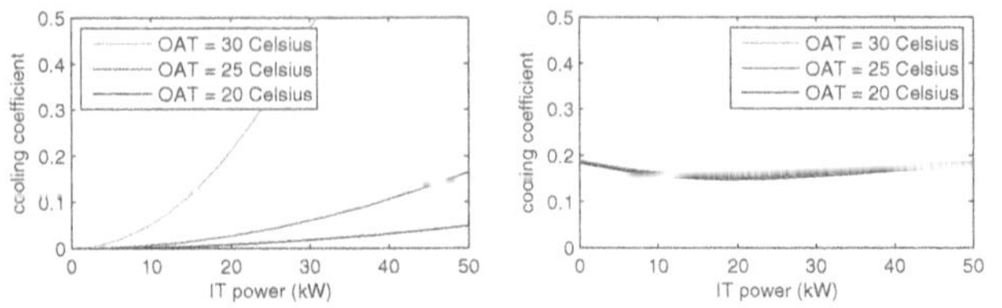

(a) Outside air cooling (b) Chiller cooling

Figure 5: Cooling coefficient comparison, for conversion, 20°C=68°F, 25°C=77°F, 30°C=86°F

theory, where t_{OA} is the outside air temperature (OAT) and t_{RA} is the temperature of the (hot) exhausting air from the IT racks. The maximum capacity of this cooling system can be modeled as $\bar{d} = C(t_{RA} - t_{OA})$. The parameter $C > 0$ is the maximum capacity of the air, which is proportional to the maximal outside air mass flow rate when the blowers run at the highest speed. As one example, Figure 5(a) shows the cooling coefficient for an outside air cooling system (assuming the exhausting air temperature is 35°C/95°F) under different outside air temperatures.

Chilled Water Cooling

First-principle models of chilled water cooling systems, including the chiller plant, cooling towers, pumps and heat exchangers, are complicated [27, 13, 25]. In this paper, we consider an empirical chiller efficiency model that was built on actual measurement of an operational chiller [25]. Figure 5(b) shows the cooling coefficient of the chiller. Different from the outside air cooling, the chiller cooling coefficient does not change much with OAT and the variation over different IT load is much smaller than that under outside air cooling. In the following analysis, the chiller power consumption is approximated as $f_c(d) = \gamma d$, where d is again the IT power and $\gamma > 0$ is a constant depending on the chiller. Our analysis also applies to the case of any arbitrary strictly increasing and convex chiller cooling function [28].

Cooling optimization

As shown in Figure 5, the efficiency of outside air cooling is more sensitive to IT load and the OAT than is that of chiller cooling. Furthermore, the cost of outside air cooling is higher than that of the chiller when the IT load exceeds a certain value because its power increases very fast (super-linearly) as the IT power increases, in particular for high ambient temperatures. The heterogeneous cooling efficiencies of the two approaches and the varying properties along with air temperature and heat load provide opportunities to optimize the cooling cost by using proper cooling capacity from each cooling supply as we discuss below, or by manipulating the heat load through demand shaping as we show in later sections.

For a given IT power d and outside air temperature t_{OA}, there exists an optimal cooling capacity allocation between outside air cooling and chiller cooling. Assume the cooling capacities provided by the chiller and outside air are d_1 and d_2 respectively ($d_1 = d - d_2$). From the cooling models introduced above, the optimal cooling power consumption is

$$c(d) = \min_{d_2 \in [0, \bar{d}]} \gamma(d - d_2)^+ + kd_2^3 \tag{1}$$

This can be solved analytically, which yields

$$d_2^* = \begin{cases} d & \text{if } d \le d_s \\ d_s & \text{otherwise} \end{cases}$$

where $d_s = \min\left\{\sqrt{\gamma/3k}, \bar{d}\right\}$, and the optimal outside air cooling capacity is $d_1^* = d - d_2^*$. So,

$$c(d) = \begin{cases} kd^3 & \text{if } d \le d_s \\ kd_s^3 + \gamma(d - d_s) & \text{otherwise} \end{cases} \tag{2}$$

is the cooling power of the optimal substructure, which is used for the optimization in later sections. Figure 6 illustrates the relationship between cooling power and IT load for different ambient temperatures. We see that the cooling power is a convex function of IT power, higher with hotter outside air. We also prove that the optimal $c(d)$ is a convex function of d in [28], which is important for using this as a component of the overall optimization for workload management.

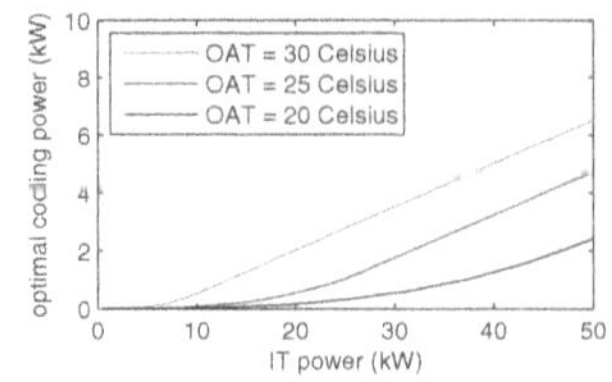

Figure 6: Optimal cooling power

3.2 System Model

We consider a discrete-time model whose timeslot matches the timescale at which the capacity provisioning and scheduling decisions can be updated. There is a (possibly long) time period we are interested in, $\{1, 2, ..., T\}$. In practice, T could be a day and a timeslot length could be 1 hour. The management period can be either static, e.g., to perform the scheduling every day for the execution of the next day, or dynamic, e.g., to create a new plan if the old scheduling differs too much from the actual supply and demand. The goal of the workload management is at each time t to:

(i) Make the scheduling decision for each batch job;

(ii) Choose the energy storage usage;

(iii) Optimize the cooling infrastructure.

We assume the renewable supply at time t is $r(t)$, which may be a mix of different renewables, such as wind and PV solar. We denote the grid power price at time t by $p(t)$ and assume $p(t) > 0$ without loss of generality. If at some time t we have negative price, we will use up the total capacity at this timeslot, then we only need to make capacity decisions for other timeslots, see [28] for more details. To model energy storage, we denote the energy storage level at time t by $es(t)$ with initial value $es(0)$ and the discharge/charge at time t by $e(t)$, where positive or negative values mean discharge or charge, respectively. Also, there is a loss rate $\rho \in [0, 1]$ for energy storage. We therefore have the relation $es(t + 1) = \rho(es(t) - e(t))$ between successive timeslots and we require $0 \le es(t) \le ES, \forall t$, where ES is the energy storage capacity. Though there are more complex energy storage models [29], they are beyond the scope of the paper.

Assume that there are I interactive workloads. For interactive workload i, the arrival rate at time t is $\lambda_i(t)$, the mean service rate is μ_i and the target performance metrics (e.g., average delay, or 95th percentile delay) is rt_i. In order to satisfy these targets, we need to allocate interactive workload i with IT capacity $a_i(t)$ at time t. Here $a_i(t)$ is derived from analytic models (e.g., M/GI/1/PS, M/M/k) or system measurements as a function of $\lambda_i(t)$ because performance metrics generally improve as the capacity allocated to the workload increases, hence there is a sharp threshold for $a_i(t)$. Note that our solution is quite general and does not depend on a particular model.

Assume there are J classes of batch jobs. Class j batch jobs have total demand B_j, maximum parallelization MP_j, starting time S_j and deadline E_j. Let $b_j(t)$ denote the amount of capacity allocated to class j jobs at time t. We have $0 \le b_j(t) \le MP_j, \forall t$ and $\sum_t b_j(t) \le B_j$. Given the above definitions, the total IT demand at time t is given by

$$d(t) = \Sigma_i a_i(t) + \Sigma_j b_j(t). \quad (3)$$

When taking into consideration the server power model, we can further transform $d(t)$ into power demand, as in Section 4.1. We assume the total IT capacity is D, so $0 \le d(t) \le D, \forall t$. Note here $d(t)$ is not constant, but instead time-varying as a result of dynamic capacity provisioning.

3.3 Cost and Revenue Model

The cost of a data center includes both capital and operating costs. Our model focuses on the operational electricity cost. Meanwhile, by servicing the batch jobs, the data center can obtain revenue. We model the data center cost by combining the energy cost and revenue from batch jobs. Note that, to simplify the model, we do not include the switching costs associated with cycling servers in and out of power-saving modes; however, the approach of [3] provides a natural way to incorporate such costs if desired.

To capture the variation of the energy cost over time, we let $g(t, d(t), e(t))$ denote the energy cost of the data center at time t given the IT power $d(t)$, optimal cooling power, renewable generation, electricity price, and energy storage usage $e(t)$. For any t, we assume that $g(t, d(t), e(t))$ is non-decreasing in $d(t)$, non-increasing in $e(t)$, and jointly convex in $d(t)$ and $e(t)$.

This formulation is quite general, and captures, for example, the common charging plan of a fixed price per kWh plus an additional "demand charge" for the peak of the average power used over a sliding 15 minute window [30], in which case the energy cost function consists of two parts:

$$p(t)\left(d(t) + c(d(t)) - r(t) - e(t)\right)^+$$

and

$$p_{peak}\left(\max_t \left(d(t) + c(d(t)) - r(t) - e(t)\right)^+\right),$$

where $p(t)$ is the fixed/variable electricity price per kWh, and p_{peak} is the peak demand charging rate. We could also include a sell-back mechanism and other charging policies. Additionally, this formulation can capture a wide range of models for server power consumption, e.g., energy costs as an affine function of the load, see [1], or as a polynomial function of the speed, see [4, 31].

We model only the variable component of the revenue[2], which comes from the batch jobs that are chosen to be run. Specifically, the data center gets revenue $\mathcal{R}(\mathbf{b})$, where $\mathbf{b}$ is the matrix consisting of $b_j(t), \forall j, \forall t$. In this paper, we focus on the following, simple revenue function

$$\mathcal{R}(\mathbf{b}) = \Sigma_j R_j \left(\Sigma_{t\in[S_j,E_j]} b_j(t)\right),$$

where R_j is the per-job revenue. $\left(\Sigma_{t\in[S_j,E_j]} b_j(t)\right)$ captures the amount of class j jobs finished before their deadlines.

3.4 Optimization Problem

We are now ready to formulate the renewable and cooling aware workload management optimization problem. Our optimization problem takes as input the renewable supply $r(t)$, electricity price $p(t)$, optimal cooling substructure $c(d(t))$, and IT workload demand $a_i(t), B_j$ and related information (the starting time S_j, deadline E_j, maximum parallization MP_j), IT capacity D, energy storage capacity ES and loss rate ρ, and generates an optimal schedule of each timeslot for batch jobs $b_j(t)$ and energy storage usage $e(t)$, according to the availability of renewable power and cooling supply such that specified SLAs (e.g., deadlines) and operational goals (e.g., minimizing operational costs) are satisfied.

[2]Revenue is also derived from the interactive workload, but for the purposes of workload management the amount of revenue from this workload is fixed.

This is captured by the following optimization problem:

$$\min_{\mathbf{b},\mathbf{e}} \Sigma_t g(t, d(t), e(t)) - \Sigma_j R_j \left(\Sigma_{t\in[S_j,E_j]} b_j(t)\right) \quad (4a)$$

$$\begin{aligned}
\text{s.t.} \Sigma_t b_j(t) &\le B_j, & \forall j \quad (4b)\\
es(t+1) &= \rho(es(t) - e(t)), & \forall t \quad (4c)\\
0 \le b_j(t) &\le MP_j, & \forall j, \forall t \quad (4d)\\
0 \le d(t) &\le D, & \forall t \quad (4e)\\
0 \le es(t) &\le ES. & \forall t \quad (4f)
\end{aligned}$$

Here $d(t)$ is given by (3). (4b) means the amount of served batch jobs cannot exceed the total demand, and could become $\Sigma_t b_j(t) = B_j$ if finishing all class j batch job is required. (4c) updates the energy storage level of each timeslot. We also incorporate constraints on maximum parallelization (4d), IT capacity (4e), and energy storage capacity (4f). We may have other constraints, such as a "net zero" constraint that the total energy consumed be less than the total renewable generation within $[1, T]$, i.e. $\sum_t (d(t) + c(d(t))) \le \sum_t r(t)$. Note that, though highly detailed, this formulation does ignore some important concerns of data center design, e.g., reliability and availability. Such issues are beyond the scope of this paper; nevertheless, our designs merge nicely with proposals such as [32] for these goals.

In this paper, we restrict our focus from optimization (4a) to (5a), but the analysis can be easily extended to other convex cost functions.

$$\min_{\mathbf{b},\mathbf{e}} \Sigma_t p(t)(d(t) + c(d(t)) - r(t) - e(t))^+ - \Sigma_j R_j \left(\Sigma_{t\in[S_j,E_j]} b_j(t)\right) \quad (5a)$$

$$\begin{aligned}
\text{s.t.} \Sigma_t b_j(t) &\le B_j, & \forall j \quad (5b)\\
es(t+1) &= \rho(es(t) - e(t)), & \forall t \quad (5c)\\
0 \le b_j(t) &\le MP_j, & \forall j, \forall t \quad (5d)\\
0 \le d(t) &\le D, & \forall t \quad (5e)\\
0 \le es(t) &\le ES. & \forall t \quad (5f)
\end{aligned}$$

Note that this optimization problem is jointly convex in $b_j(t)$ and $e(t)$ and can therefore be efficiently solved.

Given the significant amount of prior work approaching data center workload management via convex optimization [16, 17, 18, 19, 3, 11, 20], it is important to note the key difference between our formulation and prior work–our formulation is the first, to our knowledge, to incorporate renewable generation, storage, an optimized cooling micro grid, and batch job scheduling with consideration of both price diversity and temperature diversity. Prior formulations have included only one or two of these features. This "universal" inclusion is what allows us to consider truly integrated workload management.

3.5 Properties of the optimal workload management

The usage of the workload management optimization described above depends on more than just the ability to solve the optimization quickly. In particular, the solutions must be practical if they are to be adopted in actual data centers.

In this section, we provide characterizations of the optimal solutions to the workload management optimization, which highlight that the structure of the optimal solutions facilitates implementation. Specifically, one might worry that the optimal solutions require highly complex scheduling of the batch jobs, which could be impractical. For example, if a plan schedules too many jobs at a time, it may not be practical because there is often an upper limit on how many workloads can be hosted in a physical server. The following results here show that such concerns are unwarranted.

Energy usage and cost

Although it is easily seen that the workload management optimization problem has at least one optimal solution,[3] in general, the optimal solution is not unique. Thus, one may worry that the optimal solutions might have very different properties with respect to energy usage and cost, which would make capacity planning difficult. However, it turns out that the optimal solution, though not unique, has nice properties with respect to energy usage and cost.

In particular, we prove that all optimal solutions use the same amount of power from the grid at all times. Thus, though the scheduling of batch jobs and the usage of energy storage might be very different, the aggregate grid power usage is always the same. This is a nice feature when considering capacity planning of the power system. Formally, this is summarized by the following theorem proved in [28].

Theorem 1. *For the simplified energy cost model (5a), suppose the optimal cooling power $c(d)$ is strictly convex in d. Then, the energy usage from the grid, $(d(t) + c(d(t)) - r(t) - e(t))^+$, at each time t is common across all optimal solutions.*

Though Theorem 1 considers a general setting, it is not general enough to include the optimal cooling substructure discussed in Section 3.1, which includes a strictly convex section followed by a linear section (while in practice, the chiller power is usually strictly convex in IT power, and satisfies the requirement of Theorem 1). However, for this setting, there is a slightly weaker result that still holds–the marginal cost of power during each timeslot is common across all optimal solutions. This is particularly useful because it then provides the data center operator a benchmark for evaluating which batch jobs are worthy of execution, i.e., provide revenue larger than the marginal cost they would incur. Formally, we have the following theorem proved in [28].

Theorem 2. *For the simplified energy cost model (5a), suppose $c(d)$ is given by (2). Then, the marginal cost of power, $\partial\left(p(t)(d(t) + c(d(t)) - r(t) - e(t))^+\right)/\partial(d(t))$, at each time t is common across all optimal solutions.*

Complexity of the schedule for batch jobs

A goal of this work is to develop an efficient, implementable solution. One practical consideration is the complexity of the schedule for batch jobs. Specifically, a schedule must not be too "fragmented", i.e., have many batch jobs being run at the same time and batch jobs being split across a large number of time slots. This is particularly important in virtualized server environments because we often need to allocate a large amount of memory for each virtual machine and the number of virtual machines sharing a server is often limited by the memory available to virtual machines even if the CPUs can be well shared. Additionally, there is always overhead associated with hosting virtual machines. If we run too many virtual machines on the same server at the same time, the CPU, memory, I/O and performance can be affected. Finally, with more virtual machines, live migrations and consolidations during runtime management can affect the system performance.

[3]This can be seen by applying Weierstrass' theorem [33], since the objective function is continuous and the feasible set is compact subset of $\mathbb{R}^n$.

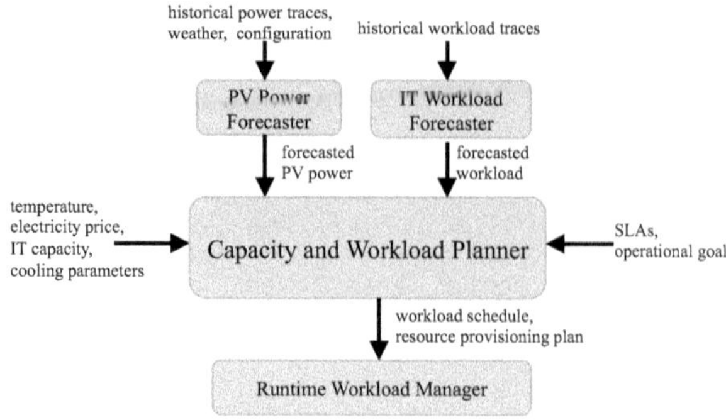

Figure 7: System Architecture

However, it turns out that one need not worry about an overly "fragmented" schedule, since there always exists a "simple" optimal schedule. Formally, we have the following theorem, which is proved in [28].

Theorem 3. *There exists an optimal solution to the workload management problem with at most $(T + J - 1)$ of the $b_j(t)$ are neither 0 nor MP_j.*

Informally, this result says that there is a simple optimal solution that uses at most $(T+J-1)$ more timeslots, or corresponding active virtual machines, in total than any other solutions finishing the same number of jobs. Thus, on average, for each class of batch job per timeslot, we run at most $\frac{(T+J-1)}{TJ}$ more active virtual machines than any other plan finishing the same amount of batch jobs. If the number of batch job classes is not large, on average, we run at most one more virtual machine per slot. In our experiments in Section 5, the simplest optimal solution only uses 4% more virtual machines. Though Theorem 3 does not guarantee that every optimal solution is simple, the proof is constructive. Thus, it provides an approach that allows one to transform an optimal solution into the simplest optimal solution.

In addition to Theorem 3, there are two other properties of the optimal solution that highlight its simplicity. We state these without proof due to space constraints. First, when multiple classes of batch jobs are served in the same timeslot, all of them except possibly the one with the lowest revenue are finished. Second, in every timeslot, the lowest marginal revenue of a batch job that is served is still larger than the marginal cost of power from Theorem 2.

4. SYSTEM PROTOTYPE

We have designed and implemented a supply-aware workload and capacity management prototype in a production data center based on the description in the previous section. The data center is equipped with on-site PV power generation and outside air cooling. The prototype includes workload and capacity planning, runtime workload scheduling and resource allocation, renewable generation and IT workload demand prediction. Figure 7 depicts the system architecture. The predictors use the historical traces of supply and demand information to predict the available power of an on-site PV, and the expected interactive workload demand. The capacity planner takes the predicted energy supply and cooling information as inputs and generates an optimal capacity allocation scheme for each workload. Finally, the runtime workload manager executes the workload plan.

The remainder of this section provides more details on each component of the system: capacity and workload planning, PV and workload prediction, and runtime workload management.

4.1 Capacity and Workload Planner

The data center has mixed energy sources: on-site photovoltaic (PV) generation tied to grid power. The cooling infrastructure has a cooling micro grid, including outside air cooling and chiller cooling. The data center hosts interactive applications and batch jobs. There are SLAs associated with the workloads. Though multiple IT resources can be used by IT workloads, we focus on CPU resource management in this implementation. We use a virtualized server environment where different workloads can share resources on the same physical servers.

The planner takes the following inputs: power supply (time varying PV power and grid power price data), interactive workload demand (time varying user request rates, response time target), batch job resource demands (CPU hours, arrival time, deadline, revenue of each batch job), IT configuration information (number of servers, server idle and peak power, capacity) and cooling configuration parameters (blower capacity, chiller cooling efficiency) and operational goals. We use the optimization (5a) in Section 3.4 with the following additional details.

We first determine the IT resource demand of interactive workload i using the M/GI/1/PS model, which gives $\frac{1}{\mu_i - \lambda_i(t)/a_i(t)} \leq rt_i$. Thus, the minimum CPU capacity needed is $a_i(t) = \frac{\lambda_i(t)}{\mu_i - 1/rt_i}$, which is a linear function of the arrival rate $\lambda_i(t)$. We estimate μ_i through real measurements and set the response time requirement rt_i according to the SLAs. While the model is not perfect for real-world data center workloads, it provides a good approximation. Although important, performance modeling is not the focus of this paper. The resulting average CPU utilization of interactive workload i is $1 - \frac{1}{\mu_i rt_i}$, therefore its actual CPU usage at time t is $a_i(t)\left(1 - \frac{1}{\mu_i rt_i}\right)$, the remaining $a_i(t)\frac{1}{\mu_i rt_i}$ capacity can be shared by batch jobs. For a batch job j, assume at time t it shares $n_{ji}(t) \geq 0$ CPU resource with interactive workload i and uses additional $n_j(t) \geq 0$ CPU resource by itself, then its total CPU usage at time t is $b_j(t) = \Sigma_i n_{ji}(t) + n_j(t)$, which is used to update Constraint (5b) and (5d). We have an additional constraint on CPU capacity that can be shared $\Sigma_j n_{ji}(t) \leq a_i(t)\frac{1}{\mu_i rt_i}$. Assume the data center has D CPU capacity in total, so the IT capacity constraint becomes $\Sigma_i a_i(t) + \Sigma_j n_j(t) \leq D$. Although our optimization (5a) in Section 3.4 can be used to handle IT workload with multi-dimensional demand, e.g., CPU, memory, here we restrict our attention to CPU-bound workloads.

The next step is to estimate the IT power consumption, which can be done based on the average CPU utilization

$$P_{server}(u) = P_i + (P_b - P_i) * u$$

where u is the average CPU utilization across all servers, P_i and P_b are the power consumed by the server at idle and their fully utilized state, respectively. This simple model has proved very useful and accurate in modeling power consumption since other components' activities are either static or correlate well with CPU activity [1]. Assuming each server has Q CPU capacity, using the above model, we estimate the IT power as follows[4]:

$$d(t) = \frac{\Sigma_i a_i(t)}{Q}\left(P_i + (P_b - P_i) * u_i\right) + \frac{\Sigma_j n_j(t)}{Q} P_b,$$

where $u_i = \left(1 - \frac{1}{\mu_i rt_i} + \frac{\Sigma_j n_{ji}(t)}{a_i(t)}\right)$.

The cooling power can be derived from the IT power according to the cooling model (2) described in Section 3.1.

[4] Since the number of servers used by an interactive workload or a class of batch jobs is usually large in data centers, we treat it as continuous.

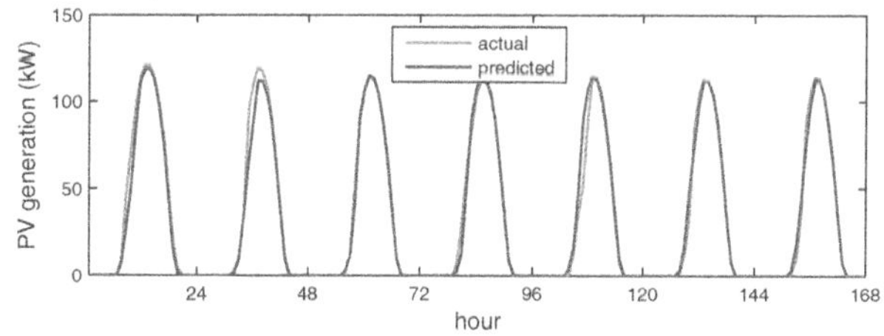

Figure 8: PV prediction

By solving the cost optimization problem (5a), we then obtain a detailed capacity plan, including at each time t the capacity allocated to each class j of batch jobs $b_j(t)$ (from $n_{ji}(t)$ and $n_j(t)$), and interactive workload i $a_i(t)$, energy storage usage $e(t)$, as well as optimal cooling configuration (i.e., capacity for outside air cooling and chiller cooling).

It follows from Section 3.4 that this problem is a convex optimization problem and hence there exist efficient algorithms to solve this problem. For example, disciplined convex programming [34] can be used. Under this approach, convex functions and sets are built up from a small set of rules from convex analysis, starting from a base library of convex functions and sets. Constraints and objectives that are expressed using these rules are automatically transformed to a canonical form and solved. In our prototype, the algorithm is implemented using Matlab CVX [34], a modeling system for convex optimization.

We then utilize the Best Fit Decreasing (BFD) method [35] to decide how to place and consolidate the workloads at each timeslot. More advanced techniques exist for optimizing the workload placement [5], but they are out this paper's scope.

4.2 PV Power Forecaster

A variety of methods have been used for fine-grained energy prediction, mostly using classical auto-regressive techniques [36, 37]. However, most of the work does not explicitly use the associated weather conditions as a basis for modeling. The work in [38] considered the impact of the weather conditions explicitly and used an SVM classifier in conjunction with a RBF kernel to predict solar irradiation. We use a similar approach for PV prediction in our prototype implementation. In order to predict PV power generation for the next day, we use a k-nearest neighbor (k-NN) based algorithm. The prediction is done at the granularity of one-hour time periods. The basic idea is to search for the most "similar" days in the recent past (using one week worked well here[5]) and use the generation during those days to estimate the generation for the target hour. The similarity between two days is determined using features such as ambient temperature, humidity, cloud cover, visibility, sunrise/sunset times on those days, etc. In particular, the algorithm uses weighted k-NN, where the PV prediction for hour t on the next day is given by $\hat{y}_t = \frac{\Sigma_{i \in N_k(\mathbf{x}_t, \mathcal{D})} y_i / d(\mathbf{x}_i, \mathbf{x}_t)}{\Sigma_{i \in N_k(\mathbf{x}_t, \mathcal{D})} 1/d(\mathbf{x}_i, \mathbf{x}_t)}$, where $\hat{y}_t$ is the PV predicted output at hour t, $\mathbf{x}_t$ is the feature vector, e.g., temperature, cloud cover, for the target hour t obtained from the weather forecast, y_i is the actual PV output for neighbor i, $\mathbf{x}_i$ is the corresponding feature vector, d is the distance metric function, $N_k(\mathbf{x}_i, \mathcal{D})$ are k-nearest neighbors of $\mathbf{x}_i$ in $\mathcal{D}$. k is chosen based on cross-validation of historical data.

Figure 8 shows the predicted and actual values for the PV supply of the data center for one week in September 2011. The average prediction errors vary from 5% to 20%. The prediction accuracy depends on occurrence of similar weather conditions in the recent past and the accuracy of the weather forecast. The results in [28] show that a ballpark

[5] If available, data from past years could also be used.

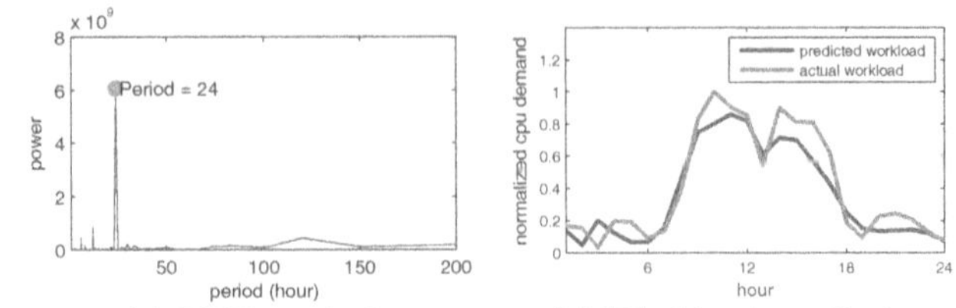

(a) FFT analysis (b) Workload prediction

Figure 9: Workload analysis and prediction

approximation is sufficient for planning purposes and our system can tolerate prediction errors in this range.

4.3 IT Workload Forecaster

In order to perform the planning, we need knowledge about the IT demand, both the stochastic properties of the interactive application and the total resource demand of batch jobs. Though there is large variability in workload demands, workloads often exhibit clear short-term and long-term patterns. To predict the resource demand (e.g., CPU resource) for interactive applications, we first perform a periodicity analysis of the historical workload traces to reveal the length of a pattern or a sequence of patterns that appear periodically. Fast Fourier Transform (FFT) can be used to find the periodogram of the time-series data. Figure 9(a) plots the time-series and the periodogram for 25 work days of a real CPU demand trace from an SAP application. From this we derive periods of the most prominent patterns or sequences of patterns. For this example, the peak at 24 hours in the periodogram indicates that it has a strong daily pattern (period of 24 hours). Actually, most interactive workloads exhibit prominent daily patterns. An auto-regressive model is then used to capture both the long term and short term patterns. The model estimates $w(d,t)$, the demand at time t on day d, based on the demand of the previous N days as $w(d,t) = \Sigma_{i=1}^{N} a_i * w(d-i,t) + c$. The parameters are calibrated using historical data.

We evaluate the workload prediction algorithm with several real demand traces. The results for a Web application trace are shown in Figure 9(b). The average prediction errors are around 20%. If we can use the previous M time points of the same day for the prediction, we could further reduce the error rate.

The total resource demand (e.g., CPU hours) of batch jobs can be obtained from users or from historical data or through offline benchmarking [39]. Like supply prediction, a ballpark approximation is good enough, as we will see in [28].

4.4 Runtime Workload Manager

The runtime workload manager schedules workloads and allocates CPU resource according to the plan generated by the planner. We implement a prototype in a KVM-based virtualized server environment [40]. Our current implementation uses a KVM/QEMU hypervisor along with control groups (Cgroups), a new Linux feature, to perform resource allocation and workload management [40]. In particular, it executes the following tasks according to the plan: (1) create and start virtual machines hosting batch jobs; (2) adjust the resource allocation (e.g., CPU shares or number of virtual CPUs) to each virtual machine; (3) migrate and consolidate virtual machines via live migration. The workload manager assigns a higher priority to virtual machines running interactive workloads than virtual machines for batch jobs via Cgroups. This guarantees that resources are available as needed by interactive applications, while excess resources can be used by the batch jobs, improving server utilization.

5. EVALUATION

To highlight the benefits of our design for renewable and cooling aware workload management, we perform a mixture of numerical simulations and experiments in a real testbed. We first present trace-based simulation results in Section 5.1, and then the experimental results on the real testbed implementation in Section 5.2.

5.1 Case Studies

We begin by discussing evaluations of our workload and capacity planning using numerical simulations. We use traces from real data centers. In particular, we obtain PV supply, interactive IT workload, and cooling data from real data center traces. The renewable energy and cooling data is from measurements of a data center in California. The data center is equipped with 130kW PV panel array and a cooling system consisting of outside air cooling and chiller cooling. We use the real-time electricity price of the data center location obtained from [41]. The total IT capacity is 500 servers (100kW). The interactive workload is a popular web service application with more than 85 million registered users in 22 countries. The trace contains average CPU utilization and memory usage as recorded every 5 minutes. Additionally, we assume that there are a number of batch jobs. Half of them are submitted at midnight and another half are submitted around noon. The total demand ratio between the interactive workload and batch jobs is 1:1.5. The interactive workload is deemed critical and the resource demand must be met while the batch jobs can be rescheduled as long as they finish before their deadlines. The plan period is 24-hours and the capacity planner creates a plan for the next 24-hours at midnight based on renewable supply and cooling information as well as the interactive demand. The plan includes hourly capacity allocation for each workload. We assume perfect knowledge about the workload demand and renewable supply, and the results in [28] validate our solution works well with prediction errors and different mixes of interactive and batch workloads.

Here we explore: (i) How valuable is renewable and cooling aware workload management? (ii) Is net zero possible under renewable and cooling aware workload management? (iii) What portfolio of renewable sources is best?

How valuable is renewable and cooling aware workload management?

We start with the key question for this paper: how much energy cost/CO_2 savings does renewable and cooling aware workload management provide? In this study, we assume half of batch jobs must be finished before noon and another half must be finished before midnight. We compare the following four approaches: (i) *Optimal*, which integrates supply and cooling information and uses our optimization algorithm to schedule batch jobs; (ii) *Night*, which schedules batch jobs at night to avoid interfering with critical workloads and to take advantage of idle machines (this is a widely used solution in practice); (iii) *Best Effort (BE)*, which runs batch jobs immediately when they arrive and uses all available IT to finish batch jobs as quickly as possible; (iv) *Flat*, which runs batch jobs at a constant rate within the deadline period for the jobs.

Figure 10 shows the detailed schedule and power consumption for each approach, including IT power (batch and interactive workloads), cooling, and supply. As shown in the figure, compared with other approaches, *Optimal* reshapes the batch job demand and fully utilizes the renewable supply, and uses non-renewable energy, if necessary, to complete the batch jobs during this 24-hour period. These additional batch jobs are scheduled to run between 3am and 6am or 11pm and midnight, when the outside air cooling is most efficient and/or the electricity price is lower. As a result, our

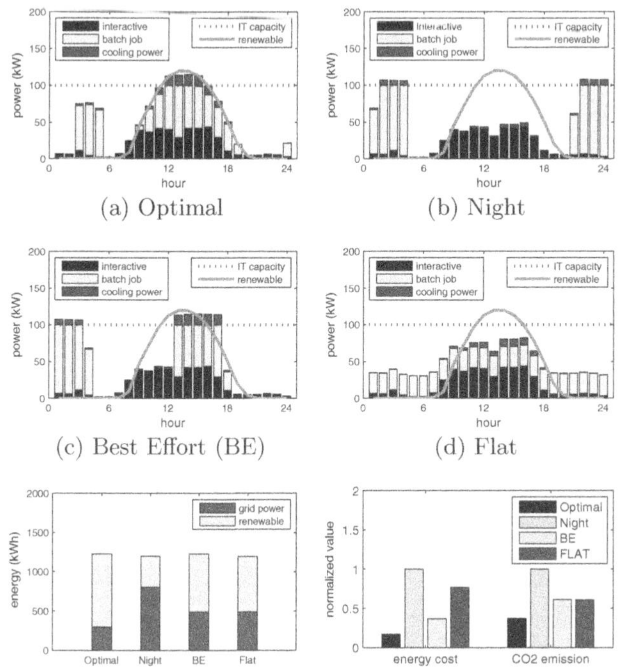

(a) Optimal (b) Night

(c) Best Effort (BE) (d) Flat

(e) Power usage comparisons (f) Efficiency comparisons

Figure 10: Power cost minimization while finishing all jobs

solution reduces the grid power consumption by 39%-63% compared to other approaches (Figure 10(e)). Though not clear in the figure, the optimal solution does consume a bit more total power (up to 2%) because of the low cooling efficiency around noon. Figure 10(f) shows the average recurring electricity cost and CO_2 emission per job. The energy cost per job is reduced by 53%-83% and the CO_2 emission per job is reduced by 39%-63% under the *Optimal* schedule. The adaptation of workload management to renewable availability is clear in Figure 10. Less clear is the importance of managing the workload in a manner that is "cooling aware".

The importance of cooling aware scheduling: As discussed in Sections 2.2 and 3.1, the cooling efficiency and capacity of a cooling supply often vary over time. This is particularly true for outside air cooling. One important component of our solution is to schedule workloads by taking into account time varying cooling efficiency and capacity. To understand the benefits of cooling integration, we compare our optimal solution as shown in Figure 10(a) with two solutions that are renewable aware but handle cooling differently: (i) *Cooling-oblivious* ignores cooling power and considers IT power only, (ii) *Static-cooling* uses a static cooling efficiency (assuming the cooling power is 30% of IT power) to estimate the cooling power from IT power and incorporates the cooling power into workload scheduling.

Figures 11(a) and 11(b) show *Cooling-oblivious* and *Static-cooling* schedules, respectively. As shown in the figures, both schedules integrate renewable energy into scheduling and run most batch jobs when renewables are available. However, because they do not capture the cooling power accurately, they cannot fully optimize workload schedule. In particular, by ignoring the cooling power, *Cooling-oblivious* underestimates the power demand and runs more jobs than the available PV supply and hence uses more grid power during the day. This is also less cost-efficient because the electricity price peaks at that time. On the other hand, by overestimating the cooling power demand, *Static-cooling* fails to fully utilize the renewable supply and results in inefficiency, too. Figures 11(c) and 11(d) compare the total power usage and energy efficiency,

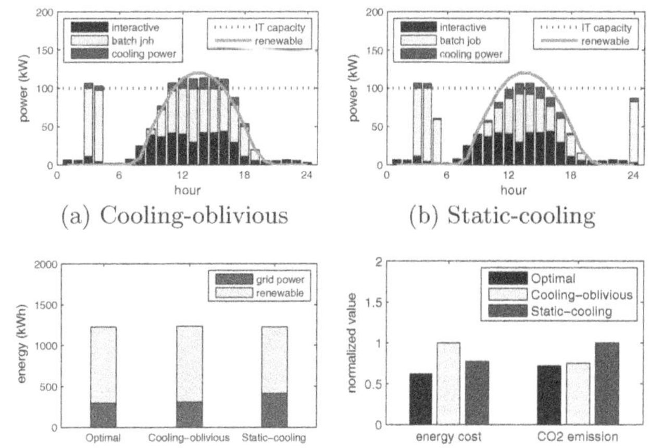

(a) Cooling-oblivious (b) Static-cooling

(c) Power usage comparisons (d) Efficiency comparisons

Figure 11: Benefit of cooling integration

i.e., normalized energy cost and carbon emission per batch job of these two approaches and *Optimal*, respectively. By accurately modeling the cooling efficiency and adapting to time variations in cooling efficiency, our solution reduces the energy cost by 20%-38% and CO_2 emission by 4%-28%.

The importance of optimizing the cooling micro-grid: Optimizing the workload scheduling based on cooling efficiency is only one aspect of our cooling integration. Another important aspect is to optimize the cooling micro-grid, i.e, using the proper amount of cooling capacity from each cooling resource. This is important because different cooling supplies exhibit different cooling efficiencies as the IT demand and external conditions such as OAT changes. Our solution takes this into account and optimizes the cooling capacity management in addition to IT workload management.

We compare: (i) *Optimal* adjusts the cooling capacity for outside air cooling and chiller cooling based on the dynamic cooling efficiency, which is determined by IT demand and outside air temperature; (ii) *Binary Outside Air (BOA)* uses outside air cooling at its full capacity if OAT exceeds some threshold (25°C) or interactive demand is too low (less than 10% of the IT capacity) and does not use it at all otherwise; (iii) *Chiller only* uses the chiller cooling only. All three solutions are renewable and cooling aware and schedule workload according to the renewable supply and cooling efficiency. They finish the same number of batch jobs. The difference is how they manage cooling resources and capacity.

Figure 12 shows the cooling capacity from outside air cooling and chiller cooling for these three solutions. As shown in this figure, *Optimal* uses outside air only during night when it is more efficient, and combines outside air cooling and chiller cooling during other times. In particular, our solution uses less outside air cooling and more chiller cooling between 1pm and 4pm as outside air cooling is less efficient due to high IT demand and outside air temperature at that time. In contrast, *BOA* runs outside air at full capacity except the hours around noon when the outside air is less efficient. Figures 12(g) and 12(h) compare the power, cost, and cooling consumption of the three approaches. By optimizing the cooling substructure, our solution reduces the cooling power by 66% over *BOA* and 48% over *Chiller only*.

Is net zero energy consumption possible with renewable and cooling aware workload management?

Now, we switch our goal from minimizing the cost incurred by the data center to minimizing the environmental impact of the data center. Net zero is often used to describe a building with zero net energy consumption and zero carbon emission annually. Recently, researchers have envisioned how net zero

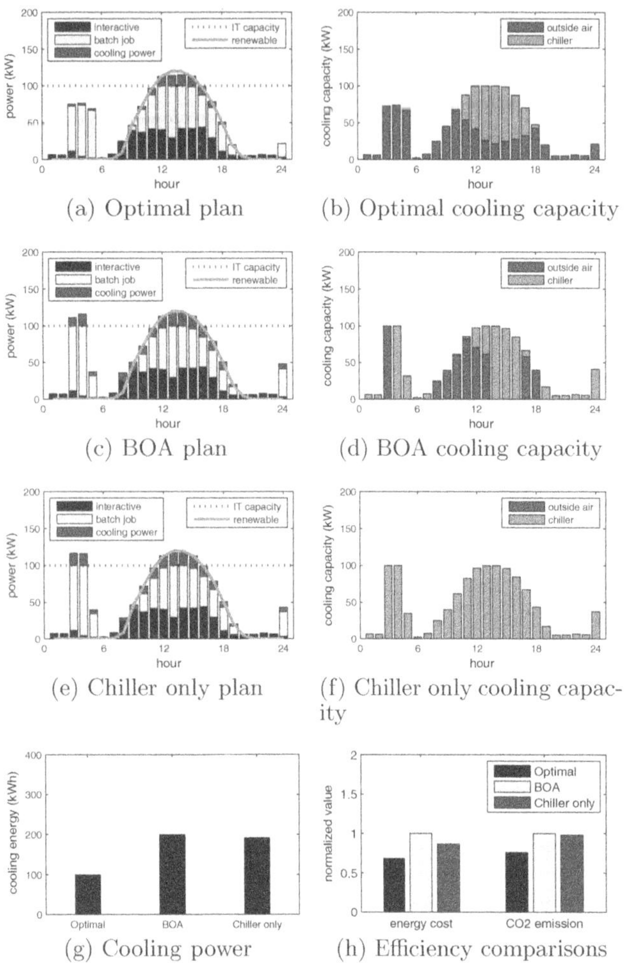

(a) Optimal plan (b) Optimal cooling capacity

(c) BOA plan (d) BOA cooling capacity

(e) Chiller only plan (f) Chiller only cooling capacity

(g) Cooling power (h) Efficiency comparisons

Figure 12: Benefit of cooling optimization

building concepts can be effectively extended into the data center space to create a net zero data center, whose total power consumption is less than or equal to the total power supply from renewable. We explore if net zero is possible with renewable and cooling aware workload management in data centers and how much it will cost.

By adding a net-zero constraint (i.e., total power consumption $\leq$ total renewable supply) to our optimization problem, our capacity planner can generate a net-zero schedule. Figure 13(a) shows our solution (*Net-zero1*) for achieving a net zero operation goal. Similar to the optimal solution shown in Figure 10(a), *Net-zero1* optimally schedules batch jobs to take advantage of the renewable supply; however, batch jobs are only executed when renewable energy is available and without exceeding the total renewable generation, and thus some are allowed to not finish during this 24 hour period. In this case, about 40% of the batch jobs are delayed till a future time when a renewable energy surplus may exist. Additionally, some renewable energy is reserved to offset non-renewable energy used at night for interactive workloads. This excess renewable power is reserved in the afternoon when the outside air temperature peaks, thus minimizing the energy required for cooling.

A key to achieving net zero is energy storage. By maximizing renewable usage directly, *Net-zero1* reduces the dependency on storage and hence the capital cost. To understand the benefit, we compare *Net-zero1* with another schedule, *Net-zero2*, which runs the same amount of batch jobs but distributes the batch jobs over 24-hours as shown in Fig-

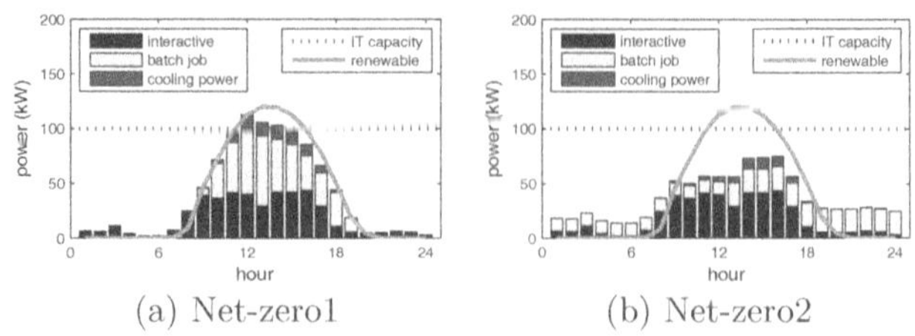

(a) Net-zero1 (b) Net-zero2

Figure 13: Net Zero Energy

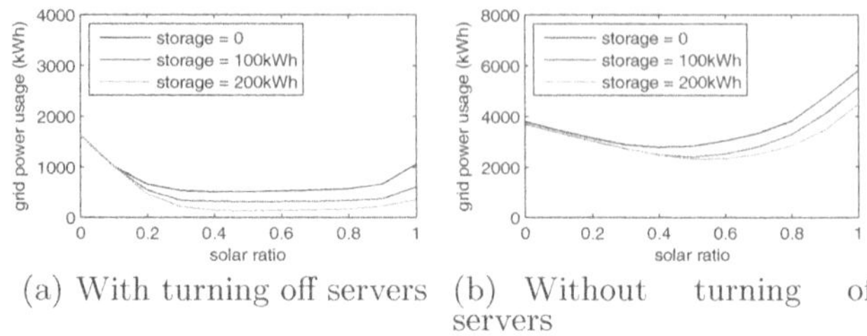

(a) With turning off servers (b) Without turning off servers

Figure 14: Optimal renewable portfolio

ure 13(b). Both approaches achieve the net-zero goal, but *Net-zero2* uses 287% more grid power compared to our solution *Net-zero1*. As a result, the energy storage sizes of *Net-zero1* and *Net-zero2* are 82kWh and 330kWh, respectively. Using an estimated cost of 400$/kWh [22], this difference in energy demand results in $99,200 more energy storage expenditure for *Net-zero2*.

What portfolio of renewable sources is best?

To this point, we have focused on PV solar as the sole source of renewable energy. Since wind energy is becoming increasingly cost-effective, a sustainable data center will likely use both solar and wind to some degree. The question that emerges is which one is better source from the perspective of optimizing data center energy efficiency. More generally, what is the optimal portfolio of renewable sources?

We conduct a study using the wind and solar traces depicted in Figure 2. Assuming an average renewable supply of 200kW, we vary the mix of solar and wind in the renewable supply. For each mix, we use our capacity management optimization algorithm to generate an optimal workload schedule. We compare the non-renewable power consumption for different renewable mixes for two cases (turning off unused servers and without turning off unused servers). Figure 14 shows the results as a function of percentage of solar with different storage capacity. As shown in the figure, the optimal portfolio contains more solar than wind because solar is less volatile and the supply aligns better with IT demand.

However, wind energy is still an important component and a small percentage of wind can help improve the efficiency. For example, the optimal portfolio without storage consists of about 60% solar and 40% wind. When we do not turn off unused servers, wind becomes more valuable due to the significant power consumption during night even when the server utilization is low.

In summary, solar is a better source for local data centers in sunny areas such like Palo Alto and a small addition of wind can help improve energy efficiency. The optimal portfolio varies for different areas. Additionally, recent work has shown that the value of wind increases significantly when geographically diverse data centers are considered [17, 20].

5.2 Experimental Results on a Real Testbed

The case studies described in the previous section highlight the theoretical benefits of our approach over existing solutions. To verify our claims and ensure that we have a practical and robust solution, we experimentally evaluate our prototype implementation on a real data center testbed and contrast it with a current workload management approach.

5.2.1 Experiment Setup

Our testbed consists of four high end servers (each with two 12-core 1.8GHz processors and 64 GB memory) and the following workloads: one interactive Web application, and 6 batch applications. Each server is running Scientific Linux. Each workload is running inside a KVM virtual machine. The interactive application is a single-tier web application running multiple Apache web servers and batch jobs are sysbench [42] with different resource demands. httperf [43] is used to replay the workload demand traces in the form of CGI requests, and each request is directed to one of the Web servers. The PV, cooling data, and interactive workload traces used in the case study are scaled to the testbed capacity. We measure the power consumption via the server's built-in management interfaces, collect CPU consumption through system monitoring and obtain response times of Web servers from Apache logs.

5.2.2 Experiment Results

We compare two approaches: (i) *Optimal* is our optimal design, (ii) *Night*, which runs batch jobs at night. For each plan, the runtime workload manager dynamically starts the batch jobs, allocates resources to both interactive and batch workloads and turns on/off servers according to the plan. Figures 15(a) and 15(b) shows the CPU allocation of our optimal solution and the actual CPU consumption measured in the experiment, respectively. The results show that actual resource usage closely follows the power generated by the capacity planner. The results for *Night* are similar. We further compare the predicted power usage in the plan and the actual power consumption in the experiment for both approaches. From Figures 15(c) and 15(d), we see that the actual power usage is close to the power plan.

We then compare the power consumption and performance of the two approaches. Figure 16(a) shows the power consumption. *Optimal* does more work during the day when the renewable energy source is available. *Night* uses additional servers from midnight to 6am to run batch jobs while our solution starts batch jobs around noon by taking advantage of renewable energy. Compared with *Night*, our approach reduces the grid power usage by 48%. One thing worth mentioning is that the total power is not quite proportional to the total CPU utilization as a result of the large idle part of the server power. This is most noticeable when the number of servers is small, as we see in the experimental results, Figures 15(b) and 15(c). When the total number of servers increases, the impact of idle power decreases and *Optimal* will save even more grid power.

One reason that batch jobs are scheduled to run at night is to avoid interfering with interactive workloads. Our approach runs more jobs during the day when the web server demand is high. To understand the impact of this on performance, we compare the average response time of the web server. The results show that both approaches are almost identical: 153.0ms for *Optimal*, compared to 156.0ms for *Night*. See [28] for more details. This is because both solutions satisfy web server demand and Linux KVM/Cgroups scheduler is preemptive and enables CPU resources to be effectively virtualized and shared among virtual machines [40]. In particular, assigning a much higher priority to virtual machines hosting the web servers guarantees that resources are available as needed by the web servers.

In summary, the real experiment results demonstrate that (i) the optimization-based workload management scheme can translate effectively into a prototype implementation, (ii) compared with traditional workload management solution,

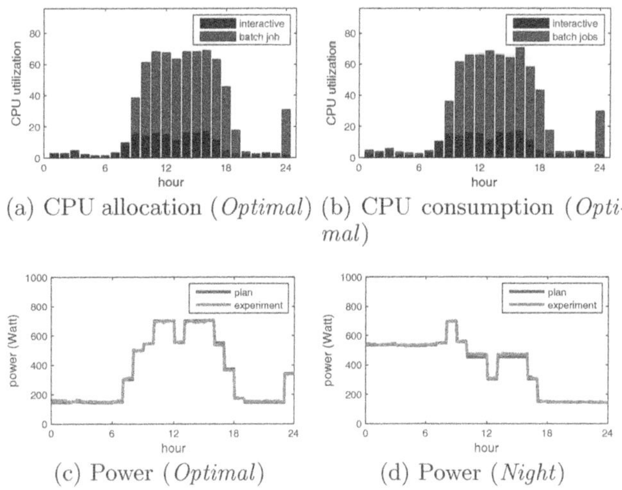

(a) CPU allocation (*Optimal*) (b) CPU consumption (*Optimal*)

(c) Power (*Optimal*) (d) Power (*Night*)

Figure 15: Comparison of plan and experimental results

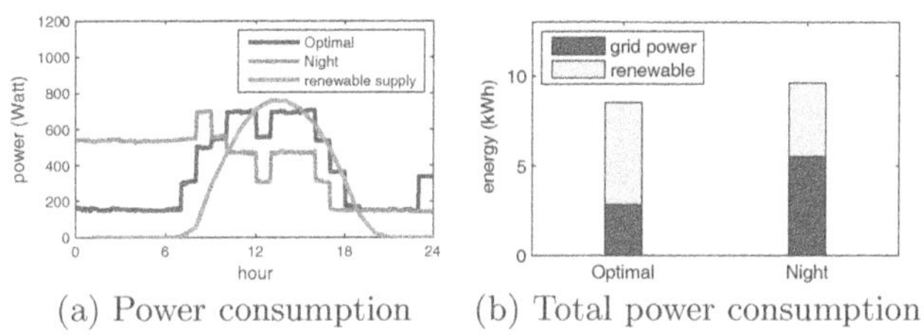

(a) Power consumption (b) Total power consumption

Figure 16: Comparison of optimal and night

Optimal significantly reduces the use of grid power without degrading the performance of critical demand.

6. CONCLUDING REMARKS

Our goal in this paper is to provide an integrated workload management system for data centers that takes advantage of the efficiency gains possible by shifting demand in a way that exploits time variations in electricity price, the availability of renewable energy, and the efficiency of cooling. There are two key points we would like to highlight about our design.

First, a key feature of the design is the integration of the three main data center silos: cooling, power, and IT. Though a considerable amount of work exists in optimizing efficiencies of these individually, there is little work that provides an integrated solution for all three. Our case studies illustrate that the potential gains from an integrated approach are significant. Additionally, our prototype illustrates that these gains are attainable. In both cases, we have taken case to measurements from a real data center and traces of real applications to ensure that our experiments are meaningful.

Second, it is important to point out that our approach uses a mix of implementation, modeling, and theory. At the core of our design is a cost optimization that is solved by the workload manager. Care has been taken in designing and solving this optimization so that the solution is "practical" (see the characterization theorems in Section 3.5). Building an implementation around this optimization requires significant measurement and modeling of the cooling substructure, and the incorporation of predictors for workload demand and PV supply. We see one role of this paper as a proof of concept for the wide-variety of "optimization-based designs" recently proposed, e.g., [16, 17, 18, 19, 3, 11, 20].

There are a number of future directions building on this work including integrating reliability and a more detailed study of the role of storage. But, perhaps the most exciting direction is the potential to consider renewable and cooling aware workload management of geographically diverse data centers as opposed to the local workload management considered here. As illustrated in [17, 20], geographical diversity can be a significant aid in handling the intermittency of renewable sources and electricity price fluctuations. For example, the fact that fluctuations in wind energy are nearly uncorrelated for significantly distant locations means that wind can provide a nearly constant baseline supply of energy if workload can be adapted geographically. Another future direction we would like to highlight is to understand the impact of workload management on the capacity planning of a data center, e.g. the size of renewable infrastructure, the capacity of IT and cooling infrastructure, and the capital expense and to minimize the Total Cost of Ownership (TCO).

Acknowledgements

We are grateful to many members of Sustainable Ecosystem Research Group at HP Labs. Chandrakant Patel has provided great support and guidance at various stages of this work. Niru Kumari provided valuable information on chiller cooling models. Martin Arlitt, Amip Shah, Sergey Blagodurov and Alan McReynolds offered helpful feedback. We also thank the anonymous reviewers and our shepherd, Christopher Stewart, for their valuable comments and help.

7. REFERENCES

[1] X. Fan, W.-D. Weber, and L. A. Barroso, "Power provisioning for a warehouse-sized computer," in *Proc. of ACM ISCA*, 2007.

[2] A. Gandhi, M. Harchol-Balter, and C. L. R. Das, "Optimal power allocation in server farms," in *Proc. of ACM Sigmetrics*, 2009.

[3] M. Lin, A. Wierman, L. L. H. Andrew, and E. Thereska, "Dynamic right-sizing for power-proportional data centers," in *Proc. of INFOCOM*, 2011.

[4] A. Wierman, L. L. H. Andrew, and A. Tang, "Power-aware speed scaling in processor sharing systems," in *Proc. of INFOCOM*, 2009.

[5] J. Choi, S. Govindan, B. Urgaonkar, and A. Sivasubramaniam, "Power consumption prediction and power-aware packing in consolidated environments," *IEEE Transactions on Computers*, vol. 59, no. 12, 2010.

[6] R. Raghavendra, P. Ranganathan, V. Talwar, Z. Wang, and X. Zhu, "No "power" struggles: Coordinated multi-level power management for the data center," in *Proc. of ASPLOS*, 2008.

[7] Z. Wang, A. McReynolds, C. Felix, C. Bash, and C. Hoover, "Kratos: Automated management of cooling capacity in data centers with adaptive vent tiles," in *Proc. of IMECE*, 2009.

[8] C. E. Bash, C. D. Patel, , and R. K. Sharma, "Dynamic thermal management of aircooled data centers," in *Proc. of ITHERM*, 2006.

[9] W. Huang, M. Allen-Ware, J. Carter, E. Elnozahy, H. Hamann, T. Keller, C. Lefurgy, J. Li, K. Rajamani, and J. Rubio, "Tapo: Thermal-aware power optimization techniques for servers and data centers," in *Proc. of IGCC*, 2011.

[10] J. Moore, J. Chase, P. Ranganathan, and R. Sharma, "Making scheduling cool: Temperature-aware workload placement in data centers," in *Proc. of USENIX ATC*, 2005.

[11] E. Pakbaznia and M. Pedram, "Minimizing data center cooling and server power costs," in *Proc. of ISLPED*, 2009.

[12] Y. Chen, D. Gmach, C. Hyser, Z. Wang, C. Bash, C. Hoover, and S. Singhal, "Integrated management of application performance, power and cooling in data centers," in *Proc. of NOMS*, 2010.

[13] T. Breen, E. Walsh, J. Punch, C. Bash, and A. Shah, "From chip to cooling tower data center modeling: Influence of server inlet temperature and temperature rise across cabinet," *Journal of Electronic Packaging*, vol. 133, no. 1, 2011.

[14] D. Gmach, J. Rolia, C. Bash, Y. Chen, T. Christian, A. Shah, R. Sharma, and Z. Wang, "Capacity planning and power management to exploit sustainable energy," in *Proc. of CNSM*, 2010.

[15] "Clean urban energy: Turn buildings into batteries." 2011.

[16] K. Le, O. Bilgir, R. Bianchini, M. Martonosi, and T. D. Nguyen, "Capping the brown energy consumption of internet services at low cost," in *Proc. IGCC*, 2010.

[17] Z. Liu, M. Lin, A. Wierman, S. H. Low, and L. L. H. Andrew, "Greening geographical load balancing," in *Proc. ACM Sigmetrics*, 2011.

[18] L. Rao, X. Liu, L. Xie, and W. Liu, "Minimizing electricity cost: Optimization of distributed internet data centers in a multi-electricity-market environment," in *Proc. of INFOCOM*, 2010.

[19] P. Wendell, J. W. Jiang, M. J. Freedman, and J. Rexford, "Donar: decentralized server selection for cloud services," in *Proc. of ACM Sigcomm*, 2010.

[20] Z. Liu, M. Lin, A. Wierman, S. H. Low, and L. L. H. Andrew, "Geographical load balancing with renewables," in *Proc. ACM GreenMetrics*, 2011.

[21] M. Lin, Z. Liu, A. Wierman, and L. L. Andrew, "Online algorithms for geographical load balancing." http://http://www.cs.caltech.edu/ zliu2/onlineGLB.pdf.

[22] *Electricity Energy Storage Technology Options: A White Paper Primer on Applications, Costs and Benefits.* 2010.

[23] "Report to congress on server and data center energy efficiency." 2007.

[24] R. Zhou, Z. Wang, A. McReynolds, C. Bash, T. Christian, and R. Shih, "Optimization and control of cooling microgrids for data centers," in *Proc. of ITherm*, 2012.

[25] C. Patel, R. Sharma, C. Bash, and A. Beitelmal, "Energy flow in the information technology stack," in *Proc. of IMECE*, 2006.

[26] F. Bleier, *Fan Handbook: Selection, Application and Design*. New York: McGraw-Hill, 1997.

[27] J. Holman, *Heat Transfer. 8th ed.* New York: McGraw-Hill, 1997.

[28] Z. Liu, Y. Chen, C. Bash, A. Wierman, D. Gmach, Z. Wang, M. Marwah, and C. Hyser, "Renewable and cooling aware workload management for sustainable data centers," Tech. Rep. HPL-2012-73, HP Labs, April 2012.

[29] R. Urgaonkar, B. Urgaonkar, M. Neely, and A. Sivasubramaniam, "Optimal power cost management using stored energy in data centers," in *Proc. of ACM Sigmetrics*, 2011.

[30] S. Ong, P. Denholm, and E. Doris, "The impacts of commercial electric utility rate structure elements on the economics of photovoltaic systems," Tech. Rep. NREL/TP-6A2-46782, National Renewable Energy Laboratory, 2010.

[31] L. L. H. Andrew, M. Lin, and A. Wierman, "Optimality, fairness and robustness in speed scaling designs," in *Proc. of ACM Sigmetrics*, 2010.

[32] E. Thereska, A. Donnelly, and D. Narayanan, "Sierra: a power-proportional, distributed storage system," Tech. Rep. MSR-TR-2009-153, Microsoft Research, 2009.

[33] D. P. Bertsekas, *Nonlinear Programming*. Athena Scientific, 1999.

[34] http://cvxr.com/cvx/

[35] V. Vazirani, *Approximation Algorithms*. Springer, 2003.

[36] D. R. Cox, "Prediction by exponentially weighted moving averages and related methods," 1961.

[37] A. Kansal, J. Hsu, S. Zahedi, and M. B. Srivastava, "Power management in energy harvesting sensor networks," 2007.

[38] N. Sharma, P. Sharma, D. Irwin, and P. Shenoy, "Predicting solar generation from weather forecasts using machine learning," in *Proc. of SmartGridComm*, 2011.

[39] Y. Becerra, D. Carrera, and E. Ayguade, "Batch job profiling and adaptive profile enforcement for virtualized environments," in *Proc. of ICPDNP*, 2009.

[40] "Kvm kernel based virtual machine." http://www.redhat.com/f/pdf/rhev/DOC-KVM.pdf.

[41] http://www.ferc.gov/market-oversight/mkt electric

[42] "Sysbench: a system performance benchmark." http://sysbench.sourceforge.net/.

[43] http://www.hpl.hp.com/research/linux/httperf/

Energy Storage in Datacenters: What, Where, and How much?

Di Wang, Chuangang Ren, Anand Sivasubramaniam, Bhuvan Urgaonkar, and Hosam Fathy*
Dept. of Computer Science and Engineering, *Dept. of Mechanical and Nuclear Engineering
The Pennsylvania State University
{diw5108, cyr5126, anand, bhuvan}@cse.psu.edu, hkf2@engr.psu.edu

ABSTRACT

Energy storage - in the form of UPS units - in a datacenter has been primarily used to fail-over to diesel generators upon power outages. There has been recent interest in using these Energy Storage Devices (ESDs) for demand-response (DR) to either shift peak demand away from high tariff periods, or to shave demand allowing aggressive under-provisioning of the power infrastructure. All such prior work has only considered a single/specific type of ESD (typically re-chargeable lead-acid batteries), and has only employed them at a single level of the power delivery network. Continuing technological advances have provided us a plethora of competitive ESD options ranging from ultra-capacitors, to different kinds of batteries, flywheels and even compressed air-based storage. These ESDs offer very different trade-offs between their power and energy costs, densities, lifetimes, and energy efficiency, among other factors, suggesting that employing hybrid combinations of these may allow more effective DR than with a single technology. Furthermore, ESDs can be placed at different, and possibly multiple, levels of the power delivery hierarchy with different associated trade-offs. To our knowledge, no prior work has studied the extensive design space involving multiple ESD technology provisioning and placement options. This paper intends to fill this critical void, by presenting a theoretical framework for capturing important characteristics of different ESD technologies, the trade-offs of placing them at different levels of the power hierarchy, and quantifying the resulting cost-benefit trade-offs as a function of workload properties.

Categories and Subject Descriptors: C.0 [Computer Systems Organization]: General

Keywords: Datacenters, Power Provisioning, Energy Storage, Cost Reduction.

1. INTRODUCTION

Datacenter power consumption is raising serious cost, environmental footprint, and scalability concerns. A large datacenter may spend millions of dollars in annual operational expenditures (op-ex) paying its electricity bills. An even larger capital expenditure (cap-ex) goes into provisioning the power delivery network to accommodate the peak power draw, even if this draw never/rarely occurs (see Figure 1). In fact, the peak power draw also impacts op-ex, because utility tariffs typically dis-incentivize high peak power draws (especially when they come simultaneously from numerous customers) with time-of-day pricing, peak-based pricing, etc. Demand-Response (DR) mechanisms are commonly deployed for modulating the power draws in electrical grids to address these concerns, and such mechanisms are also being adopted in the datacenter context. Datacenter DR primarily uses IT-based knobs - consolidation, scheduling, migration, and power state modulation - to shape power draw. One common mechanism - energy storage - that is used in grids (and other domains) [2, 45] to hoard power when available and draw from it when needed (to address supply-demand mismatch) has only recently drawn attention for datacenter DR [18, 20, 43].

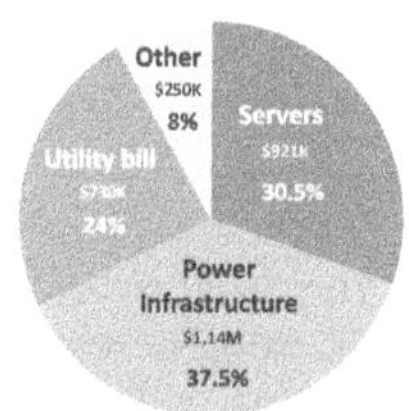

Figure 1: Amortized *Monthly* Costs for Physical Infrastructure of a 10MW Datacenter. Source: [3, 21, 32].

Energy storage in the datacenter has been primarily used as a back-up mechanism to temporarily handle power outages until diesel generators are brought online. This typically takes a few seconds (at most a couple of minutes), and most datacenters provision UPS devices with lead-acid batteries of possibly 2X-3X this capacity. Many datacenters also have multiple (e.g., N+1 redundancy) UPS units for enhancing availability. Recently some proposals have been made to leverage either these devices, or add additional storage capacities, for DR within a datacenter [18, 20, 43].

Concurrently, newer high-density datacenters are being built with "distributed" ESDs, e.g., server-level UPS units in Google [17], rack and power distribution unit (PDU) level units in Facebook [12] and Microsoft [31]. The primary motivation for such decentralization is to reduce energy losses: centralized UPS units cause a double-conversion wherein they convert from AC → DC → AC which is distributed to the servers and then converted back to DC by server-level power supplies. Moving the UPS units close to the server can help avoid losses due to such double-conversion (another alternative is to build DC-based datacenters as in [42]). In

SIGMETRICS'12, June 11–15, 2012, London, England, UK.

all these cases, the ESD - whether at a server or in a rack - is still used only for handling power outages.

While recent research has shown the benefits of lead-acid battery based UPS for datacenter DR - whether it be in shaving peaks to under-provision the power infrastructure [18, 20] or for shifting demand away from high tariff periods [43], all such prior work has only considered a single type of ESD, placed at a single location in the datacenter power hierarchy. Provisioning and placement of energy storage is a complex problem, with (i) a plethora of ESD options, (ii) each option with its idiosyncracies in cost, density, wear, and operational characteristics, (iii) a multitude of choices when placing them at different - possibly multiple - levels of the power hierarchy, and (iv) controlling their usage based on workload characteristics. This paper presents a formal framework for modeling and optimizing these design choices. Specifically, we address the following questions in the provisioning and operation of ESDs:

- Which ESDs should we employ? With a plethora of technologies available today, we need to model the trade-offs in cost, density, wear/health, efficiency and other operational characteristics when provisioning.
- Why should we be restricted to any one ESD technology? Given diversity in load demands temporally and spatially (across regions of the datacenter), should we consider multiple options given that different technologies are suited for different kinds of workloads?
- Where should these ESDs be placed? Why should we restrict them to any one level of the datacenter power hierarchy (e.g., central or server-level)? Does a multi-level energy storage hierarchy make sense given the statistical multiplexing effects (less burstiness) as we move up the hierarchy? An important consideration is the amount of space/volume that can be devoted for such ESDs, since datacenter real-estate is expensive.

While this paper provides specific answers to these questions (e.g., (i) single technologies suffice when there is little temporal/spatial heterogeneity, though the choice of technology would depend on the workload (ultra-capacitors and flywheels for tall and narrow workload peaks, but compressed air and/or batteries for wide peaks); (ii) regions of diversity in workload characteristics where hybrid ESD options are attractive; (iii) the benefits of multi-level ESD solutions, and the impact of volumetric constraints on these solutions), the more important contribution is a modeling and optimization framework that can take a range of input workload specifications, operating conditions, and power-related costs to derive ESD provisioning and dispatch solutions towards reducing cap-ex and op-ex. Using a combination of synthetic workloads which exercise the intricacies of ESD operation, and loads reported in 4 real datacenters, we demonstrate how this framework can be used to answer the above questions. We believe our framework can be very helpful when designing and operating a datacenter power infrastructure that leverages ESDs for DR.

2. BACKGROUND

Power Hierarchy: Figure 2 shows a typical datacenter power hierarchy. At the highest layer, a switchgear scales down the voltage of utility power, which then passes through centralized UPS units (with redundancy for availability). The UPS units also get another feed from backup diesel generators. Power then goes through Power Distribution Units (PDUs) which route it to different racks. At the next level, each rack may have regulated power distributors/outlets, with power then going down finally to the power supply units within each server (lowest level). In all, there are 4 levels shown in this particular hierarchy, though for simplicity we generally use 3 levels (datacenter, rack, and server) in this paper.

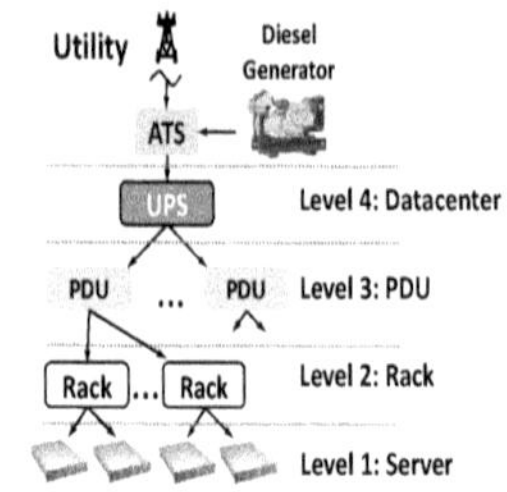

Figure 2: Typical Datacenter Power Hierarchy.

ESDs to Lower Power Costs: The cap-ex of provisioning the power infrastructure is reported to cost between \$10-20 per watt [3, 21]. For safety reasons, it needs to be provisioned for the peak draw that may ever happen (even if it is a rare event). Shaving peak draws can, therefore, reduce cap-ex costs. Furthermore, shaving at the bottom/lower layers of the hierarchy benefits a larger portion of the hierarchy compared to shaving only at the top level - shaving at a level allows all the equipment in that level and above to be provisioned for a smaller peak. The op-ex that goes into paying the monthly power bills can have different tariff structures depending on the utility. Since peak draws at the utility scale are bound by the capacity of the grid and the generation capacity of power plants, utility companies disincentivize high peak draw with either (i) time-of-day pricing [5] (high prices occur when everyone is expected to have high draws), and/or (ii) peak slab based pricing [11] (where the maximum draw is separately tracked and priced for each watt of this draw). Thus, reducing the peak draw can also reduce op-ex. ESDs can hoard energy during a "valley" (period of low power draw), which can then be used to supplement the utility when a peak occurs - in effect, hiding a portion of the peak from higher up in the hierarchy (and the utility) - to provide both cap-ex and op-ex savings.

Centralized vs. Distributed and Hierarchical ESDs: ESDs, while continuing their role in handling outages, can be introduced at each level of the hierarchy. Most current datacenters use centralized UPS units, i.e., only at the datacenter level, which are typically lead-acid based with enough capacity to sustain the datacenter needs for a few minutes. Newer high-density datacenters are starting to avoid centralized UPS, and are going for de-centralized options, e.g., rack-level in Facebook [12], Microsoft [31], or server-level as in Google [17]. Whether centralized or distributed, all these are still single-level ESD placement options. We could have ESDs (possibly different technologies) simultaneously present at different layers hierarchically. We note the following qualitative comparisons between centralized vs. distributed/hierarchical placement options:

- Distributed ESD placement, particularly deep down (e.g., server level), allows cap-ex savings in a larger portion of the hierarchy.
- There is an analogy with issues in shared vs. private caches in chip-multiprocessors. While a shared (centralized ESD) cache allows better resource utilization when there is imbalance across different users, resource contention can become a problem leading to potential unfairness. Private (distributed ESDs) caches are isolated from each other from this perspective. For example, two server-level ESDs that can each shave a single peak, could do so

for their respective servers. It is possible that when replacing them with a single ESD at the higher level (with sum of their capacities), this ESD ends up shaving two peaks of 1 server and none of the other (becoming unfair).

- As noted earlier, a completely distributed server-level ESD option can help avoid double-conversion related energy losses compared to centralized placement.
- A centralized ESD solution may not have a serious volume/real estate constraint. In fact, many facilities place such ESDs outside of the datacenter itself (e.g., separate room of shelves with lead-acid batteries, flywheels, basements of buildings for compressed air, etc.), since datacenter floor/rack space is precious (running to thousands of dollars per square foot). A distributed/hierarchical solution would need real-estate within the datacenter.

Consequently, it would be interesting to find distributed and/or hierarchical ESD solutions, provided we can stipulate volume constraints for the ESDs at each level.

Availability Issues: Prior work [18, 19, 27] has shown that ESDs can be used for DR without affecting their ability to handle power outages, as long as a few residual minutes of capacity is always retained. We could either adopt this option, or have separate sets of ESDs (one set for handling outages and the other for DR). This relieves us of concerns of our ESD-based DR hurting datacenter availability.

3. ENERGY STORAGE DEVICES (ESD)

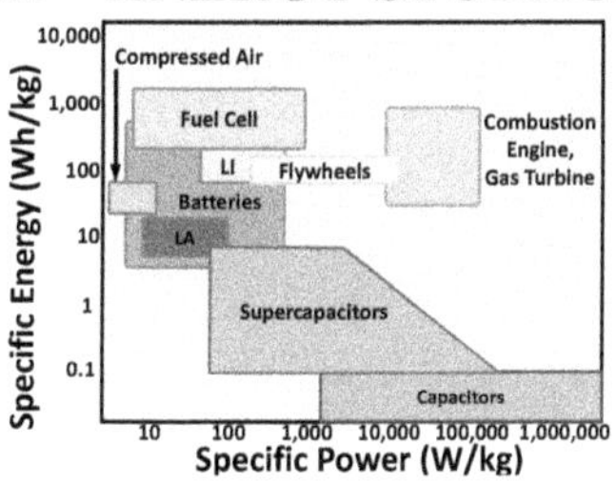

Figure 3: Ragone Plot.

Significant advances have been made in energy storage technologies, both in extending the practicality of their applications (by boosting densities, increasing lifetimes, lowering cost, etc.), as well as in bringing new technologies to the market. A broad spectrum of energy storage options exists, as is typically depicted using Ragone plots [36], such as the one shown in Figure 3. A Ragone plot compares different ESD technologies in terms of their power densities and energy densities, where "density" can be either volumetric or mass-based. As can be seen in Figure 3, there are sharp differences between various ESDs. For instance, compressed air-based energy storage (CAES), has a relatively high specific energy but a low specific power, implying that it is better suited for holding a large amount of energy as long as this energy does not need to be discharged very fast. On the other hand, capacitors have high power densities, albeit they are unable to sustain a large power draw for an extended period of time. In addition to this broad characterization, there are numerous other factors that can impact ESD suitability for DR, which we discuss below. In the interest of space and clarity, we use the following representative ESD technologies (which are also gradually finding their way into the datacenter [29]) from the Ragone design space in our discussions:

- *Ultra/Super-capacitors (UC):* These improve on conventional capacitors using double-layer electrochemistry between the electrodes, allowing a thousand-fold increase in energy stored. While the double-layer restricts it to low voltage operation, these capacitors can be connected in series for higher voltage needs. There has been nearly two orders of magnitude improvement in their cost per Farad over the past decade, and we are already seeing some commercial offerings of these products [28] for the datacenter market as UPS devices. We use this ESD as representative of the lower right end of the Ragone plot.
- *Compressed Air Energy Storage (CAES):* Air can be compressed (with compressors which consume energy) in confined spaces, and this pressurized air can subsequently be used to drive turbines for electricity generation. Since compression and decompression generate and absorb heat respectively, heat exchange mechanisms are needed to ensure proper operation. More importantly, CAES [9] may require significant real-estate to create such confined spaces, and the cost/availability of such real-estate needs to be taken into consideration (e.g., building basements, tanks in parking lots, etc.). We use CAES as representative of the upper left end of the Ragone plot.
- *Flywheels (FW):* The momentum of a rotating wheel/cylinder is gaining acceptance [47] as a UPS device for the datacenter, to temporarily handle the load until diesel generators kick in. Even though they are not intended for extended operation (somewhat inferior to even batteries from this perspective), they can provide the high power needs in the brief interlude between the outage and generator start-up.
- *Batteries (LA or LI):* These (particularly lead-acid) are the most commonly used storage devices in datacenters, where the electrochemical reactions (of the appropriate chemistry within), is used to store and generate electricity. There are several kinds of batteries [10] - lead-acid, lead-carbon, lithium-ion, vanadium flow, sodium-sulphur, etc., and we will consider lead-acid (LA) and lithium-ion (LI), which are more prevalent and representive of two ends of battery spectrum on the Ragone plot, and with very different costs, in our evaluations.

While some consider fuel cells, diesel generators, and other captive sources as ESDs, in this work we do not consider these options and limit ourselves to these 5 technologies.

ESD	LA	LI	UC	FW	CAES
Energy Cost C_k^{eng} (\$/kWh)	200	525	10000	5000	50
Power Cost C_k^{pow} (\$/kW)	125	175	100	250	600
Energy Density v_k^{eng} (Wh/L)	80	150	30	80	6
Power Density v_k^{pow} (W/L)	128	450	3000	1600	0.5
Discharge:Charge Rate γ_k	10	5	1	1	4
Life Cycle $Lcyc_k$ (# discharges x 1000)	2	5	1000	200	15
Max. DoD DoD_k^{max} (%)	80	80	100	100	100
Float Life T_k^{max} (years)	4	8	12	12	12
Energy Efficiency η_k (%)	75%	85%	95%	95%	68%
Self-discharge μ_k per Day	0.3%	0.1%	20%	100%	low
Ramp Time T_k^{ramp} (sec)	0.001	0.001	0.001	0.001	600

Table 1: ESD parameter values [9, 10, 38, 39].

We now explain the different factors that need to be taken into consideration when incorporating such ESDs into the datacenter. In Table 1, we quantify relevant parameters for the 5 technologies that we evaluate.

Cost (Energy and Power): When optimizing electricity costs with ESDs, we need to account for the costs of the ESDs themselves. The cost of ESD depends on 2 factors -

the total energy that is to be stored/discharged, and the rate (power) at which the energy is to be charged/discharged. This is somewhat indicated by where the device falls on the Ragone plot. Rows 1 and 2 of Table1 show these two components of the cost for the 5 ESDs under consideration. As can be expected, from the energy point of view, CAES is the least expensive (50 \$/kWh) with ultra-capacitors at the other end of the spectrum at 200X this cost. On the other hand, with respect to power, ultra-capacitors are the most attractive option with CAES being 6X more expensive. Batteries offer a good compromise between these extremes.

Density (Energy and Power): Beyond costs, it is also important to consider the densities of these technologies required to provide a certain energy and power demand. Density determines the "volume" (real-estate) that needs to be provisioned in the datacenter to sustain the demands. Since datacenter real-estate is very precious - whether it be rack space or floor space, volume constraints may need to be imposed when provisioning ESDs. ESDs which may be attractive based on energy or power costs may not necessarily be suitable because of space constraints. For instance, CAES - the most cost-attractive option - is the worst from the density viewpoint even if we are only trying to cater to energy demands (and willing to tolerate the slow discharge rate offered by CAES). In fact, as we will find, trying to provide CAES for each server (or even a rack), is prohibitive in real-estate demands. At best, we can consider CAES at a datacenter scale, where basements, sealed tanks in parking lots, etc., may be options.

Discharge/Charge Rate Ratio: Since ESDs alternate between charging and discharging, it is important that there be sufficient charging time to hoard the required capacity before the next discharge. We can capture this by the discharge/charge ratio, which is larger than 1 (i.e., it takes longer to charge than discharge) for many ESDs. Ultra-capacitors and flywheels may come close to this ideal behavior, while batteries (particularly LA) are not as attractive.

Replacement Costs (Charge/Discharge cycles and Lifetime): We need to consider the costs of ESD replacement, since the datacenter infrastructure may itself have a much longer lifetime (e.g., 12 years as suggested in [21]). The lifetime of an ESD, especially batteries, depends (among other factors) on the number of charge-discharge cycles and the Depth-of-Discharge (DoD) of each discharge [9]. In addition, the internal chemistry itself has certain properties such as lead-out, which can also impact the lifetime orthogonal to usage. Row 8 of Table 1 gives the average lifetime (in years) of these ESDs based on typical usage. Batteries typically need replacement while our other technologies can possibly match the expected datacenter lifetime. It is not that batteries stop working abruptly - rather, their capacity for holding charge degrades over time, and replacement is done when it drops below 80% of the original capacity.

Energy Efficiency: The energy used to charge an ESD is higher than what can be drawn out subsequently, implying losses. Ultra-capacitors and flywheels are very energy efficient, while batteries can incur losses of 15-25% based on their chemistries. The efficiency of CAES is even worse.

Self-Discharge Losses: ESDs can lose charge even when they are not being discharged, with the loss proportional to the time since the last charge. Fly-wheels can be poor from this perspective, and so are ultra-capacitors. Consequently, it may be desirable that such devices be charged just before a discharge, rather than hoarding the charge for a long time.

Ramp Rate: While power density is one factor influencing the rate at which energy can be drawn, the ramp rate is another consideration in some ESDs. One can view the ramp rate as a start up latency to change the power output (analogous to how combustion engines of automobiles can accelerate from zero to a given speed in a certain amount of time, and then sustain it at that speed). In most ESDs we consider the ramp rate is very high (i.e., it takes at most a few milliseconds to start supplying requisite power draw), except in CAES where it can take several minutes. Hence, CAES cannot instantaneously start sustaining any desired draw, requiring either (i) anticipating the draw and taking pro-active measures, or (ii) using some other ESD until CAES becomes ready to sustain the draw.

4. EFFICACY OF DIFFERENT ESDS

To achieve effective selection and placement of ESDs in the datacenter, it is important to understand the efficacy of each ESD technology in shaping a given power demand time-series, and use this to understand the trade-offs across these technologies. Towards this, we intentionally keep the power demand representation simplistic at this stage (more extensive representations and real loads are considered later): it is simply an ON-OFF series where the ON periods correspond to a high demand value ("peaks") while the OFF periods correspond to a low demand value ("valleys"). We denote the mean amplitude ("height") and duration ("width") of the peaks and valleys of this time-series as (h_{peak},w_{peak}) and (h_{valley},w_{valley}), respectively. Note that both the cap-ex and op-ex costs grow with the tallest peak of the series as discussed in Section 2. Hence to understand the efficacy of an ESD, we focus on finding its size/cost that is needed to "shave" a certain specified portion of *all* the peaks (rather than any one peak) in the time-series. We develop a simple model to compare their cost-efficacy in shaping different kinds of power demands.

4.1 Model for a single ESD

We denote the portion (amplitude) of the peak that is to be shaved as h_{shave}. It is important that h_{shave} be assigned a "realizable" value, e.g., clearly we must have $h_{shave} < h_{peak} - h_{valley}$, since an ESD capacity is finite and it needs to be charged at some point (in a valley). We denote the "frequency" of peak occurrences as $f_{peak} = \frac{1}{w_{peak}+w_{valley}}$. We use $k \in \{1, 2, ..., K\}$, to denote an ESD technology (so $K = 5$ in our evaluations). We can now translate the ESD properties in Table 1 into the following constraints to calculate the cost of ESD k (C_k^{total}) that must be provisioned to shave h_{shave} from the demand.

First, the power and energy densities of technology k impose these lower bounds on the required ESD capacity (cost):

$$\frac{C_k^{total}}{C_k^{pow}} \geq h_{shave}; \quad \frac{C_k^{total}}{C_k^{eng}} \times DoD_k^{max} \geq h_{shave} \times w_{peak}.$$

Next, the device must possess enough energy at the beginning of a peak to shave h_{shave} of it. It may have to acquire all of this energy by re-charging during the preceding valley, implying the following dependence on the discharge/charge rate ratio (γ_k). (Note that this re-charging will increase the power drawn during the valley making it higher than h_{valley}, but this increased value would still be less than $h_{peak}-h_{shave}$

by our "realizability" assumption above):

$$\frac{C_k^{total}}{C_k^{pow}} \times w_{valley} \times \frac{1}{\gamma_k} \geq h_{shave} \times w_{peak}.$$

Finally, the cost of ESD replacement should also be factored. This is governed by its expected float-life (T_k^{max}), as well as (i) the wear caused by repeated discharges and (ii) the extent/depth of each these discharges. Except for batteries, the other 3 ESDs have a large enough T_k^{max} to be less affected. To quantify the effect of wear on the lifetime, we can de-rate the expected number of lifetime charge-discharge cycles ($Lcyc_k$) which is calculated pessimistically at a Depth-of-Discharge of DoD_k^{max}, by the actual depth to which it is discharged DoD_k^{actual}, to get the expected lifetime of the ESD k as

$$Life_k = min\left(\frac{1}{f_{peak}} \times Lcyc_k \times \frac{DoD_k^{max}}{DoD_k^{actual}}, T_k^{max}\right).$$

This expected lifetime can be used to find the amortized cost (yearly) as per each of the above three requirements (energy needs, power needs, re-charging rates), and the cost of the employed ESD k is given by the maximum of these three requirements:

$$max\left(\frac{h_{shave}C_k^{pow}}{Life_k}, \frac{h_{shave}w_{peak}C_k^{eng}}{Life_k \times DoD_k^{max}}, \frac{h_{shave}w_{peak}\gamma_k C_k^{pow}}{w_{valley}Life_k}\right).$$

4.2 ESD Suitability for Different Demands

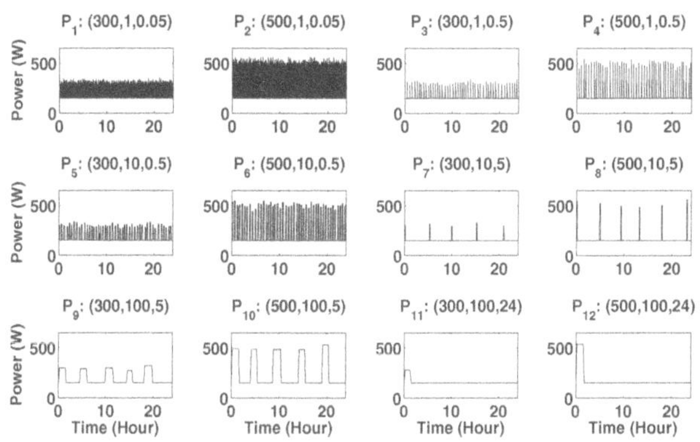

Figure 4: Power demand building blocks with mean values of (h_{peak} watt, w_{peak} min, $\frac{1}{f_{peak}}$ hour)

4.2.1 Model Evaluation Methodology

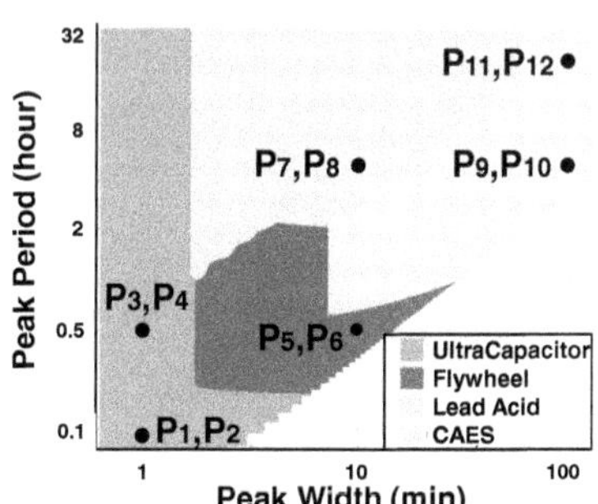

Figure 5: Most cost-effective ESD for different Peak types.

Since at this stage our goal is to evaluate the match between ESD properties and workload characteristics, we begin with synthetic power demands (using our ON-OFF series described above) for which we vary the parameters over a wide range. We use normal distributions for each of these parameters with specified mean and variance. We pick a set of 12 different combinations of means (2 each for peak height and frequency, 3 for peak width, and 1 for valley height) that we use as our synthetic workload "building blocks". Figures 4 (P_1-P_{12}) shows the 12 resulting power demands. For each of these 12 power demands, we choose an h_{shave} that is realizable for that demand. Using the model described in previous subsection, we compute the (peak width, peak frequency) region over which each of the 5 ESDs under consideration is the most cost-effective (since h_{shave} is set to be the same for all ESDs, the resulting cap-ex and op-ex savings are identical, and hence we need only compare the ESD costs). We show these regions in Figure 5, together with where our 12 workloads fall.

4.2.2 Key Findings from our Evaluation

No Single Technology Always Best: For each storage technology, there is a portion of the workload region, where it is cost-superior to other technologies. For example, ultra-capacitor is best when we have extremely narrow peaks (tens of seconds to a minute) as in P_1-P_4. Among the 5 technologies, ultra-capacitors offer the cheapest cost/power draw ($/kW). They can also re-charge fast enough within the high frequency of peak occurrence in these demands. Although they are the most expensive in terms of cost/unit energy ($/kWh), this does not become prohibitive since the peaks to be shaved for these demands require only small amounts of energy. At the other end, CAES is an attractive option for demands P_9-P_{12}, which are more "energy-demanding" with wide peaks (and ultra-capacitors are high cost options for these demands). CAES, on the other hand, requires very high capacities (and costs) to handle the narrow high power peaks where ultra-capacitors are attractive. There are regions in the middle where batteries (P_7-P_8) and flywheels (P_5-P_6) are the better options. *Therefore, a datacenter may need to consider these workload idiosyncrasies and variances over its lifetime in provisioning ESDs rather than always employing a fixed technology.*

Hybrid ESDs May Be Desirable: Certain technologies appear complementary to each other in terms of their pros and cons. The most stark contrast is between ultra-capacitors and CAES: while ultra-capacitors are the most cost-effective for P_1-P_4, CAES turns out to be the most prohibitive; the reverse holds for P_9-P_{12}. Such complementary behavior is also seen, to different degrees, for other pairs of technologies as well. *Therefore, when a datacenter may house different kinds of workloads - either across its different spatial regions or temporally over its lifetime - it may be worthwhile to consider hybrid ESD options.*

Multi-level ESD May Be Desirable: Within a datacenter, the nature of the power demand seen at different levels of its power hierarchy can be different, e.g., higher averages and smaller variances because of statistical multiplexing effects as we move up. When we compare a power demand with smaller average but higher variance (e.g, P_1) against those with higher average but smaller variance (e.g., P_{10}), we find different technologies being the most cost-effective. Whereas P_1 is best shaped using ultra-capacitors, CAES is the best choice for P_{10}. *Therefore, it may be desirable to employ appropriate (possibly different) ESD technologies at multiple - server, rack, and datacenter - levels of the power hierarchy. Furthermore, pushing ESDs deeper down the hierarchy can allow higher cap-ex savings.*

5. A FRAMEWORK FOR PROVISIONING AND CONTROL OF ESDS

Motivated by these insights, we develop an optimization

framework for provisioning ESDs within a datacenter. In particular, we design it to allow for multiple kinds of ESD technologies as well as the possibility of having them at multiple locations within the datacenter. Such placement should also take into consideration the volumetric/real-estate constraints that may restrict the usage/capacity of the ESDs at these locations (servers and racks) in the datacenter. Provisioning is closely tied with the associated control problem: how should these ESDs be used (i.e., charged/discharged) for a given datacenter configuration, utility tariffs, and power needs of various servers? Consequently, we design our framework to jointly address the provisioning and control problems. The goal is to determine an ESD based solution that maximizes the amortized net cost savings (i.e., cost savings in power-related cap-ex and op-ex minus cost of procuring and operating the ESDs).

5.1 Inputs

Workload (Power Demand): There is considerable prior work on characterizing and predicting server workloads (e.g., [1]) and properties such as time-of-day effects, etc., have been observed. For this work, we are concerned with a time-series of power draws at different levels of the datacenter. Since we already have a lot of ground to cover, we assume that prior work on load prediction can be leveraged, and combined with power modeling work (e.g., [4]), to derive a reasonable, accurate time-series of power draws at a server granularity over the given optimization horizon (e.g., a day). Further, our work is intended to provide guidelines when building (ESD solutions for) datacenters, at which point some estimate of load characteristics is in any case assumed for right-sizing of IT and power equipment. A more detailed treatment of these issues can be considered in future work. Specifically, for server i, we assume its power demand time-series given by $P_{1,i,t}, t \in \{1, ..., T\}$, where $T \times \delta$ represents our optimization horizon. We will consider different such time-series - both synthetic and real workloads - in our evaluations.

Power Infrastructure (Cap-Ex): We assume L levels (e.g., datacenter, rack, server) in the power hierarchy and use the variable $l \in \{1, ..., L\}$ to denote a particular level, with $l = L$ corresponding to the highest level and $l = 1$ corresponding to the server-level. Within a level l, we denote the number of power supply equipment (e.g., transformers, switchgear, and centralized UPS at datacenter level, and so on until individual power supplies at the server level) by n_l. The equipment also includes any ESDs we may need to provision at that level, and we begin with homogeneous equipment at a level for simplicity, though this can be generalized (particularly when we have different parts of the datacenter running different workloads as in some of our experiments). Prior work has pointed to cap-ex costs ranging between \$10-20 per watt of power provisioning (i.e., for our set of $\sum_l n_l$ equipment). Though the costs are not explicitly stated for power provisioning at each level of the hierarchy, it is typically more effective to start under-provisioning from deep down the hierarchy (i.e., $l = 1$) since it would allow larger portion of the hierarchy to benefit from cap-ex savings. We consider a conservative cap-ex saving of \$10/watt resulting from peak shaving as a starting point, and go as low as \$1/watt in our experiments. This is the saving that would be obtained by reducing a watt from the maximum draw P_L^{max}. The power draw under l at any time is given by the sum of the power draws of all servers under this sub-hierarchy, and the maximum of this sum over our optimization horizon is denoted as P_l^{max}.

Utility Tariffs (Op-Ex): Utilities base their tariffs on the actual energy consumption (say a \$/kWh), and the need to sustain the maximum power draw across all their customers within the constraints of their existing capacity. To address the latter concern, utilities dis-incentivize high power draws (especially simultaneously from multiple customers) by two mechanisms: (i) vary a (say as $a(t)$) based on the time-of-day [5]; and/or (ii) track the peak draw (typically averaged over 15 minute windows) and impose a cost of b \$/watt (e.g., as in [11]). Our framework is generic enough to accommodate either, and we simply use mechanism (ii) in our discussions/evaluations. Consequently, we need to track P_L^{max} (i.e. the maximum power draw at any time at the datacenter scale), and associate a b \$/watt cost to it.

5.2 Optimization Problem Formulation

Decision Variables: Given our goal to jointly address provisioning and subsequent control, we choose decision variables that capture the operational aspects of ESDs as well as the decisions about their sizing and placement. In the subsequent discussions, the subscripts l and i of the variables indicate the level in the datacenter hierarchy, and the index of associated equipment instance at that level, respectively. E.g., at the leaf level, $l = 1$ and i can take values from 1 to the number of servers; at rack level, $l = 2$ and i can take values from 1 to the number of racks and so on. In general, the tuple (l,i) denotes the root of the sub-hierarchy governing a certain set of servers. A server can source its power only from the ESDs that are in the path from itself to the root. Subscript k is used to denote the ESD technology.

First, let $S_{k,l,i}$ denote the "size" - the energy capacity of an ESD of type k placed at (l,i). Second, for each such device, to capture its "usage", we use variables $D_{k,l,i,t}$ and $R_{k,l,i,t}$ to represent the discharge and re-charge rate, respectively, during time slot t. To carry over the residual ESD energy capacity from one time slot to the next, we use $E_{k,l,i,t}$, which is the energy left in this device at the beginning of time slot t. Finally, $P_{l,i}^{realize}$ denotes the realized peak as a result of our shaving in sub-hierarchy (l,i).

Objective: We can now express various components of our overall objective function. All of these have been normalized/amortized to the horizon of our time series. The expected cap-ex savings in power infrastructure due to under-provisioning is given as $CapExSavings = \sum_{l=1}^{L} \sum_{i=1}^{n_l} \alpha_{l,i} \times (P_{l,i}^{max} - P_{l,i}^{realize})$, where $\alpha_{l,i}$ is the savings for each watt of under-provisioning at level l. The expected op-ex savings can be expressed as $OpExSavings = (\sum_{k=1}^{K} \sum_{l=1}^{L} \sum_{i=1}^{n_l} \sum_{t=1}^{T} a \times (D_{k,l,i,t} - \frac{R_{k,l,i,t}}{\eta_k})) + b \times (P_{L,1}^{max} - P_{L,1}^{realize})$, where a and b are the unit costs for energy and peak power draw in the utility tariff explained in previous subsection. Finally, the additional cost of ESDs themselves is given by $EStoreCost = \sum_{k=1}^{K} \sum_{l=1}^{L} \sum_{i=1}^{n_l} (S_{k,l,i} \times C_{k,l,i})$. Here $C_{k,l,i}$ is the normalized cost of ESD k per unit energy adjusted to its actual lifetime, which depends on how the device is used (e.g., the same battery would last longer if it undergoes shallow discharges), and hence is itself unknown. Rather than dealing with a non-linear program in which $C_{k,l,i}$ is treated as an unknown, we keep our program linear and run it successively with the value of $C_{k,l,i}$ yielded by one run fed into the next run till convergence is achieved.

Finally, putting these components together, we have our objective as:
Maximize $(CapExSaving + OpExSaving - EStoreCost)$.
Constraints: We assume that all ESDs are fully charged at the beginning of the time-series, and need to leave them in the same state at the end of the time-series. In any time slot, an ESD may only hold energy between a lower threshold allowed by its recommended DoD and its maximum capacity. To capture these we have:

$$E_{k,l,i,1} = E_{k,l,i,T+1} = S_{k,l,i}, \forall k, l, i, (1a)$$

$$(1 - DoD_k^{max}) \times S_{k,l,i} \leq E_{k,l,i,t} \leq S_{k,l,i}, \forall k, l, i, t, (1b)$$

For each ESD, the amount of energy that can be discharged or stored is bounded by the product of its provisioned size and corresponding discharge ($r_k^{discharge}$) and recharge ($r_k^{recharge}$) rates:

$$0 \leq D_{k,l,i,t} \leq S_{k,l,i} \times r_k^{discharge}, \forall k, l, i, t, (2a)$$

$$0 \leq R_{k,l,i,t} \leq S_{k,l,i} \times r_k^{recharge}, \forall k, l, i, t, (2b)$$

We account for the conversion losses (energy efficiency η_k) of an ESD, during the charging process as

$$P_{l,i,t} = \sum_{j=1}^{n_{l-1,i}} \left(P_{l-1,j,t} + \sum_{k=1}^{K} \frac{R_{k,l-1,j,t}}{\eta_k} - \sum_{k=1}^{K} D_{k,l-1,j,t} \right), \forall l \geq 2, i, j, t, (3a)$$

Furthermore, when charging we should still ensure that the net power draw (including the power for all the equipment under l) is bound by $P_{l,i}^{realize}$ (which is in turn less than $P_{l,i}^{max}$). This gives us:

$$0 \leq P_{l,i,t} + \sum_{k=1}^{K} \frac{R_{k,l,i,t}}{\eta_k} - \sum_{k=1}^{K} D_{k,l,i,t} \leq P_{l,i}^{realize}, \forall l, i, t, (3b)$$

$$0 \leq P_{l,i}^{realize} \leq P_{l,i}^{max}, \forall l, i, (3c)$$

To account for energy losses due to self-discharge (μ_k) characteristics, we have

$$E_{k,l,i,t} = E_{k,l,i,t-1} + R_{k,l,i,t-1}\delta - D_{k,l,i,t-1}\delta - E_{k,l,i,t-1}\mu_k, \forall k, l, i, t \geq 2, (4)$$

The ramp-up properties of ESDs pose restrictions on how fast the rate of discharge can itself increase over time (recall the analogy of car acceleration). We capture this as:

$$\frac{D_{k,l,i,t+1} - D_{k,l,i,t}}{\delta} \leq \frac{S_{k,l,i} \times r_{k,l,i,t}^{discharge}}{T_k^{ramp}}, \forall k, l, i, t, (5)$$

Our final constraints restricts the volume ($V_{l,i}^{max}$) within which the ESDs must be accommodated at various levels:

$$\sum_{k=1}^{K} \left(\frac{S_{k,l,i}}{v_k^{eng}} \right) \leq V_{l,i}^{max}, \forall l, i, (6a)$$

and

$$\sum_{k=1}^{K} \left(\frac{S_{k,l,i} \times r_k^{discharge}}{v_k^{pow}} \right) \leq V_{l,i}^{max}, \forall l, i, (6b)$$

Discussion: When solving for a large datacenter with thousands of servers, this strategy can become intractable. We exploit the homogeneity of load across servers to appropriately scale down the number of decision variables, together with associated parameters. Finally, it should be noted that our framework automatically allows one ESD to charge by discharging another ESD instead of only using utility power.

6. EXPERIMENTS AND EVALUATION

6.1 Experimental Setup and Methodology

Max. Power	4 MW
# racks	256
# servers	8192
V_2^{max}	20% of rack vol.
V_1^{max}	10% of server vol.
Cap-ex (α)	\$10,\$1/Watt
Op-ex energy (a)	\$0.05/kWh
Op-ex peak (b)	\$12/kW/Month

Table 2: Parameter Values.

Configuration and Parameters: Our evaluations use a 4 MW datacenter of 8192 servers (placed in racks of 32 servers/rack), each with a 500W power supply, organized in a hierarchy as in Figure 2. We choose three levels for placing ESDs (L=3): top of the hierarchy (l=3, as in most datacenters today), rack-level (l=2, corresponding to some reported datacenters of Facebook [12] and Microsoft [31]), and server-level (l=1, as in some reported datacenters of Google [17]). Again note that these reported datacenters still place their ESDs at only one level, and not as a multi-level hierarchy which we allow.

We present results for $K = 5$ ESD technologies discussed earlier (however, LI based solutions do not explicitly appear in the results since whenever LI comes up on top of LA, the CAES option does even better). As discussed in Section 2, we use an op-ex cost model (Table 2) that is representative of that charged by Duke Electric [11], which has a monthly peak component charge of \$12/kW/month in addition to the energy usage charge. We consider cap-ex cost of \$10/W for the datacenter power infrastructure which is at the lower end of the \$10-20/W range reported in literature [3, 21]. Since it is difficult to quantify the cap-ex benefits for peak reduction only at a lower level of the hierarchy, we also consider sensitivity experiments where we push cap-ex costs as low as \$1/W in our technical report [48]. Note that even a cent of difference in additional cap-ex savings (i.e., $\alpha_{l+1} - \alpha_l > \epsilon$) when we push ESDs deeper down the hierarchy, will automatically enable our formulation to place ESDs deeper down the hierarchy as allowed by volume constraints. The cap-ex (12 year datacenter lifetime), op-ex (typically charged monthly), and ESD costs (appropriate actual lifetimes) are amortized for the horizon of the time series.

ESD Placement/Configurations: For comparison, we use 3 existing baseline strategies which are all "non-hybrid & single-level" placement styles (i.e., only one ESD technology x used at only one level in a given solution): $B_{dc,x}$, $B_{rack,x}$, $B_{server,x}$. Though these represent some datacenter ESD placement styles in use today, note that x=lead-acid batteries in most of them, and their capacities are chosen just for power outages. Our solutions will consider other options for x together with higher capacities. We compare these baselines with: (i) "hybrid & single-level," where we allow multiple technologies to be provisioned at a fixed level - centralized ($HybSin_{dc}$), rack-level ($HybSin_{rack}$), or server-level ($HybSin_{server}$), and (ii) "hybrid & multi-level," where we allow multiple technologies to be provisioned at possibly all of these levels ($HybMul$).

Workloads (Power Demands): To stress and understand the impact of workload parameters, we take the individual synthetic power demands P_1 ... P_{12} described earlier in section 4 and combine them in interesting ways (pair-wise) to bring out the impact of homogeneity and heterogeneity of workload behavior on ESD provisioning (section 6.2). Each resulting server-level power demand time-series spans a day, with each point in the series corresponding to the power needs over a one minute duration. Broadly, we refer to the peaks with mean width upto a minute as "narrow," 1-10 minutes as "medium," and higher (10 minutes to 2 hours) as "wide." In addition, Section 6.3 studies these issues with power demands of real-world datacenters and clusters (for Google [13], TCS [44], MSN [8] and stream media clusters [23]), reported in prior studies.

6.2 Synthetic Workload Experiments

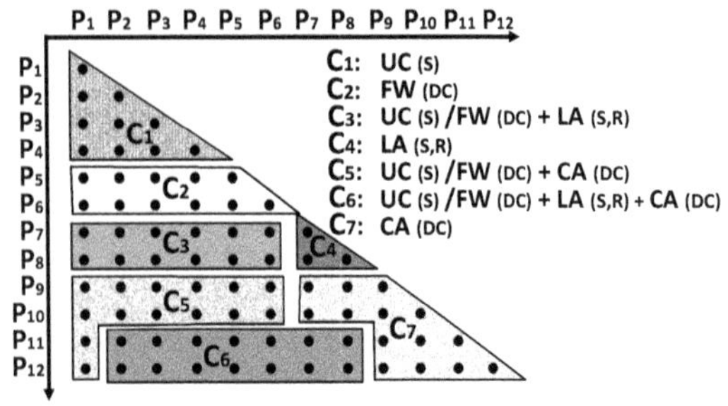

Figure 6: **Results for the 78 synthetic workload combinations grouped in Clusters of "Best Configuration". The element (P_i, P_j) shows the ESD configuration when the per-server power demand is $P_{i,j}$.**

While in Section 4 we had considered power demands that were homogeneous in time and in space (i.e., across servers) to get an overall idea of which single technology is better suited for a workload characteristic, we now use pair-wise combinations of the P_1 ... P_{12} time-series to study whether (i) hybrid combinations make sense, and (ii) whether multi-level ESDs are promising. This results in a 78-combination design-space of experiments to capture a large range of peak widths, heights and frequencies. This combination can create temporal heterogeneity. For example, Figure 7 shows one such power demand ($P_{2,9}$): it has two "phases" with significantly different properties. We will later see that this kind of workload is representative of some real world behavior with multi time-scale variations, e.g., time-of-day effects of load change at a macro-scale, with finer scale variations at each of these loads (as in the MSN workload). Dealing with such "temporal" heterogeneity, may mandate different solutions (hybrid or multi-level) compared to spatial heterogeneity, where different regions of the datacenter/racks may have different behaviors.

Results at a Glance: Figure 6 presents a simple way of viewing the results from our design space of experiments, by showing the best (or comparable to the best) ESD configurations for various $P_{i,j}$. For ease of discussion, we group these into "iso-configuration" clusters. The exact sizing decisions for various ESD technologies may vary across elements of a cluster. With a few exceptions, we find that our power demands fall into seven different clusters, and we present the ESD configuration for each cluster. For example, C_6 is best served by an ESD configuration which uses a combination of (i) ultra-capacitors at server level or fly-wheel at datacenter, plus (ii) lead-acid batteries at server and/or rack levels, plus (iii) CAES at datacenter level. We find such a representation easier to parse, than go through every data point in the results. The savings from such ESD provisioning are typically between 10-40% of total datacenter power-related costs, after factoring in the cost of ESD provisioning itself. Below we discuss the provisioning choices made by our framework for each cluster, and give detailed cost savings results for the $P_{2,9}$ workload.

Temporal Homogeneity (Peak Widths are all Narrow or Medium or Wide): Recall that our analysis in Section 4 had suggested that ultra-capacitors are the most cost-effective in dealing with narrow peaks (P_1-P_4 in Figure 4) due to their low power cost, superior lifetime, and excellent charge/discharge ratio. With the additional volume constraints, self-discharge, and energy efficiency that our optimization framework captures, ultra-capacitors continue to serve as the most cost-effective ESD technology for such power demands, and suffice by themselves without requiring any other ESD technology. The capacity can be met right at the server-level, within its volume constraints (thereby providing higher cap-ex savings in the hierarchy). This set of results is depicted by cluster C_1 in Figure 6.

At the other end of the spectrum, we find that a solely CAES-based ESD design is best for demands whose peaks are wide (P_9-P_{12}), again in agreement with our model. However, the volume constraints mandate that its capacity be provisioned at the datacenter level, rather than rack/server levels. This set of results is depicted by cluster C_7.

However, in the middle of the spectrum, lead-acid battery at the server-level and/or rack-level is the most cost-effective ESD in dealing with less frequent medium width peaks (cluster C_4). However, when the frequency of such peaks increases, the lifetime deterioration of lead-acid batteries comes into play, making flywheel at the datacenter-level as the better option (cluster C_2).

Note that homogeneous peak widths of pair-wise collation of P_is refers to the region close to the diagonal in Figure 6. In these regions, creating power demand mixes is not significantly changing the individual demand properties, keeping these results in agreement with those in Section 4.

Temporal Heterogeneity (Mix of Narrow, Medium and Wide Peaks):

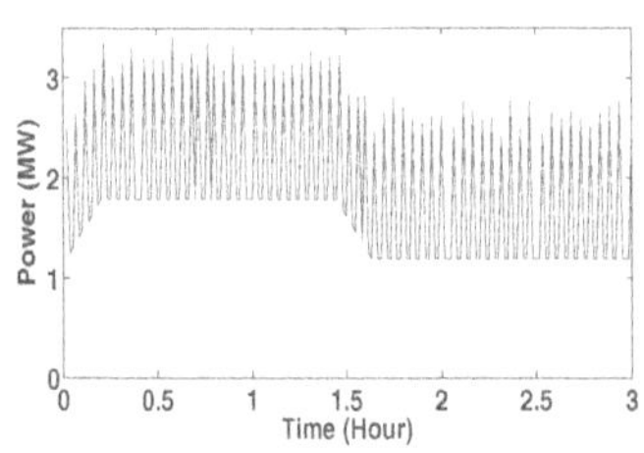

Figure 7: **$P_{2,9}$ demand.**

Clusters C_3, C_5 and C_6 bring out the need for hybrid, and possibly multi-level, ESD solutions. E.g., C_3 suggests both lead-acid batteries and ultra-capacitors at the server-level, or lead-acid batteries at server-level and flywheels at the datacenter-level; C_5 suggests CAES at the datacenter-level and ultra-capacitors at the server-level or both CAES and flywheel at the datacenter-level. In addition to the peak characteristics, the cap-ex savings when pushing ESDs deeper down the hierarchy as well as the associated volumetric constraints lead to these more extensive options rather than a single-level single-technology solution. To understand these issues in detail, we take $P_{2,9}$ (shown pictorially in Figure 7) and examine savings and ESD costs for different options in Table 3. We have the following observations and key take-aways from these results:

	B_ (savings, cost)	HybSin_ (savings, cost)	HybMul (savings, cost)
Datacenter	LA (2.6k,0.5k)	UC+FW+CAES (3.0k, 0.2k)	FW+CAES
Rack	LA (2.3k,0.3k)	UC+LA (3.0k,0.2k)	-
Server	LA (1.7k,0.1k)	UC+LA (3.0k,0.2k)	UC (3k,0.2k)

Table 3: **$P_{2,9}$: (Savings($/day), ESD costs($/day)). Total cost without ESD is $10K/day.**

- Even the baselines B_- (i.e., current datacenters endowed with sufficient lead-acid battery capacities) can offer substantial cost savings (16-25% even after factoring in the storage cost). In this case, the savings are better with a centralized ESD that does not have volume constraints as opposed to restricted capacity sizes deeper in the hierarchy, since we do not have explicit cap-ex savings values when shaving peaks at each level of the power hierarchy. This lack of additional cap-ex information about savings when we go deeper down the hierarchy (which is conservatively set to ϵ) is also the reason why the cost savings with $HybMul$ are not different from those of $HybSin_{dc}$ (though in reality the savings are likely to be higher for $HybMul$).
- For datacenters with centralized ESD, CAES (in combination with flywheels or ultra-capacitors if there are tall and narrow peaks to compensate for the slow ramp rate of CAES) appears to be a better option if space is not a problem. For instance, CAES-based hybrid datacenter level solutions provide 15% better savings than just a lead-acid centralized solution.
- The improvements that our `HybSin_` techniques offer over their corresponding baselines improve as we go down the hierarchy ($HybSin_{dc}$ offers 15% more cost savings that B_{dc} while $HybSin_{server}$ offers over 75% more cost savings than B_{server}). This results from the more stringent volume constraints at lower levels, where hybrid solutions that include ESDs with higher power and/or energy density offer larger gains. This may suggest that recent datacenters with distributed ESDs, like those at Google, Facebook and Microsoft, may benefit further from a move to hybrid ESDs.

Spatial Heterogeneity: Until now, we have only discussed spatially homogeneous power demands (i.e., all servers across the datacenter experience the same power demands). However, our techniques can address heterogeneous demands, and in fact hybrid and multi-level ESDs make even more sense in such environments. Many datacenters host different applications, with diverse power demands, e.g. a search engine may have applications which directly cater to Internet requests along with crawlers running in the background. These may not necessarily run on the same servers, and may even fall in different power sub-hierarchies in the datacenter. In the interest of space, we summarize one result to illustrate this point. When half the servers run P_1 and the other half run P_{12}, and we compare our $HybSin_{server}$ which uses ultra-capacitors and lead-acid batteries in the two sets of servers respectively, it provides over 50% more cost savings than both homogeneous ESD baselines $B_{server,UC}$ and $B_{server,LA}$.

6.3 Real Workload Experiments

In this section, we construct power demands to mimic behavior reported previously in four different real-world datacenters/clusters.

6.3.1 TCS

Figure 8(a) presents the power demand based on measurements reported from a TCS cluster [44] (that runs a range of many standard enterprise class applications) scaled to our assumed 4 MW datacenter. This power demand has an extremely small peak (the peak to average ratio is about 1.1), which lasts roughly 2 hours each day. We find that the net savings offered by any ESD configuration is small (just 2%, though still off-setting the cost of the storage provisioning).

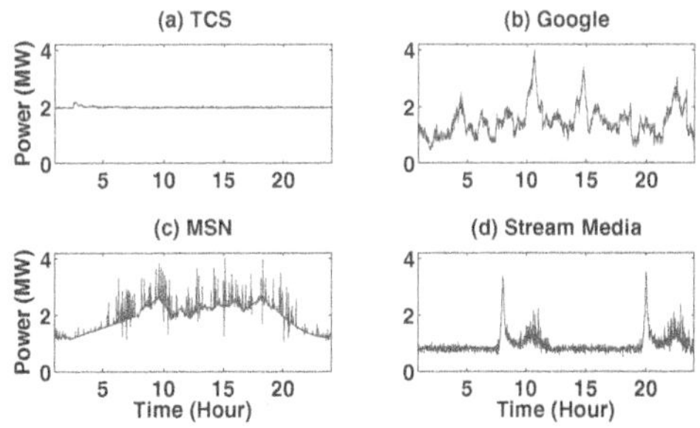

Figure 8: Real-world power profiles

6.3.2 Google

Figure 8(b) presents the power demand from a Google cluster [13] scaled to our assumed datacenter. This power demand shows several peaks during the day with high variances in the power demand, suggesting that ESDs can help. Furthermore, given that server-level LA ESDs are reportedly employed in their datacenters, we would like to examine whether we can improve upon them.

	B_ (savings, cost)	HybSin_ (savings, cost)	HybMul (savings, cost)
Datacenter	CAES (4.9k,0.4k)	FW+LA+CAES (5.2k,0.3k)	FW+CAES
Rack	LA (4.7k,0.3k)	UC+LA (4.8k,0.3k)	-
Server	LA (3.9k,0.2k)	UC+LA (4.7k,0.5k)	LA (5.2k,0.3k)

Table 4: Google Workload: (Savings($/day), ESD costs($/day). Total cost without ESD is $12K/day.

Table 4 presents results for the ESD configurations under consideration. First, we see that if we are to use just a single technology, single-level solution, a datacenter level provisioning (using CAES) does provide considerably higher savings (nearly 25%) than using only lead-acid batteries at each server. The volume constraint does play an important role in limiting the benefits of ESDs in the lower levels of the hierarchy. However, considerations such as double-conversion, and more significant cap-ex benefits (than what we have conservatively used) across the layers, may be reasons for going with a server-level option as in Google. Our framework suggests that even if we are restricted to a server-level placement, a hybrid option of ultra-capacitors together with lead-acid batteries can mitigate the volume constraints to bridge this 25% cost savings gap. If we can remove restrictions even further and explore multi-level hybrid options, our framework suggests flywheel and CAES at the datacenter level, together with lead-acid batteries at the server level to provide as much as 30% benefits over just server-level batteries. As can be seen in Figure 8(b), this workload shows burstiness at different time scales, allowing a richer set of ESD options to shape this power profile.

6.3.3 MSN

Figure 8(c) shows the load in a MSN facility [8], which has been translated to a power demand for our 4 MW datacenter. Table 5 shows the cost savings with the different ESD configurations. To a large extent, the results/savings are similar to those in the Google workload - capacity limitations and conservative cap-ex cost assumptions limit the extent of savings with just server-level lead-acid batteries, and CAES/flywheels can better augment the power needs centrally. The main difference is that this workload has very diverse sets of peaks - some last as long as 8 hours per day, and some which are at most a few minutes. The short and bursty tall power spikes favor a ultra-capacitor based solution at the server level, whether it be in $HybSin_{server}$ or *HybMul*. Overall we find *HybMul* giving around 30% and 20% better savings than server level alone, or rack-level alone placement of lead-acid batteries.

	B_ (savings, cost)	HybSin_ (savings, cost)	HybMul (savings, cost)
Datacenter	LA (4.0k,0.5k)	UC+FW+CAES (4.4k,0.3k)	FW+CAES
Rack	LA (3.8k,0.3k)	UC+LA (4.3k,0.3k)	-
Server	LA (3.4k,0.1k)	UC+LA (4.2k,0.2k)	UC (4.4k,0.3k)

Table 5: MSN Workload: (Savings($/day), ESD costs($/day). Total cost without ESD is $15K/day.

Until now, we have presented only overall summary results. In order to give more detailed facets of ESD operation, we zoom in on a small time window of the MSN power profile and show the operation of different ESDs for *HybMul* in Figure 9. For instance, the horizontal straight line shows the draw from the "utility", and we can see that despite the "demand" varying over time (which is also shown in this figure), the draw from the utility remains constant. To bridge this gap, the lines at the bottom show the charge (negative values of power in the y-axis), and discharge (positive values in y-axis) of the ESDs. We can see that CAES takes a bulk of the gap for significant portions of the time. However, when there is a sudden spike, the ultra-capacitor meets the difference. In order to charge this ultra-capacitor, we see that its curve goes through a negative spike just before it serves the required surge. Note that this negative spike is served by the energy sourced from the CAES, rather than pose an additional load on "utility".

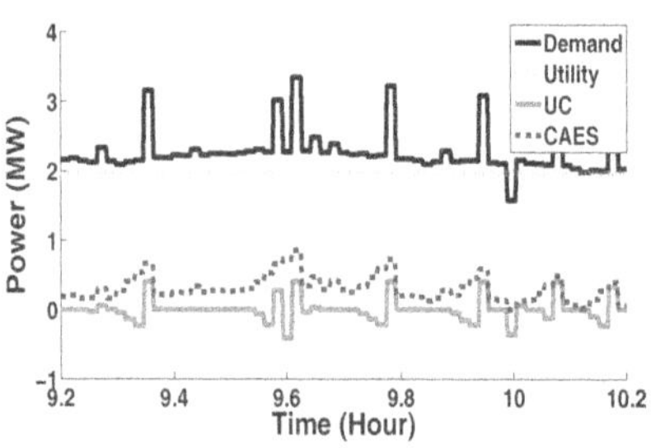

Figure 9: ESD charge/discharge control for the MSN power demand.

Next, we focus on $HydSin_{rack}$ to take a closer look at the impact of device lifetime and charge/discharge ratio on provisioning efficacy. As in the Google environment, we arrive at a hybrid solution that combines ultra-capacitors with lead-acid batteries. Of the three main ways in which ultra-capacitors are better than lead-acid batteries - lifetime, charge/discharge ratio, and power density - we would like to understand which precise ones allow ultra-capacitors to complement lead-acid batteries so well. To do this, we relaxed the constraints related to each of these one at a time, and compared those results with the solution in Table 5. Though not explicitly shown here, we note that all three aspects have a role to play in why this particular hybrid solution was suggested. We show sensitivity results of these aspects in our technical report [48].

6.3.4 Streaming Media

Temporal heterogeneity can also occur at shorter (than MSN) time-scales, as in a server running a streaming media server where there is a power spike once every hour or few hours when new clients login to start watching a new show. We see this in the Media server load [23] shown in Figure 8(d), which has again been scaled for our 4 MW datacenter. Table 6 shows the correspond savings with ESD options.

	B_ (savings, cost)	HybSin_ (savings, cost)	HybMul (savings, cost)
Datacenter	LA (5.6k,0.2k)	FW+LA+CAES (5.7k, 0.2k)	FW+CAES
Rack	LA (5.6k,0.2k)	LA (5.6k,0.2k)	LA
Server	LA (4.0k,0.1k)	UC+LA (5.4k,0.1k)	LA (5.7k,0.2k)

Table 6: Streaming media: (Savings($/day), ESD costs($/day)). Total cost without ESD is $10K/day.

As before, if considering a single level and single technology provisioning, the savings are better at the higher levels because of the restrictions we have imposed. However, even the server level hybrid provisioning (comprising lead-acid batteries and ultra-capacitors) does as well as any centralized provisioning, since the peaks are not as wide as in the MSN workload - benefits of ultra-capacitors can out-weigh any volume constraints of lead-acid batteries. Adding higher level storage capacities does not buy much more (just around 6% improvement).

6.4 Key Insights from Evaluation

1. ESDs help reduce power-related cap-ex and op-ex by up to 50%, even accounting for their provisioning costs.
2. With a single-level restriction, real-estate constraints limit the savings that we can get with server/rack level distributed solutions. In such cases, centralized ESD placement is a better option (e.g. 25% better in the Google workload).
3. Allowing hybrid ESD technologies even at the server level, improves the savings by upto 35% (e.g. in MSN workload) compared to a single ESD option.
4. Overall, a multi-level multi-ESD solution provides the best savings, giving improvements between 10-30% with respect to the best single-level single-ESD solution.

7. RELATED WORK

While there has been considerable work on datacenter energy and peak power management (summarized below), energy storage has been discussed mainly from the viewpoint of handling utility failures and/or intermittent power availability (e.g. with renewables [22, 24, 40, 41]). Exploiting energy storage for DR has been studied in battery-powered embedded, mobile, sensor domains [6, 35]), with such DR in datacenters only recently emerging [18, 20, 43].

Reducing Datacenter Energy Consumption: Much of the early work on datacenter power focused on reducing energy consumption by: (i) exploiting server-level performance knobs (e.g., DVFS-capable CPUs [15]), (ii) scheduling, placement/consolidation, and migration of computation across servers [7, 14, 26], (iii) reducing energy losses within the overall power infrastructure [30], and (iv) improving the energy consumed by the cooling infrastructure [37].

Cost-aware Provisioning and DR for Datacenters: Recent work [13, 16, 33] has proposed ideas to reduce provisioning costs or improve power infrastructure utilization with underprovisioning and statistically multiplexing it among workloads of complementary power needs. Such work relies upon reactive power control mechanisms to ensure safety and limit performance overheads during such emergencies [37]. DR techniques have been explored to reduce the utility bill by adapting power consumption to the vagaries of electricity cost and availability. These include: (i) across datacenters - dynamic workload redistribution to datacenter sites with cheaper prices or power availability [34, 46] and (ii) within a datacenter - complementing the utility draw with energy storage during periods when energy is expensive or unavailable [43], workload scheduling/postponement to match electricity price [25], etc.

8. CONCLUSIONS AND FUTURE WORK

For the first time, this paper has investigated the novel problem of energy storage provisioning - what, where and how much - in the datacenter for Demand Response (DR) purposes. With a plethora of energy storage options, intricacies in their characteristics, pros and cons of placing them in different layers of the power hierarchy, and their suitability to diverse workload characteristics, there are numerous design choices when provisioning and dispatching power from these energy storage devices. We have presented a detailed treatise on energy storage technologies/characteristics impacting their operation in the datacenter. We have presented a simple model to gauge the suitability of a given technology to different workload power profiles, and used this to identify the regions where each becomes cost-effective. We have then formalized a systematic framework for capturing the different intricacies of ESD operations, and developed a generalized optimization platform for ESD placement and control in the datacenter. This platform can be invaluable in datacenter design, capturing a whole spectrum of costs, constraints and workload demands.

Using a wide spectrum of synthetic workloads that stress different aspects of these ESDs, we have shown (i) homogeneous ESD technologies suffice when there is not much heterogeneity in the workload, though the region of operation will decide which ESD should be deployed (e.g., narrow, tall and frequent peaks suited for ultra-capacitors/flywheels vs. broad and infrequent peaks better suited for compressed air and possibly batteries); (ii) even when placing ESDs in a single layer of the power hierarchy, considerations such as how much of the power hierarchy to optimize, volume constraints deciding storage capacity, and statistical multiplexing effects of the workload, influence where (server, rack or datacenter levels) the ESDs should be placed; (iii) even at a single layer of the power hierarchy, hybrid ESD solutions employing multiple technologies can offset the limitations of these constraints to provide substantial benefits (e.g., 25% improvement in cost savings in MSN at the server level); (iv) even if a hybrid ESD option is not employed at each level, a multi-layer hybrid solution can provide as much, if not better, savings across the spectrum of workloads that we have studied. The hybrid and multi-level ESD solutions are even more beneficial when the temporal (over different time scales) and spatial (across regions of the datacenter) heterogeneity in the workload increases.

We are building a small scale prototype with actual ESDs to study these issues experimentally. Further, we are looking to improve control/dispatch algorithms of the ESDs available in the datacenter based on continuously evolving properties. Our contributions are analogous to those in capacity planning of IT load for provisioning computing equipment in the datacenter, with the difference being that we are focusing on power provisioning. Such planning usually involves awareness of the workload, to help in right-sizing of the equipment. We believe this paper provides the valuable tools toward right-sizing the power infrastructure (when a datacenter is built) given workload characteristics.

9. ACKNOWLEDGMENTS

This work was supported, in part, by NSF grants CNS-0720456, CNS-0615097, CAREER award 0953541, and research awards from Google and HP.

10. REFERENCES

[1] M. F. Arlitt and C. L. Williamson. Internet Web Servers: Workload Characterization and Performance Implications. *IEEE Trans. Netw.*, 5(5):631–645, 1997.

[2] A. Bar-Noy, M. P. Johnson, and O. Liu. Peak Shaving Through Resource Buffering. In *Workshop On Approximation and Online Algorithms*, 2008.

[3] L. A. Barroso and U. Holzle. *The Datacenter as a Computer: An Introduction to the Design of Warehouse-Scale Machines.* Morgan and Claypool Publishers, 2009.

[4] D. Brooks, V. Tiwari, and M. Martonosi. Wattch: a framework for architectural-level power analysis and optimizations. In *Proceedings of ISCA*, 2000.

[5] California ISO Open Access Same-time Information System Hourly Average Energy Prices, Nov. 2011. `http://oasishis.caiso.com/`.

[6] Q. Cao, D. Kassa, N. Pham, Y. Sarwar, and T. Abdelzaher. Virtual Battery: An Energy Reserve Abstraction for Embedded Sensor Networks. In *Proceedings of RTSS*, 2008.

[7] J. Chase, D. Anderson, P. Thakur, and A. Vahdat. Managing Energy and Server Resources in Hosting Centers. In *Proceedings of SOSP*, 2001.

[8] G. Chen, W. He, J. Liu, S. Nath, L. Rigas, L. Xiao, and F. Zhao. Energy-aware Server Provisioning and Load Dispatching for Connection-intensive Internet Services. In *Proceedings of NSDI*, 2008.

[9] H. Chen, T. N. Cong, W. Yang, C. Tan, Y. Li, and Y. Ding. Progress in Electrical Energy Storage System: A Critical Review. *Progress in Natural Science*, 19(3), 2009.

[10] K. C. Divya and J. Stergaard. Battery Energy Storage Technology for Power Systems - An Overview. *Electric Power Systems Research*, 79(4), 2009.

[11] Duke Utility Bill Tariff, Oct. 2011. `http://www.duke-energy.com/pdfs/scscheduleopt.pdf`.

[12] Facebook Open Compute Project, Nov. 2011. `opencompute.org`.

[13] X. Fan, W.-D. Weber, and L. A. Barroso. Power Provisioning for a Warehouse-Sized Computer. In *Proceedings of ISCA*, 2007.

[14] A. Gandhi, V. Gupta, M. Harchol-Balter, and M. Kozuch. Optimality Analysis of Energy-Performance Trade-off for Server Farm Management. In *Proceedings of SIGMETRICS*, 2010.

[15] A. Gandhi, M. Harchol-Balter, R. Das, and C. Lefurgy. Optimal Power Allocation in Server Farms. In *Proceedings of SIGMETRICS*, 2009.

[16] D. Gmach, J. Rolia, C. Bash, Y. Chen, T. Christian, A. Shah, R. K. Sharma, and Z. Wang. Capacity

Planning and Power Management to Exploit Sustainable Energy. In *Proceedings of CNSM*, 2010.
[17] Google Server-level UPS for Improved Efficiency, Apr. 2009. http://news.cnet.com/8301-1001_3-10209580-92.html.
[18] S. Govindan, A. Sivasubramaniam, and B. Urgaonkar. Benefits and Limitations of Tapping into Stored Energy For Datacenters. In *Proceedings of ISCA*, 2011.
[19] S. Govindan, D. Wang, L. Chen, A. Sivasubramaniam, and B.Urgaonkar. Towards Realizing a Low Cost and Highly Available Datacenter Power Infrastructure. In *Workshop on HotPower*, 2011.
[20] S. Govindan, D. Wang, A. Sivasubramaniam, and B. Urgaonkar. Leveraging Stored Energy for Handling Power Emergencies in Aggressively Provisioned Datacenters. In *Proceedings of ASPLOS*, 2012.
[21] J. Hamilton. Internet-scale Service Infrastructure Efficiency, ISCA 2009, Keynote. http://perspectives.mvdirona.com/.
[22] K. Le, R. Bianchini, T. D. Nguyen, O. Bilgir, and M. Martonosi. Capping the Brown Energy Consumption of Internet Services at Low Cost. In *Proceedings of IGCC*, 2010.
[23] B. Li, G. Y. Keung, S. Xie, F. Liu, Y. Sun, and H. Yin. An Empirical Study of Flash Crowd Dynamics in a P2P-Based Live Video Streaming System. In *Proceedings of GLOBECOM*, 2008.
[24] C. Li, A. Qouneh, and T. Li. Characterizing and Analyzing Renewable Energy Driven Data Centers. In *Proceedings of SIGMETRICS*, 2011.
[25] J. Li, Z. Li, K. Ren, X. Liu, and H. Su. Towards Optimal Electric Demand Management for Internet Data Centers. *IEEE Trans. on Smart Grid*, 2011.
[26] Z. Liu, M. Lin, A. Wierman, S. H. Low, and L. L. H. Andrew. Greening Geographical Load Balancing. In *Proceedings of SIGMETRICS*, 2011.
[27] M. Marwah, P. Maciel, A. Shah, R. Sharma, T. Christian, V. Almeida, C. Araújo, E. Souza, G. Callou, B. Silva, S. Galdino, and J. Pires. Quantifying the Sustainability Impact of Data Center Availability. *SIGMETRICS Performance Evaluation Review*, 37(4), 2010.
[28] Maxwell Ultracapacitor Uninterruptible Power Supply Solutions, Oct. 2011. http://www.maxwell.com/products/ultracapacitors/industries/.
[29] S. McCluer and J. F. Christin. APC White Paper: Comparing Data Center Batteries, Flywheels, and Ultracapacitors, Oct. 2011. http://www.apcmedia.com/salestools/DBOY-77FNCT_R2_EN.pdf.
[30] D. Meisner, C. M. Sadler, L. A. Barroso, W. Weber, and T. F. Wenisch. Power Management of Online Data-intensive Services. In *Proceedings of ISCA*, 2011.
[31] Microsoft Reveals its Specialty Servers, Racks, Apr. 2011. http://www.datacenterknowledge.com/archives/.
[32] M. K. Patterson, D. G. Costello, P. F. Grimm, and M. Loeffler. Data Center TCO; A Comparison of High-density and Low-density Spaces. In *Proceedings of THERMES*, 2007.
[33] S. Pelley, D. Meisner, P. Zandevakili, T. F. Wenisch, and J. Underwood. Power Routing: Dynamic Power Provisioning in the Data Center. In *Proceedings of ASPLOS*, 2010.
[34] A. Qureshi, R. Weber, H. Balakrishnan, J. Guttag, and B. Maggs. Cutting the Electric Bill for Internet-Scale Systems. In *Proceedings of SIGCOMM*, 2009.
[35] M. Ra, J. Paek, A. Sharma, R. Govindan, M. H. Krieger, and M. J. Neely. Energy-delay Tradeoffs in Smartphone Applications. In *Proceedings of the International Conference on Mobile Systems, Applications, and Services*, 2010.
[36] D. V. Ragone. *Review of Battery Systems for Electrically Powered Vehicles*. Society of Automotive Engineers, 1968.
[37] P. Ranganathan, P. Leech, D. Irwin, and J. Chase. Ensemble-level Power Management for Dense Blade Servers. In *Proceedings of ISCA*, 2006.
[38] D. Rastler. Electricity Energy Storage Technology Options. Technical Report 1020676, Electric Power Research Institue, 2010.
[39] S. M. Schoenung and W. V. Hassenzahl. Long- vs. Short-Term Energy Storage Technologies Analysis. A Life-Cycle Cost Study. A Study for the DOE Energy Storage Systems Program. Technical Report SAND2003-2783, Sandia National Laboratories, 2003.
[40] N. Sharma, S. Barker, D. Irwin, and P. Shenoy. Blink: Managing Server Clusters on Intermittent Power. In *Proceedings of ASPLOS*, 2011.
[41] C. Stewart and K. Shen. Some Joules Are More Precious Than Others: Managing Renewable Energy in the Datacenter. In *Workshop on HotPower*, 2009.
[42] M. Ton, B. Fortenbery, and W. Tschudi. DC Power for Improved Data Center Efficiency, Mar. 2008. http://hightech.lbl.gov/dcpowering/about.html.
[43] R. Urgaonkar, B. Urgaonkar, M. J. Neely, and A. Sivasubramaniam. Optimal Power Cost Management Using Stored Energy in Data Centers. In *Proceedings of SIGMETRICS*, 2011.
[44] A. Vasan, A. Sivasubramaniam, V. Shimpi, T. Sivabalan, and R. Subbiah. Worth Their Watts? - An Empirical Study of Datacenter Servers. In *Proceedings of HPCA*, 2010.
[45] P. Ven, N. Hegde, L. Massoulie, and T. Salonidis. Optimal Control of Residential Energy Storage Under Price Fluctuations. In *Proceedings of the International Conference on Smart Grids, Green Communications and IT Energy-aware Technologies*, 2011.
[46] A. Verma, P. De, V. Mann, T. Nayak, A. Purohit, D. Gargi, and K. Ravi. BrownMap : Enforcing Power Budget in Shared Data Centers. In *Proceedings of the USENIX International Middleware Conference*, 2010.
[47] VYCON: Flywheel Based UPS System in Data Centers, Nov. 2011. http://www.vyconenergy.com/pq/ups.htm.
[48] D. Wang, C. Ren, A. Sivasubramaniam, B.Urgaonkar, and H. Fathy. Energy Storage in Datacenters: What, Where, and How much? Technical Report CSE-11-016, The Pennsylvania State University, November 2011.

Rumor Centrality: A Universal Source Detector

Devavrat Shah
Massachusetts Institute of Technology
Cambridge, Massachusetts
USA
devavrat@mit.edu

Tauhid Zaman
Wharton School, University of Pennsylvania
Philadelphia, Pennsylvania
USA
tzaman@wharton.upenn.edu

ABSTRACT

We consider the problem of detecting the source of a rumor (information diffusion) in a network based on observations about which set of nodes possess the rumor. In a recent work [10], this question was introduced and studied. The authors proposed *rumor centrality* as an estimator for detecting the source. They establish it to be the maximum likelihood estimator with respect to the popular Susceptible Infected (SI) model with exponential spreading time for regular trees. They showed that as the size of infected graph increases, for a line (2-regular tree) graph, the probability of source detection goes to 0 while for d-regular trees with $d \geq 3$ the probability of detection, say α_d, remains bounded away from 0 and is less than $1/2$. Their results, however stop short of providing insights for the heterogeneous setting such as irregular trees or the SI model with non-exponential spreading times.

This paper overcomes this limitation and establishes the effectiveness of rumor centrality for source detection for generic random trees and the SI model with a generic spreading time distribution. The key result is an interesting connection between a multi-type continuous time branching process (an equivalent representation of a generalized Polya's urn, cf. [1]) and the effectiveness of rumor centrality. Through this, it is possible to quantify the detection probability precisely. As a consequence, we recover all the results of [10] as a special case and more importantly, we obtain a variety of results establishing the *universality* of rumor centrality in the context of tree-like graphs and the SI model with a generic spreading time distribution.

Categories and Subject Descriptors

G.2.2 [**Graph Theory**]: Network problems, Graph algorithms; G.2.1 [**Combinatorics**]: Combinatorial algorithms, Counting problems, Permutations and combinations

General Terms

Theory, Performance, Security, Algorithms

SIGMETRICS '12, June 11–15, 2012, London, England, UK.

Keywords

Epidemics, Estimation

1. INTRODUCTION

Imagine a rumor spreads through a network, and after a certain amount of time, we only know who has heard the rumor and the underlying network structure. With only this information, is it possible to determine who was the rumor source? Finding rumor sources is a very general type of problem which arises in many different contexts. For example, the rumor could be a computer virus on the Internet, a contagious disease in a human population, or some trend in a social network. In each of these scenarios, detection of the source is of interest as this source may be a malicious agent, patient zero, or an influential person.

There is limited prior work on the question of finding the source of a rumor. However, there has been much work done to understand conditions under which a rumor becomes an epidemic and how to use these insights to stop the spread [7],[9],[4]. In a thematically related problem of reconstruction, the interest is in predicting the state of the source based on the noisy observations about this state that are available in the network. Like the reconstruction problem, the source detection problem is quite complex: the signal of interest, the state of source for reconstruction problem and the rumor source here is extremely 'low-dimensional' while the observations, the noisy versions of the state in reconstruction problem and infected nodes here, lie in a very 'high-dimensional' setting. This makes the estimation or detection quite challenging[1]. It is not surprising that even to obtain meaningful answers for the reconstruction problem for tree or tree-like graphs, sophisticated techniques have been required, cf.[3],[8], [5].

There are two key challenges that need to be addressed to resolve the rumor source detection problem. First, how does one actually construct the rumor source estimator? The estimator would naturally need to incorporate the topology of the underlying network, but it is not obvious in what manner. Second, what are the fundamental limits to this rumor source detection problem? In particular, how well can one find the rumor source, what is the distribution of the error, and how does the network structure affect one's ability to find the rumor source?

In a recent work [10], the authors introduced and studied the problem of rumor source detection in networks. They proposed *rumor centrality*, a graph-score function, for ranking the importance of nodes as the source. They showed that the node with maximal rumor centrality is the maximum likelihood (ML) estimation in the context of regular trees and the SI model with homogeneous exponential spreading times. They showed the effectiveness of this

[1]The phrase *finding needle in a haystack* seems quite appropriate.

estimator by establishing that the rumor source is found with non-trivial probability for regular trees and geometric trees under this setting. The model and precise results from [10] are described in Section 2.

The key limitations of this prior work are : (i) the results do not quantify the exact detection probability, say α_d, for d-regular graphs, under the proposed maximum likelihood estimator other than $\alpha_2 = 0$, $\alpha_3 = 0.25$ and $0 < \alpha_d \leq 0.5$ for $d \geq 4$ for the SI model with exponential spreading times; (ii) the results do not quantify the magnitude of the error in the event of not being able to identify the source; and more generally, (iii) the results do not provide any insights into how the estimator behaves for generic heterogeneous tree (or tree-like) graphs under the SI model with a generic spreading time distribution.

1.1 Summary of results

The primary reason behind the limitations of the results in [10] is the fact that the analytic method employed there is quite specific to regular trees with homogeneous exponential spreading times. To overcome these limitations, as the main contribution of this work we introduce a novel analysis method that utilizes connections to the classical multi-class Markov branching process (MCMBP) (equivalently, generalized Polya's urn (GPU)). As a consequence of this, we are able to quantify the probability of the error event precisely and thus eliminate the shortcomings of the prior work. The following is a summary of the key results (see Section 3 for precise statements):

1. *Regular tree, SI model with exponential spreading time*: we characterize α_d, the detection probability for d-regular trees, for all d. Specifically, for $d \geq 3$
$$\alpha_d = dI_{1/2}\Big(\frac{1}{d-2}, \frac{d-1}{d-2}\Big) - (d-1).$$
In above $I_x(\alpha, \beta)$ is the incomplete beta function with parameters α, β evaluated at $x \in [0, 1]$ (see (3.1)). This implies that $\alpha_d > 0$ for $d \geq 3$ with $\alpha_3 = 0.25$ and $\alpha_d \to 1 - \ln 2$ as $d \to \infty$. Further, we show that the probability of rumor centrality estimating the kth infected node as the source decays as $\exp(-\Theta(k))$. The precise results are stated as Theorem 3.1, Corollaries 1 and 2.

2. *Generic random tree, SI model with exponential spreading time*: for generic random trees (see Section 3.2 for precise definition) which are expanding, we establish that there is strictly positive probability of correct detection using rumor centrality. Furthermore, the probability of rumor centrality estimating the kth infected node as the source decays as $\Theta(1/k)$. The precise results are stated as Theorem 3.2 and Theorem 3.3.

3. *Geometric tree, SI model with spreading time with finite moment generating function*: for any geometric tree (see Section 3.2.2 for precise definition), we establish that the probability of correct detection goes to 1 as the number of infected nodes increases. The precise result is stated as Theorem 3.4.

4. *Generic random tree, SI model with generic spreading time*: for generic expanding random tree with generic spreading time (see Section 3.2 for definition), we establish that the probability of correct source detection remains bounded away from 0. The precise result is stated as Theorem 3.2.

The above results collectively establish that, even though, rumor centrality is an ML estimator only for regular tree and the SI model with exponential spreading times, it is universally effective with respect to heterogeneity in the tree structure and spreading time distributions. It's effectiveness for generic random trees immediately implies its utility for finding sources in sparse random graphs that are locally tree-like. Examples include Erdos-Renyi and random regular graphs. A brief discussion to this effect can be found in Section 3.3.

2. MODEL, PROBLEM STATEMENT AND RUMOR CENTRALITY

We start by describing the model and problem statement followed by a quick recall of the precise results from [10]. In the process, we shall recall the definition of rumor centrality and source estimation as introduced in [10].

2.1 Model

Let $\mathcal{G} = (\mathcal{V}, \mathcal{E})$ be a possibly infinite connected graph. Let $v \in \mathcal{V}$ be a rumor source from which a rumor starts spreading at time, say 0. As per the classical Susceptible Infected (SI) model the rumor spreads in the graph. Specifically, each edge say $e = (u_1, u_2)$, has a spreading time, say S_e, associated with it. If node u_1 gets infected at time t_1, then at time $t_1 + S_e$ the infection spreads from u_1 to u_2. A node, once becoming infected, remains infected. The spreading times associated with edges are independent random variables with identical distribution. Let $F : \mathbb{R} \to [0, 1]$ denote the cumulative density function of the spreading time distribution. We shall assume that the distribution is non-negative valued, i.e. $F(0) = 0$ and it is non-atomic at 0, i.e. $F(0^+) = 0$. Since it is a cumulative density function, it is non-decreasing and $\lim_{x\to\infty} F(x) = 1$. The simplest, homogeneous SI model has exponential spreading times with parameter $\lambda > 0$ with $F(x) = 1 - \exp(-\lambda x)$ for $x \geq 0$. In [10], the results were restricted to this homogeneous exponential spreading time setting. In this paper, we shall develop results for arbitrary spreading time distributions consistent with the above assumptions.

Problem statement.

Given the above spreading model, we observe the rumor infected graph $G = (V, E)$ at some time $t > 0$. We do not know the value of t or the realization of the spreading times on edges $e \in E$; we only know the rumor infected nodes $V \subset \mathcal{V}$ and edges between them $E = V \times V \cap \mathcal{E}$. The goal is to find the rumor source (among V) given G.

2.2 Rumor centrality: an estimator

To solve this problem, the notion of rumor centrality was introduced in [10]. Rumor centrality is a 'graph score' function. That is, it takes $G = (V, E)$ as input and assigns a positive number or score to each of the vertices. Then the estimated source is the one with maximal (ties broken uniformly at random) score or rumor centrality. The estimated source is called the 'rumor center'. We start with the precise description of rumor centrality for a tree[2] graph G: the rumor centrality of node $u \in V$ with respect to $G = (V, E)$ is

$$R(u, G) = \frac{|V|!}{\prod_{w\in V} T_w^u}, \tag{2.1}$$

where T_w^u is the size of the subtree of G that is rooted at w and points away from u. For example, in Figure 1, let u be node 1. Then $|V| = 5$; the subtree sizes are $T_1^1 = 5, T_2^1 = 3, T_3^1 = T_4^1 = T_5^1 =$

[2]We shall call an undirected graph a *tree*, if it is connected and it does not have any cycles.

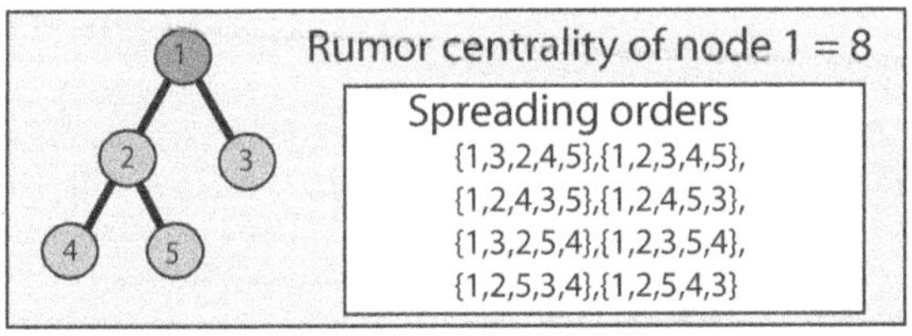

Figure 1: Example of rumor centrality calculation for a 5 node network. The rumor centrality of node 1 is 8 because there are 8 spreading orders that it can originate, which are shown in the figure.

1 and hence $R(1, G) = 8$: exactly equal to the number of distinct spreading orders starting from 1. In [10], a linear time algorithm is described to compute the rumor centrality of all nodes building on the relation $R(u, G)/R(v, G) = T_u^v/T_v^u$ for neighboring nodes $u, v \in V$ ($(u, v) \in E$).

The rumor centrality of a given node $u \in V$ for a tree given by (2.1) is precisely the number of distinct spreading orders that could lead to the rumor infected graph G starting from u. This is equivalent to computing the number of linear extensions of the partial order imposed by the graph G due to causality constraints of rumor spreading. Under the SI model with homogeneous exponential spreading times and a regular tree, it turns out that each of the spreading orders is equally likely. Therefore, the rumor centrality turns out to be the Maximum Likelihood (ML) estimator for the source in this specific setting (cf. [10]). In general, the likelihood of each node $u \in V$ being the source given G is proportional to the weighted summation of the number of distinct spreading orders starting from u, where weight of a spreading order could depend on the details of the graph structure and spreading time distribution of the SI model. Now for a tree graph and SI model with homogeneous exponential spreading times, as mentioned above, such a quantity can be computed in linear time. But in general, this could be complicated. For example, computing the number of linear extensions of a given partial order is known to be #P-complete [2]. While there are algorithms for approximately sampling linear extensions given a partial order [6], [10] proposed a simpler alternative for general graphs.

Definition 1 (Rumor Centrality)**.** *Given node $u \in V$ in graph $G = (V, E)$, let $T \subset G$ denote the breadth-first search tree of u with respect to G. Then, the rumor centrality of u with respect to G is obtained by computing it as per* (2.1) *with respect to T. The estimated rumor source is the one with maximal rumor centrality (ties broken uniformly at random).*

2.3 Prior results

In [10], the authors established that rumor centrality is the maximum-likelihood estimator for the rumor source when the underlying graph $\mathcal{G}$ is a regular tree. They studied the effectiveness of this ML estimator for such regular trees. Specifically, suppose we observe the $n(t)$ node rumor infected graph G after time t, which is a subgraph of $\mathcal{G}$. Let $C_{n(t)}^k$ be the event that the source estimated as per rumor centrality is the kth infected node, and thus $C_{n(t)}^1$ corresponds to the event of correct detection. The following are key results from [10]:

Theorem 2.1 ([10])**.** *Let $\mathcal{G}$ be a d-regular infinite tree with $d \geq 2$. Let*

$$\alpha_d^L = \liminf_{t\to\infty} \mathbf{P}\Big(C_{n(t)}^1\Big) \leq \limsup_{t\to\infty} \mathbf{P}\Big(C_{n(t)}^1\Big) = \alpha_d^U. \quad (2.2)$$

Then,

$$\alpha_2^L = \alpha_2^U = 0, \quad \alpha_3^L = \alpha_3^U = \frac{1}{4}, \quad (2.3)$$

$$\text{and} \quad 0 < \alpha_d^L \leq \alpha_d^U \leq \frac{1}{2}, \ \forall\, d \geq 4. \quad (2.4)$$

3. MAIN RESULTS

We state the main results of this paper. In a nutshell, our results concern the characterization of the probability of $C_{n(t)}^k$ for any $k \geq 1$ for large t when $\mathcal{G}$ is a generic tree. As a consequence, it provides a characterization of the performance for sparse random graphs.

3.1 Regular tree, SI model with exponential spreading time

We first look at rumor source detection on regular trees with degree $d \geq 3$, where rumor centrality is an exact ML estimator when the spreading times are exponentially distributed. Our results will utilize properties of Beta random variables. We recall that the regularized incomplete Beta function $I_x(a, b)$ is the probability that a Beta random variable with parameters a and b is less than $x \in [0, 1]$,

$$I_x(a,b) = \frac{\Gamma(a+b)}{\Gamma(a)\Gamma(b)} \int_0^x t^{a-1}(1-t)^{b-1}dt, \quad (3.1)$$

where $\Gamma(\cdot)$ is the standard Gamma function. For regular trees of degree ≥ 3 we obtain the following result.

Theorem 3.1. *Let $\mathcal{G}$ be d-regular infinite tree with $d \geq 3$. Assume a rumor spreads on $\mathcal{G}$ as per the SI model with exponential distribution with rate λ. Then, for any $k \geq 1$,*

$$\lim_{t\to\infty} \mathbf{P}\Big(C_{n(t)}^k\Big) = I_{1/2}\left(k-1+\frac{1}{d-2}, 1+\frac{1}{d-2}\right) + (d-1)\left(I_{1/2}\left(\frac{1}{d-2}, k+\frac{1}{d-2}\right)-1\right). \quad (3.2)$$

For $k = 1$, Theorem 3.1 yields that $\alpha_d^L = \alpha_d^U = \alpha_d$ for all $d \geq 3$ where

$$\alpha_d = dI_{1/2}\left(\frac{1}{d-2}, \frac{d-1}{d-2}\right) - (d-1). \quad (3.3)$$

More interestingly,

Corollary 1.

$$\lim_{d\to\infty} \alpha_d = 1 - \ln 2 \approx 0.307. \quad (3.4)$$

For any $d \geq 3$, we can obtain a simple upper bound for Theorem 3.1 which provides the insight that the probability of error in the estimation decays exponentially with error distance (not number of hops in graph, but based on chronological order of infection) from the true source.

Corollary 2. *When $\mathcal{G}$ is a d-regular infinite tree, for any $k \geq 1$,*

$$\lim_{t\to\infty} \mathbf{P}\Big(C_{n(t)}^k\Big) \leq k(k+1)\left(\frac{1}{2}\right)^{k-1} \sim \exp\Big(-\Theta(k)\Big).$$

To provide intuition, we plot the asymptotic error distribution $\lim_{t\to\infty} \mathbf{P}\left(C_{n(t)}^k\right)$ for different degree regular trees in Figure 2. As can be seen, for degrees greater than 4, all the error distributions fall on top of each other, and the probability of detecting the kth infection as the source decays exponentially in k. We also plot the upper bound from Corollary 2. As can be seen, this upper bound

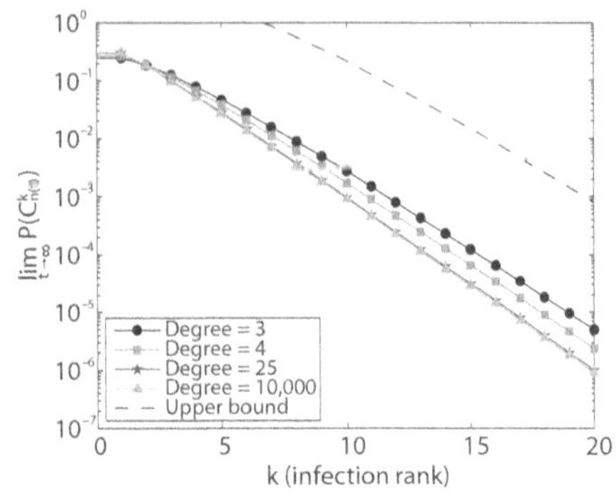

Figure 2: (left) $\lim_{t\to\infty} \mathbf{P}\left(C^k_{n(t)}\right)$ **versus** k **for regular trees of different degree.**

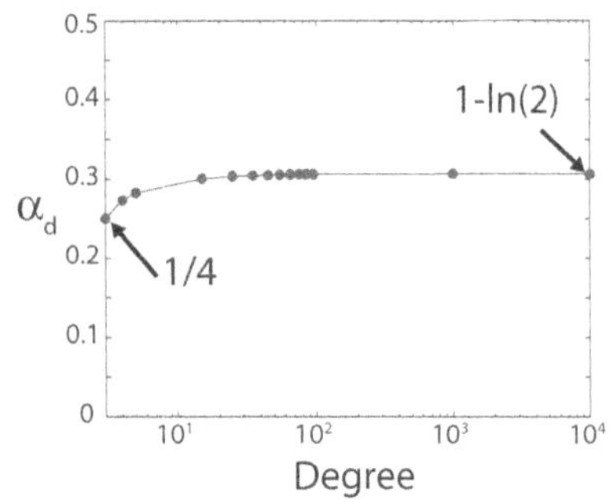

Figure 3: α_d **versus degree** d **for regular trees.**

captures the rate of decay of the error probability. Thus we see tight concentration of the error for this class of graphs. Figure 3 plots the asymptotic correct detection probability α_d versus degree d for these regular trees. It can be seen that the detection probability starts at $1/4$ for degree 3 and rapidly converges to $1 - \ln(2)$ as the degree goes to infinity.

3.2 Generic random tree, SI model with general spreading time distribution

The above precise results were obtained using the memoryless property of the exponential distribution and the regularity of the trees. Next, we wish to look at a more general setting both in terms of tree structures and spreading time distributions. In this more general setting, while we cannot obtain precise values for the detection and error probabilities, we are able to make statements about the non-triviality of the detection probability of rumor centrality. When restricted to exponential spreading times for generic trees, we can identify bounds on the error probability as well. Let us start by defining what we mean by generic random trees through a generative model.

Definition 2 (Random Trees). *A random tree is generated as follows. Starting with a root node, add a random number of children, say η_0 to the root with $\eta_0 \in \{0, 1 \ldots\}$ having some distribution $\mathcal{D}_0$. If $\eta_0 \neq 0$, then to each child of the root, add a random number of children chosen as per distribution $\mathcal{D}$ over $\{0, 1, \ldots\}$. Recursively, to each newly added node, add independently a random number of nodes as per distribution $\mathcal{D}$. When 0 children are added to a node, that branch of the tree terminates there.*

The generative model described above is precisely the standard Galton-Watson branching process if $\mathcal{D}_0 = \mathcal{D}$. If we take $\mathcal{D}_0$ and $\mathcal{D}$ to be deterministic distributions with support on d and $d-1$ respectively, then it gives the d-regular tree. For a random d-regular graph on n nodes, as n grows the neighborhood of a randomly chosen node in the graph converges (in distribution, locally) to such a d-regular tree. If we take $\mathcal{D}_0 = \mathcal{D}$ as a Poisson distribution with mean $c > 0$, then it asymptotically equals (in distribution) the local neighborhood of a randomly chosen node in a sparse Erdos-Renyi graph as the number of nodes grows. Recall that a (sparse) Erdos-Renyi graph on n nodes with parameter c is generated by selecting each of the $\binom{n}{2}$ edges to be present with probability c/n independently. Effectively, random trees as described above capture the local structure for sparse random graphs reasonably well. For that reason, establishing the effectiveness of rumor centrality for source detection for such trees provide insights into its effectiveness for sparse random graph models.

We shall consider spreading time distributions to be generic: let $F : \mathbb{R} \to [0, 1]$ be the cumulative density function of spreading time distribution. Then $F(0) = 0$, $F(0^+) = 0$ and $\lim_{t\to\infty} F(t) = 1$. We state the following result about the effectiveness of rumor centrality with a generic spreading time distribution.

Theorem 3.2. *Let η_0, distributed as $\mathcal{D}_0$, be such that $\Pr(\eta_0 \geq 3) > 0$ and let η, distributed as per $\mathcal{D}$, be such that $\mathbf{E}[\eta^2] < \infty$, $\mathbf{E}[\eta] > 1$. Suppose the rumor starts from the root of the random tree generated as per distributions $\mathcal{D}_0$ and $\mathcal{D}$ as described above and spreads as per the SI model with generic spreading time distribution as discussed above. Then,*

$$\liminf_{t\to\infty} \mathbf{P}\left(C^1_{n(t)}\right) > 0.$$

The above result says that irrespective of the structure of the random trees, spreading time distribution and time elapsed, there is non-trivial probability of detecting the root as the source by rumor centrality. The interesting aspect of the result is that this non-trivial detection probability is established by studying events when the tree grows without bound. In specific models (e.g. Poisson distribution of $\mathcal{D}_0$, $\mathcal{D}$), one may derive such a bound by identifying the probability of having an empty tree to be non-trivial. But, indeed, such events are trivial and are not of much interest to us (neither mathematically, nor motivationally).

3.2.1 Generic random tree, SI model with exponential spreading time distribution

Extending the results of Theorem 3.2 for explicitly bounding the probability of error event, $\mathbf{P}\left(C^k_{n(t)}\right)$, for generic spreading time distribution seems rather challenging. Here we provide a result for generic random trees with exponential spreading times.

Theorem 3.3. *Consider the setup of Theorem 3.2 with spreading times being homogeneous exponential distributions with (unknown, but fixed) parameter $\lambda > 0$. In addition, let $\mathcal{D}_0 = \mathcal{D}$. Let (with some abuse of notation) η_i denote the number of children of ith infected node. Then conditioned on the event that, (i) $\eta_k \geq 2$, and (ii) $\sum_{i=1}^{k-1} \eta_i \geq ck\eta_k$ for some $c > 1$,*

$$\mathbf{P}\left(C^k_{n(t)}\right) \leq \frac{1}{k}. \tag{3.5}$$

The above result establishes an explicit upper bound on the error event under the occurrence of a specific event. The bound is relatively weaker ($1/k$ versus $\exp(-\Theta(k))$) and holds under specific conditions. However, it applies to essentially any generic random tree and demonstrates that the probability of (mis-)estimating later infected nodes decreases.

3.2.2 Geometric trees

The trees considered thus far, d-regular tree with $d \geq 3$ or random tree with $\mathbf{E}[\eta] > 1$, grow exponentially in size with the diameter of the tree. This is, in contrast with line graphs or d-regular trees with $d = 2$ which grow only linearly in diameter. It can be easily seen that the probability of correct detection, $\mathbf{P}(C^1_{n(t)})$ will scale as $\Theta(1/\sqrt{t})$ for line graphs as long as the spreading time distribution has non-trivial variance (see [10] for proof of this statement for SI model with exponential spreading times). In contrast, the results of this paper stated thus far suggest that the expanding trees allow for non-trivial detection as $t \to \infty$. Thus, qualitatively line (tree) graphs and expanding trees are quite different – one does not allow detection while the other does. To understand where the precise detectability threshold lies, here we study the polynomially growing *geometric* trees.

Definition 3 (Geometric Tree). *This family of rooted, non-regular trees are parameterized by constants α, b, and c, with $0 < b \leq c$ and a root v^*. Let d^* be the degree of this root v^* and let the d^* neighboring subtree of v^*, be denoted by $T_1, \ldots, T_{d^*}$. Consider the ith subtree T_i, $1 \leq i \leq d^*$. Let v be any node in T_i and let $n^i(v, r)$ be the number of nodes in T_i at distance exactly r from the node v. Then we require that for all $1 \leq i \leq d^*$ and $v \in T_i$*

$$br^{\alpha} \leq n^i(v, r) \leq cr^{\alpha}. \tag{3.6}$$

The condition imposed by (3.6) states that each of the neighboring subtrees of the root should satisfy polynomial growth (with exponent $\alpha > 0$) and regularity properties. The parameter $\alpha > 0$ characterizes the growth of the subtrees and the ratio c/b describes the regularity of the subtrees. If $c/b \approx 1$ then the subtrees are somewhat regular, whereas if the ratio is much greater than 1, there is substantial heterogeneity in the subtrees. Note that the line graph is a geometric tree with $\alpha = 0$, $b = 1$, and $c = 2$.

We shall consider the scenario where the rumor starts from the root node of a rooted geometric tree. We shall show that rumor centrality detects the root as the source with asymptotic probability of 1 for a generic spreading time distribution with exponential tails. This is quite interesting given the fact that rumor centrality is an ML estimator only for regular tree with exponential spreading time. The precise result is stated next.

Theorem 3.4. *Let $\mathcal{G}$ be a rooted geometric tree as described above with parameters $\alpha > 0$, $0 < b \leq c$ and root node v^* with degree d^* such that*

$$d_{v^*} > \max\left(2, \frac{c}{b} + 1\right).$$

Suppose the rumor starts spreading on $\mathcal{G}$ starting from v^* as per the SI model with generic spreading time distribution whose cumulative density function $F : \mathbb{R} \to [0, 1]$ is such that (a) $F(0) = 0$, (b) $F(0^+) = 0$, and (c) if X is a random variable distributed as per F then $\mathbf{E}[\exp(\theta X)] < \infty$ for $\theta \in (-\varepsilon, \varepsilon)$ for some $\varepsilon > 0$. Then

$$\lim_{t} \mathbf{P}(C^1_{n(t)}) = 1.$$

A similar theorem was proven in [10], but only for the SI model with an exponential distribution. We have now extended this result to arbitrarily distributed spreading times. Theorem 3.4 says that $\alpha = 0$ and $\alpha > 0$ serve as a threshold for non-trivial detection: for $\alpha = 0$, the graph is essentially a linear graph, so we would expect the detection probability to go to 0 as $t \to \infty$ as discussed above, but for $\alpha > 0$ the detection probability converges to 1 as $t \to \infty$.

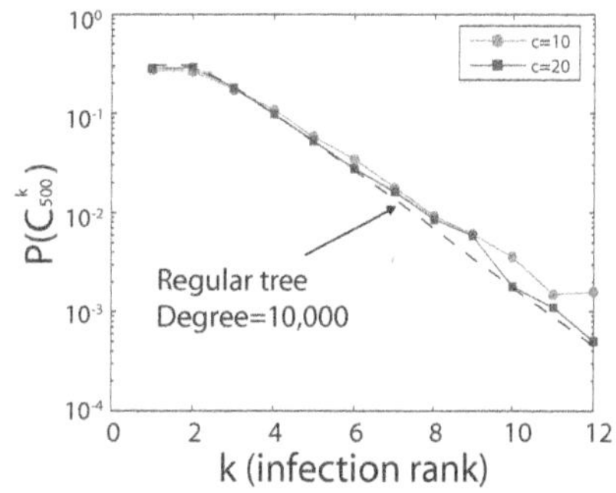

Figure 4: $\mathbf{P}\left(C^k_{500}\right)$ versus k for Erdos-Renyi graphs with mean degree 10 and 20. Also shown with a black dashed line is $\lim_{t\to\infty} \mathbf{P}\left(C^k_{n(t)}\right)$ for a degree 10,000 regular tree.

3.3 Locally tree-like graphs: discussion

The results of the paper stated are primarily for all sorts of tree structured graphs. On one hand, they are specialized. On the other hand, they do serve as local approximations for a variety of sparse random graph models. As discussed earlier, for a random d-regular graph over m nodes, a randomly chosen node's local neighborhood (say up to distance $o(\log m)$) is a tree with high probability. Similarly, consider an Erdos-Renyi graph over m nodes with each edge being present with probability $p = c/m$ independently for any $c > 0$ ($c > 1$ is an interesting regime due to existence the of a giant component). Then again, a randomly chosen node's local neighborhood (up to distance $o(\log m)$) is a tree and distributionally equivalent (in the large m limit) to a random tree with Poisson degree distribution.

Given such 'locally tree-like' structural properties, if a rumor spreads on a random d-regular graph or sparse Erdos-Renyi graph for time $o(\log m)$ starting from a random node, then rumor centrality can detect the source with guarantees given by Theorems 3.1 and 3.2. Thus, effectively though the results of this paper are for tree structured graphs, they do have meaningful implications for tree-like sparse graphs.

For the purpose of illustration, we conducted some simulations for Erdos-Renyi graphs that are reported in Figure 4. We generated graphs with $m = 50,000$ nodes and edge probabilities $p = c/m$ for $c = 10$ and $c = 20$. The rumor graph contained $n = 500$ nodes. We ran $10,000$ rumor spreading simulations to obtain the empirical error distributions plotted in Figure 4. As can be seen, the error drops of exponentially, very similar to the regular tree error distribution. In fact, we also plot the distribution for regular tree of degree $10,000$ and it can be seen that the error decays at similar, exponential rates. This indicates that even though there is substantial randomness in the graph, the asymptotic rumor source detection error distribution behaves as though it were a regular tree graph. This result also suggests that the bounds in Theorem 3.3 are loose for this graph.

4. PROOFS

Here proofs of the results stated in Section 3 are presented. We establish results for d-regular trees by connecting rumor spreading with Polya urn models and branching processes. Later we extend this novel method to establish results for generic random trees under arbitrary spreading time distributions. After this, we prove Theorem 3.4 using standard Chernoff's bound and the polynomial growth property of geometric trees.

4.1 Proof of Theorem 3.1: d-regular trees

4.1.1 Setup, notations

Let $\mathcal{G} = (\mathcal{V}, \mathcal{E})$ be an infinite d-regular tree and let the rumor start spreading from a node, say v_1. Without loss of generality, we view it as a randomly generated tree, as described in Section 3, with v_1 being the root with d children and all the subsequent nodes with $d-1$ children (hence each node has degree d). We shall be interested in $d \geq 3$. Now suppose the rumor is spread on this tree starting from v_1 as per the SI model with exponential distribution with rate $\lambda > 0$.

Initially, node v_1 is the only rumor infected node and its d neighbors are potential nodes that can receive the rumor. We will denote the set of nodes that are not yet rumor infected but neighbors of rumor infected nodes as the *rumor boundary*. Thus, initially the rumor boundary consists of the d neighbors of v_1. Under the SI model, each edge has an independent exponential clock of mean $1/\lambda$. The minimum of d independent exponentials of mean $1/\lambda$ is an exponential random variable (of mean $1/(d\lambda)$) and hence one of the d nodes (chosen uniformly at random) in the rumor boundary gets infected after an exponential amount of time (of mean $1/(d\lambda)$). Upon this infection, this node gets removed from the boundary but adds it's $d-1$ children to the rumor boundary. That is, each infection effectively adds $d-2$ new nodes to the rumor boundary. In summary, let $Z(t)$ denote the number of nodes in the rumor boundary at time t, then $Z(0) = d$ and $Z(t)$ evolves as follows: each of the $Z(t)$ nodes has an exponential clock of mean $1/\lambda$; when it ticks, it dies and replaces itself with $d-2$ new nodes which in turn start their own independent exponential clocks of mean $1/\lambda$ and so on. The thus described $Z(t)$ is precisely the multi-class Markov branching process (MCMBP): the multi-class comes when we think of the contributions of each of the d subtress of the root v_1 to the rumor boundary separately and hence effectively having d branching processes each starting at time 0 with initial value equal to 1: let $u_1, \ldots, u_d$ be the children of v_1; let $Z_i(t)$ denote the number of nodes in the rumor boundary that belong to the subtree $T_i(t)$ that is rooted at u_i with $Z_i(0) = 1$ for $1 \leq i \leq d$; $Z(t) = \sum_{i=1}^{d} Z_i(t)$. With an abuse of notation, let $T_i(t)$ also denote the total number of nodes infected in the subtree rooted at u_i at time t; initially $T_i(0) = 0$ for $1 \leq i \leq d$. Since each infected node add $d-2$ nodes to the rumor boundary, it can be easily checked that $Z_i(t) = (d-2)T_i(t) + 1$ and hence $Z(t) = (d-2)T(t) + d$ with $T(t)$ being the total number of infected nodes at time t (excluding v_1, i.e. $T(0) = 0$).

4.1.2 Probability of correct detection $\mathbf{P}\left(C^1_{n(t)}\right)$

Suppose we observe the rumor infected nodes at some time t which we do not know. That is, we observe the rumor infected graph $G(t)$ which contains the root v_1 and its d infected subtrees $T_i(t)$ for $1 \leq i \leq d$. We recall the following result of [10] that characterizes the rumor center (the node(s) with maximal rumor centrality).

Lemma 1 ([10]). *Given a rumor infected tree $G = (V, E)$, there can be at most two rumor centers. Specifically, a node $v \in V$ is a rumor center if and only if*

$$T_i^v \leq \frac{1}{2}\Big(\sum_{j \in \mathcal{N}(v)} T_j^v \Big), \quad \forall\, i \in \mathcal{N}(v), \tag{4.1}$$

where $\mathcal{N}(v) = \{u \in V : (u,v) \in E\}$ are neighbors of v in G and T_j^v denotes the sub-tree of G that is rooted at node $j \in \mathcal{N}(v)$ that includes all nodes that are away from node v (i.e. the subtree does not include v). The node v is the unique rumor center if the inequality in (4.1) *is strict for all $i \in \mathcal{N}(v)$.*

This immediately suggests the characterization of the event that node v_1, the true source, is identified by rumor centrality at time t: v_1 is a rumor center only if $2T_i(t) \leq \sum_{j=1}^{d} T_j(t)$ for all $1 \leq i \leq d$, and if the inequality is strict then it is indeed the rumor center. Now if $n(t)$ is the total number of infected nodes at time t, then as per our earlier notation, $C^1_{n(t)}$ is the event of correct detection at time t. Let $E_i = \{2T_i(t) < \sum_{j=1}^{d} T_j(t)\}$ and $F_i = \{2T_i(t) \leq \sum_{j=1}^{d} T_j(t)\}$. Then,

$$\begin{aligned}\mathbf{P}\left(C^1_{n(t)}\right) &\geq \mathbf{P}\left(\cap_{i=1}^{d} E_i\right) = 1 - \mathbf{P}\left(\cup_{i=1}^{d} E_i^c\right) \\ &\overset{(a)}{\geq} 1 - \sum_{i=1}^{d} \mathbf{P}\left(E_i^c\right) \overset{(b)}{=} 1 - d\mathbf{P}\left(E_1^c\right). \end{aligned} \tag{4.2}$$

Above, (a) follows from the union bound of events and (b) from symmetry. Similarly, we have

$$\begin{aligned}\mathbf{P}\left(C^1_{n(t)}\right) &\leq \mathbf{P}\left(\cap_{i=1}^{d} F_i\right) = 1 - \mathbf{P}\left(\cup_{i=1}^{d} F_i^c\right) \\ &\overset{(a)}{=} 1 - \sum_{i=1}^{d} \mathbf{P}\left(F_i^c\right) \overset{(b)}{=} 1 - d\mathbf{P}\left(F_1^c\right). \end{aligned} \tag{4.3}$$

Above, (a) follows because events $F_1^c, \ldots, F_d^c$ are disjoint and (b) from symmetry. Therefore, the probability of correct detection boils down to evaluating $\mathbf{P}(E_1^c)$ and $\mathbf{P}(F_1^c)$ which, as we shall see, will coincide with each other as $t \to \infty$ (equivalently, $n(t) \to \infty$). Therefore, the bounds of (4.2) and (4.3) will provide the exact evaluation of the correct detection probability as $t \to \infty$.

4.1.3 $\mathbf{P}(E_1^c)$, $\mathbf{P}(F_1^c)$ and Polya's urn

Effectively, the interest is in the ratio $T_1(t)/(\sum_{i=1}^{d} T_i(t))$ especially as $t \to \infty$ (implicitly we are assuming that this ratio is well defined for a given t or else by definition there is only one node infected which will be v_1, the true source). It can be easily verified that as $t \to \infty$, $T_i(t) \to \infty$ for all i almost surely and hence $Z_i(t) = (d-2)T_i(t) + 1$ goes to ∞ as well. Therefore, it is sufficient to study the ratio $Z_1(t)/(\sum_{j=1}^{d} Z_j(t))$ as $t \to \infty$ since we shall find that this ratio converges to a random variable with density on $[0,1]$. In summary, if we establish that the ratio $Z_1(t)/(\sum_{j=1}^{d} Z_j(t))$ converges in distribution on $[0,1]$ with a well defined density, then it immediately follows that $\mathbf{P}(E_1^c) = \mathbf{P}(F_1^c)$ as $t \to \infty$ and we can use $Z_1(t)/(\sum_{j=1}^{d} Z_j(t))$ in place of $T_1(t)/(\sum_{j=1}^{d} T_j(t))$ to evaluate $\mathbf{P}(E_1^c)$ as $t \to \infty$.

With these in mind, let us study the ratio $Z_1(t)/(\sum_{j=1}^{d} Z_j(t))$. For this, it is instructive to view the simultaneous evolution of $(Z_1(t), Z_{\neq 1}(t))$ ($Z_{\neq 1}(t) \triangleq \sum_{j=2}^{d} Z_j(t)$) as that induced by the standard, discrete time, Polya's urn: initially, $\tau_0 = 0$ and there is one ball of type 1 representing $Z_1(\tau_0) = 1$ and $d-1$ balls of type 2 representing $Z_{\neq 1}(\tau_0) = d-1$ in a given *urn*; the nth event happens at time τ_n when one of the $Z_1(\tau_{n-1}) + Z_{\neq 1}(\tau_{n-1})$ ($= d + (n-1)(d-2)$) balls chosen uniformly at random is thrown out of the urn and new $d-2$ balls of its type are added to the urn. If we set $\tau_n - \tau_{n-1}$ equal to an exponential random variable with mean $1/(\lambda(d + (n-1)(d-2)))$, then it is easy to check that the fraction of balls of type 1 is identical in law to that of $Z_1(t)/(\sum_{j=1}^{d} Z_j(t))$ (here we are using the *memoryless* property of exponential random variables crucially). Therefore, for our purposes, it is sufficient to study the limit law of fraction of balls of type 1 under this Polya's urn model.

It is well understood that the fraction of balls of type 1 at time τ_n, which is equal to $Z_1(\tau_n)/(Z_1(\tau_n) + Z_{\neq 1}(\tau_n))$, is a martingale with value in $[0, 1]$. By the standard martingale convergence theorem, it converges to a well defined random variable almost surely. Further, the law of this limiting random variable in our particular case turns out to be the Beta distribution with parameters $a = 1/(d-2)$ and $b = (d-1)/(d-2)$. (See chapter on generalized Polya's urn in [1], for example, for proof details of this statement; a more general version of this result will be utilized later in the context of general random trees).

From the above discussion, we conclude that the ratio $Z_1(t)/(\sum_{i=1}^{d} Z_i(t))$ converges to a Beta random variable with parameters $a = 1/(d-2)$ and $b = (d-1)/(d-2)$. Since the Beta distribution has density on $[0, 1]$, from the above discussion it follows that as $t \to \infty$ (equivalently, $n(t) \to \infty$), $\mathbf{P}(E_1^c) = \mathbf{P}(F_1^c)$ and hence from (4.2), (4.3)

$$\lim_{t\to\infty} \mathbf{P}\Big(C^1_{n(t)}\Big) = 1 - d\Big(1 - I_{1/2}\Big(\frac{1}{d-2}, 1 + \frac{1}{d-2}\Big)\Big), \quad (4.4)$$

where recall that $I_{1/2}(a, b)$ is the probability that a Beta random variable with parameters a and b takes value in $[0, 1/2]$. Note that this establishes the result of Theorem 3.1 for $k = 1$ in (3.2).

4.1.4 *Probability of* $C^k_{n(t)}$

Thus far we have established Theorem 3.1 for $k = 1$, the probability of the rumor center being the true source. The probability of the event $C^k_{n(t)}$ (the kth infected node being the rumor center) is evaluated in an almost identical manner with a minor difference. For this reason, we present an abridged version of the proof.

Let $v_k, k \geq 2$ be the kth infected node when the rumor starts from v_1. We will evaluate the probability of identifying v_k as the rumor center. As before, let us suppose we observe the infected tree G at time t with $n(t) \geq k$ nodes. Let $w_1, \ldots, w_d$ be the d neighbors of v_k with respect to $\mathcal{G}$. Note that one of the neighbors of v_k is infected before it. Equivalently, viewing the tree being rooted at v_1, this neighbor is the 'parent' of v_k. We shall denote it by w_1 and let $w_2, \ldots, w_d$ be the $d-1$ 'children' of v_k. Let $T_i^k(t)$ be the subtrees of G rooted at w_i if we imagine v_k as the root of G: therefore, $T_1^k(t)$ is rooted at w_1 and includes $v_1, \ldots, v_{k-1}$; $T_i^k(t)$ are rooted at w_i for $2 \leq i \leq d$ and contain nodes in G that are away from v_k; none of the $T_i^k(t)$ for $1 \leq i \leq d$ include v_k. By definition $T_1^k(t)$ is never empty, but $T_i^k(t)$ can be empty if w_i is not infected, for $2 \leq i \leq d$. As before, with abuse of notation, we shall denote $T_i^k(t)$ as the size of the subtree as well. As per Lemma 1, v_k is identified as a rumor center if and only if all of its d subtrees are balanced, i.e.

$$2T_i^k(t) \leq \sum_{j=1}^{d} T_j^k(t), \ \forall\, 1 \leq i \leq d. \quad (4.5)$$

Therefore, as before,

$$\begin{aligned}\mathbf{P}\Big(C^k_{n(t)}\Big) \geq \mathbf{P}\Big(\cap_{i=1}^{d} E_i\Big) &= 1 - \mathbf{P}\Big(\cup_{i=1}^{d} E_i^c\Big)\\ &\geq 1 - \sum_{i=1}^{d} \mathbf{P}\Big(E_i^c\Big),\end{aligned} \quad (4.6)$$

and

$$\begin{aligned}\mathbf{P}\Big(C^k_{n(t)}\Big) \leq \mathbf{P}\Big(\cap_{i=1}^{d} F_i\Big) &= 1 - \mathbf{P}\Big(\cup_{i=1}^{d} F_i^c\Big)\\ &= 1 - \sum_{i=1}^{d} \mathbf{P}\Big(F_i^c\Big).\end{aligned} \quad (4.7)$$

Above, $E_i = \{2T_i^k(t) < \sum_{j=1}^{d} T_j^k(t)\}$ and $F_i = \{2T_i^k(t) \leq \sum_{j=1}^{d} T_j^k(t)\}$.

To evaluate these probabilities, as before, we shall study the evolution of the rumor boundaries in each tree. Unlike the earlier situation where all events had the same probability, we need to be a bit careful for $k \geq 2$. Specifically, note that the time when the kth node, v_k gets infected, the tree $T_1^k(\cdot)$ has size $k-1$ and it's rumor boundary, $Z_1^k(\cdot)$, is of size $(d-2)(k-1)+1$. But for $2 \leq i \leq d$, $T_i^k(\cdot)$ is empty and has its rumor boundary, $Z_i^k(\cdot)$, of size 1. Beyond this difference in initial values, the evolution is the same as before and therefore the limiting laws of the ratios of the sizes of rumor boundaries can be evaluated as before as the limit of the fraction of balls of a given type in a Polya's urn model with different initial number of balls of two types. Specifically, to evaluate E_1^c (and F_1^c), we consider a Polya's urn in which we start with $(d-2)(k-1)+1$ balls of type 1 (corresponding to $Z_1^k(\cdot)$) and $d-1$ balls of type 2 (corresponding to $\sum_{j=2}^{d} Z_j^k(\cdot)$). With these initial conditions, the limit law of fraction of balls of type 1 turns out to be (see [1] for details) a Beta distribution with parameters $a = ((d-2)(k-1)+1)/(d-2) = (k-1) + 1/(d-2)$ and $b = (d-1)/(d-2) = 1 + 1/(d-2)$. In summary, the fraction of balls of type 1 equals the ratio $Z_1^k(t)/(\sum_{j=1}^{k} Z_j^k(t))$ which is equal to the ratio of $T_1^k(t)/(\sum_{j=1}^{d} T_j^k(t))$ as $t \to \infty$, since these quantities go to infinity as $t \to \infty$ and $Z_i^k(t)$ is linearly related to $T_i^k(t)$ for $1 \leq i \leq d$. Since the limit law of the fraction of balls of type 1 has density on $[0, 1]$, we conclude that as $t \to \infty$

$$\mathbf{P}\Big(E_1^c\Big) = \mathbf{P}\Big(F_1^c\Big) = 1 - I_{1/2}\Big(k - 1 + \frac{1}{d-2}, 1 + \frac{1}{d-2}\Big). \quad (4.8)$$

To evaluate E_i^c (and F_i^c) for $2 \leq i \leq d$, in the corresponding Polya's urn model, we start with 1 ball of type 1 and $k(d-2)+1$ balls of type 2. Therefore, using an identical sequence of arguments, we obtain that for $2 \leq i \leq d$ as $t \to \infty$,

$$\mathbf{P}\Big(E_i^c\Big) = \mathbf{P}\Big(F_i^c\Big) = 1 - I_{1/2}\Big(\frac{1}{d-2}, k + \frac{1}{d-2}\Big). \quad (4.9)$$

From (4.6)-(4.9), it follows that

$$\begin{aligned}\lim_{t\to\infty} \mathbf{P}\Big(C^k_{n(t)}\Big) =& I_{1/2}\Big(k - 1 + \frac{1}{d-2}, 1 + \frac{1}{d-2}\Big)\\ &+ (d-1)\Big(I_{1/2}\Big(\frac{1}{d-2}, k + \frac{1}{d-2}\Big) - 1\Big).\end{aligned} \quad (4.10)$$

This establishes (3.2) for all k and hence completes the proof of Theorem 3.1.

4.2 Proof of Corollary 1

Simple analysis yields Corollary 1. We start by defining the asymptotic probability for a d-regular tree as $\lim_{t\to\infty} \mathbf{P}\left(C^1_{n(t)}\right) = \alpha_d$. This quantity then becomes

$$\begin{aligned}\alpha_d =& d\left(I_{1/2}\left(\frac{1}{d-2}, 1 + \frac{1}{d-2}\right)\right) - d + 1\\ =& 1 - d\frac{\Gamma(1 + \frac{2}{d-2})}{\Gamma(\frac{1}{d-2})\Gamma(1 + \frac{1}{d-2})} \int_{\frac{1}{2}}^{1} t^{\frac{1}{d-2}-1}(1-t)^{\frac{1}{d-2}} dt\end{aligned}$$

We then take the limit as d approaches infinity.

$$\lim_{d\to\infty} \alpha_d = \lim_{d\to\infty} 1 - d\frac{\Gamma(1+\frac{2}{d-2})}{\Gamma(\frac{1}{d-2})\Gamma(1+\frac{1}{d-2})}\int_{\frac{1}{2}}^{1} t^{\frac{1}{d-2}-1}(1-t)^{\frac{1}{d-2}}dt$$
$$=1-\lim_{d\to\infty}\frac{d\Gamma(1+\frac{2}{d-2})}{(d-2-\gamma+O(d^{-1}))\,\Gamma(1+\frac{1}{d-2})}$$
$$\int_{\frac{1}{2}}^{1} t^{\frac{1}{d-2}}(1-t)^{\frac{1}{d-2}}\,dt$$
$$=1-\int_{\frac{1}{2}}^{1} t^{-1}dt = 1-\ln(2)$$

Above, γ is the Euler-Mascheroni constant and we have used the following approximation for $\Gamma(x)$ for small x: $\Gamma(x) = x^{-1} - \gamma + O(x)$.

4.3 Proof of Corollary 2

Corollary 2 follows from (3.2) and monotonicity of the Γ function over $[1, \infty)$ as follows: for $k \geq 2$,

$$\lim_{t\to\infty} \mathbf{P}\left(C^k_{n(t)}\right) \leq I_{1/2}\left(k-1+\frac{1}{d-2}, 1+\frac{1}{d-2}\right)$$
$$=\frac{\Gamma(k+\frac{2}{d-2})}{\Gamma(k-1+\frac{1}{d-2})\Gamma(1+\frac{1}{d-2})}$$
$$\int_0^{\frac{1}{2}} t^{k+\frac{1}{d-2}-2}(1-t)^{\frac{1}{d-2}}dt$$
$$\stackrel{(a)}{\leq}\frac{\Gamma(k+\frac{2}{d-2})}{\Gamma(k-1+\frac{1}{d-2})\Gamma(1+\frac{1}{d-2})}\int_0^{\frac{1}{2}} t^{k-2}dt$$
$$\stackrel{(b)}{\leq}\frac{4e^2\Gamma(k+2)}{\Gamma(k-1)\Gamma(1)}\int_0^{\frac{1}{2}} t^{k-2}dt$$
$$\leq\frac{4e^2 k(k+1)}{k-1}\left(\frac{1}{2}\right)^{k-1}$$
$$=\exp\Big(-k\ln 2+\varepsilon(k)\Big) = \exp\big(-\Theta(k)\big),$$

where $\varepsilon(k) = \Theta(\log k)$. In above (a) follows from the fact that $t < 1$ and hence $t^{k-2+1/(d-2)} \leq t^{k-2}$. For (b), we need to use property of the Γ function carefully. It is well known that Γ achieves minimum value in $[1, 2]$, $\Gamma(1) = \Gamma(2) = 1$, and $\Gamma(x)$ increases for $x \geq 2$. Now the minimum value of Γ function is at least $1/(2e)$. Since $d \geq 3$, $1 + 1/(d-2) \in [1, 2]$. Therefore, $\Gamma(1+1/(d-2)) \leq \Gamma(1)/(2e)$. Similarly, $\Gamma(k-1+1/(d-2)) \geq \Gamma(k-1)/(2e)$ for all $k \geq 2$ and $d \geq 3$. Therefore, (b) follows.

4.4 Proof of Theorem 3.2: correct detection for random trees

The goal is to establish that there is a strictly positive probability of detecting the source correctly as the rumor center when the rumor starts at the root of a generic randomly generated tree: this is with respect to the joint probability distribution induced by the tree construction and the SI rumor spreading model with independent spreading times with distribution $F(t)$. We establish this result along the lines of the proof for Theorem 3.1. However, it requires additional details due to the irregularity and randomness in the node degrees in the tree and the arbitrary spreading time distribution $F(t)$.

4.4.1 Notations

We quickly recall some notations. To start with, as before let v_1 be the root node of the tree. It has η_0 children distributed as per $\mathcal{D}_0$. By assumption of Theorem 3.2, $\mathbf{P}(\eta_0 \geq 3) > 0$. We shall condition on this positive probability event that $\eta_0 \geq 3$ and let $d = \eta_0$ for the remainder of the proof. Let $u_1, \ldots, u_d$ be the d children of v_1. The random tree $\mathcal{G}$ is constructed by adding a random number of children to $u_1, \ldots, u_d$ recursively as per distribution $\mathcal{D}$ as explained in Section 3.2. The rumor starts at v_1 at time 0 and spreads as per SI model on $\mathcal{G}$ with spreading times whose cumulative density function $F: \mathbb{R} \to [0, 1]$ is such that $F(0) = 0$, $F(0^+) = 0$ and $\lim_{t\to\infty} F(t) = 1$.

Let G be the sub-tree of $\mathcal{G}$ that is infected at time t, let $n(t)$ be the number of nodes in G at time t, and let $T_i(t)$ denote the subtree of G rooted at node u_i at time t, for $1 \leq i \leq d$. We shall abuse notation as before by using $T_i(t)$ as the subtree size as well. By definition $T_i(0) = 0$ for $1 \leq i \leq d$. Let $Z_i(t)$ denote the size of the rumor boundary of $T_i(t)$; initially $Z_i(0) = 1$.

Since we are interested in evaluating the probability of detection with respect to the joint distribution over the tree generation and SI spreading model, we model the evolution of $Z_i(\cdot)$ and $T_i(\cdot)$ as follows. Each node in the rumor boundary has its own independent clock with distribution $F(t)$. When the clock of a particular node ticks, it dies and it is replaced by η new nodes where η is an independent random variable distributed as per $\mathcal{D}$. If the node that died belonged to $Z_i(\cdot)$ (i.e. tree $T_i(\cdot)$), then the new nodes are added to $Z_i(\cdot)$. Therefore, each $Z_i(\cdot)$ is a general time branching process with $Z_i(0) = 1$ for all $1 \leq i \leq d$. Now we recall some facts about branching processes that will be useful for establishing the non-triviality of the probability of correct detection for such randomly generated trees.

First we define what is known as the Malthusian parameter for the branching process.

Definition 4. *[1, pp. 146] The Malthusian parameter for a constant γ and a distribution F is the root, provided it exists, of the equation*

$$\gamma\int_0^\infty e^{-\alpha y}dF(y) = 1. \qquad (4.11)$$

We denote it by $\alpha = \alpha(\gamma, F)$.

For any $\gamma > 1$ the Malthusian parameter always exists. The Malthusian parameter characterizes the growth rate of a general time branching process. Consider for example a Markov branching process with exponential spreading times of rate λ and let $\mathbf{E}[\eta] = m > 1$. The spreading time distribution is $F(t) = 1 - e^{-\lambda t}$ Then the Malthusian parameter for this process $\alpha(m, F)$ is given by

$$m\int_0^\infty e^{-\alpha y}\lambda e^{-\lambda y}dy = 1$$
$$m\frac{\lambda}{\alpha+\lambda} = 1$$
$$\lambda(m-1) = \alpha.$$

This is exactly the growth rate for the mean of a Markov branching process [1]. The Malthusian parameter also describes the growth of the mean of general time branching processes, as the following theorem shows.

Theorem 4.1. *[1, Theorem 3A, pp. 152] Let $Z(\cdot)$ be a continuous time branching process as described above: $Z(0) = 1$; each node in $Z(t)$ has an independent clock with distribution whose CDF is F as described above, and it dies upon the tick of the clock; upon death of a node, it is replaced by η new nodes chosen independently for each node, and so on. If $\mathbf{E}[\eta] = m > 1$ then as $t \to \infty$,*

$$\lim_{t\to\infty}\frac{\mathbf{E}\left[Z(t)\right]}{c'e^{\alpha t}} = 1,$$

where α is the Malthusian parameter for (m, F) and

$$c' = \frac{m-1}{\alpha m^2 \int_0^\infty y e^{-\alpha y} dF(y)}.$$

This theorem says that the mean of the branching process $Z(t)$ has exponential growth with rate given by the Malthusian parameter $\alpha(m, F)$. As an example of this general theorem, consider again the Markov branching process with exponential spreading times with rate λ. Then we have already seen that the Malthusian parameter $\alpha = \lambda(\mathbf{E}[\eta] - 1)$. The constant c' evaluates to

$$\begin{aligned} c' &= \frac{m-1}{\alpha m^2 \int_0^\infty y e^{-\alpha y} \lambda e^{-\lambda y} dy} \\ &= \frac{(m-1)(\alpha+\lambda)^2}{\lambda \alpha m^2} \\ &= \frac{(m-1)(\lambda(m-1)+\lambda)^2}{\lambda^2(m-1)m^2} \\ &= \frac{(m-1)\lambda^2 m^2}{\lambda^2(m-1)m^2} = 1 \end{aligned}$$

Therefore, we have that for the Markov branching process, $\mathbf{E}[Z(t)] = e^{\lambda(\mathbf{E}[\eta]-1)}$, a well known result [1]. For the general time branching process, we have the following result.

Theorem 4.2. *[1, Theorem 2, pp. 172] Let $Z(\cdot)$ be a continuous time branching process as described above: $Z(0) = 1$; each node in $Z(t)$ has an independent clock with distribution whose CDF is given by F and it dies upon the tick of the clock; upon death of a node, it is replaced by η new nodes chosen independently for each node, and so on. Let α be the Malthusian parameter for $(\mathbf{E}[\eta], F)$ and c' be defined as in Theorem 4.1. If $\mathbf{E}[\eta] > 1$ and $\mathbf{E}[\eta \log \eta] < \infty$, then*

$$Z(t)/c' e^{\alpha t} \to W, \qquad \textit{in distribution},$$

where W is such that

$$\mathbf{P}(W = 0) = q, \tag{4.12}$$

$$\mathbf{P}(W \in (x_1, x_2)) = \int_{x_1}^{x_2} w(y) dy, \quad \textit{for} \quad 0 < x_1 < x_2 < \infty, \tag{4.13}$$

where $q \in (0,1)$ is the smallest root of the equation $f_\eta(s) = s$ in $[0,1]$ and $w(\cdot)$ is absolutely continuous with respect to the Lebesgue measure so that $\int_0^\infty w(y)dy = 1 - q$. Here $f_\eta(s) = \sum_{k=0}^\infty s^k \mathbf{P}(\eta = k)$.

As we will see, this theorem will be key to proving Theorem 3.2.

4.4.2 Correct detection

Recall from the proof for regular trees, the probability of the event of correct detection at time t, $C^1_{n(t)}$, is lower bounded as

$$\mathbf{P}\Big(C^1_{n(t)}\Big) \geq \mathbf{P}\Big(\cap_{i=1}^d \Big\{2T_i(t) < \sum_{j=1}^d T_j(t)\Big\}\Big). \tag{4.14}$$

We shall establish a non-trivial lower bound for the right hand side of (4.14) using Theorem 4.2. This will be done in the two steps: (i) identify an event $\mathcal{E} \subset \cap_{i=1}^d \Big\{2Z_i(t) < \sum_{j=1}^d Z_j(t)\Big\}$ and then establish a non-trivial lower bound on $\mathcal{E}$ using Theorem 4.2; (ii) establish that as $t \to \infty$, $\mathcal{E} \subset \cap_{i=1}^d \Big\{2T_i(t) < \sum_{j=1}^d T_j(t)\Big\}$. This will immediately imply that $\mathbf{P}(\mathcal{E})$ is a non-trivial lower bound on $\mathbf{P}\Big(C^1_{n(t)}\Big)$.

4.4.3 A non-trivial event

The event $2Z_i(t) < \sum_{j=1}^d Z_j(t)$ is equivalent to $\frac{Z_i(t)c'^{-1}e^{-\alpha t}}{\sum_{j=1}^d Z_j(t)c'^{-1}e^{-\alpha t}} < 1/2$, with the Malthusian parameter α and c' defined as in Theorem 4.1. For any $x > 0$, define event $\mathcal{E}(x)$ as

$$\mathcal{E}(x) = \cap_{i=1}^d \Big\{Z_i(t)c'^{-1}e^{-\alpha t} \in (x, (d-1)x)\Big\}. \tag{4.15}$$

Under event $\mathcal{E}(x)$, since each $Z_i(t)c'^{-1}e^{-\alpha t}$ is at least x and at most $(d-1)x$, it follows immediately that

$$\begin{aligned} \mathcal{E}(x) &\subset \Big\{2 \max_{i=1}^d Z_i(t) < \sum_{j=1}^d Z_j(t)\Big\} \\ &\subset \cap_{i=1}^d \Big\{2Z_i(t) < \sum_{j=1}^d Z_j(t)\Big\}. \end{aligned} \tag{4.16}$$

Now $Z_i(\cdot)$ are independent across $1 \leq i \leq d$. By Theorem 4.2 it follows that $Z_i(t)c'^{-1}e^{-\alpha t}$ converges to W_i (because $\mathbf{E}[\eta^2] < \infty$ and hence $\mathbf{E}[\eta \log \eta] < \infty$) which are independent across i and W_i are distributed as per (4.12)-(4.13). From this it follows that as $t \to \infty$,

$$\mathbf{P}\Big(\mathcal{E}(x)\Big) = p(x)^d, \qquad \text{where} \quad p(x) \triangleq \int_x^{(d-1)x} w(y)dy > 0. \tag{4.17}$$

From the above discussion, it follows that as $t \to \infty$

$$\mathbf{P}\Big(\cap_{i=1}^d \Big\{2Z_i(t) < \sum_{j=1}^d Z_j(t)\Big\}\Big) \geq \Big(\sup_{x>0} p(x)\Big)^d > 0. \tag{4.18}$$

4.4.4 Equivalence of boundary and tree processes

For regular trees, the fractions $Z_i(t)/(\sum_{j=1}^d Z_j(t))$ and $T_i(t)/(\sum_{j=1}^d T_j(t))$ converge to the same limit primarily because each of them converge to ∞ and $Z_i(t)$ and $T_i(t)$ are related linearly. Such a relation does not exist for the random tree. However, with an additional, careful argument we shall establish the same fact for random trees as well under the event $\mathcal{E}(x)$ for $x > 0$.

To that end, for $1 \leq i \leq d$ and $n \geq 0$, define

$$M^i_{n+1} = M^i_n + Q^i_{n+1}(\eta_{n+1} - \mu), \tag{4.19}$$

where Q^i_{n+1} is the probability that the $n+1$ rumor infected node is added to the tree $T_i(\cdot)$, η_{n+1} is the number of children of this infected node, and $\mu = \mathbf{E}[\eta]$. We define $M^i_0 = 0$. It can be checked that M^i_n is a martingale with respect to the filtration $\mathcal{F}_n$, where $\mathcal{F}_n$ contains all the information about the part of the graph $\mathcal{G}$ to which the rumor has spread including the rumor boundary. Now M^i_n is a martingale with respect to $\mathcal{F}_n$ because, (a) Q^i_{n+1} is a binary random variable with its probability of being 1 determined by $\mathcal{F}_n$, and (b) η_{n+1} is independent of $\mathcal{F}_n$ and distributed as per $\mathcal{D}$. Now $|M^i_{n+1} - M^i_n| \leq \eta_{n+1}$ and η_{n+1} has a well defined mean and finite second moment. By the property of the martingale, therefore it follows that

$$\mathbf{E}[(M^i_n)^2] \leq n\mathbf{E}[\eta^2].$$

Therefore, a straightforward application of Chebychev's inequality will lead to the following 'weak law of large numbers':

$$\frac{1}{n} M^i_n \to \mathbf{E}[M^i_0] = 0, \qquad \text{in probability}. \tag{4.20}$$

Now under event $\mathcal{E}(x)$ (for any $x > 0$), $Z_i(t)$ scales like $e^{\alpha t}$ for all $1 \leq i \leq d$. Therefore, it can be checked that $T_i(t)$ also scales like

$e^{\alpha t}$ (since $Z_i(t)$ represents the 'rate' at which $T_i(t)$ is growing). Precisely, we have that

$$\mathbf{E}[Z_i(t)] = 1 + \mathbf{E}\left[\sum_{l \in T_i(t)} \eta_l\right] = 1 + \mu \mathbf{E}[T_i(t)]$$

Now using Theorem 4.1, we have that

$$\lim_{t\to\infty} \frac{\mathbf{E}[T_i(t)]}{c' e^{\alpha t}} = \frac{1}{\mu} \lim_{t\to\infty} \frac{\mathbf{E}[Z_i(t)]}{c' e^{\alpha t}} - \frac{1}{c' e^{\alpha t}} = \frac{1}{\mu}$$

Therefore, we see that the means of both $Z_i(t)$ and $T_i(t)$ grow as $e^{\alpha t}$.

Since d is finite, it further follows that $n(t)$, the number of rumor infected nodes till time t, or equivalently $\sum_{i=1}^{d} T_i(t)$ scales like $e^{\alpha t}$. Using these facts under event $\mathcal{E}(x)$ and an application of (4.20) with n replaced by $n(t)$ (and taking $t \to \infty$ or equivalently $n(t) \to \infty$), we obtain that for $1 \le i \le d$ as $t \to \infty$,

$$\frac{T_i(t)}{n(t)}\Big(\frac{1}{T_i(t)} M^i_{n(t)}\Big) \to 0. \tag{4.21}$$

Since under event $\mathcal{E}(x)$, $T_i(t)/n(t)$ remains bounded away from 0 as $t \to \infty$, from (4.21), it follows that

$$\frac{1}{T_i(t)} M^i_{n(t)} \to 0. \tag{4.22}$$

But

$$M^i_{n(t)} = \sum_{j \in T_i(t)} (\eta_j - \mu) = T_i(t)\Big(\frac{1}{T_i(t)} \sum_{j \in T_i(t)} \eta_j - \mu\Big). \tag{4.23}$$

From (4.22) and (4.23), it follows that under event $\mathcal{E}(x)$, $x > 0$ for $1 \le i \le d$, as $t \to \infty$,

$$\frac{1}{T_i(t)} \sum_{j \in T_i(t)} \eta_j \to \mu. \tag{4.24}$$

Now we are ready to conclude the proof of Theorem 3.2 by establishing that under the event $\mathcal{E}(x)$, $x > 0$, $Z_i(t)/(\sum_{j=1}^{d} Z_j(t))$ and $T_i(t)/(\sum_{j=1}^{d} T_j(t))$ converge to the same quantity. To that end, observe that for $1 \le i \le d$,

$$\frac{Z_i(t)}{\sum_{j=1}^{d} Z_j(t)} = \frac{1 + \sum_{\ell \in T_i(t)} \eta_\ell}{d + \sum_{\ell'=1}^{n(t)} \eta_{\ell'}} = \frac{T_i(t)}{n(t)} \frac{\frac{1}{T_i(t)} + \frac{1}{T_i(t)}\Big(\sum_{\ell \in T_i(t)} \eta_\ell\Big)}{\frac{d}{n(t)} + \frac{1}{n(t)}\Big(\sum_{\ell'=1}^{n(t)} \eta_{\ell'}\Big)}. \tag{4.25}$$

Now as $t \to \infty$, under the event $\mathcal{E}(x)$, $x > 0$, the right most term in (4.25) goes to 1 since the numerator and denominator both go to μ due to $T_i(t), n(t) \to \infty$ and (4.24) (with its application to all the subtrees). This concludes that under event $\mathcal{E}(x)$, the ratio $Z_i(t)/(\sum_{j=1}^{d} Z_j(t))$ and $T_i(t)/(\sum_{j=1}^{d} T_j(t))$ are asymptotically equal as $t \to \infty$. Therefore, from (4.18) and the fact that the initial conditioned event $\mathbf{P}(\eta_0 \ge 3)$ has strictly positive probability, it follows that

$$\liminf_{t\to\infty} \mathbf{P}(C^1_{n(t)}) > 0.$$

This concludes the proof of Theorem 3.2.

4.5 Proof of Theorem 3.3

To obtain the upper bound in Theorem 3.3 for $\lim_{t\to\infty} \mathbf{P}\left(C^k_{n(t)}\right)$ we assume that after time t at least k nodes have been infected ($n(t) \ge k$), with the kth infected node being defined as v_k which has degree d. The number of children of v_k is $\eta_k = d - 1 \ge 2$. $C^k_{n(t)}$ is the event that v_k is the rumor center after time t. To upper bound the probability of this event, we will use the memoryless property of the exponential spreading times crucially. There are d subtrees neighboring v_k. We define the time when v_k is infected as $t_k < t$. We define the size of the rumor boundary at t_k as $Z(t_k)$ which consists of all uninfected nodes neighboring infected nodes. We have that $Z(t_k) = 1 + \sum_{i=1}^{k} (\eta_i - 1)$. Because of the memoryless property of the exponential spreading times and the way in which the random tree is constructed, at time t_k each node in the rumor boundary is an independent copy of identically distributed subtree random processes which we will refer to as $X_j(t)$, for $1 \le j \le Z(t_k)$ in the rumor boundary.

We now use the notation from Section 4.1.4 for the subtree processes. Specifically, let us imagine the node v_k as the global root and with respect to it, let $T^k_1(t)$ denoted the size of the subtree rooted at v_{k-1} at time t. Let $T^k_i(t)$ for $i = 2, ..., d$ be the other subtrees rooted at the children of v_k (which were not infected at time t_k but were only part of the rumor boundary). Then, we have that $T^k_1(t_k) = k - 1$ and $T^k_i(t_k) = 0$ for $2 \le i \le d$. In $T^k_1(t_k)$, there are $Z(t_k) - \eta_k$ nodes on the rumor boundary, each of which will be the source for i.i.d. subtree process $X_j(t)$, $1 \le j \le Z(t_k) - \eta_k$ starting at $t = t_k$. Therefore,

$$T^k_1(t) = k - 1 + \sum_{j=1}^{Z(t_k)-\eta_k} X_j(t) \tag{4.26}$$

Now, we will upper bound $\mathbf{P}\left(C^k_{n(t)}\right)$ as follows.

$$\begin{aligned}
\mathbf{P}\left(C^k_{n(t)}\right) &\le \mathbf{P}\left(\cap_{i=1}^{d}\Big\{2T^k_i(t) \le \sum_{j=1}^{d} T^k_j(t)\Big\}\right) \\
&\le \mathbf{P}\left(T^k_1(t) \le \sum_{j=2}^{d-1} T^k_j(t)\right) \\
&\le \mathbf{P}\left(k - 1 + \sum_{i=1}^{Z(t_k)-\eta_k} X_i(t) \le \sum_{j=Z(t_k)-\eta_k+1}^{Z(t_k)} X_j(t)\right) \\
&\le \mathbf{P}\left(\sum_{i=1}^{Z(t_k)-\eta_k} X_i(t) \le \sum_{j=Z(t_k)-\eta_k+1}^{Z(t_k)} X_j(t)\right)
\end{aligned}$$

By the condition of Theorem 3.3, we have that $Z(t_k) \ge (ck+1)\eta_k$ for some $c > 1$. Define $X'_i(t) = \sum_{j=(i-1)\eta_k+1}^{i\eta_k} X_j(t)$. Then

$$\begin{aligned}
\mathbf{P}\Big(C^k_{n(t)}\Big) &\le \mathbf{P}\left(\sum_{i=1}^{\lfloor (ck+1)\rfloor \eta_k} X_i(t) \le \sum_{j=Z(t_k)-\eta_k+1}^{Z(t_k)} X_j(t)\right) \\
&\le \mathbf{P}\left(\sum_{i=1}^{\lfloor (ck+1)\rfloor} X'_i(t) \le X'_{\lfloor (ck+1)\rfloor+1}(t)\right) \\
&\le \mathbf{P}\left(\bigcap_{i=1}^{\lfloor (ck+1)\rfloor} \{X'_i(t) \le X'_{\lfloor (ck+1)\rfloor+1}(t)\}\right) && (4.27) \\
&\le \frac{1}{\lfloor (ck+1)\rfloor + 1} \le \frac{1}{k} && (4.28)
\end{aligned}$$

Above we have used the fact that for any fixed $t > t_k$, there are in total $\lfloor (ck+1) \rfloor + 1$ independent copies of the random variables $X_i'(t)$ and the probability in equation (4.27) is the probability that one of these random variables is larger than rest, which is $\frac{1}{\lfloor (ck+1) \rfloor + 1}$ by symmetry. The above bound is independent of t, so this establishes Theorem 3.3.

4.6 Proof of Theorem 3.4: geometric trees

The proof of Theorem 3.4 uses the characterization of the rumor center provided by Lemma 1. That is, we wish to show that for all n large enough, the probability of the event that the size of the d^* rumor infected sub-trees of the source v^* are essentially 'balanced' with high enough probability. To establish this, we shall use coarse estimations on the size of each of these sub-trees using the standard concentration property of renewal processes along with geometric growth. This will be unlike the proof for regular trees where we had to necessarily delve into very fine detailed probabilistic estimates of the size of the sub-trees to establish the result. This relatively easier proof for geometric trees (despite heterogeneity) brings out the fact that it is fundamentally much more difficult to analyze expanding trees than geometric structures as expanding trees do not yield to generic concentration based estimations as they necessarily have very high variances.

To that end, we shall start by obtaining sharp estimations on the size of each of the rumor infected d^* sub-trees of v^* for any given time t. We are assuming here that the spreading times have distribution with CDF F with mean $\mu > 0$ and exponential tail (precisely, if X is random variable with F as its CDF, then $\mathbf{E}[\exp(\theta X)] < \infty$ for $\theta \in (-\varepsilon, \varepsilon)$ for some $\varepsilon > 0$). Initially, at time 0 the source node v^* has the rumor. It starts spreading along its d^* children (neighbors). Let $T_i(t)$ denote the size of the rumor infected subtree, denoted by $G_i(t)$, rooted at the ith child (or neighbor) of node v^*. Initially, $T_i(0) = 0$. The $T_i(\cdot)$ is a renewal process with time-varying rate: the rate at time t depends on the 'boundary' of the tree as discussed earlier. Due to the balanced and geometric growth conditions assumed in Theorem 3.4, the following will be satisfied: for small enough $\epsilon > 0$ (a) every node within a distance $\frac{t}{\mu}(1-\epsilon)$ of v^* is in one of the $G_i(t)$, and (b) no node beyond distance $\frac{t}{\mu}(1+\epsilon)$ of v^* is in any of the $G_i(t)$. Such a tight characterization of the 'shape' of $G_i(t)$ along with the polynomial growth will provide sharp enough bound on $T_i(t)$ that will result in establishing Theorem 3.4. This result is summarized below with its proof omitted due to space constraints.

Proposition 1. *Consider a geometric tree with parameters $\alpha > 0$ and $0 < b \leq c$ as assumed in Theorem 3.4 and let the rumor spread from source v^* starting at time 0 as per the SI model with spreading time distribution whose cumulative density function is F such that the mean is μ and $\mathbf{E}[\exp(\theta X)] < \infty$ for $\theta \in (-\varepsilon, \varepsilon)$ for some $\varepsilon > 0$ where X is distributed as per F. Define $\epsilon = t^{-1/2+\delta}$ for any small $0 < \delta < 1/2$. Let $G(t)$ be the set of all rumor infected nodes in the tree at time t. Let $\mathcal{G}_t$ be the set of all sub-trees rooted at v^* (rumor graphs) such that all nodes within distance $\frac{t}{\mu}(1-\epsilon)$ from v^* are in the tree and no node beyond distance $\frac{t}{\mu}(1+\epsilon)$ from v^* is in the tree. Then*

$$\mathbf{P}(G_t \in \mathcal{G}_t) = 1 - O\left(e^{-t^{\delta}}\right) \xrightarrow{t \to \infty} 1.$$

Define $\mathcal{E}_t$ as the event that $G_t \in \mathcal{G}_t$. Under event $\mathcal{E}_t$, consider the sizes of the sub-trees $T_i(t)$ for $1 \leq i \leq d_{v^*}$. Due to the polynomial growth condition and $\mathcal{E}_t$, we obtain the following bounds on each $T_i(t)$ for all $1 \leq i \leq d_{v^*}$:

$$\sum_{r=1}^{\frac{t}{\mu}(1-\epsilon)-1} br^{\alpha} \leq T_i(t) \leq \sum_{r=1}^{\frac{t}{\mu}(1+\epsilon)-1} cr^{\alpha}.$$

Now bounding the summations by Riemann's integrals, we have

$$\int_0^{L-1} r^{\alpha} dr \leq \sum_{r=1}^{L} r^{\alpha} \leq \int_0^{L+1} r^{\alpha} dr.$$

Therefore, it follows that under event $\mathcal{E}_t$, for all $1 \leq i \leq d_{v^*}$

$$\frac{b}{1+\alpha}\left(\frac{t}{\mu}(1-\epsilon) - 2\right)^{\alpha+1} \leq T_i(t) \leq \frac{c}{1+\alpha}\left(\frac{t}{\mu}(1+\epsilon)\right)^{\alpha+1}.$$

In the most 'unbalanced' situation, $d_{v^*} - 1$ of these sub-trees have minimal size $T_{\text{min}}(t)$ and the remaining one sub-tree has size $T_{\text{max}}(t)$ where

$$T_{\text{min}}(t) = \frac{b}{1+\alpha}\left(\frac{t}{\mu}(1-\epsilon) - 2\right)^{\alpha+1},$$

$$T_{\text{max}}(t) = \frac{c}{1+\alpha}\left(\frac{t}{\mu}(1+\epsilon)\right)^{\alpha+1}.$$

Since by assumption $c < b(d_{v^*} - 1)$, there exists $\gamma > 0$ such that $(1+\gamma)c < b(d_{v^*} - 1)$. Therefore, for any choice of $\epsilon = t^{-1/2+\delta}$ for some $\delta \in (0, 1/2)$, we have

$$\begin{aligned}
\frac{(d^*-1)T_{\text{min}}(t) + 1}{T_{\text{max}}(t)} &= \frac{b(d_{v^*}-1)}{c}\left(\frac{\frac{t}{\mu} - t^{\frac{1}{2}+\delta} - 2}{\frac{t}{\mu} + t^{\frac{1}{2}+\delta}}\right)^{\alpha+1} \\
&+ \frac{1+\alpha}{c}\left(\frac{1}{\frac{t}{\mu} + t^{\frac{1}{2}+\delta}}\right)^{\alpha+1} \\
&\overset{(i)}{>} (1+\gamma)\left(\frac{1 - t^{-\frac{1}{2}+\delta}\mu - 2\mu t^{-1}}{1 + t^{-\frac{1}{2}+\delta}\mu}\right)^{\alpha+1} \\
&+ \frac{1+\alpha}{c}\left(\frac{1}{\frac{t}{\mu} + t^{\frac{1}{2}+\delta}}\right)^{\alpha+1} \\
&> 1 + \gamma > 1,
\end{aligned}$$

for t large enough since as $t \to \infty$ the first term in inequality (i) goes to 1 and the second term goes to 0. From this, it immediately follows that under event $\mathcal{E}_t$ for t large enough

$$\max_{1 \leq i \leq d_{v^*}} T_i(t) < \frac{1}{2}\left(\sum_{i=1}^{d_{v^*}} T_i(t) + 1\right).$$

Therefore, by Lemma 1 it follows that the rumor center is unique and equals v^*. We also have that $\mathcal{E}_t \subset C^1_{n(t)}$. Thus, from above and Proposition 1 we obtain

$$\lim_t \mathbf{P}(C^1_{n(t)}) \geq \lim_t \mathbf{P}(\mathcal{E}_t) = 1.$$

This completes the proof of Theorem 3.4.

5. CONCLUSION

Finding the source of a rumor in a network is an important and challenging problem. Here we characterized the performance of the rumor source estimator known as rumor centrality for generic tree graphs. Our analysis was based upon multi-type continuous time branching processes/generalized Polya's urn models. As an implication of this novel analysis method, we recovered all the previous results for regular trees [10] as a special case. We also showed that for rumor spreading on a random regular graph, the probability that the estimated source is more than k hops away from the true source decays exponentially in k. Additionally, we showed that for general random trees and hence for sparse random graphs like Erdos-Renyi graph, there is a strictly positive probability of correct rumor source detection. In summary, we have established the universality of rumor centrality as a source estimator across a variety of tree structured graphs and across variety of SI spreading time distributions.

6. ACKNOWLEDGMENTS

We would like to acknowledge the support of the AFOSR Complex Networks Project, MURI on Tomography of Social Networks and the MIT-Shell Graduate Student Fellowship.

7. REFERENCES

[1] K. B. Athreya and P. E. Ney. *Branching Processes*. Springer-Verlag, 1972.

[2] G. Brightwell and P. Winkler. Counting linear extensions is# p-complete. In *Proceedings of the twenty-third annual ACM symposium on Theory of computing*, pages 175–181. ACM, 1991.

[3] W. Evans, C. Kenyon, Y. Peres, and L. Schulman. Broadcasting on trees and the Ising model. *Ann. Appl. Prob.*, 10:410–433, 2000.

[4] A. Ganesh, L. Massoulie, and D. Towsley. The effect of network topology on the spread of epidemics. In *Proc. 24th Annual Joint Conference of the IEEE Computer and Communications Societies (INFOCOM)*, volume 2, pages 1455–1466, 2005.

[5] A. Gerschenfeld and A. Montanari. Reconstruction for models on random graphs. In *Proc. 48th IEEE Symp. Found. Comp. Sci. (FOCS)*, pages 194–204, 2007.

[6] A. Karzanov and L. Khachiyan. On the conductance of order markov chains. *Order*, 8(1):7–15, 1991.

[7] C. Moore and M. E. J. Newman. Epidemics and percolation in in small-world networks. *Phys. Rev. E*, 61:5678–5682, 2000.

[8] E. Mossel. Reconstruction on trees: Beating the second eigenvalue. *Ann. Appl. Prob.*, 11:285–300, 2001.

[9] R. Pastor-Satorras and A. Vespignani. Epidemic spreading in scale-free networks. *Phys. Rev. Lett.*, 86:3200–3203, 2001.

[10] D. Shah and T. Zaman. Finding sources of computer viruses in networks: Theory and experiment. In *Proc. ACM Sigmetrics*, volume 15, pages 5249–5262, 2010.

Learning the Graph of Epidemic Cascades

Praneeth Netrapalli
Dept. of Electrical and Computer Eng.
The University of Texas at Austin
Austin, TX-78712
praneethn@utexas.edu

Sujay Sanghavi
Dept. of Electrical and Computer Eng.
The University of Texas at Austin
Austin, TX-78712
sanghavi@mail.utexas.edu

ABSTRACT

We consider the problem of finding the graph on which an epidemic spreads, given *only* the times when each node gets infected. While this is a problem of central importance in several contexts – offline and online social networks, e-commerce, epidemiology – there has been very little work, analytical or empirical, on finding the graph. Clearly, it is impossible to do so from just one epidemic; our interest is in learning the graph from a small number of independent epidemics.

For the classic and popular "independent cascade" epidemics, we analytically establish sufficient conditions on the number of epidemics for both the global maximum-likelihood (ML) estimator, and a natural greedy algorithm to succeed with high probability. Both results are based on a key observation: the global graph learning problem decouples into n local problems – one for each node. For a node of degree d, we show that its neighborhood can be reliably found once it has been infected $O(d^2 \log n)$ times (for ML on general graphs) or $O(d \log n)$ times (for greedy on trees). We also provide a corresponding information-theoretic lower bound of $\Omega(d \log n)$; thus our bounds are essentially tight.

Furthermore, if we are given side-information in the form of a super-graph of the actual graph (as is often the case), then the number of epidemic samples required – in all cases – becomes independent of the network size n.

Categories and Subject Descriptors

G.2.2 [**Graph Theory**]: Graph algorithms; G.3 [**Probability and Statistics**]: Stochastic processes

General Terms

Epidemics, cascades, graph structure learning, theory

1. INTRODUCTION

Epidemic cascades: Initially developed as a way to study disease propagation, epidemic cascades have recently emerged as popular and useful models in a wide range of application areas. Examples include
(a) peer-to-peer networks: epidemic protocols, where users sending and receiving (pieces of) files in a random uncoordinated fashion, form the basis for many popular peer-to-peer content distribution, caching and streaming networks [9, 1].
(b) social networks: epidemic cascades provide natural models for understanding both the consumption of online media (e.g. viral videos, news articles[8]) and spread of ideas and opinions (e.g. trending of topics and hashtags on Twitter/Facebook[16], keywords on blog networks[4])
(c) e-commerce: understanding epidemic cascades (and, in this case, finding influential nodes) is crucial to viral marketing [5], and predicting/optimizing uptake on social buying sites like Groupon, LivingSocial etc.
(d) security and reliability: epidemic cascades model both the spread of computer worms and malware [6], and cascading failures in infrastructure networks [7, 15] and complex organizations [12].

Structure Learning: The vast majority of work on epidemic cascades has focused on understanding how the graph structure of the network (e.g. power laws, small world, expansion etc.) affects the spread of epidemics. We focus on the *inverse problem:* if we only observe the states of nodes as the cascades spread, can we infer the underlying graph ? Structure learning is the crucial first step before we can *use* network structure; for example, before we find influential nodes in a network (e.g. for viral marketing) we need to know the graph. Often however we may only have crude, prior information about what the graph is, or indeed no information at all.
For example, in online social networks like Twitter or Facebook, we may have access to a *nominal* graph of all the friends of a user. However, clearly not all of them have an equal effect on the user's behavior; we would like to find the sub-graph of important links. In several other settings, we may have no a-priori information; examples include information forensics that study the spread of worms, and offline settings like real-world epidemiology and social science. The standard practice seems to be to use crude/nominal subgraphs if they exist (e.g. Twitter), or find graphs by other means (e.g. surveys). We propose to take a *data-driven* approach, finding graphs from observations of the epidemic cascades themselves.

While structure learning from cascades is an important primitive, there has been very little work investigating it (we summarize below). There are two related issues that need to be addressed: *(a) algorithms:* what is the method, and

SIGMETRICS'12, June 11–15, 2012, London, England, UK.

its complexity, and *(b) performance:* how many observations are needed for reliable graph recovery? The main intellectual contribution of this paper is characterizing the performance of two algorithms we develop, and a lower bound showing they perform close to optimal. Ours is the first paper (that we know of) to do any performance analysis for graph learning for epidemics.

1.1 Summary of Our Results

We present two algorithms, and information-theoretic lower bounds, for the problem of learning the graph of an epidemic when we are given prior information of a super-graph. It is not possible to learn the graph from a single epidemic; we study the number of epidemics required for reliable learning. Key outcomes of our results are that *(i)* epidemic graph learning can be done in a fast, distributed fashion, *(ii)* with a number of samples that is close to the lower bound.

Our results:

(a) Maximum Likelihood: We show that, via a suitable change of variables, the problem of finding the graph most likely to generate the epidemics we observe *decouples* into n convex problems – one for each node, and requiring as input only the infection times of that nodes' super-neighborhood (i.e., its neighborhood in the super-graph). Our main result here is to establish that for this efficient algorithm, the number of times a node i needs to be infected to find its size-d_i true neighborhood from size-D_i super-neighborhood with probability greater than $1-\delta$ is $O(d_i^2 \log \frac{D_i}{\delta})$, for a general graph.

(b) Greedy algorithm: We also consider a natural greedy algorithm which iteratively adds to the estimated neighborhood nodes that provide the best incremental explanation for the infections of a node. We show that if the graph is a tree, then this is able to find the true neighborhood with probability greater than $1-\delta$ with only $O(d \log \frac{D}{\delta})$ samples.

(c) Lower bounds: We establish an information-theoretic lower bound on the number of epidemics needed in a general setting, and specialize it to show that reliable recovery needs at least $\Omega(d \log \frac{D}{d})$ samples.

A nice feature of our results is that both the algorithms, and the lower bounds, work on a *node by node basis.* Thus for recovering the neighbors of a node we only need information about its super-neighborhood, and solve a local problem. Similarly, the number of samples required to recover the neighborhood of a node depends only on the sizes of its own neighborhood and super-neighborhood. We can use union bound along with the node by node guarantees above to obtain sufficient conditions on the number of samples required for recovering the entire graph correctly. In the full version of this paper[11], we also establish the relationship between the graph of an epidemic and its Markov random field. Due to lack of space, we do not provide proofs of all the results in this paper. For complete proofs of all the results in this paper, please refer [11].

Directly related work: While structure learning from epidemics is an important primitive, there has been very little work investigating it:

(a) algorithms: A recent paper [14] investigates learning graphs from infection times for the independent cascade model (similar setting as our paper). However, they take an approach that results in an NP-hard combinatorial optimization problem, which they show can be approximated. Another paper [10] shows max-likelihood estimation in the independent cascade model can be cast as a decoupled convex optimization problem (albeit a different one from ours). Another recent paper [13] shows that the likelihood function for the entire graph decouples into n likelihood functions, one for each node and that it is convex for some general models of epidemics. Though the paper shows that the maximum likelihood estimator is consistent, it does not analytically investigate the number of infections required for consistent estimation. *(b) performance:* On this, there has been no work we are aware of; indeed, this is the main focus of our paper.

2. SYSTEM MODEL

Most of the analytical results of this paper are for the classic and popular *independent cascade* model; in particular we will consider the simple one-step model first proposed in [3] and recently popularized by Kempe, Kleinberg and Tardos [5].

Standard independent cascade epidemic model [5]: The network is assumed to be a *directed* graph $G = (V, E)$; for every directed edge (i, j) we say i is a parent and j is a child of the corresponding other node. Let $\mathcal{V}_i := \{j : (j, i) \in E\}$ denote the set of parents of each node i. Epidemics proceed in discrete time; all nodes are initially in the *susceptible* state. At time 0, each node tosses a coin and independently becomes *active*, with probability p_{init}. This set of initially active nodes are called *seeds.* In every time step each active node probabilistically tries to infect its susceptible children; if node i is active at time t, it will infect each susceptible child j with probability p_{ij}, independently. Correspondingly, a node j that is susceptible at time t will become active in the next time step, i.e. $t+1$, if *any one* of its parents infects it. Finally, a node remains active for only *one* time slot, after which it becomes *inactive:* it does not spread the infection, and cannot be infected again. Thus some nodes remain forever susceptible because the epidemic never reaches them, while others transition according to:
susceptible $\rightarrow$ active for one time step $\rightarrow$ inactive.

Observation model: For a cascade u that spreads over a graph, we observe for each node i the time t_i^u when i became active. If i is one of the seed nodes of epidemic u then $t_i^u = 0$, and for nodes that are never infected in u we set $t_i^u = \infty$. Let t^u denote the vector of infection times for epidemic u. We observe more than one epidemic on the same graph; let $\mathcal{U}$ be the set of cascades, and $m = |\mathcal{U}|$ be the number, which we will often refer to as the *sample complexity.* Each cascade is assumed to be generated and observed as above, independent of all others.

(possible) Super-graph information: In several applications, we (may) also have prior knowledge about the network, in the form of a directed *super-graph*[1] of G. We find it convenient to represent super-graph information as follows: for each node i, we are given a set $\mathcal{S}_i \subset V$ of nodes that contain its true parents; i.e. $\mathcal{V}_i \subset \mathcal{S}_i$ for all i. In terms of edge probabilities, this means that $p_{ji} > 0$ (strictly) for $j \in \mathcal{V}_i$, and $p_{ji} = 0$ for $j \in \mathcal{S}_i \backslash \mathcal{V}_i$. Of course if no super-graph is available we can set $\mathcal{S}_i = V$, the set of all nodes; so from now on we assume a $\mathcal{S}_i$ is always available.

Problem description: Using the vectors of infection times $\{t^u\}$ we are interested in finding the parental neigh-

[1]For example, on social networks like Facebook or Twitter, we may know the set of all friends of a user, and from these we want to find the ones that most influence the user.

borhood $\mathcal{V}_i$, for some or all of the nodes i. Clearly, this is not possible when we only observe a single epidemic; we will thus be interested in learning the graph from *as few epidemics as possible.*

Note that multiple seeds begin each epidemic $u \in \mathcal{U}$; thus, for a single epidemic even at time step 1 we will not be able to say with surety which seed infected which individual.

Correlation decay: Loosely speaking, random processes on graphs are said to have "correlation decay" if far away nodes have negligible effects. For our problem, this means that the epidemic from each seed does not travel too far. Formally, all the results in this paper assume that there exists a number $\alpha > 0$ such that for every node i, the sum of all probabilities of incoming edges satisfies $\sum_k p_{ki} < 1-\alpha$. The following lemma clarifies what this assumption means for the infection times of a node.

LEMMA 1. *For any node i and time t, we have*

$$\mathbb{P}\left[T_i = t\right] \leq (1-\alpha)^{t-1} p_{init}$$

Thus, the probability $\mathbb{P}[T_i < \infty]$ that a node is infected satisfies $p_{init} < \mathbb{P}[T_i < \infty] < \frac{p_{init}}{\alpha}$. Also, the average distance from a node to any seed that infected it is at most $\frac{1}{\alpha}$. We discuss the case where there is no correlation decay in the Discussion section.

Interpreting the results: Each epidemic we observe provides some information about the graph. Suppose we want to infer the presence, or absence, of the directed edge (i, j) (i.e. if $p_{ij} > 0$ or not). Note that if the parent i is not infected in an epidemic, then *that epidemic provides no information* about (i, j): since the parent was never infected, no infection attempt was made using that edge; the "edge activation variable" was never sampled. While our theorems are in terms of the total number m of epidemics needed for graph estimation, for a meaningful interpretation of this number one needs to realize that the expected number of times we get *useful* information about any edge is, on average, between mp_{init} and mp_{init}/α.

We provide both upper bounds (via two learning algorithms), and (information theoretic) lower bounds on the sample complexity. Note that the *execution* of our algorithms does not require knowledge of these parameters like p_{init}, α etc.; these are defined only for the *analysis.*

3. MAXIMUM LIKELIHOOD

The graph learning problem can be interpreted as a parameter estimation problem: for each epidemic, the vector T of infection times is a set of random variables that has a joint distribution which is determined by a set of parameters $p_{ji} \geq 0$ for every i and $j \in \mathcal{S}_i$. We want to find these parameters, or more specifically the identities of the edges where they are non-zero, from samples t^u, $u \in \mathcal{U}$. Each choice of parameters has an associated probability, or likelihood, of generating the infection times we observe. The classical *Maximum-likelihood (ML) estimator* advocates picking the parameter values that maximize this likelihood.

Our crucial insight in this section is that, with an appropriate change of variables the likelihood function has a particularly nice (decoupled, convex) form, enabling both efficient implementation and analysis. In particular, define $\theta_{ij} := -\log(1-p_{ij})$; note that $p_{ij} = 0 \Leftrightarrow \theta_{ij} = 0$.

Further, for each node i let $\theta_{*i} := \{\theta_{ji}\,; j \in \mathcal{S}_i\}$ be the set of parameters corresponding to the possible parents $\mathcal{S}_i$ of node i. Let θ be the set of all parameters of the graph. Note that $\theta \geq 0$ (i.e. every parameter is positive or zero). Finally, we define the *log-likelihood* of a vector t of samples to be

$$\mathcal{L}(t;\theta) \;:=\; \log\left(\Pr_\theta[T = t]\right)$$

The proposition below shows how $\mathcal{L}$ decouples into convex functions with this change of variables.

PROPOSITION 1 (CONVEXITY & DECOUPLING). *For any vector of parameters θ, and infection time vector t, the log-likelihood is given by*

$$\mathcal{L}(t;\theta) \;=\; \log(p_{init}^{s}(1-p_{init})^{n-s}) + \sum_i \mathcal{L}_i(t_{\mathcal{S}_i};\theta_{*i})$$

where s is the number of seeds (i.e. nodes with $t_i = 0$), and the node-based term

$$\mathcal{L}_i(t_{\mathcal{S}_i};\theta_{*i}) \;:=\; -\sum_{j:t_j \leq t_i - 2} \theta_{ji} + \log\left(1 - \exp\left(-\sum_{j:t_j = t_i - 1} \theta_{ji}\right)\right)$$

Furthermore, $\mathcal{L}_i(t;\theta_{*i})$ is a concave function of θ_{*i}, for any fixed t.

Proof: Please see appendix.

Remark: The overall log-likelihood $\mathcal{L}(t;\theta)$ has now decoupled because it is the sum of n terms of the form $\mathcal{L}_i(t_{\mathcal{S}_i};\theta_{*i})$ (which will hence forth be referred to as $\mathcal{L}_i(t;\theta_{*i})$ for ease of notation), each of which depend on a *different* set of variables θ_{*i}. Thus each one can be optimized, and analyzed, in isolation.

The *algorithmic* implications of this proposition are:
(a) if we are only interested in a small subset of nodes, we can find their parental neighborhood by solving a separate $|\mathcal{V}_i|$-variable convex program for each one,
(b) even if we want to find the entire graph, the decoupling allows for parallelization, and speedup: solving n convex programs with n variables each is much faster than solving one program with n^2 variables.
(c) The function $\mathcal{L}_i$ is fully determined by the times $t_{\mathcal{S}_i}$ of the node's super-neighborhood; it does not need knowledge of the infection times of other nodes.

Proposition 1 is equally crucial *analytically,* as it enables us to derive bounds on the number of epidemics required for us to reliably select the neighborhood, via analysis of the first-order optimality conditions of the convex program. In particular, we will see that complementary slackness conditions from convex programming, and concentration results, are key to proving our results on the sample complexity of the ML procedure.

The ML algorithm for finding the parental neighborhood of node i is formally stated below. it involves solving the convex program corresponding to the max-likelihood, and setting small values of θ_{ji} to 0. The threshold for this cut-off is η, which is an input to the procedure.

Our main analytical result of this section is a characterization of the performance of this ML algorithm, in terms of the number of epidemics it needs to reliably estimate the parental neighborhood of any node i.

THEOREM 1. *Consider a node i with true parental degree $d_i := |\mathcal{V}_i|$, and super-graph degree $D_i := |\mathcal{S}_i|$. Let $p_{i,min} = \min_{j \in \mathcal{V}_i} p_{ji}$ be the strength of the edge from the*

Algorithm 1 ML Algorithm for Node i

1: Find

$$\widehat{\theta}_{*i} := \arg\max_{\theta_{*i}} \sum_u \mathcal{L}_i(t^u, \theta_{*i})$$

where $\mathcal{L}_i(t; \theta_{*i})$ is as defined in Prop. 1.

2: Estimate the parental neighborhood to be

$$\widehat{\mathcal{V}}_i := \{j : \widehat{\theta}_{ji} \geq \eta\}$$

3: Output $\widehat{\mathcal{V}}_i$.

weakest parent. Assume $d_i p_{init} < \frac{1}{2}$. Then, for any $\delta > 0$, if the number of epidemics $m = |\mathcal{U}|$ satisfies

$$m > \frac{c}{p_{init}} \left(\frac{1}{\alpha^7 \eta^2 p_{i,min}^2} \right) d_i^2 \log \left(\frac{D_i}{\delta} \right) \quad (1)$$

Then, with probability greater than $1 - \delta$, the estimate $\widehat{\mathcal{V}}_i$ from the ML algorithm with threshold η will have
(a) no false neighbors, i.e. $\widehat{\mathcal{V}}_i \subset \mathcal{V}_i$, and
(b) all strong enough neighbors: if $j \in \mathcal{V}_i$ and $p_{ji} > \frac{8}{\alpha}(e^{2\eta} - 1)$, then $j \in \widehat{\mathcal{V}}_i$ as well.
Here c is a number independent of any other system parameter.

Remarks:

(a) This is a *non-asymptotic* result that holds for *all* values of the system variables $d_i, p_{init}, \alpha, p_{i,min}, \eta$ and δ. Appropriate asymptotic results can be derived as corollaries, if required. Note that this result on finding the nodes that influence node i *does not depend on n*.

(b) We can learn the entire neighborhood, i.e. $\widehat{\mathcal{V}}_i = \mathcal{V}_i$, by choosing the threshold $\eta \leq \frac{1}{2}\log(1 + \frac{\alpha p_{i,min}}{8})$ low enough, and the corresponding number of epidemic samples m according to (1). Thus, the number of times node i needs to be infected before we can reliably (i.e. with a fixed small error probability) learn its neighborhood scales as $O(d_i^2 \log D_i)$ (for fixed values of other system variables). Our result allows for learning stronger edges with fewer samples.

(c) If we want to learn the structure of the *entire* graph with probability greater than ϵ, we can set $\delta = \epsilon/n$ and then take a union bound over all the nodes. So, for example, if every node has true degree at most $|\mathcal{V}_i| \leq d$, and super-graph degree $|\mathcal{S}_i| \leq D$, then the number of samples needed to learn the entire graph (with probability at least $1 - \epsilon$) scales as $O(d^2 \log \frac{Dn}{\epsilon})$ (for fixed values of other system variables).

(d) The average number of parents of i that are seeds is $d_i p_{init}$. If this is large, then in every epidemic there will be a reasonable probability of one of them being seeds, and infecting i in the next time slot. This makes it hard to discern the neighborhood of i; the (mild) assumption $d_i p_{init} < \frac{1}{2}$ is required to counter this effect. Indeed, in most applications p_{init} is likely to be quite small.

4. GREEDY ALGORITHM

We now analyze the sample complexity of a simple iterative greedy algorithm – for the case when the graph is a tree[2]. The algorithm is of course defined for general graphs.

[2]We believe (especially since we have correlation decay) that our results can be easily extended to the case of "locally tree-like" graphs; e.g. random graphs from the Erdos-Renyi, random regular or several other popular models.

The idea is as follows: suppose we want to find the parents of node i from a given set of epidemics $\mathcal{U}$. In each epidemic u, the set of nodes that could have possibly infected i is the set of nodes j for which $t_j^u = t_i^u - 1$. In the first step, the algorithm thus picks the j which has $t_j^u = t_i^u - 1$ for the largest number of observed epidemics. It then *removes* those epidemics from further consideration (since they have been "accounted for") and proceeds as before on the remaining epidemics, stopping when all epidemics are exhausted.

Algorithm 2 Greedy Algorithm for Node i

1: Initialize unaccounted epidemics $U = \mathcal{U}$
2: Initialize $\widehat{\mathcal{V}}_i = \emptyset$
3: **while** $U \neq \emptyset$ **do**
4: Find $k = \arg\max_{j \in \mathcal{S}_i} |\{u \in U : t_j^u = t_i^u - 1\}|$
5: Add it : $\widehat{\mathcal{V}}_i \leftarrow \widehat{\mathcal{V}}_i \cup k$
6: Remove epidemics : $U \leftarrow U \setminus \{u : t_k^u = t_i^u - 1\}$
7: **end while**
8: Output $\widehat{\mathcal{V}}_i$

Our main result for this section is below.

THEOREM 2. *Suppose the graph G is a tree, and the degree of node i is $d_i := |\mathcal{V}_i|$. Suppose also that $p_{init} < \frac{\alpha^2 p_{min}}{16 e d_i}$. If Algorithm 2 is given a super-neighbhorhood of size $D_i := |\mathcal{S}_i|$, then for any $\delta > 0$ if the number of samples satisfies*

$$m > \frac{c}{p_{init}} \left(\frac{1}{p_{min}} \right) d_i \log \frac{D_i}{\delta}$$

then with probability at least $1 - \delta$ the estimate from the greedy algorithm will be the same as the true neighborhood, i.e. $\widehat{\mathcal{V}}_i = \mathcal{V}_i$. Here c is a constant independent of any other system parameter.

5. LOWER BOUNDS

We now turn our attention to establishing lower bounds on the number of epidemics that need to be observed for even approximately learning graph structure, using *any* algorithm. Clearly, we now cannot focus on learning just one graph, since in that case we could come up with an "algorithm" tailored to find precisely that one graph. Instead, as is standard practice in information-theoretic lower bounds, we need to consider a collection (or "ensemble") of graphs, and study how many epidemics are needed to (approximately) find *any one* graph from this collection.

We first state a lower bound in a general setting, for any pre-defined ensemble and notion of approximate recovery. We then provide two corollaries specializing it to our independent cascade epidemic model, edit distance approximation, and two natural graph ensembles.

General Setting: Consider any general epidemic process generating infection times $\{T_i\}$. Let $\mathcal{G}$ be a fixed collection of graphs and corresponding edge probabilities, and let G be a graph chosen uniformly at random from this collection. We then generate a set $\mathcal{U}$, with $|\mathcal{U}| = m$, of independent epidemics, and observe infection times $T^{\mathcal{U}}$. Let $\widehat{G}(T^{\mathcal{U}})$ be a graph estimator that takes the observations as an input and outputs a graph. Finally, we say that a graph G' approximately recovers graph G if $G \in \mathcal{B}(G')$, where $\mathcal{B}(G') \subseteq \mathcal{G}$ is any pre-defined set of graphs, with one such set defined for every G'.

So for example, if we are interested in exact recovery, we would have $\mathcal{B}(G') = \{G'\}$, i.e. the singleton. If we were interested in edit distance of s, we would have $\mathcal{B}(G')$ be the set of all graphs within edit distance s of G'.

We define the probability of error of a graph estimator $\widehat{G}(\cdot)$ to be

$$P_e(\widehat{G}) \ := \ \mathbb{P}[G \notin \mathcal{B}(\widehat{G}(T^{\mathcal{U}}))]$$

where the probability is calculated over the randomness in the choice of G itself, and the generation of infection times in this G. Note that the definition defines error to be when approximate recovery (as defined by the sets $\mathcal{B}$) fails.

THEOREM 3. *In the general setting above, for any graph estimator to have a probability of error of P_e, we need*

$$m \ \geq \ \frac{(1-P_e)\log\frac{|\mathcal{G}|}{\sup_{G'}|\mathcal{B}(G')|} - 1}{\sum_{i\in V} H(T_i)}$$

where $H(\cdot)$ is the entropy function.

PROOF. To shorten notation, we will denote $\widehat{G}(T^{\mathcal{U}})$ simply by $\widehat{G}$. The proof uses several basic information-theoretic inequalities, which can be found e.g. in [2]. In the following $H(\cdot)$ denotes entropy and $I(\cdot;\cdot)$ denotes mutual information.

We can see that the following diagram forms a Markov chain

$$G \longleftrightarrow T^{\mathcal{U}} \longleftrightarrow \widehat{G}$$

We have the following series of inequalities:

$$\begin{aligned} H(G) &= I(G;\widehat{G}) + H(G \mid \widehat{G}) \\ &\overset{(\varsigma_1)}{\leq} I(G;T^U) + H(G \mid \widehat{G}) \\ &\overset{(\varsigma_2)}{\leq} H(T^U) + H(G \mid \widehat{G}) \\ &\overset{(\varsigma_3)}{\leq} mH(T) + H(G \mid \widehat{G}) \\ &\overset{(\varsigma_4)}{\leq} m\sum_{i\in V} H(T_i) + H(G \mid \widehat{G}) \end{aligned}$$

where (ς_1) follows from the data processing inequality, (ς_2) follows from the fact that the mutual information between two random variables is less than the entropy of either of them, (ς_3) and (ς_4) follows from the subadditivity of entropy. Since G is sampled uniformly at random from $\mathcal{G}$, we have that $H(G) = \log|\mathcal{G}|$. We now use Fano's inequality to bound $H(G \mid \widehat{G})$.

$$\begin{aligned} H(G \mid \widehat{G}) &\overset{(\varsigma_1)}{\leq} H(G, Err \mid \widehat{G}) \\ &\overset{(\varsigma_2)}{=} H(Err \mid \widehat{G}) + H(G \mid Err, \widehat{G}) \\ &\overset{(\varsigma_3)}{\leq} H(Err) + H(G \mid Err, \widehat{G}) \\ &\overset{(\varsigma_4)}{\leq} 1 + P_e \log|\mathcal{G}| + (1-P_e)\log\sup_{\widehat{G}}|\mathcal{B}_s(\widehat{G})| \end{aligned}$$

where Err is the error indicator random variable (i.e., is 1 if $G \notin \mathcal{B}(\widehat{G})$ and 0 otherwise), so that $P_e = \mathbb{E}[Err]$. (ς_1) follows from the monotonicity of entropy, (ς_2) follows from the chain rule of entropy, (ς_3) follows from the monotonicity of entropy with respect to conditioning and (ς_4) follows from Fano's inequality[2]. Combining the above two results, we obtain

$$\begin{aligned} m\sum_{i\in V} H(T_i) &\geq (1-P_e)\log\frac{|\mathcal{G}|}{\sup_{\widehat{G}}|\mathcal{B}(\widehat{G})|} - 1 \\ \Rightarrow m &\geq \frac{(1-P_e)\log\frac{|\mathcal{G}|}{\sup_{\widehat{G}}|\mathcal{B}(\widehat{G})|} - 1}{\sum_{i\in V} H(T_i)} \end{aligned} \tag{2}$$

□

To apply this result to a particular ensemble $\mathcal{G}$ and notion of approximation $\mathcal{B}$, we need to find a lower bound on $|\mathcal{G}|$, and upper bounds on $|\mathcal{B}(G')|$ for all G' and $H(T_i)$ for all i. The following lemma states an upper bound on $H(T_i)$ for our independent cascade model when we have correlation decay coefficient α. Both our corollaries assume this is the case for all graphs in their respective ensembles.

LEMMA 2. *For any graph with correlation decay coefficient α, for any node i, and when $p_{init} < \frac{1}{e}$, we have that*

$$\begin{aligned} H(T_i) \ &\leq \ \frac{p_{init}}{1-\alpha}\left(\log\frac{1}{p_{init}} + \left(\frac{1-\alpha}{\alpha}\right)^2 \log\frac{1}{1-\alpha}\right) \\ &\quad - \left(1 - \frac{p_{init}}{\alpha}\right)\log\left(1 - \frac{p_{init}}{\alpha}\right) \\ &=: \ p_{init}\overline{H}(\alpha, p_{init}) \end{aligned}$$

Note that the *edit distance* between two graphs is the number of edges present in only one of the two graphs but not the other (i.e. the number of edges in the symmetric difference of the two graphs). Our first corollary is for the case when there is no super-graph information, and we want to approximate in global edit distance.

COROLLARY 1. *Let $\mathcal{G}_d$ denote the set of all graphs with in-degrees bounded by d, and $\mathcal{B}_\gamma(G')$ be the set of all graphs within edit distance γ of G'. Let $p_{init} < \frac{1}{e}$. Then for any algorithm to have a probability of error of P_e, we need*

$$m \ > \ \frac{(1-P_e)}{p_{init}}\frac{1-\alpha}{\overline{H}(\alpha, p_{init})}\left(d\log\frac{n}{d} - \frac{\gamma}{n}\log\frac{n^2}{\gamma}\right) - 1$$

PROOF. We have that

$$\log|\mathcal{G}_d| = \log\binom{n}{d}^n = (1+o(1))\,nd\log\frac{n}{d}$$

$$\log|\mathcal{B}_\gamma(G')| \leq \log\binom{\binom{n}{2}}{\gamma} \leq \gamma\log\frac{n^2}{\gamma}$$

Using the above two equations along with Theorem 3 and Lemma 2 gives us the result. □

Note that the number of times a node is infected thus needs to be $\Omega((d - \frac{2\gamma}{n})\log n)$ (since it is of the same order as mp_{init}). For exact recovery, i.e. $\gamma = 0$, we see that our result on the performance of our ML algorithm – specialized to the no prior information case $D = n$ – is off by just a factor d in terms of the number of samples required.

The second corollary is for the case when we do have prior supergraph information. In particular, we assume that we are given sets $\mathcal{S}_i$, of size $|\mathcal{S}_i| = D$, for each node i. We consider the ensemble $\mathcal{G}_{D,d}$ of all in-degree-d *subgraphs of this fixed supergraph.* Thus for each node, we need to learn the d parents it has, from a given super-set of size D. Finally, for each node i we allow s_i errors; let $\mathcal{B}_s(G')$ be the corresponding set of all subgraphs of the given supergraph.

COROLLARY 2. *For any estimator to have a probability of error of P_e in the setting above, the number of samples m must be bigger than*

$$\left[\frac{(1-P_e)}{p_{init}}\frac{1-\alpha}{\overline{H}(\alpha, p_{init})}\times \left(d\log\frac{D}{d} - \frac{1}{n}\sum_i s_i \log\frac{eD}{s_i} + \log\max(s_i,1)\right)\right] - 1$$

Remark: Specializing this result to exact recovery (i.e. $s_i = 0$) removes dependence on n, and again shows us that the ML algorithm is within a factor d of optimal for the case when we have a super-graph.

PROOF. We have the following bound on the size of the ensemble:

$$\log|\mathcal{G}_d| = \log\binom{D}{d}^n = (1+o(1))\, nd\log\frac{D}{d}$$

Similarly,

$$\begin{aligned}\log|\mathcal{B}_s(\widehat{G})| &\leq \log\prod_{i\in V}\left(\sum_{l=0}^{s_i}\binom{D}{l}\right)\\ &\leq \log\prod_{i\in V}\left(\max(1,s_i)\binom{D}{s_i}\right)\\ &\leq \sum_{i\in V}\log\left(\max(1,s_i)\left(\frac{De}{s_i}\right)^{s_i}\right)\\ &= \sum_{i\in V}\log\max(1,s_i) + \sum_{i\in V} s_i\log\frac{De}{s_i} \qquad (3)\end{aligned}$$

where

$$\mathcal{B}_s(\widehat{G}) = \{\widetilde{G}\in\mathcal{G}_d : \widetilde{\mathcal{V}}_i \,\triangle\, \widehat{\mathcal{V}}_i \leq s_i\ \forall\, i\in V\}$$

Note that in the second inequality we assume $s_i \leq \frac{D}{2}$ because otherwise if $d < \frac{D}{2}$, we can choose $\widehat{\mathcal{V}}_i = \Phi$ and if $d \geq \frac{D}{2}$, we can choose $\widehat{\mathcal{V}}_i = \mathcal{V}_i$. Using Theorem 3, (3) and Lemma 2 gives us the first part of the result. □

6. EXPERIMENTS

In this section, we will present experimental evaluations of both the ML and Greedy algorithms on synthetic and real world graphs.

6.1 Synthetic graphs

Grids: First, we present the results of both ML and Greedy algorithms on grids. For each grid size, edge parameters are chosen so as to satisfy the assumptions of Theorem 1. Using these parameters, independent infections are generated by simulating the independent cascade model on the graph. Both ML and Greedy algorithms are given these infections as input to obtain an estimate of the grid. A graph is said to be recovered if the output parent set of *each* node is the same as the parent set of that node in the original graph. Given m infections, a trial executes the algorithm with those infections. The probability of recovery for m infections is calculated empirically as the fraction of trials which recover the parent set of every node of the graph exactly out of a total of 20 trials. Figure 1 shows the probability of recovery of a graph versus the total number of infections. We can see that as the number of infections increases, both the algorithms recover the graph exactly with higher probability. We also note that the number of infections needed to obtain a given probability of exact recovery increases as the graph size increases. On the other hand, Figure 2 shows the probability of recovery versus the *average number of times a node is infected.* One remarkable fact to note is that the plots for recovery almost line up on top of each other for various problem sizes. This indicates that in a grid, the probability of recovery is dependent only on the average number of infections experienced by a node irrespective of the problem size.

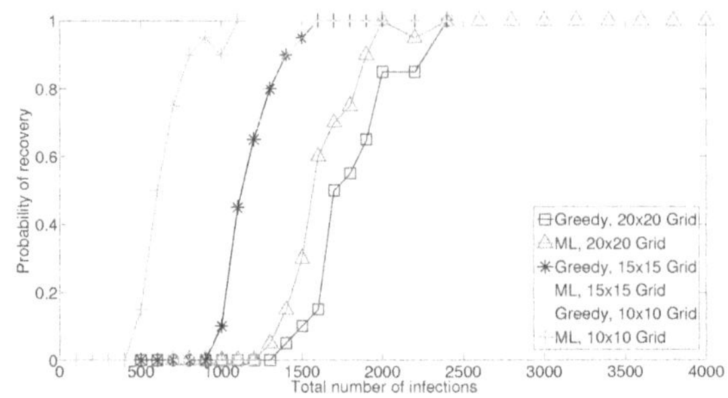

Figure 1: Recovery of grids with total number of infections: This plot shows the probability of recovery versus the total number of infections for various grid sizes.

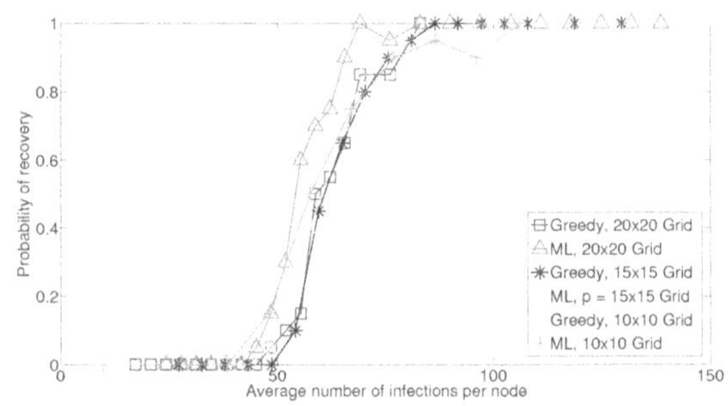

Figure 2: Recovery of grids with average infections per node: This plot is from the same experiment as Figure 1. The only (and crucial) difference is that the x-axis in this plot denotes the average number of times a node is infected.

Random Regular Graphs: We now present the results of ML and Greedy algorithms on random regular graphs of degree 4. A random regular graph is first sampled and appropriate values are chosen for the edge parameters. Independent infections are then sampled by simulating the independent cascade model. Figure 3 shows the plot of probability of recovery versus the average number of infections per node for different sizes of graphs for both the ML and Greedy algorithms. Figure 4 shows the comparison between the ML and Greedy algorithms when there is a super graph as opposed to when there is no super graph. The underlying graph is a random 4-regular 200 node graph. Both the ML and Greedy algorithms are run on varying number of infections. For each number of infections, two versions of

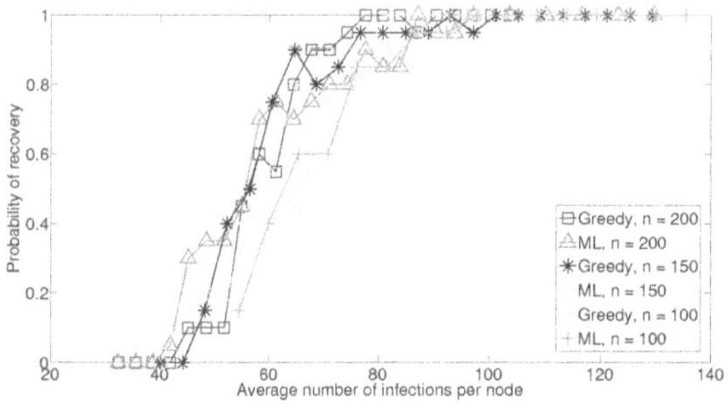

Figure 3: Random 4-regular graph: This figure plots the probability of recovery versus the average number of infections per node for both the ML and Greedy algorithms for different sizes of random regular graphs.

each algorithm were executed - one that has a super graph and the other that does not have a super graph. The y-axis denotes the fraction of those graphs that the algorithm recovered exactly. The x-axis denotes the average number of times a node is infected. Our analytical results suggest that the non availability of a super graph does not affect the sample complexity drastically. We can see that the above plot corroborates this claim.

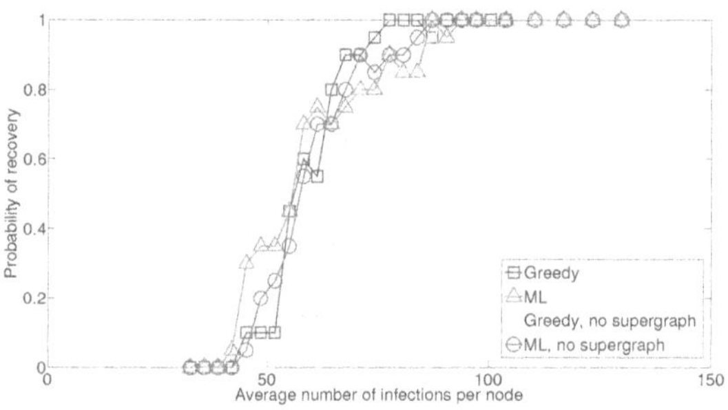

Figure 4: Super graph/No super graph: comparison between the ML and Greedy algorithms when there is a super graph as opposed to when there is no super graph.

6.2 Twitter Graph

We present the results of two experiments on Twitter graph. In the first experiment, a connected 1000 node subgraph of the Twitter follower-following graph was extracted. Even on this small subgraph, some nodes have high in-degree and/or out-degree. To emulate people who "officially" follow many other people but are really influenced by a few of them, for each node, only a few of the in-edges of that node were assigned positive edge parameters (corresponding to those who actually influence the current node) and the rest are assigned an edge parameter of zero. Infections were then sampled by simulating the independent cascade model using the above assignment of edge parameters. Both the ML and Greedy algorithms were given infections and the entire 1000 node graph as a super graph. Figure 5 shows the plot of fraction of nodes recovered versus the average number of infections of a node.

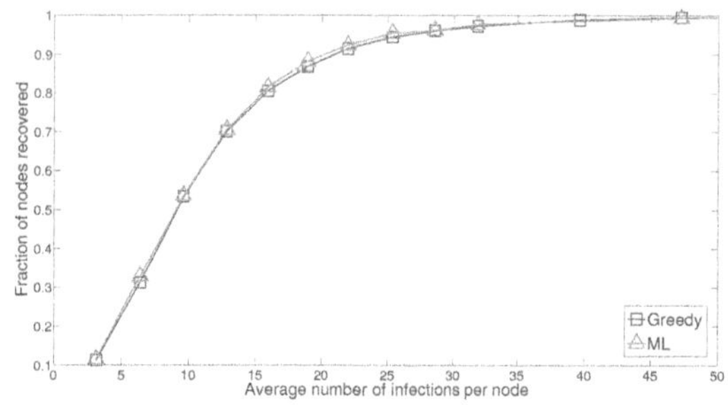

Figure 5: Twitter sub-graph with a few important parents.

In the second experiment, a 300 node subgraph of the Twitter graph was extracted. As was the case in the 1000 node sub graph, even in the 300 node subgraph, there were nodes of high in-degree and/or out-degree. For each node, all parents were assigned equal edge parameters. Infections were sampled according to the independent cascade model using these edge parameters. Both the ML and Greedy algorithms were given these infections as input without any super graph information. Figure 6 shows a scatter plot of the number of infections taken by a node for its neighborhood to be estimated correctly versus the degree of that node. Each scatter point corresponds to a node in the graph - the value of the x-axis is the degree of that node and the value of the y-axis is the number of infections of that node so that the algorithm estimated its neighborhood correctly. Note that the sample complexity increases super-linearly with degree for the ML algorithm where as the dependence of the sample complexity on the degree is almost linear for the Greedy algorithm.

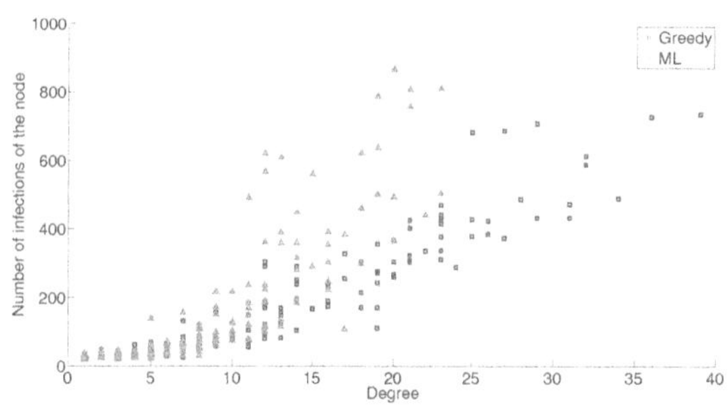

Figure 6: Twitter sub-graph with high degree: Complexity of learning the neighborhood vs degree of the node

7. ACKNOWLEDGMENTS

This research was supported by NSF grants 0954059 (CAREER) and 1017525.

8. REFERENCES

[1] T. Bonald, L. Massoulié, F. Mathieu, D. Perino, and A. Twigg. Epidemic live streaming: optimal performance trade-offs. *SIGMETRICS Perform. Eval. Rev.*, 36:325–336, June 2008.

[2] T. M. Cover and J. A. Thomas. *Elements of Information Theory (Wiley Series in Telecommunications and Signal Processing)*. Wiley-Interscience, 2006.

[3] J. Goldenberg, B. Libai, and E. Muller. Talk of the network: A complex systems look at the underlying process of word-of-mouth. *Marketing Letters*, 12:211–223, 2001.

[4] D. Gruhl, R. Guha, D. Liben-Nowell, and A. Tomkins. Information diffusion through blogspace. In *Proc. 13th International Conference on World Wide Web*, WWW '04, pages 491–501, New York, NY, USA, 2004. ACM.

[5] D. Kempe, J. Kleinberg, and E. Tardos. Maximizing the spread of influence through a social network. In *Proc. 9th ACM SIGKDD international conference on Knowledge discovery and data mining*, KDD '03, pages 137–146, New York, NY, USA, 2003. ACM.

[6] J. O. Kephart and S. R. White. Directed-graph epidemiological models of computer viruses. *Security and Privacy, IEEE Symposium on*, 0:343, 1991.

[7] D. Kosterev, C. Taylor, and W. Mittelstadt. Model validation for the august 10, 1996 wscc system outage. *Power Systems, IEEE Transactions on*, 14(3):967 –979, aug 1999.

[8] K. Lerman and R. Ghosh. Information contagion: An empirical study of the spread of news on Digg and Twitter social networks. In *Proc. International AAAI Conference on Weblogs and Social Media*, 2010.

[9] L. Massoulié and A. Twigg. Rate-optimal schemes for peer-to-peer live streaming. *Performance Evaluation*, 65(11-12):804 – 822, 2008.

[10] S. A. Myers and J. Leskovec. On the convexity of latent social network inference. In *Proc. Neural Information Processing Systems (NIPS)*, 2010.

[11] P. Netrapalli and S. Sanghavi. Finding the graph of epidemic cascades, 2012. http://arxiv.org/abs/1202.1779.

[12] C. Perrow. *Normal Accidents: Living with High-Risk Technologies*. Princeton University Press, updated edition, Sept. 1999.

[13] M. G. Rodriguez, D. Balduzzi, and B. Schölkopf. Uncovering the temporal dynamics of diffusion networks. In L. Getoor and T. Scheffer, editors, *Proceedings of the 28th International Conference on Machine Learning (ICML-11)*, ICML '11, pages 561–568, New York, NY, USA, June 2011. ACM.

[14] M. G. Rodriguez, J. Leskovec, and A. Krause. Inferring networks of diffusion and influence. In *Proc. 16th ACM SIGKDD international conference on Knowledge discovery and data mining*, KDD '10, pages 1019–1028, New York, NY, USA, 2010. ACM.

[15] M. L. Sachtjen, B. A. Carreras, and V. E. Lynch. Disturbances in a power transmission system. *Phys. Rev. E*, 61:4877–4882, May 2000.

[16] Z. Zhou, R. Bandari, J. Kong, H. Qian, and V. Roychowdhury. Information resonance on Twitter: watching Iran. In *Proc. 1st Workshop on Social Media Analytics*, SOMA '10, pages 123–131, New York, NY, USA, 2010. ACM.

APPENDIX

A. CORRELATION DECAY

PROOF OF LEMMA 1. We establish this by induction on n. If $n = 1$, the lemma is clearly true. Suppose that the lemma is true for all graphs which have upto $n-1$ nodes. Consider now a graph G that has n nodes. Consider any node i. The statement of the proposition is clearly true for $t = 1$. For $t > 1$, consider the probability that i is infected by a parent $k \in \mathcal{S}_i$ at time step t. This can be upper bounded as follows:

$$\begin{aligned}\mathbb{P}_G\left[k \text{ infects } i \text{ at time } t\right] &\leq \mathbb{P}_{\widetilde{G}}\left[T_k = t-1\right] p_{ki} \\ &\leq (1-\alpha)^{t-2} p_{\text{init}} p_{ki}\end{aligned}$$

where $\widetilde{G} := G \setminus i$ is the graph without node i, $\mathbb{P}_G$ denotes the probability when the graph is G, and similarly for $\mathbb{P}_{\widetilde{G}}$. The second inequality follows from the induction assumption, and the fact that if α is the decay coefficient for G, it is also for $\widetilde{G}$. Taking a union bound over $k \in \mathcal{S}_i$, we get:

$$\begin{aligned}\mathbb{P}_G\left[T_i = t\right] &= \sum_{k \in \mathcal{S}_i} \mathbb{P}_G\left[k \text{ infects } i \text{ at time } t\right] \\ &\leq (1-\alpha)^{t-2} p_{\text{init}} \sum_{k \in \mathcal{S}_i} p_{ki} \\ &\leq (1-\alpha)^{t-1} p_{\text{init}}\end{aligned}$$

Bounds on $\mathbb{P}[T_i < \infty]$ follow from summing this series. □

B. MAXIMUM LIKELIHOOD

B.1 Proof of Prop. 1

Let $X_i(\tau) = 0$ if i is susceptible at time τ, 1 if i is active at time τ and 2 if i is inactive at time τ. Let $X(\tau), \tau = 0, \cdots, n$ be the corresponding vector process. Note that $X(\tau)$ is a Markov process, and there is a one to one correspondence between the set of infection times t and sample path $x(\tau)$ of the process $X(\tau)$.

Given t, let $x^0(\tau)$ be the corresponding vector process. In particular,

$$x_i^0(\tau) = \begin{cases} 0 & \text{if } \tau < t_i \\ 1 & \text{if } \tau = t_i \\ 2 & \text{if } \tau > t_i. \end{cases}$$

Then,

$$\begin{aligned}\mathbb{P}_\theta\left[T = t\right] &= \mathbb{P}_\theta\left[X(\tau) = x^0(\tau) \text{ for } \tau = 0, \cdots, n\right] \\ &= \mathbb{P}_\theta\left[X(0) = x^0(0)\right] \times \\ &\quad \prod_{\tau=1}^{n} \mathbb{P}_\theta\left[X(\tau) = x^0(\tau) \middle| X(\tau-1) = x^0(\tau-1)\right]\end{aligned}$$

Now, $\mathbb{P}_\theta\left[X(0) = x^0(0)\right] = p_{\text{init}}^s (1-p_{\text{init}})^{n-s}$. Also,

$$\begin{aligned}&\mathbb{P}_\theta\left[X(\tau) = x^0(\tau) \middle| X(\tau-1) = x^0(\tau-1)\right] \\ &= \prod_{i \in V} \mathbb{P}_\theta\left[X_i(\tau) = x_i^0(\tau) \middle| X(\tau-1) = x^0(\tau-1)\right]\end{aligned}$$

because each node gets infected independently from each of

its currently active neighbors. Thus we have that

$$\mathbb{P}[T=t]=p_{\text{init}}^{s}(1-p_{\text{init}})^{n-s}\prod_{i\in V}\left(\prod_{\tau=1}^{n}a_i(\tau)\right) \quad (4)$$

where $a_i(\tau)=\mathbb{P}_\theta\left[X_i(\tau)=x_i^0(\tau)\middle|X(\tau-1)=x^0(\tau-1)\right]$. It is clear that for $\tau>t_i$, $a_i(\tau)=1$. For $\tau=t_i$, $a_i(\tau)$ is the probability that at least one of its active nodes at time t_i-1 infected node i. Thus,

$$a_i(t_i)=1-\prod_{j:t_j=t_i-1}\exp(-\theta_{ji}) \quad (5)$$

Finally, for each $\tau<t_i$, $a_i(\tau)$ is the probability that active nodes at time $\tau-1$ failed to infect node i. The set of all nodes that were active but failed to infect susceptible node i is $\{j:t_j\le t_i-2\}$. So we have

$$\prod_{\tau<t_i}a_i(\tau)=\prod_{j:t_j\le t_i-2}\exp(-\theta_{ji}) \quad (6)$$

Putting (4), (5) and (6) together and taking log gives the result.

Concavity follows from the fact that $\log(1-\exp(-x))$ is a concave function of x, and the fact that if any function $f(x)$ is a concave function of x then $f(\sum_i\theta_i)$ is jointly concave in θ. ■

B.2 Proof of Theorem 1

For brevity, we denote θ_{*i} by θ, $\mathcal{V}_i$ by $\mathcal{V}$ and $\mathcal{S}_i$ by $\mathcal{S}$. Let θ^* be the true parameter values. Define

$$\widehat{L}(\theta):=\frac{1}{m}\sum_u\mathcal{L}_i(t^u;\theta)$$

Note that the ML algorithm finds $\widehat{\theta}=\text{argmax}_\theta\,\widehat{L}(\theta)$. Also let $L(\theta):=\mathbb{E}_{\theta^*}[\mathcal{L}_i(T,\theta)]$.

Idea : Note that as m increases, $\widehat{L}\to L$. Also, we know that $\theta^*=\arg\min_\theta L(\theta)$; this is just stating that the expected value of the likelihood function is maximized by the true parameter values, a simple classical result from ML estimation. Thus when $\widehat{L}\simeq L$, θ^* will approximately minimize $\widehat{L}$ as well. This means it will be close to $\widehat{\theta}$.

Implementing the above roadmap involves showing concentration results and some tricks from convex analysis. Since our analysis is based on first-order methods (i.e., using the gradient), we prove a characterization of the gradient of the log likelihood function. For any j, let $\nabla_j\widehat{L}(\theta)$ be the partial derivative of $\widehat{L}(\theta)$ with respect to θ_j.

PROPOSITION 2.

$$\nabla_jL(\theta^*)=-\mathbb{P}[T_i>T_j;T_k\neq T_j\forall k\in\mathcal{V}] \quad (7)$$

PROOF. Taking the derivative of $L(\cdot)$ with respect to θ_j, we obtain

$$\nabla_j\,L(\theta)=\mathbb{E}\left[-\mathbb{1}_{\{T_j\le T_i-2\}}+\frac{\mathbb{1}_{\{T_j=T_i-1\}}}{\exp\left(\sum_{k:\,T_k=T_i-1}\theta_k\right)-1}\right]$$

Let $\mathcal{F}_{T_j}$ be the σ-algebra with information up to the (random) time T_j. By iterated conditioning, we obtain

$$\nabla_j\,L(\theta^*)$$
$$=-\mathbb{E}\left[\mathbb{E}\left[\mathbb{1}_{\{T_j\le T_i-2\}}-\frac{\mathbb{1}_{\{T_j=T_i-1\}}}{\exp\left(\sum_{k:\,T_k=T_i-1}\theta_k^*\right)-1}\,\middle|\,\mathcal{F}_{T_j}\right]\right] \quad (8)$$

Since the event $\{T_i\le T_j\}$ is measurable in $\mathcal{F}_{T_j}$, we have

$$\mathbb{E}\left[\mathbb{1}_{\{T_j\le T_i-2\}}-\frac{\mathbb{1}_{\{T_j=T_i-1\}}}{\exp\left(\sum_{k:\,T_k=T_i-1}\theta_k^*\right)-1}\,\middle|\,\mathcal{F}_{T_j}\right]$$
$$=0\text{ if }T_i\le T_j \quad (9)$$

On the other hand, if $\{T_i>T_j\}$, we have

$$\mathbb{E}\left[\mathbb{1}_{\{T_j\le T_i-2\}}-\frac{\mathbb{1}_{\{T_j=T_i-1\}}}{\exp\left(\sum_{k:\,T_k=T_i-1}\theta_k^*\right)-1}\,\middle|\,\mathcal{F}_{T_j}\right]$$
$$=\mathbb{P}\left[T_i\ge T_j+2\,\middle|\,\mathcal{F}_{T_j}\right]-$$
$$\mathbb{E}\left[\frac{\mathbb{1}_{\{T_j=T_i-1\}}}{\exp\left(\sum_{k:\,T_k=T_i-1}\theta_k^*\right)-1}\,\middle|\,\mathcal{F}_{T_j}\right]$$

Considering the two terms above separately, we see that

$$\mathbb{P}\left[T_i\ge T_j+2\,\middle|\,\mathcal{F}_{T_j}\right]=\exp\left(-\sum_{k:\,T_k=T_j}\theta_k^*\right)$$

which follows from the fact that the probability that (active) j failed to infect (susceptible) i is equal to the probability that all the nodes that were active at T_j failed to infect i. For the second term, we have

$$\mathbb{E}\left[\frac{\mathbb{1}_{\{T_j=T_i-1\}}}{\exp\left(\sum_{k:\,T_k=T_i-1}\theta_k^*\right)-1}\,\middle|\,\mathcal{F}_{T_j}\right]$$
$$=\mathbb{E}\left[\frac{\mathbb{1}_{\{T_j=T_i-1\}}}{\exp\left(\sum_{k:\,T_k=T_j}\theta_k^*\right)-1}\,\middle|\,\mathcal{F}_{T_j}\right]$$
$$\overset{(\varsigma_1)}{=}\frac{1}{\exp\left(\sum_{k:\,T_k=T_j}\theta_k^*\right)-1}\mathbb{E}\left[\mathbb{1}_{\{T_j=T_i-1\}}\,\middle|\,\mathcal{F}_{T_j}\right]$$
$$\overset{(\varsigma_2)}{=}\frac{\left(1-\exp\left(-\sum_{k:\,T_k=T_j}\theta_k^*\right)\right)\mathbb{1}_{\{\exists k\in\mathcal{V}\text{ s.t. }T_k=T_j\}}}{\exp\left(\sum_{k:\,T_k=T_j}\theta_k^*\right)-1}$$
$$=\exp\left(-\sum_{k:\,T_k=T_j}\theta_k^*\right)\mathbb{1}_{\{\exists k\in\mathcal{V}\text{ s.t. }T_k=T_j\}}$$

where (ς_1) follows from the fact that $\{k:T_k=T_j\}$ is measurable in $\mathcal{F}_{T_j}$ and (ς_2) follows from the fact that $T_i=T_j+1$ if and only if at least one of the parents of i were active at T_j and succeeded in infecting i. Combining the above two equations, we obtain

$$\mathbb{E}\left[\mathbb{1}_{\{T_j\le T_i-2\}}-\frac{\mathbb{1}_{\{T_j=T_i-1\}}}{\exp\left(\sum_{k:\,T_k=T_i-1}\theta_k^*\right)-1}\,\middle|\,\mathcal{F}_{T_j}\right]$$
$$=\mathbb{1}_{\{T_k\neq T_j\;\forall\,k\in\mathcal{V}\}}\text{ if }T_i>T_j \quad (10)$$

Combining (8), (9) and (10)

$$\nabla_j L(\theta^*) = -\mathbb{P}\left[T_i > T_j; T_k \neq T_k \forall k \in \mathcal{V}\right] \quad (11)$$

□

An easy corollary of Proposition 2 is that if j is a parent of i, then the gradient with respect to θ_j is zero since the probability above needs none of the parents of i to be infected at the same time as j. On the other hand, if j is not a parent of i, the gradient is strictly negative since the probability on the right hand side is strictly positive.

$$\nabla_j L(\theta^*) = 0 \text{ if } j \in \mathcal{V} \quad (12)$$
$$\nabla_j L(\theta^*) < 0 \text{ if } j \notin \mathcal{V} \quad (13)$$

We now state our concentration results. For $j \in \mathcal{V}$, let

$$m_{1,j} :\ = \left|\{u : t_j^u = t_i^u - 1 \ \&\ t_k^u \neq t_i^u - 1 \ \forall\, k \in \mathcal{V} \setminus j\}\right|$$

be the number of epidemics where j is the sole infector of node i and

$$m_{2,j} :\ = \left|\{u : t_j^u \leq t_i^u - 2\}\right|$$

be the number of epidemics where j is infected at least two time units before i.

LEMMA 3. *For* $m > \frac{c}{p_{init}}\left(\frac{1}{\alpha^7\eta^2 p_{i,min}^2}\right) d_i^2 \log\left(\frac{D_i}{\delta}\right)$, *we have that*

(a) $\left|\nabla_j \widehat{L}(\theta^*)\right| < a$ *for* $j \in \mathcal{V}$ *where* $a :\ = \frac{\alpha^3 \eta p_{init}}{144d}$

(b) $\nabla_j \widehat{L}(\theta^*) < -b$ *for* $j \notin \mathcal{V}$ *where* $b :\ = \frac{\alpha p_{init}}{16}$

(c) $\xi_1 p_j^* < m_{1,j} < \bar{\xi}_1$ *for* $j \in \mathcal{V}$ *where* $\xi_1 :\ = \frac{c}{4}\log\frac{D}{\delta}$, $\bar{\xi}_1 :\ = \frac{2c}{\alpha}\log\frac{D}{\delta}$ *and* $p_j^* :\ = 1 - \exp(-\theta_j^*)$

(d) $\xi_2 < m_{2,j} < \bar{\xi}_2$ *for* $j \in \mathcal{V}$ *where* $\xi_2 :\ = \frac{c\alpha}{4}\log\frac{D}{\delta}$ *and* $\bar{\xi}_2 :\ = \frac{2c}{\alpha}\log\frac{D}{\delta}$

with probability greater than $1 - \delta$.

PROOF. For simplicity of notation we denote the number of samples as $m = \frac{C \log \frac{D}{\delta}}{p_{\text{init}}}$ where $C = \frac{cd_i^2}{\alpha^7\eta^2 p_{i,min}^2}$ and $D = D_i$. We will first prove (c). First, we note the following bounds for independent Bernoulli random variables X_l where μ is the mean of the sum of X_l.

$$\mathbb{P}\left[\sum_l X_l < (1-\kappa)\mu\right] < \left(\frac{\exp(-\kappa)}{(1-\kappa)^{(1-\kappa)}}\right)^{\mu} \quad (14)$$

$$\mathbb{P}\left[\sum_l X_l > (1+\kappa)\mu\right] < \left(\frac{e^{\frac{\kappa}{1+\kappa}}}{1+\kappa}\right)^{(1+\kappa)\mu} \quad (15)$$

So as to be able to use the above inequalities, we first establish bounds on the expected value of $m_{1,j}$.

$$\mathbb{E}\left[m_{1,j}\right] \geq m p_{\text{init}}(1-p_{\text{init}})^d p_j^* \geq 2\xi_1 p_j^*$$

where the bound uses the probability that j is infected at time 0 and neither i nor any of its other neighbors are infected at time 0 and j infects i at time 1. Similarly, we have

$$\mathbb{E}\left[m_{1,j}\right] \leq m\mathbb{P}\left[T_j < \infty\right] \leq \frac{\bar{\xi}_1}{2}$$

where we use Lemma 1. Now applying (14) to $m_{1,j}$ we obtain

$$\mathbb{P}\left[m_{1,j} < (1-\frac{1}{2})2\xi_1 p_j^*\right] < \left(\frac{\exp\left(-\frac{1}{2}\right)}{\left(\frac{1}{2}\right)^{\frac{1}{2}}}\right)^{2\xi_1 p_j^*} < \frac{\delta}{8D}$$

Similarly applying (15) to $m_{1,j}$ gives us

$$\mathbb{P}\left[m_{1,j} > (1+1)\frac{\bar{\xi}_1}{2}\right] < \left(\frac{\sqrt{e}}{2}\right)^{\bar{\xi}_1} < \frac{\delta}{8D}$$

This proves (c). The proof of (d) is similar.

We will now prove (a). Fix any $j \in \mathcal{V}$. Let $\mathcal{U}_j = \{u \in \mathcal{U} : T_j^u < \infty\}$. Since $\mathbb{E}\left[|\mathcal{U}_j|\right] \geq p_{\text{init}} m = C \log\frac{D}{\delta}$, using (14), we obtain

$$\mathbb{P}\left[|\mathcal{U}_j| < \frac{C\log\frac{D}{\delta}}{2}\right] < \frac{\delta}{16D} \quad (16)$$

Similarly since $\mathbb{E}\left[|\mathcal{U}_j|\right] \leq \frac{p_{\text{init}}}{\alpha} m = \frac{C}{\alpha}\log\frac{D}{\delta}$, using (15), we obtain

$$\mathbb{P}\left[|\mathcal{U}_j| > \frac{2C\log\frac{D}{\delta}}{\alpha}\right] < \frac{\delta}{16D} \quad (17)$$

Define the random variable

$$Z_j = -1_{\{T_j \leq T_i - 2\}} + \frac{1_{\{T_j = T_i - 1\}}}{\exp\left(\sum_{k: T_k = T_i - 1} \theta_k^*\right) - 1}$$

Note that we have the following absolute bound on Z_j

$$|Z_j| < 1 + \frac{1}{\exp(\theta_j^*) - 1} = \frac{1}{p_j^*} \quad (18)$$

where $p_j^* = 1 - \exp\left(-\theta_j\right)$ and also

$$\nabla_j \widehat{L}(\theta^*) = \frac{1}{m}\sum_{u \in \mathcal{U}} Z_j^u = \frac{1}{m}\sum_{u \in \mathcal{U}_j} Z_j^u$$

where Z_j^u is the realization of Z_j on infection u.

$$\mathbb{P}\left[\left|\nabla_j \widehat{L}(\theta^*)\right| \geq a\right]$$
$$= \mathbb{P}\left[\frac{1}{m}\left|\sum_{u\in\mathcal{U}} Z_j^u\right| \geq a\right] = \mathbb{P}\left[\left|\sum_{u\in\mathcal{U}} Z_j^u\right| \geq ma\right]$$

At this point we could apply Azuma-Hoeffding inequality to bound the above probability. However, the scaling factor in the exponent will be ma^2 which gives us an extra p_{init}. To avoid this, we bound the above quantity as follows:

$$\mathbb{P}\left[\left|\sum_{u\in\mathcal{U}} Z_j^u\right| \geq ma\right]$$
$$\leq \mathbb{P}\left[|\mathcal{U}_j| > \frac{2C\log\frac{D}{\delta}}{\alpha} \text{ or } |\mathcal{U}_j| < \frac{C\log\frac{D}{\delta}}{2}\right]$$
$$+ \sum_{s=\frac{C\log\frac{D}{\delta}}{2}}^{\frac{2C\log\frac{D}{\delta}}{\alpha}} \mathbb{P}\left[|\mathcal{U}_j| = s; \left|\sum_{u\in\mathcal{U}} Z_j^u\right| \geq ma\right]$$
$$\overset{(\varsigma_1)}{\leq} \frac{\delta}{8D} +$$
$$\sum_{s=\frac{C\log\frac{D}{\delta}}{2}}^{\frac{2C\log\frac{D}{\delta}}{\alpha}} \sum_{U_j:|U_j|=s} \mathbb{P}\left[\mathcal{U}_j = U_j\right]\mathbb{P}\left[\left|\sum_{u\in U_j} Z_j^u\right| \geq ma \,\middle|\, \mathcal{U}_j = U_j\right] \tag{19}$$

where U_j varies over all the subsets of $\mathcal{U}$ and (ς_1) follows from (16) and (17). Focusing on the last term, we first note that Z_j^u are still independent random variables for $u \in U_j$. Since $\mathbb{E}[Z_j] = 0$ from (12), we can apply Azuma-Hoeffding inequality and using (18) we obtain

$$\mathbb{P}\left[\left|\sum_{u\in U_j} Z_j^u\right| \geq ma \,\middle|\, \mathcal{U}_j = U_j, |U_j| = s\right]$$
$$\leq 2\exp\left(\frac{-(ma)^2}{2s\left(\frac{1}{p_j^*}\right)^2}\right) < \frac{\delta}{16D} \tag{20}$$

where (ς_1) follows from the fact that $s \leq \frac{2C\log\frac{D}{\delta}}{\alpha}$. The proof of (b) is on the same lines after noting that for any $j \notin \mathcal{V}$,

$$\mathbb{E}[Z_j] = \nabla_j L(\theta^*) \overset{(\varsigma_1)}{=} -\mathbb{P}[T_i > T_j; T_j \neq T_k \;\forall\, k \in \mathcal{V}]$$
$$\overset{(\varsigma_2)}{<} -p_{\text{init}}(1-p_{\text{init}})^{d+1} \overset{(\varsigma_3)}{<} -\frac{p_{\text{init}}}{2} \tag{21}$$

where (ς_1) follows from Proposition 2, (ς_2) follows from the fact that the probability when j is infected before i and none of the parents of i are infected at the same time can be lower bounded by the case where j is infected at time 0 and neither i nor any of its parents are infected at time 0. (ς_3) follows from the assumption that $p_{\text{init}} < \frac{1}{2d}$ and hence $(1-p_{\text{init}})^{d+1} > \frac{1}{2}$. Using (21) and Lemma 1, we obtain

$$\mathbb{E}[Z_j \mid T_j < \infty] = \frac{\mathbb{E}[Z_j] - \mathbb{E}\left[Z_j 1_{\{T_j=\infty\}}\right]}{\mathbb{P}[T_j < \infty]} \leq \frac{-\alpha}{2} \tag{22}$$

Using (19) it suffices to show that

$$\mathbb{P}\left[\sum_{u\in U_j} Z_j^u \geq -mb \,\middle|\, \mathcal{U}_j = U_j, |U_j| = s\right] < \frac{\delta}{16D}$$

for $\frac{C\log\frac{D}{\delta}}{2} \leq s \leq \frac{2C\log\frac{D}{\delta}}{\alpha}$. An application of Azuma-Hoeffding inequality gives us the required bound as follows.

$$\mathbb{P}\left[\sum_{u\in U_j} Z_j^u \geq -mb \,\middle|\, \mathcal{U}_j = U_j, |U_j| = s\right]$$
$$\overset{(\varsigma_1)}{=} \mathbb{P}\left[\sum_{u\in U_j} Z_j^u - s\mathbb{E}[Z_j] \geq \frac{-C\alpha\log\frac{D}{\delta}}{16} - s\mathbb{E}[Z_j] \,\middle|\, \mathcal{U}_j = U_j, |U_j| = s\right]$$
$$\overset{(\varsigma_2)}{\leq} \mathbb{P}\left[\sum_{u\in U_j} Z_j^u - s\mathbb{E}[Z_j] \geq \frac{C\alpha\log\frac{D}{\delta}}{8} \,\middle|\, \mathcal{U}_j = U_j, |U_j| = s\right]$$
$$\overset{(\varsigma_3)}{\leq} \exp\left(\frac{\left(\frac{C\alpha\log\frac{D}{\delta}}{8}\right)^2}{2\left(\frac{2C\log\frac{D}{\delta}}{\alpha}\right)\left(\frac{1}{p_j^*}\right)^2}\right) \leq \frac{\delta}{16D}$$

where (ς_1) follows by subtracting $s\mathbb{E}[Z_j]$ from both sides of the inequality for which we are bounding the probability, (ς_2) follows from the fact that $s \geq \frac{C\log\frac{D}{\delta}}{2}$ and (22) and (ς_3) is an application of the Azuma-Hoeffding inequality using (18) and the fact that $s \leq \frac{2C\log\frac{D}{\delta}}{\alpha}$. □

We will use the quantities defined in Lemma 3 in what follows. Recall we need to show $\widehat{\theta}_j < \eta$ for $j \notin \mathcal{V}$ and $\widehat{\theta}_j > \eta$ for $j \in \mathcal{V}$ and $\theta_j^* > -\log\left(1 - \frac{8}{\alpha}(e^{2\eta} - 1)\right)$.

LEMMA 4. $\max_{j\in\mathcal{V}} \widehat{\theta}_j < \frac{\bar{\xi}_1}{\xi_2}$

PROOF. Let $k = \operatorname{argmax}_{j\in\mathcal{V}} \widehat{\theta}_j$. If $\widehat{\theta}_k = 0$, we are done. So assume $\widehat{\theta}_k > 0$. By the optimality of $\widehat{\theta}$, we see that

$$\nabla_k \widehat{L}(\widehat{\theta}) = 0 \tag{23}$$

On the other hand, we have

$$\nabla_k \widehat{L}(\widehat{\theta})$$
$$= \frac{1}{m}\left(-m_{2,k} + \sum_u 1_{\{t_i^u<\infty\}}\left(\exp\left(\sum_{j:t_j^u=t_i^u-1} \widehat{\theta}_j\right) - 1\right)^{-1}\right)$$
$$\overset{(\varsigma_1)}{\leq} \frac{1}{m}\left(-m_{2,k} + \frac{1}{\exp(\widehat{\theta}_k) - 1} m_{1,k}\right)$$
$$\overset{(\varsigma_2)}{\leq} \frac{1}{m}\left(-\xi_2 + \frac{1}{\exp(\widehat{\theta}_k) - 1}\bar{\xi}_1\right) \leq \frac{1}{m}\left(-\xi_2 + \frac{1}{\widehat{\theta}_k}\bar{\xi}_1\right) \tag{24}$$

where (ς_1) follows from the definition of $m_{1,k}$ and the fact that on the infections corresponding to $m_{1,k}$, we have

$$\sum_{j:t_j^u=t_i^u-1} \widehat{\theta}_j \geq \widehat{\theta}_k$$

and (ς_2) follows from Lemma 3. Putting (23) and (24) together, we obtain the result. □

LEMMA 5. $\sum_{j\notin\mathcal{V}} \widehat{\theta}_j \leq \frac{ad}{b}\left(\frac{\bar{\xi}_1}{\xi_2} + \log\frac{1}{\alpha}\right)$

PROOF. Since $\widehat{L}(\theta)$ is concave, the subgradient condition at θ^* gives us the following

$$\begin{aligned}\widehat{L}(\widehat{\theta}) - \widehat{L}(\theta^*) &\leq \left\langle \nabla \widehat{L}(\theta^*), \widehat{\theta} - \theta^* \right\rangle \\ &\overset{(\varsigma_1)}{=} \left\langle \nabla_{\mathcal{V}^c} \widehat{L}(\theta^*), \widehat{\theta}_{\mathcal{V}^c} \right\rangle + \left\langle \nabla_{\mathcal{V}} \widehat{L}(\theta^*), \widehat{\theta}_{\mathcal{V}} - \theta^*_{\mathcal{V}} \right\rangle \\ &\overset{(\varsigma_2)}{\leq} -b||\widehat{\theta}_{\mathcal{V}^c}||_1 + a||\widehat{\theta}_{\mathcal{V}} - \theta^*_{\mathcal{V}}||_1 \\ &\leq -b||\widehat{\theta}_{\mathcal{V}^c}||_1 + ad\left(||\widehat{\theta}_{\mathcal{V}}||_\infty + ||\theta^*_{\mathcal{V}}||_\infty\right) \quad (25)\end{aligned}$$

where (ς_1) follows from the fact that $\theta^*_{\mathcal{V}^c} = 0$ and (ς_2) follows from the fact that $\widehat{\theta} > 0$ and Lemma 3. The optimality of $\widehat{\theta}$ gives us

$$\widehat{L}(\widehat{\theta}) - \widehat{L}(\theta^*) \geq 0 \quad (26)$$

Finally we have the following bound on $||\theta^*_{\mathcal{V}}||_\infty$:

$$\theta^*_j = -\log\left(1 - p^*_j\right) \leq \log \frac{1}{\alpha} \quad (27)$$

Using (25), (26), (27) and Lemma 4 gives us the result. □

Note that $\eta > \frac{ad}{b}\left(\frac{\xi_1}{\xi_2} + \log\frac{1}{\alpha}\right)$ and hence we have that $\widehat{\theta}_j < \eta$ for all $j \notin \mathcal{V}$. Turning now to $j \in \mathcal{V}$, we have the following:

LEMMA 6. *$\widehat{\theta}_j > \log\left(1 + \frac{p^*_j \xi_1}{\xi_2}\right) - \eta$ where $p^*_j = 1 - \exp(\theta^*_j)$ for every $j \notin \mathcal{V}$*

PROOF. Since $\widehat{\theta}_j \geq 0$, by the optimality of $\widehat{\theta}$ we have

$$\nabla_j \widehat{L}(\widehat{\theta}) \leq 0 \quad (28)$$

On the other hand, we have the following bound on the gradient

$$\begin{aligned}&\nabla_j \widehat{L}(\widehat{\theta}) \\ &= \frac{1}{m}\left(-m_{2,j} - \sum_u 1_{\{t^u_i < \infty\}}\left(\exp\left(\sum_{k:t^u_k = t^u_i - 1} \widehat{\theta}_k\right) - 1\right)^{-1}\right) \\ &\overset{(\varsigma_1)}{\geq} \frac{1}{m}\left(-m_{2,j} + \frac{1}{\exp\left(\widehat{\theta}_j + ||\widehat{\theta}_{\mathcal{V}^c}||_1\right) - 1} m_{1,k}\right) \\ &\overset{(\varsigma_2)}{\geq} \frac{1}{m}\left(-\xi_2 + \frac{1}{\exp\left(\widehat{\theta}_j + ||\widehat{\theta}_{\mathcal{V}^c}||_1\right) - 1} p^*_j \xi_1\right) \quad (29)\end{aligned}$$

where (ς_1) follows from the fact that on the infections corresponding to $m_{1,k}$, we have

$$\sum_{k:t^u_k = t^u_i - 1} \widehat{\theta}_k \leq \widehat{\theta}_j + ||\widehat{\theta}_{\mathcal{V}^c}||_1$$

and (ς_2) follows from Lemma 3. Combining (28), (29) and Lemma 5 gives us the result. □

Thus we see that if the true parameter θ^*_j satisfies $\theta^*_j > -\log\left(1 - \frac{8}{\alpha}(e^{2\eta} - 1)\right)$, then $\widehat{\theta}_j > \eta$ and thus will be in the estimated neighborhood $\widehat{\mathcal{N}}_i$. This completes the proof of Theorem 1.

C. LOWER BOUNDS

PROOF OF LEMMA 2. Recall from Lemma 1 that $\mathbb{P}[T_i = t] \leq (1-\alpha)^{t-1} p_{\text{init}}$. The proof just involves using this to bound $H(T_i)$. Since $p_{\text{init}} < \frac{1}{e}$, we have the following

$$\begin{aligned}H(T_i) &= -\sum_{t=1}^{n} \mathbb{P}[T_i = t] \log \mathbb{P}[T_i = t] \\ &\quad -\mathbb{P}[T_i = \infty] \log \mathbb{P}[T_i = \infty] \\ &\leq -\sum_{t=1}^{n} (1-\alpha)^{t-1} p_{\text{init}} \log (1-\alpha)^{t-1} p_{\text{init}} \\ &\quad -\left(1 - \frac{p_{\text{init}}}{\alpha}\right) \log\left(1 - \frac{p_{\text{init}}}{\alpha}\right) \\ &\overset{(\varsigma_1)}{\leq} \frac{p_{\text{init}}}{1-\alpha}\left(\log\frac{1}{p_{\text{init}}} + \left(\frac{1-\alpha}{\alpha}\right)^2 \log\frac{1}{1-\alpha}\right) \\ &\quad -\left(1 - \frac{p_{\text{init}}}{\alpha}\right) \log\left(1 - \frac{p_{\text{init}}}{\alpha}\right)\end{aligned}$$

where (ς_1) follows from some algebraic manipulations. □

Network Forensics: Random Infection vs Spreading Epidemic

Chris Milling
The University of Texas at Austin
Austin, TX 78712, USA
cmilling@mail.utexas.edu

Constantine Caramanis
The University of Texas at Austin
Austin, TX 78712, USA
caramanis@mail.utexas.edu

Shie Mannor
Technion, Israel Institute of Technology
Haifa 32000, Israel
shie@ee.technion.ac.il

Sanjay Shakkottai
The University of Texas at Austin
Austin, TX 78712, USA
shakkott@mail.utexas.edu

ABSTRACT

Computer (and human) networks have long had to contend with spreading viruses. Effectively controlling or curbing an outbreak requires understanding the dynamics of the spread. A virus that spreads by taking advantage of physical links or user-acquaintance links on a social network can grow explosively if it spreads beyond a critical radius. On the other hand, random infections (that do not take advantage of network structure) have very different propagation characteristics.

If too many machines (or humans) are infected, network structure becomes essentially irrelevant, and the different spreading modes appear identical. When can we distinguish between mechanics of infection? Further, how can this be done efficiently? This paper studies these two questions. We provide sufficient conditions for different graph topologies, for when it is possible to distinguish between a random model of infection and a spreading epidemic model, with probability of misclassification going to zero. We further provide efficient algorithms that are guaranteed to work in different regimes.

Categories and Subject Descriptors

G.3 [**Probability and Statistics**]: Stochastic Processes

Keywords

epidemic process, network inference

1. INTRODUCTION

The degree of interconnection in communication and social networks is unprecedented, and by now, well-documented. While interconnection speeds the spread of information and ideas — another exhaustively studied research topic — it inevitably contributes to the spread of viruses. This is true not only because of (what we might now call) old-fashioned contact networks, but increasingly true thanks to social networks, and the fact that many computer (and human) viruses exploit the relaxed filters we all employ when in virtual or physical contact with friends and acquaintances – neighbors on our social network. The prevalence of (thus far, apparently relatively harmless) Facebook spam [1] is but one testament to this fact. Yet, while many viruses can spread in various manners through social networks, it is not difficult with only minor sophistication, for a virus to disguise its path, namely, how it arrived at a particular machine, and where it spread from there. To make matters worse, analogous to the setting where not all sick people immediately go to a doctor for diagnosis, for a variety of reasons we may not even have access to the identity of all infected nodes, let alone be able to determine the spreading mechanism. Nevertheless, distinguishing between an infection that spreads through a particular network, and one that affects nodes without the help of that network, can be critical: it offers opportunities to react accordingly, including quarantining portions of the network, as well as possibly predicting the extent of the spread.

This motivates us to study this basic problem in social-network-forensics, in the most dire setting: suppose that at a single snapshot in time, we are informed that a given subset of nodes has a particular virus. Initial sickness times are not available, nor are we able to observe the evolution of the sick-reporting process. Given (for now) complete knowledge of the network topology, the problem is to determine if the virus is an epidemic, spreading through the network, or if nodes have become infected via an independent infection mechanism that is external to the network being considered, and not propagated through the edges of the graph. These issues apply not only to "sickness" spreading in human/online social networks, but more generally as well. As a concrete example of these two different modes of "sickness", consider a computer network that undergoes cascaded failures due to to virus/worm propagation (the epidemic) vs. random failures due to misconfiguration whose stochastic behavior is external to the network itself (independent in-

SIGMETRICS'12, June 11–15, 2012, London, England, UK.

fections). When a small subset of nodes report failure, the objective is to determine which of these two modes has occurred.

We study this problem in four regimes: for a d-dimensional grid, for uniformly branching tree, and critically and also highly connected Erdös-Renyi graphs. Grids are in a sense local connectivity models, lacking long-range edges. They model contact networks that are very correlated with geography. They are characterized by slow spreading and small neighborhood growth. Trees model explosive (exponential) neighborhood growth. Also, while contact networks are rarely trees, they are often (locally) tree-like. Erdös-Renyi graphs are on the opposite extreme to grid graphs: there is no notion of near and far when it comes to an edge, as all edges are equally likely. They model contact networks with large neighborhoods, and small diameter.

As is to be expected, if too many nodes are infected, then the effect of network structure is washed away: it is effectively impossible to distinguish between a random infection model independent of the network, and a network-spread epidemic. Also, from a practical perspective, we are interested in detecting if there is an epidemic at an early-stage where only "few" nodes are infected, so that appropriate intervention strategies can be deployed to quell the epidemic. An interesting general finding is that the results are quite delicate, depending both on the topology of the graph, and the level of infection. What is meant by "too many infected nodes" crucially depends on both the topology of the network, as well as the algorithm used. Thus using carefully designed algorithms with performance guarantees in terms of their detection capability, is critical.

The intuition behind distinguishing the infection mechanism is simple: if the sick nodes are uniformly spread out on the network, a random infection is likely at work, while if they are "clustered" in some appropriate sense, then it is more likely that we have an infection on our hands. As we see, not all measures of "clustering" are equally powerful. Thus, finding efficiently computable and maximally discriminating measures of clustering is, in a sense, the heart of the problem. The main contribution of this paper is to provide the analysis of this problem for several different regimes, and to provide two efficiently implementable algorithms that each compute a particular measure of "spread." We call them the "Ball Algorithm" and the "Tree Algorithm" (they are described explicitly below). The Ball Algorithm considers the smallest ball that contains all the reporting sick nodes, and the Tree Algorithm considers the smallest tree connecting all reporting sick nodes (the Steiner tree). Both algorithms then declare "infection" or "random sickness" based on a threshold test. We analyze both algorithms, showing analytically and empirically where each is strongest. Figure 1 shows examples of this problem on a grid and an Erdös-Renyi graph.

Related Work

The infection model we consider here is the susceptible-infected (SI) model [3]. Most of the work on this model has focused on the analytic side, characterizing the spread of the infection in different settings, e.g., for graphs with multiple mixing distances (that is, local and global spreading) [4], and where the infected nodes are mobile [5]. There are other approaches to modeling infection, and while interesting to extend the current ideas and analysis there, we do not consider these in the present work.

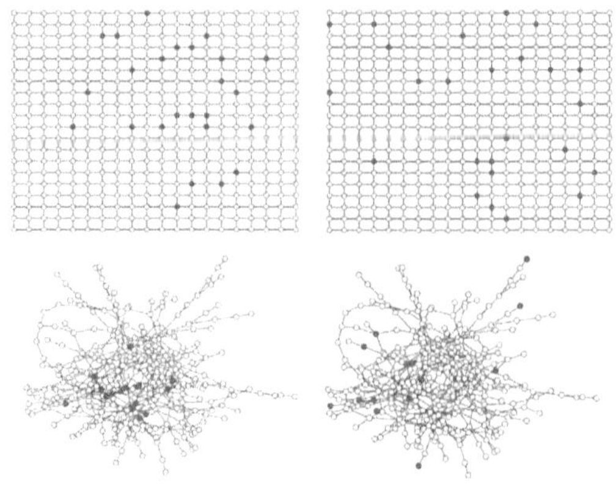

Figure 1: This figure shows infection (left) vs random sickness (right) on the grid and the Erdös-Renyi graph. The figures have been generated using NetworkX [2].

On the inference side, work in [6] provides a Bayesian inference approach for estimating the transmission rates of the infection. Alternatively, one can use MCMC methods to estimate the model parameters [7], [8]. A similar problem is considered in [9, 10], where, given a set of infected nodes, one seeks to determine which node is most likely to be the original source of the infection. These results typically involve approximation, at least for general graphs, due to the difficulty of exact inference for infections.

Several of our results here are related to first-passage percolation [11]. In the first-passage percolation basic formulation, there is a (lattice) graph of infinite size. For each edge, an independent random variable is generated that represents the time taken to traverse that edge. Some node is denoted the source, and the time taken to reach another node is the minimum of the total time to traverse a path over all paths between the source and that destination. This is equivalent to an infection traveling through the network as considered here. Work has been done to analyze interesting properties of this percolation, such as the shape of the infection and the rate at which it spreads. In particular, there are strong results on trees [12] and lattices [11] which we leverage.

Outline of the Paper and Notation

The remainder of the paper is organized as follows. In Section 2, we precisely define the statement of the problem, and the two infection models which we later attempt to distinguish. We also give the Ball and Tree Algorithms whose performance we analyze in the sequel. Section 3 considers infections and node sickness in a grid topology. Section 4 then analyzes trees. Section 5 considers Erdös-Renyi graphs, where we find more complex behavior exhibited. Finally, we numerically illustrate our results and the performance of our algorithms on different graph topologies, in Section 6. Figure 1 shows examples of the infection on these graphs.

2. PROBLEM STATEMENT

This paper considers the spread of a virus or an infection among interconnected agents, that might represent computers, or perhaps humans. We model the interconnections via edges in a graph, with an edge representing interaction between two nodes. This could be physical interaction as in a contact model, or it might denote an acquaintance relationship as in a social network. The setting we have in mind is when the interaction represented by these nodes has the potential to spread certain types of viruses. In contact networks this might be due to direct infection, while in a social network this might be because the virus exploits the implicit trust represented by links (e.g., click-through more likely for a malicious link sent from a friend's account than from a stranger's).

We note that while this paper uses the language of *infection* and *virus*, our results could equally well be understood in the context of *information* or some other abstract quality (e.g., owns an iPhone), where the mechanism of spread or acquisition is of interest (e.g., television commercials, or word-of-mouth). While we do not consider weighted graphs here, the related questions are clearly relevant, and are natural extensions of the work we present.

Node Sickness Models

As discussed, we assume there are two possible causes of the sickness: *Random sickness*, where the sickness spreads randomly and uniformly over the network and in particular the network plays no role in spreading the sickness; and *Infectious spread*, where the sickness is caused through a contagion that spreads through the network, with one node infecting its neighbors with some probability. We wish to distinguish between these two modes of sickness, *when only a small sub-collection of nodes report sick.* More precisely, we have:

> *Random Sickness*: Each node becomes sick with probability $\hat{q}_1$, independently of all other nodes. At a fixed time t each sick node reports sickness to a central authority with probability $\hat{q}_2$, again independently of all other nodes. Thus on average, a fraction $\hat{q}$ of the network reports sick, where we let $\hat{q} = \hat{q}_1 \cdot \hat{q}_2$.
>
> *Infectious Spread*: At time 0, a randomly selected node in the network becomes infected. When a node becomes infected, we start a clock for each outgoing edge attached to an adjacent node that is not already infected, with expiration time exponentially distributed with unit mean (independent of any other event). Upon expiration of a edge's clock, the corresponding node becomes infected (if by then it is not already infected through some other neighbor), and in-turn begins infecting its neighbors. Alternatively, the infection can be said to travel at rate 1 along the edges of the graph. In this way, the infection spreads through the graph for time t. At this time, as in the network-free sickness model, sick nodes report the sickness independently with probability q. For $q = 1$, the reporting sick nodes form a connected component, making the detection problem trivial. For small values of $q < 1$, however, reporting nodes need not be adjacent, and can in fact be far from other reporting sick nodes.

Naturally, the problem is of most interest when the probabilities of sickness, reporting, and also time that the sicknesses are collectively reported/discovered in the spreading model, are such that the expected numbers of sick nodes and reporting sick nodes are equal under both models, as this is when the discrimination problem is most challenging. We refer to "infected nodes," denoted by I, when the model is an infection, and "sick nodes," denoted by S, when the model is a random sickness. We use I_r and S_r to denote the subset of reporting sick nodes in each setting. The case of most interest is thus when $\mathbb{E}[S_r] = \mathbb{E}[I_r]$. When only a few (say, two or three) nodes report sick, distinguishing between the two models is easy. On the other extreme, when all or nearly all of the network is infected, distinguishing the two modes of sickness is impossible. Thus one way to talk about the power of a given algorithm on a given graph topology, is according to how many nodes can report sick and still have successful discrimination between the two models. Equivalently, we talk about the "time" t, and normalize such that at this fixed time t, $\mathbb{E}[S_t] = \mathbb{E}[I_t]$. While we explicitly use the knowledge of t in the algorithms and results, we note that it is possible to *estimate* this parameter t using only the number of sick people reporting, and knowledge of spreading and reporting rates. It turns out, this does not materially change the convergence results up to poly-log factors (i.e., the estimates appropriately concentrates to the true value in the large n setting). However, in this paper, we simply assume that t is known for ease of discussion.

Accordingly, in our analysis below, we seek to provide bounds on precisely this: what is the maximum number of reporting sick nodes we can have, while still maintaining correct detection with probability one (asymptotically). We assume that the *a priori* probabilities of each type of sickness are equal, and define the event *error* as incorrectly identifying the type of sickness. Then using this notation, we would like *upper* bounds on t, or equivalently $\mathbb{E}[S_r]$ (which scales with graph size), for which we can guarantee that if the sickness is discovered before time t, or before $\mathbb{E}[S_r]$ nodes are infected, then we can discriminate between the two spreading mechanisms, i.e., $P(error) \to 0$ as $n \to \infty$. We note again that we consider the problem where we have no knowledge of the evolution of the sick-reporting process. This is an interesting direction, which would surely enable *more powerful* algorithms that can exploit this additional time-evolution information.

The Ball and Tree Algorithms

We consider two algorithms for solving this problem. We compare their error rates analytically in Sections 3, 4 and 5, and then empirically in Section 6. These algorithms examine the set of reporting sick nodes and calculate a 'score' that rates in their respective ways how clustered the sick nodes are. They take as a parameter a threshold m and if the score is no more than that threshold, they report that the sick nodes appear to come from an infection. The threshold parameter m is topology-dependent, and we provide values for it in each relevant section below. We denote the distance between nodes u and v by $dist(u, v)$.

We term the first algorithm the 'Ball Algorithm'. We find the center of the reporting sick nodes, and then compute the radius of the ball containing all reporting sick nodes. If this distance is no more than m, we call the sickness an infection because it appears clustered. Otherwise, we call it a random sickness.

The second algorithm is called the 'Tree Algorithm.' We find a tree with the smallest number of nodes that connects each reporting node – this is called the Steiner tree [13]. If the number of nodes in the tree is less than the (again topology-dependent) threshold m, we call the sickness an

Algorithm 1 Ball Algorithm

Input: Set of reporting sick nodes S; Threshold m
Output: INFECTION or RANDOM

```
k ← ∞
for all v ∈ V do
  d ← 0
  for all u ∈ S do
    if dist(u, v) > d then
      d ← dist(u, v)
    end if
  end for
  if d < k then
    k ← d
  end if
end for
if k ≤ m then
  return INFECTION
else
  return RANDOM
end if
```

infection. Otherwise, we call it a random sickness. Finding the minimum Steiner tree is an NP-hard problem, though there are efficient algorithms that give approximate solutions, guaranteeing no more than twice the optimum number of nodes or better [14].

We analyze this inference problem and in particular the performance of our two algorithms, on three types of graphs. First, we consider an infection on a d-dimensional grid. In this case, both our algorithms are able to (asymptotically) eliminate Type I and Type II error, for up to a constant fraction of sick nodes, even when only a logarithmic fraction report sick. Orderwise, this is the best any algorithm (regardless of computational complexity) can hope to achieve. Our empirical results verify this performance, and also show that the Ball Algorithm outperforms the Tree Algorithm on the grid.

Algorithm 2 Tree Algorithm

Input: Set of reporting sick nodes S; Threshold m
Output: INFECTION or RANDOM

```
T = SteinerTree(G, S)
k = card(T)
if k ≤ m then
  return INFECTION
else
  return RANDOM
end if
```

Next we consider tree graphs. Here we show that the Tree Algorithm can correctly discriminate between infections and random sickness for larger numbers of reporting sick nodes than the Ball Algorithm is able to handle. Finally, we analyze Erdös-Renyi graphs under two different connectivity regimes: a low-connectivity with edge probability close to the regime when the giant component emerges; and a high connectivity regime the produces densely connected graphs. Again, we show that each algorithm can identify an infection with probabilities of error that decay to 0 as the network size goes to infinity, for appropriate ranges of parameters. Not surprisingly, the more densely connected, the more difficult it becomes to obtain a good measure of 'clustering.' Consequently, in those latter regimes, we find that one needs to intercept the sickness much earlier, i.e., with many fewer reporting sick nodes, in order to hope to accurately discriminate between the two potential sickness mechanisms. In the Erdös-Renyi setting, we are unable to find direct analytic results to compare our two algorithms. However, in Section 6 we evaluate them empirically and find that the Ball Algorithm tends to perform better, despite its relative algorithmic simplicity.

3. MULTIDIMENSIONAL GRIDS

The phenomenon of a sickness that is "going around" the office, the neighborhood, the school, is an instance of a contact network that is geographic – distance on the graph is closely related to geographic distance, and thus there are no 'long hops' in the graph. A canonical graph from this family is the d-dimensional grid, and we consider this first. Thus, let the graph G be such a grid network with n nodes and side length $n^{1/d}$. To avoid edge effects, we let the opposite edges of the grid connect, so that the graph forms a torus. Now due to the symmetrical structure of the grid, the initial source of an infection does not change the behavior of the infection.

Now we establish that both our algorithms work very well on this graph, even in the case of very low reporting rates. First we consider the Ball Algorithm. It turns out this performs very well on this very structured graph, in part because it matches well with the expected shape of an infection on a grid. The Tree Algorithm can also be shown to work on this graph for smaller infections, though this proof has been omitted for brevity and because it is heavily outperformed by the Ball Algorithm in this setting.

The next theorem gives conditions on the performance of the Ball algorithm, when time t has elapsed (recall that this is equivalent to fixing the expected size of the infection, and we assume for now that this is known). The number of reporting nodes can be arbitrary, but must be above $\log n$. Note that this requirement, along with the time t, implicitly constrains the underlying parameters of the problem setup, namely q. We use μ to denote the expected rate that an infection travels along an axis on the grid, which is only a function of the dimension of the graph, since we assume the spreading rate to be normalized. We have the following.

THEOREM 1. *Consider the Ball algorithm (Algorithm 1) with threshold $m = 1.1d\mu t$. Suppose that the expected number of reporting nodes scales at least as $\log n$. Then there exists constant C_1 such that for sufficiently large n, if the expected number of infected nodes is less than $C_1 n$,*

$$P(error) \to 0.$$

In other words, an infection can be identified with probability approaching 1 as n tends to infinity.

To prove this theorem, we use a previous result that characterizes the spread of an infection. Since we model the time it takes the infection to traverse an edge as an independent exponentially distributed random variable, the time a node is infected is the minimum sum of these random variables over all paths between the infection origin and that node.

This simply phrases the infection process in terms of first-passage percolation on this graph. This allows us to use a result characterizing the 'shape' of an infection on this graph (see [11]). Let $I(t)$ be the set of infected nodes at time t. Imagining the graph as the integer lattice embedded in $\mathbb{R}^d$ with the infection starting at the origin, let us put a small ℓ^∞-ball around each infected node. This allows us to simply state inner and outer bounds for the shape of the infection. To this end, define this expanded set as $B(t) = I(t) + [-1/2, 1/2]^d$.

LEMMA 1 ([11]). *There exists a set B_0 and constants C_1 to C_5 such that for $x \le \sqrt{t}$,*

$$P\{(B(t)/t \subset (1 + x/\sqrt{t})B_0)\} \ge 1 - C_1 t^{2d} e^{-C_2 x}$$

and

$$P\{(1 - C_3 t^{-1/(2d+4)}(\log t)^{1/(d+2)})B_0 \subset B(t)/t\}$$
$$\ge 1 - C_4 t^d \exp(-C_5 t^{(d+1)/(2d+4)}(\log t)^{1/(d+2)}).$$

That is, the shape of the infected set $B(t)$ can be well-approximated by the region tB_0.

Moreover, one can show that this set B_0 is regular in that it contains an ℓ^1-ball and is contained in an ℓ^∞ ball: $\{x : \|x\|_1 \le \mu\} \subset B_0 \subset [-\mu, \mu]^d$, where $\mu \triangleq \sup_x\{(x, 0, ..., 0) \in B_0\}$, effectively the rate the infection spreads along an axis [11]. Note that μ does not depend on the *realization*. This result says that the expected shape of the infection is "nearly" a ball, in the sense described above. Therefore it is not surprising that our Ball Algorithm should do well.

Now we turn back to the finite grid with side length $n^{1/d}$ to present the proof our theorem.

PROOF OF THEOREM 1. To prove this theorem, we prove the following more general statement. Let m be the threshold for the Ball Algorithm and suppose $(2m/d + 1) < n^{1/d}$. If for some $\epsilon > 0$,

$$t < \frac{m}{d\mu(1+\epsilon)},$$

the Type II error probability decreases to 0 as t, m, and n increase. In addition, the Type I error probability also decreases to 0 in the limit if

$$t^d q \left(\frac{n^{1/d} - 2m/d - 1}{n^{1/d}}\right) = \omega(\log n).$$

We begin with the Type II error probability, which we denote by E_{II}: the probability we mistake an infection process for a random sickness. As long as m is chosen as in the statement of the theorem, we are guaranteed that if the sickness is in fact from an infection, then using the above lemma, the spread of the infection is limited to the sub-grid $[-m/d, m/d]^d$ with high probability, where the origin is set to be the original infected node. Consequently, all nodes must be within m steps of the origin since the grid is d-dimensional. That is, we have

$$E_{II} < 1 - P\{B(t) \subset [-m/d, m/d]^d\}$$
$$< C_1 t^{2d} e^{-C_2 t^{-1/2}(m/(d\mu) - t)},$$

from Lemma 1, where we use $x = \min(t^{-1/2}(m/(d\mu) - t), t^{1/2})$. Therefore, given $\epsilon > 0$, $t < \frac{m}{d\mu(1+\epsilon)}$, indeed the error goes to 0 as t and n increase.

Next, we consider Type I error, E_I: the probability we mistake a random sickness for an infection process. This happens if all the reporting sick nodes happen to fall inside the ball of radius m/d. Recall that our problem is only of interest if the two processes yield roughly the same number of sick nodes reporting. We can get a lower bound on this number for the infection process (and hence for the random sickness process) this time using the inner bound on B_0. For the infection process, the second part of Lemma 1 asserts that the infected region contains all nodes within the $l1$-ball of radius $w = (1 - C_3 t^{-1/(2d+4)}(\log t)^{1/(d+2)})\mu t$ with probability at least $1 - P_1$, where

$$P_1 = C_4 t^d \exp(-C_5 t^{(d+1)/(2d+4)}(\log t)^{1/(d+2)}).$$

Therefore at least $2\lfloor w \rfloor^d$ nodes will be sick with that probability, and hence there will be on average, at least $2q\lfloor w \rfloor^d$ sick nodes reporting. What is the probability that the random sickness model with (at least) this many sick nodes will have all reporting nodes inside the sub grid $[-m/d, m/d]^d$? There are $L = (2m/d + 1)^d$ nodes in that region. Evidently, any given sick node satisfies that property with probability L/n, so they all satisfy it with probability at most $(L/n)^{2qw^d}$. Note that any dependence between sick nodes only reduces the probability. After this, we use a union bound to find that the probability no such region contains all sick nodes is at most $P_2 = n(L/n)^{2qw^d}$.

Putting it all together, we have,

$$E_I < 1 - (1 - P_1)(1 - P_2) < P_1 + P_2$$
$$< C_4 t^d \exp\left(-C_5 t^{(d+1)/(2d+4)}(\log t)^{1/(d+2)}\right)$$
$$+ n\left(\left(\frac{2m/d + 1}{n^{1/d}}\right)^d\right)^{2qw^d}.$$

and

$$2w^d \ge 2\mu^d t^d (1 - dC_3 t^{-1/(2d+4)}(\log t)^{1/(d+2)}).$$

Note that P_2 dominates as n increases. We want to find the regime when this probability tends to 0. That is, we want

$$n \exp(2\mu^d t^d q d \ln\left(1 - \frac{n^{1/d} - 2m/d - 1}{n^{1/d}}\right)$$
$$(1 - dC_3 t^{-1/(2d+4)}(\log t)^{1/(d+2)})) \to 0.$$

Using a Taylor expansion and some simplification, we find a sufficient condition for this is that

$$t^d q \left(\frac{n^{1/d} - 2m/d - 1}{n^{1/d}}\right) = \omega(\log n).$$

This completes the proof of the general statement. In addition, the Type I error can be shown to dominate in the range of interest. Theorem 1 follows immediately using the threshold provided.

□

4. TREES

We now turn to the problem on tree graphs. Trees have different (exponential) spreading rates from grids, and hence manifest fundamentally different behavior. Indeed, while simple, tree graphs convey the key conceptual point of this section: the difficulty of distinguishing an epidemic from a random sickness on graphs where the infection spreads quickly. In addition, while the results do not immediately carry over, the behavior on a tree provides an intuition for the behavior of an infection on an Erdös-Renyi graph, which we cover in the next section.

Thus, let G be a balanced tree with n nodes, constant branching ratio c, and a single root node a. In the case of an infection, instead of choosing a node at random to be the original source of the infection, we always choose the root of the tree. This is the most interesting case, since otherwise a constant fraction of the nodes are very far from the infection source and bottlenecked by the root node. Also, this precisely models the scenario for locally tree-like graphs, such as Erdös-Renyi graphs.

First we examine the performance of the Ball Algorithm on this graph. Again recall the meaning of t: it is the time at which the sicknesses are reported, and also a proxy for the expected number of infected nodes.

THEOREM 2. *Consider the Ball algorithm (Algorithm 1). Suppose that the expected number of reporting nodes scales at least as* $\log n$. *Then there exist constants* b, β *such that if the threshold* $m = 1.1bt$ *and the expected number of infected nodes is less than* n^β,

$$P(error) \to 0.$$

In other words, an infection can be identified with probability approaching 1 *as* n *tends to infinity.*

PROOF. To prove this theorem, we prove the following more general statement:

For some constant $\beta < 1$, if $qE[I] = \omega(1)$ and $E[I] < n^{beta}$, then the Type I error probability tends to 0. Next, there exists a constant b such that if $b_0 > b$ and the threshold $m > b_0 t$ for all n, then the Type II error probability converges to 0 asymptotically, as the tree size scales.

The Type II error bound follows from results in first passage percolation [15]. In particular, one can compute the fastest-sustainable transit rate. This quantity is basically the time from the root to the leaves, normalized for depth, as the size of the tree scales. Formally (again, see [15] for details), let us consider a limiting process of trees whose size grows to infinity, with Γ_n denoting the balanced tree on n nodes, and $\delta(\Gamma_n)$ denoting the set of paths from the root to the leaves, and for a node $v \in p$ for some path $p \in \delta(\Gamma_n)$, let X_v denote the time it takes the infection to reach node v. Then the *fastest-sustainable transit rate* is defined as: $\lim_n \inf_{p\in\delta(\Gamma_n)} \limsup_{v\in p} \frac{X_v}{\text{depth}(v)}$. Basic results [15] show that this quantity exists, and thus shows that the rate at which an infection travels, defined as the maximum distance of the infection from the root over time, converges to a constant b that depends on the branching ratio. The probability that an infection travels at a faster rate converges to 0 in the size of the tree. This establishes the Type II result.

The Type I error result follows simply as well. Given the branching ratio, c, there are $\frac{c^{m+1}-1}{c-1}$ nodes within a distance m from the root. Again letting S_r denote the number of reporting sick nodes, the probability of a Type I error is (approximately) $(\frac{c^m}{n})^{S_r}$ – the probability that the randomly sick nodes are closer than the threshold m to the root. Then if c^m is $o(n)$, it is sufficient that the probability that $S_r = 0$ goes to 0. This occurs if the expected number of reporting sick nodes is $\omega(1)$. That is, we need $qE[I] = qe^{(c-1)t} = \omega(1)$, calculating $E[I]$ with a simple differential equation. Alternatively, if $c^m = \alpha n$ for some constant $\alpha < 1$, then we require S_r to increase with n with probability 1. The same condition as before is sufficient for this to be true. This completes the Type I result.

Using both these results, there is a choice of m such that both error types become rare as long as $c^{b_0 t} < \alpha n$, so $c^t < (\alpha n)^{1/b_0}$. The theorem follows using a particular threshold. □

Next, we consider the Tree Algorithm on this graph. The threshold here depends on $E[I]$ instead of depending explicitly on t, but as discussed previously, these are essentially equivalent.

THEOREM 3. *Consider the Tree algorithm (Algorithm 2) with reporting probability* $q > \log\log n/\log n$ *and threshold* $m = E[I]\log\log n$. *Suppose that the expected number of reporting nodes scales at least as* $\log n$. *Then for any constant* $\alpha < 1$, *if the expected number of infected nodes scales as less than* n^α,

$$P(error) \to 0.$$

In other words, an infection can be identified with probability approaching 1 *as* n *tends to infinity.*

PROOF. We prove the following generalization of the theorem: The Type I error probability converges to 0 for any choice of the threshold $m = o(qE[I]\log n)$ with $qE[I] = O(n^\alpha)$ for some $\alpha < 1$. In addition, the Type II error probability converges to 0 if $m = \omega(E[I])$.

To prove the Type II error result (mistaking an infection for a random sickness), note that the size of the infection is $E[S] \leq e^{(c-1)t}$. Since the Steiner tree containing the reporting nodes can be no larger than the infection itself, the Type II error converges to 0 as long as we use a threshold $m = \omega(E[I])$ from Markov's inequality. Next, we evaluate the Type I error probability (mistaking a random sickness for an infection). This requires estimating the size of the Steiner tree containing the reporting sick nodes. Suppose there is an $\alpha < 1$ such that $E[S_r] = O(n^\alpha)$. Since the number of sick nodes increases with n, the probability that there are sick nodes on at least two subtrees of the root node goes to 1, hence the root of the tree is in the Steiner tree connecting the randomly sick nodes with high probability. Given this, we see that a node is in the Steiner tree if and only if it is infected or a node below it in the tree is infected. Let $N = S_r$. Since $E[S_r]$ is $\omega(1)$, N is $\omega(1)$ with high probability. Choose the first level in the tree that has at least N/c nodes. Then there are between N/c and N subtrees below that level. It is straightforward to show that each sick node in the tree has at least a $1/2$ probability of being a leaf node since $c \geq 2$. Since at least N nodes are sick, at least $N/4$ of the leaf nodes are sick and distributed independently among the at most N subtrees. Therefore, the total number of subtrees with sick nodes at the bottom is at least $N/(8c)$. In addition, each leaf node in a separate subtree requires a path at least up to the aforementioned level in the Steiner tree. This gives us the following high probability bound on the Steiner tree size.

$$\begin{aligned}\text{Steiner Tree Size} &> \frac{N}{8c}(\log_c n - \log_c N)\\ &> N\frac{(1-\alpha)\log_c n}{8c}\\ &= S_r\frac{(1-\alpha)\log_c n}{8c}.\end{aligned}$$

For any $w = o(E[S_r])$, we know that $S_r > w$ with probability approaching 1, since $E[S_r] = E[I_r]$. Also, if $E[S_r] = O(n^\alpha)$, then $S_r = O(n^\alpha)$ with high probability. Therefore, if $m = o(qw \log_c n)$, which is equivalent to $m = o(E[S_r] \log n)$, the Type I error probability tends to 0. □

Note that the Ball Algorithm succeeds until the farthest infected node reaches the edge of the graph. At this point, the ball radius can increase no further, thus there is no hope of distinguishing an infection from a random sickness. Since this farthest point travels at a faster rate than the bulk of the infection, the Ball Algorithm can only work up to some time $\log_c n/b$. However, the Tree Algorithm can still correctly identify an infection with high probability nearly to the point where $\Theta(n)$ nodes are sick. This includes infection times close to $\log_c n$, the time it takes for every node to be infected. From this, we see that the Tree Algorithm works for a wider range of times compared to the Ball Algorithm. This is demonstrated by simulations in Section 6.

5. ERDÖS-RENYI GRAPHS

In this section, we consider Erdös-Renyi graphs. A notable difference in the topology of Erdös-Renyi graphs and grids is that the diameter of the former scales much more slowly (logarithmically) with graph size. That is, Erdös-Renyi graphs are more highly connected, in the sense that no two nodes are too far apart. These model contact graphs that are not tightly correlated to geographic proximity. For example, one might consider physical proximity forced by an event (a concert) attended by neighbors and non-neighbors alike, or a virtual network where edges are formed independent of geography.

We consider two connectivity regimes: the regime where the giant component first emerges, and each node has a constant expected number of edges, and then a much more highly connected regime, where the graph demonstrates different local properties, and discrimination between random sickness and infection is harder still.

5.1 Detection with Constant Average Degree

We first consider Erdös-Renyi graphs with constant average degree. Define the graph $G = G(n,p)$ to be the graph with n nodes and for each pair of nodes, there is an edge between them with probability p. In the section above, we used c to denote the branching ratio. We overload notation and use it again to measure the spread of the graph, but here as the expected degree: let $p = c/n$ with $c > 1$. In this regime, the graph is almost surely disconnected, but there is a giant component. Since this problem would be trivial on a disconnected graph, we limit both the infection and random sick nodes to the giant component. We show that unlike the case of trees, we are unable to distinguish infection from random sickness for close to a constant fraction of nodes. Instead, we consider infections that cover only $o(n)$ nodes. As is well-known (e.g., [16]) in this connectivity regime, the graph is locally tree-like, and hence tree-like in the infected region. This allows us to leverage some results from the previous section, although direct translation is not possible, particularly in the analysis of our second algorithm.

Again we note that in the next two theorems, the threshold depends on t and $E[I]$, respectively. As discussed, these are essentially equivalent, and the choice amounts to ease of notation and exposition.

THEOREM 4. *Consider the Ball algorithm (Algorithm 1). Suppose that the expected number of reporting nodes scales at least as* $\log n$. *Then there exist constants* b, β *such that if the threshold* $m = 1.1bt$ *and the expected number of infected nodes is less than* n^β,

$$P(error) \to 0.$$

In other words, an infection can be identified with probability approaching 1 as n tends to infinity.

PROOF. The proof follows similar lines as in the previous section, so we omit most details. In particular, we show the following: Using a threshold $m < \frac{\log n}{2 \log c}$ and $qE[I] = \omega(1)$, the probability of a Type I error is at most $o(n^{-1})$. In addition, the probability of a Type II error converges to 0 as long as $m > bt$ for a constant b specified in the proof.

To control the probability of a Type I error, we have to bound the probability that all randomly sick nodes are within a ball of radius m on the graph. A sufficient condition for this is that all nodes are within distance $2m$ from a given sick node, or there are 0 nodes sick. The latter probability is simply $(1-q)^n$ which decays exponentially. Also, with probability $1 - o(n^{-1})$, the number of nodes within a distance $2m$ from a given sick node is no more than $16m^3c^{2m} \log n$ [17]. Then the error probability in this case is at most $\left(1 - \frac{16m^3c^{2m}\log n}{n}\right)^n$. Then this decays exponentially as long as $c^{2m} = o(n)$, which occurs when $m < \frac{\log n}{2 \log c}$. Thus we find in total, the Type I error probability is $o(n^{-1})$.

We bound the probability of a Type II error again using the notion of the fastest sustainable transit rate from first-passage percolation [15]. As in Theorem 2, the constant b comes from the calculation of the infection spreading rate, and the results follow similarly. □

The Tree Algorithm is more complex to analyze for this graph. The more delicate analysis comes from the challenge of bounding the size of the Steiner tree for the random sickness process, needed to control Type I error.

THEOREM 5. *Consider the Tree algorithm (Algorithm 2) with reporting probability* $q > \log\log n/\log n$ *and threshold* $m = E[I]\log\log n$. *Suppose that the expected number of reporting nodes scales at least as* $\log n$. *Then for any constant* $\alpha < 1/2$, *if the expected number of infected nodes scales as less than* n^α,

$$P(error) \to 0.$$

In other words, an infection can be identified with probability approaching 1 as n tends to infinity.

PROOF. We show the following more general statement: The Type II error probability decays to 0 if the threshold is chosen as $m = \omega(E[I])$ and $E[I] = o(n)$. The Type I error probability goes to 0 when $m < kqE[I]$ for some constant $k = o(\log(n/(qE[I])^2))$ and $qE[I] = o(\sqrt{n})$.

First, if the sickness is from an infection, the smallest tree connecting the reporting sick nodes must have size no more than the actual number of sick nodes. Hence, to bound the Type II error, it is sufficient to bound the probability the number of infected nodes is over a certain size. This probability decreases to 0 as long as m is $\omega(E[I])$ when $E[I] = o(n)$. To see this, recall that in this regime, the graph looks locally tree-like. Consequently, we can bound the maximum number of infected nodes using bounds on the distance an infection can travel (e.g., see [15]). Again, Markov's inequality provides the exact error bound in the theorem statement.

To control Type I error probability, that a random sickness is mistaken for an infection, we must lower bound the size of the Steiner tree of a random sickness. Call this minimum value r. Again, let S denote the number of sick nodes, and $\mathcal{S}$ the set of sick nodes. For $A \in \mathcal{S}$, let d_A denote the distance from that node to the nearest other sick node. First we show that $\sum_{A \in \mathcal{S}} d_A \leq 2r$. Note that the bound is attained for some graphs, such as a star graph with the central node uninfected.

Consider the Steiner tree subgraph, and duplicate all edges on it. Since the degree of each node in the subgraph is even, there is a cycle that connects all these nodes. Naturally, the length of this cycle, which is twice the size of the Steiner tree, is larger than the length of the smallest cycle connecting all sick nodes. In addition, the length of this cycle is at least $\sum_{A \in \mathcal{S}} d_A$, since the distance from one sick node to the next sick node in the cycle is clearly no smaller than the distance from that sick node to the closest sick node. This establishes that $\sum_{A \in \mathcal{S}} d_A \leq 2r$.

Now we simply need to bound d_A. To do this, we need an understanding of the neighborhood sizes in a $G(n, p)$ graph. We provide an interesting way to visualize the distance distribution $f(d)$ – the distribution for the number of nodes at distance d. Then, using a CLT result, we provide a lower bound on the distance between one random node and the nearest sick node. To do this, we leverage concentration results for spreading processes on graphs. In order to not confuse this process with the sickness/infections we have been discussing, we follow standard terminology (e.g., [16]) and call a node "checked" if it has been reached by the infection, and "active" if it is checked but its neighbors are not all checked. Our process evolves as follows. At each time slot, we pick an active node at random, add its unchecked neighbors to the set of active nodes, and remove it from the active node set. If the set of active nodes ever becomes empty before the entire graph has been checked, we pick an unchecked node at random and make it active. This process continues until the whole graph is checked. Thus, at any time t we have checked nodes C_t, active nodes A_t, and the remaining nodes U_t.

The following CLT result for this process is established in [16]. Define ρ to be the solution to $\rho = \exp(c(\rho - 1))$. For any constant α such that αn is an integer, define $u_{\alpha n} = \text{card}(U_{\alpha n})$. Then, for $0 < \alpha < \rho$, $u_{\alpha n}$ converges to $ne^{-\alpha c}$. In particular,

$$(u_{\alpha n} - ne^{-\alpha c})/\sqrt{n} \xrightarrow{d} N(0, e^{-\alpha c} - c^{-2\alpha c}).$$

Now we illustrate how to use this result to determine the distance distribution for this graph. First, note that we can replace the random selection of an active node by always picking the closest node to the original node at each step in the process, and the CLT result remains unchanged. Thus, the process effectively performs a breadth first search of the graph. Eventually, we reach a state where the set C_t of checked nodes contains all nodes at distance at most d from the original node, A. Label the time this occurs t_d. Note that the number of nodes at distance $d+1$ is the set of active nodes, and $\text{card}(A_{t_d}) = n - u_{t_d} - t_d$. Then the time that we check all nodes within distance $d+1$ will be at

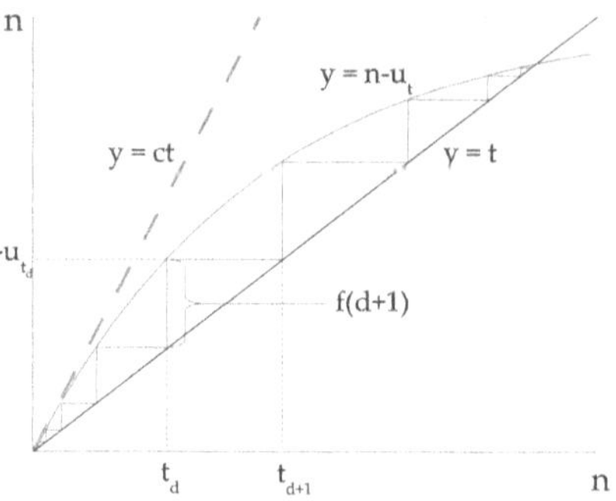

Figure 2: Diagram illustrating how the limiting curve of this process can be used to determine the distance distribution.

$t_d + (n - u_{t_d} - t_d) = n - u_{t_d}$. This can be used to calculate the distance distribution. Letting time go to infinity and plotting on the graph with spacing $1/t$, we can think of u_t as a curve. Using the above CLT result, the curve $y = n - u_t$ can be approximated by $y = ct$ for small t. That is, the distance distribution is close to that of a tree graph with the same branching ratio, c. Now we can calculate $f(d)$, the number of nodes at distance d. Let $\epsilon > 0$. It is simple to calculate by comparison of the two curves above, that with this branching process, $f(d+1) < (1+\epsilon)cf(d)$. Therefore, there are no more than $((1+\epsilon)c)^d$ nodes within distance d when the process is close to its limit, which occurs with high probability provided that $d = \omega(1)$. Figure 2 illustrates how $f(d)$ is determined from these curves.

Now assume the number of sick nodes satisfies $S = o(\sqrt{n})$. Let $\epsilon > 0$ and $m = \epsilon n/S^2$. We let k be a distance from an arbitrarily chosen sick node, A, within which there are at most m nodes. Using the distance distribution calculation above, we find $k = o(\log(n/S^2))$ is sufficient for this condition. As the sick nodes are randomly selected, the probability that none of these are within a distance k from A is approximately $(1 - S/n)^m \to e^{-\epsilon/S} \to 1 - \epsilon/S$. Thus the distance to the closest sick node to A is at least k, i.e., $d_A > k$, with high probability, and using a simple union bound, the same is true, simultaneously, for all sick nodes. Hence the Steiner tree joining the set of *reporting* sick nodes will be of size at least $r \geq (1/2)\sum d_A = (1/2)kqE[I]$, with probability decaying to zero. Again we have used the fact that $E[I] = E[S]$. Therefore, the Type I error probability tends to 0 as long as the threshold satisfies $m < kqE[I]$, for $k = o(\log(n/(qE[I])^2))$. Using this result, we find that the Tree Algorithm can succeed so long as $q\log(n/(qE[T])^2) = \omega(1)$. This is a complex condition, though the conditions given in the theorem are sufficient for it to be true. □

5.2 Detection on Dense Graphs

Now we consider the case of an Erdös-Renyi graph with a denser set of edges. Higher connectivity means the infection spreads faster, making it more difficult to distinguish between spreading mechanisms. The performance depends critically on the exact scaling regime. We consider the regime where there exists $d \in \mathbb{Z}$ and constants $\epsilon, h \in \mathbb{R}$ such that $\epsilon < n^{d-1}p^d < h$ holds for all n as $n \to \infty$ (see also [18] for further discussion of this scaling regime and properties of these dense graphs). The next result bounds the size of the Steiner tree on a random collection of nodes, and is the key result for bounding of Type I error.

LEMMA 2. *Suppose nodes are independently sick, with probability $n^{1/d}/n$, so that the expected number of reporting sick nodes is $qn^{1/d}$. Further suppose our graph is a $G(n,p)$ whose parameters satisfy $\epsilon < n^{d-1}p^d < h$ for $d > 4$. Let Z be the size of the minimum Steiner tree connecting the reporting sick nodes. Also, let $m < (d-3)qn^{1/d}/2$ be the threshold for the Steiner tree size in the Tree Algorithm. Then Z satisfies the following probabilistic limit: $\lim_{n\to\infty} Pr(Z < m) = 0$.*

PROOF. Using precisely the same argument as above, we can lower-bound the size of the Steiner tree by $\sum d_A \leq 2Z$, where the sum is over all reporting sick nodes, and as before, d_A denotes the minimum distance from a reporting sick node A to the nearest other reporting sick node. To lower bound the size of this sum, we rely on a result from [18] that shows that in this scaling regime, the asymptotic distribution of the distance between two random nodes is positive on only d and $d+1$. That is, *almost all nodes* are either at distance d or $d+1$ from any given source node A, and thus the function $f(d)$ defined previously, concentrates around d. To put this another way, let $F(d)$ be the probability that a random node is at distance more than d from A. Then for any $\hat{d} > 1$, if $n^{\hat{d}-1}p^{\hat{d}} < h$, we have

$$\lim F_{\hat{d}} = \exp^{-n^{\hat{d}-1}p^{\hat{d}}}.$$

Now we condition on the number of sick nodes, S. Note $E[S] = n^{1/d}$ and the number of reporting sick nodes is just q times this. We can compute the probability that the closest node is at distance more than $\hat{d}$ from A simply as $F^I_{\hat{d}} \to \exp^{-(I/n)(np)^{\hat{d}}}$. Using our scaling regime, we know that $(\epsilon n)^{1/d} < np < (hn)^{1/d}$. To simplify notation, let $h' = h^{1/d}$. We have

$$\begin{aligned} F^I_{d-3} &\to 1 - I/n(np)^{d-3} \\ &> 1 - I/h'nn^{(d-3)/d}. \end{aligned}$$

Using a simple union bound, we find that the probability that some reporting sick node is within distance $d-3$ of another reporting sick node is at most $S^2/h'nn^{(d-3)/d}$. Since S is a binomial random variable, it concentrates about its mean: for any $\epsilon' > 0, Pr((1-\epsilon')E[S] < S < (1+\epsilon')E[S]) \to 1$. Within this range, we find that $\sum d_A > (d-3)(1-\epsilon')E[S]$ with probability at least $1 - (1+\epsilon')^2 h' E[S]^2 n^{-3/d} > 1 - Cn^{-1/d}$ for some constant C. This converges to 1 for large enough n. Thus, we have shown the desired result. □

Now the probability of error calculations and hence the proof of correctness for the Tree Algorithm follows directly from the above.

THEOREM 6. *For G as above, suppose the expected number of reporting sick nodes in either model is $qn^{1/d}$. Then the Tree Algorithm with threshold m, the probability of a Type I error converges to 0, as long as the threshold satisfies $m < (d-3)qn^{1/d}/2$. The probability of a Type II error upper bounded by $2/(d-3-\epsilon)$ as long as the threshold satisfies $m > (d-3-\epsilon)qn^{1/d}/2$, for any value of $\epsilon > 0$ such that $\epsilon + 3 < d$. This bound converges to 0 as $d \to \infty$.*

PROOF. Consider first the probability of a Type I error. This is the probability that a random sickness has a Steiner tree of size less than m. From Theorem 2, this probability converges to 0 if $E[I] = O(n^{1/d})$.

Second, consider the probability of a Type II error. As we have argued before, the size of this tree is no more than the total number of infected nodes, so it is sufficient to find the probability there are more than m infected nodes. Using Markov's Inequality, this goes to zero when m is an increasing factor greater than the mean number of infected nodes. □

6. SIMULATIONS

In this section we provide simulation-based evidence of the theoretical results of the previous sections. The simulations aim to demonstrate, in particular, two facts. First, the thresholds specified in the previous sections do actually work empirically, and as the graph size increases, the probability of both types of error decrease to zero. In addition, this provides insight into how quickly the probability of error decays. While our results include rate estimates given as part of the proof of correctness, we have not made an effort to optimize these in this work. Next, we seek to describe the relative performance of each algorithm, and show that it is as described above. Thus, we show that the Ball Algorithm outperforms the Tree Algorithm on a grid; the Tree Algorithm performs better than the Ball Algorithm on a balanced tree; and on an Erdos-Renyi graph, the performances are similar, with the Ball Algorithm performing slightly better. We accomplish this by determining the probability of error for a range of infection times. We call an algorithm superior if it works in a wider range of times.

We note that to perform our simulations, it was necessary to use an approximate Steiner tree algorithm to perform the Tree Algorithm in a reasonable time frame. Naturally, since the exact problem is NP-hard, this would be required in any practical use of this algorithm at the moment. However, as a consequence, the empirical results may differ from the true theoretical result that would be obtained by employing an exact algorithm. Nevertheless, approximation algorithms typically have reasonable performance and we do not expect significant deviation from the correct results. The approximation algorithm we use is the Mehlhorn 2-approximation algorithm provided by the Goblin library [19]. This algorithm is an efficient algorithm which produces a Steiner tree with no more than twice the optimal number of edges.

Each of the points in these results represents the average of 10,000 runs. The average infection size, which is used to normalize the expected infection size in a random sickness, was determined by averaging the results of 10,000 infections. For each simulation, we use a reporting probability $q = 0.25$, and other parameters (n, t and m) as specified in each section below. Finally, the graphs are plotted with error bars at 95% confidence.

6.1 Error Rate Versus Graph Size

Though our theoretical results have characterized the range for which each algorithm works, naturally we wish to see empirically the error probability for each algorithm and the rate at which the error decreases as graph size increases. Both Type I and Type II error probabilities were determined for each algorithm and graph topology. For this section, we have chosen time to keep the fraction of infected nodes at a consistent scaling. In particular, $t = 0.2\sqrt{n}$ for the grid, and $t = 0.5\log(0.5n)$ with $p = 2/n$ for the Erdös-Renyi graph.

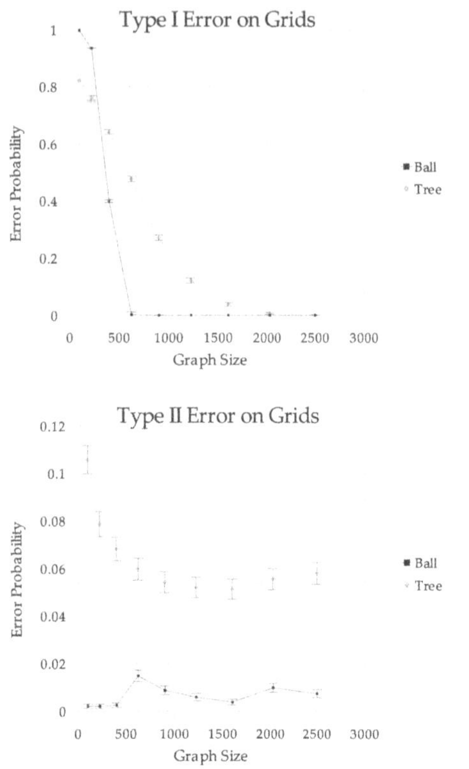

Figure 3: Empirical Type I and Type II error probability vs graph size for grid graphs. The sample size is $10,000$ and infection size scales linearly with n.

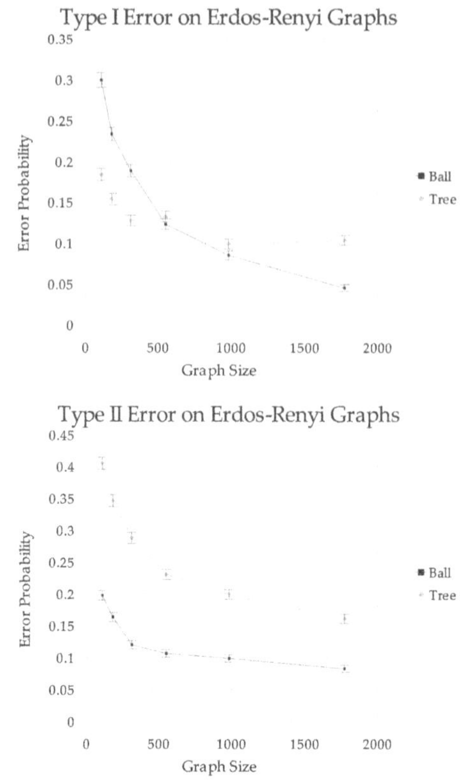

Figure 4: Empirical Type I error probability vs graph size for graphs $G(n, 2/n)$. The sample size is $10,000$ and infection size scales orderwise as $\sqrt{n}$.

The exact constants for these scalings were chosen empirically so that the problem was tractable, and the Type I and Type II errors were as balanced as possible. The thresholds m were also chosen with the same scaling, according to our theoretical results. To be exact, for the grid, the Ball algorithm used threshold $m = 0.75\sqrt{n}$ and the Tree algorithm used threshold $m = 0.28n$. For the Erdös-Renyi graphs, the Ball algorithm used threshold $m = 0.69 \log(4.33n)$ and the Tree algorithm used threshold $m = 0.03\sqrt{n \log n} \log n$.

Figure 3 presents our results for grid graphs. The error probability of the Ball Algorithm on a grid is very low, while the tree algorithm performs relatively poorly. This is expected since the Ball Algorithm is closely aligned with the true shape of an infection on this graph. The Tree Algorithm has a much higher error probability which decays slowly with n, in particular Type II error.

Next, the results for Erdös-Renyi graphs are in Figure 4. Here we see again that the Ball Algorithm performs better than the Tree Algorithm, at least for larger n, and that the error probability also seems to be decreasing faster for the Ball Algorithm as well. Though a tree more closely matches the infection shape on an Erdös-Renyi graph, it is also easier for a random sickness to mimic a small tree, especially for small world graphs like Erdös-Renyi graphs. This causes the Ball Algorithm to be ultimately superior. The Tree Algorithm is superior for larger infection sizes on bottle necked graphs (such as trees) where the random sickness can be easily distinguished, as we see in Section 6.2.

6.2 Error Rate Versus Infection Time

Next, we examine empirically how the infection duration affects the probability of error for each of our algorithms. Since we are comparing the two algorithms by the range of infection sizes for which they work, we say an algorithm is superior if it maintains a lower probability of error for a wider time frame. We use thresholds that empirically minimize the overall probability of error. That is, the sickness was chosen to be either an infection or simply random with equal probability, and the threshold with minimum probability of error from the simulations was chosen.

These results are presented in Figure 5 for grids, trees, and Erdös-Renyi graphs. For each of the graph topologies, we used a graph size of $n = 1600$. The error probability is plotted against the average infection size from the simulation for a variety of infection times. This choice better conveys how infection size affects the error rate, which is the chief question of interest.

These charts allow us to compare the performance of the algorithms. It is clear that the error probability of the Ball Algorithm is less than that of the Tree Algorithm on both the grid and Erdös-Renyi graphs. On these graphs, the Ball Algorithm performs uniformly better at all timescales. However, the results on a tree are more complex. For low time scales where the infection is small, the Ball Algorithm has superior performance. However, for higher time scales, the Tree Algorithm has better performance. The larger timescales represent a larger infection, which would generally be considered a harder problem, especially since the

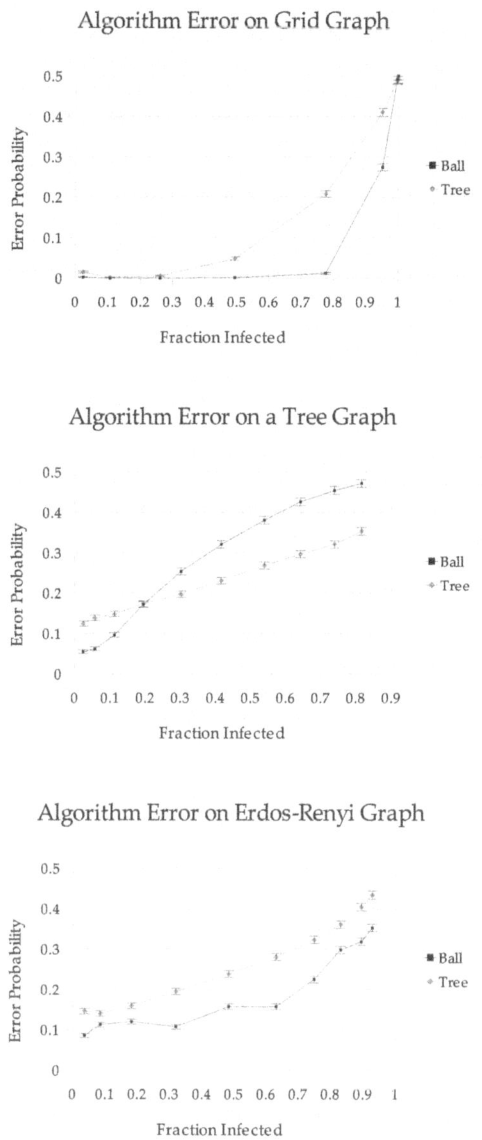

Figure 5: This figure shows the overall error probability for each algorithm, for each of the three topologies we consider.

infection is likely to have reached some of the leaves by this time. Then the Tree Algorithm is superior for this graph under this viewpoint. In addition, the Tree Algorithm maintains a fairly low error for a wider range of infection times. However, many practical applications of these algorithms would occur when the infection is still of limited size, in which case the Ball Algorithm would perform better. The best algorithm would depend on the circumstances.

It is particularly interesting to ask how these results extend to real-world graphs, as opposed to random (or highly regular) graphs that we have constructed. To this end, we used the call-graph from an Asian telecom network. In this graph, each node is a cell customer, and there is an edge between two users if they contacted each other over this network during a certain range of time. Since the original

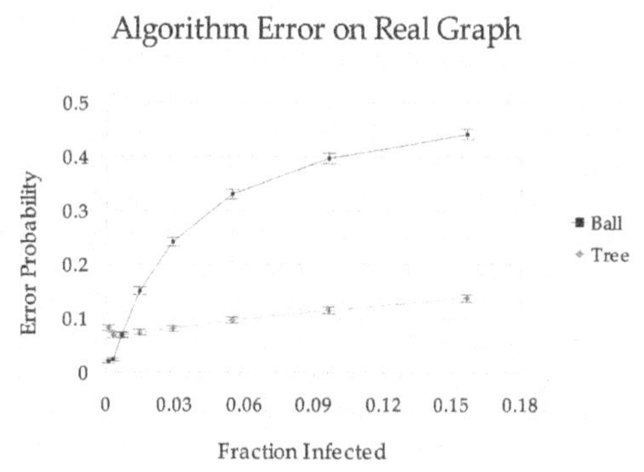

Figure 6: This figure shows the overall error probability for each algorithm on a real world graph.

graph was too large for practical simulation times, we cut out a partial subset. We chose a random node and all nodes with a distance 9 and used the induced subgraph generated by these nodes. The resulting graph had size $n = 13189$. The probability of error for a range of times are present in Figure 6. We see that the results are similar to those for a Tree graph, where the Ball algorithm performs better on small infections, but it is out performed by the Tree algorithm at larger times. In particular, we see that the Ball algorithm performs particularly poorly for larger values of the infected fraction of nodes. This is to be expected, as the intuition for the Ball algorithm stems from the geometry of spatial grid-like networks. The call-graph here is very much tree-like (however, with very small diameter and high degree), and infections are unlikely to propagate to the same depth across various leaves. This will result in poor Ball "fits", especially as the infected fraction of nodes grow. This intuition is indeed borne out in the simulations.

The exact parameters for each point in the plots in Figure 5 and 6 are as follows.

Grid graph: (% infected, time (t), Ball threshold (m), Tree threshold (m)) – (2%, 2, 10, 40), (11%, 4, 21, 137), (26%, 6, 27, 267), (49%, 8, 31, 400), (78%, 10, 34, 525), (95%, 12, 35, 594), (99%, 14, 36, 631), (100%, 16, 37, 625).

Tree graph: (2%, 3, 4, 24), (6%, 4, 5, 48), (11%, 5, 5, 96), (19%, 6, 5, 160), (30%, 7, 5, 228), (42%, 8, 5, 296), (54%, 9, 5, 359), (64%, 10, 5, 425), (74%, 11, 5, 468), (82%, 12, 5, 508).

Erdös-Renyi graph: (4%, 3, 7, 35), (8%, 4, 8, 80), (18%, 5, 9, 156), (32%, 6, 10, 245), (48%, 7, 11, 337), (63%, 8, 11, 400), (75%, 9, 11, 459), (83%, 10, 12, 496), (89%, 11, 12, 513), (93%, 12, 12, 533).

Real world graph: (0.1%, 3, 7, 25), (0.3%, 4, 8, 87), (0.7%, 5, 8, 180), (1.4%, 6, 8, 350), (2.9%, 7, 8, 591), (5.4%, 8, 8, 959), (9.6%, 9, 8, 1396), (15.6%, 10, 8, 1896).

7. CONCLUSIONS

In this paper, we seek to answer the question: given a set of people reporting a sickness, how can you distinguish between a sickness spreading like an epidemic, or simply a illness that is occurring at random? To answer this question, we develop two natural algorithms which rate the likelihood a sickness is an infection by either the size of smallest ball or smallest tree containing the reporting sick nodes. We provide theoretical guarantees on the range of infection times and other parameters for which these algorithms succeed for several standard graph topologies. These have been supported by simulation data that provide insight into the true probability of error. As a high-level summary of our results, our work demonstrates both theoretically and empirically that the ball algorithm is superior on a grid, and the tree algorithm is superior on a tree graph.

There are several directions in which this work could be extended in the future. One natural direction is to ask the question, if you see the infection over a range of times, can you better estimate whether the sickness is a spreading epidemic or a simple random infection over the nodes? In particular, what is the best way to use the new information gained in this way? Another extension is considering that the sickness is spreading on one of two different networks (with potentially different epidemic models on each network), and we wish to determine which network the infection is traveling on.

8. ACKNOWLEDGMENTS

This work was partially supported by NSF Grants CNS-1017525, CNS-0721380, EFRI-0735905, EECS-1056028, DTRA grant HDTRA 1-08-0029 and Army Research Office Grant W911NF-11-1-0265. We also gratefully acknowledge Profs. Sujay Sanghavi and Sriram Vishwanath at The University of Texas at Austin for providing access to the (anonymized) call-graph data.

9. REFERENCES

[1] G. Brown, T. Howe, M. Ihbe, A. Prakash, and K. Borders, "Social networks and context-aware spam," in *Proceedings of the 2008 ACM conference on Computer supported cooperative work*, ser. CSCW '08. ACM, 2008, pp. 403–412.

[2] NetworkX: http://networkx.lanl.gov.

[3] A. J. Ganesh, L. Massoulié, and D. F. Towsley, "The effect of network topology on the spread of epidemics," in *INFOCOM*, 2005, pp. 1455–1466.

[4] F. Ball and P. Neal, "Poisson approximation for epidemics with two levels of mixing," *The Annals of Probability*, vol. 32, no. 1B, pp. 1168–1200, 2004.

[5] A. Gopalan, S. Banerjee, A. K. Das, and S. Shakkottai, "Random mobility and the spread of infection," in *INFOCOM 2011*, 2011, pp. 999–1007.

[6] N. Demiris and P. D. O'Neill, "Bayesian inference for epidemics with two levels of mixing," *Scandinavian Journal of Statistics*, vol. 32, pp. 265–280, 2005.

[7] G. Streftaris and G. J. Gibson, "Statistical inference for stochatic epidemic models," in *Proc. 17th International Workshop on Statistical Modeling*, 2002, pp. 609–616.

[8] N. Demiris and P. D. O'Neill, "Bayesian inference for stochastic multitype epidemics in structured populations via random graphs," *Journal of the Royal Statistical Society Series B*, vol. 67, no. 5, pp. 731–745, 2005.

[9] D. Shah and T. Zaman, "Detecting sources of computer viruses in networks: Theory and experiment," *SIGMETRICS Perform. Eval. Rev.*, vol. 86, pp. 203–214, 2010.

[10] ——, "Rumors in a network: Who's the culprit?" *IEEE Transactions on Information Theory*, vol. 57, August 2011.

[11] H. Kesten, "On the speed of convergence in first-passage percolation," *The Annals of Applied Probability*, vol. 3, no. 2, pp. 296–338, 1993.

[12] R. Lyons and R. Pemantle, "Random walk in a random environment and first-passage percolation on trees," *The Annals of Probability*, vol. 20, no. 1, pp. 125–136, 1992.

[13] F. K. Hwang and D. S. Richards, "Steiner tree problems," *Networks*, vol. 22, no. 1, pp. 55–89, 1992.

[14] C. Gröpl, S. Hougardy, T. NierHoff, and H. J. Proömel, *Approximation Algorithms for the Steiner Tree Problem in Graphs*. Kluwer Academic Publishers, 2000, pp. 235–279.

[15] I. Benjamini and Y. Peres, "Tree-indexed random walks on groups and first passage percolation," *Probability Theory and Related Fields*, vol. 98, pp. 91–112, 1994.

[16] R. Durrett, *Random Graph Dynamics*. Cambridge University Press, 2007.

[17] F. Chung and L. Lu, "The diameter of sparse random graphs," *Adv. in Appl. Math*, vol. 26, pp. 257–279, 2001.

[18] V. D. Blondel, J.-L. Guillaume, J. M. Hendrickx, and R. M. Jungers, "Distance distribution in random graphs and application to network exploration," *Physical Review*, vol. 76, no. 066101, 2007.

[19] K. Mehlhorn, "A faster approximation algorithm for the steiner problem in graphs," *Information Processing Letters*, vol. 27, pp. 125–128, 1988.

What is a Good Buffer Cache Replacement Scheme for Mobile Flash Storage?

Hyojun Kim
Georgia Institute of Technology
Altanta, GA
hyojun.kim@cc.gatech.edu

Moonkyung Ryu
Georgia Institute of Technology
Altanta, GA
mkryu@gatech.edu

Umakishore Ramachandran
Georgia Institute of Technology
Altanta, GA
rama@cc.gatech.edu

ABSTRACT

Smartphones are becoming ubiquitous and powerful. The Achilles' heel in such devices that limits performance is the storage. Low-end flash memory is the storage technology of choice in such devices due to energy, size, and cost considerations.

In this paper, we take a critical look at the performance of flash on smartphones for mobile applications. Specifically, we ask the question whether the state-of-the-art buffer cache replacement schemes proposed thus far (both flash-agnostic and flash-aware ones) are the right ones for mobile flash storage. To answer this question, we first expose the limitations of current buffer cache performance evaluation methods, and propose a novel evaluation framework that is a hybrid between trace-driven simulation and real implementation of such schemes inside an operating system. Such an evaluation reveals some unexpected and surprising insights on the performance of buffer management schemes that contradicts conventional wisdom. Armed with this knowledge, we propose a new buffer cache replacement scheme called *SpatialClock*.

Using our evaluation framework, we show the superior performance of SpatialClock relative to the state-of-the-art for mobile flash storage.

Categories and Subject Descriptors

C.4 [**Computer Systems Organization**]: Performance of Systems—*Measurement techniques*; D.4.2 [**Software**]: Operating Systems—*Storage Management*

Keywords

buffer management, page cache, flash storage

1. INTRODUCTION

Over the past decade, mobile computing devices, particularly smartphones, are finding increasing use in our daily lives. According to a recent Gartner report, within the next three years, mobile platforms will surpass the PC as the most common web access device worldwide [10]. By 2013, over 40% of the enhanced phone installed-base will be equipped with advanced browsers [28].

Although mobile systems have become unbelievably popular today, only few studies have been conducted for deep understanding of mobile systems. Mobile systems are not just miniatures of personal computer systems, and thus, the previous research insights from desktop and server systems should not be simply applied to mobile systems without careful reexamination. For example, a recent study reveals that the storage subsystem has a much bigger performance effect on application performance on smartphones than it does on conventional computer systems [21]. Considering the rapid growth of mobile systems, it is time to move our focus to the mobile system components.

CPU power and main memory capacity are increasing very fast; the latest smartphone has a quad core 1.4 GHz processor (Tegra3 [26]) as well as 1 GB of main memory capacity. On the other hand, the technology used for storage on mobile platforms lags significantly behind that used on regular computers. Flash storage is the norm for smartphones because of the limitations of size, cost, and power consumption. Flash storage exhibits very different performance characteristics relative to the traditional Hard Disk Drive (HDD); plus current operating systems (owing to their legacy of assuming HDD as the primary storage technology) are not engineered to support flash storage adequately. Consequently, flash storage is the Achilles' heel when it comes to performance of mobile platforms [21]. While high-end flash based Solid-State Drives (SSDs) are available and used in regular and enterprise class machines, adoption of such storage for mobile platforms is infeasible for reasons of cost, size, and energy consumption. Write buffering can be used to solve the small write problem both in enterprise storage servers using disk arrays [11] and inside flash storage devices [22]. However, this solution approach has its limitations, especially for a smartphone environment for a variety of reasons, most notably, loss of reliability due to unexpected power losses (e.g., battery getting unhitched from the phone due to accidental dropping of the phone). Therefore, we argue that operating system level software support is critically needed for low-end flash storage to achieve high performance on mobile platforms, and thus, we focus our attention on inexpensive flash storage in this study. Specifically, we are con-

SIGMETRICS'12, June 11–15, 2012, London, England, UK.

cerned with the buffer cache replacement schemes for mobile platforms using inexpensive flash storage.

OS buffer cache is the focal point for actions regarding how to enhance the performance for OS generated write operations to the storage device. Therefore, we are interested in revisiting the page replacement algorithm used by the OS buffer cache. The primary goal of the OS buffer cache is ensuring a good hit-ratio for the subsystems that sit on top of it. It is well-known that Least Recently Used (LRU) or some variant thereof that preserves temporal locality is a good choice for a page replacement algorithm from the point of ensuring a good hit-ratio. However, such algorithms tend to be agnostic about the performance characteristics of the primary storage backing the buffer cache.

The first step is to take stock of the state-of-the-art in buffer cache management schemes proposed and or used in current operating systems and evaluate their efficacy for flash storage used in smartphones. LRU , Clock [5], Linux2Q [6] are three well-known *flash-agnostic* buffer cache replacement schemes. Clean First LRU (CFLRU) [27], LRU Write Sequence Reordering (LRUWSR) [19], Flash based Operation aware Replacement (FOR) [24], Flash-Aware Buffer management (FAB) [17] are previously proposed four *flash-aware* buffer cache replacement schemes. Even though most of these proposed schemes are aiming for general flash storage rather than the inexpensive ones found in mobile platforms, they are a step in the right direction. We would like to understand the performance potential of these schemes (both flash-agnostic and flash-aware ones) for mobile flash storage.

What is the best evaluation strategy for answering this question? Analytical modeling, simulation, and real implementation are the traditional approaches to performance evaluation of computer systems. Specifically, in the context of OS buffer cache replacement schemes, two techniques have been extensively used: *real implementation* in an operating system, and *trace-driven simulation*. Clearly, real implementation inside an operating system would reveal the true performance potential of any buffer cache replacement scheme. But such an approach is fraught with a number of difficulties and downsides. A real implementation of even a single scheme would require a huge amount of effort. This is because changing the core functionality of an operating system such as the buffer cache replacement scheme is non-trivial since it affects all the subsystems that live on top of it (e.g., VM, file systems). Also, to have a side by side comparison, such an approach would require the implementation of all the competing schemes in the operating system. Besides these difficulties, there are also downsides to this approach. It may be difficult to assess the true performance benefit of the scheme being evaluated due to performance noise from other parts of the operating system. Further, it would be difficult to ask a variety of "what if" questions with a real implementation, without re-engineering the implementation to answer such questions. Perhaps, most importantly the barrier to trying out new ideas will be too high if it has to be implemented first in an operating system to get an estimate of its performance potential. It would stifle creativity.

Trace-driven simulation has been extensively used for buffer cache related studies sometimes together with real implementation [14, 15, 27], and many other times just by itself [8, 12, 16, 17, 18, 23, 24, 25]. Typically, storage access traces are collected first from real applications on an existing system or synthesized from a workload model of applications. These traces are then used as inputs to a buffer cache simulator to gather metrics of interest for performance evaluation. Hit-ratio is the most popular metric, but some studies also measure the I/O operation completion time. The virtues of trace-driven simulation include time to getting useful results compared to real implementation, repeatability of results, isolation of performance benefits from other noises, and the ability to have useful "what if" knobs (additional input parameters) in addition to the traces serving as the workload for the evaluation. However, the main drawback of trace-driven simulation is that the results may not accurately capture all the metrics of interest pertinent to the real system. This is especially true with flash storage due to the complicated and often opaque mapping layer inside such devices. Device manufacturers do not publish such internal details; thus these devices have to necessarily be treated as black boxes. Therefore, any simulator can only make a best effort guess as to what is happening inside the device making the veracity of trace-driven simulation results for flash storage questionable.

In this paper, we propose a novel buffer cache evaluation framework, which is a hybrid between trace-driven simulation and real implementation. Basically, our method expands the existing trace-driven simulation by adding one more step with a *real* storage device. It allows us to see the real performance effect of cache replacement schemes without actually implementing the algorithm into an operating system.

We collect *before-cache* storage access traces from a real Android smartphone while running popular applications such as Web browser and YouTube player. By using the traces and our proposed evaluation framework, we evaluate seven state-of-the-art buffer cache replacement schemes, and report very surprising results. The most previously proposed flash-aware schemes are not better (sometimes much worse) than flash-agnostic schemes at least with the smartphone workloads that we have evaluated them with. A careful analysis of the results using our new framework reveals the source of this disconnect between previous studies and our surprising new results, namely, not respecting *spatial adjacency* for write operations to inexpensive flash storage. Armed with this new insight, we propose a new buffer cache replacement scheme called *SpatialClock* for mobile flash storage. By comparing SpatialClock to the state-of-the-art buffer cache replacement schemes using our evaluation framework, we show that SpatialClock delivers superior storage performance on real mobile flash storage while not degrading the cache hit-ratio.

We make the following three contributions through this work. First, we propose a new buffer cache evaluation framework. Second, we collect *before-cache* storage access traces from an Android platform, and make them available for other researchers[1] The third and final contribution is the SpatialClock buffer cache replacement algorithm.

The rest of the paper is structured as follows. Section 2 explains previously proposed flash-aware cache replacement schemes. Section 3 introduce the new cache evaluation framework, and Section 4 describes SpatialClock algorithm. Section 5 and Section 6 provide evaluation results and our conclusions.

[1]https://wiki.cc.gatech.edu/epl/index.php/S-Clock

2. FLASH-AWARE CACHE SCHEMES

Ever since the appearance of NAND flash memory based solid state storage devices, multiple flash-aware buffer cache replacement schemes have been proposed. One of the earliest schemes is CFLRU [27]. Due to its very nature, flash memory incurs less time for servicing a read operation in comparison to a write operation. In other words, to reduce the total I/O operation time of flash, it is desirable to reduce the total number of write operations. To this end, CFLRU tries to evict a clean page rather than a dirty page because a dirty page must be written back to the storage during the eviction process. However, such a biased policy could fill the cache with mostly dirty pages at the expense of not holding frequently accessed clean pages. This is clearly undesirable as it will bring down the overall cache hit-ratio. To mitigate this problem, CFLRU divides the LRU cache list into two parts (as done in the 2Q algorithm [18]), and applies the clean-first policy only to the lower part of LRU list. The authors claim that choosing the partition size intelligently will result in shorter total operation time for flash storage.

LRUWSR [19] shares the same motivation with CFLRU. It also tries to give higher priority to dirty pages, but it uses a different method. Instead of partitioning the LRU list into two parts, LRUWSR adds a *cold bit* to each cache frame, and gives a second chance to a dirty page frame to remain in the cache. When a page is selected as a potential victim, its dirty and cold bits are checked first. If the page is dirty and its cold bit is zero, then the algorithm decides not to choose it as a victim. Instead it sets the cold bit for this page to indicate that the page has gotten its second chance to stay in the cache. The authors argue that LRUWSR is better than CFLRU both in terms of usability (because it does not require any workload dependent parameters) and performance.

One of the latest flash-aware cache replacement scheme is FOR [24]. It also focuses on the asymmetric read and write operation time of flash storage. In addition, it combines *inter operation distance (IOD)* (the core idea of the Low Inter Reference Recency [16]) together with the recency attribute of the LRU algorithm. IOD is the number of distinct operations performed between two consecutive "identical operations" on one page including the operation itself. Further, FOR calculates the IOD and recency values separately for read and write operations. By considering all these factors, FOR calculates the weight of each page, and evicts the page having the minimal weight value. The results reported by the authors show 20% improvement for database workloads for FOR over other schemes.

Flash-Aware Buffer (FAB) management scheme [17] was proposed especially for portable media players to generate more sequential writes. It clusters cache pages in blocks and maintains an LRU list in units of blocks. By choosing and flushing the victim block having the highest number of pages, FAB produces large sequential writes, which are desirable for flash storage. To verify the performance effect of existing cache replacement schemes on mobile systems, we decided to evaluate these four flash-aware schemes as well as three flash-agnostic schemes: LRU, Clock, and Linux2Q. Linux2Q is the page replacement scheme used in Linux kernel. Compared to the original 2Q algorithm [18], it introduces the *active bit*, which makes the transition between the active and inactive queues more strict.

3. A NOVEL CACHE EVALUATION FRAMEWORK

Flash memory is different from conventional magnetic storage. To overcome the physical limitations of flash storage, every flash storage device includes a Flash Translation Layer (FTL) [13, 20] in addition to the storage elements. FTL is a special software layer emulating sector read and write functionalities of an HDD to allow conventional disk file systems to be used with flash memory without any modifications. FTLs employ a *remapping technique* to use the storage cells more judiciously. When FTL receives a request to overwrite a sector, it redirects the new content to an empty page, which is already erased, and modifies the mapping table to indicate the new physical page address where the logical sector has been written.

The FTL algorithm employed by a flash storage device is usually opaque, making it difficult to simulate a flash storage device. The performance of a flash storage device critically depends on the algorithms used internally by the FTL. Thus it is pretty much impossible to accurately simulate the internal architecture of a flash device for performance evaluation purposes. While it is always possible to simulate a given FTL algorithm (assuming the details are known) for a specific flash storage, it is impossible to generalize and use it for other flash devices that we want to compare it against, since the performance characteristics of a flash device is so intimately tied to its specific FTL algorithm. Trace-driven simulation may still be good enough to understand the performance potential of a buffer cache management scheme with respect to certain metrics of interest (e.g., hit-ratio). However, we believe, it is not good enough for evaluating all the metrics of interest (e.g., completion time of I/O operations) in understanding the performance potential of a buffer cache scheme on a specific flash storage.

3.1 Evaluation Framework

The new buffer cache evaluation framework (Figure 1) is a hybrid between trace-driven simulation and real implementation. First, we give the big picture and then drill down to the details. We collect traces of read/write accesses to the buffer cache from an Android platform running popular Apps. We call this the *before-cache* traces. We use these traces as the workload on a simulator that implements the seven different buffer cache management policies that we alluded to in the previous section. The output of this simulator is two-fold: *hit-ratio* for the chosen cache scheme; and *after-cache* storage access trace for each cache scheme. The latter is the sequence of read/write requests that would be issued to the actual storage since the buffer cache does not have these pages. We have developed a tool called *Workload Player* that takes the *after-cache* trace as its input, sends the read/write requests in the trace to a real storage device, and reports the total elapsed time for performing the read/write operations. Since the times gathered by the Workload Player are the actual elapsed times for the requests, they account for the internal architecture of the flash storage on which the trace is being played. Thus, this hybrid evaluation framework is a faithful reproduction of the combined performance characteristic of the buffer cache algorithm and the real flash storage.

To contrast our hybrid approach to the traditional trace-driven simulator, the latter stops with reporting the observed hit-ratio for a given scheme and generating the ac-

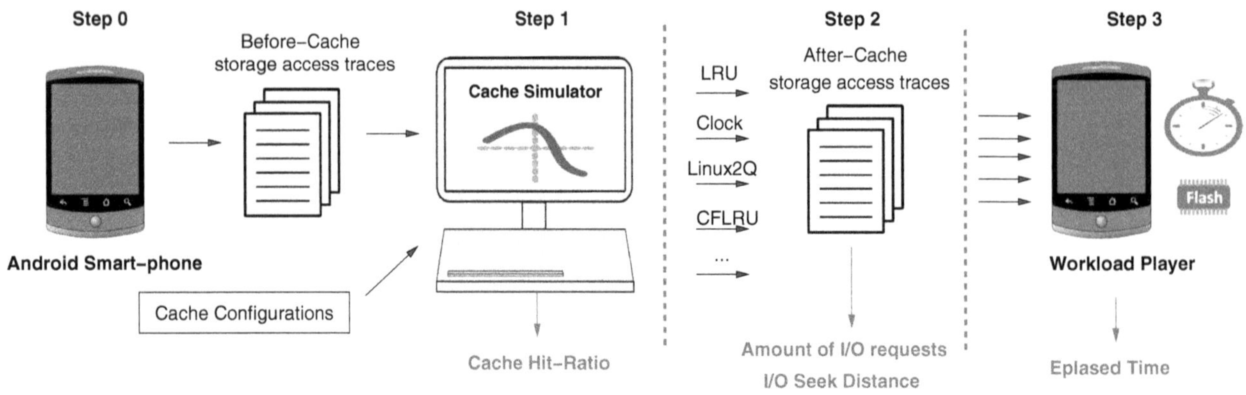

Figure 1: The evaluation framework for buffer cache replacement schemes: *Traditional trace-driven simulations stop with Step 1 or 2. Enhancing the framework with Step 3 allows us to do an accurate evaluation of the performance implications of different cache replacement schemes on real flash storage devices.*

tual storage access traces corresponding to the misses. Some studies may take the actual storage access traces to compute the expected completion of I/O requests based on published static read/write/block-erase times of a given flash storage device. By actually playing the *after-cache* traces on a storage device we are able to get the real I/O completion times.

To collect the *before-cache* traces, we have instrumented the Android OS running on a smartphone. We have used Google Nexus-One smartphone with Android version 2.3.7 Gingerbread. This in itself is a non-trivial piece of engineering. We modified the *init procedure* of Android for our purpose, and also patched Linux kernel page cache related sources. We developed the buffer cache simulator for the seven schemes discussed in Section 2 to run on a standard desktop Linux platform. The Workload Player runs both on the smartphone and the desktop, and collects performance statistics of playing the *after-cache* traces on flash storage. Our experimental setup includes multiple smartphone storage devices to run the *after-cache* traces.

3.2 A Surprising Result

We first present a representative result for the seven buffer cache management schemes using a microSD card on Google Nexus-One phone. The traces are generated from mobile Apps (such as web browsing and video streaming) running on the Android phone. The result is summarized in Table 1. This result is a good sample of the overall trend we observed for most of the test cases (different flash storage devices and different cache sizes), which we elaborate in Section 5 (with more details about the workloads that are used to generate the traces). At this point our goal is to reveal a surprising result that emerged from the evaluation of these seven schemes.

All the schemes show remarkably higher hit-ratios with 64 MB cache size than with 4 MB cache size as expected. However, despite the fact that higher hit ratios implies a reduction in storage activity, the measured *elapsed times* on a real storage device tells a different story. Note for example from Table 1 that the measured *elapsed times* for LRU, Linux2Q, CFLRU, LRUWSR, and FOR are worse than those for Clock and FAB. This is surprising because hit-ratio is the overarching metric used to evaluate the effectiveness of buffer cache replacement schemes.

Besides, all four flash-aware schemes fail to reduce the number write operations. Recall that the main focus of flash-aware schemes (except FAB) is to reduce the number of write requests to the storage device. Given this focus, it is interesting that the amount of write operations generated by the flash-aware schemes is not that different from the flash-agnostic ones.

What is interesting from this representative result is that we cannot differentiate the relative merits of these cache replacement strategies using a conventional metric such as hit-ratio. Incidentally, this result also highlights the limitation of a pure trace-driven simulator since hit-ratio and read/write traffic to the storage device are the metrics that can be generated by such a simulator.

Our hybrid approach helps understand the performance potential of the schemes better by letting us measure the elapsed time for playing the *after-cache* traces on a real flash storage device. Surprisingly, three of the four flash-aware schemes show slower performance than the Clock scheme. This is interesting because Clock is not designed for flash storage, and the observed performance differences cannot be explained either by hit-ratios or by the number of generated read/write operations. The surprising result is the fact that the latest flash-aware schemes are not performing as well as one would have expected on a mobile flash storage (Section 5 shows this is true for a variety of flash storage devices). More importantly, this result establishes our first contribution in this paper, namely, the power of the hybrid evaluation framework for performance analysis of buffer cache replacement strategies for flash storage

3.3 Explaining the surprising result

A more intriguing question is why the three out of the four flash-aware schemes are not performing as well as one would expect. A careful investigation reveals the source of this puzzling anomaly. The short answer to this puzzle is *not respecting spatial adjacency* for the write requests that are generated to the flash storage. To fully appreciate this phenomenon, we need to understand some basics of flash storage.

Flash storage is based on semiconductor technology, and hence shows very different performance characteristics when compared to the traditional magnetic disk. A number of studies have reported on the special performance character-

Table 1: Evaluation results for seven cache replacement schemes: Mixed workload on Patriot 16GB microSDHC card / Nexus One with 4 / 64MB cache size

		LRU	Clock	Linux2Q	CFLRU	LRUWSR	FOR	FAB
4MB	Hit-Ratio	0.7592	0.7583	0.7665	0.7584	0.7580	0.7529	0.7497
	Generated Read Operation Count	13,735	13,917	12,709	14,067	14,125	15,418	14,549
	Generated Write Operation Count	44,600	44,650	44,096	44,413	44,450	44,261	46,131
	Measured Elapsed Time (second)	**234.69**	**234.78**	**261.69**	**241.68**	**229.78**	**236.62**	**292.48**
64MB	Hit-Ratio	0.8863	0.8860	0.8876	0.8860	0.8857	0.8829	0.8860
	Generated Read Operation Count	1,861	2,745	1,605	1,909	1,927	2,523	1,681
	Generated Write Operation Count	26,064	25,833	25,998	26,062	26,060	26,120	26,327
	Measured Elapsed Time (second)	**236.86**	**183.57**	**277.44**	**237.87**	**231.43**	**291.22**	**129.30**

Table 2: Comparison of an HDD (3.5" 7200 RPM HDD) vs. three flash storage devices (Patriot 16GB microSD, two eMMC devices used in Nokia N900 and Google Nexus-S smartphones (KB/sec): *write ordering is important but read ordering is not important on flash storage.*

Storage	Read(KB/sec)		Write(KB/sec)	
	Sorted	Scattered	Sorted	Scattered
HDD	6,498.4	537.6	4,836.6	1,004.0
microSD	4,852.7	4,836.6	545.2	8.3
eMMC-1	5,100.1	4,444.6	470.9	16.1
eMMC-2	3,124.5	2,551.5	566.4	259.1

istics of flash storage [4, 7, 9]. It is well known that flash storage devices show a relatively low write-throughput for small, scattered (random) requests and a higher throughput for large, sequential write requests. At the same time, they are insensitive to the order of read requests, showing almost unchanging performance for sequential and random read requests. We ourselves have performed simple measurements to identify these differences in performance.

Table 2 compares the measured read and write throughput of an HDD and three flash storage devices. We use four synthetic workloads. All four workloads use the same number of requests (32,768), with request sizes of 4KB (typical page size in most virtual memory systems) within a 1 GB address space (typical process virtual address space). Two of these workloads use random read and write requests, respectively. The remaining two workloads use, respectively, read and write requests that are sorted by the sector number (thus resulting in accessing sequentially ordered sectors on the storage device).

On an HDD, both read and write throughputs are highly influenced by the sequence of the requests because it has seek-delays of the mechanically moving magnetic head. In contrast, the read throughput of flash storage is not much influenced by request ordering because there is no seek delay. For the write requests, flash devices show uniformly lower throughput than the HDD, and their scattered write throughputs are lower than the sorted write throughputs even though there is no moving parts inside flash storage devices. The reason for the lower throughput for scattered writes is due to the way data updating happens internally in a NAND flash memory chip. In other words, not respecting the spatial adjacency for consecutive write requests can result in a huge performance penalty in flash storage. This result suggests that write request ordering can make a huge performance difference, and the disparity between sorted and scattered writes demonstrates that the *ordering* is perhaps more important than the *number* of write requests.

Of the flash-aware schemes evaluated, only FAB respects spatial adjacency while the others (CFLRU, LRUWSR, and FOR) are focused on reducing the total number of write requests to the flash storage. As Table 2 shows, the penalty for ignoring spatial adjacency (i.e., sending scattered write requests to the storage) is huge. This is the reason we see elapsed time differences among the cache replacement schemes even though they all generate roughly the same amount of read/write requests (see Table 1). As is evident from Table 1, FAB has the least elapsed time compared to the other schemes (for 64 MB cache size) since it is the only scheme that explicitly cares about spatial adjacency. However, FAB, owing to its focus on supporting media player workload, is biased too much towards write performance optimization for flash storage to the detriment of overall buffer hit-ratio, which is an important figure of merit for a general-purpose OS buffer cache. This becomes apparent especially at smaller cache sizes and other diverse workloads. For example, it can be seen in Table 1 that FAB has the worst performance (both elapsed time and hit ratio) with a 4 MB cache size compared to the other schemes. Further, it has some inherent complexities for implementation as a general-purpose OS buffer cache scheme, which we discuss in Section 5.5.

4. SPATIALCLOCK

We have seen that even the flash-aware general-purpose OS buffer cache replacement algorithms proposed thus far do not pay attention to the spatial adjacency (or lack thereof) of the pages being evicted from the OS buffer cache (FAB is an exception but as we noted earlier it does this at the expense of cache hit-ratio and so it is not general-purpose enough for OS buffer cache). Given the discussion in Section 3.3, this is a missed opportunity that hurts the performance of flash storage. Therefore, we propose a new algorithm *SpatialClock* that respects the spatial adjacency of the pages being evicted from the OS buffer cache without loosing cache hit-ratio remarkably.

There are two important points we want to address head on before we delve into describing SpatialClock:

1. Page replacement algorithms are an age-old topic. However, from the point of view of the storage technology that is currently being used and will be used for the foreseeable future in mobile platforms, we believe it is time to revisit this topic. From our discussion Section 3.3, we can distill a couple of observations regarding

flash storage that strengthen our belief: (a) respecting spatial adjacency for writes is very important, and (b) read and write operations are independent of each other due to the nature of the flash technology, in contrast to traditional storage devices such as an HDD (due to the absence of the mechanical head movement).

2. The OS buffer cache is deeply entrenched in the software stack of the operating system. Therefore it is not prudent to overburden this layer with device-specific optimizations (such as write reordering), which would require a significant architectural change of the entire OS software stack. What we are proposing in this section is a localized change only to the page replacement algorithm of the OS buffer cache, which does not affect the other functionalities of this layer. Further, as we will see shortly, the proposed algorithm is not storage specific; it merely respects the *logical* spatial adjacency of the pages being evicted from the buffer in addition to temporal locality

4.1 Main Idea

The key question is how to design a new page replacement scheme to achieve the two different objectives simultaneously: high cache hit-ratio and sequentially ordered write requests. One commonly used approach is dividing cache memory space into multiple partitions, and applying different cache management policies to the distinct cache partitions [15, 25, 27]. However, this partitioning approach introduces another difficult problem: how to adaptively adjust the partition sizes for various workloads. Further, such a partitioning approach is too major a change to this critical layer of the operating system. Therefore in designing SpatialClock, we take a different approach rather than partitioning the OS buffer.

Before we describe SpatialClock, let us briefly review LRU and Clock algorithms. In LRU, page references are kept in a sorted temporal order by the OS buffer cache. When a page frame is accessed, the frame needs to be moved to the Most Recently Used (MRU) position. The operation may require obtaining a global lock to protect the data structure from concurrent accesses. Because page references are very common, such frequent rearrangement of the data structure is expensive. Further, true LRU is difficult to implement in practice since it requires hardware assistance at individual memory reference granularity to track page frame accesses from the VM subsystem. Nevertheless, true LRU is used in memory system studies as a *standard* to compare other practical page replacement algorithms.

Clock is an approximation to the true LRU algorithm and is often referred to as *second-chance* replacement algorithm. Clock relies on a simple hardware assist common to all processor architectures supporting virtual memory, namely, a per-page *reference bit* (usually part of the page table entry for that page). The reference bit can be set by the hardware and cleared by the software. The hardware sets the associated reference bit when a page frame is accessed unbeknownst to the software (i.e., the operating system). The Clock algorithm keeps the page frames as a circular list in FIFO order of their arrival into the OS buffer cache from the storage device. The victim selection works as follows. The algorithm sweeps the circular list of page frames skipping over the frames whose reference bits are set (clearing the reference bits as it sweeps) and stops at the page frame

```
/* Victim selection */
pageframe*
spatialclock_choose_victim()
{
  /* sweeping until find a victim */
  while (1)
  {
    /* circular movement */
    if (cur_pointer == NULL)
      cur_pointer =
        avltree_move_to_first();

    victim      = current_pointer;
    cur_pointer =
      avltree_move_to_next(cur_pointer);

    if (victim->referenced == 0) break;
    victim->referenced = 0;
  }
  return victim;
}
```

Figure 2: SpatialClock victim selection algorithm

whose reference bit is not set. This page frame is chosen as the victim for eviction from the OS buffer cache. Clock does not keep the precise reference order like LRU; hence it is simpler and does not require global locks for maintaining its data structure. Despite its impreciseness in maintaining the page reference history, the good news is that the performance of Clock approximates LRU in most cases. Therefore, Clock has been widely used especially for virtual memory systems, which require low overhead lookup of the buffer cache.

In SpatialClock, we follow the basic rules of the Clock algorithm with only one difference. Page frames are arranged by the *logical* sector number of the storage system that contains the page frame. Consequently, page frames are chosen as victims for eviction in the sequential order of the sectors that contain these frames, and thus, frames are implicitly chosen sequentially with respect to the storage device. This results in preserving/respecting spatial locality during victim selection when the chosen frames happen to be dirty as well. Figure 2 shows the victim selection algorithm of SpatialClock.

Figure 3 shows an example of the victim selection in the SpatialClock algorithm. Each row represents a page frame, and the left cell in the row represents the containing sector number for that page frame, the right cell indicates the reference bit value. The page frames are pre-arranged in sorted order with respect to the containing sector numbers for the page frames. To choose a victim page, page frames are scanned from the current pointer position to find a page frame, which has a '0' for the reference bit value. In the given example, the sweep stops at page frame whose containing sector number is 80, while clearing the reference bits of the page frames having 40 and 72 as the containing sector numbers, respectively.

Respecting and checking the reference bits gives SpatialClock the advantage of an approximate LRU for victim selection. Arranging the page frames in a spatially adjacent manner gives an opportunity to enforce write ordering for the evicted page frames. Giving more importance to phys-

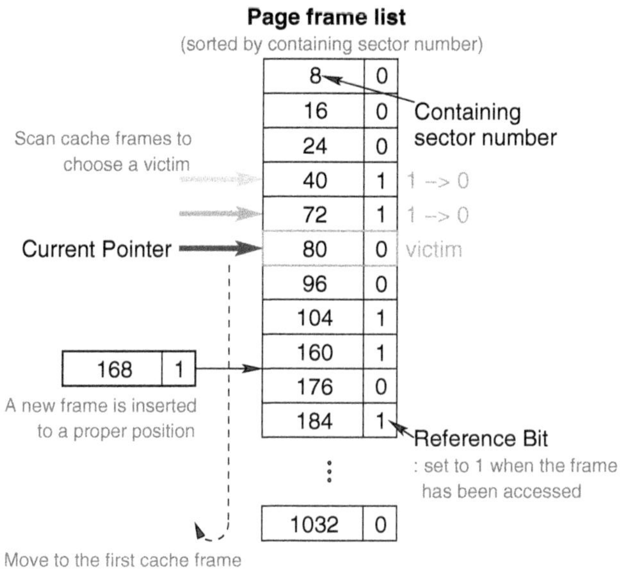

Figure 3: Victim Selection in SpatialClock: *SpatialClock maintains and scans page frames in the order of the containing sector numbers to generate ordered write requests.*

ical adjacency than the recency of access could affect the hit-ratio. However, our evaluation results show that this is not the case at least for the traces we studied. More importantly, we argue that paying attention to the elapsed time for storage access is crucial for achieving good performance on flash storage.

Compared to the original Clock scheme, SpatialClock requires maintaining page frames in a sorted manner, and we use an AVL tree [3] for the purpose. However, the burden is only for a page frame insertion operation, which is a relatively rare operation as long as the hit-ratio is high. The more common reference operation of the OS buffer cache remains exactly the same as in the original Clock algorithm. Besides, the AVL tree can be used for page look up purpose, which is mandatory for buffer cache maintenance.

We have implemented SpatialClock using an AVL tree to bound the page frame insertion time to be $\log N$, where N is the number of page frames. We associate logical sector numbers with each frame (obtained from the storage map maintained by the OS buffer cache) to organize the circular list respecting spatial adjacency.

5. EVALUATION

We focus our evaluation on the following two key points:

- Hit-Ratio Comparison: SpatialClock is designed to produce sequentially ordered write requests, and often disobeys the philosophy of Clock and LRU policies. Will it degrade cache hit-ratio remarkably? We will answer this question by comparing cache hit-ratios with multiple traces and cache sizes.
- Performance effect on flash storage: We will verify the performance effect of SpatialClock on real flash storage devices.

We compare SpatialClock head to head with the seven schemes we introduced already: (1) LRU, (2) Clock, (3) Linux2Q, (4) CFLRU, (5) LRUWSR, (6) FOR, and (7) FAB.

5.1 Experimental Setup

5.1.1 Trace Collection from Android Smartphone

We collected *before-cache* storage access traces from a real Android smartphone. Even though many disk access traces are available in the public domain, most of them are *after-cache* traces, and some traces used in previous studies (for example, LIRS [16]) do not separate read and write accesses. More importantly, we want to use the traces that came from a real smartphone while running popular mobile Apps.

We used a Google's Android reference phone, Nexus-One [2] with Android Open Source Project (AOSP) [1] 2.3.7, Gingerbread version. We modified the init procedure of Android to use the partitions on an external microSD card with EXT3 file system instead of the internal NAND flash memory with YAFFS2 file system because it is not possible to collect general block level traces from YAFFS2 file system. We also had to modify the page cache related parts of Linux kernel (version 2.6.35.7) to collect the *before-cache* accesses.

Since we do not have standard workloads for smartphones, we have tried to use typical workloads for data usage on smartphones. Of the three workloads used in this study, the first two, namely, W1 (web browsing) and W2 (video streaming), are very typical but with vastly different characteristics in terms of storage access. The third workload is a mix of several popular applications that are run today on smartphones.

- **W1: Web Browsing.** We collected storage access traces while doing web browsing for multiple hours. Web browsing may be the most common activity on today's mobile platforms such as smartphones and Internet tablets. When we visit web pages, web browser downloads web resources like image files into local storage to reduce network traffic. Therefore, while doing web browsing, small files are continually read and written, and storage performance influences user's web browsing experience. The collected amount of traces is smaller than our expectation because Android web browser is directed to the mobile web pages, which are optimized to minimize network and I/O traffic.

- **W2: Video Streaming.** We collected storage access traces while watching various YouTube video clips for multiple hours. When we watch Internet streaming video like YouTube, video data are buffered into local storage to provide stable video watching quality. This is another very popular activity on mobile platforms, and generates very different storage access pattern compared to web browsing. This workload has the highest amount of write traffic among the three workloads studied.

- **W3: Mixed App Workload.** In this workload, we collected storage access traces for several hours while running multiple Apps sometimes together and sometimes separately. Following Apps were used: Facebook, Twitter, Maps, Pandora, Angry Birds (game), Fruit Ninja (game), OfficeSuite, Camera, Internet Browser, YouTube, Gallery, Android Market, etc. We believe this workload is the best one to reflect a realistic usage of the smartphone.

Table 3 shows the number of read and write operations in the collected mobile traces. Note that there are only few read requests in the video streaming trace (W2). This could

Table 3: Trace Information

	Read Operation		Write Operation	
	Count	Amount (MB)	Count	Amount (MB)
W1	23,666	92.4	47,350	185.0
W2	67	0.3	387,701	1,514.5
W3	134,910	527.0	105,796	413.3

Table 4: Flash Storage Devices

Smartphone	Type	Chip Maker	Size
Nexus One	microSDHC	Patriot(Class 10)	16 GB
N900	eMMC	Samsung	30 GB
Nexus S	eMMC	SanDisk	15 GB

very well be due to the limitation of our trace collection method since it is not possible to collect in-memory accesses for a memory mapped file without hardware support[2]. Even though the collected traces may not be a perfectly faithful reproduction of the I/O activity in these Apps (since they are missing the accesses to memory mapped files), we note that this situation is unfortunately unavoidable and will happen even if we profile a real operating system. Thus, we believe that the traces are valid and proper for our evaluation. Besides, since all the cache replacement schemes are compared with the same set of traces, the comparison is fair.

5.1.2 Parameters for Cache Replacement Schemes

Some of the buffer cache replacement schemes require setting some algorithm specific parameters. For Linux2Q, we set the active vs. inactive queue ratio to be 3:1 (this is similar to the setting in the Linux kernel). For CFLRU, the Clean-First window size is set to be 25% of total cache size. For FOR, we use an alpha value of 0.5 as recommended by the authors of the paper, and read and write operation cost as 100us and 800us, respectively. Lastly for FAB, we set the number of pages per block as 64, which is the same as in the author's own evaluation of their scheme.

5.1.3 Flash Storage Devices

Two different types of flash storage are popularly used in smartphones today: microSD cards and eMMC devices. Due to space limitation, we choose to present the result of three devices. Table 4 shows the list of the chosen flash devices: one microSD card (with Google Nexus-one phone) and two (one slower and the other faster) eMMC devices (internal to each of a Nokia N900 and Google Nexus-S phones, respectively).

5.1.4 Workload Player

Workload Player simply receives a trace file, performs the I/O operations specified in the trace file on a real storage device, and reports the elapsed time for performing the operations. We run Workload Player on real smartphones. Google Nexus-One is used to evaluate the microSD card, and a Nokia N900 and a Google Nexus-S are used respectively, to evaluate their internal eMMC devices. The Workload Player is written as a regular C program running on Linux, and the buffer cache is bypassed by using `O_DIRECT` option.

[2] ARM processor in the Nexus-One phone does not provide this functionality.

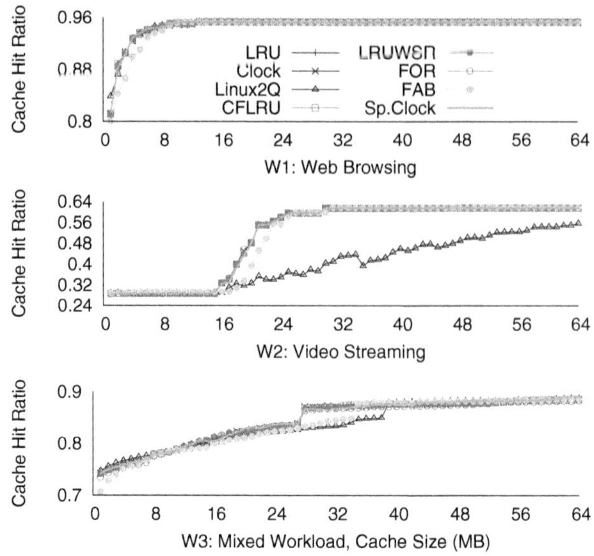

Figure 4: Hit-Ratio Comparison: *SpatialClock shows comparable hit-ratios to other schemes.*

5.2 Hit-ratio Comparison

Figure 4 shows simulated buffer cache hit-ratios[3] with 4-64 MB cache sizes[4] for the eight cache replacement schemes using the three traces. Except Linux2Q and FAB, other six schemes are not much different from one another in terms of hit-ratio. Linux2Q shows lower hit-ratio than the others for the video streaming workload (middle graph) while showing relatively higher hit-ratios when cache size is small. Meanwhile, FAB shows remarkably lower hit-ratios when the cache size is small. It will be very interesting to analyze the reason for the poor performance of Linux2Q and FAB but it is not the focus of this study. We can clearly verify that SpatialClock and other flash-aware schemes except FAB show comparable (not remarkably low, at least) hit-ratios to non-flash-aware schemes even though they sometimes disobey LRU philosophy for the sake of accommodating the performance quirks of flash storage.

5.3 I/O Operation Cost Analysis

Existing flash-aware buffer replacement schemes are mainly focusing on the asymmetric read and write operation costs. Prior cache replacement performance studies have calculated the total cost of the I/O operation by applying a simple mathematical equation using the differential read/write times. We have done a similar calculation. To this end,

[3] Cold-miss ratios are 0.05, 0.38, 0.11 for W1, W2, and W3, respectively; since most of the evictions stemming from misses are due to on-demand paging, there is significant opportunity for SpatialClock to improve the performance of the storage system.

[4] Even though modern smartphones have more than 512 MB main memory, a significant portion of the memory is used for other purposes such as kernel heap / stacks and application heap, and only a limited portion of the memory is available for page / buffer cache. Besides, our study shows that the hit-ratio saturates with 64MB cache size (except in one case: Linux2Q, W2) irrespective of the caching scheme or the workload. This is the reason for choosing 64 MB as the maximum cache size in our real storage evaluation.

we count the number of read and write operations for each buffer management scheme, and calculate the total cost by using a simple cost model for a flash chip as is done in the FOR paper [24] (100us and 800us for read and write I/O operations, respectively).

Figure 5 shows the calculated times. Similar to the hit-ratio comparison results, no obvious differences are seen except for the Linux2Q and FAB cases. Based on this calculated result, it would appear that none of the flash-aware algorithms (including SpatialClock) are any better in reducing the total I/O cost compared to the flash-agnostic ones. We show in the next subsection that such a conclusion would be erroneous.

5.4 Performance Effect on Real Flash Storage

It is hard to show write ordering effect of buffer cache replacement algorithms without using real flash storage devices. Therefore, we collect *after-cache* traces generated by the cache simulator (Figure 1), and play them on real smartphones.

Figure 6-8 show the elapsed time on real flash storage devices. The measured time is represented by the bars in the graph, and shorter bars imply better performance. Unlike the mathematically calculated performance result shown in Figure 5, we can see clear differences among the seven buffer replacement schemes through this exercise of running the *after cache* traces on real flash storage devices[5].

In each cluster of the graphs, the right most red bar represents the elapsed time of SpatialClock. In general across all the mobile flash storage devices used in the evaluation, SpatialClock shows remarkable performance gains with the Web Browsing workload (W1) and Mixed workload (W3). Linux2Q and FOR algorithms show very poor performances with the Video Stream workload (W2). SpatialClock is significantly better than Linux2Q and FOR but does not show any significant performance advantage over the other cache replacement algorithms for the Video Streaming workload (W2).

As already shown in Table 2, eMMC-2 in the Nexus-S smartphone is less sensitive to write ordering, and thus, SpatialClock shows the smallest performance gains for this flash storage (Figure 8) while it shows huge performance gains for eMMC-1 (Figure 7). This is because this eMMC-2 chip is specially designed to provide good random write performance similar to a high-end SSD, and hence the limited performance gain with SpatialClock. This result also implies that the interface of the eMMC devices to the host is not a differential point in the observed results. It is an interesting point to note that SpatialClock consistently performs better with the inexpensive microSD card than on the other the two eMMC chips, which appear to be high-end ones given their superior performance for dealing with scattered writes. One way of interpreting this result is that if the flash storage already is well positioned to handle scattered writes, then the additional performance advantage due to SpatialClock is small. However, SpatialClock does better than the other cache replacement schemes even on the eMMC-2 (24% re-

[5]Please note that the absolute calculated numbers in Figure 5 are very different from what we obtained from measurements shown in Figure 6-8. This is because the parameters used for the calculation (directly obtained from [24]) are most certainly different from the actual internal chip-level timing values to which we have no access.

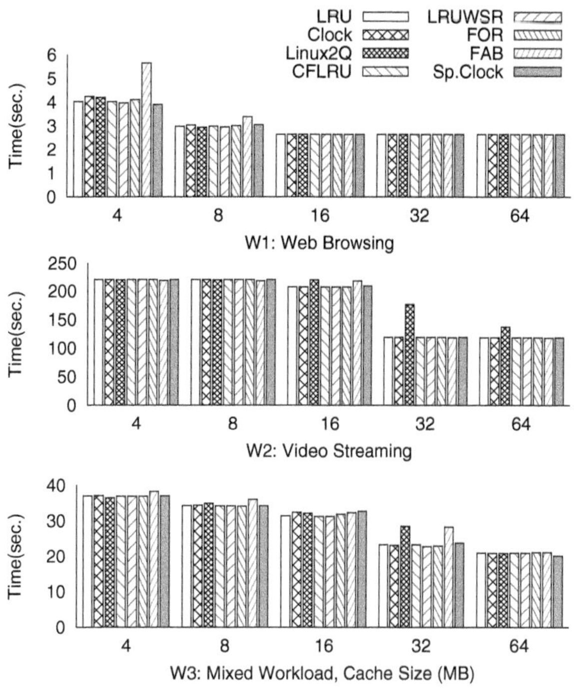

Figure 5: Calculated elapsed time based on the number of read and write operations in after-cache traces: *the results are almost indistinguishable for the different schemes.*

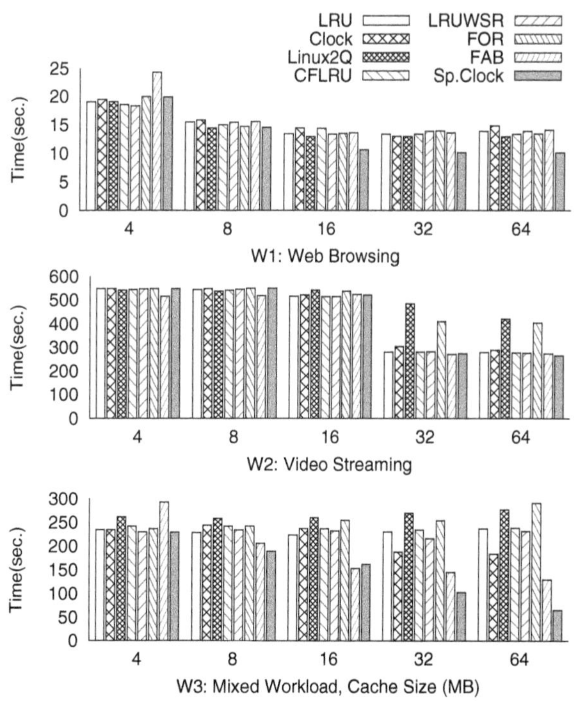

Figure 6: Patriot microSD: *SpatialClock shows -8.6-31.9%(W1), -6.4-43.4% (W2), and -5.4-77.7% (W3) elapsed time reduction compared to the other schemes.*

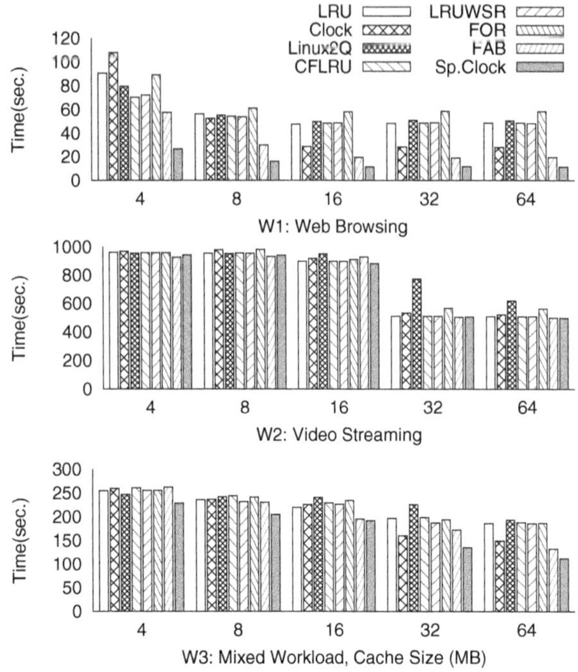

Figure 7: eMMC-1 (N900): *SpatialClock shows shows 0-80.5% (W1), -1.5-34.4% (W2), and 0-42.3% (W3) elapsed time reduction compared to the other schemes.*

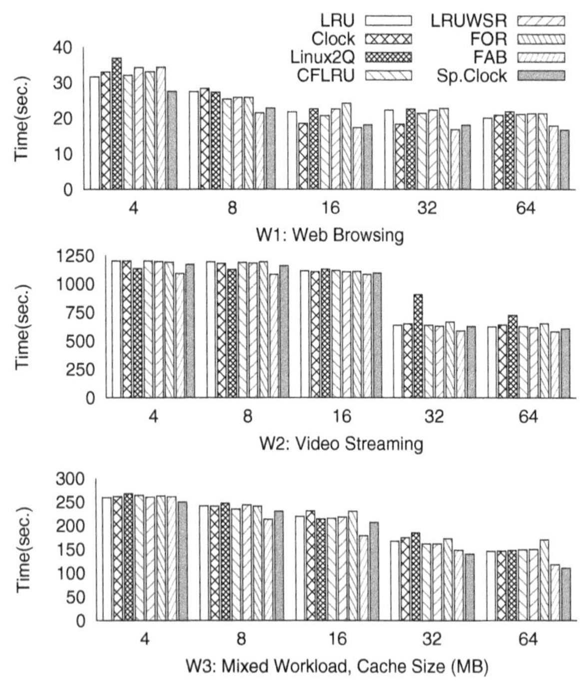

Figure 8: eMMC-2 (Nexus-S): *SpatialClock shows -7.4-25.4% (W1), -7.4-30.9% (W2), and -15.4-34.9% (W3) elapsed time reduction compared to the other schemes.*

duction in elapsed time compared to LRU for W3 workload and 64 MB cache).

There is another very surprising and interesting insight stemming from this performance result. With 64 MB cache and W3 workload the elapsed times for LRU are: microSD: 236.9, eMMC-1: 186.3, eMMC-2: 146.0 seconds. For the same configuration, the SpatialClock elapsed times are: microSD: 64.9, eMMC-1: 111.8, eMMC-2: 110.8 seconds. That is, the best absolute elapsed time (64.9 seconds) for this workload is achieved by using SpatialClock on the cheaper microSD card! Compare this with using the standard cache replacement scheme available in commercial operating systems running on a souped up flash storage such as eMMC and still being nearly 2.2 times slower than SpatialClock on an inexpensive flash. In other words, with the right OS support (SpatialClock), we can achieve better performance than using a hardware solution (eMMC) to circumvent the performance issues of mobile flash storage. SpatialClock is the third contribution of this paper, presenting a compelling case for revisiting the replacement scheme used for the buffer cache in smartphones.

5.5 Discussion

By using three different workload traces and three different flash storage devices, we show the superior performance of our proposed SpatialClock replacement scheme. We look more into some of the finer details concerning SpatialClock.

5.5.1 *FAB vs. SpatialClock*

According to the evaluation results, FAB shows comparable performances to our SpatialClock. FAB is also designed to respect spatial adjacency, which we know is very important on low-end mobile storage devices. However, there are important differences between SpatialClock and FAB from the point of view of a viable buffer cache replacement scheme for a general-purpose OS.

FAB clusters cache pages in blocks and maintains an LRU list in units of blocks. By choosing and flushing the victim block having the highest number of pages, FAB produces large sequential writes, which are desirable for flash storage. However, such a policy sacrifices temporal locality to maximize spatial locality, and results in lower cache hit-ratio as shown in Figure 4, and also can cause performance issue when cache size is small (see Figure 6, wherein it can be seen that FAB displays even worse performance than flash-agnostic schemes). Note that SpatialClock does not have hit-ratio issue nor performance issue with small cache size.

Besides, FAB would also incur a significant computation overhead in any reasonable implementation. Inspecting the pseudo-code provided by the authors of FAB [17], the implementation of the algorithm needs to check all blocks to find a victim block that has the most number of sectors to be written in it. This would undoubtedly result in a significant performance penalty especially with large caches. In other words, for small cache sizes FAB suffers from poor hit-ratio; and for large cache sizes FAB will result in significant performance penalties in terms of computation overhead. Interestingly, FAB reveals a limitation of our cache evaluation framework. As we pointed out, FAB has CPU computation overhead issue, but unfortunately our evaluation framework does not measure the computation overhead. Consequently in a real implementation, the performance results of FAB will be worse than what we have reported in this paper.

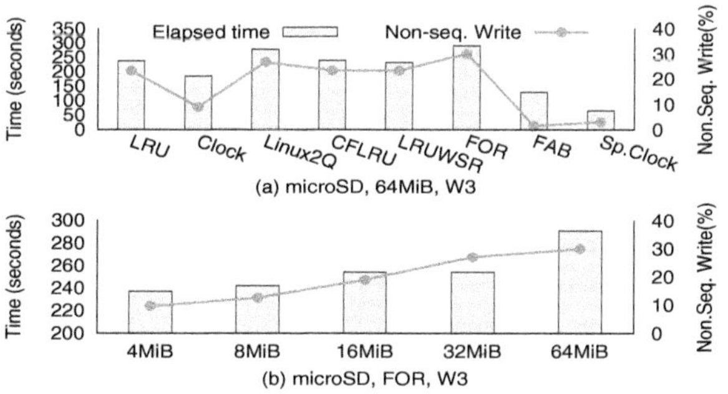

Figure 9: Correlation between the elapsed time and portion of non-sequential write operations in after-cache traces (microSD card)

5.5.2 *Result with Video Streaming*

SpatialClock shows significant performance gains with W1 (Web Browsing) and W3 (Mixed) workloads. However, for W2 (Video Streaming) workload we see almost no gain with SpatialClock. This is easily explained by understanding the video streaming workload. Recall that SpatialClock is geared to respect spatial locality for write requests to the flash storage. Most of the write requests generated by the video streaming workload are sequential in nature (except for a few metadata accesses). The traces are already flash-friendly, thus obviating the need for any special handling by the cache replacement algorithms.

5.5.3 *Verification of Sequentiality*

We claim that SpatialClock generates more sequentially ordered write requests than the other schemes, and that is the reason why it achieves better performance. How can we verify it is actually doing that? To answer this question, we analyze the generated traces for each cache replacement scheme for one chosen test-case (64 MB, W3, microSD). We count the number of non-sequential write operations from the generated trace, and show the portion of non-sequential writes as a percent of all the write requests together with the measured elapsed times in Figure 9 for the different buffer management schemes (Figure 9-(a)), and FOR (Figure 9-(b)). Figure 9-(a) shows that SpatialClock meets its design goal of respecting spatial adjacency for write requests.

5.5.4 *Performance Anomalies*

It is interesting to note the performance anomaly in Figure 9-(b) for the FOR cache replacement scheme. The figure shows that the performance (in terms of elapsed time for the I/O operations) actually becomes worse with larger cache size. This defies conventional wisdom! The reason once again can be linked to the increase in the amount of non-sequential writes to the storage, which as can be seen in Figure 9-(b), increases with the cache size. FOR chooses a victim page using a complex weighted function that takes into account operation cost, recency, and inter-operation distance. With such a choice, it is conceivable that the chosen victim page might be the best one for statistical reasons, but quite a bit distant spatially from the previously chosen victim, thus affecting the performance on a mobile flash memory.

In our studies, we noticed similar anomalies for the other flash-aware cache replacement schemes as well. In general, such schemes that give preferential treatment to dirty pages shielding them from eviction to reduce the I/O cost seem to work well when there is memory pressure. With large buffer caches, the memory pressure goes away and the lack of attention to spatial adjacency for writes in these schemes starts dominating the total I/O cost making them perform worse.

5.5.5 *Limitation of Our Evaluation Framework*

Although our evaluation framework allows us to see the performance effects of application workloads on real storage devices, it has its limitations. As we already mentioned in Section 5.5.1, it does not measure the computation overhead of the cache schemes being compared. Besides, the elapsed time for storage completion reported by our framework may not necessarily translate to comparable gains or losses at the application level, since performance at the application level is influenced by additional factors such as CPU computation overhead and user input.

6. CONCLUSION

Recent studies have shown that flash storage may be the performance bottleneck for the performance of common Apps on mobile devices. Due to size, power, and cost considerations, smartphones will continue to deploy low-end flash memories as the primary storage. Therefore, it is important to consider what can be done in the OS to enhance the performance of flash based storage systems. In particular, since the buffer cache is the point of contact between the upper layers of the OS software stack and the I/O subsystem, this paper re-examines the buffer cache replacement schemes with respect to their suitability for mobile flash storage. We make three contributions through this work. First, we develop a novel performance evaluation framework that is a hybrid between trace-driven simulation and real implementation. Second, we gather *before cache* storage traces for popular Apps running on an Android phone that can be used in the study of cache replacement schemes. We use this and the evaluation framework to study seven different cache replacement strategies. We made some surprising findings through this study, and the insight drawn from the study paved the way for our new buffer cache replacement scheme, SpatialClock. The key insight is the need to pay attention to spatial locality for writes to the flash storage to reduce the overall I/O time, a crucial metric to enhance the storage performance, and hence the application performance on smartphones.

Our future work includes considering the actual implementation of SpatialClock in the Android OS and fully understanding its performance potential in the presence of other OS entities such as the dirty page flusher.

7. ACKNOWLEDGMENTS

We thank the anonymous reviewers for their insightful comments, which helped us tremendously in revising the manuscript. Our shepherd, Mustafa Uysal, has been very helpful in guiding us with the revision adding his own thoughtful comments augmenting those of the reviewers. We also thank the members of our Embedded Pervasive Lab for their support and feedback. This work was supported in part by the NSF award: NSF-CSR-0834545.

8. REFERENCES

[1] Android Open Source Project. http://source.android.com/index.html.

[2] Google Nexus One. http://en.wikipedia.org/wiki/Nexus_One.

[3] G. Adelson-Velskii and E. M. Landis. An algorithm for the organization of information. In *Proc. of the USSR Academy of Sciences*, 1962.

[4] N. Agrawal, V. Prabhakaran, T. Wobber, J. D. Davis, M. Manasse, and R. Panigrahy. Design tradeoffs for SSD performance. In *Proc. of the USENIX Annual Technical Conf.*, ATC'08, pages 57–70, Berkeley, CA, USA, 2008. USENIX Association.

[5] A. Bensoussan, C. Clingen, and R. C. Daley. The Multics Virtual Memory: Concepts and Design. *Communications of the ACM*, 15:308–318, 1972.

[6] D. Bovet and M. Cesati. *Understanding The Linux Kernel.* Oreilly & Associates Inc, 2005.

[7] F. Chen, D. A. Koufaty, and X. Zhang. Understanding intrinsic characteristics and system implications of flash memory based solid state drives. In *Proc. of the international joint conf. on Measurement and modeling of computer systems*, SIGMETRICS'09, pages 181–192, New York, NY, USA, 2009. ACM.

[8] J. Choi, S. H. Noh, S. L. Min, and Y. Cho. Towards application/file-level characterization of block references: a case for fine-grained buffer management. In *Proc. of the international conf. on Measurement and modeling of computer systems*, SIGMETRICS'00, pages 286–295, New York, NY, USA, 2000. ACM.

[9] C. Dirik and B. Jacob. The performance of PC solid-state disks (SSDs) as a function of bandwidth, concurrency, device architecture, and system organization. In *Proc. of the international symposium on Computer architecture*, ISCA'09, pages 279–289, New York, NY, USA, 2009. ACM.

[10] Gartner. Gartner Highlights Key Predictions for IT Organizations and Users in 2010 and Beyond. http://www.gartner.com/it/page.jsp?id=1278413.

[11] B. S. Gill and D. S. Modha. WOW: wise ordering for writes - combining spatial and temporal locality in non-volatile caches. In *Proc. of the USENIX conf. on File and stroage technologies*, FAST'05, pages 10–10, Berkeley, CA, USA, 2005. USENIX Association.

[12] G. Glass and P. Cao. Adaptive page replacement based on memory reference behavior. In *Proc. of the international conf. on Measurement and modeling of computer systems*, SIGMETRICS'97, pages 115–126, New York, NY, USA, 1997. ACM.

[13] Intel Corporation. Understanding the Flash Translation Layer (FTL) Specification. White Paper, http://www.embeddedfreebsd.org/Documents/Intel-FTL.pdf, 1998.

[14] S. Jiang, F. Chen, and X. Zhang. CLOCK-Pro: an effective improvement of the CLOCK replacement. In *Proc. of the USENIX Annual Technical Conf.*, ATC'05, pages 35–35, Berkeley, CA, USA, 2005. USENIX Association.

[15] S. Jiang, X. Ding, F. Chen, E. Tan, and X. Zhang. DULO: an effective buffer cache management scheme to exploit both temporal and spatial locality. In *Proc. of the USENIX Conf. on File and Storage Technologies*, FAST'05, pages 8–8, Berkeley, CA, USA, 2005. USENIX Association.

[16] S. Jiang and X. Zhang. LIRS: an efficient low inter-reference recency set replacement policy to improve buffer cache performance. In *Proc. of the international conf. on Measurement and modeling of computer systems*, SIGMETRICS'02, pages 31–42, New York, NY, USA, 2002. ACM.

[17] H. Jo, J.-U. Kang, S.-Y. Park, J.-S. Kim, and J. Lee. FAB: flash-aware buffer management policy for portable media players. *IEEE Transactions on Consumer Electronics*, 52(2):485–493, 2006.

[18] T. Johnson and D. Shasha. 2Q: A Low Overhead High Performance Buffer Management Replacement Algorithm. In *Proc. of the International Conf. on Very Large Data Bases*, VLDB '94, pages 439–450, San Francisco, CA, USA, 1994. Morgan Kaufmann Publishers Inc.

[19] H. Jung, H. Sim, P. Sungmin, S. Kang, and J. Cha. LRU-WSR: Integration of LRU and Writes Sequence Reordering for Flash Memory. *IEEE Transactions on Consumer Electronics*, 54(3):1215–1223, 2008.

[20] A. Kawaguchi, S. Nishioka, and H. Motoda. A flash-memory based file system. In *Proc. of the USENIX Technical Conference*, TCON'95, pages 13–13, Berkeley, CA, USA, 1995. USENIX Association.

[21] H. Kim, N. Agrawal, and C. Ungureanu. Revisiting storage for smartphones. In *Proc. of the USENIX conf. on File and stroage technologies*, FAST'12, Berkeley, CA, USA, 2012. USENIX Association.

[22] H. Kim and S. Ahn. BPLRU: a buffer management scheme for improving random writes in flash storage. In *Proc. of the 6th USENIX conf. on File and Storage Technologies*, 2008.

[23] J. M. Kim, J. Choi, J. Kim, S. H. Noh, S. L. Min, Y. Cho, and C. S. Kim. A low-overhead high-performance unified buffer management scheme that exploits sequential and looping references. In *Proc. of the conf. on Symposium on Operating System Design & Implementation*, OSDI'00, pages 9–9, Berkeley, CA, USA, 2000. USENIX Association.

[24] Y. Lv, B. Cui, B. He, and X. Chen. Operation-aware buffer management in flash-based systems. In *Proc. of the international conf. on Management of data*, SIGMOD '11, pages 13–24, New York, NY, USA, 2011. ACM.

[25] N. Megiddo and D. S. Modha. ARC: a self-tuning, low overhead replacement cache. In *Proc. of the USENIX conf. on File and stroage technologies*, FAST'13, pages 115–130, Berkeley, CA, USA. USENIX Association.

[26] Nvidia. Tegra 2 and Tegra 3 Super Professors. http://www.nvidia.com/object/tegra-3-processor.html.

[27] S.-y. Park, D. Jung, J.-u. Kang, J.-s. Kim, and J. Lee. CFLRU: a replacement algorithm for flash memory. In *Proc. of the international conf. on Compilers, architecture and synthesis for embedded systems*, CASES '06, pages 234–241, New York, NY, USA, 2006. ACM.

[28] Richard Pentin (Summary). Gartner's Mobile Predictions. http://ifonlyblog.wordpress.com/2010/01/14/gartners-mobile-predictions/.

Versatile Refresh: Low Complexity Refresh Scheduling for High-throughput Multi-banked eDRAM

Mohammad Alizadeh, Adel Javanmard, Shang-Tse Chuang[†], Sundar Iyer[†], and Yi Lu[‡]
Stanford University [†]Memoir Systems [‡]University of Illinois at Urbana-Champaign
{alizade, adelj}@stanford.edu, {dachuang, sundaes}@memoir-systems.com, yilu4@illinois.edu

ABSTRACT

Multi-banked embedded DRAM (eDRAM) has become increasingly popular in high-performance systems. However, the data retention problem of eDRAM is exacerbated by the larger number of banks and the high-performance environment in which it is deployed: The data retention time of each memory cell decreases while the number of cells to be refreshed increases. For this, multi-bank designs offer a concurrent refresh mode, where idle banks can be refreshed concurrently during read and write operations. However, conventional techniques such as periodically scheduling refreshes—with priority given to refreshes in case of conflicts with reads or writes—have variable performance, increase read latency, and can perform poorly in worst case memory access patterns.

We propose a novel refresh scheduling algorithm that is low-complexity, produces near-optimal throughput with universal guarantees, and is tolerant to bursty memory access patterns. The central idea is to decouple the scheduler into two simple-to-implement modules: one determines which cell to refresh next and the other determines when to force an idle cycle in all banks. We derive necessary and sufficient conditions to guarantee data integrity for all access patterns, with any given number of banks, rows per bank, read/write ports and data retention time. Our analysis shows that there is a tradeoff between refresh overhead and burst tolerance and characterizes this tradeoff precisely. The algorithm is shown to be near-optimal and achieves, for instance, 76.6% reduction in worst-case refresh overhead from the periodic refresh algorithm for a 250MHz eDRAM with $10\mu s$ retention time and 16 banks each with 128 rows. Simulations with Apex-Map synthetic benchmarks and switch lookup table traffic show that VR can almost completely hide the refresh overhead for memory accesses with moderate-to-high multiplexing across memory banks.

Categories and Subject Descriptors: B.3.1 [**Memory Structures**]: Semiconductor Memories—*Dynamic memory (DRAM)*; C.4 [**Performance of Systems**]: Design studies

General Terms: Algorithms, Design, Performance

Keywords: Embedded DRAM, Multi-banked, Memory Refresh Scheduling

SIGMETRICS'12, June 11–15, 2012, London, England, UK.

1. INTRODUCTION

Multi-banked embedded DRAM (eDRAM) is widely used in high-performance systems; for example, in packet buffers and control path memories in networking [24], L3 caches in multi-processor cores [8, 1], and internal memories for select communication and consumer applications [19, 23]. Multi-banked eDRAM offers higher performance, lower power and smaller board footprint in comparison to embedded SRAM and discrete memory solutions [21, 9, 10]. For instance, a typical 1Mb SRAM running up to 1GHz occupies $0.5mm^2$-$1mm^2$ in area, and consumes 70-200mW in leakage power on a 45nm process node. Both the low density and high leakage power limit the total amount of SRAM that can be embedded on-chip. In contrast, eDRAMs run at about $1/2$-$1/3^{rd}$ the speed of SRAMs, but are two to three times as dense, and have an order of magnitude lower leakage per bit as compared to SRAMs. For instance, a typical 1Mb eDRAM running up to 500 MHz occupies $0.15mm^2$-$0.25mm^2$ in area, and consumes 6mW-10mW in leakage power on a 45nm process node. Currently, eDRAMs are offered by a number of leading ASIC and foundry vendors, such as IBM, TSMC, ST and NEC.

However, eDRAMs have a memory retention problem: The data in each memory cell wears out over time and needs to be *refreshed* periodically to avoid loss. This is not specific to eDRAMs; the retention issues with discrete DRAMs are also well-known. Traditionally, memory refresh is handled by using an internal counter to periodically refresh all the cells within a particular eDRAM instance. This is done by forcing a refresh operation and giving it highest priority causing conflicting reads or writes to the same bank to be queued. The policy is widespread due to its simplicity. Historically, the penalties due to refresh were low enough to not warrant additional complexity.

However, the memory retention problem is getting worse over time and is exacerbated by the multi-banked design of eDRAMs and the high-performance environments in which they are deployed:

1. Shorter data retention time. The typical data retention time of eDRAM cells at 75°C-85°C is $50\mu s$-$200\mu s$, during which every memory cell needs to be refreshed. With high performance applications such as networking, the operating temperature increases to about 125°C and consequently the data retention time decreases super-linearly to $15\mu s$-$100\mu s$. Also, shrinking geometry means less capacitance on an eDRAM bit cell which further lowers the data retention time. As refreshing a memory cell prevents concurrent read or write accesses, shorter data retention time results in more throughput loss.

2. Larger number of memory cells. Multi-banked eDRAMs achieve high density by assembling multiple banks of memory with a common set of I/O and refresh ports. This drastically increases the potential refresh overhead as an order of magnitude more memory cells need to be refreshed sequentially within the same data retention time. In addition, the manufacturing of memory banks with a larger number of rows (for higher density) increases refresh overhead even further.

In this paper we propose a novel refresh scheduling algorithm, Versatile Refresh (VR), which is simple to implement, provides universal guarantees of data integrity and produces near-optimal throughput. VR exploits *concurrent refresh* [11], a capability in multi-banked eDRAM macros that allows an idle bank to be refreshed during a read/write operation in other banks. The central idea in VR is to decouple the scheduler into two separate modules, each of which is simple to implement and complements each other to achieve high-throughput scheduling. The "Tracking" module consists of a small number of pointers and addresses the question *which* cells to refresh next. The "Back-pressure" module consists of a small bitmap and addresses the question *when* to force an idle cycle in all banks by back-pressuring memory accesses. In order to provide worst-case guarantees with a low-complexity algorithm, we ask the question:

Given a fixed number of slots (Y), how many (X) idle cycles in every consecutive Y slots are necessary and sufficient to guarantee data integrity, that is, all memory cells are refreshed in time?

The X idle cycles include those resulting from the workload itself when there are no read/write operations, as well as the idle cycles forced by the scheduler. A larger Y increases the flexibility of placement of the X idle cycles and helps improve the goodput of bursty workloads by deferring refresh operations longer.

Our main contributions are as follows:

(i) We give an explicit expression of the relationship of X and Y to the question above for the VR algorithm in a general setting, that is, for any given number of banks, rows per bank, read/write ports and data retention time. This allows an efficient scheduling algorithm with a worst-case guarantee on the refresh overhead.

(ii) We lower-bound the worst-case refresh overhead of any refresh scheduling algorithm that guarantees data integrity and show that the proposed algorithm is very close to optimal. It achieves, for instance, 76.6% reduction in worst-case refresh overhead compared to the conventional periodic refresh algorithm for a 250MHz eDRAM with $10\mu s$ retention time and 16 banks each with 128 rows.

(iii) The VR algorithm displays a tradeoff between worst-case refresh overhead and burst tolerance: To tolerate larger bursts (allow refreshes to be deferred longer), a higher worst-case refresh overhead is necessary. We analytically characterize this tradeoff and provide guidelines for optimizing the algorithm for different workloads.

(iv) We simulate the algorithm with Apex-Map [17] synthetic benchmarks and switch lookup table traffic. The simulations show that VR has almost no refresh overhead for memory access patterns with moderate-to-high multiplexing across memory banks.

Organization of the paper. We describe the refresh scheduling problem in §2, and present the VR algorithm for a single read/write port in §3 and its analysis in §4. The algorithm and analysis are generalized for multiple read/write ports in §5. We independently corroborate our analytical results using a formal verification property checking tool in §6. Our performance evaluation using simulations is presented in §7. We discuss the related work in §8 and conclude in §9.

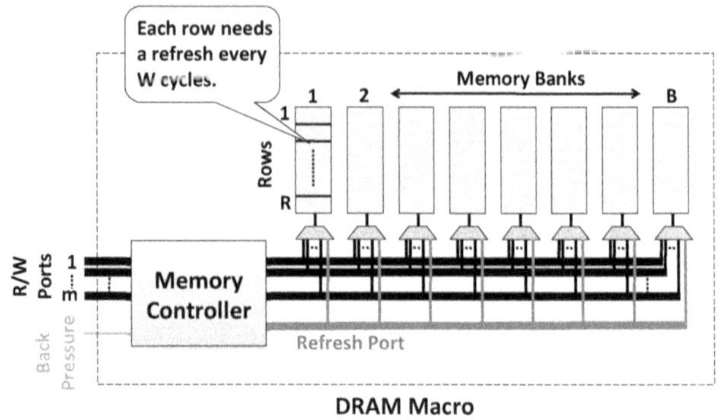

Figure 1: Schematic diagram of a generic eDRAM macro with concurrent refresh capability. Note that in every time slot, each bank can be accessed by only one read/write or refresh port.

2. REFRESH SCHEDULING PROBLEM

In this section we describe the refresh scheduling problem and the main requirements for a refresh scheduling algorithm.

2.1 Setup

We consider a generic eDRAM macro composed of $B \geq 2$ banks, each with R rows,[1] as shown Figure 1. The macro has $1 \leq m < B$ read/write ports and one internal refresh port (typically $m = 1, \ldots, 4$ in practice). A row loses its data if it is not refreshed at least once in every W time slots (W is equal to the retention time, tREF, times the clock frequency). In each time slot, the user may read or write data from up to m rows in different banks. All read/write and refresh operations take one time slot.

A bank being accessed by a read/write port is *blocked*, meaning it cannot be refreshed. In this case, the memory controller can refresh a row from a non-blocked bank using the internal refresh port. This is called a *concurrent refresh* operation. Alternatively, the memory controller may choose to *back-pressure* user I/O and give priority to refresh. This forces pending memory accesses to be suspended/queued until the next time slot. Back-pressure effectively results in some loss of memory bandwidth and additional latency when a read operation gets queued. Write latency can sometimes be hidden since writes can typically be cached or posted later, but we do not consider such optimizations in this paper since we are designing for the worst case (all accesses may be reads).

Remark 1. It is important to note that our model is for a typical eDRAM with a SRAM-like interface [20, 2]. Conventional discrete DRAM chips are more complex and have a large number of timing constraints that specify when a command can be legally issued [6]. For example, a refresh operation usually takes more than one clock cycle in DRAMs [18].

2.2 Requirements

There are three main requirements for a refresh scheduling algorithm:

- **Data Integrity:** This is the most important requirement. Refreshes must always be in time so that no data is lost.
- **Efficiency:** The algorithm must make judicious use of back-pressure so that the throughput (and latency) penalty associated with refresh is low.

[1] Memory vendors sometimes bunch multiple physical rows into one 'logical' row which are all refreshed in one operation [14]. In this paper, R refers to the number of 'logical' rows.

- **Low Complexity:** It is not uncommon for large chips to have hundreds of embedded memory instances, all of which will require their own refresh memory controller. Therefore, it is crucial that the algorithm be lightweight in terms of implementation complexity.

Periodic Refresh. In anticipation of our proposed solution, we briefly consider a conventional refresh scheduling algorithm, henceforth referred to as *Periodic Refresh*. The algorithm schedules refreshes to all the rows according to a fixed periodic schedule. Refreshes are done, in round-robin order across banks, every W/RB time slots to ensure that all RB rows are refreshed in time. Since refresh is a blocking operation, memory accesses to that particular bank are back-pressured. Note that concurrent accesses to other idle banks are allowed.

This is the most straight-forward refresh scheduling algorithm and is commonplace due to its very low implementation complexity. However, since all refresh operations can result in back-pressure in case of conflict with memory accesses, the throughput loss with Periodic Refresh is as high as RB/W in the worst case. Historically, this hasn't been much of a concern since the memory bandwidth lost has typically been ~1-3%. However, as previously described (§1), because of decreasing retention time (smaller W) and increasing density (larger B and R), the memory bandwidth loss can be unacceptably large in high-performance eDRAM macros.

3. VERSATILE REFRESH

In this section we describe the Versatile Refresh (VR) algorithm. The VR algorithm provides very high throughput (in fact, it is provably close to optimal) and it has a low implementation complexity.

3.1 Basic Design

The VR algorithm simplifies managing refreshes by decoupling the refresh controller into two separate components: The *Tracking* and the *Back-pressure* modules. The Tracking module keeps track of which row needs to be be refreshed in each time slot. It operates under the assumption that the memory access pattern contains (at least) X idle slots where no bank is being accessed in *any* Y consecutive time slots (X and Y are parameters of the algorithm). This condition is enforced by the Back-pressure module which back-pressures memory accesses whenever necessary.

In the following, we describe the two modules in detail.

3.1.1 Back-pressure module

The Back-pressure module simply consists of a bitmap of length Y and a single counter that sums the 1's in the bitmap. At any time, the bits that are 1 correspond to the idle slots and the counter provides the total number of idle slots in the last Y slots. The Back-pressure module guarantees that there are at least X idle slots in any consecutive Y slots by back-pressuring pending memory accesses if the value of the counter is about to drop below X.

Flexibility. It is important to note that the Back-pressure module imposes no restrictions on the exact placement of the idle slots; so long as there are X idle slots *anywhere* in every sliding window of Y slots, the memory access pattern is valid. In particular, if the user memory access pattern itself satisfies this constraint, back-pressure is not needed. This affords the user of the memory the flexibility to supply idle slots when a memory access is not needed, and, consequently, access the memory in bursts without any stalls for refresh. In fact, larger X and Y imply more freedom in distributing the idle slots. For example, the constraint $X = 10, Y = 100$ has the same fraction of idle slots as $X = 1, Y = 10$. However, the former constraint allows for much longer bursts of consecutive memory accesses (up to 90 slots) than the latter (up to 9 slots).

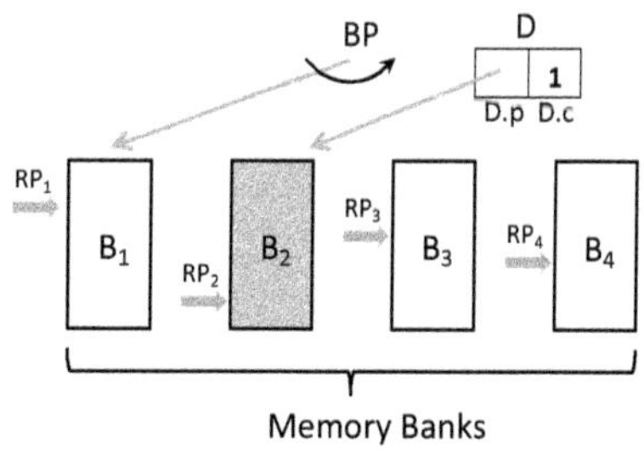

Figure 2: Block diagram of the VR Tracking module. In this example, bank B_2 has a deficit of one refresh.

3.1.2 Tracking module

The Tracking module determines the schedule at which rows are refreshed. In normal operations, it attempts to refresh the rows in a round-robin order. If a row is blocked and cannot be refreshed on its turn, a *deficit counter* is incremented for that row's bank. The algorithm gives priority to refreshes for the bank with deficit, until its deficit is cleared.

We now formally describe the algorithm. For simplicity, we assume the case of a single read/write port ($m = 1$; see Figure 1). The general version of the algorithm for any m is given in §5.1. The Tracking module maintains the following state:

- A row pointer per bank, $1 \leq RP_i \leq R$ (for $i = 1, \ldots, B$).
- A single bank pointer, $1 \leq BP \leq B$.
- A deficit register, D, which consists of a counter, $0 \leq D_c \leq D_{MAX}$, and a bank pointer $1 \leq D_p \leq B$.

The row pointers move in round-robin fashion across the rows of each bank and the bank pointer moves round-robin across the banks. These pointers keep track of which row is to be refreshed next according to round-robin order, skipping the refreshes that are blocked due to a conflicting memory access. The deficit register, D, records which bank, if any, has a deficit of refreshes and its deficit count (see Figure 2 for an illustration). The value of the deficit counter is capped at:

$$D_{MAX} = X + 1, \qquad (1)$$

where X is the parameter from the constraint imposed on memory accesses by the Back-pressure module (at least X idle slots in every Y slots). This choice for the maximum deficit is based on the analysis of the algorithm that is presented in §4.

In each time slot, the bank that should be refreshed, B^*, is chosen according to Algorithm 1. The algorithm first checks whether the bank with a deficit (if one exists) is idle, and if so, it chooses this bank to refresh and decrements the deficit counter (Lines 1-3). Next, the algorithm tries to refresh the bank BP which is next in round-robin order (Lines 4-6). Finally, if the bank BP is blocked, it is skipped over, the deficit register is associated with it, and the deficit counter is incremented (Lines 7-11). Note that the deficit register may already be associated with bank BP in which case Line 9 is superfluous.

Once a bank B^* is chosen for refresh, its row pointer RP_{B^*} determines which of its rows to refresh. After the refresh, RP_{B^*} is incremented. All increments to row and bank pointers are modulo R and B respectively.

Algorithm 1 Versatile Refresh Scheduling Algorithm ($m = 1$)

Input: BP, D, currently blocked bank $\hat{B}$.
Output: B^*, the bank from which a row should be refreshed in this time slot.

if $D_c > 0$ **and** $D_p \neq \hat{B}$ **then**
    $B^* \leftarrow D_p$ {Refresh the bank with deficit.}
    $D_c \leftarrow D_c - 1$
else if $BP \neq \hat{B}$ **then**
    $B^* \leftarrow BP$ {Refresh the bank in round robin order.}
    $BP \leftarrow BP + 1$
else
    $B^* \leftarrow BP + 1$ {Skip blocked bank and increment deficit.}
    $D_p \leftarrow BP$
    $D_c \leftarrow \min(D_c + 1, D_{MAX})$
    $BP \leftarrow BP + 2$
end if

A simple but important property is that at most one bank can have a deficit of refreshes at any time. Therefore, only a single deficit register is required. This is because with one read/write port ($m = 1$), at most one bank can be blocked in each time slot. In general, m deficit registers are required (§5.1).

Example. The timing diagram in Figure 3 shows an example of the operation of the refresh scheduling algorithm with $B = 4$, $X = 1$, and $Y = 7$. During the first 6 clock cycles, bank B_2 is continuously accessed and the algorithm chooses B^* in round-robin order, skipping over B_2 at time slots $t = 2$ and $t = 5$. The deficit counter, D_c, is also incremented at these time slots and D_p points to B_2. Time slot $t = 7$ is an idle slot,[2] and subsequently, bank B_3 is accessed. Hence, the algorithm refreshes bank B_2 at time slots $t = 7$ and $t = 8$ reducing its deficit to zero. Note that in these time slots, the bank pointer, BP, does not advance. With the deficit counter at zero, the refreshes continue in round-robin order according to BP.

3.2 Enhancement

In the basic design, we required that the Back-pressure module guarantee (at least) X idle time slots in every sliding window of Y time slots. Here, we briefly discuss a simple enhancement that allows us to relax this requirement and improve system throughput.

In each time slot, the Tracking module has a bank that it *prefers* to refresh, ignoring potential conflicting memory accesses. The preferred bank is either the bank with a deficit, if one exists, or the bank pointed to by the bank pointer. Now the main observation is that any time slot with a memory access to a bank other than the preferred bank is equivalent to an idle slot for the refresh scheduling algorithm. In both cases, the preferred bank is refreshed. We refer to such time slots as *no-conflict* slots. For example, in Figure 3, time slot $t = 8$ is a no-conflict even though there is a memory access to bank B_3, because the preferred bank, B_2, is idle. In fact, all the time slots $t = 1, 2, 7, 8, 9, 10$ are no-conflict slots in this example.

Therefore, instead of requiring the Back-pressure module to enforce idle slots, it suffices that it guarantee that there are (at least) X no-conflict slots in every Y consecutive slots. This can be done using exactly the same bit-map structure as before. The only difference is that the Tracking module needs to inform the Back-pressure module which slots are no-conflict slots. The memory access is

[2]Note that this is necessary (and will be enforced by the Back-pressure module) to ensure that there is at least $X = 1$ idle slot in every $Y = 7$ slots.

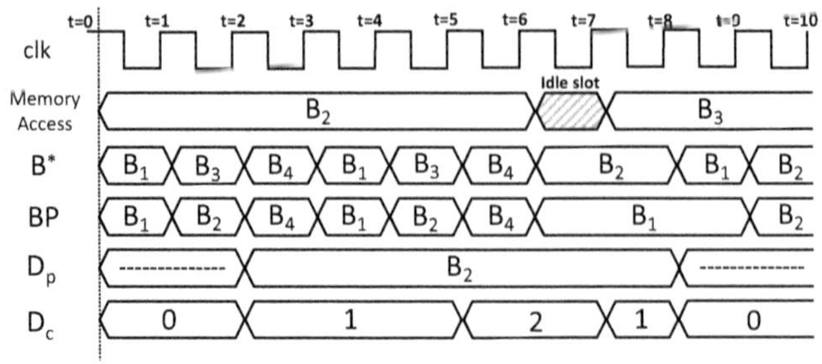

Figure 3: Timing diagram for the VR algorithm with $B = 4$, $X = 1$, and $Y = 7$. The algorithm chooses bank B^* for refresh in each cycle.

back-pressured only if the number of no-conflict slots in the last Y cycles is about to drop below X.

This enhancement can greatly reduce the amount of back-pressure required for workloads that multiplex memory accesses across multiple banks, because even without idle slots, there may be adequate no-conflict slots. In fact, as our simulations in §7 show, even with moderate levels of multiplexing, the overhead of refresh can almost entirely be hidden.

Note: In the rest of the paper, we always consider Versatile Refresh with the 'no-conflict' enhancement.

Remark 2. It is important to note that a *strong adversary* who knows the internal state of the algorithm at each step can always create conflicts by accessing the preferred bank. In this case, the no-conflict slots are exactly the idle slots that are enforced by back-pressure and the enhancement does not provide any benefits. Hence, in the *worst case*, there are exactly X back-pressures required in every Y cycles.

3.3 Implementation Complexity

The VR algorithm has a very low state requirement. The tracking module needs $B + 1$ pointers (B row pointers and one bank pointer), and an extra counter and pointer for tracking deficits. The implementation of Algorithm 1 is a simple state-machine. The back-pressure module also requires a Y-bit bitmap and a counter. Overall, the complexity is $O(B + Y)$. (The next section discusses the choice of X and Y in detail). We estimate that a typical instantiation of VR requires ~10K gates and occupies ~0.02mm^2 in area on a 45nm process node. Even on a relatively small instantiation with say 1Mb eDRAM, this is only ~2.5% of the eDRAM area.

4. ANALYSIS OF THE VERSATILE REFRESH ALGORITHM

In this section we provide a mathematical analysis of the VR algorithm. The aim of our analysis is to determine the conditions under which the algorithm can guarantee data integrity—always refresh all rows in time—*for any input memory access pattern*. By virtue of our analysis, we discuss how the parameters X and Y should be chosen based to the macro configuration and the workload characteristics. We further show that the VR algorithm is nearly optimal in the sense of worst-case refresh overhead by proving a lower-bound on the refresh overhead of any refresh scheduling algorithm that ensures data integrity.

Notation: In this paper, $\lfloor x \rfloor$ and $\lceil x \rceil$ denote the floor and ceiling functions respectively. Also, $\mathbb{1}(\cdot)$ is the indicator function.

4.1 Data integrity for the VR algorithm

As previously mentioned, the back-pressure module ensures that there are (at least) X no-conflict slots in any Y consecutive time

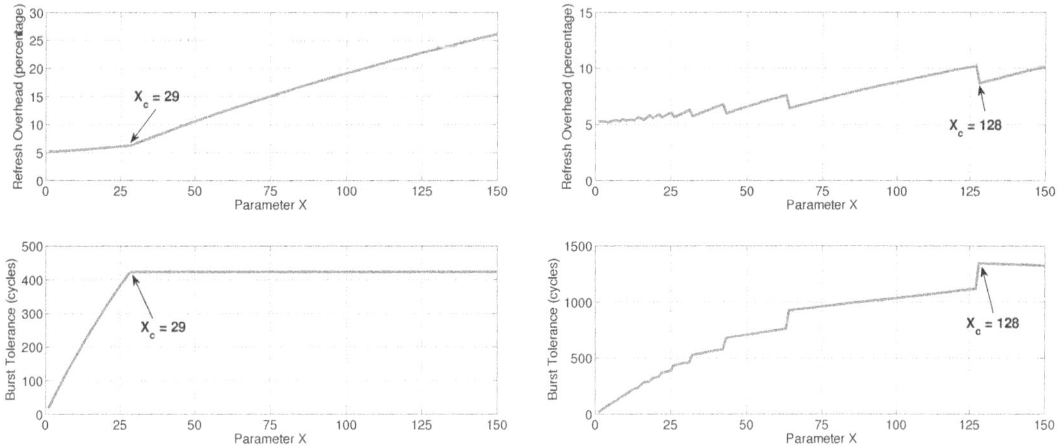

(a) $B = 16 < \frac{W}{R}$ (b) $B = 8 < \frac{W}{2R}$

Figure 4: Worst case refresh overhead and burst tolerance for VR algorithm in Example 1. Note the different scales of the y-axes in the plots.

slots. The analysis proceeds by considering arbitrarily fixed X and Y, and finding the smallest W for which the algorithm can ensure each row is refreshed at least once in every W time slots.

Theorem 1. *Consider the VR algorithm with parameters X and Y. Let $R = aX + b$, where $1 \leq b \leq X$. Then $W \geq W_{VR}$ is necessary and sufficient for the VR Algorithm to refresh all rows in time, where:*

$$W_{VR} = \begin{cases} RB + Y - X + \lceil \frac{Y-X}{B-1} \rceil & \text{if } Y \leq BX, \\ (a+1)Y + bB + 1 & \text{if } Y > BX. \end{cases} \quad (2)$$

The proof of Theorem 1 is given in §4.3.

4.1.1 Choosing the parameters X and Y

In practice, we are typically given B and R. The amount of time we have to refresh each row, W, can also be determined using the retention time specifications of the eDRAM (this typically depends on the vendor, the technology, and the maximum operating temperature). We need to choose X and Y for the VR algorithm.

We consider the following two performance metrics:
(i) **Worst-case Refresh Overhead: $\mathbf{OV = X/Y}$.** Since there are at most X back-pressures in every Y consecutive slots, the throughput loss due to refresh is at most OV.
(ii) **Burst Tolerance: $\mathbf{Z = Y - X}$.** This is the longest burst of memory accesses to a particular bank without back-pressure. It is a measure of the flexibility the algorithm has in postponing refreshes during bursts of memory accesses.

Ideally, we want a small refresh overhead and a large burst tolerance. However, we will see that there is a tradeoff between these two metrics.

For any choice of X, we can use Theorem 1 to find the largest Y for which the VR algorithm can successfully refresh the banks. Denote this by Y^*. Using Eq. (2), we can derive:

$$Y^* = \begin{cases} W - (B-1)R - \left\lceil \frac{W}{B} \right\rceil + X & \text{if } RB \leq W \leq (R+X)B, \\ \left\lfloor \frac{W - bB - 1}{a+1} \right\rfloor & \text{if } W > (R+X)B. \end{cases} \quad (3)$$

Note that for a given X, $OV_X = X/Y^*$ is the smallest refresh overhead, and $Z_X = Y^* - X$ is the largest burst tolerance.

Refresh Overhead vs Burst Tolerance tradeoff. Our analysis indicates that, overall, the flexibility afforded in postponing refreshes by having a large burst tolerance results in a larger worst-case refresh overhead. The parameter X controls this tradeoff. We briefly summarize our findings. The derivation of these facts is simple and omitted.

- **Minimizing Refresh Overhead:** The refresh overhead is not a monotone function of X in general. However, the overall trend is that the refresh overhead is higher for large values of X. In fact, the refresh overhead with $X = 1$, given by:

$$OV_1 = \begin{cases} \frac{1}{W - BR} & \text{if } RB < W \leq (R+1)B, \\ \frac{1}{\lfloor (W - B - 1)/R \rfloor} & \text{if } W > (R+1)B, \end{cases} \quad (4)$$

  is very close to the smallest possible value.[3]

- **Maximizing Burst Tolerance:** The burst tolerance increases with X and attains its largest value for all $X_c \leq X \leq R$, where:

$$X_c = \min\{R, \lceil \frac{W}{B} \rceil - R\}. \quad (5)$$

  In fact, $X > X_c$ only results in higher refresh overhead, without any benefit in burst tolerance and should not be used. The maximum value of burst tolerance is given by:

$$\max\{W - R(B+1) - 1, W - R(B-1) - \lceil \frac{W}{B} \rceil\}. \quad (6)$$

Example. Consider two eDRAM macros with $B = 16$ and $B = 8$ banks. Each bank has $R = 128$ rows. The rows must be refreshed at most every $10\mu s$. Assume clock frequency 250MHz, corresponding to every row requiring a refresh every $W = 2500$ time slots. Note that the first macro corresponds to scenarios with W slightly larger than $RB = 2048$, while the second macro corresponds to scenarios with W moderately larger than $RB = 1024$. We vary X from 1 to 150 (corresponding to increasing levels of flexibility in the refresh pattern), and use Eq. (3) to determine the best Y, and the worst-case refresh overhead and burst tolerance in each case. The results are shown in Figure 4.

Overall, the refresh overhead and burst tolerance both increase as X increases. For the case $B = 16$, the refresh overhead increases

[3]It is easy to show that the refresh overhead of any X is bounded by: $OV_X \geq OV_1/(1 + OV_1)$.

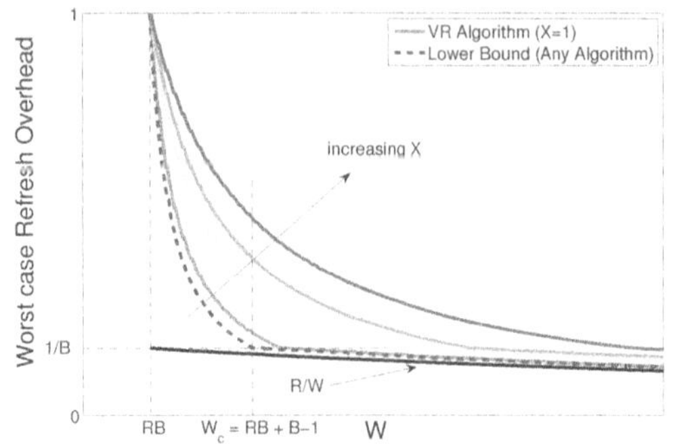

Figure 5: Behavior of the worst-case refresh overhead for different X as W varies.

from 5.3% to over 25%, and the burst tolerance increases from 18 to 423 cycles, as X varies from 1 to 150. Note that at $X = X_c = 29$, the burst tolerance reaches its maximum (see Eq. (5)). Also, the refresh overhead at $X = 29$ is 6.4%, only 1.1% higher than at $X = 1$. Therefore, unless the lowest refresh overhead is crucial, $X = 29$ is a good choice in this case. For $B = 8$, the refresh overhead is smallest for $X = 4$ at 5.19%; it is 5.26% at $X = 1$. The largest value of the burst tolerance (1347 cycles) is achieved at $X = X_c = 128$, which has a refresh overhead of 8.68%.

Recall that the refresh overhead for the Period Refresh algorithm (§2.2) is as high as RB/W in the worst case, amounting to 81.9% of memory bandwidth in the $B = 16$ case, and 40.9% in the $B = 8$ case. Hence, compared to Periodic Refresh, the refresh overhead for the VR algorithm (in the best setting) is 76.6% lower in the $B = 16$ case, and 35.71% lower in the $B = 8$ case.

4.2 Near-optimality of the VR algorithm

In this section we demonstrate that the VR algorithm is near-optimal in the sense of worst-case refresh overhead. The following theorem provides a lower bound for the worst-case refresh overhead of *any* algorithm that guarantees data integrity. This allows us to quantify how far the VR algorithm is from the 'optimal' algorithm.

Theorem 2. *The worst-case refresh overhead for any algorithm that ensures data integrity is lower bounded by :*

$$OV_{LB} = \max\{\frac{1}{W - BR + 1}, \frac{R}{W - B + 1}\}. \quad (7)$$

The proof of Theorem 2 is deferred to Appendix D. Comparing Eq. (7) with Eq. (4) shows that the VR algorithm with $X = 1$ (small X) achieves a near-optimal worst case overhead.

Figure 5 illustrates the behavior of the necessary refresh overhead (the lower bound), and the overhead of the VR algorithm for different choices of X as we vary W. Note that this plot is for a fixed B, and R. An obvious requirement to refresh all the rows in time is $W \geq RB$. It is important to note the two distinct regimes for W: (i) $RB \leq W \leq W_c$ and (ii) $W > W_c$, where:

$$W_c = RB + B - 1. \quad (8)$$

For $RB \leq W \leq W_c$, the necessary refresh overhead rapidly drops to $1/B$. For larger W, the necessary overhead decreases much more gradually and is very close to the trivial bound of R/W (the required refresh overhead when a single bank is always read.). Observe that for small values of X, the refresh overhead of the VR algorithm is close to the necessary lower bound for any algorithm. Larger values of X increase the worst-case refresh overhead of the algorithm. However, they also increase the burst tolerance, allowing larger burst of memory accesses without back-pressure. We explore this tradeoff in choosing the value of X further in §7 using simulations.

4.3 Proof of Theorem 1

In order to prove that $W \geq W_{VR}$ is necessary, we introduce a special (adversarial) memory access pattern and prove that $W \geq W_{VR}$ is necessary to refresh all rows in time for this pattern. We refer to the full version of this paper [25] for the details.

In the following, we prove that $W \geq W_{VR}$ is sufficient. We first establish some definitions and lemmas.

Definition 1. *The bank pointer progress during an interval J, denoted by $P(J)$, is the total number of bank positions it advances in the interval. For example, if the bank pointer is at bank 1 at the start of J, and ends at bank 2 after one full rotation across the banks, $P(J) = B + 1$. Furthermore, the number of times the bank pointer passes some bank $\tilde{B}$ is denoted by $p_{\tilde{B}}(J)$. In the previous example, $p_1(J) = 2$ and $p_{\tilde{B}}(J) = 1$ for $2 \leq \tilde{B} \leq B$.*

The following lemma is the key ingredient in the proof. It provides a precise characterization of the number of refreshes to each bank in a given time interval.

Lemma 1. *Consider an interval J, spanning $T \geq 1$ time slots. Let C_0 and C_1 be the initial and final values of the deficit counter for J, and assume these deficits correspond to banks B_0 and B_1 respectively. If the deficit counter does not reach $D_{MAX} = X + 1$ at any time during J, then:*

$$P(J) = T + C_1 - C_0. \quad (9)$$

Furthermore, the number of refreshes to any bank, $\tilde{B}$, during J is exactly:

$$f_{\tilde{B}}(J) = p_{\tilde{B}}(J) + C_0\mathbb{1}\{\tilde{B} = B_0\} - C_1\mathbb{1}\{\tilde{B} = B_1\}. \quad (10)$$

PROOF. In each time slot, the bank pointer advances by either zero, one, or two positions. Let N_0, N_1, and N_2 denote the number of times each of these occur in the interval J. Hence,

$$N_0 + N_1 + N_2 = T. \quad (11)$$

Since the deficit counter never reaches D_{MAX} during J, it is incremented exactly N_2 times and decremented exactly N_0 times. Therefore, we must have:

$$C_0 + N_2 - N_0 = C_1. \quad (12)$$

Using (11) and (12), we obtain:

$$P(J) = N_1 + 2N_2 = T + C_1 - C_0.$$

Now consider an arbitrary bank, $\tilde{B}$. Note that the deficit for $\tilde{B}$ varies from $C_0\mathbb{1}\{\tilde{B} = B_0\}$ to $C_1\mathbb{1}\{\tilde{B} = B_1\}$ during J. In each of the $p_{\tilde{B}}(J)$ times the bank pointer passes $\tilde{B}$, it either skips over it (if it's blocked), or refreshes it. Let s be the number of times it skips over it. The deficit for bank $\tilde{B}$ is incremented exactly s times (since it never reaches D_{MAX}). Therefore, it must also have been decremented exactly $C_0\mathbb{1}\{\tilde{B} = B_0\} + s - C_1\mathbb{1}\{\tilde{B} = B_1\}$ times.

Note that the refreshes which decrement the deficit for $\tilde{B}$ are different from those due to the bank pointer passing $\tilde{B}$, since the bank pointer does not advance in the former while it advances in the latter. As discussed, bank $\tilde{B}$ is refreshed $C_0\mathbb{1}\{\tilde{B} = B_0\} + s - C_1\mathbb{1}\{\tilde{B} = B_1\}$ times in the first manner. Also, it is refreshed $(p_{\tilde{B}} - s)$ times in the second manner. This results in a total of $p_{\tilde{B}}(J) + C_0\mathbb{1}\{\tilde{B} = B_0\} - C_1\mathbb{1}\{\tilde{B} = B_1\}$ refreshes to bank $\tilde{B}$ during J. □

The gist of the proof of Theorem 1 is to divide the evolution of the system into appropriate intervals, so that Lemma 1 can be applied to bound the number of refreshes for a given bank, relative to the length of each interval. For the rest of the proof, we focus on an arbitrary bank, $\tilde{B}$.

Definition 2. *At time t, the* state *of the VR scheduling system, $S(t)$, is the current values of the bank pointer and deficit register; i.e., $S(t) = (BP(t), D_p(t), D_c(t))$. The system is in state S_D (for **Deficit State**), if bank $\tilde{B}$ has a positive deficit: $D_p(t) = \tilde{B}$ and $D_c(t) > 0$. The system is in state S_{ND} (for **No Deficit State**), if bank $\tilde{B}$ does not have a deficit and is next in turn for a refresh according to the bank pointer: either $D_c(t) = 0$ or $D_p(t) \neq \tilde{B}$, and $BP(t) = \tilde{B}$.*

Definition 3. *Assume at time t_0, the system is in one of the states S_D or S_{ND}. An* epoch, *starting at t_0, proceeds until bank $\tilde{B}$ either gets at least one refresh and the system is in state S_{ND}, or bank $\tilde{B}$ gets X refreshes and the system is in S_D. Hence, the duration of the epoch, starting at $t_0 = 0$ is given by:*

$$T = \min\{t \geq 1 | f(t) \geq 1, S(t) = S_{ND}; \text{ or } f(t) = X, S(t) = S_D\}, \tag{13}$$

where $f(t)$ is the number of refreshes to bank $\tilde{B}$ until time t.

First note that T is finite. To see this, assume $T = \infty$, and consider the time slot t such that $f(t) = X$. There are two cases: (i) The system is currently at state S_D. (ii) $D_c(t) = 0$ or $D_p(t) \neq \tilde{B}$. In the latter case, when bank $\tilde{B}$ is met by BP for the next time, it still has no deficit and the system reaches the state S_{ND}. Therefore, after a finite time, there is a transition either to S_D or S_{ND}, showing that T is finite. Second, the same argument implies that the number of refreshes to bank $\tilde{B}$ in each epoch is at most X. In the following lemma, we use Lemma 1 to bound the duration of an epoch relative to how many refreshes occur to bank $\tilde{B}$. We defer its proof to Appendix A.

Lemma 2. *Consider an epoch starting at state $S_0 \in \{S_D, S_{ND}\}$ and ending at state $S_1 \in \{S_D, S_{ND}\}$. Let C_0 and C_1 be the values of the deficit counter at the beginning and the end of the epoch respectively. Also, let δ be the epoch duration and f be the number of refreshes to bank $\tilde{B}$ during this epoch. Then f and δ satisfy:*

$$\begin{array}{lll} f \in \{1, \ldots, X\} & \delta \leq C_0 + fB - C_1 & \text{if } (S_0, S_1) = (S_{ND}, S_{ND}), \\ f = X & \delta \leq C_0 + Y & \text{if } (S_0, S_1) = (S_{ND}, S_D), \\ f \in \{1, \ldots, X\} & \delta \leq fB - C_1 & \text{if } (S_0, S_1) = (S_D, S_{ND}), \\ f = X & \delta \leq Y & \text{if } (S_0, S_1) = (S_D, S_D). \end{array}$$

The following lemma extends the result of Lemma 2 to a sequence of consecutive epochs.

Lemma 3. *Consider a sequence of consecutive epochs starting at state $S_0 \in \{S_D, S_{ND}\}$. Let $S_l \in \{S_D, S_{ND}\}$ be the state of the system and C_l be the value of the deficit counter at the end of the lth epoch. Also, let F_l be the total number of refreshes to bank $\tilde{B}$ and Δ_l be the total number of slots during the first l epochs. If $F_l = \psi_l X + \xi_l$, where $0 \leq \xi_l \leq X - 1$. Then:*

$$\Delta_l \leq \begin{cases} C_0 + F_l B - C_l \mathbb{1}\{S_l = S_{ND}\} & \text{if } Y \leq BX, \\ C_0 + \psi_l Y + \xi_l B - C_l \mathbb{1}\{S_l = S_{ND}\} & \text{if } Y > BX. \end{cases} \tag{14}$$

The proof of Lemma 3 is straight forward by induction and is given in Appendix B. The following lemma provides a tight bound on the maximum value of the deficit counter. Its proof is given in Appendix C.

Lemma 4. *At any time, the deficit counter satisfies the bound:*

$$D_c(t) \leq \begin{cases} \lceil \frac{Y-X}{B-1} \rceil & \text{if } Y \leq BX, \\ X + 1 & \text{if } Y > BX. \end{cases} \tag{15}$$

We are now ready to prove the theorem.

PROOF OF THEOREM 1 (SUFFICIENCY). We will show that at any time, the number of slots it takes for all the rows of $\tilde{B}$ to get refreshed (equivalently, for $\tilde{B}$ to get R refreshes) is at most W_{VR}. Since $\tilde{B}$ is an arbitrary bank, this proves the sufficiency part.

Assume the system is in an arbitrary initial state and the value of the deficit counter is C_i. It is easy to see that it takes

$$\Delta_i \leq C_i + B - 1 - C_0 \tag{16}$$

slots for the system to enter state $S_0 \in \{S_D, S_{ND}\}$ for the first time, where C_0 is the value of the deficit counter in S_0. Now consider a sequence of epochs beginning in state S_0, and define F_l and Δ_l as in Lemma 3. Let

$$l^* = \max\{l | F_l < R\}. \tag{17}$$

Since the number of refreshes to bank $\tilde{B}$ in one epoch is at most X, we have $F_{l^*} = R - e$, where $1 \leq e \leq X$. Let

$$b + X - e = uX + v, \tag{18}$$

where $u \in \{0, 1\}$ and $0 \leq v \leq X - 1$. We obtain:

$$F_{l^*} = (a-1)X + b + X - e = (a + u - 1)X + v. \tag{19}$$

Now, invoking Lemma 3, we can bound the total number of slots for the l^* epochs as:

$$\Delta_{l^*} \leq \begin{cases} C_0 + (R-e)B - C_{l^*}\mathbb{1}\{S_{l^*} = S_{ND}\} & \text{if } Y \leq BX, \\ C_0 + (a+u-1)Y + vB - C_{l^*}\mathbb{1}\{S_{l^*} = S_{ND}\} & \text{if } Y > BX. \end{cases} \tag{20}$$

Bank $\tilde{B}$ has received $R - e$ refreshes until the end of the $(l^*)^{th}$ epoch. We only need to bound how long it takes for it to receive the next e refreshes. Let this take Δ_e slots. By definition of l^* (see Eq. (17)), all e refreshes must occur during the $(l^* + 1)^{th}$ epoch. This implies that the deficit for bank $\tilde{B}$ cannot be zero after it gets refresh $j < e$ during epoch $l^* + 1$. Otherwise, the next time BP meets $\tilde{B}$, the system transits to S_{ND}, and the $(l^* + 1)^{th}$ epoch contains only j refreshes. Therefore, if $S_{l^*} = S_D$, then the next e subsequent no-conflict slots will refresh bank $\tilde{B}$. If $S_{l^*} = S_{ND}$, at most C_{l^*} slots can be initially spent reducing the deficit of some bank other than $\tilde{B}$ before the first refresh to bank $\tilde{B}$ occurs. (Note that $BP(l^*) = \tilde{B}$). Afterward, any subsequent no-conflict slots will refresh bank $\tilde{B}$ until its eth refresh. Since it takes at most $Y - X + e$ slots to get e no-conflict slots, we have:

$$\Delta_e \leq C_{l^*}\mathbb{1}\{S_{l^*} = S_{ND}\} + Y - X + e. \tag{21}$$

The total number of slots for bank $\tilde{B}$ to receive R refreshes is bounded using (16), (20), (21) by:

$$\Delta_i + \Delta_{l^*} + \Delta_e \leq \begin{cases} C_i + RB + Y - X + (B-1)(1-e) & \text{if } Y \leq BX, \\ C_i + (a+1)Y + bB - X & \text{if } Y > BX. \\ +(u-1)(Y - BX) + (B-1)(1-e) & \end{cases} \tag{22}$$

For the $Y > BX$ case in the above, we have used (18) to write $v = b - e - (u-1)X$.

Consider the two cases separately:

1)$\mathbf{Y} \leq \mathbf{BX}$: Using $(B-1)(1-e) \leq 0$ (because $1 \leq e \leq X$), and Lemma 4 to bound C_i, we have:

$$\Delta_i + \Delta_{l^*} + \Delta_e \leq RB + Y - X + \lceil \frac{Y-X}{B-1} \rceil = W_{VR}. \quad (23)$$

2)$\mathbf{Y} > \mathbf{BX}$: Using $(u-1)(Y-BX) \leq 0$ (since $u \in \{0,1\}$), and $(B-1)(1-e) \leq 0$, and Lemma 4, we have:

$$\Delta_i + \Delta_{l^*} + \Delta_e \leq (a+1)Y + bB + 1 = W_{VR}. \quad (24)$$

Therefore, it takes at most W_{VR} slots for bank $\tilde{B}$ to get R refreshes. Since bank $\tilde{B}$ was arbitrary, $W \geq W_{VR}$ is sufficient for the VR algorithm to refresh all the rows in time. □

5. GENERALIZATION TO MULTIPLE READ/WRITE PORTS

We describe how the VR algorithm can be modified for the general setting with $m > 1$ read/write ports, and extend our analysis to derive the conditions under which the algorithm can refresh all rows in time for any input memory access pattern using m read/write ports (extension of Theorem 1). We also lower bound the worst case refresh overhead of any algorithm (extension of Theorem 2) in this setting to the determine the optimality gap of the Generalized VR (GVR) algorithm.

5.1 VR with multiple read/write ports

With $1 < m < B$ read/write ports, the user can potentially block multiple banks at each time slot. The GVR algorithm is obtained by modifying VR as follows. The Tracking module maintains the state of m deficit registers, $D^{(1)}, \cdots, D^{(m)}$. The registers keep track of which banks have been recently blocked and have a deficit of refreshes. In addition, a new pointer, CP, is needed to choose which bank to refresh. At any time, CP points to one of the banks with a positive deficit (if one exists). The bank that should be refreshed, B^*, is chosen as follows:

- If the bank that CP points to is blocked, then B^* is chosen according to the BP pointer.
- If the bank that CP points to is not blocked, then it is refreshed and its deficit is decremented. The pointer CP then advances to the next bank (in round robin order) with a deficit. This bank is found by consulting the deficit registers.

The Back-pressure module ensures that there are (at least) X no-conflict slots in every Y consecutive slots, similar to the case $m = 1$.

The following properties of the algorithm are worth noting:

(i) If at a time slot the banks $BP, BP+1, \cdots, BP+j-1$ are blocked ($1 \leq j \leq m$), then BP advances by $j+1$ positions and each of the corresponding deficit counters are incremented in that time slot.

(ii) At each time slot, the *preferred bank* for refresh is the bank pointed to by CP, if one exists, or the bank pointed to by the bank pointer, BP. Then, a no-conflict slot is a slot that the preferred bank is not blocked by any of the m read/write ports.

(iii) While a bank has a positive deficit, it is guaranteed to be refreshed at least once in every m no-conflict slots. This is because every no-conflict slot advances the CP pointer to the next bank with a deficit in round-robin order, and there are at most m such banks at any time.

5.2 Analysis

The following theorem provides a sufficiency condition for the GVR algorithm to ensure data integrity. Its proof proceeds along the same lines as for the case $m = 1$ (Theorem 1) and is omitted.

Theorem 3. *Consider the GVR algorithm with parameters X and Y. Let $mR = aX + b$, $b = pm + q$, and $m = gX + h$, where $1 \leq b \leq X$, $1 \leq q \leq m$ and $1 \leq h \leq X$. Then $W \geq W_{VR}$ is sufficient for the GVR Algorithm to refresh all rows in time, where:*

$$W_{VR} = \begin{cases} RB + (g+1)Y - X + \frac{B}{m}(h-1) & \text{if } mY \leq BX, \\ +m\lceil \frac{Y-X}{B-m} \rceil + m - 1 & \\ & \\ (a+1)Y + (p+1)B - X & \text{if } mY > BX. \\ +\frac{B}{m}(q-1) + m(X+1) & \end{cases} \quad (25)$$

Note that the lower bound obtained on W in Theorem 1 (case $m = 1$) is both necessary and sufficient. However, for multiple read/write ports, Theorem 3 only provides a sufficiency bound.

We can use Theorem 3 to determine the largest Y for a given X such that the GVR algorithm can ensure data integrity, following the same approach discussed in §4.1.1 for the $m = 1$ case. Also, the parameter X controls the same tradeoff between worst-case refresh overhead and burst tolerance as before.

Lower bound on refresh overhead of any algorithm. The result of Theorem 2 can also be extended for the setting of m read/write ports. This allows us to quantify the gap between the refresh overhead of the GVR algorithm and the optimal refresh overhead.

Theorem 4. *The worst case refresh overhead of any algorithm that ensures data integrity is lower bounded by:*

$$OV_{LB} = \max\{\frac{m}{W - BR + m}, \frac{mR}{W - B + m}\}. \quad (26)$$

For any choice of X, the worst case refresh overhead of the GVR algorithm can be found using Theorem 3. For example, with $X = 1$, after some simple algebraic manipulations, we have:

$$OV_1 \leq \max\left\{\frac{1}{\lfloor \frac{W-RB}{m} \rfloor - 2}, \frac{1}{\lfloor \frac{W-B-2m+1}{mR} \rfloor}\right\}. \quad (27)$$

By comparing Eqs. (26) and (27), it is evident that the GVR algorithm with $X = 1$ (more generally, small X) achieves a near optimal worst case refresh overhead; especially when $W - RB \gg m$, which is the case in practice.

6. FORMAL VERIFICATION

In this section we use the formal property checking tool Magellan [3] to independently verify our analytical results for an implementation of the VR algorithm. Magellan formally verifies user-specified properties for a given design. Properties are specified using SystemVerilog [15] assertions and Magellan's formal property checkers try to mathematically prove whether the behavior of a particular design conforms to the given assertions. If the assertions are static properties (i.e. invariants) of the design, and if Magellan can validate that these properties are universally true (irrespective of the input parameters), then this leads to a formal proof that a particular design works.

The tool either returns a `Proven` or `Falsified` outcome when it converges. The `Proven` outcome means that the design has the correct behavior for any input satisfying the assertions. The `Falsified` outcome returns a counter example in which the design violates the given property. However, if the state space is large, the formal tool may not converge. The key is to identify and isolate static properties that are independent of each other in order to facilitate convergence.

Y	1	2	3	4	5	6	7	8	9	10	11	12
Formal tool (m=1)	128	130	131	132	133	134	135	136	153	169	185	201
Analysis (m=1)	128	130	131	132	133	134	135	136	153	169	185	201
Formal tool (m=2)	128	133	135	138	171	203	235	267	299	331	363	395
Analysis (m=2)	130	134	136	138	171	203	235	267	299	331	363	395

Table 1: Comparison of the smallest feasible W for the VR algorithm derived by the Formal tool and analysis. The parameters used are $B = 8$, $R = 16$, $X = 1$, $m = 1, 2$ and $Y = 1, \ldots, 12$.

For the VR algorithm, we isolate the behavior of one row and one bank. We create an abstract model for memory, and track the time since the last refresh for every memory row in every bank. In our particular example, we consider a macro with $B = 8$ banks, $R = 16$ rows per bank, and $m = 1$ or 2 read/write ports. We develop RTL for the VR algorithm with $X = 1$ in Verilog. For a given value of Y and W, the formal tool verifies whether the RTL satisfies the constraint that each row is refreshed in every W cycles (as well as several intermediate constraints).

We use the formal tool to determine the smallest value of W for which the VR algorithm, with $X = 1$ and $Y = 1, \ldots, 12$, can successfully refresh the banks in time for any memory access pattern. This is done by sweeping W for each Y and finding the W for which the formal tool returns `Proven` with W, and `Falsified` with $W - 1$. In Table 1, we compare the results from the formal tool with the bound obtained by our analysis (Theorems 1 and 3). The results of the formal tool agree with the predictions from analysis. As previously discussed, with $m = 1$, the bound in Eq. (2) is tight (both necessary and sufficient). With $m = 2$, in some cases, our analysis gives a slightly larger lower bound for W than necessary, as proven by the formal tool.

Remark 3. The formal tool cannot be used to verify VR when the state space is large (e.g., large X or Y). For example, the formal tool did not converge even after 48 hours for $Y \geq 13$ in this design. This highlights the usefulness of having an exact formula that immediately shows whether a design is feasible, greatly simplifying the design process and reducing verification time.

7. PERFORMANCE EVALUATION

The analytical results of the previous sections determined the worst-case refresh overhead of the VR algorithm and showed that for small values of X, it is very close to a lower bound for any algorithm. It was also shown that increasing X results in an increase in the worst case refresh overhead, but provides tolerance to larger bursts of memory accesses because of increased flexibility in postponing refreshes. In this section we use simulations to explore the consequences of this tradeoff in choosing the value of X for a number of (non-adversarial) synthetic and trace-driven workloads.

7.1 Apex-Map Synthetic Benchmarks

Apex-Map [17] is a synthetic benchmark that generates memory accesses with parametrized degrees of spatial and temporal locality. Spatial locality is the tendency to access memory addresses near other recently accessed addresses and temporal locality refers to accessing the same memory addresses that have been recently referenced [22]. Apex-Map has been used to characterize various scientific and HPC workloads [16, 5].

The workload generated by Apex-Map is based on a stochastic process defined using two parameters, L and α. These parameters respectively control the degree of spatial and temporal locality, and can be varied independently between extreme values. Memory accesses occur in strides (contiguous blocks) of length L. When one stride is complete, a new one begins at a random starting address sampled from the distribution:

$$X = Mu^{\frac{1}{\alpha}}, \tag{28}$$

where M is the total memory size and u is uniform on (0, 1). Note that with $\alpha = 1$, the starting addresses are uniformly spread, and as $\alpha \to 0$ they become increasingly clustered near address 0, leading to higher temporal locality.

Simulation Setup. We consider a 1Mb eDRAM macro organized as $B = 8$ banks of $R = 128$ rows. Each row has 8 words of 128 bits. The macro has $M = 8192$ words in total. The eDRAM operates at 250MHz and has a retention time of 10μs, giving $W = 2500$ cycles. We generate memory access patterns according to Apex-Map with $L = 1, 64, 4096$ and $\alpha = 0.001, 0.01, 0.1, 0.25, 0.5, 1$. Each simulation continues until 100,000 memory accesses have been completed. We measure the total memory overhead for refresh (the fraction of cycles with a back-pressure). The results presented in each case are the average of 20 runs.

Schemes Compared. As a baseline, we consider the conventional Periodic Refresh scheme which periodically performs a high-priority refresh operation (see §2.2). We use two configurations for Versatile Refresh: $X = 4, Y = 77$ and $X = X_c = 128, Y = 1475$. These values are derived based on the analysis in §4.1.1. The first configuration gives the lowest worst-case refresh overhead of 5.19%. The second configuration has a refresh overhead of 8.68% in the worst-case, but maximizes the burst tolerance by allowing refreshes to be postponed the longest.

The results are shown in Figure 6. The refresh overhead for Periodic Refresh is fairly consistent around 6.25%. VR with $X = 4$ achieves a lower refresh overhead than Periodic Refresh in all cases (at most 5.19%). VR with $X = 128$ has a higher refresh overhead than the other schemes when memory accesses are highly concentrated on a single bank, but has the lowest overhead when memory accesses are (even moderately) multiplexed across banks. For example, with $\alpha = 0.001$ and $L = 1, 64$, essentially all memory accesses are to the first bank and the refresh overhead for both VR schemes is almost the same as the worst case overhead. But with $\alpha \geq 0.1$ or $L = 4096$, VR with $X = 128$ shows almost no refresh overhead. This is because with $X = 128$, VR can tolerate up to 1347 consecutive memory accesses to a single bank without back-pressuring. (For $X = 4$, a back-pressure is forced after only 73 consecutive memory accesses to one bank.)

Note: The Apex-Map memory access patterns do not cause the worst-case refresh overhead for the Periodic Refresh algorithm. Indeed, the worst-case overhead for Periodic Refresh occurs if memory accesses become synchronized with the periodic refreshes, requiring a back-pressure for each refresh. In this case, the refresh overhead of Periodic Refresh would be $RB/W \approx 41\%$, while the overhead with VR is *always* at most 5.19% with $X = 4$, and 8.68% with $X = 128$.

Remark 4. Conventional DRAMs exploit locality in memory accesses by using a Fast page mode (or page mode), where a row can be kept "open" in a row buffer so that successive reads or writes

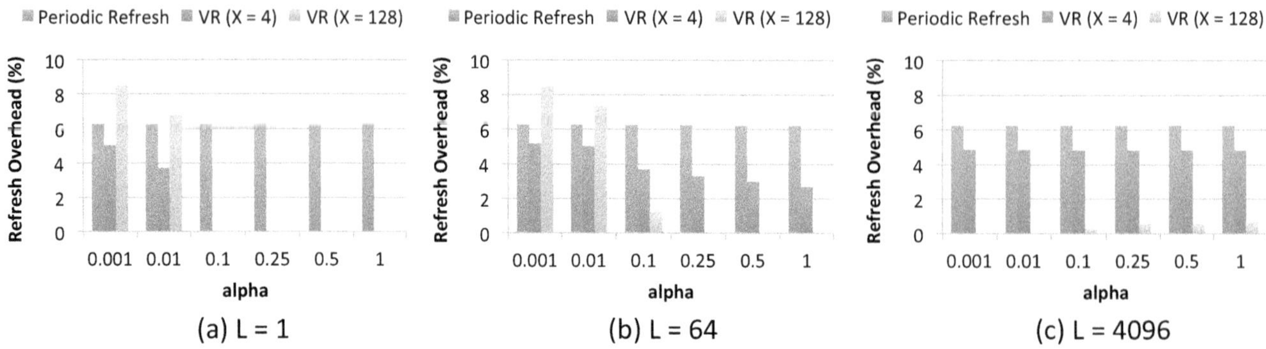

Figure 6: Apex-Map synthetic benchmark results. The results are the average of 20 runs and are within 0.1% of the true value with 95% confidence. Note that in some experiments the refresh overhead is zero and the bar is not visible.

within the row do not need to access the DRAM core and, therefore, do not suffer the delay of precharge. However, because of the wide IO typically used in eDRAM (128 bits or more), page mode is less effective and is not supported in recent eDRAM macros [10]. Therefore, we do not consider page mode in our simulations.

7.2 Switch Lookup Table

Embedded DRAM is extensively used in networking gear for packet buffers and lookup tables [24, 9, 10]. In this section we evaluate the performance implications of refresh for a lookup table stored in eDRAM in a high speed switch. We consider a 1Mb macro similar to the previous section ($B = 8, R = 128, W = 2500$), and use publicly available enterprise packet traces [12] to derive the memory access pattern. We assume a simple L2 lookup based on destination MAC address. For each packet, the destination MAC address is hashed to get the address that needs to be read from the lookup table.

The entire trace consists of 125,244,082 packets. We choose 10 random blocks of 1 million consecutive packets, and simulate the corresponding memory accesses. We assume one packet arrives every clock cycle requiring a lookup and measure the total overhead for refreshes (the fraction of cycles with a back-pressure) over each block. Table 2 shows the results with Periodic Refresh and Versatile Refresh with $X = 4$ and $X = 128$. The VR algorithm shows almost no refresh overhead. As suggested by the Apex-Map benchmark (§7.1), this is because the packet lookups are sufficiently multiplexed across the memory banks to allow VR to hide the refreshes. In fact, with $X = 128$, we did not observe even a single back pressure for the 10 million packet lookups simulated.

	Periodic Refresh	VR ($X = 4$)	VR ($X = 128$)
Refresh Overhead	6.65%	0.39%	0%

Table 2: Lookup table memory refresh overhead.

8. RELATED WORK

The research literature has mostly focused on the problems associated with refresh for DRAMs. We briefly discuss the most relevant work.

Concurrent refresh. Kirihata *et. al.* proposed concurrent refresh [11] to allow simultaneous memory access and refresh operations at different banks of an eDRAM. They also describe a concurrent refresh scheduler for a macro with 16 banks and one read/write port. However, the refresh scheduling algorithm is not fully analyzed and not readily generalizable to arbitrary configurations (e.g. multiple read/write ports). Moreover, the algorithm relies on a periodic external refresh signal to guarantee data integrity, which may unnecessarily increase refresh overhead. In contrast, VR is flexible in the placement of refreshes and allows configurable burst tolerance through the parameter X.

Delayed refresh. The JEDEC DDRx standards allow flexibility in the spacing of refresh operations. In the current DDR3 standard, it allows a maximum of eight refresh operations to be delayed [13] as long as the average refresh rate is maintained. Elastic Refresh [18] takes advantage of the flexibility and improves performance by delaying refreshes based on the predicted workload; it also uses the rule of thumb given in the standard for maximum number of refreshes. Our algorithm allows similar flexibility in refreshes to avoid clashes with read/write operations, while prescribing universal bounds on necessary number of refreshes and giving worst-case guarantees. Hence it improves performance by optimizing the minimum number of refreshes.

Per-word monitoring. Another approach to reducing refresh overhead is to monitor each memory cell, or a combination of cells, to decide a refresh schedule. For instance, Smart Refresh [4] keeps a time-out counter next to each memory row to monitor its urgency for refreshes. It uses this to eliminate unnecessary refreshes to rows that are automatically refreshed during a recent read or write operation. ESKIMO [7] uses program semantics information to decide which memory rows are inconsequential to the correct execution of the program (e.g. have been freed) and avoid refreshing them. These methods can improve throughput or save power for specific workloads, but require complex memory cell monitoring and application analysis. Our algorithm is orthogonal to these approaches and can benefit all workloads.

9. FINAL REMARKS

We introduced the Versatile Refresh (VR) algorithm, which exploits concurrent refresh to solve the eDRAM refresh scheduling problem. Our work can potentially be extended in a number of directions: (i) We could consider its applicability for DRAMs. This would mean adapting it to fit within the instantaneous power budget of a DRAM, and possibly slowing down the rate at which VR performs concurrent refreshes. (ii) We could consider the case where the refresh takes more than one cycle (as is common in current DRAMs). This can be easily incorporated in our analysis.

Our work lays a mathematical foundation in understanding the memory refresh scheduling problem. It can be used as an additional analytical tool by design engineers to complement system performance evaluation using simulations and workload analyses.

Acknowledgments

Mohammad Alizadeh and Adel Javanmard are supported by the Caroline and Fabian Pease Stanford Graduate Fellowship. We would like to thank Rob Busch from IBM Microelectronics; and also the anonymous reviewers for their helpful comments.

10. REFERENCES

[1] J. Barth, D. Plass, E. Nelson, C. Hwang, G. Fredeman, M. Sperling, A. Mathews, T. Kirihata, W. Reohr, K. Nair, and N. Caon. A 45 nm SOI Embedded DRAM Macro for the POWER7TM Processor 32 MByte On-Chip L3 Cache. *Solid-State Circuits, IEEE Journal of*, 46(1):64 –75, jan. 2011.

[2] C.-M. Chang, M.-T. Chao, R.-F. Huang, and D.-Y. Chen. Testing Methodology of Embedded DRAMs. In *Test Conference, 2008. ITC 2008. IEEE International*, pages 1 –9, oct. 2008.

[3] Magellan Formal Verification Tool. http://www.synopsys.com/tools/verification/functionalverification/pages/magellan.aspx.

[4] M. Ghosh and H.-H. S. Lee. Smart Refresh: An Enhanced Memory Controller Design for Reducing Energy in Conventional and 3D Die-Stacked DRAMs. In *Proceedings of the 40th Annual IEEE/ACM International Symposium on Microarchitecture*, MICRO 40, pages 134–145, Washington, DC, USA, 2007. IEEE Computer Society.

[5] K. Ibrahim and E. Strohmaier. Characterizing the Relation Between Apex-Map Synthetic Probes and Reuse Distance Distributions. In *Parallel Processing (ICPP), 2010 39th International Conference on*, pages 353 –362, sept. 2010.

[6] E. Ipek, O. Mutlu, J. F. Martń?nez, and R. Caruana. Self-Optimizing Memory Controllers: A reinforcement learning approach. In *International Symposium on Computer Architecture*, page 39?50, 2008.

[7] C. Isen and L. K. John. ESKIMO: Energy savings using Semantic Knowledge of Inconsequential Memory Occupancy for DRAM subsystem. In *Proc. of MICRO 42*, MICRO 42, pages 337–346, New York, NY, USA, 2009. ACM.

[8] S. S. Iyer, J. E. Barth, Jr., P. C. Parries, J. P. Norum, J. P. Rice, L. R. Logan, and D. Hoyniak. Embedded DRAM: Technology platform for the Blue Gene/L chip. *IBM Journal of Research and Development*, 49(2.3):333 –350, march 2005.

[9] D. Keitel-Schulz and N. Wehn. Embedded DRAM Development: Technology, Physical Design, and Application Issues. *IEEE Design and Test of Computers*, 18:7–15, 2001.

[10] T. Kirihata. High performance embedded dynamic random access memory in nano-scale technologies. In K. Iniewski, editor, *CMOS Processors and Memories*, volume 0 of *Analog Circuits and Signal Processing*, pages 295–336. Springer Netherlands, 2010.

[11] T. Kirihata, P. Parries, D. Hanson, H. Kim, J. Golz, G. Fredeman, R. Rajeevakumar, J. Griesemer, N. Robson, A. Cestero, B. Khan, G. Wang, M. Wordeman, and S. Iyer. An 800-MHz embedded DRAM with a concurrent refresh mode. *Solid-State Circuits, IEEE Journal of*, 40(6):1377 – 1387, June 2005.

[12] LBNL/ICSI Enterprise Tracing Project. http://www.icir.org/enterprise-tracing.

[13] Micron, TN-47-16 Designing for High-Density DDR2 Memory Introduction, 2005.

[14] L. Minas and B. Ellison. The problem of power consumption in servers. *Intel Press Report*, 2009.

[15] C. Spear. *SystemVerilog for Verification, Second Edition: A Guide to Learning the Testbench Language Features*. Springer Publishing Company, Incorporated, 2nd edition, 2008.

[16] E. Strohmaier and H. Shan. Architecture Independent Performance Characterization and Benchmarking for Scientific Applications. In *Proceedings of the The IEEE Computer Society's 12th Annual International Symposium on Modeling, Analysis, and Simulation of Computer and Telecommunications Systems*, pages 467–474, Washington, DC, USA, 2004. IEEE Computer Society.

[17] E. Strohmaier and H. Shan. Apex-Map: A Global Data Access Benchmark to Analyze HPC Systems and Parallel Programming Paradigms. In *Proceedings of the 2005 ACM/IEEE conference on Supercomputing*, SC '05, pages 49–, Washington, DC, USA, 2005. IEEE Computer Society.

[18] J. Stuecheli, D. Kaseridis, H. C.Hunter, and L. K. John. Elastic Refresh: Techniques to Mitigate Refresh Penalties in High Density Memory. In *Proc. of MICRO 43*, pages 375–384. IEEE Computer Society, 2010.

[19] M. Takahashi, T. Nishikawa, M. Hamada, T. Takayanagi, H. Arakida, N. Machida, H. Yamamoto, T. Fujiyoshi, Y. Ohashi, O. Yamagishi, T. Samata, A. Asano, T. Terazawa, K. Ohmori, Y. Watanabe, H. Nakamura, S. Minami, T. Kuroda, and T. Furuyama. A 60-MHz 240-mW MPEG-4 videophone LSI with 16-Mb embedded DRAM. *Solid-State Circuits, IEEE Journal of*, 35(11):1713 –1721, nov 2000.

[20] S. Thoziyoor, J. H. Ahn, M. Monchiero, J. B. Brockman, and N. P. Jouppi. A Comprehensive Memory Modeling Tool and Its Application to the Design and Analysis of Future Memory Hierarchies. In *Proceedings of the 35th Annual International Symposium on Computer Architecture*, ISCA '08, pages 51–62, Washington, DC, USA, 2008. IEEE Computer Society.

[21] N. Wehn and S. Hein. Embedded DRAM architectural trade-offs. In *Design, Automation and Test in Europe, 1998., Proceedings*, pages 704 –708, feb 1998.

[22] J. Weinberg, M. O. McCracken, E. Strohmaier, and A. Snavely. Quantifying Locality In The Memory Access Patterns of HPC Applications. In *Proceedings of the 2005 ACM/IEEE conference on Supercomputing*, SC '05, pages 50–, Washington, DC, USA, 2005. IEEE Computer Society.

[23] C.-W. Yoon, R. Woo, J. Kook, S.-J. Lee, K. Lee, and H.-J. Yeo. An 80/20-MHz 160-mW multimedia processor integrated with embedded DRAM, MPEG-4 accelerator and 3-D rendering engine for mobile applications. *Solid-State Circuits, IEEE Journal of*, 36(11):1758 –1767, nov 2001.

[24] NEC Electronics Embedded DRAM over 10 Gbps SONET/SDH and Ethernet takes off. http://www2.renesas.com/process/ja/pdf/eDRAM-SPI4.2.pdf.

[25] M. Alizadeh, A. Javanmard, S.T. Chuang, S. Iyer, and Y. Lu. Versatile Refresh: Low Complexity Refresh Scheduling for High-throughput Multi-banked eDRAM. http://simula.stanford.edu/papers/VR-full.pdf.

APPENDIX

A. PROOF OF LEMMA 2

We prove the statement for the case $S_0 = S_D$. The case $S_0 = S_{ND}$ is similar. With $S_0 = S_D$, the deficit is initially $C_0 \geq 1$ for bank $\tilde{B}$. Consider the following cases.

• **Case 1**: The fth refresh to bank $\tilde{B}$, with $f \leq X$, reduces its deficit to zero. (Note that $C_0 \leq f$). Assume this occurs at the tth time slot of the epoch. In this case, the next time $\tilde{B}$ is met by BP, the system transits to $S_1 = S_{ND}$. Let δ be the epoch duration. Firstly, note that although the deficit for bank $\tilde{B}$ is zero at the end of the epoch, some other bank may have non zero deficit, i.e., C_1. Secondly, the deficit counter did not reach $D_{MAX} = X + 1$ during the epoch; otherwise, $f \leq X$ refreshes were not adequate to reduce the deficit for bank $\tilde{B}$ to zero. Hence, we can apply Lemma 1 to the epoch. Using (9), the progress of the bank pointer during the epoch is:

$$P = \delta + C_1 - C_0. \tag{29}$$

Also, using (10), we have:

$$f = p_{\tilde{B}} + C_0, \tag{30}$$

where $p_{\tilde{B}}$ is the number of times the bank pointer passes bank $\tilde{B}$. This implies $P \leq (f - C_0)B + B - 1$, since if $P \geq (f - C_0 + 1)B$, the bank pointer will pass $\tilde{B}$ at least $f - C_0 + 1$ times; i.e., $p_{\tilde{B}} \geq f - C_0 + 1$, which along with (30) leads to a contradiction. Therefore, using (29), we have:

$$\begin{aligned} \delta &= P + C_0 - C_1 \\ &\leq (f - C_0)B + B - 1 + C_0 - C_1, \\ &= fB - C_1 + (B-1)(1 - C_0), \\ &\leq fB - C_1, \end{aligned} \tag{31}$$

proving the desired result.

• **Case 2**: The deficit for bank $\tilde{B}$ remains positive, up to and after it receives its Xth refresh in the epoch. Then $S_1 = S_D$ and the epoch ends right after the Xth refresh to $\tilde{B}$. Hence, $f = X$. Also, every no-conflict slot during the epoch is guaranteed to refresh $\tilde{B}$ because it has positive deficit. Since there are at least X no-conflict slots in every Y time slots, $\delta \leq Y$. The result follows. □

B. PROOF OF LEMMA 3

The proof is by induction on l. For $l = 1$ the statement follows from Lemma 2. Assume it's true for $l \geq 1$, we prove it for $l + 1$.

Let δ be the duration of the $(l+1)^{th}$ epoch, and f be the number of refreshes to bank $\tilde{B}$ in this epoch. Consider the following two separate cases.

1)$\mathbf{Y} \leq \mathbf{BX}$: Clearly, $F_{l+1} = F_l + f$. Also, the values of the deficit counter at the beginning and the end of $(l+1)^{th}$ epoch are respectively C_l and C_{l+1}. Applying Lemma 2 in conjunction with the assumption $Y \leq BX$ yields

$$\delta \leq C_l \mathbb{1}\{S_l = S_{ND}\} + fB - C_{l+1}\mathbb{1}\{S_{l+1} = S_{ND}\}. \quad (32)$$

Therefore:

$$\begin{aligned} \Delta_{l+1} &\leq \Delta_l + \delta \\ &\leq C_0 + (F_l + f)B - C_{l+1}\mathbb{1}\{S_{l+1} = S_{ND}\} \quad (33) \\ &= C_0 + F_{l+1}B - C_{l+1}\mathbb{1}\{S_{l+1} = S_{ND}\}. \end{aligned}$$

2)$\mathbf{Y} > \mathbf{BX}$: Let $f + \xi_l = uX + v$, with $0 \leq v \leq X - 1$. Note that $F_{l+1} = F_l + f = \psi_{l+1}X + \xi_{l+1}$, where $\psi_{l+1} = \psi_l + u$ and $\xi_{l+1} = v$. There are two cases:

- $S_{l+1} = S_D$: In this case $f = X$, $u = 1$, $v = \xi_l$. Therefore: $\psi_{l+1} = \psi_l + 1$, $\xi_{l+1} = \xi_l$. Also, using Lemma 2, $\delta \leq C_l \mathbb{1}\{S_l = S_{ND}\} + Y$. Hence:

$$\begin{aligned} \Delta_{l+1} &\leq \Delta_l + \delta \\ &\leq C_0 + \psi_l Y + \xi_l B - C_l \mathbb{1}\{S_l = S_{ND}\} \\ &\quad + C_l \mathbb{1}\{S_l = S_{ND}\} + Y \quad (34) \\ &= C_0 + (\psi_l + 1)Y + \xi_l B \\ &= C_0 + \psi_{l+1}Y + \xi_{l+1}B. \end{aligned}$$

- $S_{l+1} = S_{ND}$: In this case $\delta \leq C_l \mathbb{1}\{S_l = S_{ND}\} + fB - C_{l+1}$, and we have:

$$\begin{aligned} \Delta_{l+1} &\leq \Delta_l + \delta \\ &\leq C_0 + \psi_l Y + (\xi_l + f)B - C_{l+1} \\ &= C_0 + \psi_l Y + uBX + vB - C_{l+1} \quad (35) \\ &\leq C_0 + (\psi_l + u)Y + vB - C_{l+1} \\ &= C_0 + \psi_{l+1}Y + \xi_{l+1}B - C_{l+1}. \end{aligned}$$

In all cases, we have shown (14) holds for $l+1$. ☐

C. PROOF OF LEMMA 4

Consider the evolution of $D_c(t)$. Its value starts from zero and is always nonnegative. Assume an interval of time slots, $J = [t_0, t_1]$, such that $D_c(t_0) = 0$ and D_c is (strictly) positive for $t_0 < t \leq t_1$. Clearly, it suffices to prove the bound only for $t \in J$, since the timeline can be partitioned into so many of these intervals. We further assume that $t_0 = 0$, and $D_p = B_1$ during J, with no loss of generality.

For $0 < t \leq t_1$, let $I(t)$ be the number of no-conflict slots in $[1, t]$. In the following, we bound the number of increments and decrements to D_c in the interval $[1, t]$ separately, whence we obtain a bound on the value of $D_c(t)$.

Since $D.c$ is positive over the interval $[1, t]$, any no-conflict slot in this interval is used to reduce the deficit counter. Therefore, there are at most $t - I(t)$ slots in which D_c is potentially increased. To get a bound on the maximum increments to D_c, we track the bank pointer. Since the bank pointer does not advance in the no-conflict slots, we confine ourselves to the $t - I(t)$ slots. In these slots, D_c is increased by one every time the bank pointer meets B_1 and it is blocked. Since the bank pointer advances in a round robin fashion, it skips bank B_1 at most once in every $B - 1$ slots. Consequently, D_c is increased at most once in every $B - 1$ slots, implying that the maximum increments to D_c is $\lceil \frac{t - I(t)}{B-1} \rceil$. On the other hand, since D_c is always positive in the interval $[1, t_1]$, any no-conflict slot yields a decrease in the value of D_c. Accordingly, the value of counter at time t is bounded as follows.

$$D_c(t) \leq \left\lceil \frac{t - I(t)}{B - 1} \right\rceil - I(t) = \left\lceil \frac{t - BI(t)}{B - 1} \right\rceil. \quad (36)$$

Let $I(t) = k$, and write $k + 1 = k_q X + k_r$ with $1 \leq k_r \leq X$. Note that the $(k+1)^{th}$ no-conflict slot occurs by the $n(k+1)^{th}$ slot, where:

$$n(k+1) = (k_q + 1)Y - X + k_r. \quad (37)$$

This is because there are at least X no-conflict slots in every Y consecutive time slots. Hence, we have

$$t \leq n(k+1) - 1. \quad (38)$$

Otherwise, we get $I(t) \geq k + 1$. Substituting for t and $I(t)$ in Eq. (36), we obtain

$$D_c(t) \leq \left\lceil \frac{(Y - X) + k_q(Y - BX) - (B-1)(k_r - 1)}{B - 1} \right\rceil.$$

If $Y \leq BX$, the above bound is clearly at most $\lceil \frac{Y-X}{B-1} \rceil$. For the case $Y > BX$, we have the trivial bound $X + 1$ on $D_c(t)$ as set by the algorithm. The result follows. ☐

D. PROOF OF THEOREM 2

We propose two adversarial patterns each of which provides a lower bound on the worst case refresh overhead. Throughout, t_0 is sufficiently large such that all the rows have distinct ages from t_0 onward.

First pattern: At time slot t_0, consider the youngest row in each bank. Denote the oldest row among them by r^* and its bank by B^*. Clearly, $Age(r^*) \geq B - 1$. The adversary blocks bank B^* in the subsequent slots. By time $t_1 = t_0 + W - B + 1$, the algorithm must back pressure the memory at least R times. Otherwise, one of the rows in bank B^* is not refreshed in the interval $[t_0, t_1]$, and loses its data by time t_1. (Note that all the rows in bank B^* have age at least $Age(r^*) \geq B - 1$ at time slot t_0). Now, repeat this pattern starting at the first time slot $\hat{t}_0 \leq t_1$ that bank B^* is refreshed R times. At time slot $\hat{t}_0$, let r^* be the oldest row in the set of the youngest rows in each bank, and let B^* be its bank. By a similar argument to the above, the memory is back pressured at least R times within the next $W - B + 1$ time slots, and so on. Accordingly, the refresh overhead for this input read pattern is at least $R/(W - B + 1)$.

Second pattern: At time slot t_0, let r^* be the oldest row and let B^* be its bank. Therefore, $Age(r^*) \geq BR - 1$. The adversary blocks bank B^* in the following slots. By time $t_1 = t_0 + W - BR + 1$, the algorithm must back pressure the memory at least once. Otherwise, r^* loses its data. Now, repeat this pattern starting at the first time slot $\hat{t}_0 \leq t_1$ that row r^* is refreshed. At time slot $\hat{t}_0$, consider the oldest row, r^*, and its bank B^*. The adversary blocks bank B^* in the subsequent slots. Therefore, the memory is back pressured at least once within the next $W - BR + 1$ slots, and so on. Hence, the refresh overhead for this input pattern is at least $1/(W - BR + 1)$.

A refresh scheduling algorithm that ensures data integrity for any input pattern must satisfy both bounds, completing the proof. ☐

Does Lean Imply Green? A Study of the Power Performance Implications of Java Runtime Bloat

Suparna Bhattacharya
Indian Institute of Science

Karthick Rajamani
IBM Research

K. Gopinath
Indian Institute of Science

Manish Gupta
IBM Research

ABSTRACT

The presence of software bloat in large flexible software systems can hurt energy efficiency. However, identifying and mitigating bloat is fairly effort intensive. To enable such efforts to be directed where there is a substantial potential for energy savings, we investigate the impact of bloat on power consumption under different situations.

We conduct the first systematic experimental study of the joint power performance implications of bloat across a range of hardware and software configurations on modern server platforms. The study employs controlled experiments to expose different effects of a common type of Java runtime bloat, excess temporary objects, in the context of the SPECPower_ssj2008 workload. We introduce the notion of equi-performance power reduction to characterize the impact, in addition to peak power comparisons. The results show a wide variation in energy savings from bloat reduction across these configurations. Energy efficiency benefits at peak performance tend to be most pronounced when bloat affects a performance bottleneck and *non-bloated resources have low energy-proportionality.* Equiperformance power savings are highest when *bloated resources have a high degree of energy proportionality.*

We develop an analytical model that establishes a general relation between resource pressure caused by bloat and its energy efficiency impact under different conditions of resource bottlenecks and energy proportionality. Applying the model to different "what-if" scenarios, we predict the impact of bloat reduction and corroborate these predictions with empirical observations. Our work shows that the prevalent software-only view of bloat is inadequate for assessing its power-performance impact and instead provides a full systems approach for reasoning about its implications.

Categories and Subject Descriptors

D.2.8 [**Software Engineering**]: Metrics—*performance measures*; C.4 [**Performance of Systems**]: Measurement techniques, Modeling techniques—*energy efficiency*

Keywords

software bloat, power, energy-efficiency, energy proportional

1. INTRODUCTION

Power-efficient software is being proposed as an important tool [25, 36] in energy optimization of server systems. Meanwhile, in the software engineering domain, researchers have observed that large framework based applications can suffer from runtime inefficiencies due to "software bloat" [21, 35]. "Bloat" is the resource overhead induced by the presence of excess functionality and objects, typically due to the use of highly general components standardized around deeply layered frameworks.

Excess resource usage from bloat could lead to energy inefficiency and reduced performance [35]. Energy savings from reducing bloat are anticipated via both direct and indirect effects (e.g., server consolidation opportunity) of reducing excess resources. However, reducing bloat is non-trivial, particularly because its origin is linked to the same software development trends [21] that have been extremely successful in fueling the growth and widespread impact of redeployable software. Hence, there is a need to develop approaches to assess cost-benefit implications of reducing bloat and focus these efforts where they matter the most.

While reduction of bloat is expected to (obviously) have an impact on power-performance, we find that the inherent slack in large scale IT solution architectures and the presence of elements in the system that are not energy proportional[1] may require this intuition to be qualified.

Is the effect of bloat more pronounced or less pronounced in the presence of energy proportional hardware? Should we expect an increase or a decrease in peak power consumption with lower bloat? In two different experiments on the same hardware platform, but involving different kinds of bloat, one with Apache DayTrader and another with a microbenchmark, we obtained opposite answers. Even with the same workload and same de-bloating optimization, we have seen wide variations in the effects with different hardware and software characteristics. There is, therefore, a need for empirical and analytical studies that validate intuitions and provide a deeper understanding of the relationships between measures of bloat and energy consumption.

Conducting a systematic study of the effects of bloat is challenging, in part due to the same reasons why addressing bloat is non-trivial. Not only does finding and fixing bloat

[1]energy proportional [2] hardware consumes power in proportion to actual resource utilization

involve manual effort and domain expertise, the nature of bloat varies from case to case and its impact can be very workload and system specific. This can make it difficult to arrive at generalizable conclusions from such a study.

In order to conduct a systematic investigation of the impact of bloat on power-performance, we focus on a detailed study of single type of bloat that is very common in Java applications, the presence of excess temporary objects, that is relatively easy to find/vary, but exhibits a diversity of effects impacting multiple system resources. We devise a methodology for systematically varying bloat and hardware and software characteristics to manifest these effects in the context of a standard server side Java power-performance benchmark, SPECPower_ssj2008.

Our experimental findings reveal a wide variation in the impact of bloat, indicating that a software only view is inadequate for assessing the energy-efficiency benefits from bloat reduction. We develop an abstract model to enable a generalized exploration of the effect of bloat on power-performance, from a whole system perspective.

The complexity of modern software and system layers make it impractical to compute the exact power-performance impact of run-time bloat (reduction) analytically. However, our analytical model is still useful in reasoning about implications of reducing bloat. It surfaces certain aspects of the complex behavior that determine the impact of bloat, by abstracting operational relationships at bottleneck zones. This creates a foundation for reasoning quantitatively about the impact of bloat reduction on system power, performance and energy-efficiency. For example, energy proportionality of a bloat-impacted resource can amplify benefits of reducing bloat but energy proportionality of other resources can shrink those benefits when bloat affects a bottleneck.

Contributions:.

(1) We conduct the first systematic empirical study of the joint power-performance implications of software bloat, using SPECpower_ssj2008, across a range of server hardware and software configurations covering different processors/system designs, levels of power management, multi-threading, cache sizes, and heap sizes. We undertake controlled experiments varying the degree of bloat for one prevalent type of Java runtime bloat, excess temporary objects, and the system/software characteristics to investigate the power-performance effects. Using multiple metrics for evaluating the impact of bloat - peak power, equi-performance power, peak performance, and resulting energy efficiency measures - we systematically analyze and expose the effect of energy proportionality and bottleneck resources on the impact of bloat reduction.

(2) We develop a simplified analytical model for studying the implications of runtime bloat on power and energy efficiency under different situations. The model takes into account bottlenecks in the system as well as the energy proportionality characteristics of hardware in the system. It provides a generalized abstraction to enable bloat impact estimation (or trends) for different scenarios. Analyzing different scenarios with the model enables us to put our experimental results in perspective, with the experimental results re-affirming the effects predicted by our model in real systems.

(3) We show that a whole system perspective is required for an informed assessment of the impact of bloat and its

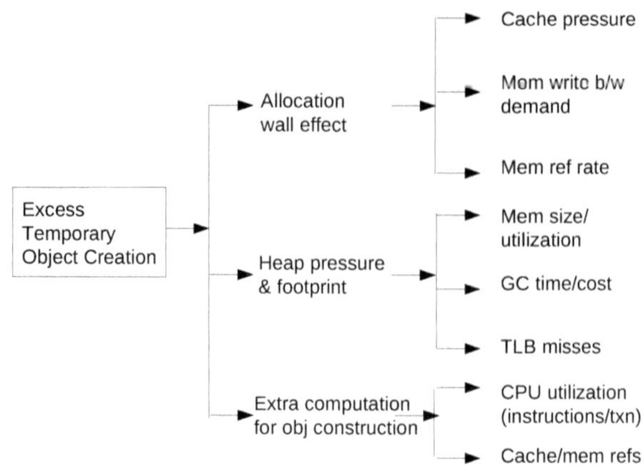

Figure 1: Effects of Java temporary object creation bloat

reduction. The nature and extent of impact is dependent on whether a bloat-impacted resource is a bottleneck resource as well as on the energy proportionality of not just the bloat-impacted resource but other key resources as well.

The paper is organized as follows. Section 2 details different effects of Java temporary object bloat and resources they impact. Section 3 describes our empirical study and summarizes the findings. Section 4 and section 5 describe the model, its implications and their corroboration by our experimental observations. Section 6 covers related work and Section 7 concludes.

2. TEMPORARY (JAVA) OBJECT CHURN BLOAT AND ITS EFFECTS

In Java, the programming model encourages the creation of many short-lived objects - these are allocated on the heap[2] and may be passed across framework layers, only to be used briefly and eventually garbage collected. For example, temporary objects are generated repeatedly during data transformations required for framework based reuse.

This can lead to the problem of object churn, i.e. a high volume of temporary objects [26] spreading out the memory footprint of the application (because the memory is not reused until after the next garbage collection cycle). Excessive allocation of these temporary objects, which we refer to henceforth as temporary objects bloat, is a common type of Java runtime bloat; it causes excess memory usage and has deep and pervasive effects on the performance of a system. We find it a good representative of bloat for our empirical studies, as it exercises multiple hardware resources including the CPU and the memory system.

Figure 1 depicts some of the potential effects of temporary objects bloat in Java. We discuss these briefly.

2.1 Allocation wall effect

Researchers have previously observed [37] that a large volume of temporary object allocations causes high memory write bandwidth consumption which limits scalability of cer-

[2]state of the art escape analysis techniques in modern production JVMs can only optimize a small fraction of these allocations [26]

tain classes of Java programs on multi-core platforms. The term "allocation wall" has been used to describe this phenomenon, as this slowdown is due to allocation overheads and not garbage collection cost.

2.2 Heap pressure effect

Creating many temporary objects can increase garbage collection overhead. Given a sufficiently sized JVM heap (typical in well-tuned JVM configurations) and a generational garbage collector, the percentage time spent in GC[3] becomes small enough that it could be ignored in comparison to other effects. Even so, de-bloating software to reduce temporary object allocation can reduce its footprint by enabling lower heap sizes to be used for the same application. Heap size reductions are beneficial from a power-performance perspective, when the memory footprint savings is significant enough to (i) enable inactive memory ranks to be switched to a low power mode (ii) enable use of a smaller memory configuration of the system for cost and power savings, or (iii) enable allocation of spared memory to another virtual partition for improved workload consolidation with same system configuration/power envelope.

2.3 Object construction computation overhead

If the construction of a temporary object involves a costly initialization sequence for setting up its fields, object creation can also have a significant instruction pathlength impact. Object construction computation overhead manifests as an increased CPU utilization due to increased instructions per transaction. It may or may not have a significant effect on CPI depending on the nature of instructions added.

2.4 Influence of system configuration

A single category of bloat may have multiple effects as described above, each of which, in turn, impacts physical resource utilization in different ways. A given effect may have a low impact in one situation but can become crucial under a different set of system/workload characteristics.

For example, the "allocation wall" effect [37] is observable in the presence of bottlenecks caused by constraints in memory system resources like cache, memory bandwidth and latency. In this situation, it leads to increased (effective) CPU utilization through its impact on the CPI. This increased utilization impacts power consumption. However, if the system is configured with a processor DVFS[4] algorithm that is memory slack aware [31], it could exploit the available slack to run the processor at a slower speed; hence, the change in CPI may have a relatively lower impact on the effective (scaled) CPU utilization and power consumption.

In other situations with relatively large on-chip caches and powerful memory subsystems, where memory performance is not a constraint, the allocation wall can effectively become irrelevant. Reducing bloat can still be beneficial in this case, due to another effect. Lower temporary object allocation rates enable a Java application to be configured to use a smaller heap size without an increase in GC time. If this heap size reduction is sufficient to enable the working set of the application to be entirely contained in a (huge) on-chip cache (a realistic possibility in the future, with 3D integration), off-chip memory accesses may be avoided altogether, potentially leading to significant power savings.

[3]garbage collection

[4]dynamic voltage and frequency scaling

3. EXPERIMENTAL STUDY

We conduct a systematic study on the quantitative impact of bloat reduction on power and performance in the context of varying system characteristics and bottleneck scenarios with the following methodology:

- Adopt SPECPower_ssj2008 as the evaluation workload as it has well defined performance measures, power measurement methodology, load variation and both detailed result reports and a composite energy-efficiency measure over a full range of system loads.
- Create lower bloat and higher bloat variants of the baseline code using different degrees of object reuse to vary the extent of bloat.
- Conduct experiments across multiple platforms with differing energy proportionality and memory system characteristics to understand their impact on bloat reduction's benefits. Further vary software/system characteristics to examine the impact of the availability of key resource(s) on the benefit of bloat reduction.

3.1 SPECPower_ssj2008 and Metrics

SPECpower_ssj2008 is a server side Java ("ssj") energy-efficiency benchmark. As the first commercial workload benchmark from SPEC [27] requiring power consumption and energy efficiency reports across the full range of system loads, it is well-suited for controlled experiments to study the power-performance impact of software runtime bloat in the context of server-side Java. Additionally the benchmark offers relatively easy means to vary the amount of temporary object allocation bloat, giving us the means to study the impact of the extent of bloat (or its reduction).

There are 11 measurement intervals; starting from 100% load as measured during calibration, the intensity drops by 10% for each subsequent interval, finishing with an idle interval. During the entire run, the system power consumption is measured. The benchmark metric is an energy-efficiency score composed of the ratio of the sum of the transaction throughput of every load interval to the sum of the average power of every load interval (including the idle period). This is a fixed time rather than a fixed work benchmark, i.e. each load level is maintained for a fixed time. For our analysis, in addition to the energy-efficiency score across the load-levels we also use comparisons of peak performance, power at peak performance and power at *equi-performance* points.

An equi-performance power comparison between two alternatives compares power measurements taken at the same performance level (application throughput) for the two alternatives. It also serves as an energy-efficiency measure at constant performance, useful in assessing relative efficiency impact of bloat reduction when there is also a change in performance as result of bloat (reduction). For SPECPower_ssj2008, we utilize the availability of measurement results over the different load levels to derive equi-work or equi-performance comparisons (interpolating for power between the load levels, if necessary).

3.2 Varying extent of bloat

To understand the impact of the extent of bloat, we introduce variation in temporary object bloat in SPECPower_ssj2008 application by increasing or decreasing the degree of object reuse. Object reuse is a well-known coding technique for reducing object creation in Java. As it is non-trivial to automate [37], we had to implement the variants by inspecting the benchmark code and making manual code changes[5].

We employ three code variants for different extent of bloat (or of bloat reduction):

- AllocOrig: the baseline SPECPower_ssj2008 code.
- AllocLess: a lower bloat variant obtained by implementing object reuse to eliminate more than half of the temporary object memory allocations in the original code. This reduces temporary object allocations from 8KB/transaction to 3KB/transaction on the systems running a 64 bit JVM, and from 6.9KB/transaction to 1.8KB/transaction on the system running a 32-bit JVM. The form of object reuse here only reuses the memory allocation, and not object content, hence it does not save object construction computation costs for initializing fields.
- AllocMore: a higher bloat variant obtained by turning off object reuse in the original code, introducing excess temporary object allocations with object construction computation overheads. AllocOrig had an explicit optimization to maintain a pool of previously constructed objects for reuse, where the content of many fields of the objects in question could be reused without being overwritten, thus saving on object construction cost in addition to memory savings. Turning off this optimization raises the temporary object allocations from 8KB/transaction to 11KB/transaction on the systems running a 64 bit JVM and from 6.9KB/ transaction to 9.8KB/transaction on the system running a 32-bit JVM. While a code change was necessary to introduce bloat in this workload, it often occurs in practice when optimization opportunities are not all exploited.

The volume of temporary objects given for each variant was computed by post processing garbage collection logs. Table 1 summarizes the specific effects of temporary objects bloat (described in the previous section) in terms of the variants and configuration constraints under which they could be manifested.

Bloat in Variant	No constraint	Memory constraint	Low heap constraint
AllocOrig vs AllocLess	Effect not perceptible	Allocation wall	Heap pressure
AllocMore vs AllocOrig	Computation overhead (field initialization)	Allocation wall + computation overhead	Heap pressure + computation overhead

Table 1: Effects of temporary objects bloat observable by comparing specific code variants under specific configuration constraints

3.3 Experimental setup

Our experiments were conducted on three platforms to explore cross-platform differences in the impact of software bloat. Table 2 describes the three system configurations.

All systems are instrumented for obtaining system-level power measurements from the on-board service processors at

[5]the technique has recently been automated [3] for select object types

System	Processor Config	Cache	Mem	JVM
IBM Power 750 AIX 6.1	IBM POWER7 4/8/4	32MB	64GB DDR3	J9 32b
IBM HS21 Blade Linux 2.6.33	Intel Xeon E5450 2/4/1	12MB	8GB DDR2	J9 64b
IBM x3650 M2 Linux 2.6.33	Intel Xeon X5570 2/4/2	8MB	64GB DDR3	J9 64b

Table 2: Systems Configurations: Processor Config is Sockets/ Cores per Socket/ Threads per Core. Cache size is for the last-level per socket.

fine-grained, periodic intervals for reliable power and energy-efficiency metric calculations. The Power 750 system also additionally provided processor and memory sub-system level measurements, processor throughput and memory bandwidth information at fine-grain, periodic intervals.

The Power 750 system uses the IBM POWER7 processor [29] with EnergyScale firmware [19] employing new dynamic voltage and frequency saving (DVFS) algorithms for aggressive load-based energy savings [24]. The x3650 M2 system with the Intel Xeon X5570 processor uses the Linux `CPUfreq ondemand` governor[6] also exploiting DVFS for load-based energy savings. The HS21 blade system with Intel Xeon E5450 processors was employed without any active power management.

3.4 Multi-platform experiments and results

Figure 2(a) presents the results of comparing the baseline variant *AllocOrig* with the lower and higher bloat variants, *AllocLess* and *AllocMore*, on the test platforms. The energy efficiency scores are based on full benchmark runs for the Power 750 and x3650-M2 system and the 100% load level measurement for the HS21 blade system. All results are normalized with respect to the original (default) implementation, *AllocOrig*.

We note a wide variation in power-performance impact of bloat. On the HS21 system *AllocLess* shows 1.59X the energy-efficiency of *AllocOrig* from reduction in bloat and *AllocMore* shows 0.61X the energy-efficiency of *AllocOrig* because of increase in bloat. The relatively poorer off-chip memory system of the HS21 blade system is responsible for a pronounced "allocation wall" effect which combined with the poor energy-proportionality characteristic (no active power management enabled) results in the biggest energy-efficiency impact for bloat (reduction) among the three configurations.

On the two larger server systems with more powerful memory subsystems and power management, i.e. the Power 750 and x3650-M2 systems, there is a lower but still significant impact from bloat. *AllocMore* shows 0.76X and 0.85X the performance of *AllocOrig* (from increased bloat) and *AllocLess* shows 1.06X and 1.11X the performance of *AllocOrig* (from reduced bloat) on the Power 750 and x3650-M2 platforms, respectively.

Figure 2(b) shows the impact on equi-performance power and power at the different peak performances (peak power) across the Power 750 and x3650 M2 systems. The equi-performance power graph shows the relative power of *AllocMore* and *AllocLess* both compared to *AllocOrig* at a con-

[6]When utilization rises above a threshold, the ondemand governor sets the frequency to the highest available. When utilization falls below the threshold, it gradually decreases the frequency as long as the system remains underutilized.

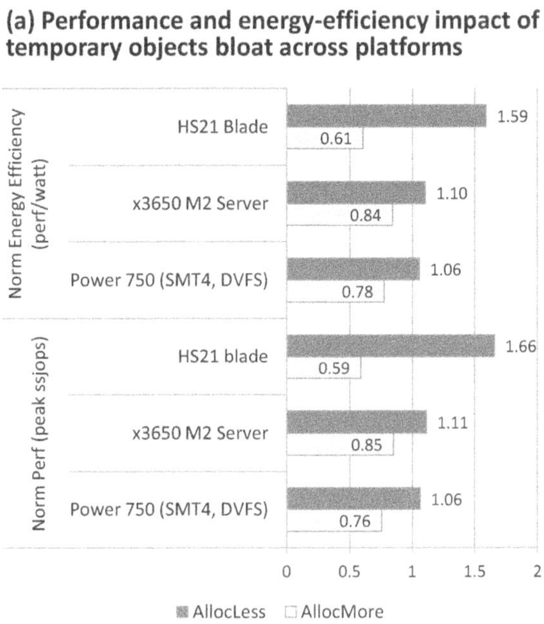

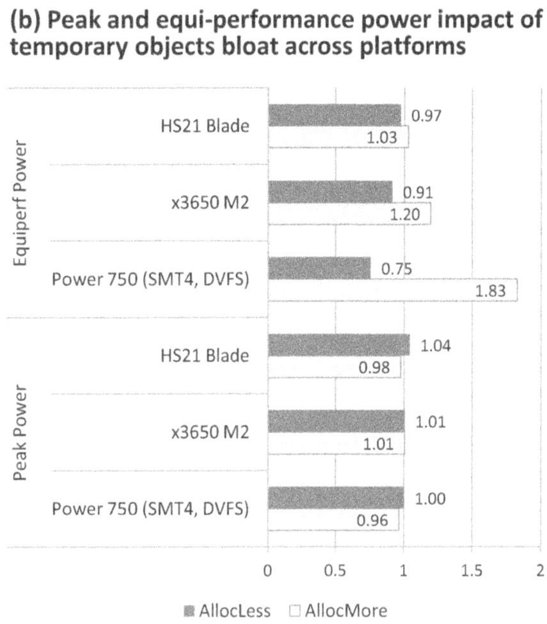

Figure 2: Cross-platform comparison: All results are normalized with respect to the corresponding *AllocOrig* measurement

stant performance point - in the former case it is the lower peak throughput of *AllocMore* (compared to *AllocOrig*) and in the latter case it is at the lower peak throughput of *AllocOrig* compared to *AllocLess*.

The equi-performance power numbers indicate the synergistic impact of DVFS and bloat reduction. As bloat is lowered from *AllocMore* to *AllocOrig* and from *AllocOrig* to *AllocLess*, for a given performance more slack is introduced. The DVFS algorithm then works on the slack to translate that to increased power reduction and energy-efficiency. Additionally, one can see how the effectiveness of the DVFS capability magnifies the impact of bloat reduction by comparing *the larger equi-perf power reduction for Power 750 when reducing bloat compared to x3650 M2*, the former platform having a bigger take-down in power with load reduction (cubic vs quadratic) as seen in Figure 6.

An interesting observation from the cross platform results is that *even though the energy efficiency score improvement with* AllocLess *is smaller on Power 750 than the x3650 as shown in Fig 2 (a), the corresponding equiperformance power results in Fig 2 (b) shows a higher (25%) savings on Power 750 than on x3650(9%).* The efficiency score improvements in Fig 2 (a) are at different performance levels. Equi-performance comparisons in Fig 2 (b), by normalizing to the same performance, show the true impact on energy-efficiency of bloat reduction. Bloat reduction decreases wasted resource usage and a more energy proportional system converts the saved resource usage into higher power reduction/energy savings.

The power numbers at peak are comparable across the bloat options. At peak performance, the numbers corre-

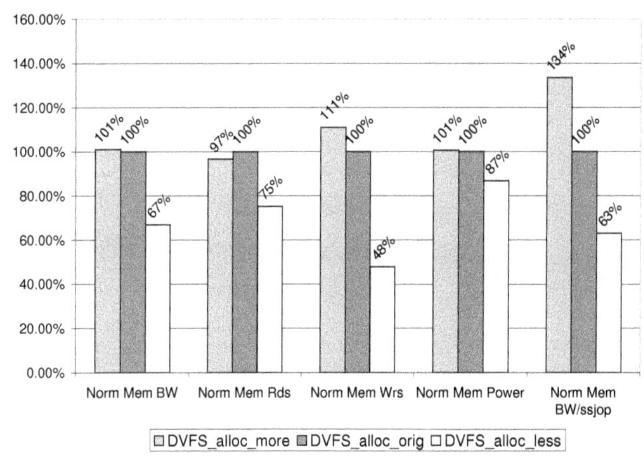

Figure 3: Memory Statistics for SPECpower_ssj2008 on Power 750 in SMT4 mode (normalized wrt *AllocOrig*)

spond to roughly the same processor activity across the bloat options and consequently roughly the same processor power. Figure 3 shows the impact of bloat on the memory controller and memory power statistics for SMT4 mode on the Power750 system. Reducing bloat reduces memory traffic to 67% resulting in a lowering of memory power consumption to 87%. The memory bandwidth per ssjop dropped to 63%. However, the power impact of this is marginalized by the signficantly lower power consumption of the memory sub-system in this configuration.

3.4.1 Object construction computation overhead

The *AllocMore* variation showed significant performance degradation compared to *AllocOrig* (e.g. 0.59X for HS21 blade, 0.76X for Power 750). However when we measured the reduction in IPC for *AllocMore*, it was very small (around 6% on HS21 blade, even smaller on Power 750). The instructions per transaction, on the other hand had increased by over 25%. This extra computation is a manifestation of the object construction costs that are involved when the object is not reused across iterations. We did not see any computation cost savings in the *AllocLess* case because it involved only a memory allocation reuse and not content reuse.

To probe further, we created a variant that combines the two changes *AllocLess* and *AllocMore* - this variant reduces the allocation wall effect (relative to *AllocMore*) but maintains the same object construction overhead. On the HS21 blade system this showed a high gain in IPC, resulting in performance improvement of 8% over *AllocOrig*, despite the extra instruction costs; on Power 750 too, the hybrid variant had a significant improvement in performance over AllocMore but was still 15% below AllocOrig (AllocMore being 25% below). This indicates that the allocation wall effect is the dominant overhead for the HS21 blade (with a relatively poorer memory system) whereas the object construction computation overhead is a sizeable component of the impact of bloat with *AllocMore* on the Power 750.

3.4.2 Heap size and memory pressure effect

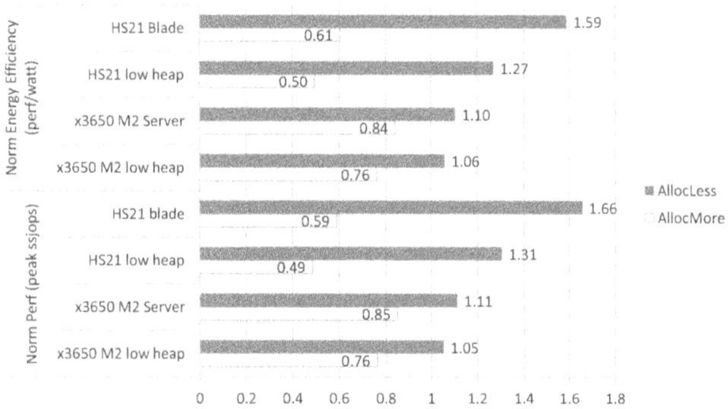

Figure 4: Heap size reduction impact with decrease/increase in bloat: All results are normalized with respect to the corresponding *AllocOrig* measurement at full heap size

The experiments discussed so far were executed with a sufficiently large JVM heap size (typical in well-tuned JVM configurations) in order to isolate the "allocation wall" and object construction computation effects of bloat from the heap pressure effects. We now turn our attention to heap pressure effects on impact of bloat.

Figure 4 shows the results on the HS21 blade and x3650-M2 system with significantly reduced heap sizes. Reducing the heap size lowers base performance on both platforms. The benefit from bloat reduction is more pronounced with reduced heap sizes (bars shown are normalized to the *AllocOrig* numbers for the full heap size). Further, even with a substantially smaller heap size, *AllocLess low heap* shows 27% improvement in energy-efficiency over the original full heap configuration on the HS21 blade and 6% improvement on the x3650 M2 server. This suggests that as an additional benefit of bloat reduction one can get good performance even with reduced heap sizes which would allow more instances of the workload (virtual machines) to be run in the same physical memory foot print.

3.4.3 Cache Pressure Effect

Cache resources of a microprocessor often have a key impact on a workload's performance. Runtime bloat can reduce the effectiveness of the caches leading to lower performance. Alternatively, the impact of bloat reduction can vary with the shortage/plentifullness of cache capacity of the microprocessor. Here we examine the impact of cache pressure by varying it on a single platform (Power750) to better isolate its impact from other characteristics. We increase cache pressure by increasing the degree of hardware multi-threading from 2-way (SMT2) to 4-way (SMT4) and further by reducing the cache size to half (SMT4-halfcache).

In Figure 5 we see the impact of bloat reduction (for *AllocLess* over *AllocOrig*) as cache capacity per thread is progressively halved from SMT2 (2MB/thread) to SMT4 (1MB/thread) to SMT4-halfcache (512KB/thread). The SMT modes are changed through the OS facilities for setting the mode and SMT4-halfcache is realized by booting the system with reduced L3 cache sizes. Difference in energy proportionality characteristics is examined by doing the runs at `fixed frequency` as well as with DVFS.

Bloat reduction shows highest benefit when cache capacity is most constrained, for SMT4-halfcache and benefits decrease going to SMT4 and then SMT2, as cache capacity becomes more plentiful. There is actually an increase in peak power (negative power savings) with bloat reduction as the underutilized compute resources are utilized more improving throughput. This power increase is higher when using DVFS for adaptive power management than with fixed frequency operation because of the superlinear power characteristics with DVFS. Consequently, the energy-efficiency improvement mirrors the performance improvement for `fixed frequency` while energy-efficiency improvements are lower than the performance improvements for `DVFS`. As earlier, savings in equi-performance power (and equi-performance energy efficiency increase) is higher than the improvement in energy-efficiency at peak performance. The savings in equi-performance power is highest for SMT4-halfcache as bloat reduction is most effective when the cache pressure is maximum (more severe a performance bottleneck).

With the lowest cache-constraint, SMT2, the performance impact is the lowest and we actually observe a slight decrease in system power consumption (positive power savings), which is more pronounced at `fixed frequency`. Using the memory power statistics (not shown), we find an 18% reduction in memory power consumption, which translates to a lower overall system power savings because the memory component contributes to a small fraction of system power.

3.5 Experiments with other workloads

The degree of impact of temporary objects reduction on

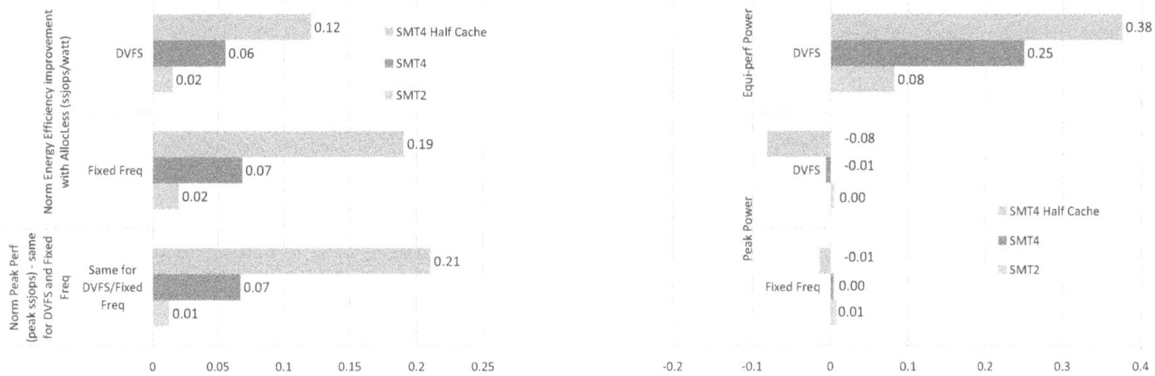

Figure 5: Cache capacity effect on improvement from bloat reduction (on Power750): SMT2 has most cache resource/thread, SMT4 has half SMT2's capacity/thread, SMT4-halfcache has half SMT4's capacity/thread. For energy-efficiency and peak performance the numbers show the percentage improvement (increase) for *AllocLess* relative to *AllocOrig*. For Equi-perf Power and Peak Power the quantities shown are percentage saving (decrease) for *AllocLess* relative to *AllocOrig*. For all cases, a positive number signifies an improvement for that quantity with bloat reduction.

performance is workload dependent, as has been established from results on object churn reduction in prior work [37, 26]. In addition to our systematic studies with SPECPower_ssj2008 we conducted some smaller studies with other workloads.

Microbenchmark Experiments: We chose a simple microbenchmark, called "AllocMark", from [37] and extended this to create a microbenchmark called "AllocReuseMark" that uses different degrees of object reuse as a way of varying temporary object allocation bloat. Power and allocation rate measurements were collected for different levels of object reuse. We notice that reducing bloat by 75% improved the effective performance by 287%. This improvement was associated with a 19% increase in power consumption, which was relatively smaller than the performance gain, resulting in a net gain in energy efficiency.

Apache DayTrader Experiments: Temporary objects bloat is often an indication of other inefficiencies like excessive data transformations. To gain an assessment of potential power-performance implications of complex patterns of bloat in large server workloads, we ran comparisons of the DaCapo [5] *tradesoap* and *tradebeans* benchmarks[7]. Both *tradebeans* and *tradesoap* execute the same underlying workload, except that *tradesoap* uses indirect calls through SOAP[8] from the client (like many real workloads do) while *tradebeans* executes direct calls on the server. Comparing these two configurations is useful for studying the additional costs of fine grained messaging, layering and transformations that are needed for interoperability in the *tradesoap* implementation. Such excess costs are typical in patterns of software bloat observed in real applications. We observe a 15% increase in power consumption on the x3650 M2 system running *tradesoap* vs *tradebeans*, with 2X slowdown in performance.*tradesoap* generated almost 10X higher footprint of temporary objects and caused a significant increase in CPU utilization. This shows that finer grain messaging and associated transformations (in *tradesoap*) can have a significant power efficiency cost, especially for small, high volume transactions.

Comparing the two sets of experiments above, we make an interesting observation. We see an increase in power consumption with *lower bloat* in AllocReuseMark and an increase in power consumption with *higher bloat* in DayTrader. In AllocReuseMark, bloat affects a bottleneck resource (stresses the memory hierarchy). In DayTrader, in addition to memory resources, bloat also affected a non-bottleneck (or underutilized) resource (the CPU), as was observed from increased utilization for *tradesoap* over *tradebeans*.

3.6 Key observations

Reducing runtime software bloat in the form of excess temporary objects has significant energy-efficiency impact, with upto 59% improvement at peak load seen on a memory performance constrained HS21 blade (1.59X energy-efficiency for *AllocLess* over *AllocOrig*) and 45% equi-performance power savings on a energy proportional Power 750 (1.83X equi-perf power for *AllocMore* compared to *AllocOrig*). The extent of impact was dependent on the bottleneck pressure with respect to the memory hierarchy resources and energy proportionality of the physical resources.

- Energy efficiency benefits at peak performance tend to be most pronounced when bloat affects a performance bottleneck and underutilized resources are less energy proportional (e.g. HS21 system), while equi-performance power savings are highest when impacted resources are super-linearly energy proportional (e.g. Power 750 DVFS).

[7]Based on the Apache DayTrader J2EE workload, included in DaCapo v9.12; executed within the Geronimo application server utilizing the Derby in-memory database.
[8]Simple Object Access Protocol

- Higher degrees of energy proportionality (e.g. power management in the form of processor DVFS) has a complementary impact wrt addressing software bloat. On the one hand it can reduce the peak energy-efficiency degradation caused by bloat working on underutilized resources. On the other, it magnifies the equiperformance energy efficiency improvements brought about by reduction in bloat working on the resources that get freed up from bloat reduction.
- Performance effects of bloat are most acute when memory hierarchy resources are already strained, e.g., bottlenecks due to low off-chip memory bandwidth as with HS21, low allocated memory or cache pressure with smaller caches or higher degree of multi-threading.
- Power consumption at peak performance may increase or decrease with bloat reduction depending on the impact on resources underutilized in the presence of bloat.

Addressing runtime software bloat was also found to facilitate heap size reductions. The reduced bloat alternative performs better even with significantly reduced heap sizes.

4. QUANTIFYING POWER-EFFICIENCY IMPACT OF BLOAT: A SIMPLE ABSTRACT MODEL

Could our experimental observations be a manifestation of certain general implications that are valid for any category of bloat? In this section, we construct an abstract analytical model to better understand the power performance implications of reducing bloat and when its effects are more pronounced. This is a highly simplified model relating the hardware resource pressure caused by bloat and its impact on system energy efficiency using a few fundamental operational laws [8, 17] of queueing theory [9]. Hence, it is generally applicable to any kind of resource bloat irrespective of its category.

Applications use a variety of hardware resources on any given system, e.g., processor cores, on-chip caches, off-chip memory and disk storage. An imbalanced use of these resources can cause a performance bottleneck at one resource and under utilization of others. For example high cache miss rates caused by profligate use of objects due to bloat can cause under-utilization of the processor cores. The power efficiency characteristics differ in nature and magnitude across resources types, e.g., CPU with a super-linear power versus load characteristic when using dynamic voltage and frequency scaling (DVFS) versus main memory with a linear power characteristic and high standby power. This difference leads to a very different impact on energy-efficiency for bloat reduction depending on which resource(s) is impacted by bloat and which are under utilized.

When a resource becomes the performance bottleneck because of bloat, reduction of bloat can increase power consumption because of increase in throughput. The varied and sometimes non-linear power characteristics of resources with load can make the impact of bloat reduction on power difficult to assess when compared across different throughput levels. To enable comparison on an equal footing before and after bloat reduction, we also analyze comparisons of power at *equiperformance* levels with and without bloat.

4.1 The Model

Let $R_i, i = 1..N$, be various types of resources with service demands (time) D_i in the software without bloat. Let $b_i, i = 1..N$, be the overhead due to bloat introduced in each of these resources in the bloated software, changing the service demands to $D_i(1 + b_i)$.

Using asymptotic bounds based on bottleneck analysis [17] to approximate achievable performance, peak throughput is given by $X = min_i(1/D_i)$ whereas peak throughput with bloat, $X_b = min_i(1/((1 + b_i)D_i))$.

Let $P_i(U_i)$ be the power consumed by resource R_i with utilization U_i (the exact relationship between utilization and power can be different for different resources). Utilization U_i of resource R_i is D_iX [17], when running the non-bloated software and $D_i(1 + b_i)X_b$ with the bloated software.

Power without bloat, $P = \Sigma(P_i(U_i)) = \Sigma(P_i(D_iX))$
Power with bloat, $P_b = \Sigma(P_i(D_i(1 + b_i)X_b))$

Power efficiency (perf/watt metric) without bloat,

$$E = X/P = \frac{min_i(1/D_i)}{\Sigma(P_i(D_iX))}$$

Power efficiency with bloat,

$$E_b = X_b/P_b = \frac{min_i(1/((1 + b_i)D_i))}{\Sigma(P_i(D_i(1 + b_i)X_b))}$$

We are primarily interested in quantifying potential improvements from bloat reduction. Hence, we define the metrics of interest for relative throughput, peak power, power-efficiency and equiperformance power of the non-bloated software *normalized with respect to that of the bloated software.*

Relative throughput with bloat reduction (> 1 is good),

$$\phi_x = (X/X_b) = \frac{min_i(1/D_i)}{min_i(1/((1 + b_i)D_i))} \quad (1)$$

Relative peak power with bloat reduction (< 1 is good),

$$\phi_p = \frac{P}{P_b} = \frac{\Sigma(P_i(D_iX))}{\Sigma(P_i(D_i(1 + b_i)X_b))} \quad (2)$$

Relative power-efficiency[10] with bloat reduction (> 1 is good),

$$\phi_e = \frac{X/P}{X_b/P_b} = (X/X_b)\frac{\Sigma(P_i(D_i(1 + b_i)X_b))}{\Sigma(P_i(D_iX))} = \frac{\phi_x}{\phi_p} \quad (3)$$

Relative equiperformance power with bloat reduction (i.e. comparing power consumed by original and bloated software at the same throughput X_b) (< 1 is good)

$$\phi_q = \frac{\Sigma(P_i(D_iX_b))}{\Sigma(P_i(D_i(1 + b_i)X_b))} \quad (4)$$

[9]The laws used express basic operational relationships, such as the utilization law/equality, hence widely applicable and general enough to hold without any assumptions about interarrival or service times; we do not use any additional assumptions from operational analysis beyond these laws, e.g. we do not rely on product form queuing network conditions and do not assume closed loop networks.

[10]Notice that in the case of SPECPower_ssj2008, the analysis extends to the energy-efficiency score across load levels (and not just the peak load), as the load levels are scaled by a fixed percentage with respect to achievable peak performance.

4.1.1 *Effect of degrees of energy proportionality*

An energy proportional hardware resource consumes power in proportion to actual resource utilization (a desirable property of server systems). In the presence of certain power management schemes (e.g. DVFS), this relationship may be super-linear; we characterize this with an exponent which we call the degree of energy proportionality of the resource.

Let us model the power consumed by each resource as $P_i(U_i) = a_i U_i^{\alpha_i} + c_i$, where α_i = degree of energy proportionality of resource R_i.

Let $P_{static} = \Sigma(c_i)$, be the static power of the hardware system, $P_{dyn} = \Sigma(a_i U_i^{\alpha_i})$ be the total dynamic (load dependent) power consumption. (α_i would be zero if resource R_i is non-energy proportional)

Let $L_i = a_i U_i^{\alpha_i}$ be the load-dependent power for resource R_i. Thus $P_{dyn} = \Sigma(L_i)$, $P = P_{static} + P_{dyn}$.

Relative peak power impact with bloat reduction:

$$\phi_p = \frac{\Sigma(L_i(D_i X_b)\phi_x^{\alpha_i}) + P_{static}}{\Sigma(L_i(D_i X_b)(1+b_i)^{\alpha_i}) + P_{static}}$$

Defining f_i = fraction of load dependent power consumed by resource R_i (wrt total system power) when running bloated software, f_s = fraction of static power consumed with the bloated software ($f_s + \Sigma f_i = 1$), the above can be re-written as:

$$\phi_p = \Sigma(f_i(\frac{\phi_x}{1+b_i})^{\alpha_i}) + f_s \quad (5)$$

As for the relative equiperformance power,

$$\phi_q = \Sigma(\frac{f_i}{(1+b_i)^{\alpha_i}}) + f_s \quad (6)$$

4.2 System Bottlenecks and Bloat: A Curious Interaction

Consider the situation where bloat primarily affects the demand for a single resource. Let R_k be the bloated resource, then $b_k > 0$ and $b_i = 0, \forall i \neq k$. We show how the impact of bloat reduction depends on where the primary bottleneck is relative to the bloat site. Table 3 summarizes the impact on performance, peak power, and equiperformance power.

Bloat at non-bottleneck resource.

When bloat does not affect the bottleneck resource, $\phi_x = 1$, i.e. there is *no change in performance with bloat reduction.* Substituting in equation 5, we obtain:

$$\phi_p = \frac{f_k}{(1+b_k)^{\alpha_k}} + \Sigma_{i \neq k} f_i + f_s \leq 1$$

Peak power *decreases* with bloat reduction, showing a higher improvement when the bloated resource has a steeper (larger α_k) power-to-load characteristic and consumes a higher fraction of system power (larger f_k).

Since there is no change in performance $\phi_e = 1/\phi_p$, i.e., the relative power-efficiency improves with bloat reduction. And $\phi_q = \phi_p$, i.e., the relative equiperformance power is the same as the relative power at peak performance.

Bloat at Bottleneck Resource.

If bloat affects the bottleneck resource, i.e. $k = argmin_i(1/D_i)$, then $\phi_x = 1 + b_k > 1$, i.e. *throughput improves with bloat reduction*, maximum improvement being $1 + b_k$ when bloat is eliminated. Substituting in equation 5

$$\phi_p = f_k + \Sigma_{i \neq k}(f_i(1+b_k)^{\alpha_i}) + f_s \geq 1$$

Peak power *increases* or remains the same depending on the power characteristics of the *non-bloated resources*, in contrast with the previous case. Reducing bloat allows more productive use of the bottleneck resource, improving peak throughput. If this increase in throughput increases the usage of resources that were under-utilized earlier because of the bloat-affected bottleneck, and this increases their power consumption, then the power consumed by the application at peak throughput can increase.

$$\phi_e = (1+b_k)/\phi_p <= 1 + b_k$$

Relative power efficiency improvement is less than or equal to the throughput gain. A steeper energy proportionality characteristic of the other (non bloated) resources lowers the efficiency improvement from bloat reduction, especially if their power consumption is significant compared to the power consumption of the bloat-impacted bottleneck resource. The highest improvement from bloat reduction occurs in the case when the non-bottleneck resources are non-energy proportional (when $\alpha_i = 0, \forall i \neq k$).

Bloat reduction shifts bottleneck.

If reducing bloat causes the bottleneck to shift from R_k to R_l, then, $1 < \phi_x < 1 + b_k$, i.e. throughput improves with bloat reduction (but to a lower extent than the previous case). Let us term $b_{eff} = \phi_x - 1$ as the effective bloat factor. Now the analysis for peak power and power efficiency are similar to the previous case, adjusting for b_{eff}.

Equiperformance power is impacted to the same extent in all the three cases above.

4.3 Summary

The extent to which bloat impacts power-performance may not always be obvious because bloat shifts the relative usage of different resources, some of which may have a non-linear power-vs-load variation. Performance and equiperformance power are generally improved with bloat reduction. However, power at peak performance can increase with bloat reduction as a result of increased throughput following reduced pressure at a bottleneck resource. The degree of increase depends on the energy proportionality characteristics of the resources which are not bloated. Reducing bloat can also cause a shift in bottleneck from the bloated resource to another resource. In general, bloat can involve multiple resources, so we need to use equations 5 and 6 to assess the combined impact of these conditions.

5. CORROBORATING THE MODEL WITH EXPERIMENTAL OBSERVATIONS

5.1 Experimental study in perspective

Our model provides a generalized frame-work for relating the power-performance impact of bloat reduction to resource bottlenecks and system energy proportionality. It highlights two important factors that determine the extent to which bloat impacts power-performance: (a) the relative energy proportionality of the system resources and (b) the extent to which the resource's usage is a bottleneck to performance.

Figure 6 shows the power characteristics with load for the different systems used in our experimental study with

	Rel Peak perf ϕ_x	Rel power at peak perf. ϕ_p	Rel equi-perf power ϕ_q
Bloat at non-bottleneck resource	1 (no improvement)	$\frac{f_k}{(1+b_k)^{\alpha_k}} + \Sigma_{i \neq k} f_i + f_s \leq 1$ (same if $\alpha_k = 0$, else decreases)	$\frac{f_k}{(1+b_k)^{\alpha_k}} + \Sigma_{i \neq k} f_i + f_s \leq 1$ (same if $\alpha_k = 0$, decreases o/w)
Bloat at bottleneck resource	$1 + b_k$ (improves)	$f_k + \Sigma_{i \neq k}(f_i(1+b_k)^{\alpha_i}) + f_s > 1$ (same if $\alpha_i = 0, \forall i \neq k$, else increases)	ditto as above
Bloat reduction shifts bottleneck	$1 + b_{eff}$ (improves, but less)	$f_k(\frac{1+b_{eff}}{1+b_k})^{\alpha_k} + \Sigma_{i \neq k}(f_i(1+b_{eff})^{\alpha_i}) + f_s$ (can increase or decrease or stay same)	ditto as above

Table 3: Effect of bloat reduction in different scenarios when bloat affects a single resource R_k

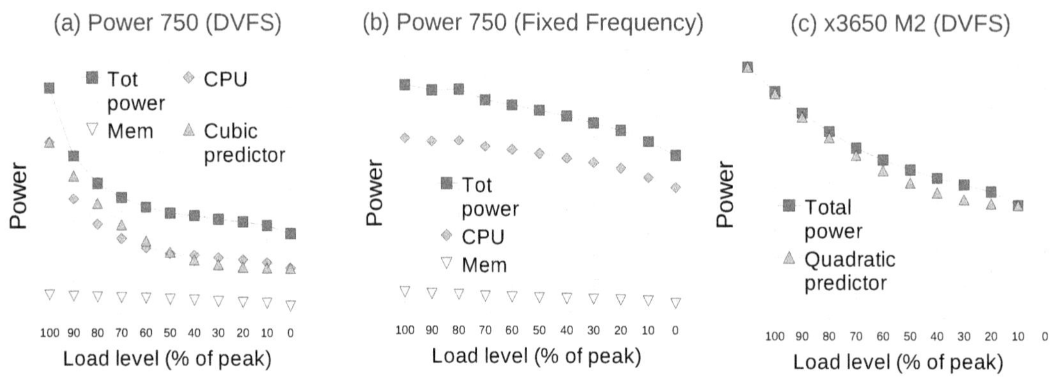

Figure 6: Hardware energy proportionality differences: (a) The Power 750 system employing new DVFS algorithms shows an *approximately cubic* relationship for CPU power; *memory power increases linearly but as a much smaller fraction of system power* on the test configuration (which uses adequate memory for SPECPower_ssj2008, but far below the system's memory capacity of 512GB). (b) Without DVFS the relationship for the Power 750 system is *almost linear*, similar for HS21. (c) The x3650 M2 system has a *near quadratic* characteristic for the full system power (we do not have CPU and memory power measurements in this case).

SPECPower_ssj2008. The energy proportionality goes progressively higher from HS21 blade/Power750 system (6(b), near linear) with no adaptive power management to x3650 M2 with DVFS (6(c), quadratic) to the Power750 system with DVFS (6(a), cubic).

In our study the memory hierarchy resources are the ones primarily affected by bloat and serve as the bottleneck resource on different occasions, e.g., memory bandwidth and capacity being relatively limited for the HS21 (section 3.4), main memory being limited with reduced heap sizes (section 3.4.2), and on-chip cache being limited (section 3.4.3).

System	Mem stress	Degree of energy proportionality	Peak Perf/ Eff. Score impact	Equi-perf power impact
HS21 (noDVFS)	High	Low	High	Low
x3650 M2 (DVFS)	Low	Med	Med	Med
Power750 (DVFS)	Low	High	Low	High

Table 4: Trends from cross-platform experiments

Table 4 summarizes the trends seen in cross-platform experimental observations of the impact of bloat reduction (Section 3) through object memory reuse (i.e. from *AllocOrig* to *AllocLess*), in the context of memory constraint (bottleneck strain) and energy proportionality differences between platforms.

The higher the degree of energy proportionality (higher α_k), higher the equi-perf power savings from bloat reduction in Table 3. This is supported by the increasing impact on equi-performance power in Table 4 going from HS21 to Power750. On the other hand, the higher the extent of bottleneck, higher the performance improvement with bloat reduction in Table 3, consequently the higher the increase in efficiency. This is supported by the higher impact on energy-efficiency for HS21 over x3650 M2 and Power 750.

5.2 Specific model predictions and corroborating experimental results

1. Peak power can *increase or decrease* with reduction in bloat depending on whether it affects the bottleneck resource or other resources. In the situation where bloat affects the bottleneck, *the degree of impact can depend on the steepness of energy proportionality characteristic of the resources which are not bloated.* and the fraction of system power consumed by them.

In our cache pressure experiments (Figure 5), bloat induced cache pressure causes under-utilization of the compute resources for SMT4 and HC, hence throughput increases with bloat reduction. Consequently peak power actually rises (negative peak power savings) with reduction in bloat. This effect is more pronounced for the steeper power characterstics with DVFS than for fixed frequency. On the other hand, reducing bloat also reduces memory references and consequently memory power (by 13% in Power750, SMT4 mode, as shown in Figure 3, and 18% in SMT2); the overall system power reduction due to this effect, however, is small as memory consumes a low fraction of system power on this system. In the SMT2 case, where the performance impact of bloat is lowest, this reduction translates into a slight reduction in overall system power.

2. The energy-efficiency improvement from reducing bloat is likely to be most pronounced when bloat affects a bottleneck resource and the non-bottleneck resources are not very energy proportional as per Table 3. *Energy proportional hardware mitigates the effect of bloat on energy efficiency at peak performance* - Figure 5 confirms this, showing the gains in energy efficiency are greater when running the cores at fixed frequency than with DVFS. Similar behavior can be seen in Figure 2 with HS21 getting a higher improvement in energy-efficiency with bloat reduction (Efficiency of AllocLess/Efficiency of AllocOrig = 1.59) than x3650 M2 (1.1) or Power 750 (1.06).

3. While energy efficiency improvement at peak performance is higher with non-energy-proportional resources, *the improvement at equal performance can be significantly higher for energy proportional hardware.* This can be seen as significantly higher **equiperformance power savings** for DVFS in Figure 5 compared to the energy efficiency improvements at peak. The same figure also shows that having more energy proportional resources (DVFS) can yield significantly higher equi-performance energy savings (compared to fixed frequency).

6. RELATED WORK

Analysis and measurement of software bloat.

Mitchell, Sevitsky and Srinivasan [23] define metrics based on modeling runtime information flow to classify and characterize the nature and volume of data transformations executed, but these measures have not been automated till date. The notion of data structure health signatures proposed by Mitchell and Sevitsky [22] has been used very effectively in characterization and automated measurement [20] of Java memory bloat in long lived heap objects.

For some categories of bloat, including the problem of temporary objects bloat which we investigate in our empirical study, an explicit model may not always be available for distinguishing overhead from necessary data or activity. Researchers have therefore used different measures of excesses like excessive volumes of temporary objects, data copies and heavy object creation costs to recognize the presence of bloat [12, 33, 34]. A summary of the state of the art in research on software bloat analysis and solutions is covered in [35]; to the best our knowledge, we are the first to investigate the power-performance implications of bloat.

Java energy characterization.

Much prior work on energy (and power) characterization of the Java runtime and applications [28, 14, 18] have been simulator based studies or primarily conducted on embedded platforms. Contreras and Martonosi [11] used real system power measurements (like we do) on some mobile platforms to show that a significant proportion of energy is consumed by the JVM, particularly components like the classloader, JIT and garbage collector. Recently, Esmaeilzadeh et al [13] examined measured power and performance of Java benchmarks across hardware generations of Intel based processors and find Java multithreaded benchmarks to be more power-intensive than their single threaded counterparts: the differences may be explained by noting that complex Java workloads are likely to be memory bound and more sensitive to cache size than clock speed. Our work differs in its focus on the impact of a specific category of bloat on full system power-performance for a given workload on large server systems running a production JVM.

Object churn analysis, impact and solutions.

Compiler and runtime optimizations like escape analysis [10, 6, 15, 30], escape detection and improvements in memory management and garbage collection [1] have been developed to reduce the overheads of allocating and reclaiming temporary objects. However, Shankar et al [26] found that even a sophisticated escape analysis implementation in a high performance production JVM typically eliminates less than 10% of allocations in component based applications, which matches our observations. Techniques have also been proposed for ensuring faster reclamation of temporary objects [9, 16, 32] and for guiding programmers in eliminating excess temporaries [12, 7]. In our controlled experiments, we apply object reuse manually for de-bloating excess temporaries - the technique has recently been automated [3] for certain object types (container and string objects).

Our work complements such efforts by studying the actual systems level power-performance impact under different conditions, to help determine which optimization opportunities are most worthwhile. We believe that we are the first to perform such a study, particularly with real power measurements on large scale server systems with dynamic power management capabilities. As we find, in many situations, an improvement in peak performance need not translate to an equivalent improvement in equi-performance power savings and vice-versa. This paper is an extended version of our previous workshop paper [4] which described the model and a small subset of experimental observations. The major addition here is the systematic multi-platform empirical study of the power-performance effects of temporary objects bloat, covering our methodology and key findings from conducting a detailed set of controlled experiments of the impact of bloat on real systems.

Zhao et al [37] analysed the implications of object allocation on scalability and performance. We were able to reproduce similar results during our experimentation, particularly on the HS21 blade server which appears to be closest in configuration to their experimental setup. However, power-efficiency was not a consideration in their work.

7. CONCLUSIONS

Software bloat is fast being recognized as an impediment to performance and efficiency of systems. Many studies have been undertaken to understand the nature and source of bloat and devise solutions to address them. In this paper, we present the first systematic empirical study analyzing the power-performance implications of software runtime bloat. With a methodology using the SPECPower_ssj2008 energy-efficiency benchmark for suitable injection/reduction of temporary object bloat and a detailed multi-platform analysis we establish the quantitative power-performance impact of bloat reduction in the context of system energy proportionality and resource bottlenecks. We then present a simplified abstract model for relating the power-performance impact of bloat reduction to energy proportionality and resource bottlenecks for "what-if" analysis. We further corroborate our model with the findings from our in-depth experimental study. Our work provides the first detailed insight into the varying impact of software runtime bloat on the power-performance characteristics of systems. We conclude with lean does usually imply green, but to tell the shade, a whole system analysis like ours is necessary.

8. ACKNOWLEDGMENTS

We thank Kazuaki Ishizaki, Gary Sevitsky, Vaidyanathan Srinivasan, Hong Hua, Dibyendu Das, Amar Devegowda, Ankita Goel, Derek Inglis and Varsha Apte.

9. REFERENCES

[1] D. F. Bacon, P. Cheng, and V. T. Rajan. A unified theory of garbage collection. In *OOPSLA'04*.

[2] L. A. Barroso and U. Hölzle. The case for energy-proportional computing. *Computer*, 40(12), 2007.

[3] S. Bhattacharya, M. G. Nanda, K. Gopinath, and M. Gupta. Reuse, recycle to de-bloat software. In *ECOOP'11*.

[4] S. Bhattacharya, K. Rajamani, K. Gopinath, and M. Gupta. The interplay of software bloat, hardware energy proportionality and system bottlenecks. In *HotPower'11*.

[5] S. M. Blackburn and et. al. The DaCapo benchmarks: Java benchmarking development and analysis. In *OOPSLA '06*.

[6] B. Blanchet. Escape analysis for object-oriented languages: application to java. In *OOPSLA'99*.

[7] D. Buytaert, K. Beyls, and K. De Bosschere. Hinting refactorings to reduce object creation in java. In *ACES*, 2005.

[8] J. P. Buzen. Fundamental laws of computer system performance. In *SIGMETRICS'76*.

[9] S. Cherem and R. Rugina. Uniqueness inference for compile-time object deallocation. In *ISMM '07*.

[10] J.-D. Choi, M. Gupta, M. Serrano, V. C. Sreedhar, and S. Midkiff. Escape analysis for java. In *OOPSLA'99*.

[11] G. Contreras and M. Martonosi. Techniques for real-system characterization of java virtual machine energy and power behavior. *IISWC'06*.

[12] B. Dufour, B. G. Ryder, and G. Sevitsky. A scalable technique for characterizing the usage of temporaries in framework-intensive java applications. In *SIGSOFT '08/FSE-16*, pages 59–70.

[13] H. Esmaeilzadeh, S. Blackburn, L. Yang, and K. S. McKinley. Power and performance of native and java benchmarks on 130nm to 32nm process technologies. In *MoBS'10*.

[14] K. I. Farkas, J. Flinn, G. Back, D. Grunwald, and J. M. Anderson. Quantifying the energy consumption of a pocket computer and a java virtual machine. *SIGMETRICS Perform. Eval. Rev.*, 2000.

[15] D. Gay and B. Steensgaard. Fast escape analysis and stack allocation for object-based programs. In *CC '00*.

[16] H. Inoue, H. Komatsu, and T. Nakatani. A study of memory management for web-based applications on multicore processors. In *PLDI '09*.

[17] R. Jain. Operational laws, ch 33. In *The Art of Computer Systems Performance Analysis, Wiley India Edition*, pages 555–567.

[18] S. Lafond and J. Lilius. Energy consumption analysis for two embedded java virtual machines. *J. Syst. Archit.*, 53(5-6):328–337, 2007.

[19] H. Y. McCreary and et. al. EnergyScale for IBM POWER6 microprocessor-based systems. *IBM JRD*, 51(6):775–786, November 2007.

[20] N. Mitchell, E. Schonberg, and G. Sevitsky. Making sense of large heaps. In *ECOOP'09*.

[21] N. Mitchell, E. Schonberg, and G. Sevitsky. Four trends leading to java runtime bloat. *IEEE Software*, Jan 2010.

[22] N. Mitchell and G. Sevitsky. The causes of bloat, the limits of health. In *OOPSLA '07*.

[23] N. Mitchell, G. Sevitsky, and H. Srinivasan. Modeling runtime behaviour in framework based applications. In *ECOOP'06*.

[24] K. Rajamani and et. al. Power-Performance Management on an IBM POWER7 Server.

[25] E. Saxe. Power efficient software. *Communications of the ACM*, 53(2):44–48, Feb 2010.

[26] A. Shankar, M. Arnold, and R. Bodik. Jolt: lightweight dynamic analysis and removal of object churn. In *OOPSLA '08*.

[27] Standard Performance Evaluation Corporation. http://www.specbench.org.

[28] N. Vijaykrishnan, M. Kandemir, S. Kim, S. Tomar, A. Sivasubramaniam, and M. J. Irwin. Energy behavior of java applications from the memory perspective. In *JVM'01*.

[29] M. Ware and et. al. Architecting for power management: The IBM POWER7 approach. In *HPCA-16*, January 2010.

[30] J. Whaley and M. Rinard. Compositional pointer and escape analysis for java programs. In *OOPSLA'99*.

[31] Q. Wu and et. al. Dynamic-compiler-driven control for microprocessor energy and performance. In *IEEE Micro*, 2006.

[32] F. Xian, W. Srisa-an, and H. Jiang. Microphase: an approach to proactively invoking garbage collection for improved performance. In *OOPSLA '07*.

[33] G. Xu, M. Arnold, N. Mitchell, A. Rountev, and G. Sevitsky. Go with the flow: profiling copies to find runtime bloat. In *PLDI '09*.

[34] G. Xu and et. al. Finding low-utility data structures. In *PLDI '10*.

[35] G. Xu, N. Mitchell, M. Arnold, and G. Sevitsky. Software bloat analysis: Finding, removing, and preventing performance problems in modern large-scale object-oriented applications. In *FoSER'10*.

[36] Z. Xu, Y. Tu, and X. Wang. Exploring power performance tradeoffs in database systems. In *ICDE'10*.

[37] Y. Zhao and et. al. Allocation wall: a limiting factor of java applications on emerging multi-core platforms. In *OOPSLA '09*.

D-Factor: A Quantitative Model of Application Slow-Down in Multi-Resource Shared Systems

[1]Seung-Hwan Lim*, [2]Jae-Seok Huh, [2]Youngjae Kim, [2]Galen M. Shipman, and [1]Chita R. Das

[1]The Pennsylvania State University
University Park, PA 16802
{seulim, das}@cse.psu.edu

[2]Oak Ridge National Laboratory
Oak Ridge, TN 37831
{huhj, kimy1, gshipman}@ornl.gov

ABSTRACT

Scheduling multiple jobs onto a platform enhances system utilization by sharing resources. The benefits from higher resource utilization include reduced cost to construct, operate, and maintain a system, which often include energy consumption. Maximizing these benefits comes at a price – resource contention among jobs increases job completion time. In this paper, we analyze slow-downs of jobs due to contention for multiple resources in a system; referred to as *dilation factor*. We observe that multiple-resource contention creates non-linear dilation factors of jobs. From this observation, we establish a general quantitative model for dilation factors of jobs in multi-resource systems. A job is characterized by a vector-valued loading statistics and dilation factors of a job set are given by a quadratic function of their loading vectors. We demonstrate how to systematically characterize a job, maintain the data structure to calculate the dilation factor (loading matrix), and calculate the dilation factor of each job. We validate the accuracy of the model with multiple processes running on a native Linux server, virtualized servers, and with multiple MapReduce workloads co-scheduled in a cluster. Evaluation with measured data shows that the D factor model has an error margin of less than 16%. We also show that the model can be integrated with an existing on-line scheduler to minimize the makespan of workloads.

Categories and Subject Descriptors

C.4 [**Computer System Organization**]: Performance of systems—*modeling techniques, performance attributes*

General Terms

Management, Performance

*Currently, the author is affiliated with Oak Ridge National Laboratory.

Keywords

Shared resource management; Cloud computing; Performance modeling; Application running time

1. INTRODUCTION

Sharing a system with multiple workloads enhances system utilization, thereby lowering the economic [10] and environmental dent [33]. Recent advents in server virtualization bolster this sharing policy since it allows multiple operating system instances to share a physical machine [4]. However, sharing a system comes at a price – contention for system resources. Contention for system resources leads to high variance in performance, which would deter hosting latency sensitive applications that require tight performance guarantees [3]. The high variance in performance is often considered as unpredictable performance [3], due to the deficient understanding of performance variation of a workload from contention for multiple resources [13, 17]. This in turn would make the usual, but costly over-provisioning design more attractive, thereby defeating the whole concept of resource consolidation and cloud computing. Therefore, performance quantification of jobs (or performance degradation) in a multi-resource shared platform is essential to both facilitate co-hosting of applications and meet the service requirements. However, performance prediction in such an environment is admittedly a challenging problem and to our knowledge, no efficient technique is available today.

We may capture the performance variation of jobs in shared systems with slow-down due to resource contention. Let *dilation factor* denote the slow-down of a job due to resource contention. Prior efforts to estimate dilation factor falls into two groups – modeling based solutions [21, 24] or measurements based solutions [13, 16, 18, 20]. Modeling based solutions often use resource usage statistics of each job to construct the model. For example, queuing theory based approaches use system parameters like job arrival rates and service rates of resources [21], while control theory based approaches use the relationship between allocated amount of resources and workload behavior [24]. However, resource access behavior of a job depends on co-located jobs and specific hardwares, especially when both jobs and machines are heterogeneous [17,28,35]. For instance, co-located jobs can alter cache hit ratio of a job in multi-core environments [17,27] or disk access latencies in shared storage systems [35], which can change resource access statistics of a job. Therefore, in order to improve the accuracy of a model, prior modeling based approaches require detailed resource access behavior of each job.

In order to address such challenges, measurement based approaches have been proposed [13,16,18,20]. Koh *et al.* [18] predicted the performance degradation of co-located workloads using recorded similar workloads in terms of their resource usage statistics, similar to program similarity analysis [16]. Recently, Govindan *et al.* [13] and Mars *et al.* [20] independently proposed techniques that employ probe jobs to infer behavior of workloads when they are co-located, which does not require resource usage statistics. However, those approaches do not provide generic strategies to estimate dilation factors of co-located jobs. Therefore, we desire to develop a simple, but generic model to estimate dilation factors of co-located jobs, without depending on detailed description on research access behavior of each job.

In order to develop such a model, we may start from a simple model, linear sum of original completion times of jobs, which has been used to obtain makespan of jobs in scheduling algorithms [30]. With linear sum, we may obtain dilation factor of each job from dividing the makespan by individual completion time of each job. The benefit of the linear sum model is that it only relies on the completion times of jobs. However, linear sum may not be able to provide desired accuracy due to non-linearity between individual completion times and makespan in multi-resource shared environments [5,11,17]. For example, completing two co-hosted jobs – one 100 *sec* CPU-job with one 100 *sec* I/O-job – will take less than 200 *sec*, contradict to estimation from the linear sum of completion times of both jobs. The deficiency of linear sum model is the lack of ability to consider multiple resources at the same time. Thus, we propose a model that extends the linear sum model to consider multiple shared resources, which only relies on the completion times of jobs instead of resource usage statistics. With the proposed model, we overcome challenges in using prior analytical model based approaches to estimate dilation factors of co-located jobs. Also, we provide a mathematical foundation on using well-known workloads, probe jobs in [13, 20], to infer behavior of co-located workloads.

To provide accurate estimation of slow-down of jobs due to resource contention in shared environments like data centers/cloud computing platforms, we propose a generic quantitative model for dilation factors of n-jobs contending for m-resources, called the *dilation factor model* (*D-factor model*). We view *a job* as a sequence of accessing one of the system resources and a shared system as a collection of resources. For this, we characterize the resource access statistics of a job by a vector-valued loading statistics, *a loading vector*. We obtain the factor of dilated completion time, the *dilation factor*, of each job from a quadratic relation of loading vectors for jobs in the system, which can be utilized in optimization problems such as job scheduling. In addition, the proposed D-factor model can profile a job by only measuring completion time of a job, which does not require any instrumentations such as monitoring tools and modifying software/hardware infrastructures as have been used in prior studies [13]. This is an important characteristic for cloud environment, where application operators on virtual machines often cannot monitor physical resources.

We validated the proposed model with actual measurements on cluster infrastructures running native Linux and Xen Hypervisor [4], with synthetic workloads, FileBench [2],

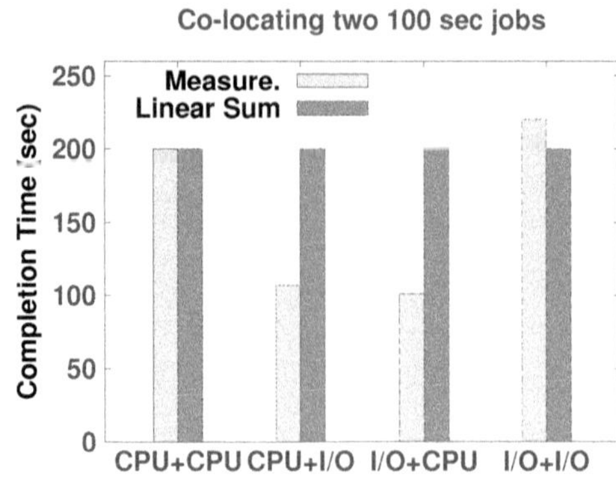

Figure 1: Non-linearity in slow-down of a job in a multi-resource system. CPU represents a CPU-bound job and IO represents an I/O-bound job. Each bar represents the completion time of job A when job B is colocated. For example, CPU+IO denotes the completion time of the CPU-bound job when the I/O-bound job is co-located.

and MapReduce. The experimental results from synthetic workloads indicate that the average error rates of the estimations from the proposed model are 7% for a system on native Linux and 10.3% for a virtualized system. However, the estimation error from the linear completion time model could be up to 98% in the worst case. For the FileBench benchmark, the proposed model estimates the completion time of workloads within a 6.0% error. We used three popular applications to benchmark MapReduce– `Sort`, `Grep`, and `PiEstimator`. In experiments with MapReduce, we increased the number of instances of each MapReduce application up to four and co-hosted three different MapReduce applications. The margins of errors are about 16% for identical MapReduce applications and 11% for heterogeneous MapReduce applications. We also demonstrate how the D-factor model can extend a scheduler for single-resource systems into a scheduler for multi-resource systems for reducing the makespan of workloads by about 20%.

This paper is organized as follows: Section 2 provides the motivation of this work. In Section 3, we present the underlying theoretical concepts for developing the D-factor model. Section 4 describes the experimental settings of this study. The validation results with both synthetic and realistic test samples are presented in Section 5, followed by an example application to a scheduling algorithm in Section 6. Related work is presented in Section 7, followed by concluding remarks in Section 8.

2. MOTIVATION

Interference due to sharing resources results in slow-down of workloads [9], depending on the characteristics of co-located workloads [13, 17]. Prior findings have suggested non-linear dilation factors when we consider multiple system resources; co-located applications on multi-core processors [5, 11], co-located processes in an operating system [9], co-located virtual machines in a physical machine [6], and co-located workloads in a data center [10].

Figure 1 highlights the non-linearity in slow-downs of workloads due to multiple resource contention. Here, we created two different types of jobs – a CPU-bound job, which consists of arithmetic operations and an I/O-bound job, which randomly reads two 2GB files. Both jobs take 100*sec* without the presence of other jobs. Experiments are done in a

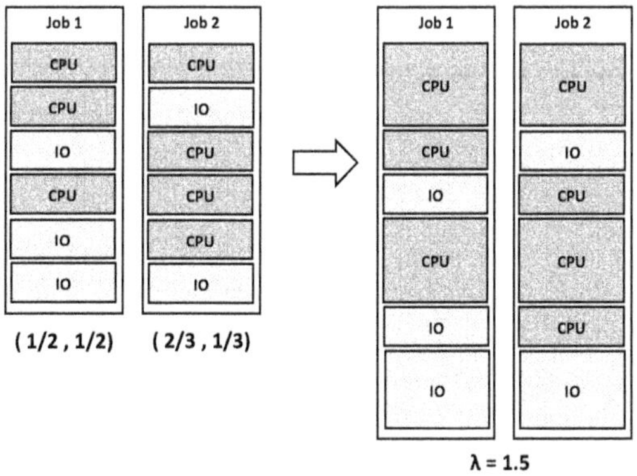

Figure 2: Dilation factor model describes slow-down of each job when multiple jobs are contending for multiple resources. (Left) Job-slices in their neutral states, where loading vectors are (1/2, 1/2) and (2/3, 1/3), respectively for CPU and I/O. (Right) The processing times of job slices will be dilated when they request the same resource at the same time. As described in Property 2 in Section 3, when two jobs are competing, their dilation factors, λ, are identical.

machine with two single-core CPUs that run Linux. However, we turned off one CPU to ensure that both jobs are accessing the same CPU. More details of the experimental platform are described in Section 4. We measured completion time of each job with another job in order to understand the interference between jobs. When the same type of jobs coexist in the system, we observe a linear relationship between total completion time and individual completion times. However, for different types of jobs in the system, a non-linear relationship is observed. This example suggests that we may reduce the performance interference among co-located jobs by considering multiple resources in a system. An empirical study on a large scale data center has shown that multiplexing workloads leads to higher efficiency since each workload utilizes different system resources [10].

A simple truth is that a better estimation results in better performance, which brings in the first fundamental question to be answered in this work:

Question 1. *What is the general quantitative model for performance of systems with multiple-resource contention?*

The previous simple example implies that, in a realistic environment, a machine or a system consists of multiple resources and hosts jobs that can request any of the resources, as shown in Figure 2. Recall, when we assume that a job accesses a single resource such as a processing unit, we may characterize a job by its completion time to estimate interference as shown in Figure 1. For multiple resources, on the contrary, a job cannot simply be measured by the time duration between the start and the end of the job; we need more information on the request distribution of the job for each of the resources. Thus, we need to find the answer to the following question:

Question 2. *How can a job that requests multiple resources be quantitatively modeled?*

In this work, we consider a job as a scheduling unit such as a process. We model a job as a sequence of hypothetical *job slices*, each of which is devoted to a single resource in order to approximate the behavior of real workloads. A job, *i.e.* the entire sequence of job slices, is statistically characterized by the probability of requesting/accessing each resource by a (random) single slice. The result is a vector-valued probability of resource-requests. Each job will be characterized by this *loading vector*. Note that the loading vector represents the portion of time to access each resource during the execution of a job, which should be dependent on the hardware that a job runs.

As for approximating a real job with job slices and characterizing a real job with a loading vector, three major issues need to be addressed: simultaneous access of resources; dynamically varying resource access patterns; and multiple resources of the same type such as multi-core CPUs. Since loading vector represents the statistical characteristics to access each resource – average intensity to access each resource, simultaneous resource accesses can be approximated. Specifically, we show that our model reasonably captures a mixture of I/O workloads and CPU workloads in Section 5. We may approximate a dynamic workload as a series of static workloads, each of which can be represented by a loading vector. In this study, we will focus on static workloads since treating time-varying parameters requires additioal effort. As for n-core processors, we may reserve one element for each core in a loading vector. More details will be discussed in Section 3.

Finally, in order to formulate the *model* for question 1, the behavior of a machine with multiple resources should be concretely defined.

Question 3. *What is the quantitative model of a machine with multiple resources?*

We model a machine as a collection of *resource-queues* – one queue for each shared resource. A slice of a job on a machine is assumed to be queued in one of the resource-queues with the probability given by the loading vector.

Multiple jobs on a machine will populate the resource-queues, hence, a job-slice can be slowed down due to the waiting time for a resource-queue. A quadratic function of loading vectors will be established to determine the dilation of jobs. Eventually, the resource contention by a job set on a machine will be described in terms of *dilation factors* – referred to as slow-down of job completion time under the presence of other jobs.

3. MATHEMATICAL MODELING

As illustrated by the simple example in Section 2, if jobs on a single machine compete over multiple shared resources, the dilation of their completion times can exhibit complicated behavior. Recall, for a single-resource machine, time-sharing jobs slow down uniformly and proportionally to the number of competing jobs, which is not true any more if they compete over multiple resoueces; jobs can even have different dilation factors. To clearly describe this phenomenon, we need the modeling of machines with multiple resources.

3.1 Modeling: machines and jobs

A machine with multiple resources can be viewed as a collection of multiple resource-queues; each resource corresponds to a queue and requests from jobs running on the machine compete for the resources. Let a machine have m resources, i.e. m-queues. We assume a resource-request from a job can be issued only after the previous request from the same job is completed. In order to describe this behavior, we introduce the concept of *job-slices* – a hypothetical atomic unit of work which is characterized by the following assumptions; (i) a job-slice requests for and can be processed by only a single resource, thus, it is also an atomic unit of request for the resource queues. (ii) It takes 1 (hypothetical) time-unit for a job-slice to be processed by the resource in which it is queued, independent of the type of resource.

A job is considered as a sequence of job-slices each of which requests a single resource. If a job consists of ℓ job slices, its *neutral* (which means undisturbed by other jobs) completion time is ℓ time-units. A request is viewed as the submission of a slice into one of the resource-queues. The job can proceed to the next slice only if the current slice in a queue is completed. For n concurrent jobs on the machine, we make the following two assumptions: (iii) there are at most n slices (including the one in service) in any one of the m queues. (iv) At any time, there are total n slices in all the queues. Assumption (iii) implies that the time for a slice to be completed is at most n time-units.

Remark 1. *Notice that the actual amount of work during a unit time such as the amount (in MB) of file processed during the time depends on the system configuration; for example, if the operating system utilizes I/O buffer cache, some of the I/O requests turn effectively into memory requests. Thus, it might not be feasible to generally estimate the actual amount of work for multiple-resource workloads by investigating the program source and hardware specification. Characteristics of workloads will be obtained by probe processes or by regression analysis of their completion times, which will be illustrated in this paper.*

Based on assumption (ii), we are actually proposing a unified measure of work done by different resources; Instead of counting the amount of work done by resources by their native measure such as the number of instructions (for CPU) and the file size in MB (for I/O), we represent the amount of work by the the time spent by any resource for the task. Thus, one unit of work is the amount of work that can be done by any resource in unit time. This allows us to compare the workloads of different kinds using a common unit.

Recall the only required information for the linear sum model for single-resource machines is the neutral completion time of the job. For a multiple-resource model, additional information is required: the request–resource-queue correspondence. The amount of information increases with the size of the system, the number of resource types to be considered, and the number of workloads if we want to obtain the complete description as with queuing model approaches. Hence, we take a statistical approach.

3.2 The loading vector

In this paper, we characterize a job by the statistical pattern of its resource requests. In general, a deterministic resource-access pattern in time is difficult to obtain except for very specific applications of known structures. Instead, we assume a job has, for each resource, a unique probability of a slice to be queued for the resource; that is, we view that the number of job-slices queued for each resource divided by the number of total slices of the job is a statistical invariant of a job. Thus, in an m-resource model, the workload of a job is characterized by an m-dimensional vector, which we call the *loading vector* $\boldsymbol{p}$ of the job.

Remark 2 (MULTICORE SYSTEMS). *In order to avoid possible confusion, we present the theory and experimental results for single-core systems since there exists a variety of multi-core processor architectures and process scheduling policies. However, the application of the presented model to multicore systems would be possible. For example, as many operating systems treat, a dual-core system can be considered as a machine with 2 CPU-resources independent of each other. Thus, if we consider CPU and I/O resources in the model, the resulting loading vector can be 3 dimensional – namely, CPU1, CPU2, and I/O. Then, we can apply the presented model to identify the 3 dimensional loading vector of a job.*

Thus, without any other competing job (in our terms, in the neutral condition), p_i are given by

$$p_i = \frac{\text{the time spent at the resource-}i}{\text{the total completion time}} \geq 0. \tag{1}$$

Also, p_i can be interpreted as the probability of a job-slice being queued for queue-i. Obviously,

$$\|\boldsymbol{p}\|_1 = \sum_{i=1}^{m} p_i \leq 1. \tag{2}$$

Notice the inequality; we allow a job to have slices that do not request any resource. Such an *idling* slice simply spends a time-unit without populating any of the m queues. We define two classes of jobs: a job is

1. *idle* if $\sum_{i=1}^{m} p_i < 1$ and
2. *busy* if $\sum_{i=1}^{m} p_i = 1$.

Given a set of n jobs, we denote $\boldsymbol{p}_j$ as the loading vector of job-j and p_{ij} as the ith component of $\boldsymbol{p}_j$. An m by n matrix can be formed with p_{ij} as its elements. We call this matrix the *loading matrix* of the job set. Each column vector of the loading matrix is the loading vector of the corresponding job. The loading vector and the loading matrix are our statistical characterizations of the workload of a job and a job set, respectively.

3.3 The dilation factor

Consider n jobs on an m-resource machine characterized by a given m by n loading matrix. Suppose a slice of job-j is queued at queue-i. Then, the expected waiting time of the job-slice (of job-j) is the expected number of job-slices (from other jobs) in the queue. Hence, the conditional expectation of the dilated completion time of the single slice of job-j, on the condition that it is in queue-i, is given by

$$1 + \sum_{\substack{k=1 \\ k \neq j}}^{n} p_{ik} = 1 + \sum_{k=1}^{n} p_{ik} - p_{ij}\,, \tag{3}$$

where the additional 1 time-unit is the service time.

Since p_{ij} is the probability of queuing a slice of job-j at queue-i, the expectation of the dilated completion time T_j of job-j is given by

$$\begin{aligned} T_j &= \tau_j \left(\left(1 - \sum_{i=1}^{m} p_{ij}\right) + \sum_{i=1}^{m} p_{ij} \left(1 + \sum_{k=1}^{n} p_{ik} - p_{ij}\right)\right) \\ &= \tau_j \left(1 + \sum_{i=1}^{m} p_{ij} \sum_{k=1}^{n} p_{ik} - \sum_{i=1}^{m} p_{ij}^2\right) \end{aligned} \tag{4}$$

where τ_j is the neutral completion time of job-j. Notice, the term $(1 - \sum_{i=1}^{m} p_{ij})$ represents the probability of idling that causes no dilation. Let us define the total loading vector $\overline{\boldsymbol{p}}$ by $\overline{\boldsymbol{p}} = \sum_{j=1}^{n} \boldsymbol{p}_j$. The above relation can be rewritten in vector notation by $T_j = \tau_j \left(1 + \boldsymbol{p}_j \cdot \overline{\boldsymbol{p}} - \boldsymbol{p}_j \cdot \boldsymbol{p}_j\right)$. Thus, a job j is slowed down by the factor of T_j/τ_j due to resource contention. We summarize the result by introducing the dilation factor $\lambda_j = T_j/\tau_j$ as follows:

Definition 1. *Given a job set on a machine characterized by the loading vectors $\boldsymbol{p}_j$ $(j = 1, \ldots, n)$, the dilation factors $\lambda_j = T_j/\tau_j$ $(j = 1, \ldots, n)$ are given by*

$$\lambda_j = 1 + \boldsymbol{p}_j \cdot \overline{\boldsymbol{p}} - \boldsymbol{p}_j \cdot \boldsymbol{p}_j \,. \tag{5}$$

Remark 3. *The above formula distinguishes our model from other applications of queuing theory. Combined with the representation of loading statistics by the loading matrix presented above, we can describe the average slow-down of a job in a closed formula. Also, the formula can be viewed as a statistical description of the interaction between jobs running on the same machine in terms of mutual interference.*

For identical jobs, the formula can be simplified as follows:

Property 1. *If all of n jobs are identical ($\boldsymbol{p}_j = \boldsymbol{p}$), the dilation factors are identical ($\lambda_j = \lambda$) and are given by $\lambda = 1 + (n-1)\,\boldsymbol{p} \cdot \boldsymbol{p}$.*

The above property can be utilized to obtain experimentally the loading vector of a job; (1) we obtain the loading factor by measuring the dilated time of n identical jobs for $n = 1$ to a sufficient number. (2) The data for various n can be analyzed by regression to obtain $\boldsymbol{p}$.

The dilation factors are also identical in another situation. By applying $n = 2$ and $\overline{\boldsymbol{p}} = \boldsymbol{p}_1 + \boldsymbol{p}_2$ to Equation (5),

Property 2. *If there are 2 jobs, the dilation factors are identical ($\lambda_1 = \lambda_2 = \lambda$) and given by $\lambda = 1 + \boldsymbol{p}_1 \cdot \boldsymbol{p}_2$.*

If we create a synthetic process which requests only a single resource, this reference (or *probe*) process can be utilized to compute the loading vector of a job. The primary benefit of the probe processes is that we can identify the loading vector of a job when we cannot control the execution of a job in the system.

Property 3. *Suppose there are two jobs – one that we want to identify its loading vector p and the other that uses only resource-i, a probe process. By Property 2, they share the same λ and the ith component of p is given by $p_i = \lambda - 1$.*

3.4 Special case: 1-resource-busy jobs (the linear sum model)

In this section, we illustrate that the linear completion time model is actually a special case of our general model, where all the jobs compete for the same resource.

Lemma 1. *Assume 1-resource-busy jobs: $p_{kj} = 0$ for any $j = 1, \ldots, n$ and for every $k = 1, \ldots, m$ except an index $1 \le i \le m$, and $\|\boldsymbol{p}_j\|_1 = 1$. Then, the dilation factors are identical ($\lambda_j = \lambda$) for all jobs and given by*

$$\lambda = n \tag{6}$$

Proof. Since all the jobs are busy, $p_{ij} = 1$ and $p_{kj} = 0$ for any $k \neq i$. Hence, all jobs are identically given by $\boldsymbol{p}_j = \boldsymbol{p}$. Then, $\boldsymbol{p} \cdot \boldsymbol{p} = 1$ and, by Property 1 in the previous section, the dilation factors are identical and given by $\lambda = 1 + (n-1)\,\boldsymbol{p} \cdot \boldsymbol{p} = 1 + (n-1) = n$ □

Let τ_j denote the neutral completion time of job-j in a job set of size n. We define the total completion time T of the job set as the time duration from the starting time of the first initiated job to the ending time of the last completed job. For 1-resource-busy jobs, $T = \sum_{j=1}^{n} \tau_j$.

Theorem 1. *Suppose during the total completion time, there is no idling gap, i.e. the machine is always populated by at least one job. Then, the total completion time is the sum of individual neutral completion times independent of the starting and ending times of the jobs, that is,*

$$T = \sum_{j=1}^{n} \tau_j \,. \tag{7}$$

Proof. Please refer to [19]. □

Note that Lemma 1 and Theorem 1 assume that jobs are fully overlapped for estimating completion times.

Remark 4. *In general cases, such a simple formula for total completion time does not exist. Consider a 2-job system with $\boldsymbol{p}_1 = (1,0)$ and $\boldsymbol{p}_2 = (0,1)$. Then, $\lambda_1 = \lambda_2 = 1$, that is, there is no dilation of completion time. Let $\tau_1 = \tau_2 =$ 1minute. If the two jobs started at the same time, they will be completed at the same time after 1 minute. If one of them started first and the other job started at the time of completion of the first job, the total completion time will be 2 minutes. Depending on the overlap, the total completion time can vary from 1 minute to 2 minutes. But, still the linear model estimate becomes the upper bound of the total completion time in any case.*

Remark 5. *(1-resource-idling jobs) Even if there's only one requested resource, the linear model cannot be applied to a job set with an idling job. Consider a simple job set of n identical jobs requesting only resource-i. Then, the loading vectors can be represented by a single scalar parameter $p < 1$. Then, $\lambda = 1 + (n-1)\,p^2 = (1-p^2)\,1 + p^2\,n$, that is, λ is a linear interpolation of 1 and n with respect to p^2, since $p < 1$ and $\lambda < n$.*

3.5 Special case: 2-resource-busy jobs

The usefulness of this model comes from the fact that each loading vector $\boldsymbol{p}_j$ can be represented by a single scalar parameter p_j. Without loss of generality, we can remove non-requested resources from considerations and assume $\boldsymbol{p}_j = (p_j, 1-p_j)$. Then, $\overline{\boldsymbol{p}} = (\overline{p}, n - \overline{p})$ where $\overline{p} = \sum_{j=1}^{n} p_j$, and

$$\begin{aligned}\lambda_j &= 1 + p_j\overline{p} + (1-p_j)(n-\overline{p}) - p_j^2 - (1-p_j)^2 \\ &= 1 + n - \overline{p} - n\,p_j + 2\,p_j\,\overline{p} - p_j^2 - (1-p_j)^2 \,. \end{aligned} \tag{8}$$

The result can be further simplified if the jobs are identical, i.e. $p_j = p$. Then, $\overline{p} = n\,p$ and, for any $j = 1, \ldots, n$,

$$\lambda_j = 1 + n - 2\,n\,p + 2\,n\,p^2 - p^2 - (1-p)^2 \tag{9}$$

$$= 1 + n(1 - 2\,p + p^2) + (n-1)\,p^2 - (1-p)^2 \tag{10}$$

$$= 1 + (n-1)\,\left(p^2 + (1-p)^2\right) \,. \tag{11}$$

To emphasize the convenience of the formula, we summarize the result as a theorem.

Theorem 2. *Assume 2-resource-busy identical jobs with the loading vector given by $(p, 1-p)$. Then, the dilation factors are identically given by*

$$\lambda = 1 + (n-1)\,\left(p^2 + (1-p)^2\right) \tag{12}$$

In other words, if the dilation factor is known, we can obtain the loading vector by the formula:

$$p = \frac{1}{2}\left(1 \pm \sqrt{1 - 2\frac{n-\lambda}{n-1}}\right) \quad (13)$$

PROOF. The derivation is given above. □

Notice that there are two possible solutions for p and the model does not distinguish them.

The above relation suggests a simple experimental strategy to obtain the loading vector using Algorithm 1. Notice that we can characterize jobs only from their completion times, which does not require resource monitoring or kernel instrumentation. However, by utilizing system resource monitor, we can enhance the accuracy of the model.

Algorithm 1 Constructing the loading vector of a job in 2-resource model.

1: Measure τ by running job j alone.
2: Measure T, the dilated completion time of job j when n instances of job j are running concurrently in the system.
3: Evaluate the dilation factor $\lambda_j = T/\tau$.
4: From Equation 13, obtain $p_i = \frac{1}{2}\left(1 \pm \sqrt{1 - 2\frac{n-\lambda}{n-1}}\right)$
5: Obtain loading vector $\boldsymbol{p}_j = (p_i, 1 - p_i)$

3.6 The total dilation factor

One of the potential benefits of D-factor model is the capability to extend existing schedulers for single-resource machines into schedulers for multi-resource machines. Towards this end, we define the total dilation factor $\overline{\lambda}$ by the sum of λ_j for all jobs. Then, by the formula given in Definition 1,

$$\overline{\lambda} = \sum_{j=1}^{n} \lambda_j = n + \|\overline{\boldsymbol{p}}\|_2^2 - \sum_{j=1}^{n} \|\boldsymbol{p}_j\|_2^2. \quad (14)$$

Notice, this simple formula involves only the L^2 norms of the loading vectors; informally the absolute values of the loading vectors. For details, refer to [19]. With the total loading vector, we can state a new objective function for a certain class of scheduling problems as follows:

Definition 2. Given a new job with the loading vector $\boldsymbol{p}'$, find an assignment to machine μ which minimizes

$$\boldsymbol{p}' \cdot \overline{\boldsymbol{p}}_\mu \quad (15)$$

where $\overline{\boldsymbol{p}}_\mu = \sum_{\forall j \in \mu} \boldsymbol{p}_j$ is the current total loading vector of machine-μ.

4. EXPERIMENTAL ENVIRONMENT

This section describes the experimental settings designed to validate the proposed D-factor model.

4.1 Target system overview

We experimented with clusters in two environments – native Linux and Xen-based virtualized environments [4]. Table 1 shows the detailed specifications of experimental settings for the native Linux and virtualized environment. In the native Linux environment, each node is running only one Linux operating system (OS). On the contrary, in the VM environment, each node can host multiple OS instances. The overview of the VM environment is shown in Figure 3.

Table 1: Specifications for experimental environment

CPU	Two single-core 64-bit AMD 2.4Ghz
RAM	4GB
Shared Storage	NFS (disk images for Xen)
Local Storage	Ultra320 SCSI
Network	1Gbps Ethernet, 10Gbps Infiniband
vCPU (Dom0)	Runs on both CPUs
vCPU (VMs)	Runs on one CPU
RAM/VM	256MB
I/O (VM)	Tap:aio (bypasses buffer cache of Dom-0)
Kernel	Linux 2.6.18
Hypervisor	Xen 3.4.2

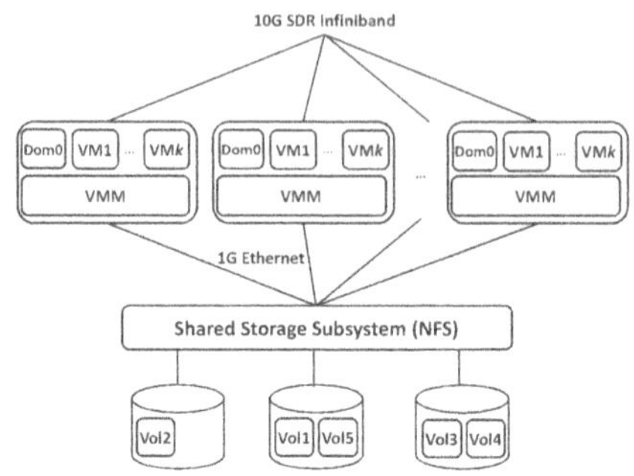

Figure 3: Virtualized experimental environment

Applications running on a virtual machine have an illusion that they exclusively access the virtualized resources. A special guest machine, Dom-0, can directly access physical resources, especially I/O devices. The Virtual Machine Monitor (VMM) manages the shared resources such as processors, memory, I/O subsystems and network devices. All the access requests to the hardware resources from applications running on a virtual machine flow into the VMM and then Dom-0, if necessary. Each node in the native Linux environment accesses local SCSI disks whereas the virtual hard disks of guest virtual machines are located in a Network File System (NFS) partition. Thus, I/O requests from guest machines may invoke network traffic. We employed varying number of applications on each node in the native Linux environment. In the VM environment, we run one application per virtual machine, but we varied the number of virtual machines.

4.2 Description of workloads

We used a mixture of synthetic and realistic workloads to validate the proposed D-factor model on a variety of workload environments. For synthetic workloads, we employed *standard jobs* (the details of which will be described later) and file compressions that use both CPU and I/O resources. For realistic workloads, we used I/O-bound workloads (FileBench [2]) and MapReduce workloads. Table 2 summarizes resource usage profile of workloads in this study.

Synthetic workloads – standard jobs and file compression. We have created standard jobs for two purposes. The first is to demonstrate that the proposed model can capture completion times of synthetic workloads using only one system resource. The second is to illustrate a method to profile workloads. *Standard job* is a workload that uses only one resource without any idle period. The completion time of a

Table 2: Resource Usage Profile of Workloads

Type	Name	CPU	I/O
Synthetic	STD-CPU	High	Low
Synthetic	STD-IO	Low	High
Synthetic	FileComp	High	Med
FileBench	FileServer	Low	High
FileBench	VarMail	High	Med
MapReduce	PiEstimator	High	Low
MapReduce	Sort	Med	Med
MapReduce	Grep	Med	Med

standard job should be consistent, provided that the standard job is running alone in the system. For example, the completion time of a standard job for disk I/O should not depend on the current size of free memory or the current status of buffer cache. In this study, we created two standard jobs – a standard job for CPU (**STD-CPU**) and a standard job for disk I/O (**STD-IO**). **STD-CPU** is a workload that repeats integer arithmetic calculations. **STD-IO** is a workload that opens two 4GB files on the local disk in the synchronous mode and, then, reads 1MB from random positions of both files, while avoiding to access the buffer cache using the POSIX library, specifically **posix_fadvise**.

We have created a workload, **FileComp** to show that we can profile a CPU-I/O workload with standard jobs. **FileComp** compresses 2,560 files, each of 256KB size. The neutral completion time of **FileComp** τ is 78.08*sec*. With **STD-CPU** of the duration of 200*sec*, the completion time of **FileComp** T is 123.67*sec*. If we assume that a system consists of two resources – CPU and I/O, we may consider **FileComp** as a two-resource-busy job. Since **STD-CPU** is a CPU-only job, the loading vector is $(CPU, IO) = (1, 0)$. Let the loading vector of **FileComp** be $\boldsymbol{p} = (p, 1-p)$. According to Property 2 in Section 3, the dilation factor $\lambda = 1 + p$. λ can be calculated by $T/\tau = 123.67/78.08 = 1.58$, which yields $p = 0.58$. Hence, the loading vector of **FileComp**, $\boldsymbol{p} = (0.58, 0.42)$. We used **FileComp** for evaluating our model in the native Linux environment. In this example, we profiled a job using standard jobs. However, it is non-trivial to implement these standard jobs due to their dependence on the system configuration. Thus, with FileBench workloads, we demonstrate an alternative way to profile a job – Algorithm 1.

Realistic workloads – FileBench and MapReduce. We experimented with FileBench in a virtualized environment. We employed two predefined workloads in FileBench, **fileserver** and **varmail**. FileBench is an application benchmark that mimics the typical behavior of workloads. We employed one FileBench workload per VM and varied the number of VMs. According to Algorithm 1, both workloads are profiled by $\boldsymbol{p}_{file} = (0.02, 0.98)$ and $\boldsymbol{p}_{mail} = (0.10, 0.90)$.

We experimented with three MapReduce workloads : **Sort**, **Grep**, and **PiEstimator** in the native Linux environment. MapReduce job consists of multiple tasks that are hosted in parallel on different cluster nodes. We run these MapReduce workloads on a dedicated 17-node native Linux cluster with Hadoop 0.20.1 [1]. Each workload generates two map-and-reduce tasks on each node. Each task accesses the local disk and exhibits insignificant communication between each other. The completion time of an application is determined by the completion time of the slowest task. For these experiments, we confirmed that the variance of completion times between tasks for one application is insignificant. Since our experimental platform consists of two single-core CPUs, increasing the number of instances of an application creates resource contention for each CPU. We conducted two experiments; (i)increasing the number of instances of each application from 1 to 4 and (ii) co-locating three different MapReduce workloads in the system. Applications are initiated at the same times and we used the Hadoop fair scheduler [1] to allocate system resources to these applications.

In order to estimate the completion times with the D-factor model, we profiled each workload with **STD-CPU**, similar to the **FileComp** workload. The loading vector, $\boldsymbol{p} = (CPU, \textit{other resources})$, and the neutral completion time, τ, of each application are $\boldsymbol{p}_{Sort} = (0.9, 0.1)$, $\tau_{Sort} = 56.0sec$, $\boldsymbol{p}_{Grep} = (0.5, 0.5)$, $\tau_{Grep} = 95.0sec$, $\boldsymbol{p}_{Pi} = (0.5, 0.5)$, $\tau_{Pi} = 90.0sec$. Then, the loading matrix is given by

$$P = \begin{bmatrix} 0.9 & 0.5 & 0.5 \\ 0.1 & 0.5 & 0.5 \end{bmatrix}.$$

Note that the loading vector represents the probability of accessing each resource instead of the utilization. Thus, resource usage does not necessarily match with the loading vector. For example, regardless of high CPU usage, some other factors may dominate the execution time of **PiEstimator**, which is captured in the loading vector representation.

Methodologies. We compare the estimated total completion time from the D-factor model and the linear sum model with actual measurements. We compare D-factor with linear sum since both methods do not require information of request arrival rate and service rate as in queuing analysis. For two jobs i and j when $\tau_i > \tau_j$, we can calculate the actual completion times of two jobs, T_i and T_j, from the dilation factors, λ_i and λ_j, obtained by $T_i = \lambda_j\tau_j + \left(1 - \frac{\lambda_j\tau_j}{\lambda_i\tau_i}\right)\tau_i$, $T_j = \lambda_j\tau_j$. Since job j finishes at $\lambda_j\tau_j < \lambda_i\tau_i$, $1 - \frac{\lambda_j\tau_j}{\lambda_i\tau_i}$ of job i will be executed without interference with job j. Similarly, we can calculate the actual completion times of more than two jobs. Note that in Remark 4, we have already discussed the difficulty of calculating completion time of jobs when jobs are partially overlapped during their executions. We believe that an efficient method for such a general case deserves a seperate effort.

What our model computes is the dilation factor, λ_j for job j, which is given by $\lambda_j = 1 + \boldsymbol{p}_j \cdot \overline{\boldsymbol{p}} - \boldsymbol{p}_j \cdot \boldsymbol{p}_j$, where $\boldsymbol{p}_j$ is the jth column vector of the loading matrix and $\overline{\boldsymbol{p}} = \boldsymbol{p}_1 + \boldsymbol{p}_2$ in the two-resource-busy model. To compute the dilation factor, we obtain the loading vector or loading matrix using either Algorithm 1 or Property 2 (Refer to Section 3).

5. MODEL VALIDATION

In this section, we validate the proposed D-factor model while illustrating the procedure to profile a job and to estimate the completion time of a job when it is co-hosted with other jobs. Experimental results in this section indicate that the D-factor model captures the behavior of each job in shared systems. The D-factor model provides (1) more accurate estimation of the completion times of co-hosted jobs than the linear sum model, (2) more efficient utilization of the system resources and (3) better predictable performance with existing scheduling algorithms than with the linear sum. Note that all numbers are averaged over 40 runs since dilation factor model actually aims to predict average completion time of jobs, not to predict variance of completion time of jobs. Numbers in parenthsis represent

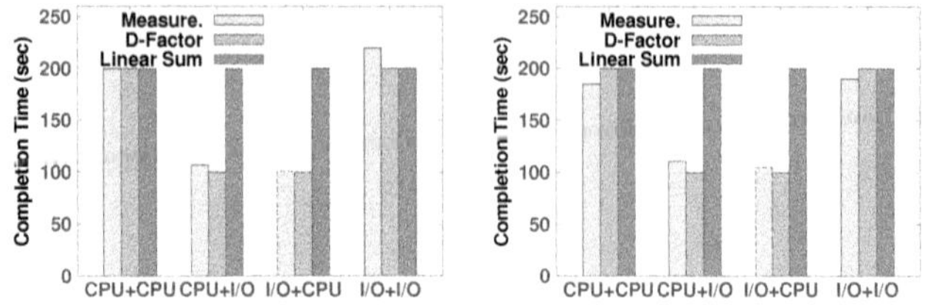

(a) Native Linux (b) Virtualized Environment

Figure 4: Experiments with standard jobs show the average errors from dilation factor are 7% for the native Linux and 10.3% for the virtualized environment. CPU represents STD-CPU and I/O represent STD-IO. We hosted two processes in (a) and two VMs in (b).

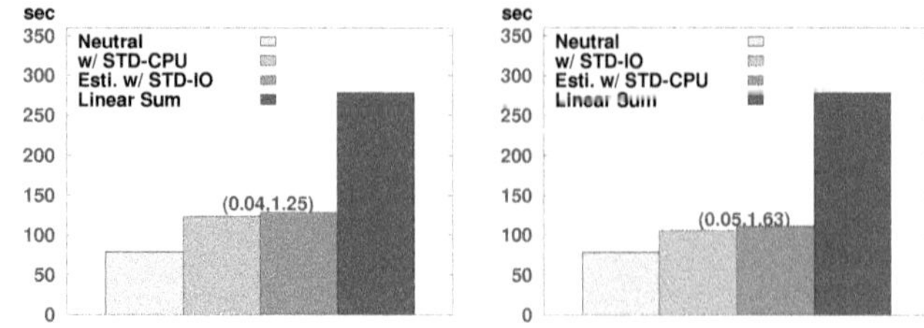

(a) FileComp with STD-CPU. (b) FileComp with STD-IO.

Figure 5: Estimated completion times of FileComp (a) using the loading vector of FileComp from measurements with STD-CPU; and (b) using the loading vector to predict the completion time with STD-IO. The numbers in parenthesis represent relative errors from D-factor and linear sum, respectively.

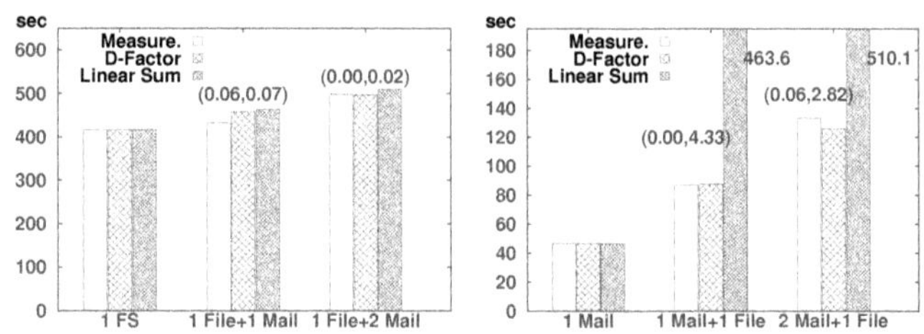

(a) fileserver (b) varmail

Figure 6: Completion times for various combinations of FileBench workloads on one physical machine with up to 3VMs. The loading vectors are obtained as to Algorithm 1.

the relative error of the estimation given by $|(\hat{T} - T)/\hat{T}|$, where $\hat{T}$ is from measurement and T is from estimation.

5.1 Synthetic workloads

Standard jobs. As shown in Figure 4, the experiments with both STD-CPU and STD-IO confirm that the proposed model estimates the slow-downs of completion times of jobs due to multiple resource contention in shared systems. Since each standard job uses only one resource, we may consider STD-CPU characterized by $\boldsymbol{p} = (1, 0)$ and STD-IO by $\boldsymbol{p} = (0, 1)$. With the given loading vectors, we obtain $\lambda = 1$ for two different standard jobs and $\lambda = 2$ for two identical standard jobs according to Theorem 1. When we set the duration of each standard job to $100sec$, the total completion time of two different standard jobs will be $100sec$ and that of two identical standard jobs will be $200sec$. Hence, we may observe that the completion time of a job in a shared multi-resource system is not linearly proportional to the completion times of individual jobs.

The gist of the dilation factor theorem is that multiple resource contention results in a non-linear waiting time, proportional to their probabilities of accessing the system resources. In contrast, the linear sum model estimates the total completion time as the linear sum of completion times of individual jobs. The linear sum fits when the system owns one resource or serves each job after completing the previously assigned jobs. Experiments from standard jobs indicate the average errors from D-factor model are 7% for the native Linux and 10.3% for the virtualized environment. However, the linear model shows a 98% error in the worst case.

Figure 4a shows completion time of each co-located workload in the native Linux (two processes) and Figure 4b for the virtualized environment (two VMs). These experiments confirm that D-factor model accurately captures the completion times of jobs with multiple shared resources in both native Linux and virtualized environments. In addition, we show that we can construct a standard job to profile workloads according to the proposed model in actual systems. However, we observe a significant error for two identical STD-IO, which is attributed to variance in disk access latencies to perform the same operations according to the sequence of access requests [31].

File compression. Now, we demonstrate that the proposed model can estimate the completion time of a workload with both CPU and disk I/O accesses, FileComp (refer to Figure 5). In these experiments, we set the duration of STD-CPU and STD-IO to $200sec$. For the loading vector of FileComp, $\boldsymbol{p} = (0.58, 0.42)$, the estimated completion time will be $78.1 \times (1 + 0.42) = 110.9sec$ since we assume that the loading vector of the I/O standard is $(0, 1)$. From actual measurements for FileComp with the I/O standard, we obtain the completion time as $105.50sec$, resulting in a 5.1% error. We have shown the accuracy of estimation from D-factor model with synthetic workloads. Next, we show the validation results with realistic workloads.

5.2 Realistic workloads

FileBench in a virtualized environment. Experimental results with FileBench are shown in Figure 6. We confirm that the D-factor model well explains the dilated completion times for collocated I/O workloads in a virtualized environment as well.

With the provided loading vectors for both workloads, we estimate the completion time as $458.1sec$ when we co-locate one varmail and one fileserver in the same physical machine, compared to $433.1sec$ with actual measurements. In this situation, we estimate the running time of varmail to be $87.62sec$, which shows an error of less than 1% with actual measurements. However, the linear model cannot estimate the completion time of each workload. With the linear model, if we consider the total completion time of all the workloads in the system as the completion time of each job, the completion time of varmail becomes $463.6sec$.

From Figure 6, we can observe that for one instance of fileserver and two instances of varmail, the respective average running times are $133.5sec$ and $498.3sec$. The corre-

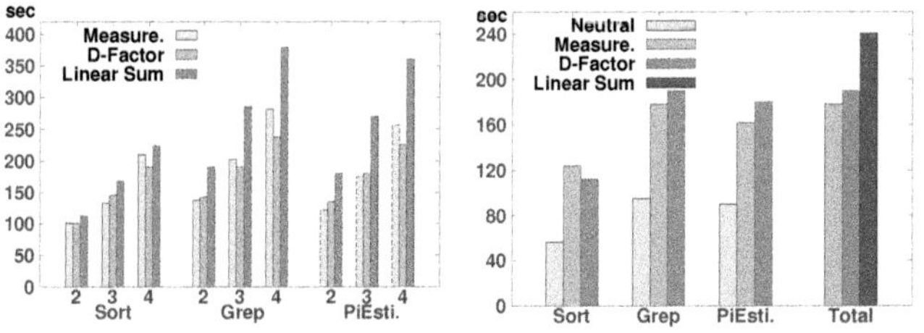

(a) Identical MapReduce (b) Heterogeneous MapReduce

Figure 7: (a) Total completion time of each MapReduce application against the number of instances. The maximal errors are 9.4% for `Sort`, 15.78% for `Grep`, and 12.1% for `PiEstimator`. (b) With the loading vectors of each of three applications, we can estimate the completion time of each hetorogeneous MapReduce application. Both experiments used a 17-node cluster.

sponding average running times from estimation are 133.48*sec* and 497.2*sec*. From the experimental results with FileBench, the estimation from the D-factor model shows 6.0% error. Next, we show more complex examples of identical MapReduce applications and heterogeneous MapReduce applications in a system.

Identical MapReduce applications. Experiments with identical mapreduce applications on a 17-node cluster demonstrate the accuracy of the D-factor model as the number of instances increases up to four. In Figure 7a, the estimation from dilation factor theorem shows 9.4% error for `Sort`, 15.78% for `Grep`, and 12.1% for `PiEstimator` in the worst case. Compared with the D-factor model, the linear model shows larger margin of errors for all the considered workloads, 26%, 38%, and 54% for `Sort`, `Grep`, and `PiEstimator`, repsectively. We observe that applications with substantial I/O accesses tend to show larger errors as we increase the number of instances in the system. We speculate that this trend stems from the variance in disk latencies similar to what we observed for `STD-IO` cases. We plan to model this behavior in future work.

Heterogeneous MapReduce applications. Figure 7b shows that the D-factor model estimates the completion times of three co-hosted MapReduce applications within 11% error. Loading vector and neutral completion time of each application remain the same as identical MapReduce experiments.

This experiment contrasts the D-factor model with the linear model in terms of the ability of estimating completion times of individual workloads when they are hosted in a shared system. The linear model accounts for the total completion time without considering the completion times of individual jobs. However, the D-factor model obtains the total completion time based upon the completion times of individual workloads. The ability to estimate completion time of each workload is practically useful in shared systems. In our experiment, we observe that `Sort` completes in about 120*sec*. Using the linear model, a new job will be scheduled to the system after all the previous workloads are completed; 241*sec* later since we cannot estimate that `Sort` will be completed before that (refer to Figure 7b). However, the D-factor model can estimate that `Sort` will be completed in 110*sec*. Thus, we may schedule another workload at 110*sec* after initiating all the applications.

We notice that the measured completion times of `Grep` and `PiEstimator` are smaller than the estimation. In this analysis, we assumed two-resource-busy jobs, which means there is no idle period in processing the given workloads and consumes only two resources. Since `Grep` and `PiEstimator` have substantial I/O activities, we may have idle wait times for completing I/O accesses. When we multiplex I/O workloads with other types of workloads, operating systems may utilize idle wait times. Thus, the completion time of `Grep` and `PiEstimator` could be smaller than the estimation when they are co-hosted. We have briefly discussed how to handle jobs with idle periods in Section 3.4 (refer to Remark 5).

To summarize, through experiments, we demonstrated that the D-factor model can estimate the total completion time of jobs when they share multiple system resources. In this section, we experimented with synthetic workloads – standard jobs and file compression as well as realistic workloads – MapReduce and FileBench. We demonstrated that the D-factor model well describes the behavior of both the native Linux and virtualized systems since the model is a high-level statistical abstraction of system behaviors. We showed that the D-factor model does not only estimate the total completion time, but also estimates the completion times of individual jobs. We can observe that the D-factor model can quantitize the performance of multiplxed workloads, given the workload profiles. Also, we showed the process to use the D-factor model to estimate the completion times of given workloads: construct standard jobs, probe the target workloads using the standard jobs, and estimates completion times of given workloads.

Experiments in this section suggest that we may predict I/O performance for cloud services [3] using the D-factor model. In the following section, we demonstrate an example for exploiting the D-factor model to enhance actual system performance with a scheduling algorithm.

6. EXTENDING SCHEDULERS FOR SINGLE RESOURCE SYSTEMS

This section describes practical benefits from the proposed D-factor model by applying it to an existing scheduling algorithm. We selected the on-line parallel machine scheduling problem [30] that addresses the problem of scheduling jobs on parallel machines without the knowledge of the sequence and the size of future jobs. This problem can be translated into the on-line bin packing problem [26], which is most widely considered in assigning virtual machines to physical machines [23,32,34]. We acknowledge that it would be challenging to apply the D-factor model to other classes of scheduling problems that consider flow control of jobs or machines such as open-shop, flow-shop, and job-shop [29] since the model assumes independent jobs.

One of the initial studies on on-line parallel machine scheduling problems is the list scheduler [14], an on-line greedy scheduler, which decides schedule S of a new job j with size p_j by

$$min \left\{ p_j + \sum_{i \in J_\mu} p_i \right\}, \forall \mu \in M \,, \qquad (16)$$

where J_μ is the set of jobs that is currently running in the machine μ and M is the set of machines. For breaking a tie, the lowest indexed machine is chosen. Although this algorithm is simple, competitive ratio of list scheduler is 2, while the best result known to date is 1.9201-competitive algo-

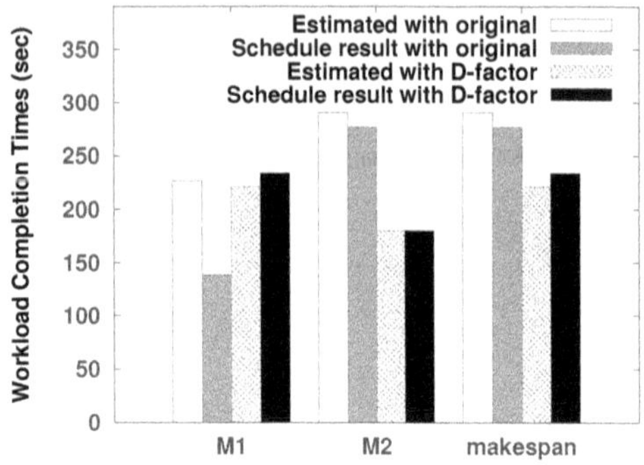

Figure 8: Adopting D-factor as objective function in Graham's on-line scheduler [14] shortens the makespan by 20.5%, compared with the original algorithm.

Table 3: Job profiles for the scheduling example.

workload	completion time	loading vector
W_1	110.56 sec	(1,0)
W_2	115.83 sec	(0,1)
W_3	180.0 sec	(1,0)
W_4	110.56 sec	(1,0)

rithm for deterministic algorithms [12] and 1.58-competitive algorithm for randomized algorithms [7]. Thus, we selected this algorithm to demonstrate the performance enhancement by adopting the D-factor model in scheduling algorithms, though we do not claim any theoretical improvements in scheduling problems.

Here, we created four jobs using synthetic workloads, `STD-CPU` and `STD-IO`, which run on two machines on the same experimental platform described in Section 4. We consider a situation that three jobs (W_1, W_2, W_3) are already in the system and a new job, W_4, arrives at the system $60sec$ later. The size, completion time and loading vector, of each job are shown in Table 3. Experimental results shown in Figure 8 demonstrate that the makespan with D-factor is 20.5% shorter than that with the original list scheduler, which is a significant enhancement since the theoretical lower bound of deterministic on-line parallel machine scheduling problem is 1.88-competitive [25], which is a 12% enhancement (1.88 compared to 2). However, with the multi-resource contention model, performance enhancement may exceed the theoretical bound for single-resource machines.

Let us explain the rationale behind this performance improvement. The original list scheduler schedules the first three jobs as follows:

$$\begin{array}{lll} Machine1 & : W_1 \quad W_2 & (226.4sec) \\ Machine2 & : W_3 & (180.0sec)' \end{array}$$

where the numbers in the parenthesis represent estimated completion times of jobs in each machine. When the fourth job, W4 with job size of $p_4 = 110.56sec$, arrives $60sec$ later, list scheduler schedules the fourth job to Machine 2, expecting $180.0 + 110.56sec$ of total completion time. Thus,

$$\begin{array}{lll} Machine1 & : W_1 \quad W_2 & (226.39sec) \\ Machine2 & : W_3 \quad W_4 & (290.56sec)' \end{array}$$

By augmenting the objective function (Equation 16) to Equation 15, we can use vector-valued size, loading vectors. Then, the list scheduler with loading vectors schedules the first three jobs as follows:

$$\begin{array}{lll} Machine1 & : W_1 \quad W_2 & (\overline{p} = (1,1), 115.83sec) \\ Machine2 & : W_3 & (\overline{p} = (1,0), 180.0sec)' \end{array}$$

where $\overline{p}$ is the total loading vector and the numbers are estimated total completion times based upon D-factor model. Notice that, for the same configuration of machine 1, the estimated completion time with D-factor model is $115.83sec$, compared to $226.4sec$ with the original list scheduler based upon linear sum. Actual measurement of this schedule was $138.65sec$, which confirms that the D-factor model provides better estimation of total completion time. This will lead to a contrasting schedule when W_4 arrives $60sec$ later. For W_4 with $\boldsymbol{p}_4 = (1,0)$, the schedule becomes

$$\begin{array}{lll} Machine1 & : W_1 \quad W_2 \quad W_4 & (\overline{p} = (2,1), 221.2sec) \\ Machine2 & : W_3 & (\overline{p} = (1,0), 180.0sec)' \end{array}$$

which results in 20.5% enhancement in makespan.

In this example, we demonstrated that the same scheduling algorithm may show significant performance gain by evaluating the total completion time of candidate schedules with the D-factor model. In general, we can expect better scheduling results with the D-factor model when workloads access multiple resources and they are independent since the D-factor model considers multiple resources contention among independent jobs. In order to consider multiple resources in a system, we may consider other types of scheduling problems such as open-shop, flow-shop, or job-shop scheduling problems. Instead, the D-factor model can augment existing on-line parallel machine scheduling algorithms that assume a machine as one resource, to consider multiple resources in a machine. Hence, when a system uses on-line parallel machine scheduler or on-line bin packing algorithms, we could augment the system without significant changes in software/hardware to reduce the makespan of workloads.

7. RELATED WORK

Despite the importance of estimating dilation factor of each co-located job for providing predictable performance in shared environments, there is no established generic approach to estimate dilation factor of workloads in shared envionments [13, 20]. The main difficulty to estimate the dilation factor of each job is that it depends on the behavior of co-located jobs, which is often described as non-deterministic behavior [17] and a critical problem in Cloud platforms [3].

As an attempt to estimate dilation factor, Govindan *et al.* [13] and Mars *et al.* [20] proposed an empirical method for sharing memory subsystems. Especially, Mars *et al.* demonstrated that they could predict dilation factors up to three co-located Google's workloads in Google's infrastructure. Both studies created a probe program to measure the sensitivity of each workload for sharing memory/cache. Based upon the empirical sensitivity analysis, they estimated slow-down of workloads with different co-located workloads. With our model, both works can be considered as an example of two-resource busy model to express the slow-down of co-located applications. Their concepts of sensitivity of each application and pressure on shared resources are captured in our statistical job characteristics – loading vector. In addition, we suggested probe jobs for other resources such as CPU and disk I/O. We believe that loading vector can be constructed using probe jobs in [13, 20] in order to consider spatial characteristics of memory systems.

The closest problem setting to our model is the bin packing problem, specifically the multi-bin packing problem. Bin packing problem finds a solution to pack items into single or multiple bins so as to minimize the number of bins used [8]. In the bin packing problem, the total size of packed items is the linear sum of the sizes of individual items. However, this study mentions that obtaining the actual size of all the packed items might be smaller than the total size of each item. In multi-bin packing, we model bins and the sizes of items as vectors, but it does not consider the contention across resources when we place items to bins. Thus, it cannot express the non-linearity of dilation factors of workloads in shared environments. Since most of prior virtual machine placement methods are based upon on-line bin packing algorithms [23, 32, 34] or similar linear relations [15], they are inherently difficult to reflect non-linear slow-down of a job due to multiple resource contention.

Unlike the prior work, we provide a model that can predict the performance of applications in shared environments. With mixed workloads in data centers, we can achieve more graceful performance degradation [10, 22]. In addition, the issue raised from I/O-bound work in [3] implies that we need to consider the importance of multiple resource requests in processing a job. Therefore, we proposed a performance model that estimates the performance impact on a job by other collocated jobs running together in a server.

8. CONCLUSIONS

In this study, we derived a novel completion time model of jobs for shared service systems. We estimate the completion time of jobs on a system by considering that multiple shared resources may be involved to process a job. The resource usage of a job is represented by a loading vector, which in turn is used to estimate the dilation in individual job completion times. Based upon the proposed model, we profiled a job and estimate the overall completion time of jobs in shared service systems. In contrast to queuing theory based models that require parameters of each resource such as service rates and request arrival rates, the D-factor model only needs to the completion times to profile a job, from which the model can estimate the completion times of co-located jobs. We validate the proposed D-factor model with experiments using synthetic and real workloads. From the validation results using synthetic workloads, the average relative errors are 7% in the native Linux environment and 10.3% in a VM environment. With realistic workloads, the D-factor model also predicts the completion time of co-existing workloads within a 16% error.Also, we presented an example to extend a scheduler based upon single-resource model, which reduces the makespan by 20.5%.

Calculating the overall completion times of the assigned jobs is the fundamental operation in designing or evaluating a scheduling algorithm. We can use the D-factor model to estimate the completion time more accurately or conveniently than previous models. The required overhead is to find the loading vector of a job to obtain the expected total completion time. As described in section 3, we can obtain the loading vectors by comparing the total completion time of multiple instances of identical jobs with the neutral completion time of the job. One of the assumptions made in this study is that the resource access pattern of each job is independent to each other. Otherwise, we cannot easily calculate the probability of the resource contention by the inner product of loading vectors.

Since sharing multiple resources among jobs is a common practice in computing systems, we can find a plenty of applications for the proposed D-factor model. Some of possible applications are as follows: Estimating the total completion time of jobs when we have heterogeneous processors such as CPU and GPU might be possible. CPUs and GPUs can be treated as different types of resources to be shared among jobs and the total completion time of a job depends on the portion of accessing times of each processor. Similarly, when we have multiple layers of caches and want to find the total completion time of a job, we can apply the D-factor model.

Although we successfully demonstrated the potential of D-factor model, several diretions are possible to further enhance the D-factor model. These include:

- Extending the model for the space-shared resources like memory systems: the working set behavior of each co-located job will modify the loading vector of each job. In order to use the model for the space-shared resources, we need to establish a model that identifies the modifier of the loading vector of each job due to the working set behavior. The authors believe such an extention can consider in-processor cache and shared system memory, which will make the D-factor model more useful in modern many-core environments.
- An algorithm to compute the dilation factor for n partially overlapped jobs: this can be discussed in the context of job scheduling since the initialization and completion of jobs are dependent on job schedulers. As breifly mentioned in the section 6, developing a job scheduler with the D-factor model is one of the eventual goals of this study.
- Overcoming the dependency of the loading vector of a job on the measured platform: since the loading vector of a job is obtained from measurements, it is dependent on a specific hardware-operating system combination. However, the D-factor model requires relatively smaller effort than prior analytical models. One possible direction to work around this would be a method to convert the loading vector of a job in one system to other systems.

In a sense, although the proposed D-factor model is not the most perfect model to explain shared resource contention, the model provides an insight to understand contention for multiple shared resources. In addition, the D-factor model allows to extend many existing scheduling algorithms for single resources into scheduling algorithms for multiple resources.

9. ACKNOWLEDGMENTS

We thank to the shepherd Xiaoyun Zhu of VMware Inc. and the anonymous reviewers for their detailed comments that improved the quality of this paper.

This research was supported in part by NSF grants CNS-0721479, CNS-1152449, and CCF-1147388. This manuscript has been authored by UT-Battelle, LLC, under contract DE-AC05-00OR22725 with the U.S. Department of Energy. The United States Government retains and the publisher, by accepting the article for publication, acknowledges that the United States Government retains a non-exclusive, paid-up, irrevocable, world-wide license to publish or reproduce the published form of this manuscript, or allow others to do so, for United States Government purposes. This research used resources of the Center for Computational Sciences at Oak Ridge National Laboratory, which is supported by the Office of Science of the U.S. Department of Energy under Contract No. DE-AC05-00OR22725.

10. REFERENCES

[1] Apache Hadoop. http://hadoop.apache.org.

[2] FileBench. http://www.solarisinternals.com/wiki/index.php/FileBench.

[3] Michael Armbrust, Armando Fox, Rean Griffith, Anthony D. Joseph, Randy Katz, Andy Konwinski, Gunho Lee, David Patterson, Ariel Rabkin, Ion Stoica, and Matei Zaharia. A view of cloud computing. *Commun. of the ACM*, 53(4), 2010.

[4] Paul Barham, Boris Dragovic, Keir Fraser, Steven Hand, Tim Harris, Alex Ho, Rolf Neugebauer, Ian Pratt, and Andrew Warfield. Xen and the art of virtualization. In *SOSP*, 2003.

[5] Ramazan Bitirgen, Engin Ipek, and Jose F. Martinez. Coordinated management of multiple interacting resources in chip multiprocessors: A machine learning approach. In *MICRO*, 2008.

[6] N. Bobroff, A. Kochut, and K. Beaty. Dynamic placement of virtual machines for managing SLA violations. In *10th IFIP/IEEE International Symposium on Integrated Network Management*, 2007.

[7] Bo Chen, AndrÃľ van Vliet, and Gerhard J. Woeginger. A lower bound for randomized on-line scheduling algorithms. *Information Processing Letters*, 51(5), 1994.

[8] E. G. Coffman, Jr., M. R. Garey, and D. S. Johnson. *Approximation algorithms for bin packing: a survey.* PWS Publishing Co., Boston, MA, USA, 1997.

[9] Peter J. Denning. The working set model for program behavior. *Commun. of the ACM*, 11(5):323–333, 1968.

[10] Xiaobo Fan, Wolf-Dietrich Weber, and Luiz Andre Barrose. Power provisioning for a warehouse-sized computer. In *ISCA '07*.

[11] Alexandra Fedorova, Sergey Blagodurov, and Sergey Zhuravlev. Managing contention for shared resources on multicore processors. *Commun. of the ACM*, 2010.

[12] Rudolf Fleischer and Michaela Wahl. Online scheduling revisited. In *Algorithms - ESA 2000*. 2000.

[13] Sriram Govindan, Jie Liu, Aman Kansal, and Anand Sivasubramaniam. Cuanta: Quantifying effects of shared on-chip resource interference for consolidated vitual machines. In *ACM SOCC*, 2011.

[14] R.L. Graham. Bounds on multiprocessing timing anomalies. *SIAM Journal on Applied Mathematics*, 17(2):416–429, 1969.

[15] Fabien Hermenier, Xavier Lorca, Jean-Marc Menaud, Gilles Muller, and Julia Lawall. Entropy: a consolidation manager for clusters. In *VEE*, 2009.

[16] Kenneth Hoste, Aashish Phansalkar, Lieven Eeckout, Andy Georges, Lizy K. John, and Koen De Bosschere. Performance prediction based on inherent program similarity. In *PACT*, 2006.

[17] Ravi Iyer, Li Zhao, Fei Guo, Ramesh Illikkal, Srihari Makineni, Don Newell, Yan Solihin, Lisa Hsu, and Steve Reinhardt. Qos policies and architecture for cache/memory in cmp platforms. In *ACM SIGMETRICS*, 2007.

[18] Younggyun Koh, R. Knauerhase, P. Brett, M. Bowman, Zhihua Wen, and C. Pu. An analysis of performance interference effects in virtual environments. In *ISPASS*, 2007.

[19] Seung-Hwan Lim, Jae-Seok Huh, Youngjae Kim, Galen M. Shipman, and Chita R. Das. A quantitative analysis of performance of shared service systems with multiple resource contention. Technical Report CSE-10-010, The Pennsylvania State University, 2010.

[20] Jason Mars, Lingjia Tang, Robert Hundt, Kevin Skadron, and Mary Lou Soffa. Bubble-up: Increasing utilization in modern warehouse scale computers via sensible co-locations. In *Micro*, 2011.

[21] D.A. Menasce. Two-level iterative queuing modeling of software contention. In *10th IEEE MASCOTS*, 2002.

[22] Xiaoqiao Meng, Canturk Isci, Jeffrey Kephart, Li Zhang, Eric Bouillet, and Dimitrios Pendarakis. Efficient resource provisioning in compute clouds via vm multiplexing. In *ICAC*, 2010.

[23] Xiaoqiao Meng, Vasileios Pappas, and Li Zhang. Improving the scalability of data center networks with traffic-aware virtual machine placement. In *INFOCOM*, 2010.

[24] Ripal Nathuji, Aman Kansal, and Alireza Ghaffarkhah. Q-clouds: managing performance interference effects for qos-aware clouds. In *Eurosys*, 2010.

[25] III Rudin, John F., and R. Chandrasekaran. Improved bounds for the online scheduling problem. *SIAM J. Comput.*, 32:717–735, March 2003.

[26] Peter Sanders, Naveen Sivadasan, and Martin Skutella. Online scheduling with bounded migration. *Mathematics of Operations Research*, 34(2), 2009.

[27] Akbar Sharifi, Shekhar Srikantaiah, Asit K. Mishra, Mahmut Kandemir, and Chita R. Das. Mete: meeting end-to-end qos in multicores through system-wide resource management. In *ACM SIGMETRICS*, 2011.

[28] Bikash Sharma, Victor Chudnovsky, Joseph Hellerstein Rasekh Rifaat, and Chita R. Das. Modeling and synthesizing task placement constraints in google computer clusters. In *ACM SOCC*, 2011.

[29] D. B. Shmoys, Clifford Stein, and Joel Wein. Improved approximation algorithms for shop scheduling problems. *The second annual ACM-SIAM symposium on discrete algorithms*, 1991.

[30] D.B. Shmoys, J. Wein, and D.P. Williamson. Scheduling parallel machines on-line. *IEEE Symposium on Foundations of Computer Science*, 1991.

[31] Elizabeth Shriver, Arif Merchant, and John Wilkes. An analytic behavior model for disk drives with readahead caches and request reordering. In *ACM SIGMETRICS*, 1998.

[32] Aameek Singh, Madhukar Korupolu, and Dushmanta Mohapatra. Server-storage virtualization: integration and load balancing in data centers. In *SC '08*.

[33] ENERGY STAR Program U.S. Environmental Protection Agency. EPA report to congress on server and data center energy efficiency, August 2007.

[34] Akshat Verma, Gargi Dasgupta, Tapan Kumar Nayak, Pradipta De, and Ravi Kothari. Server workload analysis for power minimization using consolidation. In *USENIX Annual Technical Conference*, 2009.

[35] Matthew Wachs, Lianghong Xu, Arkady Kanevsky, and Gregory R. Ganger. Exertion-based billing for cloud storage access. In *HotCloud*, 2011.

ADP: Automated Diagnosis of Performance Pathologies Using Hardware Events

Wucherl Yoo, Kevin Larson, †Lee Baugh, Sangkyum Kim, Roy H. Campbell
Department of Computer Science, University of Illinois at Urbana-Champaign, †Intel Corp.
{wyoo5, klarson5, kim71, rhc}@illinois.edu, †lee.w.baugh@intel.com

ABSTRACT

Performance characterization of applications' hardware behavior is essential for making the best use of available hardware resources. Modern architectures offer access to many hardware events that are capable of providing information to reveal architectural performance bottlenecks throughout the core and memory hierarchy. These events can provide programmers with unique and powerful insights into the causes of the resource bottlenecks in their applications. However, interpreting these events has been a significant challenge. We present an automated system that uses machine learning to identify an application's performance problems. Our system provides programmers with insights about the performance of their applications while shielding them from the onerous task of digesting hardware events. It uses a decision tree algorithm, random forests on our micro-benchmarks to fingerprint the performance problems. Our system divides a profiled application into functions and automatically classifies each function by the dominant hardware resource bottlenecks. Using the classifications from the hotspot functions, we were able to achieve an average speedup of 1.73 from three applications in the PARSEC benchmark suite. Our system provides programmers with a guideline of where, what, and how to fix the detected performance problems in applications, which would have otherwise required considerable architectural knowledge.

Categories and Subject Descriptors

C.4 [**Performance of Systems**]: Measurement techniques, Modeling techniques, Performance attributes; D.0 [**Software**]: General

Keywords

Performance analysis, micro-benchmark, fingerprint, resource bottleneck, hardware event, machine learning

1. INTRODUCTION

The performance of applications can be negatively affected by two phenomena: poor selection of algorithms and inefficient usage of hardware resources. Although both algorithmic and hardware-oriented performance tuning can be essential to improve performance, many programmers have overlooked hardware-oriented performance tuning. This tendency has been encouraged by a long-standing and powerful trend of hardware abstraction. For instance, where once programmers had to be keenly aware of their program's memory usage or the underflow of their computations, now they can assume practically unbounded virtual memory and significant accuracy for very small numerical values. Many of the underlying hardware's resource limitations and design tradeoffs are made intentionally opaque to simplify the job of programmers. Seemingly suitable programs can run correctly, but may suffer from hidden hardware bottlenecks that can severely hinder performance. We have coined the term hardware *performance pathologies*, which we define as program-level behaviors that encounter hardware resource bottlenecks. Traditional identification of these pathologies involved much guesswork and time-consuming experimentation. The present hardware trends moving towards multi-core machines with more elaborate interconnects and memory hierarchies only exacerbate this challenge.

Modern microprocessors provide hardware events that had been primarily intended for processor verification. These events provide low level details about architectural components such as the core pipelines, execution units, memory hierarchy, and interconnects. These events can provide insights into how a program's execution utilizes hardware resources and provide opportunities to detect resource bottlenecks. However, it is challenging for developers to directly use these hardware events for performance tuning. We identify five major reasons for this:

- **Lack of standardization.** Different manufacturers, and even different product lines from the same manufacturer, have offered significantly different sets of hardware events.
- **Poor documentation / validation.** Historically, the hardware events have not been well documented, or have been documented at an inaccessible level to most users. In addition, they have not been well validated.
- **Inadequate tools.** Historically, the tools supporting hardware-monitoring-based performance tuning have been paltry for all but architectural experts.
- **Lack of micro-architectural knowledge.** Significant micro-architectural understanding has generally been required to understand and interpret the hardware events.

For these reasons, using the raw hardware events does not - and perhaps cannot - provide an effective performance tuning solution for most programmers. We argue that a more effective approach to hardware performance tuning would be *pathology-based*, in which programmers profile their applications using hardware events but receive user-friendly feedback in terms of the performance pathologies that their code exhibits. For example, a function could be described as having 'inefficient memory accesses on large working set', instead of the raw event data, which might appear as, 'a MEM_LOAD_RETIRED.LLC_MISS count of 793,320,000'. In this paper, we present a system, *ADP* (Automated Diagnosis of Performance pathology), which can automatically analyze and discover patterns of hardware events and identify those patterns in applications as user-understandable program-level performance pathologies.

Our mechanism relies on the notion of *hardware event fingerprints*. Suppose that there exists a hardware-related performance pathology, which significantly affects performance during an interval of some application's execution. This execution consequently incurs a significant change in the values of those predominant hardware events associated with the pathology. We have observed that different executions, which suffer from the same hardware pathology, tend to have similar patterns of predominant hardware events; we call these patterns of events that mark a performance pathology its *fingerprint*. In Section 5, we show that these fingerprints can reliably identify pathologies resident in well-known applications. In order to generate these fingerprints, we build micro-benchmarks that exhibit the presence or absence of particular performance pathologies.[1] We currently employ 10 micro-benchmarks, each of which codifies and represents a single known pathology. Factoring in the existence or lack of a pathology of each micro-benchmark and three working set size labels (for the 5 memory-bound micro-benchmarks), there are presently 40 pathology labels.

In order to classify the performance pathologies characterized by these fingerprints, we use a machine learning mechanism, decision tree classification. ADP has two phases: the *training phase* and the *classification phase*. In the training phase, decision trees are trained by the profiled measurements of hardware events generated by our micro-benchmarks. ADP profiles the micro-benchmarks by collecting a selected subset of hardware events identified as significant by correlation-based feature selection (CFS) [17]. We call this subset the *key events*. Once the key events for the execution have been collected, ADP splits the profiled events from the micro-benchmarks into segments representing durations of the execution. We refer to these segments as *time-slices*. Each time-slice is a vector comprised of aggregated event counts, and shares a pathology label determined by the intended pathological behavior. These time-slices are used as the training data set for constructing the decision trees. After the trained decision trees are constructed, they can classify pathology labels from the vectors of key events.

In the classification phase, ADP uses the decision trees from the training phase in order to detect performance pathologies exhibited by the functions of target applications. It measures the same key events used in the training phase by executing target applications. Then, it aggregates the measured events by grouping them by the functions of the applications. We refer to these segments as *function-slices*. For each function-slice, ADP uses the decision trees to assign a pathology label that represents their behaviors. The underlying intuition is that similar patterns of events occur if both the application and the micro-benchmark are exposed to the same hardware resource bottleneck. If the label of a function-slice is classified to be a *pathological* case, ADP directs programmers to the function responsible and provides suggestions to resolve the pathology. To study the effectiveness of our decision trees against frequently used applications, we experiment with the subset of the SPEC CPU2006 integer and floating-point benchmarks [19] written in C and C++, and the PARSEC benchmarks [3] as target applications. The applications from both benchmarks represent a set of well-known single-threaded applications, parallel applications, and scientific simulation applications.

We present an automated system, ADP that can fingerprint and detect the performance pathologies of applications. ADP is designed to identify hardware resource bottlenecks within a single machine. It supports both serial and parallel applications. However, bottlenecks involving OS-level resources or network interactions are not yet supported, e.g., lock contention, or the delay of web services. The micro-benchmarks characterize a variety of common patterns of bottlenecks in the memory hierarchy and the CPU resources. It is challenging for developers to use well-known machine learning tools on hardware events due to the large number of hardware events, noises from sampling, dependencies of hardware resources, and various behaviors of applications. Our contributions are:

- **Constructed micro-benchmarks.** The micro-benchmarks characterize the presence or lack of hardware performance pathologies.
- **Automated key event selection.** ADP can automatically select key events regardless of their standardization, documentation, or validation.
- **Automated pathology classification.** ADP can classify pathology labels from the profiled functions of a target application. This label can provide developers with high-level optimization suggestions without requiring the analysis of raw hardware events or knowledge of hardware architectures.

Section 2 introduces previous research. Section 3 describes attribute selection algorithms and decision tree algorithms. Section 4 demonstrates our system, ADP detecting the performance pathologies from the applications of the benchmarks. Section 5 shows how our system works by analyzing the identified cases of the performance pathologies and Section 6 concludes.

2. RELATED WORKS

Modern processors provide hardware events that are helpful for determining the performance of applications [8]. Oprofile [23] samples the hardware events; however it can only collect a limited number of events simultaneously. Similar to the work of Azimi et al. [2], Intel VTune Amplifier XE [21] supports *multiplexing* the performance monitoring hardware, which allows it to effectively collect an arbitrary number of hardware events. It also supports statistical event sampling, which allows estimated event counts to be associated with specific code contexts such as functions. Extending our previous work [44], we present ADP, an automated system that fingerprints the pathological patterns of hardware events and identifies them in applications.

Bitirgen et al. [4] present a framework that manages shared resources on chip multiprocessors. Their framework uses a machine learning mechanism to formulate a predictive model of the resource allocation. Curtis-Maury et al. [12] propose an online power-performance prediction model built around the identification of parallel application execution phases. Heath et al. [18] use hardware events to manage thermal emergencies in server clusters by emulating temperature. Stoess et al. [38] present a power management framework using hardware events in a virtualized environment. Schneider et al. [35] use hardware events for adaptive optimizations in compilers and runtime systems. Ould-Ahmed-Vall et al. [28] use regression model trees to predict CPI using hardware events. Shen et al. [36] use hardware events to construct a model of user requests of a concurrent server environment. Xu et al. [43] use

[1]These micro-benchmarks are written, if possible, in a high-level language. This ensures that the performance pathology is expressible at the program level, rather than the micro-architectural level; it also provides a reference sample of the pathology for programmers to use to better understand and resolve the performance pathology.

data mining to analyze console logs in order to detect anomalies in large-scale systems.

Vetter [41] proposes to use a decision tree trained from micro-benchmarks to identify Message Passing Interface (MPI) specific performance problems. He uses instrumentation mechanisms to trace the performance data of MPI applications. Paradyn [33] automates instrumentation and diagnoses bottlenecks in parallel applications such as waiting in MPI communication. Casas et al. [10] propose signal processing techniques to automatically identify phases and structures of MPI applications. They use the instrumentation environment of Paraver [29] to gather execution traces from MPI applications. Böhme et al. [13] present an automatic mechanism which performs instrumentation during compilation in order to identify the causes of waiting periods in MPI applications. When compared with hardware event sampling, instrumentation mechanisms [24] have much greater effects on the execution of applications and cause more overhead. As the hardware event collection mechanisms of ADP are separate from the main execution hardware, events can be collected at nearly full execution speed, without the overhead of instrumentation mechanisms.

Paraver [29], VAMPIR [27], Jumpshot [45], PAPI [7] Perfsuite [22], and Paradyn [33] provide performance data collection and visualizations to identify performance bottlenecks such as MPI communication inefficiencies. Tau [37] supports monitoring parallel applications by automatically inserting instrumentation routines. Performance tuning tools such as Oprofile [23] and Intel VTune [21] profile hardware events and visualize them. While these tools help architectural experts and developers find performance problems, in order to analyze the information they provide, significant manual interpretation is required. ADP imposes no instrumentation overhead.

Periscope [15], Perfexpert [9], and HPCToolkit [1] are automated tools that detect performance bottlenecks in parallel applications using hardware events. Perfexpert [9] also suggests solutions for the detected bottlenecks. In addition, HPCToolkit [1] also uses compiler data to suggest source modifications for parallel applications. The detection mechanisms from these tools are heavily dependent on manually created metrics and rules. In addition, these tools are mostly targeted at MPI and OpenMP based parallel applications. ADP can complement these tools to diagnose and classify hardware resource bottlenecks.

3. PRELIMINARIES

3.1 Attribute Selection

Correlation-based Feature selection (CFS) [17] is a scheme that searches subsets of attributes (hardware events in ADP) by selecting those highly correlated with classes (represented by pathology labels) and those less inter-correlated with each other. CFS uses a heuristic based on the hypothesis that good attributes have high correlation with classes and less inter-correlation with each other [16]. The "merit" heuristic of an attribute subset S containing k attributes, is defined as

$$Merit_S = \frac{k \cdot \overline{r_{ca}}}{\sqrt{k + (k-1) \cdot \overline{r_{aa}}}} \quad (1)$$

where $\overline{r_{ca}}$ is the average attribute-class correlation, and $\overline{r_{aa}}$ is the average attribute-attribute inter-correlation. By this heuristic, CFS discards irrelevant attributes as they have low correlation with the classes. In addition, CFS discards redundant attributes as they have high inter-correlation with the other attributes. For the numeric valued event data, CFS discretizes them using a mechanism suggested by Fayyad and Irani [14]. CFS iterates through subsets of attributes to find the subset with a local maximum for the "merit" heuristic in Equation 1. We use the best-first search method [42], which considers local changes by adding or removing an event to the current subset in order to find a better subset with a higher "merit". If the path being explored looks less promising, the search can backtrack to a more promising previous subset.

3.2 Decision Tree

The decision tree algorithm is a machine learning technique used for classification where patterns of input attribute vectors are analyzed to create a predictive model. A decision tree consists of non-leaf nodes that represent tests of attributes (hardware events in ADP), branches between nodes that represent the outcomes of the tests, and leaf nodes that hold the class labels (pathology labels). Constructing the most optimal and accurate decision tree is usually NP-hard for a given set of class-labeled training attribute vectors [20] [32]. To construct a decision tree, most practical algorithms use a greedy approach with heuristics such as *information gain* [30] or *gain ratio* [31]. Using a heuristic, the training set is recursively partitioned into smaller subsets. Random forests [6] consist of multiple decision trees that are constructed by randomly chosen attributes with a predefined size s. The random forests classify a label by voting. Because of the law of large numbers, random forests do not overfit as more trees are added. Additionally, the generalization error converges to a limited value.

In our case, the purpose of constructing a decision tree from the training dataset is to iteratively select the event with the highest splitting criterion for the classification of pathology labels. In this iteration, the best splitting threshold for this event is also chosen. This selected event minimizes the information needed to classify the data in the resulting partitions of datasets and reflects the least randomness in these partitions.

4. ADP

We have built an automated system, ADP, which models, detects, and provides suggestions of how to fix performance pathologies. ADP provides the programmer with an automated and intuitive assessment of the software, using profiled hardware events that are characterized as 40 different labels. Additionally, it provides a comprehensive analysis and requires less effort than manual approaches. ADP is suitable where one does not need to know what the specific architectural events mean, but wants to detect specific performance problems.

Figure 1 shows the procedures for experts and users to use ADP. In order to provide reference samples of performance pathologies with which to construct the decision trees, we codify performance pathologies as micro-benchmarks, which are specifically implemented to expose a particular hardware resource bottleneck or a set of related resource bottlenecks. The execution of each pathological micro-benchmark produces a characteristic pattern of the hardware events by repeatedly stressing a set of hardware resources; ADP then extracts the fingerprints from these patterns of events and uses them to formulate decision trees that model the relationship between the hardware events and the performance pathologies. Then, the decision trees can diagnose target applications according to the fingerprints of the pathologies. ADP features the *training phase* for experts and the *classification phase* for users; we describe each in Section 4.1 and Section 4.2.

4.1 Training Phase

The procedures of the training phase are shown in Figure 1.(a)$\sim$(d). In this phase, ADP:

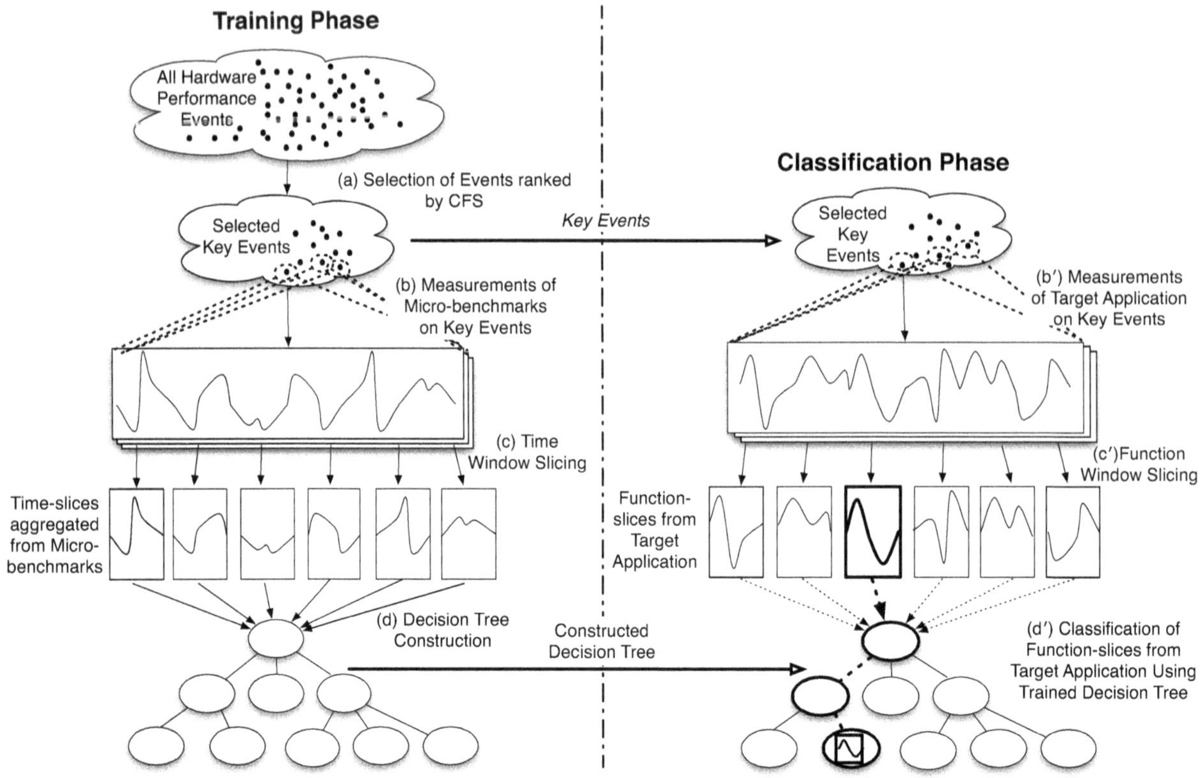

Figure 1: ***The Processing Flow.*** **(a) The pathology-bearing micro-benchmarks are profiled to determine the most relevant events (*key events*). (b) They are profiled again, measruing only the key events. (c) The profiled results are divided into time-slices. (d) The time-slices are used to construct decision trees. (b′) To identify those pathologies in the target application, the key events are measured during the execution of the application. (c′) The measured events are divided into function-slices. (d′) Each function-slice is compared in the decision trees to identify the most relevant pathology.**

1. Codifies hardware performance pathologies in micro-benchmarks that strongly and consistently exhibit those pathologies
2. Measures all the available hardware events from profiling runs of the micro-benchmarks and uses CFS analysis to select the key events that are most highly correlated (either negatively or positively) with performance (Figure 1.a);
3. Measures the key events from profiling runs of the micro-benchmarks (Figure 1.b);
4. Divides the resulting profile into time-slices (Figure 1.c); and
5. Uses those time-slices to construct decision trees that can classify the performance pathologies. (Figure 1.d);

4.1.1 Micro-benchmarks

The training phase of ADP begins with the construction of micro-benchmarks in order to characterize known performance pathologies. Using the micro-benchmarks, ADP measures every hardware event from their runs. The measurement of hardware events imposes nearly no overhead and results in no perturbation of execution. Table 1 describes some of the micro-benchmarks. We use 10 micro-benchmarks that provide 40 different combinations of labels. Each micro-benchmark fingerprints pathological and non-pathological patterns from one or more resource bottlenecks. Separate labels from the same micro-benchmark fingerprint those different patterns. We believe that current set of our micro-benchmarks covers the most common hardware resource bottlenecks related to CPU and memory subsystems in our environments. However, this set is not complete and micro-benchmarks can be added to improve this coverage, e.g., a micro-benchmark to characterize Non-Uniform Memory Access (NUMA). Our analysis and automated mechanisms are based on the combinations of labels with many profiled hardware events. Thus, the diagnosis of the performance pathologies involves a large search space that requires considerable effort. The purpose of the micro-benchmarks is not to characterize the most complex and obscure performance problems, but to present simple abstractions to help automate hardware performance tuning for average programmers. The micro-benchmarks provide reference samples of performance pathologies based on the fingerprints of their predominant hardware events. The fingerprinted pathologies also help programmers understand their code and resolve the detected pathologies.

Each micro-benchmark features an initialization phase and an execution phase. The initialization phase sets up any data the execution may require. The execution phase actually exhibits the pathology and can be executed repeatedly in order to provide whatever execution duration is required. As we are only interested in this execution phase, we filter out any execution pertaining to the initialization in the event measurements. Each micro-benchmark is designed to codify at least a representative pathology as well as the *lack* of that pathology, while otherwise keeping the execution as similar as possible. For example, a micro-benchmark encoding the branch misprediction pathology can be configured to produce two nearly-identical execution streams whose only significant differences are whether the branches are mostly predicted by the branch predictor or not.

Micro-Benchmark	Pathology Label	Pathology Description
Array	**P**_Array_**L2/L3/M**	Inefficient (random) accesses on arrays that incur heavy cache misses over L2 / L3 / Memory resident working sets
	N_Array_**L2/L3/M**	Efficient (linear) accesses on arrays over L2 / L3 / Memory resident working sets
LList	**P**_LList_**L2/L3/M**	Inefficient (random) accesses on linked list incurring heavy cache misses over L2 / L3 / Memory resident working sets
	N_LList_**L2/L3/M**	Efficient (linear) accesses on linked list over L2 / L3 / Memory resident working sets
Pointer	**P**_Pointer_**L2/L3/M**	Inefficient pointer chasing accesses that incur heavy sequential cache misses over L2 / L3 / Memory resident working sets
	N_Pointer_**L2/L3/M**	Efficient (linear) accesses on pointer-linked data over L2 / L3 / Memory resident working sets
BrMis	**P**_BrMis	Heavy branch misprediction
	N_BrMis	Light branch misprediction
FPU	**P**_FPU	Heavy software emulation of floating point instructions
	N_FPU	Efficient usage of Floating Point Units

Table 1: Description of Performance Pathologies Modeled by Micro-benchmarks.

Array and Pointer are memory-bound micro-benchmarks. P_Array characterizes heavy cache misses on array data and P_Pointer models sequential cache misses raised by pointer chasing access patterns. Since applications may have varying memory footprints, even the same micro-benchmark can show different patterns of hardware events depending on the working set size. Thus, we collect a range of different pathologies from memory-bound micro-benchmarks by adjusting their working set sizes. For example, the micro-benchmark Array can be configured either to iterate over the working set in a random order (pathological) or a strided sequential order (non-pathological). In addition, Array can characterize at least three kinds of pathologies, each with its complement. We prepend P_ to the names of micro-benchmarks (base labels) configured to exhibit their pathology, and prepend N_ to the base labels configured *not* to exhibit that pathology. The non-pathological case characterizes the same but efficient execution compared with the pathological case. In addition, we add a suffix, L2, L3, or M after the base labels to indicate a working set resident in L2, L3, or Memory respectively; i.e., P_Array_L3 for pathology-enabled Array on L3-resident data. BrMis and FPU are CPU-bound micro-benchmarks. P_BrMis models poor prediction from the branch predictor. P_FPU models heavy software emulation of floating point instructions instead of using dedicated Floating Point Units (FPU). Since CPU-bound micro-benchmarks are independent of the working set size, they do not have the additional suffixes. The labels given to pathologies (or non-pathologies) are used as classes for the classifications made by the decision trees.

4.1.2 Key Events Selection

In ADP, the data space is comprised of hundreds of hardware events, most of which may be weakly correlated with the performance pathologies and are irrelevant for identifying the pathologies. Furthermore, some of the events may be highly inter-correlated with each other; thus, they are redundant. Using every event to train decision trees often results in classification degradation either from the redundant events or from noise effects from the irrelevant events. For these reasons, by only sampling the set of the events highly correlated with the performance pathologies, we can yield better classification accuracies from decision trees and further decrease their training and classification time.

ADP uses the Correlation-based Feature Selection (CFS) [17] in order to select a subset of the hardware events that are strongly correlated with the performance pathologies and weakly inter-correlated with each other. If we pick the events with high *gain ratios* [31], we may have highly inter-correlated events in the selected subset. The aggregated counts of these events can have nearly the same values or they can show strong inter-correlation among them. For instance, LONGEST_LAT_CACHE.MISS and MEM_LOAD_RETIRED.LLC_MISS events are similarly measured, showing L3 cache misses in our experiments. Thus, we need to select a subset of the hardware events strongly correlated to the performance pathologies while removing highly inter-correlated events in the selected subset. CFS searches the subsets of the hardware events with high "merit" heuristic values from Equation 1 in Section 3. Combining a best-first greedy search strategy with CFS, ADP finds a subset that has a local optimum of the "merit". The size of selected subset is decided when the search terminates at the chosen iteration values (100,000 in our experimentation).

4.1.3 Time Window Slicing

The performance monitoring hardware triggers an event when the number of the events overflows a certain threshold. It is easy for the hardware events to be represented as aggregated counts. ADP aggregates all the measured events within each *time-slice*. The time slicing mechanism helps to increase the classification accuracy of the trained decision trees by providing more training points and reducing event sampling noise. As our micro-benchmarks repeatedly execute the pathological or non-pathological behaviors in a loop, the patterns of measured hardware events are similar among the time-slices from the same execution. The time-slices from the same execution of a micro-benchmark share the same pathology label. Furthermore, ADP normalizes the time-slices by dividing the aggregated event values within a time-slice by the number of clock cycles in that time-slice. With this normalization, the event data collected from different time-slices can be treated equally in the decision trees. Our current implementation of ADP uses the time-slices of equal durations. It drops the last time-slice as it often has a shorter duration than the other time-slices.

4.1.4 Decision Tree

ADP uses decision tree algorithms to identify the performance pathologies resident in applications. The decision tree algorithms are used to construct a comprehensive model that can fingerprint and identify the performance pathologies. Compared with other classification algorithms *e.g.*, support vector machine (SVM) [40], neural network [34] and bayesian [11], decision tree algorithms have two merits:

- The constructed models are easy to understand, thus they help to analyze the identified performance pathologies.
- They show relatively short classification times as well as short training times.

Once the decision trees are constructed from the time-slices of the micro-benchmarks, they are not changed in the classification phase.

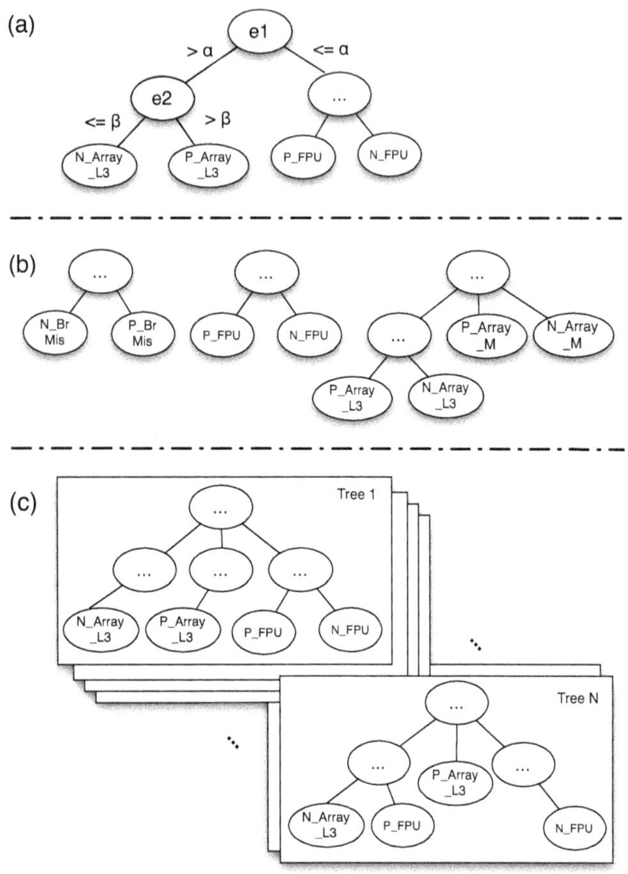

Figure 2: ***Abstract View of the Decision Trees.*** **(a) One decision tree is trained from all the time-slices of every micro-benchmark. (b) Multiple decision trees are trained from groups of time-slices. Each decision tree is designated to one micro-benchmark. (c) Random forests consisting of decision trees are created from randomly selected subsets of the key events; each tree can classify all the pathology labels with different viewpoints of the pathology model.**

Decision tree algorithms automatically pick the events for the non-leaf nodes and the thresholds to compare in branches as explained in Section 3.2. Each path through the decision tree ends on a unique leaf node, which has a pathology label. There may exist multiple leaf nodes sharing the same pathology label. The paths from the root to these leaf nodes can be considered classification rules that fingerprint patterns of hardware events for that label. Constructed classification rules can provide useful information from the combination of fingerprinted hardware events. Generating classification rules traditionally required considerable manual effort from domain experts. ADP instead provides an automated mechanism to construct these rules. In addition, it can detect pathologies that are difficult to be discovered by inspecting individual events. For instance, the classification of pathologies and non-pathologies characterized from memory-bound micro-benchmarks requires inspecting the combinations of multiple hardware events such as cache or TLB hit/miss and the stalls of read/write buffers. Separately inspecting these events would not achieve the same quality of the classification

There are three possible ways to construct decision trees; first, as shown in Figure 2.(a), we can construct a single tree trained from all the time-slices measured from every micro-benchmark. Each time-slice has one of the pathology labels described in Table 1. After training, this single decision tree can classify every pathology label from the vectors of the key events of the time-slices. In Figure 2.(a), when event *e1* is greater than a threshold, α and event *e2* is less than or equal to β for a time-slice, the time-slice is classified as `N_Array_L3`. Second, as shown in Figure 2.(b), we can construct multiple decision trees, each of which is trained using time-slices from a separate micro-benchmark. Each trained tree can classify the pathology labels characterized from specific micro-benchmarks. For instance, a decision tree trained from micro-benchmark `FPU`, can classify two pathology labels, `P_FPU` and `N_FPU`. Third, as shown in Figure 2.(c), we construct random forests [6] consisting of various decision trees (random trees) constructed from randomly selected subsets of hardware events. In our experiments, the size of those subsets is two thirds of the key events. Each random tree is trained from all the time-slices, similarly to the tree in Figure 2.(a), but with a different (randomly selected) subset of events from the key events. The label classified by the most random trees is the classification result selected by the random forests. This process is called *voting*. The voting ratio is $\frac{\text{the number of trees with classified label}}{\text{the number of random trees}}$.

While the tree in Figure 2.(a) is simple and requires the least time to construct and identify the pathologies from target applications, it may lose classification accuracy of a decision tree due to having too many classes when combining all the training data. The trees in Figure 2.(b) are useful for classifying multiple performance pathologies for a time-slice or a function-slice. However, the trees cannot decide which pathology is dominant. In addition, training each tree by only one micro-benchmark can lead to overfitting; it can fit the particularities of the training set, such as random fluctuation due to small samples. ADP uses random forests in Figure 2.(c) that do not lose classification accuracy as they are resistant to overfitting. This is because multiple random trees, which are constructed from the randomly selected events can model the performance pathologies from different viewpoints. In our experiments, we use 1,000 random trees, which yields consistent classification results as well as sufficient randomness. The pathology selected by voting is the most dominant behavior and is the most likely to be limited by the resource bottleneck characterized by that pathology. Therefore, the voting ratio can be used as a confidence factor for how strongly the respective patterns of hardware events are associated with a classified pathology label.

4.2 Classification Phase

ADP allows programmers to identify the types of the performance pathologies caused by specific hardware resource bottlenecks and pinpoints their locations in the code. The procedures of the classification phase are shown in Figure 1.(b′)∼(d′). In this phase, ADP:

1. Measures the key events selected in the training phase during the execution of a target application (Figure 1.b′);
2. Divides the collected the key events into *function-slices* (Figure 1.c′); and
3. Uses the vectors of key events to traverse the decision trees constructed in the training phase and classifies pathologies for the respective functions (Figure 1.d′).

Similarly to the time window slicing in Section 4.1.3, ADP aggregates and normalizes the key events by the code context of the function in which they were produced, which we term *function-slices*. The function-slice aggregation considerably reduces the effort required to locate the code responsible for the performance pathologies. We believe the function-slices reflect the average behaviors of their respective functions. A dominant (frequently executed) performance pathology, if it exists, strongly affects the patterns of the events for a period of significant time. The hardware events that are strongly correlated with a performance pathology affect the aggregated events within the time-slices or the function-slices. Thus, there is high probability that a dominant pathology makes noticeable event patterns and can be identified by ADP.

The classification phase uses the same key events selected in the training phase, because the key event selection is based on the hardware resource bottlenecks characterized by the micro-benchmarks. If a target application experiences a dominant resource bottleneck and that bottleneck is fingerprinted by a micro-benchmark, ADP does not need to adjust the key events. This is because the seemingly different behaviors of target applications are affected by the dominant resource bottleneck and the affected patterns of hardware events can be identified by the fingerprints using the key events related to the bottleneck.

ADP automatically classifies a performance pathology in a function-slice. Using the decision trees, it classifies a pathology label whose fingerprints are similar to the patterns of key events in the function-slices of target applications. The classification for a function-slice is determined by traversing a path from the decision tree's root node to one of the leaf nodes. The traversal is comprised of a series of tests on the vectors of key events. The tests at non-leaf nodes are determined by comparing these event counts with the thresholds selected in the training phase. As the leaf nodes have been assigned a pathology label, the respective function-slice is classified as the label at the leaf node selected by the traversal. As ADP uses random forests, the classification is chosen by voting from the random trees used in random forests. Once a function with a performance pathology label is identified, using the characterized information from the label, the programmer can make adjustments to the code to mitigate or to eliminate the problem.

5. EXPERIMENTAL RESULTS

5.1 Experimental Setup

To evaluate the applicability of ADP on different generations of CPU architectures, experiments were conducted on two environments: `E1` and `E2`. `E1` has one 3.4 Ghz quad-core Intel Core i7 2600 CPU with 8MB L3 cache, 256KB L2 cache, and 8GB memory. `E2` has two 2.4 Ghz quad-core Intel Xeon E5620 CPUs, each with 12M L3 cache, 1M L2 cache, and 12GB memory. We confined the execution of the single-thread applications of the SPEC CPU2006 benchmarks to one core and ran them with the "ref" data sets. For executing PARSEC benchmarks, we used their "native" data sets and used two different numbers of worker threads (dedicated to separate cores); 1 and 8. We call these environments `E2.1` and `E2.8` when experimented in `E2`. The hardware events of the applications' user-level execution were measured using the kernel module of Intel VTune Amplifier XE [21] in Linux 2.6.35. This measurement imposes almost no overhead for the execution time of applications (2.4% in `E1` and 0.8% in `E2`). We used `gcc` and `g++` to compile the micro-benchmarks and applications with the "-O2" optimization.

5.2 Training Phase

As described in Section 4.1.2, CFS [17] selects 41 events in `E1` and 35 events in `E2` as the *key events*. The execution time for CFS is 176s in `E1` and 219s in `E2`. As *Multiplexing* groups consist of eight events in `E1` and four events in `E2`, six multiplexing groups are required to measure the 41 events in `E1`. We set the duration of a time-slice to one iteration of every multiplexing group. In our experiments, transitions between the multiplexing groups occur every 100M clock ticks. With the 3.4Ghz CPU clock frequency in `E1`, each multiplexing group was measured for almost 29.4ms before being replaced by the next multiplexing group. To measure six multiplexing groups, the duration of a time-slice must be approximately 176ms (375ms in `E2`).

In `E1`, the working set sizes of the micro-benchmarks range from 128KB to 256KB for L2-resident data, from 4MB to 8MB for L3-resident data, and from 128MB to 256MB for Memory-resident data. We selected these working set sizes in order to sufficiently fill the respective caches or memory. By filling at least half of the upper level cache/memory hierarchy, we can characterize a hardware resource bottleneck mostly related to lower level cache misses. For instance, `P_Array_L3` can model a resource bottleneck related to lower level L2 cache misses by assessing sufficiently filled L3-resident data. The profiling of the micro-benchmarks made up most of the training phase, which took approximately 2 hours. The only manual effort that is required is that of configuring the data set sizes for the memory-bound micro-benchmarks, which are trivially derived from cache sizes. We observed the average differences in execution time between pathologies and non-pathologies were a factor of 4.6 for memory-bound micro-benchmarks and a factor of 6.1 for CPU-bound micro-benchmarks.

Cross-validation of Decision Trees

We performed 10-fold cross-validation to estimate the classification accuracy of the decision trees constructed in the training phase. Cross-validation is a broadly accepted technique used to estimate the classification accuracy of decision trees. We randomly divided the measured time-slices from the micro-benchmarks into ten sets. Then, nine of the sets were used as training sets for the decision trees. The last one was used as the test set for the decision trees. The vectors of the hardware events from a *time-slice* were used for traversing the decision trees. While the behaviors in the time-slices of the same label are homogeneous, variances exist in the hardware event counts of those time-slices due to sampling noise, OS intervention, out-of-order execution, different levels of cache or TLB interactions, and hardware assists. Using cross-validation, we assessed the accuracy of the classifications of ADP and whether these classifications were robust to the variances of the measured hardware event counts.

Table 2 shows the 10-fold cross-validation accuracy of the decision trees trained from the micro-benchmarks. We compared two decision tree algorithms, CART [5] and C4.5 [31] with random forests [6]. While this result shows comparably high accuracies from the decision tree algorithms, the incorrect classifications of the random forest are slightly lower. This result shows the time-slices of micro-benchmarks have identifiable patterns of hardware events and the decision tree algorithms can correctly classify them.

5.3 Performance Pathology Classification

If the specific pathology of each function-slice from a target application was known, we could have directly computed the classification error of the decision trees. However, we could not find a broadly acknowledged set of applications that included classified performance pathologies at the *function-level*. Since we could not directly calculate the classification accuracy of the decision trees during the classification phase, we searched for an indirect mechanism to analyze the correctness of the classified labels. We first considered Student t-test on the average Instruction Per Cycles

Algorithm	E1			E2		
	Accuracy	CC	IC	Accuracy	CC	IC
CART [5]	99.84%	11678	19	99.85%	6176	9
C4.5 [31]	99.92%	11588	9	99.87%	6177	8
Random forests [6]	99.97%	11594	3	99.97%	6183	2

Table 2: 10-fold Cross Validation Accuracy of Decision Trees for the Micro-benchmarks. CC **is the number of correctly classified time-slices.** IC **is the number of incorrectly classified time-slices.** *Accuracy (%)* **is** $\frac{CC}{CC+IC}$**.**

(IPC) of the time-slices from each pathology label represented in the micro-benchmarks and the average IPC of the function-slices from target applications classified with a corresponding label. However, this statistical validation on IPC could result in coincidental matching. One event or one derived event may not represent all performance characteristics; we observed that time-slices or function-slices with similar IPC could have different dominant pathologies and could show completely different patterns of hardware events. Instead, we need comparisons of the patterns of multiple hardware events between the training set and the test set. For this purpose, we first evaluated whether the classified pathologies could be used to classify the applications as CPU-bound or memory-bound. Previous research [26] classified the types of bounds of the applications in SPEC CPU2006. Using the constructed random forests, we classify whether the SPEC CPU2006 applications are CPU or memory bound from the labels of the function-slices and evaluate the classification accuracy in Section 5.3.1. In Section 5.3.2, we evaluate the classified performance pathologies of the function-slices from PARSEC by analyzing the functions and conducting case studies about performance improvement. For these classifications, ADP used random forests consisting of 1,000 random trees, whose training time is 128.2s. Using the random forests, it took ADP 3.2s to classify all 19 SPEC CPU2006 applications.

5.3.1 Classification Results of SPEC CPU2006

We evaluate the ability of the random forests to determine whether the SPEC CPU2006 applications are CPU-bound or memory-bound. Our micro-benchmarks have bottlenecks either in the memory (resources related to the memory subsystem) or CPU (other core resources such as the ALU). Our intuition is that an application is memory-bound if the majority of the hotspot functions (functions contributing most to the total runtime) of the application are classified as labels from memory-bound micro-benchmarks. We think that these automated classifications provide indirect confidence about the classified pathologies.

Table 3 describes some of the SPEC CPU2006 applications and their top 3 hotspot functions as well as their pathology labels and voting ratio. In order to classify whether the application was memory or CPU bound, we computed a weighted sum of each bound, weighting them by application coverage. For this classification, all labels with working set size suffixes were considered to be memory-bound regardless of whether they were pathological or non-pathological. For instance, *bzip2* was identified as CPU-bound as more hotspot functions are identified as CPU-bound. ADP correctly classified the bound type from 18 applications in `E1` and 17 in `E2` out of the 19 SPEC CPU2006 applications that we used. *Norm_L3Mis* and *Norm_BranchMis* [2] represent normalized penalties in clock cycles from L3 cache load misses and from branch mispredictions. They are weighted by their respective stall cycles and normalized by clock cycles. In `E2`, an L3 cache miss results in approximately 100 cycles of stalls and a branch mis-prediction results in approximately 15 cycles of stalls. By weighting the normalized event counts by these factors, they show the fraction of the time that the pipeline is spent stalling from these events. As the fingerprints of ADP contain every key event, analyzing only a subset of hardware events can distort the meaning of the results. However, the stalls from both events provide rough confirmation about the pathology labels.

For example, the `BZ2_compressBlock` function of *bzip2* was identified as `P_BrMis` in both environments; this function exhibited heavy branch mispredictions. We found that this function included many *if* statements about the state of the block being compressed. The top 3 hotspot functions of *mcf* were mostly classified as `P_Array_M` and `P_LList_L3`; these functions contained inefficient accesses on memory-bound and L3-bound working sets respectively. As its hotspot functions were classified as memory-bound, *mcf* was classified as memory-bound. We observed that these functions included many memory reads and writes within *for* loops. We think `N_FPU` label of `primal_bea_mpp` in `E1` was a mis-classification due to its frequent memory accesses. `Do_play_move` of *gobmk* was classified as `P_BrMis`. We observed that this function had many logic statements to compute the next move for the game *Go*. While *soplex* was classified as memory-bound in `E1`, it was classified as CPU-bound in `E2`. We suspect that this classification was due to either large cache sizes in `E2` or the insufficient coverage of the hotspot functions of *soplex*.

We observed increased confidence in the pathology labels of hotspot functions when the voting ratio of random forests was higher. A high voting ratio means that the decision trees strongly classify the pathologies from separate viewpoints of the hardware events. Those pathologies almost never changed when we selected key event subsets with different random seeds. Instead, the labels with low voting ratios sometimes changed to similar pathologies, e.g., the `BZ2_compressBlock` function of *bzip2*. This is because infrequently executed functions cannot trigger sufficient hardware events to fingerprint consistent patterns, and the ratios between their measured events deviate more. We suspect some functions were classified with low voting ratios, because they either did not exhibit a dominant resource bottleneck or showed patterns of hardware events different from those of micro-benchmarks. Rather than set a threshold for the voting ratio, we simply have less confidence in the classified labels with low voting ratios.

5.3.2 Classification Results of PARSEC and Case Studies about Performance Improvement

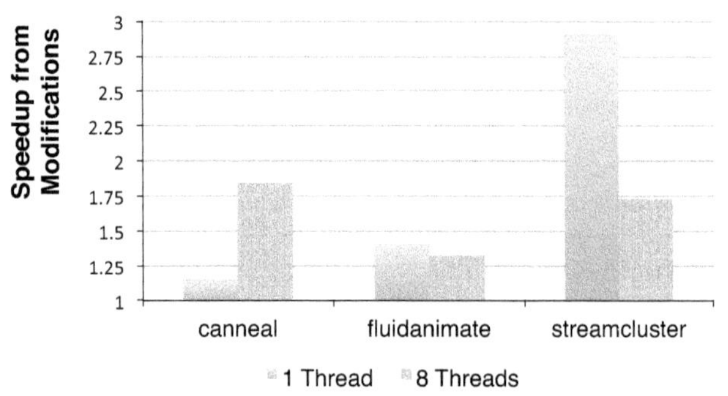

Figure 3: Speedup of PARSEC Applications after ADP-directed Tuning In `E2`. Speedup $=\frac{\text{The Runtime of Unmodified Version}}{\text{The Runtime of Modified Version}}$

[2] ADP did not use these manually created metrics about approximated penalties, instead it used measured hardware events.

Name	Env.	Functions	Cov. (%)	Pathologies	Ratio	Norm-BranchMis	Norm-_L3Mis	Mem./CPU	Correct
bzip2	E1	BZ2_blockSort	65.4	N_Div	0.87	0.268	0.014	CPU	Y
		mainGtU		N_Div	0.72	0.211	0.003		
		BZ2_compress-Block		P_BrMis	0.56	0.147	0.006		
	E2	mainGtU	64.4	N_Array_L2	0.19	0.119	0.000	CPU	Y
		mainSort		P_BrMis	0.31	0.243	0.000		
		BZ2_compress-Block		P_BrMis	0.31	0.132	0.000		
mcf	E1	primal_bea_mpp	76.9	N_FPU	0.71	0.001	1.270	Mem.	Y
		replace_weaker_arc		P_Array_M	0.44	0.000	1.305		
		refresh_potential		P_LList_L3	0.43	0.000	0.640		
	E2	primal_bea_mpp	75.7	P_Array_M	0.30	0.064	0.282	Mem.	Y
		replace_weaker_arc		P_Array_M	0.48	0.008	0.866		
		refresh_potential		P_LList_L3	0.73	0.035	1.604		
gobmk	E1	do_play_move	21.2	P_BrMis	0.81	0.367	0.001	CPU	Y
		dfa_matchpat_loop		N_LList_M	0.76	0.164	0.019		
		fastlib		P_BrMis	0.87	0.369	0.001		
	E2	do_play_move	21	P_BrMis	0.62	0.346	0.001	CPU	Y
		fastlib		P_BrMis	0.76	0.353	0.001		
		do_dfa_matchpat		P_Array_L3	0.32	0.142	0.009		
soplex	E1	entered4X	42	P_Array_L3	0.32	0.111	0.510	Mem.	Y
		setup		N_Div	0.32	0.264	0.008		
		assign2productFull		P_Pointer_L2	0.41	0.037	1.016		
	E2	entered4X	44	N_ITLB	0.22	0.1001	0.459	CPU	N
		setup		N_ITLB	0.46	0.225	0.011		
		assign2productFull		P_Pointer_L2	0.52	0.044	0.792		

Table 3: Classification of SPEC CPU2006 Pathology Labels and the Accuracy of Memory-bound and CPU-bound Labels. *Env.* is the experimental environment. *Functions* are the top 3 hotspot functions (most instructions executed in descending order). *Cov.* is the total coverage of these functions among the entire execution in terms of retired instructions. *Pathologies* are the classified results. *Ratio* is the voting ratio of the random forests for that pathology. *Mem./CPU* is whether the application is classified as memory-bound or CPU-bound. *Correct* is the correctness of the classification. *Norm_BranchMis* is the approximated penalty due to branch misprediction in cycles: 20 × BR_MISP_RETIRED.ALL_BRANCHES ÷ CPU_CLK_UNHALTED.THREAD (CLK) in `E1` and 15 × BR_MISP_EXEC.ANY ÷ CLK in `E2`. *Norm_L3Mis* is the approximated penalty due to L3 cache load miss in cycles: 180 × MEM_LOAD_UOPS_MISC_RETIRED.LLC_MISS ÷ CLK in `E1` and 100 × MEM_LOAD_RETIRED.LLC_MISS ÷ CLK in `E2`.

To verify ADP's ability to find performance issues in real code examples, we used the classified pathology labels of PARSEC benchmarks to improve performance. After profiling the applications of PARSEC, ADP produced a list of their hotspot functions and labeled each with its predominant pathology (or lack of a pathology). Each hotspot function labeled with a pathology was examined to find its causes. We selected the subset that had pathology labels that were easy for us to resolve. In *canneal*, *fluidanimate*, and *streamcluster*, there were hotspot functions with both high coverage as well as high voting ratios which were labeled as exhibiting a pathological behavior. We had no prior experience with these applications; however, in each of their hotspot functions, we were able to use the labeled pathology to modify the code to significantly reduce the runtime of the applications. These case studies are our samples of how ADP can be used to fix a pathology. In Figure 3, we show the speedup that this process obtained relative to the original PARSEC code. On both single- and multi-threaded execution in `E2`, our targeted performance tuning yielded from 1.15x to 2.91x speedup. The remainder of this section describes the specific issues detected by ADP, the performance issues uncovered by our analysis, and our resolutions of these issues accompanied by ADP analysis of the performance-improved workloads.

Table 4 shows three applications from PARSEC, their classified pathologies, and representative hardware events. We executed the PARSEC applications with one worker thread and with 8 worker threads in `E2`; these environments are denoted by `E2.1` and `E2.8` respectively. The function-slice for the `netlist` function of the *canneal* benchmark was classified as `P_LList_L3` in both `E2.1` and `E2.8`. This label fingerprints inefficient accesses on L3 resident data with a similar structure to a linked list, which implies this function has a similar resource bottleneck. Our investigation discovered that these functions were shown to exhibit the pathologies associated with inefficient pointer accesses. While the execution is looping, the `netlist` function calls the `create_elem_if_necessary` function, repeatedly searching a hash-map (tree-like structure) for elements to check the necessity of creating these elements. This check involves frequent pointer comparisons and heavy cache misses. As the elements in this map have unique names, we were able to store them in a array sorted alphabetically by their names. We changed the map structure to an array, which was accessed by an index calculated from each element name. Our modifications of the `netlist` function reduced the CPU time by 95.4% and the *L3Mis* count by 94.2% in `E2.8`. In addition, the usage of the array structure simplified the element search and resulted in a 1.84x speedup of the *canneal* benchmark in `E2.8` (74.9s improved to 40.6s). Interestingly, the identified labels of the modified `netlist` function became `P_Array_M`, and had a higher *Ratio*. As the modified *netlist* created a larger array than the unmodified version, we think that this classification is reasonable. In the unmodified *netlist*, the inefficient accesses to the map structure share some degrees of similarity with the inefficient accesses to a linked list. However, the dissimilarity between the

Name	Functions	Env.	Ratio	Pathologies	CPU Time (s)	Inst	BranchMis	L3Mis	Norm_-BranchMis	Norm-_L3Mis
canneal	netlist	E2.1	0.19	P_LList_L3	34.15	1.03×10^{10}	2.79×10^{8}	2.19×10^{8}	0.051	0.536
		E2.1 (M)	0.42	P_Array_M	1.62	1.56×10^{9}	4.18×10^{6}	1.98×10^{7}	0.016	0.746
		E2.8	0.20	P_LList_L3	34.11	1.01×10^{10}	2.85×10^{8}	2.23×10^{8}	0.051	0.544
		E2.8 (M)	0.49	P_Array_M	1.58	1.61×10^{9}	4.40×10^{6}	1.29×10^{7}	0.017	0.680
fluid-animate	Compute-ForcesMT Compute-DensitiesMT	E2.1	0.33	P_BrMis	258.22	1.01×10^{12}	7.44×10^{9}	6.73×10^{7}	0.176	0.032
			0.27	P_BrMis	177.91	7.63×10^{11}	4.00×10^{9}	4.97×10^{7}	0.136	0.038
		E2.1 (M)	0.31	P_BrMis	174.35	7.13×10^{11}	3.52×10^{9}	9.5×10^{7}	0.126	0.045
			0.30	P_BrMis	124.22	5.52×10^{11}	2.69×10^{9}	6.22×10^{7}	0.136	0.042
		E2.8	0.32	P_BrMis	262.04	1.03×10^{12}	7.72×10^{9}	9.08×10^{7}	0.184	0.030
			0.31	P_BrMis	183.32	7.71×10^{11}	4.42×10^{9}	5.85×10^{7}	0.149	0.026
		E2.8 (M)	0.33	P_BrMis	181.64	7.28×10^{11}	4.05×10^{9}	1.22×10^{8}	0.139	0.056
			0.34	P_BrMis	130.95	5.57×10^{11}	3.16×10^{9}	7.56×10^{7}	0.151	0.048
stream-cluster	dist	E2.1	0.28	P_LList_L3	957.41	9.97×10^{11}	2.46×10^{8}	1.83×10^{9}	0.002	0.159
		E2.1 (M)	0.39	P_LList_L3	174.35	7.13×10^{11}	3.52×10^{9}	9.50×10^{7}	0.004	0.398
		E2.8	0.23	P_LList_L3	842.73	9.96×10^{11}	3.04×10^{8}	2.10×10^{9}	0.002	0.207
		E2.8 (M)	0.61	P_LList_L3	181.64	7.28×10^{11}	4.05×10^{9}	1.22×10^{8}	0.004	0.314

Table 4: Classification of PARSEC Pathology Labels. *Env.* is the experimental environment. `E2.1` executes the PARSEC applications with a single worker thread and `E2.8` uses 8 worker threads. *(M)* represents our modifications. *Functions* are the hotspot functions used for performance optimization. *Ratio* is the voting ratio from random forests. *CPU Time* is the sum of CPU time (CPU clock cycles $\div$ clock rate) in each executed core in seconds (s): CPU_CLK_UNHALTED.THREAD (CLK) $\div$ (2.4×10^{9}). *Inst* is the sum of executed instructions: INST_RETIRED.ANY. *BranchMis* is the number of mispredicted branch instructions: BR_MISP_EXEC.ANY. *L3Mis* is the number of L3 cache load misses: MEM_LOAD_RETIRED.LLC_MISS. *Norm_BranchMis* is the approximated penalty due to branch misprediction in clock cycles: 15 $\times$ BR_MISP_EXEC.ANY $\div$ CLK. *Norm_L3Mis* is the approximated penalty due to L3 cache load miss in clock cycles: 100 $\times$ MEM_LOAD_RETIRED.LLC_MISS $\div$ CLK.

map and linked list structures resulted in a low *Ratio*, around 0.2. As the usage of the array structure in the modified *netlist* was more directly associated with the `P_Array_M` pathology, it had a higher *ratio*, resulting from similar patterns of hardware events.

The *fluidanimate* benchmark was noted to exhibit bad branch prediction. The function-slices for `ComputeDensitiesMT` and `ComputeForcesMT` were classified as `P_BrMis` in both `E2.1` and `E2.8`. We verified that they exhibited heavy branch mispredictions that resulted from a comparison inside nested loops. The end condition for the iterations (a comparison of pointers) is checked too frequently, and is responsible for excessive branch misprediction. Optimizing the iteration logic in both functions of the *fluidanimate* benchmark resulted in 1.32x speedup (71.3s over 53.9s) in `E2.8`. Both modified functions remained branch misprediction bound, which were classified as `P_BrMis`. However, they showed a reduction in the *BranchMis* count, by 47.5% and 28.5% respectively. Their CPU times were also reduced by 30.7% and 28.7%. While the *L3Mis* count was increased by around 30% in both functions, this did not degrade performance, which helped confirm that heavy branch misprediction was still the dominant pathology. Manual inspection of the counts of the *BranchMis* could likely detect branch misprediction pathologies. However, this process would require considerable time and effort in order to find a representative event for every architecture as well as a good threshold for each event with which to judge the pathology. Even if this manual effort is successful, it would also be difficult to answer whether branch misprediction is the dominant hardware bottleneck. ADP automatically performs this task and determines the pathology that arises from the dominant resource bottleneck.

The execution of the *streamcluster* benchmark was shown to have inefficient pointer accesses. The `dist` hotspot function was identified as exhibiting the `P_LList_L3` behavior. While execution is looping, this function computes the distance between vectors, which consist of 4 floating point values. Optimization of this function through a combination of loop unrolling, prefetching, and Single Instruction Multiple Data (SIMD) operations achieved 1.73x speedup (133.1s over 77.1s) in `E2.8`. In the modified `dist` function, the *L3Mis* count was reduced by 94.2% and *CPU Time* was reduced by 78.4%, while the *BranchMis* count was increased by 33.2%. While this optimization reduced the overall runtime and the *L3Mis* count of the `dist` function, the *Norm_L3Mis* was increased. This increase of *Norm_L3Mis* is reasonable as the vectorized SIMD instructions increase memory pressure by requiring higher memory bandwidth during a reduced runtime. Additionally, the increase of *Norm_L3Mis* is a likely explanation for the increased *Ratio*.

The optimizations in Figure 3 were also applied to `E1` and showed similar performance improvement although `E1` and `E2` were in different generations of CPU architectures. In addition, these results show that ADP can identify a pathology involving interactions and contentions between hardware resources in a multi-threaded application. While it would require further experimentation, we believe our mechanisms can be applied to the execution of multiple (possibly heterogeneous) co-located applications. The current implementation of ADP can separately measure co-located applications. The classification of their pathologies would not require modification of the trained decision trees as they are based on the hardware resource bottlenecks characterized from the micro-benchmarks. Despite the fact that our experiments run on x86 architecture, our mechanisms are applicable to any architecture that exposes sufficient hardware events; this is because our automated mechanism does not require explicit information, such as the written descriptions of the hardware events. Without interpreting the specific hardware events, CFS effectively selects a meaningful subset of events that are highly correlated with performance pathologies, and decision trees classify performance pathologies resident in applications. Thus, ADP can operate regardless of poor documentation, poor validation, and the lack of standardization of hardware events.

During the performance tuning processes, the information provided by ADP considerably simplified our search for performance pathologies. ADP automatically classifies labels against hotspot functions that exhibit event patterns indicative of hardware bottlenecks. Each classified label represents a dominant resource bottleneck, which help to guide what needed to be improved in the function. Despite our unfamiliarity with these functions, we were able to improve the performance of each of these applications in only a few hours. Because ADP's decision trees expose the dominant performance pathologies as easy-to-understand labels, the interpretation of these labels does not require architectural knowledge, and the barrier-to-entry for hardware performance tuning is significantly reduced.

6. CONCLUSION

Performance characterization of hardware bottlenecks is essential to effectively tailor algorithms to architectures. Different architectures manifest different performance bottlenecks – for example, branch misprediction is different on out-of-order processors and in-order processors. Even similar architectures may vary in affliction from the same performance bottlenecks, depending on properties like the sizes and configurations of their caches, the latency and degree of pipelining of their functional units, and their pipeline depth and issue width. Thus, tuning applications to specific architectures can be difficult. One of the best resources available to support this tuning is events from performance monitoring hardware. However, it is challenging to choose an appropriate set of hardware events to collect and to interpret those results.

In order to simplify the identification of performance bottlenecks or pathologies using hardware events, we design and implement an automated system, ADP. It uses micro-benchmarks developed by architecture experts to model the performance pathologies that exhibit event patterns to expose resource bottlenecks. ADP selects a refined subset of the hardware events that are highly correlated with the performance pathologies. Random forests of decision trees are trained with the selected key events in order to fingerprint the characteristics of the performance pathologies and their related hardware resource bottlenecks. The fingerprints and decision trees can identify the performance pathologies in a target application. ADP is effective for applications if they incur a hardware resource bottleneck and the bottleneck is fingerprinted by a micro-benchmark. It matches the behaviors of applications with respect to hardware resources against those of micro-benchmarks and provides a level of confidence that this match is not coincidental. As a result, it is possible to have false positives and false negatives. As ADP provides guidelines to interpret the resource bottlenecks, we believe false positives and false negatives are evident to the users.

As long as an architecture has multiplexing support for the performance monitoring hardware and has a sufficient set of hardware performance events, we believe our mechanisms are applicable to any architecture. ADP automatically classifies the performance pathology labels for an application's hotspot functions. Using these labels, we were able to speedup the execution times of three PARSEC applications by an average of 1.73. Our next step is to investigate mechanisms to determine false positive and false negative ratios for the decision trees. We also intend to explore pathologies related to additional hardware resources and as well a communication delays between these resources.

7. ACKNOWLEDGMENTS

We would like to thank Diwakar Krishnamurthy, Robert Kuhn, Wonsun Ahn, and the anonymous reviewers for their comments and suggestions. This work is supported by a grant from Intel.

8. REFERENCES

[1] L. Adhianto, S. Banerjee, M. Fagan, M. Krentel, G. Marin, J. Mellor-Crummey, and N. R. Tallent. Hpctoolkit: tools for performance analysis of optimized parallel programs http://hpctoolkit.org. *Concurr. Comput. : Pract. Exper.*, 22:685–701, April 2010.

[2] R. Azimi, M. Stumm, and R. Wisniewski. Online performance analysis by statistical sampling of microprocessor performance counters. In *Proc. of International Conference on Supercomputing*, pages 101–110. ACM, 2005.

[3] R. Bagrodia, R. Meyer, M. Takai, Y. Chen, X. Zeng, J. Martin, and H. Song. Parsec: A parallel simulation environment for complex systems. *Computer*, 31(10):77–85, 1998.

[4] R. Bitirgen, E. Ipek, and J. Martinez. Coordinated management of multiple interacting resources in chip multiprocessors: A machine learning approach. In *Proc. of IEEE/ACM International Symposium on Microarchitecture*, pages 318–329. IEEE Computer Society, 2008.

[5] L. Breiman. *Classification and regression trees*. Chapman & Hall/CRC, 1984.

[6] L. Breiman. Random forests. *Machine learning*, 45(1):5–32, 2001.

[7] S. Browne, J. Dongarra, N. Garner, G. Ho, and P. Mucci. A portable programming interface for performance evaluation on modern processors. *International Journal of High Performance Computing Applications*, 14(3), 2000.

[8] S. Browne, J. Dongarra, N. Garner, K. London, and P. Mucci. A scalable cross-platform infrastructure for application performance tuning using hardware counters. In *Proc. of ACM/IEEE Conference on Supercomputing*. IEEE Computer Society, 2000.

[9] M. Burtscher, B.-D. Kim, J. Diamond, J. McCalpin, L. Koesterke, and J. Browne. Perfexpert: An easy-to-use performance diagnosis tool for hpc applications. In *Proc. of International Conference for High Performance Computing, Networking, Storage and Analysis*, SC '10, pages 1–11. IEEE Computer Society, 2010.

[10] M. Casas, R. M. Badia, and J. Labarta. Automatic phase detection and structure extraction of mpi applications. *Int. J. High Perform. Comput. Appl.*, 24:335–360, August 2010.

[11] P. Cheeseman and J. Stutz. Bayesian classification (AutoClass): Theory and results. In *Advances in knowledge discovery and data mining*. American Association for Artificial Intelligence, 1996.

[12] M. Curtis-Maury, F. Blagojevic, C. Antonopoulos, and D. Nikolopoulos. Prediction-based power-performance adaptation of multithreaded scientific codes. *IEEE Transactions on Parallel and Distributed Systems*, pages 1396–1410, 2008.

[13] B. David, M. Geimer, F. Wolf, and L. Arnold. Identifying the root causes of wait states in large-scale parallel applications. In *Proc. of International Conference on Parallel Processing*. IEEE Computer Society, 2010.

[14] U. Fayyad and K. Irani. Multi-interval discretization of continuous-valued attributes for classification learning. In *Proc. of International Joint Conference on Artificial Intelligence*, pages 1022–1029, 1993.

[15] M. Gerndt and M. Ott. Automatic performance analysis with periscope. *Concurr. Comput. : Pract. Exper.*, 22:736–748, 2010.

[16] E. Ghiselli. *Theory of psychological measurement*. McGraw-Hill, 1964.

[17] M. A. Hall. Correlation-based feature selection for discrete and numeric class machine learning. In *Proc. of International Conference on Machine Learning*, pages 359–366, 2000.

[18] T. Heath, A. Centeno, P. George, L. Ramos, Y. Jaluria, and R. Bianchini. Mercury and freon: temperature emulation and management for server systems. In *Proc. of International Conference on Architectural Support for Programming Languages and Operating Systems*, pages 106–116. ACM, 2006.

[19] J. Henning. SPEC CPU2006 benchmark descriptions. *ACM SIGARCH Computer Architecture News*, 34(4):1–17, 2006.

[20] L. Hyafil and R. Rivest. Constructing optimal binary decision trees is NP-complete. *Information Processing Letters*, 5(1):15–17, 1976.

[21] Intel. Vtune Amplifier XE. *Web site: www.intel.com/software/products/vtune*, 2011.

[22] R. Kufrin. Perfsuite: An accessible, open source performance analysis environment for linux. In *The International Conference on Linux Clusters*, volume 151, 2005.

[23] J. Levon and P. Elie. Oprofile: A system profiler for linux. *Web site: http://oprofile.sourceforge.net*, 2011.

[24] C. Luk, R. Cohn, R. Muth, H. Patil, A. Klauser, G. Lowney, S. Wallace, V. Reddi, and K. Hazelwood. Pin: building customized program analysis tools with dynamic instrumentation. *ACM SIGPLAN Notices*, 40(6):190–200, 2005.

[25] D. T. Marr, F. Binns, D. L. Hill, G. Hinton, D. A. Koufaty, J. A. Miller, and M. Upton. Hyper-threading technology architecture and microarchitecture. *Intel Technology Journal*, 6(1):1–12, 2002.

[26] A. Merkel, J. Stoess, and F. Bellosa. Resource-conscious scheduling for energy efficiency on multicore processors. In *Proc. of European conference on Computer systems*, EuroSys, pages 153–166. ACM, 2010.

[27] W. E. Nagel, A. Arnold, M. Weber, H.-C. Hoppe, and K. Solchenbach. Vampir: Visualization and analysis of mpi resources. *SUPERCOMPUTER*, 12:69–80, 1996.

[28] E. Ould-Ahmed-Vall, J. Woodlee, C. Yount, K. Doshi, and S. Abraham. Using model trees for computer architecture performance analysis of software applications. *IEEE International Symmposium on Performance Analysis of Systems and Software*, 0:116–125, 2007.

[29] V. Pillet, J. Labarta, T. Cortes, and S. Girona. Paraver: A tool to visualize and analyze parallel code. *IN WOTUG-18*, pages 17–31, 1995.

[30] J. Quinlan. Induction of decision trees. *Machine learning*, 1(1):81–106, 1986.

[31] J. Quinlan. *C4. 5: programs for machine learning*. Morgan Kaufmann, 1993.

[32] J. R. Quinlan and R. L. Rivest. Inferring decision trees using the minimum description length principle. *Inf. Comput.*, 80:227–248, 1989.

[33] P. C. Roth and B. P. Miller. On-line automated performance diagnosis on thousands of processes. In *Proc. of Symposium on Principles and Practice of Parallel Programming*, pages 69–80. ACM, 2006.

[34] D. Rumelhart. *Learning internal representations by error propagation*. MIT Press, 1986.

[35] F. Schneider, M. Payer, and T. Gross. Online optimizations driven by hardware performance monitoring. In *Proc. of Conference on Programming Language Design and Implementation*, pages 373–382. ACM, 2007.

[36] K. Shen, M. Zhong, S. Dwarkadas, C. Li, C. Stewart, and X. Zhang. Hardware counter driven on-the-fly request signatures. *ACM SIGOPS Operating Systems Review*, 42(2), 2008.

[37] S. S. Shende and A. D. Malony. The tau parallel performance system. *Int. J. High Perform. Comput. Appl.*, 20:287–311, 2006.

[38] J. Stoess, C. Lang, and F. Bellosa. Energy management for hypervisor-based virtual machines. In *Proc. of the USENIX Annual Technical Conference*, page 1. USENIX Association, 2007.

[39] D. M. Tullsen, S. J. Eggers, and H. M. Levy. Simultaneous multithreading: maximizing on-chip parallelism. In *Proc. of International Symposium on Computer Architecture*, ISCA '95, pages 392–403. ACM, 1995.

[40] V. Vapnik. An overview of statistical learning theory. *Neural Networks, IEEE Transactions on*, 10(5):988–999, 1999.

[41] J. Vetter. Performance analysis of distributed applications using automatic classification of communication inefficiencies. In *Proc. of International Conference on Supercomputing*, pages 245–254. ACM, 2000.

[42] L. Xu, P. Yan, and T. Chang. Best first strategy for feature selection. In *International Conference on Pattern Recognition*, pages 706 –708 vol.2, 1988.

[43] W. Xu, L. Huang, A. Fox, D. Patterson, and M. Jordan. Detecting large-scale system problems by mining console logs. In *Proc. of ACM Symposium on Operating Systems Principles*, pages 117–132. ACM, 2009.

[44] W. Yoo, K. Larson, S. Kim, W. Ahn, R. Campbell, and L. Baugh. Automated Fingerprinting of Performance Pathologies Using Performance Monitoring Units (PMUs). In *Proc. of USENIX Workshop on Hot topics in parallelism*. USENIX Association, 2011.

[45] O. Zaki, E. Lusk, W. Gropp, and D. Swider. Toward scalable performance visualization with jumpshot. *International Journal of High Performance Computing Applications*, 13(3), 1999.

Providing Fairness on Shared-Memory Multiprocessors via Process Scheduling

Di Xu[1,2], Chenggang Wu[1]*, Pen-Chung Yew[3,4], Jianjun Li[1], and Zhenjiang Wang[1]
[1]State Key Laboratory of Computer Architecture, Institute of Computing Technology, Chinese Academy of Sciences
[2]Graduate University of Chinese Academy of Sciences, Beijing, China
[3]Department of Computer Science and Engineering, University of Minnesota at Twin-Cities, Minnesota, USA
[4]Institute of Information Science, Academia Sinica, Taiwan
{xudi, wucg, lijianjun, wangzhenjiang}@ict.ac.cn, yew@cs.umn.edu

ABSTRACT

Competition for shared memory resources on multiprocessors is the most dominant cause for slowing down applications and makes their performance varies unpredictably. It exacerbates the need for Quality of Service (QoS) on such systems. In this paper, we propose a *fair-progress process scheduling* (FPS) policy to improve system fairness. Its strategy is to force the equally-weighted applications to have the same amount of slowdown when they run concurrently. The basic approach is to monitor the progress of all applications at runtime. When we find an application suffered more slowdown and accumulated less effective work than others, we allocate more CPU time to give it a better parity. Our policy also allows different weights to different threads, and provides an effective and robust tuner that allows the OS to freely make tradeoffs between system fairness and higher throughput.

Evaluation results show that FPS can significantly improve system fairness by an average of 53.5% and 65.0% on a 4-core processor with a private cache and a 4-core processor with a shared cache, respectively. The penalty is about 1.1% and 1.6% of the system throughput. For memory-intensive workloads, FPS also improves system fairness by an average of 45.2% and 21.1% on 4-core and 8-core system respectively at the expense of a throughput loss of about 2%.

Categories and Subject Descriptors

D.4.1 **[Operating Systems]**: Process Management – *scheduling*

General Terms

Management, Design, Performance

Keywords

Process Scheduling, Performance Fairness, Memory Bandwidth

1. INTRODUCTION

Shared-memory multi-core processors are the most prevalent platforms used today. When applications run concurrently on such systems, the competition for the shared memory resources such as on-chip caches and DRAM subsystems could degrade their performance unpredictably (compared to when they run alone on the same system). Figure 1 shows the effect of resource contention on the performance of four equally-weighted and concurrently running applications, *perl*, *bwaves*, *milc* and *libquantum*, all from SPEC2006. They run on a 4-core CMP with private cache (details are in Section 4.1). Compared to the isolated run, the execution time of *perl* increases to 1.10X, while the execution time of *libquantum* increases to 1.62X because *libquantum* is memory-intensive and suffers more slowdown due to off-chip main memory contention. If we replace the last two co-runners with *leslie3d* and *soplex*, the relative slowdown of *bwaves* changes from 1.19X to 1.47X. It shows that the performance of an application highly depends on its co-runners and can change unpredictably due to resource contention. It violates the assumption of weight-based CPU time allocation policy in the OS, and exacerbates the need for quality of service (QoS) on such systems.

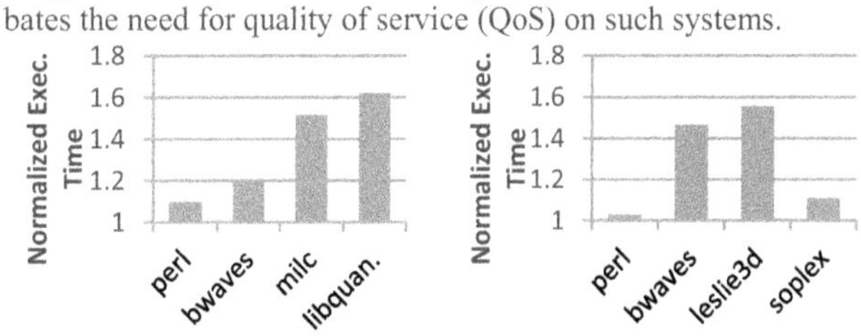

Figure 1. Performance variations of concurrent applications

In order to provide performance fairness to concurrently running applications, some prior works tried to guarantee the applications their fair share of system resources, such as cache space [8] and/or memory bandwidth [10]. Some tried to maintain fair performance on demanded resources, such as cache miss rates [3, 20] and memory-related stall time [6]. However, there still exist gaps between the share of demanded resources or the resource-performance and the real application performance (e.g. IPC). In this paper, we assume that, for equally-weighted applications, a system is *fair* if all applications' experienced slowdowns are the same. This assumption is based on application performance rather than on resource related metrics. It has also been used in several prior works [2, 9, 11].

In this paper, we propose a *fair-progress scheduling (FPS)* policy, a process scheduling policy that ensures fairness among applications running concurrently. The basic mechanism is: at runtime, we use the data gathered from the performance monitoring unit (PMU) and an analytical model to derive the amount of its *forward progress* after the execution of a time quantum. If we find an application suffered more slowdown (thus accumulated less *progress*) than others within the same time quantum, we would allocate more time quanta to the application and allow it to make the same *forward progress* as others.

To calculate the *forward progress* of an application, the greatest challenge is to estimate its performance if it runs alone on the system, while it is actually running simultaneously with others [2,

*To whom correspondence should be addressed

SIGMETRICS'12, June 11–15, 2012, London, England, UK.

6]. In this paper, we proposed a software-based approach. Firstly, we classify all executed time quanta into phases [14 17]. The performance in the time quanta of the same phase is very similar. In each phase, we estimate its run-alone performance via identifying the *low-contention* time quanta (Section 4.1), in which its performance is close to its run-alone performance. We then incorporate the information to other time quanta in the same phase and estimate their *forward progress*.

For a phase without such *low-contention* time quanta, we force a time quantum to run with the desired *low-contention* co-runners by turning it into a *training* quantum (Section 4.3). Training improves the accuracy of run-alone performance estimation and the system fairness significantly at the expense of some CPU idleness and system throughput degradation. To mitigate the problem, we proposed techniques that can effectively reduce the training overhead. In addition, by setting an upper-bound on the training overhead, FPS provides the OS with an effective and robust tuner to tradeoff between system fairness and throughput. It makes FPS adaptive to different fairness objectives.

Our experiments are on a commercial server with Intel multicore processors. Evaluations show that compared to the native OS scheduler, FPS could reduce 53.5% and 65.2% of system unfairness on a 4-core private-cache system and a 4-core share-cache system with a throughput degradation of 1.1% and 1.6%, respectively. For memory-intensive workloads, FPS reduces the system unfairness by an average of 45.2% and 21.1% on 4-core and 8-core systems respectively when capping the training overhead to 2%. Even without any training, FPS still gets 15% better fairness than the default OS scheduler, and the change in throughput is quite negligible.

Our contributions are as follow:

- We propose a scheduling policy to provide performance fairness on commodity systems. The policy can significantly improve system fairness at the expense of slightly decreased throughput, and it also enforces thread priorities/weights.
- We propose a practical, phase-based run-time scheme to obtain the run-alone performance of an application while it actually runs simultaneously with others. It is software-based and does not need any special hardware support.
- An effective and robust tuner is provided to let the user freely make tradeoffs between system-fairness and higher throughput.

The rest of this paper is organized as follow: Section 2 introduces the related work. Section 3 shows the overview of our policy. The run-alone-performance estimation scheme is introduced in Section 4. In Section 5, we briefly discuss the system software support. Second 6 and Section 7 introduce the evaluation methodology and results, respectively. Finally, we conclude this paper in Section 8.

2. RELATED WORK

The techniques to provide performance fairness on multiprocessors have been widely studied, and memory resource contention was identified as the primary cause for unfairness [2, 3, 6-8, 21]. There are mainly three different ways to target fairness [7], i.e., using (1) resource usage (RUM), (2) resource performance (RPM) and (3) overall performance (OPM) as a metric.

Techniques using RUM try to allocate the demanded amount of resources to applications. R. Iyer et al. [12] designed cache partition techniques to make sure that high-priority applications get more cache space. Kyle J. Nesbit et al. [14] proposed fair queuing on the memory controller to ensure that each thread receives its allocated fraction of memory bandwidth. However, providing different applications with the same amount of resources does not necessarily produce fair performance because the demand for resources is highly application-dependent. Techniques using RPM try to guarantee the applications a certain level of resource performance. O. Mutlu and T. Moscibroda designed a memory access scheduling policy to let equally-weighted applications have the same increase in memory-related stall time [6]. A. Fedorova et al. [3] proposed a thread scheduling policy to let the threads achieve execution times if they have the same miss rate on shared cache. However, other complementary techniques are still needed to bridge the gap between the resource-performance and the final application-performance (e.g. IPC). By comparison, FPS targets application performance directly using the OPM objectives.

For using OPM and RPM, the most challenging task is to estimate what the situation *would* be if the application runs alone while it actually runs simultaneously with others. For example, in [6], authors added special hardware counters and triggers in memory controller to estimate what the memory stall time is if the application runs alone. Similar hardware support is used in their follow-up work [2], in which the shared-cache contention is also counted. Because of the complicated working mechanism in memory devices and their interactions with the processor pipeline, precise analytical modeling of performance is still very difficult. In this paper, in order to estimate what the application performance (IPC) would be if it runs alone, we proposed a totally different runtime approach: we make use of the phase behavior of applications and identify its IPC_{alone} directly by constructing a *low-contention* environment for it. Our approach is software based and does not need any special hardware support.

In order to provide system fairness, most prior works manage the shared resources and change the behavior of applications when they share the resources. In this paper, we use a process scheduling approach to deal with the problem. Although contention-aware thread scheduling policies have been widely studied, most of them focus on system throughput [4, 5, 12, 13]. A fairness-oriented thread scheduling policy has been proposed in [3]. It targets shared-cache contention and uses RPM as its objective. By comparison, FPS mainly targets main memory contention, which has been identified as the most dominated cause for an application's performance degradation [1], and it uses OPM.

3. POLICY OVERVIEW

3.1 Specifying the Fairness Target

Similar to previous works [2, 6, 9, 11], we assume a system is *fair* if equally-weighted applications have the same slowdown when they run concurrently on system. As shown in Equations (1) and (2), on a system with N applications, the slowdown of application i is T^i_{shared}/T^i_{alone}, where T^i_{shared} and T^i_{alone} are the execution time when the application runs concurrently with others and runs alone, respectively. In the context of process scheduling, an application's execution time T includes both the time when it executes on a CPU and the time when it is swapped out. System unfairness is defined as the ratio between the maximal and minimal slowdown among the N applications. An unfairness of 1 means the system is perfectly fair.

$$slowdown_i = T^i_{shared}/T^i_{alone} \tag{1}$$

$$unfairness = \frac{MAX\{slowdown_0, \dots, slowdown_{N-1}\}}{MIN\{slowdown_0, \dots, slowdown_{N-1}\}} \tag{2}$$

3.2 Basic Ideas

FPS tries to guarantee the equally-weighted applications to experience the same slowdown when they run concurrently. In another word, the applications should accomplish the same amount of *effective work* (measured in T_{alone}) within the same time period. We define the *forward progress* to quantitatively measure the *effective work* that an application has done. Assume that when an application runs *alone* for C_{unit} cycles, it makes a *progress* of 1. When it runs concurrently with others, its *progress* can be calculated as:

$$progress = \sum_{q=1}^{Q} \frac{C_{alone}^{q}}{C_{unit}} = \sum_{q=1}^{Q} \left(\frac{I^{q}}{IPC_{alone}^{q}} \times \frac{1}{C_{unit}} \right) \qquad (3)$$

For a time quantum q, C_{alone}^{q} is the number of CPU cycles if the application runs alone. The application's *progress* is the accumulation of C_{alone}^{q} in each executed time quantum (from 1 to Q) normalized to C_{unit}. For example, an application runs simultaneously with others for C_{unit}*2 cycles but suffers 4X slowdown, it has only made a *progress* of 0.5, while another application runs for C_{unit} cycles but does not have any slowdown, it has made a *progress* of 1.

In calculating *progress*, I^{q} is the number of executed instructions in quantum q. It can be obtained directly from PMU. The main challenge is to estimate IPC_{alone}^{q}. In Section 4, we will describe our proposed method in more detail.

Algorithm 1: Overview of Policy

```
Initialize task-queue: run-queue, wait-queue
while task remains do
   run all apps in run-queue
   wait for a quantum
   // apps run, and then the scheduler resumes here:
   for each app in run-queue do
      pause execution
      move app to wait-queue
      process with PMU data
      estimate IPC_alone of this quantum
      progress+= I/IPC_alone × 1/C_unit
   end for
   // schedule for fairness:
   for each available CPU core do
      find app with smallest progress in wait-queue
      move app to run-queue
   end for
end while
```

In order to impose equally-weighted applications the same slowdown, FPS tries to let them achieve the same *progress* within the same given time when they run concurrently. Algorithm 1 shows the basic steps of FPS. Each time we need to schedule applications, we update the *progress* of each application according to the runtime information gathered from PMU and the estimated IPC_{alone}^{q}. We then repeatedly schedule the application with the smallest *progress* on each available CPU core.

4. ESTIMATING RUN-ALONE PERFORMANCE

To estimate the run-alone performance in each executed quantum, we make use of the phase behavior in applications. Firstly, we group executed quanta into phases, and use the attribute that the performance of the quanta in the same phase should be similar [14-17]. If we know IPC_{alone}^{q} of at least one quantum q in a phase, we can apply the information to other quanta in the same phase.

How to estimate IPC_{alone} of a given phase? An intuitive solution is to select some quanta in that phase and let them run alone. But, this method would result in large CPU idleness if there are many applications and each has many different phases. Fortunately, we found that in some situations, even when an application run concurrently with others, its performance is still the same as (or very similar to) that of when it runs alone. In which case, we can get the estimated IPC_{alone}^{q} without running the application alone.

4.1 Identifying *Low-Contention* Applications in a Quantum

Competition for shared memory resource is the primary cause for performance variations [2, 3, 6-8, 20, 21]. Even if contention happens in an unpredictable way, we observed that at least in three cases, the execution of an application suffers little or minor interference. Hence, we could assume that $IPC_{alone}^{q} \approx IPC_{shared}^{q}$ in those cases.

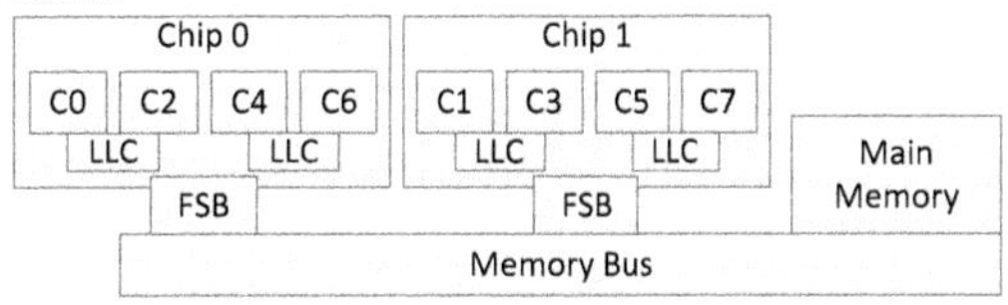

Figure 2. Architecture overview of the evaluation system.

In this section, we use measured results on real systems to better explain the phenomenon. Figure 2 shows the evaluation system. The system is equipped with two Intel Xeon E5410 quad-core processors. Each core has a private L1 data cache, and each 2 cores share one L2 data cache (LLC) on the chip. The benchmarks are from SPEC2006 suite, compiled by Intel Compiler with flag -O3, and use the reference input set. We generate 10 random benchmark mixes. To evaluate the contention on the main memory, we run benchmarks on cores 0, 1, 4 and 5 to isolate the impact of the shared cache. We also evaluate the situation in which both cache and main memory are shared by executing them on cores 0, 1, 2 and 3. We use Bus Transaction Rate (BTR) to characterize the memory-bandwidth requirement of the execution. BTR is defined as the number of full-cache-line bus transactions per microsecond. The realistic peak BTR of the memory bus is 120 trans./usec, and that of the FSB is 80 trans./usec. The OS is Linux, kernel version v2.6.29.

In this paper, we call the execution part of an application during a scheduling time quantum an *application segment*, or *segment* for short. In each segment, its IPC_{shared}^{q} can be obtained via PMU. We also get its real IPC_{alone}^{q} by querying an offline performance profiling file, which is generated by executing the application *alone* on the same system. At last we can calculate its speedup as $IPC_{shared}^{q}/IPC_{alone}^{q}$. Note the method of obtaining IPC_{alone}^{q} by profiling is only for our evaluation and analysis purpose. It is not a part of our scheduling policy.

Memory Bandwidth Contention: We associate the speedup of each segment s with two memory-bandwidth related metrics: $SelfBTR_s$, i.e., the BTR of s when running with others, and $SysWideBTR_s$, i.e., the total BTR of s and all of its co-runners within the quantum. To show the correlation among the metrics, Figures 3(a) and 3(b) plot the evaluation results of the same randomly selected and representative 1k segments in private-cache mode. Figure 3(c) shows a subset of them. The three *low-contention* cases are as follows:

- The bandwidth requirement of a segment is extremely low (Criterion 1). In this case, its performance degradation due

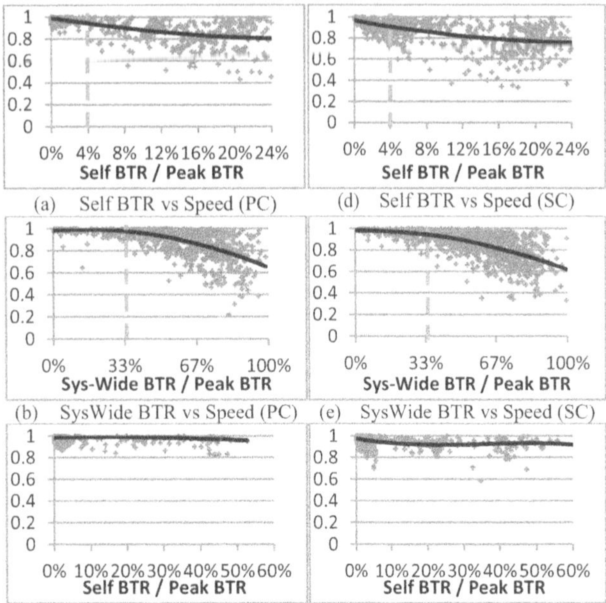

(a) Self BTR vs Speed (PC) (d) Self BTR vs Speed (SC)

(b) SysWide BTR vs Speed (PC) (e) SysWide BTR vs Speed (SC)

(c) The Criterion 3 Subset(PC) (f) The Criterion 3 Subset(SC)

Figure 3. Speedup over alone run on private cache mode (PC) and shared cache mode (SC). X-axes are the percentage of measured BTR compared to peak BTR. Y-axes are speedups, 1 means no slowdown. The solid lines show the curve-fitting of the points. The dashed lines illustrate the thresholds.

to bandwidth contention is always small, no matter what applications it runs with. Evaluation results shown in Figure 3(a) confirm that memory-intensive segments generally suffer more slowdown than less intensive ones [1]. In this paper, we set a threshold $BTR_{SelfLow}$ to 4% of the peak BTR. If BTR of a segment is smaller than the threshold, we assume its IPC^q_{shared} is similar to IPC^q_{alone}.

- The system wide bandwidth utilization is low (Criterion 2). In [4], authors found that even when the average bandwidth requirement of concurrent segments is lower than the realistic peak bandwidth of bus, contentions still happen because of the fluctuation in memory intensity within the segments. Only when the system bandwidth utilization is much lower than peak, the remaining available bandwidth could tolerate the fine-grained contention and that results in a relatively smaller slowdown. In this paper, we set a system-wide BTR threshold $BTR_{SyswideLow}$ to be one third of the peak BTR. If the system-wide BTR is smaller than $BTR_{SyswideLow}$, we can assume IPC^q_{shared} is similar to IPC^q_{alone} for *all* the concurrent segments.
- The system wide BTR is larger than $BTR_{SyswideLow}$ but only one of the concurrent segments is memory-intensive, i.e., whose BTR is larger than $BTR_{SelfLow}$ (Criterion 3). Severe contention only happens when there are at least *two* memory intensive segments that are fighting against each other. Figure 3(c) shows a subset of evaluated segments that belong to this case. Compare it with Figure 3(a), we found using this criterion could successfully pick up those quanta that have inherently high memory requirement but suffer relatively small slowdown.

Cache and Bandwidth Contention: Similarly, Figures 3(d,e,f) show the execution results in shared-cache mode. Compared to the results in private-cache mode, we have the following observations. First, the performance degradation of the application segments could become more severe because of the added shared cache contention. Second, the tendency of performance variations is quite similar to that of the private-cache mode. Previous work also shows that contention for shared cache is not the dominant cause for performance degradation, but the contention in many components of the main-memory is [1]. Although the segments selected according to the abovementioned three criteria would have a bigger performance degradation compared to that in the private-cache mode, their performance degradation is still relatively small. As will be shown later, the information gathered from such co-scheduled applications will help to estimate the IPC^q_{alone} in each executed quantum.

4.2 Phase Identification and Performance Information Management

Program phase behavior has been studied extensively. In this paper, we use a runtime basic block vector (BBV)-based [14-17] phase identification scheme to classify similarly behaved quanta into a phase. BBV analysis has been shown to be an effective method of identifying phases in programs [14, 15].

During the execution of each application segment, we use PMU to sample its instruction pointers (IP) and construct a BBV. Each element of the BBV maps to a static basic block, and its value is increased by 1 when an IP sample falls into it, so the BBV reflects the distribution of the sampled IPs in the application's code space. We quantify the similarity of two normalized BBVs by calculating their *Manhattan Distance*, as shown in Equation (4), where x_i and y_i is the element of vector X and Y respectively, and N is the number of static basic blocks in application binary. If the Manhattan Distance of two BBVs is smaller than a threshold, the corresponding segments are in the same phase.

$$ManhattanDistance(X,Y) = \sum_{i=1}^{N} |x_i - y_i| \qquad (4)$$

Evaluations on PMU sampling overhead and phase identification accuracy are in Section 7.2 and 7.7.

Table 1. Per-Phase Performance Info Update Method

Exec. history	IPC^q_{shared} of current quantum	Updated IPC_{phase}
None	Valid/Invalid	$IPC_{phase} = IPC^q_{shared}$
#valid=0	Invalid	$IPC_{phase}=$ $(IPC_{phase} * n + IPC^q_{shared})/(n+1)$
	Valid	$IPC_{phase} = IPC^q_{shared}$
#valid >=1	Invalid	*Unchanged*
	Valid	$IPC_{phase}=$ $(IPC_{phase} * n + IPC^q_{shared})/(n+1)$

For each application, we maintain a phase table to record the performance information of its phases. The goal is to estimate the run-alone-performance of a given phase, denoted as IPC_{phase}. After the execution of a quantum q, firstly we do phase identification and calculate some basic performance metrics such as BTR^q_{shared}, IPC^q_{shared} and system-wide BTR according to the PMU data. We then check whether the application's execution meets one of the three *low-contention* criteria. If it meets, its performance data is considered *valid*, otherwise, it is *invalid*. In any case, we update the performance information in the phase table following the method shown in Table 1. Before a phase gets its first valid execution, IPC_{phase} is the average of all *invalid* histories. After the phase gets its first valid execution, the intended value of IPC_{phase} is the average of all valid histories. The method provides the phase with a running estimate, and the three *low-*

contention criteria work as a filter to let only suitable data participate in the estimation of IPC_{phase}.

Finally, the estimated IPC^{q}_{alone} for this quantum is the larger one between IPC_{phase} and IPC^{q}_{shared}, because we assume the IPC of a simultaneously running segment could not be larger than that of when it runs alone.

4.3 Training Quantum

During execution, a phase of an application may never have a quantum that fits any of the three *low-contention* cases, and it degrades the accuracy of the estimation. In that case, we can temporarily change the scheduling policy and inject a *training* period to create necessary *low-contention* situations for the phase.

For each application, we use a Markov predictor to predict its phase changes based on its full histories. To tolerate incorrect prediction, the predictor reports several phases that are most likely to appear in next quantum according to their transferring probabilities. If one of the predicted phases has appeared at least twice in history and we have not obtained its valid IPC_{alone} yet, that application will become a training-target-candidate. A training target selection policy will be used to determine the final training target if there are multiple candidates (Section 4.5), then FPS transfers the scheduling policy to *training* in next quantum

Algorithm 2: Scheduling Algorithm - Training

01 // schedule the training target app *t*
02 move app *t* to *run-queue*
03 $BTR_{remain} = BTR_{SyswideWeak} - BTR^{t}_{required}$
04 $CORE_{remain} = \#cores$-1
05 // limit system-wide BTR (to meet criterion 2)
06 **while** BTR_{remain}>0 **do**
07   **for** each app *p* in *wait-queue* **do**
08         $FITNESS^{P} = \frac{1}{\left|\frac{BTR_{remain}}{CORE_{remain}} - BTR^{P}_{required}\right|}$
09   **end for**
10   find app with maximal *fitness* → app *f*
11     $BTR_{remain} -= BTR^{f}_{required}$
12   **if** ($BTR_{remain} > 0$) **then**
13   move app *f* to *run-queue*
14         $CORE_{remain} --$
15   **end if**
16 **end while**
17 // meet criterion 3
18 **if** *#mem-intensive* in *run-queue* is no larger than 1 **then**
19   **for** each app *p* in *wait-queue* **do**
20   **if** ($BTR^{p}_{required} \leq BTR_{self}$ && $CORE_{remain} > 0$)
21   move app *p* to *run-queue*
22             $CORE_{remain} --$
23   **end for**
24 **end if**

Algorithm 2 shows the training algorithm. Firstly, the training target is selected to run. The policy then selects proper co-runners to let the system-wide bandwidth requirement close to but not exceeding $BTR_{SyswideLow}$ (to meet Criterion 2). To do so, it goes through all un-selected applications to compute their *fitness*, and the application whose bandwidth requirement is closest to the remaining bandwidth per remaining core has the highest priority to be scheduled. Similar fitness calculation has been used in previous works [4, 12, 13] as a throughput-oriented scheduling policy. After that, the policy selects other non-memory-intensive applications, if possible, to meet Criterion 3. Finally, there may be remaining CPU cores, but we cannot assign applications to them because of the bandwidth constraints. In Section 5, we will discuss the impact of such CPU idleness on the system throughput.

Task color: If some applications always be selected as co-runner of the training target, it would upset the desired system fairness. So we improve the training policy with a task-coloring mechanism. At runtime, we classify the applications into 2 exclusive categories (colors). The application with maximal *progress* currently and those whose *progress* would become the maximal if it executes in the next quantum (predicted according to the histories in phase table) are colored as black. Others are non-black. Scheduling a black application may make its *progress* even larger than current maximal *progress* and degrade system fairness. So the improved training policy first finds the best-fit application among the non-black ones (Line 07 of Algorithm 2 is changed to "**for** each non-black app *p* in *wait-queue* **do**"). The black applications will not be scheduled unless the number of non-black applications is smaller than the number of CPU cores.

Reduction of Training Period: For some phases, such as iterative execution of the body of a loop (so called loop-dominated phases), the performance of part of its execution already represent that of the entire run. This phenomenon gives us an opportunity to further reduce the CPU idleness caused by training. In this paper, we set the length of a training quantum to one-quarter of a normal quantum. If the trained phase is loop-dominated, the distribution of the sampled IPs should remain the same for the rest of the quantum, and the partial execution could still get valid IPC_{alone}. If the phase is not loop-dominated, partial execution would result in a very different IP sampling distribution, and the executed quantum would be recognized as different phases. It will not mislead the IPC_{alone} estimation of the targeted phase.

4.4 Training for Applications with Phase Fluctuation

Training by phase prediction requires phases to be correctly predicted. If the accuracy of prediction is low, many training quanta will be wasted, and it also misses the training opportunities for other phases. Figure 4 shows the phase patterns of two different applications that result in different prediction accuracy. Phases of *bwaves* appear in long and stable periods, so the Markov predictor would work well on it. In contrast, the phases of *leslie3d* fluctuate greatly. The reason is its executed code region changes frequently, and when it runs concurrently with others, contention and partial training make the quantum boundary shift unpredictably compared to when it runs alone. As a result, the BBV of each quantum looks different, and forms a hard-to-predict phase sequences.

So we introduce another training trigger for applications with fast fluctuating phases. In the beginning, the training is still guided by phase prediction. For an application, if we find the prediction accuracy of quanta is getting very low, the application is identified as having fluctuating phases. It is changed to a sequential training mode: the application is trained continuously in the next N quanta (N=6 in our studies). The motivation is that, if its phases fluctuate, a continuous execution of N quanta is very likely to cover most of the static phases and obtain their valid IPC_{alone}. The scheduling algorithm is unchanged, but the length of training is forced to a full quantum.

4.5 Distribution of Training Quanta Among the Applications

Training could always improve the accuracy of IPC_{alone} estimation of applications. But we found that in a particular case, although the estimation accuracies are improved for some applica-

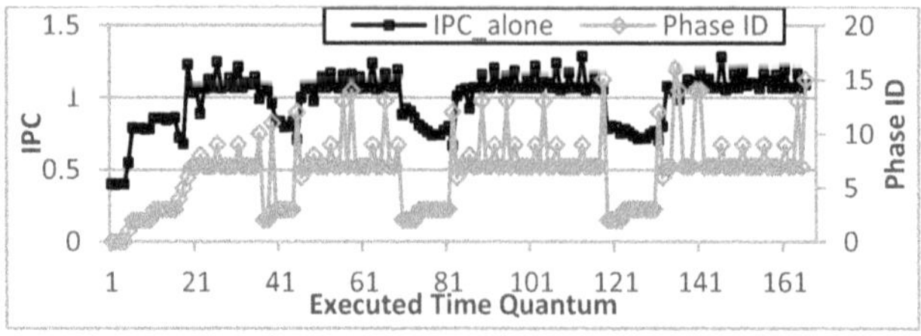

(a) 410.bwaves – run with random co-runners

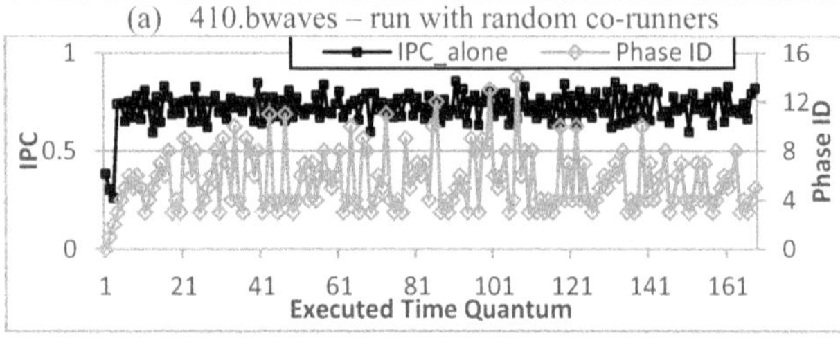

(b) 437.leslie3d – run with random co-runners

Figure 4. Applications with different phase behaviors.

tions, it may lead to system fairness degradation because the training quanta are not properly distributed among the applications.

Figure 5 shows such an example. Consider a situation where all the applications in a workload are memory intensive, and all of them will experience large slowdown due to memory contention. The application with maximal and minimal slowdown are B and A respectively, as shown in case 1, and the system unfairness is determined by the difference of their slowdowns. Case 2 shows that when we have sufficient training quanta, the IPC_{alone} estimation accuracies of all applications will improve and approach the upper bound of 100%, and the gap between the estimated maximal and minimal slowdowns becomes smaller and system fairness improves. However, if FPS doesn't have enough training quanta, and they are not properly distributed among the applications, e.g., applications A used most of the trainings to improve its own IPC_{alone} estimation accuracy, while that of the others' remains nearly unchanged, as a result, the gap between the estimated maximal and minimal slowdowns becomes larger, and system fairness degrades (Case 3). What we expect is shown in case 4, where the trainings are properly distributed, so IPC_{alone} estimation accuracies of *all* applications could improve. Intuitively, the improvement of B is larger because it has larger slowdown, and system fairness improves.

In this paper, we propose a training distribution policy. In FPS, an application segment can get its valid estimated IPC^{q}_{alone} from the *low-contention* executions, or from other segments that belong to the same phase. There also exist some segments that have not got their valid IPC^{q}_{alone} estimation. We define the *valid data coverage* of an application to be the ratio between the number of segments that have a valid IPC^{q}_{alone} estimation and the number of all executed time quanta. At runtime, FPS updates the *coverage* metric for each application during its execution. When it is going to insert a *training* quantum, firstly it checks all the applications and finds all the training-target-candidates, and finally, it selects the one with minimal *coverage* among them as the training target. The purpose is to let the applications keep similar *valid data coverage* during execution.

Under this distribution policy, all applications will have chances to use a training quantum, and intuitively the one with larger slowdown will get more training opportunities because it has relatively smaller *valid data coverage*. Note that this policy is always applied in FPS, no matter what the current workload is, we found it especially effective when the workload is memory-intensive and

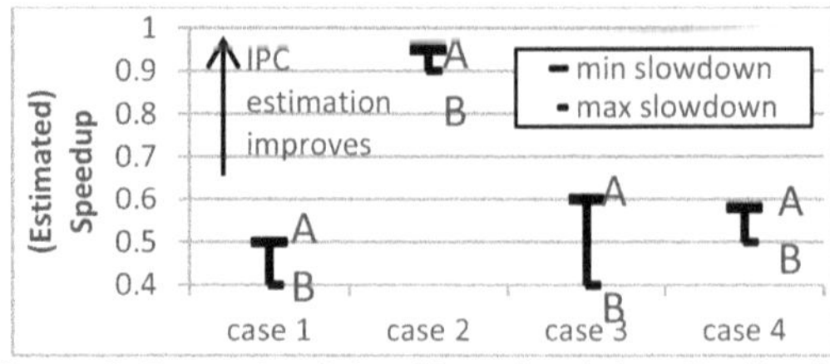

Figure 5. Example of the effect of training distribution

the number of training period is limited, because it could avoid the unbalanced IPC_{alone} estimation accuracy improvement among the applications.

4.6 Shared Cache Considerations

Unlike bandwidth contention, there is no easily identifiable situation in which we can assume the cache contention is small and only depends on simple performance statistics. There may be 2 ways to address the shared cache contention. First, train an application on an unified cache, but this method would involve huge overhead because we need to train at least once for each phase of each application, and at least one CPU core have to be idle. Second, use stack-distance analysis [18-20], but it needs actual memory access traces, which is hard to obtain at runtime without expensive instrumentations.

Nevertheless, we still applied some techniques that could mitigate as much cache contention as possible without introducing further overheads. First, during normal execution in which all CPU cores are used, we adapt the Distributed Intensity Online (DIO) thread-CPU mapping policy [1] to schedule high miss-rate applications to different caches, so that the miss rate is evenly distributed among the caches. Second, when it is in a training period in which at least one CPU core is idle, we will leave the core that shares the same LLC with the training target idle. The remaining applications are assigned to other cores using the DIO policy. Our evaluation shows that, the accuracy of the estimate for IPC_{alone} on a shared-cache system also improves significantly, and system fairness improvement is no less than that on a private cache system.

5. SYSTEM SOFTWARE SUPPORT

A Fairness-Throughput Tuner: Training could improve the accuracy of IPC_{alone} estimation and benefit system fairness, but the side effect is CPU idleness and throughput degradation. We quantify the overhead caused by training using Equation (5):

$$Overhead_{train} = \frac{C_{TrainWaste}}{C_{working}} = \frac{\sum_{for\ each\ training\ quantum\ t}(\#cores - TrainPara^{t}) \times C^{t}_{shared}}{\sum_{for\ each\ app}\sum_{for\ each\ quantum\ q} C^{q}_{shared}} \quad (5)$$

$C_{TrainWaste}$ is the number of cycles wasted in training quanta. It is further calculated as the sum of wasted cycles by each idle CPU core in each training quantum t. $TrainPara^{t}$ is the training parallelism, i.e., the number of simultaneously running applications in training quantum t, and C^{t}_{shared} is number of cycles it lasts. $C_{working}$ is the number of cycles that all CPU cores are executing a job. It is the sum of the number of executed cycles in each quantum q (denoted as C^{q}_{shared}) of each application.

Recall that in FPS, we reduce the number of training quanta and increase training parallelism by identifying the *low-contention* executions. FPS also uses shorter training quanta. As a result, the overhead of training could be significantly reduced. In addition, by measuring the training overhead and setting a limitation, FPS provides an effective and robust interface to the OS, and it allows

Table 2. Evaluation System Setups

Setup name	CPU cores used	LLC	Bandwidth bottleneck @	Per-core LLC Size (MB)	Per-core BTR (trans./usec)
4core-private-cache (PC)	0, 1, 4, 5	Private	Memory Bus	6	120/4=30
4core-shared-cache-diff-chip (SC-1)	0, 1, 2, 3	Shared	Memory Bus	3	120/4=30
4core-shared-cache-same-chip (SC-2)	0, 2, 4, 6	Shared	Front Side Bus	3	80/4=20
8core	0-7	Shared	Memory Bus	3	120/8=15

tradeoff between system fairness and throughput: the more training we do, the more accurate the estimated run-alone performance becomes, and the more fairness improvement we could get, while the expense is more CPU idleness. It makes FPS adapted to different fairness objectives. Relevant evaluation results will be shown in Section 7.4 and 7.5.

Thread Weight: The policy we have described so far assumes that all applications are of the same priority. The policy can be easily extended to support different thread weights and differentiated performance. We assume a higher weight will result in a higher performance. We define $WeightedProgress = Progress/Weight$. The policy uses *weighted progress* instead of measured *progress*, so an application with a higher weight would appear to achieve less progress than it really does. As a result, it will obtain more time quanta and result in a higher performance.

Task Submission and Completion: Real applications are different in execution time, and they may enter or exit from the system at any time. As a result, not all parts of applications keep running concurrently, so in this situation, FPS does not try to guarantee a fair slowdown of the *entire* run of each application respectively. Instead, we divide the execution into multiple *concurrent regions*. *Concurrent regions* transfer from one to another when the composition of concurrent applications changes, i.e., when a new application start to run on the system, or an old application terminates. The idea of FPS is to guarantee the fairness *within* each *concurrent region*. When a new application is submitted, its *progress* should be initialized to zero. At the same time, for each old application *i* that is still running on the system, its *progress* should be recalculated as $progress^i = progress^i - progress_{min}$, where $progress_{min}$ is the smallest *progress* among all the old applications. The old applications get reduced *progress* to avoid being throttled. When an application exits from the system, the *progress* of other applications remain unchanged.

6. METHODOLOGY

Scheduler Implementation: In order to evaluate the effectiveness of our scheduling policy, we implemented a user-level process scheduler on Linux. The scheduler itself executes as a daemon. When a job is submitted, the scheduler forks out the process and creates a PMU sampling context for it. The scheduler sets a real-time timer to count the scheduling time quanta. When the timer expires, the scheduler is notified by a signal and it enters the scheduling routine. The main steps have been described in Section 3.2. The applications are paused by PTRACE_ATTACH, so that they will not be scheduled by the Linux kernel. At the end, we let the selected applications continue to run using PTRACE_DETACH, reset the quantum timer and let the scheduler sleep to wait for the next notification.

System Setup: We use the same system described in Section 4.1. Table 2 shows the system setups for our evaluations. When evaluated on a 4-core system, we use different CPU cores to create different scenarios of resource contention. When all used cores are on the same chip, the shared front-side bus becomes the bottleneck because its realistic peak bandwidth (80 trans./usec) is smaller than that of the memory bus (120 trans./usec). When the cores are on different chips, the potential pressure from the 2 FSB's to the memory bus is 160 trans./usec. It is larger than the realistic peak bandwidth of the memory bus, so the memory bus becomes the bottleneck. Unless stated otherwise, Table 3 shows the parameters used in our evaluation.

Table 3. Parameters setup of scheduler

Scheduling quantum length	100ms
PMU sampling period	500k instructions
BBV similarity threshold	0.7
Training overhead limitation	Unlimited
Sequential training trigger	#failed training>5 && failure ratio>60%

Workloads: The workloads are constructed using the SPEC CPU 2006 suite. Firstly, we do length normalization. We run each benchmark alone for 10 seconds, and record the number of instructions executed. The same part of execution will be added when a benchmark is selected to run. Job normalization eliminates the variation of the application length. It results in a fair measure of system unfairness because almost all parts of benchmarks keep running concurrently. It also gives fair measurement of system throughput because if the applications are different in length, load balancing could influence the results significantly [4].

In reality, the execution times of applications are different, as we discussed in Section 5, FPS divides the execution into multiple *concurrent regions*, and guarantee the fairness *within* each *region*. The *progress* of applications are recalculated when *region* changes, so the scheduling results of *regions* are relatively independent of each other, and we can focus on the results of some specific and representative *regions* that created by length normalization.

It is more challenging to evaluate the first 10 seconds than in a longer run because the number of quanta in each phase becomes relatively smaller, so the workloads' throughput becomes more vulnerable to the CPU idleness due to training. *483.Xalancbmk* is excluded from the benchmark pool because it has a long initialization period so its behavior in the first 10 seconds changes monotonically and does not have a repeated phase. Our current implementation does not handle this situation, but it can be extended in the future to detect such an application: it counts the times that each phase appears, and if most of the phase does not repeat, we would let it run under a regular scheduling policy.

To evaluate the generality of FPS, we use 10 randomly generated multiprogramming workloads, as shown in Table 4. There are 8 to 16 randomly selected benchmarks in each workload for our 4-core experiments. We use the metric *Ideal Average Bandwidth Requirement* (called IABW for short) defined in [4] to characterize the average bandwidth requirement of a workload, and the workloads are reordered by their IABW in ascending order. When evaluated on the 8-core system, we use the same benchmark combination but each benchmark is spawned twice. We also use other manually constructed memory-intensive workloads for evaluation purposes. The details are in Section 7.5.

Table 4. Random SPEC workloads. The benchmarks in a workload are listed according their run-alone-BTR from high to low. The expression appx(n) means there are n parallel instance of appx in the workload.

WL index	IABW	Composition
WL#05	47.1	leslie(2) zeusmp(1) soplex(1) wrf(1) gobmk(1) perl(1) hmmer(2) namd(2) gamess(1) tonto(1)
WL#02	49.3	libquantum(1) leslie(1) lbm(1) sphinx3(1) soplex(1) wrf(2) sjeng(2) gobmk(1) gromacs(1) dealII(1) h264ref(1) gamess(2) tonto(1)
WL#01	49.9	milc(1) lbm(1) cactusADM(1) astar(1) omnetpp(1) hmmer(1) dealII(1) namd(1)
WL#08	60.0	leslie(1) lbm(2) sphinx3(2) soplex(1) mcf(1) gcc(1) omnetpp(1) wrf(1) gobmk(1) perl(2) dealII(1) gamess(1)
WL#10	65.0	GemsFDTD(1) lbm(1) zeusmp(1) soplex(1) astar(1) calculix(1) gobmk(1) povary(1)
WL#07	65.4	leslie(1) GemsFDTD(1) milc(1) sjeng(1) calculix(2) dealII(2) povary(1)
WL#09	67.4	libquantum(1) GemsFDTD(2) zeusmp(1) gcc(1) astar(1) bzip2(1) perl(1) hmmer(2) dealII(1) h264ref(1)
WL#06	76.6	libquantum(1) milc(1) lbm(2) zeusmp(1) mcf(1) cactusADM(1) astar(1) omnetpp(2) calculix(1) h264ref(1)
WL#04	78.5	libquantum(1) bwaves(1) GemsFDTD(1) sphinx3(1) zeusmp(1) soplex(2) gcc(1) astar(1) hmmer(1) gromacs(1) namd(1) h264ref(1)
WL#03	90.6	libquantum(1) leslie(1) bwaves(1) milc(2) zeusmp(3) mcf(2) cactusADM(1) wrf(2) sjeng(1) perl(1) hmmer(1)

Metrics: We compare the results of FPS to the native Linux scheduler (kernel v2.6). In order to show fairness improvement, we measure system unfairness as defined in Section 3.1. We use 2 metrics to evaluate the impact of FPS to system throughput: *workload turnaround time*, i.e., the time from all applications start at the same time to the last application finishes, and *extended weighted speedup (EWSpeedup)*. The original *weighted speedup* [11] was commonly used to measure the throughput of multiprocessors systems on which the number of concurrent threads does not exceed the number of CPU cores. It is calculated as the sum of the speedups of all concurrent applications. However, a job scheduling policy may pathologically improve this metric by forcing all jobs run serially so that each job suffers no slowdown. So we define extended weighted speedup as shown in equation (6).

$$EWSpeedup = \sum_{i=0}^{N-1} \frac{C_{alone}^{i}}{C_{shared}^{i} + C_{wasted}^{i}} \tag{6}$$

The key to the definition is that, when calculating the speedup of applications *i*, if any CPU core is idle before the number of remaining applications becomes smaller than the number of available cores, the wasted cycles on the idle CPU core are also counted as its execution time. In our policy, CPU idles are caused by the training quanta, and we attribute the wasted cycles to the training target in the corresponding training quantum.

Prior works use Harmonic Mean of Speedups [13] to give a combined measure for both fairness and throughput. We don't use this metric because it is determined by applications' individual IPCs, while our process scheduling technique is not to give the applications fair IPC during execution, but to adjust the CPU time distribution to achieve fair execution time.

7. EVALUATION RESULTS

7.1 4-core System Results

Figure 6 shows the average performance of 10 random workloads on the 4-core systems. We evaluate 3 different scheduling policies: the native OS, FPS and Optimal. The optimal policy uses our fairness-oriented scheduling algorithm but IPC_{alone} of each quantum comes from offline profiling runs instead of runtime estimation, as described in Section 4.1.

In the private-cache mode, the unfairness under OS scheduler ranges from 1.08 to 1.23, the average is 1.14. FPS improves fairness on all workloads. The average of unfairness is decreased to 1.06, and about 53.5% of the unfairness is eliminated. On the shared-cache-diff-chip mode, the system peak bandwidth is unchanged but cache contention is added. Cache contention and the resulted higher pressure to bandwidth let the system unfairness under OS increased to 1.22. About 65.0% of the unfairness is eliminated by FPS, and it decreased to 1.08. On the shared-cache-same-chip mode, bandwidth contention is further increased. The unfairness under OS is decreased to 1.29. The unfairness under FPS is 1.10. FPS eliminates about 65.8% of the unfairness. Results show that FPS is effective in eliminating unfairness on both private- and shared-cache systems.

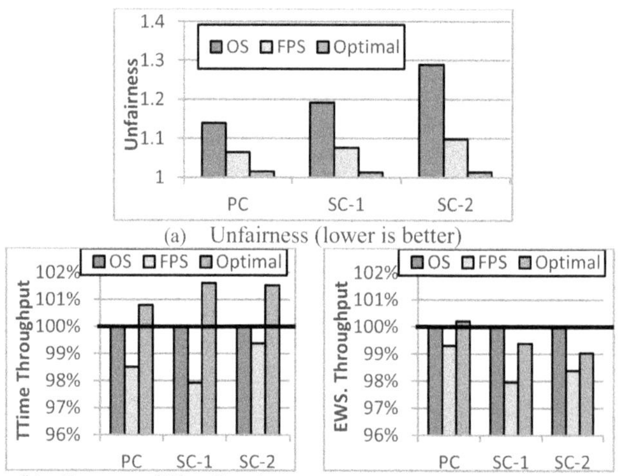

(a) Unfairness (lower is better)

(b) Turnaround Time Speedup over OS (higher is better)

(c) EWSpeedup over OS (higher is better)

Figure 6. Average performance on 4-core systems

For all the evaluated modes, the most severe system throughput degradation is about 2% compared to OS, no matter whether it was measured in workload turnaround time or EWSpeedup. The average decrease is 1.1%, 2.06% and 1.12% respectively for the three execution modes. The main sources of the degradation is PMU sampling and CPU idleness caused by training.

In every situation, the optimal policy achieves almost perfect fairness on all workloads and the best throughput. It shows the effectiveness of the fairness-oriented scheduling algorithm.

7.2 IPC_{alone} Estimation Accuracy

To give an insight into why FPS improves system fairness, we analyze the accuracy of our IPC_{alone} estimation scheme in this section. We use the evaluation results on the shared-cache-same-chip mode because the resource contention is the most severe among all 4-core modes.

Application Level: For a given benchmark, estimation on each of its quanta has a cumulative effect on the IPC_{alone} estimation accuracy of the entire execution, which is evaluated using Equations

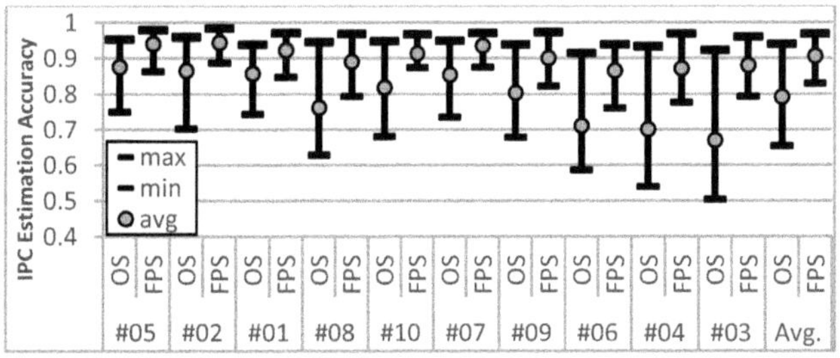

(a) Application-level IPC_{alone} estimation accuracy (1 is best)

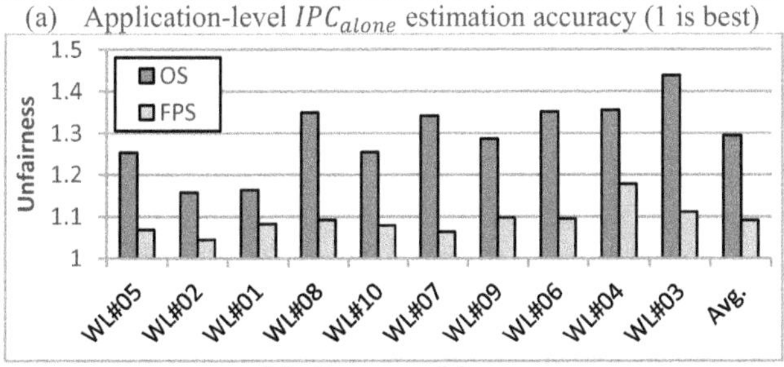

(b) System unfairness

Figure 7. 4-core shared-cache-same-chip evaluation results

(7, 8). If we always use ICP_{shared} as IPC_{alone} in our policy, all applications will appear to make the same progress in all quanta. Hence, FPS will allocate the same number of quanta to applications, which has the same effect as using the native OS scheduler. We compare our estimation accuracy to that in this situation.

$$IPC_{esti\_alone} = \frac{\sum_{q=1}^{Q} I^q}{\sum_{q=1}^{Q}\left(I^q / IPC_{esti\_alone}^{q}\right)} \quad (7)$$

$$EstiAcc = \frac{IPC_{esti\_alone}}{IPC_{alone}} \quad (8) \qquad EstiAcc_{OS} = \frac{IPC_{shared}}{IPC_{alone}} \quad (9)$$

Figure 7(a) reports the maximal, minimal and average estimation accuracy of the benchmarks in each workload respectively. Figure 7(b) report the corresponding system unfairness. As the bandwidth requirement of workloads increase, the slowdowns of applications also increase significantly, e.g., *libquantum* inWL#03 suffers a slowdown of 1.99X, while that of others may be no more than 1.1X. The huge gap between the maximal and minimal slowdown in a workload illustrates the cause of unfairness. The average accuracy of our IPC_{alone} estimation scheme is about 90% for all workloads, and the gap between maximal and minimal is reduced. As a result, system fairness is improved when we further allocate proper fraction of time quanta according to the estimation.

Quantum Level: There are two necessary requirements to achieve high estimation accuracy in each quantum. First, the IPC_{shared} of an application in the low-contention co-schedule and its IPC_{alone} should be as close as possible. We have discussed and evaluated it in Section 4.1. Second, performance of quanta in the same phase should be as similar as possible. The accuracy of phase identification is application-dependent. To evaluate, we run each benchmark for 10 seconds under our phase identification scheme. For each identified phase, we compute the *relative standard deviation (%RSD)* of the IPC_{alone} for the quanta within the phase. Smaller *%RSD* means the *IPCs* of quanta that in the same phase are similar, and is better. Finally, we report the application's phase identification accuracy by calculating the *weighted %RSD* of all phases, as shown in Equation (10).

$$WRSD = \sum_{for\ each\ phase\ p} w_p \times RSD_p\text{, } where\ w_p = \frac{n_p}{\sum_{for\ each\ phase\ i} n_i} \quad (10)$$

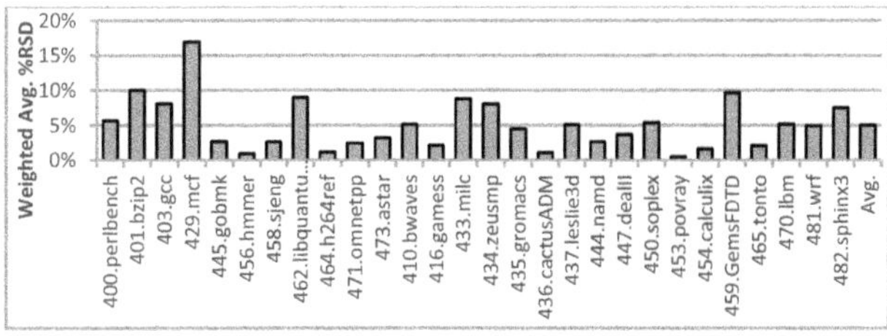

Figure 8. Phase Identification: Weighted Relative Standard Deviation (lower is better)

n_p is the number of quanta that belong to phase p. Each phase is assigned with a weight w_p. Figure 8 shows the phase accuracy of all benchmarks. The average *WRSD* is 5%, which shows that the phase identification scheme could successfully classify the executed quanta so that the performance in each phase is quite similar.

7.3 Effectiveness of Training

A segment could get its *valid* IPC_{alone} from one of the following sources: the three *low-contention* executions during normal quantum, or training trigged by phase prediction and sequential training. For each application, we compute the distribution of all valid IPC_{alone} sources, and report the average of all applications in a workload, as shown in Figure 9(a). As the bandwidth requirement of the workload increases, the number of *low-contention* execution in normal quanta is reduced. On average, the *valid data coverage* is 90%. About 30% of the quanta get its valid IPC_{alone} via training. 60% are from spontaneous low-contention executions.

However, the contribution to the IPC_{alone} estimation accuracy is different. We evaluate the contribution of each data source in an application as follow: the total IPC_{alone} estimation improvement is $IPC_{esti\_alone} - IPC_{shared}$. To calculate the contribution of source x, we find all quanta that use source x to estimate IPC_{alone}^{q}, and replace their $IPC_{esti\_alone}^{q}$ with IPC_{shared}^{q}. The purpose is to simulate the situation in which if we did not get a valid IPC_{alone} for this quantum, and have to use IPC_{shared} instead. We recalculate the estimated IPC_{alone} of the entire application in this case as $IPC_{alone}^{esti\_without\_x}$, and the contribution of x is calculated as $\frac{IPC_{esti\_alone} - IPC_{alone}^{esti\_without\_x}}{IPC_{esti\_alone} - IPC_{shared}}$. Figure 9(b) shows the contribution breakdown. It shows that, for most workloads, training plays an important role on improving the accuracy of IPC_{alone}. It is because training deals with those quanta that have inherently high memory intensity, so they have a higher potential to suffer a bigger slowdown that could cause larger system unfairness.

The average contribution of sequential training appears small because it only deals with applications with fluctuating phases, such as *leslie3d*, *milc* and *zeusmp* in SPEC suite. However, it is important to improve their *coverage* and the IPC_{alone} estimation accuracy. For example, sequential training contributes 28.8% of the estimation accuracy improvement for *leslie3d* in WL#03 and it improves the estimation *coverage* from 88.2% to 93.7% and improves the estimation accuracy from 86.8% to 90.9%, compared to the situation when sequential training is turned off. Significant estimation improvements are also seen in *leslie3d* in WL#02, *milc* in WL#04 and *GemssFDTD* in WL#10, etc. Sequential training can also reduce the number of training quanta because phase prediction accuracy is low for those applications. Sequential training is triggered in 9 applications in the 10 workloads, and on average, it improves the IPC_{alone} estimation accuracy by 2.1% and reduce the number of training quanta by 11%.

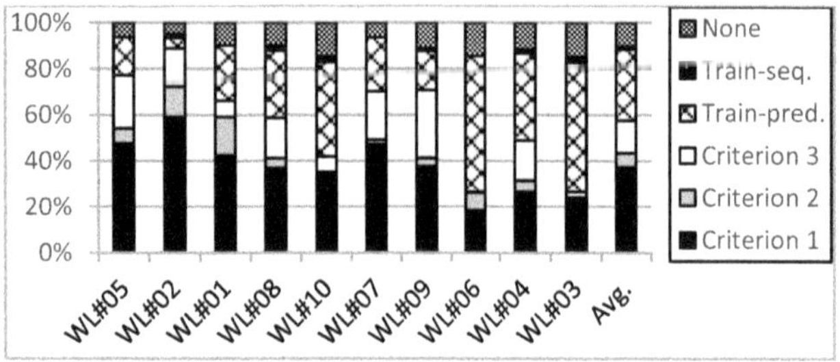

(a) Quantum number breakdown

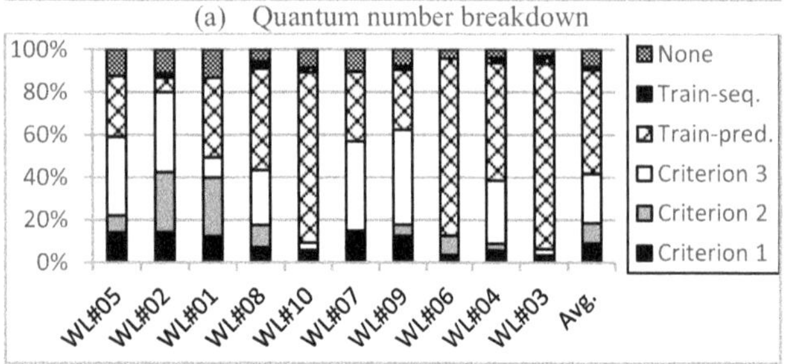

(b) Contribution breakdown

Figure 9. Breakdown of valid IPC^q_{shared} source

Note phases that never get a valid IPC_{alone} also contribute slightly, recall their estimated IPC_{phase} is the average of all invalid histories (refer to Table 1), so it still improves the estimation accuracy for the quanta whose IPC^q_{shared} is smaller than IPC_{phase}.

Table 5 shows the statistics of training on a 4-core system. *Avg. Training Parallelism* is the average number of co-scheduled applications in all the training quanta. Memory intensive workloads suffer more overhead than less memory-intensive ones because there are less spontaneous *low-contention* quanta in the former, so they require more training. WL#03 is the most memory intensive one among the random workloads, about 25.9% of its executed quanta are training, but we can finally reduce the overhead to 4.5% because we reduce the length of a training quantum and increase the training parallelism as much as possible. The average of overhead of all workloads is as low as 1.6%.

Table 5. Training Overheads

WL	#Exec. Quantum	#Train-Pred.	#Train-Seq.	Avg. Training Parallelism	Overhead
#05	376	21	0	2.8	0.5%
#02	472	14	6	3.8	0.1%
#01	246	19	0	2.7	0.8%
#08	498	32	6	2.6	0.9%
#10	266	36	6	2.4	2.4%
#07	274	21	0	3.0	0.6%
#09	413	68	24	3.0	1.8%
#06	468	79	0	2.3	2.3%
#04	504	73	12	2.7	2.3%
#03	715	167	18	2.3	4.5%
Avg.	423.2	53	7.2	2.8	1.6%

7.4 8-core system results

Figure 10 shows the average performance of the 10 workloads on 8-core system. System unfairness under the native OS increases to 1.55 compared to the 4-core modes. FPS could eliminate about 15% of the unfairness even without any training, because it uses the data from spontaneous *low-contention* execution. The overhead is quite negligible. When we gradually relax the training overhead limitation, the fairness improves significantly and system throughput degrades slightly. When the training overhead is unlimited, FPS eliminates 70% of system unfairness at the expense of 4.5% system throughput degradation. Compared to the results on 4-core systems, throughput degradation is slightly larger because the number of available CPU cores is doubled but the training parallelism is nearly unchanged. Hence, more CPU idleness is incurred due to training. Evaluation shows that our fairness-throughput tuner is effective and robust.

7.5 Results on Memory-Intensive Workloads

Memory intensive workloads would result in more training quanta than non-memory-intensive ones. If all applications in a workload are memory-intensive, training overhead may become unacceptable, and the accuracy of IPC_{alone} estimation may also be affected. In this section, we evaluate the effectiveness of FPS on 5 manually constructed and representative memory-intensive workloads. Firstly we use a workload that only includes the top 5 applications with the largest BTR in SPEC suite, i.e., *libquantum, leslie3d, bwaves, GemsFDTD* and *milc*. There are 2 concurrent instances for each application. As a result, the IABW of the workload is as high as 196 trans./usec. This workload is denoted as WL-M. And then, we pick up another 4 less-memory-intensive benchmarks: *lbm, mcf, astar* and *gamess*. Their average BTRs vary from 27 trans./usec to nearly zero. We add one of them to WL-M respectively to form another 4 workloads. We run the 5 workloads on 4 system setups. The evaluation results are shown in Table 6. By comparing the results of the workloads and the results on different system setups, we have the following interesting observations.

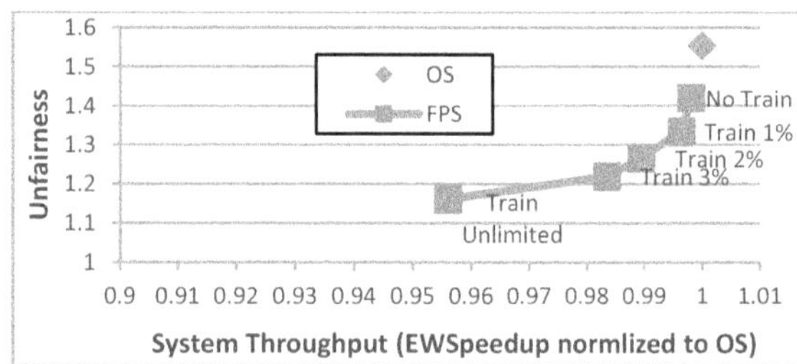

Figure 10. Effect of different training limitation

System unfairness under OS: For an extremely memory-intensive workload where all concurrent applications are memory-intensive, although all of the applications would experience large slowdown, the system unfairness remains relatively small because the difference among the applications' slowdowns is small. For example, When WL-M runs under 4-core-private-cache mode, the maximal and minimal slowdown is 1.92X (for *libquantum*) and 1.65X (for *milc*) respectively, and the system unfairness under OS is only 1.13. Similar results are observed on other 3 system setups, in which the unfairness are 1.12, 1.17 and 1.25, respectively. They are all below the corresponding average of the random workloads. We conclude that severe unfairness is likely to exist when there are both memory-intensive and non-memory-intensive applications. Evaluation results confirmed that when we gradually add a less memory-intensive application into WL-M, the less-memory-intensive application would suffer much smaller slowdown than the memory-intensive ones, and the system unfairness become larger. In the extreme case when WL-M+*gamess* runs in 8-core mode, the unfairness is as high as 4.08, which is the largest among all the workloads that we have evaluated throughout the paper.

Effect of FPS: When the workloads run under FPS and training is not limited, FPS could still effectively eliminate system unfairness even for WL-M where the fairness improvement potential is already small. The average unfairness elimination on the 4 system setups are 59.7%, 66.0%, 61.4% and 71.1% respectively. But the

Table 6. Evaluation results of memory-intensive workloads (positive/negative values are compared to the OS)

System Setup	Workload	OS Unfair-ness	FPS-train-unlimited					FPS-train-limited-2%				
			Unfairness	Training Overhead	T.Time Speedup	EW-Speedup	Unfairness-No Training Distribution	Unfairness	Training Overhead	T.Time Speedup	EW-Speedup	Unfairness-No Training Distribution
PC	WL-M	1.13	1.06 (-52.7%)	17.61%	-11.93%	-10.64%	1.08 (-43.3%)	1.10 (-25.9%)	1.99%	-2.82%	-1.79%	1.47 (+246.9%)
	WL-M+lbm	1.21	1.14 (-34.5%)	20.77%	-14.58%	-13.20%	1.16 (-22.2%)	1.16 (-24.7%)	2.10%	-2.64%	-2.14%	1.44 (+107.0%)
	WL-M+mcf	1.28	1.13 (-53.3%)	15.76%	-10.94%	-9.60%	1.18 (-35.9%)	1.20 (-30.1%)	1.96%	-1.98%	-1.31%	1.34 (+19.9%)
	WL-M+astar	1.44	1.08 (-80.9%)	19.52%	-14.18%	-11.02%	1.12 (-72.9%)	1.25 (-41.9%)	1.97%	-2.85%	-1.86%	1.41 (-6.8%)
	WL-M+gamess	1.65	1.15 (-76.9%)	15.25%	-13.32%	-10.53%	1.16 (-75.2%)	1.28 (-56.5%)	2.02%	-3.10%	-1.83%	1.41 (-37.0%)
	Average	1.34	1.11 (-59.7%)	17.78%	-12.99%	-11.00%	1.14 (-49.9%)	1.20 (-35.8%)	2.01%	-2.68%	-1.79%	1.41 (+66.0%)
SC-1	WL-M	1.12	1.11 (-13.3%)	13.6%	-9.56%	-10.97%	1.11 (-10.3%)	1.10 (-19.1%)	1.98%	-1.58%	-2.49%	1.60 (+383.9%)
	WL-M+lbm	1.32	1.08 (-74.7%)	18.9%	-14.44%	-15.94%	1.07 (-77.4%)	1.19 (-40.7%)	1.97%	-3.91%	-3.90%	1.44 (+36.1%)
	WL-M+mcf	1.31	1.08 (-74.5%)	14.4%	-9.28%	-10.76%	1.08 (-72.5%)	1.12 (-60.8%)	2.02%	-1.43%	-2.50%	1.50 (+61.6%)
	WL-M+astar	1.63	1.10 (-83.8%)	17.7%	-12.01%	-11.10%	1.14 (-78.1%)	1.28 (-56.4%)	2.11%	-2.23%	-2.08%	1.38 (-39.5%)
	WL-M+gamess	1.69	1.11 (-83.8%)	15.3%	-12.13%	-11.21%	1.12 (-83.0%)	1.39 (-43.3%)	2.00%	-2.71%	-3.03%	1.44 (-36.0%)
	Average	1.41	1.10 (-66.0%)	15.98%	-11.48%	-12.00%	1.10 (-64.3%)	1.22 (-44.0%)	2.02%	-2.37%	-2.80%	1.47 (+81.2%)
SC-2	WL-M	1.17	1.15 (-13.4%)	10.60%	-6.02%	-6.95%	1.19 (+9.1%)	1.13 (-22.5%)	1.98%	-1.90%	-2.68%	1.53 (+208.6%)
	WL-M+lbm	1.36	1.15 (-57.3%)	9.45%	-5.46%	-5.17%	1.16 (-54.1%)	1.15 (-56.8%)	1.99%	-1.98%	-1.56%	1.37 (+4.2%)
	WL-M+mcf	1.37	1.17 (-53.7%)	6.92%	-4.39%	-4.41%	1.18 (-51.6%)	1.10 (-74.3%)	2.00%	-1.40%	-1.64%	1.55 (+48.2%)
	WL-M+astar	1.86	1.06 (-92.5%)	9.11%	-5.50%	-4.72%	1.18 (-79.0%)	1.22 (-75.1%)	1.97%	-2.09%	-1.97%	1.32 (-63.5%)
	WL-M+gamess	2.46	1.15 (-90.0%)	9.89%	-6.30%	-5.37%	1.20 (-86.4%)	1.73 (-50.2%)	2.01%	-1.93%	-2.39%	1.40 (-72.4%)
	Average	1.64	1.14 (-61.4%)	9.19%	-5.53%	-5.32%	1.18 (-67.8%)	1.27 (-55.8%)	1.99%	-1.86%	-2.05%	1.43 (+25.0%)
8-core	WL-M	1.25	1.14 (-42.5%)	15.58%	-8.75%	-10.19%	1.17 (-30.8%)	1.19 (-22.6%)	1.80%	-1.84%	-0.68%	1.29 (+15.8%)
	WL-M+lbm	1.51	1.14 (-73.8%)	13.27%	-8.08%	-8.41%	1.14 (-73.0%)	1.49 (-4.1%)	1.77%	-1.39%	-0.51%	1.48 (-7.2%)
	WL-M+mcf	1.29	1.12 (-59.4%)	32.5%	-15.75%	-13.42%	1.17 (-42.1%)	1.24 (-14.9%)	1.93%	-2.57%	-1.19%	1.23 (-18.1%)
	WL-M+astar	2.57	1.13 (-91.6%)	24.2%	-11.54%	-12.08%	1.12 (-92.1%)	2.15 (-26.8%)	1.87%	-0.86%	-2.57%	2.17 (-25.7%)
	WL-M+gamess	4.08	1.36 (-88.2%)	11.0%	-7.32%	-7.15%	1.30 (-90.1%)	2.94 (-37.0%)	1.78%	-2.25%	-2.39%	2.98 (-35.6%)
	Average	2.14	1.18 (-71.1%)	19.31%	-10.29%	-10.25%	1.18 (-65.6%)	1.80 (-21.1%)	1.83%	-1.78%	-1.47%	1.83 (-14.2%)

training overhead is much larger than those random workloads because there are much less spontaneous *low-contention* executions. For example, when WL-M executes in SC-2 mode, the average *valid data coverage* of all applications is only 2% if training is not allowed. If training is not limited, the overheads are between 10% and 20% for the workloads, and the system throughput degradations are between 10% and 15% (as shown in the "T.Time Speedup" and "EWSpeedup" columns). However, we can always use the proposed fairness-throughput tuner to limit the training overhead. It is especially suitable when the unfairness under OS is already relatively small but training is potentially very expensive. For example, FPS could eliminate system unfairness by an average of 35.8%, 44.1%, 55.8% and 21.1% respectively for the 4 system setups when training overhead limitation is set to 2%.

Effect of training distribution: Table 6 also shows the unfairness achieved by FPS when we turn off the proposed training distribution method, which is shown in the "Unfairness-No-Training-Distribution" column. Instead of keeping similar *valid data coverage* of the applications, the compared method always selects the first training candidate that we meet in the run-queue as the final training target. Evaluation results show that, when training is not limited, there is not much difference no matter training distribution is turned on or off, because when there are sufficient training quanta to use, the *valid data coverage* of applications would all approach their upper bound respectively. While the training overhead is limited, different quanta distribution methods would have significant influence on system fairness. We take WL-M running on SC-2 mode as an example. Under OS, the maximal and minimal IPC slowdowns are 3.20X (for *libquantum*) and 2.15X (for *milc*) respectively. When training distribution is off, the unbalanced training resulted in vastly differing *valid data coverage* from 2% (for *GemsFDTD*) to 93% (for *libquantum*). As a result, their estimated IPC slowdowns becomes 2.39X and 1.08X respectively, and the unfairness increases from 1.17 to 1.53. By comparison, when training distribution is on, the maximal and minimal *valid data coverage* is 77% and 53% respectively, and it makes the maximal and minimal estimated IPC slowdowns more similar, which is 1.52X and 1.80X respectively, and system unfairness decreased to 1.13.

7.6 Thread Weight Support

To evaluate the effects of threads with different weights (i.e. priorities), we select 4 different benchmarks whose bandwidth requirements vary greatly from nearly 0% to 46% of the peak, and run 2 concurrent instances for each benchmark and evaluate them on a 4-core shared-cache-diff-chip mode. Figure 11 shows the results. The first set of bars show the performances of benchmarks under the native OS with the same weight. It shows the performance variation due to resource contention. When assigning different weights of 1, 1, 2 and 4 respectively to the applications, OS would allocate proportional number of quanta to application with a higher weight (weighted round robin). The results are shown in the second set of bars. *CactusADM* still runs 21% slower than *gamess* even though they have the same weight, and *bwaves*'s performance is still 1.5% smaller than *gamess* even its number of executed time quanta is doubled compared to the latter. The third set of bars shows the results of FPS. FPS enforces thread weight better because the applications with the same weight have quite similar performance, and the performances of other applications are proportional to their weights.

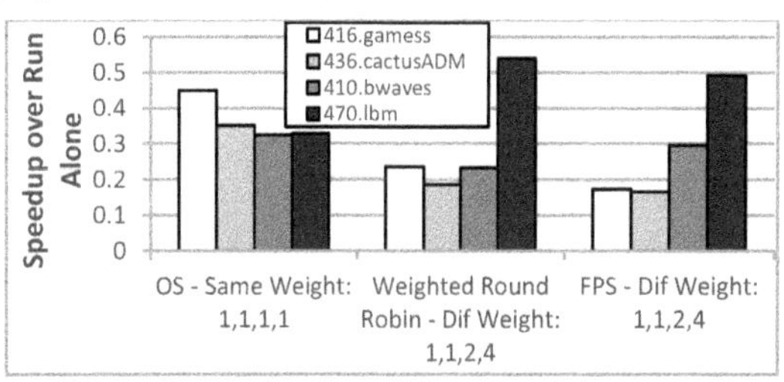

Figure 11. Evaluation of thread weight support

7.7 Overhead of the Scheduler

Compared to the runs under OS, FPS involves overhead mainly from the PMU sampling (interrupt handler) and the scheduling routine (includes the process of PMU data and scheduling). To evaluate the overhead, we run 4 identical applications simultaneously on 4 cores. Compared to OS, execution time under FPS increases 2.87% in total. The overhead from the scheduling routine is 1.68%, and the main source of this part is from PMU and phase related work (overhead from the scheduling algorithm itself is less than 2‰.). Our current user-level scheduler is single-threaded, but PMU data processing for each running application can be naturally distributed to the core on which it executed. Hence, this part of the overhead can be further reduced and made scalable. The remaining 1.19% overhead comes from the PMU sampling, which is distributed among applications, so it is also scalable when the number of cores increases.

8. CONCLUSIONS AND FUTURE WORK

We proposed a *fair progress scheduling policy (FPS)* to provide performance fairness on shared-memory multiprocessors. The basic idea is that, given the same amount of CPU time, if an application did less effective work than others because it suffers bigger slowdown due to resource contention, FPS would allocate extra time quanta to it.

To monitor system unfairness, we define the *forward progress* to quantitatively measure the effective work of an application. The challenge when calculating the *progress* at runtime is to estimate the run-alone performance in each executed quantum while the application is actually running simultaneously with others. Our solution is to classify the execution quanta of application into phases, and obtain their estimated IPC_{alone} by constructing and identifying the *low-contention* co-scheduled applications. We then extend the performance information to other quanta that belong to the same phase in order to help estimating their *progress*.

FPS does not need any special hardware support. Evaluation results show that the IPC_{alone} estimation accuracy is high and it can significantly improve system fairness at the expense of slightly decreased throughput. FPS supports different thread weights. It also provides an effective tuner to let OS freely tradeoff system fairness and higher throughput. Combined with the training distribution policy, it is especially suitable for the memory-intensive workloads where the fairness improvement is smaller but the potential training is expensive.

As a future work, we plan to seek a low-overhead solution to address the issue of cache contention and further improve the estimation accuracy. We also plan to design proper metrics and methodology to address the I/O contention issues.

9. ACKNOWLEDGEMENTS

This research is supported by the Innovation Research Group of NSFC under the grant 60921002, the National Basic Research Program of China (973 program) under the grant 2011CB302504, the National High Technology Research and Development Program of China (863 program) under the grant 2007AA01Z110, 2012AA010901 and 2012AA010902, the National Science and Technology Major Project of China under the grant 2009ZX01036-001-002, and by the U.S. National Science Foundation under the grant CNS-0834599 and CCF-0708822, the Taiwan National Science Council under the grant 100-2220-E-001-001 and 99-2221-E-001-004.

10. REFERENCES

[1] S. Zhuravlev, S. Blagodurov, and A. Fedorova. Addressing shared resource contention in multicore processors via scheduling. In ASPLOS-19, 2010.

[2] E. Ebrahimi, C. J. Lee, O. Mutlu, and Y. N. Patt. Fairness via source throttling: a configurable and high-performance fairness substrate for multi-core memory systems. In ASPLOS-19, 2010.

[3] A. Fedorova, M. Seltzer, and M. D. Smith. Improving Performance Isolation on Chip Multiprocessors via an Operating System Scheduler. In PACT-16, 2007.

[4] D. Xu, C. Wu, and P. C. Yew. On mitigating memory bandwidth contention through bandwidth-aware scheduling. In PACT-19, 2010.

[5] H. Y. Cheng, C. H. Lin, J. Li, and C. L. Yang. Memory Latency Reduction via Thread Throttling. In MICRO-43, 2010.

[6] O. Mutlu and T. Moscibroda. Stall-Time Fair Memory Access Scheduling for Chip Multiprocessors. In MICRO-40, 2007.

[7] R. Iyer, L. Zhao, F. Guo, R. Illikkal, S. Makineni, D. Newell, Y. Solihin, L. Hsu, and S. Reinhardt. QoS policies and architecture for cache/memory in CMP platforms. In SIGMETRICS, 2007.

[8] R. Iyer. CQoS: a framework for enabling QoS in shared caches of CMP platforms. In ICS-18, 2004.

[9] K. Luo, J. Gummaraju, and M. Franklin. Balancing throughput and fairness in SMT processors. In ISPASS, 2001.

[10] K. J. Nesbit, N. Aggarwal, J. Laudon, and J. E. Smith. Fair Queuing Memory Systems. In MICRO-39, 2006.

[11] A. Snavely and D. M. Tullsen. Symbiotic job scheduling for a simultaneous multithreaded processor. In ASPLOS-9, 2000.

[12] C. D. Antonopoulos, D. S. Nikolopoulos, and T. S. Papatheodorou. Scheduling algorithms with bus bandwidth considerations for smps. In ICPP, 2003.

[13] E. Koukis and N. Koziris. Memory and network bandwidth aware scheduling of multiprogrammed workloads on clusters of SMPs. In ICPADS-12, 2006.

[14] T. Sherwood, E. Perelman, G. Hamerly, and B. Calder. Automatically characterizing large scale program behavior. In ASPLOS-10, 2002.

[15] A. S. Dhodapkar and J. E. Smith. Comparing program phase detection techniques. In MICRO-36, 2003.

[16] T. Sherwood, S. Sair, and B. Calder. Phase tracking and prediction. In ISCA-30, 2003.

[17] T. Sherwood, E. Perelman, B. Calder. Basic Block Distribution Analysis to Find Periodic Behavior and Simulation Points in Applications. In PACT-10, 2001.

[18] D. Chandra, F. Guo, S. Kim, and Y. Solihin. Predicting Inter-Thread Cache Contention on a Chip Multi-Processor Architecture. In HPCA-11, 2005.

[19] C. CaBcaval and D. A. Padua. Estimating cache misses and locality using stack distances. In ICS-17, 2003.

[20] S. Kim, D. Chandra, and Y. Solihin. Fair Cache Sharing and Partitioning in a Chip Multiprocessor Architecture. In PACT-13, 2004.

[21] O. Mutlu and T. Moscibroda. Parallelism-Aware Batch Scheduling: Enhancing both Performance and Fairness of Shared DRAM Systems. In ISCA-35, 2008

Characterizing Continuous Time Random Walks on Time Varying Graphs

Daniel Figueiredo
COPPE
Federal Univ. of Rio de Janeiro
Rio de Janeiro, Brazil
daniel@land.ufrj.br

Philippe Nain
INRIA
Sophia Antipolis,France
philippe.nain@inria.fr

Bruno Ribeiro
Dept. of Computer Science
UMASS Amherst
Amherst, MA
ribeiro@cs.umass.edu

E. de Souza e Silva
COPPE
Federal Univ. of Rio de Janeiro
Rio de Janeiro, Brazil
edmundo@land.ufrj.br

Don Towsley
Dept. of Computer Science
UMASS Amherst
Amherst, MA
towsley@cs.umass.edu

ABSTRACT

In this paper we study the behavior of a continuous time random walk (CTRW) on a stationary and ergodic time varying dynamic graph. We establish conditions under which the CTRW is a stationary and ergodic process. In general, the stationary distribution of the walker depends on the walker rate and is difficult to characterize. However, we characterize the stationary distribution in the following cases: i) the walker rate is significantly larger or smaller than the rate in which the graph changes (time-scale separation), ii) the walker rate is proportional to the degree of the node that it resides on (coupled dynamics), and iii) the degrees of node belonging to the same connected component are identical (structural constraints). We provide examples that illustrate our theoretical findings.

Categories and Subject Descriptors

G.3 [**PROBABILITY AND STATISTICS**]: Stochastic processes

Keywords

Random Walks, Dynamic Graphs, Time Varying Graphs, Continuous Time Random Walks, Stationary Distribution, Time Scale Separation

This work was supported by the NSF grant CNS-0721779 and ARL Cooperative Agreement W911NF-09-2-0053. The views and conclusions contained in this document are those of the authors and should not be interpreted as representing the of official policies, either expressed or implied of the NSF, ARL, or the U.S. Government. The U.S. Government is authorized to reproduce and distribute reprints for Government purposes notwithstanding any copyright notation hereon. The work of E. de Souza e Silva and D. Figueiredo was partially supported by grants from CNPq and Faperj.

SIGMETRICS'12, June 11–15, 2012, London, England, UK.

1. INTRODUCTION

During the last decade, there has been a wide interest in characterizing and modeling the structure of various networks, from neural networks, to the web, to Facebook friends. Real networks are inherently dynamic in the sense that both nodes and edges come and go over some time-scale. However, most efforts consider the network as either a single static graph or as a pre-defined sequence of graph configurations.

Random walks are an important building blocks for characterizing networks. Their simple behavior on static networks has been explored to devise algorithms for various purposes, from ranking to searching (details in Section 5). However, very little is known about the long-term behavior of random walks on dynamic networks.

In this paper, we study continuous time random walks (CTRWs) on stationary and ergodic dynamic graphs. We make the following contributions towards this goal:

- We consider stationary and ergodic dynamic graphs where nodes are always present in the network but edges are allowed to come and go over time, including the cases where the network consists of several connected components. We introduce the notion of T-connectivity and show that if the dynamic graph is stationary, ergodic and T-connected then the CTRW is also stationary and ergodic. In the full generality of our framework, the stationary distribution of the walker depends on the walker rate and is difficult to characterize. However,
- we characterize the stationary distribution of the random walk for several cases: *(i)* **Time-scale separation**: the walker rate is significantly larger or smaller than the rate in which the graph changes; *(ii)* **Coupled dynamics**: the walker rate is proportional to the degree of the node that it resides on; *(iii)* **Structural constraints**: the degrees of nodes within any connected components are identical (but can vary among different components).
- We evaluate numerically several examples to support our theoretical results and illustrate their applicability. We also present a simple illustrative DTN application.

The remainder of this paper is organized as follows. Section 2 presents the proposed modeling framework together with some definitions and properties. Section 3 presents the stationary distribution of CTRW when the walker rate (for being too fast or too slow in respect to the speed the graph changes) allows a time scale decomposition of the combined walker and graph processes; we also present conditions under which the CTRW stationary distribution is invariant under time scale changes. Section 4 presents the numerical examples and applications. In Section 5 we discuss the related work. Finally, Section 6 concludes the paper.

2. MODEL FORMULATION

In this section we define important concepts that will be used throughout this paper. We define a dynamic graph as a simple marked point process. A continuous time random walk (CTRW) over a dynamic graph is also a marked point process. We define the concept of T-connectivity to express the ability of nodes to be connected in time. We also define conditions for stationarity of the graph process and the CTRW process. We start by defining the graph dynamics.

DEFINITION 2.1 (DYNAMIC GRAPH). *The time evolution of the graph under consideration is given by the (possibly simultaneous) addition and deletion of edges. Let V denote a finite set of n nodes and let $\mathcal{A}$ denote a finite set of m adjacency matrices $\mathcal{A} = \{A_k\}_{k=1}^m$, where A_k is an $n \times n$ unweighted symmetric adjacency matrix. A dynamic graph is a simple Random Marked Point Process (RMPP) $\Psi = \{(X_i, S_i)\}_{i\in\mathbb{Z}}$, where $\mathbb{Z}$ is the set of all integers, $X_i \in \mathcal{A}$ denotes the i-th graph configuration and S_i is the time that the network spends in that configuration.*

Because Ψ is simple, $P(S_i = 0) = 0$ for all i. Moreover, we assume $0 < E[S_i] < \infty$, $i \in \mathbb{Z}$. We use G_k to denote the graph configuration that has adjacency matrix A_k, $k = 1, \ldots, m$. Throughout this work we use A_k and G_k interchangeably. To simplify our analysis we focus on unweighted adjacency matrices. However, edge weights can be easily accounted for in the walker rates and thus our results are also applicable to weighted dynamic graphs. We define the process $\{A(t)\}_{t\in\mathbb{R}}$, as

$$A(t) = \sum_{i\in\mathbb{Z}} X_i \mathbf{1}_{\{T_i \le t < T_{i+1}\}}, \qquad (1)$$

where by convention $\cdots < T_{-1} < T_0 \le 0 < T_1 < \cdots$ are the successive times at which the graph switches to another configuration with $S_i := T_{i+1} - T_i$, $i \in \mathbb{Z}$, i.e., $A(t)$ denotes the adjacency matrix of the graph at time t; $A(t)$ is right-continuous.

ASSUMPTION 2.1. *The graph process Ψ is stationary and ergodic.*

Throughout this paper we assume that Assumption 2.1 holds. The following proposition shows that the ergodicity and stationarity of $\Psi = \{X_i, S_i\}_{i\in\mathbb{Z}}$ implies $\{A(t)\}_{t\in\mathbb{R}}$ is also stationary and ergodic.

PROPOSITION 2.1. *Under Assumption 2.1, $\{A(t)\}_{t\in\mathbb{R}}$ is stationary and ergodic.*

In what follows we provide a result that will be useful in our proofs:

THEOREM 2.1. *Under Assumption 2.1,*

$$\lim_{t\to\infty} \frac{1}{t}\int_0^t \mathbf{1}_{\{A(x)=A_k\}} dx = \sigma_k\,, \quad P\text{-a.s.}, \qquad (2)$$

where $\sigma_k > 0$.

The proofs of Proposition 2.1 and Theorem 2.1 are found in our technical report [5]. We refer to $\sigma = (\sigma_1, \ldots, \sigma_m)$ as the stationary distribution of $\{A(t)\}_{t\ge0}$. We note in passing that under Birkhoff's ergodic theorem (Shiryaev [19, pg. 409, Theorem 1]), $\sigma_k = E[\mathbf{1}_{\{X_i=A_k\}} S_i]/E[S_i]$, for all i.

Another important property of Ψ that we use throughout this work is the uniform convergence of the time average regardless of the initial conditions if Ψ is stationary and ergodic.

PROPOSITION 2.2 (UNIFORM MIXING). *Under Assumption 2.1,*

$$\lim_{t\to\infty} \frac{1}{t}\int_0^t P(A(x) = A_k|\mathcal{B})dx = \sigma_k\,, \quad k = 1, \ldots, m, \qquad (3)$$

for any Borel set $\mathcal{B}$ such that $P(\mathcal{B}) > 0$. Furthermore, the convergence is uniform with respect to any $\mathcal{B}$.

Proof. A short proof is presented. An extended proof can be found in our technical report [5]. Stationarity and ergodicity imply (2). Integrating both sides of (2) w.r.t. $dP(\omega)$ for $\omega \in \mathcal{B}$ and using the bounded convergence theorem, Fubini's theorem and Egorov's theorem [11, pg. 290, Theorem 12] gives (3) uniformly in $\mathcal{B}$ for any Borel set $\mathcal{B}$ such that $P(\mathcal{B}) > 0$. □

It is possible for one or more graph configurations to consist of two or more disconnected components, in which case we have to be concerned about whether a walker can move from any node to any other node over time. In what follows we introduce the concept of connectivity over time between two nodes (denoted as T-connectivity).

DEFINITION 2.2 (T-CONNECTIVITY). *Two nodes u and v are said to be T-connected in Ψ, if they are connected in the graph induced by adjacency matrix $A = \vee_k A_k$.*

T-connectivity can also be stated as a graph property.

DEFINITION 2.3 (T-CONNECTED GRAPH). *A dynamic graph is said to be T-connected if all pairs of nodes are T-connected.*

We now define a Continuous Time Random Walk (CTRW) over the dynamic graph, starting at time $t = 0$.

DEFINITION 2.4 (CTRW). *A continuous time random walk (CTRW) on a dynamic graph $\{A(t)\}_{t\in\mathbb{R}}$ associated with RMPP Ψ, is a process $\{(A(t), U(t))\}_{t\ge0}$, where $U(t) \in V$ is the position (node) of the walker at time t. The times between CTRW steps are independent and exponentially distributed. The rate at which the walker makes a step at node $U(t) = v$ when $A(t) = A_k$ is $\gamma_{k,v}$. At the time the walker leaves v, it chooses one of its currently connected neighbors in A_k (if any) uniformly at random. When v has no neighbors in A_k the walker stays at v until the next step event.*

Let $\Gamma = \{\gamma_{k,v}\}$ denote the set of walker rates associated with $\{A(t)\}_{t\ge0}$. We will find it useful to express $\gamma_{k,v}$ as $\gamma_{k,v} = \beta_{k,v}\gamma$, $k = 1, \ldots, m$ and $v \in V$. Walker rates of interest to us include $\beta_{k,v} = 1$ (denoted *CTRW with constant walker rate*) and $\beta_{k,v} = d_{k,v}$, where $d_{k,v}$ is the degree of v given adjacency matrix A_k (denoted *CTRW with degree dependent walker rate*).

The above framework is general enough to describe several more particular dynamic graph models, such as renewal processes and Markovian processes. In a Markovian process S_i is exponentially distributed and $P[X_i = x_i | X_{i-1} = x_{i-1}, X_{i-2} = x_{i-2}, \dots] = P[X_i = x_i | X_{i-1} = x_{i-1}]$, $x_i \in V$, $i = 0, 1, \dots$.

Notation Summary

$\Psi = \{(X_i, S_i)\}_{i\in\mathbb{Z}}$	dynamic graph process (in events)
$\{A(t)\}_{t\in\mathbb{R}}$	dynamic graph process (in time)
$\{(A(t), U(t))\}_{t\geq 0}$	CTRW process
$\sigma = (\sigma_1, \dots, \sigma_m)$	stationary distribution of $\{A(t)\}_{t\geq 0}$
$\gamma_{k,v} = \beta_{k,v}\gamma$	*walker rate* of the CTRW at node v at configuration A_k

3. CHARACTERIZING RWS: STATIONARY BEHAVIOR

In this section we focus on the stationary behavior of a RW on a dynamic graph, in particular the steady state fraction of time the walker spends in each node of the network: $\boldsymbol{\pi} = (\pi_1, \dots, \pi_n)$.

The steady state distribution $\boldsymbol{\pi}$ is trivial if the graph is static and T-connected, i.e., $A(t) = A'$, $\forall t \geq 0$, where A' is a symmetric $(0, 1)$-adjacency matrix of a connected graph. The stationary distribution is unique and given by

$$\pi_v = \frac{d_v/\gamma_v}{\sum_w d_w/\gamma_w}, \quad v \in V,$$

where d_v denotes the degree of node v and γ_v is the walker rate at node v. Characterization on a dynamic graph is much more challenging. How can we characterize $\boldsymbol{\pi}$ on dynamic graphs? When does $\boldsymbol{\pi}$ converge for dynamic graphs? When can we give an expression for $\boldsymbol{\pi}$? We focus on three cases where we are able to characterize this behavior.

We begin our study of the stationary behavior of the process $\{U(t)\}$ with the following.

THEOREM 3.1. *If the RMPP Ψ is T-connected, stationary, and ergodic, then the process $\{(A(t), U(t))\}_{t\geq 0}$ is stationary, and the stationary distribution is unique.*

Proof. We create a new marked point process, $\{(X'_i, S'_i)\}_0^\infty$ that is a superposition of the graph process $\{(X_j, S_j)\}_0^\infty$ and a Poisson process having rate $\gamma_{\max} = \max_{r\in\Gamma} r$ (recall that Γ is the set of walker rates). To simplify our proof we shall assume $P[T_0 = 0] = 1$, where T_0 is as defined in (1), although the proof is valid for any $T_0 \leq 0$. We associate the mark "0" with each point of the Poisson process, Hence $X'_i \in \{0\} \cup \{A_1, \dots, A_m\}$. As both the graph and Poisson processes are event stationary, the new merged process is also event stationary [6, Section 1.3.5]. Let $t'_0 < t'_1 < \cdots < t'_i \leq \cdots$ denote the times associated with this new process, $\{(X'_i, S'_i)\}_0^\infty$. Consider the process $\{(A'_i, U_i)\}_0^\infty$ where U_i denotes the walker position at time t'_i and A'_i denotes the adjacency matrix during the period $[t'_i, t'_{i+1})$. Note that $(A'_i, U_i) \in \mathcal{A} \times V$ takes values from a finite set. $\{(A'_i, U_i)\}$ is described by a stochastic recursion of the form $(A'_i, U_i) = \phi(U_{i-1}, X'_i, R_i)$ where

$$A'_i = \phi_a(U'_{i-1}, X'_i, R_i) = \mathbf{1}\{X'_i = 0\}A'_{i-1} + \mathbf{1}\{X'_i \neq 0\}X'_i,$$
$$U_i = \phi_b(U'_{i-1}, X'_i, R_i),$$

for all $i = 0, \dots$. Here X'_i, S'_i are as previously defined and $\{R_i\}$ is an iid sequence of uniformly distributed rvs in $[0, 1]$ independent of $\{(X'_i, S'_i)\}$. These auxiliary rvs are used to choose the neighbor to which the walker goes or to remain stationed at its current node. Note that $\{(X'_i, S'_i, R_i)\}$ is stationary. ϕ_b is defined so that when $X'_i \neq 0$, the walker does not move ($U_i = U_{i-1}$) but the graph changes to configuration X'_i. If $X'_i = 0$, the walker moves from U_i with probability $\gamma_{X'_i, U_i}/\gamma_{\max}$, moving to one of its neighbors (in configuration A'_{i-1}) chosen uniformly at random (using R_i).

Theorem 1 in [13] states that if there exists a random subset, $B \subseteq \mathcal{A} \times V$ such that a sample path monotonicity condition ((5) in [13]) holds and the existence of a finite non-empty sample path absorbing set ((9) in [13]) exists, then it is possible to construct process $\{X'_i, S'_i, A'_i, U_i\}$ that is event stationary as is $\{U_i\}$. In our case, because our state space is finite, these conditions trivially hold by taking $B = \mathcal{A} \times V$. Since $\{X'_i, S'_i, A'_i, U_i\}$ is event stationary, $\{A'(t), U(t)\}$ is also stationary. It follows from our construction that $\{A(t)\} = \{A'(t)\}$; hence $\{A(t), U(t)\}$ is also stationary.

We now address the question of uniqueness through a coupling argument. Consider two random walks $\{\{U_1(t)\}_{t\geq 0}$ and $\{U_2(t)\}\}_{t\geq 0}$ that differ in their starting locations at time $t = 0$, $U_1(0) = u_1$ and $U_2(0) = u_2$. We are interested in establishing that the time, T at which they meet, is finite a.s.. After time T the processes couple, i.e., for $t > T$, $U_1(t) = U_2(t)$. This is possible because the times between steps are exponentially distributed random variables. Thus, when T is finite, the above coupling argument implies that $\{U_1(t)\}$ and $\{U_2(t)\}$, which we have shown to be time asymptotic stationary, have the same stationary distribution.

It is left to show is that T is finite. We sketch the argument here and relegate the details to the our technical report [5]. The basic idea is to identify intervals of time of length $T' < \infty$ starting at times $iT' \geq 0$, $i = 0, 1, \dots$, and based on the ergodicity and time stationarity of the graph process to establish a lower bound, p_0, on the probability of two walkers coupling during interval $[iT', (i+1)T']$. The probability that the walkers do not couple within the interval $[0, jT_0)$ is upper bounded by $(1 - p_0)^j$. Thus the walkers couple in finite time a.s.. □

Note that if the graph process is not T-connected, then it is possible for the system to exhibit multiple stationary regimes that depend on the initial position of the walker. Next we characterize $\boldsymbol{\pi}$ when there is a time-scale separation of the walker and graph dynamics.

3.1 Stationary Behavior under Time-scale Separation

Consider a scenario where the walker is either much faster or much slower relative to the rate that the graph changes configurations. In this case, we have a time-scale separation between the two processes that allows us to characterize $\boldsymbol{\pi}$.

3.1.1 *The Fast Walker*

Let us first assume that the walker rate is much larger than the rate at which the graph changes. For a sufficiently large γ, the steady state probabilities of the random walk $\boldsymbol{\pi}$ is a linear combination of the corresponding probabilities of the adjacency matrices $A_1, \dots, A_m$. Theorem 3.2 formalizes this argument for the case that every adjacency matrix in

$\mathcal{A}$ is connected. We will describe, under certain conditions, how to relax this assumption later.

In preparation, let $\gamma_{k,v} = \beta_{k,v}\gamma$ and let $\boldsymbol{\pi}^{(k)}(\gamma) = (\pi_1^{(k)}(\gamma), \ldots, \pi_n^{(k)}(\gamma))$ denote the steady state distribution of a random walk on the undirected graph with adjacency matrix A_k as a function of $\gamma > 0$. It is given by

$$\pi_v^{(k)}(\gamma) \equiv \pi^{(k)} = \frac{d_{k,v}/\beta_{k,v}}{\sum_{j\in V} d_{k,j}/\beta_{k,j}}, \quad v \in V; k = 1, \ldots, m. \tag{4}$$

independent of γ. Let

$$\boldsymbol{\pi}^{(k)}(\gamma, t, w) = (\pi_1^{(k)}(\gamma, t, w), \ldots, \pi_n^{(k)}(\gamma, t, w))$$

denote the distribution of the CTRW on A_k at time $t \geq 0$ starting from node w. Assume A_k is irreducible, $k = 1, \ldots, m$, i.e., the graph with adjacency matrix A_k is connected. Because the random walk with adjacency matrix A_k is described by a time-reversible Markov chain, $\boldsymbol{\pi}^{(k)}(\gamma, t, w)$ can be expressed as

$$\boldsymbol{\pi}^{(k)}(\gamma, t, w) = \boldsymbol{\pi}^{(k)} + \sum_{j=2}^{n} \mathbf{c}_{j,w}^{(k)} e^{\lambda_{kj}\gamma t}, \quad w \in V,\ t > 0, \tag{5}$$

where $0 = \lambda_{k1} > \lambda_{k2} \geq \cdots \geq \lambda_{km}$ are the eigenvalues associated with $Q_k(\gamma)/\gamma$ where $Q_k(\gamma)$ is the infinitesimal generator associated with the random walk with parameter γ on the graph with adjacency matrix A_k, and $\{\mathbf{c}_{j,w}^{(k)}\}$ are vectors related to the j-th eigenvector of the random walk and the initial condition that the walker begins at node w.

THEOREM 3.2. *If the graph process Ψ is T-connected, stationary, ergodic, and the configurations are always connected, then in the limit as $\gamma \to \infty$, the stationary distribution $\boldsymbol{\pi}$ of the random walk is given by*

$$\boldsymbol{\pi} = \sum_{k=1}^{m} \sigma_k \boldsymbol{\pi}^{(k)}. \tag{6}$$

Proof. We show that the walker steady state distribution $\boldsymbol{\pi}(\gamma) \to \boldsymbol{\pi}$ as $\gamma \to \infty$ where $\boldsymbol{\pi}$ is given in (6).

We focus on the i-th graph configuration, X_i, $i \geq 0$. To simplify our proof we shall assume $P[T_0 = 0] = 1$, where T_0 is as defined in (1). Let $F_i^{(k)}(x) = P(S_i \leq x | X_i = A_k)$ and define $\boldsymbol{\eta}_i^{(k)}(\gamma)$ to be the stationary distribution of the CTRW while the graph is in state $X_i = A_k$. Let $P_{i,w}(\gamma)$ denote the initial walker distribution when the process first enters graph configuration X_i. $\boldsymbol{\eta}_i^{(k)}(\gamma)$ is defined as

$$\begin{aligned}
&\boldsymbol{\eta}_i^{(k)}(\gamma) \\
&= \sum_{w\in V} P_{i,w}(\gamma) \int_0^\infty \frac{1}{t}\int_0^t \boldsymbol{\pi}^{(k)}(\gamma, x, w)dx\, dF_i^{(k)} \\
&= \boldsymbol{\pi}^{(k)} + \sum_{w\in V} P_{i,w}(\gamma) \int_0^\infty \frac{1}{t}\int_0^t \sum_{j=2}^{n} \mathbf{c}_w^{(k)} e^{\lambda_{kj}\gamma x} dx\, dF_i^{(k)},
\end{aligned}$$

where the second equality follows from (5). We focus on the second term, henceforth denoted as C_γ, which we show goes to zero as $\gamma \to \infty$. We focus first on the singularity of the $1/t$ term due to the first integral starting from zero,

$$\begin{aligned}
|C_\gamma| &< F_i^{(k)}(\gamma^{-1/4})\mathbf{e} \\
&+ \sum_{w\in V} P_{i,w}(\gamma) \int_{\gamma^{-1/4}}^\infty \frac{1}{t}\int_0^t \sum_{j=2}^{n} |\mathbf{c}_w^{(k)}| e^{\lambda_{kj}\gamma x} dx\, dF_i^{(k)},
\end{aligned}$$

where $|\mathbf{c}|$ is the vector whose components are the absolute values of the components of $\mathbf{c}$ and $\mathbf{e}$ is a vector of all ones. Evaluating the second integral and recognizing that $1/t \leq \gamma^{1/4}$ for $t \geq \gamma^{-1/4}$ yields

$$\begin{aligned}
|C_\gamma| &< F_i^{(k)}(\gamma^{-1/4})\mathbf{e} \\
&\quad + \gamma^{1/4} \sum_{w\in V} P_{i,w}(\gamma) \sum_{j=2}^{n} \int_{\gamma^{-1/4}}^\infty \frac{|\mathbf{c}_w^{(k)}|}{\lambda_{kj}\gamma}(e^{\lambda_{kj}\gamma t} - 1)dF_i^{(k)} \\
&\leq F_i^{(k)}(\gamma^{-1/4})\mathbf{e} \\
&\quad + \frac{1}{\gamma^{3/4}} \sum_{w\in V} P_{i,w}(\gamma) \sum_{j=2}^{n} \int_{\gamma^{-1/4}}^\infty \frac{|\mathbf{c}_w^{(k)}|}{(-\lambda_{kj})} dF_i^{(k)} \\
&\leq F_i^{(k)}(\gamma^{-1/4})\mathbf{e} \\
&\quad + \frac{1}{\gamma^{3/4}} \sum_{w\in V} P_{i,w}(\gamma) \sum_{j=2}^{n} -\frac{|\mathbf{c}_w^{(k)}|}{\lambda_{kj}}(1 - F_i^{(k)}(\gamma^{-1/4})).
\end{aligned}$$

Both terms go to zero as $\gamma \to \infty$. Consequently $C_\gamma \to 0$ and

$$\lim_{\gamma\to\infty} \boldsymbol{\eta}_i^{(k)}(\gamma) = \boldsymbol{\pi}^{(k)}, \quad \forall k$$

This holds for all i; therefore it holds when the graph is in steady state and removal of the conditioning on the graph configuration yields (6). □

We now focus on the case where one or more of the graph configurations consists of disconnected components. We relabel the nodes in each graph configuration in order to easily identify the disconnected components. For each of the original m adjacency matrices, A_k, we rearrange the n nodes into subsets of connected components. In other words, consider graph configuration G_k associated with adjacency matrix A_k. Partition the set of nodes in G_k into o_k sets, each containing only connected nodes. The o_k sets correspond to o_k adjacency matrices, $\{A_{k,1}, \ldots, A_{k,o_k}\}$ and graph configurations $\{G_{k,1}, \ldots, G_{k,o_k}\}$. Let $V_{k,l}$ denote the set of nodes in configuration $G_{k,l}$.

Let $\boldsymbol{\psi}(\gamma) = (\psi_{1,1}(\gamma), \ldots, \psi_{m,o_m}(\gamma))$ denote the vector of stationary probabilities that the walker is in the different components of all of the configurations when the rate parameter is γ. Because the CTRW process is ergodic, this vector exists and is given by

$$\psi_{k,l}(\gamma) = \lim_{t\to\infty} \frac{1}{t}\int_0^t \sum_{v\in V_{k,l}} \mathbf{1}_{\{A(s)=A_k, U(s)=v\}} ds, \quad \forall k, l.$$

Define

$$\boldsymbol{\psi} = \lim_{\gamma\to\infty} \boldsymbol{\psi}(\gamma). \tag{7}$$

We will describe conditions under which $\boldsymbol{\psi}$ can be computed later. In what follows we show that if $\boldsymbol{\psi}$ exists then we obtain the stationary distribution $\boldsymbol{\pi}$ of the random walk in the limit as $\gamma \to \infty$.

Let $\boldsymbol{\pi}^{(k,l)}$ be the steady state distribution of a random walk on the undirected graph with adjacency matrix $A_{k,l}$. Similar to equation (4)[1],

$$\pi_v^{(k,l)} = \frac{d_{k,v}/\beta_{k,v}}{\sum_{j\in V_{k,l}} d_{k,j}/\beta_{k,j}}, \quad v \in V_{k,l},$$

and $k = 1, \ldots, m, l = 1, \ldots, o_k$.

[1]If the denominator is zero (i.e., there are isolated nodes) we simplify our notation assuming the ratio $0/0 = 1$.

We let $\boldsymbol{\pi}^{(k)}$ be the concatenation of vectors $\boldsymbol{\pi}^{(k,l)}$, that is, $\boldsymbol{\pi}^{(k)} = (\boldsymbol{\pi}^{(k,1)}\| \dots \|\boldsymbol{\pi}^{(k,o_k)})$ and

$$\hat{\boldsymbol{\pi}}^{(k)} = (\psi_{k,1}\boldsymbol{\pi}^{(k,1)}\| \dots \|\psi_{k,o_k}\boldsymbol{\pi}^{(k,o_k)}).$$

Note that vectors $\hat{\boldsymbol{\pi}}^{(k)}$ for all $1 \leq k \leq m$ have the same cardinality.

We have the following result.

THEOREM 3.3. *If the graph process Ψ is T-connected, stationary, and ergodic, and $\boldsymbol{\psi}$ exists, then in the limit as $\gamma \to \infty$, the stationary distribution $\boldsymbol{\pi}$ of the random walk when graph configurations may be disconnected is given by*

$$\boldsymbol{\pi} = \sum_{k=1}^{m} \hat{\boldsymbol{\pi}}^{(k)}. \tag{8}$$

Proof. The proof is similar to that for the case where all graphs are connected. □

In general $\boldsymbol{\psi}$ is difficult to compute. The difficulty here lies in that the walker state at time t_0 can now depend on $\{A(t)\}_0^{t_0}$, something that was not possible when all configurations were connected. However, $\boldsymbol{\psi}$ is easily characterized when the underlying transitions between configurations are described by a Markov chain and the times that the graph remain in a configuration correspond to mutually independent sequences of iid random variables; one sequence for each configuration. Let $\mathbf{P} = [p_{ij}]$ denote the $m \times m$ transition probability matrix for the graph configurations at the time of transitions between graphs and, with an abuse of notation, let $\{S_{k,i}\}_0^\infty$, $k = 1, \dots m$, denote the mutually independent iid sequences of configuration holding times for the graph configurations.

We focus now on transitions that the walker makes between connected components in two different graph configurations, say the j_1-th connected component in configuration G_{k_1} and the j_2-th connected component in configuration G_{k_2}. We define a transition probability matrix $\hat{\mathbf{P}} = [\hat{p}_{k_1,j_1;k_2,j_2}]$ as follows

$$\hat{p}_{k_1,j_1;k_2,j_2} = p_{k_1,k_2} \frac{\sum_{v \in V_{k_1,j_1} \cap V_{k_2,j_2}} d_{k_1,v}/\beta_{k_1,v}}{\sum_{w \in V_{k_1,j_1}} d_{k_1,w}/\beta_{k_1,w}}. \tag{9}$$

The first term accounts for transitions between graph configurations and the second term accounts for the walker dynamics. Here $\hat{\mathbf{P}}$ can be thought of as the transition probability matrix for a discrete time Markov chain that characterizes the subgraphs visited by a random walk at graph transitions in the limit as $\gamma \to \infty$. This chain is irreducible provided the graph is T-connected. Let $\boldsymbol{\psi}^* = (\psi^*_{1,1}, \dots, \psi^*_{m,l_m})$ denote the stationary distribution of this MC. The earlier introduced probability distribution $\boldsymbol{\psi}$ can be expressed in terms of $\boldsymbol{\psi}^*$ as follows

$$\psi_{k,l} = \frac{\psi^*_{k,l} E[S_k]}{\sum_{i=1}^{m} \sum_{j=1}^{o_i} \psi^*_{i,j} E[S_i]}, \quad A_k \in \mathcal{A}; l = 1, \dots, o_k\,, \tag{10}$$

Note that the above characterization depends on the independence and identical distribution assumptions of the configuration holding times. This, along with (8) fully characterizes the stationary distribution of the walker in the fast walker regime for the Markovian environment.

3.1.2 The Slow Walker

In this section we consider the walker stationary distribution, $\boldsymbol{\pi}$, at the other timescale decomposition, namely where the graph dynamics speed up relative to the walker. Consider a walker with the set of walker rates Γ walking a dynamic graph Ψ. We consider the RMPP $\Psi^{(a)} = \{(X_i, aS_i)\}_{i \in \mathbb{Z}}$ that is a speed up of the RMPP Ψ by a factor of a, $0 < a < 1$, and characterize the CTRW on $\Psi^{(a)}$ as $a \to 0$. We denote by $A^{(a)}(t)$ the state at time t of the dynamic graph corresponding to the RMMP $\Psi^{(a)}$. We do this in two steps. We first consider an observer of $\Psi^{(a)}$, who makes observations according to a renewal process with the property that it has a continuous non-increasing probability density function with finite mean. We then determine conditions under which the observer is guaranteed to observe independent instances of the graph with probability given by the stationary distribution of the graph. Finally, we consider a Poisson observer and couple the walker with it in order to characterize the stationary distribution of the walker.

We introduce a renewal process $\{W_j\}_1^\infty$ where W_j denotes the time between the $(j-1)$-th and j-th observations with CDF $G(x)$ (with PDF $g(x)$) satisfying the following assumption.

ASSUMPTION 3.1. *The pdf $g(x) := dP(W_i < x)/dx$ is differentiable with $g'(x) = dg(x)/dx$, non-increasing, non-negative, with (i) $g(0) < \infty$, (ii) $\int_0^\infty g(x)dx = 1$ and (iii) $E[W_j] = \int_0^\infty xg(x)dx := D < \infty$. As a consequence of the previous assumptions (iv) $\int_0^\infty xg'(x)dx = -1$ (Hint: use an integration by part and note that $\lim_{x\to\infty} xg(x) = 0$ thanks to (iii)).*

Assumption 3.1 holds if W_i is exponentially distributed with parameter $\gamma < \infty$. It also holds if W_i has a Pareto distribution with Pareto index strictly larger than one. We will now observe the graph at the renewal instants $\sum_{k=1}^{j} W_k$, $j \geq 1$.

We denote by $A^{(a)}(t)$ the state at time $t \in \mathbb{R}$ of the graph associated with the RMPP $\Psi^{(a)}$, namely,

$$A^{(a)}(t) = \sum_{i=-\infty}^{\infty} X_i \mathbf{1}(aT_i \leq t < aT_{i+1}), \tag{11}$$

so that $A^{(a)}(t) = A(t/a)$ for all $t \in \mathbb{R}$, where T_i is as defined in (1). We denote by $A^{(a)}_{(j)} = A^{(a)}(W_1 + \cdots + W_j)$ the graph configuration of $A^{(a)}(t)$ at the j-th renewal instant ($j \geq 1$).

LEMMA 3.1. *Let $\Psi^{(a)}$ be the RMPP associated with the stationary and ergodic dynamic graph Ψ. If the observation process satisfies Assumption 3.1, then for any $i \geq 1$, $k = 1, \dots, m$,*

$$\lim_{a \to 0} P\left(A^{(a)}_{(i+1)} = A_k \mid A^{(a)}_{(j)} = A_{l_j}, j = 1, \dots, i\right) = \sigma_k. \tag{12}$$

Proof. Throughout $i \geq 1$ is fixed and so are $k, l_1, \dots, l_i \in \{1, \dots, m\}$. Define the set $I_i = \{1, \dots, i\}$ and let $g_a(x) := ag(ax)$.

Conditioning on $W_j = y_j$ for $j \in I_i$ and $W_{i+1} = x$ and using the independence assumption between the process $\{A(t)\}$ and the iid rvs $(W_j)_j$ with pdf $g(\cdot)$, gives

$$P\left(A^{(a)}_{(i+1)} = A_k \,|\, A^{(a)}_{(j)} = A_{l_j}, j \in I_i\right) - \sigma_k =$$
$$\int_{[0,\infty)^i} \int_{x=0}^{\infty} (P(A((x_i + x)/a) = A_k \,|\, A(x_j/a) = A_{l_j}, j \in I_i) - \sigma_k) g(x) dx \prod_{j\in I_i} g(y_j) dy_j$$
$$= \int_{[0,\infty)^i} \int_{x=0}^{\infty} (P(A(x_i + x) = A_k \,|\, A(x_j) = A_{l_j}, j \in I_i) - \sigma_k) g_a(x) dx \prod_{j\in I_i} g_a(y_j) dy_j$$
$$= \int_{[0,\infty)^i} \int_{x=0}^{\infty} (P(A(x) = A_k \,|\, A(x_j - x_i) = A_{l_j}, j \in I_i) - \sigma_k) g_a(x) dx \prod_{j\in I_i} g_a(y_j) dy_j \quad (13)$$

with $x_j := \sum_{l=1}^{j} y_l$, $j \in I_i$, where we have used the stationarity of the process $\{A(t)\}_{-\infty}^{\infty}$ to derive (13). Define

$$\mathbf{x}^i := (x_1, \ldots, x_i),$$
$$f(u, \mathbf{x}^i) := P(A(u) = A_k \,|\, A(x_j - x_i) = A_{l_j}, j \in I_i)) - \sigma_k\,,$$
$$F(x, \mathbf{x}^i) := \int_0^x f(u, \mathbf{x}^i) du.$$

Note that $|f(u, \mathbf{x}^i)| \leq 1$ for any $u, \mathbf{x}^i$ so that $|F(x, \mathbf{x}^i)| \leq x$ for any $x, \mathbf{x}^i$. In this notation (13) rewrites

$$P\left(A^{(a)}_{(i+1)} = A_k \,|\, A^{(a)}_{(j)} = A_{l_j}, j \in I_i\right) - \sigma_k =$$
$$= \int_{[0,\infty)^i} \int_{x=0}^{\infty} f(x, \mathbf{x}^i) g_a(x) dx \prod_{j\in I_i} g_a(y_j) dy_j. \quad (14)$$

Integrating by parts and using the definition of $g_a(x)$ and Assumption 3.1 yields

$$\int_0^{\infty} f(s, \mathbf{x}^i) g_a(x) dx$$
$$= \left[g_a(x) F(x, \mathbf{x}^i)\right]_0^{\infty} - \int_0^{\infty} F(x, \mathbf{x}^i) g_a'(x) dx$$
$$= \lim_{x\uparrow\infty} g_a(x) F(x, \mathbf{x}^i) - a^2 \int_0^{\infty} F(x, \mathbf{x}^i) g'(ax) dx \quad (15)$$
$$= -a^2 \int_0^{\infty} F(x, \mathbf{x}^i) g'(ax) dx\,, \quad (16)$$

where the limit in (15) is zero since $0 \leq g_a(x) F(x, \mathbf{x}^i) \leq g_a(x) x$ and $\lim_{x\to\infty} x g(x) = 0$ (see Assumption 3.1). Combining (14) and (16) gives

$$P\left(A^{(a)}_{(i+1)} = A_k \,|\, A^{(a)}_{(j)} = A_{l_j}, j \in I_i\right) - \sigma_k = \quad (17)$$
$$-a^2 \int_{[0,\infty)^i} \int_{x=0}^{\infty} F(x, \mathbf{x}^i) g'(ax) dx \prod_{j\in I_i} g_a(y_j) dy_j.$$

Fix $\epsilon > 0$. By Prop. 2.2 we know that there exists $0 < T_\epsilon < \infty$, denoted as T from now on, such that for all $x > T$, $|F(x, \mathbf{x}^i)/x| < \epsilon/2$, uniformly in $\mathbf{x}^i$ or, equivalently, uniformly in $y_1, \ldots, y_i \in [0, \infty)$. We have (Hint: use Assumption 3.1 and inequality $|F(x, \mathbf{x}^i)| \leq x$)

$$\left|\int_0^{\infty} F(x, \mathbf{x}^i) g'(ax) dx\right| \leq -\int_0^T F(x, \mathbf{x}^i) g'(ax) dx$$
$$- \int_T^{\infty} \left|\frac{F(x, \mathbf{x}^i)}{x}\right| x g'(ax) dx$$
$$\leq -T \int_0^T g'(ax) dx - \frac{\epsilon}{2} \int_T^{\infty} x g'(ax) dx$$
$$\leq -T \int_0^{\infty} g'(ax) dx - \frac{\epsilon}{2} \int_0^{\infty} x g'(ax) dx$$
$$= \frac{Tg(0)}{a} + \frac{\epsilon}{2a^2} \quad (18)$$

so that, from (17),

$$\left|P\left(A^{(a)}_{(i+1)} = A_k \,|\, A^{(a)}_{(j)} = A_{l_j}, j \in I_i\right) - \sigma_k\right| \leq$$
$$= \left(aTg(0) + \frac{\epsilon}{2}\right) \int_{[0,\infty)^i} \prod_{j\in I_i} g_a(y_j) dy_j$$
$$= aTg(0) + \frac{\epsilon}{2}. \quad (19)$$

We observe from (19) that

$$\left|P\left(A^{(a)}_{(i+1)} = A_k \,|\, A^{(a)}_{(j)} = A_{l_j}, j \in I_i\right) - \sigma_k\right| < \epsilon$$

for any $0 < a < \epsilon/(2Tg(0))$, which completes the proof since ϵ is arbitrary. □

Application of the chain rule yields the following result.

PROPOSITION 3.1. *As $a \to 0$ the sequence $\{A^{(a)}_{(j)}\}_{j\geq 1}$ converges to an iid sequence with distribution $P\left(A^{(a)}_{(j)} = A_k\right) = \sigma_k$, $k = 1, \ldots, m$.*

It is now straightforward to describe the behavior of a constant rate walker. Take the observation process to be Poisson with rate $\gamma' > \gamma$ (recall that γ is the walker rate of our constant rate walker), namely $P(W_j < x) = 1 - e^{-\gamma' x}$. Consider the dynamic graph $\{A^{(a)}(t)\}_{t\in\mathbb{R}}$ associated with the RMPP $\Psi^{(a)}$ (see (11)). We embed the times that the walker takes a step into the observation process. At each observation the walker takes a step with probability γ/γ'; otherwise it does not with probability $(\gamma' - \gamma)/\gamma'$. Let $U_j^{(a)} \in \{1, \ldots, n\}$ denote the position of the walker immediately after the j-th observation of the observation process ($j \geq 1$), and let $U_0^{(a)}$ be the walker position at time $t = 0$. We assume that $\lim_{a\to 0} P(U_0^{(a)} = v)$ exists for all $v = 1, \ldots, n$. This is the case, for instance, if $U_0^{(a)}$ is constant for any $a > 0$.

The following equation describes the behavior of $\pi_j^{(0)}(v) = \lim_{a\to 0} P(U_j^{(a)} = v)$, the fraction of *observations* after which the walker resides at node $v \in V$. Assume first that this limit exists for any $j \geq 1$ and $v = 1, \ldots, n$. Let $\mathbf{P} := [\mathbf{P}(u, v)]$ be an n-by-n stochastic matrix with (u, v)-entry given by

$$\mathbf{P}(u, v) = \begin{cases} \frac{\gamma}{\gamma'} \sum_{k=1}^{m} \sigma_k \frac{A_k(u,v)}{d_{k,u}}\,, & \text{if } d_{k,u} > 0,\ u \neq v \\ \frac{\gamma'-\gamma}{\gamma'} + \frac{\gamma}{\gamma'} \sum_{k=1}^{m} \sigma_k \mathbf{1}_{\{d_{k,u}=0\}}\,, & \text{if } u = v\,, \\ 0\,, & \text{otherwise,} \end{cases} \quad (20)$$

$u, v = 1, \ldots, n$. We have

$$\begin{aligned}
\pi_j^{(0)}(v) &= \lim_{a\to 0}\sum_{u=1}^{n}\sum_{k=1}^{m} P\left(A_{(j)}^{(a)} = A_k, U_{j-1}^{(a)} = v\right) \quad (21)\\
&\times \sigma_k\left(\frac{A_k(u,v)}{d_{k,u}}\mathbf{1}(d_{k,u}>0) + \mathbf{1}(u=v)\mathbf{1}(d_{k,u}=0)\right)\\
&= \sum_{u=1}^{n}\sum_{k=1}^{m} \lim_{a\to 0} P\left(A_{(j)}^{(a)} = A_k\right) \lim_{a\to 0} P\left(U_{j-1}^{(a)} = v\right)\\
&\times \sigma_k\left(\frac{A_k(u,v)}{d_{k,u}}\mathbf{1}(d_{k,u}>0) + \mathbf{1}(u=v)\mathbf{1}(d_{k,u}=0)\right)\\
&= \sum_{u=1}^{n} \mathbf{P}(u,v)\pi_{j-1}^{(0)}(u), \quad (22)
\end{aligned}$$

for $j \geq 1$ and $v = 1, \ldots, n$, where $d_{k,u}$ is the degree of node $u \in V$ in graph configuration A_k and $A_k(u, v)$ is the (u, v)-entry of the adjacency matrix A_k (i.e. $A_k(u, v) = 1$ if there is a link between vertices u and v in configuration k and zero otherwise). The second and third equalities follow from Proposition 3.1.

The existence of $\lim_{a\to 0} P(U_j^{(a)} = v)$ for all $j \geq 1$ and $v = 1, \ldots, n$ can be shown by induction on j based on (22).

Define $\pi_j^{(0)} := (\pi_j^{(0)}(1), \ldots, \pi_j^{(0)}(n))$. With these definitions (22) rewrites in the following matrix form

$$\pi_j^{(0)} = \pi_{j-1}^{(0)}\mathbf{P}, \quad j \geq 1,$$

with $\pi_0^{(0)}$ the n-dimensional vector where all entries are equal to zero except entry $U_0^{(a)}$ that is equal to 1. To show that $\pi^{(0)}$ is unique, we prove that $\mathbf{P}$ is irreducible. The definition of T-connectivity and the fact that $\sigma_k > 0$, $k = 1, \ldots, m$ imply that $\mathbf{P}$ is an adjacency matrix of a strongly connected directed graph and strong connectivity of this graph is equivalent to the irreducibility of $\mathbf{P}$ [9, Theorem 6.2.24], the details of this proof are found in our technical report [5]. As $\mathbf{P}$ is also aperiodic, as the diagonal elements of $\mathbf{P}$ are non-zero, then the associated discrete-time Markov chain is ergodic since the state-space is finite so that, by Markov chain theory, the limit $\pi^{(0)} = \lim_{j\to\infty} \pi_j^{(0)}$ exists and is given by the unique solution of

$$\pi^{(0)} = \pi^{(0)}\mathbf{P}, \quad \sum_{u=1}^{n} \pi^{(0)}(u) = 1.$$

Because of the PASTA property the steady state probability $\pi^{(0)} = \lim_{j\to\infty} \pi_j^{(0)}$ on the observation events is also the distribution in time, i.e., in the limit as $a \to 0$, $\boldsymbol{\pi} = \pi^{(0)}$.

The case where the walker rate depends on the node and graph configuration in which the walker resides yields a similar characterization.

PROPOSITION 3.2. *Let Ψ be a stationary, ergodic, and T-connected dynamic graph and let $\{(A(t), U(t))\}_{t\geq 0}$ be an associated CTRW with walker rates $\Gamma = \{\beta_{k,v} : k = 1, \ldots, m, v \in V\}$. Let $\beta_{\max} > \sup(\Gamma)$. Then, in the limit as $a \to 0$, the stationary walker position distribution $\boldsymbol{\pi}$ satisfies*

$$\boldsymbol{\pi} = \boldsymbol{\pi}\mathbf{P},$$

where

$$\mathbf{P}(u,v) = \begin{cases} \sum_k \sigma_k \frac{\beta_{k,v}}{\beta_{\max}}\frac{A_{k,vu}}{d_{k,v}}, & d_{k,u} > 0,\ v \neq u \\ \sum_k \sigma_k\left(1 - \frac{\beta_{k,v}}{\beta_{\max}} + \frac{\beta_{k,v}}{\beta_{\max}}\mathbf{1}_{\{d_{k,u}=0\}}\right), & v = u. \end{cases} \quad (23)$$

The proof is similar to that given for the constant rate walker case and is omitted. The assumption that $\beta_{\max} > \sup(\Gamma)$ ensures that $\mathbf{P}$ is aperiodic and the assumption of T-connectivity ensures that $\mathbf{P}$ is irreducible.

Proposition 3.2 shows, as $a \to 0$, the steady state distribution of a walker with state dependent rates to be just a function of $\boldsymbol{\sigma}$ (the stationary distribution of $\{A(t)\}_{t\geq 0}$), the set of configurations $\mathcal{A}$, and the walker rates $\vec{\beta}$, regardless of the graph dynamics.

3.2 Time-scale Invariant Stationary Distribution

In this section we turn our attention to a sufficient condition where the CTRW stationary distribution is invariant to the walker time scale γ. Consider a CTRW $\{(A(t), U(t))\}_{t\geq 0}$ with non-zero walker rates on a stationary, ergodic, and T-connected graph Ψ.

The key insight into our sufficient condition is the following: If there exists a $\boldsymbol{\pi}$ that is the CTRW stationary distribution given any (static) configuration $A_1, \ldots, A_m$, then once the CTRW reaches distribution $\boldsymbol{\pi}$ it remains with distribution $\boldsymbol{\pi}$ independent of the graph dynamics. The key challenge is to show that the CTRW always converges to distribution $\boldsymbol{\pi}$, irrespective of the graph dynamics. We see that this is true if Ψ is stationary, ergodic, and T-connected. However, we also believe that the following results can be extended to some families of non-stationary dynamic graphs.

We first present the notation used in this section. It will be useful to describe the walker rates as a row vector $\vec{\gamma}(\gamma) = (\gamma\beta_{k,v})_{v\in V, k=1,\ldots,m}$.

The CTRW confined to a given configuration A_k is a Markov chain, $k = 1, \ldots, m$. Let

$$Q(A_k, \vec{\gamma}(\gamma)) = \begin{cases} A_k(i,j)\gamma\beta_{k,i}/d_{k,i}, & \text{if } i \neq j, \\ -\sum_{j\in V} A_k(i,j)\gamma\beta_{k,i}/d_{k,i}, & \text{if } i = j, \end{cases}$$

where $A_k(i, j)$ is the element (i, j) of A_k, be the infinitesimal generator of $\{U(t)\}_{t\geq 0}$ given configuration A_k.

ASSUMPTION 3.2 (FIXED POINT $\boldsymbol{\pi}^\star$). *Let $\mathcal{A}$ be the set of graph configurations of Ψ and $\vec{\gamma}$ be a set of walker rates such that there exists a $\boldsymbol{\pi}^\star \in [0, 1]^n$, $\sum_{v\in V} \boldsymbol{\pi}^\star(v) = 1$, that is a fixed point solution to*

$$\mathbf{0} = \boldsymbol{\pi}^\star Q(M, \vec{\gamma}), \quad \forall M \in \mathcal{A}. \quad (24)$$

In what follows we show that if $\mathcal{A}$ and $\vec{\gamma}$ satisfy Assumption 3.2, then $\lim_{t\to\infty} P[U(t) = v] = \boldsymbol{\pi}^\star(v)$, $\forall v \in V$. Moreover, we show that $\boldsymbol{\pi}^\star$ is independent of γ. We are now ready for the main result of this section.

THEOREM 3.4. *Let graph process Ψ be a stationary, ergodic, and T-connected graph with configuration set $\mathcal{A}$. Let $\{(A(t), U(t))\}_{t\geq 0}$ be a CTRW on the dynamic graph $\{A(t)\}_{t\in\mathbb{R}}$ associated with Ψ. The CTRW has walker rates $\vec{\gamma}(\gamma) = \{\gamma\beta_{k,v}\}, v \in V, k = 1, \ldots, m, \gamma > 0$. If $\mathcal{A}$ and $\vec{\gamma}(1)$ satisfy Assumption 3.2, then*

$$\lim_{t\to\infty} P[U(t) = v] = \boldsymbol{\pi}^\star(v), \quad \forall v \in V,$$

where $\boldsymbol{\pi}^\star$ solves (24). Moreover, $\boldsymbol{\pi}^\star$ does not depend on γ.

Proof. For now assume $\gamma = 1$. Let $\Pi(t) = (P[U(t) = v])_{v \in V}$. The Kolmogorov forward equation gives

$$\frac{d\Pi(t)}{dt} = \Pi(t) Q(A(t), \vec{\gamma}(1)). \tag{25}$$

From Assumption 3.2 there exists $\boldsymbol{\pi}^\star$ is that is a solution to (24). Hence, $\Pi(t) = \boldsymbol{\pi}^\star$ is also a solution to (25) where $d\Pi(t)/dt = 0$. It follows from Theorem 3.1 that there is no other solution to (25) and therefore $\lim_{t\to\infty} P[U(t) = v] = \boldsymbol{\pi}^\star(v), \forall v \in V$. To show that $\boldsymbol{\pi}^\star$ does not depend on γ, note that for any $\alpha > 0$ and $k = 1, \ldots, m$

$$\mathbf{0}\alpha = \boldsymbol{\pi}^\star Q(A_k, \vec{\gamma}(1))\alpha = \boldsymbol{\pi}^\star Q(A_k, \vec{\gamma}(\alpha)).$$

□

Examples of adjacency matrix sets $\mathcal{A} = \{A_k : k = 1, \ldots, m\}$ that satisfy Assumption 3.2 for a constant rate walker, $\vec{\gamma}(\gamma) = (\gamma, \ldots, \gamma)$ include:

- **Regular graphs**: A_i, $i = 1, \ldots, m$, consists of $C_i \geq 1$ connected components where the j-th connected component ($j = 1, \ldots, C_i$) is a $d_j^{(i)}$-regular graph ($d_j^{(i)} >= 0$).
- **Nodes $v \in V$ alternate between isolated and connected with constant degree, i.e., $d_k(v) \in \{0, d(v)\}$, $d(v) > 0$, $k = 1, \ldots, m$.** Figure 1 illustrates a dynamic graph that satisfies these requirements.

Conditions imposed on the walker rates $\vec{\gamma}(\gamma)$ can also guarantee that Assumption 3.2 is valid for any set of graph configurations $\mathcal{A}$, as long as $\{A(t)\}_{t\in\mathbb{R}}$ is T-connected. Consider the coupled CTRW and graph dynamics that satisfies Assumption 3.2 in the following proposition, stated without a proof:

PROPOSITION 3.3 (DEGREE PROPORTIONAL WALKER). *Let $\mathcal{A} = \{A_k : k = 1, \ldots, m\}$ be a set of graph configurations. If the walker rates are $\vec{\gamma}(\gamma) = (\gamma d_{k,v})_{v\in V, k=1,\ldots,m}$, where $d_{k,v}$ is the degree of node v at configuration k. Then Theorem 3.4 is satisfied. Moreover, $\boldsymbol{\pi}^\star = (\frac{1}{n}, \ldots, \frac{1}{n})$.*

Proposition 3.3 has an interesting application. We can uniformly sample nodes (in time) without knowing the underlying topologies, $\mathcal{A}$, or graph dynamics, $\{A(t)\}_{t\in\mathbb{R}}$, as long as $\{A(t)\}_{t\in\mathbb{R}}$ is stationary, ergodic, and T-connected. So far we have focused on conditions that allow us to obtain the stationary distribution of the walker. In what follows we present some case studies solved numerically.

4. CASE STUDIES

In previous sections we characterized the stationary behavior of an RW on a broad class of dynamic graph processes $\{(X_i, S_i)\}_{i\geq\mathbb{Z}}$. In this section, we focus mostly on random walks on *Markovian dynamic graphs* where $\{X_i\}_{i\geq 0}$ forms a Markov chain and $\{S_i\}_{i\geq 0}$ is a sequence of independent and exponentially distributed random variables. Note that this model allows state dependent graph holding times to be taken into account in the Markov chain $\{X_i\}_{i\geq 0}$. In what follows we provide several examples and numerical evaluations. Later in the section, we also show how the proposed framework can be applied to a Delay-Tolerant Network (DTN) scenario.

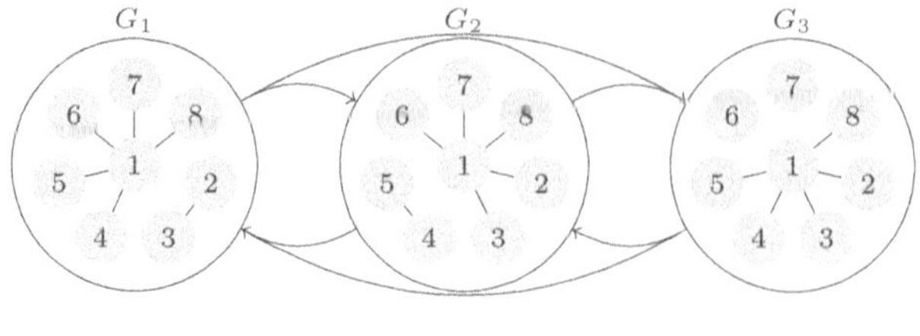

Figure 1: Illustration of a dynamic graph whose node degrees are either kept constant in all graph configurations or there are isolated nodes. We make no assumption about the holding times of each graph configuration except that the graph is T-connected.

4.1 Markovian dynamic graph examples

In this section we present numerical results for some toy Markovian dynamic graph examples, that illustrate the non-trivial behavior of random walks on dynamic graphs and that support our theoretical findings.

4.1.1 *Star-circle example*

We begin by considering a very simple model, consisting of just two graph snapshots: a star and a circle, as illustrated in Figure 2a. The graph transits from one snapshot to another with rates $\lambda_{12} = \lambda_{21} = 1$. Thus, the average time in each graph is 1/2. Note however, that edges (1,2) and (1,10) are always present, since they exist in both configurations.

We investigate the steady state solution of the CTRW on this dynamic graph. Figure 2b shows the steady state distribution of the random walk as a function of the walker rate (for clarity, only a subset of the states are shown). Note that the stationary distribution of the walker depends on the walker rate and converges to different distributions as the walker moves faster or slower. Indeed, the numerical results obtained are in agreement with the theoretical distributions for the fast and slow walker given in Sections 3.1.1 and 3.1.2, respectively. Finally, we note that in a graph with n nodes, node one alternates between degrees $n-1$ and two. As n increases the dependence on the walker speed is magnified.

4.2 Edge Markovian model and examples

In this section we consider some particularities of random walks on a special class of dynamic graphs called edge Markovian graphs. Start with a fixed adjacency matrix A and attach an independent On-Off process to each edge with exponentially distributed holding times. In edge Markovian graphs, edges alternate between being present and absent from the graph according to independent On-Off processes. Let E be the set of edges in the graph described by A. Let $\Lambda_0(e)$ and $\Lambda_1(e)$ denote the rate at which edge $e \in E$ changes from the On to the Off state and from the Off to the On state, respectively, which can vary from edge to edge.

A few observations on the model follows. Let A_k be a particular configuration of the dynamic graph model. In particular, the edge Markovian model induces a total of $m = 2^{|E|}$ configurations, which represent all possible labeled subgraphs over an edge set with $|E|$ edges. Moreover, consider any transition between two configurations induced by the model. The graphs corresponding to these two configurations differ by exactly one edge, since the on-off processes associated with the edges are continuous in time. Moreover,

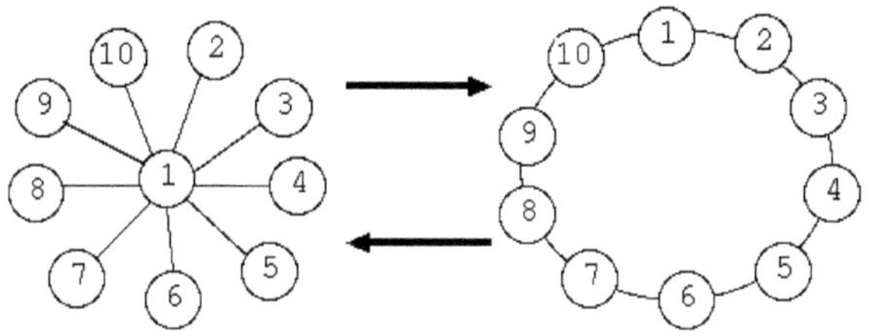

(a) The star-circle graph dynamics.

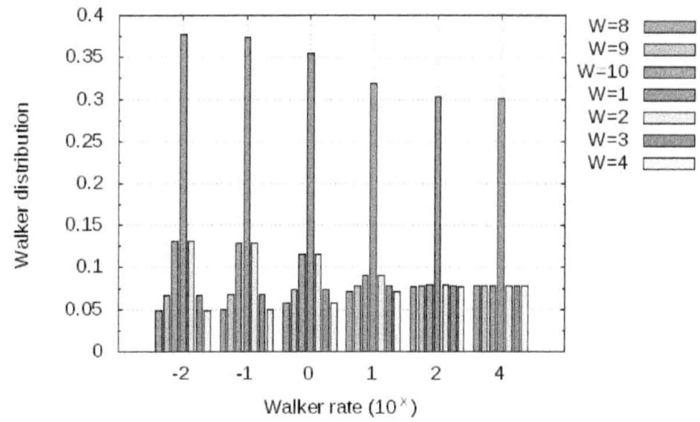

(b) Steady state distribution of walker as a function of walker rate (nodes 5, 6 ,7 not shown for clarity).

Figure 2: The star-circle graph dynamics and behavior of CTRW as a function of walker rate.

the rate associated with this graph transition is given by the corresponding rate of the edge (either its On rate or Off rate).

Let q_{uv} denote the stationary fraction of time that edge $(u, v) \in E$ is On, which is simply given by

$$q_{uv} = \Lambda_1(u, v)/(\Lambda_0(u, v) + \Lambda_1(u, v)).$$

Let σ_k denote the steady state fraction of time that the edge Markovian model spends in configuration A_k, $k = 1, \ldots, 2^{|E|}$. In particular, we have

$$\sigma_k = \prod_{(u,v)\in E} \mathbf{1}\{A_k(u, v)\}q_{uv} + (1 - \mathbf{1}\{A_k(u, v)\})(1 - q_{uv}) \tag{26}$$

Note that σ_k is given by the product of the probabilities the egdes that define A_k are present while all other edges are absent. Since all edges are independent, this is trivially obtained as shown above. Edge Markovian graphs are of interest due to their simple description and structure. However, as we will soon see in our numerical results, the steady state distribution of a constant rate random walk on this model depends on the walker rate. It is an open problem whether the walker steady state distribution can be obtained in closed form.

4.2.1 *Edge Markovian:* $n = 3$

Consider the edge Markovian graph model over a complete graph with 3 nodes. The number of different configurations is $2^3 = 8$, out of which 4 have at least one isolated vertex (graph not connected). Moreover, let $\Lambda_1(1, 2) = \Lambda_0(1, 2) = 10^4$, $\Lambda_1(1, 3) = \Lambda_0(1, 3) = 1$, $\Lambda_1(2, 3) = \Lambda_0(2, 3) = 1$. Thus, $p_e = 0.5$ for every edge (i.e., all edges have the same time average), and thus, all configurations have the same time average probability of $1/8$, as given by equation (26).

Figure 3a shows the exact steady state distribution of the random walk as a function of the walker rate. Interestingly, while all edges have the same time average and all configurations A_k, $k = 1, \ldots, 2^{|E|}$, have the same σ_k, the walker steady state distribution still depends on the walker rate. Moreover, the behaviors of the fast and slow walkers differ. While the slow walker converges to a uniform distribution over the nodes, the fast walker always favors node 3, the node not incident to the fastest changing edge $(1, 2)$. Despite the relatively small differences in the walker distribution ($P[W = 3]$ varies by 7%), the point of this example is to illustrate that such differences can arise even in small and simple models.

Figure 3b also shows the maximum absolute difference between our theoretical results for the fast and slow walker and the actual distribution obtained exactly. In particular, we present the *total variation distance* between the two distributions, defined as $\max_{i=1,\ldots,n} |\pi(i) - \pi'(i)|$, where π is the exact walker distribution and π' is either the fast or slow walker distribution, and n is the number of nodes in the graph. For walker rates greater than one, the theoretical results for the fast walker were used (π' as defined in Section 3.1.1), while for rates smaller than one the results for the slow walker were used (π' as defined in Section 3.1.2). Note that as the walker slows down or speeds up, the total variation decreases (graph in log-log scale). Our numerical results indicate that the fast and slow walker become close to our asymptotic results as their rates increase and decrease, respectively. When the timescales of the walker and graph dynamics are similar, the total variation distance between the asymptotic cases and the steady state distribution is relatively larger, as expected.

Moreover, if we consider the "degree-time distribution" of a given node, namely, the fraction of time that node $v \in V$ has degree $0, 1, \ldots$, we note that all three nodes have identical degree-time distributions but the fraction of time the walker spends on each node varies. This indicates that the degree-time distribution is insufficient to characterize the walker steady state. This is also like true for transient metrics as well.

4.2.2 *Edge Markovian: 6-node kite*

Now consider an edge Markovian process over the "kite graph" illustrated in Figure 4a. In particular, let all thin edges e have On-Off rates $\Lambda_1(e) = \Lambda_0(e) = 1$. Similarly, let all thick edges e' have On-Off rates $\Lambda_1(e') = 100, = \Lambda_0(e') = 10$. Note that locally all nodes are connected through identical and independent On-Off processes, two thin edges (On-Off rates equal to one) and one thick edge (On-Off rates equal to one hundred). Thus, in some sense, "locally" all nodes are indistinguishable. Surprisingly, even in this case the behavior of the walker depends on its rate, as shown

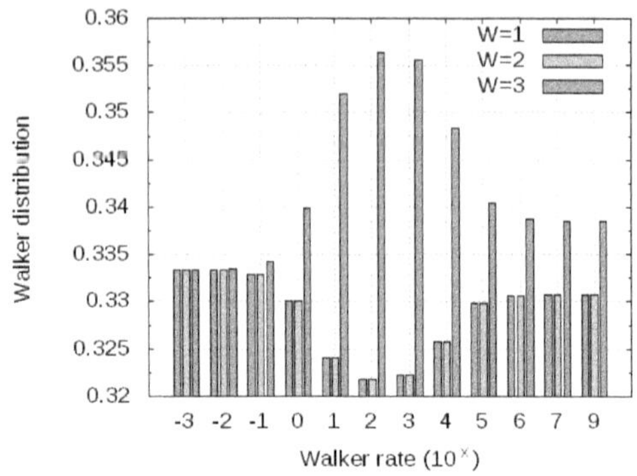

(a) Steady state distribution of walker as a function of walker rate.

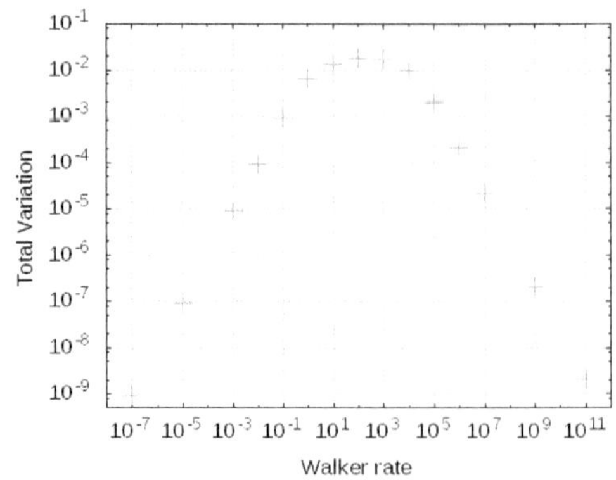

(b) Total variation distance between theoretical results for fast and slow walker when compared to exact walker distribution.

Figure 3: Characteristics of random walks on a K_3 edge Markovian graph model.

in Figure 4b. Clearly, the structure of the graph plays an important role, as illustrated in this example, as the fast and the slow walkers have different time stationary distributions for different nodes. This indicates the difficulty of characterizing the exact behavior of random walks in general graph dynamics, even if we limit ourselves to the class of edge Markovian graphs.

4.3 A simple vehicular DTN

In this section we consider an application of our modeling framework to a simple vehicular disruption-tolerant networks (DTN) model. Our model captures some essential characteristics of DTNs. Consider a set of buses equipped with wireless routers moving around according to their routes. Two buses establish communication when they are within the coverage radius of the wireless routers. Buses belonging to the same line (route) move from one bus stop to another following a predefined sequence of stops in a circular fashion. The following notation is used to describe the model: $S = \{s_1, \ldots, s_o\}$ is the set of bus stops across all bus lines, where o is the number of different stops; $L_i \in S^{n_i}$ is a vector with the sequence of stops for bus line i, and n_i is the number of stops at bus line i; l denotes the number of different bus lines and b_i is the number of different buses operating in line $i = 1, \ldots, l$; Assume that both ξ_k^i, the amount of time line i bus stays at stop k, and ζ_{kl}^i, the amount of time it takes line i bus to move from stop k to l, are exponentially distributed random variables, but can have different parameter values for any i, k, l. In addition, buses move independently of each other, including those in the same line.

The bus routes and the coverage radius of the wireless router allow two or more buses to exchange information when buses are at the same stop. Thus, if two or more different bus lines share at least one bus stop in their route, then buses from these lines will be able to communicate at the shared bus stops. Moreover, two or more buses from the same line can communicate in any stop of their line, as they can always meet at these stops. Finally, we assume that the communication radius is smaller than the distance between bus stops, such that buses only communicate when located at a shared bus stop.

Figure 5a shows an example with 11 bus stops, three bus lines ($l = 3$), defined by $L_1 = (s_1, s_2, s_3, s_4, s_5)$, $L_2 = (s_3, s_4, s_6, s_7, s_8)$ and $L_3 = (s_7, s_9, s_{10}, s_{11})$, and four buses: $b_1 = 1$, $b_2 = 1$, $b_3 = 2$ (line three has two buses). Note that lines 1 and 2 share two bus stops (s_3 and s_4) and that lines 2 and 3 share one bus stop (s_7).

Consider a continuous-time random walker (CTRW) moving around the buses with rate γ. The goal is to determine the fraction of time that the walker spends in each bus or in each bus line. This problem can be formulated and solved using the modeling framework proposed in this paper. The first step is to construct a dynamic connectivity graph model from the movement of the buses in their respective lines. In particular, each bus is a node in the graph, since this corresponds to a possible location for the random walk. Moreover, each possible configuration of buses on their stops will define a connectivity graph, where nodes (buses) in the same stop are all within communication radius of one another. Note that each connectivity graph is composed of connected components that are all cliques (fully connected subgraph), since all buses in the same stop can communicate.

Consider the example in Figure 5a and the possible connectivity graphs that can be created, which are illustrated in Figure 5b. The connectivity graph has four nodes, corresponding to the four buses. Each bus can be in a different stop, thus yielding a connectivity graph with no edges. Also, bus in line 2 can be at stop s_7 at the same time as the two buses from line 3, yielding a connectivity graph where these three buses are all connected. Finally, note that not all graphs with four nodes are possible, since different lines may not have stops in common such as lines 1 and 3, for instance.

The transitions between graph configurations are shown in Figure 5b. In our model, buses cannot simultaneously leave a stop. As a consequence, the number of allowed transitions is reduced. Once the dynamic graph model is constructed, we can obtain the state holding times for each graph configuration. This is possible if the holding times at bus stations and the amount of time it takes a bus to move from a station to another are exponentially distributed. However, this is non-trivial in the general case, since buses can move along their routes without changing the connectivity graph. Moreover, totally different bus configurations over the set of stops can lead to the same connectivity graph. Since our modeling framework makes no assumption on the state (static graph)

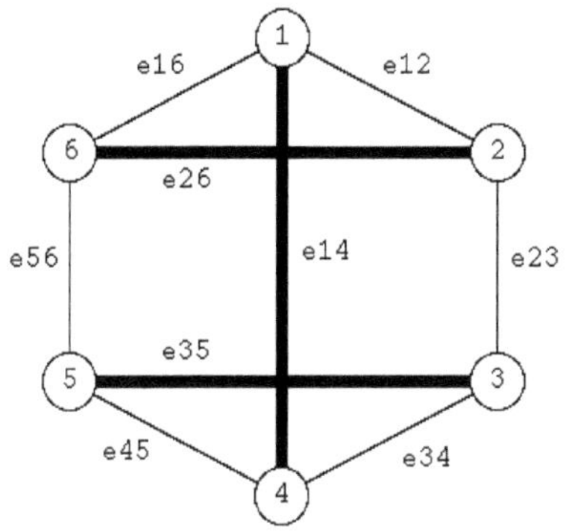

(a) The edge Markovian model over the 6-node kite graph where edges belong to one of two On-Off processes.

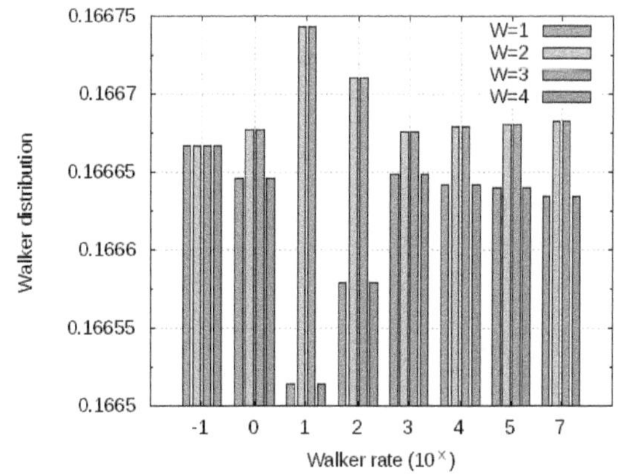

(b) Steady state distribution of walker as a function of walker rate (nodes 5 and 6 not shown, but are identical to nodes 2 and 3).

Figure 4: Characteristics of random walks on a 6-node kite edge Markovian graph model.

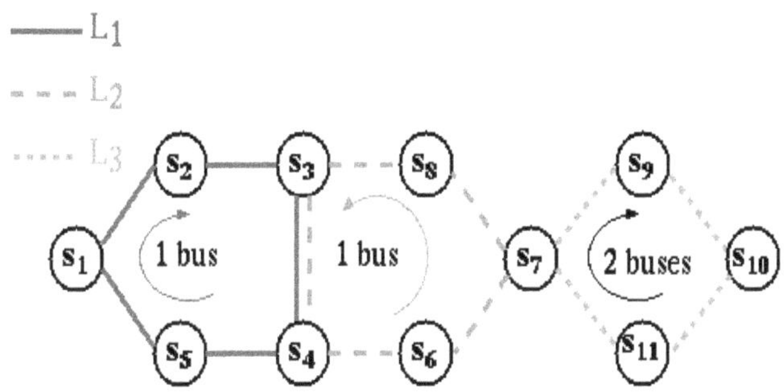

(a) Example of a vehicular DTN with eleven bus stops, three bus lines and four buses (line 3 has 2 buses).

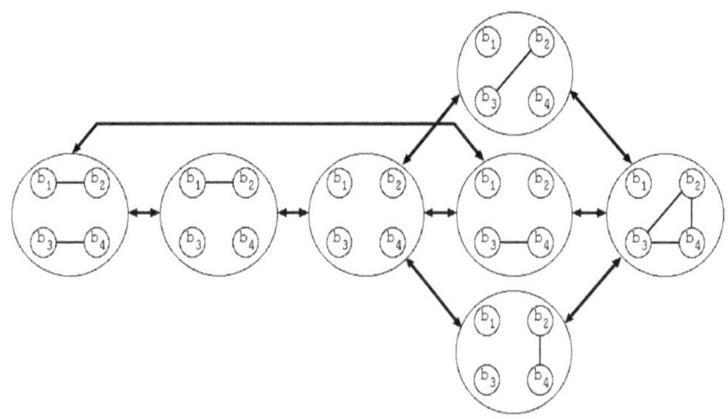

(b) Connectivity graphs and transitions between them according to the bus system illustrated in Figure 5a.

Figure 5: Example of a simple bus system (a) and the induced dynamic graph model (b).

holding times of the dynamic graph model we can extend the exponential assumption considering general distributions for the holding times *at each graph configuration*, assuming only that the expected holding time is finite for all static graphs and that dynamic graph process is stationary, ergodic and T-connected.

The model constructed from this scenario matches the case studied in Section 3.2 in which the stationary distribution of the random walk is time-scale invariant and uniform over the set of nodes in the graph, independent of graph dynamics (see Theorem 3.4). This occurs since every connected component of every possible graph configuration is a clique, thus, having identical degree within each component. Therefore, the fraction of time the walker spends in any given bus is simply $1/\sum_j b_j$, while the fraction of time spent in bus line i is simply $b_i/\sum_j b_j$. Thus, CTRWs could find applications in searching for information or sampling properties in such systems, as its steady state does not depend on the graph dynamics.

5. RELATED WORK

Random walks have been widely used to understand and characterize graphs due to their well understood steady state behavior. By leveraging the steady state distribution of random walks, principled mechanisms for characterizing and estimating vertex-related properties have been devised [7, 12, 14, 16, 17].

It follows that random walks can potentially be used to understand and characterize dynamic graphs. In fact, efforts in this direction concerning time-independent dynamic graphs (i.e., each snapshot is independent of the previous) have appeared in the literature [3, 8, 10, 15], mainly in the context of determining upper and lower bounds for the cover time of random walks. More recently, proposals to define time-dependent dynamic graph models as well as characterize random walks in them have also appeared in the literature [1,2,4]. However, these efforts have focused on discrete-time dynamic graph models with a goal of computing the cover time of random walks either in special graph structures [2], in specific dynamic graph models [4], or through numerical evaluations [1]. Our work differs from these in the sense that we consider continuous-time dynamic graph models and continuous-time random walks with the goal of analytically characterizing the steady state behavior of the walker. Moreover, our prior work on this topic considered only Markovian dynamics and characterized the steady state behavior of the walker only under time-scale separation [18].

Finally, random walks have also been used as a sampling mechanism to estimate characteristics of vertices (e.g., fraction of vertices of a particular kind) in large static graphs [7, 12, 17]. More recently, efforts to measure characteristics of vertices in dynamic graphs have also appeared in the literature [16, 20]. However, these are mostly preliminary and exploratory papers, indicating potential pitfalls and biases introduced by fast changing dynamic graphs. In contrast, our works is a first step at providing a theoretical foundation that can then be applied to estimate characteristics of vertices in dynamic graphs.

6. CONCLUSION

Understanding the long-term behavior of CTRW over dynamic graphs is an important step towards a comprehensive study of dynamic graphs. Since the steady state distribution of random walks on static graphs is arguably the most important characteristic of these processes, it is of vital importance to characterize the CTRW steady state distribution for a broad class of dynamic graph processes. Unlike random walks on static graphs, CTRWs on dynamic graphs have a non-trivial behavior. The walker rate as well as the process that governs the graph dynamics both impact the asymptotic time stationary distribution of the walker (the amount of time a walker spends on each node).

Our main results assume the graph process to be asymptotically stationary, ergodic and T-connected. We make no independence assumptions concerning the times the process resides in each of the graph configurations or the particular distribution of these residence times. In other words, the time spent in a given graph configuration can be dependent on the residence time at other configurations and, in addition, the distribution of the time the network spends in a configuration can be general. Moreover, the dynamic graph can have temporarily disconnected nodes as long as the dynamic graph is T-connected.

Under this general scenario, we have obtained the steady state distribution of cases in which the walker is either much faster or much slower as compared to the rate of changes in graph configurations. We have obtained a sufficient condition for the CTRW stationary distribution to be invariant to the walker rate and presented examples that illustrate models in which these results are applicable. In this context, additional application examples for the constant degree constraint can be found in P2P networks where peers maintain a nearly fixed number of connections. Hence, Theorem 3.4 helps explain why sampling these dynamic networks using random walks leads to meaningful results [20].

The examples in this paper serve mainly for illustrative purposes. However, we believe that the theory we developed will find applications in many important areas. Examples of promising application areas are in sampling DTN and P2P networks.

7. REFERENCES

[1] Utku Günay Acer, Petros Drineas, and Alhussein A. Abouzeid. Random walks in time-graphs. In *MobiOpp*, pp. 93–100, 2010.

[2] C. Avin, M. Koucky, and Z. Lotker. How to explore a fast-changing world. (on the cover time of dynamic graphs). In *ICALP*, pp. 121–132, 2008.

[3] Andrea E. F. Clementi, Francesco Pasquale, Angelo Monti, and Riccardo Silvestri. Communication in dynamic radio networks. In *PODC*, pp. 205–214. 2007.

[4] Andrea E.F. Clementi, Claudio Macci, Angelo Monti, Francesco Pasquale, and Riccardo Silvestri. Flooding time in edge-markovian dynamic graphs. In *PODC*, pp. 213–222. ACM, 2008.

[5] Daniel Figueiredo, Philippe Nain, Bruno Ribeiro, Edmundo de Souza e Silva, and Don Towsley. Characterizing random walks on general time varying graphs. Technical Report UM-CS-2012-011, 2012.

[6] P. Franken, D. Konig, U. Arndt, and V. Schmidt. *Queues and Point Processes*. J. Wileyl, 1982.

[7] M. Gjoka, M. Kurant, C. Butts, and A. Markopoulou. A walk in Facebook: Uniform sampling of users in online social networks. In *INFOCOM*, 2010.

[8] S.M. Hedetniemi, S.T. Hedetniemi, and A.L.Liestman. A survey of gossiping and broadcasting in communication networks. *Networks*, 18(4):319–349, 1988.

[9] R. Horn and C. Johnson. Matrix analysis. Technical report, Cambridge University Press, 1985.

[10] D. Kempe and J. Kleinberg. Protocols and impossibility results for gossip-based communication mechanisms. In *FOCS*, pp. 471–480, 2002.

[11] A. N. Kolmogorov and S. V. Fomin. *Introductory Real Analysis*. Dover, 1975.

[12] Laurent Massoulié, Erwan Le Merrer, Anne-Marie Kermarrec, and Ayalvadi Ganesh. Peer counting and sampling in overlay networks: random walk methods. In *PODC*, pp. 123–132, 2006.

[13] P. Moyal. A generalized backwards scheme for solving non monotonic stochastic recursions. *Arxiv preprint arXiv:1009.1235*, Sept. 2010.

[14] M.E.J. Newman. A measure of betweenness centrality based on random walks. *Social Networks*, 27(1):39–54, 2005.

[15] B. Pittel. On spreading a rumor. *SIAM Journal on Applied Mathematics*, 47(1):213–223, 1987.

[16] A. H. Rasti, M. Torkjazi, R. Rejaie, N. Duffield, W. Willinger, and D. Stutzbach. Respondent-driven sampling for characterizing unstructured overlays. In *INFOCOM Mini-Conference*, 2009.

[17] B. Ribeiro and D. Towsley. Estimating and sampling graphs with multidimensional random walks. In *SIGCOMM IMC*, Nov 2010.

[18] Bruno Ribeiro, Daniel Figueiredo, Edmundo de Souza e Silva, and Don Towsley. Characterizing continuous-time random walks on dynamic networks. *SIGMETRICS*, 39(1):343–344, June 2011.

[19] Albert N. Shiryaev. *Probability*. Springer, 2nd edition, 1995.

[20] Daniel Stutzbach, Reza Rejaie, Nick Duffield, Subhabrata Sen, and Walter Willinger. On unbiased sampling for unstructured peer-to-peer networks. *IEEE/ACM Trans. Netw.*, 17:377–390, April 2009.

Beyond Random Walk and Metropolis-Hastings Samplers:
Why You Should Not Backtrack for Unbiased Graph Sampling

Chul-Ho Lee Xin Xu Do Young Eun
Department of Electrical and Computer Engineering
North Carolina State University
Raleigh, NC 27695
{clee4,xxu5,dyeun}@ncsu.edu

ABSTRACT

Graph sampling via crawling has been actively considered as a generic and important tool for collecting uniform node samples so as to consistently estimate and uncover various characteristics of complex networks. The so-called simple random walk with re-weighting (SRW-rw) and Metropolis-Hastings (MH) algorithm have been popular in the literature for such unbiased graph sampling. However, an unavoidable downside of their core random walks – slow diffusion over the space, can cause poor estimation accuracy. In this paper, we propose non-backtracking random walk with re-weighting (NBRW-rw) and MH algorithm with delayed acceptance (MHDA) which are *theoretically guaranteed* to achieve, at *almost no additional cost*, not only unbiased graph sampling but also higher efficiency (smaller asymptotic variance of the resulting unbiased estimators) than the SRW-rw and the MH algorithm, respectively. In particular, a remarkable feature of the MHDA is its applicability for *any* non-uniform node sampling like the MH algorithm, but ensuring better sampling efficiency than the MH algorithm. We also provide simulation results to confirm our theoretical findings.

Categories and Subject Descriptors: G.3 [Probability and Statistics]: Probabilistic algorithms, Stochastic processes

General Terms: Theory, Algorithms, Performance

Keywords: unbiased graph sampling, random walks, non-reversible Markov chains, asymptotic variance

1. INTRODUCTION

Estimating various nodal and topological properties of complex networks such as online social networks (OSNs), peer-to-peer (P2P) networks, and the world wide web (WWW) has recently attracted much attention from research community because of their ever-increasing popularity and importance in our daily life. However, the estimation of network characteristics is a non-trivial task, as these networks are typically too large to measure, making a complete picture of the network hard to obtain and even its size unknown. It is thus infeasible to perform 'independence sampling' which obtains uniform node samples (for unbiased estimation) directly and independently from such a large, unknown network. Instead, graph crawling techniques – graph sampling via crawling, have been widely used for that purpose. In particular, random walk-based graph sampling methods (or Markov chain samplers) have become popular, as they are simple and implementable in a distributed fashion and also able to provide *unbiased* graph sampling, unlike the breadth-first-search (BFS) and its variants leading to unknown bias [12, 20].

In the literature, the most popular random walk-based graph sampling methods are the so-called simple random walk with re-weighting (SRW-rw) [29, 12] and Metropolis-Hastings (MH) algorithm [25, 16, 34, 29, 12, 15]. The former launches a simple random walk (SRW) over a graph $\mathcal{G}$, which moves from a node to one of its neighbors chosen uniformly at random, to collect random node samples, followed by a re-weighting process in order to eliminate the bias caused by the non-uniform stationary distribution of the SRW. The other method is to rely on a Metropolis-Hastings random walk (MHRW) crawling over $\mathcal{G}$ – a random walk achieving a unform distribution constructed by the famous MH algorithm [25, 16], to obtain uniform node samples.

Motivation and Contributions: While the SRW-rw and MH algorithm ensure unbiased graph sampling, the core components – SRW and MHRW, suffer from their slow diffusion over the space, which can in turn lead to poor estimation accuracy. In particular, their fully random nature in selecting the next node, when making a transition, often cause them to go back to the previous node from where they just came. This produces many duplicate samples for a short to moderate time span, thereby reducing estimation accuracy. It is apparently desirable to avoid such backtracking transitions whenever possible, so as to steer them toward 'unvisited' places (or to obtain new node samples), as long as such a modification does not affect the unbiased estimation.

However, it is still uncertain how to achieve this *at almost no additional cost* and whether it really results in better estimation accuracy. We provide affirmative answers for these questions. Specifically, we propose non-backtracking random walk with re-weighting (NBRW-rw) and MH algorithm with delayed acceptance (MHDA), and prove that each of them guarantees not only *unbiased* graph sampling but also *higher efficiency* (smaller asymptotic variance of the estimators) than the SRW-rw and the MH algorithm, respec-

SIGMETRICS'12, June 11–15, 2012, London, England, UK.

tively. A notable feature of our MHDA is its generic purpose: the MHDA is theoretically guaranteed to enhance the standard MH algorithm for constructing a random walk or a Markov chain with *any* arbitrarily given stationary distribution under the constraints of graph structure. Thus, the MHDA is applied, as 'a special case', to construct a random walk crawling over a graph $\mathcal{G}$ achieving a uniform stationary distribution, leading to higher efficiency than the MHRW while ensuring the unbiased estimation. To the best of our knowledge, this is the first theoretical result to improve, with proven guarantee, *both* SRW-rw and the MH algorithm for unbiased graph sampling.

Related Work: Very recently, there have been a few attempts to improve the estimation accuracy against the SRW-rw (not the MH algorithm) through multiple dependent random walks [30], a random walk on a weighted graph (with a priori estimate of network information) [20], and the addition of random jumps (to anywhere in the graph) [5]. The corresponding Markov chains are time-reversible, whereas the main kernel of our proposed methods is transforming 'any' reversible Markov chain to its related non-reversible chain which avoids backtracking transitions and also achieves the same stationary distribution. Thus, our work is complementary to their approaches.

On the other hand, there is a body of research works across many disciplines for speeding up a random walk, or Markov chain, on a graph $\mathcal{G}$ in terms of its mixing time, hitting time, and/or cover time. The fastest mixing (reversible) Markov chain on a graph is obtained in [8] with complete knowledge of entire graph. [9, 10] showed that certain 'lifted' (non-reversible) Markov chains converge to their stationary distributions faster than their related reversible chain, and [19, 23] subsequently applied this idea to design a fast and efficient average consensus algorithm. It is, however, still unknown how to construct such a 'lifted' Markov chain in a distributed or decentralized manner for a general graph.

[3, 7, 17] recently undertook speeding up a SRW based only on local information, but did not provide any direct implication to the unbiased graph sampling. As the MH algorithm is the most popular method of Markov Chain Monte Carlo (MCMC) simulations or samplers, it has been an active research topic to improve the MH algorithm in terms of the sampler performance (asymptotic variance) in the MCMC literature (e.g., [26, 14, 35]). However, most works toward more efficient MCMC samplers (including [26, 14, 35]) do not take into account graph-topological constraints in that transition from node i to $j \neq i$ is allowed only when they are neighbors of each other, and thus cannot be directly applicable to unbiased graph sampling.

Organization: The rest of the paper is organized as follows. We first provide an in-depth overview on generic Markov chain samplers for unbiased graph sampling in Section 2, and then briefly review the SRW-rw and MH algorithm in Section 3. In Section 4, we present a general recipe for the transformation of a time-reversible Markov to its related non-reversible Markov chain, which forms a common building block for our proposed NBRW-rw and MHDA. We then explain the details of the NBRW-rw and MHDA, and provide relevant analysis. In Section 5, we provide simulation results obtained based on real graphs to support our theoretical findings. We finally conclude in Section 6.

2. PRELIMINARIES

2.1 Unbiased Graph Sampling

Consider a *connected, undirected* graph $\mathcal{G} = (\mathcal{N}, \mathcal{E})$ with a set of nodes (vertices) $\mathcal{N} = \{1, 2, \ldots, n\}$ and a set of edges $\mathcal{E}$. We assume that $3 \leq |\mathcal{N}| = n < \infty$. We also assume that the graph $\mathcal{G}$ has no self-loops and no multi-edges. Let $N(i) \triangleq \{j \in \mathcal{N} : (i,j) \in \mathcal{E}\}$ be the set of neighbors of node $i \in \mathcal{N}$, and $d(i) \triangleq |N(i)|$ be the degree of node i.

Unbiased graph (or node) sampling, via crawling, is to consistently estimate nodal or topological properties of a target graph $\mathcal{G}^*$ (e.g., an overlay network or an OSN) based upon *uniform* node samples obtained by a random walk (or possibly multiple random walks) crawling over the graph $\mathcal{G}$. The goal here is to unbiasedly estimate a proportion of the nodes with a specific characteristic. Thus, the unbiased, uniform graph sampling is, in principle, developing a random walk-based "estimator" or a Markov chain sampler for the expectation of any given, desired function f with respect to a uniform distribution, i.e., $\mathbb{E}_{\boldsymbol{u}}(f) \triangleq \sum_{i \in \mathcal{N}} f(i)/n$, where $\boldsymbol{u} \triangleq [u(1), u(2), \ldots, u(n)] = [1/n, 1/n, \ldots, 1/n]$. Note that a nodal (or topological) characteristic of interest can be specified by properly choosing a function f. For example, for a target graph $\mathcal{G}$, if one is interested in estimating its degree distribution (say, $\mathbb{P}\{D_{\mathcal{G}} = d\}, d = 1, 2, \ldots, n-1$), then choose a function f such that $f(i) = \mathbf{1}_{\{d(i)=d\}}$ for $i \in \mathcal{N}$, i.e., $f(i) = 1$ if $d(i) = d$, and $f(i) = 0$ otherwise.

We below review a basic Markov chain theory which serves as the mathematical foundation for unbiased graph sampling via a (Markovian) random walk crawling over a graph $\mathcal{G}$. Define a random walk or a finite discrete-time Markov chain $\{X_t \in \mathcal{N}\}_{t \geq 0}$ on the nodes of the graph $\mathcal{G}$ with its transition matrix $\mathbf{P} \triangleq \{P(i,j)\}_{i,j \in \mathcal{N}}$ in which $P(i,j) = \mathbb{P}\{X_{t+1} = j | X_t = i\}, i, j \in \mathcal{N}$, and $\sum_j P(i,j) = 1$ for all i. Each edge $(i,j) \in \mathcal{E}$ is associated with a transition probability $P(i,j) \geq 0$ with which the chain (or random walk) makes a transition from node i to node j. We allow the chain to include self-transitions, i.e., $P(i,i) > 0$ for some i, although $\mathcal{G}$ has no self-loops. Clearly, $P(i,j) = 0$ for all $(i,j) \notin \mathcal{E}$ $(i \neq j)$. We then assume that the Markov chain $\{X_t\}$ is irreducible, i.e., every node in $\mathcal{N}$ is reachable in finite time with positive probability, such that the chain has a unique stationary distribution $\boldsymbol{\pi} \triangleq [\pi(1), \pi(2), \ldots, \pi(n)]$.

For any function $f : \mathcal{N} \to \mathbb{R}$, define an estimator

$$\hat{\mu}_t(f) \triangleq \frac{1}{t} \sum_{s=1}^{t} f(X_s) \tag{1}$$

for the expectation of the function f with respect to $\boldsymbol{\pi}$ which is given by $\mathbb{E}_{\boldsymbol{\pi}}(f) \triangleq \sum_{i \in \mathcal{N}} f(i)\pi(i)$. Then, the following Strong Law of Large Numbers (SLLN) (a.k.a., ergodic theorem) has been a fundamental basis for most of the random walk-based graph sampling methods in the literature [34, 29, 12, 15, 30, 5, 20], and more generally, MCMC samplers [28, 26, 35, 18, 31, 27].

THEOREM 1. *[18, 31] Suppose that $\{X_t\}$ is a finite, irreducible Markov chain with its stationary distribution $\boldsymbol{\pi}$. Then, for any initial distribution $\mathbb{P}\{X_0 = i\}, i \in \mathcal{N}$, as $t \to \infty$,*

$$\hat{\mu}_t(f) \to \mathbb{E}_{\boldsymbol{\pi}}(f) \text{ almost surely (a.s.)}$$

for any function f with $\mathbb{E}_{\boldsymbol{\pi}}(|f|) < \infty$. □

*A target graph for sampling may be time-varying due to node join/leave, which is beyond the scope of this paper.

The SLLN ensures that the estimator $\hat{\mu}_t(f)$ based on any finite, irreducible Markov chain with the same π can serve as a valid and unbiased approximation of $\mathbb{E}_\pi(f)$.

2.2 Central Limit Theorem and Asymptotic Variance

For a given graph $\mathcal{G}$, there are potentially many (finite) irreducible Markov chains (or different random walks) preserving the same stationary distribution π, all of which can be used to obtain asymptotically unbiased estimates of $\mathbb{E}_\pi(f)$, and also of $\mathbb{E}_{\boldsymbol{u}}(f)$, together with proper re-weighting if $\pi \neq \boldsymbol{u}$. One important question would then be how to compare these 'competing' Markov chains, or rather, which one is 'better' or more efficient than the others as a Markov chain sampler for unbiased graph sampling.

Mixing time [8, 22] can perhaps be a criterion to compare several irreducible, aperiodic Markov chains, all with the same stationary distribution. If the speed of convergence to the stationary distribution is a primary concern, then the mixing time is surely the right metric to compare different Markov chains with the same stationary distribution. However, this is not the case for the unbiased graph sampling. Random walk-based graph sampling methods typically adopt an initial burn-in period over which (initial) sampled values are discarded to get rid of the dependence on the initial position of a random walk [12]. After such a burn-in period, the Markov chain (or random walk) will be close to its stationary regime (well mixed), but many samples are still yet to be obtained from this point onward. Therefore, the primary concern should be, instead, the *efficiency* of the estimator $\hat{\mu}_t(f)$ in deciding how many random samples are required to achieve a certain accuracy of $\hat{\mu}_t(f)$ in regard to $\mathbb{E}_\pi(f)$ (and eventually to $\mathbb{E}_{\boldsymbol{u}}(f)$ after proper re-weighting if necessary).

To that end, we define by $\sigma^2(f)$ the asymptotic variance of the estimator $\hat{\mu}_t(f)$ based on an irreducible Markov chain $\{X_t\}$ with its stationary distribution π, which is given by

$$\sigma^2(f) \triangleq \lim_{t\to\infty} t \;\; \mathrm{Var}\left(\hat{\mu}_t(f)\right) = \lim_{t\to\infty} \frac{1}{t}\mathbb{E}\left\{\left[\sum_{s=1}^{t}(f(X_s) - \mathbb{E}_\pi(f))\right]^2\right\} \quad (2)$$

for any function f with $\mathbb{E}_\pi(f^2) < \infty$, where the initial position (state) X_0 is drawn from the stationary distribution π, i.e., $X_0 \sim \pi$. Note that the asymptotic variance $\sigma^2(f)$ is, in fact, *independent* of the distribution of the initial state X_0 [28, 31]. Not only for the well-known case with *i.i.d.* samples (or random variables), the Central Limit Theorem (CLT) holds also for Markov chains, as given below.

THEOREM 2. *[18, 31] For a finite, irreducible Markov chain $\{X_t\}$ with its stationary distribution π,*

$$\sqrt{t}\cdot[\hat{\mu}_t(f) - \mathbb{E}_\pi(f)] \;\overset{d}{\Longrightarrow}\; \mathrm{N}(0, \sigma^2(f)), \;\; as\ t\to\infty,$$

for any function f with $\mathbb{E}_\pi(f^2) < \infty$ regardless of any initial distribution, where $\overset{d}{\Longrightarrow}$ denotes convergence in distribution and $\mathrm{N}(0,\sigma^2(f))$ is a Gaussian random variable with zero mean and variance $\sigma^2(f)$ given by (2). □

Note that Theorems 1–2 (SLLN and CLT) do not require any assumption of aperiodicity [31]. However, for simplicity, we do not consider periodic Markov chains in our analysis throughout the paper. In addition, we focus on *bounded* functions f (and thus $\mathbb{E}_\pi(f^2) < \infty$), which is typical in graph sampling applications.

The CLT says that the distribution of $\hat{\mu}_t(f)$ is asymptotically normal with variance $\sigma^2(f)$, and thus allows one to evaluate the asymptotic variance $\sigma^2(f)$ in order to decide approximately how many (correlated) samples are required to achieve a certain accuracy of the estimator $\hat{\mu}_t(f)$. Hence, the asymptotic variance $\sigma^2(f)$ has been an important criterion to rank the *efficiency* among competing Markov chains with the same π for the MCMC samplers [28, 26, 35, 18, 31, 27], although quantifying $\sigma^2(f)$ may not be easy. In particular, by noting that the asymptotic variance is independent of any initial distribution for which the CLT holds, the efficiency ordering over competing Markov chains with the same π (the smaller the asymptotic variance, the better the estimator performance) is still in effect even when the competing Markov chains are already in their stationary regimes (already 'mixed'). Observe that from $X_0 \sim \pi$, $X_t \sim \pi$ for all t (the chain $\{X_t\}$ is in the stationary regime), and thus (2) becomes

$$\sigma^2(f) = \mathrm{Var}(f(X_0)) + 2\sum_{k=1}^{\infty}\mathrm{Cov}(f(X_0), f(X_k)), \quad (3)$$

where $\mathrm{Cov}(f(X_0), f(X_k)) = \mathbb{E}\{f(X_0)f(X_k)\} - \mathbb{E}_\pi^2(f)$ denotes the covariance between $f(X_0)$ and $f(X_k)$. As a special case, if the samples $\{X_t\}$ are *i.i.d.* and drawn directly from π, then $\sigma^2(f) = \mathrm{Var}(f(X_0))$. Also, even if the competing Markov chains are already in their stationary regimes, the correlation structure over random samples given by each of these Markov chains can vary and significantly affect their asymptotic variances. Observe that reducing the temporal correlation over random samples can lead to smaller asymptotic variances. This intuition can be leveraged to improve the existing Markov chain samplers for unbiased graph sampling.

Motivated by the effectiveness of the asymptotic variance with its connection to the CLT, in this paper, we consider the asymptotic variance as a primary performance metric, and develop two random walk-based graph sampling methods, each of which guarantees the unbiased graph sampling with smaller asymptotic variance than its corresponding counterpart in the current networking literature. Before going into details, we next briefly review the existing two random walk-based graph sampling methods.

3. RANDOM WALK-BASED SAMPLING

3.1 Simple Random Walk with Re-weighting

We first review the SRW-rw, a.k.a., respondent-driven sampling [33], which has been recently used in [29, 12] for unbiased graph sampling. This method operates based upon a sequence of (correlated) random samples obtained by a SRW, together with a proper re-weighting process to ensure the unbiased sampling. It is essentially a special case of the importance sampling (a Monte Carlo method) applied for random samples generated by a Markov chain [6, 24, 13].

Consider a SRW on $\mathcal{G}$ that moves from a node to one of its neighbors chosen uniformly at random (u.a.r.). Specifically, let $\{X_t\}$ be the Markov chain representing the sequence of visited nodes by the SRW, with its transition matrix $\mathbf{P} = \{P(i,j)\}_{i,j\in\mathcal{N}}$ given by $P(i,j) = 1/d(i)$ if $(i,j)\in\mathcal{E}$, and $P(i,j) = 0$ otherwise. It is well known that $\mathbf{P}$ is irreducible, and reversible with respect to a unique stationary distribution $\boldsymbol{\pi}$ for which $\pi(i) = d(i)/(2|\mathcal{E}|), i \in \mathcal{N}$ [2].

Suppose that there are t random samples $\{X_s\}_{s=1}^{t}$ from the SRW. Then, for a function of interest f, choose a weight function $w : \mathcal{N} \to \mathbb{R}$ such that $w(i) = u(i)/\pi(i) = 2|\mathcal{E}|/(nd(i))$, $i \in \mathcal{N}$. Observe that from the SLLN in Theorem 1, as $t \to \infty$,

$$\hat{\mu}_t(wf) = \frac{1}{t}\sum_{s=1}^{t} w(X_s)f(X_s) \;\to\; \mathbb{E}_{\boldsymbol{\pi}}(wf) = \mathbb{E}_{\boldsymbol{u}}(f) \text{ a.s.}$$

and thus the estimator $\hat{\mu}_t(wf)$ is unbiased for $\mathbb{E}_{\boldsymbol{u}}(f)$. However, this estimator itself is not practical, since n and $|\mathcal{E}|$ are typically unknown a priori. Instead, another estimator $\hat{\mu}_t(wf)/\hat{\mu}_t(w)$ is often used as an unbiased estimator for $\mathbb{E}_{\boldsymbol{u}}(f)$. Indeed, Theorem 1 asserts that $\hat{\mu}_t(wf)$ and $\hat{\mu}_t(w)$ converge to $\mathbb{E}_{\boldsymbol{u}}(f)$ and 1 almost surely, as $t \to \infty$, respectively. This yields

$$\frac{\hat{\mu}_t(wf)}{\hat{\mu}_t(w)} = \frac{\sum_{s=1}^{t} w(X_s)f(X_s)}{\sum_{s=1}^{t} w(X_s)} \to \mathbb{E}_{\boldsymbol{u}}(f) \text{ a.s.}$$

Hence, the estimator $\hat{\mu}_t(wf)/\hat{\mu}_t(w)$ can be made in such a way that we need to know $w(i)$ only up to a multiplicative constant. That is, if we set $w(i) = 1/d(i)$, $i \in \mathcal{N}$, then the estimator $\hat{\mu}_t(wf)/\hat{\mu}_t(w)$ remains intact, and is more practical as an unbiased estimator for $\mathbb{E}_{\boldsymbol{u}}(f)$. Throughout this paper, we refer to the estimator $\hat{\mu}_t(wf)/\hat{\mu}_t(w)$ with $w(i) = 1/d(i)$ $(i \in \mathcal{N})$ as the unbiased estimator for $\mathbb{E}_{\boldsymbol{u}}(f)$ in the SRW-rw [29, 12].

3.2 Metropolis-Hastings Algorithm

The MH algorithm [25, 16] was developed to construct a transition matrix $\mathbf{P}$ of a time-reversible Markov chain $\{X_t\}$ with a given, desired stationary distribution $\boldsymbol{\pi}$. Here, we only discuss the MH algorithm under the topological constraints of a graph $\mathcal{G}$ in that transition from node i to $j \neq i$ is allowed only when they are neighbors of each other. The MH algorithm is defined as follows. At the current state i of X_t, the next state X_{t+1} is proposed with a *proposal* probability $Q(i,j)$, which is a state transition probability of an arbitrary irreducible Markov chain on the state space $\mathcal{N}$, where $Q(i,j) > 0$ if and only if $Q(j,i) > 0$, and $Q(i,j) = 0$ for all $(i,j) \notin \mathcal{E}$ $(i \neq j)$. Let $\mathbf{Q} \triangleq \{Q(i,j)\}_{i,j\in\mathcal{N}}$ be a proposal (transition) matrix. The proposed state transition to $X_{t+1} = j$ is accepted with an *acceptance* probability

$$A(i,j) = \min\left\{1, \frac{\pi(j)Q(j,i)}{\pi(i)Q(i,j)}\right\}, \tag{4}$$

and rejected with probability $1 - A(i,j)$ in which case $X_{t+1} = i$. Thus, the transition probability $P(i,j)$ becomes, for $i \neq j$,

$$P(i,j) = Q(i,j)A(i,j) = \min\left\{Q(i,j), Q(j,i)\frac{\pi(j)}{\pi(i)}\right\}, \tag{5}$$

with $P(i,i) = 1 - \sum_{j\neq i} P(i,j)$, which ensures that $\mathbf{P}$ is reversible with respect to $\boldsymbol{\pi}$. Note that the uniqueness of $\boldsymbol{\pi}$ is granted due to the irreducibility of $\mathbf{Q}$ (so is $\mathbf{P}$) and the finite state space.

The MH algorithm, in addition to its popular applications for MCMC simulation, has been also widely used as a means for unbiased graph sampling [34, 29, 12, 15]. Specifically, the MH algorithm has been applied to construct a MHRW on $\mathcal{G}$ achieving a uniform stationary distribution, i.e., $\boldsymbol{\pi} = \boldsymbol{u}$. This is done with transition probabilities of a SRW as the proposal probabilities, i.e., $Q(i,j) = 1/d(i)$ if $(i,j) \in \mathcal{E}$, and $Q(i,j) = 0$ otherwise. The resulting transition probability of the MHRW on $\mathcal{G}$ becomes

$$P(i,j) = \begin{cases} \min\left\{\frac{1}{d(i)}, \frac{1}{d(j)}\right\} & \text{if } (i,j) \in \mathcal{E}, \\ 0 & \text{if } (i,j) \notin \mathcal{E}, i \neq j, \end{cases} \tag{6}$$

and $P(i,i) = 1 - \sum_{j\neq i} P(i,j)$. Thus, $\mathbf{P}$ is reversible with respect to $\boldsymbol{\pi} = \boldsymbol{u}$, implying that for any function f, the estimator $\hat{\mu}_t(f)$ based upon random samples by the MHRW is unbiased for $\mathbb{E}_{\boldsymbol{u}}(f)$. This version of MH algorithm is summarized in Algorithm 1, where $X_t \in \mathcal{N}$ denotes the location of the MHRW at time t, and $d(X_t)$ denotes the degree of node X_t. Here, X_0 can be arbitrarily chosen.

Algorithm 1 MH algorithm for MHRW (at time t)

```
Choose node j u.a.r. from neighbors of X_t, i.e., N(X_t)
Generate p ~ U(0, 1)
if p ≤ min{1, d(X_t)/d(j)} then
    X_{t+1} ← j
else
    X_{t+1} ← X_t
end if
```

Remark 1. *The MH algorithm (Algorithm 1) does not need to know the self-transition probabilities $P(i,i)$ explicitly, nor does it require all the neighbors' degree information of the current node X_t at each time t. Instead, only the degree information of the randomly chosen neighbor j is enough for making decision whether or not to move to j.*

Recall that the above unbiased estimators are based on t random, consecutive samples obtained under SRW or MHRW, respectively. Observe that the SRW, currently at node i at time s can 'backtrack' to the previously visited node with probability $1/d(i)$, i.e., $X_{s+1} = X_{s-1}$, trapping the SRW temporarily in a local region. The situation can be worse for the regions in which nodes have small degrees (so higher chance of backtracking). Similarly, the MHRW at node i can also backtrack to the previously visited node after staying at node i for some random time. This slow 'diffusion' of SRW/MHRW over the space can, in turn, lead to highly duplicated random samples for a short to moderate time duration, thereby increasing the variance of the unbiased estimators. Recall that the asymptotic variance in (3) involves covariance terms $\mathrm{Cov}(f(X_0), f(X_k))$. Thus, it would be beneficial for both SRW and MHRW (or precisely, their variants) to avoid backtracking to the previously visited node up to the extent possible in order to reduce the temporal correlation over random consecutive samples, while maintaining the same stationary distribution so that the aforementioned mathematical framework for the unbiased estimation remains intact. Thus motivated, for the rest of this paper, we investigate how to achieve this at *almost no additional cost*, and rigorously prove that our proposed sampling methods give smaller (no worse) asymptotic variance than the SRW (with re-weighting) and MHRW-based ones, respectively.

4. AVOID BACKTRACKING TO PREVIOUSLY VISITED NODE

In this section, we propose two random walk-based graph sampling methods – **(i) non-backtracking random walk**

with re-weighting and **(ii) MH algorithm with delayed acceptance**, each of which *theoretically guarantees* unbiased graph sampling with smaller asymptotic variance than the SRW-rw and the (original) MH algorithm, respectively. In particular, our proposed sampling methods require almost no additional cost, or more precisely, just remembering where the underlying random walk came from, when compared to the conventional methods. The reasoning behind the improvement of asymptotic variance is to modify each of SRW and MHRW, when making a transition from the current node to one of its neighbors, to reduce bias toward the previous state (one of the neighbors of the current node), while maintaining the same stationary distribution. Note that such directional bias breaks the time-reversibility of the SRW and MHRW. Thus, a common building block for our proposed sampling methods will be, for a given reversible Markov chain with its stationary distribution $\boldsymbol{\pi}$, to construct a *non-reversible* Markov chain preserving the same $\boldsymbol{\pi}$ while avoiding (to the extent possible) transitions that backtrack to the state from which the chain just came. Our challenge here is to construct such a non-reversible chain with only one-step memory and theoretical guarantee for higher efficiency (smaller asymptotic variance). In what follows, we first explain a basic setup for this transformation and several relevant issues, and then present the details of our proposed methods.

4.1 From Reversible To Non-reversible Chains

Consider a generic random walk on $\mathcal{G}$, or a finite, irreducible, *time-reversible* Markov chain $\{X_t \in \mathcal{N}\}_{t\geq 0}$, with its transition matrix $\mathbf{P} = \{P(i,j)\}_{i,j\in\mathcal{N}}$ and stationary distribution $\boldsymbol{\pi} = [\pi(i), i \in \mathcal{N}]$. Our goal here is to construct its related new random walk or a finite, irreducible, *non-reversible* Markov chain with the same $\boldsymbol{\pi}$ which avoids backtracking to the previously visited node, which in turn produces a smaller asymptotic variance than the original reversible chain. An important requirement is that this transformation should be done at no additional cost and in a distributed manner. It is worth noting that there have been other works [9, 10] showing that certain non-reversible Markov chains or lifted Markov chains mix substantially faster than their related reversible chains. While this concept has been also applied to design a fast and efficient average consensus algorithm [19, 23], it is still unknown how to construct such a non-reversible chain or lifted Markov chain in a fully distributed or decentralized fashion, not to mention how to do so for any arbitrarily given target stationary distribution $\boldsymbol{\pi}$.

A general recipe for constructing a non-reversible Markov chain in an augmented state space: Let $X'_t \in \mathcal{N}$, $t = 0, 1, 2\ldots$, be the location of a new random walk at time t. At the current node X'_t, the next node X'_{t+1} is decided based upon not only the current node X'_t but also the previous node X'_{t-1} so as to avoid backtracking. Due to the dependency (memory) to the previous node, $\{X'_t\}_{t\geq 0}$ itself cannot be a Markov chain on the state space $\mathcal{N}$, regardless of the choice of transition matrix. This walk, however, can still be made Markovian on an augmented state space instead, defined by

$$\Omega \triangleq \{(i,j) \,:\, i,j \in \mathcal{N} \text{ s.t. } P(i,j) > 0\} \subseteq \mathcal{N}\times\mathcal{N} \quad (7)$$

with $|\Omega| < \infty$, and $Z'_t \triangleq (X'_{t-1}, X'_t) \in \Omega$ for $t \geq 1$. For notational simplicity, let e_{ij} denote state $(i,j) \in \Omega$. Note that $e_{ij} \neq e_{ji}$. It is also possible that $e_{ii} \in \Omega$ for some i. A similar interpretation of a weighted random walk (or a reversible Markov chain) on the augmented state space can be also found in [2, Ch.3], although its purpose is not for the construction of a related non-reversible chain.

Let $\mathbf{P'} \triangleq \{P'(e_{ij}, e_{lk})\}_{e_{ij},e_{lk}\in\Omega}$ be the transition matrix of an irreducible Markov chain $\{Z'_t \in \Omega\}_{t\geq 1}$ on the state space Ω. Here, by definition, $P'(e_{ij}, e_{lk}) = 0$ for all $j \neq l$. If the unique stationary distribution $\boldsymbol{\pi}' \triangleq [\pi'(e_{ij}), e_{ij} \in \Omega]$ of the chain $\{Z'_t\}$ is given by

$$\pi'(e_{ij}) = \pi(i)P(i,j), \qquad e_{ij} \in \Omega, \quad (8)$$

implying that $\pi'(e_{ij}) = \pi'(e_{ji})$ from the reversibility of the original chain $\{X_t\}$, then the probability of the new random walk $\{X'_t\}$ being at node j in the *steady-state* is the same as $\pi(j)$ for all j (the stationary distribution of the original reversible chain $\{X_t\}$). To see this, note that

$$\sum_{i\in\mathcal{N}:e_{ij}\in\Omega} \pi'(e_{ij}) = \sum_{i\in\mathcal{N}} \pi(i)P(i,j) = \pi(j), \ \forall j \in \mathcal{N}, \quad (9)$$

where the first equality follows from $P(u,v) = 0$, $\forall (u,v) \notin \Omega$. In particular, for any original function of interest $f : \mathcal{N} \to \mathbb{R}$, choose another function $g : \Omega \to \mathbb{R}$ such that $g(e_{ij}) = f(j)$, and observe

$$\begin{aligned}\mathbb{E}_{\pi'}(g) &= \sum_{e_{ij}\in\Omega} g(e_{ij})\pi'(e_{ij}) = \sum_{j\in\mathcal{N}}\sum_{i\in\mathcal{N}} f(j)\pi(i)P(i,j) \\ &= \sum_{j\in\mathcal{N}} f(j)\pi(j) = \mathbb{E}_{\pi}(f).\end{aligned}$$

Then, the SLLN in Theorem 1 gives

$$\frac{1}{t}\sum_{s=1}^{t} g(Z'_s) = \frac{1}{t}\sum_{s=1}^{t} f(X'_s) \ \to\ \mathbb{E}_{\pi'}(g) = \mathbb{E}_{\pi}(f) \ \text{ a.s.}, \quad (10)$$

i.e., $\sum_{s=1}^{t} g(Z'_s)/t$ is a valid unbiased estimator for $\mathbb{E}_{\pi}(f)$. We thus define, for any given function $f : \mathcal{N} \to \mathbb{R}$,

$$\hat{\mu}'_t(f) \triangleq \frac{1}{t}\sum_{s=1}^{t} f(X'_s) \quad (11)$$

to be clearly distinguished from $\hat{\mu}_t(f)$ in (1) defined based on the original chain $\{X_t\}$, while $\hat{\mu}'_t(f)$ and $\hat{\mu}_t(f)$ are both unbiased estimators for $\mathbb{E}_{\pi}(f)$. In addition, the CLT in Theorem 2 implies

$$\begin{aligned}\sqrt{t}\cdot\left[\frac{1}{t}\sum_{s=1}^{t} g(Z'_s) - \mathbb{E}_{\pi'}(g)\right] &= \sqrt{t}\cdot[\hat{\mu}'_t(f) - \mathbb{E}_{\pi}(f)] \\ &\xrightarrow{d} \mathrm{N}(0, {\sigma'}^2(f)), \quad (12)\end{aligned}$$

where ${\sigma'}^2(f)$ denotes the asymptotic variance of $\hat{\mu}'_t(f)$ (and also of $\sum_{s=1}^{t} g(Z'_s)/t$). Throughout the paper, we use the prime symbol ($'$) for any notation related to a newly defined process (e.g., $\{X'_t\}$) to differentiate it from its counterpart defined on the original process (e.g., $\{X_t\}$).

While there are infinitely many different transition matrices $\mathbf{P}'$ leading to the unbiased estimator $\hat{\mu}'_t(f)$ for $\mathbb{E}_{\pi}(f)$, our primary goal is, at (almost) no additional cost and in a distributed manner, to find a transition matrix $\mathbf{P}'$ that also guarantees smaller asymptotic variance. Under a rather restricted setting, R. Neal gave a partial answer to this in [27] saying that less backtracking (rendering the resulting

Markov chain $\{Z'_t\}$ non-reversible) can result in a smaller asymptotic variance. We restate his finding below.

THEOREM 3. *[27, Theorem 2] Suppose that $\{X_t\}$ is an irreducible, reversible Markov chain on the state space $\mathcal{N}$ with transition matrix $\mathbf{P} = \{P(i,j)\}$ and stationary distribution $\boldsymbol{\pi}$. Construct a Markov chain $\{Z'_t\}$ on the state space Ω with transition matrix $\mathbf{P}' = \{P'(e_{ij}, e_{lk})\}$ in which the transition probabilities $P'(e_{ij}, e_{lk})$ satisfy the following two conditions: for all $e_{ij}, e_{ji}, e_{jk}, e_{kj} \in \Omega$ with $i \neq k$,*

$$P(j,i)P'(e_{ij}, e_{jk}) = P(j,k)P'(e_{kj}, e_{ji}), \tag{13}$$

$$P'(e_{ij}, e_{jk}) \geq P(j,k). \tag{14}$$

Then, the Markov chain $\{Z'_t\}$ is irreducible and non-reversible with a unique stationary distribution $\boldsymbol{\pi}'$ in which $\pi'(e_{ij}) = \pi(i)P(i,j)$, $e_{ij} \in \Omega$. Also, for any function f, the asymptotic variance of $\hat{\mu}'_t(f)$ is no greater than that of $\hat{\mu}_t(f)$, i.e., $\sigma'^2(f) \leq \sigma^2(f)$. □

REMARK 2. *The condition in (13) ensures that the resulting transition matrix $\mathbf{P}'$ is stationary with respect to $\boldsymbol{\pi}'$ in (8) and, in turn, leads to the unbiased estimator $\hat{\mu}'_t(f)$ for $\mathbb{E}_{\boldsymbol{\pi}}(f)$. Together with this condition, the condition in (14) – less backtracking to the previously visited node, brings out the improvement of asymptotic variance.*

Theorem 3 is quite versatile and provides a guideline on how to choose the transition matrix $\mathbf{P}'$ of a Markov chain $\{Z'_t\}$ leading to smaller asymptotic variance, and thus will play an essential role in developing our graph sampling methods and subsequent analysis. Despite this large degree of freedom, it is still uncertain how to choose such a transition matrix $\mathbf{P}'$ *at no additional cost.* While R. Neal suggested a procedure to find $\mathbf{P}'$, it generally poses significant cost, especially for improving the MH algorithm, as admitted in [27]. (See pp. 9–10 therein.) Recall that the MH algorithm (Algorithm 1) for MHRW only needs the degree information of a randomly chosen neighbor j of the current node X_t to decide whether or not to move j, as mentioned in Remark 1.[†] However, the procedure by R. Neal necessitates the *explicit knowledge* of all $P(i,i)$'s [27]. That is, the corresponding modified MHRW would require all the neighbors' degree information of the current node X'_t at each time t in order to choose the next node X'_{t+1}. Imagine such modified MHRW crawling over an OSN (say, Facebook) and located at a certain user's page. To simply decide where to go, the walk would have to visit all his/her friends' pages first and collect all their degree information (i.e., the number of friends) before making decision to move. This is clearly impractical for our graph sampling purpose. Therefore, in this paper, we set out to develop our own graph samplers with higher efficiency *without any such overhead*, by leveraging Theorem 3 as a building block.

4.2 Non-backtracking Random Walk with Re-weighting

We first introduce non-backtracking random walk with re-weighting (NBRW-rw) that ensures unbiased graph sampling, and then prove that NBRW-rw guarantees a smaller asymptotic variance than SRW-rw. The non-backtracking random walk (NBRW) is a discrete-time random walk which 'never' backtracks (thus named non-backtracking) to the previous node (whenever possible) while preserving the same stationary distribution as that of a SRW. Thus, the proposed sampling method is to use an NBRW, instead of a SRW, to collect a sequence of samples by crawling over a target $\mathcal{G}$, and at the same time, to employ the same re-weighting process as is done for SRW in order to eliminate sampling bias induced from its non-uniform stationary distribution.

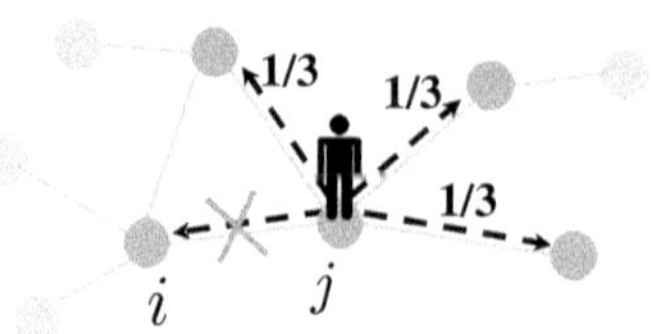

Figure 1: Illustrating the transitions of an NBRW. The walker is currently located at node j (with $d(j)=4$) and just came from node i. From j, it will move to one of its neighbors except node i with equal probability.

Consider an irreducible, reversible Markov chain $\{X_t\}_{t\geq 0}$ (a sequence of visited nodes) by the SRW, with its transition matrix $\mathbf{P}$ and stationary distribution $\boldsymbol{\pi}$. Then, the NBRW is defined as follows. A (discrete-time) random walk at the current node j with $d(j)\geq 2$ moves to the next node k, chosen u.a.r. from the neighbors of node j except the previous node i. If the current node j has only one neighbor ($d(j)=1$), the walk always returns to the previous node i. Figure 1 depicts this non-backtracking nature of the NBRW in its transitions over the nodes of $\mathcal{G}$. Here, an initial position of the NBRW can be arbitrarily chosen. The NBRW initially moves from the initial position to one of its neighbors with equal probability due to the absence of its 'previous node', and then proceeds as defined above thereafter.

Let $X'_t \in \mathcal{N}$, $t=0,1,2,\ldots$, be the location of an NBRW. As before, we construct a Markov chain $\{Z'_t = (X'_{t-1}, X'_t)\}_{t\geq 1}$ with its transition matrix $\mathbf{P}' = \{P'(e_{ij}, e_{lk})\}_{e_{ij},e_{lk}\in\Omega}$ given by, for all $e_{ij}, e_{jk} \in \Omega$ with $i \neq k$ ($d(j) \geq 2$),

$$P'(e_{ij}, e_{jk}) = \frac{1}{d(j)-1} > \frac{1}{d(j)} = P(j,k), \tag{15}$$

implying that $P'(e_{ij}, e_{ji}) = 0$. Also, $P'(e_{ij}, e_{ji}) = 1$ for any j with $d(j) = 1$. All other elements of $\mathbf{P}'$ are zero. Clearly, $\mathbf{P}'$ satisfies the conditions in (13)–(14). From Theorem 3, the Markov chain $\{Z'_t\}$ is irreducible and non-reversible with a unique stationary distribution

$$\pi'(e_{ij}) = \pi(i)P(i,j) = \frac{1}{2|\mathcal{E}|}, \quad e_{ij} \in \Omega. \tag{16}$$

That is, the probability of the NBRW being at node j in the steady-state is the same as $\pi(j)$. See (9). From (10)–(11) and Theorem 3, we also know that for any given function f of interest, $\hat{\mu}'_t(f)$ and $\hat{\mu}_t(f)$ are both unbiased estimators for $\mathbb{E}_{\boldsymbol{\pi}}(f)$, and the asymptotic variance of $\hat{\mu}'_t(f)$ (based on the random samples by the NBRW) is no larger than that of $\hat{\mu}_t(f)$ (by the SRW), i.e., $\sigma'^2(f)\leq\sigma^2(f)$.

However, both unbiased estimators $\hat{\mu}'_t(f)$ and $\hat{\mu}_t(f)$ are for $\mathbb{E}_{\boldsymbol{\pi}}(f)$, not $\mathbb{E}_{\boldsymbol{u}}(f)$. It is unclear whether such improvement for the asymptotic variance remains true even after a proper re-weighting to obtain *unbiased* samples. As explained in Section 3.1, the SRW-rw is to use the estimator $\hat{\mu}_t(wf)/\hat{\mu}_t(w)$ with $w(i)=1/d(i)$ ($i\in\mathcal{N}$) in order to consis-

[†]More generally, in the MH algorithm with any proposal matrix $\mathbf{Q}$, it is often unnecessary to know self-transition probabilities $P(i,i)$ explicitly, or does not require summing the probabilities of rejection for all possible proposals just to compute $P(i,i)=Q(i,i)+\sum_{j\neq i} Q(i,j)(1-A(i,j))$.

tently estimate $\mathbb{E}_{\boldsymbol{u}}(f)$. Since the stationary distribution of the NBRW remains the same as that of the SRW, we can also use the estimator $\hat{\mu}'_t(wf)/\hat{\mu}'_t(w)$ with the same weight function w, as a valid approximation of $\mathbb{E}_{\boldsymbol{u}}(f)$. Let $\sigma^2_{\mathrm{W}}(f)$ and $\sigma'^2_{\mathrm{W}}(f)$ denote the asymptotic variances of the estimators $\hat{\mu}_t(wf)/\hat{\mu}_t(w)$ and $\hat{\mu}'_t(wf)/\hat{\mu}'_t(w)$, respectively. To proceed, we need the following.

THEOREM 4 (SLUTSKY'S THEOREM). *[4, pp.332] Let $\{A_t\}$ and $\{B_t\}$ be the sequences of random variables. If $A_t \xrightarrow{d} A$, and B_t converges in probability to a non-zero constant b, then $A_t/B_t \xrightarrow{d} A/b$.* □

Now we state our main result.

THEOREM 5. *For any function $f : \mathcal{N} \to \mathbb{R}$, the asymptotic variance of $\hat{\mu}'_t(wf)/\hat{\mu}'_t(w)$ is no larger than that of $\hat{\mu}_t(wf)/\hat{\mu}_t(w)$, i.e., $\sigma'^2_{\mathrm{W}}(f) \leq \sigma^2_{\mathrm{W}}(f)$, where the weight function w is given by $w(i) = 1/d(i)$, $i \in \mathcal{N}$.* □

PROOF. Since the estimator $\hat{\mu}_t(wf)/\hat{\mu}_t(w)$ remains invariant up to a constant multiple of w, without loss of generality, we can set $w(i) = u(i)/\pi(i) = 2|\mathcal{E}|/(nd(i))$. For any given f, observe that

$$\sqrt{t}\left[\frac{\hat{\mu}_t(wf)}{\hat{\mu}_t(w)} - \mathbb{E}_{\boldsymbol{u}}(f)\right] = \sqrt{t}\left[\frac{\sum_{s=1}^t w(X_s)f(X_s)}{\sum_{s=1}^t w(X_s)} - \mathbb{E}_{\boldsymbol{u}}(f)\right]$$
$$= \frac{t}{\sum_{s=1}^t w(X_s)}\sqrt{t}\left[\frac{\sum_{s=1}^t w(X_s)(f(X_s)-\mathbb{E}_{\boldsymbol{u}}(f))}{t}\right]. \quad (17)$$

Define another function $h : \mathcal{N} \to \mathbb{R}$ such that

$$h(i) \triangleq w(i)(f(i) - \mathbb{E}_{\boldsymbol{u}}(f)), \qquad i \in \mathcal{N},$$

implying $\mathbb{E}_\pi(h) = \sum_{i\in\mathcal{N}} h(i)\pi(i) = 0$. Then, from Theorems 1 and 2, we have, as $t \to \infty$,

$$\frac{1}{t}\sum_{s=1}^t w(X_s) \to 1 \text{ a.s., and } \sqrt{t}\left[\frac{1}{t}\sum_{s=1}^t h(X_s)\right] \xrightarrow{d} \mathrm{N}(0, \sigma^2(h)).$$

Since almost sure convergence implies convergence in probability [4], by Slutsky's theorem, from (17), we have

$$\sqrt{t}\left[\frac{\hat{\mu}_t(wf)}{\hat{\mu}_t(w)} - \mathbb{E}_{\boldsymbol{u}}(f)\right] \xrightarrow{d} \mathrm{N}(0, \sigma^2(h)), \text{ as } t \to \infty.$$

Together with (10) and (12), following the same lines above, we similarly have

$$\sqrt{t}\left[\frac{\hat{\mu}'_t(wf)}{\hat{\mu}'_t(w)} - \mathbb{E}_{\boldsymbol{u}}(f)\right] \xrightarrow{d} \mathrm{N}(0, \sigma'^2(h)), \text{ as } t \to \infty.$$

Hence, for a given f, the asymptotic variance of the estimator $\hat{\mu}_t(wf)/\hat{\mu}_t(w)$ is nothing but $\sigma^2_{\mathrm{W}}(f) = \sigma^2(h)$. Similarly, $\sigma'^2_{\mathrm{W}}(f) = \sigma'^2(h)$. Therefore, since Theorem 3 says that for any function f, $\sigma'^2(f) \leq \sigma^2(f)$, we also have $\sigma'^2_{\mathrm{W}}(f) \leq \sigma^2_{\mathrm{W}}(f)$. That is, the asymptotic variance of $\hat{\mu}'_t(wf)/\hat{\mu}'_t(w)$ is no larger than that of $\hat{\mu}_t(wf)/\hat{\mu}_t(w)$. ■

REMARK 3. *In [3], the NBRW was originally considered for regular graphs with $d(i) = d > 3$, $\forall i \in \mathcal{N}$, and shown to lead to faster mixing rate (i.e., faster rate of convergence to its stationary distribution) than that of the SRW. In contrast, for any general (connected, undirected, not necessarily regular) graph $\mathcal{G}$, we show that the NBRW-rw ensures not only the unbiased graph sampling but also smaller asymptotic variance than the SRW-rw.*

4.3 Metropolis-Hastings Algorithm with Delayed Acceptance

We turn our attention to improving the MH algorithm. For any given, desired stationary distribution $\boldsymbol{\pi}$, we propose Metropolis-Hastings algorithm with delayed acceptance (MHDA), which theoretically guarantees smaller asymptotic variance than the (generic) MH algorithm with proposal matrix $\mathbf{Q}$ that constructs a reversible Markov chain with arbitrary $\boldsymbol{\pi}$. In particular, we demonstrate that MHDA can be applied, as a special case, to construct a (non-Markovian) random walk on a graph $\mathcal{G}$ which not only achieves a uniform stationary distribution $\boldsymbol{\pi} = \boldsymbol{u}$ for unbiased graph sampling, but leads to higher efficiency than MHRW by the MH algorithm (Algorithm 1). We emphasize that the only additional overhead here is remembering the previously visited node (one of the neighbors of the current node) from which the random walk came.

Interpreting a reversible MH Markov chain as a semi-Markov chain: Consider an irreducible, reversible Markov chain $\{X_t \in \mathcal{N}\}_{t\geq 0}$ by the MH algorithm with its transition matrix $\mathbf{P} = \{P(i,j)\}_{i,j\in\mathcal{N}}$ given by (5), and any arbitrarily given target stationary distribution $\boldsymbol{\pi}$. Recall that the MH algorithm is nothing but a repetition of proposing a state transition with proposal probability $Q(i,j)$ that is then accepted with an acceptance probability $A(i,j)$ in (4) or rejected otherwise. Observe that the process $\{X_t\}$, after entering into state (node) i, stays at state i for a geometrically distributed time duration with mean $1/(1 - P(i,i))$, and then moves to another state $j \in N(i)$. Formally, define a Markov chain $\{\tilde{X}_m \in \mathcal{N}\}_{m\geq 0}$ with its transition matrix $\tilde{\mathbf{P}} \triangleq \{\tilde{P}(i,j)\}_{i,j\in\mathcal{N}}$ given by, for $j \neq i$,

$$\tilde{P}(i,j) = \frac{P(i,j)}{1 - P(i,i)} = \frac{Q(i,j)A(i,j)}{\sum_{j\neq i} Q(i,j)A(i,j)}$$
$$= \frac{\min\{Q(i,j), Q(j,i)\pi(j)/\pi(i)\}}{\sum_{j\neq i}\min\{Q(i,j), Q(j,i)\pi(j)/\pi(i)\}}, \quad (18)$$

with $\tilde{P}(i,i) = 0$. It is not difficult to see that the chain $\{\tilde{X}_m\}$ is irreducible, and reversible with respect to a unique stationary distribution $\tilde{\boldsymbol{\pi}} \triangleq [\tilde{\pi}(i), i\in\mathcal{N}]$, given by

$$\tilde{\pi}(i) \propto \pi(i)(1 - P(i,i)), \quad i \in \mathcal{N}.$$

Also, we define a function $\gamma : \mathcal{N} \to \mathbb{R}$ such that, for $i \in \mathcal{N}$,

$$\gamma(i) \triangleq 1 - P(i,i) = \sum_{j\neq i}\min\{Q(i,j), Q(j,i)\pi(j)/\pi(i)\}, \quad (19)$$

and define a sequence $\{\xi_m\}_{m\geq 0}$ for which ξ_m depends solely on $\{\tilde{X}_m\}_{m\geq 0}$ and is geometrically distributed with parameter $\gamma(\tilde{X}_m)$. It thus follows that $\mathbb{E}\{\xi_m|\tilde{X}_m = i\} = 1/\gamma(i)$, $i \in N$. The process $\{X_t\}$ can now be interpreted as a *semi-Markov* chain with *embedded* Markov chain $\{\tilde{X}_m\}$ and respective sojourn times $\{\xi_m\}$. Suppose that the random walk by the MH algorithm (or the process $\{X_t\}$) enters node j of a graph $\mathcal{G}$, depicted in Figure 2, at time $t = 1$ ($X_1 = j$). If we consider a sample path $(X_1, X_2, \ldots, X_7) = (j, j, j, i, i, j, k)$, then we have corresponding sequences $(\tilde{X}_1, \tilde{X}_2, \tilde{X}_3, \tilde{X}_4) = (j, i, j, k)$ and $(\xi_1, \xi_2, \xi_3) = (3, 2, 1)$. Note that the standard definition of a semi-Markov process allows the sojourn time ξ_m to depend on both $\tilde{X}_m$ and $\tilde{X}_{m+1}$ (and so we are dealing with a special case). From the theory of semi-Markov processes (e.g., [32]), one can easily recover the stationary

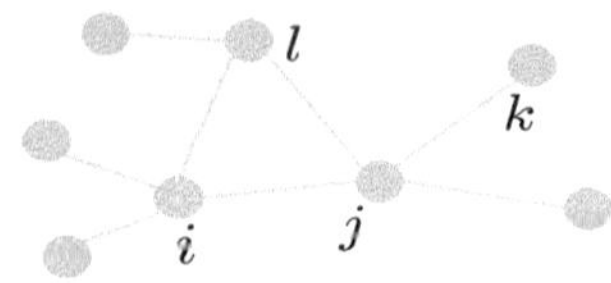

Figure 2: An example graph $\mathcal{G}$

distribution $\boldsymbol{\pi}$ as

$$\pi(i) \propto \tilde{\pi}(i)/\gamma(i), \quad i \in \mathcal{N}. \tag{20}$$

The above interpretation has been similarly given in the MCMC literature [24, 11]. In particular, it is known that, for any given function $f : \mathcal{N} \to \mathbb{R}$,

$$\hat{\mu}_{m,\mathsf{MH}}(f) \triangleq \frac{\sum_{l=1}^{m} \xi_l f(\tilde{X}_l)}{\sum_{l=1}^{m} \xi_l} \tag{21}$$

converges almost surely to $\mathbb{E}_\pi(f)$, as $m \to \infty$, and thus $\hat{\mu}_{m,\mathsf{MH}}(f)$ is also an unbiased estimator for $\mathbb{E}_\pi(f)$ [24]. This definition of $\hat{\mu}_{m,\mathsf{MH}}(f)$ enables more tractable analysis on its asymptotic variance, denoted as $\sigma^2_{\mathsf{MH}}(f)$, by connecting it to its counterpart in the importance sampling for Markov chains [24, 11]. Note that for sufficiently large t (also m), the (original) unbiased estimator $\hat{\mu}_t(f) = \sum_{s=1}^{t} f(X_s)/t$ can be written as $\hat{\mu}_{m,\mathsf{MH}}(f)$ plus some negligible term (after setting the same initial point $\tilde{X}_1 = X_1$), because it is always possible to find m such that $\sum_{l=1}^{m} \xi_l \leq t < \sum_{l=1}^{m+1} \xi_l$. Also, in the limit $t, m \to \infty$, $\hat{\mu}_t(f)$ and $\hat{\mu}_{m,\mathsf{MH}}(f)$ are the same. We thus focus on estimators in the form of $\hat{\mu}_{m,\mathsf{MH}}(f)$ in our subsequent analysis.

Consider a sequence of pairs $(\tilde{X}_m, \xi_m)$. From the success in the NBRW-rw, one may ask what if the reversible embedded Markov chain $\{\tilde{X}_m\}_{m\geq 0}$ is replaced by a related stochastic process $\{\tilde{X}'_m \in \mathcal{N}\}_{m\geq 0}$, or more precisely, a non-reversible Markov chain $\{(\tilde{X}'_{m-1}, \tilde{X}'_m)\}_{m\geq 1}$ on the augmented state space Ω, which avoids backtracking transitions to the extent possible, while preserving the same stationary distribution $\tilde{\boldsymbol{\pi}}$. Another question can be whether this transformation guarantees that the estimator in (21) based on $(\tilde{X}'_m, \xi_m)$ remains *unbiased* for $\mathbb{E}_\pi(f)$ and also have *higher efficiency* than the original one. Our answer is in the affirmative, and this is the reasoning behind the improvement of our proposed MHDA over the standard MH algorithm. We stress here that, in contrast to the NBRW, backtracking transitions in the process $\{\tilde{X}'_m\}$ should be *avoided only up to the extent possible*[‡] so as to maintain the arbitrarily given original stationary distribution $\tilde{\boldsymbol{\pi}}$. Thus, the extension from the MH algorithm to our proposed MHDA becomes necessarily more involved than the case of NBRW.

Description of MHDA: Let $X'_t \in \mathcal{N}$, $t = 0, 1, 2, \ldots$, be the position of a random walk (or the state of a stochastic process). We also define the augmented state space Ω in (7) based on the reversible embedded Markov chain $\{\tilde{X}_m\}$, where $\tilde{P}(i,i) = 0$ and so $e_{ii} \notin \Omega$ for all i.

MHDA is described as follows. Suppose that node i is the previous node from which the walk came. MHDA first operates just like the MH algorithm. At the current node (state) $X'_t = j \neq i$, the next node $X'_{t+1} = k \in N(j)$ is proposed with probability $Q(j,k)$ $(j \neq k)$. Then, the proposed transition to k is accepted with probability $A(j,k)$ in (4), and rejected with probability $1 - A(j,k)$ in which case $X'_{t+1} = j$. Here, in contrast to the MH algorithm, MHDA renders the accepted transition to $X'_{t+1} = k$ temporarily *pending*, and applies another procedure to proceed with the actual transition to k.[§]

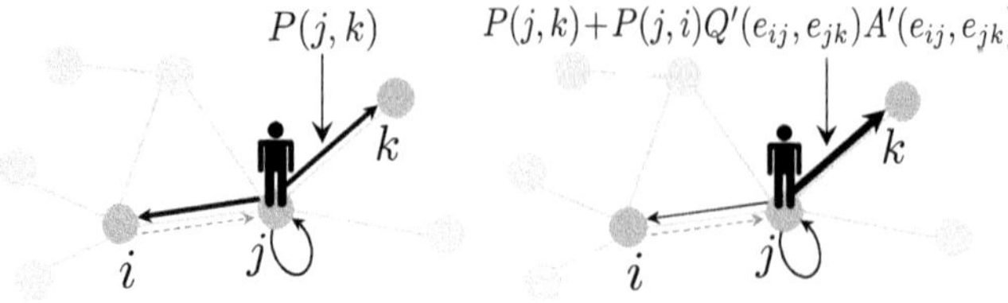

(a) MH algorithm (b) MHDA

Figure 3: Illustrating a difference between MH algorithm and MHDA: a walker moves from node j to node k with probability $P(j,k)$ in the MH algorithm, but with larger probability $P(j,k) + P(j,i)Q'(e_{ij}, e_{jk})A'(e_{ij}, e_{jk})$ in the MHDA.

Specifically, for the accepted transition to k, if $k \neq i$, then the 'actual' transition takes place, i.e., $X'_{t+1} = k$, with probability $P(j,k) = Q(j,k)A(j,k)$ as in the MH algorithm. On the other hand, if $k = i$, then the transition to node i is *delayed* (thus named 'delayed acceptance'). The next node X'_{t+1} is again proposed with another proposal probability $Q'(e_{ij}, e_{jk})$, which is a transition probability of an arbitrary Markov chain on the state space Ω, where $Q'(e_{ij}, e_{lk}) = 0$ for all $j \neq l$, and $Q'(e_{ij}, e_{jk}) > 0$ if and only if $Q'(e_{kj}, e_{ji}) > 0$. The (second) proposed transition to $X'_{t+1} = k$ is accepted with another acceptance probability $A'(e_{ij}, e_{jk})$, and rejected with probability $1 - A'(e_{ij}, e_{jk})$ in which case $X'_{t+1} = i$ (backtracking occurs). That is, transition probability $P(j,i) = Q(j,i)A(j,i)$ in the MH algorithm is leveraged to create another transition opportunity from j to $k \neq i$ in the MHDA. So, the transition from j to $k \neq i$ occurs with larger probability $P(j,k) + P(j,i)Q'(e_{ij}, e_{jk})A'(e_{ij}, e_{jk})$ than the MH algorithm (w.p. $P(j,k)$). This is also illustrated in Figure 3 where the thickness of arrows represents the corresponding transition probabilities from node j to other node (including self-transition). The new acceptance probability $A'(e_{ij}, e_{jk})$ will be specified shortly.

In summary, under MHDA, the walker stays at each node for the same random amount of time as it would be under the MH algorithm, while reducing the bias toward the previous node when making transitions to one of its neighbors.

Analysis of MHDA: Let $\tilde{X}'_m$, $m \geq 0$, be the sequence of nodes visited by the walk, which moves over $\mathcal{G}$ according to the MHDA. The process $\{\tilde{X}'_m\}$ is clearly different from the reversible, embedded Markov chain $\{\tilde{X}_m\}$ for the MH algorithm. Also, let ξ'_m, $m \geq 0$, be the respective sojourn time at node $\tilde{X}'_m$. Note that the MHDA behaves differently from the MH algorithm (performs the additional procedure) only when a proposed transition from node j to node $k \neq j$ (occurring with probability $Q(j,k)$) is accepted with probability $A(j,k)$ in the MH algorithm. Thus, ξ'_m is also geometrically distributed with parameter $\gamma(\tilde{X}'_m)$. See (19) for $\gamma(\cdot)$. That is, given that $\tilde{X}'_{m_1} = \tilde{X}_{m_2} = i$, the sojourn times ξ'_{m_1} and ξ_{m_2} have identical distributions. There-

‡If $\{\tilde{X}'_m\}$ is made purely non-backtracking just like we did for NBRW, then we lose unbiasedness for the resulting MH-based estimator in general.

§If the transition to $k = j$ was accepted after a proposal with $Q(j,j) > 0$, then the MHDA accepts the transition as in the MH algorithm without any further action.

fore, the MHDA, similar to the MH algorithm, can be also characterized by a sequence of the pairs $(\tilde{X}'_m, \xi'_m)$. As an example, if the random walk by the MHDA (or the process $\{X'_t\}$) enters node i in Figure 2 at time $t=1$ ($X'_1 = i$) and $(X'_1, X'_2, \ldots, X'_7) = (i,i,l,j,j,j,k)$, then we consequently have $(\tilde{X}'_1, \tilde{X}'_2, \tilde{X}'_3, \tilde{X}'_4) = (i,l,j,k)$ and $(\xi'_1, \xi'_2, \xi'_3) = (2,1,3)$. We define, for any given $f : \mathcal{N} \to \mathbb{R}$,

$$\hat{\mu}'_{m,\mathsf{MHDA}}(f) \triangleq \frac{\sum_{l=1}^{m} \xi'_l f(\tilde{X}'_l)}{\sum_{l=1}^{m} \xi'_l}. \qquad (22)$$

We prove below that $\hat{\mu}'_{m,\mathsf{MHDA}}(f)$ converges almost surely to $\mathbb{E}_{\pi}(f)$, implying that $\hat{\mu}'_{m,\mathsf{MHDA}}(f)$ is an unbiased estimator for $\mathbb{E}_{\pi}(f)$. We also prove that, after showing the CLT holds for $\hat{\mu}'_{m,\mathsf{MHDA}}(f)$, the asymptotic variance of $\hat{\mu}'_m(f)$, denoted as $\sigma'^2_{\mathsf{MHDA}}(f)$, is smaller than its counterpart $\sigma^2_{\mathsf{MH}}(f)$ for the MH algorithm.

To this end, we first explain how to properly choose the new acceptance $A'(e_{ij}, e_{jk})$ so that the process $\{\tilde{X}'_m\}$ has the same stationary distribution as that of the reversible embedded chain $\{\tilde{X}_m\}$, while, at the same time, the process $\{\tilde{X}'_m\}$ reduces backtracking transitions. Instead of the process $\{\tilde{X}'_m\}$, we deal with its related non-reversible Markov chain defined on the augmented state space Ω by consulting the general recipe for this purpose in Section 4.1. Recall the state space Ω in (7) obtained from the transition matrix $\tilde{\mathbf{P}} = \{\tilde{P}(i,j)\}$ of the chain $\{\tilde{X}_m\}$. We define $\tilde{Z}'_m \triangleq (\tilde{X}'_{m-1}, \tilde{X}'_m) \in \Omega$ for $m \geq 1$, and $\tilde{\mathbf{P}}' \triangleq \{\tilde{P}'(e_{ij}, e_{lk})\}_{e_{ij}, e_{lk} \in \Omega}$ to be the transition matrix of a Markov chain $\{\tilde{Z}'_m\}_{m \geq 1}$. For instance, consider a sample path $(\tilde{X}'_1, \tilde{X}'_2, \tilde{X}'_3, \tilde{X}'_4) = (i,l,j,k)$ in the above example. We have $(\tilde{Z}'_2, \tilde{Z}'_3, \tilde{Z}'_4) = ((i,l),(l,j),(j,k))$. If the chain $\{\tilde{Z}'_m\}$ has a unique stationary distribution $\tilde{\boldsymbol{\pi}}' \triangleq [\tilde{\pi}'(e_{ij}), e_{ij} \in \Omega]$ given by

$$\tilde{\pi}'(e_{ij}) = \tilde{\pi}(i)\tilde{P}(i,j), \qquad e_{ij} \in \Omega, \qquad (23)$$

implying that $\tilde{\pi}'(e_{ij}) = \tilde{\pi}'(e_{ji})$ from the reversibility of the embedded chain $\{\tilde{X}_m\}$, then the *steady-state* probability of the process $\{\tilde{X}'_m\}$ being at node j is the same as $\tilde{\pi}(j)$ for all j. From the description of MHDA, observe that, for all $e_{ij}, e_{jk} \in \Omega$ with $i \neq k$ ($d(j) \geq 2$),

$$\tilde{P}'(e_{ij}, e_{jk}) = \tilde{P}(j,k) + \tilde{P}(j,i)Q'(e_{ij}, e_{jk})A'(e_{ij}, e_{jk}), \quad (24)$$

while $\tilde{P}'(e_{ij}, e_{ji}) = 1 - \sum_{k \neq i} \tilde{P}'(e_{ij}, e_{jk})$, as is also shown in Figure 3(b). Note that $\tilde{P}'(e_{ij}, e_{jk})$ specifies the next node of the random walk by MHDA, *given that* the walk has to move from the current node to one of its neighbors (its sojourn time is over). Thus, $\tilde{P}(j,k)$ and $\tilde{P}(j,i)$ are used here instead of $P(j,k)$ and $P(j,i)$, respectively. In addition, for any j with $d(j) = 1$, we have $\tilde{P}'(e_{ij}, e_{ji}) = \tilde{P}(j,i) = 1$, $(i,j) \in \mathcal{E}$, since $Q'(e_{ij}, e_{ji}) = 1$ (due to the stochastic matrix $\{Q'(e_{ij}, e_{lk}\})$ and $A'(e_{ij}, e_{ji}) = 1$ which is shown below.

Among many possible choices for the acceptance probability $A'(e_{ij}, e_{jk})$ in the MHDA, we have the following.

Proposition 1. *For any given $\{Q'(e_{ij}, e_{lk})\}$, suppose that the acceptance probability $A'(e_{ij}, e_{jk})$ is given by*

$$A'(e_{ij}, e_{jk}) = \min\left\{1, \frac{P^2(j,k)Q'(e_{kj}, e_{ji})}{P^2(j,i)Q'(e_{ij}, e_{jk})}\right\}. \qquad (25)$$

Then, the resulting transition matrix $\tilde{\mathbf{P}}'$, and $\tilde{\mathbf{P}}$ satisfy conditions (13)–(14). □

Proof. See our technical report [21]. ■

From Theorem 3 and Proposition 1, the Markov chain $\{\tilde{Z}'_m\}$ with its transition matrix $\tilde{\mathbf{P}}'$ as in (24) and (25), is irreducible and non-reversible with a unique stationary distribution $\tilde{\boldsymbol{\pi}}'$ in (23). This also implies that the process $\{\tilde{X}'_m\}$ has the same stationary distribution $\tilde{\boldsymbol{\pi}}$, as explained before. We now present our main result.

Theorem 6. *Consider a given, desired stationary distribution $\boldsymbol{\pi} = [\pi(i), i \in \mathcal{N}]$. Under the MHDA with any given $\{Q'(e_{ij}, e_{lk})\}$ and its corresponding $A'(e_{ij}, e_{jk})$ in (25), for any given function $f : \mathcal{N} \to \mathbb{R}$, as $m \to \infty$, $\hat{\mu}'_{m,\mathsf{MHDA}}(f)$ converges almost surely to $\mathbb{E}_{\pi}(f)$, and also the asymptotic variance of $\hat{\mu}'_{m,\mathsf{MHDA}}(f)$ is no larger than that of $\hat{\mu}_{m,\mathsf{MH}}(f)$, i.e., $\sigma'^2_{\mathsf{MHDA}}(f) \leq \sigma^2_{\mathsf{MH}}(f)$.* □

Proof. See our technical report [21]. ■

An application of MHDA for unbiased graph sampling: We explain how MHDA can be applied for unbiased graph sampling applications. In particular, we present how to construct a (discrete-time) random walk by MHDA, named Metropolis-Hastings Random walk with Delayed Acceptance (MHRW-DA), on $\mathcal{G}$ that achieves the uniform stationary distribution, i.e., $\boldsymbol{\pi} = \boldsymbol{u}$. The MHRW-DA here operates as an extension of Algorithm 1 with the following choice of $\{Q'(e_{ij}, e_{lk})\}$: for all $e_{ij}, e_{jk} \in \Omega$ with $i \neq k$ ($d(j) \geq 2$),

$$Q'(e_{ij}, e_{jk}) = 1/(d(j)-1), \qquad (26)$$

implying that $Q'(e_{ij}, e_{ji}) = 0$. Also, $Q'(e_{ij}, e_{ji}) = 1$ for any j with $d(j) = 1$. All other elements are zero. While $\{Q'(e_{ij}, e_{lk})\}$ is the same as the transition matrix of NBRW, a 'Metropolizing' step, which is done with $A'(e_{ij}, e_{jk})$ in (25), must follow in order to ensure that the stationary distribution is uniform and the resulting estimator is unbiased. In other words, $A'(e_{ij}, e_{jk})$ in (25) becomes

$$A'(e_{ij}, e_{jk}) = \min\left\{1, \min\left\{\frac{1}{d(j)^2}, \frac{1}{d(k)^2}\right\} \Big/ \min\left\{\frac{1}{d(j)^2}, \frac{1}{d(i)^2}\right\}\right\}.$$

This version of the MHDA is summarized in Algorithm 2, where $X'_t \in \mathcal{N}$ is the location of MHRW-DA at time t and $Y_t \in \mathcal{N}$ indicates the previous node from which the MHRW-DA came ($Y_t \neq X'_t$). Here, X'_0 can be chosen arbitrarily. Since there is no notion of 'previous node' Y_0 at time $t=0$, MHRW-DA initially behaves the same as MHRW until it moves from the initial position to one of its neighbors, and then proceeds as described in Algorithm 2 thereafter.

Theorem 6 states that the MHDA works for any given stationary distribution $\boldsymbol{\pi}$, while allowing us to freely choose the new proposal probabilities $\{Q'(e_{ij}, e_{lk})\}$ as desired. Thus, Algorithm 2 for MHRW-DA is nothing but a 'special case' of the MHDA. Theorem 6 asserts that MHRW-DA produces unbiased samples with higher efficiency than the corresponding MHRW (Algorithm 1). Again, we emphasize that the only additional overhead for MHRW-DA, compared to the MHRW, is *remembering where it came from*, Y_t. Note that the degree of the previous node Y_t is already known and can easily be retrieved, while the degree information of another randomly chosen neighbor is also necessary anyway even in the MH algorithm (to decide whether or not to move there).

5. SIMULATION RESULTS

In this section, we present simulation results to support our theoretical findings. To this end, we use the following

Algorithm 2 MHDA for MHRW-DA (at time t)

Choose node i u.a.r. from neighbors of X'_t, i.e., $N(X'_t)$
Generate $p \sim U(0,1)$
if $p \leq \min\left\{1, \frac{d(X'_t)}{d(i)}\right\}$ **then**
  if $Y_t = i$ and $d(X'_t) > 1$ **then**
    Choose node k u.a.r. from $N(X'_t) \setminus \{i\}$
    Generate $q \sim U(0,1)$
    if $q \leq \min\left\{1, \min\left\{1, \left(\frac{d(X'_t)}{d(k)}\right)^2\right\} \max\left\{1, \left(\frac{d(i)}{d(X'_t)}\right)^2\right\}\right\}$ **then**
      $X'_{t+1} \leftarrow k$ and $Y_{t+1} \leftarrow X'_t$
    else
      $X'_{t+1} \leftarrow i$ and $Y_{t+1} \leftarrow X'_t$
    end if
  else
    $X'_{t+1} \leftarrow i$ and $Y_{t+1} \leftarrow X'_t$
  end if
else
  $X'_{t+1} \leftarrow X'_t$ and $Y_{t+1} \leftarrow Y_t$
end if

real-world network datasets [1]: **AS-733** – an undirected graph of autonomous systems (ASs) composed of 6474 nodes and 13233 edges, where nodes represent ASs and edges exist according to AS-AS peering relationships; **Road-PA** – a road network of Pennsylvania, forming an undirected graph with 1088092 nodes and 3083796 edges, where nodes represent intersections and endpoints and edges represent the roads connecting them; **Web-Google** – a directed web graph with 875713 nodes and 5105039 edges, where nodes represent web pages and directed edges represent hyperlinks between them. For our simulation, we use an undirected version of this web graph. To ensure graph connectivity, we also use the largest connected component (LCC) of each graph, where the LCC sizes of AS-733, Road-PA, and Web-Google graphs are 6474, 1087562, and 855802, respectively. Here, the average degrees of AS-733, Road-PA, and Web-Google graphs are 4.09, 2.83, and 10.03, while their maximum degrees are 1459, 9, and 6332, respectively.

As a test case, we consider the estimation of the degree distribution of each graph – $\mathbb{P}\{D_{\mathcal{G}} = d\}$ (pdf) and $\mathbb{P}\{D_{\mathcal{G}} > d\}$ (ccdf), to evaluate and compare our proposed NBRW-rw and MHRW-DA (MHDA in Algorithm 2) against SRW-rw and MHRW (MH algorithm in Algorithm 1), respectively. As mentioned before, to estimate $\mathbb{P}\{D_{\mathcal{G}} = d\}$, we just need to choose a function $f(i) = \mathbf{1}_{\{d(i)=d\}}$, $i \in \mathcal{N}$, for the corresponding estimators. Similarly, we choose $f(i) = \mathbf{1}_{\{d(i)>d\}}$ for $\mathbb{P}\{D_{\mathcal{G}} > d\}$. To measure the estimation accuracy, we use the following normalized root mean square error (NRMSE) [5, 30, 20], $\sqrt{\mathbb{E}\{(\hat{x}(t) - x)^2\}}/x$, where $\hat{x}(t)$ is the estimated value out of t samples and x is the (ground-truth) real value. ($x = \lim_{t\to\infty} \hat{x}(t)$ from unbiasedness.) In all simulations, an initial position of each random walk is drawn from its stationary distribution as similarly used in [5], unless otherwise specified. In practical implementations, one can employ a 'burn-in' period to drive the random walk close to its steady-state [12]. Each data point reported here for AS-733 graph is obtained from 10^4 independent simulations, while, for Road-PA and Web-Google graphs, the data points are based on 10^5 and $5 \cdot 10^5$ simulations, respectively.

We first present the simulation results for AS-733 graph whose 'actual' degree distribution is almost a 'power-law' as depicted in Figure 5 (insets). Figure 4 shows that NBRW-rw

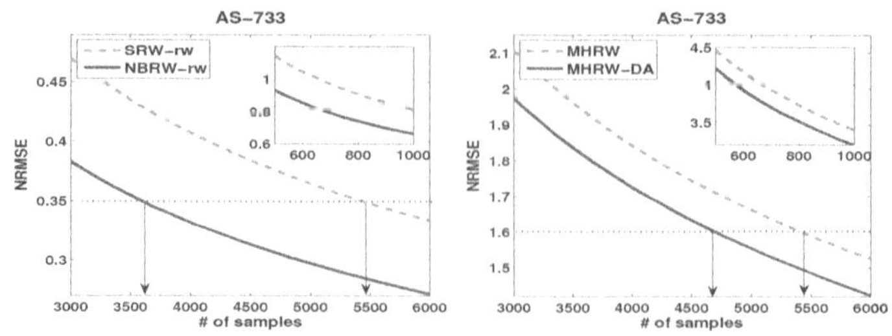

(a) SRW-rw vs. NBRW-rw (b) MHRW vs. MHRW-DA

Figure 4: AS-733 graph. NRMSE (averaged over all possible degrees d) of the estimator of $\mathbb{P}\{D_{\mathcal{G}} = d\}$, when we vary the number of samples; the insets are for smaller samples.

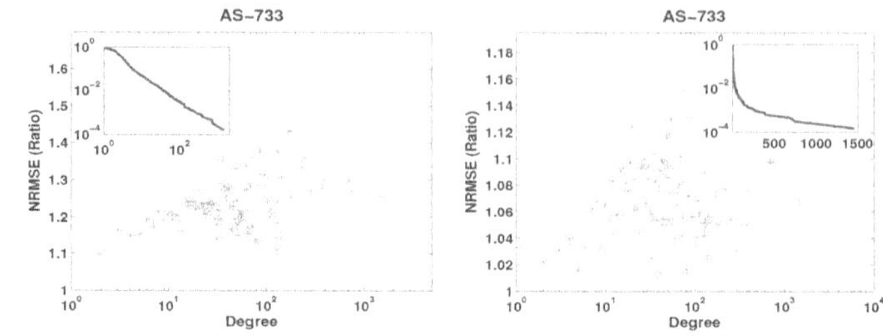

(a) SRW-rw vs. NBRW-rw (b) MHRW vs. MHRW-DA

Figure 5: AS-733 graph. NRMSE ratio (per degree d) when estimating $\mathbb{P}\{D_{\mathcal{G}} = d\}$ with 10^4 samples; the insets represent the 'actual' degree distribution (ccdf) in (a) log-log scale, (b) semi-log scale.

(resp. MHRW-DA) outperforms SRW-rw (resp. MHRW) in terms of the required number of samples (cost) to achieve the same level of estimation error when estimating $\mathbb{P}\{D_{\mathcal{G}} = d\}$, as expected from our theoretical results. Here, the NBRW-rw (resp. MHRW-DA) brings out about 35% (resp. 14%) cost saving on average, when compared to the SRW-rw (resp. MHRW). In addition, we plot, in Figure 5, the NRMSE ratio of SRW-rw (resp. MHRW) to the case of NBRW-rw (resp. MHRW-DA) for every degree d when estimating $\mathbb{P}\{D_{\mathcal{G}} = d\}$ with 10^4 samples. It clearly shows the improvement of our proposed methods for each degree d (all data points are above one). We also provide the NRMSE curve (with its ratio), in Figure 6, for the comparison between NBRW-rw (resp. MHRW-DA) and SRW-rw (resp. MHRW) when estimating $\mathbb{P}\{D_{\mathcal{G}} > d\}$ with 10^4 samples, which is again clearly consistent with our theoretical findings. In addition, we conduct another simulation to see the impact of non-stationary start for each random walk on the sampling accuracy, for which an initial position of each SRW and NBRW is drawn from a uniform distribution, while the initial position for MHRW and MHRW-DA is chosen with a probability proportional to node degree. Under this setting, we measure NRMSE of the estimator of $\mathbb{P}\{D_{\mathcal{G}} = d\}$, and observe that NBRW-rw and MHRW-DA still outperform SRW-rw and MHRW, respectively, as shown in Figure 7. Note that there is not much difference between the stationary start and non-stationary start cases. (See Figures 4 and 7.)

We next present the simulation results for Road-PA graph in which every node has small degree, ranging from 1 to 9, and the actual degree distribution (pdf) is given in Figure 9 (inset). As seen from Figure 8, SRW-rw (resp. MHRW) requires *more than twice larger samples* than the case of NBRW-rw (resp. MHRW-DA) to attain the same level of accuracy for the estimation of $\mathbb{P}\{D_{\mathcal{G}} = d\}$. Specifically, the

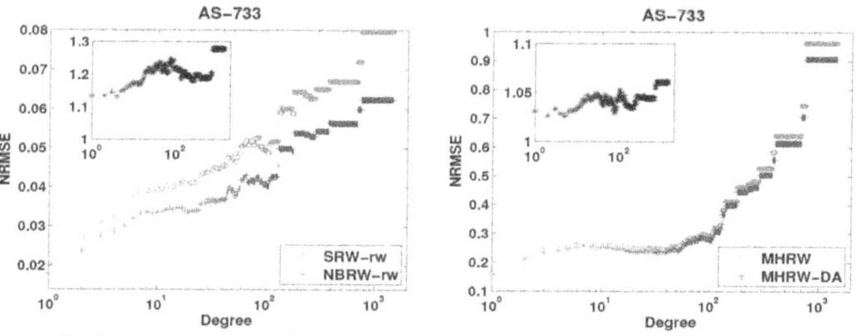

(a) SRW-rw vs. NBRW-rw (b) MHRW vs. MHRW-DA

Figure 6: AS-733 graph. NRMSE (per degree d) when estimating $\mathbb{P}\{D_\mathcal{G} > d\}$ with 10^4 samples; the insets show NRMSE ratio.

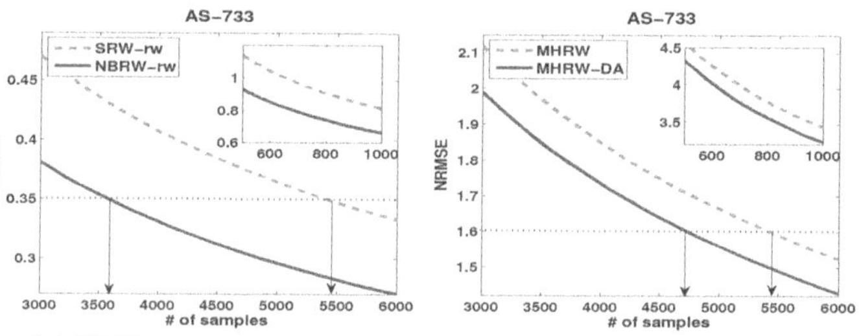

(a) SRW-rw vs. NBRW-rw (b) MHRW vs. MHRW-DA

Figure 7: AS-733 graph. NRMSE (averaged over all possible d) of the estimator of $\mathbb{P}\{D_\mathcal{G} = d\}$, when each random walk does not start in the stationary regime.

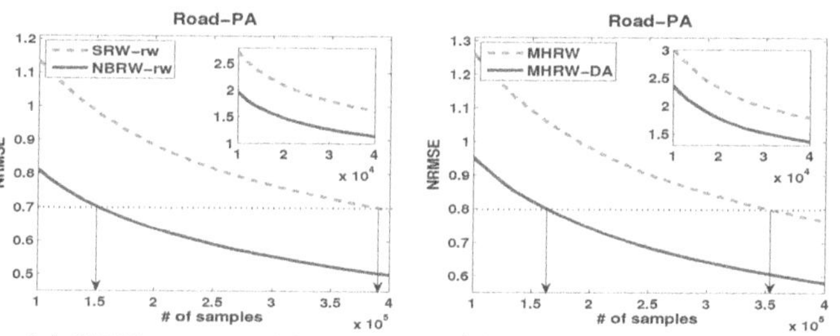

(a) SRW-rw vs. NBRW-rw (b) MHRW vs. MHRW-DA

Figure 8: Road-PA graph. NRMSE (averaged over all possible d) of the estimator of $\mathbb{P}\{D_\mathcal{G} = d\}$, while varying the number of samples; the insets are for smaller samples.

NBRW-rw and MHRW-DA leads to about 60% and 54% cost saving on average. Also, as before, Figure 9 shows the NRMSE ratio of SRW-rw (resp. MHRW) to the case of NBRW-rw (resp. MHRW-DA) for every degree d when estimating $\mathbb{P}\{D_\mathcal{G} = d\}$ with $5 \cdot 10^5$ samples, and Figure 10 depicts the NRMSE curve (with its ratio) for the estimation of $\mathbb{P}\{D_\mathcal{G} > d\}$ with $5 \cdot 10^5$ samples, which are all in good agreement with our theoretical findings. We observe that the NBRW-rw and MHRW-DA are remarkably effective for Road-PA graph, as the graph structure with small node degrees makes the less-backtracking feature more favorable.

We finally provide the simulation results for Web-Google graph whose actual degree distribution is more like a power-law as shown in Figure 12 (insets). Figure 11 demonstrates that NBRW-rw (resp. MHRW-DA) surpasses SRW-rw (resp. MHRW) overall for the estimation of $\mathbb{P}\{D_\mathcal{G} = d\}$, although their improvements are not as large as before. Again, Figure 12 shows the NRMSE ratio of SRW-rw (resp. MHRW) to the case of NBRW-rw (resp. MHRW-DA) for every degree d in estimating $\mathbb{P}\{D_\mathcal{G} = d\}$ with $5 \cdot 10^5$ samples, and Figure 13 depicts the NRMSE curve (with its ratio) for the estimation of $\mathbb{P}\{D_\mathcal{G} > d\}$ with $5 \cdot 10^5$ samples. Clearly, NBRW-rw per-

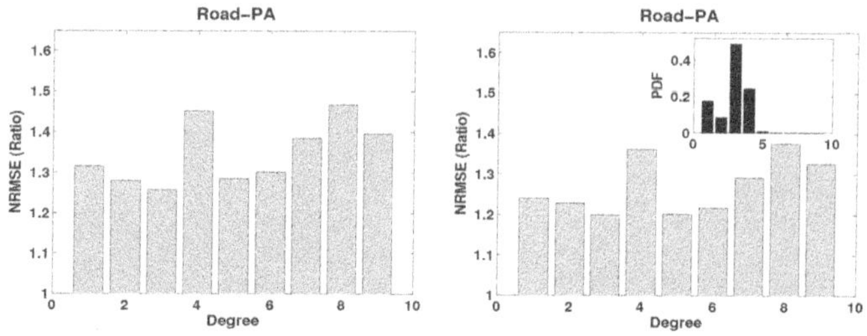

(a) SRW-rw vs. NBRW-rw (b) MHRW vs. MHRW-DA

Figure 9: Road-PA graph. NRMSE ratio (per degree d) when estimating $\mathbb{P}\{D_\mathcal{G} = d\}$ with $5 \cdot 10^5$ samples; the inset represents the 'actual' degree distribution (pdf).

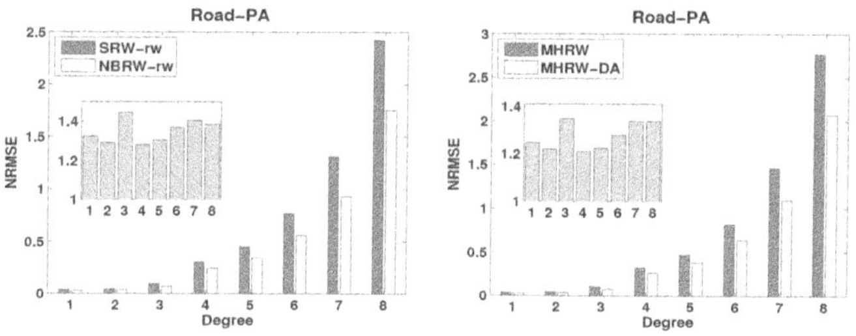

(a) SRW-rw vs. NBRW-rw (b) MHRW vs. MHRW-DA

Figure 10: Road-PA graph. NRMSE (per degree d) for the estimation of $\mathbb{P}\{D_\mathcal{G} > d\}$ with $5 \cdot 10^5$ samples; the insets show NRMSE ratio.

forms better than SRW-rw for each degree d (all data points are above one), as expected from our theoretical results. We also observe similar results when comparing MHRW-DA and MHRW. There is, however, just one data point below one (in the ratio) for the estimation of $\mathbb{P}\{D_\mathcal{G} = d\}$. We admit that such an 'outlier' may be possible, since our theoretical results hold in the asymptotic sense. Nonetheless, MHRW-DA leads to an overall performance improvement (over all possible d). Due to space constraints, we refer to our technical report [21] for more simulation results including the impact of non-stationary start for each random walk on the estimation accuracy under Road-PA and Web-Google graphs.

It is also worth noting that a direct comparison between SRW-rw (or NBRW-rw) and MH algorithm (or MHDA) may not be appropriate. Recently, [12] numerically shows a counter-example that MHRW can be more efficient, although SRW-rw has been shown to be better than the MHRW over several numerical simulations [29, 12]. In addition, [6] proved, through several examples, that there is no clear winner between the importance sampling for reversible Markov chains (whose special case is the SRW-rw) and the MH algorithm. The MH algorithm also is valuable because it can be used to construct a reversible chain with any given stationary distribution. We thus have focused on improving each of the SRW-rw and the MH algorithm separately.

6. CONCLUDING REMARKS

We demonstrated, in theory and simulation, that our proposed NBRW-rw and MHDA guarantee unbiased graph sampling, while also achieving higher sampling efficiency than SRW-rw and MH algorithm, respectively. While the focus of this paper was on the unbiased graph sampling, we cannot stress enough the versatile applicability of the MHDA for *any* non-uniform node sampling (e.g., intentionally creating a known bias toward preferable nodes), not to mention

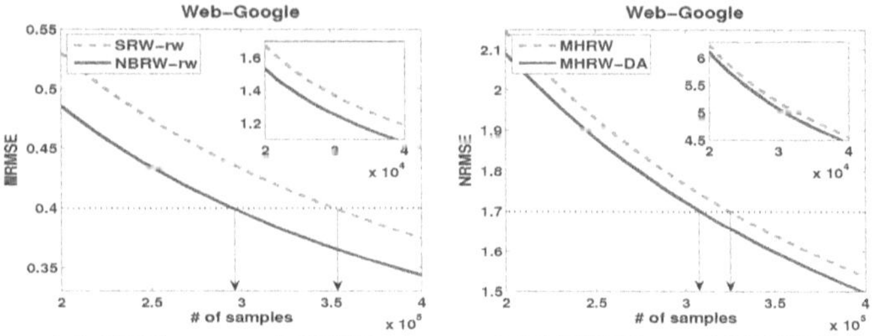

(a) SRW-rw vs. NBRW-rw (b) MHRW vs. MHRW-DA

Figure 11: Web-Google graph. NRMSE (averaged over all possible d) of the estimator of $\mathbb{P}\{D_{\mathcal{G}}=d\}$ with different number of samples; the insets are for smaller samples.

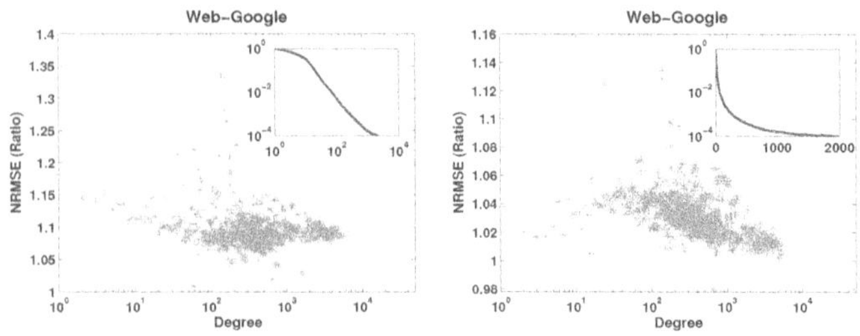

(a) SRW-rw vs. NBRW-rw (b) MHRW vs. MHRW-DA

Figure 12: Web-Google graph. NRMSE ratio (per degree d) when estimating $\mathbb{P}\{D_{\mathcal{G}}=d\}$ with $5 \cdot 10^5$ samples; the insets represent the 'actual' degree distribution (ccdf) in (a) log-log scale, (b) semi-log scale.

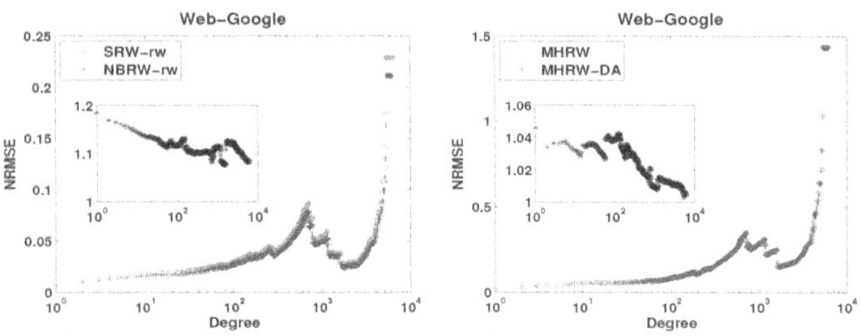

(a) SRW-rw vs. NBRW-rw (b) MHRW vs. MHRW-DA

Figure 13: Web-Google graph. NRMSE (per degree d) when estimating $\mathbb{P}\{D_{\mathcal{G}}>d\}$ with $5 \cdot 10^5$ samples; the insets show NRMSE ratio.

its improvement over the famous MH algorithm in sampling efficiency. We expect that the MHDA can be applied to many other problems beyond the unbiased graph sampling.

Acknowledgement

The authors thank the anonymous reviewers and especially our shepherd, Don Towsley, for many constructive comments and suggestions that greatly improved the quality of this paper. This work was supported in part by NSF CNS-0545893.

7. REFERENCES

[1] Stanford Large Network Dataset Collection. http://snap.stanford.edu/data/.

[2] D. Aldous and J. Fill. *Reversible Markov Chains and Random Walks on Graphs.* monograph in preparation.

[3] N. Alon, I. Benjamini, E. Lubetzky, and S. Sodin. Non-backtracking random walks mix faster. *Communications in Contemporary Mathematics*, 9(4):585–603, 2007.

[4] R. B. Ash and C. A. Doléans-Dade. *Probability and measure theory.* Academic Press, second edition, 2000.

[5] K. Avrachenkov, B. Ribeiro, and D. Towsley. Improving random walk estimation accuracy with uniform restarts. In *WAW*, 2010.

[6] F. Bassetti and P. Diaconis. Examples comparing importance sampling and the Metropolis algorithm. *Illinois Journal of Mathematics*, 50(1):67–91, 2006.

[7] P. Berenbrink, C. Cooper, T. R. R. Elsässer, and T. Sauerwald. Speeding up random walks with neighborhood exploration. In *ACM SODA*, 2010.

[8] S. Boyd, P. Diaconis, and L. Xiao. Fastest mixing markov chain on a graph. *SIAM Review*, 46(4):667–689, 2004.

[9] F. Chen, L. Lovász, and I. Pak. Lifiting markov chains to speed up mixing. In *ACM STOC*, 1999.

[10] P. Diaconis, S. Holmes, and R. M. Neal. Analysis of a nonreversible markov chain sampler. *Annals of Applied Probability*, 10(3):726–752, 2000.

[11] R. Douc and C. P. Robert. A vanilla Rao-Blackwellization of Metropolis-Hastings algorithms. *Annals of Statistics*, 39(1):261–277, 2011.

[12] M. Gjoka, M. Kurant, C. T. Butts, and A. Markopoulou. Practical recommendations on crawling online social networks. *IEEE JSAC*, 2011.

[13] S. Goel and M. J. Salganik. Respondent-driven sampling as Markov chain Monte Carlo. *Statistics in Medicine*, 28(17):2202–2229, 2009.

[14] P. J. Green and A. Mira. Delayed rejection in reversible jump metropolis-hastings. *Biometrika*, 88(4):1035–1053, 2001.

[15] M. A. Hasan and M. J. Zaki. Output space sampling for graph patterns. In *VLDB*, 2009.

[16] W. K. Hastings. Monte carlo sampling methods using markov chains and their applications. *Biometrika*, 57(1):97–109, 1970.

[17] S. Ikeda, I. Kubo, and M. Yamashita. The hitting and cover times of random walks on finite graphs using local degree information. *Theoretical Computer Science*, 410(1):94–100, January 2009.

[18] G. L. Jones. On the Markov chain central limit theorem. *Probability Surveys*, 1:299–320, 2004.

[19] K. Jung and D. Shah. Fast gossip via nonreversible random walk. In *IEEE ITW*, 2006.

[20] M. Kurant, M. Gjoka, C. T. Butts, and A. Markopoulou. Walking on a graph with a magnifying glass: stratified sampling via weighted random walks. In *ACM SIGMETRICS*, 2011.

[21] C.-H. Lee, X. Xu, and D. Y. Eun. Beyond random walk and Metropolis-Hastings samplers: Why you should not backtrack for unbiased graph sampling. Technical report, Dept. of ECE, North Carolina State University, April 2012.

[22] D. A. Levin, Y. Peres, and E. L. Wilmer. *Markov chains and mixing times.* American Mathematical Society, 2009.

[23] W. Li and H. Dai. Accelerating distributed consensus via lifting markov chains. In *IEEE ISIT*, 2007.

[24] S. Malefaki and G. Iliopoulos. On convergence of properly weighted samples to the target distribution. *Journal of Statistical Planning and Inference*, 138(4):1210–1225, 2008.

[25] N. Metropolis, A. W. Rosenbluth, M. N. Rosenbluth, A. H. Teller, and E. Teller. Equation of state calculations by fast computing machines. *Journal of Chemical Physics*, 21(6):1087–1092, 1953.

[26] A. Mira. Ordering and improving the performance of monte carlo markov chains. *Statistical Science*, 16(4):340–350, 2001.

[27] R. M. Neal. Improving asymptotic variance of MCMC estimators: non-reversible chains are better. Technical report, No. 0406, Dept. of Statistics, University of Toronto, July 2004.

[28] P. H. Peskun. Optimum monte-carlo sampling using markov chains. *Biometrika*, 60:607–612, 1973.

[29] A. H. Rasti, M. Torkjazi, R. Rejaie, N. Duffield, W. Willinger, and D. Stutzbach. Respondent-driven sampling for characterizing unstructured overlays. In *INFOCOM*, 2009.

[30] B. Ribeiro and D. Towsley. Estimating and sampling graphs with multidimensional random walks. In *IMC*, 2010.

[31] G. O. Roberts and J. S. Rosenthal. General state space Markov chains and MCMC algorithms. *Probability Surveys*, 1:20–71, 2004.

[32] S. M. Ross. *Stochastic processes.* John Wiley & Son, second edition, 1996.

[33] M. J. Salganik and D. D. Heckathorn. Sampling and estimation in hidden populations using respondent-driven sampling. *Sociological Methodology*, 34:193–239, 2004.

[34] D. Stutzbach, R. Rejaie, N. Duffield, S. Sen, and W. Willinger. On unbiased sampling for unstructured peer-to-peer networks. *IEEE/ACM Transactions on Networking*, 17(2):377–390, 2009.

[35] S. S. Wu and M. T. Wells. An extension of the metropolis algorithm. *Communications in Statistics – Theory and Methods*, 34(3):585–596, 2005.

Clustered Embedding of Massive Social Networks

Han Hee Song[§], Berkant Savas[§*], Tae Won Cho[†], Vacha Dave[§],
Zhengdong Lu[‡], Inderjit S. Dhillon[§], Yin Zhang[§], Lili Qiu[§]
The University of Texas at Austin[§] AT&T Labs[†] Microsoft Research Asia[‡] Linköping University[*]
Austin, TX, USA Florham Park, NJ, USA Beijing, P. R. China Linköping, Sweden
{hhsong,berkant,vacha,inderjit,yzhang,lili}@cs.utexas.edu, twcho@research.att.com, zhengdol@microsoft.com

Abstract — The explosive growth of social networks has created numerous exciting research opportunities. A central concept in the analysis of social networks is a proximity measure, which captures the closeness or similarity between nodes in the network. Despite much research on proximity measures, there is a lack of techniques to efficiently and accurately compute proximity measures for large-scale social networks. In this paper, we embed the original massive social graph into a much smaller graph, using a novel dimensionality reduction technique termed *Clustered Spectral Graph Embedding*. We show that the embedded graph captures the essential clustering and spectral structure of the original graph and allow a wide range of analysis to be performed on massive social graphs. Applying the clustered embedding to proximity measurement of social networks, we develop accurate, scalable, and flexible solutions to three important social network analysis tasks: proximity estimation, missing link inference, and link prediction. We demonstrate the effectiveness of our solutions to the tasks in the context of large real-world social network datasets: Flickr, LiveJournal, and MySpace with up to 2 million nodes and 90 million links.

Categories and Subject Descriptors

H.3.5 [**Information Storage and Retrieval**]: Online Information Services—*Web-based services*; J.4 [**Computer Applications**]: Social and Behavioral Sciences—*Sociology*

General Terms

Algorithms, Human Factors, Measurement

Keywords

Social Network, Graph Clustering, Graph Embedding, Proximity Estimation, Missing Link Inference, Link Prediction

1. INTRODUCTION

Motivation. Social networks have gained tremendous popularity recently. Social networking sites, such as MySpace, Facebook, YouTube, Twitter and LiveJournal have each attracted tens of millions of visitors each month [32] and are among the most popular sites on today's Internet [3]. The explosive growth of social networks creates exciting research opportunities in network security (*e.g.*, fighting spam [12], defending against Sybil attacks [43, 45]), systems research (*e.g.*, constructing socially aware overlay networks [33] and systems), information technology (*e.g.*, improving Internet search [27] and content recommendation [5]), business (*e.g.*, fraud detection [8], viral marketing [15]), and social sciences (*e.g.*, modeling complex networks [4, 9]).

A central concept in the analysis of social networks is a *proximity measure*, which quantifies the closeness or similarity between nodes in a social network. Intuitively, socially "close" users are often more trustworthy (which is useful for fraud detection [8], spam mitigation [12], and Sybil attack defense [43,45]), and tend to have similar interests (which is useful for improving Internet search [27] and content recommendation [5]). A variety of effective proximity measures have been proposed, such as the number of common neighbors, the Katz measure [16], rooted PageRank [25], and escape probability [42]. Despite their effectiveness, however, many proximity measures have high computational complexity and are considered prohibitive for large social networks [37, 42].

In our previous work [40], we made significant progress on scalable proximity estimation in large social networks. Its key observation is that for certain proximity measures, such as the Katz measure, while the complete proximity matrix (which specifies the proximity between all node pairs) is massive (with millions of rows and columns), it can be accurately approximated as the product of two factor matrices with much smaller size. In other words, the proximity matrix has a good *low-rank approximation*. Similar ideas based on low-rank approximation have also been successfully exploited in network coordinate systems to approximate delay between Internet hosts (*e.g.*, [26, 31]), and in network compressive sensing to infer missing elements of a network data matrix [46].

Challenges. Despite much progress in low-rank approximation of massive network matrices, three significant challenges remain: (i) *Accuracy*. Existing low-rank approximation techniques are only effective when the matrix of interest has a comparatively low rank. For example, the proximity estimation techniques in [40] use factor matrices with rank 60. Similarly, existing network coordinate systems typically use low-rank approximation with rank below 20. Unfortunately, given the massive scale and enormous complexity of social networks, such few dimensions may not capture enough information about the underlying social structure. Indeed, as shown in [40], proximity measures, such as rooted PageRank [25] and escape probability [42], have much higher intrinsic dimensionality and thus cannot be approximated accurately by existing techniques. (ii) *Scalability*. Existing techniques require computing a large number of rows and columns within the proximity matrix (also known as "landmarks") in order to derive the low-rank ap-

SIGMETRICS'12, June 11–15, 2012, London, England, UK.

proximation. Such preprocessing becomes increasingly expensive as the size of the network grows. Our results in Section 5.2 suggest that with just 2.5% of MySpace's user accounts, the preprocessing already takes over 5 hours. Further scaling up the method poses significant scalability challenges. (iii) *Flexibility.* As shown in [40], no proximity measure performs consistently well across different social networks. Their effectiveness is also sensitive to the choice of control parameters, which is difficult to tune for unclear network characteristics each social graph has. It is desirable to have a flexible technique that automatically learns the optimal parameter configuration and performs consistently better than other measures.

Approach and contributions. To address the above challenges, we develop a novel dimensionality reduction technique, called *clustered spectral graph embedding (CSGE)*, which embeds the original highly sparse but massive social graph into a dense but much smaller graph. In this paper we make the following contributions: (1) We show that CSGE improves performance in a wide range of social network analysis tasks. In particular, CSGE captures essential clustering and spectral structure of the original massive graph and improves proximity measure estimates, performance of link prediction, and missing link inference, even in cases when the considered matrix does not have a low-rank structure. (2) Social network analysis often involves functions of the adjacency matrix of a graph. We show that by incorporating CSGE into these functions, we can analyze and work with functions of huge graphs in a computationally efficient and scalable manner. In addition, the methods are memory efficient and can easily be implemented on a parallel computer. (3) We further generalize the CSGE approach by optimizing for model parameters with supervised learning, by accommodating asymmetric link structure, and by coping with dynamic networks that have incremental updates.

We use three large real-world social network datasets (Flickr, LiveJournal, and MySpace with up to 2 million nodes and 90 million links) to experimentally demonstrate the effectiveness of our CSGE based proximity estimation. In particular, we evaluate its accuracy, scalability and flexibility in the context of three important social network analysis tasks: (i) proximity estimation (*i.e.*, approximating well-known proximity measures proposed in the literature), (ii) *missing link inference* (*i.e.*, inferring the locations of unobserved links based on observed links), and (iii) *link prediction* (*i.e.*, predicting which node pairs will become connected based on past snapshots of the social network).

In the context of proximity estimation, our new technique results in nearly an order of magnitude speedup over the state-of-the-art proximity estimation techniques [40]. More importantly, with the same memory requirement, our technique is able to create approximations when the rank is an order of magnitude higher than previous methods. As a result, our technique results in dramatic improvement on the approximation accuracy of proximity measures, such as rooted PageRank and escape probability, which are not low-rank and thus cannot be approximated accurately by previous methods. In the context of missing link inference, our technique results in several-fold reduction in the false positive rate subject to the same false negative rate. In the context of link prediction, our technique yields a novel *supervised proximity measure* that significantly improves link prediction accuracy by learning optimal parameter configurations and consistently yielding better accuracy than the previously proposed proximity measures across the three social network datasets. These results clearly demonstrate the effectiveness of our approach.

Organization. The remainder of the paper is organized as follows. In Section 2, we provide background on proximity measures, spectral embedding and clustering. In Section 3, we present details on our clustered spectral graph embedding approach. In Section 4, we explore three important applications: proximity estimation, missing link inference, and link prediction, and then evaluate the effectiveness of our methods on these applications in Section 5. In Section 6, we survey the related work, and conclude in Section 7.

2. PRELIMINARIES

A social network can naturally model the explicit friendship or trust relationship among users in a social networking site. A social network can also be defined implicitly to quantify the interaction levels among users. For example, one can construct a social network based on the past (non-spam) email exchanges between users [12], or the traffic volumes transmitted between Internet hosts.

Formally, we denote a social network as a graph $G = (\mathcal{V}, \mathcal{E})$, where $\mathcal{V} = \{1, 2, \ldots, |\mathcal{V}|\}$ is a set of vertices, and $\mathcal{E} = \{e_{ij} \mid i, j \in \mathcal{V}\}$ is a set of edges. In particular, if there is an edge between vertex i and vertex j, then e_{ij} denotes the weight of this edge. The *adjacency matrix* A of the graph G is an $m \times m$ matrix with $m = |\mathcal{V}|$:

$$a_{ij} = A[i, j] = \begin{cases} e_{ij}, & \text{if there is an edge between } i \text{ and } j, \\ 0, & \text{otherwise.} \end{cases}$$

Below we define some of the most commonly used proximity measures, all of which can benefit from our new dimensionality reduction technique. We then introduce three important concepts – *graph embedding*, *spectral graph embedding*, and *graph clustering* – essential for understanding our graph embedding technique.

2.1 Proximity measures

Proximity measures are important for many social network applications. Most proximity measures can be divided into two broad categories: (1) direct measures that are based on shortest graph distances or maximum information flow between two nodes or node neighborhoods, *e.g.*, *common neighbors*; and (2) more sophisticated measures that include infinite sums over ensembles of all paths between two nodes, *e.g.*, *Katz measure* [16], *rooted PageRank* [25], and *escape probability* [42]. It has been shown that the path-ensemble based proximity measures capture much more information about the underlying network compared to the direct measures and are generally more effective at performing various tasks [25, 42]. The above measures are defined as follows:

Common neighbors. Let N_i be the neighbor set of vertex i. Then, the common neighbors proximity measure is $P_{\mathsf{cn}}[i, j] = |N_i \cap N_j|$. If the number of common neighbors is high between vertices i and j, then it is more likely they will get connected. For an *unweighted* graph (*i.e.*, $e_{ij} = 1$ for all edges), the common neighbor matrix for all vertex pairs is simply given by $P_{\mathsf{cn}} = A^2$.

Katz measure. Let $p_{ij}^{(k)}$ denote the number of paths of length k between vertices i and j. Then, the Katz measure is

$$P_{\mathsf{kz}}[i, j] = \sum_{k=1}^{\infty} \beta^k p_{ij}^{(k)},$$

where β is a damping parameter. A high value of the Katz measure between two vertices signifies a stronger relationship. Using the adjacency matrix A, we may write the Katz measure for all vertex pairs simultaneously as

$$P_{\mathsf{kz}} = \sum_{k=1}^{\infty} \beta^k A^k = (I - \beta A)^{-1} - I,$$

where I is an identity matrix and $\beta < 1/\|A\|$.

Rooted PageRank. The rooted PageRank measure (rooted at vertex i) is the probability of landing at vertex j in a random walk with a probability α of jumping to vertex i in each step, and with a probability $1-\alpha$ that the process continues to a random neighbor. As an irreducible, finite, and aperiodic Markov chain, the probabilities that rooted PageRank yield are stationary and converge to an equilibrium distribution regardless of the starting distribution.

Let D be the diagonal *degree matrix* given by $D[i,i]=\sum_j A[i,j]$. Let $T=D^{-1/2}AD^{-1/2}$ be the normalized adjacency matrix. The stationary probability of the rooted PageRank for all vertex pairs is

$$\begin{aligned}P_{\mathsf{rpr}} &= (1-\alpha)(I-\alpha D^{-1}A)^{-1}\\ &= (1-\alpha)D^{-1/2}(I-\alpha T)^{-1}D^{1/2}\\ &= (1-\alpha)D^{-1/2}\Big(\sum_{k=0}^{\infty}\alpha^k T^k\Big)D^{1/2}.\end{aligned}$$

Escape probability. The escape probability $P_{\mathsf{ep}}[i,j]$ from vertex i to j is the probability that a random walker (who started from i) will visit j before returning back to i. With α being the random jump probability, the measure is derivable from rooted PageRank by $P_{\mathsf{ep}}[i,j]=f(P_{\mathsf{rpr}},i,j)$, where the function f is defined as

$$f(P,i,j)=\frac{(1-\alpha)P[i,j]}{P[i,i]P[j,j]-P[i,j]P[j,i]}. \quad (1)$$

2.2 Graph embedding

Let A be an $m\times m$ adjacency matrix of a graph. For simplicity, we assume that A is symmetric. In section 3.2 we will demonstrate how to extend the concepts to non-symmetric adjacency matrices. A *graph embedding* can bemathematically formalized as the decomposition

$$A_{m\times m}\approx U_{m\times r}L_{r\times r}U^{\mathsf{T}}_{m\times r}=ULU^{\mathsf{T}}, \quad (2)$$

where U is an $m\times r$ orthonormal matrix (*i.e.*, $U^{\mathsf{T}}U=I_r$ is an identity matrix), and L is an $r\times r$ matrix. U represents a basis for the *embedding subspace* and L represents the *embedded adjacency matrix* of the original graph. Since U is orthonormal, Eq. (2) can be applied to approximate any matrix power A^k by

$$A^k\approx(ULU^{\mathsf{T}})^k=UL^kU^{\mathsf{T}}. \quad (3)$$

As a special case, with $k=2$, we get the frequently used common neighbor proximity measure $P_{\mathsf{cn}}=A^2\approx UL^2U^{\mathsf{T}}$. Many functions of A can be approximated using a sum of matrix powers through the Taylor series expansion. Using Eq. (3) we can approximate these functions with corresponding functions on L. This can significantly reduce the computational cost as typically $r\ll m$ and most of the calculations will involve the $r\times r$ matrix L instead of the $m\times m$ matrix A. For example, using Eq. (2) and Eq. (3), we can approximate the Katz measure as

$$P_{\mathsf{kz}}\approx\sum_{k=1}^{\infty}\beta^kUL^kU^{\mathsf{T}}=U\left((I_r-\beta L)^{-1}-I_r\right)U^{\mathsf{T}}.$$

2.3 Spectral graph embedding

The best rank-r approximation of A, in terms of squared approximation error, is given by the r-dimensional *spectral graph embedding* (SGE):

$$A\approx U\Lambda U^{\mathsf{T}}, \quad (4)$$

where Λ is a diagonal matrix with the r largest (in magnitude) eigenvalues of A, and U contains the corresponding eigenvectors. Figure 1(a) shows an illustration of SGE.

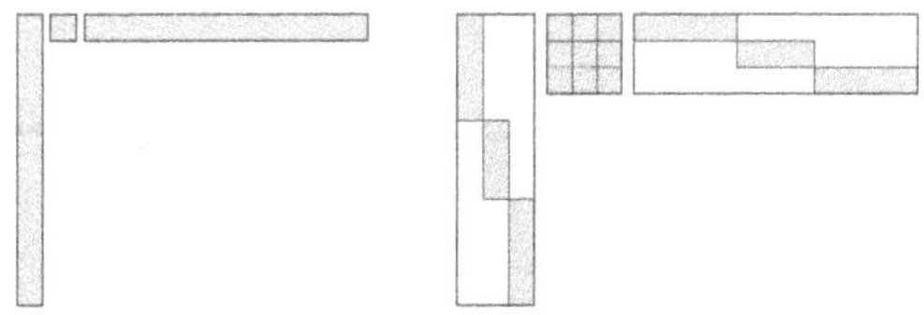

(a) Regular SGE (b) CSGE

Figure 1: Illustration of (a) regular SGE $A\approx U\Lambda U^{\mathsf{T}}$ and (b) CSGE $A\approx VSV^{\mathsf{T}}$ in Eq. (7) with $c=3$ clusters.

Over the past several decades, eigendecomposition and spectral graph embedding have been important research tools for achieving dimensionality reduction on large matrices and graphs. Although there are computationally efficient algorithms [20, 21] to compute the spectral embedding of large sparse matrices, they are still quite expensive on massive social networks with millions of nodes. As a result, SGE can only afford to work with a relatively small r, which may not capture sufficient social/network structure of very large social networks and thus yields poor approximation accuracy (see Section 5).

2.4 Graph clustering

Graph clustering in itself is not the focus of this paper, however, efficient clustering or partitioning algorithms are crucial to the methods we are proposing. Given a graph $G=(\mathcal{V},\mathcal{E})$ there are various objective functions that measure the quality of the clustering, *e.g.*, *ratio cut* [14] and *normalized cut* [39]. Although these graph clustering objectives are NP-hard to optimize [44], there are several efficient clustering algorithms that often produce good quality results, *e.g.*, Graclus [10], METIS [1], SPAR [34], and "modularity" optimization [6].

Assume that we have a clustering of $G(\mathcal{V},\mathcal{E})$ into c disjoint clusters specified by the vertex sets $\mathcal{V}_i$, $i=1,\ldots,c$, *i.e.*, $\bigcup_{i=1}^{c}\mathcal{V}_i=\mathcal{V}$ and $\mathcal{V}_i\cap\mathcal{V}_j=\emptyset$ for all $i\neq j$. Let $m_i=|\mathcal{V}_i|$. Without loss of generality, we can assume that the vertices in $\mathcal{V}_1,\ldots,\mathcal{V}_c$ are in a strictly increasing order. Then the adjacency matrix A will have the following form

$$A=\begin{bmatrix}A_{11} & \cdots & A_{1c}\\ \vdots & \ddots & \vdots\\ A_{c1} & \cdots & A_{cc}\end{bmatrix}, \quad (5)$$

where each diagonal block A_{ii} is an $m_i\times m_i$ matrix, that can be considered as a local adjacency matrix for cluster i. The off-diagonal blocks A_{ij} ($i\neq j$) are $m_i\times m_j$ matrices that contain the set of edges with vertices belonging to two different clusters. In an ideal scenario with perfect clustering, the off-diagonal blocks will not contain any edges, so $A_{ij}=0$, and the graph will have c connected components. On the other hand, in the more general scenario of A comprised of a single connected component with a clear clustering structure, a naive approximation of the original graph could be obtained through its diagonal blocks $A\approx\operatorname{diag}(A_{11},\ldots,A_{cc})$. By further introducing low-rank approximations $A_{ii}\approx V_i\Lambda_iV_i^{\mathsf{T}}$, we have $A\approx\operatorname{diag}(V_1\Lambda_1V_1^{\mathsf{T}},\ldots,V_c\Lambda_cV_c^{\mathsf{T}})$.

3. CLUSTERED SPECTRAL GRAPH EMBEDDING

In this section, we describe the baseline *clustered spectral graph embedding (CSGE)* and suggest extensions suitable for dealing with large, dynamic social networks. Then we analyze advantages of our proposed CSGE over regular spectral graph embedding (SGE) in terms of computational efficiency and accuracy.

3.1 Basic algorithm

Our baseline algorithm, *clustered spectral graph embedding* (CSGE) improves the efficiency and accuracy of approximating

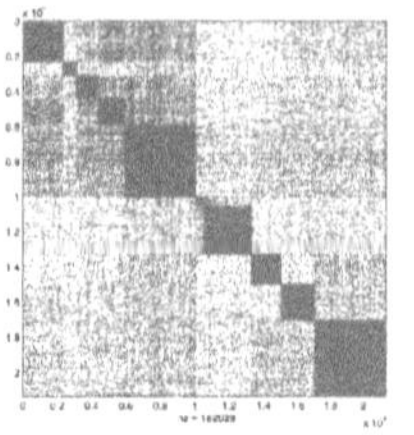

Figure 2: Sparsity pattern of an adjacency matrix with $c = 10$ clusters; 80% of the edges are within the diagonal blocks.

various proximity measures by effectively combining clustering with spectral graph embedding. Recall that A is the adjacency matrix of a graph. We will assume that the graph has been partitioned into c clusters and that the vertices are ordered so that the diagonal blocks A_{ii}, $i = 1, \cdots, c$, correspond to the local adjacency matrices for the different clusters as in Eq. (5). Since the block partitioning of A is obtained through clustering of the graph, it follows that most of the edges are within the diagonal blocks. Only a small fraction of the edges are between clusters and are consequently located in the off-diagonal blocks. Figure 2 shows the typical sparsity pattern of an adjacency matrix after a clustering step. In this particular case, we have clustered the graph into $c = 10$ clusters and 80% of the edges are within the diagonal blocks. Computing the best rank-r_i approximations through spectral graph embedding for every cluster (diagonal block), we get

$$A_{ii} \approx V_i \Lambda_i V_i^{\mathsf{T}}, \quad i = 1, \dots, c, \tag{6}$$

where Λ_i is a diagonal matrix and contains the r_i largest eigenvalues of A_{ii} (in magnitude), and V_i is an orthonormal matrix with the corresponding eigenvectors. Due to the orthonormality of V_i it can be shown that the matrix $V = \mathrm{diag}(V_1, \dots, V_c)$ is also orthonormal. We can now use this block-diagonal matrix V to obtain a graph embedding for the entire adjacency matrix A. The graph embedding may be written as $A \approx VSV^{\mathsf{T}}$. Since V is orthonormal, it follows that the optimal S, in least squares sense, is

$$S = V^{\mathsf{T}}AV = \begin{bmatrix} S_{11} & \cdots & S_{1c} \\ \vdots & \ddots & \vdots \\ S_{c1} & \cdots & S_{cc} \end{bmatrix},$$

where $S_{ij} = V_i^{\mathsf{T}} A_{ij} V_j$, for $i, j = 1, \dots, c$. Using Eq. (6) we can verify that $S_{ii} = \Lambda_i$ are diagonal. The off-diagonal blocks S_{ij}, on the other hand, capture interactions between different clusters. We obtain the following approximation

$$A \approx VSV^{\mathsf{T}} = \tag{7}$$

$$\mathrm{diag}(V_1, \dots, V_c) \begin{bmatrix} S_{11} & \cdots & S_{1c} \\ \vdots & \ddots & \vdots \\ S_{c1} & \cdots & S_{cc} \end{bmatrix} \mathrm{diag}(V_1, \dots, V_c)^{\mathsf{T}},$$

which we call *clustered spectral graph embedding* (CSGE). For example, with $c = 3$ we can write

$$A \approx \begin{bmatrix} V_1 & 0 & 0 \\ 0 & V_2 & 0 \\ 0 & 0 & V_3 \end{bmatrix} \begin{bmatrix} S_{11} & S_{12} & S_{13} \\ S_{21} & S_{22} & S_{23} \\ S_{31} & S_{32} & S_{33} \end{bmatrix} \begin{bmatrix} V_1 & 0 & 0 \\ 0 & V_2 & 0 \\ 0 & 0 & V_3 \end{bmatrix}^{\mathsf{T}}.$$

Figure 1 shows an illustration of SGE compared to CSGE. Using analogous terminology SGE, we denote $V = \mathrm{diag}(V_1, \cdots, V_c)$ as a basis for the *clustered embedding subspace*, and S as the *embedded adjacency matrix* for CSGE. Note that with $c = 1$, CSGE becomes the regular SGE. In related preliminary evaluation, we explored the benefit of combining clustering with different local (within-cluster) low rank approximation schemes from the viewpoint of numerical accuracy on a few static graphs [38]. However, higher numerical accuracy in matrix approximations does not necessarily translate to benefits in end applications, such as link prediction. Additionally, social network analysis requires more than matrix approximation in order to accommodate scalability and flexibility for various algorithms. In the subsequent sections, we develop and validate CSGE in the context of large, dynamic social networks.

3.2 Extensions

Different social networks exhibit different link structure, density, and dynamic behavior as their purpose, characteristics, and demography vary. In this section, we propose the following extensions to the basic CSGE algorithm aiming to better accommodate various networks: (i) asymmetric adjacency matrix computation to flexibly accommodate networks with asymmetric link relationships, (ii) further embedding to scalably handle larger networks, (iii) incremental updates to cope with dynamic nature of social networks, and (iv) parallel/distributed computation to balance the computation load.

Asymmetric adjacency matrices. There are two possible strategies to cope with an asymmetric adjacency matrix A:

(1) When the fraction of asymmetric edges (*i.e.*, vertex pairs (i, j) such that $A[i, j] \neq A[j, i]$) is not high, we can simply derive the basis of the clustered embedding subspace (*i.e.*, the V matrix) using a symmetrized version of A, *e.g.*, $A_{\mathrm{sym}} = \frac{1}{2}(A + A^{\mathsf{T}})$ or $A_{\mathrm{sym}} = \max(A, A^{\mathsf{T}})$. We can then capture the asymmetry of A by solving $\min_S \|A - VSV^{\mathsf{T}}\|_F$ which yields $S = V^{\mathsf{T}}AV$, where $\|X\|_F = \sqrt{\sum_{ij} X[i,j]^2}$ is the Frobenius norm of X.

(2) Alternatively, we can apply singular value decomposition [13] to compute the best rank-r_i approximation for every cluster (diagonal block), yielding $A_{ii} \approx U_i \Sigma_i V_i^{\mathsf{T}}$ for $i = 1, \dots, c$, where Σ_i is a diagonal matrix containing the r_i largest singular values of A_{ii}, U_i and V_i are orthonormal matrices with the corresponding left and right singular vectors, respectively. Due to the orthonormality of U_i and V_i, $U \triangleq \mathrm{diag}(U_1, \dots, U_c)$ and $V \triangleq \mathrm{diag}(V_1, \dots, V_c)$ are also orthonormal. We can then use the block-diagonal matrices U and V to obtain an asymmetric clustered graph embedding for the entire adjacency matrix A, which is written as $A \approx USV^{\mathsf{T}}$. The optimal S, in least squares sense, is

$$S = U^{\mathsf{T}}AV = \begin{bmatrix} S_{11} & \cdots & S_{1c} \\ \vdots & \ddots & \vdots \\ S_{c1} & \cdots & S_{cc} \end{bmatrix},$$

where $S_{ij} = U_i^{\mathsf{T}} A_{ij} V_j$, for $i, j = 1, \dots, c$. The asymmetric graph embedding $A \approx USV^{\mathsf{T}}$ has properties very similar to that of the symmetric graph embedding. For example, it can be applied to efficiently approximate matrix powers $A^k \approx (USV^{\mathsf{T}})^k = U(SV^{\mathsf{T}}U)^{k-1}SV^{\mathsf{T}}$.

Further embedding. With a large number of clusters, and larger ranks in the approximations, the size of S could become too large. To reduce memory usage, we can further compute SGE of the embedded adjacency matrix S. That is, we further approximate S by keeping the largest eigenvalues (in magnitude), *i.e.*, $S \approx \bar{Q}\bar{\Lambda}\bar{Q}^{\mathsf{T}}$, where $\bar{\Lambda}$ contains the largest eigenvalues of S and $\bar{Q}$ contains the corresponding eigenvectors. The combined approximation is then $A \approx V\bar{Q}\bar{\Lambda}\bar{Q}^{\mathsf{T}}V^{\mathsf{T}}$. Note that we can directly derive SGE $S \approx \bar{Q}\bar{\Lambda}\bar{Q}^{\mathsf{T}}$ without having to explicitly compute the dense matrix S (which requires extra computation and memory). All we need is to treat $S = V^{\mathsf{T}}AV$ as an operator acting on a vector. Thus, for a given vector v we compute $Sv = (V^\top AV)v = V^\top(A(Vv))$. Since V is block diagonal, and A is sparse, computing matrix-vector products with both V and A is efficient. State-of-the-art algorithms for sparse eigendecomposition (*e.g.*, [21, 22]) can then efficiently compute SGE $S \approx \bar{Q}\bar{\Lambda}\bar{Q}^\top$ using such matrix-vector products.

Incremental updates. Because many social networks are highly dynamic, it is desirable to cheaply update the graph embedding equation $A \approx VSV^\top$ under the new adjacency matrix $A' = A + \Delta_A$ when Δ_A has only few non-zero elements. A simple strategy is to keep V stable while updating S with

$$S' = V^\top A'V = V^\top(A+\Delta_A)V = S + V^\top\Delta_A V \triangleq S + \Delta_S, \quad (8)$$

where $\Delta_S = V^\top\Delta_A V$ contains the updates to S and can be efficiently computed due to the sparsity of Δ_A. The embedding for the new adjacency matrix A' is then $A' \approx VS'V^\top$.

Parallel/distributed computation. For the applications with pre-clustered input, CSGE is naturally suited for parallel/distributed computation. For example, consider the email exchange graph of a large corporation, which may consist of a number of organizations. Instead of requiring a separate clustering step, we can directly partition users based on their natural organizational boundaries. Each organization (*i.e.*, cluster) i can then derive V_i locally based on its internal email exchange subgraph A_{ii} according to $A_{ii} \approx V_i\Lambda_i V_i^\top$. Each pair of organizations i and j can jointly compute the block S_{ij} of the embedded adjacency matrix S based on their V_i, V_j and the inter-organization email exchange subgraph A_{ij}, which can again be locally monitored. The ability to support parallel/distributed computations can further improve the efficiency in parallel/distributed computational environments.

3.3 Advantages

Compared with the rank-r SGE $A \approx U\Lambda U^\top$, the CSGE $A \approx VSV^\top$ can achieve much higher accuracy while using a comparable amount of memory. In many cases, CSGE is also computationally more efficient. To simplify the discussion for CSGE, we use r-dimensional graph embeddings for each cluster A_{ii} (*i.e.*, $r_i = r$).

3.3.1 Efficiency

Memory usage of the final embedding. From the block-diagonal structure of V, we immediately observe that we have a cr-dimensional embedding in CSGE, while only an r-dimensional embedding in SGE. Thus, there are c times more columns in $V_{m\times cr}$ than in $U_{m\times r}$. However, $V_{m\times cr}$ has exactly the same $O(mr)$ memory usage as $U_{m\times r}$, because we only store the diagonal blocks V_i, and not the off-diagonal blocks, which are all zeros (see Figure 1). Comparing the embedded adjacency matrices S from CSGE and Λ from SGE, we see that the $cr \times cr$ matrix S is larger and dense, while the Λ is $r \times r$ and diagonal. Therefore, CSGE uses $O(mr + c^2r^2)$ total memory and SGE uses $O(mr + r)$. For large graphs with millions of vertices, the memory complexity is dominated by U or V because we have $m \gg r$ and $m \gg cr$. For example, in the LiveJournal dataset $m = 1,770,961$. With (typical values) $r = 100$ and $c = 50$, S accounts for only 12% of the total memory usage of CSGE. As shown in Section 3.2, we can further reduce the memory usage of S through another embedding. So the total memory usage of CSGE is comparable to that of SGE.

Memory usage for deriving the embedding. With state-of-the-art algorithms for computing a small number of eigenvectors of a large and sparse matrix (*e.g.*, [21,22]), SGE has a memory complexity of $O(m(r + p))$, where p is a user specified parameter and usually $p \approx r$. A smaller p requires less memory but the convergence becomes slower, and vice versa. For CSGE, the approximation of the different clusters is independent of one another and thus the computation of each cluster can be done using the entire memory space. Because the size of each cluster $m_i = |\mathcal{V}_i|$ may be orders of magnitude smaller than $m = \sum_{i=1}^{c} m_i$, we can compute the per-cluster spectral graph embedding with a much larger dimension than the embedding on the entire m. When $c = 10$, for example, the average cluster size would be about $m/10$. Allowing CSGE to fully utilize the entire memory space would increase the maximum computable dimensions from r to $10r$.

Computational efficiency. The time complexity for computing CSGE or SGE is dominated by the cost of eigendecomposition. State-of-the-art algorithms (*e.g.*, [21,22]) for sparse eigendecomposition are typically iterative; their time complexity for each iteration scales linearly with respect to the number of non-zeros in the input matrix, whereas the number of iterations required to achieve convergence depends on the gap between adjacent eigenvalues. Thus, it typically takes many more iterations to decompose the normalized adjacency matrix $T = D^{-1/2}AD^{-1/2}$ than the original adjacency matrix A because eigenvalues of T have smaller gaps.

It is easy to see that the number of non-zeros in the global adjacency matrix A is larger than the total number of non-zeros from all of the per-cluster adjacency matrices A_{ii}. Hence, the per-iteration cost for decomposing A is higher than the total per-iteration cost for decomposing all the A_{ii}. In addition, our experience suggests that it often takes a larger number of iterations for the global eigendecompositon to converge. As a result, it is often much faster to compute many r-dimensional graph embeddings of smaller matrices A_{ii} than it is for a single r-dimensional graph embedding computation of a large A. Our experimental results in Section 5 show that even after including the initial clustering time of the graph as well as the computation time for S, CSGE is still much faster than SGE. In the specific case when the normalized adjacency matrix T is used, CSGE is an order of magnitude faster than SGE. Moreover, with parallel/distributed computation of clusters detailed in Section 3.2, we can further improve the timing efficiency of CSGE.

3.3.2 Accuracy

An important consequence of explicitly focusing on each cluster of the network is that, using the same amount of memory, CSGE yields a significantly smaller residual than the residual for the regular SGE, *i.e.*, $\|A - VSV^\top\|_F < \|A - U\Lambda U^\top\|_F$. Recall that SGE is optimal with respect to the dimension of the embedding (or with respect to the rank in the approximation), but in terms of memory consumption, CSGE gives significantly better embedding (see Section 5).

The accuracy benefit of CSGE is most significant when we are able to transform (using permutations) a given adjacency matrix so that most of the non-zeros are contained within the diagonal blocks. This property is closely related to a graph forming good clusters. Many, if not all, real-world graphs and social networks exhibit this property of forming reasonably good clusters [23]. This is certainly the case for the datasets we consider in this paper.

Interestingly, even if the original graph does not form good clusters or if the clustering algorithm performs poorly, CSGE can still achieve a lower residual error than the regular SGE. The following theorem establishes this guarantee for the special case with $c = 2$ clusters [1].

THEOREM 1. *Let $A \approx U\Lambda U^\top$ be the r-dimensional SGE. Split U into any two parts $U^\top = [U_1^\top\ U_2^\top]$. Let $U_i = Q_iR_i$ be the QR decomposition [13] of U_i, where Q_i is orthonormal (i.e., $Q_i^\top Q_i =$*

[1] The proof of the theorem is provided in the technical report version of this paper [41].

I_r) and R_i is upper triangular. Let $V = \mathrm{diag}(Q_1, Q_2)$ and let $S = V^\mathsf{T} A V$. We have $\|A - VSV^\mathsf{T}\|_F \le \|A - U\Lambda U^\mathsf{T}\|_F$.

The theorem can be easily generalized to the case with $c > 2$ clusters. Therefore, under any arbitrary clustering of the original graph, there always exists CSGE that has a lower residual error than the regular SGE.

4. APPLICATION TO SOCIAL NETWORKS

In this section, we describe how we apply CSGE to three significant social network analysis tasks. In proximity estimation, we provide detailed description on estimation techniques to a number of proximity measures. In missing link inference, we leverage CSGE in determining unobserved interactions in the well appreciated network analysis problem. And in link prediction, we develop novel parameter learning schemes aimed at automatically optimizing for the best parameter configuration for targeted networks.

4.1 Proximity estimation

In Section 2.1 we defined four proximity measures: common neighbors, Katz measure, rooted PageRank, and escape probability. Each of these proximity measures can be computed or approximated using three different approaches: (i) direct computation; (ii) approximation using SGE $A \approx U\Lambda U^\mathsf{T}$ from Eq. (4); and (iii) approximation using CSGE $A \approx VSV^\mathsf{T}$ from Eq. (7). We obtain 12 different proximity measures as summarized in Table 1. Note that following [40], the summation for the Katz measures are truncated to only include $k_{\max} = 6$ terms (*i.e.*, at most length-6 paths are taken into account). This truncation is necessary to compute the real proximity measures that do not use any graph embedding [40]; these serve as the ground truth for accuracy evaluation when we compare approximated measures from (ii) and (iii). In the rooted PageRank measures where we truncate the summation to only include $k_{\max} = 20$ terms, we have $T \triangleq D^{-1/2}AD^{-1/2} \approx \bar{U}\bar{\Lambda}\bar{U}^\mathsf{T}$ (from SGE) and $T \approx \bar{V}\bar{S}\bar{V}^\mathsf{T}$ (from CSGE). Finally, the escape probability measures are computed from the rooted PageRank measures using the function f defined in Eq. (1).

4.2 Missing link inference

Missing link inference aims to infer additional links that, while not directly visible, are likely to exist (based on directly observed links). Missing link inference falls into the general realm of compressive sensing, which aims to reconstruct missing data based on indirect, partial observations. Compressive sensing has many applications in networking [46] and beyond, and has attracted considerable research attention recently (*e.g.*, [7, 11, 35, 46]).

Problem definition. Let $G = (\mathcal{V}, \mathcal{E})$ be a social network with a binary adjacency matrix A. Let $\mathcal{O}$ be the set of observed edges or links and $\mathcal{M} = \mathcal{E} \setminus \mathcal{O}$ be the set of missing or unobserved links. Let $A_\mathcal{O}$ be the incomplete adjacency matrix containing the set of observed links. $A_\mathcal{O}$ is defined as

$$A_\mathcal{O}[i,j] = \begin{cases} A[i,j], & \text{if } (i,j) \in \mathcal{O}; \\ 0, & \text{otherwise.} \end{cases}$$

Let $A_\mathcal{M} = A - A_\mathcal{O}$. Given $A_\mathcal{O}$, the goal of missing link inference is to infer non-zeros in $A_\mathcal{M}$ as they correspond to the set of missing links in $\mathcal{M}$.

Inference algorithm. Despite much progress on compressive sensing, we are not aware of any existing compressive sensing algorithm that can scale to massive social networks with millions of vertices. Therefore, in this paper we explore the following simple but much more scalable heuristic. We first compute proximity measures based on the observed incomplete adjacency matrix $A_\mathcal{O}$ (*e.g.*, those given in Section 4.1), and then assume that the high values in these proximity measures will correspond to the set of missing links, *i.e.*, non-zeros in $A_\mathcal{M}$. The threshold for determining high proximity measure values can be varied to achieve different trade-offs between false positives and false negatives.

4.3 Link prediction

Link prediction [25] refers to the task of predicting which vertex pairs in a social network will become connected. An accurate link predictor can provide valuable insights for constructing meaningful network evolution models [4, 9]. It also allows social networks to make high-quality recommendations on potential new friends, making it easier for individual users to expand their social neighborhood. Link prediction also has direct applications in cyber security. For example, it allows one to conjecture that certain individuals in a terrorist network are working together even though their interaction has not been directly observed [18]. In this section, we show how CSGE and supervised learning together can facilitate more accurate link prediction with no parameter configurations.

4.3.1 Problem specification

A natural setting for evolving social networks, or networks in general, is to introduce discrete time steps $t = 1, \cdots, t_{\max}$ at which "snapshots" $G_t = (\mathcal{V}_t, \mathcal{E}_t)$ of the graph are taken. Denote the corresponding adjacency matrices with A_t. To ease the analysis and notation, we will restrict ourselves and only use $\mathcal{V}_1$ for all time steps, *i.e.*, $\mathcal{V}_k = \mathcal{V}_1 \triangleq \mathcal{V}$. It is clear that the evolution of the graph is incremental. In terms of the adjacency matrices, we can express this as $A_{t+1} = A_t + \Delta_t$, where Δ_t contains the edges or links that are formed between time t and $t+1$ (for simplicity, we assume no edges are removed).

In the link prediction problem, given A_t, we try to find the non-zeros in Δ_t as they correspond to newly formed links. The standard heuristic is to first compute some proximity measures based on A_t (*e.g.*, those given in Section 4.1) and then assume that the high scores in these proximity measures will correspond to new links, *i.e.*, non-zeros in Δ_t. In the following, we present several supervised proximity measures that explicitly target Δ_t and construct graph specific models for link prediction. To clarify the problem setting, we use three snapshots, A_1, A_2, and A_3, in the order of data collection time. The first two will be used to learn the model and the third one will be used to validate the obtained model. Extending to more than three snapshots is straightforward.

4.3.2 Link prediction models and framework

Link prediction models. The models we propose have generic prediction scores, obtained from a low dimensional embedding

$$P_* = W_* F_*(x) W_*^\mathsf{T},$$

where W_* represents the basis for a graph embedding, and $F_*(x)$ is a small matrix with the model parameters x that will be learned. In particular, we will consider the following two models that are characterized by the particular form of the embedded adjacency matrix $F_*(x)$ and the kind of graph embedding (spectral or clustered spectral) that is used.

- *Spectral learning.* In this model, we set $W_{\text{sl-sge}} = U_t$, where $A_t \approx U_t \Lambda_t U_t^\mathsf{T}$ is SGE of the adjacency matrix A_t. We then let the parameter matrix be of the form

$$F_{\text{sl-sge}}(x) = \mathrm{diag}(x_1, \cdots, x_r).$$

- *Clustered spectral learning.* Here we set $W_{\text{sl-csge}} = V_t$, where $A_t \approx V_t S_t V_t^\mathsf{T}$ is CSGE of the adjacency matrix A_t as

Abbreviation	Method name	Definition
cn	Common neighbor	$P_{\mathsf{cn}} = A^2$
cn-sge	Common neighbor with spectral graph embedding	$P_{\mathsf{cn\text{-}sge}} = U\Lambda^2 U^\top$
cn-csge	Common neighbor with clustered spectral graph embedding	$P_{\mathsf{cn\text{-}csge}} = VS^2V^\top$
kz	Katz measure	$P_{\mathsf{kz}} = \sum_{k=1}^{k_{\max}} \beta^k A^k$
kz-sge	Katz measure with spectral graph embedding	$P_{\mathsf{kz\text{-}sge}} = U\big(\sum_{k=1}^{k_{\max}} \beta^k \Lambda^k\big)U^\top$
kz-csge	Katz measure with clustered spectral graph embedding	$P_{\mathsf{kz\text{-}csge}} = V\big(\sum_{k=1}^{k_{\max}} \beta^k S^k\big)V^\top$
rpr	Rooted PageRank	$P_{\mathsf{rpr}} = (1-\alpha)D^{-1/2}\big(\sum_{k=0}^{k_{\max}} \alpha^k T^k\big)D^{1/2}$
rpr-sge	Rooted PageRank with spectral graph embedding	$P_{\mathsf{rpr\text{-}sge}} = (1-\alpha)D^{-1/2}\big(I + \bar{U}\big(\sum_{k=1}^{k_{\max}} \alpha^k \bar{\Lambda}^k\big)\bar{U}^\top\big)D^{1/2}$
rpr-csge	Rooted PageRank with clustered spectral graph embedding	$P_{\mathsf{rpr\text{-}csge}} = (1-\alpha)D^{-1/2}\big(I + \bar{V}\big(\sum_{k=1}^{k_{\max}} \alpha^k \bar{S}^k\big)\bar{V}^\top\big)D^{1/2}$
ep	Escape probability	$P_{\mathsf{ep}}[i,j] = f(P_{\mathsf{rpr}}, i, j)$
ep-sge	Escape probability with spectral graph embedding	$P_{\mathsf{ep\text{-}sge}}[i,j] = f(P_{\mathsf{rpr\text{-}sge}}, i, j)$
ep-csge	Escape probability with clustered spectral graph embedding	$P_{\mathsf{ep\text{-}csge}}[i,j] = f(P_{\mathsf{rpr\text{-}csge}}, i, j)$

Table 1: Description of the proximity measures.

in Eq. (7). The parameter matrix has the form

$$F_{\mathsf{sl\text{-}csge}}(x) = Q_t \operatorname{diag}(x_1, \cdots, x_{cr}) Q_t^\top,$$

where orthogonal matrix Q_t is obtained from the full eigendecomposition $S_t = Q_t \Lambda_{S_t} Q_t^\top$. Recall that V_t is block diagonal and S_t is a dense matrix that captures interactions among all clusters. The number of parameters to be learned is cr, where c is the number of clusters and r is the embedding dimension.

Framework. Our basic framework for supervised link prediction consists of the following two phases:

1. *Supervised learning.* We compute the basis matrix W_* from either SGE or CSGE of the first snapshot A_1. We then learn the parameter matrix $F_*(x)$ by performing linear regression on $\Delta_1 = A_2 - A_1$ (which contains the links newly formed between snapshots A_1 and A_2) with respect to $F_*(x)$.
2. *Link prediction.* We compute the basis matrix $\bar{W}_*$ from either SGE or CSGE of the second snapshot A_2. We then use $P_* = \bar{W}_* F_*(x) \bar{W}_*^\top$ as the prediction score matrix to predict $\Delta_2 = A_3 - A_2$, which contains the set of new links that are formed between snapshots A_2 and A_3.

4.3.3 Supervised learning

Because different networks exhibit different link structures, performance of link prediction schemes vary to their characteristics ([40]). Moreover, because the characteristics tend to be unclear, it is not easy to pick one that will perform the best. To flexibly accommodate diverse networks, we develop a series of supervision schemes that seek for the most favorable model parameters.

Problem setup. At each time step t, there are three associated sets: the set of existing edges $\mathcal{E}_t$; a positive set $\mathcal{P}_t$ containing vertex pairs that form new links in the time interval $(t, t+1]$; and a negative set $\mathcal{N}_t$ containing vertex pairs without edges at time step $t+1$. Using adjacency matrices A_t and A_{t+1}, we can write

$$\mathcal{E}_t = \{(i,j) \mid A_t[i,j] \neq 0\},$$
$$\mathcal{P}_t = \{(i,j) \mid A_t[i,j] = 0 \text{ and } A_{t+1}[i,j] \neq 0\},$$
$$\mathcal{N}_t = \{(i,j) \mid A_t[i,j] = 0 \text{ and } A_{t+1}[i,j] = 0\}.$$

It is straightforward to see that $\mathcal{E}_{t+1} = \mathcal{E}_t \cup \mathcal{P}_t$, and that the three sets $\mathcal{E}_t, \mathcal{P}_t, \mathcal{N}_t$ are mutually disjoint.

Supervised learning of model parameters. We perform linear regression on Δ_1 to learn the parameter matrix $F_*(x)$. Specifically, we learn x by solving the following least squares problem:

$$\min_x \sum_{(i,j)\in\mathcal{S}} \left([W_* F_*(x) W_*^\top]_{i,j} - \Delta_1[i,j]\right)^2, \quad (9)$$

where W_* is obtained from either SGE or CSGE of A_1, $F_*(x)$ is one of the parameter matrices from Section 4.3.2 (for time step $t=1$), $\Delta_1 = A_2 - A_1$ contains the new links, the notation $[\,\cdot\,]_{i,j}$ denotes the i,j entry of the argument, and $\mathcal{S}$ is a sample set (see discussions below). Care must be taken in order to solve this least squares problem efficiently. In the interest of brevity, we will defer the details of the solution process to the technical report [41].

Choice of the sample set $\mathcal{S}$. In an ideal case, the model parameters in the vector x should be learned only over the positive set $\mathcal{P}_1$ and the negative set $\mathcal{N}_1$, thus setting $\mathcal{S} = \mathcal{P}_1 \cup \mathcal{N}_1$. With this approach, the edges that already exist in $\mathcal{E}_1$, *i.e.*, the non-zeros in A_1, will not contribute to the learning process. The reason behind this choice of the sample set is that we only want to target links that will form during the next time interval and we do not want to target links that already exist. Unfortunately, for the social networks we consider, the choice $\mathcal{S} = \mathcal{P}_1 \cup \mathcal{N}_1$ would yield a sample set of the order $|\mathcal{V}|^2$ and this is practically impossible to work with. To make the problem manageable, we choose $\mathcal{S}$ to contain a fraction of $\mathcal{P}_1$ and a fraction of $\mathcal{N}_1$. In addition $|\mathcal{S}|$ should not only be large enough to capture the essence of the model, but also have a manageable size. In our experiments we have $|\mathcal{V}| \approx 2 \cdot 10^6$ and we choose $|\mathcal{S}| \approx 5 \cdot 10^5$ (see Section 5).

4.3.4 Link prediction

Different link prediction models are validated by predicting the new links in A_3. The prediction scores are based on

$$P_* = \bar{W}_* F_* \bar{W}_*^\top,$$

where $\bar{W}_*$ is obtained from a SGE or CSGE based on A_2 (as opposed to A_1 which is used in the model learning step). Specifically, let SGE of A_2 be $U_2 \Lambda_2 U_2^\top$, then the prediction scores for sl-sge can be written as

$$P_{\mathsf{sl\text{-}sge}} = U_2 F_{\mathsf{sl\text{-}sge}}(x) U_2^\top = U_2 \operatorname{diag}(x_1, \cdots, x_r) U_2^\top,$$

where the parameter vector $x = [x_1, \cdots, x_r]^\top$ is learned by solving Eq. (9). Similarly, let CSGE of A_2 be $V_2 S_2 V_2^\top$, then the prediction scores for sl-csge are given by

$$P_{\mathsf{sl\text{-}csge}} = V_2 F_{\mathsf{sl\text{-}csge}}(x) V_2^\top = V_2 Q_2 \operatorname{diag}(x_1, \cdots, x_{cr}) Q_2^\top V_2^\top,$$

where Q_2 is obtained from the eigendecomposition $S_2 = Q_2 \Lambda_{S_2} Q_2^\top$, and the parameter vector $x = [x_1, \cdots, x_{cr}]^\top$ is learned by solving the least squares problem in Eq. (9).

5. EVALUATION

In this section we present experimental results that evaluate accuracy, scalability, and flexibility of CSGE in the context of the three applications on massive scale social network datasets.

	c	$\mu = \sum_i m_i/c$	Links in A_{ii}	links in $A_{ij}, i \neq j$
Flickr	18	110,563	71.8%	28.2%
LiveJournal	17	106,241	72.5%	27.5%
MySpace	17	125,721	51.9%	48.1%

Table 2: Clustering results with Graclus; c is the number of clusters and μ is the average cluster size.

5.1 Dataset description

In our experiments, we use three large real-world online social networks with millions of nodes: Flickr (1,990,149 nodes, 41,302, 536 links), LiveJournal (1,770,961 nodes, 83,663,478 links) and MySpace (2,137,264 nodes, 90,333,122 links) From the dataset, we see that the majority (80%) of links in the positive set $\mathcal{P}_1$ are between user pairs who are two-hops away, whereas the fraction of new links between users who are 4 or more hops away is very small [2]. All users in the datasets are connected to at least one other user and for simplicity, we do not consider rare occasions of link deletions. Links in MySpace are undirected because it requires mutual agreement for users to become friends. Although Flickr and LiveJournal allow directed 'follower/followee' relations, the majority is symmetric. For simplicity, we make Flickr and LiveJournal undirected.

Flickr is a photo-sharing website, where users can connect to each other by indicating a relationship. This dataset was gathered by a breadth-first search on the graph starting from a few seed nodes. To allow most nodes to be discovered, we use the first few months as a bootstrap period, and create three snapshots when most nodes have been discovered and link growth has stabilized. Because of this crawling method, we observe that even though the snapshot dates are just ten days apart, there is 2% growth in the number of links.

LiveJournal is a blogging site, where members can become "fans" of other members. The dataset was collected by listening to the RSS server, which sends out recent update information. The statistics suggest that LiveJournal users are more active in forming links than users in other networks.

MySpace is a social networking site for people to interact with their acquaintances by posting on each other's personal pages. We collected the friendships of the first 10 million users. MySpace assigns user IDs chronologically. Since the first few million IDs we crawled are also the oldest IDs, they have already formed most of the links and are relatively dormant in forming new ones (*i.e.*, the fraction of new links is smaller than those of other networks).

5.2 Scalability

In this section, we compare various aspects of the computational efficiency of CSGE, SGE, and *proximity embedding* introduced in [40]. All benchmarks were done using an Intel Xeon[tm] E5440 machine with 32GB memory, running Ubuntu Linux Kernel v2.6.

Graph clustering: In our experiments we use both GRACLUS [10] and METIS [1] to partition the social networks. The two software packages produce different clusterings as they minimize different objective functions: METIS attempts to produce clusters with equal size, regardless of the inherent clustering structure of the network, whereas GRACLUS produces more balanced clusters. Both software produce good quality partitioning in a relatively short period of time. All experiments are conducted on the largest connected component of each graph, which results in only a very small fraction of users (5.1%) and links (0.5%) being discarded. Table 2 gives an example of clustering results on each data set. In this particular case the clustering was performed using GRACLUS in a recursive way until all cluster sizes were smaller than 1/10 of the original network size. We observe that more than 70% of the links in Flickr and LiveJournal are within the same clusters, while only 51.9% of the links in MySpace are within the same clusters.

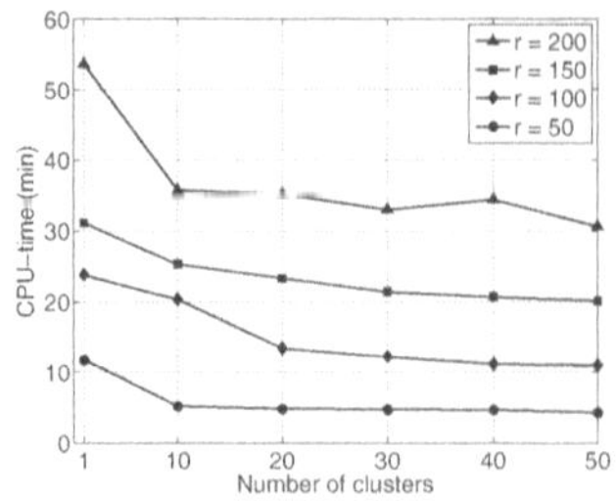

Figure 3: Comparison of eigendecomposition times (on LiveJournal).

Timing benchmarks: Approximation of proximity measures involves two stages: (1) *preparation* of the embedded matrix and (2) *querying* proximity of user pairs from the embedded matrix. We evaluate the timing performance of CSGE by comparing it against other algorithms for each of these stages.

In the first stage of preparing an embedded matrix, we compare CSGE against SGE and Proximity Embedding from [40]. In the case of CSGE, the preparation involves three sub-stages: (i) clustering; (ii) SGE of each cluster; and (iii) computation of the embedded adjacency matrix S. We compare CSGE and SGE for embedding both the adjacency matrix A and the normalized adjacency matrix $T = D^{-1/2}AD^{-1/2}$ in each of these sub-stages. For Proximity Embedding, which does not directly approximate A or T, we instead generate models to compute approximations of P_{kz} and P_{rpr} with relatively few (1,600) "landmark" nodes so that they are comparable to the embeddings of A and T, respectively.

Table 3 summarizes the preparation timing benchmarks for the three approximation algorithms for all three data sets. The number of clusters is set to be $c = 20$ and the rank in SGE and CSGE is set to be $r = r_i = 100$. We see that CSGE outperforms the other two algorithms in most cases; in the approximation of A, CSGE is up to 30% faster than the other algorithms. In the approximation of T, the timing difference between CSGE and SGE becomes even higher, resulting in over an order of magnitude difference. The convergence of iterative spectral methods is influenced by the size of the "gap" in the eigenvalues [21]. Because the eigenvalues of T are normalized to be between 1 and -1 with very small gaps between them, the computation times for T are expected to become much longer than that of A; therefore, the difference in timing performance becomes more dramatic. In an extreme case of Flickr dataset where all 100 dominant eigenvalues of T (and T_{ii}) are very close to 1, the computation of T by CSGE is 20% slower than the computation of rooted PageRank by Proximity Embedding due to the aforementioned reasons.

Among the three sub-stages of CSGE, the majority of time is spent in SGE for each of the A_{ii} and T_{ii}. Figure 3 further analyzes the SGE time of LiveJournal dataset with varying numbers of clusters and sizes of embedding dimensions within each cluster. As Flickr and MySpace exhibit similar trends, we omit them here for brevity. The timing results for $c = 1$ are simply SGE on the entire A (because A is a single connected component). The timings for $c > 1$ are the sum of SGE times for all A_{ii}. We observe from the graph that, for any given r, the aggregate times of cluster-wise approximations are significantly less than the SGE time without clustering. It is also evident that computational time generally decreases with increasing number of clusters. Furthermore, from these results, we can estimate the potential amount of time improvement when we parallelize the per-cluster SGE computation (as discussed in Sec. 3.2).

[2] A detailed description of the three datasets is provided in our technical report [41].

Dataset	Proximity Embedding		SGE		CSGE							
	Katz	Rooted PageRank	A	T	clustering	SGE of all A_{ii}	S	Total	SGE of all T_{ii}	S	Total
Flickr	216	276	19.9	2,821	1.4	12.0	2.3	**15.7**	327	3.1	**331.5**
LiveJournal	324	456	23.8	420	1.4	12.8	2.4	**16.6**	33.0	2.5	**36.9**
MySpace	330	588	22.8	546	2.6	14.4	2.9	**19.9**	48.1	3.5	**54.2**

Table 3: Comparison of preparation times ($c = 20$ and $r = r_i = 100$). All timings are in minutes.

Dataset	Direct Method		Proximity Embedding	SGE		CSGE		
	cn	kz	kz-prox.embed.	cn-sge	kz-sge	cn-csge	kz-csge	sl-csge
Flickr	15.9ms	8040ms	0.051ms	0.042ms	0.045ms	2.72ms	2.76ms	5.59ms
LiveJournal	23.5ms	14790ms	0.045ms	0.038ms	0.036ms	5.45ms	2.03ms	4.57ms
MySpace	24.5ms	16655ms	0.076ms	0.040ms	0.036ms	2.60ms	2.65ms	4.73ms

Table 4: Comparison of query times ($r = r_i = 100$, 0.6 million samples).

	A_{FL}	B	C
m	2,000,000	6,000,000	12,000,000
Numbers of links	40,000,000	239,000,000	598,000,000
c	18	52	104
Timing	22.6 min	116.3 min	391.2 min
Memory usage	74 MB	546 MB	1,197 MB

Table 5: Computational time and memory usage for CSGE. Network size m and number of links are approximate.

In the second stage of querying proximity of user pairs, we compare the average query times of 600,000 randomly sampled node pairs for the three embedding algorithms (*i.e.*, CSGE, SGE, and Proximity Embedding) as well as directly calculated common neighbor and Katz scores. We consider the direct calculation in the query stage but not in the preparation stage because the storage of exact proximity measures for all m^2 node pairs in preparation stage is prohibitive. From Table 4, we observe that all three embeddings are orders of magnitude faster than the direct calculations. While all three embedding algorithms exhibit a millisecond level of fast query time, CSGE is slightly slower than the other two. This is because CSGE is dependent on the size of its dense core matrix S. While the query time of CSGE is already several folds faster than that of Proximity Embedding, in a time-sensitive online application, the query time can be further improved by either using a smaller S or applying low-rank approximation on S (*c.f.*, further embedding in Sec. 3.2).

Scalability of graph embedding: While CSGE has more efficient precomputation, its major advantage is lower memory usage so that it can achieve higher accuracy for a fixed memory cost. In Section 3.3.1, we discussed the memory usage of CSGE. To show the scalability, both in computational time and memory efficiency, we present some measurements on even bigger (artificial) networks. Let A_{FL}, A_{LJ}, and A_{MS} be the adjacency matrices for Flickr, LiveJournal and MySpace, respectively. Then we form $B = \text{diag}(A_{\text{FL}}, A_{\text{LJ}}, A_{\text{MS}}) + A_{\text{Off}}$ where A_{Off} contains a small fraction of links in the off-diagonal part so that B becomes connected. We also form C in a similar way, $C = \text{diag}(B, B) + B_{\text{Off}}$. One may consider that the constructed datasets correspond to some real-world social networks. The approximate size, number of links, and number of clusters are presented in the upper half of Table 5.

The lower part of Table 5 shows the memory required to store $V = \text{diag}(V_1, \cdots, V_c)$ and the embedded adjacency matrix S. Corresponding computational times are also given. We fix $r_i = 100$ in all cases and examine the behavior by increasing the number of clusters c rather than the size of individual clusters. The memory and time required to create the embedded adjacency matrix S not only grows quadratically with the number of clusters c, but also with the rank r_i. Despite the fact that the size of S is inherently quadratic in c, CSGE is able to handle the largest network with 12 million users and 598 million links - with only 1.2 GB of memory. On the other hand, regular SGE is unable to load U for B network, confirming that S is indeed not a limiting factor of memory usage in CSGE, and that it has higher spatial scalability than SGE.

5.3 Proximity measure estimation

Next, we compare the accuracy of Katz, rooted PageRank, and escape probability when they are combined with SGE and CSGE. For the sake of brevity, we present results only for LiveJournal.

5.3.1 *Evaluation methodology*

Since it is expensive to compute and store the actual proximity measures for all m^2 user pairs, we instead evaluate SGE and CSGE using sampled user pairs $\mathcal{S}$, which consists of 100 columns randomly chosen from the proximity matrix. This gives roughly 180,000,000 sample points. For each pair $(i, j) \in \mathcal{S}$ we let p_{ij} denote the 'true' value of a proximity measure and $\hat{p}_{ij}$ to be an 'estimate'. For example, we may have $p_{ij} = P_{\text{kz}}[i, j]$ while $\hat{p}_{ij} = P_{\text{kz-sge}}[i, j]$. The true proximity measures were computed for comparison purpose using the methodology outlined in [40]. Regarding the accuracy measure, we use the *normalized absolute error* $e_{ij} = |p_{ij} - \hat{p}_{ij}|/\mu$, where $\mu = \sum_{(i,j)\in\mathcal{S}} p_{ij}/|\mathcal{S}|$. We plot the *cumulative distribution function* (CDF) to compare the error.

In all Katz computations, we use $\beta = 0.0005$ and $k_{\max} = 6$. For computing the rooted PageRank and the escape probability, we use $\alpha = 0.15$ and $k_{\max} = 20$ (*c.f.*, Table 1). The embedding subspace dimensions in SGE and within each cluster in CSGE are set to $r = 100$. Clustering of the datasets is done on A while the graph embedding is based on A for Katz and $T = D^{-1/2}AD^{-1/2}$ for rooted PageRank and escape probability.

5.3.2 *Accuracy evaluation*

Approximating low-rank matrix. Figure 4 (a) plots the CDF of the normalized absolute errors in approximating Katz measure with $P_{\text{kz-sge}}$ and $P_{\text{kz-csge}}$. We make two observations: (1) for most samples, the error is small: with 85% of the node pairs having an error of 0.2 or less; and (2) the error for CSGE is lower than SGE with the gap in error as little as 2%. A likely reason for SGE and CSGE yielding similar performance is that P_{kz} has a low intrinsic dimensionality and that both SGE and CSGE have reached a point where $r = 100$ is enough for the low-rank approximation of Katz.

Approximating non low-rank matrix. In Figure 4 (b) we present the CDF of normalized absolute errors in approximating the rooted PageRank measure with $P_{\text{rpr-sge}}$ and $P_{\text{rpr-csge}}$. We observe that clustering gives a considerable improvement in the accuracy of the rooted PageRank measure. For over 95% of the samples, the normalized absolute error is less than 0.01. On the other hand, SGE exhibits a relatively higher error: above 0.6 error for 95% of the samples. It can be verified that the normalized adjacency matrix T, for which we compute SGE and CSGE, has a much higher intrinsic dimensionality than A. The improved accuracy in $P_{\text{rpr-csge}}$ may be explained by the fact that 100 dimensional embeddings on

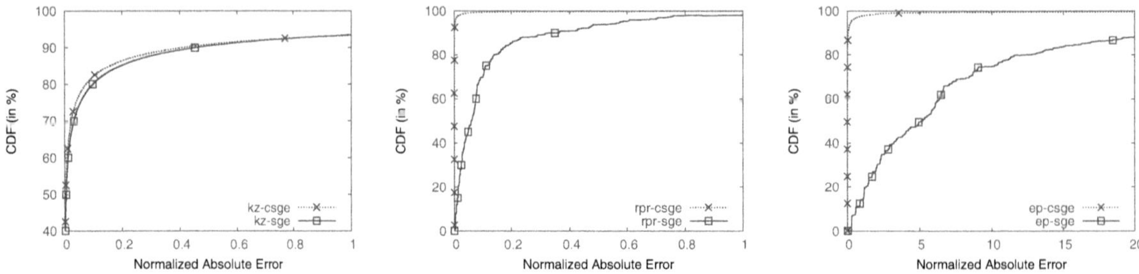

(a) Katz measure (b) Rooted PageRank (c) Escape Probability

Figure 4: Accuracy of proximity estimation for LiveJournal dataset.

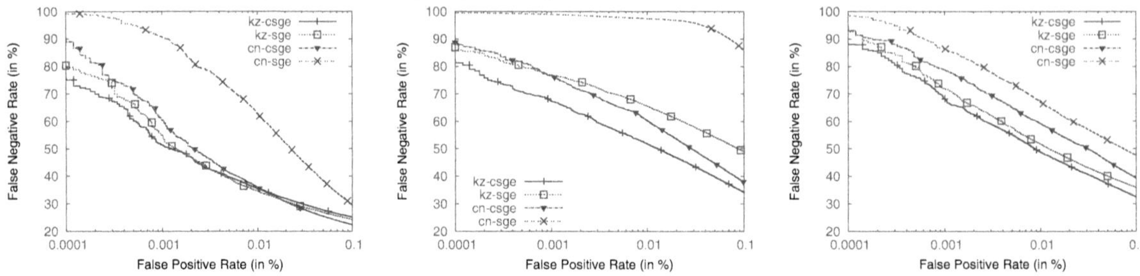

(a) Flickr (b) LiveJournal (c) MySpace

Figure 5: Missing link inference accuracy for different proximity measures.

each cluster (CSGE) captures a much larger fraction of variance compared to an $r = 100$ embedding on the entire matrix (SGE). Figure 4 (c) shows the CDFs of normalized absolute error for escape probability measure $P_{\text{ep-sge}}$ and $P_{\text{ep-csge}}$. Again, using clustering significantly improves the accuracy. This improvement is to be expected because the escape probability is based on the rooted PageRank measure. While CSGE provides a normalized absolute error less than 0.1 for more than 95% of the samples, SGE exhibits a much higher error of over 20 for the same 95% of the samples.

Summary. Our proximity estimation evaluation shows that CSGE is not only effective in approximating proximity measures on A, but also performs well on matrices with high intrinsic dimension such as the normalized adjacency matrix T. Compared with SGE, CSGE can accurately approximate the rooted PageRank and escape probability despite the general difficulty in approximating these metrics.

5.4 Missing link inference

Here, we compare the amount of correctly inferred missing links among proximity measures with and without clustering.

5.4.1 Evaluation methodology

Metrics. The accuracy of link prediction is quantified by computing *false positive rates* (FPR $= \frac{\#\text{of incorrectly predicted friend links}}{\#\text{of non-friend links}}$), and *false negative rates* (FNR $= \frac{\#\text{ of missed friend links}}{\#\text{ of new-friend links}}$) of all user pairs in a sample set. Note that the denominator of the FPR is the number of user pairs who are not friends. This number is usually very large, *e.g.*in MySpace, we have $2 \times 10^6 \times 2 \times 10^6 - 90 \times 10^6 \approx 10^{12}$. Since we are more interested in picking up small number of correct friendships (as opposed to finding as many new friendship links as possible), we present trade-off curves with an emphasis to small FPR area by displaying the x-axis in log-scale.

Experimental setup. From the first snapshots, A_1, of all three datasets, we randomly mask half of the links as missing $\mathcal{M}$. The adjacency matrix with the remaining links is considered as an incomplete adjacency matrix with observed links $A_{\mathcal{O}}$. The trade-off curve between FPR and FNR is plotted for all user pairs given the non-zero of $A_{\mathcal{M}}$ (*i.e.*, $A_{\mathcal{M}}$ being used as the ground truth).

5.4.2 Accuracy evaluation

In Figure 5, we present the performance of $P_{\text{cn-sge}}$, $P_{\text{cn-csge}}$, $P_{\text{kz-csge}}$ and $P_{\text{kz-csge}}$. We observe that using CSGE in both proximity measures consistently outperforms SGE in all three datasets. Comparing across different measures, we observe that Katz measure with CSGE generally performs the best. For instance, in LiveJournal, for a given FPR, $P_{\text{kz-csge}}$ yields 10% or less FNR than $P_{\text{kz-sge}}$.

5.5 Link prediction evaluation

In this section, we compare the link prediction accuracy of supervised learning combined with CSGE, supervised learning with SGE, and unsupervised proximity measures.

5.5.1 Evaluation methodology

Training and testing steps. From each dataset, we take three snapshots of social graphs, A_1, A_2, and A_3, with 1-2% (600,000 - 1,300,000) increment in links from the previous snapshot. To learn the model parameters in the two supervised models, we devise the training step to use a graph embedding of A_1 and minimize Eq. (9) by explicitly targeting newly formed links in A_2. In the next step of testing, we use an embedding of A_2 with the learned model parameters to predict new links in A_3. We validate the prediction against the ground truth of A_3.

Because of the size of our datasets, we randomly select a fraction of the positive and negative samples. Specifically, for training, we select 100,000 user pairs from the positive links $\mathcal{P}_1$, and 500,000 from the negative links $\mathcal{N}_1$. For testing, we pick a different sample set of the same size as before but now from $\mathcal{P}_2$ and $\mathcal{N}_2$.

In a second experiment, we learn the model parameters based on a sample set of user pairs that are connected by *two hops*. This practical scenario focuses on link prediction for user pairs who are already close in the network (likely to be friends but not friends yet) and thus require proximity algorithms to consider only a small set of user pairs. These are user pairs that will form a triangle with a common friend, if they become friends.

Metrics. The accuracy of link prediction is quantified using the FPR and FNR introduced in Section 5.4. In the context of link prediction, the "true" and "estimated" links refer to the links in

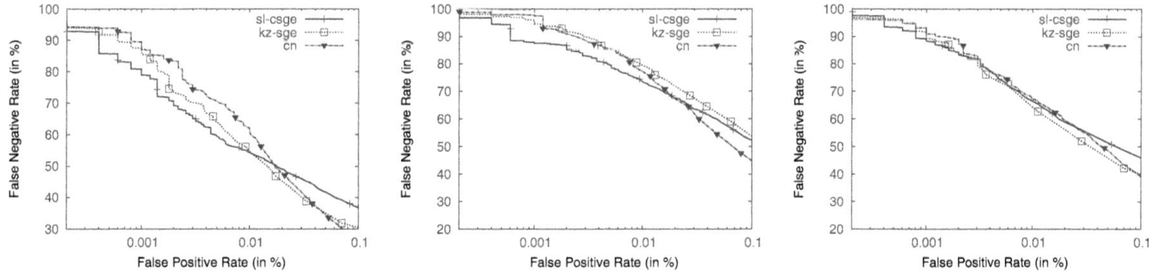

(a) Flickr (b) LiveJournal (c) MySpace

Figure 6: Link prediction accuracy of different measures.

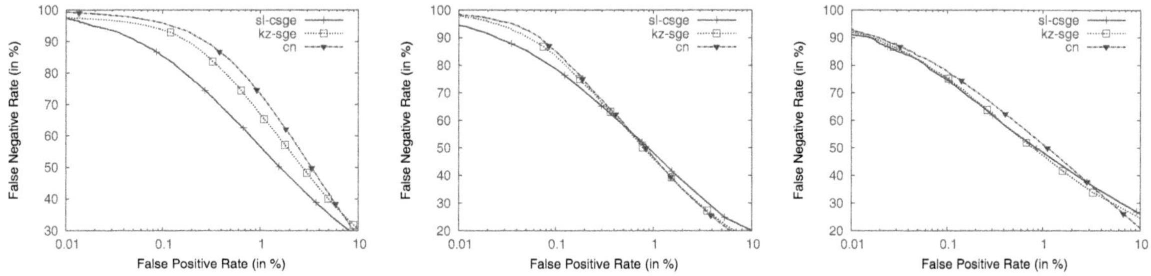

(a) Flickr (b) LiveJournal (c) MySpace

Figure 7: Link prediction accuracy with 2-hop scenario.

$\mathcal{P}_2$. As in missing link inference, the raw count of non-friend pairs in FPR is extremely large, and thus we present the performance measures with x-axis in log-scale.

Link predictors. We have conducted an extensive set of experiments, with numerous methods. In the interest of brevity, we present link prediction results based on three link models: P_{cn}, $P_{\text{kz-sge}}$ and the supervised $P_{\text{sl-csge}}$.

5.5.2 *Accuracy evaluation*

Clustered Spectral Graph Embedding. Figure 6 presents the link prediction accuracy of P_{cn}, $P_{\text{kz-sge}}$ and $P_{\text{sl-csge}}$. We see that, the spectral learning with CSGE performs the best in all datasets, followed by the Katz measure with SGE. For example, at an FPR of 0.001, spectral learning with CSGE reduces FNR by more than 10% in both Flickr and LiveJournal. In MySpace, the performance of clustered spectral learning is still better than the other two measures albeit by a smaller margin.

Two hop user pairs. In Figure 7, we evaluate link predictors for user pairs who are only two hops apart. Our spectral learning model again outperforms other measures by up to 20% in the Flickr dataset, and 10% in the LiveJournal dataset. For MySpace, the performance of Katz with SGE and spectral learning with CSGE is better than common neighbor by about 4%.

Note that there is no significant difference among predictors in MySpace. We speculate that this is an artifact of the data collection technique. Since this data set contains first 10 million users [40], these users have been in the network the longest time, and seem to already have a large number of friends, and thus are less active in creating new relationships. An indication of the claim is in the relatively small rate of link increase in MySpace (0.7% on average) compared to Flickr (1.2%) and LiveJournal (1.8%). Another possible reason is the large number of inter-cluster links in MySpace, as shown in Table 2. Taking into account that 48% of the links are outside the clusters, the benefit of the clustering approach may have diminished, as almost half the links in the network are not used when computing the cluster-wise embeddings.

Summary. Through the comparison between supervised and unsupervised learning methods, we verify that learning model parameters in a supervised way is indeed helpful in improving accuracy. Also, comparing the two supervised learning methods, we find sl-csge consistently out-performs sl-sge across different datasets.

6. RELATED WORK

Social network analysis. Traditionally, studies on social networks often focus on relatively small social networks (*e.g.*, [25] examine co-authorship networks with about 5000 nodes). The recent explosion of online social networks, however, has given rise to large-scale social networks with billions of links. A number of measurement studies characterize the topological structure, information propagation and user behavior of online social networks [2,28,29]. In [38], we explore the use of graph clustering with a few different within clusters dimensionality reduction schemes. In this paper, we develop the CSGE and demonstrate its effectiveness on large scale social network analysis tasks, and illustrate its ability to cope with temporal dynamics present in real world applications.

Proximity estimation. Given their importance in social network applications, proximity measures have received considerable research attention (*e.g.*, [16,17,25,30,36,37,42]). A number of proximity measures have been proposed, such as common neighbors, the Katz measure [16], rooted PageRank [25], and escape probability [42]. Despite their effectiveness in a multitude of social network applications (*e.g.*, fraud detection [8], viral marketing [15], and link prediction [25]), many existing proximity measures are computationally prohibitive for large social networks [37,42]. In our previous work [40], we proposed scalable techniques for approximating proximity measures in online social networks based on the idea of low-rank approximation. In Section 5, we compare our new technique with [40] and show that the new approach is not only much more scalable, it is much more accurate when the proximity measures of interest have a high intrinsic dimensionality.

Link prediction. The problem with link prediction in social networks was first introduced in [24] and a number of proximity measures have been considered for link prediction in [24,25]. A decision tree based link predictor that combines multiple proximity measures has been studied in [40]. There has also been some recent work on using supervised learning methods for link prediction in diverse networks such as hyperlink and citation graphs [19]. As shown in Section 5.5, our supervised link prediction technique can achieve good performance in link prediction accuracy without requiring network-specific parameter configurations.

Missing link inference. The problem of missing link inference is closely related to link prediction and was also mentioned in [24,25]. Missing link inference falls into the general realm of compressive sensing, which has broad applicability in computer science [7, 11, 35, 46]. However, we are unaware of any existing compressive sensing techniques that can scale to massive social networks with millions of vertices. To this end, we focus on simple inference algorithms based on proximity measures, which are much more scalable and can directly benefit from our CSGE technique.

7. CONCLUSION

In this paper, we develop a novel dimensionality reduction technique termed *clustered spectral graph embedding (CSGE)* to embed a massive original graph into a much smaller, dense graph and show its potential in social network analysis. The existing techniques often require the underlying graph to have good low-rank approximations. CSGE, in contrast, can easily cope with massive graphs that have much higher intrinsic dimensionalities and improves both accuracy and computational efficiency.

On three large-scale real-world social network datasets (*i.e.*, Flickr, LiveJournal and MySpace) with up to 2 million vertices and 90 million edges, we employ CSGE to explore three important social network analysis tasks – for proximity estimation, we achieve up to an order of magnitude improvement in computation time and memory usage, and up to several orders of magnitude improvement in accuracy when the proximity measures of interest have high intrinsic dimensionality. For missing link inference, CSGE consistently yields better inference on unobserved links across different datasets. For link prediction, our novel *supervised learning* automatically learns parameter configurations optimal to target networks, achieving the best accuracy among proximity measures being compared.

Acknowledgments: This research is supported in part by NSF grants CCF-0916309 and CCF-1117009. We thank Vijay Erramilli and anonymous reviewers for their valuable comments.

8. REFERENCES

[1] A. Abou-Rjeili and G. Karypis. Multilevel algorithms for partitioning power-law graphs. In *Proc. of IEEE IPDPS*, 2006.

[2] Y.-Y. Ahn, S. Han, H. Kwak, S. Moon, and H. Jeong. Analysis of topological characteristics of huge online social networking services. In *WWW*, 2007.

[3] Alexa global top 500 sites. `http://www.alexa.com/site/ds/top_sites`.

[4] A. L. Barabasi, H. Jeong, Z. Néda, E. Ravasz, A. Schubert, and T. Vicsek. Evolution of the social network of scientific collaboration. *Physica A: Statistical Mechanics and its Application*, 2002.

[5] R. M. Bell, Y. Koren, and C. Volinsky. Chasing $1,000,000: How we won the Netflix Progress Prize. *Statistical Computing and Statistical Graphics Newsletter*, 2007.

[6] V. D. Blondel, J.-L. Guillaume, R. Lambiotte, and E. Lefebvre. Fast unfolding of communities in large networks. *Journal of Statistical Mechanics: Theory and Experiment*, 7(10), 2008.

[7] E. J. Candès and B. Recht. Exact matrix completion via convex optimization. *Foundations of Computational Mathematics*, 9(6):717–772, 2009.

[8] C. Cortes, D. Pregibon, and C. T. Volinsky. Communities of interest. *Intelligent Data Analysis*, 6(3):211–219, 2002.

[9] J. Davidsen, H. Ebel, and S. Bornholdt. Emergence of a small world from local interactions: Modeling acquaintance networks. *Physical Review Letters*, 2002.

[10] I. S. Dhillon, Y. Guan, and B. Kulis. Weighted graph cuts without eigenvectors: A multilevel approach. *IEEE Trans. Pattern Anal. Mach. Intell.*, 29(11):1944–1957, 2007.

[11] D. Donoho. Compressed sensing. *IEEE Trans. on Information Theory*, 52(4):1289–1306, Apr. 2006.

[12] S. Garriss, M. Kaminsky, M. J. Freedman, B. Karp, D. Mazieres, and H. Yu. RE: Reliable Email. In *Proc. of NSDI*, 2006.

[13] G. H. Golub and C. F. Van Loan. *Matrix Computations*. Johns Hopkins Studies in the Mathematical Sciences. Johns Hopkins University Press, 1996.

[14] L. Hagen and A. Kahng. New spectral methods for ratio cut partitioning and clustering. *Computer-Aided Design of Integrated Circuits and Systems, IEEE Transactions on*, 11(9):1074–1085, Sep 1992.

[15] S. Hill, F. Provost, and C. Volinsky. Network-based marketing: Identifying likely adopters via consumer networks. *Statistical Science*, 2006.

[16] L. Katz. A new status index derived from sociometric analysis. *Psychometrika*, 1953.

[17] Y. Koren, S. C. North, and C. Volinsky. Measuring and extracting proximity graphs in networks. *ACM Trans. Knowl. Discov. Data*, 2007.

[18] V. Krebs. Mapping networks of terrorist cells. *Connections*, 24(3):43–52, Winter 2002.

[19] J. Kunegis and A. Lommatzsch. Learning spectral graph transformations for link prediction. In *ICML*, 2009.

[20] R. Larsen. Lanczos bidiagonalization with partial reorthogonalization. Technical Report DAIMI PB-357, Dept. of Comp. Sci., Aarhus Univ., 1998.

[21] R. Lehoucq, D. Sorensen, and C. Yang. *Arpack Users' Guide: Solution of Large Scale Eigenvalue Problems with Implicitly Restarted Arnoldi Methods*. SIAM, Philadelphia, 1998.

[22] R. B. Lehoucq and D. C. Sorensen. Deflation techniques for an implicitly restarted arnoldi iteration. *SIAM Journal on Matrix Analysis and Applications*, 17(4):789–821, 1996.

[23] J. Leskovec, K. J. Lang, A. Dasgupta, and M. W. Mahoney. Statistical properties of community structure in large social and information networks. In *Proc. of WWW*, pages 695–704, New York, NY, USA, 2008. ACM.

[24] D. Liben-Nowell and J. Kleinberg. The link prediction problem for social networks. In *CIKM*, 2003.

[25] D. Liben-Nowell and J. Kleinberg. The link-prediction problem for social networks. *J. Am. Soc. Inf. Sci. Technol.*, 2007.

[26] Y. Mao and L. K. Saul. Modeling distances in large-scale networks by matrix factorization. In *Proc. of IMC*, 2004.

[27] A. Mislove, K. P. Gummadi, and P. Druschel. Exploiting social networks for Internet search. In *Proc. of HotNets-V*, 2006.

[28] A. Mislove, H. S. Koppula, K. Gummadi, P. Druschel, and B. Bhattacharjee. Growth of the Flickr social network. In *Proc. of WOSN*, 2008.

[29] A. Mislove, M. Marcon, K. P. Gummadi, P. Druschel, and S. Bhattacharjee. Measurement and analysis of online social networks. In *Proc. of IMC*, 2007.

[30] T. Murata and S. Moriyasu. Link prediction of social networks based on weighted proximity measures. In *Proc. of Int. Conf. Web Intelligence*, 2007.

[31] T. E. Ng and H. Zhang. Predicting internet network distance with coordinate-based appoaches. In *INFOCOMM*, 2002.

[32] Nielson Online. Fastest growing social networks for September 2008. `http://blog.nielsen.com/nielsenwire/wp-content/uploads/2008/10/press_release24.pdf`.

[33] J. A. Patel, I. Gupta, and N. Contractor. JetStream: Achieving predictable gossip dissemination by leveraging social network principles. In *Proc. of IEEE Network Computing and Applications (NCA)*, 2006.

[34] J. M. Pujol, V. Erramilli, G. Siganos, X. Yang, N. Laoutaris, P. Chhabra, and P. Rodriguez. The little engine(s) that could: scaling online social networks. In *Proc. of ACM SIGCOMM 2010*.

[35] B. Recht, W. Xu, and B. Hassibi. Necessary and sufficient conditions for success of the nuclear norm heuristic for rank minimization. In *Proc. of 47th IEEE Conference on Decision and Control*, Dec. 2008.

[36] M. Richardson and P. Domingos. The intelligent surfer: Probabilistic combination of link and content information in pagerank. In *NIPS*, 2002.

[37] P. Sarkar, A. W. Moore, and A. Prakash. Fast incremental proximity search in large graphs. In *Proc. of ICML '08*, 2008.

[38] B. Savas and I. S. Dhillon. Clustered low rank approximation of graphs in information science applications. In *SIAM Conference on Data Mining (SDM)*, pages 164–175, 2011.

[39] J. Shi and J. Malik. Normalized cuts and image segmentation. *IEEE Transactions on Pattern Analysis and Machine Intelligence*, 22:888–905, 2000.

[40] H. H. Song, T. W. Cho, V. Dave, Y. Zhang, and L. Qiu. Scalable proximity estimation and link prediction in online social networks. In *Proc. of IMC*, 2009.

[41] H. H. Song, B. Savas, T. W. Cho, V. Dave, Z. Lu, I. S. Dhillon, Y. Zhang, and L. Qiu. Clustered embedding of massive social networks. Technical Report TR-12-06, Department of Computer Science, U. of Texas at Austin, 2012.

[42] H. Tong, C. Faloutsos, and Y. Koren. Fast direction-aware proximity for graph mining. In *Proc. of KDD '07*, 2007.

[43] B. Viswanath, A. Post, K. P. Gummadi, and A. Mislove. An analysis of social network-based Sybil defenses. In *Proc. of ACM SIGCOMM*, 2010.

[44] D. Wagner and F. Wagner. Between min cut and graph bisection. In *Proc. of MFCS*, pages 744–750, London, UK, 1993. Springer-Verlag.

[45] H. Yu, M. Kaminsky, P. B. Gibbons, and A. Flaxman. SybilGuard: Defending against Sybil attacks via social networks. In *Proc. of SIGCOMM*, 2006.

[46] Y. Zhang, M. Roughan, W. Willinger, and L. Qiu. Spatio-temporal compressive sensing and Internet traffic matrices. In *Proc. of ACM SIGCOMM*, 2009.

Don't Let The Negatives Bring You Down: Sampling from Streams of Signed Updates

Edith Cohen
AT&T Labs–Research
180 Park Avenue
Florham Park, NJ 07932, USA
edith@cohenwang.com

Graham Cormode
AT&T Labs–Research
180 Park Avenue
Florham Park, NJ 07932, USA
graham@research.att.com

Nick Duffield
AT&T Labs–Research
180 Park Avenue
Florham Park, NJ 07932, USA
duffield@research.att.com

ABSTRACT

Random sampling has been proven time and time again to be a powerful tool for working with large data. Queries over the full dataset are replaced by approximate queries over the smaller (and hence easier to store and manipulate) sample. The sample constitutes a flexible summary that supports a wide class of queries. But in many applications, datasets are modified with time, and it is desirable to update samples without requiring access to the full underlying datasets. In this paper, we introduce and analyze novel techniques for sampling over dynamic data, modeled as a stream of modifications to weights associated with each key.

While sampling schemes designed for stream applications can often readily accommodate positive updates to the dataset, much less is known for the case of negative updates, where weights are reduced or items deleted altogether. We primarily consider the turnstile model of streams, and extend classic schemes to incorporate negative updates. Perhaps surprisingly, the modifications to handle negative updates turn out to be natural and seamless extensions of the well-known positive update-only algorithms. We show that they produce unbiased estimators, and we relate their performance to the behavior of corresponding algorithms on insert-only streams with different parameters. A careful analysis is necessitated, in order to account for the fact that sampling choices for one key now depend on the choices made for other keys.

In practice, our solutions turn out to be efficient and accurate. Compared to recent algorithms for L_p sampling which can be applied to this problem, they are significantly more reliable, and dramatically faster.

Categories and Subject Descriptors

G.3 [**Probability and Statistics**]: Probabilistic Algorithms

Keywords

sampling, deletions, data streams, updates

SIGMETRICS'12, June 11–15, 2012, London, England, UK.

1. INTRODUCTION

Random sampling has repeatedly been proven to be a powerful and effective technique for dealing with massive data. The case for working with samples is compelling: in many cases, to estimate a function over the full data, it suffices to evaluate the same function over the much smaller sample. Consequently, sampling techniques have found applications in areas such as network monitoring, database management, and web data analysis. Complementing this, there is a rich theory of sampling, based on demonstrating that different techniques produce unbiased estimators with low or optimal variance.

Initial work on sampling from large datasets focused on a random access model: the data is static, and disk resident, and we want to build an effective sample with a minimal number of probes to the data. However, in modern applications we do not think of the data as static, but rather as constantly changing. In this setting, we can conceive of the data as being defined by a stream of transactions, and we get to see each transaction that modifies the current state. For concreteness we describe some motivating scenarios:

- First, we consider the case when the stream is a sequence of financial transactions, each of which updates an account balance. It is important to be able to maintain a sample over current balances, which describes the overall state of the system, and to provide a snapshot of the system against which to quickly test for anomalies without having to traverse the entire account database.

- Internet Service Providers (ISPs) witness streams in the form of network activities. These can set up or tear down (stateful) network connections. It is not practical for the ISP to centrally keep a complete list of all current and active connections. It is nevertheless helpful to draw a sample of these connections, so that the ISP can keep statistics on quality of service, round-trip delay, nature of traffic in its network and so on. Such statistics are needed to show that its agreements with customers are being met, and for traffic shaping and planning purposes.

- Updates to a database generate a stream of transactions, to insert or delete records to tables. The database management system needs to keep statistics on each attribute within a table, to determine what indices to keep, and how to optimize query processing. Currently, deployed systems track only simple aggregates online (e.g. number of records in a table), and must periodically rebuild more complex statistics with a complete scan, which makes this approach unsuitable for (near) real-time systems.

In all these examples, and others like them, we can extract a central problem. We are seeing a stream of weighted updates to a set of keys, and we wish to maintain a sample that reflects the current weights of the keyset. Specifically, we aim to support queries over the total weight associated with a subset of keys (subset-sum queries), which are the basis of most complex queries [6]. If the set of keys ever seen is tiny, then we could just retain the weights of these keys, but in general there are many active keys at any one time, and so we want to maintain just a small sample. From this sample, we should be able to accurately address the problems in the above examples, such as fraud detection, finding anomalies, and reporting behavior trends.

The core problem of sampling from a stream of distinct, unweighted keys is one of the earliest examples of what we now think of as streaming algorithms [22]. In this paper, we tackle a much more general version of the problem: each key may appear multiple times in the stream. Each occurrence is associated with a weight, and the total weight of a key is the sum of its associated weights. Moreover, the updates to the weights are allowed to be *negative*. This models various queuing and arrival/departure processes which can arise in the above applications. Despite the naturalness and generality of this problem, there has been minimal study of sampling when the updates may be negative. Through our analysis, we are able to show that there are quite intuitive algorithms to maintain a sample under such updates, that offer unbiased estimators, and whose performance can be bounded in terms of the performance of a comparable algorithm on an update stream with positive updates only. We next make precise the general model of streams we adopt in this paper, and go on to describe prior work in this area and why it does not provide a satisfactory solution. At the end of this section, we summarize our contributions in this work, and outline our approach.

Streaming Model. We primarily consider the *turnstile stream* model, where each entry is a (positive or negative) update to the value of a key i. Here, the data is a stream of updates of the form (i, Δ), where i is a key and $\Delta \in \mathbb{R}$. The value v_i of key i is initially 0 and is modified with every update, but we do not allow the aggregate value to become negative. Formally, the value of key i is initially $v_i = 0$ and after update (i, Δ),

$$v_i \leftarrow \max\{0, v_i + \Delta\} \ . \quad (1)$$

1.1 Prior Work on Stream Sampling

The simplest form of sampling is Bernoulli sampling, where each occurrence of an (unweighted) key is included in the sample with probability q. More generally, Poisson sampling includes key i in the sample with probability q_i (depending on i but independent of other keys). The expected sample size is $\sum_i q_i$. However, typically we wish to fix a desired sample size k, and draw a sample of exactly this size.

To draw a uniform sample of size k from a stream of (distinct) keys, the so-called reservoir sampling algorithm chooses to sample the ith key with probability $1/i$, and overwrite one of the existing k keys uniformly [18]. This algorithm, attributed to Waterman, was refined and extended by Vitter [22].

Gibbons and Matias proposed two generalizations in the form of counting samples and concise samples for when the stream can contain multiple occurrences of the same (unit weight) key [14]. Concise samples are Bernoulli samples where multiple occurrences of the same key are replaced in the sample with one occurrence and a count, obtaining a larger effective sample. This approach is used in networking as the basis of the "sampled netflow" format (`http://www.cisco.com/en/US/docs/ios/12_0s/feature/guide/12s_sanf.html`). In the case of counting samples, however, the sampling scheme is altered to count all subsequent occurrences of a sampled key. The same idea was referred to as Sample and Hold (SH) by Estan and Varghese, who applied it to network data with integral weights, and provided unbiased estimators [10].

In detail, the SH algorithm maintains a *cache* S of keys and a counter c_i for each cached key $i \in S$. The (true) value v_i of a key i is initially zero and each stream occurrence increments v_i. When an increment of key i is processed, then if $i \in S$ (the key is already cached), its counter is incremented $c_i \leftarrow c_i + 1$. Otherwise, i is inserted into the cache with (fixed) probability q and c_i is initialized to 0. Clearly, the probability that a key is not cached is $(1-q)^{v_i}$ and when cached the distribution of $v_i - c_i$ is geometric with parameter q. SH is particularly effective when multiple occurrences are likely. Because once a key is cached, all subsequent occurrences are counted, the resulting sample is more informative than "packet" sampling, where only a q fraction of the updates are sampled and the count of each key is the number of sampled updates for this key. It therefore offers lower variance than a concise sample for the same cache size k.

A drawback of SH is the fixed sampling rate q, which means that it is not possible to exactly control cache size. An adaptive version of sample and hold (aSH) was proposed in [14, 10] where subsampling is used to adaptively decrease q so that the number of cached keys does not exceed some fixed limit k. Subsampling is applied to the current cache content and the result mimics an application of SH with respect to the new lower $q' < q$. A very similar idea with geometric step sizes was proposed by Manku and Motwani in the form of "sticky sampling" [19].

Estan and Varghese [10] showed that with SH, $\hat{v}_i = 1/q + c_i - 1$ if $i \in S$ and 0 otherwise is an unbiased estimate of v_i. Thus, an unbiased estimate on the total value of selected keys (based on a selection predicate P) is the sum of $\hat{v}_i$ over cached (sampled) keys that satisfy P. With aSH, however, the analysis is complicated by dependence of the rate adjustments in the randomization. Only in subsequent work were unbiased estimators for aSH presented, as well as estimators over SH and aSH counts for other queries including "flow size" distribution and secondary weights [6, 5]. The technique used to get around the dependence was to consider each key after "fixing" the randomization used for other keys. This could then be used to establish that the dependence actually works in the method's favor, as correlations are zero or non-positive.

We review (increment-only) aSH as presented in [6, 5]: new keys are cached until the cache contains $k+1$ keys. The sampling rate is then "smoothly" decreased, such that the cache content simulates the lower rate, until one key is ejected. Subsequent processing of the stream is subjected to the new rate. When a new key is cached, the sampling rate is again decreased until one key is ejected. The sampling rate of this process is monotone non-increasing. The set of keys cached by aSH is a PPSWR sample (sampling probability proportional to size without replacement), also known as bottom-k (order) sampling with exponentially distributed ranks [21, 7, 8]. Here, keys are successively sampled with probability proportional to their value and without replacement until k keys are selected. Since (when there are multiple updates per key) the exact values v_i of sampled keys are not readily available, we need to apply different (weaker) estimators than PPSWR estimators.

All the stream sampling techniques described so far, however, rely on the fact that all weights are positive: they do not allow the negative weights that arise in the motivating examples. In fact, there has been only very limited prior work on sampling in the turnstile model, also known as sampling with deletions. Gemulla *et al.* gave a generalization of reservoir sampling for the unweighted, distinct key case [12]. They subsequently studied maintaining a SH-style sample under *signed* unit updates [13], and proposed an algorithm that resembles SH and adds support for unit decrements by maintaining an additional "tracking counter" for each cached key. Our results are more general, and apply to arbitrary updates as well as to the much harder adaptive Sample and Hold case.

Other models. Under the regime of "distinct" sampling (also known as L_0 sampling), the aim is to draw a sample uniformly over the set of keys with non-zero counts [15]. This can be achieved under a model allowing increments and decrements of weights by maintaining data structures based on hashing, but this requires a considerable overhead, with factors logarithmic in the size of the domain from which keys are drawn [9, 11].

More recently, the notions of "L_p sampling" and "precision sampling" have been proposed, which allow each key to be sampled with probability proportional to the pth power of its weight ($0 < p < 2$) [20, 1, 17]. These techniques rely on sketch data structures to recover keys and can tolerate arbitrary weight fluctuations. Our problem can be seen as related to the $p = 1$ case. In our setting, we do not allow the aggregate weight of a key to fall below 0. In contrast, the sketch-based techniques for L_p sampling can sample a key whose aggregate weight is negative, with probability proportional to the pth power of the absolute value of the aggregate weight.

The sketch-based sampling techniques have limitations even when the aggregate weights do not fall below zero: They incur space factors logarithmic in the size of the *domain* of keys, which is not favorable for applications with structured key domains (IP addresses, flow keys) that are much larger than the number of active keys. Extracting the sample from the sketches is a very costly process, since it requires enumerating the entire domain for each sketch. Our methods operate in a comparison model, and so can work on keys drawn from arbitrary domains, such as strings or real values (although they do still need to store the sampled keys) and the space usage is proportional to the sample size. The space factors in the sketch-based methods also grow polynomially with the inverse of the bias, whereas our samples are *unbiased*, and thus allow the relative error to diminish with aggregation. Lastly, the weighted sampling performed is "with replacement," which suffers when the weights are highly skewed compared with our "without replacement" sampling. Consequently, sketch-based methods are very slow to work with, and require a lot of space to provide an accurate sample, as we see in our later experimental study.

A different model of deletions arises from the "sliding window" model. In the time-based case, keys above a fixed age are considered deleted, while in the sequence-based case, only the W most recent keys are considered active [2, 3]. However, results in this model are not comparable to the model we study, which has explicit modifications to key weights.

1.2 Our Results

We present a turnstile stream sampling algorithm that efficiently handles signed weighted updates, where the number of cached keys is at most k. The presence of negative updates, the efficient handling of weighted (versus unit) updates, and an adaptive implementation which allows for full utilization of bounded storage, pose several challenges and we therefore develop our algorithm in two stages:

- **SH with signed weighted updates.** (Section 2) We first provide a generalization of Sample and Hold which allows arbitrary updates. When working with weighted updates, we find it convenient to work with a parameter we call the *sampling threshold*, which corresponds to the inverse of the sampling rate when updates are one unit ($\tau \equiv 1/q$). The sampling threshold is an unbiased estimator on the portion of the total value that is not accounted for in c_i.

  We quantify the impact of negative updates on performance, and specifically on the storage used. Although the final sample only depends on v_i, the occupancy of the sample at intermediate points may be much larger, due to keys which are subject to many decrements. We relate the probability that a key is cached at some point but not at the end to the aggregate sum of positive updates.

  When restricted to signed unit weight updates, our algorithm maintains a single counter c_i for each cached key $i \in S$ and the distribution of the counter c_i is exactly the same as (increment-only) SH with value v_i. This gives the benefit of using "off the shelf" SH estimators, and simplifies and improves over the previous efforts of Gemulla *et al.* [13].

- **aSH with signed weighted updates.** In Section 3 we present aSH with signed weighted updates. Our algorithm generalizes reservoir sampling [22] (single unit update for each key), PPSWR sampling (single weighted positive update for each key) [21, 7, 8] and aSH [14, 10, 6, 5] (multiple unit positive updates for each key).

  We work with a bounded size cache which can store at most k keys. At the same time, we want to ensure that we obtain maximum benefit of this cache by keeping it as full as possible. Hence, we allow the "effective" sampling threshold for entering the cache to vary: it increases after processing positive updates but can also decrease after processing negative updates. At the extreme, when negative updates cause ejections so there are fewer than k cached keys, the "effective" sampling threshold is zero.

As a precursor to presenting the adaptive algorithm, we study sampling changes that are randomization-independent. Specifically, we show how to efficiently subsample weighted data, that is, how to modify counter values of cached keys (possibly ejecting some keys) so that we mimic an increase in the sampling threshold from (fixed) τ to a (fixed) $\tau' > \tau$.

The analysis of our aSH with signed weighted updates is delicate and complicated by the dependence of the "effective" sampling threshold on the randomization, on other keys, and on the implementation of "smooth" adaptation of sampling threshold to facilitate ejecting exactly one key when the cache is full. Nevertheless, we show that it provides unbiased estimates with bounded variance that is a function of the effective sampling rate. Along the way, we show how to handle a varying sampling threshold that can decrease as well as increase. When the sampling threshold decreases, we cannot "recover" information about keys which have gone by, but we can "remember" the effective sampling threshold for the keys which are stored in the cache. Then for subsequent keys, a lower threshold makes it is easier for them to enter the cache.

To better understand the behavior of these algorithms, we perform an experimental study in Section 4. We compare the more general solution, aSH with signed weighted updates, to the only comparable technique, L_1 sampling, over data drawn from a networking application. We show that, given the space budget, aSH is more accurate, and faster to process streams and extract samples.

Lastly, in Section 5, we conclude by briefly remarking upon alternate models of stream updates, where instead of incrementing values, a reappearance of a key "overwrites" the previous value. In contrast to many other problems in this streaming model, we note some positive results for sampling.

2. SH WITH SIGNED WEIGHTED UPDATES

We present an extension of the SH procedure to the case when the stream consists of signed, weighted updates. The algorithm maintains a cache S of keys and associated counters c_i, based on a sampling rate $q \equiv 1/\tau$. Increments to key i are handled in a similar way as arrivals in the original (unweighted) SH setting: if i is already in S, then its counter c_i is incremented. Otherwise, i is included in S if Δ exceeds a draw from an exponential distribution with parameter $1/\tau$.

Processing a decrement of key i can be seen as undoing prior increments. If i is not in the cache S, no action is needed. But if i is in the cache, we decrement its associated counter c_i. If this counter becomes negative, we remove i from S. The estimation procedure is unchanged from the increment-only case. This procedure is formalized in Algorithm 1.

To simplify exposition, every key i is associated with a count c_i: keys that are not cached ($i \notin S$) have $c_i = 0$. To show the unbiasedness of this procedure, we derive the distribution of c_i and show that it depends only on v_i, and not any other function of the pattern of updates.

THEOREM 2.1. *The distribution of c_i for a key i with value v_i is*

$$[v_i - \text{EXP}_\tau]^+ \tag{2}$$

Algorithm 1 Sample and Hold with signed weighted updates. Sampling rate $q \equiv 1/\tau$

procedure UPDATE(i, Δ) ▷ $v_i \leftarrow [v_i + \Delta]^+$
  if $i \subset S$ **then**
    $c_i \leftarrow c_i + \Delta$
    if $c_i \leq 0$ **then**
      $S \leftarrow S \setminus \{i\}$ ▷ eject i from cache
  else ▷ case $i \notin S$
    $r \leftarrow \text{EXP}_\tau$
      ▷ Exponential distribution with mean τ
    if $r < \Delta$ **then**
      $S \leftarrow S \cup \{i\}$, $c_i \leftarrow \Delta - r$

procedure SUBSETSUMEST(P)
  ▷ Estimate $\sum_{i:P(i)} v_i$ for a selection predicate P
  $s \leftarrow 0$
  for $i \in S$ **do**
    if $P(i)$ **then**
      $s \leftarrow s + \tau + c_i$
return s

where EXP_τ *is exponentially distributed with mean* τ. *We make use of the notation* $[x]^+$ *to indicate the function* $\max\{x, 0\}$

PROOF. We establish the result by computing the changes in c_i in response to the updates of v_i. We consider a fixed key i, whose label we henceforth omit, and let $\{\Delta_{(n)} : n = 1, 2, \ldots\}$ be its updates, yielding corresponding values $v_{(0)} = 0$ and $v_{(n+1)} = [v_{(n)} + \Delta_{(n)}]^+$. The value of v_i at a given time is the cumulative result of the updates that have occurred up to that time.

According to Algorithm 1, the corresponding counter values are $c_{(0)} = 0$ with

$$c_{(n+1)} = \text{I}(c_{(n)} > 0)[c_{(n)} + \Delta_{(n)}]^+ + \text{I}(c_{(n)} = 0)[\Delta_{(n)} - \text{EXP}_{(n)}]^+ \tag{3}$$

where the $\{\text{EXP}_{(n)} : n = 0, 1, 2, \ldots\}$ are i.i.d. exponential random variables of mean τ, and I is the indicator function. Recall that a counter value $c = 0$ of zero corresponds to the counter not being maintained for the key in question. In particular, $c_{(n)} = 0$ corresponds to no counter being kept prior to the update $\Delta_{(n)}$, while taking the positive part $[c_{(n)} + \Delta_{(n)}]^+$ encodes that when the update due to $\Delta_{(n)}$ yields a non-positive counter value, that counter is deleted from storage.

We show that for each $n = 0, 1, \ldots,$

$$c_{(n)} =^d [v_{(n)} - \text{EXP}]^+ \tag{4}$$

where $=^d$ denotes equality in distribution, and EXP is another exponential random variable of mean τ independent of $\{\text{EXP}_{(n')} : n' \geq n\}$. (4) is trivially true for $n = 0$. We establish the general case by induction. Assuming (4), then by (3)

$$\begin{aligned} c_{(n+1)} = \tilde{c}_{(n+1)} := &\text{I}(v_{(n)} > \text{EXP})[v_{(n)} - \text{EXP} + \Delta_{(n)}]^+ \\ &+ \text{I}(v_{(n)} \leq \text{EXP})[\Delta_{(n)} - \text{EXP}_{(n)}]^+ \end{aligned} \tag{5}$$

To complete the proof, we need to show that

$$\tilde{c}_{(n+1)} =^d c'_{(n+1)} =^d [[v_{(n)} + \Delta_{(n)}]^+ - \text{EXP}']^+$$

where EXP' is an independent copy of EXP. When $v_{(n)} + \Delta_{(n)} \leq 0$ then $c'_{(n+1)} = \tilde{c}_{(n+1)} = 0$. When $v_{(n)} + \Delta_{(n)} > 0$, the complementary cumulative distribution function (CCDF) of $c'_{(n+1)}$ is

$$\begin{aligned}\Pr[c'_{(n+1)} > z] &= \Pr[\text{Exp} < [v_{(n)} + \Delta_{(n)} - z]^+]) \\ &= 1 - e^{-[v_{(n)}+\Delta_{(n)}-z]^+/\tau}, \text{ for } z \geq 0.\end{aligned}$$

The CCDF of $\tilde{c}_{(n+1)}$ can be derived from (5) as

$$\begin{aligned}\Pr[\tilde{c}_{(n+1)} > z] = &\Pr[\text{Exp} < \min\{v_{(n)}, [v_{(n)} + \Delta_{(n)} - z]^+\}] + \\ &\Pr[v_{(n)} \leq \text{Exp}] \Pr[\text{Exp}_{(n)} < [\Delta_{(n)} - z]^+]\end{aligned} \quad (6)$$

When $\Delta_{(n)} < z$, the first term in (6) is

$$\Pr[\text{Exp} < [v_{(n)} + \Delta_{(n)} - z]^+] = \Pr[c'_{(n+1)} > z]$$

and the second is zero. When $\Delta_{(n)} \geq z$, then

$$\begin{aligned}&\Pr[\tilde{c}_{(n+1)} > z] \\ &= \Pr[\text{Exp} < v_{(n)}] + \Pr[\text{Exp} \geq v_{(n)}) \Pr[\text{Exp}_{(n)} < \Delta_{(n)} - z] \\ &= (1 - e^{-v_{(n)}/\tau}) + e^{-v_{(n)}/\tau}(1 - e^{-(\Delta_{(n)}-z)/\tau}) \\ &= 1 - e^{-(v_{(n)}+\Delta_{(n)}-z)/\tau} \\ &= 1 - e^{-[v_{(n)}+\Delta_{(n)}-z]^+)/\tau} \\ &= \Pr[c'_{(n+1)} > z]\end{aligned}$$

□

Theorem 2.1 shows that the distribution of the counter c_i depends only on the actual sum v_i, and is exactly captured by a truncated exponential distribution. This is a powerful result, since it means that the sampling procedure is identical in distribution to one where each key is unique, and occurs only once with weight v_i. From this, we can provide unbiased estimators for subset sums and bound the variance. In SubsetSumEst (Algorithm 1), each key is assigned an adjusted weight $\hat{v}_i$, which is $\tau + c_i$ if $i \in S$, and 0 otherwise. Using the convention $c_i = 0$ for deleted counters, this can be expressed succinctly as

$$\hat{v}_i = \mathrm{I}(c_i > 0)(c_i + \tau)$$

Given a selection predicate P, we estimate the subset sum $\sum_{i:P(i)} v_i$ with $\sum_{i:P(i)} \hat{v}_i$, the sum of adjusted weights of keys in the cache which satisfy P. It suffices to show $\hat{v}_i$ is an unbiased estimate of v_i.

Lemma 2.2. *$\hat{v}_i$ is an unbiased estimate of v_i.*

Lemma 2.2 turns out to be a special case of the more general Theorem 3.1 that we state and prove later in context.

2.1 Special case: unit updates

We briefly consider the special case of unit updates, i.e. where each $\Delta \in \{-1, +1\}$. In this case, we can adopt a simplified variant: note that the test of Δ against an exponential distribution succeeds only when $\Delta = +1$, and does so with probability $q = 1/\tau$. When this occurs, we choose to initialize $c_i = 0$. Here, c_i is integral and can be initialized with value ≥ 0 or uninitialized (when i is not cached). It is easy to see the correctness of this procedure: observe that if an i is sampled, then it will only remain in the cache if there is no corresponding decrement later in the stream. Thus we can "pair off" increments which are erased by decrements, and leave only v_i "unpaired" increments. The key i only remains in the cache if it is sampled during one of these unpaired increments, and therefore has count c_i with probability $q(1-q)^{v_i - c_i}$, and is not sampled with probability $(1-q)^{v_i}$. That is, it exactly corresponds to a SH procedure on an increment-only input. Correctness, and unbiasedness of the SubsetSumEst procedure follows immediately as a result. This improves over the result of [13], by removing the need to keep additional tracking counters for cached keys.

2.2 Cache occupancy

From our analysis, it is clear that the distribution of the final count c_i depends only on v_i. In particular, the probability that the key is cached at termination is $1 - \exp(-v_i/\tau)$. With the presence of negative updates in the update stream, however, a key may be cached at some point during the execution and then ejected. The key i is never cached if and only if the independent exponential random variables r generated at line 7 of Algorithm 1 all exceed their corresponding update $\Delta_{(n)}$. This observation immediately establishes:

Lemma 2.3. *The probability that key i is cached at some point during the execution is $1 - \exp(-\Sigma\Delta^+(i)/\tau)$, where $\Sigma\Delta^+(i) \equiv \sum_t \max\{0, \Delta_{(n)}\}$ is the sum of positive updates for key i.*

When $\Sigma\Delta^+(i) \ll \tau$, the probability that a key ever gets cached is small, and is approximately $\Sigma\Delta^+(i)/\tau$. The probability that it is cached at termination is $\approx v_i/\tau$. Summing over all keys, the worst-case cache utilization (which is observed after all negative updates occur at the end), is the ratio of the sum of positive updates to the sum of values, $\sum \Delta^+(i) : v_i$.

3. ASH WITH SIGNED WEIGHTED UPDATES

In this section, we describe an adaptive form of Sample and Hold (aSH), generalized to allow updates that are both weighted and signed, while ensuring that the total number of keys cached does not exceed a specified bound k.

3.1 Increasing the sampling threshold

In order to bound the number of keys cached, we need a mechanism to eject keys, by effectively increasing the sampling threshold τ. We show how to efficiently increase from τ_0 to $\tau_1 > \tau_0$ so that we achieve the same output distribution as if the sampling threshold had been τ_1 throughout. Algorithm 2 shows the procedure for a single key $i \in S$. With probability τ_0/τ_1, no changes are made; otherwise c_i is reduced by a value drawn from an exponential distribution with mean τ_1, and ejected if this is now below 0. We can formalize this as follows. Let $c \geq 0$, $0 \leq \tau_0, \tau_1$, u be a random variable uniformly distributed in $(0, 1]$, and Exp_{τ_1} be an exponential random variable of mean τ_1 independent of u. Then define the random variable

$$\Theta(c, \tau_0, \tau_1) = \mathrm{I}(u\tau_1 > \tau_0)[c - \text{Exp}_{\tau_1}]^+ + \mathrm{I}(u\tau_1 \leq \tau_0)c$$

Note $\Theta(c, \tau_0, \tau_1) = c$ when $\tau_1 \leq \tau_0$. We give an algorithmic formulation of Θ in Algorithm 2 as SampThreshInc, which replaces c_i by the value $\Theta(c_i, \tau_0, \tau_1)$ if this value is positive, and otherwise deletes the key i.

We now show that Θ preserves unbiasedness, and in particular that the distribution of an updated count c_i under Θ is that of a fixed-rate SH procedure with threshold τ_1:

Theorem 3.1. *Let $0 \leq \tau_0 < \tau_1$ and $\tilde{c} = \Theta(c, \tau_0, \tau_1)$.*

Algorithm 2 Adjust sampling threshold from τ_0 to τ_1 for key i

Require: $\tau_1 > \tau_0$, $i \in S$

procedure SampThreshInc(i, c_i, τ_0, τ_1)
  $u \leftarrow$ RAND()
  if $\tau_1 > \frac{\tau_0}{u}$ **then**
    $z \leftarrow$ RAND()
    $r \leftarrow (-\ln(z))\tau_1$ ▷ $r \leftarrow \text{Exp}_{\tau_1}$
    $c_i \leftarrow c_i - r$
    if $c_i \leq 0$ **then** $S \leftarrow S \setminus \{i\}$

(i) $\mathsf{E}[\mathrm{I}(\tilde{c} > 0)(\tilde{c} + \tau_1)|c] = c + \tau_0$

(ii) If $c =^d [v - \text{Exp}_{\tau_0}]^+$, *then* $\tilde{c} =^d [v - \text{Exp}_{\tau_1}]^+$.

Proof. (i)

$$\begin{aligned} &\mathsf{E}[\mathrm{I}(\tilde{c} > 0)(\tilde{c} + \tau_1)|c] \\ &= (1 - \tau_0/\tau_1) \int_0^c e^{-x/\tau_1}(c - x + \tau_1)\, dx + (\tau_0/\tau_1)(c + \tau_1) \\ &= (1 - \tau_0/\tau_1)c + (\tau_0/\tau_1)(c + \tau_1) = c + \tau_0 \end{aligned}$$

(ii) Let $c =^d [v - \text{Exp}_{\tau_0}]^+$. Then $\Theta(c, \tau_0, \tau_1)$ can be rewritten as $[v - W]^+$ where

$$W = \mathrm{I}(\tau_1 u > \tau_0)(\text{Exp}_{\tau_0} + \text{Exp}_{\tau_1}) + \mathrm{I}(\tau_1 u \leq \tau_0)\text{Exp}_{\tau_1}$$

A direct computation of convolution of distributions shows that $\text{Exp}_{\tau_0} + \text{Exp}_{\tau_1}$ has distribution function

$$x \mapsto (\tau_1 \text{Exp}_{\tau_1}(x) - \tau_0 \text{Exp}_{\tau_0}(x))/(\tau_1 - \tau_0).$$

Hence, using $\Pr[\tau_1 u > \tau_0] = 1 - \tau_0/\tau_1$, one computes that W has distribution function

$$\begin{aligned} W(x) &= \Pr[\tau_1 u > \tau_0](\text{Exp}_{\tau_0} + \text{Exp}_{\tau_1})(x) + \\ &\quad + \Pr[\tau_1 u \leq \tau_0]\text{Exp}_{\tau_1}(x) \\ &= \text{Exp}_{\tau_1}(x) \end{aligned}$$

□

Proof of Lemma 2.2.
From Theorem 2.1, $c_i =^d [v_i - \text{Exp}_\tau]^+ = \Theta(v_i, 0, \tau)$. Hence $\mathsf{E}[\hat{v}_i] = \mathsf{E}[\mathrm{I}(c_i > 0)(c_i + \tau)] = v_i$ as a special case of Theorem 3.1(i). □

3.2 Maintaining a fixed size cache

We are now ready to present Algorithm 3, which maintains at most k cached keys at any given time. For each cached key i, the algorithm stores a count c_i and the key's effective sampling threshold τ_i. This τ_i is set to the sampling threshold in force during the ejection following the most recent entry of that key into the cache. It may also be adjusted upward due to the ejection of another key, a process we explain below.

When the cache is not full, a new key i is admitted with sampling threshold $\tau_i = 0$. When the cache is full, in the sense that it contains k keys, a new key is provisionally admitted, then one of the $k + 1$ keys is selected for ejection. The procedure EjectOne adjusts the minimum sampling threshold τ^* to the lowest value for which one key will be ejected. This is implemented by considering the potential action of SampThreshInc on all counts c_i simultaneously, fixing a independent randomization of the variates u_i, z_i for each i, and finding the smallest threshold τ^*

Algorithm 3 aSH with signed weighted updates

1: **procedure** Update(i, Δ)
  ▷ Update weight of key i by Δ
2:   **if** $i \in S$ **then**
3:     $c_i \leftarrow c_i + \Delta$
4:     **if** $c_i \leq 0$ **then**
5:       $S \leftarrow S \setminus \{i\}$ ▷ i ejected from cache.
6:   **else if** $\Delta > 0$ **then** ▷ $i \notin S$
7:     $S \leftarrow S \cup \{i\}$, $\tau_i \leftarrow 0$, $c_i \leftarrow \Delta$
    ▷ Insert i with sampling threshold 0
8:     **if** $|S| = k + 1$ **then**
9:       EjectOne(S)

10: **procedure** SubsetSumEst(P) ▷ Estimate $\sum_{i:P(i)} v_i$
11:   $s \leftarrow 0$
12:   **for** $i \in S$ **do**
13:     **if** $P(i)$ **then**
14:       $s \leftarrow s + \tau_i + c_i$ ▷ estimate
  return s

15: **procedure** EjectOne(S)
  ▷ Subroutine to increase sampling threshold so one key is ejected
16:   **for** $i \in S$ **do**
17:     $u_i \leftarrow$ RAND(), $z_i \leftarrow$ RAND()
18:     $T_i \leftarrow \max\{\frac{\tau_i}{u_i}, \frac{c_i}{-\log(z_i)}\}$
    ▷ T_i is the sampling threshold that would eject i
19:   $\tau^* \leftarrow \min_{i \in S} T_i$
    ▷ τ^* is the new minimum sampling threshold
20:   **for** $i \in S$ **do**
21:     **if** $T_i = \tau^*$ **then** $S \leftarrow S \setminus \{i\}$
22:     **else**
23:       **if** $\tau_i \leq \tau^*$ **then**
24:         **if** $\tau^* u_i > \tau_i$ **then**
25:           $c_i \leftarrow c_i + \tau^* \log z_i$
  ▷ Given $T_i > \tau^*$ and $\tau^* u_i > \tau_i$, then $c_i + \tau^* \log z_i > 0$
  ▷ Given $T_i > \tau^*$ and $\tau^* u_i \leq \tau_i$, then c_i is unchanged.
26:           $\tau_i \leftarrow \tau^*$

for which $\tilde{c}_i = \Theta(c_i, \tau_i, \tau^*) = 0$ for some i. This key is ejected, while the thresholds of surviving keys are adjusted as $(c_i, \tau_i) \leftarrow (\tilde{c}_i, \tau^*)$ if $\tau_i \leq \tau^*$, and are otherwise left unchanged.

Lemma 3.2. *$\hat{v}_i$ retains its expectation under the action of* EjectOne.

Proof. We choose a particular key i, and fix all c_j, and also fix for $j \neq i$ the random variates u_j, z_j from line 17 of Algorithm 3. This fixes the effect of random past selections and updates. Let $T_j = \max\{\tau_j/u_j, c_j/(-\log z_j)\}$ and $\tau' = \min_{j \neq i} T_j$, which are hence also treated as fixed. Then the update to c_i is $\tilde{c}_i = \Theta(c_i, \tau_i, \tau')$; we will establish that $\tilde{v}_i = \mathrm{I}(\tilde{c}_i > 0)(\tilde{c}_i + \tau')$ is a (conditionally) unbiased estimator of v_i **for any fixed** τ', and hence unbiased.

We first check $\tilde{c}_i$ corresponds to the action on c_i described in Algorithm 3. For clarity we state

$$\tilde{c}_i = \mathrm{I}(\tau' u_i > \tau_i)[c_i - \text{Exp}_{\tau'}]^+ + \mathrm{I}(\tau' u_i \leq \tau_i)c_i$$

and observe that $-\tau' \log z_i$ is the random variable $\text{Exp}_{\tau'}$ employed. When $T_i < \tau'$, i is selected for deletion. This corresponds to the case $\{\tau' > \tau_i/u_i\} \cap \{\tau' > c_i/(-\log z_i)\}$.

The condition $\tau' > \tau_i/u_i$ selects the first term in the expression for $\tilde{c}_i$, while the condition $\tau' > c_i/(-\log z_i)$ makes that term zero, i.e. $\tilde{c}_i = 0$ and the key is deleted. Otherwise, if $T_i \geq \tau'$, the first or second term in $\tilde{c}_i$ may be selected, but both cannot be zero.

Let $\tilde{v}_i$ denote the estimate of v_i based on $\tilde{c}_i = \Theta(c_i, \tau_i, \tau')$. Then from Theorem 3.1(i)

$$\mathsf{E}[\tilde{v}_i|\tau', c_i > 0] = \mathsf{E}[\mathrm{I}(\tilde{c}_i > 0)(\tilde{c}_i + \tau')|\tau', c_i > 0] = c_i + \tau_i$$

independent of τ'. Hence

$$\mathsf{E}[\tilde{v}_i] = \mathsf{E}[\mathrm{I}(c_i > 0)(c_i + \tau_i)] = v_i.$$

□

THEOREM 3.3. *$\hat{v}_i$ is an unbiased estimator of v_i*

PROOF. Initially, the cache is empty and both $v_i = 0$ and $\hat{v}_i = 0$. We need to show that the estimate remains unbiased after an update operation. The first part of a positive update $\Delta > 0$ clearly preserves the expectation: τ_i is not modified (or initialized to 0 if i was not cached) and c is increased by Δ. Hence $\hat{v}_i$ increases by exactly Δ. Unbiasedness under the second part, performing EJECTONE if the cache is full, follows from Lemma 3.2.

To conclude the proof of the unbiasedness of the estimator, we invoke Lemma 3.6(i), which is stated and proved below. This Lemma uses a 'pairing' argument to pair off the negative update with a prior positive update, and so reduces to a stream with only positive updates, which yields the same $\hat{v}_i$. Therefore, the result follows from the above argument on positive updates. □

3.3 Estimation Variance

It is important to be able to establish likely errors on the unbiased estimators $\hat{v}_i$ resulting from Algorithm 3. A straightforward calculation shows that when $c_i =^d [v_i - \text{EXP}_\tau]^+$, the unbiased estimate $\hat{v}_i = \mathrm{I}(c_i > 0)(c_i + \tau_i)$ has variance

$$\mathsf{Var}[\hat{v}_i] = \tau_i^2(1 - e^{-v_i/\tau_i})$$

Moreover, $\mathsf{Var}[\hat{v}_i]$ itself has an unbiased estimator s_i^2 that does not depend explicitly on the value v_i:

$$s_i^2 = \mathrm{I}(c_i > 0)\tau_i^2.$$

The intuition behind s_i^2 is clear: for a key in S, the uncertainty concerning v_i is determined by the estimated unsampled increments, which are exponentially distributed with mean τ_i and variance τ_i^2. Observe that both $\mathsf{Var}[\hat{v}_i]$ and s_i^2 are increasing functions of τ_i.

Note that the estimated variance associated with a given key is non-decreasing while the key is stored in the cache, then drops to zero when the key is ejected, possibly growing again after further updates for that key. Since s_i^2 is increasing in τ_i, a simple upper bound on the variance is obtained using the maximum threshold encountered over all instances of EJECTONE. This is because one of these instances must have given rise to the largest threshold associated with each particular key.

LEMMA 3.4. *For any two keys $i \neq j$, $\mathsf{E}[\hat{v}_i\hat{v}_j]$ is invariant under* EJECTONE.

PROOF. Reusing notation from the proof of Lemma 3.2, let $T_j = \max\{\tau_j/u_j, c_j/(-\log z_j)\}$. We fix c_j and $\tau' = \min_{h\neq i,j} T_h$. The update to c_h ($h \in \{i, j\}$) is $\tilde{c}_h = \Theta(c_h, \tau_h, \tau')$, and (when $\tilde{c}_h > 0$) the update to τ_h is $\tilde{\tau}_h = \min\{\tau', T_i, T_j\}$. It suffices to show that

$$\begin{aligned}&\mathsf{E}[\mathrm{I}(\tilde{c}_i > 0, \tilde{c}_j > 0)(\tilde{c}_i + \tilde{\tau}_i)(\tilde{c}_j + \tilde{\tau}_j)] \\ &\quad = \mathrm{I}(c_i > 0, c_j > 0)(c_i + \tau_i)(c_j + \tau_j)] .\end{aligned}$$

We observe that

$$\begin{aligned}&\mathsf{E}[\mathrm{I}(\tilde{c}_i > 0, \tilde{c}_j > 0)(\tilde{c}_i + \tilde{\tau}_i)(\tilde{c}_j + \tilde{\tau}_j)] \\ &\quad = \mathsf{E}[\mathrm{I}(\tilde{c}_i > 0, \tilde{c}_j > 0)(\tilde{c}_i + \tau')(\tilde{c}_j + \tau')],\end{aligned}$$

which holds because there can be a positive contribution to the expectation only when $T_i, T_j > \tau'$. Under this conditioning, however, τ' essentially functions as a fixed threshold. Thus, we can apply Theorem 3.1 (i) and obtain

$$\begin{aligned}&\mathsf{E}[\mathrm{I}(\tilde{c}_i > 0, \tilde{c}_j > 0)(\tilde{c}_i + \tau')(\tilde{c}_j + \tau')] \\ &\quad = \mathrm{I}(c_i > 0, c_j > 0)(c_i + \tau_i)(c_j + \tau_j).\end{aligned}$$

□

Consequently, we are able to show that the covariance between the estimates of any pair of distinct keys is zero.

THEOREM 3.5. *For any two keys $i \neq j$, $\mathsf{Cov}[\hat{v}_i, \hat{v}_j] = 0$.*

PROOF. We show inductively on the actions of UPDATE in Algorithm 3 that $\mathsf{E}[\hat{v}_i\hat{v}_j] = v_i v_j$.

For a positive update (i, Δ), the claim is clear following $c \leftarrow c + \Delta$ (line 3 in Algorithm 3), when i is in the cache. Both v_i and $\hat{v}_i = I(c_i > 0)\tau_i + c_i$ increase by Δ and both v_j and $\hat{v}_j$ are unchanged. Hence, if prior to the update we had $\mathsf{E}[\hat{v}_i\hat{v}_j] = v_i v_j$ then this holds after the update. A positive update may also result in EJECTONE and we apply Lemma 3.4 to show that $\mathsf{E}[\hat{v}_i\hat{v}_j]$ is unchanged.

To complete the proof, we also need to handle negative updates. We argue that the expectation $\mathsf{E}[\hat{v}_i\hat{v}_j]$ is the same as if we remove the negative update and a prior matching positive update, leaving a stream of positive updates only. The details of this argument are provided in Lemma 3.6(ii). □

A consequence of this property is that the variance on subset sum estimate is the sum of single-key variances, just as with independent sampling: $\mathsf{Var}[\sum_{i:P(i)} \hat{v}_i] = \sum_{i:P(i)} \mathsf{Var}[\hat{v}_i]$. In particular, $\sum_{i:P(i)} \mathrm{I}(c_i > 0)\tau_i^2 = \sum_{i\in S:P(i)} \tau_i^2$ is an unbiased estimate on $\sum_{i:P(i)} v_i$.

3.4 Analysis of negative updates under aSH

Our analysis in Theorems 3.3 and 3.5 relies on replacing a stream with a mixture of positive and negative weight updates with one which has positive weight updates only, and then arguing that certain properties of this positive stream match those of the original input. This generalizes the "pairing" argument outlined in Section 2.1 for the special case of unit weighted updates. In this section, we provide more details of this pairing transformation, and prove that this preserves the required properties of the estimates.

Pairing Process. In our pairing process, each negative update is placed in correspondence ("paired") with preceding, previously unpaired, positive updates. We then go on to relate the state to that on a stream with both paired updates omitted. Figure 1 gives a schematic view of the pairing process for a key, which we describe in more detail below.

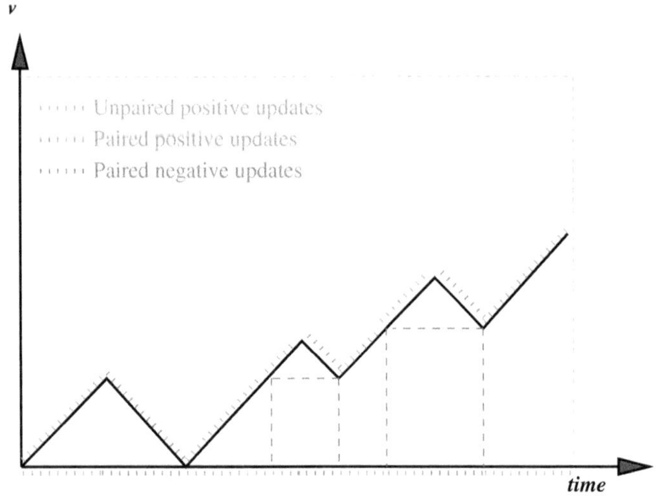

Figure 1: Value of key with time. Unpaired and paired positive update and paired negative updates are marked.

Specifically, a negative update of key i is paired with the most recent unpaired positive update of i. If there is no such update, the negative update is unpaired. This occurs when the aggregate weight before the update is zero, in which case according to (1), v_i remains zero, and we can ignore this update.

Since updates are weighted, a negative update $(i, -\Delta)$ may be paired with multiple positive updates, or with a fraction of a positive update. Without loss of generality, each negative update will be paired with a "suffix" of a positive update, followed by zero or more "complete" positive updates. If $v_i < \Delta$, the negative update only has its v_i "prefix" paired and $v_i - \Delta$ "suffix" unpaired.

To aid analysis, we observe that we can "split" updates without altering the state distribution. More precisely, let σ be an update stream terminating with an update (i, Δ). Let σ' be the same stream with the last update replaced by two consecutive updates (i, Δ_1) and (i, Δ_2) such that $\Delta_1 + \Delta_2 = \Delta$, and $\text{sign}(\Delta_1) = \text{sign}(\Delta_2) = \text{sign}(\Delta)$. Then the distribution of the state of the algorithm after processing σ or σ', conditioned on the initial state, is the same. This means that by splitting updates, we can replace the original sequence by another sequence (where each original update is now a subsequence of updates), on which the algorithm has the same final state but all updates are fully paired or fully unpaired.

We next prove the lemma we require to replace the original stream with a positive-only stream.

LEMMA 3.6. *Consider an update stream where the ℓ'th update is a negative update $(i, -\Delta)$ and a modified stream with the negative update, and all positive update(s) paired with it (if any) omitted. Then*

(i) $\mathsf{E}[\hat{v}_i]$ *and*

(ii) for $j \neq i$, $\mathsf{E}[\hat{v}_i \hat{v}_j]$

are the same for both streams.

PROOF. We observe that a negative update can be unpaired if and only if $v_i = 0$ just prior to the current negative update. Since the counter $c_i \leq v_i$, this means that i is not cached and thus the processing of the unpaired negative update has no effect on the state of the algorithm.

For paired negative updates, let σ_0 be the prefix of the stream up to the corresponding paired positive update, σ be the suffix including and after the positive update, and $\sigma' \subset \sigma$ be an alternative suffix with the negative update and its paired positive update all omitted. Fix the execution of the algorithm on σ_0. To complete the proof, we show that

(i) The distributions of (τ_i, c_i) for key i after processing σ and σ' are the same.

(ii) For a key $j \neq i$, if $c_i > 0$, then the distribution of (τ_j, c_j) conditioned on the final (τ_i, c_i) when $c_i > 0$ is the same: $(\tau_j, c_j)|\sigma, \tau_i, c_i =^d (\tau_j, c_j)|\sigma', \tau_i, c_i$

Since the actual splitting point of updates does not affect the state distribution, we can treat v_i as defined by the update stream projected on i as a contiguous function of "time". Initially, before any updates of i are processed, the time is 0. If the time is t_0 prior to processing an update (i, Δ), then for $t \in [t_0, t_0 + |\Delta|]$, we interpolate the value v_i as a function of time as $v_i(t) = [v_i(t_0) + t - t_0]^+$. After processing the update, the time is $t_0 + |\Delta|$. Any point in time now has a gradient, depending on whether v_i is increasing or decreasing at that time. Pairing is between intervals of equal size and opposite gradient. Figure 1 shows the value v_i as a function of time and distinguishes between updates that are paired and unpaired with respect to the final state.

Tracking the state of key i during execution, we map an interval $[0, c_i]$ to positive update intervals in a length-preserving manner. The mapping corresponds to the positive updates which contributed to the count c_i, that is, the most recent unpaired positive update intervals of (total) length c_i. We refer to the point that 0 is mapped to as the (most recent) *entry point* of key i into the cache. Upon a positive update, the counter is incremented by $\Delta > 0$. The mapping of $[0, c_i]$ is unchanged and the interval $[c_i, c_i + \Delta]$ maps to the interval $[t_0, t_0 + \Delta]$ of the current update on the time axis. An EJECTONE operation which reduces the counter c_i by r removes an r "prefix" of the counter interval: a positive update time previously paired with $y \in [0, c]$ such that $y > r$ is paired with the point $y - r$ in the updated interval. A negative update of Δ results in $c \leftarrow [c - \Delta]^+$. A Δ "suffix" of $[0, c]$ is removed (reflecting that the positive update points this suffix was mapped to are now paired) and the mapping of the remaining $[0, [c - \Delta]^+]$ prefix is unchanged. Note that the positive update interval removed is the one that is paired with the negative update just processed.

We now consider a negative update of Δ, and compare the execution of the algorithm on suffixes σ and σ'.

- If i is not cached after σ_0, then it would not be cached after any execution of either σ or σ', since all positive updates of i are paired. If i was cached at the end of σ_0 and ejected during σ, we fix the randomization in each EJECTONE performed when processing σ. We then look at executions of σ' that follow that randomization until (and if) the set of cached keys diverges. Under σ', i has a lower c value (by Δ) than under σ. Thus, when i is removed by an EJECTONE at σ, it would also be removed under σ', unless it was removed already under a prior EJECTONE. As all positive updates of i in σ and σ' are paired, once i is removed, then even if it re-enters the cache it will not be cached at termination for either σ' or σ. Thus, the outcome for i under σ and σ' is the same.

- If i is cached after σ, its most recent entry point must be in σ_0. We again fix the execution of the algorithm on σ, fixing all random draws when performing EJECTONE procedures. We will show that if the execution of σ' follows these random draws, then i will not be ejected and will have the same τ_i, c_i values at termination of σ'. Consider the execution of the algorithm on σ' and let τ'_i, c'_i be the parameters for i. Initially, $c'_i = c_i - \Delta$. Clearly, any EJECTONE where c is not changed, retains i under both σ and σ'. If c is reduced under σ, it still must be such that $c_i > \Delta$ for i to be cached at the end, since all subsequent positive updates are paired, and the last update is of $-\Delta$. Thus, it would also remain cached under the corresponding EJECTONE in σ'. Moreover, all other keys cached under σ would also be cached (and have the same (τ_j, c_j) values) under σ'.

Lastly, we consider (τ_j, c_j) for $j \neq i$ conditioned on (τ_i, c_i) when $c_i > 0$. If i is not cached after σ, it is also not cached under σ' and thus $c_i = 0$. If i is cached after σ, it has the same state (τ_i, c_i) as under σ' (fixing randomization). Furthermore, the state (τ_j, c_j) for any key and $j \neq i$ is the same.

From these observations, we can conclude that the expectation of the estimate for any key, and for any pair of distinct keys (and likewise for higher moments), are the same for both streams. □

Note that once we have the above lemma, we can apply it repeatedly to remove all negative updates, and result in a "positive-only" stream. The distributions of the state of algorithm on these paired streams are identical.

4. EXPERIMENTS

In this section we exhibit the action of aSH on a stream of signed updates, and compare its performance against a comparable state-of-the-art method, namely L_p sampling.

4.1 Implementation Issues.

Our reference comparison was with L_p sampling. The L_p sampling procedure builds on the idea of sketch data structures, which summarize a d-entry vector x. A sketch built with parameter ε can provide an estimate of any x_i with error $\varepsilon\|x\|_2$, using space $O(\varepsilon^{-2} \log d)$ [4]. In outline, for L_1 sampling, we build a sketch of the vector $x_i = v_i/u_i$, where v_i are the aggregate weights for key i, and each u_i is a fixed uniform random variable in the range $[0, 1]$ [17]. To draw a sample, we find the entry of this vector which is estimated as having largest x_i value by the sketch. To obtain the correct sampling distribution, we have to reject samples whose x_i value does not exceed a fixed threshold as a function of $\|v\|_1$, which in our case is just the sum of all update weights. As a result, the procedure requires a lot of space per sample: $O(\log^2 d)$, even using a large constant value of ε. Further, the time to extract a sample can be high, since we have to enumerate all keys in the domain. The search time could be reduced using standard tricks, but this would increase the space by further factors of $\log d$. We implemented both L_1 sampling and our adaptive Sample and Hold algorithm in interpreted languages (Perl, Python); we expect optimized implementations to have the same relative performance, but improved scalability. To ensure comparability, we fix the space used by aSH to draw a sample of size k (i.e. k tuples of $(i, c_i, \tau_i, u_i, z_i)$), and allocate this much space to L_p sampling to be used for sketch data structures. Based on our parameter settings, the sketch used by L_p sampling to extract a single sample equates to the space for 10 samples under aSH.

4.2 Data Description

We tested our methods on data corresponding to the ISP network monitoring scenario described in the Introduction. The update stream was derived from arrival and departures at a queue. The queue was driven by a synthetic arrival process, comprising keyed items with sizes drawn independently from a Pareto(1.1) distribution. The arrival times and key values were derived from an IP network trace of 10^6 packets. We simulated a FIFO queue in which each item remains at the head of the queue for a time equal to its size, and converted the trace into a stream of 2×10^6 updates (i, s), where i is a key and s is positive for an arriving item and negative of the same magnitude when that item has completed service for a departure, the stream items having the corresponding event order as for the queue. Thus the values v_i correspond to the total size of items of key i in the queue at a given time. We evaluate the methods based on their ability to accurately summarize the queue occupancy distribution of different subsets of keys.

4.3 Parametrization

We parametrized different runs of the simulation as follows.

- *Key Granularity:* The trace contained about 110,000 unique keys. These were mapped to smaller keys sets as $i \mapsto \beta = h(i) \mod b$ with h a hash function and b taking values $1,000$, $10,000$ and $100,000$. This is the granularity of keys in the sample set. Note that the time for our aSH algorithm does not depend explicitly on the key granularity, but L_p sampling incurs a cost linear in b; hence, we focus on moderate values of b to bound the experimental duration.

- *Query Granularity:* For determination of estimation accuracy, we divide the keyspace into a different classes, and use the recovered sample to estimate the weight distribution across these classes. Specifically, we assigning each key β to a bin by $\beta \mapsto \alpha = \beta \mod a$. (Note that the sampling methods are not aware of this fixed mapping, and so are unable to take advantage of it.) We used values $10, 100$, and $1,000$ for a.

- *Sample Size:* we selected roughly geometric sample sizes k from $30, 100, 300$ and $1,000$ for aSH, and allocated the equivalent space to L_p sampling, as described above.

Our subsequent experiments compare the performance in time and accuracy across the different combinations of these settings of a, b, and sample size k.

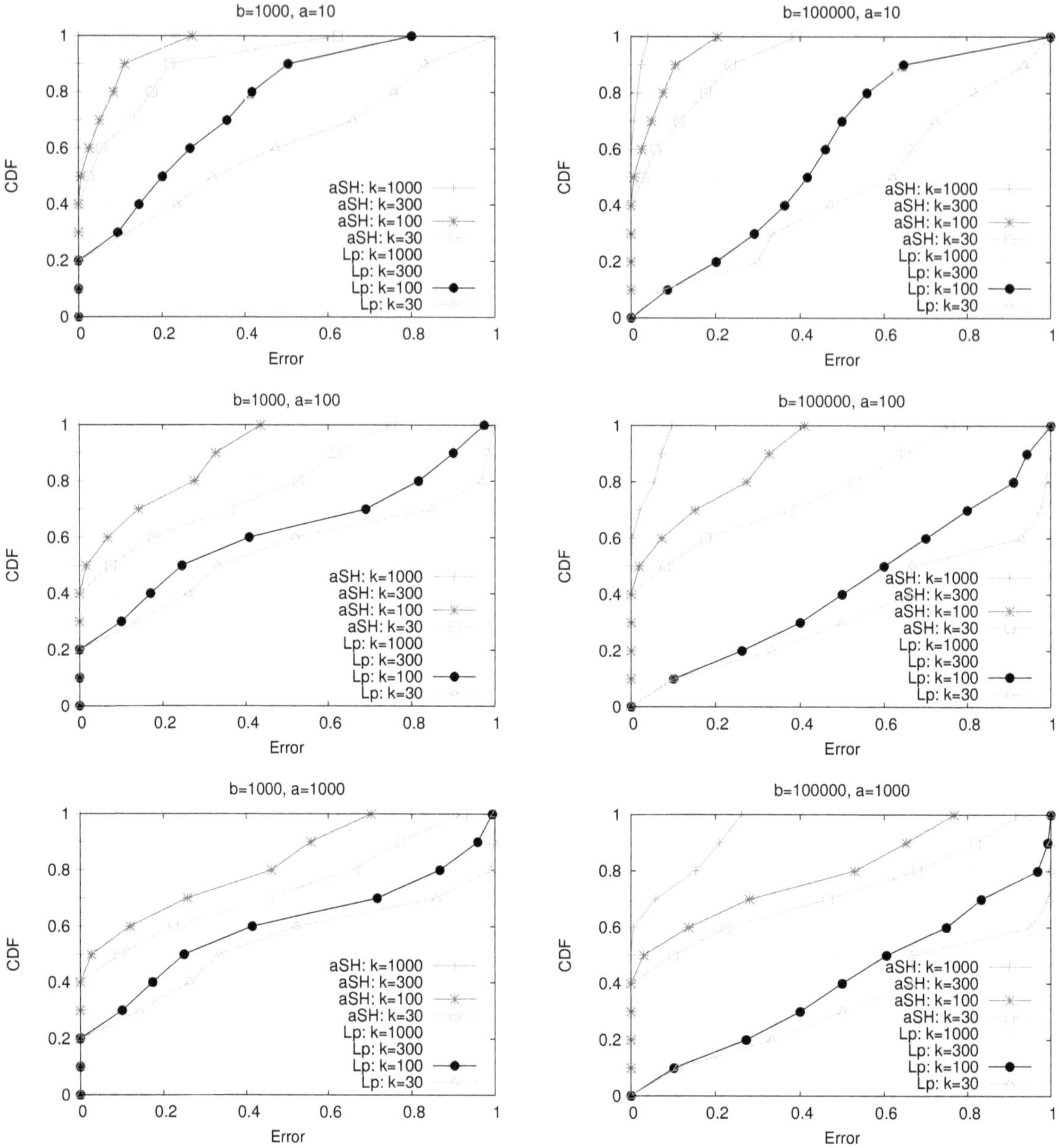

Figure 2: CDF of Estimation Error as a function of sample size k for aSH and L_p; key granularity $b = 1,000$ and $100,000$. Query granularity $a = 10, 100$ and $1,000$. aSH is consistently more accurate than L_p.

4.4 Results

Query Accuracy. Each time we probe the samples, we obtain the estimated weights of the a different bins. We measure the accuracy by comparing the induced frequency distribution to the true distribution computed offline. That is, let $w(\alpha)$ and $\hat{w}(\alpha)$ the total and estimated weighted in each query aggregate labeled by $\alpha = 1, 2 \ldots a$. Then accuracy is measured by the distribution error

$$\frac{1}{2} \sum_{\alpha} \left| \frac{w(\alpha)}{W} - \frac{\hat{w}(\alpha)}{\hat{W}} \right| \in [0, 1] \tag{7}$$

where $W = \sum_\alpha w(\alpha)$ and $\hat{W} = \sum_\alpha \hat{w}(\alpha)$.

This distribution error was computed for each positive update for aSH and every 1000 updates in L_p sampling. Figure 2 shows the empirical cumulative distributions of the errors computed for each method, using key granularity $b = 1,000$ and $100,000$ and query granularity $a = 10, 100$ and $1,000$.

On these plots, an ideal summary reaches the top left hand corner (i.e. if all queries have zero error). For aSH with k=1000, this is indeed achieved in the case $b = 1000$. That is, when there are only 1000 distinct keys, the sample of size 1000 is able to represent this distribution exactly, and hence can answer any query perfectly. In more realistic situations, k is less than b (often, much less than b). However, we see even for $k = 100$, corresponding to 10% of the active keys, we see that aSH does a good job of answering the query. This holds even for $b = 100,000$, meaning the sample can capture

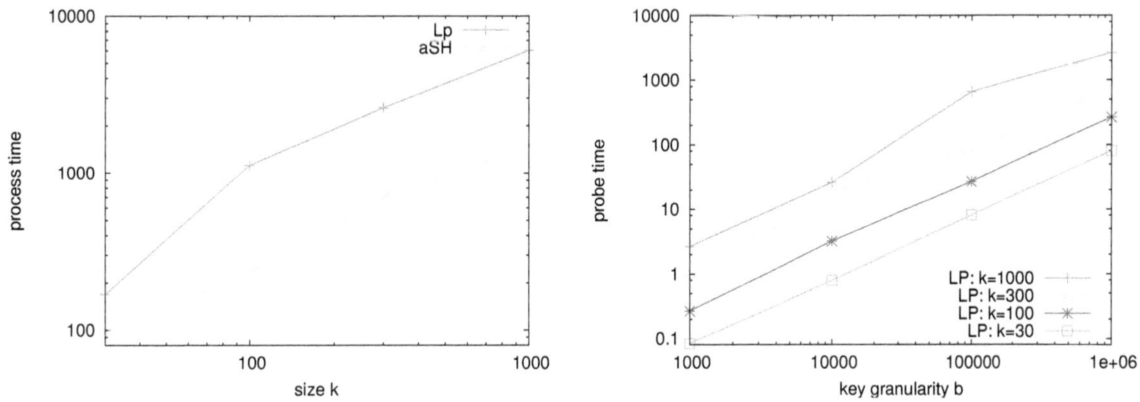

(a) Update Processing Time (in seconds) as a function of sample size k for aSH and L_p.

(b) Query Probe Time (in seconds) as a function of key granularity b for L_p.

Figure 3: Timing results for stream processing and querying

only 0.1% of the keyspace. We note the accuracy tends to improve as a decreases, meaning that there are fewer bins for the query, and hence more keys in each bin. In this case, almost every query is answered with high accuracy.

In contrast, the accuracy from L_p sampling is quite low. The main reason is the much higher space overhead of this method. As noted above, even with space corresponding to $k = 1000$, L_p sampling only has room to recover up to 100 samples. Moreover, each attempt to recover a sample from the sketch fails with constant probability (this is an integral part of the method, which is needed to achieve the correct sample distribution). In practice, we were only able to recover a small number of samples, often only in the single figures. As a result, we observe that L_p sampling with space for $k = 1000$ is often outperformed by aSH with $k = 30$, i.e. aSH is more accurate even with a much smaller summary size.

Update Processing Time. Both aSH and L_p sampling were run using interpreted languages on the same system. We measured the total processing time associated with processing the update stream. The update processing times is largely independent of key granularity, and was observed to grow roughly linearly as a function of the sample size k; see Figure 3(a) which shows the cost on logarithmic axes. Under this implementation, L_p sampling is roughly half an order magnitude (i.e. five times) slower than aSH.

Asymptotically, L_p sampling is truly linear in k: it updates $O(k)$ different sketches, taking constant time for each. Hence, we do not expect to be able to improve substantially on this. The time cost for aSH includes the time to perform EJECTONE for every update. We note that the update time could be improved for aSH, at the expense of slightly increased space, by deferring this step. That is, suppose we buffer c arrivals, then perform c steps of EJECTONE, one after another. This can be shown to be equivalent to determining a new threshold τ_c^* which is sufficient to eject c keys. Then we can perform a single pass over the $c+k$ keys and track the c'th largest threshold in a heap. Thus, setting $c = O(k)$ means that the update time could be reduced to $O(\log k)$, allowing larger samples to be drawn efficiently.

Query Answering Time. For the aSH summary, answering queries is trivial: we just have to read the explicitly maintained counts and thresholds, and use these within the SUBSETSUMEST routine. In our experiments, this time was essentially nil. However, this is not the case for the L_p sampling case, due to the need to test the sketch-estimated count each potential key value. Figure 3(b) displays the time to answer perform this extraction as a function of key granularity b for different buffer sizes k. The results are in accordance with the asymptotic cost, growing as $O(bk)$. At the extreme end, the cost is of the order of 45 minutes to extract a sample over a domain of $b = 10^6$, making real time analysis infeasible. We would argue that this is not a particularly large domain (e.g. IP addresses span a domain 3 orders of magnitude larger). From this, we conclude that the time cost of working with L_p sampling is too high for anything above a moderate sized domain. In contrast, the time cost for working with aSH sampling is independent of b.

5. CONCLUDING REMARKS

In many situations, data is presented in the form of streams of updates which can include negative weights. When these streams become large, it is important to be able to accurately maintain a sample over them. We have introduced an aSH sampling technique for such streams of weighted, signed updates, which is unbiased and has zero co-variance between estimated keys. The procedure is easy to implement. In our experimental study, we observed that its performs substantially better than the L_p sampling technique based on sketches: given the same amount of space, aSH is more accurate, faster to process the stream, and dramatically faster to answer queries.

Looking beyond this work, we note that other models of streaming arrivals are also of interest, but have similarly received relatively little attention. One important case is that of the *overwrite streams* model, where an update of the form (i, v) means that the weight associated with key i is updated to v. The update $(i, 0)$ corresponds to deletion of the key. This model captures a simple notion of "updating" information about a key. It is also of interest since many natural streaming problems are hard in this setting, meaning that they require space linear in the size of the input; see e.g. [16].

In contrast, a sampling algorithm for constant rate $q = 1/\tau$ is straightforward: if a key is observed which is already stored in the cache, eject it. Then independently decide whether to retain the current key, based on its weight v and τ. Correctness—i.e., that this is distributed as a Poisson sample on the final values for each key—is immediate. It is more challenging to manage a fixed-sized cache S. Here, again, overwrites deplete the cache, but arrivals can cause the cache size to be exceeded. In this case, we must choose a key to eject, in a similar way to EJECTONE, based on a local τ_i for each. We leave further study of this model to future work.

6. REFERENCES

[1] A. Andoni, R. Krauthgamer, and K. Onak. Streaming algorithms from precision sampling. Technical Report 1011.1263, arXiv, 2010.

[2] B. Babcock, M. Datar, and R. Motwani. Sampling from a moving window over streaming data. In *ACM-SIAM Symposium on Discrete Algorithms*, pages 633–634, 2002.

[3] V. Braverman, R. Ostrovsky, and C. Zaniolo. Optimal sampling from sliding windows. In *ACM Principles of Database Systems*, 2009.

[4] M. Charikar, K. Chen, and M. Farach-Colton. Finding frequent items in data streams. In *Proceedings of the International Colloquium on Automata, Languages and Programming (ICALP)*, pages 693–703, 2002.

[5] E. Cohen, N. Duffield, H. Kaplan, C. Lund, and M. Thorup. Algorithms and estimators for accurate summarization of Internet traffic. In *Proceedings of the 7th ACM SIGCOMM conference on Internet measurement (IMC)*, 2007.

[6] E. Cohen, N. Duffield, H. Kaplan, C. Lund, and M. Thorup. Sketching unaggregated data streams for subpopulation-size queries. In *Proc. of the 2007 ACM Symp. on Principles of Database Systems (PODS 2007)*. ACM, 2007.

[7] E. Cohen and H. Kaplan. Summarizing data using bottom-k sketches. In *Proceedings of the ACM PODC'07 Conference*, 2007.

[8] E. Cohen and H. Kaplan. Tighter estimation using bottom-k sketches. In *Proceedings of the 34th VLDB Conference*, 2008.

[9] G. Cormode, S. Muthukrishnan, and I. Rozenbaum. Summarizing and mining inverse distributions on data streams via dynamic inverse sampling. In *International Conference on Very Large Data Bases*, 2005.

[10] C. Estan and G. Varghese. New directions in traffic measurement and accounting. In *Proceedings of the ACM SIGCOMM'02 Conference*. ACM, 2002.

[11] G. Frahling, P. Indyk, and C. Sohler. Sampling in dynamic data streams and applications. In *Symposium on Computational Geometry*, June 2005.

[12] R. Gemulla, W. Lehner, and P. J. Haas. A dip in the reservoir: Maintaining sample synopses of evolving datasets. In *VLDB*, pages 595–606, 2006.

[13] R. Gemulla, W. Lehner, and P. J. Haas. Maintaining bernoulli samples over evolving multisets. In *PODS 2007*, pages 93–102. ACM, 2007.

[14] P. Gibbons and Y. Matias. New sampling-based summary statistics for improving approximate query answers. In *SIGMOD*. ACM, 1998.

[15] P. Gibbons and S. Tirthapura. Estimating simple functions on the union of data streams. In *Proceedings of the 13th Annual ACM Symposium on Parallel Algorithms and Architectures*. ACM, 2001.

[16] M. Hoffmann, S. Muthukrishnan, and R. Raman. Streaming algorithms for data in motion. In *ESCAPE*, pages 294–304, 2007.

[17] H. Jowhari, M. Saglam, and G. Tardos. Tight bounds for Lp samplers, finding duplicates in streams, and related problems. In *PODS*, pages 49–58, 2011.

[18] D. E. Knuth. *The Art of Computer Programming, Vol 2, Seminumerical Algorithms*. Addison-Wesley, 2nd edition, 1998.

[19] G. Manku and R. Motwani. Approximate frequency counts over data streams. In *International Conference on Very Large Databases (VLDB)*, pages 346–357, 2002.

[20] M. Monemizadeh and D. P. Woodruff. 1-pass relative-error l_p-sampling with applications. In *Proc. 21st ACM-SIAM Symposium on Discrete Algorithms*. ACM-SIAM, 2010.

[21] B. Rosén. Asymptotic theory for successive sampling with varying probabilities without replacement, I. *The Annals of Mathematical Statistics*, 43(2):373–397, 1972.

[22] J. Vitter. Random sampling with a reservoir. *ACM Trans. Math. Softw.*, 11(1):37–57, 1985.

Efficient Rank Aggregation Using Partial Data

Ammar Ammar
Massachusetts Institute of Technology
32 Vassar St.
Cambridge, USA
ammar@mit.edu

Devavrat Shah*
Massachusetts Institute of Technology
32 Vassar St.
Cambridge, USA
devavrat@mit.edu

ABSTRACT

The need to rank items based on user input arises in many practical applications such as elections, group decision making and recommendation systems. The primary challenge in such scenarios is to decide on a global ranking based on partial preferences provided by users. The standard approach to address this challenge is to ask users to provide explicit numerical ratings (cardinal information) of a subset of the items. The main appeal of such an approach is the ease of aggregation. However, the rating scale as well as the individual ratings are often arbitrary and may not be consistent from one user to another. A more natural alternative to numerical ratings requires users to compare pairs of items (ordinal information). On the one hand, such comparisons provide an "absolute" indicator of the user's preference. On the other hand, it is often hard to combine or aggregate these comparisons to obtain a consistent global ranking.

In this work, we provide a tractable framework for utilizing comparison data as well as first-order marginal information (see Section 2) for the purpose of ranking. We treat the available information as partial samples from an unknown distribution over permutations. We then reduce ranking problems of interest to performing inference on this distribution. Specifically, we consider the problems of (a) finding an aggregate ranking of n items, (b) learning the mode of the distribution, and (c) identifying the top k items. For many of these problems, we provide efficient algorithms to infer the ranking directly from the data *without* the need to estimate the underlying distribution. In other cases, we use the Principle of Maximum Entropy to devise a concise parameterization of a distribution consistent with observations using only $O(n^2)$ parameters, where n is the number of items in question. We propose a distributed, iterative algorithm for estimating the parameters of the distribution. We establish the correctness of the algorithm and identify its rate of convergence explicitly.

*This work was supported in parts by AFOSR Complex Networks Program, MURI on Tomography of Social Networks and NSF CMMI Program. We would like to acknowledge useful conversations with Vivek Farias, Srikanth Jagabathula, and Andrea Montanari.

SIGMETRICS'12, June 11–15, 2012, London, England, UK.

Categories and Subject Descriptors

G.3 [**Information Systems Applications**]: Statistical Computing

Keywords

Ranking, Aggregation, Maximum Entropy

1. INTRODUCTION

Judging, rating, or ranking objects is omnipresent: whether it be restaurants in a city, movies on Netflix, books on Amazon, candidates interviewed for faculty positions or papers submitted to the ACM Sigmetrics conference. In all such instances, a global ranking of objects is achieved based on the inputs about partial rankings provided by a large number of people.

The current practice is to seek input in terms of scores, e.g. assign between 1 to 5 stars to a restaurant/movie or score between 1 to 5 for a paper. The key advantage of seeking such quantitative input is that it is easy to achieve global aggregation: in Sigmetrics, for example, each paper may receive scores from, say 5 TPC reviewers, between 1 to 5; the average of these scores will lead to the global ranking of all the submitted papers to assist in making the final acceptance/rejection decisions in the TPC meeting.

On the flip side, the key disadvantage stems from the fact that scores are *relative*: the score of 4, for example, may be interpreted differently by different individuals. Furthermore, the same individual may score objects differently depending upon the contextual details, such as the order in which s/he reviewed the assigned papers. While one may argue that it could be possible to correct for such reviewer "biases" using auxiliary information, such an approach is somewhat adhoc and even not feasible when the ratings are obtained anonymously.

An alternative approach of seeking input,which we advocate in this paper, is qualitative [1] : for example, ask reviewers explicitly to compare the papers they reviewed (score assignments do not necessarily achieve this as there could

[1]We believe that in an ideal system, inputs of both forms should be obtained for better decision making. In this paper, we focus on qualitative inputs primarily to understand what sorts of information, on its own, does it contain.

be a tie and in the context of anonymous ratings, this is totally different from quantitative rating). One key advantage of seeking such information is that it is more *absolute*: when two individuals say they like A over B, they do mean the same; or a reviewer is likely to compare two papers in the same way despite the order in which they review them. It is no surprise that some polling sites (e.g. Washington Post [1]) have started using such interfaces to collect information. Further, in many settings data is naturally available in this form; for instance, customers reveal their preferences among items on display at a store by purchasing one of them, cf. [15].

The key challenge with qualitative information arises in the aggregation phase, due to possible contradictions: for three items A, B and C, we could have a scenario where one person prefers A over B, another prefers B over C, and two people prefer C over A as shown in Figure 1. Such apparent conflicts have created challenges for aggregation over the centuries starting with the celebrated work of Condorcet [9]; also see work on impossibility of existence of rankings pioneered by Arrow [5]. Unlike the standard setting of the, so called, ranked elections considered in the literature following the works [9] [5], in our context, we have access to partial ranking information of objects: in general, we have a fraction of population comparing a given pair of objects unlike in the standard ranked election literature where each individual provides complete ranking.

The main contribution of this paper lies in a proposal of a novel method for aggregation of such partial (qualitative) ranking information to come up with a global ranking. The key insight is to view the collected data as the partial information about an underlying distribution over complete orderings of all objects. For example, the votes shown on the left in Figure 1 could have originated from the complete user preferences shown on the right.

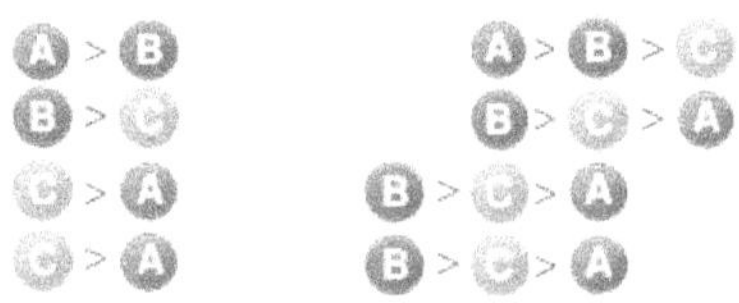

Figure 1: Data and Underlying Distribution

That said, the problem of aggregation reduces to making certain inferences on the underlying distribution. For many aggregation tasks, these inferences can be made directly from the data, with or without making assumptions about the underlying distribution. For other tasks, learning the distribution is necessary. Both cases are presented, and when the latter is the case, our approach involves finding the distribution with maximal entropy (near) consistent with the observed data. The inference problems and our solutions are summarized in the table below.

Problem	First-Order	Comparison
Aggregate Ranking	From Data	From Data
Mode	From Data	Max-Ent
Top-K Ranking	From Data	Max-Ent

Table 1: Summary of results.

In Table 1, we use "From Data" to indicate the combination of data type and problem that can be solved directly from the data, and "Max-Ent" to indicate those where learning an underlying distribution (a maximum entropy one in our case), is necessary. Before we describe these contributions in further detail, we quickly recall related work.

Related Work. The question of learning distribution over permutations from partial or limited information has been well studied in the recent literature. Notably, in the work of Huang, Guestrin and Guibas [18], the task of interest is to infer the most likely permutation of identities of objects that are being tracked through noisy sensing by maintaining distribution over permutations. To deal with the 'factorial blowup', authors propose to maintain only the first-order marginal information of the distribution (essentially corresponding to certain Fourier coefficients), then use the Fourier inversion formula to recover the distribution and subsequently predict its mode as the likely assignment. In the work by Jagabathula and Shah [19], authors took a different approach to the same problem where they proposed to learn the distributed over permutations by finding the sparsest distribution consistent with the observed partial information. Finally, this approach was further extended and integrated with the decision making in the context of revenue management in work by Farias, Jagabathula and Shah [15]. None of these works, however, deals with the question of aggregation or achieving ranking. While the mode of the distribution is a candidate for such a ranking, it might not necessarily be a robust one. It should also be noted that, through maximum entropy distribution learning, we are trying to be maximally unconstrained subject to observed data, unlike the above cited approaches which implicitly or explicitly impose additional constraints (e.g. sparsity).

The task of ranking objects or assigning scores has been of great interest over the past decade or so with similar concerns. There is a long list of works, primarily in the context of bipartite ranking, including the RankBoost by Freund et al. [16], label ranking by Dekel et al. [11], Crammer and Singer [10], Shalev-Shwartz and Singer [25] as well as analytic, learning results on bipartite ranking including those of Agarwal et al. [3], Usunier et al. [27] and Rudin and Schapire [24]. The algorithm that will be closest to our proposal is the p-norm push algorithm by Rudin [23] which uses ℓ_p norm of information to achieve ranking.

The algorithmic view on rank aggregation was revived in work by Dwork et al [13] where they consider design of approximation algorithms to find 'optimal' ranking with respect to a specific metric on permutations. Very recently, a high-dimensional statistical inference view for learning distribution over permutations based on comparison data has been introduced by Mitliagkas et al [22].

The maximum entropy approach for learning distribution is a classical one dating back to the work of Boltzman. The maximum entropy (max-ent) distribution, a member of an appropriate exponential distribution family, is maximum likelihood estimation of the parameters in that family (cf. see [29]). Indeed, the use of exponential family distribution over rankings has been around for more than few decades now (cf. see [12, Chapter 9]). We provide a careful analysis of a stochastic sub-gradient algorithm for learning the parameters of this max-entropy distribution. This algorithm is distributed and iterative. It directly builds upon the algorithm used in [21] for distributed wireless scheduling. It is worth taking note of use of maximum entropy distribution over permutation based on given marginal information to learn the "missing" marginals by Agrawal et al [4] in the context of parimutuel betting.

Our contributions. The primary contribution of this paper is the use of the framework of distributions over permutations as means to reach rank aggregation from collection of partial preferences.

In our setting, the data available for ranking comes in two different flavors: (a) pair-wise comparison data (e.g. item i is preferred to item j), and (b) first-order marginal data (e.g. item i is ranked in position k). Given data in either form, we focus our attention on three aggregation problems: (1) finding an aggregate ranking over a collection of items (e.g. NetFlix movies), (2) finding the most likely ordering of the items (e.g. object tracking a la [18]), and (3) identifying the top-k items in a collection (e.g. selecting accepted papers for Sigmetrics 2012, such as this one). We solve (1) by introducing a general method which gives each item a score that reflects its importance according to the distribution. We then present a specific instance of this method which allows us to compute the desired scores from the data (comparison or first-order marginal) directly, without the need to learn the distribution. More importantly, we show that the ranking induced by this scoring method is equivalent to the ranking obtained from the family of Thurstone (1927, [26]; also see [12, Ch 9]) models, a popular family of parametric distributions used in a wide range of applications (e.g. online gaming and airline ticket pricing). For (2), we use the principle of maximum entropy to derive a concise parameterization of an underlying distribution (most) consistent with the data. Given the form of the max-ent distribution (an exponential family), computing the mode reduces to solving a maximum-weight matching problem on a bipartite graph with weights induced from the parameters. For the case of first-order marginals, this is an easy instance of the network-flow problem (can be solved, for example, using belief propagation [6]). Furthermore, we propose a heuristic for mode computation as well that bypasses the step of learning the max-ent parameters but uses directly the available partial preference data. Such a heuristic, for example, can speed up computation of [18] drastically. Somewhat curiously, we show that this heuristic is first-order approximation of the mode finding of the max-ent distribution. For pair-wise comparisons representation, the problem is not known to be solvable in polynomial time. We propose a simple randomized scheme that is a 2-approximation of it. We solve problem (3) using another distribution-based scoring scheme where the scores can be computed directly from the data for first order marginals, or by learning a max-ent distribution in the case of comparisons.

We present a stochastic gradient algorithm for learning the max-ent distribution needed for some of the aforementioned problems. This algorithm is derived from [21], however the proof is different (and simpler). It provides explicit rate of convergence for both data types (comparisons and first-order marginals). In both cases, the algorithm uses an oracle to compute intermediate marginal expectations of the max-ent distibution. We prove that the exact computation of such marginal expectations is $\#P$-hard. Using standard MCMC methods and their known mixing time bounds, our analysis suggests that for a collection of n items, the computation time scales exponentially in n and polynomially in n respectively for the pair-wise comparisons and first-order marginals respectively. Two remarks are in order: first, the result for first-order marginals also suggests a distributed scheduling algorithm for input-queued switches with polynomial time learning complexity (unlike exponential for wireless network model). Second, the standard stochastic approximation based approaches cf. [8] do not apply as is (due to compactness of domain related issues).

2. MODEL AND PROBLEM STATEMENT

Model. We consider a universe of n available items, $\mathcal{N} = \{1, 2, ..., n\}$. Each user has preference order, represented as permutation, over these n items. Specifically, if σ is the permutation, the user prefers item i over j if $\sigma(i) < \sigma(j)$. We assume that there is a distribution, say μ, over the space of permutations of n items, S_n, that defines the collective preferences of the entire user population.

Data. We consider scenarios where we have access to partial or limited information about μ. Specifically, we shall restrict our attention to two popular types of data: first-order ranking and comparisons. Each of these two types correspond to some sort of marginal distribution of μ as follows:

First-order marginals: For any $1 \leq i, k \leq n$, the fraction of population that ranks item i as their kth choice is the first-order marginal information for distribution μ. Specifically,

$$m_{ik} \triangleq \mathbb{P}_\mu[\{\sigma(i) = k\}] = \sum_{\sigma \in S_n} \mu(\sigma)\mathbb{I}_{\{\sigma(i)=k\}} \qquad (1)$$

where $\mathbb{I}_{\{E\}}$ denotes the indicator variable for event E. Collectively, we have the $n \times n$ matrix $[m_{ij}]$ of the first-order marginals, that we shall denote by M. This is the type of information that was maintained for tracking agents in the framework introduced by Huang, Guestrin and Guibas [18].

Comparison Data: For any $1 \leq i, j \leq n$, the fraction of population that prefers item i over item j is the comparison marginal information. Specifically,

$$c_{ij} \triangleq \mathbb{P}_\mu[\{\sigma(i) < \sigma(j)\}] = \sum_{\sigma \in S_n} \mu(\sigma)\mathbb{I}_{\{\sigma(i)<\sigma(j)\}}. \qquad (2)$$

Collectively, we have access to the $n \times n$ matrix $[c_{ij}]$ of comparison marginals, denoted by C. Such data is available through customer transactions in many businesses, cf. [15].

Remarks. First, while we assume m_{ik} (resp. c_{ij}) available for all i, k (resp. i, j), if only a subset of it is available, the algorithm with that information works equally well, with the obvious caveat that the quality of the output is dependant on the richness of our data. Second, we shall assume that $m_{ik} \in (0, 1)$ for all i, k (resp. $c_{ij} \in (0, 1)$ for all i, j). Finally, in practice one may have a noisy version of M or C data. However, the procedures we describe are inherently robust (as they are simple continuous functions of the observed data) with respect to small noise in the data. Therefore, for the purpose of conceptual development, such an idealized assumption is reasonable.

Goal. Roughly speaking, the goal is to utilize data of type M or C to obtain various useful rankings of the objects of interest. Specifically, we are interested in (a) finding an aggregate or representative ranking over the items in question,

(b) finding 'most likely' (or mode) ranking, and (c) finding a ranking that emphasizes the top k objects.

To address these questions, we propose the following approach: (a) assume that the data originates from some underlying distribution over permutations. (b) Use the data to answer the question directly, without learning the distribution, whenever possible. (c) Otherwise, learn a distribution that is consistent with the data (M or C), and use said distribution to answer the question. In principle, there could be multiple, possibly infinitely many, distributions that are consistent with the observed data (M or C, assuming it is generated by a consistent underlying unknown distribution). As mentioned earlier, we shall choose the max-ent distribution that is consistent with the observed data.

Result outline. Here we provide somewhat detailed explanation of the results summarized in the table presented earlier. Specifically, we solve problems (a), (b), and (c) as follows. To find an aggregate ranking (Section 3.1), we assign each item a score derived from the distribution over permutations. We then propose an efficient algorithm to compute said score directly from the data, without learning the distribution . We show that the ranking induced by the computed scores is equivalent to the ranking induced by the parametric family of Thurstone models [26][12, Ch 9] (Section 3.1), a popular family of distributions used in applications ranging from online gaming to airline ticket pricing. Effectively, our result implies that if one learns *any* of the distributions in this family from the data, and uses the learned parameters to obtain a ranking, then this ranking is *identical* to the ranking we obtain directly from the data (i.e. no need to learn the distribution)!

As for the mode of the distribution, we assume a maximum entropy underlying model, and derive a concise parameterization of the model using $O(n^2)$ parameters (Section 3.2). We also show that finding the mode of the distribution is equivalent to solving an optimization problem on these parameters. In the case of First-Order Marginals (see [18]), this problem is easy and can be solved using max-weight matching on a bipartite graph. We also provide an efficient heuristic for finding the mode in the case of first-order marginal data directly from the data, without learning the max-ent distribution. In the case of comparison data, the problem is more challenging. In this case, we provide an 2-approximation algorithm for finding the mode. In Section 3.3, for the top-k ranking problem, we propose a score that emphasizes the top-k items. We show that this score can be computed exactly and directly from First-Order Marginal data, and approximated using the max-ent distribution in the case of comparison data.

3. MAIN RESULTS

Before we get into the details of estimation the distribution, lets consider the problem of ranking given said distribution. More precisely, lets assume that we are given a distribution over permutations μ, and asked to obtain an ordered list of the items of interest that reflects the collective preference implied by the distribution. A classical approach in this setting is the axiomatic one. In this approach one comes up with a set of axioms that the ranked list should satisfy, and then try to come up with a ranking function or algorithm that satisfies these axioms. Unfortunately, seemingly natural axioms cannot be satisfied by any algorithm [5].

In this section, we opt for a non-axiomatic approach to aggregate preferences. We address the problems of finding: (a) an overall aggregate ranking of all items, (b) the mode of the distribution, and a (c) top-k ranking. These problems demonstrate the utility of having or assuming an underlying distribution, and give rise to situations where one can bypass the learning step and use the data directly for ranking. In the latter situation, one can make the conceptual use of assuming a distribution, without performing complicated computations to obtain a ranking.

3.1 Aggregate Ranking

Here we propose a method to obtain an entire ranking of all objects. Building on the intuition followed by popular voting rules, the basic premise is that the objects that are ranked higher more frequently should be getting higher ranking. This can be formalized as follows: for any monotonically strictly increasing non-negative function $f : \mathbb{N} \to [0, \infty]$, define score $S_f(i)$ for object i as

$$S_f(i) = \sum_{k=1}^{n} f(n-k)\mathbb{P}(\sigma(i) = k). \quad (3)$$

The choice of $f(x) = x^p$ assigns the pth norm of the distribution of $\sigma(i)$ as score to object i.

One can take this line of reasoning further by noting that the exponential function for a given $\Theta > 0$, $f_\Theta(x) = \exp(\Theta x)$, effectively captures the combined effect of all p-norms. Therefore, we propose, what we call the Θ-ranking, with scores defined as:

$$S_\Theta(i) = \sum_{k=1}^{n} \exp(-\Theta k)\mathbb{P}(\sigma(i) = k). \quad (4)$$

By selection $\Theta \approx \ln k$, the scores are effectively capturing the occurrence of objects in top k positions only; and for Θ near 0 they are capturing the effect of lower p moments more prominently. Furthermore, intermediate choices of Θ give effective ranking for various scenarios.

We focus our attention on the case where $p = 1$, and present a score that can take us directly from the data to the ranking, without the intermediate step of learning the distribution. We refer to this ranking as the ℓ_1 ranking.

ℓ_1 *Ranking*

The ℓ_1 score is given by:

$$S_1(i) = \sum_{k=1}^{n} (n-k) \cdot \mathbb{P}[\sigma(i) = k]$$

In the case of first-order marginal data, this score can be computed in a straightforward way. For comparison data, however, the marginals $\mathbb{P}[\sigma(i) = k]$ are not available, without having the distribution. Fortunately, the score above can be computed from the data directly in the following form:

$$S(i) = \frac{1}{n-1} \sum_{j \neq i} \mathbb{P}[\sigma(i) < \sigma(j)] = \frac{1}{n-1} \sum_{j \neq i} c_{ij}$$

using the following lemma:

LEMMA 1. *Given the definition of $S(i)$ and $S_1(i)$ above, we have*

$$S_1(i) = S(i)$$

A proof of this lemma is provided in Section 6. One interesting aspect of this shortcut is that the equivalence between the different scores does not assume any particular distribution. It only assumes that the underlying distribution is consistent with the data. This suggests that the produced ranking should work with different distributions. One family of such distributions is the one based on the celebrated model of Thurstone [26][12, Ch 9], as we shall see in the next section.

Why ℓ_1 Ranking?

Here we demonstrate the utility of our ℓ_1 ranking by showing its equivalence to the ranking obtained using a Thurstone model. In a Thurstone model, preferences over n items come from a "hidden" process as follows: the "favorability" of each item i is a random variable $X_i = u_i + Z_i$, where u_i is an unknown parameter (also known as the skill parameter), and Z_i is a random variable with some distribution. Furthermore, the random variables $Z_1, ..., Z_n$ are identically distributed. If we take the tuple $(x_1, x_2, ..., x_n)$ to be the outcome of some trial, then item j is ranked in position k if x_j is ranked kth among the values $x_1, ..., x_n$. Equivalently, item i is preferred to item j if $x_i > x_j$. In a typical application of such models one observes these comparisons or positional rankings, and uses these observations to infer the values of the unkown parameters $u_1, ..., u_n$. These values are then used to find a ranking over all items. More precisely, items $i > j > ... > k$ if $u_i > u_j > ... > u_k$.

As it turns out, the ranking obtained by following the algorithm based on ℓ_1 scores is equivalent to the ranking one would get by fitting a Thurstone model. The formal statement is as follows:

THEOREM 1. *Let u_i and u_j be the (skill) parameters assigned to item i and j (respectively) in a Thurstone model, and let $S(i)$ and $S(j)$ be the score assigned to the same items using our method (ℓ_1 scores), then:*

$$u_j \leq u_i \qquad \Leftrightarrow \qquad S(j) \leq S(i) \qquad \forall i, j \tag{5}$$

A proof of this theorem is provided in Section 6. Thurstone models have been used in a wide range of applications such as revenue management in airline ticket sales, and player ranking in online gaming platforms (e.g. a variant of this model is used in Microsoft's TrueSkill [17]).

3.2 The Mode

Given a distribution over permutations that is consistent with the data, in the context of object tracking (a la Huang et al. [18]) one would like to find the most likely permutation under said distribution, or the mode. It is easy to see that the mode of a distribution over permutations is hard to compute in general. To address this difficulty, one might want to follow some criteria for selecting a tractable class of distributions to deal with. Ideally, we would like distributions from this class to obey the constraints given by the data, without imposing any additional structure. This intuitive requirement is captured by the Maximum Entropy criterion, whereby we choose a distribution that maximizes the information entropy while satisfying the data constraints. In the following section, we provide a formal derivation of the maximum entropy distribution along those lines.

The Maximum Entropy Model

Formally, the observations M or C impose the constraints that the distribution, μ, should belong to class $\mathcal{M}$:

$$\sum_{\sigma \in S_n} \mu(\sigma) \mathbb{I}_{\{\sigma(i)=k\}} = m_{ik}, \quad \forall i, k \in \mathcal{N} \tag{6}$$

or class $\mathcal{C}$:

$$\sum_{\sigma \in S_n} \mu(\sigma) \mathbb{I}_{\{\sigma(i)<\sigma(j)\}} = c_{ij}, \quad \forall i, j \in \mathcal{N} \tag{7}$$

with the the normalization and non-negativity constraints in both cases.

$$\sum_{\sigma \in S_n} \mu(\sigma) = 1, \quad \mu(\sigma) \geq 0, \quad \forall \sigma \in S_n. \tag{8}$$

$\mathcal{M}$ (resp. $\mathcal{C}$) is non-empty only if M (resp. C) is generated by a distribution over S_n to begin with. For clarity of exposition, we will assume that this is the case. When this is not the case, The algorithm that we shall present is based on the solving the Lagrangian dual of an appropriate optimization problem in which the constraints imposed by M (resp. C) are "dualized". Therefore, by construction such algorithm is robust.

Now $|S_n| = n!$ and the data of type M (resp. C) imposes $O(n^2)$ constraints. Therefore, there could be multiple solutions. The max-ent principle suggests that we choose the one that has maximal entropy in the class $\mathcal{M}$ (resp. $\mathcal{C}$). Philosophically, we follow this approach since we wish to utilize the information provided by the data and nothing else, i.e. we do not wish to impose any additional structure beyond what data suggests. It is also well known that such a distribution provides maximum likelihood estimation over certain class of exponential family distributions (cf. [29]). In effect, the goal is to find the distribution that solves the following optimization:

$$\begin{aligned} \max_{\nu} \quad & H_{\text{ER}}(\nu) \triangleq - \sum_{\sigma \in S_N} \nu(\sigma) \log \nu(\sigma) \\ & \nu \in \mathcal{M} \quad \text{or} \quad \mathcal{C}. \end{aligned} \tag{9}$$

It can be checked that the Lagrangian dual of this problem is as follows (since all entries of M, C in $(0, 1)$): let λ_{ik} be the dual variables associated with marginal consistency constraint for $\mathcal{M}$ in (6). Then, the dual takes the following form:

$$\max_{\lambda} \sum_{i,k} \lambda_{ik} m_{ik} - \log \Big(\sum_{\sigma} \exp \Big(\sum_{ik} \lambda_{ik} \mathbb{I}_{\{\sigma(i)=k\}} \Big) \Big) \tag{10}$$

It can be shown that this is a strictly concave optimization and has a unique optimal solution. Let it be $\lambda^* = [\lambda^*_{ik}]$. Then the corresponding primal optimal solution of (9) (with $\mathcal{M}$) is given by

$$\mu(\sigma) \propto \exp \Big(\sum_{i,k \in \mathcal{N}} \lambda^*_{ik} \cdot \mathbb{I}_{\{\sigma(i)=k\}} \Big). \tag{11}$$

Similarly, for the comparison data, the dual optimization takes the form

$$\max_{\lambda} \sum_{i,j} \lambda_{i<j} c_{ij} - \log\Big(\sum_{\sigma} \exp\Big(\sum_{ij} \lambda_{i<j} \mathbb{I}_{\{\sigma(i)<\sigma(j)\}}\Big)\Big), \quad (12)$$

and the optimal primal of (9) given optimal dual $\lambda^* = [\lambda^*_{i<j}]$ is

$$\mu(\sigma) \propto \exp\Big(\sum_{i\neq j\in\mathcal{N}} \lambda^*_{i<j} \cdot \mathbb{I}_{\{\sigma(i)<\sigma(j)\}}\Big). \quad (13)$$

As can be seen, in either case the maximum entropy distribution is parameterized by at most n^2 parameters, which is the same as the degrees of freedom of the received data. For future purposes and with a slight abuse of notation, we shall use $F(\lambda)$ to represent the objective of both Lagrangian dual optimization problems (10) and (12).

Computing the Mode

Having restricted our attention to the maximum entropy distribution, we now proceed to compute the mode. We begin by providing an algorithm for computing the mode exactly in the case of First-Order Marginal data. We then present a more efficient algorithm for approximating the same mode directly from the data without the need to learn the max-ent distribution. Finally, we present an algorithm that uses the max-ent distribution to compute a 2-approximation of the mode in the general case.

Recall that under the maximum-entropy distribution, the logarithm of the probability of a permutation σ is proportional to $\sum_{i,k} \lambda_{ik}\mathbb{I}_{\{\sigma(i)=k\}}$ for first-order marginal data, and $\sum_{i,j} \lambda_{i<j}\mathbb{I}_{\{\sigma(i)<\sigma(j)\}}$ for comparison data. Since the log function is monotone, finding the mode, in both cases, boils down to finding:

$$\sigma^* \in \arg\max_{\sigma\in S_n} \Big(\sum_{i,k} \lambda_{ik}\mathbb{I}_{\{\sigma(i)=k\}}\Big) \quad (14)$$

$$\sigma^* \in \arg\max_{\sigma\in S_n} \Big(\sum_{i,j} \lambda_{i<j}\mathbb{I}_{\{\sigma(i)<\sigma(j)\}}\Big) \quad (15)$$

Solving the problem in (14) exactly is equivalent to the following maximum weight matching problem: consider an $n \times n$ complete bipartite graph with edge between node i on left and node k on right having weight λ_{ik}. A matching is a subset (of size n) edges so that no two edges are incident on same vertext. Let the weight of the matching be the summation of the weights of the edge chosen by it. Then the maximum weight matching in this graph is precisely solving (14). This is a well known instance of the classical network flow problem and has strongly polynomial time algorithms [14]. It also allows for distributed iterative algorithm for finding it including the auction algorithm of Bertsekas [7] and the recently popular (max-product) belief propagation [6]. Thus, overall finding the mode of the distribution for the case of first-order marginal is *easy* and admits distributed algorithmic solution.

Next, we describe a (heuristic) method for finding the mode without requiring the intermediate step of finding the max-ent parameters λ in the case of first-order marginal data. Declare the solution of the following optimization as the mode:

$$\max \sum_{i,k} m_{ik}\mathbb{I}_{\{\sigma(i)=k\}}.$$

That is, in place of λ_{ik}, use m_{ik}. The intuition is that λ_{ik} is higher if m_{ik} is and vice versa. While there is no direct relation between this heuristic and mode of the max-ent approximation, we state the following result which establishes the heuristic to be a 'first-order' approximation. A proof is provided in Section 6.

THEOREM 2. *For $\lambda = [\lambda_{ik}]$ in small enough neighborhood of $\mathbf{0} = [0]$,*

$$m_{ik} \approx \frac{1}{n} + \frac{1}{n-1}\lambda_{ik}.$$

For comparison data, the problem in (15) is also equivalent to a combinatorial problem with the space of objects being the matchings. However, it does not admit the nice representation as above. One way to represent the matchings in comparison form is $n \times n$ matrices, say $B = [B_{ij}]$ with (a) each entry B_{ij} being $+1$ or -1 for all $1 \le i, j \le n$, (b) for all $1 \le i, j \le n$, $B_{ij} + B_{ji} = 0$ (anti-symmetric), and (c) if $B_{ij} = B_{jk} = 1$, then $B_{ik} = 1$ for all $1 \le i, j, k \le n$. The goal is to find B so that $\sum_{ij} B_{ij}\lambda_{i<j}$ is maximized. It is not clear if this is an easy problem.

To address this problem, we have the following 2-approx. algorithm to compute the mode using the parameters of the max-ent distribution: choose L permutatations uniformly at random, compute their weights (defined as per (15)) and select the one with maximal weight among these L permutations. For L large enough, this is essentially with $1/2$ weight of the maximum weight. This requires λ to have all non-negative components. This is not an issue since given the structure of the permutations (each having equal number comparisons, $\sigma(i) < \sigma(j)$, correct) and hence an affine transformation of λ by vector with all components being same constant does change the distribution. Therefore, in principle, we could require the subgradient algorithm to be restricted to the non-negative domain (projected verison). The formal statement about this algorithm is stated below.

THEOREM 3. *Let $\lambda = [\lambda_{i<j}]$ be non-negative vector. Let OPT be the maximum of $\sum_{ij} \lambda_{i<j}\mathbb{I}_{\{\sigma(i)<\sigma(j)\}}$ among all permutation $\sigma \in S_n$. Then in the above described randomized algorithm, if we choose $L \ge \frac{1}{2\delta}\ln\frac{1}{\epsilon}$, then*

$$\mathbb{P}\Big[W(\hat{\sigma}) < \frac{1}{2}(1-\delta)OPT\Big] < \epsilon$$

A proof of this theorem is included in Section 6. To complete the solution, we only need to estimate the parameters of the max-ent distribution. An algorithm is provided in Section 4.

3.3 Top-K Ranking

Here the interest is in finding a ranking that emphasizes the top k objects (the favorites). To do this, we can compute the aggregate ranking, or the mode, and then declare the top k ranked objects in resulting list. We propose a natural way to emphasize the favorites. Intuitively, if an object is ranked among top k positions by a large fraction (probability-wise) of the permutations in the distribution, then it ought to be among favorites. This suggests that for a distribution λ, each object i can be given a score $S_k(i)$, defined as

$$S_k(i) = \mathbb{P}_\lambda[\sigma(i) \le k],$$

In the case of first-order marginal data, this score is nothing but $\sum_{\ell \leq k} m_{i\ell}$, and can be computed directly from the data. In the case of comparison data, this score can be inferred from the max-ent distribution, which can be learned by the procedure outlined in Section 4. Finally, once the score is computed, we can now declare the top k objects with highest scores as per $S_k(\cdot)$ as the result of top k.

4. LEARNING THE MAX-ENT MODEL

Here we describe an iterative, distributed sub-gradient algorithm that solves the dual optimization problems (10), (12). First, we describe an idealized procedure that calls certain oracle that estimates marginals of distribution from exponential family. We can, in general, only hope to estimate these marginals approximately because the exact estimation, as we show later, is #*P*-hard. Therefore, the main result that we state is for a sub-gradient algorithm based on such an approximate oracle. In a later section, we shall describe how to design such an approximate oracle in a distributed manner along with its associated computational cost.

Algorithm 1 MaxEnt Estimation: Using Ideal Oracle

Require: Ranking data m_{ik} $\forall i, k$.

1: **Initialize:** $\lambda^0_{ik} = 0 \; \forall i, k$.
2: **for** $t = 1 \to T$ **do**
3: $\quad \lambda^{t+1}_{ik} \leftarrow \lambda^t_{ik} + \frac{1}{\sqrt{t}}\left(m_{ik} - \mathsf{E}_{\lambda^t}[\mathbb{I}_{\{\sigma(i)=k\}}]\right)$
$\quad$ ($\mathsf{E}_{\lambda^t}[\mathbb{I}_{\{\sigma(i)=k\}}]$ is provided by an oracle)
4: **end for**
5: Choose $\tau \in \{1, \ldots, T\}$ at random so that $\mathbb{P}(\tau = t) \propto 1/\sqrt{t}$
6: **return** λ^τ

Here, $\mathsf{E}_{\lambda^t}[\mathbb{I}_{\{\sigma(i)=k\}}] = \sum_{\sigma \in S_n} \mathbb{P}_{\lambda^t}(\sigma)\mathbb{I}_{\{\sigma(i)=k\}}$ where

$$\mathbb{P}_{\lambda^t}(\sigma) = \frac{1}{Z(\lambda^t)} \exp\Big(\sum_{i,k} \lambda^t_{ik}\mathbb{I}_{\{\sigma(i)=k\}}\Big),$$

with normalizing constant (partition function) defined as:

$$Z(\lambda^t) = \sum_{\sigma \in S_n} \exp\Big(\sum_{i,k} \lambda^t_{ik}\mathbb{I}_{\{\sigma(i)=k\}}\Big)$$

Instead of $\mathsf{E}_{\lambda^t}[\mathbb{I}_{\{\sigma(i)=k\}}]$, we will use a randomized estimation, $\tilde{\mathsf{E}}_{\lambda^t}(i,k) = \tilde{\mathsf{E}}_{\lambda^t}[\mathbb{I}_{\{\sigma(i)=k\}}]$, such that the error vector $\mathbf{e}(t) = [\mathbf{e}_{ik}(t)]$ where each component

$$\mathbf{e}_{ik}(t) = \mathsf{E}_{\lambda^t}[\mathbb{I}_{\{\sigma(i)=k\}}] - \tilde{\mathsf{E}}_{\lambda^t}(i,k)$$

is sufficiently small. We state the following result about the convergence of this algorithm.

THEOREM 4. *Suppose that each iteration of the sub-gradient algorithm uses an approximate estimate $\tilde{E}.(\cdot,\cdot)$ such that $\|\mathbf{e}(t)\|_1 \leq \frac{1}{A(t)+\|\lambda^*\|_\infty + \|\lambda^*\|_2^2}$, where $A(t) = \sum_{s=1}^t 1/\sqrt{s}$ and λ^* is a solution of the optimization problem. Then, for any $\gamma > 0$, for choice of $T = \Theta\Big(\epsilon^{-2-\delta}\big(n^2 + \|\lambda^*\|_\infty + \|\lambda^*\|_2^2\big)^{2+\delta}\Big)$, we have*

$$\mathsf{E}\Big[F(\lambda^\tau)\Big] \geq F(\lambda^*) - \epsilon,$$

where $F(\cdot)$ is the objective of dual optimization (10). The identical result holds for the comparison information (12).

A proof of this theorem is included in Section 6.

An Approximate Oracle

Theorem 4 relies on existence of an oracle that can produce an estimation of marginals approximately with appropriate accuracy for each time step t. Computing marginals exactly is computationally hard. For first-order marginal data, this follows from [4]. We prove a similar result for comparison data. Both results are summarized by the following theorem:

THEOREM 5. *Given a max-ent distribution λ, computing $\mathsf{E}_\lambda[\mathbb{I}_{\{\sigma(i)=k\}}]$ and $\mathsf{E}_\lambda[\mathbb{I}_{\{\sigma(i)<\sigma(j)\}}]$ is #P-hard.*

We skip the proof due to space constraint. We now describe an approximate oracle. We shall restrict our description to the Markov Chain Monte Carlo (MCMC) based oracle. In principle, one may use heuristics like Belief Propagation to estimate these marginals instead of MCMC (of course, this may lead to the loss of the performance guarantee).

Now the computation of marginals requires computing $\mathbb{P}_{\lambda^t}(\sigma)$ for any $\sigma \in S_n$. From its form, the basic challenge is in computing the partition function $Z(\lambda^t)$. The partition function $Z(\lambda^t)$ is the same as computation of permanent of a non-negative valued matrix $A = [A_{ik}]$ where $A_{ik} = \mathbf{e}^{\lambda_{ik}}$. In an amazing work, Jerrum, Sinclair and Vigoda [20] have designed Fully Polynomial Time Randomized Approximation Scheme (FPRAS) for computing permanent of any non-negative valued matrix. That is, $Z(\lambda^t)$ (hence $\mathbb{P}_{\lambda^t}(\sigma)$) can be computated within multiplicative accuracy $(1 \pm \varepsilon)$ in time polynomial in $1/\varepsilon, n, \log(1/\delta)$ with probability at least $1 - \delta$. Therefore, it follows that the desired guarantee in Theorem 4 can be provided for all timesteps (using union bound) with probability at least $1 - 1/n$ within polynomial in n building upon the algorithm of [20].

For the case of comparison information, however no such FPRAS algorithm for computing the partition function is known. Therefore, we suggest a simple MCMC based algorithm and provide the obvious (exponential) bound for it. To that end, define $W_\lambda(\sigma) = \sum_{i,k \in \mathcal{N}} \lambda_{ik} \cdot \mathbb{I}_{\{\sigma(i)<\sigma(j)\}}$, and construct a Markov chain, $\mathfrak{M}(\lambda)$, whose state space is the set of all permutations, S_n, and whose transitions from a given state σ to a new state σ' are given as follows:

1: With probability $\frac{1}{2}$ let $\sigma' = \sigma$.
2: Otherwise, construct σ' as follows:

- Choose two elements i and j uniformly at random; set $\tilde{\sigma}(i) = \sigma(j)$, $\tilde{\sigma}(j) = \sigma(i)$ and $\tilde{\sigma}(k) = \sigma(k)$ for all $k \neq i, j$.
- Set $\sigma' = \tilde{\sigma}$ with probability $\min\{1, \exp\big(W_\lambda(\tilde{\sigma}) - W_\lambda(\sigma)\big)\}$; else set $\sigma' = \sigma$.

Using this Markov chain, we estimate $\mathsf{E}_\lambda[\mathbb{I}_{\{\sigma(i)<\sigma(j)\}}]$ as follows: starting from any initial state, run the Markov chain for T_m steps and then record the state of the Markov chain, say σ^{T_m}. If $\sigma^{T_m}(i) < \sigma^{T_m}(j)$, then record 1 else record 0. Repeat this for S times and obtain the empirical average of the recorded 0/1 values. Declare this as the estimate of $\mathsf{E}_\lambda[\mathbb{I}_{\{\sigma(i)<\sigma(j)\}}]$. Indeed, one simultaneously obtains such estimates for all i, j. We have the following bound on T_c, which we establish in Section 6:

THEOREM 6. *The above stated Markov chain has stationary distribution μ^* so that*

$$\mu^*(\sigma) \propto \exp\Big(W_\lambda\Big).$$

Let $\mu(t)$ be the distribution of the Markov chain after t steps starting from any initial condition. Then for any given $\delta > 0$, there exists

$$T_c = \Theta\Big(\exp\Big(\Theta(n^2\|\lambda\|_\infty + n\log n)\Big)\log\frac{1}{\delta}\Big),$$

such that for $t \geq T_c$,

$$\Big\|\frac{\mu(t)}{\mu^*} - 1\Big\|_{2,\mu^*} < \delta,$$

where $\|\cdot\|_{2,\mu}$ is the χ^2 distance.

Now the total variation distance between $\mu(t)$ and μ^* is smaller than the χ^2 distance between them. Therefore, by Theorem 6, it follows that the estimation error of $\mathbb{P}_\lambda(\sigma)$ using $\mu(t)$ will be at most δ. From Chernoff's bound, by selecting S (mentioned above) to be $O(\delta^{-2}\log n)$ (with large enough constant), it will follow that the estimated empirical marginals for all i, j components must be within error $O(\delta)$ with probability $1 - 1/\text{poly}(n)$. Given that increment in each component of λ as part of the sub-gradient algorithm is $O(\sqrt{T})$ by time T, from Theorem 4, it follows that the $\|\lambda\|_\infty = O\big((n + \|\lambda^*\|_\infty + \|\lambda^*\|_2^2)^{1+\gamma}\big)$ (for any choice of $\gamma > 0$ in Theorem 4). Finally, the smallest δ required in Theorem 4 is an inverse polynomial in n, ϵ, from above discussion it follows that the overall cost of the approximate oracle required for the comparisons effectively scales exponentially in $n^{3+\gamma}$ (ignoring other smaller order terms).

5. EXPERIMENTS AND SCALABILITY

Here we provide results from a simple experiment to demonstrate that the ranking produced by our ℓ_1 algorithm converges to the right ranking for the Multinomial Logit Model, an instance of Thurstone model (choose Z_is to be i.i.d. logit distribution). Specifically, we sample distinct items i and j from $1, ..., n$ uniformly at random as per the distribution. We then consult an MNL model, defined using n parameters, for the value of $\mathbb{I}_{\{\sigma(i)<\sigma(j)\}}$. All the samples are then combined into a matrix $[c_ij]$, which is used to find the ℓ_1 ranking. In Figure 2, we show a plot of the error measured using the normalized number of discordant pairs versus the number of samples used for $n = 10$. As we can see, beyond 500 samples, the error induced is extremely small.

To test the scalability of our method, we implemented a voting/survey tool that enables a large number of participants to vote on any number of items in real time. By doing so, we had the following two questions in mind: in addition to being theoritically interesting, can our algorithm be applied in real time? is comparison based voting practical and simple enough for adoption? through this exeperiment, we believe the answer to both questions to be affirmative.

Our tool was installed in voting booths that were made available to the visitors of the MIT150 event [2], a university-wide public open house. Voting categories included movies, actors, musicians, atheletes, among others, and the results at any time were continuously displayed on a large screen. The participation was impressive, and the feedback was mostly positive, which makes us believe that adopting comparison as form of voting is worth a serious consideration.

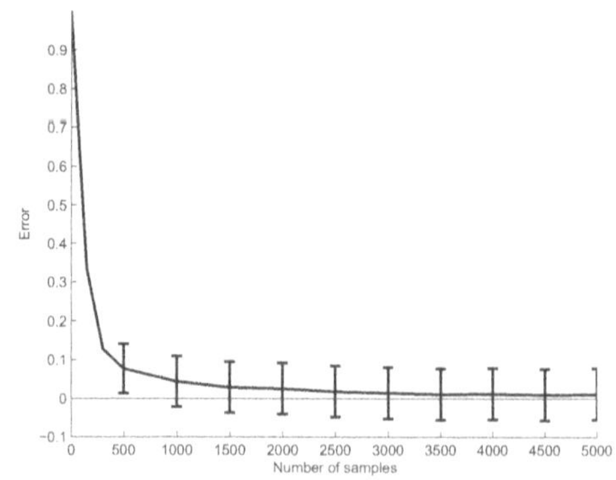

Figure 2: Plot of the error induced by ℓ_1 ranking algorithm for the MNL model, a specific instance of Thurstone's model.

6. PROOFS

This section provides detailed proofs of all the results stated earlier in the paper. Due to space constraints, proof of Theorems 5 and 6 are omitted from this version. [2].

6.1 Proof of Lemma 1

With some arithmetic manipulation, we get

$$\begin{aligned}
S(i) &= \frac{1}{n-1}\sum_{j\neq i}\sum_{\sigma_l\in S_n}\mathbb{P}[\sigma(i)<\sigma(j)|\sigma=\sigma_l]\mathbb{P}[\sigma=\sigma_l] \\
&= \frac{1}{n-1}\sum_{\sigma_l\in S_n}\sum_{j\neq i}\mathbb{P}[\sigma(i)<\sigma(j)|\sigma=\sigma_l]\mathbb{P}[\sigma=\sigma_l] \\
&= \frac{1}{n-1}\sum_{\sigma_l\in S_n}(n-\sigma_l(i))\mathbb{P}[\sigma=\sigma_l] \\
&= \frac{1}{n-1}[n-\mathsf{E}[\sigma(i)]] = \sum_{k=1}^{n}(n-k)^1\cdot\mathbb{P}[\sigma(i)=k] \\
&= S_1(i)
\end{aligned}$$

□

6.2 Proof of Theorem 1

Recall that, under Thurstone's model, each item i has "skill" parameter u_i associated with it. The random "favorability" $X_i = u_i + Z_i$ where Z_i are i.i.d. random variables with some distribution. Our algorithm, with access to exact partial marginal data (first-order or comparison), computes scores for each item i: $S_1(i)$ using first-order data and $S(i)$ using comparison data. As proved in Lemma 1, these two scores are equivalent. Therefore, if we establish that $u_i > u_j$ if and only if $S(i) > S(j)$, it is equivalent to being $S_1(i) > S_2(j)$ as well. We shall establish this statement in two parts: (a) $u_i > u_j$, and (b) $u_i = u_j$.

[2]A full version of this paper is available at `web.mit.edu/ammar/www/rankaggregation2012full.pdf`

Let us start with the first case, $u_i > u_j$. Recall that, score for an item i is

$$S(i) = \frac{1}{n-1}\sum_{k\neq i}\mathbb{P}[X_i > X_k]$$

Therefore, for $i \neq j$,

$$\begin{aligned} S(i) - S(j) &\propto \Big(\sum_{k\neq i}\mathbb{P}[X_i > X_k]\Big) - \Big(\sum_{\ell\neq j}\mathbb{P}[X_j > X_\ell]\Big) \\ &= \Big(\mathbb{P}[X_i > X_j] - \mathbb{P}[X_j > X_i]\Big) + \\ &\quad \Big(\sum_{\ell\neq i,j}\Big(\mathbb{P}[X_i > X_\ell] - \mathbb{P}[X_j > X_\ell]\Big)\Big) \\ &= \Big(\mathbb{P}[X_j \leq X_i] - \mathbb{P}[X_i \leq X_j]\Big) + \\ &\quad \Big(\sum_{\ell\neq i,j}\Big(\mathbb{P}[X_j \leq X_\ell] - \mathbb{P}[X_i \leq X_\ell]\Big)\Big). \quad (16) \end{aligned}$$

Recall that $X_i = u_i + Z_i$ and $X_j = u_j + Z_j$ where u_i, u_j are the "skill" parameters of i and j respectively while Z_i, Z_j are i.i.d. random variables with some distribution. Define, $W_{ij} = Z_i - Z_j$. Then for all i, j, W_{ij} are identically distributed, say with distribution similar to a random variable W which has CDF given by F_W, i.e. $F_W(x) = \mathbb{P}[W \leq x]$. Since W is difference of independent and identically distributed random variables, by definition it is 'symmetric' around 0. That is, for any $x \geq 0$,

$$\mathbb{P}[W < -x] = \mathbb{P}[W > x]. \quad (17)$$

Given these notations, it follows that

$$\begin{aligned} \mathbb{P}[X_i \leq X_j] &= \mathbb{P}[W_{ij} \leq u_j - u_i] \\ &= F_W(u_j - u_i). \end{aligned} \quad (18)$$

Similarly,

$$\begin{aligned} \mathbb{P}[X_j \leq X_i] &= F_W(u_i - u_j) \\ \mathbb{P}[X_i \leq X_\ell] &= F_W(u_\ell - u_i) \\ \mathbb{P}[X_j \leq X_\ell] &= F_W(u_\ell - u_j). \end{aligned} \quad (19)$$

Since $u_i > u_j$, we have $u_\ell - u_j > u_\ell - u_i$ for any $\ell \neq i, j$. Since F_W is a CDF and hence monotonically non-decreasing, i.e. $F_W(x) \leq F_W(y)$ for all $x \leq y$,

$$F_W(u_\ell - u_j) - F_W(u_\ell - u_i) \geq 0, \quad (20)$$

for all ℓ. Also, let $\delta = u_i - u_j > 0$. Then, from above discussion, (16) becomes

$$\begin{aligned} S(i) - S(j) &\propto \Big(F_W(\delta) - F_W(-\delta)\Big) + \\ &\quad \Big(\sum_{\ell\neq i,j}\Big(F_W(u_\ell - u_j) - F_W(u_\ell - u_i)\Big)\Big) \end{aligned} \quad (21)$$

Now,

$$\begin{aligned} F_W(\delta) - F_W(-\delta) &= \mathbb{P}[W \in (-\delta, \delta]] \\ &\geq \mathbb{P}[|W| \leq \delta/2]. \end{aligned} \quad (22)$$

As we shall show next, for any distribution of Zs, W is such that for any $\gamma > 0$,

$$\mathbb{P}[|W| \leq \gamma] > 0. \quad (23)$$

From (20)-(23) (and $\gamma = \delta/2$ in last equation), it follows that if $u_i > u_j$, then

$$S(i) - S(j) > 0. \quad (24)$$

Now we establish (23). For this note that due to Z (distributed as Z_i, Z_j) being a distribution, there exists (tightness) $[-a, a] \subset \mathbb{R}$ for some $a > 0$ so that $\mathbb{P}\Big[Z \in [-a, a]\Big] > \frac{1}{2}$. Given any $\gamma > 0$, partition this interval into at most $N = \lceil \frac{4a}{\gamma} \rceil$ disjoint contiguous intervals, each of length $\gamma/2$. One of these intervals must have probability at least $1/2N$. Call this interval I. That is, $\mathbb{P}[Z \in I] \geq 1/2N$. Since Z_i, Z_j are distributed independently and identically distributed manner with distribution same as that of Z, we have that

$$\mathbb{P}[Z_i \in I, Z_j \in I] \geq \frac{1}{4N^2} > 0. \quad (25)$$

But when both Z_i and Z_j are in I, their difference $W = Z_i - Z_j$ must be withint $[-\gamma/2, \gamma/2]$. This completes the justification of (23).

For the case (b), $u_i = u_j$, using identical arguments as above, one can argue that $S(i) = S(j)$. This complete the proof of Theorem 1.

□

6.3 Proof of Theorem 2

Let λ be in neighborhood of $\mathbf{0} = [0]$. We shall establish claim by means of Taylor's expansion of m as function of λ around $\mathbf{0}$. For simplicity, let us denote $\sigma_{ij} = \mathbb{I}_{\{\sigma(i)=j\}}$. Then

$$m_i j(\lambda) = \sum_{\sigma\in S_n}\sigma_{ij}\frac{1}{Z(\lambda)}\exp\Big(\sum_{kl}\lambda_{kl}\sigma_{kl}\Big),$$

where partition function $Z(\lambda) = \sum_{\sigma\in S_n}\frac{1}{Z(\lambda)}\exp\big(\sum_{k,l}\lambda_{kl}\sigma_{kl}\big)$. For $\lambda = \mathbf{0}$, we have $m_{ij}(\mathbf{0}) = \frac{1}{n}$ for all i, j. By the first-order Taylor expansion, for λ near 0.

$$m_{ij}(\lambda) \approx m_{ij}(\mathbf{0}) + \sum_{kl}\lambda_{kl}\frac{\partial m_{ij}(\star)}{\partial\lambda_{kl}}\Big|_{\star=\mathbf{0}}. \quad (26)$$

By the property of exponential family (see [29] for example), it follows that

$$\begin{aligned} \frac{\partial m_{ij}(\lambda)}{\partial\lambda_{kl}} &= \mathsf{E}_\lambda[\sigma_{ij}\sigma_{kl}] - E_\lambda[\sigma_{ij}]E_\lambda[\sigma_{kl}] \\ &= \mathsf{E}_\lambda[\sigma_{ij}\sigma_{kl}] - m_{ij}(\lambda)m_{kl}(\lambda). \end{aligned} \quad (27)$$

From (26) and (27), it follows that for λ near $\mathbf{0}$,

$$m_{ij}(\lambda) \approx \frac{1}{n} + \Big(\sum_{k,l}\lambda_{kl}\mathsf{E}_\lambda[\sigma_{ij}\sigma_{kl}]\Big) - \frac{1}{n^2}\Big(\sum_{k,l}\lambda_{kl}\Big) \quad (28)$$

We state the following proposition.

Proposition 1. *All distributions can be represented by λ s.t.*

$$\sum_k \lambda_{ik} = 0, \qquad \sum_k \lambda_{kj} = 0, \quad \text{for } 1 \leq i, j \leq n. \quad (29)$$

Proof. Consider a λ such that (29) is not satisfied. We will transform λ to ν which satisfies (29) but induces exactly the same distribution. Specifically, we shall prove that for each $\sigma, \tilde{\sigma} \in S_n$

$$\sum_{k,l}\nu_{kl}(\sigma_{kl} - \tilde{\sigma}_{kl}) = \sum_{k,l}\lambda_{kl}(\sigma_{kl} - \tilde{\sigma}_{kl}).$$

To that end, define

$$\nu_{ij} = \lambda_{ij} - \frac{1}{n}\lambda_{i\cdot} - \frac{1}{n}\lambda_{\cdot j} + \frac{1}{n^2}\lambda_{\cdot\cdot},$$

where

$$\lambda_{i\cdot} = \sum_{k=1}^{n}\lambda_{ik} \quad , \quad \lambda_{\cdot j} = \sum_{k=1}^{n}\lambda_{kj} \quad , \quad \lambda_{\cdot\cdot} = \sum_{k,l=1}^{n}\lambda_{kl}. \tag{30}$$

Then,

$$\sum_{k=1}^{n}\nu_{ik} = \sum_{k=1}^{n}\lambda_{ik} - \frac{1}{n}\lambda_{i\cdot}\sum_{k=1}^{n}1 - \frac{1}{n}\sum_{k=1}^{n}\lambda_{\cdot k} + \frac{1}{n^2}\lambda_{\cdot\cdot}\sum_{k=1}^{n}1$$
$$= \lambda_{i\cdot} - \lambda_{i\cdot} - \frac{1}{n}\lambda_{\cdot\cdot} + \frac{1}{n}\lambda_{\cdot\cdot} = 0, \qquad \forall i.$$

Similarily, we can check $\sum_{k=1}^{n}\nu_{kj}$ for all j. Now we have:

$$\sum_{k,l}\nu_{kl}\sigma_{kl} = \sum_{k,l}\lambda_{kl}\sigma_{kl} - \frac{1}{n}\sum_{k}\lambda_{k\cdot}(\sum_{l=1}^{n}\sigma_{kl})$$
$$- \frac{1}{n}\sum_{l}\lambda_{\cdot l}(\sum_{k=1}^{n}\sigma_{kl}) + \frac{1}{n^2}\lambda_{\cdot\cdot}(\sum_{k,l}\sigma_{kl})$$
$$= \sigma_{kl}\lambda_{kl}\sigma_{kl} - \frac{1}{n}\sum_{k=1}^{n}\lambda_{k\cdot} - \frac{1}{n}\sum_{l=1}^{n}\lambda_{\cdot l} + \frac{n}{n^2}\lambda_{\cdot\cdot}$$

$$= \sum_{kl}\lambda_{kl}\sigma_{kl} - \frac{2}{n}\lambda_{\cdot\cdot} + \frac{1}{n}\lambda_{\cdot\cdot} = \sum_{kl}\lambda_{kl}\sigma_{kl} - \frac{1}{n}\lambda_{\cdot\cdot}$$

Therefore:

$$\sum_{kl}\nu_{kl}(\sigma_{kl} - \tilde{\sigma}_{kl}) = \sum_{kl}\lambda_{kl}(\sigma_{kl} - \tilde{\sigma}_{kl}) - \frac{1}{n}\lambda_{\cdot\cdot} + \frac{1}{n}\lambda_{\cdot\cdot}$$
$$= \sum_{kl}\lambda_{kl}(\sigma_{kl} - \tilde{\sigma}_{kl}).$$

This implies that the distributions induced by λ and ν are identical. □

Given Proposition 1, we shall assume λ satisfying (29) without loss of generality. Then, from (28)

$$m_{ij}(\lambda) = \frac{1}{n} + \sum_{k,l}\lambda_{kl}\mathsf{E}[\sigma_{ij}\sigma_{kl}] - \frac{1}{n}\lambda_{\cdot\cdot}$$
$$= \frac{1}{n} + \sum_{k,l}\lambda_{kl}\mathsf{E}[\sigma_{ij}\sigma_{kl}] \tag{31}$$

Now,

$$\mathsf{E}[\sigma_{ij}\sigma_{kl}] = \begin{cases} \frac{1}{n} & : k = i, j = l \\ \frac{1}{n(n-1)} & : k \neq i, j \neq l \\ 0 & : k = i, j \neq l \end{cases}$$

Then from (31)

$$m_{ij} = \frac{1}{n} + \frac{1}{n}\lambda_{ij} + \sum_{k\neq i, l\neq j}\frac{1}{n(n-1)}\lambda_{kl}. \tag{32}$$

Focusing on the last term, we have

$$\sum_{k\neq i,l\neq j}\frac{1}{n(n-1)}\lambda_{kl} = \frac{1}{2n(n-1)}\Big[\sum_{k\neq i}(\sum_{q=1,q\neq j}^{n}\lambda_{kq})$$
$$+\sum_{l\neq j}(\sum_{q=1,q\neq i}^{n}\lambda_{ql})\Big]$$
$$= \frac{1}{2n(n-1)}\Big[\sum_{k\neq i}(\lambda_{k\cdot} - \lambda_{kj}) +$$
$$\sum_{l\neq j}(\lambda_{\cdot l} - \lambda_{il})\Big]$$
$$= -\frac{1}{2n(n-1)}\Big[\sum_{k\neq i}\lambda_{kj} + \sum_{l\neq j}\lambda_{il}\Big]$$
$$= -\frac{1}{2n(n-1)}\Big[\lambda_{\cdot j} = \lambda_{ij} + \lambda_{i\cdot} - \lambda_{ij}\Big]$$
$$= -\frac{1}{2n(n-1)}(-2\lambda_{ij}) = \frac{\lambda_{ij}}{n(n-1)}$$

Combining this with (32), we get

$$m_{ij}(\lambda) = \frac{1}{n} + \lambda_{ij}(\frac{1}{n} + \frac{1}{n(n-1)}) = \frac{1}{n} + \frac{1}{n-1}\lambda_{ij},$$

as desired. □

6.4 Proof of Theorem 3

Denote the difference between the weight of a permutation, σ^i, and the mode by Δ_i, defined as:

$$\Delta_i \triangleq W(\sigma^*) - W(\sigma^i)$$

Since the permutations $\sigma^1, \ldots, \sigma^k$ are drawn uniformly at random, for each permutation σ^i we have:

$$\mathsf{E}[W(\sigma^i)] = \sum_{i,j}\lambda_{i<j}\mathsf{E}[\sigma_{i<j}] = \frac{1}{2}\sum_{i,j}\lambda_{i<j} \geq \frac{1}{2}W(\sigma^*)$$

And therefore,

$$\mathsf{E}[\Delta_i] = W(\sigma^*) - \mathsf{E}[W(\sigma^i)] \leq \frac{1}{2}W(\sigma^*)$$

Since $\hat{\sigma}$ is chosen to have the maximum weight $W(\cdot)$ of all permutations, and since these permutations are drawn independently, we have:

$$\mathbb{P}\Big[W(\hat{\sigma}) < (\frac{1}{2} - \delta)W(\sigma^*)\Big] = \prod_{i=1}^{k}\mathbb{P}\Big[W(\sigma^i) < (\frac{1}{2} - \delta)W(\sigma^*)\Big]$$
$$= \prod_{i=1}^{k}\mathbb{P}\Big[\Delta_i > (\frac{1}{2} + \delta)W(\sigma^*)\Big]$$

Using the Markov inequality we get:

$$\mathbb{P}\Big[W(\hat{\sigma}) < (\frac{1}{2} - \delta)W(\sigma^*)\Big] \leq \prod_{i=1}^{k}\frac{1}{1+2\delta} \approx \prod_{i=1}^{k}(1-2\delta)$$
$$\leq \prod_{i=1}^{k}\mathrm{e}^{-2\delta} \leq \mathrm{e}^{-2\delta k}$$

Where the approximation is valid for sufficiently small δ. Setting $k > \frac{1}{2\delta}\log\frac{1}{\epsilon}$, we have:

$$\mathbb{P}\Big[W(\hat{\sigma}) < (\frac{1}{2} - \delta)W(\sigma^*)\Big] < \epsilon$$

6.5 Proof of Theorem 4: subgradient algorithm

We shall establish result for the first-order marginal. The proof for comparison is identical. To that end, recall that the optimization problem of interest is

$$\max_{\lambda} \quad F(\lambda) \triangleq \sum_{i,k} \lambda_{ik} m_{ik} - \log\Big(\sum_{\sigma} \exp\Big(\sum_{ik} \lambda_{ik} \mathbb{I}_{\{\sigma(i)=k\}}\Big)\Big). \tag{33}$$

Let λ^* be an optimizer of the objective function with optimal value $F(\lambda^*)$. Now $F(\cdot)$ is a concave function. As before, we shall use t as the index of algorithm's iteration, λ^t be parameter value in iteration t, g^t be the subgradient of $F(\lambda^t) = m - \mathsf{E}_{\lambda^t}[[\mathbb{I}_{\{\sigma(i)=k\}}]]$ and $e(t)$ be the error in this subgradient. Then

$$\begin{aligned}
\|\lambda^{t+1} - \lambda^*\|^2 &= \|\lambda^t + \alpha_t(g^t + e(t)) - \lambda^*\|^2 \\
&= \|\lambda^t - \lambda^*\|^2 + \alpha_t^2\|g^t + e(t)\|^2 \\
&\quad + 2\alpha_t\langle g^t, \lambda^t - \lambda^*\rangle + 2\alpha_t\langle e(t), \lambda^t - \lambda^*\rangle \\
&\leq \|\lambda^t - \lambda^*\|^2 + \alpha_t^2\|g^t + e(t)\|^2 \\
&\quad + 2\alpha_t(F(\lambda^t) - F(\lambda^*)) + 2\alpha_t\langle e(t), \lambda^t - \lambda^*\rangle
\end{aligned}$$

where the last inequality follows from the fact that g^t is a subgradient of F at λ^t. Applying this inequality recursively, and keeping in mind that $\|\cdot\| \geq 0$, we get:

$$\begin{aligned}
0 \leq \|\lambda^0 - \lambda^*\|^2 &+ 2\sum_{s=0}^{t} \alpha_s(F(\lambda^s) - F(\lambda^*)) \\
&+ \sum_{s=0}^{t} \alpha_s^2\|g^s + e(s)\|^2 + 2\sum_{s=0}^{t} \alpha_s\langle e(s), \lambda^s - \lambda^*\rangle
\end{aligned}$$

Therefore

$$\begin{aligned}
2\sum_{s=0}^{t} \alpha_s(F(\lambda^*) - F(\lambda^s)) \leq \|\lambda^0 - \lambda^*\|^2 \\
+ \sum_{s=0}^{t} \alpha_s^2\|g^s + e(s)\|^2 \\
+ 2\sum_{s=0}^{t} \alpha_s\langle e(s), \lambda^s - \lambda^*\rangle
\end{aligned}$$

Let λ be chosen to be λ^s with probability $p_s = \frac{\alpha_s}{\sum q=1^t \alpha_q}$. Then on average, we have

$$\begin{aligned}
\mathsf{E}\big[F(\lambda^*) - F(\lambda)\big] \leq \frac{\|\lambda^0 - \lambda^*\|^2 + \sum_{s=0}^{t} \alpha_s^2\|g^s + e(s)\|^2}{2\sum_{s=0}^{t} \alpha_s} \\
+ \frac{2\sum_{s=0}^{t} \alpha_s\langle e(s), \lambda^s - \lambda^*\rangle}{2\sum_{s=0}^{t} \alpha_s}.
\end{aligned} \tag{*}$$

To simplify the term in $(*)$, note that $g^s + e(s)$ is a vector whose elements are in $[-1, 1]$. Therefore $\|g^s + e(s)\| \leq n^2$, where n is the dimension of the vector. Furthermore, the term $\langle e(s), \lambda^s - \lambda^*\rangle$ can be bounded as follows:

$$\begin{aligned}
\langle e(s), \lambda^s - \lambda^*\rangle &\leq |\langle e(s), \lambda^s - \lambda^*\rangle| \leq \|e(s)\|_1\|\lambda^s - \lambda^*\|_\infty \\
&\leq \|e(s)\|_1(\|\lambda^s - \lambda^0\|_\infty + \|\lambda^0 - \lambda^*\|_\infty)
\end{aligned}$$

And,

$$\|\lambda^s - \lambda^0\|_\infty \leq \sum_{q=0}^{s} \alpha_q\|\Delta_q\|_\infty \leq \sum_{q=0}^{s} \alpha_q$$

where Δ_q is the change in the value of λ at step q. Combining this with the previous inequality, we get:

$$\langle e(s), \lambda^s - \lambda^*\rangle \leq \|e(s)\|_1(\sum_{q=0}^{s} \alpha_s + \|\lambda^0 - \lambda^*\|_\infty)$$

Combining this with $(*)$, and letting
$B = \max\{\|\lambda^0 - \lambda^*\|_\infty, \|\lambda^0 - \lambda^*\|^2\}$, we get:

$$\begin{aligned}
\mathsf{E}\big[F(\lambda^*) - F(\lambda)\big] &\leq \frac{B + \sum_{s=0}^{t} \alpha_s^2 n^2}{2\sum_{s=0}^{t} \alpha_s} \\
&+ \frac{2\sum_{s=0}^{t} \alpha_s\|e(s)\|_1(\sum_{q=0}^{s} \alpha_s + B)}{2\sum_{s=0}^{t} \alpha_s}
\end{aligned}$$

Using our approximation oracle, we can choose the value of $\|e(s)\|$ to be $\frac{\alpha_s}{\sum_{q=0}^{s} \alpha_q + B}$, which yields:

$$\begin{aligned}
\mathsf{E}\big[F(\lambda^*) - F(\lambda)\big] &\leq \frac{B + \sum_{s=0}^{t} \alpha_s^2 n^2 + 2\sum_{s=0}^{t} \alpha_s^2}{2\sum_{s=0}^{t} \alpha_s} \\
&= \frac{B + (n^2 + 2)\sum_{s=0}^{t} \alpha_s^2}{2\sum_{s=0}^{t} \alpha_s}
\end{aligned} \tag{34}$$

Recall that $\alpha_s = \frac{1}{\sqrt{s}}$. Therefore, $\sum_{s=0}^{t} \alpha_s = \Theta(\sqrt{t})$ and numerator scales as $\log t$. Therefore, the quantity above converges to zero, and $F(\lambda^t)$ converges to $F(\lambda^*)$. Now (ignoring constants), the bound in (34) scales like $(B + n^2 \log t)/\sqrt{t}$. Therefore, for $t \geq T$,

$$\mathsf{E}\big[F(\lambda^*) - F(\lambda)\big] \leq \epsilon,$$

for any $\gamma > 0$,

$$T = \Theta\Big(\epsilon^{-2-\gamma}\big(\|\lambda^*\|_\infty + \|\lambda^*\|_2^2 + n^2\big)^{2+\gamma}\Big).$$

7. CONCLUSION

In this paper, we have introduced a novel approach for rank aggregation from observed partial data. The key conceptual contribution is viewing the partial data as coming from an underlying 'ground truth' that is distribution over permutations and thus providing a consistent resolution of paradoxes like that of Condorcet. We make this approach feasible by providing efficient algorithms for solving three important classes of rank aggregation problems: (a) selecting an entire ranking, (b) selection of most likely ranking as per the underlying distribution, and (c) choosing top k items. Interestingly, in many of these problems, we can devise algorithms that reach decision directly from data (without learning the underlying distribution) that is consistent with the approach in which one first learns the distribution and then processes the distribution to obtain the desired answer. This makes algorithmic solutions of this paper very attractive for designing large scale ranking systems such as recommendation systems. We strongly believe that algorithmic result of this paper will be of great practical utility across variety of applications and developing such system design could be an interesting direction going forward.

8. REFERENCES

[1] Who had the "worst year in washington"? `http://voices.washingtonpost.com/thefix/worst-week-in-washington/worst-year-in-washington.html`.

[2] MIT open house "Under the dome", 150 years of celebration, Massachusetts Institute of Technology, `http://mit150.mit.edu/open-house`.

[3] S. Agarwal, T. Graepel, R. Herbrich, S. Har-Peled, and D. Roth. Generalization bounds for the area under the roc curve. *Journal of Machine Learning Research*, 6(1):393, 2006.

[4] S. Agrawal, Z. Wang, and Y. Ye. Parimutuel betting on permutations. *Internet and Network Economics*, pages 126–137, 2008.

[5] K.J. Arrow. *Social choice and individual values.* Number 12. Yale Univ Pr, 1963.

[6] M. Bayati, D. Shah, and M. Sharma. Max-product for maximum weight matching: Convergence, correctness, and lp duality. *Information Theory, IEEE Transactions on*, 54(3):1241–1251, 2008.

[7] D.P. Bertsekas. The auction algorithm: A distributed relaxation method for the assignment problem. *Annals of Operations Research*, 14(1):105–123, 1988.

[8] V.S. Borkar. *Stochastic approximation: a dynamical systems viewpoint.* Cambridge Univ Pr, 2008.

[9] M. Condorcet. *Essai sur l'application de l'analyse á la probabilité des décisions rendues á la pluralité des voix* . l'Imprimerie Royale, 1785.

[10] K. Crammer and Y. Singer. On the algorithmic implementation of multiclass kernel-based vector machines. *The Journal of Machine Learning Research*, 2:265–292, 2002.

[11] O. Dekel, C. Manning, and Y. Singer. Log-linear models for label ranking. *Advances in neural information processing systems*, 16, 2003.

[12] P. Diaconis. *Group representations in probability and statistics*, volume 11. Inst of Mathematical Statistic, 1988.

[13] C. Dwork, R. Kumar, M. Naor, and D. Sivakumar. Rank aggregation methods for the web. In *Proceedings of the 10th international conference on World Wide Web*, pages 613–622. ACM, 2001.

[14] J. Edmonds and R.M. Karp. Theoretical improvements in algorithmic efficiency for network flow problems. *Journal of the ACM (JACM)*, 19(2):248–264, 1972.

[15] V. Farias, S. Jagabathula, and D. Shah. A data-driven approach to modeling choice. *Advances in Neural Information Processing Systems*, 22:504–512, 2009.

[16] Y. Freund, R. Iyer, R.E. Schapire, and Y. Singer. An efficient boosting algorithm for combining preferences. *The Journal of Machine Learning Research*, 4:933–969, 2003.

[17] R. Herbrich, T. Minka, and T. Graepel. Trueskilltm: A bayesian skill rating system. *Advances in Neural Information Processing Systems*, 20:569–576, 2007.

[18] J. Huang, C. Guestrin, and L. Guibas. Efficient inference for distributions on permutations. *Advances in neural information processing systems*, 20:697–704, 2008.

[19] S. Jagabathula and D. Shah. Inferring rankings under constrained sensing. *Advances in Neural Information Processing Systems (NIPS)*, 2008.

[20] M. Jerrum, A. Sinclair, and E. Vigoda. A polynomial-time approximation algorithm for the permanent of a matrix with nonnegative entries. *Journal of the ACM (JACM)*, 51(4):671–697, 2004.

[21] L. Jiang, D. Shah, J. Shin, and J. Walrand. Distributed random access algorithm: scheduling and congestion control. *Information Theory, IEEE Transactions on*, 56(12):6182–6207, 2010.

[22] I. Mitliagkas, A. Gopalan, C. Caramanis, and S. Vishwanath. User rankings from comparisons: Learning permutations in high dimensions. In *Proceedings of Allerton Conference*, 2011.

[23] C. Rudin. The p-norm push: A simple convex ranking algorithm that concentrates at the top of the list. *The Journal of Machine Learning Research*, 10:2233–2271, 2009.

[24] C. Rudin and R.E. Schapire. Margin-based ranking and an equivalence between adaboost and rankboost. *The Journal of Machine Learning Research*, 10:2193–2232, 2009.

[25] S. Shalev-Shwartz and Y. Singer. Efficient learning of label ranking by soft projections onto polyhedra. *The Journal of Machine Learning Research*, 7:1567–1599, 2006.

[26] L.L. Thurstone. A law of comparative judgment. *Psychological review*, 34(4):273, 1927.

[27] N. Usunier, M.R. Amini, and P. Gallinari. A data-dependent generalisation error bound for the auc. In *Proceedings of the ICML 2005 Workshop on ROC Analysis in Machine Learning*. Citeseer, 2005.

[28] L.G. Valiant. The complexity of computing the permanent. *Theoretical computer science*, 8(2):189–201, 1979.

[29] M.J. Wainwright and M.I. Jordan. Graphical models, exponential families, and variational inference. *Foundations and Trends® in Machine Learning*, 1(1-2):1–305, 2008.

[30] D.J.A. Welsh. *Complexity: knots, colourings and counting.* Number 186. Cambridge Univ Pr, 1993.

Fair Sampling Across Network Flow Measurements

Nick Duffield
AT&T Labs–Research
180 Park Avenue
Florham Park, NJ 07932, USA
duffield@research.att.com

ABSTRACT

Sampling is crucial for controlling resource consumption by internet traffic flow measurements. Routers use Packet Sampled NetFlow [9], and completed flow records are sampled in the measurement infrastructure [13]. Recent research, motivated by the need of service providers to accurately measure both small and large traffic subpopulations, has focused on distributing a packet sampling budget amongst subpopulations [26, 33, 40]. But long timescales of hardware development and lower bandwidth costs motivate post-measurement analysis of complete flow records at collectors instead. Sampling in collector databases then manages data volumes, yielding general purpose summaries that are rapidly queried to trigger drill-down analysis on a time limited window of full data. These are sufficiently small to be archived.

This paper addresses the problem of distributing a sampling budget over subpopulations of flow records. Estimation accuracy goals are met by fairly sharing the budget. We establish a correspondence between the type of accuracy goal, and the flavor of fair sharing used. A streaming Max-Min Fair Sampling algorithm fairly shares the sampling budget across subpopulations, with sampling as a mechanism to deallocate budget. This provides timely samples and is robust against uncertainties in configuration and demand. We illustrate using flow records from an access router of a large ISP, where rates over interface traffic subpopulations vary over several orders of magnitude. We detail an implementation whose computational cost is no worse than subpopulation-oblivious sampling.

Categories and Subject Descriptors

C.2.3 [**Computer-Communication Networks**]: Network Operations—*Network Monitoring*; G.3 [**Probability and Statistics**]: Probabilistic Algorithms

General Terms

Algorithms, Measurement, Theory

SIGMETRICS'12, June 11–15, 2012, London, England, UK.

Keywords

Sampling, Estimation, Max-Min Fairness, IP Flows, Streaming

1. INTRODUCTION

1.1 Flow Records and Network Management

Passive traffic flow measurement plays a vital role in managing communications networks [20]. Flow measurement is performed by routers, most prominently by the NetFlow [9] feature, and more flexibly by standalone measurement devices [11] observing traffic via port replication or optical splitters. The measurement data are flow records, each of which summarizes the protocol-level information of a set of packets related by having a common key—comprising IP address and TCP/UDP ports and other header fields—observed locally in time. A flow record reports the flow key and other quantities, e.g., the flow's number of packets and bytes, and timing information. Each measuring device exports a stream of flow records—either directly or through co-located mediation devices—to one or more collectors that house a database whose functions include routine reporting (e.g., large scale traffic matrices and application mix) real-time anomaly detection (of traffic patterns due to network attacks or routing anomalies), and ad hoc retrospective queries (for forensic studies or debugging); see e.g., [20, 12].

1.2 Measurement Costs and Summarization

Several architectures for flow record collection and analysis currently are used, with differences according to relative situational costs of transmission, storage, and processing the flow records. The volume of flow records is immense; a major ISP will carry 10's of PetaBytes of user traffic per day [1], potentially generating 100's of TeraBytes of flow records daily. Intelligent sampling has played, and, we argue, will continue to play, an essential role in managing this data volume. In recent practice, sampling functionality has been deployed at or close to the measurement point, with sampling of packets in routers prior to the formation of flow statistics [9], then sampling of completed flow records in mediation devices [13] that export the sampled flow records to a central collector.

The bandwidth for 100 TB of flow records daily is only about 10Gb/s. The combined effects of decreasing bandwidth costs [29] and the advent of relatively cheap standalone measurement devices that need not packet sample, coupled with the increasing needs of network management for protocol-level measurement of the complete traffic stream, have made the collection of full sets of unsampled flow records increasingly feasible and desirable for ISPs. Although much ingenuity has been devoted to packet-level approaches to measurement resource management [26, 33, 40], the relatively long development times of hardware features makes full collection of flow records a flexible and compelling approach for ISPs, since development of analysis capabilities on the collector side is both flexible and rapid.

However, the volume of flow records remains a challenge. While retaining flow records over a limited time window (e.g., one or few days) is feasible in terms of storage cost, it remains problematic both to store all flow records over longer periods and to rapidly process arbitrary database queries over even the limited time window. A solution to both these problems is to summarize the flow records at collectors through a combination of aggregation and sampling. Although summarization incurs a loss of resolution for analysis, the reduced data size enables more rapid automated identification of network events large enough to be reliably detected, potentially triggering (fast) drill-down analysis into the summary, or (slower) drill-down into the full set of flow records available within the retention window. Furthermore, the summaries can be retained to support fast retrospective analysis over longer periods than it is feasible to retain the full flow data[1]. This architecture can be realized either entirely in a central collector, or in distributed local collectors. These routinely transmit summaries to a central location for global analysis and can initiate or remotely service queries on the limited window of full flow records that they store. One hundred such collectors, each equipped with a few TeraBytes of storage, could collectively retain a day's flow records from an entire major ISP network.

Aggregation and sampling are two complementary methods of summarization. Aggregation involves partitioning the stream of flow records into disjoint *subpopulations* (SPs) according to some explicit or derived property, and computing the aggregate flow, byte and/or packet counts within each SP over successive time windows. Multiple aggregation schemes may be run in parallel, e.g., according to single fields of the flow key, such as (i) source or destination IP routing prefix; (ii) source or destination TCP/UDP port; or (iii) router interface traversed. Time series of aggregates are useful both for routine reporting and anomaly detection. But general drill-down queries concern subaggregates over finer SPs of flows, and it is not feasible to compute and store all possible subaggregates of interest due to the high cardinality of the key space. Instead, sampling provides a data summary unconstrained by the granularity of any flow key aggregation scheme, and supports estimation of arbitrary subaggregates that need not specified at the time that sampling takes place.

1.3 The Challenge of Rate Skewness

We abstract the space constraints to which any summary must conform (either for storage or rapid query) as a sampling budget, i.e., a maximum number of samples to be gathered from data arriving in a specified time period. A feasible sampling method for flow records must (i) control sample size within a sampling budget; (ii) yield sufficiently accurate estimates; and (iii) provide samples in a sufficiently timely manner for applications. In particular, the sample design must match the statistical distribution of flow features to the relevant accuracy measures for estimation. If a numerical data feature has a heavily skewed distribution, such as a Pareto or other heavy-tailed distribution, and is used for selection and/or aggregation by a query, then it is well-known that estimation from uniformly drawn samples can be highly inaccurate [7]. An example comes from the measured distribution of flow sizes in which a small fraction of the flow records report a large fraction of the bytes [19]. While uniform sampling is well adapted to estimating subpopulation sizes (i.e., a number of flows in a subset), it is poorly adapted to estimating subpopulation weight sums (i.e., the total bytes of a subset of flows), since omission of a single large flow can drastically impact estimation accuracy. Instead, weighted sampling to preferentially select records of large flows [14, 16] enables accurate byte estimation.

This paper addresses skewness of a different type, that of the distribution of traffic rates over SPs. Drill-down queries often are localized within a SP of flow records whose aggregate timeseries triggered an anomaly. In many cases of interest, the traffic rates across SPs are highly skewed. Mirroring the general observation cited above, the basic problem that we address is that estimation accuracy varies greatly across SPs when sampling is *undifferentiated* in the sense that a flow record's sampling probability does not depend on the SP of which it is a member, although it may still depend on other attributes such as flow size.

Two examples of SP rate skewness are as follows. Firstly, when flow records are partitioned according to TCP/UDP port, a small number of ports account for a majority of the traffic, due to the relative popularity of different user applications [4]. Secondly, for analysis of traffic at an access router, flow records are implicitly partitioned according to the interface that the flow traversed, in order to analyze different customers' traffic. But line rates and corresponding traffic rates can vary by several orders of magnitude over different interfaces on a large access router. In both examples, the challenge for analysis is to return accurate responses to queries on traffic in each SP regardless of the SP size. For example, traffic monitoring for security must be able to alert on and drill-down into significant traffic changes on both small and large customer interfaces.

A simple analysis is illustrative. Consider a SP comprising n flow records which are then sampled independently with probability p. Now estimate from the samples the number m of flows in some subset of flows within the population. Whereas a "needle in a haystack" query might target a subset of size m within any SP, queries often concern SPs whose size m increases with the size n of the SP of which they are part, e.g., application-level flows comprising a fraction of all flows on each interface of an access router. The relative error in estimating m is roughly $1/\sqrt{mp}$; see eq. (4) following. With fixed p, estimation accuracy decreases for smaller m of typical interest in smaller n SPs. But if the sampling probability p were differentiated by SP size n, it would be possible to make accuracy uniform in n, redistributing some of the sampling budget to SPs with small n.

1.4 Optimally Sharing The Sampling Budget

Moving beyond the example analyzed above, consider the following static problem. Given a set of SPs of flow records collected in a time window, and a sampling methodology (e.g., flow size weighted), allocate a fixed total sampling budget between the SPs in order to realize certain estima-

[1]The analytic value of full data over summaries decreases with age, which may in any case be curtailed by policy.

tion accuracy goals for subsets of traffic within each SP. This budget allocation problem can be formulated in terms of fair sharing: the allocation to any SP will depend not only on its own flow records, but also on the demands of flow records in other SPs. Each SP needs to receive sufficient budget to realize its own accuracy goals; once these are met, any remaining sampling budget can be allocated to other SPs that can use them. Several variants of fairness are in general use, the best known being Max-Min Fairness and Proportional Fairness; see [2, 24]. Which one should be used? In this paper we will see that the type of accuracy measure employed determines which variant of fairness should be used. Put another way, fair sharing of sampling resources is motivated by the need to realize specific accuracy goals.

A sampling scheme using this approach could be used offline, batches of flow records being collected over successive measurement windows, and each SP sampled at the end of each window to fit within its fair share of the budget. However the lag between collection and summarization, being the sampling processing time plus an amount as large as the window duration, may be problematic for measurement applications that must query summaries in real time. This constraint favors online sampling in order to make samples available at any time. Some type of reservoir sampling [39] is well suited to this task: a reservoir of samples is progressively maintained throughout each window and is hence available for query at any time. Each arriving flow record must either be included in the reservoir (displacing a previous sample from that window if the reservoir is full) or discarded permanently. Since the sampling budget is the reservoir size, reservoir sampling also provides (i) robustness against unexpectedly large sets of flow records that would otherwise overflow storage, and (ii) the flexibility to sample flow records at devices with limited storage budget.

The online scheme should not simply reservoir sample with some fixed allocation of sampling budget amongst the SPs, e.g., based on modeled or predicted flow record arrivals, since these allocations would not in general be fair across the actual flow record arrivals, and hence suboptimal for estimation accuracy. Furthermore, the set of SPs represented in the flow records (e.g., which TCP/UDP ports occur) may not be known in advance. Instead, the online scheme must adapt the allocation in response to the actual flows records. Those that are sampled may subsequently be discarded, either to make way for preferentially sampled records in the same SP, or if the allocation to that SP is reduced.

1.5 Contribution: Fair Sampling

In our setting, there is a population of items (e.g., flow records) each with a weight (flow bytes, packets or count), and belonging to one set of subpopulations. Items are sampled into a reservoir of finite capacity (the sampling budget), and the sampled items are used to construct unbiased estimators of weight sums over subsets within SPs. The population is presented as a stream; each item must be either selected into the reservoir or discarded permanently. Selected items may later be discarded to make way for newer items. A high-level statement of our problem is then: *How should a sampling scheme share the sampling budget amongst SPs in order to best fulfill desired goals in estimation accuracy?*

Our proposed method of *Fair Sampling* integrates ideas from fair sharing, sampling and complexity analysis to solve this problem in a provably optimal and demonstrably feasible manner. We now outline the content of the paper and, in the list below, our main new contributions. We start in Section 2 by reviewing the notions of fair allocation and the sampling methodologies that we will employ.

- Section 3 relates different types of estimation accuracy to the type of fair sharing used in an offline context. Proportional Fair sharing minimizes the average estimation variance over SPs, and achieves the same accuracy as Undifferentiated Sampling (i.e., sampling items without regard to their SP membership). Max-Min Fair Sharing minimizes average *relative* estimation variance over SPs, and the resulting Fair Sampling increases accuracy for smaller SPs at the expense of decreasing accuracy for larger SPs.
- Section 4.1 presents a Streaming Fair Allocation algorithm that progressively and fairly allocates the sampling budget amongst SPs, without advance knowledge of their demand. The allocation is Lexicographic Max-Min Fair, which inherently accommodates the discrete nature of flow records.
- Section 4.2 presents a Streaming Fair Sampling algorithm that integrates sampling as a discard step when the Streaming Fair Allocation to some SP must be decreased. The VarOpt sampling algorithm [10] is variance optimal for estimation and can be implemented efficiently.
- Section 5 describes an implementation of Fair Sampling in a single shared reservoir whose computational cost is no worse than Undifferentiated VarOpt Sampling, i.e., $O(\log k)$ per item for a reservoir of capacity k.
- Section 6 uses flow records of traffic at an access router to evaluate the accuracy of Fair Sampling relative to other approaches, and its composite with Undifferentiated Sampling. It improves estimation accuracy in 89% of cases.
- Section 7 analyzes the performance gains of Fair Sampling, and provides measurement system design criteria that include the effects of any prior packet sampling.

We discuss related work in Section 8 and conclude in Section 9. Theorems in Sections 3 & 4 are proved in Section 10.

2. REVIEW: FAIRNESS AND SAMPLING

Before presenting our contribution in Sections 3 and following, we review the notions of budget sharing that underpin our work (Section 2.1), motivation in sampling and estimation (Section 2.2), the specific sampling and estimation algorithms that we employ (Section 2.3), and how different sample sets—in our case from Fair and Undifferentiated Sampling—can be combined into a single estimator (Section 2.4). Our setting employs the following notation that is retained throughout the paper. We assume a population of n items, partitioned in disjoint subpopulations[2] (SPs) labelled by $d \in \mathcal{D}$, there being n_d items in SP d, hence $\sum_d n_d = n$. The sampling budget k is the number of items that can be sampled. Each subpopulation d is allocated some non-negative integer amount $k_d \leq n_d$ such that $\sum_d k_d \leq k$; such allocations are called *feasible*. Lastly, each item i comes equipped a weight $w_i > 0$ that determines its sampling probability within each SP. For the motivating case where items are flow records, examples of subpopulation partitions were mentioned in Section 1.3; the weights

[2]The term subpopulation will refer to both its label d and the set of items in the subpopulation

w_i may be the flow's recorded bytes, or its packets, or a unit weight, depending on the estimation accuracy goals.

2.1 Fair Allocation

Following terminology common in resource sharing, we consider the subpopulation sizes $N = \{n_d \geq 0 : d \in \mathcal{D}\}$ as a set of *demands* over which the budget k is to be partitioned according to the allocations $K = \{k_d \geq 0 : d \in \mathcal{D}\}$.

A feasible allocation K^0 is said to be *Max-Min Fair* (MMF) [18] if for any other feasible allocation K, then for all SPs d such that $k_d > k_d^0$, there exists some SP d' such that $k_{d'} < k_{d'}^0 \leq k_d^0$. In other words, allocating more than the MMF allocation to any SP, can only be done at the expense of reducing the allocation to some smaller SP.

If the allocations were not constrained to be integers, the well known progressive filling algorithm could be used to construct the MMF allocation [2]. Starting with all $k_d = 0$, all allocations are increased at the same rate until one or more of the SPs d are satisfied ($k_d = n_d$). Then the procedure repeats, dividing the remaining budget amongst the unsatisfied SPs, and so on, until either all SPs are satisfied or the budget is used up. However, the MMF allocation is not generally integral. This is problematic in our motivating example since flow records are indivisible. A possible workaround would be to use an integral allocation close to the MMF allocation. However, when allocating to a dynamic stream of demands, we must deal systematically with each discrete arrival (each flow record) rather than accumulate unfairness through successive uncontrolled approximations. Therefore, we will work with a more general notion of fairness, namely, Lexicographic Max-Min Fairness (see [3, 32]), that naturally accommodates discreteness.

Let $T(K)$ denote the elements of an allocation K sorted in non-decreasing order. K is said to be *lexicographically greater than* K', written $K \succ K'$, if the first non-zero component of $T(K)-T(K)'$ is positive. We say K is *lexicographically equal to* K' if $T(K) = T(K')$. We write $K \succeq K'$, if either $K \succ K'$ or $T(K) = T(K')$. With these definitions, the feasible allocation K^0 is *Lexicographically Max-Min Fair* (LMMF) if $K^0 \succeq K$ for any other feasible allocation K. LMMF enables handling the case where integer constraints prevent the MMF solution from existing, but several feasible allocations are close to it. As a simple example, consider a single unit budget that must accommodate two unit demands. The MMF allocation $K = (1/2, 1/2)$ is not allowed by the integer constraints, but the allocations $(1, 0)$ and $(0, 1)$ are both LMMF.

2.2 Skewness, Sampling and Estimation

Because of the observed heavy-tailed distribution of flow bytes, several streaming weighted sampling algorithms currently are used for flow record sampling, using byte size as the sampling weight. Threshold Sampling [14] performs independent weighted sampling. The related Priority Sampling [16] samples into a fixed size reservoir, and VarOpt [10]—described more completely below—does so with optimal estimation variance that is as good as any offline sampling scheme, and with computational cost smaller than previous related methods [6, 38]. All these methods can provide uniform sampling as a special case using unit weights.

All the schemes mentioned provide unbiased estimates of the sums of weights over any subset of items using the Horwitz-Thompson approach [21]. Let item i of weight w_i be sampled with marginal probability p_i. Each sampled w_i is replaced with its unbiased estimate (or adjusted weight) $\widehat{w}_i = w_i/p_i$; non-sampled items have adjusted weight 0. A generic query is to find the total weight of a subset S of items that satisfy some predicate, e.g., the total bytes of flows that use a specified protocol, The weight sum $W(S) = \sum_{i \in S} w_i$, has an unbiased estimator

$$\widehat{W}(S) = \sum_{i \in S} \widehat{w}_i = \sum_{i \in \widehat{S}} w_i/p_i \qquad (1)$$

where $\widehat{S}$ is the intersection of S with the random sample. This is a powerful construction because S need not be known at the time of sampling, enabling retrospective analysis.

2.3 Variance Optimal Sampling

Our methods use sampling to control the reservoir occupancy. Once the reservoir contains k items, any new item is provisionally added, then one random item is removed to return the occupancy to k. The weights of the surviving items are adjusted as above. This paper uses the VarOpt sampling primitive [10]. Its action VarOpt$_k$ on a set Ω of $k+1$ weights w_i is recorded as Algorithm 1 below. Sampling is IPPS (Inclusion Probability Proportional to Size), item i being sampled with probability $p_i = \min\{1, w_i/\tau\}$, where τ is the unique value for which $\sum_i p_i = k$, i.e., k items are selected. Thus all large items (those i with $w_i \geq \tau$) are sampled with probability 1, while the remaining small items are sampled with probability proportional to size. This embodies the requirement from Section 2.2 to sample larger items. (Unit weights are used when uniform sampling is required). Sampling proceeds by picking one item i for discard with probability $1-p_i$. This is achieved by dividing up the unit interval into subintervals of length $1-p_i$, (note $\sum_i(1-p_i) = 1$), and discarding the item whose interval contains a random point chosen uniformly. Each of the k remaining weights are adjusted to their new value $w_i/p_i = \max\{w_i, \tau\}$. Note that VarOpt works with the item weights presented to it. *It does not use or require any assumptions concerning the statistical distribution of item weights.*

Used recursively, VarOpt samples exactly k out of any $n > k$ items. In addition to the estimate for individual weights being unbiased, the estimate of the total is exact and VarOpt minimizes the average estimation variance over weight subsets of a given size with respect to *any* unbiased estimator, including even offline algorithms. Furthermore, it has efficient implementation; its computational cost is no worse that $O(\log k)$ for any single new item, and in fact $O(\log \log k)$ when amortized over k items.

Algorithm 1: VarOpt$_k(\Omega)$ where $|\Omega| = k + 1$.

find τ be such that $\sum_{i=1}^{k+1} \min\{1, w_i/\tau\} = k$
for $i = 1, \ldots, k+1$ **do** $p_i \leftarrow \min\{1, w_i/\tau\}$,
$w_i \leftarrow \max\{\tau, w_i\}$
generate uniformly random $r \in U(0, 1)$
maximize j such that $\sum_{1 \leq i < j}(1 - p_i) \leq r$.
delete element w_j from Ω

2.4 Combined Estimation

In current network management practice, multiple sampling schemes are applied to flow records in support of different measurement applications; see e.g., [28]. Our proposed

Fair Sampling is not expected to supplant Undifferentiated Sampling; rather, it extends the applicability of measurement applications. Undifferentiated Sampling will remain important for applications that must focus on the largest traffic subpopulations. Thus it is natural to ask: *If both fair and undifferentiated sampling are performed, can the samples be combined to form an estimator that is better than either individually?* We will investigate this question experimentally in Section 6 using a combined estimator, proposed in general from in [15], that we now describe.

Given different unbiased estimates $\{X_i\}$ of some X, with associated estimation variances $\{V_i\}$, any convex combination $\sum_i \lambda_i X_i$, $\lambda_i \geq 0$, $\sum_i \lambda_i = 1$, is also an unbiased estimate of X. Choosing $\lambda_i = 1/V_i/(\sum_j 1/V_j)$ minimizes estimation variance. But naively substituting estimated variances leads to pathologies. For VarOpt, an unbiased estimate of the variance in estimating a weight w is

$$v = w \max\{0, \tau - w\} \tag{2}$$

where τ is the sampling threshold. But large items (of weight $w \geq \tau$) have zero associated variance, while some small items may be missed, yielding a small or zero estimated variance which causes the associated estimate X_i to dominate.

Regularized variance estimators proposed in [15] avoid these pathologies. The *bounded variance estimator* exploits that, from (2), $\mathsf{Var}(X_i)$ bounded above by $\tau_i X$, where τ_i is the sampling threshold in force for X_i. This bound is tight in the limit of small weights. Approximating V_i by $\tau_i X$ results in the convex combination estimate

$$X^{(\text{reg})} = \sum_i X_i \tau_i^{-1} / \sum_i \tau_i^{-1} \tag{3}$$

This extends to uniform sampling with probability p, using an effective τ of $1/p$ times the maximum observed weight.

3. FAIR SAMPLING AND ACCURACY

3.1 Estimation Accuracy Goals

Our first contribution is to determine the relationship between the desired type of accuracy goal for estimation and the type of method used to share the sampling budget across SPs. We show that the choice between goals of controlling relative vs. absolute error in estimation leads naturally to a corresponding choice between Max-Min Fair vs. Proportional Fair sharing of the sampling budget. Furthermore, Proportional Fair Sharing offers little or no advantage over undifferentiated sampling. We first establish the result for uniform independent sampling (i.e., unit weights), then show how it extends to weighted VarOpt sampling. To be specific, we express our motivation in terms of estimation from subpopulations of flow records.

(i) *What to estimate:* The weight sum of subsets of flows that constitute at least some fraction $\beta < 1$ of the flows in a SP. Motivation: Analysis thresholds for both short-term management (e.g., anomaly detection) and long-term management (e.g., capacity planning) are both commonly expressed in terms of relative usage or changes thereof.

(ii) *Estimation accuracy:* two alternative measures of error estimating a fraction β of traffic: (ii$^{[abs]}$) the mean square *absolute* error; or (ii$^{[rel]}$) the mean square *relative* error. The importance of relative error when estimating over SPs of different sizes has been emphasized in [26].

(iii) *Balance across SPs:* to balance goals (i) and (ii) by minimizing the average error across SPs.

3.2 Fairness/Accuracy in Uniform Sampling

Consider an SP d of n_d items from which k_d on average are sampled uniformly and independently. Suppose we wish to estimate the size m_d of a subset of items satisfying some predicate. Using Horwitz-Thompson [21], an unbiased estimate for m_d is $\widehat{m}_d n_d/k_d$, where $\widehat{m}_d$ is the number of the m_d items that are sampled. The estimation variance is

$$V(n_d, k_d, m_d) = m_d \left(\frac{n_d}{k_d} - 1 \right) \tag{4}$$

Note the variance for undifferentiated sampling of the aggregate of n flows with sampling budget k is $V(n, k, m_d)$.

Theorem 1. *Consider the problem of estimating the size $m_d = \beta n_d$ of a fraction β of items in each SP d.*

(i) The average across all SPs d of the absolute estimation variances $V(n_d, k_d, \beta n_d)$ is minimized by $k_d^{[abs]} = k n_d / n$. With this allocation, the ratio of the corresponding variance to that for undifferentiated sampling from SP d is

$$\frac{V(n_d, k_d^{[abs]}, m_d)}{V(n, k, m_d)} = 1. \tag{5}$$

(ii) The average across all SPs d of the relative estimation variances $V(n_d, k_d, \beta n_d)/(\beta n_d)^2$ is minimized by the Max-Min Fair Allocation $k_d^{[rel]}$ of the budget k over the SPs $\{n_d\}$. The ratio of the corresponding variance to that for undifferentiated sampling from SP d is

$$\frac{V(n_d, k_d^{[rel]}, m_d)}{V(n, k, m_d)} \leq \frac{\max\{0, |\mathcal{D}| n_d - k\}}{n - k}, \tag{6}$$

with $V(n_d, k_d^{[rel]}, m_d) = 0$ if d is fully satisfied.

We draw two conclusions from Theorem 1. Firstly, from (5), proportional sharing does no better in terms of accuracy than undifferentiated sampling. Secondly, (6) tells us that for SPs contributing smaller than average offered load ($n_d < n/|\mathcal{D}|$), allocating equal sampling budget to each SP yields lower variance than undifferentiated sampling, while for SPs carrying larger than average load ($n_d > n/|\mathcal{D}|$) the reverse may be true.

3.3 Fairness/Accuracy in Weighted Sampling

Although Theorem 1 was proved for independent sampling with uniform weights, its conclusions extend to size-weighted sampling with a fixed budget. It is shown in [36] that in weighted VarOpt sampling of k_d from n_d items, the estimation variance of the weight of $m_d \leq n_d$, averaged over all subsets of m_d items, is bounded above by

$$U(n_d, k_d, n_d, X_d) = \frac{m_d(n_d - m_d) X_d^2}{n_d(n_d - 1) k_d} \tag{7}$$

where X_d is the total weight of the subpopulation. This bound is asymptotically tight when each item weight is $o(X_d/k)$. Assuming a common distribution of weights over items, take X_d proportional to n_d, and find $U(n_d, k_d, n_d, X_d) = a(\beta) V(n_d, k_d, m_d) + b$ where $a(\beta)$ is constant up to a term $O(1/n_d)$ and b is independent of k_d. Thus the analysis of Theorem 1 holds in the same approximation.

4. STREAMING FAIR SAMPLING

Section 3 has shown how fair allocation of the sampling budget uniformizes relative estimation variance over different subpopulations. The choice of sampling method is left open. For example, each subpopulation could be sampled offline using VarOpt to select a sample of size equal to its fair allocation. We now realize Fair Sampling as a reservoir sampling algorithm when the population is presented as a stream, and hence the demands (subpopulation sizes) are not known in advance. Section 4.1 describes a streaming fair allocation algorithm that adaptively allocates the sampling budget, while Section 4.2 uses sampling as a discard mechanism when the allocation to a SP is reduced.

4.1 Streaming Fair Allocation

Adapting our previous notation, we now assume that items arrive in a stream labeled by $i = 1, 2, \ldots, n$, with item i belonging to subpopulation $d^i \in \mathcal{D}$. From the stream we wish to select k items in total, with each SP d obtaining its fair allocation k_d of the total slots k. The allocations are computed progressively as items arrive, so that, after k initial items have arrived, the allocations at any time will be exactly consumed by the sampled items; only a single pass through the data is performed. Our Algorithm 2 can be summarized as follows: *Allocate budget to* SPs *until exhausted; thereafter accommodate new* SPs *by decrementing the allocation of a* SP *with maximal current allocation.*

Algorithm 2: Stream Fair Allocation of a Budget of Size k

```
D ← ∅;
while new item in SP d do
    if d ∉ D then
        include d in D
        k_d ← 0
    k_d ← k_d + 1
    if Σ_{d∈D} k_d > k then
        select d_* ∈ D that maximizes k_{d_*}
        k_{d_*} ← k_{d_*} − 1
```

$K = \{k_d : d \in \mathcal{D}\}$ will denote the generic allocation. Let $\mathcal{X}(N, k)$ denote the feasible allocations of the budget k to demands $N = \{n_d : d \in \mathcal{D}\}$ of the subpopulations, and let $\mathcal{X}_d(N, k) \subset \mathcal{X}(N, k)$ denote those feasible allocations in which the demand n_d is fully satisfied, i.e., $k_d = n_d$. Let $\mathbf{1}_d$ denote the unit demand from SP d. N^i is the cumulative demand due to the first i arrivals, i.e., $n^i_d = \#\{j \le i : d^j = d\}$. Let $K^i = \{k^i_d : d \in \mathcal{D}\}$ denote any allocation provided by Algorithm 2 from the first i items. Notationally, it will be convenient for $\mathcal{D}$ to be the fixed set of all possible demands, so $k^i_d = 0$ for demands d not represented in the first i items. Of course, actual implementations need only retain labels for demands currently represented in the reservoir.

Theorem 2. *For each i, K^i is LMMF for the demands $N^i = \{n^i_d : d \in \mathcal{D}\}$.*

In Algorithm 2, K^{i+1} is generated from K^i by composing two steps. Firstly, the arriving increment to demand n_d is added, then the allocation to one of the largest current demand n_{d_*} is decremented. We write these steps as

$$K \mapsto K + \mathbf{1}_{d^{i+1}} \mapsto K + \mathbf{1}_{d^{i+1}} - \mathbf{1}_{d_*} \qquad (8)$$

The proof of Theorem 2 proceeds by demonstrating that each of these two steps, subject to the conditions of our problem, maintains lexicographic order, as we now state. We will need the notation $\Sigma K = \sum_{d \in \mathcal{D}} k_d$. The proofs of all the theorems are deferred to Section 10.

Theorem 3. *Suppose $K \succeq K'$ and $k_d \le k'_d$. Then $K + \mathbf{1}_d \succeq K' + \mathbf{1}_d$.*

Theorem 4. *Let $\Sigma K \ge \Sigma K'$, $K \succeq K'$ and d_* maximize k_d. Then $K - \mathbf{1}_{d_*} \succeq K' - \mathbf{1}_d$ for all $d \in \mathcal{D}$.*

4.2 Stream Sampling and Budget Deallocation

Algorithm 2 extends to *Stream Fair Sampling* by maintaining a reservoir of size k of selected items. Each arriving item is added to the reservoir; when an allocation k_{d_*} is decremented, an item from subpopulation d_* is deleted from the reservoir. Although any method that deletes a single item could be used, sampling is a natural choice because the statistical consequences of deletion for estimation can be controlled. We use VarOpt sampling because it can delete exactly one item, can be efficiently implemented, and has minimal average variance for estimation of subset sums of a given size. For estimating bytes from flow records, the reported bytes should be used as a sampling weight. Other applications may be better served by a different assignment of weight, e..g. uniform weights for estimating flow counts.

We incorporate VarOpt as the discard step for Algorithm 2 as follows. We represent each item in the stream as a pair (d, w) where d is the subpopulation the item belongs to, and w is the weight. D is the set of subpopulations observed and Ω_d is the multiset of weights selected from subpopulation d. The sizes $|\Omega_d|$ in Algorithm 3 play the same role as the allocations k_d in Algorithm 2. Here we store only the weights w; obviously, one could store the (d, w) plus any other information carried by the item.

Algorithm 3: Stream Fair Sampling into a Reservoir of Size k

```
D ← ∅;
while new item (d, w) arrives do
    if d ∉ D then
        include d in D
        Ω_d ← ∅
    include w in Ω_d
    if Σ_{d∈D} |Ω_d| > k then
        select d_* ∈ D that maximizes |Ω_{d_*}|
        VarOpt_{|Ω_{d_*}|−1}(Ω_{d_*})
        if |Ω_{d_*}| = 0 then
            remove d_* from D
```

Online and offline fair sampling are equivalent in a statistical sense we now discuss. Concerning solely the sampling aspects, it was shown in [10] that progressively VarOpt sampling a stream of n items into a reservoir of capacity k is statistically equivalent to single VarOpt sampling of k out of n items. It should now be clear the Fair Allocation Algorithm 2 enjoys a similar recurrence property; after n items have been processed, the final allocations K^n are LMMF for the demands N. From this it is largely a matter of formalism to show that the Stream Fair Sampling Algorithm 3 satisfies an analogous property. The final sample is equivalent to

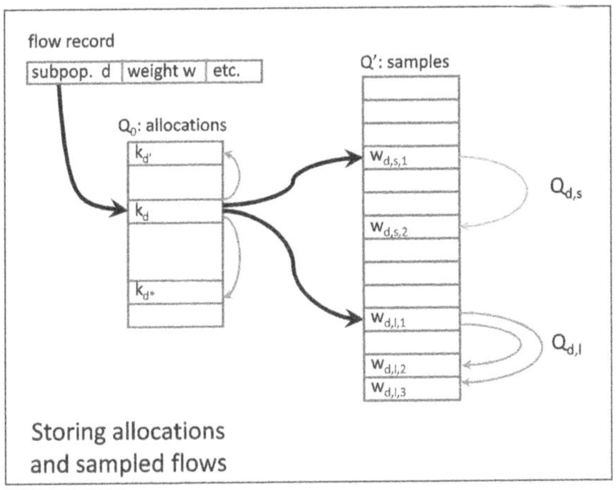

Figure 1: Data Structures for allocations k_d (in Q_0) and samples (in Q'). Thick arrows map from flow record demand d to allocation k_d in Q_0 and onward to large and small item sets $Q_{d,l}, Q_{d,s} \subset Q'$. Parent to child mappings within BSTs shown as thin arrows.

one obtained by (i) finding LMMF allocations $\{k_d\}$ for the demands $\{n_d\}$, then (ii) making a VarOpt selection of k_d out of n_d items for each subpopulation d. The equivalence is that the distribution of sampled items is the same when conditioned on obtaining the same LMMF allocations.

5. IMPLEMENTATION AND COSTS

This section describes data structures that can support Stream Fair Sampling Algorithm 3, and their associated computational costs per item. Although the collector and mediator environments are less resource stringent than on a router, in view of the high arrival rate of flow records, it is important to demonstrate that Stream Fair Sampling does not add per item time complexity above that of existing Undifferentiated Stream Sampling algorithms.

We first review the maintenance of a single VarOpt$_k$ sample set from [10]. $k+1$ storage locations are required, i.e., k for the items stored, plus 1 for the new item. Each location stores an item weight, associated properties, and address pointers needed to maintain the data structure. Summarizing from [10], the data structure comprises two Binary Search Trees (BSTs) of total size $k+1$: Q_l which stores large items (with weight greater than the current threshold τ) and Q_s for the remaining small items. The VarOpt$_k$ sampling operation involves refreshing the τ value, selecting an item for deletion, and transferring any items that change order with respect to the new threshold, between Q_l and Q_s, as appropriate. These operations cost at most $O(\log k)$ per arriving item, amortizing to $O(\log \log k)$ over k items.

For Fair Sampling, we require a data structure Q_0 that maintains the current allocations $\{k_d : d \in \mathcal{D}\}$; see Figure 1. Q_0 is organized as a k_d-descending order priority queue Q_0 of size $|\mathcal{D}|$, implemented, e.g., as a self-balancing BST. The computation time for budget allocation is no worse than $O(\log |\mathcal{D}|)$ per arriving item. The subpopulation membership represented in each arriving stream item must be mapped to the associated location in Q_0. For a fixed set $\mathcal{D}$ of known subpopulations (e.g., interface identifiers), this mapping can be generated at initialization. Otherwise, a collision free hash of the subpopulation label d into Q_0 is used.

Finally, we describe the storage of the samples themselves in a data structure Q' which maintains VarOpt samples for all SPs in $k+1$ locations. The entry in Q_0 for SP d includes its current sampling threshold τ_d and two pointers to the roots of two BSTs, $Q_{d,l}$ and $Q_{d,s}$, within Q' that maintain the large and small items for SP d. A pointer u to the unused location in Q' also is maintained. The operation of Algorithm 3 is then the following:

- *Insertion:* An arriving item with weight w from SP d is mapped to an the appropriate location in Q_0 based on its SP label d, where the item count is incremented. The item is then inserted the empty location in Q', and incorporated in either $Q_{d,l}$ or $Q_{d,s}$, depending on the order of its weight w relative to τ_d.
- *Allocation:* When storage is full, the SP d_* whose allocation is to be decremented is the next item in the priority queue of Q_0. The allocation k_{d_*} then is decremented.
- *Sampling:* One item from SP d_* is removed by operation of VarOpt using the priority queues $Q_{d_*,l}$ and $Q_{d_*,s}$. The threshold τ_{d_*} is updated.
- *Cleanup:* The unused-location pointer u is updated. If $k_{d_*} = 0$, the SP label d_* can be removed from Q_0.

Since at most k items are stored from each SP, the operation of Algorithm 3 on Q' has the same cost as VarOpt$_k$.

To summarize: The allocation cost is $O(\log |\mathcal{D}|)$, which is no worse than $O(\log k)$ even when then set of SPs $\mathcal{D}$ is not known in advance. The sampling cost is no worse than $O(\log k)$ per item. In a setting where no SP demand is fully satisfied, each has about $k/|\mathcal{D}|$ samples, so the sampling cost is in fact no worse than $O(\log k/|\mathcal{D}|)$.

6. EVALUATION: ACCESS ROUTER FLOWS

Access routers are situated at the edge of the ISP network where they provide customer access to the network, in some cases supporting hundreds of interfaces. Interface speeds can be diverse, ranging from, e.g., Gigabit Ethernet (10^9 bps) down to T1 (1.5×10^6 bps), i.e., roughly 3 orders of magnitude. The aim of this section is to illustrate the relative advantages of Fair Sampling and Undifferentiated Sampling in serving a generic class of traffic queries over the different rate interfaces. Actually, this is already determined by the performance analysis of Theorem 5 in Section 7 following. That result can be used to practically dimension measurement systems, relating traffic rates, sampling budget, and accuracy goals. Nevertheless, we will confirm its prediction on our data; see Figure 4 in Section 7.

6.1 Interface Flow Data & Heterogeneity

The evaluation used passive flow measurements on traffic traversing an access router of a major ISP. Each flow record summarized a flow that entered the router through one of 240 active customer-facing interfaces and egressed on a single uplink into the network core. The flow records, approximately 28.4 Million in all, were compiled without packet sampling by a standalone device observing the uplink during a 24-hour period in 2011. Since the flow records were not compiled at the access router, they did not report which router interfaces were traversed. Instead, this was inferred during preprocessing by longest prefix matching against the

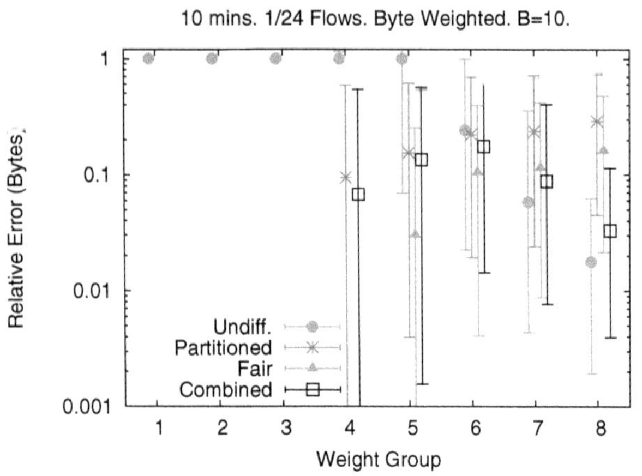

Figure 2: Byte Relative Estimation Error, Byte Weighting and average 1 in 24 flow sampling, for US, PS, FS and CS. 10 minute granularity, spatial granularity $B = 10$. Median, 10%-ile, 90-%ile.

forwarding table downloaded periodically from the access router. This preprocessing stage created a working set of derived flow records for subsequent use, that contained only anonymized versions of the IP addresses and interfaces.

The router interface line speed varied over more that three orders of magnitude. Utilization varied considerably over time and interfaces, with (non-zero) hourly utilizations varying over 5 orders of magnitude. Furthermore, large variations occurred within subsets of equal-speed interfaces. Hence, line speed is not an effective proxy for actual traffic rates, instead motivating the distribution of budget according to actual traffic demands.

This data does not represent all traffic on each access router interface, since traffic that passes directly between interfaces on the access router was not measured. However, the 5 minute average rate of interface traffic derived from SNMP polling of the access router exhibited similar variability. Furthermore, substituting forwarding tables from adjacent time periods during preprocessing scarcely changed the inferred traffic distribution, so potential staleness of the interface mapping was not an issue.

6.2 Comparisons and Reference Methods

Our principal comparison of *Fair Sampling* (FS) is with the state-of-the-art stream sampling method for completed flow records, namely *Undifferentiated Sampling* (US), in which VarOpt sampling is applied to the whole population of flow records oblivious of SP membership[3]. Two other variants are also considered. Firstly, in *Partitioned Sampling* (PS), each interface is assigned a fixed-size sampling budget in a private reservoir. The purpose of this comparison is to examine the benefits of differentially allocating the sampling budget amongst interfaces in isolation from the benefits of redistributing unused budget between interfaces.

[3]We restrict comparison to US since it is the method of *flow record* sampling on which we wish to improve in practice. Related methods described in Section 8 instead concern packet sampling, or do not allow direct expression of balanced accuracy goals over SPs, or address skewness in flow size rather than in subpopulation size.

Such an approach might conceivably be used if flow records were sampled separately at each interface. Secondly, the likely coexistence of FS and US in deployments motivates using *Combined Sampling* (CS)—see Section 2.4—to combine the two sample sets obtained from FS and US. This shows the merits of using both FS and US as opposed to using only one method but with increased budget.

6.3 Subset Sum Queries and Accuracy

Computing weight sums over subsets of flow records forms the basis of many complex database queries. One cost of sampling is reduced accuracy in estimating smaller sums. Following the accuracy goals stated in Section 3, we frame our evaluation in terms of the ability to estimate the weight of subsets of flows representing a fraction β of flows on each interface. Multiple such subsets were formed by assigning each occurring anonymized IP local address at random to one of B bins associated with the interface traversed, i.e., with $B = 1/\beta$. Let $S_{d,b}$ denote the subset of flows assigned to bin $b \in \{1, \ldots, B\}$ at interface d. Let $W_{d,b} = W(S_{d,b})$ denote the corresponding subset sum of flow weights, and $\widehat{W}_{d,b}$ its unbiased estimator. For occupied bins, the associated accuracy is the relative error $\rho_{d,b} = |1 - \widehat{W}_{d,b}/W_{d,b}|$.

Rather than focus on particular measurement applications, we abstract a detection problem: How reliably can it be detected that a weight sum $W_{d',b'}$ (within a SP d' of aggregate weight $W_{d'}$) exceeds a weight sum $W_{d,b}$ (within a SP d of aggregate weight W_d) by a factor $r > 1$, i.e., $W_{d',b'} = rW_{d,b}$. We say detection fails when $\widehat{W}_{d',b'} \leq \widehat{W}_{d,b}$.

We now compute some target detection rates for evaluation, using two bounds. Firstly, variance bounds from Section 1.5. of [10] yield $\mathsf{Var}\,\widehat{W}_{d,b} \leq W_d \cdot W_{d,b}/k_d$, and similarly for (d', b'). Secondly, Chebyshev's inequality states $\Pr[|Y - \mathsf{E}[Y]| \geq a] \leq \mathsf{Var}(Y)/a^2$ for a random variable Y and $a > 0$. Combining these, the tail distribution of the relative errors is bounded as $\Pr[\rho_{d,b} \geq \varepsilon] \leq q := W_d/(W_{d,b}k_d\varepsilon^2)$, while the probability of detection failure is bounded as

$$\frac{\mathsf{Var}\,W_{d,b} + \mathsf{Var}\,W_{d',b'}}{(W_{d,b} - W_{d',b'})^2} \leq \frac{\frac{W_d}{k_d W_{d,b}} W_{d,b}^2 + \frac{W_{d'}}{k_{d'} W_{d',b'}} W_{d',b'}^2}{(W_{d,b} - W_{d',b'})^2}$$
$$= p(q, \varepsilon, r) := q\varepsilon^2(r^2 + 1)/(r - 1)^2$$

Treating for simplicity the tail bound on $\rho_{d,b}$ as an approximation, then requiring at most a fraction q of the relative errors to exceed ε for all d, results in detection failure with probability roughly $p(q, \varepsilon, r)$. As illustrative values, we take $q = 0.1$ and $\varepsilon = 0.5$ (the 90%-ile of the relative error is to be 0.5 or less), yielding a detection failure rate of 6% for $r = 3$.

6.4 Evaluation Parameters

- *Sample Weighting:* Three variants of flow weight for VarOpt were used: byte, packet, and uniform.
- *Temporal Granularity:* 24 hours data was divided into measurement periods using either 144 windows of 10 minutes, or 24 windows of 1 hour.
- *Subset Query Granularity:* We report experiments with $B = 10$; we found the same qualitative relations amongst the performance of the sampling methods at $B = 100$, although accuracy was generally poorer.
- *Reservoir Size:* We use a constant reservoir size equivalent to a daily average flow sampling rate of 1 in 24 flows. This is

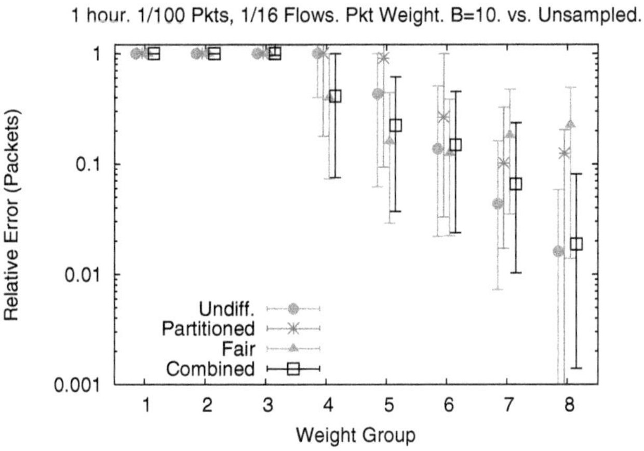

Figure 3: Packet Sampling. Relative Estimation Error for US, PS, FS, and CS. 1/100 packet sampling, 1/16 flow sampling. Packet weighting. Temporal Granularity 1 hour; Spatial: $B = 10$. Median, 10%-ile, 90-%ile.

in line with operational values and corresponds to significant reduction in both storage required and execution time for flow selection operations in database queries.

6.5 Evaluation Results

The evaluation results are presented as follows: In each parameter configuration, the experiments generated a collection of relative error statistics $\rho_{d,b}$ over all interfaces d. To break out the dependence of accuracy on subpopulation size, the errors $\rho_{d,b}$ are grouped according to true weight on their interfaces represented by the group index $g(d) = \lfloor \log_{10} W_d \rfloor$. We plot the median, 10%-ile, and 90%-ile of the $\rho_{d,b}$ values within each such weight group. In the resulting *Rangeplot* the absolute sizes are obfuscated through the adjustment $g(d) \mapsto 1 + g(d) - \min_{d'} g(d')$. A further comparison measure between sampling methods is the *Improvement Ratio*, the fraction of relative errors $\rho_{d,b}$ that are reduced, by a given sampling method, compared to another.

Figure 2 shows rangeplots of $\rho_{d,b}$ for US, PS, FS and CS under the same total budget. We see immediately:

(i) US is not able to furnish any useful estimates for medium and smaller weight groups (group 5 and lower).

(ii) FS yields negligible errors ($< 10^{-3}$) for small weight groups (2 and below) with error climbing greater than US for the largest groups, but still within target (i.e., 90%-ile relative error less than 0.5).

(iii) PS is uniformly worse than FS with error roughly twice as large for weight groups 4 and above.

(iv) CS provides a good compromise between FS and US, meeting or nearly meeting accuracy goals in all weight groups.

In terms of improvement ratios, FS improved on US in 84% of $\{d, b\}$, while the reverse held true in only 15% of cases. CS provided another 5% improvement against US mainly for a relatively small number of high weight estimates.

Space limitations preclude graphical results on two further parameter configurations. Firstly, the same general relative performance between the methods was found for uniformly weighted (as opposed to byte weighted) sampling. Secondly, the performance of CS is relatively insensitive to small to medium changes in the allocation of total budget between FS and US because (3) de-emphasizes estimates with higher thresholds τ corresponding to smaller sampling budgets.

7. ANALYSIS & PACKET SAMPLING

In our motivating example from network measurement, routers often compile flow records from a sampled packet stream, e.g., in Packet Sampled NetFlow [9]. For this reason, it is important to determine how much packet sampling offsets the advantages of downstream fair sampling of flow records for smaller SPs. To this end, we compute the relative estimation variance for a fraction β of the flows under the composition of 1 in M packet sampling followed by VarOpt flow record sampling. This extends some previous work from [13] which applied to the simpler case of threshold sampling.

THEOREM 5. *Let S be a subset of flows comprising at least a fraction β of both bytes and packets in* SP *d, subject to 1 in M packet sampling, then* VarOpt *sampling of k_d flows with byte weighting. Assume N_d total packets from all original flows in the* SP. *Then the relative estimation variance of the total bytes in S is bounded above by:*

$$R_d^2(M) = \beta^{-1}\left(k_d^{-1} + (1 + k_d^{-1})\frac{(1+r^2)(M-1)}{N_d}\right) \quad (9)$$

with r^2 the relative variance of the packet size distribution.

For system dimensioning, bounds on the relative variances of Undifferentiated (resp. Fair) Sampling are obtained by inserting $k_d^{[abs]}$ (resp. $k_d^{[rel]}$) from Theorem 1 into (9). In fact, for Fair Sampling, using $k/|\mathcal{D}|$ in place of $k_d^{[rel]}$ suffices.

We now establish the regime in which Fair Sampling is advantageous even after packet sampling. Recall from Theorem 1 the relative variance for flow record sampling alone is about $R_d^2(1) = 1/(\beta k_d)$. Assuming for simplicity that all demands can use their allocation, then Fair Sampling sets $k_d = k/|\mathcal{D}|$ while Undifferentiated Sampling has $k_d = kn_d/n$ on average, leading to lower relative variance for Fair Sampling when $n_d \leq n/|\mathcal{D}|$, or equivalently taking N_d proportional to n_d, when $N_d \leq N_{\text{tot}}/|\mathcal{D}|$, where $N_{\text{tot}} = \sum_d N_d$ is the total number of packets on all subpopulations.

But unless, due to packet sampling, the second term in (9) is smaller than the first for $k_d = k_d^{[rel]}$, then estimation variance of packet sampling will dominate that of flow sampling for all d where Fair Sampling has lower variance than Undifferentiated Sampling. Summarizing, SPs d for which

$$(1+r^2)Mk/|\mathcal{D}| < N_d < N_{\text{tot}}/|\mathcal{D}| \quad (10)$$

can expect to see a benefit from Fair Sampling. (Here we have simplified for $k, M \gg 1$). This requires the range of possible N_d be non-empty, i.e., $(1 + r^2)k < N_{\text{tot}}/M$. To conclude: *For Fair Sampling to benefit after packet sampling, the aggregate number of packets sampled in packet sampling must exceed $(1 + r^2)$ times the capacity for flows in the sampling reservoir.*

To confirm the impact of packet sampling on estimation accuracy, we repeated the experiments of Section 6 but simulating 1 in M=100 packet sampling prior to flow sampling at an average rate on 1 in 16. Since the flow data did not contain the byte sizes of individual packets, estimation focused

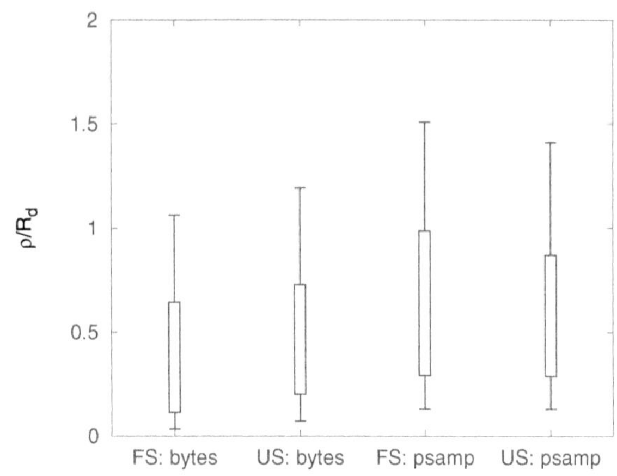

Figure 4: Ratios $\rho_{d,b}/R_d$ for FS, US in configurations of Figures 2 and 3 (w/ packet sampling). Boxplot with 25%-ile, 75%-iles, whiskers at 10%-ile and 90%-ile. Distribution near/below 1 confirms utility of (9).

instead on the number of packets in each subset $S_{d,b}$, using the number of sampled packets reported in a flow record as its sampling weight. Figure 3 compares US, PS, FS, and CS, with relative errors computed w.r.t. to the original stream before packet sampling. All methods perform badly (with relative error around 1 or greater) for small weights (groups 1–3), where only a few flows survive packet sampling. FS is more accurate than US for medium weight groups (4–6). Only CS and FS retain acceptable or near acceptable performance over weight groups 4 and higher. Estimation with FS improved on US in 46% of cases.

We now relate this behavior to the analysis of the useful regime for FS above. There were approximately N = 20 Million packets per hour, distributed over $|\mathcal{D}| = 240$ active interfaces, with $k = 10,000$ sampled flows per hour after 1 in $M = 100$ packet sampling. Thus from (10), using $r = 1$, we expect FS to improve accuracy for interface d if its hourly packet arrival rate N_d obeys: $8.4 \times 10^3 < N_d < 8.7 \times 10^5$. There were 80 such interfaces, comprising 1/3 of the total.

As a check on the predictive utility of (9) we computed the ratio $\rho_{d,b}/R_d$ over all sets $S_{d,b}$, using the actual fraction β rather than the targets $1/B$. The ratio should be distributed around or less than 1. This is confirmed in Figure 4 with boxplots of $\rho_{d,b}/R_d$ for FS and US in the configurations of Figure 2 and 3.

8. RELATED WORK

The general problem of fair resource allocation has attracted much attention in the networking context and beyond. There is extensive literature involving fairness in scheduling algorithms; see e.g., [2, 24, 30]. More recently, this approach has focused on developing areas of network management, including bandwidth allocation in wireless technologies, see e.g., [37], routing policy [31, 25], and ramifications of the choice of fairness criteria bandwidth sharing and congestion in the internet; see e.g., [23]. Some recent work that examines fairness properties of packet discard mechanisms seem somewhat suggestive of our approach [22, 27]; likewise for a recent approach to resource allocation in sensor networks [8]. However, these appear not to be directly applicable to our problem domain.

A number of papers have dealt with the differential allocation of packet sampling resources over individual flows. A starting point for these is Sample and Hold [17] in which packets are uniformly sampled, but a packet with a current cached key always is selected. Sketch Guided Sampling [26] and more recent implementations [40] counteract the inherent tendency of Sample and Hold to preferentially select longer flows, by decreasing the probability that a packet is sampled according to the currently measured flow length. The probability is chosen to uniformize the relative estimation error of different length flows. Our work is reminiscent of this general idea but different: We seek to minimize the average relative estimation error from general purpose samples of flow records of drawn from SPs of different volumes.

FlexSample [33] is a system for allocating a per-packet sampling budget over traffic SPs, including low-volume SPs, that match criteria set via a configuration language. Although the high-level motivation similar to ours, the detailed aims and context are different and lead to different approaches, as we now explain. Targeting the tight storage constraints of the router context, FlexSampling is bufferless—both packet selection and discard are final—with SP sampling probabilities dynamically adjusted according to smoothed past traffic rates. Unlike Fair Sampling, FlexSampling does not express quantitative accuracy goals for SP estimation; rather, these would depend on the SP sizes and whatever sampling probabilities the user specifies. Fair Sampling aims to yield general purpose SP flow summaries in the more resource relaxed environment typical of mediators and collectors. It does not sample packets. Working with a reservoir of provisional samples, Fair Sampling probabilities are determined by actual arrivals as a function of estimation accuracy goals. Being rate adaptive, FlexSampling distributes it budget allocation non-uniformly over the packets within a given SP, an effect which will be more pronounced after bursts of arrivals within the smoothing timescale. In contrast, Fair Sampling is uniform per unit of flow weight within each SP. Finally, the implementation of Fair Sampling is relatively simple compared with FlexSampling because it does not estimate SP rates.

Three other recent papers have dealt with broader issues of distributing sampling budget for network measurement over multiple locations. [35] and [5] considered the problem of setting rates for independent sampling in order to maximize a total utility of packets being sampled at least once. cSamp [34] uses a hash-based selection on flow keys to implicitly coordinate sampling over multiple locations in order to both partition resources over SPs and avoid duplicate measurement at different observation points.

9. CONCLUSIONS AND FUTURE WORK

In this paper, we proposed Fair Sampling as a new approach to sampling flow records derived from rate heterogeneous subpopulations of traffic, e.g., across different interfaces of an access router, or different applications. Max-Min Fair Allocation of the sampling budget was shown to be optimal for minimizing average relative estimation error over SPs of flow records generated by the different traffic components. Fair Sampling is simple, flexible and performs better than a fixed partitioning of the reservoir. Compared with undifferentiated sampling, it greatly improves estimation accuracy for all but the largest traffic components while being no more computationally complex. A combined estimator reduced relative error in 89% of cases.

General collection and analysis infrastructures can have a complex structure in which selection of an item can, in conjunction with other items, trigger downstream usage of limited resources for analysis or even further measurements. This motivates a methodological extension of fair sampling to a network of budget nodes shared by subpopulations, with items subject to resampling at multiple nodes.

10. PROOFS OF THEOREMS

PROOF OF THEOREM 1. (i) minimize $\sum_d V(n_d, k_d, \beta n_d)/|\mathcal{D}| = |\mathcal{D}|^{-1}\sum_d \beta(n_d^2/k_d - 1/n_d)$ under the constraints on the k_d. This is equivalent to

$$\begin{array}{rl} \min: & \sum_d n_d^2/k_d \\ \text{such that}: & 0 \le k_d \le n_d, \quad \sum_d k_d \le k \end{array} \tag{11}$$

Since $k \to 1/k$ is convex, an elementary convex optimization yields that k_d is proportional to n_d, and hence $k_d = kn_d/n$. The statement concerning the ratio of variance follows because $V(n_d, k_d^{[abs]}, m_d) = m_d(n_d/k_d^{[abs]} - 1) = m_d(n/k-1) = V(n, k, m_d)$.

(ii) We minimize $|\mathcal{D}|^{-1}\sum_d V(n_d, k_d, \beta n_d)/(\beta n_d)^2 = (|\mathcal{D}|\beta)^{-1}\sum_d(1/k_d - 1/n_d)$ under the constraints on the k_d. This is equivalent to

$$\begin{array}{rl} \min: & \sum_d 1/k_d \\ \text{such that}: & 0 \le k_d \le n_d, \quad \sum_d k_d \le k \end{array} \tag{12}$$

In the absence of the constraint $k_d \le n_d$, an elementary convex optimization would yield the solution the k_d is independent of $|\mathcal{D}|$ and hence $k_d = k/|\mathcal{D}|$. But when $k/|\mathcal{D}| > n_{d'}$ for the d' of minimal $n_{d'}$, this would result in a sampling probability $p_{d'} > 1$, Instead we instead set $k_{d'} = n_{d'}$, the repeat the optimization after removing the "small" interface d' from the sum and depleting the sampling resources from k to $k - n_{d'}$. We repeat until no small interfaces remain. (This must happen since $n > k$). Finally observe that the procedure we have described is just the usual progressive filling algorithm to compute the Max-Min Fair allocation of total resources k over the demands $\{n_d\}$. For "small" interfaces j whose demand is fully satisfied, the estimation variance is zero (all flows are sampled). The remaining interfaces are allocated at least $k/|\mathcal{D}|$, hence the bound follows. □

PROOF OF THEOREM 5. Let Φ_d denote the flows on interface d, and $S \subset \Phi_d$ the subset of interest. w_i is the byte size of flow i, $\widehat{w}_i$ its estimate after packet sampling, and $\widehat{y}_i$ the estimate of $\widehat{w}_i$ after flow sampling. By Lemma 1 in [13]:

$$\mathsf{Var}(\widehat{y}_i) \le \mathsf{E}[\widehat{w}_i\widehat{\tau}] + \mathsf{Var}(\widehat{w}_i) \tag{13}$$

where $\widehat{\tau}$ is now a random threshold for VarOpt that depends on all $\{\widehat{w}_i : i \in \Phi_d\}$. Setting $\widehat{W}_d = \sum_{i\in\Phi_d} w_i$:

$$k_d = \sum_{i\in\Phi_d} \min\{1, \widehat{w}_i/\widehat{\tau}\} \le \widehat{W}_d/\widehat{\tau} \tag{14}$$

Thus $\mathsf{E}[\widehat{w}_i\widehat{\tau}] \le k_d^{-1}\mathsf{E}[\widehat{w}_i\widehat{W}_d] = k_d^{-1}(w_iW_d + \mathsf{Var}(\widehat{w}_i))$. Thus so far $\mathsf{Var}(\widehat{y}_i) \le k_d^{-1}w_iW_d + (1+k_d^{-1})\,\mathsf{Var}\,\widehat{w}_i$.

A standard argument (see [13]) yields $\mathsf{Var}(\widehat{w}_i) = (M-1)\sum_j x_j^2$, summing over the sizes x_j of packets j in flow i.

From the negative covariance property of VarOpt:

$$R_d^2 = \frac{\mathsf{Var}(\sum_{i\in S}\widehat{y}_i)}{W(S)^2} \le k_d^{-1}\frac{W_d}{W(S)} + (1+k_d^{-1})\frac{\sum_j^S x_j^2}{W(S)^2}$$

with $\sum_j^S$ the sum over all $N(S)$ packets from S. The result follows since $\sum_j^S x_j^2/W(S)^2 = N(S)^{-1}\overline{x^2}/(\overline{x})^2$. □

PROOF OF THEOREM 2. Trivially $K^i = N^i$ is LMMF for $i = 1, \dots, k$ since it majorizes elementwise any feasible allocation of k. Henceforth we consider $i \ge k$ and proceed by induction. We first show that $K^{i+1} \succeq K^i$. Write the nondecreasing ordered elements of $T(K^i)$ as $k_{(1)}^i, \dots, k_{(|\mathcal{D}|)}^i$. The *index* of an element k of K will refer to its position in the vector K. The rank $r(k)$ of the element k is the lowest index of all elements with the same value k. Let D_*^i denote the set of demands that maximize $d \mapsto k_d^i + (\mathbf{1}_{d^{i+1}})_d$. If $d^{i+1} \in D_*^i$ then $T(K^{i+1}) = T(K^i)$ and we are done.

Assume now that $d^{i+1} \notin D_*^i$. Write a for rank of $k_{(d^{i+1})}^i$ in $T(K^i)$, and b for the rank of $1 + k_{d^{i+1}}^i$ is $T(K^{i+1})$. Then $T(K^{i+1})_{(j)} = k_{(j+1)}^i \ge k_{(j)}^i$ for $j = a, \dots b-1$ while $T(K^{i+1})_{(b)} = 1 + k_{(a)} \ge k_{(b)}^i$, all lower index elements being unchanged. Because $k_b^{i+1} = 1 + k_a^i$, the strict inequality $k_{a'}^{i+1} > k_{a'}^i$ must hold for some $a' \in \{a, \dots, b\}$ and hence $K^{i+1} \succ K^i$. Now $\mathcal{X}(N^i, k) \subset \mathcal{X}(N^{i+1}, k)$ since $n_d^i \le n_d^{i+1}$ for all $d \in \mathcal{D}$. Hence for each $K \in \mathcal{X}(N^i, k)$ we have shown that $K^{i+1} \succ K^i \succeq K$.

It remains only to show that $K^{i+1} \succeq K'$ for all $K' \in \mathcal{X}(N^{i+1}, k) \setminus \mathcal{X}(N^i, k)$. Any such K' must be an element of $\mathcal{X}_{d^{i+1}}(N^{i+1}, k)$, since, if not, $k'_{d^{i+1}} \le n_{d^{i+1}}^{i+1} = n_{d^{i+1}}^i - 1$ which would mean $K' \in \mathcal{X}(N^i, k)$. Hence $K' = K + \mathbf{1}_{d^{i+1}} - \mathbf{1}_d$ for some $K \in \mathcal{X}_{d^{i+1}}(N^i, k)$ and $d \neq d^{i+1} \in \mathcal{D}$. Thus it suffices to show that:

(i) $K^i + \mathbf{1}_{d^{i+1}} \succeq K + \mathbf{1}_{d^{i+1}}$ for any $K \in \mathcal{X}_{d^{i+1}}(N^i, k)$. This follows from Theorem 3 since we assume $K^i \succeq K$ for any $K \in \mathcal{X}(N^i, k)$.

(ii) $K^i + \mathbf{1}_{d^{i+1}} - \mathbf{1}_{d_*} \succeq K + \mathbf{1}_{d^{i+1}} - \mathbf{1}_d$ for any $K \in \mathcal{X}_{d^{i+1}}(N^i, k)$, $d_* \in D_*^i$ and $d \in \mathcal{D}$. Given (i), this follows from Theorem 4

□

PROOF OF THEOREM 3. Let $a = \min\{i : k_{(i)} > k'_{(i)}\}$, so that $k_{(j)} = k'_{(j)}$ for $j < i$. **Case: $k_{(a)} < k_d$.** Since $k_{(a)} < k_d \le k_{d'}$, then $T(K + \mathbf{1}_d)_{(i)} = k_{(i)}$ and $T(K' + \mathbf{1}_d)_{(i)} = k'$ for $i \le a$. Hence $K + \mathbf{1}_d \succeq K' + \mathbf{1}_d$.

Case: $k_{(a)} = k_d$. Since $k'_d \ge k_d = k_a > k'_{(a)} \ge k'_{(i)}$ for $i < a$, d is not one of the a lowest ranked demands of K'. Hence $T(K' + \mathbf{1}_d)_{(i)} = T(K')_{(i)}$ for $i \le a$ and $K + \mathbf{1}_d \succeq K' + \mathbf{1}_d$.

Case: $k_{(a)} > k_d$. Since $k'_d \ge k_d$, and $k_{(i)} = k'_{(i)}$ for $i < a$, the rank r' of k'_d in $T(K')$ is no less than the rank r of k_d in $T(K)$. If $k'_d = k_d$ then $r = r'$, and $T(K + \mathbf{1}_d)_{(i)} = T(K +' \mathbf{1}_d)_{(i)}$ for all $i < a$, except for the possible boundary case $k'_d = k'_{(a-1)} = k'_{(a)}$. In this case $T(K + \mathbf{1}_d)_{(i)} = T(K')_{(i)}$ for all $i < a$, the addition of $\mathbf{1}_d$ to K' yielding an increment of the a-ranked item. The corresponding increment to K is located at its $(a-1)$-ranked item since $k_{(a)} > k'_{(a)} = k'_{(a-1)} = k_{(a-1)}$ and so $T(K + \mathbf{1}_d)_{(i)} = T(K' + \mathbf{1}_d)_{(i)}$ for $i < a - 1$ while $T(K + \mathbf{1}_d)_{(a-1)} > T(K' + \mathbf{1}_d)_{(a-1)}$. Hence $K + \mathbf{1}_d \succeq K' + \mathbf{1}_d$. A similar argument holds if $k'_d > k_d$. □

PROOF OF THEOREM 4. **Case: $k_{(a)} < k_{d^*}$.**. Subtracting $\mathbf{1}_{d^*}$ from K leaves its a lowest ranked elements unchanged, and hence $K - \mathbf{1}_{d_*} \succeq K' \succeq K' - \mathbf{1}_d$.

Case: $k_{(a)} = k_{d^*}$. The effect of subtracting $\mathbf{1}_{d^*}$ from K is to decrement the rank a element. Thus if the rank of k'_d in K' is $\leq a$, then $T(K' - \mathbf{1}_d)_{(i)} < T(K)_{(i)} = T(K - \mathbf{1}_{d*})_{(i)}$ for one $i \in \{1, \ldots, a-1\}$ and possibly also for $i = a$, with equality for all other $i \in \{1, \ldots, a-1\}$ and the result follows.

If the rank of k'_d in K' is $> a$, we are done except if possibly $k'_{(a)}$ takes the maximum value compatible with $K \succ K'$, namely $k_{d_*} - 1$, for then the first k elements of $T(K - \mathbf{1}_{d_*})$ and $T(K' - \mathbf{1}_d)$ are equal. But then the assumption $\Sigma K \geq \Sigma K'$ implies $\Sigma_{j>a} k'_{(j)} \leq 1 + \Sigma_{j>a} k_{d_*}$. We consider the case of equality first; the unequal case follows easily. Since $k'_{(a')} \geq k'_{(a)} = k_{d_*} - 1$ for $a' > a$, either $k'_{(a')} = k_{d_*} - 1 < k_{(a)}$ holds for a' in some set $\{a+1, a+2, \ldots, \tilde{a}\}$, in which case we are done, or it holds for no such a'. In this latter case, $k'_{(a')} = k_{d_*}$ for all $a' > a$ except for $k'_{(|\mathcal{D}|} = k_{d_*} + 1$. Decrementing the largest of these yields $T(K + \mathbf{1}_{d_*}) = T(K' + \mathbf{1}_d)$ while decrementing any other yields $K + \mathbf{1}_{d_*} \succ K' + \mathbf{1}_d$. $\square$

11. REFERENCES

[1] AT&T's Global Networking Facts. http://www.corp.att.com/globalnetworking.

[2] D. Bertsekas and R. Gallager. *Data Networks*. Prentice-Hall, Englewood Cliffs, NJ, 1992.

[3] R. Bhargava, A. Goel, and A. Meyerson. Using approximate majorization to characterize protocol fairness. In *SIGMETRICS '01*, pages 330–331, New York, NY, 2001.

[4] CAIDA: The Cooperative Association for Internet Data Analysis. http://www.caida.org.

[5] G. R. Cantieni, G. Iannaccone, C. Barakat, C. Diot, and P. Thiran. Reformulating the monitor placement problem: optimal network-wide sampling. In *CoNEXT '06*, pages 5:1–5:12, New York, NY, 2006.

[6] M. T. Chao. A general purpose unequal probability sampling plan. *Biometrika*, 69(3):653–656, 1982.

[7] S. Chaudhuri, G. Das, M. Data, R. Motwani, and V. Narasayya. Overcomng limitations of sampling for aggregation queries. In *ICDE'01*, pages 534–542, 2001.

[8] S. Chen, Y. Fang, and Y. Xia. Lexicographic maxmin fairness for data collection in wireless sensor networks. *IEEE Transactions on Mobile Computing*, 6:762–776, 2007.

[9] Cisco NetFlow. http://www.cisco.com/warp/public/732/Tech/netflow.

[10] E. Cohen, N. Duffield, H. Kaplan, C. Lund, and M. Thorup. Stream sampling for variance-optimal estimation of subset sums. In *Proc. 20th ACM-SIAM Symposium on Discrete Algorithms*, 2009.

[11] C. Cranor, T. Johnson, O. Spatscheck, and V. ladislav Shkapenyuk. Gigascope: A stream database for network applications. In *Proc ACM SIGMOD*, June 2003.

[12] A. Dhamdhere, L. Breslau, N. G. Duffield, C. Ee, A. Gerber, C. Lund, and S. Sen. Flowroute: inferring forwarding table updates using passive flow-level measurements. In *IMC 2010*, pages 315–321, 2010.

[13] N. Duffield and C. Lund. Predicting resource usage and estimation accuracy in an IP flow measurement collection infrastructure. In *ACM SIGCOMM Internet Measurement Workshop*, 2003. Miami Beach, Fl, October 27-29, 2003.

[14] N. Duffield, C. Lund, and M. Thorup. Learn more, sample less: control of volume and variance in network measurements. *IEEE Transactions on Information Theory*, 51(5):1756–1775, 2005.

[15] N. Duffield, C. Lund, and M. Thorup. Optimal combination of sampled network measurements. In *Proc. ACM SIGCOMM Internet Measurement Conference (IMC)*, pages 91–104, 2005.

[16] N. Duffield, C. Lund, and M. Thorup. Priority sampling for estimation of arbitrary subset sums. *J. ACM*, 54(6):Article 32, December, 2007. Announced at SIGMETRICS'04.

[17] C. Estan and G. Varghese. New directions in traffic measurement and accounting. In *Proc. ACM SIGCOMM '2002*, Pittsburgh, PA, August 2002.

[18] J. Faffe. Bottleneck flow control. *IEEE Trans. Comm.*, 29(7):954–962, July 1981.

[19] A. Feldmann, J. Rexford, and R. Cáceres. Efficient policies for carrying web traffic over flow-switched networks. *IEEE/ACM Transactions on Networking*, 6(6):673–685, December 1998.

[20] M. Grossglauser and J. Rexford. Passive traffic measurement for IP operations. In K. Park and W. Willinger, editors, *The Internet as a Large-Scale Complex System*. Oxford University Press, 2005.

[21] D. G. Horvitz and D. J. Thompson. A generalization of sampling without replacement from a finite universe. *J. Amer. Stat. Assoc.*, 47(260):663–685, 1952.

[22] M. Hosaagrahara and H. Sethu. Max-min fair scheduling in input-queued switches. *IEEE Transactions on Parallel and Distributed Systems*, 19:462–475, 2008.

[23] F. Kelly. Charging and rate control for elastic traffic. *European Trans. Telecomm.*, 8(1):33–37, 1997.

[24] S. Keshav. *An Engineering Approach to Computer Networking*. Addison-Wesley, Reading, MA, 1997.

[25] J. Kleinberg, E. Tardos, and Y. Rabani. Fairness in routing and load balancing. *Foundations of Computer Science, Annual IEEE Symposium on*, 0:568, 1999.

[26] A. Kumar and J. Xu. Sketch guided sampling - using on-line estimates of flow size for adaptive data collection. In *INFOCOM*, 2006.

[27] N. Kumar, R. Pan, and D. Shah. Fair scheduling in input-queued switches under inadmissible traffic. In *IEEE Globecom*, volume 3, pages 1713–1717, 2004.

[28] S. Leinen. UDP Samplicator. http://www.switch.ch/network/downloads/tf-tant/samplicator.

[29] W. B. Norton. DrPeering.net. http://drpeering.net.

[30] A. K. Parekh and R. G. Gallager. A generalized processor sharing approach to flow control in integrated services networks: the single-node case. *IEEE/ACM Trans. Netw.*, 1:344–357, June 1993.

[31] M. Pioro, G. Fodor, P. Nilsson, and E. Kubilinskas. On efficient max-min fair routing algorithms. *Computers and Communications, IEEE Symposium on*, 0:365, 2003.

[32] B. Radunović and J.-Y. L. Boudec. A unified framework for max-min and min-max fairness with applications. *IEEE/ACM Trans. Netw.*, 15:1073–1083, October 2007.

[33] A. Ramachandran, S. Seetharaman, N. Feamster, and V. Vazirani. Fast monitoring of traffic subpopulations. In *Proc. Internet Measurement Conference 2008*, pages 257–270, New York, NY, USA, 2008.

[34] V. Sekar, M. K. Reiter, W. Willinger, H. Zhang, R. R. Kompella, and D. G. Andersen. cSamp: A system for network-wide flow monitoring. In *Proc. 5th USENIX NSDI*, San Francisco, CA, Apr. 2008.

[35] K. Suh, Y. Guo, J. Kurose, and D. Towsley. Locating network monitors: Complexity, heuristics and coverage. In *IEEE Infocom'05*, 2005.

[36] M. Szegedy and M. Thorup. On the variance of subset sum estimation. In *Proc. 15th ESA, LNCS 4698*, pages 75–86, 2007.

[37] L. Tassiulas and S. Sarkar. Maxmin fair scheduling in wireless networks. In *in Proceedings of IEEE INFOCOM*, pages 763–772, 2001.

[38] Y. Tillé. *Sampling Algorithms*. Springer, New York, 2006.

[39] J. Vitter. Random sampling with a reservoir. *ACM Trans. Math. Softw.*, 11(1):37–57, 1985.

[40] J. Zhang, X. Niu, and J. Wu. A space-efficient fair packet sampling algorithm. In *Proceedings of the 11th Asia-Pacific Symposium on Network Operations and Management*, APNOMS '08, pages 246–255, Berlin, Heidelberg, 2008.

TCAM-based NFA Implementation *

Kunyang Peng and Qunfeng Dong†
Institute of Networked Systems (IONS) & School of Computer Science and Technology
University of Science and Technology of China
Hefei, Anhui, People's Republic of China

Categories and Subject Descriptors

C.2.0 [**Computer-communication networks**]: General—*Security and protection(e.g.,firewalls)*; C.3 [**Special-purpose and application-based systems**]: Real-time and embedded systems

General Terms

Design, Performance, Security

Keywords

Regular Expression Matching, NFA, TCAM

1. INTRODUCTION

Regular expression matching is the core packet inspection engine of network equipments (e.g. routers, firewalls), implementing various functions of today's Internet, such as intrusion detection/prevention, worm detection, content filtering, application identification and so on. By defining patterns of interest (e.g. worm signatures) as regular expressions and searching in network traffic for pattern match, relevant information can be extracted for taking prompt actions.

Regular expression matching is performed using either DFA or NFA, each having its own drawbacks. NFA has to keep track of all possible active states, resulting in unpredictable matching speed. DFA size (i.e., the number of DFA states) can grow exponentially with regular expression pattern set size. The ideal objective of fast and scalable regular expression matching is formally defined as follows: it takes a small constant number of memory lookups — ideally one simple memory lookup (like DFA) — to match each input character and storage space growing linearly with regular expression pattern set size (like NFA) [5, 6]. Towards this ultimate goal, numerous methods have been proposed, but none has been both fast and scalable. They either require exponentially growing storage space, and/or introduce various overhead and inefficiency into the matching process.

Most recently, ternary content addressable memory (TCAM) has been considered as a promising platform for implementing DFAs to achieve high speed and memory efficient regular expression matching [2, 3, 4, 5, 6]. In this work, we propose a fundamentally different approach — TCAM-based NFA implementation — towards fast and scalable regular expression matching. An illustrative example is briefly outlined in Section 2.

*This work was supported in part by the Ministry of Education (MOE) Program for New Century Excellent Talents (NCET) in University, by the Science and Technological Fund of Anhui Province for Outstanding Youth under Grant No. 10040606Y05, by the Fundamental Research Funds for the Central Universities under Grant No. WK0110000007 and Grant No. WK0110000019, by the National Natural Science Foundation of China under Grant No. 61073184, and by Jiangsu Provincial Science Foundation under Grant No. BK2011360.

†All correspondence should be directed to Prof. Qunfeng Dong (qunfeng.dong@ieee.org).

SIGMETRICS'12, June 11–15, 2012, London, England, UK.
ACM 978-1-4503-1097-0/12/06.

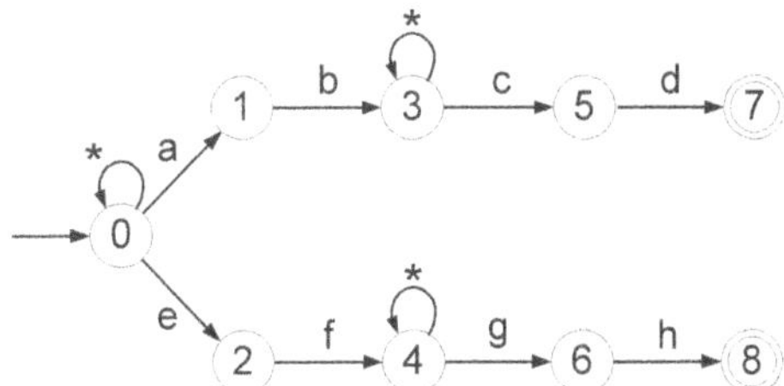

Figure 1: NFA for matching `ab.*cd` and `ef.*gh`.

2. TCAM-BASED NFA IMPLEMENTATION

To implement an NFA using TCAM, we design a TCAM encoding scheme for encoding an NFA into TCAM entries. The entire solution consists of three stages. First, we define a scheme for encoding the status of NFA. Second, we encode all NFA transitions into TCAM entries based on the encoding of NFA status. Finally, we merge the TCAM entries to obtain a more compact TCAM implementation. We illustrate our method using the NFA for matching `ab.*cd` and `ef.*gh` [7] as an example, which is shown in Figure 1.

An NFA can have multiple active states simultaneously; we refer to the set of active states as the NFA's *configuration* [7]. To encode NFA configurations, we first divide all NFA states into a number of *compatible groups* [7], where at most one state in each compatible group can be active at any moment. Each NFA state is assigned a non-zero *active code* [7] that is unique within its compatible group. For an m-state compatible group, we use an *active segment* [7] composed of $\lceil \log(m+1) \rceil$ bits to record the active code of the NFA state that is currently active in that group. (The all-zero active code is reserved for representing the case where none of the states in that group is active.) Thus, an NFA config-

TCAM					SRAM			
Source Configuration				Input	Destination Configuration			
{0}	{3}	{4}	{1,2,5,6,7,8}		{0}	{3}	{4}	{1,2,5,6,7,8}
1	0	0	000	a	0	0	0	001
1	0	0	000	e	0	0	0	010
1	0	0	000	*	0	0	0	000
1	1	0	000	a	0	0	0	001
1	1	0	000	c	0	0	0	011
1	1	0	000	e	0	0	0	010
1	1	0	000	*	0	0	0	000

Table 1: TCAM encoding of two NFA configurations {0} and {0, 3} of the NFA in Figure 1.

uration can be encoded with an *active vector* [7] formed by the concatenation of all active segments.

For example in Figure 1, the NFA states are partitioned into four compatible groups: {0}, {3}, {4}, and {1,2,5,6,7,8}. In our encoding scheme, each self-looping state (which has more than 128 transitions pointing back to itself) forms a separate compatible group. The six states in {1,2,5,6,7,8} are assigned `001` ~ `110` as their active code, respectively. The active vector for encoding the NFA's configuration is thus composed of four corresponding active segments, as shown in the `Source Configuration` and `Destination Configuration` columns of Table 1.

A TCAM chip is configured as a set of TCAM entries, each consisting of a TCAM part and an SRAM part. In our TCAM encoding scheme, each NFA transition is encoded as a TCAM entry, which is logically composed of three parts: *source configuration*, *input character* and *destination configuration*. The source configuration part represents NFA's current active states, encoded as an active vector; the destination configuration part represents NFA's active states after transition on the input character, and is also encoded as an active vector.

For example in Table 1, the first TCAM entry means when state 0 is the only active state, after processing input character `a`, the new active states (i.e., the destination configuration) will be {0,1}. Suppose state 0 is currently the only active state and input character is `a`, we combine this NFA configuration encoded as `1 0 0 000` with input character `a` to form the TCAM search key. In one clock cycle, TCAM compares the search key against the TCAM part of all TCAM entries simultaneously, and returns the highest matching entry. A ternary `*` bit in the TCAM part matches both `0` and `1` in TCAM search key. In this case, the first TCAM entry and the third TCAM entry in Table 1 will both match the search key; the first TCAM entry is returned as the first matching entry, and we correctly take its destination configuration as the new active states. (Here in the destination configuration part, to facilitate subsequent TCAM entry merging, the active segments of self-looping states encode the XOR of their values in source configuration and destination configuration.)

With this XOR encoding, the first entry and fourth entry in Table 1 can be merged into one new entry — `1 * 0 000 a 0 0 0 001`. Finally, after merging all TCAM entries encoding the NFA into a more compact yet semantically equivalent set of entries, nine TCAM entries in Table 2 have been sufficient to properly implement this 9-state NFA in Figure 1.

TCAM					SRAM			
Source Configuration				Input	Destination Configuration			
{0}	{3}	{4}	{1,2,5,6,7,8}		{0}	{3}	{4}	{1,2,5,6,7,8}
1	*	*	***	a	0	0	0	001
1	0	*	001	b	0	1	0	000
1	1	*	***	c	0	0	0	011
1	1	*	011	d	0	0	0	101
1	*	*	***	e	0	0	0	010
1	*	0	010	f	0	0	1	000
1	*	1	***	g	0	0	0	100
1	*	1	100	h	0	0	0	110
1	*	*	***	*	0	0	0	000

Table 2: TCAM encoding of the entire NFA in Figure 1 (after entry merging).

In the mean time, NFA transition on any input character is done with one single TCAM lookup (just like the TCAM-based DFA implementation methods).

3. PRELIMINARY RESULTS

We compare our TCAM-based NFA implementation method with the state-of-the-art method for TCAM-based DFA implementation [6], through experiments based on regular expression pattern sets collected from the Snort intrusion detection system [1]. In general, the number of TCAM entries used by our NFA method is consistently below DFA size, and much smaller than the number of TCAM entries used by the DFA method. Especially, the number of TCAM entries used by our method comes much closer to the linearly growing NFA size. The general trend is that, the more inflated is a DFA, the more we need to deflate it, and the higher compression ratio is obtained by our method. As the number of bits per entry used by these methods are not much different, the total number of bits used by our NFA method is much smaller than the DFA method as well.

4. REFERENCES

[1] http://www.snort.org/.

[2] M. Chen, Q. Dong, and K. Peng. TCAM-based DFA implementation: A novel approach to efficient regular expression matching. Technical report, Institute of Networked Systems (IONS), University of Science and Technology of China.

[3] M. Chen. TCAM-based high speed regular expression matching. Bachelor thesis, Institute of Networked Systems (IONS), University of Science and Technology of China, June 2010.

[4] C. R. Meiners, J. Patel, E. Norige, E. Torng, and A. X. Liu. Fast regular expression matching using small TCAMs for network intrusion detection and prevention systems. In *Proceedings of USENIX Security*, August 2010.

[5] K. Peng, Q. Dong, and M. Chen. TCAM-based DFA deflation: A novel approach to fast and scalable regular expression matching. In *Proceedings of ACM/IEEE IWQoS*, 2011.

[6] K. Peng, S. Tang, Q. Dong, and M. Chen. Chain-based DFA deflation for fast and scalable regular expression matching using TCAM. In *Proceedings of ACM/IEEE ANCS*, 2011.

[7] Y. Zu, M. Yang, Z. Xu, L. Wang, X. Tian, K. Peng, and Q. Dong. GPU-based NFA implementation for high speed memory efficient regular expression matching. In *Proceedings of ACM PPoPP*, 2012.

Stable and Efficient Pricing for Inter-domain Traffic Forwarding

Elliot Anshelevich
Computer Science Dept.
Rensselaer Polytechnic Institute
Troy, NY 12180
eanshel@cs.rpi.edu

Ameya Hate
Computer Science Dept.
Rensselaer Polytechnic Institute
Troy, NY 12180
hatea@rpi.edu

Koushik Kar
ECSE Dept.
Rensselaer Polytechnic Institute
Troy, NY 12180
koushik@ecse.rpi.edu

Michael Usher
Computer Science Dept.
Rensselaer Polytechnic Institute
Troy, NY 12180
usherm@rpi.edu

ABSTRACT

We address the question of strategic pricing of inter-domain traffic forwarding services provided by ISPs, which is also closely coupled with the question of how ISPs route their traffic towards their neighboring ISPs. Posing this question as a non-cooperative game between neighboring ISPs, we study the properties of this pricing game in terms of the existence and efficiency of the equilibrium. We observe that for "well-provisioned" ISPs, Nash equilibrium prices exist and they result in flows that maximize the overall network utility (generalized end-to-end throughput). For general ISP topologies, equilibrium prices may not exist; however, simulations on a large number of realistic topologies show that best-response based simple price update solutions converge to stable and efficient prices and flows for most topologies.

Categories and Subject Descriptors

B.2.2 [**Performance Analysis and Design Aids**]: Simulation; K.6.2 [**Installation Management**]: Pricing and resource allocation

Keywords

Internet, Next-hop Routing, Pricing, Economics

1. INTRODUCTION

The broad question we address in this paper involves determining how inter-domain traffic forwarding services should be priced. More specifically, this involves finding the "right" price that ISPs should charge for the traffic forwarding services they provide to their upstream neighbors, typically done through SLA agreements (short- or long-term) formed between neighboring ISPs or Autonomous Systems (ASes) in the Internet. As ISPs are generally interested in maximizing their individual profits, this question is naturally studied in the framework of non-cooperative game theory, as we do in this work.

Technically, our work is related to the growing body of literature on strategic pricing of bandwidth/flow/services over the Internet, although most of the existing work either uses restrictive network topology models, and/or focuses on "source routing" and pricing game models [2]. In these models, the source node of the traffic determines its entire route from the source to the destination. The efficiency of selfish flow routing by users is considered in [4]. Next-hop routing and pricing models have been considered recently in [3] and [5]. However these papers only consider a single-source single-sink network, and associate latency functions with links instead of considering link capacities.

2. CONTRIBUTION AND SIGNIFICANCE

We introduce and analyze a model of dynamic strategic pricing between ISPs, which is also closely integrated to the question of inter-domain traffic engineering. We model the Internet as an interconnected system of ISPs and represent an ISP as a *cloud*, that is composed of a set of nodes (routers) and capacitated links connected into an arbitrary topology. A subset of these nodes represents the ISP's ingress and egress nodes. At an ingress node, an ISP offers to its neighboring (upstream) ISP a per-unit price for forwarding traffic to a destination, and accepts the traffic to be forwarded. The ISP also derives utility for forwarding the traffic generated within its own network, and must decide how to forward (split) its traffic (that is offered to it by upstream neighbors, or generated inside its network) among its downstream neighbors (egress points). ISPs are assumed non-cooperative in nature, and pricing and traffic forwarding decisions are made such that they maximize the individual ISP's profit.

Although not shown in this version of the paper, we partially characterize Nash equilibria with a nice structure, and show how to compute (and the existence of) a Nash equilibrium as good as the optimum centralized solution for the case when the network is *well-provisioned*. By *well-provisioned*, we mean that bottlenecks only occur on inter-ISP links, and thus the inside of every cloud has enough

SIGMETRICS'12, June 11–15, 2012, London, England, UK.
ACM 978-1-4503-1097-0/12/06.

capacity to support whatever traffic may be required. We observe that simple price dynamics converge to stable solutions in an overwhelming majority of our simulations. Moreover, the solutions that price dynamics converge to are not only stable, but have excellent social welfare (overall utility), often within a few percent of the social optimum. Our dynamic pricing update policies, that have been observed to quickly converge and result in near-optimal flows (for most topologies), could be used to obtain these prices dynamically in a fully distributed manner.

3. SIMULATION RESULTS

Below we present results for *well-provisioned* networks. Note that our findings for general network topologies were very similar, but the simulations were more limited due to the large running time needed to perform them. We experimented with two different models of inter-ISP connectivity: (i) *Uniformly-random connectivity*, (ii) *BRITE-generated connectivity*. Details of the simulation setup will be provided in the full version of this paper but due to space limitations, we only present results for BRITE-generated topologies [1]. In these simulations, ISPs use best-response based price update strategy where each ISP increases or decreases the edge price by one if it is expected to increase the ISP's utility. The price remains the same if no gain in utility can be made.

Frequency of Convergence

We first study how frequently our pricing update policy converged to result in stable total utility/prices/flow values. Figure 1 plots the ratio of networks of a given size in which the total utility values converged, to the total number of networks tested for the BRITE-generated topology. We observed that this frequency is almost 100% in nearly all cases for BRITE-generated topologies.

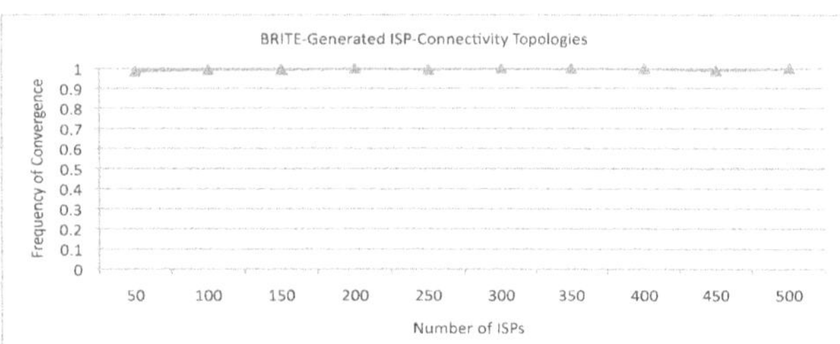

Figure 1: Frequency of Convergence (BRITE-generated connectivity).

Time of Convergence

Next we study the average convergence time, counting only the networks for which the pricing update policy converged, as discussed above. The result for BRITE-generated topology is shown in Figure 2. We observe that the average convergence time is quite short: less than 30 cycles for BRITE-generated connectivity.

Utility upon Convergence vs Optimum Utility

Next we study the network utility attained on convergence, and discuss how it compares with the optimal utility. Network utility can be viewed as generalized end-to-end throughput attained in the network. Figure 3 shows the network

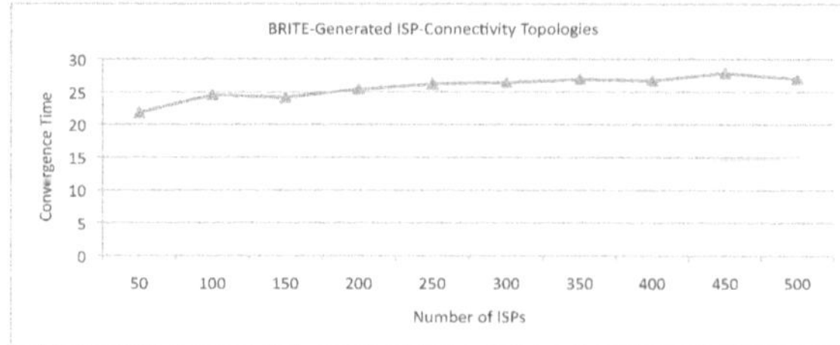

Figure 2: Convergence Time (BRITE-generated connectivity)

utility attained on convergence, as a fraction of the optimum utility for the BRITE-generated topology. The optimum utility is calculated by solving a weighted maxflow problem in the entire network (from all ISP sources to the single destination ISP). We observe that the attained utility remains quite close to the optimum, on the average, for networks up to 500 ISPs. While the ratio of attained utility and optimal utility reduces slightly as the number of ISPs increase, this reduction is quite modest – it reduces from 90% to 80% as we increase the number of ISPs from 50 to 500.

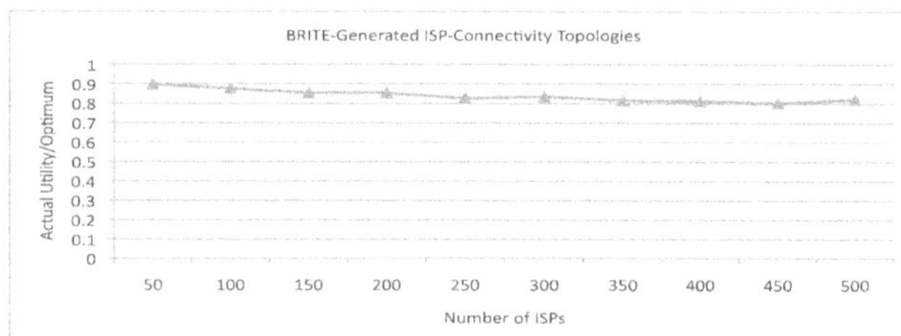

Figure 3: Ratio of Average Utility attained on convergence and Optimal Utility (BRITE-generated connectivity).

4. ACKNOWLEDGEMENTS

This work was supported in part by NSF grants CNS-1017932 and CCF-0914782.

5. REFERENCES

[1] Alberto Medina, Anukool Lakhina, Ibrahim Matta, and John Byers. `http://www.cs.bu.edu/brite/` [Accessed: 29 Mar. 2012].

[2] Asuman Ozdaglar and R. Srikant. Incentives and pricing in communication networks. In *Algorithmic Game Theory*, pages 571–591. Cambridge Press, 2007.

[3] Christos H. Papadimitriou and Gregory Valiant. A new look at selfish routing. In *Proc. of ICS*, pages 178–187, Beijing, China, 2010. Tsinghua University Press.

[4] Tim Roughgarden and Éva Tardos. How bad is selfish routing? *J. ACM*, 49:236–259, March 2002.

[5] Yufang Xi and E.M. Yeh. Pricing, competition, and routing for selfish and strategic nodes in multi-hop relay networks. In *INFOCOM 2008. The 27th Conf. on Comput. Commun. IEEE*, pages 1463 –1471, Phoenix, AZ, April 2008.

Measuring and Characterizing Home Networks

Lucas DiCioccio
Technicolor
UPMC Sorbonne Universites
lucas.dicioccio@technicolor.com

Renata Teixeira
CNRS
UPMC Sorbonne Universites
renata.teixeira@lip6.fr

Catherine Rosenberg
University of Waterloo
cath@ecemail.uwaterloo.ca

Categories and Subject Descriptors

C.2 [**Computer-Communication Networks**]: Local and Wide-Area Networks

Keywords

End-host monitoring, Home network

1. INTRODUCTION

A household today can have a variety of devices ranging from personal devices like laptops and smartphones to printers, game consoles, and media centers. These devices connect among themselves and to the Internet via a local-area network—a *home network*. A better understanding of home network performance and configuration should enable research in a number of areas, for example: home network troubleshooting and management techniques.

Unfortunately, there is little data on home networks. Most previous measurement efforts have focused on residential access links [3, 4]. The lack of data on home networks is partially due to the challenges of collecting home network data on a large scale. The vast majority of home networks are behind network-address translators, so a measurement point outside the home cannot measure the characteristics of the home network itself. Although it is feasible to deploy measurement points inside the homes of a few volunteers (as HomeMaestro did in the UK [2]), a small set of homes cannot offer a characterization of home networks at large. The effort necessary to recruit a large number of volunteers is a hurdle in itself.

We address this challenge by designing HomeNet Profiler.[1] Users run HomeNet Profiler from an end-system directly connected to their home network. HomeNet Profiler collects home network configuration and performance data. Because it runs from inside the home, HomeNet Profiler can perform a number of measurements to learn about the home network, for instance scan the local network for active devices. This paper describes the design and implementation of HomeNet Profiler. We also evaluate the performance of HomeNet Profiler – in particular how long HomeNet Profiler takes to run in real homes – and describe our initial data collection effort.

2. HomeNet Profiler DESIGN

Requirements.

The primary requirement for a home network data collection tool is that it *runs from inside the home*. The goal of measuring a large diversity of home networks and the fact that it is not possible to collect data inside a user's home without explicit user agreement and participation imposes additional requirements. HomeNet Profiler should be easy to run, even for users who are not tech-savvy. In particular, the tool should be portable and work for most home networks and end systems. Also, HomeNet Profiler should respect users' privacy: users are unlikely to run a measurement tool inside their homes if the tool collects information that they consider private. Further, we are asking home users to do us a favor by allowing us to collect data inside their homes. Hence, HomeNet Profiler must not be a burden for users, especially in terms of time and resources. Finally, HomeNet Profiler should offer an incentive for participation. Indeed, if users can get something out of the tool, then we are more likely to get a larger number of participants.

System overview.

We implement HomeNet Profiler as a client/server application. The server hosts the HomeNet Profiler website, which users visit to download the HomeNet Profiler client. Once the client finishes loading in the user's end-system, HomeNet Profiler starts in a separate window. Upon completion, the client sends all collected data to the server and redirects the web browser to a report page. Both the HomeNet Profiler client and the HomeNet Profiler website are available in French and English. A *run* refers to one execution of HomeNet Profiler in an end-system.

Measurement modules.

We select a broad range of measurements to learn as much as possible about the home network. At the same time, measurements should not take too long to execute, otherwise users might give up in the middle of the run. The HomeNet Profiler client has the following measurement modules.

Device scan: searches for active network interfaces. HomeNet Profiler sends UDP packets to all IP addresses in the end-system's LAN and then reads the ARP cache of the end-system.

Service scan: queries two commonly-used protocols to advertise services in home electronics: Zeroconf and UPnP. We opt for querying these protocols instead of a port scan per device, which is intrusive and may take several minutes to complete.

Configuration of the UPnP gateway: collects (in cases where the home gateway has UPnP) the home gateway model, the upstream connectivity type and synchronization speeds (e.g., Cable 4Mbps upload, 1Mbps download), as well as traffic counters, which report the number of bytes and packets transferred.

WiFi networks: collects the list of access points found with a WiFi scan. For each access point we collect the network name, the base station identifier, the channel number, and the received signal strength indicator.

[1] HomeNet Profiler is available at `http://cmon.lip6.fr/hnp`.

SIGMETRICS'12, June 11–15, 2012, London, England, UK.
ACM 978-1-4503-1097-0/12/06.

Netalyzr [3]: performs a number of tests related to the access network configuration, security, and performance. HomeNet Profiler invokes Netalyzr's command-line client.

Computer configuration: collects the name and version of the operating system; the end-system's network configuration, including the list of DNS servers and TCP parameters; and the list of network interfaces with the corresponding IP addresses.

Running applications: captures the list of processes running on the end-system as well as the list of TCP ports listening for incoming connections and open UDP ports. We also collect system services in MacOS and Windows.

Installed applications: lists the applications we find on the PATH environment variable. It may not reflect the full list of installed applications.

User survey: HomeNet Profiler complements and validates measurements with a user survey which runs in parallel to the measurement modules. We design the survey to be fast for users to complete and easy for us to interpret the results. Hence, all questions but one are multiple choice.

Finally, when HomeNet Profiler's server receives the client reports, it maps the client's public IP address to its geographical location and AS number using the Maxmind database.

User incentives and privacy.

As incentive to attract users, HomeNet Profiler presents a report after a measurement run.[2] The report provides some simple advice on improving home network performance. We also address privacy questions and comply with French laws by anonymizing all personally-identifiable information using SHA1. At the end of a run, HomeNet Profiler only leaves a random identifier on the user's machine to track multiple runs from the same end-system. Moreover, all measurements and the user survey are optional. As a result, users can adjust HomeNet Profiler to match their time and privacy requirements.

Pilot study.

We ran a pilot study with a small group of students, colleagues, and friends from France, Brazil, Canada, and the United States. The purpose of this study was to test measurement modules in different homes and operating systems and to adjust the survey questions. During the pilot, testers ran HomeNet Profiler 152 times from 47 different end-systems.

3. HomeNet Profiler DEPLOYMENT

Starting on April 4, 2011, we sent emails advertising HomeNet Profiler to family, friends, and colleagues as well as mailing lists of networking researchers. On April 18, 2011, we posted an announcement on Grenouille.com, a French website often accessed by people who want to monitor their ISP performance. We now evaluate how HomeNet Profiler performs in this deployment and which measurement modules are most popular.

Table 1 shows the total number of runs and end-systems that ran HomeNet Profiler between April 4, 2011 and March 21, 2012 and the number of runs per measurement module. Overall, users ran HomeNet Profiler 3634 times. Individual users ran HomeNet Profiler from 1 to 87 times, hence there are fewer end-systems than runs. Also, users skipped different measurement modules (users only select to run all measurement modules in 51% of the runs). Table 1 also shows the median and the 95th percentile duration of each module. The median time to complete the survey (3 minutes) is relatively short and reflects our desire to make the survey easy and quick to answer. The fact that different users select different measurement modules suggests that to attract a larger number of users, it is important to let users customize data collection.

Module	Runs	End systems	Homes	Duration	
				Median	95%
UPnP Gateway	3541	2692	2374	29 s.	39 s.
Netalyzr	3491	2668	2371	5 min.	7 min.
Computer conf.	3519	2687	2367	< 1 s.	3 s.
WiFi	3521	2671	2360	10 s.	11 s.
Service scan	3512	2678	2356	10 s.	21 s.
Device Scan	3533	2686	2355	1 s.	11 s.
Running apps.	3268	2485	2178	< 1 s.	4 s.
Installed apps.	3167	2402	2098	2 s.	11 s.
Survey	2142	2005	1736	3 min.	9 min.
Total	3634	2721	2432	6 min.	10 min.

Table 1: Popularity and duration of measurements.

Users may run HomeNet Profiler from enterprise or academic networks. Hence, we filter all runs from machine running outside home networks. We also ensure that we select only one run per home. In our technical report [1], we devise heuristics to perform these tasks. After applying these filtering heuristics, we infer that our data comes from a total of 2432 distinct homes. Users ran HomeNet Profiler from home networks in 46 countries and 210 different ASes. Table 2 shows the number of home networks and ASes we observe overall and for the top-five countries in our data. France dominates our data, mainly because of the announcement on the Grenouille.com website. This table shows that we obtain measurements from a fair number of different ASes in the top five countries.

Country	Homes	ASes
France	1699	33
USA	272	62
Canada	62	12
Brazil	59	10
Italy	57	6
Overall	2432	210

Table 2: Homes and ASes per country.

4. FUTURE WORK

Our future work will characterize home networks with HomeNet Profiler data. We will compare the diversity of home networks and their WiFi environment. HomeNet Profiler data will help us understand typical problems that may arise in home networks. We will complement HomeNet Profiler one-shot measurements with continuous measurements in a small number of homes.

5. ACKNOWLEDGEMENT

This work was supported by the Agence Nationale de la Recherche grant C'MON and by the European Community's Seventh Framework Programme (FP7/2007-2013) no. 258378 (FIGARO).

6. REFERENCES

[1] L. DiCioccio, R. Teixeira, and C. Rosenberg. Characterizing Home Networks With HomeNet Profiler. Technical Report CP-PRL-2011-09-0001, Technicolor, Sep 2011.

[2] T. Karagiannis, E. Athanasopoulos, C. Gkantsidis, and P. Key. HomeMaestro: Order from Chaos in Home Networks. Technical Report MSR-TR-2008-84, MSR, Redmond, WA, USA, May 2008.

[3] C. Kreibich, N. Weaver, B. Nechaev, and V. Paxson. Netalyzr: Illuminating the Edge Network. In *Proc. IMC*, Oct 2010.

[4] G. Maier, A. Feldmann, V. Paxson, and M. Allman. On Dominant Characteristics of Residential Broadband Internet Traffic. In *Proc. IMC*, Oct 2009.

[2] For an example of report please visit http://cmon.lip6.fr/hnp/example.html.

Comparing Metro-Area Cellular and WiFi Performance

[Extended Abstract]

Joel Sommers
Colgate University
jsommers@colgate.edu

Paul Barford
University of Wisconsin
pb@cs.wisc.edu

ABSTRACT

Cellular and 802.11 WiFi offer two compelling connectivity options for mobile users. The goal of our work is to better understand performance characteristics of these technologies in diverse environments and conditions. To that end, we compare and contrast cellular and Wifi performance using crowd-sourced data from `speedtest.net`. We consider spatio-temporal performance aspects (e.g., upload and download throughput and latency) using over 3 million user-initiated tests initiated in 15 different metro areas, collected over 15 weeks. In these preliminary results, we find that WiFi performance generally exceeds cellular performance, and that observed characteristics are highly variable across different locations and times of day. We also observe diverse performance characteristics resulting from the rollout of new cell access technologies and service differences among local providers.

Categories and Subject Descriptors: C.2.1 [Network Architecture and Design]: Wireless communication; C.4 [Performance of Systems]: Performance attributes

General Terms: Experimentation, Measurement, Performance

Keywords: Cellular, WiFi, throughput, latency

1. INTRODUCTION

The past five years has witnessed an explosion in the capabilities of mobile devices that are both cellular- and 802.11 WiFi-capable. The combination of a short-range, high-speed capability, and a longer-range, lower-speed capability is compelling, and has driven the development of a wide-range of new mobile applications. Consequently, there is a large and growing demand for network bandwidth by mobile users.

A vexing problem for WiFi-enabled cell phone users, service providers, and application designers is seeking out and supporting the connectivity option that provides the best and most reliable performance. Over short time scales, issues that affect performance include local network service availability, handset characteristics, and interference, among others, while over long time scales, new technology and infrastructure deployments shape achievable performance. To help users make sense of the various connectivity options available to them, a number of performance testing applications have been developed and made available. In addition to assisting users to test their network performance, the data gathered by these applications offers the possibility to provide unique insights into mobile device performance.

SIGMETRICS'12, June 11–15, 2012, London, England, UK.
ACM 978-1-4503-1097-0/12/06.

In this work, we investigate mobile device performance using crowd-sourced data provided by `speedtest.net`, one of the most popular and widely deployed mobile bandwidth testers. The goal of our study is to understand the spatio-temporal characteristics of performance of WiFi-enabled cell phones in a selection of metro areas with different population densities and diverse geographic characteristics. A longer-term goal is to formulate conclusions about the spatio-temporal aspects of mobile device network performance that will lead to improvements in the relevant protocols, configurations, and infrastructure.

Our evaluation indicates a complex set of characteristics of spatio-temporal performance of mobile devices in a metro area. As expected, we find WiFi download and upload performance to be superior to cellular performance in most areas. We also find that WiFi latency measurements are at least a factor of two lower than cell latency in all areas. However, the latency difference tends to be smaller in larger metro areas, suggesting that greater efforts have been made to optimize those cellular deployments. In our ongoing work, we plan to drill down on the data in greater detail to further examine root causes for observed behaviors, and to examine user- and provider-specific performance characteristics.

2. DATA

`Speedtest.net` is a bandwidth/performance evaluation platform that is managed and maintained by Ookla, Inc.[1] The application can be run in a web browser, and native apps are available for both Apple iOS- and Android-based devices. Over 2B performance tests have been run since `speedtest` began in 2006, with global daily tests currently exceeding 125K per day. In this work, we only consider data collected from tests initiated from the iOS and Android apps.

Each `speedtest` is initiated by the client app. Upon invocation, a test request is directed to the geographically closest `speedtest` server; there are over 600 servers deployed worldwide. Each test consists of a latency test, followed by upload and download throughput tests. At the conclusion of a test, a rich log entry is stored at the local `speedtest` server that includes information such as a timestamp, client IP, device type and OS, device geographic coordinates, measured upload and download speeds (in kb/s), latency (in milliseconds), and access type (cellular or WiFi).

The data we consider were collected from `speedtest` servers located in 15 metro areas over a period of 15 weeks from February 21, 2011 through June 5, 2011. Selection of the 15 sites was based on attempting to amass a manageable dataset, yet one that provides a broad perspective on cellular vs. WiFi performance in metro areas that are diverse in their geographic, socio-economic and behavioral characteristics. We focus on five different metro area types:

[1] `http://www.ookla.com`

three in the US (Small: Lawrence, KS; Jackson, TN; Missoula, MT; Medium: Madison, WI; Syracuse, NY; Columbia, SC; and Large: New York, NY; Chicago, IL; Los Angeles, CA), one in Europe (Belgrade, Serbia; Brussels, Belgium; Manchester, UK), and one in Asia/Pacific (Ulaanbaatar, Mongolia; Almaty, Kazakhstan; Palembang, Indonesia).

3. RESULTS

Our preliminary results reveal a wide range of characteristics of cellular and WiFi performance. The raw comparison between the two technologies shows that WiFi provides superior download performance, with maximum WiFi performance varying widely. The difference in upload performance is much smaller, yet is also highly variable. Temporal analysis reveals that performance is sensitive to time of day in the largest metro areas, with performance decreasing for both cellular and WiFi during the hours of peak use. Comparisons between metro areas shows that larger markets provide a consistently higher level of performance for both technologies, suggesting greater engineering effort and resources deployed in more populous regions. However, analysis within more localized regions shows high variability in performance for both technologies in all markets.

As an example of our results, below, we analyze the temporal characteristics of download performance for cellular and WiFi. Figure 1 shows the hourly average download performance for each technology over an 8 day period for one metro area from each of the five area types (notice the different y-axis scales for cellular (top) and WiFi (bottom)). We observe that for cellular access, the performance for all but the largest metro area is fairly similar over time; performance for the New York, NY region clearly stands above the others. This trend is similar for other metro areas in the five area types. The latency profiles we observe in the data suggest suggest that the better engineered cellular infrastructure in large metro areas has a clear impact on throughput performance. We observe that for WiFi connections, while the smallest metro areas have generally lower throughputs, the differences are not as great among the metro areas for WiFi as they are for cellular connections.

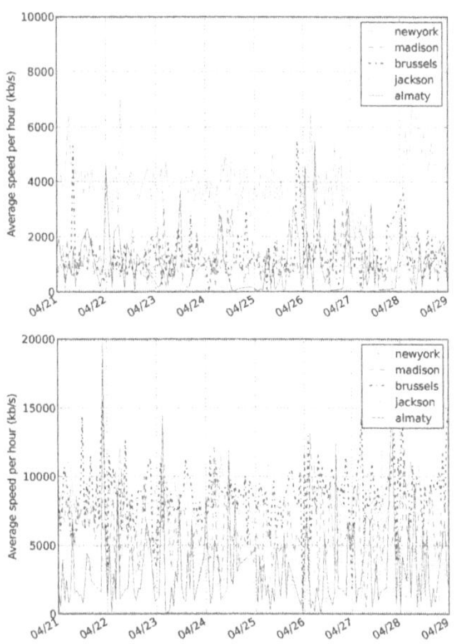

Figure 1: Average hourly performance for cellular downloads (top) and WiFi downloads (bottom) for exemplars in each of the metro areas during the week of April 21 to April 29, 2011.

4. RELATED WORK

There is a large and growing body of work that examines the behavior and characteristics of WiFi networks. Studies that are most closely related to ours have focused on analyzing mobile use characteristics in live deployments, *e.g.*, [2, 4, 5, 7]. Likewise, there is also a growing literature on empirical studies of cellular networks. Tan *et al.* describe one of the first empirical studies of 3G cellular networks in [9]; other empirical studies of behavior in cellular networks include [6, 8]. While these prior studies expand the body of knowledge on WiFi and cellular behavior individually, our work differs in objective, scope, measurement details, and the fact that we include analysis of both WiFi and cellular performance. Lastly, there are several studies that investigate both cellular and WiFi performance, primarily in vehicular settings [1,3]. Our results complement and expand this prior work by reporting client performance in diverse markets using a larger body of crowd-sourced data, and in more general (non-vehicular) settings.

5. CONCLUSIONS AND FUTURE WORK

Cellular and 802.11 WiFi are the *de facto* connectivity options for today's mobile users. The increasing availability of handsets and tablets that offer *both* connectivity options, coupled with the the explosion of applications that demand high performance means that users are sensitive to throughput performance for each technology. The objective of our study is to broadly compare and contrast the spatio-temporal aspects of performance of both technologies in 15 diverse metro areas using crowd-sourced data from `speedtest.net`.

In future work we intend to drill down on the data in greater detail in order to better understand user- and provider-specific performance, as well as variations in performance, *e.g.*, by considering related datasets such as weather conditions during test periods and cell tower/WiFi access point locations. Finally, we plan to conduct targeted, hypothesis-driven experiments in different markets using the `speedtest` application, again toward the goal of understanding the root causes of observed performance results.

Acknowledgements

The authors thank Ookla, Inc. and Andrew Bassett for generously making the `speedtest.net` data available for this study.

6. REFERENCES

[1] A. Balasubramanian, R. Mahajan, and A. Venkataramani. Augmenting Mobile 3G Using WiFi. In *Proceedings of ACM MobiSys '10*, San Francisco, CA, June 2010.

[2] V. Birk, S. Rayanchu, S. Saha, S. sen, V. Shrivastava, and S. Banerjee. A Measurement Study of a Commercial-grade Urban WiFi Mesh. In *Proceedings of ACM Internet Measurement Conference*, Vouliagmeni, Greece, October 2008.

[3] P. Deshpande, X. Hou, and S. Das. Performance Comparison of 3G and Metro-Scale WiFi for Vehicular Network Access. In *Proceedings of ACM Internet Measurement Conference*, Melbourne, Australia, November 2010.

[4] T. Henderson, D. Kotz, and I. Abyzov. The Changing Usage of a Mature Campus-wide Wireless Network. In *Proceedings of ACM MOBICOM '04*, Philadelphia, PA, October 2004.

[5] K. LaCurts and H. Balakrishnan. Measurement and Analysis of Real-World 802.11 Mesh Networks. In *Proceedings of ACM Internet Measurement Conference*, Melbourne, Australia, November 2010.

[6] X. Liu, A. Sridharan, S. Machiraju, M. Seshadri, and H. Zang. Anatomizing Application Performance on Smartphones. In *Proceedings of ACM MobiSys '10*, San Francisco, CA, June 2010.

[7] S. Sen, J. Yoon, J. Hare, J. Ormont, and S. Banerjee. Can they hear me how?: A case for a client-assisted approach to monitoring wide-area wireless networks. In *Proceedings of ACM Internet Measurement Conference*, Berlin, Germany, November 2011.

[8] M. Z. Shafiq, L. Ji, A. X. Liu, and J. Wang. Characterizing and modeling internet traffic dynamics of cellular devices. In *Proceedings of ACM SIGMETRICS '11*, San Jose, CA, June 2011.

[9] F. Lam W. Tan and W Lau. An Empirical Study on 3G Network Capacity and Performance. In *Proceedings of IEEE INFOCOM*, Anchorage, AK, May 2007.

Towards a Statistical Characterization of the Competitiveness of Oblivious Routing*

[Extended Abstract]

Gábor Németh and Gábor Rétvári
HSNLab, Dept. of Telecommunications and Media Informatics
Budapest University of Technology and Economics
Magyar tudósok körútja 2., Budapest, Hungary, H-1117
{nemethgab, retvari}@tmit.bme.hu

ABSTRACT

Oblivious routing asks for a static routing that serves arbitrary user demands with minimal performance penalty. Performance is measured in terms of the competitive ratio, the proportion of the maximum congestion to the best possible congestion. In this paper, we take the first steps towards extending this worst-case characterization to a more revealing statistical one. We define new performance metrics and we present numerical evaluations showing that, in statistical terms, oblivious routing is not as competitive as the worst-case performance characterizations would suggest.

Categories and Subject Descriptors

C.4 [**Computer-Communication Networks**]: Performance of systems—*Performance attributes*

General Terms

Performance, Theory

Keywords

oblivious ratio, performance evaluation, numerical analysis

1. INTRODUCTION

Modern networks face an increasingly complex and dynamic environment, which makes it more and more difficult to accurately measure user demands and infer reliable predictions [1]. This is a problem for network operators, as routing is usually optimized permanently with respect to the expected traffic matrix (TM). *Oblivious routing* is a method to provision routing without any *a priori* information on traffic demands at all [2]. The idea is to design a single static routing that works reasonably for all possible TMs that can appear in the network. Here, routing performance is measured in terms of the *competitive ratio* α, defined as the maximal factor between the congestion produced by oblivious routing and some ideal routing scheme, taken over all TMs. In undirected networks, the competitive ratio is upper-bounded by a logarithmic function of the number of nodes n [3], and its value usually remains under 2 in directed networks as well [4].

The competitive ratio is, by nature, a worst-case measure, as it is the maximum of the congestions experienced over *all* possible demands that determines its value. In this paper, our aim is to extend this worst-case characterization with a statistical view. We introduce two new performance metrics: the *probability of congestion* (PoC), describing the probability that congestion shows up somewhere in the network over a given demand distribution; and the *expected value of congestion* (EVoC), quantifying the anticipated extent of congestion. The main finding is that, according to numerical evaluations conducted on real networks, the performance of oblivious routing can become arbitrarily poor in terms of the new *statistical* performance metrics, in contrast to the *worst-case* characterization where there is a firm $\log(n)$ upper bound on the performance penalty.

2. NEW PERFORMANCE METRICS FOR OBLIVIOUS ROUTING

Let T denote the set of TMs that can be realized in the network with some hypothetical, optimal routing algorithm without congestion. In this paper, we make the assumption that TMs arrive from T with equal probability. In addition, let R denote the set of TMs that can be routed by oblivious routing without link overload.

DEFINITION 1. *The* probability of congestion *(PoC) η is the probability that at least one network link gets overloaded by oblivious routing:*

$$\eta = 1 - \frac{\mathrm{Vol}(R)}{\mathrm{Vol}(T)} , \qquad (1)$$

where Vol *denotes the K-dimensional volume.*

In fact, the PoC essentially tells the probability that oblivious routing overloads some link, provided that optimal routing could route input traffic matrices without congestion. This makes the PoC a revealing competitive measure.

DEFINITION 2. *The* expected value of congestion *(EVoC) μ is the mean value of the maximum link utilization produced by oblivious routing.*

*This work is connected to the scientific program of the "Development of quality-oriented and cooperative R+D+I strategy and functional model at BME" project. This project is supported by the New Hungary Development Plan (Project ID: TÁMOP-4.2.1/B-09/1/KMR-2010-0002).

SIGMETRICS'12, June 11–15, 2012, London, England, UK.
ACM 978-1-4503-1097-0/12/06.

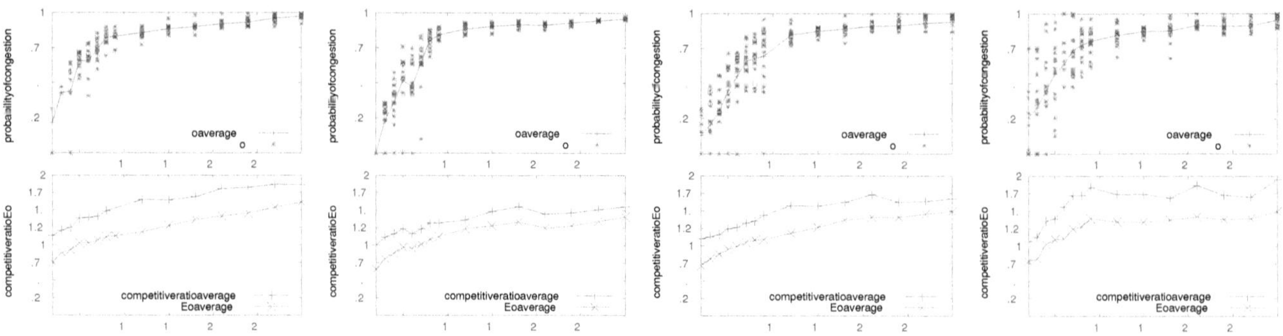

(a) NSF (dir) (b) AS3257 (dir) (c) NSF (undir) (d) AS3257 (undir)

Figure 1: The PoC, the competitive ratio, and the EVoC for the *directed* and *undirected* versions of (a) the NSF and (b) the AS3257, as the function of the number of users K, resp.

LEMMA 1. *The EVoC can be approximated as*

$$\frac{K}{K+1}\left(\frac{1}{1-\eta}\right)^{1/K} \leq \mu \leq \alpha \ , \qquad (2)$$

where K is the number of source-destination pairs.

We conducted several rounds of numerical studies to evaluate the new metrics in real networks. In particular, we used the `AS3257` ISP data map from the Rocketfuel dataset [5] and the `NSFNET Phase II` topology from [6] (other topologies gave similar results). We generated series of increasingly more complex configurations by gradually increasing the number of source-destination pairs K from 2 to 30. For each K, fifteen independent samples were generated picking the source and the destination randomly according to bimodal distribution, and in every instance two maximally node-disjoint paths were provisioned per user. For $K \leq 9$ the PoC and the EVoC can be evaluated accurately, while for larger Ks we relied on Monte-Carlo integration [7] to obtain the PoC, and Lemma 1 to estimate the EVoC. The parameters were set so that the chance of relative error larger than 10% is less than 10%. The competitive ratio was always computed accurately.

Fig. 1 depicts the exact and approximate results for the PoC, the competitive ratio, and EVoC in directed and undirected networks.

Our most important observations are as follows. Both for the directed and the undirected networks the probability of congestion grows beyond 80% for as few as about 10 users, and as the number of users enters the range of the number of nodes (about 20-30 in our cases), it surpasses 90% and approaches 100% with very high confidence. Meanwhile, the expected value of congestion grows beyond 1, indicating symptoms of grave congestion. This is despite that the competitive ratio remains relatively low (less than 1.5-1.7). An interesting further observation is that in undirected networks the variance of results is much higher than for directed ones, however, even for undirected graphs the confidence of our approximations is very good in the range where competitiveness really matters (i.e., for higher Ks).

Our numerical results suggest that one can expect the network to spend most of the time in a congested state when using oblivious routing. This is despite that an optimal adaptive routing algorithm would not produce any congestion at all in these scenarios (for such an algorithm, see [8]). This suggests that the competitiveness of oblivious routing, established in terms of the worst-case metric α, essentially vanishes under the statistical characterizations provided by the PoC η and the EVoC μ.

3. REFERENCES

[1] S. Gunnar, M. Johansson, and T. Telkamp. Traffic matrix estimation on a large IP backbone: a comparison on real data. In *ACM IMC*, pages 149–160, 2004.

[2] Harald Räcke. Minimizing congestion in general networks. In *Proceedings of the 43rd Symposium on Foundations of Computer Science*, FOCS '02, pages 43–52, 2002.

[3] Harald Räcke. Optimal hierarchical decompositions for congestion minimization in networks. In *Proceedings of the 40th annual ACM symposium on Theory of computing*, STOC '08, pages 255–264, 2008.

[4] D. Applegate and E. Cohen. Making intra-domain routing robust to changing and uncertain traffic demands: understanding fundamental tradeoffs. In *ACM SIGCOMM*, pages 313–324, 2003.

[5] R. Mahajan, N. Spring, D. Wetherall, and T. Anderson. Inferring link weights using end-to-end measurements. In *ACM IMC*, pages 231–236, 2002.

[6] B. Chinoy and H. W. Braun. The National Science Foundation network. Tech. Rep., CAIDA, available online: `http://www.caida.org/outreach/papers/1992/nsfn/nsfnet-t1-technology.pdf`, Sep 1992.

[7] M. Dyer and A. Frieze. Computing the Volume of Convex Bodies: A Case where Randomness Provably Helps. In *Proceedings of Symposia in Applied Mathematics*, volume 44, 1991.

[8] Gábor Rétvári and Gábor Németh. On optimal multipath rate-adaptive routing. In *IEEE Symposium on Computers and Communications*, ISCC'10, pages 605–610. IEEE Computer Society, 2010.

Range Tomography

Sajjad Zarifzadeh
Georgia Tech
szarifzadeh@gmail.com

Madhwaraj G K
Georgia Tech
madhwarajgk@gmail.com

Constantine Dovrolis
Georgia Tech
constantine@gatech.edu

Categories and Subject Descriptors

N w N
—*Network management, Network monitoring*

Keywords

N

1. INTRODUCTION

Analogue tomography

Boolean
tomography

%

Range Tomogra-
phy

SIGMETRICS'12, June 11–15, 2012, London, England, UK.
ACM 978-1-4503-1097-0/12/06.

range

2. A NEW TOMOGRAPHY FRAMEWORK

sensors

$p_{i,j}$ s_i s_j
$m_{i,j}$ *actual* $p_{i,j}$
f

$$m_{i,j} \quad f \quad \{x_l|\forall l \in p_{i,j}\}$$

x_l *actual* l
f *path metric function*

f
SUM

l
x_l
n
$n\,x_l$ $-x_l$ $\sqrt{}$
l

bad
δ *bad*
δ *good*

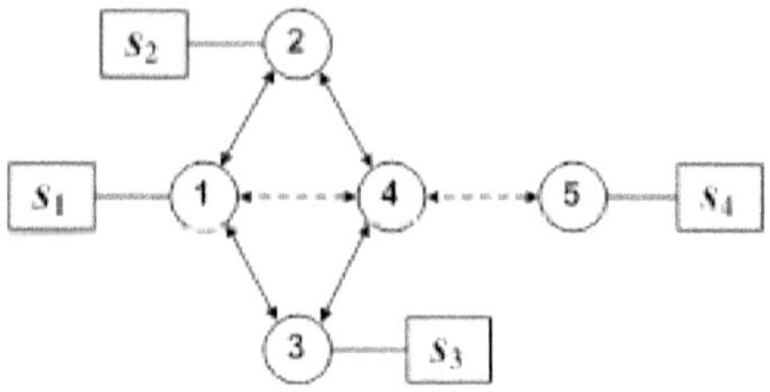

performance range

$m_{i,j}$

measured $p_{i,j}$ $p_{i,j}$

$p_{k,l}$ α *similar*

α

$$\frac{|m_{i,j} - m_{k,l}|}{min\ m_{i,j}, m_{k,l}} \leq \alpha$$

α

α

$p_{i,j}$

s_i s_j

$p_{1,4}, p_{2,4}, p_{3,4}$

% % %

α .

$p_{2,4}$ $p_{3,4}$ α

α

% % $p_{2,3}$

% %

x_l $s_l..e_l$

l l

s_l e_l $|x_l|$ x_l

$p_{i,j}$

consistent $p_{i,j}$

$m_{i,j} \simeq f\ \{x_l|\forall l \in p_{i,j}\}$,

$\forall l \in p_{i,j}, \exists t_l \in x_l$ $m_{i,j}$ $f\ \{t_l|\forall l \in p_{i,j}\}$

$p_{i,j}$ %

l_1 l_2

% %

% %

Range Tomography

(RT)

f *SUM*

N

α

any

α

3. RESULTS

N

%

N

%

4. ACKNOWLEDGEMENTS

N

5. REFERENCES

N

N

IEEE Trans. on Information Theory

N

ACM SIGCOMM Workshop on Internet Measurement

N

Proc. ACM IMC

Q N Q

N

Proc. ACM SIGMETRICS

N

Proc. ACM CoNEXT

A Scalable Architecture for Maintaining Packet Latency Measurements

Myungjin Lee[†], Nick Duffield[‡], Ramana Rao Kompella[†]
[†]Purdue University, [‡]AT&T Labs–Research

ABSTRACT

Latency has become an important metric for network monitoring since the emergence of new latency-sensitive applications (*e.g.*, algorithmic trading and high-performance computing). In this paper, to provide latency measurements at both *finer* (*e.g.*, packet) as well as *flexible* (*e.g.*, flow subsets) levels of granularity, we propose an architecture called MAPLE that essentially stores packet-level latencies in routers and allows network operators to query the latency of arbitrary traffic sub-populations. MAPLE is built using a scalable data structure called SVBF with small storage needs.

Categories and Subject Descriptors

C.2.3 [**Computer Communication Networks**]: Network management

General Terms

Measurement

1. INTRODUCTION

In recent years, *latency* has evolved into a metric that is as important as throughput in IP networks. While low latency is a desirable property for any network-based application, this obsession towards low end-to-end latency stems from the stringent requirements of many new kinds of datacenter, cloud, and wide-area applications that have become popular in the recent times. For instance, low-latency requirement exists for partition/aggregate type workloads found in search, social collaboration applications, where jobs that do not finish within a certain time are typically cancelled thus affecting the overall result, and in some cases, lost revenue [1].

Network operators managing such latency-sensitive applications need sophisticated tools for high-fidelity latency measurements at various places in the network that will help them identify root causes of SLA violations, determine offending applications that may hurt the performance of others, and so on. In light of the importance of these measurements, there has been some recent research on developing measurement mechanisms such as lossy difference aggregator (LDA) [5] and reference latency interpolation (RLI) [6]. A *key limitation* of these existing techniques is that they only obtain latency measurements at the granularity of a fixed pre-configured aggregate (*e.g.*, across all packets in LDA). By making the granularity of the aggregates for latency measurements part of the architecture, these prior architectures are quite *ossified*, lacking flexibility to obtain arbitrary latency measurements (*e.g.*, per-packet, *flow subsets*).

SIGMETRICS'12, June 11–15, 2012, London, England, UK.
ACM 978-1-4503-1097-0/12/06.

Such flexibility can be enabled with finer-grained latency measurements that are *per-packet latencies*. Thus, we propose an architecture called MAPLE that achieves these measurements in a scalable fashion. Then, any other forms of aggregation (per-flow, per-prefix, all packets), that may be of importance to network operators, are easily composable from these packet-level measurements. At its heart, MAPLE contains a scalable packet latency store (PLS) designed to simply store latencies of *all* packets in a scalable and efficient fashion. While we let readers refer to [7] for more details, we mainly discuss PLS in this paper due to interest of space.

2. PACKET LATENCY STORE

PLS stores per-packet latency measurements along with packet signatures. Thus, we first need to measure per-packet latencies somehow. For restricted settings, such as packets within a router, we can obtain approximate delays on a per-packet basis by using techniques in prior work [6]. For ease of exposition, we assume that packet headers can be modified to carry timestamps. Note that in all cases, we assume high precision time synchronization between the two measurement points, which has become feasible in modern times due to the increasing adoption of IEEE 1588 [3].

We consider two major factors in storing packet latencies: 1) storage efficiency and 2) insert/lookup times. Given a storage budget, we aim to store as many packet latencies as possible while providing fast insert and lookup operations. Simple hash table does not scale because it has high storage overhead (*e.g.*, 32 bit packet hash and 20 bit delay for a given packet) and its collision resolution methods like chaining or probing make the hash table infeasible for a high speed link (*e.g.*, an OC-192 link).

For the kind of applications we envision, such as performance diagnosis or detecting SLA violations, we can exploit the fact that *the latency values for each and every packet need not be precise, and can be approximate instead.* We can then significantly reduce the memory usage—this is the key intuition behind our approach that involves the following two steps.

Selecting representative delays. Within a given measurement interval, there are typically only a few dominant latency values (depending on the utilization) where most of the packet values are clustered. In the worst case, the latency values can be all over the entire permissible range, but in general, this is typically rare. Thus, instead of storing packets and their associated delays, we can first cluster packets into *equivalence classes* based on the delay values, and associate a single delay value, called *cluster center*, for all packets within the cluster. We use an online k-median clustering algorithm [2] to select k cluster centers dynamically. With clustering, we reduce the problem of storing $< p_i, l_i >$ tuple to $< p_i, c_i >$ where l_i is the actual latency of packet p_i and c_i is the ith center. Given a data structure, we store and lookup the center id

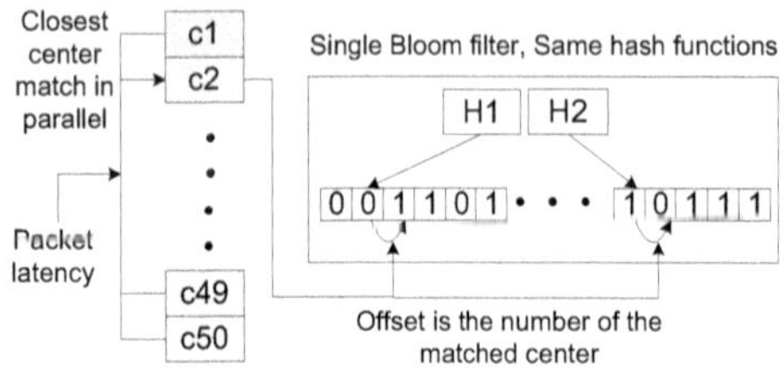

Figure 1: SVBF has $O(1)$ insert and $O(1)$ lookup assuming reading the k vector takes 1 memory access.

corresponding to a packet; the actual latency value corresponding to the center will need to be looked up in a separate table.

Storing packet delays compactly. For each cluster, we leverage approximate membership query data structures such as Bloom filters (BFs), that have gained significant prominence in networking applications recently, for better efficiency in storage (in terms of bits/packet) as well as implementation in hardware. There are several data structures to extend the basic Bloom filter such as Partitioned Bloom Filter (PBF) and Combinatorial Bloom Filters (COMB) [4]. PBF maintains BFs associated with individual centers, which makes BF provisioning difficult. In COMB, there is a trade-off between insert and lookup speeds. In order to keep up with a high line rate, insert operation must not slow down. Thus, sacrifice in lookup speed is inevitable. More detailed discussion about these data structures can be found in [7].

Our new data structure called Shared-Vector Bloom Filter (SVBF) addresses the limitations of these solutions by essentially preserving the simplicity of a single BF, but reducing the lookup complexity significantly. Specifically, we store the bits corresponding to different delay values for the same packet close-by so that during queries we can read all the bits in a burst instead of reading them sequentially from various bit positions.

Insert: The insert operation is quite similar to a regular BF, except for a small modification. In regular BF, each packet is hashed using multiple hash functions, and bits at those indices are set to 1. In SVBF, we use the hash function index as an offset into a vector of delay values. Thus, we set the bit corresponding to $h_i(s_{pkt}) + g_i$ where $g_i \in [0, k-1]$ is the group number of the packet. This is shown in Figure 1 where a packet that matches the second center $c2$ (group id 1) is added into the BF using hash functions H1 and H2. The offset at which the bit is set is 1 for this second center.

Lookup: Given a packet s_{pkt}, we first hash the packet to obtain various hash indices $h_i(s_{pkt})$. From each of these bases, we read the next set of k bits, i.e., $h_i(s_{pkt})$ to $h_i(s_{pkt}) + k - 1$, to obtain bitmap B_i. We compute the bit-wise AND across all these bitmaps, $B = B_1 \& B_2 \& \ldots$. In the final bitmap (B), the offset where a bit is set to 1 is the group id.

The biggest gain of SVBF is that, it relies on 'burst reads' which are simpler than random reads that COMB suffers from. Thus, instead of k memory accesses, we only need $\lceil k/w \rceil + 1$ memory accesses for each hash index. For example, for $k = 50$, we can obtain the bitmaps in a total of $3 \times h$ memory accesses assuming a 32-bit machine word, where h is the number of hash functions.

3. EVALUATION

This section discusses how the various data structures discussed in §2 compare in terms of their accuracy, insert and lookup complexity for a given 5Mbit storage budget. We configure the data structures to support 50 centers ($k = 50$). We use a trace in prior work [6] in which there are about 22.4M packets in a period of 60s.

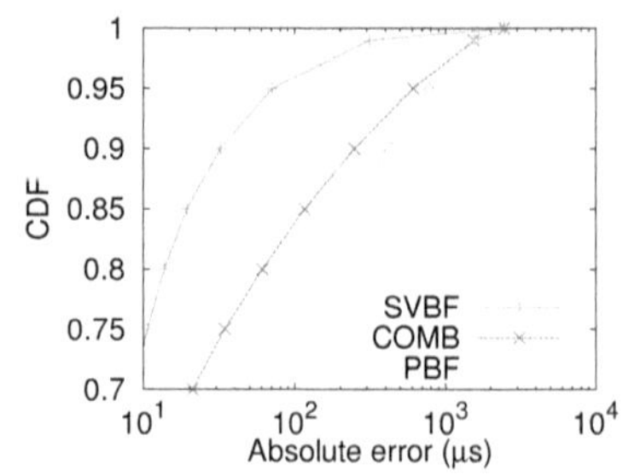

Figure 2: Analysis of estimation accuracy.

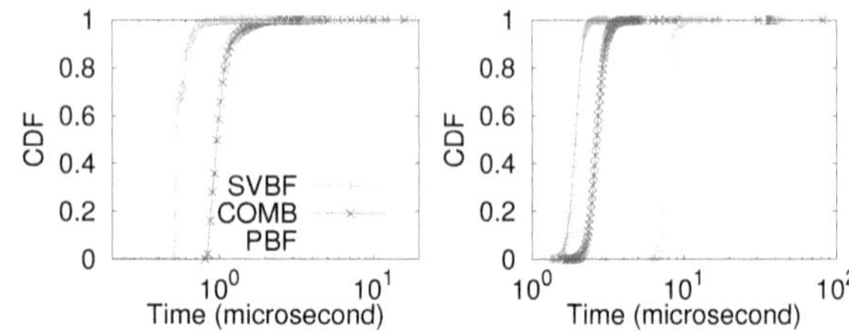

(a) Insert (b) Lookup

Figure 3: Comparison of insert and lookup times.

Accuracy of per-packet latency estimation. Figure 2 shows comparison results in terms of absolute errors of per-packet latency estimates. We show mainly the upper quartile in this graph where the difference is the most pronounced. Clearly, at lower than 75 %tile, either SVBF or COMB would return the same (correct) group id if the packet is not misclassified. We can notice that COMB and PBF suffer from much higher discrepancies as early as the 70%ile onwards, while in contrast we can see that SVBF has an absolute error that is significantly lower in comparison. For example the 85%ile absolute error for COMB is close to $116\mu s$ while SVBF has an error of $19\mu s$ at the same percentile.

Insert and lookup time complexity. We study the complexity of insert and lookup time of each data structure. We tested 0.4 million packets for insert and lookup using a Linux machine with 2.66GHz Intel CPU. Figure 3 shows the complexity in microsecond precision. From the figure, we observe that SVBF works faster than COMB in both insert (45% gain on average) and lookup (28%) operations. While PBF achieves the same performance of SVBF for insert operation, PBF is four times slower than SVBF for lookup operation on average. Note that SVBF is implemented as software and can be optimized further in hardware platform.

4. REFERENCES

[1] M. Alizadeh et al. Data center TCP (DCTCP). In *ACM SIGCOMM*, 2010.

[2] M. Charikar, L. O'Callaghan, and R. Panigrahy. Better Streaming Algorithms for Clustering Problems. In *ACM STOC*, 2003.

[3] J. Eidson and K. Lee. IEEE 1588 standard for a precision clock synchronization protocol for networked measurement and control systems. In *Sensors for Industry Conference, 2002. 2nd ISA/IEEE*, 2002.

[4] F. Hao, M. Kodialam, T. Lakshman, and H. Song. Fast multiset membership testing using combinatorial bloom filters. In *IEEE Infocom*, 2009.

[5] R. R. Kompella, K. Levchenko, A. C. Snoeren, and G. Varghese. Every MicroSecond Counts: Tracking Fine-grain Latencies Using Lossy Difference Aggregator. In *ACM SIGCOMM*, 2009.

[6] M. Lee, N. Duffield, and R. R. Kompella. Not All Microseconds are Equal: Fine-Grained Per-Flow Measurements with Reference Latency Interpolation. In *ACM SIGCOMM*, 2010.

[7] M. Lee, N. Duffield, and R. R. Kompella. Leave Them Microseconds Alone: Scalable Architecture for Maintaining Packet Latency Measurements. TR-11-013, Computer Science, Purdue University, 2011.

Modeling Randomness in Network Traffic

Markus Laner
Vienna University of Technology, Austria
mlaner@nt.tuwien.ac.at

Philipp Svoboda
Vienna University of Technology, Austria
psvoboda@nt.tuwien.ac.at

Markus Rupp
Vienna University of Technology, Austria
mrupp@nt.tuwien.ac.at

ABSTRACT

A continuous challenge in the field of network traffic modeling is to map recorded traffic onto parameters of random processes, in order to enable simulations of the respective traffic. A key element thereof is a convenient model which is simple, yet, captures the most relevant statistics.

This work aims to find such a model which, more precisely, enables the generation of multiple random processes with arbitrary but jointly characterized distributions, auto-correlation functions and cross-correlations. Hence, we present the definition of a novel class of models, the derivation of a respective closed-form analytical representation and its application on real network traffic.

Our modeling approach comprises: (i) generating statistical dependent Gaussian random processes, (ii) introducing auto-correlation to each process with a linear filter and, (iii) transforming them sample-wise by real-valued polynomial functions in order to shape their distributions. This particular structure allows to split the parameter fitting problem into three independent parts, each of which solvable by standard methods. Therefore, it is simple and straightforward to fit the model to measurement data.

Categories and Subject Descriptors

G.3 [**Probability and Statistics**]: Stochastic Processes, Random Number Generation

Keywords

Gaussian Process, Polynomial Transformation

1. INTRODUCTION

Accurate characterization of network source traffic (e.g., Video streams, VoIP, online gaming) is required for various applications, such as, traffic classification or service quality assessment. For this characterization random processes provide a useful framework, by statistically describing representative characteristics of the traffic. Probability Density Functions (PDFs), Auto-Correlation Functions (ACFs) and cross-correlations are among the most convenient measures for random processes and most often used in practice. Nevertheless, from the multitude of models proposed for network traffic, only a few are able to **jointly** characterize those measures with **arbitrary** accuracy. Examples are:

SIGMETRICS'12, June 11–15, 2012, London, England, UK.
ACM 978-1-4503-1097-0/12/06.

(i) Markov Models and respective generalizations [1], for which the fitting of PDF, ACF and cross-correlations has to be performed jointly, leading to prohibitive complexity if a high quality-of-fit is aimed.

(ii) TES Models, based on uniformly distributed random processes [3]. They rely on a separation of the fitting problem into multiple independent problems, hence, the complexity only grows linearly with the requested quality.

(iii) Modified Gaussian Models, based on the sample-wise transformations of Gaussian random processes [4], which also rely on a separation of the fitting problem.

The latter two are rather equivalent in terms of fitting complexity. Further, both suffer from the fact that there is no closed form analytic expression for the ACF.

In this work we present a specific class of Modified Gaussian Models, for which we are able to derive a closed form expression for the ACF. This strongly simplifies the fitting procedure, yielding a clear advantage over TES Models.

2. THE MODEL

The functional principle of our proposed model is depicted in Fig. 1. It consists of four main units/blocks:

[1] The generation of a real-valued Independent and Identically Distributed (I.I.D.) Gaussian random process $W[n]$ with zero mean and unit variance.

[2] A weighted addition of an arbitrary number I of such processes $W_i[n]$, introducing cross-correlation between processes, without altering the distribution and I.I.D. property of the process: $X[n] = \sum_{i=1}^{I} w_i \cdot W[n]$, with the condition that $\sum_{i=1}^{I}(w_i)^2 = 1$.

[3] An Linear Time Invariant (LTI) filter $h[m]$, which introduces auto-correlation $r_{YY}[m]$ to the process but leaves the distribution unchanged: $Y[n] = h[m] \star X[n]$, subject to the condition that $\sum_{m=-\infty}^{\infty}(h[m])^2 = 1$, where $\star$ denotes the convolution operation.

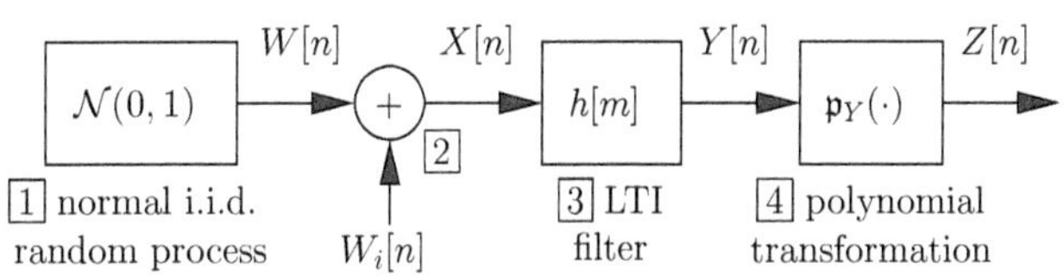

Figure 1: Proposed model for the generation of a random process with arbitrary but jointly defined PDF, ACF and cross-correlation to other processes.

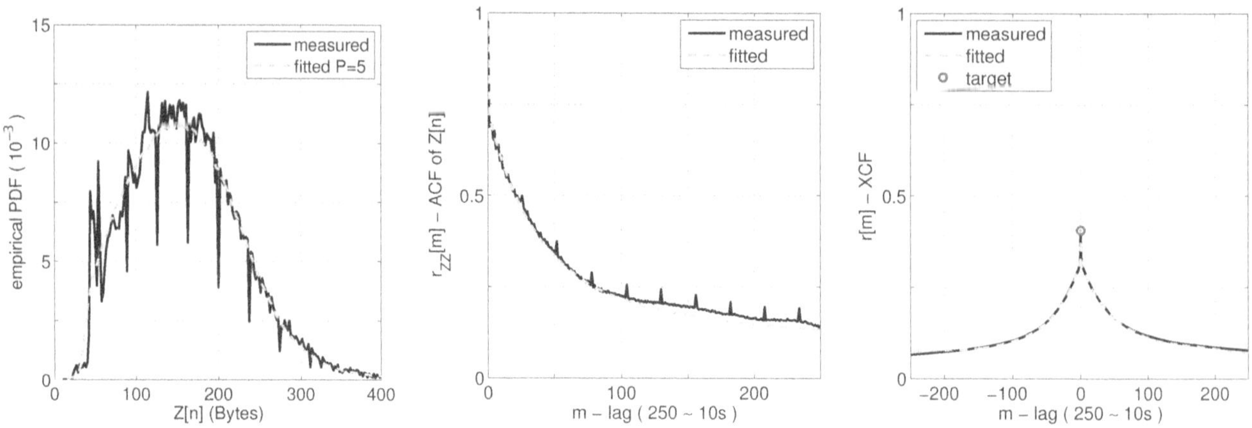

Figure 2: Data traffic of the online game *OpenArena* [5] and respective model-fit. Time series of the downlink packet size of two different players are analyzed. (left): PDF of Player 1 with fitted PDF resulting from a 5th order polynomial. (center): ACF of Player 1 with fitted ARMA(2,2) process. (right): XCF between both players. Note, that only $r_{Z_1Z_2}[0]$ (red circle) was subject to the fitting procedure.

[4] A polynomial function $\mathfrak{p}_Y(\cdot)$, transforming each sample (hence, the PDF): $Z[n] = \mathfrak{p}_Y(Y[n]) = \sum_{p=0}^{P} a_p \cdot (Y[n])^p$.

3. ANALYTICAL RESULTS

Due to the choice of a Gaussian process (closed on addition) and the conditions implied in Sec. 2, the problem of fitting this model to measurement data can be separated into the tree independent problems of fitting the distribution, the auto-correlation and the cross-correlation.

Nevertheless, the fitted parameters of Block 4 influence the fitting of Bl. 3 and, similarly, Bl. 2 is influenced by Bl. 3 and Bl. 4. This problem can be reduced to the question of *How is the auto-correlation function influenced by the polynomial*, which we are able to answer by the Theorem given below.

Note that it gives a closed form expression of the ACF with only P terms, which is crucial for efficient fitting algorithms. To the best of our knowledge, this is the first general model allowing for the exact inference of the auto-correlation function in closed form.

THEOREM: *Let $Y[n]$ denote a Gaussian random process with zero mean, unit variance and auto-correlation function $r_{YY}[m]$ and $Z[n]$ the random process obtained by the transformation of $Y[n]$ by a polynomial $\mathfrak{p}_Y(\cdot)$ according to $Z[n] = \mathfrak{p}_Y(Y[n]) = \sum_{p=0}^{P} a_p \cdot (Y[n])^p$. Then the auto-correlation function of the random process $Z[n]$ equals*

$$r_{ZZ}[m] = \mathfrak{p}_a(r_{YY}[m]) = \sum_{\rho=1}^{P} \alpha_\rho \cdot (r_{YY}[m])^\rho,$$

where $\mathfrak{p}_a(\cdot)$ denotes a polynomial with coefficients α_ρ which, for $\rho = 1, \cdots, P$, are calculated to

$$\alpha_\rho = \frac{1}{\sigma_Z^2}\rho!\Big(\sum_{p=0}^{P} a_p \cdot \binom{p}{\rho} \cdot (p-\rho-1)!! \cdot I_e(p-\rho)\Big)^2,$$

where σ_Z^2 denotes the variance of $Z[n]$, $\binom{p}{\rho}$ the binomial coefficient, $(p-\rho-1)!!$ the double factorial operator and, $I_e(p-\rho)$ the indicator function for parity (1 if even, 0 if odd).

4. FITTING TO MEAUSREMENT DATA

Due to the splitting the fitting problem into three independent standard fitting procedures, the whole process is straightforward and profits form the variety of available literature and software support. More precisely, the remaining problems are: polynomial curve fitting, ARMA modeling and the Cholesky decomposition. A detailed description of the fitting procedure as well as a software implementation can be found at [2]. As a proof of concept Fig. 2 shows the model fitted to measured online gaming traffic.

5. CONCLUSIONS

This study presents a novel class of models, which allows for the convenient generation of random processes with arbitrary but jointly defined distributions, auto-correlation functions and cross-correlations.

Compared to other models our approach allows for strongly simplified parameter fitting, due to the availability of closed form expressions for all parameters, which is unique in this field.

By fitting the model to measurements, the number of parameters can be kept small, which is vital for dissemination and reproducibility. Further, the generation of random samples according to specified model parameters shows very low complexity.

6. REFERENCES

[1] A. Dainotti et al. Internet traffic modeling by means of Hidden Markov Models. *Elsevier Computer Networks*, 52:2645–2662, 2008.

[2] Institute of Telecommunicaions, Vienna University of Technology. http://www.nt.tuwien.ac.at/downloads.

[3] B. Melamed. An Overview of TES Processes and Modeling Methodology. In L. Donatiello, editor, *Performance Evaluation of Computer and Communication Systems*, chapter 1. Springer, 1993.

[4] V. Ogorodnikov, S. Prigarin, and A. Rodionov. Quasi-Gaussian Model of Network Traffic . *Springer Automation and Remote Control*, 71(3):117–130, 2010.

[5] OpenArena. http://openarena.ws.

Performance Evaluation of the Random Replacement Policy for Networks of Caches

Massimo Gallo, Bruno Kauffmann, Luca Muscariello, Alain Simonian, Christian Tanguy
Orange Labs, France Telecom
firstname.lastname@orange.com

Categories and Subject Descriptors

C.2.1 [**Computer-Communication Networks**]: Network Architecture and Design; C.4 [**Performance of systems**]: Performance attributes

Keywords

Content Distribution Networks, Information-Centric Networking, Cache Replacement Policies, Asymptotic Analysis

1. INTRODUCTION

Caching is a key component for Content Distribution Networks and new Information-Centric Network architectures. In this paper, we address performance issues of caching networks running the RND replacement policy. We first prove that when the popularity distribution follows a general power-law with decay exponent $\alpha > 1$, the miss probability is asymptotic to $O(C^{1-\alpha})$ for large cache size C. We further evaluate network of caches under RND policy for homogeneous tree networks and extend the analysis to tandem cache networks where caches employ either LRU or RND policies. This paper is an extended abstract of the full version [2], where detailed results and proofs are provided.

2. SINGLE CACHE

Consider a cache memory of finite size which is offered requests for objects. When a request for an object cannot be satisfied (this will be called a *miss* event), the requested object is fetched from the repository server and cached locally at the expense of replacing some other object in the cache. The object replacement policy is assumed to follow the RND discipline, *i.e.*, whenever a miss occurs, the object to be replaced is chosen at random, uniformly among the objects present in the cache. Given the total number N of objects, the probability that object r, $1 \le r \le N$, is requested is defined by q_r, $1 \le r \le N$. Let $C \le N$ be the cache capacity and denote by $M(C)$ the stationary miss probability; finally, define $M_r(C)$ as the per-object miss probability, given that the requested object is precisely $r \in \{1, ..., N\}$. A general combinatorial expression of $M(C)$ has been given in ([3], Theorem 4) for any popularity distribution. We here provide asymptotics for probabilities $M(C)$ and $M_r(C)$ for large cache size C and with a Zipf popularity distribution $q_r = O(r^{-\alpha})$ for large r and exponent $\alpha > 1$.

SIGMETRICS'12, June 11–15, 2012, London, England, UK.
ACM 978-1-4503-1097-0/12/06.

PROPOSITION 2.1. *For a Zipf popularity distribution with exponent $\alpha > 1$, the miss probability $M(C)$ is asymptotic to*

$$M(C) \sim \rho_\alpha C q_C \tag{1}$$

for large C, with prefactor $\rho_\alpha = \left(\frac{\pi/\alpha}{\sin(\pi/\alpha)}\right)^\alpha$. Furthermore, given the object rank r, the per-object miss probability $M_r(C)$ is estimated by

$$M_r(C) \sim \frac{\rho_\alpha r^\alpha}{C^\alpha + \rho_\alpha r^\alpha}. \tag{2}$$

Fig. 1 depicts $M_r(C)$ as a function of the object rank r for both RND and LRU policies with fixed $C = 25$ and $\alpha = 1.7$. Numerical results confirm the asymptotic accuracy of estimate (2) for RND and the corresponding one for LRU policy [4] when compared to simulation. Besides, RND and LRU performance are very close for large enough r.

3. IN-NETWORK CACHE MODEL

We generalize the single-cache model and consider a *homogeneous tree* network, where all leaves are located at a common depth of the root, and the cache size of any node at a given level ℓ is equal to C_ℓ. Requests for content are routed towards the root of the network, until they experience a hit at some cache. Any request experiencing a miss at some cache of level k, $1 \le k \le \ell$, and an object hit at level $\ell + 1$ is copied backwards to all downstream caches on the request path. A request miss corresponds to a miss event at all levels. We assume that **(H)** *any cache considered in iso-*

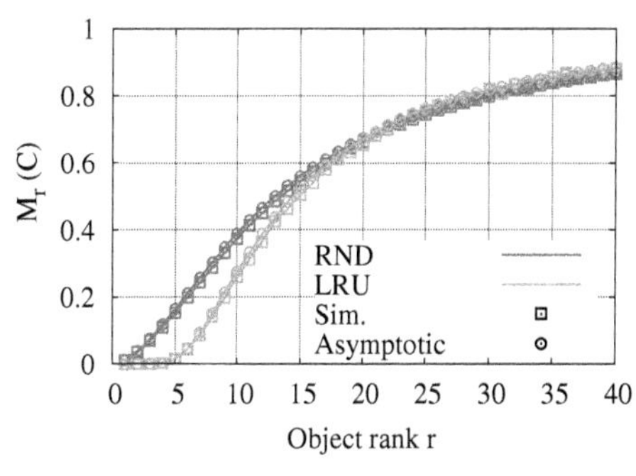

Figure 1: Asymptotic of $M_r(C)$ for a single cache with $C = 25$, $\alpha = 1.7$ for RND and LRU policies.

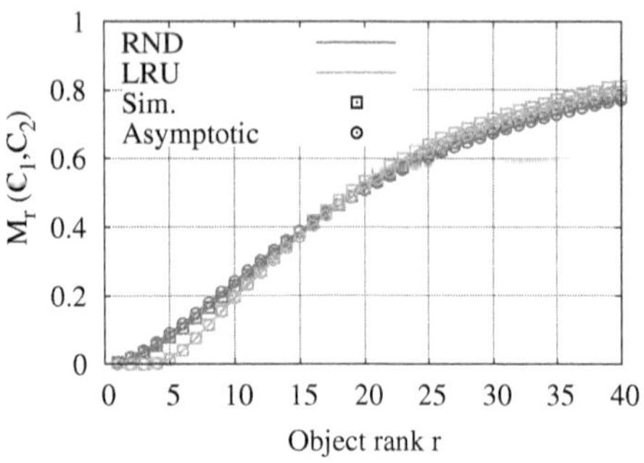

Figure 2: Asymptotics of $M_r(C_1, C_2)$ for RND and LRU policies compared to simulation for a two-level tree network with $C_1 = C_2 = 25$, $\alpha = 1.7$.

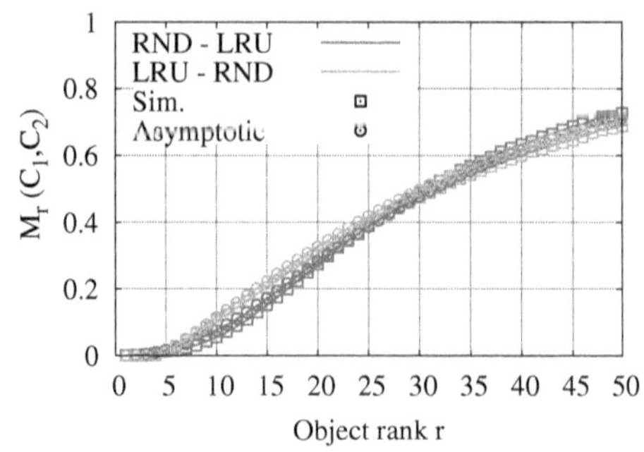

Figure 3: Asymptotic of $M_r(C_1, C_2)$ for a mixed tree cache networks with $C_1 = 25, C_2 = 50$, $\alpha = 1.7$.

lation behaves as a single cache with IRM input produced by consecutive missed requests originated by its children nodes.

PROPOSITION 3.1. *For the homogeneous tree network, suppose that the request process at the leaves is IRM with Zipf popularity distribution with exponent $\alpha > 1$, and that assumption **(H)** holds for all caches.*

For any level $\ell \in \{1, \ldots, K\}$ and cache sizes $C_1, \ldots, C_\ell$, let $M_r(C_1, \ldots, C_\ell)$ denote the "global" miss probability for request r over all caches of a route through levels $1, \ldots, \ell$. Then for large C_1, ..., C_ℓ,

$$M_r(C_1, \ldots, C_\ell) \sim \frac{\rho_\alpha r^\alpha}{\rho_\alpha r^\alpha + \sum_{1 \le j \le \ell} C_j^\alpha}. \qquad (3)$$

Fig. 2 reports miss probability $M_r(C_1, C_2)$ at the second level, *i.e.*, the probability to query an object of rank r at the repository server. We note that objects with small rank are slightly more frequently requested at the server when using RND rather than LRU, but RND is more favorable than LRU for objects with higher rank. We also be observe that the miss probability at the second level is very similar either using RND or LRU, with a slight advantage to LRU. We notice that the approximations calculated in Section 3 for RND and in [1] for LRU are very accurate.

4. MIXTURE OF RND AND LRU

This section addresses the case of a two-level tree network, where the RND replacement algorithm is used at one level while the LRU algorithm is used at the other. As in Section **3**, these results also hold in the case of a homogeneous tree.

PROPOSITION 4.1. *For the two-level tree network, suppose the request process at cache level 1 is IRM with Zipf popularity distribution with exponent $\alpha > 1$ and that assumption **(H)** for cache level 2 holds.*

***I)** When level 1(resp. level 2) uses the RND (resp. LRU) replacement policy, the global miss probability at level 2 is given by*

$$M_r(C_1, C_2) \sim \frac{\rho_\alpha r^\alpha}{\rho_\alpha r^\alpha + C_1^\alpha} \exp\left(-\frac{\rho_\alpha C_2^\alpha}{\alpha \lambda_\alpha (\rho_\alpha r^\alpha + C_1^\alpha)}\right) \qquad (4)$$

for large cache sizes C_1, C_2 and constants ρ_α, λ_α.

***II)** When level 1 (resp. level 2) uses the LRU (resp. RND) replacement policy, the global miss probability on level 2 is given by*

$$M_r(C_1, C_2) \sim \frac{\rho_\alpha r^\alpha}{\rho_\alpha r^\alpha \exp\left(\frac{C_1^\alpha}{\alpha \lambda_\alpha r^\alpha}\right) + C_2^\alpha}. \qquad (5)$$

In numerical experiments, we have simulated tree networks with 2 leaves with cache size C_1 and one root with cache size C_2. In Fig. 3, we observe that the total miss probability $M_r(C_1, C_2)$ in the two mixed tandem caches is similar, while the distribution of the objects across the two nodes varies considerably. Further numerical experiments suggest to prefer LRU at the first cache because it performs better in terms of miss probability, and to use RND at the second one in order to save significant processing time.

5. CONCLUSION

The performance of RND being reasonably close to that of LRU, RND is a good candidate for high-speed caching when the complexity of the replacement policy becomes critical. In the presence of a hierarchy of caches, caches at deep levels (i.e. access networks) typically serve a small number of requests per second which can be sustained by a cache running LRU, thus providing the best performance at the bottom level. Higher-level caches that serve many aggregated requests should use the RND policy, which yields similar performance while being less computationally expensive.

6. REFERENCES

[1] G. Carofiglio, M. Gallo, L. Muscariello, and D. Perino. Modeling data transfer in content-centric networking. In *Proc. of ITC23*, 2011.

[2] M. Gallo, B. Kauffmann, L. Muscariello, A. Simonian, and C. Tanguy. Performance evaluation of the random replacement policy for networks of caches (14 pages version). http://arxiv.org/abs/1202.4880, 2012.

[3] E. Gelenbe. A unified approach to the evaluation of a class of replacement algorithms. *IEEE Transactions on Computer*, 22(6):611–618, 1973.

[4] P. R. Jelenković and X. Kang. Characterizing the miss sequence of the LRU cache. *ACM SIGMETRICS Performance Evaluation Review*, 36:119–121, August 2008.

Saving on Cooling: The Thermal Scheduling Problem

Koyel Mukherjee
University of Maryland
College Park, USA
koyelm@cs.umd.edu

Samir Khuller
University of Maryland
College Park, USA
samir@cs.umd.edu

Amol Deshpande
University of Maryland
College Park, USA
amol@cs.umd.edu

Categories and Subject Descriptors

C.4 [**Performance of Systems**]: modeling techniques; F.2.2 [**Non-numerical Algorithms and Problems**]: sequencing & scheduling

General Terms

Algorithms, Design, Performance

Keywords

Scheduling, Parallel, Cooling energy, Data centers, Multi-core

1. INTRODUCTION

In this abstract we define some very basic scheduling problems motivated by increasing power density and consequent cooling considerations in data centers and multi-core chips. Modern data centers consist of thousands of computers closely packed in a dense space, typically arranged as hundreds of *racks* of processors. The energy costs of a data center have been compared to that of a small town, with a significant portion contributed by the cost incurred in cooling the machines [1]. The energy cost of cooling is directly driven by the *supply temperature* (denoted T_{sup}) of the cold air being blown in to cool the data center – the incoming air is often kept at a lower than necessary temperature to prevent hotspots from forming since those can damage the hardware. For instance, it has been observed that servers near the top of a rack often run hotter and are subject to higher failure rates [3]. Thermal balancing through judicious task scheduling can lead to fewer hotspots and thus lower overall cooling costs and lower failure rates. Similarly in multi-core chip architectures, the increasing density of cores and a movement toward 3D architectures [7] has made *dynamic thermal management* a key challenge. Increasing temperatures affect circuit reliability and longevity over the long term, and result in increased power consumption (because of increased leakage power) and overall high cooling costs.

In this framework we study a basic scheduling problem, called the *thermal scheduling* problem. We would like to minimize the maximum temperature of the machines in a data center while executing a set of jobs, or maximize assigned jobs while keeping the maximum temperature below a pre-specified *red-line* temperature (T_{red}). The key differentiating factor here from much of the prior work in scheduling is the notion of *spatial cross-interference*: the heat generated by jobs running on a machine raises its own temperature as well as the temperatures of nearby machines due to recirculation effects. Such effects are well-documented both for data centers [6, 5] and for multi-core chips [7]. In addition, the *geometry* of the data center plays a significant role in determining the cross-effect parameters, which are often asymmetric. Although several recent works have recognized the increasing importance of such cross-effects, that prior work (a survey can be found in [4]) has presented either reactive policies that take corrective action, or heuristics without any approximation guarantees. In this work, we initiate a formal study of the problem of thermal scheduling in presence of spatial cross-interference and present analytical results for a 1-dimensional asymmetric model where the machines are arranged in a linear array, with the cold air blowing in from one end.

SIGMETRICS'12, June 11–15, 2012, London, England, UK.
ACM 978-1-4503-1097-0/12/06.

2. PROBLEM DEFINITION AND MODEL

We base our model on the abstract heat circulation model suggested by Mukherjee et al. [5]. As with much of the prior work on thermal scheduling, we assume that the system is in steady state; i.e., we assume the jobs are long-lived, and analyse the system state when all the jobs have arrived and the temperatures have stabilized. According to the model, the temperature of a machine i is given by: $T_i = T_{sup} + D_i\mathbf{L}$, where D_i is the ith row of the heat distribution matrix D, and $\mathbf{L}$ is the load vector. The vector $\mathbf{L} = \{L_1, \cdots, L_m\}$, where m is the number of machines, denotes the loads on the machines in terms of the *power* consumed by the jobs assigned to the machine. The matrix D represents how the heat or load of any machine j affects machine i (called *cross-interference*). Since the temperature of no machine should exceed T_{red}, we have that: $T_{sup} + \max_{i\in[1,\ldots,m]} D_i\mathbf{L} \leq T_{red}$. Thus, given a set of jobs, our goal is to schedule them so as to either: (a) *maximize* T_{sup} (or equivalently, minimize $\max_{i\in[1,\ldots,m]} D_i\mathbf{L}$), or (b) given a constraint on $\max_{i\in[1,\ldots,m]} D_i\mathbf{L}$, maximize the number of assigned jobs.

For each job, we assume that we can estimate the power that will be consumed to execute it on a machine; this can be computed using the estimated resources required to execute the job, its time duration, and standard system power modeling techniques [2].

The total energy consumption is obtained by adding the energy for processing and the energy for cooling, and can be modeled as: $E = L(1 + \frac{1}{CoP(T_{sup})})$, where $L = \Sigma L_i$ is the total load on all the machines, and CoP (*coefficient of performance*) is a super linear function of the supply temperature. We formulate the problem of thermal scheduling in terms of minimizing what we call the "effective load" on a machine. Effective load on a machine is a linear combination of the load of the machine itself and the load of other machines. Specifically, given that the load of machine i is L_i, and the effect of machine j's load on machine i is captured through the **cross-interference coefficient** D_{ij}, the effective load EL_i is computed as follows: $EL_i = \sum_j D_{ij}L_j$ where $0 \leq D_{ij} \leq 1$ and $D_{ii} = 1$. Our optimization problem of minimizing the maximum temperature can now be seen as minimizing maximum effective load instead, an easier quantity to reason about.

In this abstract, we consider a model of machines in a linear array with the cold air blowing from one end (capturing either a rack in a data center, or a stack in 3D multi-core chips with a heat sink at one end). The ith machine is affected only by the heat recirculated from the machines located below it, closer to the source of the cold air. We number machines from bottom to top, in increasing order from the cold air source. Machine i is only affected by machines $j \leq i$. We assume the heat falls off in an exponential manner. Specifically, the heat felt by a machine i due to machine j is a fraction $\frac{1}{K^d}$ of the load of j, where $d = |i - j|$ is the distance between i and j and K is a constant > 1. More formally, $D_{ij} = \frac{1}{K^{|i-j|}}$. For technical reasons we assume that $K \geq 2$. The *effective load* of the ith machine, where $1 \leq i \leq m$, is then given as $EL_i = \sum_{j=1}^{i} \frac{L_j}{K^{i-j}}$.

3. RESULTS

It is NP-hard to find the optimal *integral* schedule that minimizes the effective load for a given set of jobs or that maximizes the number of jobs assigned without exceeding a certain effective load. We therefore relax the problem to the case when jobs are splittable between machines (i.e., fractional assignments are permitted), find an optimal solution, and then use this solution to devise approximations for the dual problem of maximizing the number of jobs, integrally assigned, given a hard constraint on the effective load. For the 1-D model with exponential heat fall-off, one can show that: $EL_i = L_i + \frac{EL_{i-1}}{K}$. Given this, we can show that:

LEMMA 1. *An optimal strategy for minimizing the maximum effective load for fractional assignments, with total load L, would result in uniform effective load of* $EL_i = EL = \frac{L}{m - \frac{m-1}{K}}$ $\forall i$.

The optimal strategy to minimize the effective load for a given load, would be to place a higher load on machine 1 and lower on the rest. Specifically, $L_1 = \frac{L}{m - \frac{m-1}{K}}$ and $L_i = \frac{L}{m - \frac{m-1}{K}} \left(1 - \frac{1}{K}\right)$ for $i > 1$. A non-thermal strategy on the other hand would split load uniformly in minimizing the loads of machines, and this would result in highest effective load on the last machine on the rack from the bottom.

The following theorem states the thermal savings possible.

THEOREM 1. *The reduction in effective load between a thermally aware scheduler and a naive load balanced strategy is* $\geq \frac{L}{m(K-1)+1}\left(1 - \frac{1}{K}\right)^{m-1} > 0$.

Figure 1 shows the percentage savings in effective load for different values of K and m.

The savings in maximum effective load translate into savings in energy of the cooling system. Let the maximum effective load without thermal aware scheduling be EL_{old} and the one with thermal savings be EL_{new}. Let us assume a simple function for CoP: $CoP(T) = T^{1+\delta}$, for some $\delta > 0$. The following theorem states the amount of energy savings possible.

THEOREM 2. *Let the energy consumed for cooling with a naive strategy of splitting the load uniformly without any thermal awareness be* E_{old}*, and the energy consumed by our thermally aware strategy be* E_{new}*. Let the difference be* $\Delta E = E_{old} - E_{new}$*. The fraction of energy that can be saved in cooling purposes is* $\frac{\Delta E}{E_{old}} > \frac{\Delta EL}{T_{red} - EL_{new}}$*, where,* ΔEL *is the savings in effective load,* EL_{new} *is the maximum thermal aware effective load, and* T_{red} *is the red-line temperature.*

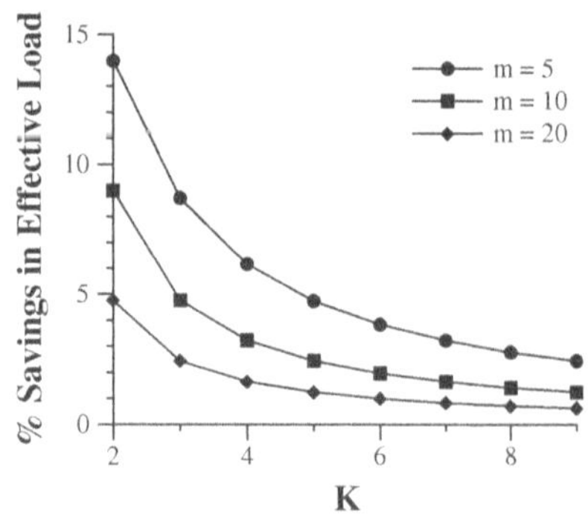

Figure 1: Percentage savings in maximum effective load for varying K and m

Now we look at the dual problem of maximizing the total assigned load, given a hard thermal or effective load constraint, which we assume is identical for all machines. Further, we assume there are no assignment restrictions. In the fractional case, by intelligently scheduling more load on the first machine than the rest, we can schedule more load overall than a non-thermally aware policy for the same effective load constraint. Let this constraint be called effective load capacity c.

LEMMA 2. *Without loss of generality, an optimal policy would assign load* c *to machine* 1 *and* $c\left(1 - \frac{1}{K}\right)$ *to all machines* $i > 1$ *till it exhausts either the load* L *or the available machines.*

THEOREM 3. *The fraction of extra load we can assign by a thermal aware strategy is* $\frac{1 - \frac{1}{K^m}}{m(K-1)} - \frac{1}{K^m}$.

The above problem becomes hard when jobs need to be assigned integrally to machines. Further, deriving the structure of the optimum fractional solution becomes much harder when we consider a 2-dimensional model with both vertical and lateral heat coupling. We show the structure of the optimum fractional solution for three different 2-dimensional heat flow models, provide analogous bounds for thermal savings, and also provide approximation algorithms for the integral assignment problem for all three heat flow models [4].

Acknowledgments: This work has been partially supported by NSF Grants CCF-0728839 and CCF-0937865.

4. REFERENCES

[1] C. Belady. In the data center, power and cooling costs more than the IT equipment it supports. *Electronics Cooling*, 2007.

[2] D. Economou, S. Rivoire, and C. Kozyrakis. Full-system power analysis and modeling for server environments. In *Workshop on Modeling Benchmarking and Simulation*, 2006.

[3] M.K. Herrlin. Gravity-assisted air mixing in data centers and how it affects the rack cooling effectiveness. *ITHERM*, 2006.

[4] K. Mukherjee, S. Khuller and A. Deshpande. Approximation Algorithms for the Thermal Scheduling Problem. URL: `http://www.cs.umd.edu/~samir/grant/thermal.pdf`, 2012

[5] T. Mukherjee, A. Banerjee, G. Varsamopoulos, S. Gupta, and S. Rungta. Spatio-temporal thermal-aware job scheduling to minimize energy consumption in virtualized heterogeneous data centers. *Computer Networks*, 53(17), 2009.

[6] R. Schmidt, E. Cruz. Raised floor computer data center: effect on rack inlet temperatures of chilled air exiting both the hot and cold aisles. In *The Eighth Intersociety Conference on Thermal and Thermomechanical Phenomena in Electronic Systems*, 2002.

[7] C. Zhu, Z. Gu, L. Shang, R.P. Dick, R. Joseph. Three-Dimensional Chip-Multiprocessor Run-Time Thermal Management. *IEEE Trans. on Computer-Aided Design of Integrated Circuits and Systems*, 2008.

Congestion Control Meets Medium Access: Throughput, Delay, and Complexity

Shreeshankar Bodas
Massachusetts Institute of Technology
Cambridge, MA 02139, USA
bodas@mit.edu

Devavrat Shah
Massachusetts Institute of Technology
Cambridge, MA 02139, USA
devavrat@mit.edu

Damon Wischik
University College London
Gower Street, London WC1E 6BT, UK
D.Wischik@cs.ucl.ac.uk

ABSTRACT

This paper looks at the problem of designing medium access algorithm for wireless networks with the objective of providing high throughput and low delay performance to the users, while requiring only a modest computational effort at the transmitters and receivers. Additive inter-user interference at the receivers is an important physical layer characteristic of wireless networks. Today's Wi-Fi networks are based upon the abstraction of physical layer where inter-user interference is considered as noise leading to the 'collision' model in which users are required to co-ordinate their transmissions through Carrier Sensing Multiple Access (CSMA)-based schemes to avoid interference. This, in turn, leads to an inherent performance trade-off [1]: it is impossible to obtain high throughput and low delay by means of low complexity medium access algorithm (unless P=NP).

As the main result, we establish that this trade-off is primarily due to treating interference as noise in the current wireless architecture. Concretely, we develop a simple medium access algorithm that allows for simultaneous transmissions of users to the same receiver by performing joint decoding at receivers, over time. For a receiver to be able to decode multiple transmissions quickly enough, we develop appropriate congestion control where each transmitter maintains a "window" of undecoded transmitted data that is adjusted based upon the "feedback" from the receiver. In summary, this provides an efficient, low complexity "online" code operating at varying rate, and the system as a whole experiences only small amount of delay (including decoding time) while operating at high throughput.

Categories and Subject Descriptors

C.2.1 [**Computer-Communication Networks**]: Network Architecture and Design—*Wireless Communication*

Keywords

Medium access, congestion control, throughput, delay, complexity

1. INTRODUCTION

The emergence of 'smart' devices will continue the enormous growth in the wireless bandwidth requirement over coming years. The wireless network resources - time and frequency - are limited. Therefore, it is essential to utilize them efficiently so as to relieve the existing bottleneck in the wireless access network.

The traditional view of wireless medium access treats simultaneous transmissions by two nearby wireless transmitters as undesired, because it leads to "collisions" between transmissions, resulting in a poor SINR[1] for all the involved transmitters. This viewpoint leads to the graphical abstraction of a wireless network, as follows: in the so-called conflict graph, the communication links in the actual (wireless) network are represented by nodes, pairs of interfering links are connected by edges, and simultaneous transmissions are possible on a set of wireless links if and only if the corresponding nodes form an independent set in the conflict graph. Given this abstraction, the Maximum Weight (MW) scheduling of Tassiulas and Ephremides [2, 3] is a high throughput and low delay medium access algorithm. But it requires solving a computationally hard combinatorial optimization problem in a centralized manner. In recent years, through a sequence of exciting results, entirely distributed and low-complexity medium access algorithms have been developed starting through two distinct independent approaches by Jiang-Walrand [4] and Rajagopalan-Shah-Shin [5]. But they result in very high delay even for modest throughput. Thus, we can obtain high throughput and low delay but with a high complexity algorithm, or high throughput and low complexity but with high delay. This trade-off was shown to be fundamental by Shah-Tse-Tsitsiklis [1]: for a wireless network of n nodes, unless P = NP, it is not possible to achieve (a) at least an $n^{\epsilon-1}$ fraction of the throughput region, for a given $\epsilon > 0$, (b) $\mathcal{O}(n^K)$ expected queue-sizes (equivalently delay) at each of the transmitters, for some integer K, and (c) $\mathcal{O}(n^M)$ computational complexity per timeslot for some integer M. The result holds even for SINR-based decoding model. Effectively, as long as the interfering transmission is treated as noise, it is not possible to have high throughput and low delay with low complexity medium access.

As the main result of this paper, we overcome this fundamental barrier in terms of the trade-off between throughput-delay-complexity for medium access algorithm. This is achieved by explicitly decoding the interfering transmissions, rather than treating them as noise. Thus the choice of treating interference as noise in the wireless architecture is the fundamental reason behind the wireless access network being currently the bottleneck, and it is necessary to do joint decoding at the receiver (not joint encoding among transmitters)

SIGMETRICS'12, June 11–15, 2012, London, England, UK.
ACM 978-1-4503-1097-0/12/06.

[1]signal-to-interference and noise ratio

to achieve the desired performance in terms of throughput-delay-complexity.

2. SETUP & MAIN RESULT

System model. We consider a system with n receivers (access points), communicating with a set of users over the wireless channel. Figure 1 shows an example of such a system with 2 access points and 3 users. The system evolves in discrete time. A user in this system is associated with a *user-class*, identified by the set of receivers within its transmission range.

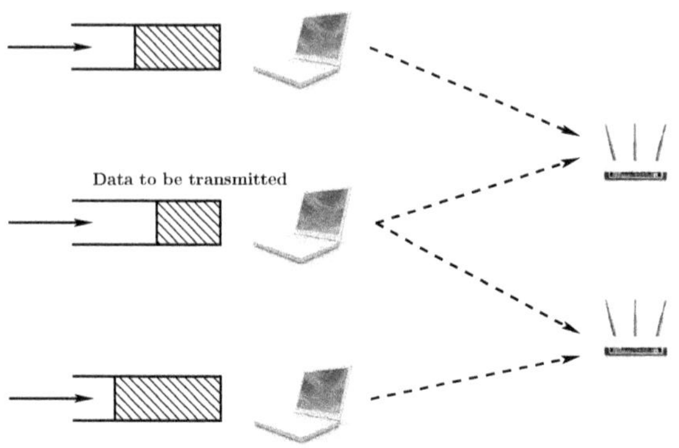

Figure 1: System Model

Physical channel model. We consider the physical description of the wireless channel. In any timeslot, a user (transmitter) transmits a real number and a receiver receives a linear combination of the transmissions of the users within its range, corrupted by additive white Gaussian noise.

External arrivals. In every timeslot, each transmitter receives a (potentially nonzero) number of "files." A file is a finite collection of bits that need to be transmitted to each one of the receivers in the transmission range.

Departure. When each one of the bits in the file has been successfully decoded by each one of the receivers within the transmitter's range, the file leaves the system. (The exact decoding mechanism is protocol-specific.)

Problem statement. Design a medium access protocol (a rule that specifies the transmission and reception/decoding for each transmitter and receiver for all times) with the following properties: (i) the protocol stabilizes (makes positive recurrent) the network Markov chain as long as the load on the system (the vector of bit-arrival rates) is within a constant fraction of the maximum possible supportable under *any* algorithm (i.e., a constant fraction of the system's throughput region), (ii) the expected backlog (number of bits) at each transmitter, and the expected decoding complexity (number of computations per timeslot) at each receiver is polynomially bounded in the system-size as long as the load is within a constant fraction of the throughput region, and (iii) the average transmit power of all the transmitters is uniformly bounded.

Discussion: why these objectives? An algorithm that satisfies the first and the third condition is essentially the best possible in terms of throughput, up to constant multiplicative factors. Combined with Little's law, the second condition requires that the symbol decoding delay at each of the receivers remains polynomially bounded in the system-size. Thus, in contrast with information theoretic capacity results which are asymptotic in the "block-length," our algorithm provides performance guarantees for finite block-lengths as well. Polynomially bounded encoding and decoding complexity of an algorithm is a desired feature from an implementation point of view. The results from [1] suggest that there does not exist a medium access algorithm that satisfies the stated throughput, delay, and complexity requirements unless P=NP. The results of [1] apply to medium access algorithms in which receivers *do not* decode transmissions jointly. We design a medium access algorithm in which a receiver decodes the interfering transmissions, and it achieves all the above goals. Thus the architectural decision of treating interference as noise is the primary reason for the fundamental barrier identified in [1], and can be overcome by exploiting the physical layer appropriately.

Main result. We develop the QNUB medium access algorithm with the above desired properties. In a nutshell, this algorithm determines the transmission rates (bits per timeslot) for each of the transmitters as a function of the backlog ("queue-length") feedback from the corresponding receivers. Each receiver performs matrix-inversion based decoding of the received linear combinations of transmissions.

3. CONCLUSION

We considered the problem of designing a medium access algorithm for a Wi-Fi-like wireless network with multiple transmitters and receivers. Our proposed algorithm simultaneously guarantees a high system throughput, low delay at each transmitter, and low encoding-decoding complexity. It exploits the additive nature of interference in the wireless medium, and the desired performance guarantees are realized by means of decoding and removing interference, rather than explicitly avoiding it or treating it as noise.

Acknowledgments

This work was supported in parts by DARPA ITMANET and AFOSR Complex Networks Program.

4. REFERENCES

[1] D. Shah, D. N. C. Tse, and J. Tsitsiklis, "Hardness of low delay network scheduling," *IEEE Trans. Inform. Theory*, vol. to appear, 2011.

[2] L. Tassiulas and A. Ephremides, "Stability properties of constrained queueing systems and scheduling policies for maximum throughput in multihop radio networks," *IEEE Trans. Automat. Contr.*, vol. 4, pp. 1936–1948, December 1992.

[3] ——, "Dynamic server allocation to parallel queues with randomly varying connectivity," *IEEE Trans. Inform. Theory*, vol. 39, pp. 466–478, March 1993.

[4] L. Jiang and J. Walrand, "A distributed csma algorithm for throughput and utility maximization in wireless networks," *IEEE/ACM Trans. Network.*, vol. 18, no. 3, pp. 960–972, Jun. 2010.

[5] S. Rajagopalan, D. Shah, and J. Shin, "Network adiabatic theorem: An efficient randomized protocol for contention resolution," in *Proc. Ann. ACM SIGMETRICS Conf.*, Jun. 2009.

Optimized Cloud Placement of Virtual Clusters Using Biased Importance Sampling

Asser N. Tantawi
IBM T.J. Watson Research Center
P.O. Box 704
Yorktown Heights, NY 10598
tantawi@us.ibm.com

ABSTRACT

We introduce an algorithm for the placement of constrained, networked virtual clusters in the cloud, that is based on importance sampling (also known as cross-entropy). Rather than using a straightforward implementation of such a technique, which proved inefficient, we considerably enhance the method by biasing the sampling process to incorporate communication needs and other constraints of placement requests to yield an efficient algorithm that is linear in the size of the cloud. We investigate the quality of the results of using our algorithm on a simulated cloud.

Categories and Subject Descriptors

K.6.4 [**Computing Milieux**]: Management of Computing and Information Systems—*System Management*

General Terms

Algorithms, Performance

Keywords

Application placement, cloud management, cross-entropy, importance sampling, virtual clusters

1. PROBLEM DESCRIPTION

As cloud computing matures, the demand for virtual resources is changing from units of virtual machines (VM) to a collection of heterogeneous VMs with communication demand among them as well as availability constraints. The problem for the cloud provider is to efficiently place such a virtual cluster on physical machines (PM), in such a way that the availability constraints are satisfied, the virtual cluster experiences good performance, and the rejection rate is kept at minimum. Further, the time to obtain a placement decision should be reasonably small and it should scale with the size of the cloud. A less constrained problem than the one considered in this paper was shown to be NP-Hard [1].

We consider a cloud system which consists of a set of PMs that are connected through switches via links. Each PM provides a set of resources, such as CPU, memory, and disk storage, with some fixed capacity. Each link provides bandwidth for communication. We assume that the switches are fast and that communication delay is solely due to link congestion.

We model the availability of the cloud as follows. Focussing on a pair of PMs, say pm_i and pm_j, let $v_{i,j}$ be the probability that at least one of pm_i or pm_j is available. We imagine a partitioning of the data center into a hierarchy of availability zones, where PMs in the same zone have similar availability characteristics. In such a case, one may model this hierarchy as a tree, where the leaves are the PMs and an intermediate node represents a zone of availability. As such, we associate an availability level, V_l, $l = 0, \cdots, L$, for a node at level l in the tree, where $l = 0$ represents the leaves and $l = L$ represents the root of the tree with height L. It follows that $V_0 < V_1 < \cdots < V_L$, since two PMs in *distant* availability zones have less common components and hence higher chance of having at least one of them available. Using this tree model, two PMs pm_i and pm_j with the lowest common ancestor at level l have $v_{i,j} = V_l$.

A virtual cluster is a collection of VMs that make up a deployable unit which we refer to as *pattern*. Each VM in the pattern is characterized by a set resource demands, one per resource type. We refer to the PM which hosts vm_i as $pm(vm_i)$. Furthermore, a pair of VMs, say vm_i and vm_j may have bandwidth demand which we denote by $\lambda_{i,j}$. Again, such demands need be satisfied by all the links along the path connecting $pm(vm_i)$ and $pm(vm_j)$. We express the availability requirements of a pattern as follows. For a subset of VMs of size n in the pattern, an availability requirement is specified as k-out-of-n VMs in this subset have to be be simultaneously available with some probability.

System performance is characterized by resource utilization and delay measures. We divide links into two types: edge links and core links. We define edge links to be the links directly connected to a PM, whereas all other links are core links. The network delay between pm_i and pm_j is the sum of the link delays along the path $h_{i,j}$. We are not concerned about absolute delay, rather delay factor as provided by a series of $M/M/1$ queues, each representing a link along the path. In comparing delay among pairs of PMs, we use a delay index metric as a value in $[0, 1]$, where $\delta_{i,j} = 0$ represents no delay and $\delta_{i,j} = 1$ represents infinite delay. A higher value of $\delta_{i,j}$ signifies more relative network congestion along the path $h_{i,j}$. We express the performance of a pattern by a weighted path length (distance) and a weighted delay index.

The overall performance objective when placing a pattern comprises two components: (1) system performance expressed as the average and skew of the utilization of the

SIGMETRICS'12, June 11–15, 2012, London, England, UK.
ACM 978-1-4503-1097-0/12/06.

various system resources and (2) pattern performance expressed as the average and skew of pattern related measures such as communication path length, communication delay, and deviation from availability requirements. The objective function is defined as a weighted sum of the average and standard deviation of the utilization of PM resources, edge and core links, and the pattern weighted path length and delay index. As far as the PM resources are concerned, we care about the imbalance through the standard deviation. As for the network, we seek to lower both the average amount of traffic as well as any imbalance among the links. Further, we need to limit the damaging impact from the imbalance in the core network than the edge links. Note that, in addition to system performance measures, the objective function includes performance measures of the pattern to be placed.

2. PLACEMENT ALGORITHM

Consider an arrival process of patterns which are to be placed in the cloud. A placed (deployed) pattern remains in the cloud for some lifetime after which the pattern departs and releases all of its resources. In this paper we focus on the handling of an arriving pattern rather than studying queueing and occupancy characteristics. As such, we are dealing with a loss system where an arriving pattern request may be lost in case the placement algorithm fails to find a mapping to place the pattern. An optimal placement algorithm attempts to find PMs in the cloud that have enough capacity to host the VMs in the pattern, while making sure that there is enough bandwidth in the network to accommodate inter-VM bandwidth requirements, as well as satisfying any pairwise VM availability constraints.

Our approach for solving this optimization problem is to find a close to optimal solution by statistically sampling mapping solutions, then using importance sampling techniques (cross-entropy) to refine the sampling process and get closer to sampling near an optimal solution. We use the communication and availability constraints to bias the sampling as we build a sample of a mapping for a pattern.

The main idea is that in order to find an optimal solution to a combinatorial (maximization) problem, one generates many samples of solutions using a parametrized probability distribution. The samples (solutions) are ordered in their attained values of the objective function. Then, the top small fraction of samples, in other words the important samples, are used to adjust the values of the parameters of the generating probability distribution so as to skew the generation process to yield samples with large objective values. The method iterates a few times until a good solution is obtained.

In our case, a sample is analogous to a mapping solution of VMs in a given pattern to PMs in the cloud. We define the parameters for the sample generation process as a matrix $\mathbf{P} = [p_{i,j}]$, where $p_{i,j}$ represents the probability of assigning vm_i in the pattern to pm_j. Starting from some initial $\mathbf{P}$, the algorithm proceeds to modify $\mathbf{P}$ until a solution is reached, represented by a dominant (close to 1) entry in each row of $\mathbf{P}$ and all other entries are negligibly small (close to 0). A simple choice for the initial $\mathbf{P}$ is such that $p_{i,j}$ is inversely proportional to the utilization of the bottleneck resource. In every iteration of the importance sampling algorithm, the entries in $\mathbf{P}$ that correspond to a large objective value are reinforced and amplified, at the cost of other solutions that are away from optimality. A straightforward implementation of the importance sampling method to our placement mapping problem would be terribly inefficient, since typically thousands of samples need to be generated at each iteration. Therefore, one needs to bias the values of $\mathbf{P}$ while building a solution so as to accelerate arriving at a solution to the problem

As we decide on the placement of a pattern we sequentially consider the VMs in the pattern without backtracking. The order of VMs in a pattern plays a role during placement. We propose to satisfy the availability constraints before satisfying communication need. Hence, we place the VMs with availability constraints ahead of the remaining VMs in the order. Further, we propose to satisfy the higher communication needs than the lower ones. Hence, we order the VMs according their pairwise communication need.

Once vm_i is placed on say pm_i, we examine any availability constraint with $vm_m, m > i$ in a look-ahead fashion. More precisely, let's say that vm_i and vm_m have an availability constraint of level l. Then, we need to bias $p_{m,j}$ positively towards $pm_j \in g_i(l)$ and negatively to all other PMs, where $g_i(l)$ is the set of PMs such that for $pm_j \in g_i(l)$ we have $v_{i,j} = V_l$. The way biasing is done is through multiplying $p_{m,j}$ by a factor and normalize the $p_{m,\cdot}$ after all biasing factors are applied.

In a similar way to biasing the probabilities to reflect availability constraints, we bias them depending on the number of hops between a given PM and the other PMs in the cloud. Once vm_i is placed on say pm_i, consider the communication demand $\lambda_{i,m}$ between vm_i and $vm_m, m > i$. In order to keep vm_m placed close to pm_i we positively bias $p_{m,j}$ towards $pm_j \in w_i(0)$, where $w_i(l)$ is the set of PMs that are l hops away from pm_i. In other words, pm_i is positively biased, then less positively towards $pm_j \in w_i(1)$, and so on until we reach a most negative bias towards $pm_j \in w_i(L)$, the farthest away PMs from pm_i. Similar to availability constraint biasing, we multiply the probabilities by a factor and normalize.

We simulated clouds ranging in size from 128 to 1,024 PMs. The placement algorithm is configured to generate 20 samples per iteration with the top 0.1 fraction used to generate the importance sampling of the subsequent iteration. We are mostly concerned with the amount of traffic on edge links, hence we wanted to force placement of VMs in the same pattern on the same PM as much as possible. As discussed earlier, we care about the imbalance in the core network than the edge network. The imbalance in CPU loading among PMs is relevant, but not as important as decreasing network traffic. Lastly, for pattern performance measures, we consider the path length to be more relevant than the delay index, which is a function of link utilization which already appears in the equation somewhere else. A full version of this paper appeared in [2].

3. REFERENCES

[1] X. Meng, V. Pappas, and L. Zhang. Improving the scalability of data center networks with traffic-aware virtual machine placement. In *INFOCOM, 2010 Proceedings IEEE*, pages 1–9, March 2010.

[2] A. N. Tantawi. Optimized cloud placement of virtual clusters using biased importance sampling. Research Report RC25248, IBM, Yorktown Heights, NY, 2012.

Power and Energy Containers for Multicore Servers

Kai Shen
University of Rochester
kshen@cs.rochester.edu

Arrvindh Shriraman
Simon Fraser University
ashriram@cs.sfu.ca

Sandhya Dwarkadas
University of Rochester
sandhya@cs.rochester.edu

Xiao Zhang*
University of Rochester
xiao@cs.rochester.edu

ABSTRACT

Power capping and energy efficiency are critical concerns in server systems, particularly when serving dynamic workloads on resource-sharing multicores. We present a new operating system facility (*power and energy containers*) that accounts for and controls the power/energy usage of individual fine-grained server requests. This facility is enabled by novel techniques for multicore power attribution to concurrent tasks, measurement/modeling alignment to enhance predictability, and request power accounting and control.

Categories and Subject Descriptors

C.5.5 [**Computer System Implementation**]: Servers; D.4.8 [**Operating Systems**]: Performance—*Measurements, Modeling and prediction*

Keywords

Multicore, server system, power and energy management.

1. INTRODUCTION

Online applications continuously evolve with new features and some (like social networks, Wiki sites, and online collaboration) rely on end users to supply content or even content-generating code. The workload diversity and dynamic client-directed processing result in large power fluctuations on modern hardware with increasing specialization and power proportionality. Recognizing the resource usage of individual requests facilitates fine-grained attribution of energy usage to clients, helping expose the full cost of web usage. Furthermore, high power-consuming tasks (or "power viruses" [2]) may either appear accidentally or be maliciously devised. Isolating per-client power attribution to identify such tasks so as to cap the system power draw in a fair fashion is desirable.

Building on our past work [3, 5] on per-request behavior characterization in a multicore server, we address the additional challenges of per-request power/energy accounting and management. Request executions in a concurrent, multi-stage server contain fine-grained activities with frequent context switches. Direct power measurements on such spatial and temporal granularities are not available on today's systems. Concurrent task executions, dynamic workload behaviors, and multicore hardware sharing lead to additional complexities in modeling per-task power behavior. Request-level power and energy management also requires agile, low-cost control to ensure isolation and achieve efficiency.

*Zhang is currently affiliated with Google.

SIGMETRICS'12, June 11–15, 2012, London, England, UK.
ACM 978-1-4503-1097-0/12/06.

We address these challenges in a new operating system facility, called *power and energy containers*, which both tracks and allows control of the power/energy usage of individual requests in multicore servers. Our power and energy containers enable fine-grained, agile management of multicore server power/energy resources in unprecedented ways. Below, we present design highlights and a brief case study, with more details in a technical report [4].

2. DESIGN HIGHLIGHTS

We support power attribution and control in two new dimensions—1) over concurrent executions on a shared-resource multicore and 2) among fine-grained requests in a multi-stage server application.

Power Attribution to Concurrent Tasks.

Bellosa [1] validated a linear model between the system power consumption and the frequency of hardware events such as instructions per cycle and memory transaction rate. This suggests that the power accounting for a task can linearly correlate with physical event rates at the CPU core that the task runs on. On a multicore processor chip with intricately shared hardware resources, however, chip-wide environmental factors also affect per-core power accounting. In particular, the maintenance of shared multicore resources (including at least clocking circuitry and voltage regulators) consumes some active power as long as one core is running. However, the power consumption does not change proportionally with core-level event rates. Our measurements show that the power increment from idle to one utilized core is much higher than further power increments, which suggests an active power component that does not scale proportionally with core-level physical events.

It is intuitive to evenly attribute the chip maintenance power at each time instant to the currently running tasks. The system utilization level fluctuates over time in production server environments. Proper accounting and attribution of shared chip maintenance power is challenging because one task's share may change depending on activities (or the lack thereof) on other cores. If a core is busy while all other siblings are idle, the full chip maintenance power should be attributed to the task on the busy core. If multiple (k) cores are busy at a moment, then each running task on one of the busy cores has $\frac{1.0}{k}$ share of the maintenance power. Note that the chip maintenance power share does not correspond to any processor hardware counter and depends instead on time-synchronized busy states across all CPU cores. The operating system must monitor all CPU busy states to accurately account for this.

Measurement Alignment for Model Recalibration.

Despite the wide uses of event-based power models [1], we found that large errors may arise in practice. Beyond superficial problems like insufficient coverage of modeled events, modeling inaccuracy also results from differing characteristics between calibration and production workloads. This is particularly the case for unusually high power-consuming production workloads that demand careful attention in server system power management. To address the modeling inaccuracy, we utilize online power measurements to adjust and recalibrate the offline-constructed power models.

The challenge is that while whole-system power measurements can be acquired through off-the-shelf meters, measurement results often arrive after some meter reporting delay and data I/O latency. On the other hand, processor event counter-based power models can be maintained at the much shorter latency of reading CPU registers and computing simple statistics. The measurement results and modeling estimates need to be properly aligned in order to identify modeling errors and recalibrate the model. Our work finds that such alignment can be enabled using signal processing cross-correlation and that the aligned measurement can effect model recalibration and improve modeling accuracy.

Request Power Accounting and Control.

We construct OS mechanisms to support request-level power/energy containers in a server system. We track request execution contexts so that power-relevant metrics can be properly attributed and control mechanisms can be properly applied. We identify a request context on-the-fly with recognized patterns on how it propagates over multiple server stages. Specifically, we recognize request context propagation events as those that indicate causal dependences through data and control flows between processes, including socket calls, IPCs, and task forking. By sampling events at propagation boundaries, our power model estimates request power consumption based on the collected event metrics. The cumulative energy usage can be simply calculated as the integral of power over time.

In addition to per-request event sampling, the on-the-fly request tracking allows us to selectively apply power and energy control mechanisms on certain requests. For example, we can apply a particular CPU duty-cycle modulation level to a given request execution. Effectively, when the request starts executing on a CPU core, the core duty-cycle level will be set appropriately. When the CPU core switches to run another request, the core duty-cycle level will be adjusted according to the policy setting of the new request. Our mechanism can limit the power consumption of selected requests without hurting the performance of others. We can similarly support request-specific dynamic voltage/frequency scaling if the multicore processor allows such scaling on a per-core basis.

3. POWER VIRUS MANAGEMENT

Our power containers enable fair power conditioning on a multicore server. While CPU duty-cycle modulation can control surging power consumption, indiscriminate full-machine throttling would lead to slowdowns of all running requests regardless of their power use. Without per-request power containers, the occurrence of a power virus could force speed reductions on all concurrently running normal requests. In a power container-controlled system, we maintain a power consumption target for each request. Those that exceed the specified target will be subject to request-specific CPU duty-cycle modulation while other requests will run at full speed. Our experiment runs a server on a quad-core Intel Nehalem machine. The workload fully utilizes all four cores on the machine. In the middle of the experimentation, we inject some high-power requests to mimic power viruses. Figure 1(A) shows that the introduction of power viruses lead to substantial power spikes. We apply our container-based fair power conditioning with a system active power target of 40 Watts. Figure 1(B) shows that our request container-enabled power conditioning can effectively keep power consumption at or below the target level despite the power viruses.

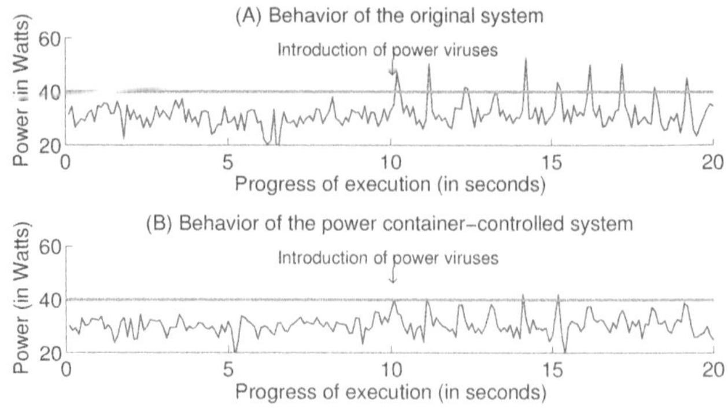

Figure 1: Measured active (full minus idle) power of a quad-core Nehalem machine. Results are for original (A) and power container-controlled (B) executions with power viruses.

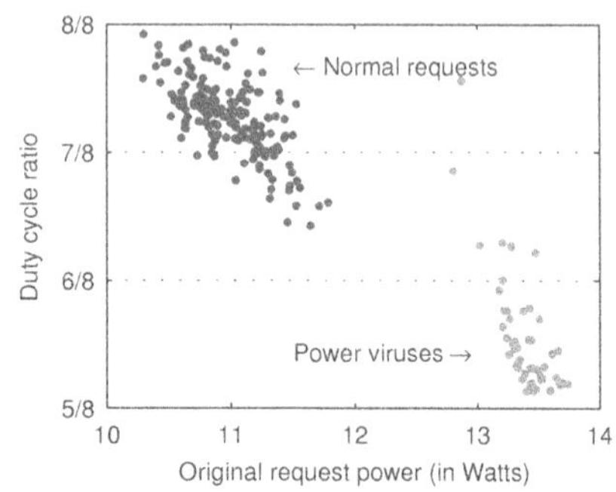

Figure 2: Each point represents a sample request (normal or power virus). X-coordinate indicates the original (before throttling) request power consumption. Y-coordinate indicates the CPU duty-cycle (slowdown) ratio applied to the request.

We next show that the CPU speed adjustment has been applied fairly to each request. Figure 2 plots the applied CPU duty-cycle ratio and original request power (before throttling) for each request. Since a request power consumption may fluctuate over its execution, different duty-cycle levels may be applied over time. We show the time-averaged duty-cycle ratio for each request. We also estimate its power consumption in the original system. Results show that the normal server requests suffer small CPU speed slowdown (averaged at about 9%). At the same time, the power viruses are subject to more substantial (31% on average) slowdown.

4. ACKNOWLEDGMENTS

This work was supported in part by the National Science Foundation (NSF) grants CCF-0448413, CNS-0834451, CCF-0937571, and CCF-1016902. Shen was also supported by an IBM Faculty Award and a Google Research Award.

5. REFERENCES

[1] F. Bellosa. The benefits of event-driven energy accounting in power-sensitive systems. In *SIGOPS European Workshop*, 2000.

[2] K. Ganesan, J. Jo, W. L. Bircher, D. Kaseridis, Z. Yu, and L. K. John. System-level max power (SYMPO): a systematic approach for escalating system-level power consumption using synthetic benchmarks. In *PACT*, 2010.

[3] K. Shen. Request behavior variations. In *ASPLOS*, 2010.

[4] K. Shen, A. Shriraman, S. Dwarkadas, and X. Zhang. Power and energy containers for multicore servers. Technical Report #970, Dept. of Computer Science, Univ. of Rochester, 2011.

[5] K. Shen, M. Zhong, S. Dwarkadas, C. Li, C. Stewart, and X. Zhang. Hardware counter driven on-the-fly request signatures. In *ASPLOS*, 2008.

Characterizing the Impact of the Workload on the Value of Dynamic Resizing in Data Centers

Kai Wang
Tsinghua University
Beijing, China
kaiphd@caltech.edu

Minghong Lin
California Institute of Technology
Pasadena, CA, USA
mhlin@caltech.edu

Florin Ciucu
T-Labs / TU Berlin
Berlin, Germany
florin@net.t-labs.tu-berlin.de

Adam Wierman
California Institute of Technology
Pasadena, CA, USA
adamw@caltech.edu

Chuang Lin
Tsinghua University
Beijing, China
chlin@tsinghua.edu.cn

ABSTRACT

Energy consumption imposes a significant cost for data centers; yet much of that energy is used to maintain excess service capacity during periods of predictably low load. Resultantly, there has recently been interest in developing designs that allow the service capacity to be dynamically resized to match the current workload. However, there is still much debate about the value of such approaches in real settings. In this paper, we show that the value of dynamic resizing is highly dependent on statistics of the workload process. In particular, both slow time-scale non-stationarities of the workload (e.g., the peak-to-mean ratio) and the fast time-scale stochasticity (e.g., the burstiness of arrivals) play key roles. To illustrate the impact of these factors, we combine optimization-based modeling of the slow time-scale with stochastic modeling of the fast time scale. Within this framework, we provide both analytic and numerical results characterizing when dynamic resizing does (and does not) provide benefits.

Categories and Subject Descriptors

C.4 [**Performance of Systems**]: Modeling techniques

Keywords

Data Centers, Dynamic Resizing, Energy Efficient IT

1. INTRODUCTION

Energy costs represent a significant, and growing, fraction of a data center's budget. Hence there is a push to improve the energy efficiency of data centers, both in terms of the components (servers, disks, network) and the algorithms. One specific aspect of data center design that is the focus of our work is dynamically resizing the service capacity of the data center so that during periods of low load some servers are allowed to enter a power-saving mode (e.g., go to sleep or shut down).

The potential benefits of this dynamic resizing have been a point of debate in the community [3, 1, 5]. On one hand, it is clear that, because data centers are far from perfectly energy proportional, significant energy is used to maintain excess capacity during periods of predictably low load when there is a diurnal workload with a high peak-to-mean ratio. On the other hand, there are also significant costs to dynamically adjusting the number of active servers. These costs come in terms of the engineering challenges in making this possible, as well as the latency, energy, and wear-and-tear costs of the actual "switching" operations involved.

The challenges for dynamic resizing highlighted above have been the subject of significant research. At this point, many of the engineering challenges associated with facilitating dynamic resizing have been resolved. Additionally, the algorithmic challenge of deciding, without knowledge of the future workload, whether to incur the significant "switching costs" associated with changing the available service capacity has been studied in depth and a number of promising algorithms have emerged.

However, despite this body of work, the question of characterizing the potential benefits of dynamic resizing has still not been properly addressed. Providing new insight into this topic is the goal of the current extended abstract. *For the full version of the work summarized here please refer to [6].*

2. METHODOLOGY

The perspective of this work is that, apart from engineering challenges, the key determinant of whether dynamic resizing is valuable is the workload, and that proponents on different sides tend to have different assumptions in this regard. In particular, a key observation, which is the starting point for our work, is that there are two factors of the workload which provide dynamic resizing potential savings:

(i) Non-stationarities at a slow time-scale, e.g., diurnal workload variations.
(ii) Stochastic variability at a fast time-scale, e.g., the burstiness of request arrivals.

The goal of this work is to investigate the impact of and interaction between these two features with respect to dynamic resizing.

To this point, we are not aware of any work characterizing the benefits of dynamic resizing that captures both of these features. There is one body of literature which provides algorithms that take advantage of (i), e.g., [4]. This work tends to use an optimization-based approach to develop dynamic resizing algorithms. There is another body of literature which provides algorithms that take advantage

SIGMETRICS'12, June 11–15, 2012, London, England, UK.
ACM 978-1-4503-1097-0/12/06.

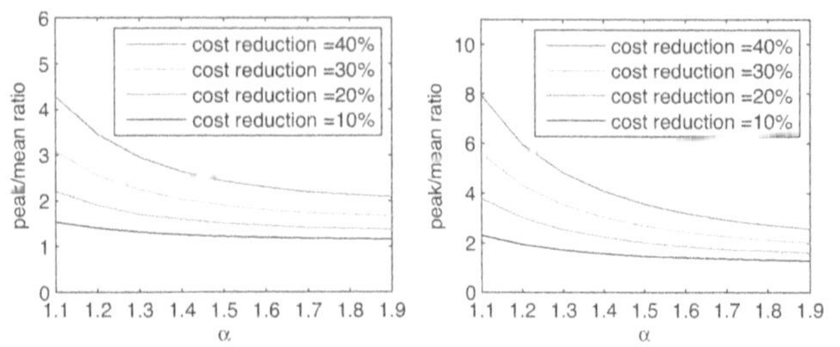

(a) Hotmail (b) MSR

Figure 1: Characterization of the cost reduction of optimal dynamic resizing under different levels of burstiness, α, and peak-to-mean ratio in the workload.

of (ii), e.g., [2]. This work tends to assume a stationary queueing model with Poisson arrivals to develop dynamic resizing algorithms.

The first contribution of our work is to provide an analytic framework that captures both effects (i) and (ii). We accomplish this by using an optimization framework at the slow time-scale, which is similar to that of [4], and combining this with stochastic network calculus and large deviations modeling for the fast time-scale, which allows us to study a wide variety of underlying arrival processes. We consider both light-tailed models and heavy-tailed models with various degrees of burstiness by varying the tail index α which describes the shape of the tail [1].

The interface between the fast and slow time-scale models happens through a constraint in the optimization problem that captures the Service Level Agreement (SLA) for the data center, which is used by the slow time-scale model but calculated using the fast time-scale model:

$$\mathbb{P}(D_k > \bar{D}) \leq \bar{\varepsilon}\,, \tag{1}$$

where we use D_k to represent the steady-state delay during frame k, and $(\bar{D}, \bar{\epsilon})$ to represent an SLA of the form "the probability of a delay larger than $\bar{D}$ must be bounded by probability $\bar{\varepsilon}$".

3. RESULTS

Using this modeling framework, we are able to provide both analytic and numerical results that yield new insight into the potential benefits of dynamic resizing. Specifically, we use trace-driven numerical simulations to study (i) the role of burstiness for dynamic resizing, (ii) the role of the peak-to-mean ratio for dynamic resizing, (iii) the role of the SLA for dynamic resizing, and (iv) the interaction between (i), (ii), and (iii). The key realization is that each of these parameters are extremely important for determining the value of dynamic resizing. In particular, for any fixed choices of two of these parameters, the third can be chosen so that dynamic resizing does or does not provide significant cost savings for the data center. Thus, performing a detailed study of the interaction of these factors is important. To that end, we provide concrete illustrations of which settings of peak-to-mean ratio, burstiness, and SLAs dynamic resizing are and are not valuable (e.g., Figure 1). Hence, debate about the *potential* value of dynamic resizing can be transformed into debate about characteristics of the workload and the SLA.

[1] A concrete example is generating jobs in every slot according to i.i.d. Pareto random variables X_i with tail distribution for all $x \geq b$: $P(X_i > x) = (x/b)^{-\alpha}$, in which smaller values of α indicate heavier tails and, thus, more burstiness.

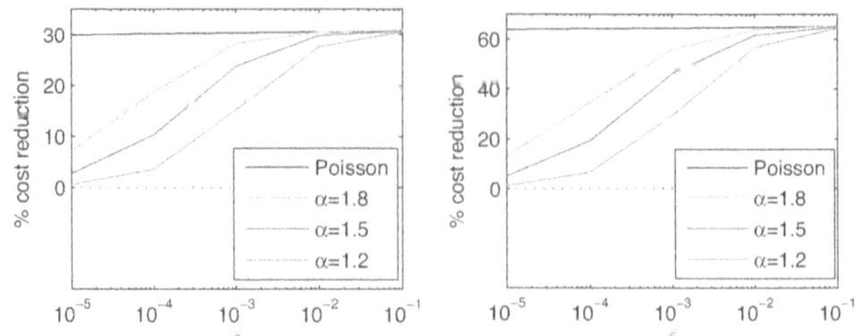

(a) Hotmail (b) MSR

Figure 2: Characterization of the impact of the SLA, $\bar{\varepsilon}$, and burstiness, α, on the cost reduction achieved by optimal dynamic resizing.

There are some interesting facts about these parameters individually that our case studies uncover. Two important examples are the following (see Figure 2). First, while one might expect that increased burstiness provides increased opportunities for dynamic resizing, it turns out the burstiness at the fast time-scale actually reduces the potential cost savings achievable via dynamic resizing. The reason is that dynamic resizing necessarily happens at the slow time-scale, and so the increased burstiness at the fast time-scale actually results in the SLA constraint requiring *more* servers to be used at the slow time-scale due to the possibility of a large burst occurring. Second, it turns out the impact of the SLA can be quite different depending on whether the arrival process is heavy- or light-tailed. In particular, as the SLA becomes more strict, the cost savings possible via dynamic resizing under heavy-tailed arrivals decreases quickly; however, the cost savings possible via dynamic resizing under light-tailed workloads is unchanged.

In addition to detailed case studies, we provide analytic results that support many of the insights provided by the numerics. In particular, we prove theorems to provide monotonicity and scaling results for dynamic resizing in the case of Poisson arrivals and heavy-tailed, self-similar arrivals.

4. ACKNOWLEDGMENTS

This research is supported by the 973 Program of China (No. 2010CB328105), the National Natural Scientific Foundation of China (No. 61020106002 and No.60973107), and NSF grant CNS 0846025 and DoE grant DE-EE0002890.

5. REFERENCES

[1] G. Chen, W. He, J. Liu, S. Nath, L. Rigas, L. Xiao, and F. Zhao. Energy-aware server provisioning and load dispatching for connection-intensive internet services. In *Proceedings of the 5th USENIX NSDI*, pages 337–350, 2008.

[2] A. Gandhi, V. Gupta, M. Harchol-Balter, and M. A. Kozuch. Optimality analysis of energy-performance trade-off for server farm management. *Performance Evaluation*, 67(11):1155–1171, 2010.

[3] A. Greenberg, J. Hamilton, D. A. Maltz, and P. Patel. The cost of a cloud: research problems in data center networks. *SIGCOMM Comput. Commun. Rev.*, 39:68–73, December 2008.

[4] M. Lin, A. Wierman, L. L. H. Andrew, and E. Thereska. Dynamic right-sizing for power-proportional data centers. In *Proceedings IEEE INFOCOM*, pages 1098–1106, 2011.

[5] D. Meisner, C. M. Sadler, L. A. Barroso, W.-D. Weber, and T. F. Wenisch. Power management of online data-intensive services. In *Proceedings of the 38th ACM International Symposium on Computer Architecture*, 2011.

[6] K. Wang, M. Lin, F. Ciucu, A. Wierman, and C. Lin. Characterizing the impact of the workload on the value of dynamic resizing in data centers. Technical report, 2012.

Provisioning for Large Scale Cloud Computing Services

Yue Tan
The Ohio State University
tan.268@osu.edu

Yingdong Lu
IBM Thomas J. Watson
Research Center
yingdong@us.ibm.com

Cathy H. Xia
The Ohio State University
xia.52@osu.edu

ABSTRACT

Resource provisioning, the task of planning sufficient amounts of resources to meet service level agreements, has become an important management task in emerging cloud computing services. In this paper, we present a stochastic modeling approach to guide the resource provisioning task for future service clouds as the demand grows large. We focus on on-demand services and consider service availability as the key quality of service constraint. A specific scenario under consideration is when resources can be measured in base instances. We develop an asymptotic provisioning methodology that utilizes tight performance bounds for the Erlang loss system to determine the minimum capacity levels that meet the service availability requirements. We show that our provisioning solutions are not only asymptotically exact but also provide better QoS guarantees at all load conditions.

Categories and Subject Descriptors: H.4 [Information Systems Applications]: Miscellaneous; D.2.8 [Software Engineering]: Metrics–*complexity measures, performance measures*
General Terms: Theory

1. INTRODUCTION

Cloud computing is rapidly gaining momentum as a new paradigm for offering computing as services via the Internet. From service providers, customers can lease infrastructure resources, such as CPU cycles, memory and disk storage, based on a "pay as you go" billing model, while providers are able to present the illusion of an infinite amount of resources to the clients via virtualization [1]. An important value proposition of cloud computing is the flexibility for customers to increase or decrease capacity on the fly to meet demand. This is especially attractive as it allows the clients to trade the high fixed costs (of owing infrastructure) for variable usage-based costs and to dynamically offload unforeseen excess demand. Cloud service offerings are typically specified in a menu of service instances or virtual machine configurations. The instances are composed of various amounts of distinct resources such as CPU, memory and storage. Clients may choose to purchase any of these instances. For example, a basic instance at Amazon EC2 [2] is comprised of 1.7 GB of memory, 1 virtual core with 1 EC2 Compute Unit, and 160 GB of instance storage. EC2 provides eight different types of virtual machine instances tailored for different user preferences. Another important component in the service offerings are the service level agreements (SLA), which specify the desired targets on various performance metrics that the service provider should meet. Violation of the SLAs typically results in significant penalty, with the potential hazard of losing customer loyalty. Resource provisioning, the task of planning sufficient amounts of resources to meet the SLAs for all cloud users, has become an important management task in modern virtualization-based service clouds. Most existing provisioning solutions typically are done individually for each user based on its peak usage, which often result in over-provisioning of resources. However, with the increasing cost on energy consumption in today's data centers, such approaches are clearly undesirable.

In this paper, we focus on *service availability*, a key performance metric specified in today's cloud service offerings, defined as the percentage of time at which new service requests can be admitted into the system with their desired amount of resources fulfilled. The objective of resource provisioning is then to plan sufficient capacity of all resource types so as to guarantee the service availability defined in the SLA. For this purpose, we present novel mathematical models that capture the key features of cloud computing: 1) services composed of multiple underlying resources, 2) customers' flexibility on upgrade/downgrade services on demand, 3) the multiplexing gains in a stochastic environment with large number of customers, and 4) the probabilistic nature of SLA violation.

SIGMETRICS'12, June 11–15, 2012, London, England, UK.
ACM 978-1-4503-1097-0/12/06.

2. PROBABILISTIC MODEL & ANALYSIS

Suppose that there are R classes of customers, each following an independent Poisson process with rate λ_r, $r = 1, \dots, R$. To capture the flexibility for customers to increase/decrease resource requirements on the fly, we consider the following probabilistic model. Assume that, after holding the service template r for a random amount of time, a class r customer upgrades/downgrades to class r' with probability $p_{rr'}$ and terminates the service with probability $1 - \sum_{r'=1}^{R} p_{rr'}$. And the holding times for class r customers are i.i.d. random variables with mean $1/\mu_r$. Suppose there are J types of resources, and each base instance consists of A_j units of type j resource, $j = 1, \dots, J$. Service template of class r contains b_r units of such base instance. Suppose for class r, there is an SLA that the service will be available with probability $1 - \epsilon_r$. If the system has an uncapacitated resource pool, it can be shown that the number of class r cus-

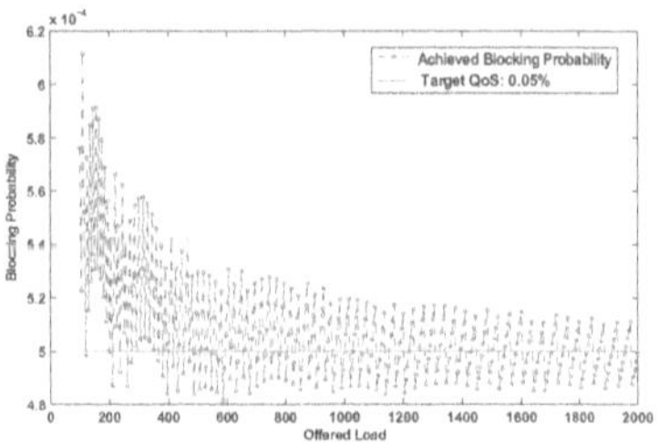

Figure 1: Blocking probability versus offered load using Normal approximation.

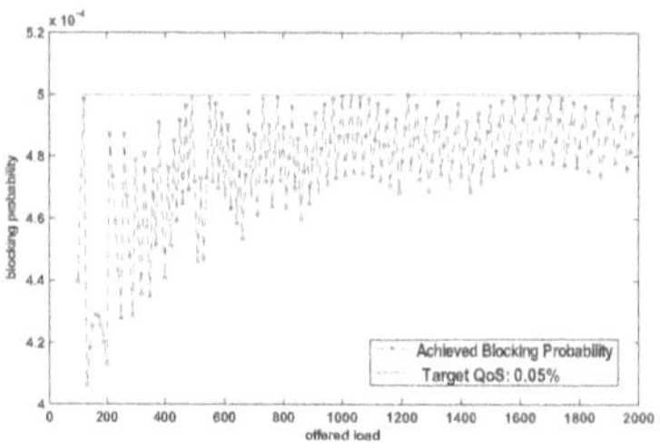

Figure 2: Blocking probability versus offered load using Poisson approximation.

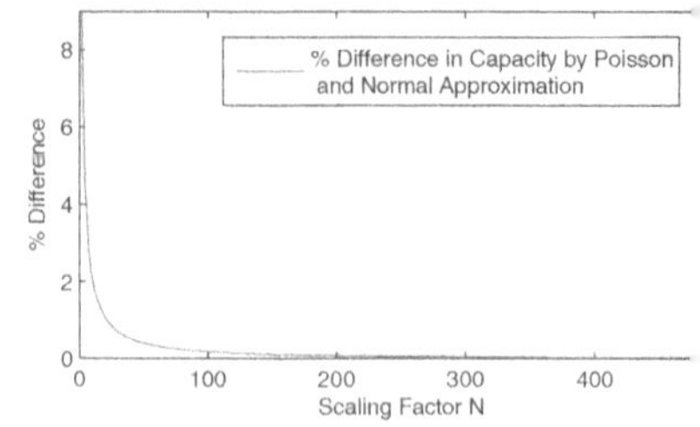

Figure 3: % difference in capacity between Normal and Poisson approximations.

tomers in steady-state, denoted by $Q_\infty^{(r)}$, called *offered load*, is Poisson distributed and independent of other classes.

1. Existing Approach: Normal Approximation

This problem can be mapped to a multi-class bandwidth model in [4]. Denote mean offered loads as $\boldsymbol{\nu} = (\nu_1, \ldots, \nu_R)$. Total offered load in terms of the number of base instances, denoted by Y, is given by $Y = \sum_{r=1}^R b_r Q_\infty^{(r)}$, with mean $\mu = \sum_{r=1}^R b_r \nu_r$ and variance $\sigma^2 = \sum_{r=1}^R b_r^2 \nu_r$. Existing approach in [4] is based on Normal approximation and an *Asymptotic Rule of Thumb* is given as follows:

$$C \geq \mu + \sigma \max_r \psi(\epsilon_r \sigma / b_r), \quad \text{where } \psi = (\phi/\Phi)^{-1}, \qquad (1)$$

and ϕ, Φ are pdf and cdf of standard normal distribution respectively. We show later that this provisioning solution provides poor SLA guarantees where QoS violation could occur at almost all load conditions.

2. New Approach: Poisson Approximation

By applying a Poisson approximation [3] to the distribution of Y, we provide the following provisioning solution that is not only asymptotically exact, but also provide better QoS guarantees than the asymptotic rule of thumb.

PROPOSITION 1. *Under large offered load $\boldsymbol{\nu}$, in order to provide service availability $1 - \epsilon_r$ for all r, it suffices to set the total capacity C such that*

$$C_* = \min\left\{C : U(k\mu, kC) \leq \frac{1}{k} \min_r \left(\frac{\epsilon_r}{b_r}\right)\right\},$$

where $k = \mu/\sigma^2$ and $U(k\mu, kC)$ is the upper bound for the Erlang-B formula given by [5]: $U(\nu, C) := \left(\frac{\Phi(\alpha)\sqrt{C}}{\phi(\alpha)} + \frac{2}{3}\right)^{-1}$, with $\alpha = sgn(1-\rho)\sqrt{-2C(1-\rho+\ln\rho)}$ and $\rho = \nu/C$. The provisioning solution C_* provides better QoS guarantees than the asymptotic rule of thumb and also becomes asymptotically exact as $\boldsymbol{\nu}$ grows larger and larger.

3. NUMERICAL RESULTS

We present two numerical examples, comparing the provisioning solutions derived using two different approximations.

Achieved QoS Comparison. Suppose a service provider only offers a single class of service, each customer requires 1 unit of the base instance upon entrance, holds it for an exponential amount of time with mean 1, then leaves. We use this example to demonstrate the difference on the achieved QoS when provisioning using (1) based on Normal approximation or using our Poisson approximation. We shall denote the resulting provisioning solutions respectively as C_n and C_p. In Figure 1 (resp. Figure 2) , we plot (in dashed line) the resulting blocking probabilities as a function of ν when the capacity C is provisioned using the Normal approximation (resp. the Poisson approximation) under a fixed target blocking probability $\epsilon = 0.05\%$ (shown as the horizontal line). As shown in Figure 1, when using the Normal approximation, although asymptotically the achieved blocking probability gets closer to the target as offered load gets larger, service level violation always happens. On the other hand, by provisioning using upper bound approach under the Poisson approximation, as shown in Figure 2, all the achieved blocking probabilities meet the desired QoS target.

Asymptotic Performance Comparison. Consider a cloud service provider that offers three different types of templates: basic, medium and large, defined as b_1, b_2, b_3 units of basic instances, respectively. Assume there is a sequence of offered loads scaled by factor N, with $\mathbf{b}^N \equiv (1000, 40, 8)$, $\boldsymbol{\nu}^N = (3.7241N, 3.1586N, 3.1172N)$ and $\boldsymbol{\epsilon}^N \equiv (1\%, 0.5\%, 0.1\%)$. Figure 3 plots the relative percentage of difference in the resulting $C_n(N)$ and $C_p(N)$. Observe that the percentage of difference diminishes as the offered load goes larger. This is consistent with the theory since the two approximations are asymptotically close to each other as the offered load grows larger. Also observe that C_p always dominates C_n, therefore when using the Poisson approximation, a large amount of penalty cost can be reduced.

4. CONCLUSION AND EXTENSIONS

We present solutions for provisioning at instance level, which generally yields better SLA guarantees. It is certainly restrictive, as all demand must be specified as multiples of the base instance. For the general scenario, we can map the provisioning problem to a link capacity planning problem in a stochastic loss network model with constraints on the blocking probabilities. It is also possible to extend the offered load process to a nonstationary Poisson process and carry out our asymptotic provisioning methodology.

5. REFERENCES

[1] M. Armbrust, A. Fox, R. Griffith, A. Joseph, R. Katz, A. Konwinski, G. Lee, D. Patterson, A. Rabkin, I. Stoica, and M. Zaharia. A view of cloud computing, April 2010.

[2] Amazon elastic compute cloud. `http://amazon.com/ec2`.

[3] M. Fay and E. Feuer. Confidence intervals for directly standardized rates: a method based on the gamma distribution. *Statistics in Medicine*, Vol. 16:791–801, 1997.

[4] R. C. Hampshire, W. A. Massey, D. Mitra, and Q. Wang. Provisioning of bandwidth sharing and exchange. *Telecommunications Network Design and Management*, 207–226, 2003.

[5] A. Janssen, J. V. Leeuwaarden, and B. Zwart. Gaussian expansions and bounds for the poisson distribution applied to the erlang b formula. *Advances in Applied Probability*, 40:122–143, 2008.

Distributed Wide-Area Traffic Management for Cloud Services

Srinivas Narayana†, Joe Wenjie Jiang†, Jennifer Rexford†, Mung Chiang*
†Department of Computer Science, and *Department of Electrical Engineering
Princeton University
{narayana, wenjiej, jrex, chiangm}@princeton.edu

ABSTRACT

The performance of interactive cloud services depends heavily on which data centers handle client requests, and which wide-area paths carry traffic. While making these decisions, cloud service providers also need to weigh operational considerations like electricity and bandwidth costs, and balancing server loads across replicas. We argue that selecting data centers and network routes independently, as is common in today's services, can lead to much lower performance or higher costs than a coordinated decision. However, fine-grained joint control of two large distributed systems—*e.g.*, DNS-based replica-mapping and data center multi-homed routing—can be administratively challenging. In this paper, we introduce the design of a system that jointly optimizes replica-mapping and multi-homed routing, while retaining the functional separation that exists between them today. We show how to construct a provably optimal distributed solution implemented through local computations and message exchanges between the mapping and routing systems.

Categories and Subject Descriptors

C.2.1 [**Computer-Communication Networks**]: Network Architecture and Design

Keywords

Request mapping, multi-homed routing, joint optimization

1. INTRODUCTION

Organizations running online services "in the cloud" worry about the end-to-end performance their customers experience, since even small increases in perceived latency can have significant impact on revenue [1]. To improve performance and reliability, cloud service providers (CSPs) typically run multiple geographically-distributed data centers (DCs), each peering with multiple ISPs. Placing servers closer to users reduces propagation delay, and path diversity resulting from multi-homing offers performance benefits. However, service providers also need to consider operational costs—*e.g.*, large services may send and receive petabytes of data traffic a day, leading to significant bandwidth costs [2], and can spend tens of millions of dollars annually on electricity [3].

CSPs adapt how they direct user requests to replicas (*request mapping*) and response traffic through peering links

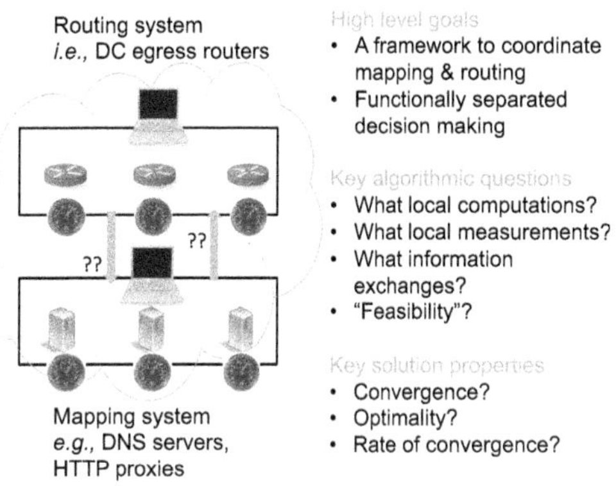

Figure 1: Summary of our high-level goals.

(*response routing*) in response to temporal variations in client demands and path performance. For example, many CSPs rely on DNS or HTTP redirection to map client requests to a particular data center, and then, the data center's edge router selects a local upstream ISP to carry response traffic back to the client. Together, these mapping and routing decisions significantly impact the the overall service performance [4] and costs [2].

Today, request-mapping and response-routing decisions are made *independently*, which can lead to bad performance and high costs. For example, the mapping system could easily direct too many requests to a data center with limited upstream bandwidth, poor performance [4] or expensive ISP connectivity, leaving the routing system no ability to rectify the problem. At human timescales, strategies like additional peering and better bandwidth provisioning may help alleviate these problems [4]. However, at shorter timescales, *jointly optimizing* mapping and routing decisions can improve performance and reduce costs through improved visibility into upstream link and path information.

Yet, we wish to *functionally separate* mapping and routing. In today's CSPs, mapping and routing are themselves performed by large distributed systems (*e.g.*, DNS) typically managed by separate groups in the same company, or may even be outsourced to third parties (*e.g.*, Akamai). Tightly coupling these systems could lead to a complex design that is difficult to administer. Instead, mapping and routing should continue to compute decisions independently, but arrive at good *joint decisions* by exchanging messages with just the "right" information (Fig. 1).

In this poster, we introduce the design of a distributed system that jointly optimizes request-mapping and response-routing. We explore an optimization framework as it provides a natural way to think about distributing computation [5]. Further, even small percentage improvements in performance or costs of large-scale systems can imply meaningful gains *e.g.*, [3]. We formulate [6] a global optimization problem that captures practical considerations like path performance, bandwidth and electricity costs, link capacity, user demands, and geo-distributed replicas. We then leverage and extend prior results on nonconvex optimization [7] to 'derive' a distributed algorithm that provably converges to an optimal solution. We are currently evaluating the practical benefits of this system on a realistic CDN dataset.

2. JOINT MAPPING AND ROUTING

Through toy examples with two DCs and one set of users *e.g.*, a single IP prefix, we highlight the challenges and our solutions to guide independent mapping and routing optimizations to good collective decisions. Our result [6] which generalizes to multiple users, DCs, and peers, shows that addressing these challenges leads to a distributed algorithm that provably converges to a globally optimal solution.

Misaligned objectives can lead to suboptimal decisions. Typically, mapping and routing systems work with different objectives—*e.g.*, mapping performs latency and load-based DC selection, while routing considers end-to-end performance and bandwidth costs to choose a peer to forward responses. Due to mismatched objectives, overall performance and cost can both suffer. In Fig. 2(a), the routing system at each DC picks the peer with the least cost per unit bandwidth, while the mapping system picks the DC with the least propagation delay given current routing choices—resulting in a situation where the service neither has globally optimal cost nor optimal latency. We argue that mapping and routing should agree on a common objective which is pareto-efficient in terms of cost and performance.

Incomplete visibility can lead to suboptimal decisions. In Fig. 2(b), the mapping and routing systems both optimize latency, and users are sending traffic at the rate of 5Gb/s. Without information on link loads and capacities, the mapping system directs too much traffic to the DC on the left, leading to large queueing delays and packet losses. If the mapping system uses information about link capacities, it could easily direct most traffic to the alternate DC with ample spare capacity, and only slightly worse latency. We argue that the routing system should share its upstream link information *i.e.*, link capacities and routing decisions, to make more globally efficient decisions.

Coupled operational constraints can lead to bad equilibria. Even if mapping and routing have aligned objectives (*e.g.*, minimize latency) and complete visibility, optimizing their decisions separately taking turns can still lead to globally suboptimal situations. In Fig. 3(a), mapping and routing are locally optimal given each other's decisions, as traffic is served through the least latency paths respecting link capacities. However, the globally optimal traffic allocation is one where all traffic is served by the DC on the right, using both peers. We identify that the coupled nonconvex constraints in our model, *i.e.*, link capacity constraints, are in fact the problematic ones. We rewrite these hard constraints into "soft" objective function penalties—thereby removing the associated saddle points—which then allows alternating optimizations to converge to a global optimum [6].

Bad routing decisions for prefixes with no traffic contribution to a DC can lead to bad equilibria. Consider the scenario in Fig. 3(b), where a mapping initialization (*e.g.*, from geo-proximity) directs all traffic to the DC on the left. No traffic from this user reaches the other DC, so all routing decisions here are equally good. Suppose this DC chooses to route traffic through the 100ms path. Then, this set of mapping and routing decisions are locally optimal to each other—preventing the routing system from exploring the globally optimal 50ms path. To avoid this anomaly, we adopt and extend the refinement from [7], which forces routing decisions to handle an "infinitesimal" amount of traffic from prefixes correctly whenever in reality there is none.

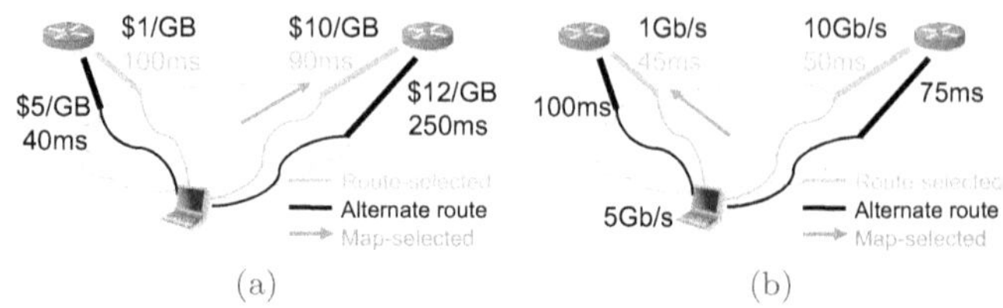

Figure 2: (a) Mapping decision is sub-optimal because of misaligned objectives (b) Mapping decision is sub-optimal because routing does not share link-related information.

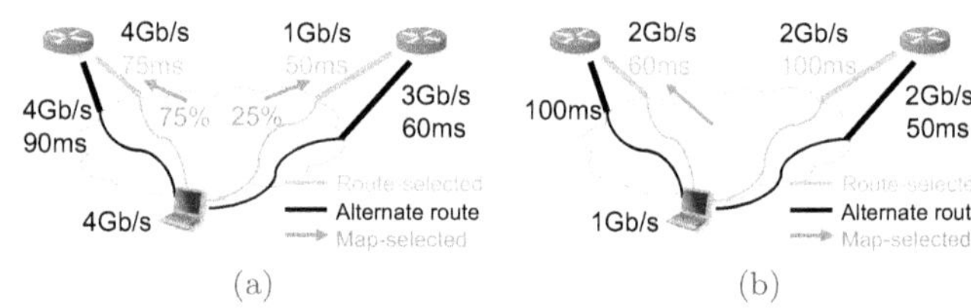

Figure 3: (a) Separate mapping and routing can be inefficient when coupled operational constraints exist; (b) Routing decision is sub-optimal when some clients send no traffic to a DC.

3. ACKNOWLEDGMENTS

We would like to thank the anonymous SIGMETRICS reviewers for comments. This work has been supported partly by AFOSR grant FA9550-09-1-0643 and a gift from Google.

4. REFERENCES

[1] J. Hamilton, "The cost of latency." `http://perspectives.mvdirona.com/2009/10/31/TheCostOfLatency.aspx`.

[2] Z. Zhang, M. Zhang, A. Greenberg, Y. C. Hu, R. Mahajan, and B. Christian, "Optimizing cost and performance in online service provider networks," in *Proc. NSDI*, 2010.

[3] A. Qureshi, R. Weber, H. Balakrishnan, J. Guttag, and B. Maggs, "Cutting the electric bill for Internet-scale systems," in *Proc. ACM SIGCOMM*, 2009.

[4] R. Krishnan, H. V. Madhyastha, S. Srinivasan, S. Jain, A. Krishnamurthy, T. Anderson, and J. Gao, "Moving beyond end-to-end path information to optimize CDN performance," in *Proc. Internet Measurement Conference*, 2009.

[5] D. Palomar and M. Chiang, "A tutorial on decomposition methods for network utility maximization," *IEEE J. on Selected Areas in Communications*, vol. 24, pp. 1439–1451.

[6] S. Narayana, J. W. Jiang, J. Rexford, and M. Chiang, "Technical report." `http://www.cs.princeton.edu/~narayana/joint-maproute.html`.

[7] D. DiPalantino and R. Johari, "Traffic engineering vs. content distribution: A game theoretic perspective," in *Proc. IEEE INFOCOM*, 2009.

On the Efficacy of Fine-Grained Traffic Splitting Protocols in Data Center Networks

Advait Dixit, Pawan Prakash, Ramana Rao Kompella, Y. Charlie Hu
Purdue University
{dixit0,pprakash,rkompella,ychu}@purdue.edu

ABSTRACT

Current multipath routing techniques split traffic at a per-flow level because, according to conventional wisdom, forwarding packets of a TCP flow along different paths leads to packet reordering which is detrimental to TCP. In this paper, we revisit this "myth" in the context of cloud data center networks which have regular topologies such as multi-rooted trees. We argue that due to the symmetry in the multiple equal-cost paths in such networks, simply spraying packets of a given flow among all equal-cost paths, leads to balanced queues across multiple paths, and consequently little packet reordering. Using a testbed comprising of NetFPGA switches, we show how cloud applications benefit from better network utilization in data centers.

Categories and Subject Descriptors

C.2.2 [**Computer Communication Networks**]: Network Protocols

General Terms

Performance

Keywords

Data centers, traffic splitting

1. INTRODUCTION

To scale the data center network to provide the level of connectivity required, most data center network fabrics are organized in the form of a multi-rooted tree topology. Further, they use multipathing between servers so that load is balanced among several alternate paths and the chances of congestion are reduced. One popular multipathing mechanism used in data centers today is equal-cost multipath (ECMP). Many recent works have identified the load imbalance that can arise due to ECMP and suggested different approaches for making the load more balanced across the different available paths.

We revisit the conventional wisdom that packet-level traffic splitting (PLTS) is inherently harmful to TCP. Specifically, our observation is grounded on the fact that many popular data center network designs such as the fat tree, or more generally, multi-rooted tree topologies are symmetric in their architecture, and spraying packets across different paths leads to a more balanced and predictable network architecture, that interacts well with TCP.

SIGMETRICS'12, June 11–15, 2012, London, England, UK.
ACM 978-1-4503-1097-0/12/06.

In the next section, we explain why we believe that PLTS will perform well in multi-rooted tree topologies. We support our hypothesis with experiments on a real testbed which show that PLTS outperforms ECMP in throughput and latency. PLTS achieve similar throughput and better latencies than MP-TCP [5] without the additional complexity and end-host changes.

2. PACKET-LEVEL TRAFFIC SPLITTING

The basic idea of packet-level traffic splitting (PLTS) is quite simple: it uses all the equal-cost shortest paths between every source and destination pair to spread all packets belonging to a given flow. Such a simple packet-level traffic splitting protocol is expected to achieve the best possible load balance for any load in a given network independent of the flow length distribution. Further, PLTS requires no changes to end hosts, and is already implemented in many commodity switches today. However, at first glance, it appears PLTS will potentially introduce a large amount of packet reordering since paths may have different latencies. We make three key observations that indicate that PLTS is unlikely to result in significant packet reordering and poor interactions with TCP in data center networks that employ multi-rooted tree topologies such as the fat-tree.

First, in a multi-rooted tree topology, links can be grouped together into *equivalence classes*. All links within each equivalence class have equal amount of load if all flows in the networks use PLTS. Thus, even though each flow is routed along several paths, each of these paths is similarly loaded and thus, the latency differential between these paths is expected to be quite small, and hence the amount of induced reordering due to PLTS is likely to be small.

Second, TCP congestion control is robust to small amount of packet reordering in the network anyway. The sender typically waits for 3 duplicate ACKs to infer that a loss event has occurred after which it performs fast retransmit and cuts its window in half.

Third, even if PLTS induces a few more fast retransmits compared to ECMP, the loss in throughput, due to the sender reducing its congestion window every time a fast retransmit event occurs, can be a small penalty compared to the better usage of the available network bandwidth. Thus, overall performance of PLTS will be better than ECMP.

3. EVALUATION

Our testbed has 36 servers connected in a 4-ary ($k = 4$) fat-tree [1] topology. All the servers are equipped with 4GB RAM, Intel Xeon 2.40GHz quad-core processors and two

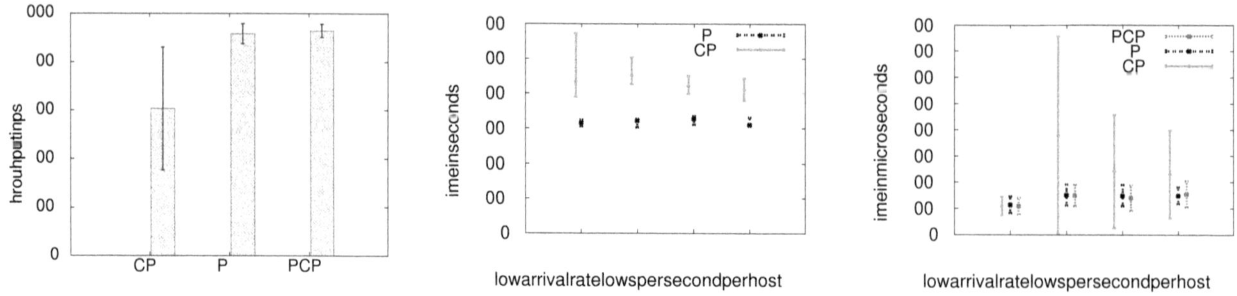

(a) Permutation matrix throughput (b) Hadoop Shuffle Time (c) Ping RTT

Figure 1: PLTS comparison with other solutions. No MP-TCP in plot (b) as it was unstable for short flows.

1Gbps Ethernet ports. We have 20 NetFPGA boards, each deployed on a server, and interconnected in a fat-tree topology via 1 Gbps Ethernet links. Rest of the 16 servers form the endhosts connected to this network. We implemented ECMP and PLTS on NetFPGA switches by modifying the code base already provided by NetFPGA. For PLTS, we generate a random number for each arriving packet to determine the output port (among all eligible output ports) to which the packet is forwarded.

Permutation traffic matrix. We first compare the throughput of PLTS with ECMP and MP-TCP using a random permutation matrix. Each host in the fat-tree is either a sender or a receiver of exactly one TCP flow. Figure 1(a) shows the average throughput of TCP flows under different schemes as a percentage of the ideal throughput (full link capacity). The low average throughput in ECMP-based forwarding can be attributed to the fact that two or more ECMP flows may be forward over the same core link which becomes a bottleneck. PLTS was able to achieve about 90% of the ideal bandwidth, an improvement of 35% over ECMP. MP-TCP also achieves about 90%. This is consistent with results reported in [5] for a similar experimental setup.

Ping RTT. We ran background traffic between 14 (out of 16) end hosts in our testbed. The flow sizes for background traffic were drawn from the distribution in [4]. The flow arrival rate followed an exponential distribution. In Figure 1(c), we varied the mean of the exponential distribution and plotted the mean RTT taken by 200 back-to-back ping packets between the two hosts that did not carry background traffic. The error bars show the mean deviation reported by ping. We observed that the latency varied widely with ECMP indicating that different paths between the two hosts different loads. Packets experience similar mean latencies with PLTS and MP-TCP but higher mean deviation with MP-TCP.

Hadoop shuffle completion time. We show that applications like Hadoop benefit from the improved network utilization done by PLTS. We run Hadoop on 4 of the 16 end hosts in our testbed (other 12 hosts have background traffic between them). We limit the bandwidth of each link to 100Mbps to mimic the scenario where the network is a bottleneck. We observe a 20% to 30% reduction in shuffle time with PLTS. Since a fat-tree is not oversubscribed, increasing background traffic intensity does not affect the shuffle completion time. We were not able to perform this experiment with MP-TCP due to bugs in the MP-TCP implementation[6].

4. RELATED WORK

The most related to our work are those mechanisms that rely on flow-level traffic splitting such as ECMP, Hedera [2] and Mahout [3]. Techniques like Hedera and Mahout, which select a path for a flow based on current network conditions suffer from a common problem: When network conditions change over time, the selected path may no longer be the optimal one. VL2[4] propose using Valiant Load Balancing (VLB) at a per-flow granularity, but they too do not split an individual flow across multiple paths.

Two research efforts propose traffic splitting at a sub-flow granularity. MP-TCP [5] splits a TCP flow into multiple flows at the end hosts. FLARE [7] exploits the inherent burstiness of TCP flows to break up a flow into bursts called flowlets. We did experiment with some simple variants of FLARE, such as forwarding a small number of consecutive packets of a flow along the same path. But we observed that, since bursts of packets may actually lead to disparity in queue lengths across different paths, they cause much more packet reordering and reduction in throughput.

5. CONCLUSION

We show that simple packet-level traffic splitting mechanims can yield significant network throughput and latency benefits in cloud data centers because these mechanism keep the network load balanced and TCP can tolerate the small amount of packet reordering induced by these mechanisms in regular network topologies. These schemes are also readily implementable and are of low complexity making them an appealing alternative to ECMP and other complicated mechanisms like Hedera or MPTCP.

6. REFERENCES

[1] Mohammad Al-Fares, Alexander Loukissas, and Amin Vahdat, "A scalable, commodity data center network architecture," *ACM SIGCOMM CCR*, 2008.

[2] Mohammad Al-fares, Sivasankar Radhakrishnan, Barath Raghavan, Nelson Huang, and Amin Vahdat, "Hedera: Dynamic flow scheduling for data center networks," in *USENIX NSDI*, 2010.

[3] Andrew Curtis, Wonho Kim, and Praveen Yalagandula, "Mahout: Low-Overhead Datacenter Traffic Management using End-Host-Based Elephant Detection," in *IEEE Infocom*, 2011.

[4] Albert Greenberg, James R. Hamilton, et al., "VL2: A Scalable and Flexible Data Center Network," in *ACM SIGCOMM*, 2009.

[5] Costin Raiciu, Christopher Pluntke, et al., "Data Centre Networking with Multipath TCP," in *HotNets-IX*, 2010.

[6] Sebastien Barr, "MultiPath TCP in the Linux Kernel," https://scm.info.ucl.ac.be/trac/mptcp/wiki/install.

[7] Shan Sinha, Srikanth Kandula, and Dina Katabi, "Harnessing TCPs Burstiness using Flowlet Switching," in *HotNets-III*, 2004.

Content-aware Traffic Engineering*

Benjamin Frank
T-Labs/TU Berlin
bfrank@net.t-labs.tu-berlin.de

Ingmar Poese
T-Labs/TU Berlin
ingmar@net.t-labs.tu-berlin.de

Georgios Smaragdakis
T-Labs/TU Berlin
georgios@net.t-labs.tu-berlin.de

Steve Uhlig
Queen Mary, University of London
steve@eecs.qmul.ac.uk

Anja Feldmann
T-Labs/TU Berlin
anja@net.t-labs.tu-berlin.de

ABSTRACT

Recent studies show that a large fraction of Internet traffic is originated by Content Providers (CPs) such as content distribution networks and hyper-giants. To cope with the increasing demand for content, CPs deploy massively distributed server infrastructures. Thus, content is available in many network locations and can be downloaded by traversing different paths in a network. Despite the prominent server location and path diversity, the decisions on how to map users to servers by CPs and how to perform traffic engineering by ISPs, are independent. This leads to a lose-lose situation as CPs are not aware about the network bottlenecks nor the location of end-users, and the ISPs struggle to cope with rapid traffic shifts caused by the dynamic CP server selection process.

In this paper we propose and evaluate Content-aware Traffic Engineering (CaTE), which dynamically adapts the traffic demand for content hosted on CPs by utilizing ISP network information and end-user location during the server selection process. This leads to a win-win situation because CPs are able to enhance their end-user to server mapping and ISPs gain the ability to partially influence the traffic demands in their networks. Indeed, our results using traces from a Tier-1 ISP show that a number of network metrics can be improved when utilizing CaTE.

Categories and Subject Descriptors

C.2.1 [**Computer-Communication Networks**]: Network Architecture and Design; C.2.3 [**Network Operations**]: Network Management

Keywords

Traffic Engineering, Content Delivery, Load Balancing, Network Optimization, ISP-CDN Collaboration.

1. INTRODUCTION

Today, a large fraction of Internet traffic is originated by a small number of Content Providers (CPs) [5]. Major CPs are highly popular rich media sites like YouTube and Netflix, One-Click Hosters (OCHs), e. g., RapidShare and MegaUpload, as well as Content Delivery Networks (CDN) such as Akamai and Limelight, and hyper-giants, e. g., Google, Yahoo!, and Microsoft. To cope with the increasing demand for content, CPs deploy massively distributed server infrastructures to replicate content and make it accessible from different locations in the Internet [2].

*A full version of this paper is available in [4].

SIGMETRICS'12, June 11–15, 2012, London, England, UK.
ACM 978-1-4503-1097-0/12/06.

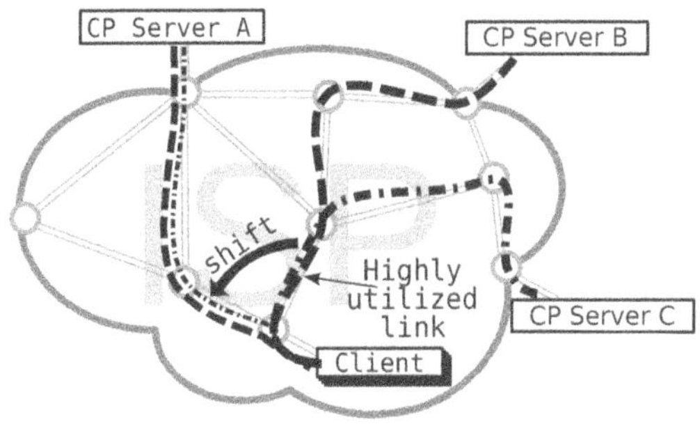

Figure 1: Content-aware traffic engineering process.

The unprecedented growth of demand for content and the resulting massive deployment of content delivery infrastructures pose new challenges both to CPs and to ISPs. For CPs, the cost of deploying and maintaining such a massive infrastructure has significantly increased during the last few years [8] and the price charged for delivering traffic to end-users has decreased due to the intense competition. Furthermore, CPs struggle to engineer and manage their infrastructures, replicate content based on end-user demand, and assign users to appropriate servers. The latter is challenging due to the mis-location of end-users [1]. Furthermore, inferring the network conditions within an ISP without direct information from the network is difficult [6].

Moreover, due to highly distributed server deployment and adaptive server assignment, the traffic injected by CPs is volatile. For example, if one of its locations is overloaded, a CP will re-assign end-users to other locations, resulting in large traffic shifts in the ISP network within minutes. Current ISP traffic engineering adapts the routing and operates on time scales of several hours [3], thus, is too slow to react to rapid traffic changes caused by CPs.

2. THE CaTE APPROACH

The pressure for cost reduction and customer satisfaction that both CPs and ISPs are confronted with, coupled with the opportunity that massively distributed server infrastructures offer, motivate us to propose a new tool in the traffic engineering landscape. We introduce *Content-aware Traffic Engineering* (CaTE). CaTE leverages the location diversity offered by CPs and, through this, enables adaptation to traffic demand shifts. In fact, CaTE relies on the observation that by selecting an appropriate server among those available to deliver the content, the path of the traffic in the network can be influenced in a desired way. Figure 1 illustrates the basic concept of CaTE. The content requested by the client is in principle available from three servers (A, B, and C) in the network.

However, the client only connects to one of the network locations. Today, the decision of where the client will connect to is solely done by the CP and is partially based on measurements and/or inference of network information and end-user location. With CaTE the decision on end-user to server assignment can be enhanced by recommendations offered by the ISP. In the illustration, a highly utilized path can be avoided by mapping users to server A and as a consequence shift traffic to less congested links.

CaTE complements the existing traffic engineering solutions by focusing on traffic demands rather than routing, by combining (i) the knowledge of CPs about their location diversity and server load, with (ii) the ISPs detailed knowledge of the network conditions and end-user location. This can be achieved without either party sharing sensitive operational information. To this end the ISP ranks candidate servers that are communicated by the CP based on the network conditions and the source of demand that can be either the resolver or the end-user [7]. CaTE offers additional traffic engineering capabilities to ISPs to better manage the volatility of CP traffic. Also, thanks to the recommendations offered by ISP networks, CPs gain the ability to better assign end-users to their servers and better amortize the cost of deploying and maintaining their infrastructure. Furthermore, the burden of measuring and inferring network topology, and the state of the network, both challenging problems, is removed from the CPs. In short, all involved parties, including the end-users, benefit from CaTE, creating a win-win situation for everyone.

Formally, we model the network as a directed graph $G(V, E)$ where V is the set of nodes and E is the set of links. An origin-destination (OD) flow f_{od} consists of all traffic entering the network at a given point $o \in V$ (origin) and exiting the network at some point $d \in V$ (destination). The traffic on a link is the superposition of all OD flows that traverse the link. The relationship between link and OD flow traffic is expressed by the routing matrix A. If $A_{ml} = 1$ the OD flow m traverses link l. The routing matrix A can be derived from routing protocols, e.g., OSPF, ISIS, BGP. Let $\mathbf{y}$ be a vector of traffic counts on links and $\mathbf{x}$ the vector of traffic counts in OD flows, then $\mathbf{y}=A\mathbf{x}$. Traditional traffic engineering reduces to controlling and optimizing the routing function and to steering traffic through the network in the most effective way. Translated into the above matrix form, traffic engineering is the process of adjusting A, given the OD flows $\mathbf{x}$, so as to influence the link traffic $\mathbf{y}$ in a desirable way. In CaTE, we revisit traffic engineering by focusing on traffic demands rather routing changes:

Definition 1: Content-aware Traffic Engineering (CaTE) is the process of adjusting the traffic demand vector $\mathbf{x}$, given a routing matrix A, so as to change the link traffic $\mathbf{y}$.

Not all traffic can be adjusted arbitrarily. Only traffic for which location diversity is available can be adjusted by CaTE. Therefore, $\mathbf{x}=\mathbf{x}_r+\mathbf{x}_s$ where $\mathbf{x}_r$ and $\mathbf{x}_s$ denote the content demands that can be adjusted and can not be adjusted (as there is only a single location) respectively. The degree of freedom in adjusting traffic highly depends on the diversity of locations from which the content can be obtained. We can rewrite the relation between traffic counts on links and traffic counts in flows as follows: $\mathbf{y}=A(\mathbf{x}_s + \mathbf{x}_r)$. CaTE adjusts the traffic on each link of the network by adjusting the content demands $\mathbf{x}_r$: $\mathbf{y}_r=A\mathbf{x}_r$ to satisfy a traffic engineering goal. In the full version of this paper [4] we show how to assign demands nearly optimal to available network locations for a number of CPs in regards to different network metrics.

3. EVALUATION

CaTE allows ISPs and CPs to optimize for a number of network metrics, such as link utilization, path length, and path delay. We quantify the effects of CaTE when using each one of these metrics individually in a large Tier-1 ISP. Note that our system design also allows for a combination of metrics. We focus on the top 10 CPs, as these have a significant share of the overall traffic [4]. To evaluate the effectiveness of CaTE, we observe network traffic and measure network quantities such as maximum link utilization as the CPs apply their server selection algorithms. We assume that the CPs follow the recommendations provided by the ISP, per request, and estimate the effects on these network quantities. Similar observations are made when applying CaTE to the top 1 and 100.

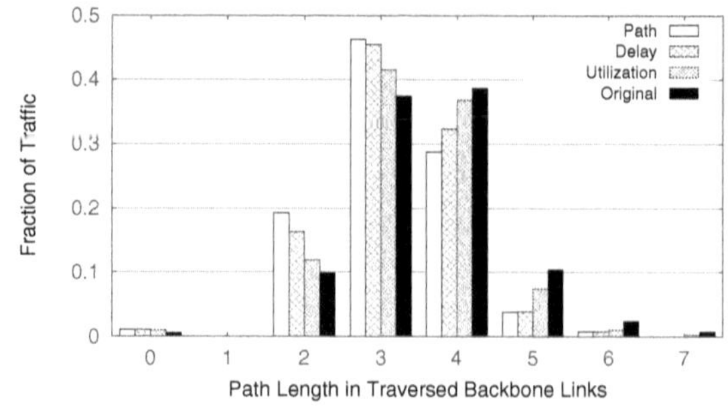

Figure 2: Traffic distribution per path length in a Tier-1 ISP.

In Figure 2, we plot the traffic distribution per path length before we apply CaTE (Original) and when we apply CaTE using one of the network metrics mentioned above. In all cases, CaTE redirects the traffic towards paths with the same or even shorter path, thus the overall traffic is reduced. Our results also show that the delay as well as the maximum link utilization are reduced as the traffic is shifted from highly utilized links to less utilized ones. In the full version of this paper [4] we present a much larger set of results and evaluate CaTE in other networks and under different demands.

4. FUTURE WORK

To capitalize on the substantial performance benefits that CaTE offers to both CPs and ISPs as well as end-users, we are currently building a system that allows all the involved parties to utilize CaTE. Moreover, we are investigating how to install CaTE in a number of ISPs and CPs and report the performance benefits for both ISPs and CPs in the wild. We are also interested in evaluating CaTE for ISP-ISP collaboration.

5. REFERENCES

[1] B. Ager, W. Mühlbauer, G. Smaragdakis, and S. Uhlig. Comparing DNS Resolvers in the Wild. In *Proc. of ACM IMC*, 2010.

[2] B. Ager, W. Mühlbauer, G. Smaragdakis, and S. Uhlig. Web Content Cartography. In *Proc. of ACM IMC*, 2011.

[3] B. Fortz and M. Thorup. Internet Traffic Engineering by Optimizing OSPF Weights. In *Proc. of IEEE INFOCOM*, 2000.

[4] B. Frank, I. Poese, G. Smaragdakis, S. Uhlig, and A. Feldmann. Content-aware Traffic Engineering. Technical University of Berlin Technical Report No. 2012-3 and CoRR arXiv e-print, `http://arxiv.org/abs/1202.1464`, 2012.

[5] A. Gerber and R. Doverspike. Traffic Types and Growth in Backbone Networks. In *Prof. of OFC/NFOEC*, 2011.

[6] E. Nygren, R. K. Sitaraman, and J. Sun. The Akamai Network: A Platform for High-performance Internet Applications. *SIGOPS Oper. Syst. Rev.*, 44:2–19, August 2010.

[7] I. Poese, B. Frank, B. Ager, G. Smaragdakis, and A. Feldmann. Improving Content Delivery using Provider-Aided Distance Information. In *Proc. of ACM IMC*, 2010.

[8] A. Qureshi, R. Weber, H. Balakrishnan, J. Guttag, and B. Maggs. Cutting the Electric Bill for Internet-scale Systems. In *Proc. of ACM SIGCOMM*, 2009.

Understanding Performance Anomalies of SSDs and Their Impact in Enterprise Application Environment

Jian Hu
University of Nebraska-Lincoln
Lincoln, Nebraska, USA
jhu@cse.unl.edu

Hong Jiang
University of Nebraska-Lincoln
Lincoln, Nebraska, USA
jiang@cse.unl.edu

Prakash Manden
VeloBit Inc.
Boxboro, Massachusetts, USA
prakash@velobit.com

ABSTRACT

SSD is known to have the *erase-before-write* and *out-of-place* update properties. When the number of invalidated pages is more than a given threshold, a process referred to as *garbage collection* (GC) is triggered to erase blocks after valid pages in these blocks are copied somewhere else. GC degrades both the performance and lifetime of SSD significantly because of the read-write-erase operation sequence.

In this paper, we conduct intensive experiments on a 120GB Intel 320 SATA SSD and a 320GB Fusion IO ioDrive PCI-E SSD to show and analyze the following important performance issues and anomalies.

(1) The commonly accepted knowledge that the performance drops sharply as more data is being written is not always true. This is because GC efficiency, a more important factor affecting SSD performance, has not been carefully considered. It is defined as the percentage of invalid pages of a GC erased block. It is possible to avoid the performance degradation by managing the addressable LBA range.

(2) Estimating the residual lifetime of an SSD is a very challenging problem because it involves several interdependent and mutually interacting factors such as FTL, GC, wear leveling, workload characteristics, etc. We develop an analytical model to estimate the residual lifetime of a given SSD.

(3) The high random-read performance is widely accepted as one of the advantages of SSD. We will show that this is not true if the GC efficiency is low.

Categories and Subject Descriptors

B.3.2 [**Design Styles**]: Mass storage

General Terms

Measurement, Performance

Keywords

SSD, anomaly

1. EVALUATIONS AND ANALYSIS

The unique physical characteristics and dynamic behaviors of SSD require different evaluation approaches than those for HDD. We follow the Solid Stage Storage Test Specification devised by SNIA to securely erase the SSD before all the tests, in light of the statefulness of SSD in that the evaluation results of one experiment run is affected by the completion status of the previous one.

SIGMETRICS'12, June 11–15, 2012, London, England, UK.
ACM 978-1-4503-1097-0/12/06.

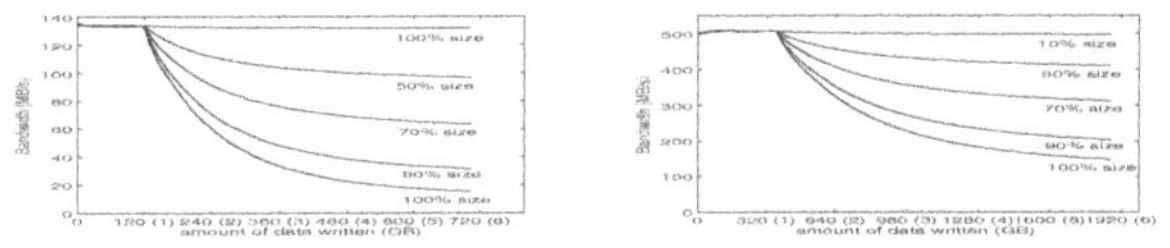

(a) 120GB Intel 320 SSD (b) 320GB Fusion IO ioDrive

Figure 1: Performance impact of GC efficiency in SSDs

1.1 Performance impact of GC efficiency

It is widely accepted that the write bandwidth of SSD drops as more data is being written because of GC. However, we will show that GC efficiency is a more important factor than GC itself. By improving GC efficiency, it is possible to avoid or control the performance degradation.

Figure 1 shows the bandwidth as a function of the amount of data written to the SSDs. We customize the workloads by issuing 64KB random write requests with their LPNs confined to 0-10%, 0-50%, 0-70%, 0-90% and 0-100% respectively of the maximal LPN range of the SSDs. The amount of data written is set to be 6 times the full capacity of the SSD. The numbers in the parentheses of the x axis indicate the amount of data written divided by the full capacity of the SSD. By customizing the workloads this way, we can control the amount of invalidated pages generated when the SSD is full.

As shown in Figure 1, before the amount of data written reaches the capacity of the SSD, the bandwidth remains unchanged and is independent of the percentage of reserved LPN range. This is because before an SSD is full, it can process the write requests immediately by using its available free pages.

However, after the SSD is full, the bandwidth drops at very different rates depending on the GC efficiency. The fastest drop rate occurs when the LPNs of write requests are within 0-100% of the LPN range, where the bandwidth drops to as low as 12% and 30% of their peak bandwidth for the Intel 320 SSD and the Fusion IO ioDrive. The reason is that LPNs of the write requests scatter all over the address space of the SSD, making it less likely for the same LPN to be updated to generate enough invalidated pages. Therefore, GC has to copy many valid pages but only collects a limited number of invalid pages when victim blocks are erased, leading to a low GC efficiency.

At the other extreme, when the LPNs of write requests are within 0-10% of the LPN range, the write bandwidth of the SSDs hardly decreases as more data is being written. This is because the LPNs of the write requests concentrate within a small percentage of the LPN range. In this case, after all the free pages are consumed, most pages are likely to have been updated multiple times. Therefore, GC can find

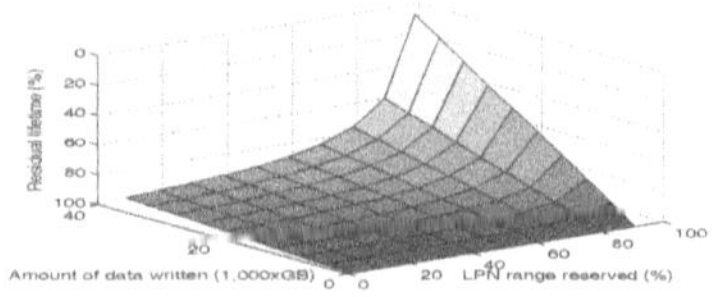

Figure 2: Analytical model of residual lifetime

victim blocks with a high percentage of invalidated pages, decreasing the number of valid pages copied and increasing the GC efficiency. The performances of the 0-50%, 0-70%, 0-90% cases fall in between the two extremes.

1.2 Residual lifetime estimation of SSD

Based on the addressable LBA range that can be controlled, we develop an analytical model to predict the residual lifetime as a function of the SSD capacity, the reserved LPN range, the amount of data written, and the maximal erase cycles of the flash memory, as shown in Equation 1.

$$ResidualLifetime = 1 - \frac{A}{S \cdot [P + (1 - P) \cdot M]} \quad (1)$$

In this equation, S denotes the SSD capacity, P_{size} the page size, $N_{page} = \frac{S}{P_{size}}$ the total number of physical pages in SSD, P the percentage of the reserved LPN range of the SSD (e.g., 0.9 if 0-90% of the full LPN range is used ($0 < P < 1$)), A the amount of data written to SSD in GB, and M maximal erase cycles.

We make the following justifiable assumptions. First, the SSD is assumed to be new to begin with and the only background operation is assumed to be GC because GC arguably dominates the background/internal operations in SSD. Second, the write requests are assumed to be random within the LPN range reserved for use, i.e., 0 to P of the full LPN range because of the high access randomness of enterprise-level applications. Therefore, the invalid pages are uniformly distributed among all blocks and the average number of invalid pages in each block is the same. We further assume that, for simplicity, when a victim block is erased, the valid pages in it are first copied somewhere else (e.g., RAM) and, after the block is erased, copied back to the same block that now contains no invalid pages.

Write requests first propagate from the 0-to-P portion of the full PPN range of the SSD and, once this portion is full, then continue to propagate the remaining $1 - P$ portion of the SSD PPN space. At this time, all the PPNs are used and the percentage of invalid pages in each block is $(1 - P) \cdot 100$ because the latter requests are all updates. Then GC starts to collect these $(1 - P) \cdot N_{page}$ invalid pages and the blocks containing these invalid pages are erased once as a result. After this point, every time $(1-P) \cdot N_{page}$ pages are written, the same number of invalid pages are generated, causing GC to be triggered to collect these invalid pages by erasing the corresponding blocks once. This process repeats until all the blocks are erased M times. Therefore, the maximal amount of data that can be written to the SSD is $N_{page} \cdot P_{size} \times P + N_{page} \cdot P_{size} \times (1 - P) \times M = S \cdot P + S \cdot (1 - P) \times M$. The residual lifetime of SSD is then calculated based on how much data is written to the SSD, as shown in Equation 1, in terms of the percentage of lifespan.

Figure 2 illustrates the predicted residual lifetime of a 100GB MLC SSD as a function of the reserved LPN range and the amount of data written based on the analytical model. We can see that when the reserved LPN range is small, say, less than 60%, the residual lifetime does not de-

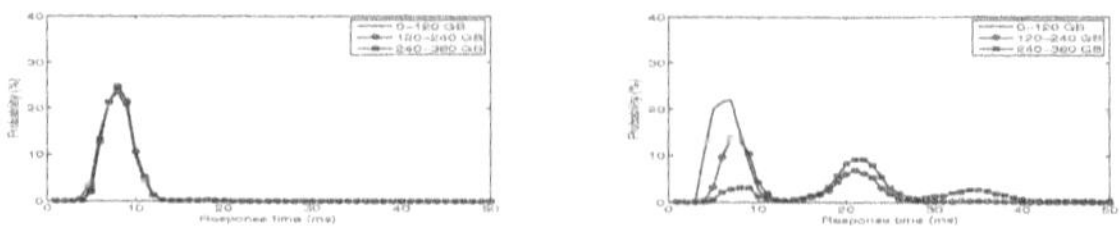

(a) 0-10% LPN is reserved (b) 0-100% LPN is reserved

Figure 3: Read latency of the Intel 320 SSD

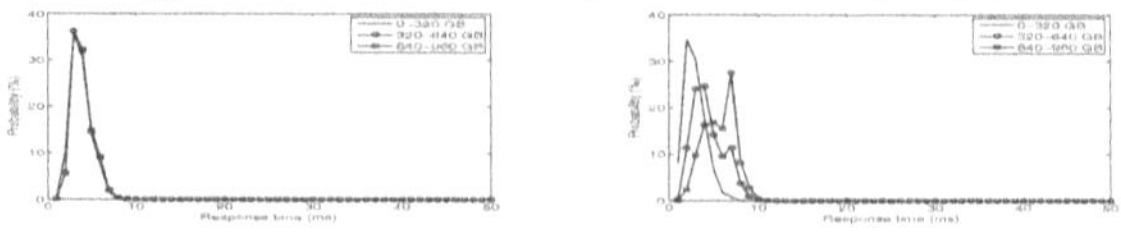

(a) 0-10% LPN is reserved (b) 0-100% LPN is reserved

Figure 4: Read latency of the Fusion IO ioDrive

crease significantly when more data is being written. However, when the reserved LPN range is more than 80%, the residual lifetime is reduced more quickly as more data is being written. Therefore, the reserved LPN range is a key factor in keeping the SSD running longer.

1.3 Unpredictability of random read

Most of the data sheets of SSDs only provide a single average value on response time of read requests. This value, however, turns out to depend highly on the GC efficiency, as revealed by our experimental evaluation.

In order to evaluate the read response time at different stages of GC, we mix the read and write requests and set the read and write requests ratio to 1:1. Both the read and write requests are random and their request size is 64KB. Further, in order to evaluate the read response time at different GC efficiencies, we customize the workloads by issuing requests with their LPNs confined to the ranges of 0-10% and 0-100% respectively of the maximal LPN range of the SSDs, as defined in Section 1.1. We write 3 times the capacity of the SSDs.

Figure 3 through Figure 4 show the response time of read requests as a function of the amount of data written to the SSDs and the percentage of the reserved LPN range of the requests. For all the SSDs, when the GC efficiency is high, as when the LPNs of requests are within 0-10% of the maximal LPN ranges of the SSDs, the response time of read requests falls into a normal distribution and is almost completely independent of the amount of data written, as shown in Figure 3(a) and Figure 4(a), which indicates that as long as GC efficiency is high, the response time of read requests is more predictable and can be kept steady no matter how much data is written to the SSDs. On the other hand, when the GC efficiency is low, as when the LPNs of requests are within 0-100% of the capacity of the SSDs, as shown in Figure Figure 3(b) and Figure 4(b), the response time of read requests increases sharply for all the three SSDs. For all the three SSDs, except for the period when the amount of data written is less than the capacity of the SSDs, the height of the curves decreases and the curves shift to the right, which indicates that the response time of read requests not only increases, but also fluctuates dramatically as the amount data written grows beyond the capacity of the SSDs.

2. ACKNOWLEDGEMENTS

This work is supported by US NSF under grants CNS-1116606, CNS-1016609, IIS-0916859 and CCF-0937993. This work is a joint work with VeloBit, Inc. The authors are also grateful to anonymous reviewers for their valuable input.

Classifying Internet One-way Traffic

[Extended Abstract]

Eduard Glatz
ETH Zurich
Zurich, Switzerland
eglatz@tik.ee.ethz.ch

Xenofontas Dimitropoulos
ETH Zurich
Zurich, Switzerland
fontas@tik.ee.ethz.ch

ABSTRACT

In this work we analyze a massive data-set that captures 5.23 petabytes of traffic to shed light into the composition of one-way traffic towards a large network based on a novel one-way traffic classifier. We find that one-way traffic makes a very large fraction of all traffic in terms of flows, it can be primarily attributed to malicious causes, and it has declined since 2004 because of relative decrease of scan traffic. In addition, we show how our classifier is useful for detecting network outages.

Categories and Subject Descriptors

C.2.3 [**Computer Systems Organization**]: Network Operations—*network monitoring*

General Terms

Design, Measurement, Security

Keywords

Internet background radiation, traffic classification

1. INTRODUCTION

A large part of Internet traffic consists of incessant noise resulting from scanning, backscatter, misconfigurations, etc. This unproductive noise is called Internet Background Radiation (IBR) and has been helpful, for example, in understanding the prevalence of DoS attacks and the propagation of worms, like Slammer and Blaster. The instrument for monitoring IBR traffic is called network telescope and is an unpopulated block of IP addresses typically of size /16 or larger that is injected in the routing system, but because it is unpopulated it only receives IBR traffic.

In this work we develop novel techniques for monitoring IBR traffic in live networks, e.g., IP address blocks that may be populated, with the two-fold goal of 1) expanding our understanding of this interesting type of traffic towards live networks as well as of 2) making IBR traffic useful for detecting network service reachability problems.

In a live network, we can separate IBR traffic from regular traffic based on the observation that the former results in one-way communication between end-hosts, while the latter in two-way communication consisting of packets in opposite direction. A *two-way flow* is the aggregate of two standard 5-tuple flows that have reverse values in the source and destination IP addresses and ports. We define an *one-way flow* as a flow that does not have a matching reverse flow. One-way traffic towards live networks is IBR traffic and results from communication errors or other unusual situations.

SIGMETRICS 12, June 11–15, 2012, London, England, UK.
ACM 978-1-4503-1097-0/12/06.

1.1 One-way Traffic Classification

To improve our understanding of one-way traffic, in this work we first introduce techniques to classify it into classes of malicious and benign causes, including traffic due to unreachable services, peer-to-peer traffic, scanning, and backscatter. Our techniques classify one-way traffic based solely on flow monitoring data, e.g., NetFlow. This enables us to monitor IBR traffic with flow monitoring technologies as opposed to deep packet inspection (DPI) approaches that have been used in the past. Flow monitoring provides fewer details but is less expensive, more generally available, and scales better to monitoring large IP address blocks than DPI. Our classifier relies on 17 rules, which encode novel heuristics as well as leverage and combine existing techniques that have been prooven effective for certain types of traffic, like the threshold random walk scan detector [1]. We associate each one-way flow with up to 15 different *flow signs*, which help dig into the causes of one-way flows. The key features of our classifier are that: 1) it relies on flow data; 2) it does not use algorithms that need to be trained to learn a target environment, which is typically a problem in deploying traffic classification tools; 3) it provides transparency into the classification process; and 4) it is easily extensible. In our on-going work we use packet-level data from an extensive monitoring infrastructure we have built in a small university campus to verify and improve the accuracy of our one-way flow-based classification.

1.2 One-way Traffic Characterization

The second contribution of our work is that we analyze a massive data-set of NetFlow records collected from the border routers of a large regional ISP between 2004 and 2010. Our flow data are collected without sampling from all the border routers of the studied network and capture in total 5.23 petabytes of traffic. To our knowledge this is one of largest network traffic data-sets that have been studied in the literature.

We first observe that one-way flows make a suprisingly large fraction of the total number of flows towards the monitored network. In the analyzed period one-way flows account for a fraction that varies between 34% and 67% of all flows. In 2010 approximately one out of every three flows

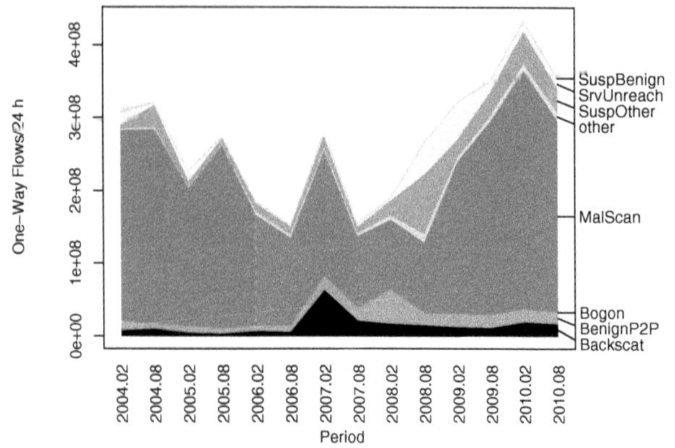

Figure 1: Composition of one-way traffic in flow counts per class.

were one-way, while in 2004 two out of every three flows were one-way. We observe that the fraction of IBR traffic decreased sharply between 2004 and 2007 and remains almost constant since then. On the other hand, we find that due to the short-lived nature of one-way flows, they correspond on average over all years to only 3.4% of the total number of packets. This observation is interesting and suggests a new conceptual model for Internet traffic. While at the flow level IBR noise accounts for a large fraction of the traffic to a live network, which may affect systems like stateful firewalls that keep per flow state, in terms of consumed bandwidth this noise is negligible.

Second, to shed light into the composition of one-way traffic, we apply our classifier on our data. Figure 1 shows how one-way traffic breaks down into different classes in terms of flows. On average the class "Malicious Scanning" accounts for 71.5% of all one-way flows. It is followed by the classes "Suspicious Other" (8.6%), "Benign P2P" (6.3%), "Backscatter" (6.0%), "Service Unreachable" (4.1%), "Other" (2.0%), "Suspected Benign" (1.4%), and "Bogon" (0.1%), where in parenthesis we show the average fraction of one-way flows per class over the seven year period. The packet perspective provides a slightly different picture. "Malicious Scanning" accounts for 49.5% of all one-way packets, "Benign P2P" for 15.1%, "Suspicious Other" for 9.1%, "Service Unreachable" for 7.2%, "Backscatter" for 7.7%, "Suspected Benign" for 7.4%, "Other" for 3.9%, and "Bogon" for 0.0%. We learn that one-way traffic viewed from the perspective of flows is clearly dominated by malicious causes, which account on average for 80.2% of the total number of one-way flows. In terms of packets, malicious causes account for a smaller fraction of 58.6% of the total number of one-way packets. This difference owes to the fact that one-way flows of malicious classes, e.g., scanning, typically consist of a single packet, whereas one-way flows of benign classes, i.e., the classes "Benign P2P" and "Service Unreachable", consist of a relatively larger number of packets per flow. This is mainly due to multi-packet UDP flows and to SYN packet retransmission attempts in the case of TCP.

1.3 Detecting Service Outages

Besides, our classifier isolates the particularly useful class of one-way traffic due to unreachable services. This class of one-way traffic can be used to monitor reachability to local network services and to detect service disruptions. Service availability monitoring typically relies on server logs or on software that periodically probes configured services. Our approach enables to passively monitor potentially a large number of local services based on flow data without inflicting network load. In addition, it does not require to manually configure services, but it automatically builds an inventory of running services.

To demonstrate the utility of one-way traffic classification for network administrators, we evaluate the extent to which traffic classified as "Service Unreachable" helps to detect outages in the production network of our academic institution. We implemented a detector that finds when a large fraction of the flows towards a service become one-way. We run our classifier on one week of NetFlow data, extracted flows towards the network of our department, and analyzed the outages and reachability of 43 detected departmental services. We met and discussed our findings with the administrators of the studied network providing them details about the availability, reachability, and outages of the services. The administrators besides confirming the validity of the discovered services, helped us investigate further a number of interesting cases.

One particularly interesting case was finding a general problem in the reachability of the department network during a particular 10 minute time interval. To learn more about this outage we analyzed three very popular services of the entire university: the main web, webmail, and software distribution services. Suprisingly at the same point in time all the services were not accessible indicating a campus-wide temporary reachability problem. During the identified outage interval, 287,583 unique clients were affected failing to access target services. Our investigation revealed that the outage occurred during a planned router software upgrade. Although, temporal disruptions due to the upgrade were expected, our analysis revealed the impact of the disruption in terms of affected clients, which was large scale.

Overall, our case study revealed a number of outages, some of which were particularly important and highlighted actions that could be taken to improve network performance.

2. CONCLUSIONS

In the past, traffic classification research has focused primarily on two-way traffic. In this work we design classification techniques for decomposing one-way traffic, which we have observed that it makes in terms of flows a significant fraction of the total traffic towards a live network. One-way traffic classification helps improve understanding of the Internet by shedding light into the composition of this large piece of traffic. In the past IBR traffic has been primarily studied with the help of a small number of large network telescopes. Our vision is to build tools that will help the administrator of any network to easily monitor the local IBR traffic and that will make IBR traffic monitoring useful for detecting service reachability problems.

3. REFERENCES

[1] J. Jung, V. Paxson, A. Berger, and H. Balakrishnan. Fast portscan detection using sequential hypothesis testing. In *Proceedings of the IEEE Symposium on Security and Privacy*, pages 211–225, 2004.

Fast Cost Efficient Designs by building upon the Plackett and Burman Method

Manish Arora
UC San Diego

Feng Wang
Qualcomm Inc.

Bob Rychlik
Qualcomm Inc.

Dean Tullsen
UC San Diego

ABSTRACT

CPU processor design involves a large set of increasingly complex design decisions, and simulating all possible designs is typically not feasible. Sensitivity analysis, a commonly used technique, can be dependent on the starting point of the design and does not necessarily account for the cost of each parameter. This work proposes a method to simultaneously analyzes multiple parameters with a small number of experiments by leveraging the Plackett and Burman (P&B) analysis method. It builds upon the technique in two specific ways. It allows a parameter to take multiple values and replaces the unit-less impact factor with cost-proportional values.

Categories and Subject Descriptors: C.4 [**Performance of Systems**][Design Studies]
General Terms: Design, Experimentation, Performance
Keywords: Plackett and Burman, Bottleneck, Cost optimized

1. INTRODUCTION

Since simulation of all design points is often not feasible; sensitivity analysis is a commonly used design exploration technique. This method varies a single parameter across its design space while keeping other parameters fixed. However, the reported importance of parameters is dependent on the choice of fixed values. The Plackett and Burman(P&B) method [2] has been proposed to address the shortcomings of sensitivity analysis [3]. P&B takes in a low value and high value for each parameter and runs a defined set of experiments. Endpoints for all parameters are varied simultaneously and an impact factor representng the percentage contribution to performance is calculated. The calculation needs O(N) experiments vs exponential brute force experiments. The method is not iterative, hence the total simulation time is bound by the longest experiment. However, existing proposals have key shortcomings. (1) There is little direction in choosing endpoint values and there is no way to get impact values for intermediate points. (2) The impact factors do not account for the resource costs of varying the parameter. We leverage P&B, but improve the technique by allowing a parameter to take multiple values and replacing the unit-less impact factor with cost-proportional values.

1.1 Plackett and Burman Method

P&B is a method for finding the dependence of some quantity to a set of independent variables, using few experiments.

SIGMETRICS'12, June 11–15, 2012, London, England, UK.
ACM 978-1-4503-1097-0/12/06.

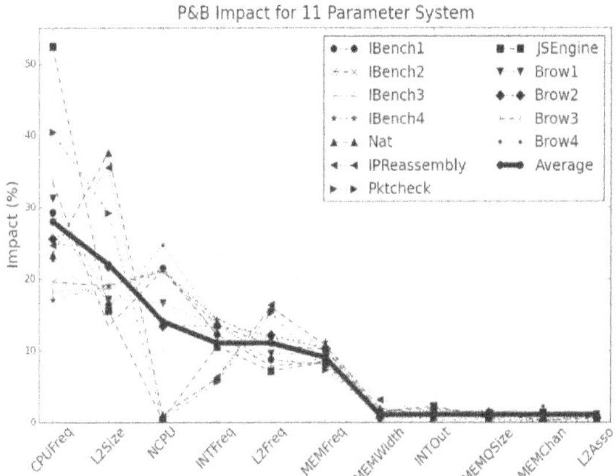

Figure 1: Impact over 12 benchmarks

Parameter	Description	Low Value (-1)	High Value (+1)	Intermediate Values
CPUFreq	CPU frequency	1GHz	2GHz	100 MHz Steps
L2Size	Shared L2 cache size	256KB	1MB	512KB
NCPU	Number of Cores	1	4	2
INTFreq	Shared interconnect frequency	200MHz	800MHz	100MHz Steps
L2Freq	Shared L2 cache frequency	1GHz	2GHz	100MHz Steps
MEMFreq	Memory system frequency	266MHz	800MHz	133MHz Steps
MEMWidth	Memory width	32 bits	64bits	-
INTOut	Interconnect queue size	4	32	-
MEMQSize	Memory controller queue size	4	16	-
MEMChan	Memory system channels	1	2	-
L2Asso	L2 cache associativity	8	32	-

Table 1: Parameter Values for our System

We use the P&B design with foldover [1], requiring 2N experiments for N parameters. For the system under test, the architect has to choose a low end value (-1) and a high end value (+1) for each parameter. Table 1 shows the values for our system. Using the chosen values, and experiments specified by the design matrix, measurements are collected. After measurements, the absolute and percentage contribution of impact of each parameter is computed as described in [3]. Figure 1 shows the impact values for our system over 12 benchmarks. CPUFreq, L2Size and NCPUs have the highest influence on performance.

2. VARYING BOUNDS

The P&B method specifies sets of experiments using combinations of +1 and -1 values but leaves the selection of the actual values up to the architect. Since typically lower bounds are more constrained, we primarily consider variations on upper bounds. Another concern with P&B is that it provides impact for the parameter over the entire range. An architect typically looks for the proverbial "knee" of the curve – if most of the marginal gain (impact) can be achieved by small increases in a parameter, we can forego the cost of fully provisioning the resource. We address this problem by setting the original upper bound to an intermediate value and rerunning the tool with a higher upper bound. This way

Description	IBench1	IBench2	IBench3	IBench4	Nat	IPReassembly	Pktcheck	JSEngine	BROW 1	BROW 2	BROW 3	BROW 4	Average
Config B vs A (% slowdown vs A)	+1.3	+5.2	+3.8	+3.4	+0.0	+0.0	+0.2	+0.6	+3.4	+0.0	+1.2	+1.3	+1.7
Config C vs A (% slowdown vs A)	+7.0	+30.8	+35.4	+30.2	+16.2	+16.3	+15.3	+16.1	+24.3	+26.5	+24.4	+41.2	+23.6
Config D vs A (% slowdown vs A)	+6.7	+19.1	+26.4	+24.9	+11.6	+11.3	+7.9	+8.8	+21.0	+18.5	+18.3	+23.8	+16.5

Table 2: Evaluating runtime performance of configurations.

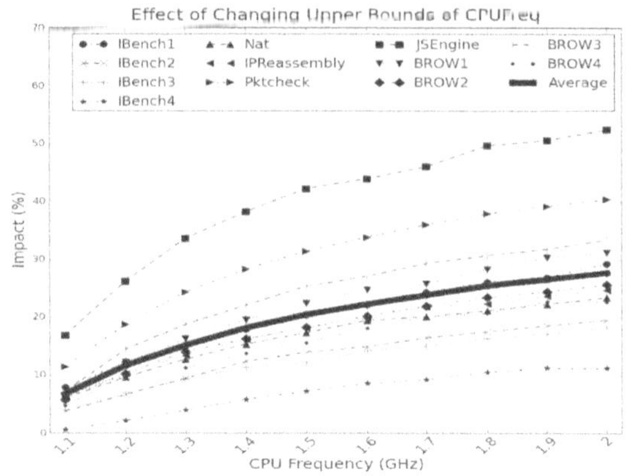

Figure 2: Impact with changing +1 values.

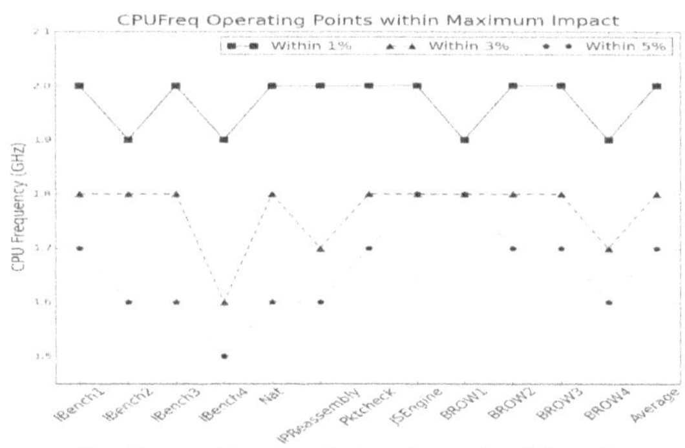

Figure 3: Operating points close to Max Impact.

we can identify the incremental impact of a parameter over various ranges and be able to identify knees. The number of extra P&B experiments for a single new max value of one parameter is N experiments. To add K design points for N parameters we require 2N + KNxN or $O(KN^2)$ experiments (far less than $O(K^N)$ exhaustive search experiments).

We add intermediate steps and analyze the impact values. Figure 2 shows results for the CPUFreq parameter. With this modification, we can determine not only what design parameters have high impact, but also what value or size of that parameter is required to get arbitrarily close to the full impact. Thus, we should be able to identify a resource-efficient design by establishing a performance threshold (e.g., within 1%, 3%, or 5% of the maximum impact), and setting each of the high-impact parameters at the lowest parameter that meets that threshold. Figure 3 shows the resulting design points varying by benchmark and within the 1/3/5% thresholds.

Based on this analysis, we can define sets of "interesting" design points. The configurations are (A) all parameters at the highest values, (B) six high impact factors set to their highest value, low impact factors set to min value (this is the design that would come out of the P&B analysis alone), (C) the six high impact factors set by the 3% threshold, (D) similar to C, but NCPU set to its highest value. Table 2 shows simulation results for these configurations relative to the execution time of the highest end system. Config B suffers only a 1.7% runtime increase versus config A. This system gives good performance, but does not allow us to compromise on resources for the high-end parameters. Cutting resources more aggressively is possible with our methodology. Config C targets the 3% operating points for the high-impact parameters. It is still within 24% of the best design, despite 5 resources being at their minimum value, and 5 of the other 6 being below their max value. Config D maximizes NCPU and goes within 17% of peak performance but has a higher energy cost despite the increased performance. Our technique allows us to navigate a very complex and dense design space with few experiments and arrive at a set of designs that provide high resource efficiency. Those designs sacrifice little in performance, yet provide significant area and energy advantages over the maximal system.

3. INCORPORATING COST MODELS

Previously we described how we can arrive at designs that use processor resources efficiently. However, we have not yet empowered the architect to make the best performance/cost decisions, since the impact factors are essentially unitless. It is difficult to compare between parameters because impact in the current form is not associated with cost required to achieve that impact. To evaluate parameters with respect to resource usage we define *cost normalized marginal impact.* Cost normalized marginal impact is defined as the P&B impact gained by moving from one design choice to another, divided by the increment of resources used at the new design. We specifically evaluate power normalized marginal impact values. Next, we formalize algorithms that utilize the cost normalized marginal impact values to derive designs that meet fixed power budgets. The algorithms work by choosing parameters with the highest cost normalized marginal impact at each step. Using our algorithm, we derive designs that consume 70% of the power but performs within 5.6% of the full design, or consume 50% of the power but perform within 19% of peak performance.

4. CONCLUSION

This work proposes a method to simultaneously analyze multiple parameters with a small number of experiments by leveraging the P&B analysis method. We extract the impact for multiple intermediate points. There is an increase in the number of experiments, but still few enough to be highly practical. With these intermediate points, we can choose incremental points in the design space that get close to full performance with a significant decrease in resources. This paper also incorporates a cost model with the P&B method. We produce results that can lead the architect directly to an architecture that sets the intermediate value of each parameter so as to maximize performance for a given cost constraint.

5. REFERENCES

[1] D. C. Montgomery. *Design and Analysis of Experiments*. John Wiley & Sons, 2006.

[2] R. L. Plackett and J. P. Burman. The design of optimum multifactorial experiments. *Biometrika*, 1946.

[3] J. Yi, D. Lilja, and D. Hawkins. A statistically rigorous approach for improving simulation methodology. In *HPCA: High Performance Computer Architecture.*, pages 281 – 291, Feb. 2003.

Multi-hop Network Tomography: Path Reconstruction and Per-hop Arrival Time Estimation from Partial Information

Matthias Keller, Jan Beutel, and Lothar Thiele
Computer Engineering and Networks Laboratory
ETH Zurich, Switzerland
{kellmatt,beutel,thiele}@tik.ee.ethz.ch

ABSTRACT

In the context of low-power wireless sensor networks, this paper presents multi-hop network tomography (MNT), a novel, non-intrusive algorithm for reconstructing the path, the per-hop arrival order, and the per-hop arrival time of individual packets at runtime. While explicitly transmitting this information over the radio would negatively impact the performance of the system under investigation, information is instead reconstructed after packets have been received at the sink.

Categories and Subject Descriptors

C.2.1 [**Computer-Communication Networks**]: Network Architecture and Design—*Wireless communication*

Keywords

Wireless Sensor Networks, Data Analysis, Tomography

1. OVERVIEW

Wireless sensor networks (WSNs) are networks of small, low-power sensor nodes that autonomously build and maintain a network structure. Running at very low duty-cycles, battery-powered sensor nodes can continuously operate for several years without being serviced. Those characteristics make WSNs well-suited for data collection applications, *e.g.*, environmental monitoring [5].

However, as significantly increasing the size or amount of packets transmitted threatens the system performance, *e.g.*, increases the packet loss rate [8], available performance metrics are usually limited to the most important health indicators, *i.e.*, end-to-end data yield, end-to-end packet delays, and battery voltage readings [7]. While those metrics are well-suited for coarsely estimating system health, understanding the root causes of an observed performance requires yet unavailable measurements taken inside the network.

For addressing this problem, this paper presents the MNT algorithm for reconstructing the path, the per-hop order, and the per-hop arrival time of individual packets. Information is reconstructed after packets arrived at the sink. Thus, the MNT algorithm allows to analyze the system performance both at runtime and at any later point in time. Without limiting the scope of this new tool, the MNT algorithm is firstly intended for the analysis of deployed systems that were continuously extended by adding nodes and new sensing modalities, *e.g.*, sensors that sample with an in the order of magnitude higher rate. Here, the interest lies in making more informed decisions when modifying an existing system configuration.

SIGMETRICS'12, June 11–15, 2012, London, England, UK.
ACM 978-1-4503-1097-0/12/06.

2. SYSTEM MODEL

We assume a multi-hop wireless sensor network that consists of a number of static sensor nodes that report to one or multiple sink nodes. All nodes produce and relay data in the sense of a data collection application. Nodes do not have access to global timing information and rely on a local clock.

Lossy channel. Communication between nodes may fail, *i.e.*, a packet transmitted is not received by the intended receiving side.

Multi-hop data collection. Each sink is the root of a multi-hop tree topology, a tree structure that consists of concatenated 1:n one-hop parent-child relations. The topology is autonomously maintained by the routing protocol used, *e.g.*, CTP [3].

FIFO send queue. All sensor nodes have the dual functionality of (i) generating data locally and (ii) forwarding packets received from other nodes. Nodes maintain a finite FIFO send queue. A packet is immediately added to this queue after generation in the local application or after arrival on the radio. If connected, a sensor nodes transmits the contents of its send queue to its parent.

Available per-packet information. For each packet k, the first-hop receiver address $p(k)$ is the address of the node to which the source node $o(k)$ forwarded the packet. The time of arrival at the sink $t_b(k)$ is measured on a precise, perfect clock, thus the order of $t_b(k)$ corresponds to the order of arrival at the sink. In contrast, the packet generation time $t_g(k)$ of a packet k is measured on clocks with imperfections, *e.g.*, low time resolution and drift, and can thus only be estimated. The maximum error of the generation time estimate $\tilde{t}_g(k)$ is bounded by $\tilde{t}_g(k) - \Delta^l(k) \leq t_g(k) \leq \tilde{t}_g(k) + \Delta^u(k)$. Worst-case clock error bounds $\Delta^{u,l}(k)$ are specific to a certain clock implementation. The unique packet index $id_M(k)$ is defined so that its order yields the order of packet generation at a node M: $id_M(u) > id_M(v)$ iff $t_g(u) > t_g(v)$. Please note that commonly found packet sequence numbers might not fulfill the required properties [6].

Observability of parent changes. Nodes can decide to switch their parent node during operation. Path changes can only be safely detected if the parent of a node is not changing more than once between the successful transmission of two consecutively, locally generated packets. Concretely, there must have been no parent change if consecutively generated packets u and v report equal first-hop receivers $p(u) \equiv p(v)$.

3. INFORMATION RECONSTRUCTION

Given a packet k, we want to reconstruct the following:

Packet path $\mathcal{N}_k$: Starting at the packet source $o(k)$, the ordered set $\mathcal{N}_k$ contains all nodes that packet k visited until arriving at the sink node S. The order of $\mathcal{N}_k$ reflects the order of visited nodes.

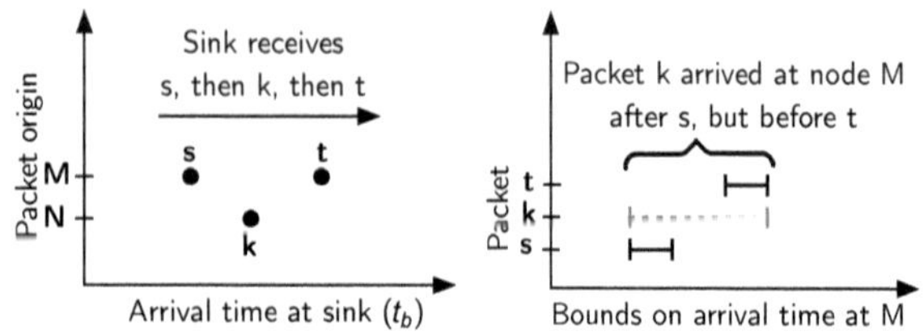

(a) Selection of s and t (b) Arrival time estimation

Figure 1: Information of a forwarded packet k is reconstructed using information from locally generated packets s and t.

Queue index $qid_N(k)$: For all nodes N that k visited, *i.e.*, $\forall N \in \mathcal{N}_k$, we want to build a queue index $qid_N(k)$ so that the order of $qid_N(k)$ reflects the order of packet arrival at N: The queue index is larger, *i.e.*, $qid_N(m) > qid_N(n)$ iff packet m arrived at N after another packet n, *i.e.*, $t_a(N, m) > t_a(N, n)$. In contrast to the already known packet index $id_N(k)$, the queue index $qid_N(k)$ provides not only the sequence of locally generated packets, but also that of forwarded packets.

Bounds on queue arrival time $t_a^{u,l}(N, k)$: For all nodes N that k visited, *i.e.*, $\forall N \in \mathcal{N}_k$, we want to bound the unknown queue arrival time $t_a(N, k)$ so that $t_a^l(N, k) \le t_a(N, k) \le t_a^u(N, k)$.

The idea is to extract missing information from locally generated packets while following the path of k through the network: While the first-hop receiver $p(k)$ of packet k is already known, *e.g.*, $p(k) := M$, the next hop after node M is extracted from two packets s and t that were generated at M. Likewise, packets s and t are used for assigning a queue index of packet k at M and for bounding the arrival time of k at M. Concretely, the queue index $qid_M(k)$ of packet k at node M must be chosen so that $qid_M(s) < qid_M(k) < qid_M(t)$. The arrival time $t_a(M, k)$ of k at M is bounded using the generation times of packets s and t, *i.e.*, $\tilde{t}_g(s) - \Delta^l(s) \le t_a(M, k) \le \tilde{t}_g(t) + \Delta^u(t)$. Ideally, this procedure is repeated until packet k has been traced up to the sink.

The question arises how can we determine corresponding packets s and t that were generated at M and that can be used to extract missing information: Packets from different sources are correlated based on their order of arrival at the sink. In the exemplary situation in Figure 1, packets s and t were consecutively generated at a node M, whereas packet k was generated at another node N. The observed order of arrival at the sink is shown in Figure 1(a), *i.e.*, packet k arrived at the sink after packet s, but before packet t. This matches with the order in which packets s, k and t arrived at the queue of the intermediate node M, see Figure 1(b).

It becomes apparent, that this approach can only yield correct information if the order of arrival at the queues of intermediate nodes matches with the observable order of arrival at the sink. The question arises how we can decide only with information available at the sink if corresponding sequences match, *i.e.*, extracting information is safe, or if packets might have been reordered while traveling through the network, and thus cannot be used. Defining $\mathcal{P}$ as the set of all packets that were received at the sink, the answer of this problem is to determine a set $\mathcal{R} \subseteq \mathcal{P}$ of "reliable" packets. The definition of a "reliable" packet is as follows: *A packet k is reliable,* i.e., $k \in \mathcal{R}$, *if it fulfills two properties: From our observations at the sink, we can guarantee that (i) packet k can only have travelled along exactly one path $\mathcal{N}_k$, and that (ii) the order relation between packet k and any other packet $m \in \mathcal{R}$ is consistent along all packet queues in the network including the sink.*

While a detailed explanation including proofs would clearly exceed the format of this paper, we can only hint on the determination of a set $\mathcal{R} \subseteq \mathcal{P}$ of "reliable" packets: First, we need to determine if there are ambiguities in the observed path of a packet, *e.g.*, a packet arrived at a node M while the parent of this node M changed. Second, we need to exclude packet reordering at each hop that k visited. Parent changes are the single cause for packets arriving at the sink out of order, *i.e.*, packets that were sent out before a parent change experience a higher delay than packets that were transmitted after the parent change. Evidence for packet reordering due to a path change at a node M is found when locally generated packets of M arrive at the sink out of order.

4. VALIDATION AND EVALUATION

For validation and evaluation purposes, the MNT algorithm is applied to traces from two state-of-the-art data collection protocols, CTP [3] and Dozer [2]. Corresponding tests are executed on up to 91 Tmote Sky nodes (TI MSP430, CC2420 radio) that are part of the TWIST testbed [4], and 25 TinyNode nodes (TI MSP430, Semtech SX1211 radio) that are part of the FlockLab testbed [1]. Ground truth information is transmitted via a second communication channel, *i.e.*, written to the serial port of the sensor nodes. When compared to ground truth, reconstructed information is correct in all cases. The reconstruction performance of the MNT algorithm is presented in Figure 2. A packet has been fully traced if its complete path was reconstructed.

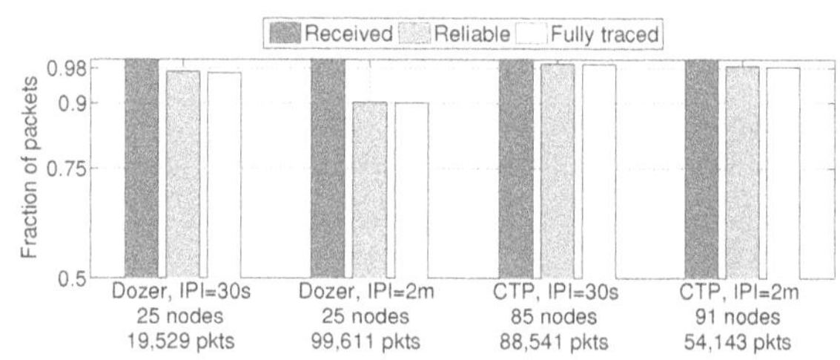

Figure 2: Performance evaluation using two well-known communication protocols with varying inter-packet intervals (IPI).

Acknowledgements. The work presented was supported by NCCR-MICS, a center supported by the Swiss National Science Foundation under grant number 5005-67322, and from the Swiss Nano-Tera.ch initiative.

5. REFERENCES

[1] J. Beutel, R. Lim, A. Meier, L. Thiele, C. Walser, M. Woehrle, and M. Yuecel. The flocklab testbed architecture. In *Proc. 7th ACM Conf. Embedded Networked Sensor Systems (SenSys '09)*, pages 415–416, 2009.

[2] N. Burri, P. von Rickenbach, and R. Wattenhofer. Dozer: ultra-low power data gathering in sensor networks. In *Proc. 6th Int'l Conf. Information Processing Sensor Networks (IPSN '07)*, pages 450–459, 2007.

[3] O. Gnawali, R. Fonseca, K. Jamieson, D. Moss, and P. Levis. Collection tree protocol. In *Proc. 7th ACM Conf. Embedded Networked Sensor Systems (SenSys '09)*, pages 1–14, 2009.

[4] V. Handziski, A. Köpke, A. Willig, and A. Wolisz. Twist: A scalable and reconfigurable testbed for wireless indoor experiments with sensor networks. In *Proc. 2nd Int'l Workshop on Multi-hop Ad Hoc Networks (REALMAN '06)*, pages 63–70, 2006.

[5] A. Hasler, I. Talzi, J. Beutel, C. Tschudin, and S. Gruber. Wireless sensor networks in permafrost research - concept, requirements, implementation and challenges. In *Proc. 9th Int'l Conf. on Permafrost (NICOP 2008)*, volume 1, pages 669–674, 2008.

[6] M. Keller, L. Thiele, and J. Beutel. Reconstruction of the correct temporal order of sensor network data. In *Proc. 10th Int'l Conf. on Information Processing in Sensor Networks (IPSN '11)*, pages 282–293, 2011.

[7] M. Keller, M. Woehrle, R. Lim, J. Beutel, and L. Thiele. Comparative performance analysis of the permadozer protocol in diverse deployments. In *Proc. of the 6th Int'l Workshop on Practical Issues in Building Sensor Network Applications (SenseApp '11)*, pages 969–977, 2011.

[8] Y. Sankarasubramaniam, I. Akyildiz, and S. McLaughlin. Energy efficiency based packet size optimization in wireless sensor networks. In *Proc. 1st Int'l Workshop on Sensor Network Protocols and Applications (SNPA '03)*, pages 1–8, 2003.

Smartphones vs. Laptops: Comparing Web Browsing Behavior and the Implications for Caching

Ioannis Papapanagiotou
ECE Dept.
NC State University
Raleigh, NC
ipapapa@ncsu.edu

Erich Nahum
IBM Research
Hawthorne, NY
nahum@us.ibm.com

Vasileios Pappas
IBM Research
Hawthorne, NY
vpappas@us.ibm.com

ABSTRACT

In this work we present the differences and similarities of the web browsing behavior in most common mobile platforms. We devise a novel Operating System (OS) fingerprinting methodology to distinguish different types of wireless devices (smartphone vs laptops) as well as operating system instances (iOS, Android, BlackBerry etc.). We showcase that most of the multimedia content in smartphone devices is delivered via Range-Requests, and a large portion of the video transfers are aborted. We also show that laptop devices have more intelligent browser caching capabilities. We investigate the impact of an additional browser cache, and demonstrate that a 10MB browser cache that is able to handle partial downloads in smartphones would be enough to handle the majority of the savings. Finally, we showcase that caching policies need to be amended to attain the maximum possible savings in proxy caches. Based on those optimizations the emulated proxy cache provides 10% – 20% in bandwidth savings.

Categories and Subject Descriptors

C.2.3 [**Computer-Communication Networks**]: Network Operations—*Network Management*

Keywords

Mobile Traffic, Network Usage, Smartphones, Caching

1. OVERVIEW

As smartphones reach the 1 billion threshold, they are already contributing more than 10% of Internet traffic [1]. Recently a number of studies have been conducted on smartphone usage [2, 3, 4, 5, 6]. Yet many aspects of smartphone traffic behavior are still not well understood. Their behavior may have implications for network design and provisioning, particularly if their traffic is significantly different from other devices, such as PCs.

This work exposes some of those differences by comparing the Web browsing behavior of smartphones with a control group, namely laptops. We do this by capturing a 3 weeks long full-packet trace in a wireless enterprise environment, composed of the traffic from over 3000 unique devices. We introduce an Operating System (OS) fingerprinting methodology based on data mining association rules. The rules are based on DHCP Request header fields, such as *Host-name*, *Vendor-Name*, *Parameter-Request* list, and the first 3-bytes

SIGMETRICS' 12, June 11–15, 2012, London, England, UK.
ACM 978-1-4503-1097-0/12/06.

Table 1: Distribution of Devices in the Trace

		DHCP		HTTP & OUI [4]	
Device	**OS**	#	%	#	%
Laptops	All	2478	79.9	2182	73.6
	Windows	2107	67.9		
	Mac OS X	333	10.7		
	Linux	38	1.2		
Smartphones	All	534	17.2	398	13.4
	iOS	440	14.2		
	Android	54	1.7		
	BlackBerry	37	1.2		
	Windows	3	0.1		
Other	All	52	1.7	484	16.3
	Cisco VoIP	15	0.5	0	0
	Unclassified	37	1.2	65	2.2
	Unknown	-	-	419	14.1
All		3064	100.0	3064	100.0

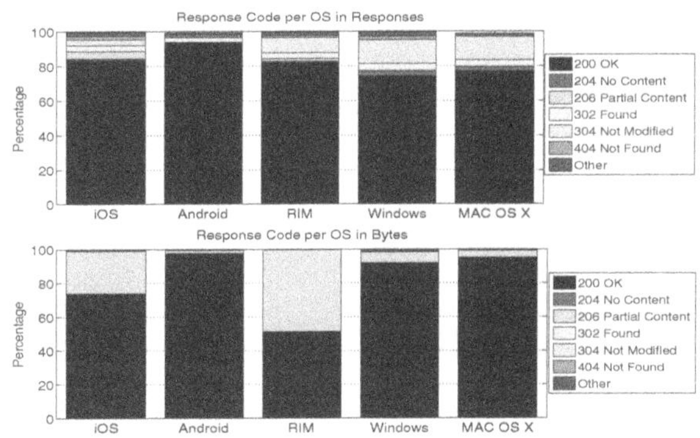

Figure 1: Response Code per Operating System

of the MAC address - also called Organization Unique Identifier (OUI) - that tend to be indicative of an OS and similar across the same device types. Table 1 shows that this OS fingerprinting algorithm can identify 98.5% of the devices in the network, as compared to 84% for earlier approaches, which were based on HTTP User-Agents and the MAC OUI.

We evaluate the Web browsing behavior of the devices, as that makes up the bulk of the traffic. Figure 1 provides an overview of the response codes per device type. We observe that while in smartphones the 304 *Not Modified* is not more than 3%, in Windows and Mac OS X it is close to 20%. This code is typically returned in response to a client generating a conditional GET request, which validates a client's cached copy of a document. If a copy is valid and up-to-date in the client's cache, the server will respond with a 304 response

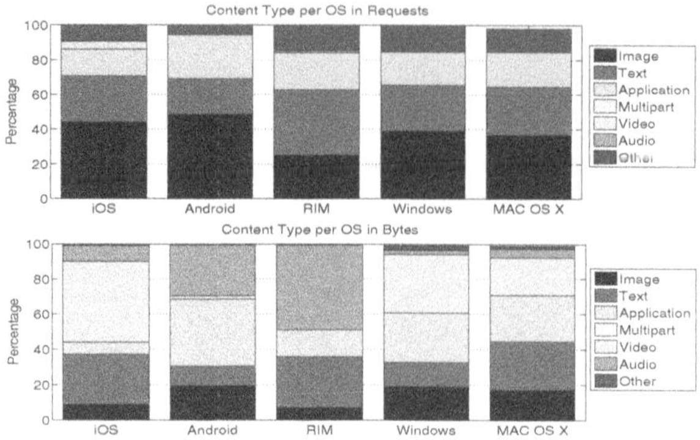

Figure 2: Content Type per Operating System

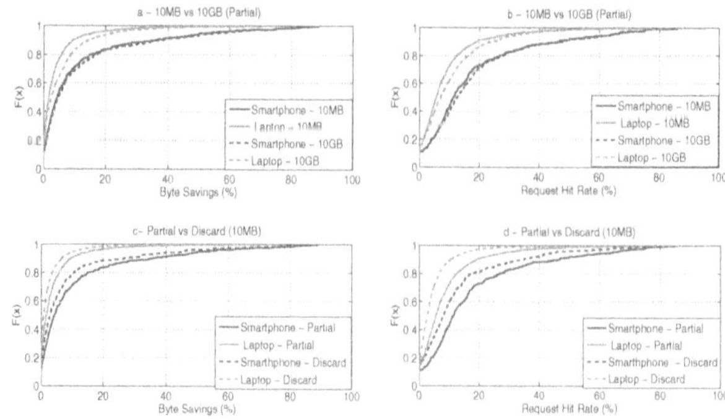

Figure 3: Comparing browser cache hit rates by varying (a-b) the size, (c-d) the storing policies.

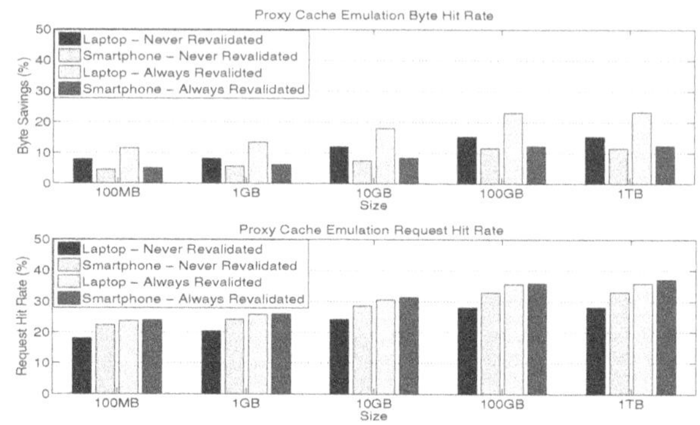

Figure 4: Proxy cache hit rate with several revalidation strategies and persistent storage sizes.

and no actual data will be transferred. Given the lack of 304 responses in the smartphones, this suggests that their browser caches are not as effective as those on the laptops.

The second observation from figure 1 is that a significant fraction of bytes downloaded by iOS and BlackBerries are returned using *206 Partial Content* responses. This status code is used when the client requests an object to be delivered in smaller chunks. For instance, such responses occur in multimedia traffic for smartphone devices, because these objects tend to be large in size. Our investigation shows that these 206 responses in iOS devices are a result of the media component *AppleCoreMedia*, which is used across different applications (we have identified more than 82 apps).

We also examine what kinds of content are downloaded by smartphones and laptops. Figure 2 shows the relative percentages of the various content types requested in the trace, both in terms of requests and in bytes. Across all platforms, a minority of requests for multimedia content (video and audio) generate the majority of the bytes transferred. Nonetheless, among the iOS requests, a higher number of video requests is associated with video objects than in other device types. In addition, 55% of the iOS bytes downloaded are multimedia, which is higher than seen on the other devices. There is also a significant portion of BlackBerry traffic that is associated with Audio. Finally, the distribution of content types on Windows and Mac OS X laptops are broadly similar.

We next turn our attention to the caching effectiveness. We study two storing policies: the *Discard* policy in which only the objects that have been downloaded in full are stored in the cache (default policy in Squid), and the *Partial* in which only the requested portion of the object is stored in the cache. We select these policies because a large portion of the objects in smartphone devices are not fully downloaded (interrupted).

In order to evaluate the browser caching we replay the trace for each device through an additional simulated cache dedicated solely to that device. If the addition of such a cache does not provide any benefits, it suggests the the browser cache is performing well. If it does provide benefits, it suggests that the browser cache is either too small or not exploiting all the available caching features of HTTP. Our results in figure 3 indicate that (a) a small browser cache size is sufficient to capture most of the savings; (b) a browser cache should be able to handle partially downloaded objects.

Finally, we evaluate the effectiveness of a Web proxy cache for our environment based on two configurations that take into account the freshness of the object in cache. In one configuration, *always revalidated*, a cached object is always assumed valid with the object at the server. In that case, the cache only revalidates the object and receives a 304 response. In the second configuration, *never revalidated*, the object is always assumed stale and the full object is retrieved via a 200 response. We show request hit rates vary from 8 to 40 percent, and bandwidth savings from 5 to 25 percent.

2. REFERENCES

[1] *Sandvine Global Internet Phenomena Report.* Spring, 2011.

[2] J. Erman, A. Gerber, K. Ramakrishnan, S. Sen, and O. Spatscheck. Over the top video: The gorilla in cellular networks. In *IMC*. ACM, 2011.

[3] H. Falaki, R. Mahajan, S. Kandula, D. Lymberopoulos, R. Govindan, and D. Estrin. Diversity in smartphone usage. In *MobiSys*. ACM, 2010.

[4] A. Gember, A. Anand, and A. Akella. A comparative study of handheld and non-handheld traffic in campus wi-fi networks. In *Passive and Active Measurement*, pages 173–183. Springer, 2011.

[5] G. Maier, F. Schneider, and A. Feldmann. A first look at mobile hand-held device traffic. In *Passive and Active Measurement*. Springer, 2010.

[6] Q. Xu, J. Erman, A. Gerber, Z. Mao, J. Pang, and S. Venkataraman. Identifying diverse usage behaviors of smartphone apps. In *IMC*. ACM, 2011.

Micro and Macro Views of Discrete-State Markov Models and their Application to Efficient Simulation with Phase-type Distributions

Philipp Reinecke
philipp.reinecke@fu-berlin.de
Freie Universität Berlin
Institute for Computer Science
Takustraße 9
14195 Berlin, Germany

Miklós Telek
telek@hit.bme.hu
Budapest University of Technology and Economics
Dept. of Telecommunications
Magyar tudósok krt. 2
1117 Budapest

Katinka Wolter
katinka.wolter@fu-berlin.de,
katinka.wolter@ncl.ac.uk
Freie Universität Berlin,
Germany, and Newcastle University, UK

Categories and Subject Descriptors

G.3 [**Mathematics of Computing**]: Probability and Statistics—*Markov processes; Random number generation; Stochastic processes*

General Terms

Performance, Reliability, Theory

Keywords

Phase-type distributions, Micro/Macro Views, Efficient Evaluation

1. DESCRIPTION OF MATERIAL

This is a proposal for a three-hour tutorial. The tutorial is split into two parts of equal length. We first talk about the distinction of the macro and micro view in modelling and illustrate its use in efficient solution methods. We then provide a hands on introduction to using phase-type simulations in discrete-event simulation, as one instance of using the distinction between the micro and macro view.

1.1 Micro and macro views of discrete state Markov models

A wide range of complex real life systems are modelled with Markov chains in order to evaluate various performance measures. There are sophisticated methodologies to compose the Markov models based on the elementary behavior of the components of the real system.

Examples of elementary behavior in a large system model include service, failure time distribution, arrival process of customers, etc. In Markov models these model elements are described with small Markov chains and the overall system model is composed by an appropriate combination of the small Markov chains.

With respect to evaluation, we may distinguish between two perspectives. If the elements of the underlying small Markov chains are known, we refer to this view as the *micro-level view* of the process. On the other hand, if we consider only the stochastic behaviour of the model elements, we call this perspective the *macro-level*. Due to the fact that the typical performance measures are related to the macro-level view of the system behaviour one can try to optimise the system representation by properly tuning the underlying small Markov chains. One interesting consequence of this optimisation procedure is that non-Markovian models can be used to compute Markovian systems in an efficient way.

The first part of the tutorial summarises the typical model elements used in discrete state system description, including phase-type distributions and Markov arrival processes. After that, it focusses on the problem of different representations. We list a few available results and a set of related open problems [3, 2, 4].

1.2 Efficient Simulation with Phase-type Distributions

Phase-type (PH) distributions are a valuable tool for representing real-world phenomena such as failure-times or response-times in an analytically tractable way. Recently, the application of phase-type distributions in simulation has received increasing attention. In simulation, phase-type distributions enable good representation of empirical distributions, even if the data does not follow one of the well-known statistical distributions. Furthermore, since phase-type distributions have Markovian representations, analytical approaches can be used to support simulation results.

In the theoretical communities, PH distributions are well-known and have been applied to derive analytical solutions in system evaluation for a long time. In contrast, they have seen little application in simulation. This is certainly partly due to the fact that the theoretical details of deriving and using PH distributions may appear rather intimidating to 'simulation guys'. A second reason may be the performance costs of generating PH-distributed random variates. Finally, the absence of support for PH distributions in popular discrete-event simulators such as OMNeT++ [10] and NS-2 [11] also constitutes a major hurdle.

In the second part we give a hands-on introduction to using PH distributions. We follow the workflow depicted in Figure 1: Given a measurement trace, a PH distribution is fitted to this data and used in simulation. We start with an accessible discussion of the essential theoretical basics.

SIGMETRICS'12, June 11-15, 2012, London, England, UK
ACM 978-1-4503-1097-0/12/06.

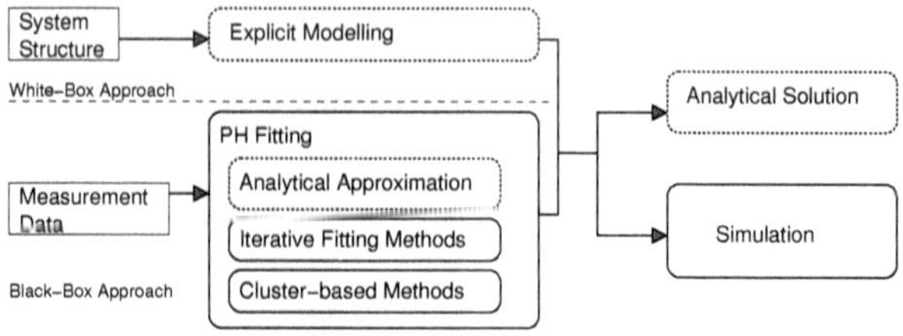

Figure 1: Basic workflow for PH distributions.

In this part we focus particularly on structural properties that are suitable for efficient fitting and simulation later on.

In the second step of this part we address the question of obtaining a PH distribution that fits a measurement trace. We focus on three important points: First, the approximating distribution must represent the data set well, second, the fitted distribution must be usable in efficient simulation, and third, fitting should be user-friendly. We will discuss several established fitting tools and illustrate how to obtain a good fit using our Hyper-* fitting tool for user-friendly and efficient cluster-based PH fitting [7].

The third step focusses on efficient random-variate generation from PH distributions. We introduce several algorithms and show how special structures can reduce the cost of random-variate generation [9]. We then discuss optimisation of PH representations with respect to simulation cost. We give results on optimal representations for the APH subclass [8] and consider extension to the general PH class [5].

In the final step we introduce the generic libphprng library for PH random-variate generation in simulation frameworks [6]. The library is part of the Butools package [1] and implements the efficient algorithms introduced in the previous part. Libphprng combines efficient methods with easy usage. Furthermore, libphrng integrates seamlessly with discrete-event simulators such as OMNeT++ without any changes to the library core. We illustrate application of the library in popular network simulators using a case-study. The case study covers evaluation of syntonisation accuracy in the precision-time protocol (PTP). We show how the use of PH distributions can tremendously reduce simulation runtimes and improve accuracy of the results.

2. BRIEF BIOGRAPHIES OF SPEAKERS

Philipp Reinecke received his Master's degree in Computer Science at the Humboldt-Universität zu Berlin in 2007. He is working in various areas of system modelling and evaluation, applying methods ranging from experiments in testbeds through simulation to analytical methods. He will submit his PhD thesis on the efficient use of phase-type distributions in the spring of 2012.

Miklós Telek graduated as an electrical engineer at the Faculty of Electrical Engineering, Technical University of Budapest in 1987. Since 1990 he has been with the Department of Telecommunications, Technical University of Budapest, where he is a professor now. His current research interests include various aspects of stochastic performance modeling and analysis of computer and communication systems.

Katinka Wolter Katinka Wolter received her Diploma and PhD degree from the Technical University Berlin in 1995 and 1999, respectively. She has worked on stochastic modelling techniques and retry mechanisms for reliability and gained her habilitation degree from Humboldt-University in 2008. Currently, she is guest-professor for Dependable Systems at Freie Universität Berlin and about to join Newcastle University, UK.

3. REFERENCES

[1] L. Bodrog, P. Buchholz, A. Heindl, A. Horváth, G. Horváth, I. Kolossváry, Z. Németh, P. Reinecke, M. Telek, and M. Vécsei. Butools: Program packages for computations with PH, ME distributions and MAP, RAP processes. http://webspn.hit.bme.hu/~butools, October 2011.

[2] P. Buchholz, A. Horvath, and M. Telek. Stochastic petri nets with low variation matrix exponentially distributed firing time. *International Journal of Performability Engineering*, 7:441–454, 2011. Special issue on Performance and Dependability Modeling of Dynamic Systems.

[3] P. Buchholz and M. Telek. On minimal representation of rational arrival processes. In *Madrid Conference on Qeueuing theory (MCQT)*, June 2010.

[4] P. Buchholz and M. Telek. Composition and equivalence of markovian and non-markovian models. In *8th International Conference on Quantitative Evaluation of SysTems (QEST)*, pages 213–222, sept 2011.

[5] G. Horváth, P. Reinecke, M. Telek, and K. Wolter. Efficient Generation of PH-distributed Random Variates. In *19th International Conference on Analytical and Stochastic Modelling Techniques and Applications (ASMTA'12)*, Grenoble, France, 4–6 July 2012. To appear.

[6] P. Reinecke and G. Horváth. Phase-type Distributions for Realistic Modelling in Discrete-Event Simulation. In *OMNeT++ Workshop 2012*. ACM, 2012. To appear.

[7] P. Reinecke, T. Krauß, and K. Wolter. Cluster-based Fitting of Phase-type Distributions to Empirical Data. *Computers and Mathematics with Applications*, 2012. To appear.

[8] P. Reinecke, M. Telek, and K. Wolter. Reducing the Costs of Generating APH-Distributed Random Numbers. In B. Müller-Clostermann, K. Echtle, and E. Rathgeb, editors, *MMB & DFT 2010*, number 5987 in LNCS, pages 274–286. Springer-Verlag Berlin Heidelberg, 2010.

[9] P. Reinecke, K. Wolter, L. Bodrog, and M. Telek. On the Cost of Generating PH-distributed Random Numbers. In G. Horváth, K. Joshi, and A. Heindl, editors, *Proceedings of the Ninth International Workshop on Performability Modeling of Computer and Communication Systems (PMCCS-9)*, pages 16–20, Eger, Hungary, September 17–18, 2009 2009.

[10] A. Varga. The OMNeT++ Discrete Event Simulation System. In *Proceedings of the European Simulation Multiconference (ESM'2001)*, June 2001.

[11] Various authors. The Network Simulator ns-2. http://www.isi.edu/nsnam/ns/. (last seen May 11, 2010).

POTRA: A Framework for Building Power Models for Next Generation Multicore Architectures

[Tutorial Overview]

Ramon Bertran
Barcelona Supercomputing Center
C. Jordi Girona 1-3
08034 Barcelona, Spain
ramon.bertran@bsc.es

Marc Gonzàlez
Universitat Politècnica de Catalunya
C. Jordi Girona 1-3
08034 Barcelona, Spain
marc@ac.upc.edu

Xavier Martorell
Barcelona Supercomputing Center
C. Jordi Girona 1-3
08034 Barcelona, Spain
xavier.martorell@bsc.es

Nacho Navarro
Barcelona Supercomputing Center
C. Jordi Girona 1-3
08034 Barcelona, Spain
nacho.navarro@bsc.es

Eduard Ayguadé
Barcelona Supercomputing Center
C. Jordi Girona 1-3
08034 Barcelona, Spain
eduard.ayguade@bsc.es

Categories and Subject Descriptors

C.4 [**Performance of Systems**]: Modeling Techniques; C.4 [**Performance of Systems**]: Measurement Techniques

General Terms

Measurement, Experimentation

Keywords

Power estimation, Performance counters, DVFS

1. INTRODUCTION

Controlling the trade-off between performance and power is a complex task that currently is addressed at different levels by hardware, firmware and system software. The effectiveness of a power management policy depends on many parameters that require an actual understanding of the power and performance levels observed for a workload to effectively turn the appropriate knobs. One key aspect of any power management solution is that of relying on meaningful data that bring this understanding and explain the power, temperature and performance levels being generated within the architecture.

Last generation multi-core chips have exposed the limitations for sensor distribution within the chip and the unfeasibility of having per-core measurements. Besides, heuristics exclusively based on sensor distribution do not allow for predicting the effect on performance of any decision at the power management level. Alternative methods are required to get power, temperature and performance estimates: for instance, the IBM POWER7 includes power models based on hardware counters collected on a per-core basis that are used by the embedded firmware to perform the power management.

SIGMETRICS'12, June 11–15, 2012, London, England, UK.
ACM 978-1-4503-1097-0/12/06.

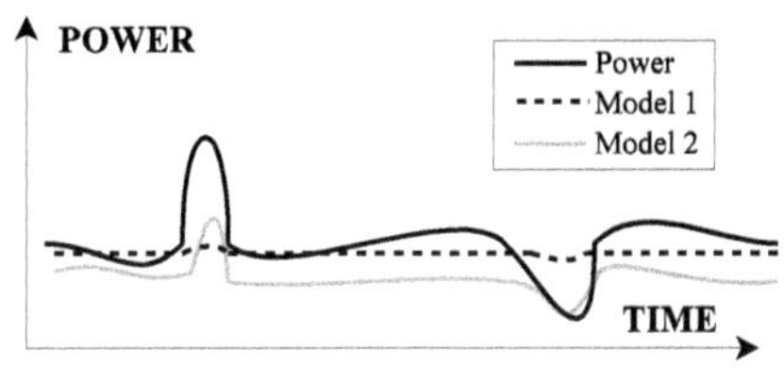

Figure 1: Power model examples. Both models show similar accuracy, but Model 2 is more responsive than Model 1.

The methods based on Performance Monitoring Counters (PMCs) have been shown to be a good solution to estimate power consumption. As a result, their applicability has been demonstrated on several fields such as power management and application profiling. PMC-based power models are used to perform live predictions of power behavior in order to guide power aware policies [2, 3, 4]. Moreover, they are also used in research for quickly exploring new approaches since they allow to profile real systems and full executions of applications, avoiding the need of performing long-time and limited simulations [5]. In the end, they have been crucial in the process of addressing power issues.

Modeling techniques to be embedded in a power management framework demand three primary features: first, simplicity and systematic generation; second, a per architectural component decomposition of the overall estimate, so that the power management decisions can be accompanied by a real understanding of the observed performance levels; and finally, accuracy and responsiveness (see Figure 1).

2. TUTORIAL OVERVIEW

The main topics covered in this tutorial are:

- A systematic methodology for producing PMC-based power models on CMP architectures [4]. The methodology ensures by definition the decomposability and the generality of the models, while at the same time it produces accurate, responsive and CMP-aware power models.

- A evaluation metric for power models: the *responsiveness*, the ability to track dynamic power variations. This metric is based on power phase detection accuracy and it allows to evaluate the suitability of the models to guide policies built on top of them.
- A case study is presented for an Intel® Core^{TM} 2 Duo. Single and multiple core models are presented for several DVFS states and an empirical evaluation of the produced models is performed using the SPECcpu2006, NAS and LMBENCH benchmark suites.

2.1 Tutorial organization

Initially we describe the basic options to generate a platform where to build a model (device for getting actual power measurements, sampling the device, getting the measurements) (*30 min*). Second, we describe how to breakdown a multicore architecture in components from where to obtain contributions on the overall power consumption (*45 min*). Third, we explain the set of counters commonly available in last generation multicore architectures and which ones better describe the activity of each architectural component (*45 min*). Fourth, we present how to linearly correlate the activity in each component with actual power. We describe a basic algorithm that uses stochastic methods to build power models (*30 min*). Finally, the tutorial describes how to validate a power model in terms of accuracy and responsiveness (*30 min*). More details of the tutorial can be found elsewhere [1].

3. ACKNOWLEDGMENTS

We thankfully acknowledge the support of the European Commission through the HiPEAC-2 Network of Excellence (FP7/ICT 217068), the support of the Spanish Ministry of Education (TIN2007-60625, andCSD2007-00050) and the Generalitat de Catalunya (2009-SGR-980).

4. REFERENCES

[1] POTRA Tutorial. `http://rbertran.site.ac.upc.edu/potra`.
[2] F. Bellosa. The benefits of event: driven energy accounting in power-sensitive systems. In *EW 9'00*, Kolding, Denmark, 2000.
[3] C. Isci *et al.* Runtime power monitoring in high-end processors: Methodology and empirical data. In *MICRO'03*, page 93, San Diego, CA, USA, 2003.
[4] R. Bertran *et al.* Decomposable and responsive power models for multicore processors using performance counters. In *ICS'10*, pages 147–158, Tsukuba, Ibaraki, Japan, June 2010. ACM.
[5] R. Bertran *et al.* Energy accounting for shared virtualized environments under dvfs using pmc-based power models. *Future Generation Computer Systems*, 28(2):457 – 468, 2012.

Biographies

Ramon Bertran received a bachelor degree in Computer Science and a master degree in Computer Architecture from Universitat Politècnica de Catalunya (UPC). Since 2005 he is a PhD student in the Computer Architecture Department at UPC. Currently, he is a resident student at Barcelona Supercomputing Center, and his research is focused on power and performance modelling of multicore architectures and energy aware computing.

Marc Gonzàlez received the Engineering degree in Computer Science in 1996 and the Computer Science PhD degree on December 2003. His research has been developed around parallel programming models and high performance computing, in particular, the OpenMP programming model. His current research is centered on this programming model and its use on heterogeneous architectures, based on accelerators and local memories. The main research activities are the design and implementation of software cache techniques for the IBM Cell BE processor as well as the implementation of runtime libraries and compiler support for the OpenMP programming model on this architecture.

Xavier Martorell received the M.S. and Ph.D. degrees in Computer Science from the Technical University of Catalunya (UPC) in 1991 and 1999, respectively. He has been an associate professor in the Computer Architecture Department at UPC since 2001, teaching on operating systems. His research interests cover the areas of paralellism, runtime systems, compilers and applications for high-performance multiprocessor systems. Since 2005 he is the manager of the team working on Parallel Programming Models at the Barcelona Supercomputing Center. He has participated in several european projects dealing with parallel environments (Nanos, Intone, POP, SARC, ACOTES). He is currently participating in the European HiPEAC2 Network of Excellence, and the ENCORE european project.

Nacho Navarro is Associate Professor at the Universitat Politècnica de Catalunya (UPC), Barcelona, Spain, since 1994, and Senior Researcher at the Barcelona Supercomputing Center (BSC). He holds a Ph.D. degree in Computer Science from UPC (1991), Spain. His current interests include: tools for evaluation of multi-core microprocessors, application-specific computer architectures, dynamic reconfigurable logic and resource management in heterogeneous environments and sensor networks. He is also doing research on the programmability and support of hardware accelerators like GPUs at the University of Illinois (IMPACT Research Group). Prof. Navarro is a member of the IEEE, the IEEE Computer Society, the ACM and USENIX.

Eduard Ayguadé received the Engineering degree in Telecommunications in 1986 and the Ph.D. degree in Computer Science in 1989, both from the Universitat Politècnica de Catalunya (UPC), Spain. Since 1987 he has been lecturing on computer organization and architecture and parallel programming models. Currently, and since 1997, he is full professor of the Computer Architecture Department at UPC. His research interests cover the areas of processor microarchitecture, multicore architectures and programming models and their architectural support. He has published more than 100 papers in these topics and participated in several research projects in the framework of the European Union and research collaborations with companies. He is associated director for research on computer sciences at the Barcelona Supercomputing Center (BSC-CNS).

Basic Theory and Some Applications of Martingales

Richard A. Hayden
Department of Computing
Imperial College London
London, SW7 2AZ, United Kingdom
rh@doc.ic.ac.uk

ABSTRACT

This tutorial surveys the fundamental results of the theory of martingales from the perspective of the performance engineer. We will present the fundamental results and illustrate their power through simple and elegant proofs of important and well-known results in performance analysis. The remainder of the tutorial will introduce the martingale functional central limit theorem and semi-martingale decomposition methodology for the characterisation and proof of heavy-traffic limit results for Markovian queueing systems.

Categories and Subject Descriptors

G.3 [**Probability and Statistics**]: Markov processes, Queueing theory, Stochastic processes

Keywords

stochastic processes, queueing theory, martingales, heavy-traffic

1. OVERVIEW

A stochastic process $X = \{X(t)\}_{t \geq 0}$ is a *martingale*[1] if:

$$\mathbb{E}[X(t+s)|(X(u))_{u \leq t}] = X(t) \text{ with probability } 1$$

for all $s, t \geq 0$.

Martingales constitute a very important class of stochastic processes about which very strong, and often intuitively surprising, general statements can be made. In addition to their interest from a purely mathematical point of view, they have key applications in applied probability, perhaps most crucially to the proof of so-called *heavy-traffic limits* of queueing systems [9, 5], and, relatedly, *mean-field* or *fluid* limits in other settings [3, 1, 6].

The aim of this tutorial is to provide an accessible introduction to the theory of martingales for the non-expert, with a specific emphasis on applications of interest to practitioners in the performance analysis community.

We will first cover the basic definitions and fundamental results, including the *optional stopping theorem*, the *maximal inequality*, the *upcrossings inequality* and the *martingale convergence theorems*. We will illustrate the practical power of even these basic results by showing how they yield simple and elegant proofs of some of the fundamental results of performance modelling, for example, the famous *PASTA (Poisson Arrivals See Time Averages)* property [12] and the fact that the best phase-type approximation to a deterministic delay is Erlang [4].

In the second part of the tutorial, our focus will be on the powerful martingale approach for establishing heavy-traffic limits of queueing networks [9, 10, 8, 11, 7]. This will rest on the decomposition of the components of the queueing processes into sums of martingales and *predictable*[2] processes according to a version of the *Doob–Meyer decomposition theorem*:

THEOREM 1 (D–M DECOMP. OF SUBMARTS. IN $\mathbb{R}_{\geq 0}$ [9]). *If X is a submartingale with paths in $\mathbb{R}_{\geq 0}$ and $\mathbb{E}[X(t)] < \infty$ for each $t \geq 0$, then there exists a predictable process A, called the* compensator *of X, such that A has non-negative, non-decreasing sample paths, $\mathbb{E}[A(t)] < \infty$ for each $t \geq 0$ and $M := X - A$ is a martingale. The compensator is unique in the sense that the sample paths of any two versions must be equal with probability 1.*

This will then allow application of the *martingale functional central limit theorem (FCLT)*, which concerns the convergence of appropriate martingales to (multi-dimensional) Brownian motion:

THEOREM 2 (MARTINGALE FCLT [9]). *For $n \geq 1$, let $\mathbf{M}^n$ be a sequence of (local) martingales in D^k with $\mathbf{M}_0^n = \mathbf{0}$.*[3] *Let $\mathbf{C} = (c_{ij})$ be a $k \times k$ non-negative-definite symmetric real matrix. Assume further that each $\mathbf{M}^n$ is (locally) square integrable so that the* predictable quadratic co-variation *processes:*

$$\langle M_i^n, M_j^n \rangle := \frac{1}{4}(\langle M_i^n + M_j^n \rangle - \langle M_i^n - M_j^n \rangle)$$

can be defined, where the predictable quadratic variation $\langle M \rangle$ of a martingale M is defined to be the unique compensator of the non-negative submartingale M^2 given in Theorem 1.

Then if the expected values of the maximum jump of $\langle M_i^n, M_j^n \rangle$ and maximum squared jump of $\mathbf{M}^n$ are asymptotically negligible as $n \to \infty$, and $\langle M_i^n, M_j^n \rangle(t) \Rightarrow c_{ij} t$ as $n \to \infty$ for each $t \geq 0$, we have:

$$\mathbf{M}^n \Rightarrow \mathbf{B} \text{ weakly in } D^k \text{ as } n \to \infty$$

[1] Or a *submartingale* if equality is replaced with $\geq$ in the definition.

[2] The value of a predictable process at time t is known given the information about the process up to (but not including) time t.

[3] D^k is the space of right-continuous functions with left limits taking values in $\mathbb{R}^k$.

SIGMETRICS'12, June 11–15, 2012, London, England, UK.
ACM 978-1-4503-1097-0/12/06.

where $\mathbf{B}$ *is a* k*-dimensional Brownian motion having mean vector* $\mathbb{E}[\mathbf{B}(t)] = \mathbf{0}$ *and covariance matrix* $\mathbb{E}[\mathbf{B}(t)\mathbf{B}(t)^T] = \mathbf{C}t$ *for* $t \geq 0$.

More concretely, in this tutorial we consider sequences of Markovian many-server queues which can be described in terms of *thinnings* of (possibly infinite) sets of Poisson processes [2]. The characterisation and proof of heavy-traffic limits then follows approximately the following recipe:

1. Decomposition of the queueing processes into sums of martingales and predictable processes (*semi-martingale decomposition*). Proof of the representation by exploiting properties of stochastic integrals such as those in [2, Page 10].

2. Verification of conditions of the martingale FCLT: proof of convergence of the *predictable quadratic variation* — usually relies on an auxiliary fluid limit result that follows from an appropriate stochastic boundedness lemma. Again, martingale inequalities are the powerful tools of choice for establishing these boundedness results.

3. Convergence to the limit process then follows by combining the FCLT with the *continuous mapping theorem (CMT)*.

We will illustrate this approach with examples taken from the literature.

2. BRIEF SPEAKER BIOGRAPHY

Richard Hayden obtained his MSci degree in mathematics and computer science from the Department of Computing at Imperial College London in 2007. He received his Ph.D. in 2011, for which he was a finalist for the 2012 INFORMS Doctoral Dissertation Award for Operations Research in Telecommunications. He currently holds a postdoctoral position at Imperial College and his research interests lie in the efficient analysis and optimisation of large-scale performance models of massively-parallel systems using mean-field analysis and related asymptotic techniques.

3. REFERENCES

[1] M. Benaïm and J.-Y. Le Boudec. A class of mean field interaction models for computer and communication systems. *Performance Evaluation*, 65(11-12):823–838, Nov. 2008.

[2] P. Brémaud. *Point processes and queues: martingale dynamics*. Springer, 1981.

[3] R. W. R. Darling and J. R. Norris. Differential equation approximations for Markov chains. *Probability Surveys*, 5:37–79, 2008.

[4] A. David and S. Larry. The least variable phase type distribution is Erlang. *Stochastic Models*, 3(3):467–473, 1987.

[5] S. Halfin and W. Whitt. Heavy-Traffic Limits for Queues with Many Exponential Servers. *Operations Research*, 29(3):567–588, May 1981.

[6] R. A. Hayden, A. Stefanek, and J. T. Bradley. Fluid computation of passage time distributions in large Markov models. *Theoretical Computer Science*, 413(1):106–141, 2012.

[7] H. Kaspi and K. Ramanan. Law of large numbers limits for many-server queues. *The Annals of Applied Probability*, 21(1):33–114, Feb. 2011.

[8] R. S. Lipster and A. N. Shiryayev. *Theory of martingales*. Kluwer, 1989.

[9] G. Pang, R. Talreja, and W. Whitt. Martingale proofs of many-server heavy-traffic limits for Markovian queues. *Probability Surveys*, 4:193–267, 2007.

[10] A. A. Puhalskii and M. I. Reiman. The multiclass $GI/PH/N$ queue in the Halfin-Whitt regime. *Advances in Applied Probability*, 32(2):564–595, June 2000.

[11] W. Whitt. Heavy-Traffic Limits for the $G/H_2^*/n/m$ Queue. *Mathematics of Operations Research*, 30(1):1–27, Feb. 2005.

[12] R. W. Wolff. Poisson Arrivals See Time Averages. *Operations Research*, 30(2):223–231, Oct. 1982.

Applications of Machine Learning to Performance Evaluation

Edmundo de Souza e Silva
Federal University of Rio de Janeiro
System Engineering and Computer Science
Rio de Janeiro, RJ
edmundo@land.ufrj.br

Daniel Sadoc Menasche
Federal University of Rio de Janeiro
Department of Computer Science
Rio de Janeiro, RJ
sadoc@land.ufrj.br

Categories and Subject Descriptors

General Terms

Keywords

1. TUTORIAL OVERVIEW

w

H v

SIGMETRICS'12, June 11–15, 2012, London, England, UK.
ACM 978-1-4503-1097-0/12/06.

Intended audience

Assumed background of attendees

2. KEY REFERENCES

3. REFERENCES

Reversible Markov chains and random walks on graphs (in preparation) http://www.stat.berkeley.edu/users/aldous/RWG/book.html

Performance Evaluation
Google's PageRank and Beyond

N *Networks: An Introduction*

Computer Networks

N
N *Network Science Workshop*

Speakers biography

E v

N

N

N

Introduction to Network Experiments using the GENI CyberInfrastructure

Jay Aikat
UNC - Chapel Hill
Brooks 314, CB#3175
Chapel Hill, NC 27599-3175
+1 919.962.1878
aikat@cs.unc.edu

Kevin Jeffay
UNC - Chapel Hill
Brooks 316, CB#3175
Chapel Hill, NC 27599-3175
+1 919.962.1938
jeffay@cs.unc.edu

ABSTRACT
In this tutorial, we will introduce the SIGMETRICS/Performance community to the vast testbeds, tools and resources openly available through the GENI (Global Environment for Network Innovations) project. We will present details about the distributed computing resources available on GENI for researchers interested in simulation as well as measurement-based performance evaluation experiments. We will demonstrate simple experiments on GENI, and leave them with information on how to run experiments for research and education using GENI resources.

Categories and Subject Descriptors
C.2.4 [**Computer Systems Organization**]: Computer-Communication Networks - Distributed Systems.

General Terms
Experimentation, Measurement, Performance.

Keywords
Network Experiments; GENI; Traffic Generation; Measurement; Modeling.

1. INTRODUCTION
For over a decade now, networking researchers have built small and large research testbeds using hardware in their laboratories, or using software tools like the Network Simulator (NS) as the primary means for performance evaluation experiments. More recently, through the largely NSF-funded Global Environment for Network Innovations (GENI) project, we have witnessed the initial deployment of customizable testbeds with vast CyberInfrastructure capabilities spread across the United States.

2. BRIEF DESCRIPTION OF MATERIAL
The presenters of this tutorial are currently working on a three-year NSF-funded project to develop education and training resources for GENI experiments. We also have the enthusiastic support of the GENI Project Office for conducting this tutorial.

GENI is a virtual laboratory at the frontiers of network science and engineering, enabling researchers to build and tear down networks and run experiments with several options for testbed topologies, instrumentation and measurement, and models for traffic generation. Through this tutorial, we would like to introduce the SIGMETRICS community to the vast testbeds, tools and resources openly available through the GENI project. This project, while still being developed and deployed, is now ready for running experiments.

This tutorial will answer the following questions:

- What is GENI?
- What are the distributed computing resources available on GENI for researchers interested in simulation as well as measurement-based performance evaluation experiments?
- Where and how do you get started if you want to run experiments on GENI testbeds?
- What are the kinds of experiments you can run on the GENI testbeds?
- What are the specific traffic generation tools available for such experiments?

We will demonstrate simple experiments that can be run using the GENI CyberInfrastructure. We will specifically address the following topics on measurement-based traffic generation:

- How do you obtain realistic Internet traffic data for your experiments?
- How do you model the application workloads that constitute this network traffic?
- How do you emulate network characteristics in your experiments?
- How can you generate realistic traffic, and run hundreds of automated experiments using slightly different variations of the same traffic input?

Using a case study of experiments for network performance evaluation, we shall walk you through the entire process from measurement of production network traffic to modeling workloads and end-to-end paths to generating this traffic for experiments using the GENI infrastructure.

This tutorial is designed for any (rookie or experienced) network researcher or network engineer who is interested in using the GENI CyberInfrastructure for their experiments. For example, these may be researchers doing performance evaluations for network components or distributed systems, testing a distributed system in a cloud environment, or testing a new protocol for wireless devices.

SIGMETRICS'12, June 11–15, 2012, London, England, UK.
ACM 978-1-4503-1097-0/12/06.

After this tutorial, the attendee will be able to run simple experiments on GENI testbeds using the tools and resources we provide. Furthermore, they will have access to resources we are currently developing (over the next year) for measurement-based realistic traffic generation on various GENI testbeds, which will include traffic data and results from GENI experiments, and several small experiment modules specifically designed for use in networking courses.

3. INTENDED AUDIENCE

The audience for whom this tutorial will be most beneficial will include the following:

- Researchers who wish to run network experiments modeling realistic traffic workloads
- Professors who wish to add simple pre-tested GENI experiment modules into their current networking courses.
- Industry researchers and engineers who run experiments to test and evaluate distributed systems or network components
- Most importantly, attendees who wish to run such experiments with very little effort at setting up the testbeds and developing tools for running experiments – i.e. GENI testbeds are available for running experiments and we will introduce you to the tools and manuals to use them.

3.1 Assumed Background of Attendees

We expect the attendee to have basic knowledge of computer networking and distributed systems, and to be interested in the research and education of empirical networking.

4. SPEAKERS' INFO

1. Jay Aikat, University of North Carolina at Chapel Hill, aikat@cs.unc.edu, 919-962-1878.
2. Kevin Jeffay, University of North Carolina at Chapel Hill, jeffay@cs.unc.edu, 919-962-1938.

Jay Aikat is a Research Assistant Professor in the Department of Computer Science at the University of North Carolina at Chapel Hill. Her interests include computer networking, measurement and modeling of Internet traffic, and experimental design and evaluation.

Kevin Jeffay is the Gillian T. Cell Distinguished Professor of Computer Science in the Department of Computer Science at the University of North Carolina at Chapel Hill. His research interests include computer networking, operating systems, real-time systems, multimedia networking, and performance evaluation.

5. REFERENCES

1. Felix Hernandez-Campos. *Generation and Validation of Empirically-Derived TCP Application Workloads*. PhD thesis, University of North Carolina at Chapel Hill, August 2006.
2. Michele C. Weigle, Prashanth Adurthi, Felix Hernandez-Campos, Kevin Jeffay, and F. Donelson Smith. A *tool for generating realistic TCP application workloads in ns-2*. ACM Computer Communication Review, 36(3):67–76, July 2006.
3. GENI: www.geni.net

Author Index